TAX, INEQUALITY, AND HUMAN RIGHTS

TAX, INEQUALITY, AND HUMAN RIGHTS

Edited by Philip Alston

AND

Nikki Reisch

OXFORD
UNIVERSITY PRESS

OXFORD
UNIVERSITY PRESS

Oxford University Press is a department of the University of Oxford. It furthers the University's objective of excellence in research, scholarship, and education by publishing worldwide. Oxford is a registered trademark of Oxford University Press in the UK and certain other countries.

Published in the United States of America by Oxford University Press
198 Madison Avenue, New York, NY 10016, United States of America.

Library of Congress Cataloging-in-Publication Data
Names: Alston, Philip, editor. | Reisch, Nikki, editor.
Title: Tax, inequality, and human rights / Philip Alston and Nikki Reisch, editors.
Description: New York: Oxford University Press, 2019. | Includes bibliographical references and index.
Identifiers: LCCN 2018038170 | ISBN 9780190882228 ((hardback) : alk. paper) |
    ISBN 9780190882235 ((pbk.) : alk. paper)
Subjects: LCSH: Taxation—Law and legislation. | Tax administration and procedure. | Equality before the law. | Taxation—Social aspects. | Tax evasion. | Tax protests and appeals. | Human rights.
Classification: LCC K4460 .T39 2019 | DDC 343.04—dc23
LC record available at https://lccn.loc.gov/2018038170

1 3 5 7 9 8 6 4 2

Paperback printed by Webcom, Inc., Canada
Hardback printed by Bridgeport National Bindery, Inc., United States of America

Note to Readers
This publication is designed to provide accurate and authoritative information in regard to the subject matter covered. It is based upon sources believed to be accurate and reliable and is intended to be current as of the time it was written. It is sold with the understanding that the publisher is not engaged in rendering legal, accounting, or other professional services. If legal advice or other expert assistance is required, the services of a competent professional person should be sought. Also, to confirm that the information has not been affected or changed by recent developments, traditional legal research techniques should be used, including checking primary sources where appropriate.

(Based on the Declaration of Principles jointly adopted by a Committee of the American Bar Association and a Committee of Publishers and Associations.)

You may order this or any other Oxford University Press publication by visiting the Oxford University Press website at www.oup.com.

CONTENTS

FOREWORD

Winnie Byanyima, Executive Director, Oxfam International*

Inequality, the global economy, and human rights—and the connections between them—lie at the center of one of the most important political debates of our time. And that debate is increasingly focused on the issue of taxation.

When people hear about tax avoidance and evasion they do not necessarily think of human rights abuses. To most people, the term "human rights abuses" evokes wrongful imprisonment, torture, freedom of speech being curtailed. It is time we widened the definition. The wealthy corporations and individuals sidestepping their obligations to pay tax are human rights abusers. Every school that is not built, every medicine that is not bought for lack of government funds due to tax dodging represents an abuse of the rights of women, children, and men across the world.

As we have learned from many of the greatest social movements in history, it is only when the moral compass of society shifts that we secure lasting change. We need to make tax dodging a moral issue—an issue of human rights. We need to see tax dodging and those who facilitate it as morally wrong, and the language and laws of human rights can help us achieve this.

There is a growing movement of people, all over the world, who want to ensure every individual and every corporation pays their fair share of taxes, who fight inequality and support human rights for all. This movement includes community leaders, activists, academics, writers, lawyers, students, artists, poets, and economists. It has a rich history. It exists in every country, from the richest to the poorest. The contributors to this important volume are part of that movement.

---

* This foreword is adapted from the keynote address that Ms. Byanyima gave at a conference on *Human Rights and Tax in an Unequal World*, held at New York University School of Law in September 2016.

Oxfam has always had human rights at its heart, and because of that, tax justice has become a greater area of focus in recent years. We know that without tax justice it is impossible to achieve our vision of a just world without poverty.

The Sustainable Development Goals (SDGs), agreed by the governments of the world in New York in 2015, set out an ambitious agenda for ending extreme poverty and hunger, ensuring equal rights for women and for marginalized communities, and much more. Delivering on these goals will cost trillions of dollars.

We know that aid will remain important for many countries for a long time to come—especially for fragile and conflict-affected states. But aid alone will not suffice. We will only achieve the SDGs if governments in poorer countries are able to mobilize their own resources, and then be held to account by their own citizens to spend those resources in a way that benefits everyone. The SDGs are achievable. The world has enough resources. The problem is that these resources are shared so unevenly: 1 percent of the people on the planet own the same amount of wealth as the other 99 percent combined. Oxfam's analysis in January 2019 showed that just twenty-six billionaires own as much same wealth as the poorest half of humanity—that's 3.8 billion people.

Faced with such extreme inequality, we must strive for tax justice, both for the revenues that can be generated and because of the urgent need to redistribute wealth—and power—from the haves to the have-nots. National tax systems must be judged on how effectively they generate revenue *and* how fairly they redistribute wealth, tackle inequalities, and enable people to claim their human rights. And the global tax system must be judged on whether it makes this possible.

Clement Attlee, the British Prime Minister who introduced the modern welfare state and the National Health Service in the United Kingdom, said: "Charity is a cold grey loveless thing. If a rich man wants to help the poor, he should pay his taxes gladly, not dole out money at a whim." Tax is the most dignified, reliable, and accountable way of ensuring we can fund the fulfillment of human rights for all. It is tax that should pay for the things we can only deliver as a society together—be it education, health services, energy infrastructure, or roads. These are not matters of charity! They are rights, and the provision of them is a duty of government and society.

The rallying call that helped spark the US War of Independence, "No taxation without representation," today seems to have been turned on its head: many of the world's wealthiest people and biggest corporations pay little or no tax, while using their wealth to exert huge influence over political decision-making, creating rules and systems that work in their favor at the expense of everybody else.

This capture and distortion of our tax system by wealthy elites is a direct attack on the principle of accountable, democratic government. The most fundamental duty of a government is to ensure the protection and fulfillment of its citizens' human rights. Through doing so, governments earn the legitimacy to raise taxes. This is the social contract upon which strong societies that respect human rights must be built. But this social contract is in danger of falling apart, unless we boldly reform how tax works at a global level and, for most countries, at a national level, too.

When governments bow to pressure from powerful corporate interests, and create regressive fiscal systems that work for the few at the expense of the many, they are fueling political, social, and economic inequalities, and they are failing in their moral and legal responsibility to protect their citizens' human rights.

Even more worryingly, governments across the world are not just favoring the interests of corporations and wealthy elites, but actively suppressing the voices of civil society actors who want to hold their governments and the private sector to account. Recently, CIVICUS World

Alliance for Citizen Participation identified serious threats to civil society in over one hundred countries—a figure that is on the rise in recent years. All human rights actors should be concerned by this.

The global tax system does not need just minor tweaks. It needs a courageous and transformational overhaul. The forces that have been allowed to shape it until now must be challenged as we seek to create a better, fairer tax system.

Firstly, we must remind ourselves that the global tax system is a symptom and a cause of a global economy that is working for a wealthy, powerful elite, at the expense of the many. In the past few decades, we have seen income and wealth inequality spiral out of control as some top corporate executives take home ever more obscene pay packets, while millions of workers are paid poverty wages. We have seen companies successfully lobby governments to reduce regulatory controls on labor rights, wages, and environmental standards. And we have seen a corporate culture develop which prioritizes shareholder returns over all else.

In the United Kingdom, for example, as the Chief Economist of the Bank of England has stated,[1] the average large company was paying out 10 percent of its profits as shareholder dividends in 1970. Now, that figure has risen to 70 percent. That is money that could be used to increase innovation or productivity, or to improve wages for ordinary workers, helping ordinary people. Instead, it is going into the pockets of mostly rich investors.

At the same time, we have seen the use of tax havens skyrocket, to the extent that the Cayman Islands can receive some 24,000 times more investment per capita than Brazil does. We have seen levels of inward investments to the British Virgin Islands of more than 66,000 percent of their GDP. The architecture of tax havens has a pervasive role in causing regressive tax and spending systems in poor countries. The international tax system encourages harmful tax competition at every level—and it drives the race to the bottom in corporate taxation.

Many countries have slashed their corporate and high marginal tax rates. The United States has recently slashed its federal corporate tax rates from 35 percent to 21 percent. We are witnessing the same trend in Europe over a longer period—most countries have reduced their corporate income tax rates—as well as in emerging or developing countries. The global average rate for corporate income tax has been falling since the early 2000s from 30 percent to close to 24 percent.

And many governments, especially in poorer countries, are being blackmailed into giving companies ludicrously generous tax breaks and incentives. Dr. Donald Kaberuka, then President of the African Development Bank, reflecting on his time as finance minister of Rwanda, recounted what it felt like to be on the receiving end of tax negotiations: "The multinational comes to you and says we want to invest in your country, but we need a 5 year tax holiday and this long list of requirements. And by the way, we only have 6 hours, and then our plane is taking us to your neighbor, who will probably agree to all of our demands."

When companies do not pay, governments are left with two basic choices: either they cut back on services—something that necessarily erodes the rights of the poorest most, hitting women and girls particularly hard—or they shift the burden onto more regressive taxes, such as value-added tax (VAT), which fall disproportionately on poor people. In sub-Saharan Africa, such indirect taxes make up on average 67 percent of tax revenues.[2]

There are two primary, interconnected causes of these alarming trends. Firstly, there is the rise of an economic consensus that took hold in the United States and the United Kingdom in the early 1980s and then rapidly spread across the world. Neoliberalism has long presented itself as the only credible economic orthodoxy in town. It is an ideology that promotes the individual above society, that argues for lower taxes and fewer regulations, that downplays any real sense of corporate social responsibility, and that makes greed not just permissible, but praiseworthy.

There is growing recognition, however, that neoliberalism has been a false prophet. A 2016 report entitled "Neo-liberalism—Oversold?" showed how and why the ideology has failed.[3] It showed that deregulating capital movement and slashing public spending has increased inequality, and harmed the level and sustainability of growth that countries could otherwise have achieved. This wasn't an Oxfam report. This came from those famous radicals at the International Monetary Fund!

Second, there is, as I have touched upon, the capture of political and economic systems by wealthy elites. The fact that those with money can use it to exert influence over decision makers creates a vicious circle. More wealth leads to more power, which in turn allows the wealthy to rig the rules so they can accrue even more wealth, leaving everyone else far behind.

Tax rules are a powerful example of this. Grassroots activists and campaigners must contend with what feels like an army of accountants and lawyers, who are employed to help the world's most powerful companies and individuals avoid paying their fair share. Imagine if we were employing thousands of people in Wall Street to travel around the United States and developing countries and actually physically destroy public buildings, schools, hospitals, or sack teachers and nurses. There would be an outcry—and people would say they are violating the human rights of those affected.

Yet that is what is effectively taking place every day in these tall glass towers full of diligent accountants, lawyers, and bankers. It is shameful. According to the Centre for Responsive Politics, the two issues that US policymakers are lobbied on most are the federal budget and appropriations, and taxes. Oxfam's report, "Rigged Reform," showed how the fifty biggest US companies—including global brands such Pfizer, Goldman Sachs, Walmart, and Apple—have stashed about $1.6 trillion dollars offshore.[4] The same fifty companies spent $2.5 billion lobbying the US government between 2009 and 2015. An estimated $352 million was spent lobbying on tax issues—helping to secure over $423 billion in tax breaks. So for every $1 spent on lobbying, these fifty companies collectively received an estimated $1,200 in tax breaks. That is a scandalous rate of return.

If the causes of our broken tax system are not unique to tax, then our solutions will not be either. Power and accountability must be central to both our concept of tax justice and to the human rights framework. That focus demands we take a critical look at who is currently making the rules. The global tax system has insufficiently evolved over many decades. Some of the underlying principles remain stuck in the past, with rules that might have worked in the 1920s but which bear little relevance in the globalized economy that we have today. Fixing this anachronistic and tangled system will take coordinated, ambitious action from the world's governments. We can take some encouragement from the fact that there have been more attempts in recent years to start to get to grips with this.

The G20 and the OECD did recognize that something had to be done about corporate tax avoidance in particular. The so-called Base Erosion and Profit Shifting (BEPS) process that they initiated has taken some welcome steps in the right direction, improving the sharing of information between tax authorities, for example. These steps do not go nearly far enough, however, particularly in addressing the needs of developing countries. That is hardly surprising as a majority of developing countries—representing two-thirds of the world's governments—had no formal role in the negotiating process.

Many issues that are priorities for developing countries are still not addressed. For example, BEPS does not address the challenge of knowing whether the price of a good or service "traded" between different parts of the same global company is fair, or how to analyze and tackle harmful tax incentives. Developing countries would also like to see a greater focus on preventing tax avoidance through more systemic actions, whether broader agreement on anti-abuse rules or on new ways to tax multinationals in the twenty-first century.

We want to see steps taken toward the creation of an inclusive, accountable multilateral tax body, in which all countries have an equal seat at the table—something that Oxfam and others have long been calling for. Based upon the existing legal responsibilities that all states have to achieve full human rights, this new body should also be empowered to sanction governments whose policies are harming the ability of other countries to raise the revenue that they need to fulfill the rights of their own populations. It should require all states to undertake assessments of the human rights implications of their tax policies, within their own borders and for other countries. The United Nations must have a central role to play in this process, facilitating inclusive intergovernmental negotiations, ensuring that the voices of rich countries aren't allowed to dominate, and bringing in the private sector, civil society, and other multilateral institutions.

Even if progressive tax systems are agreed upon, ensuring that they actually work in practice represents a significant further challenge. That is where transparency comes in. Citizens—and governments—must be able to know how money is flowing within and across borders and where tax should be levied but is actually being avoided and evaded. A number of potential measures would be both powerful and pragmatic; technical but transformative. For example, multinational companies must be required to report publicly on their turnover, profits, and taxes in every country where they operate.

Similarly, we know that many rich individuals are using tax havens to hide their wealth or as bases from which to make investments, often through opaque layers of companies. The public has a right to know who really is behind these shell companies. The Panama Papers and the Paradise Papers had a powerful effect in raising global attention to this—and people around the world responded angrily. There is growing pressure for every country to establish public registries of beneficial ownership for all companies, trusts, and partnerships held there. It has been encouraging to see a wide range of countries commit to such public registries for companies within recent years, including the United Kingdom, France, Kenya, Nigeria, and Afghanistan. The European Union has made a similar commitment requiring public registers for companies. The United Kingdom will now require its overseas territories to publish public registers for companies.

Automatic exchange of information between revenue authorities will also help, though we must avoid insisting on full reciprocity if one country simply does not have the resources or capacity to provide as much information as another. Otherwise, we again risk disadvantaging poorer countries.

State capacity is critical. Governments and their revenue authorities, especially in poorer countries, have the odds stacked against them when they are up against the armies of tax lawyers and accountants employed by major tax dodgers. Sub-Saharan African countries would need to employ more than an estimated 650,000 additional tax officials for the region to have the same ratio of tax officials to population as the OECD average. So governments in poorer countries must invest in building up effective tax revenue authorities to collect the taxes that are due and to clamp down on abuses of the system. They must be supported in this endeavor, with sufficient resources and with the ability to impose meaningful sanctions on those who commit or facilitate tax dodging.

It has been in the interests of tax dodgers, and those who facilitate tax dodging, to make sure that tax laws are as complex and opaque as possible. It is essential that we find ways to demystify tax—to get people to see that their rights are at stake, and to show them that there is something they can do about it. Tax justice can only be achieved when citizens are able to make their voices heard at all stages of the process and can hold their governments to account on both policymaking and implementation.

Human rights frameworks give us further opportunities to hold governments and corporations to account. For example, governments who are not doing all they can to generate resources for essential public services, and who are thus failing to meet the economic and social rights of their citizens, could be challenged in national courts or through international fora such as the Human Rights Council.

The same can apply to corporations too. Tax behavior should be assessed alongside companies' other commitments to sustainable development under, for example, the UN Global Compact initiative, and should be seen as relevant to a company's "corporate responsibility to respect human rights" outlined in the UN Guiding Principles for Business and Human Rights.

Well-designed tax systems that redistribute wealth and drive spending on public goods are one of the best weapons we have in the fight against inequality and poverty. Badly designed tax systems, on the other hand, exacerbate both. When judging efforts at a national level, therefore, we must ask whether or not tax reforms will serve to reduce inequalities while raising enough money to fulfill the rights and needs of their citizens. We must look at whether countries are setting progressive marginal tax rates, at whether they are relying more on direct or indirect taxes, at whether they are implementing wealth and inheritance taxes, at their corporate tax rate and the effective incidence of this.

And when assessing efforts to reform tax at a global level, we must ask ourselves whether or not the reforms are making it easier for national governments to implement these kinds of progressive, effective tax systems within their own countries, or will they still find themselves at the mercy of the big multinationals and the global super-rich?

Creating a fairer tax system continues to be an uphill battle. But there are reasons for optimism. After multiple high-profile tax scandals, and as ordinary citizens around the world are feeling the impact of an economic system that is rigged against them, governments are under pressure to act and have taken some steps in the right direction. Lasting change will occur, I believe, when we make tax dodging and those who facilitate it morally unacceptable. Let us expose more than ever how tackling tax dodging is fundamental to realizing and respecting the human rights of people all over the world, and vital to ending the injustice of poverty.

NOTES

1. D. Weldon, 'Shareholder power "holding back economic growth"', *BBC News*, 24 July 2015, available online at https://www.bbc.com/news/business-33660426.
2. IMF, *Fiscal Policy and Income Inequality*, IMF Policy Paper (2014), at Figure 8, available online at https://www.imf.org/external/np/pp/eng/2014/012314.pdf.
3. J. D. Ostry, P. Loungani, and D. Furceri, IMF, 'Neoliberalism: Oversold?', *Finance & Development* (2016), available online at https://www.imf.org/external/pubs/ft/fandd/2016/06/pdf/ostry.pdf.
4. Oxfam, *Rigged Reform* (2017), available online at https://www.oxfamamerica.org/static/media/files/Rigged_Reform_FINAL.pdf.

ACKNOWLEDGMENTS

The co-editors are very grateful to the many people who contributed to planning, running, and participating in the conference that generated the chapters in this volume. The conference was organized by the Center for Human Rights and Global Justice at New York University School of Law, and particular thanks are due to Lauren Flanagan, Pamela Mercado, Nealofar Panjshiri, Deborah Popowski, Silvia de Rosa, and Anam Salem.

We received very helpful advice in relation to topics and speakers from our colleagues in the NYU School of Law Tax Program, and especially from Daniel Shaviro and Mitchell Kane. Allison Christians and Krishen Mehta also provided important insights.

The conference was followed by a workshop on legal accountability for tax injustice, which involved a range of advocates, practitioners, and scholars from around the world. We are grateful to the Open Society Foundations, and their Public Health Program, Fiscal Governance Program, and the Open Society Justice Initiative, for financial and logistical support for the workshop, as well as their participation in its conceptualization. Thanks are due to Betsy Apple, Ben Batros, Reema Hijazi, Rosalind McKenna, and Vera Mshana.

Other groups working on issues relating to taxation and human rights also provided valuable advice and assistance in the context of both the conference and the workshop. In particular, we are grateful to the staff of the Center for Economic and Social Rights, especially Niko Lusiani, and to the staff of Tax Justice Network, especially Alex Cobham and Liz Nelson.

We are also grateful to Jessye Freeman for assistance in editing the manuscript, and to Blake Ratcliff and his colleagues at Oxford University Press.

NOTES ON CONTRIBUTING AUTHORS

Philip Alston is John Norton Pomeroy Professor of Law at New York University School of Law and is also currently UN Special Rapporteur on extreme poverty and human rights.

Reuven S. Avi-Yonah is the Irwin I. Cohn Professor of Law and director of the International Tax LLM Program at the University of Michigan Law School. He specializes in corporate and international taxation. He has served as a consultant to the US Department of the Treasury and the Organisation for Economic Co-operation and Development (OECD) on tax competition, and is a member of the steering group for OECD's International Network for Tax Research.

Joshua D. Blank is Professor of Law at the University of California, Irvine School of Law. He previously taught at New York University School of Law, where he was Professor of Tax Law, Vice Dean for Technology-Enhanced Education, and Faculty Director of the Graduate Tax Program. His scholarship focuses on tax administration and compliance, taxpayer privacy and tax transparency, and taxation of business entities.

Troels Boerrild is Head of Responsible Investments at Danish Pension fund, MP Pension. At the time of writing he was Senior Policy and Advocacy Adviser at ActionAid Denmark.

Céline Braumann is a Lecturer and Researcher in the Department of European, International, and Comparative Law at the University of Vienna. She holds an LLM from New York University School of Law, and her research focuses on international economic law and the effects of and remedies for economic and social inequality and injustice.

Winnie Byanyima is Executive Director of Oxfam International. She is a global women's rights leader, human rights defender and a global authority on economic inequality. She served eleven years in the Ugandan Parliament, and has served at the African Union Commission and as Director of Gender and Development at the UN Development Program.

Allison Christians is the H. Heward Stikeman Chair in the Law of Taxationat McGill University Faculty of Law, where she teaches and writes on national, comparative, and international tax law and policy.

Alex Cobham is chief executive of the Tax Justice Network, and a founding member of the steering group of the Independent Commission for the Reform of International Corporate

Taxation (ICRICT). Previously he was a research fellow at the Center for Global Development, and before that held posts at Christian Aid, Save the Children, and Oxford University (St Anne's College and Queen Elizabeth House).

Arthur J. Cockfield is a Professor at Queen's University Faculty of Law, where he was appointed as a Queen's National Scholar. He is a senior research fellow at Monash University, and has been a Fulbright Visiting Chair in Policy Studies at the University of Texas at Austin. His research mainly focuses on tax law.

Mary Cosgrove is a lecturer on tax and accountancy at the J.E. Cairnes School of Business and Economics, National University of Ireland, Galway, and a doctoral candidate at the Irish Centre for Human Rights. She previously worked as a tax adviser for over fifteen years, including in a "Big Four" accountancy firm and a multinational enterprise.

Bridget J. Crawford is a Professor at the Elisabeth Haub School of Law at Pace University School of Law. She is a member of the American Law Institute and the American College of Trust and Estate Counsel, and her most recent book is *Feminist Judgments: Rewritten Tax Opinions* (with Anthony C. Infanti).

Olivier De Schutter is a professor at the University of Louvain (Belgium) and at SciencesPo (France). From 2008 to 2014 he was the UN Special Rapporteur on the right to food, and since 2015, has been a member of the UN Committee on Economic, Social and Cultural Rights.

Sandra Fredman is Professor of Law at the University of Oxford, a Fellow of the British Academy, and a Queen's Council (honoris causa). She has published widely in the fields of equality, labor law, and human rights. In 2012, she founded the Oxford Human Rights Hub, of which she is the director.

Michael Hanni is an Economic Affairs Officer in the Economic Development Division of the UN Economic Commission for Latin America and the Caribbean (ECLAC).

Daniel J. Hemel is an assistant professor at the University of Chicago Law School, where he teaches tax, administrative law, and torts. He previously clerked for Judge Michael Boudin on the US Court of Appeals for the First Circuit, Judge Sri Srinivasan on the US Court of Appeals for the District of Columbia Circuit, and Associate Justice Elena Kagan on the US Supreme Court.

Monica Iyer is a human rights attorney and consultant based in Milan, Italy. She has worked on human and civil rights issues for a number of nongovernmental, state, and international organizations, including the UN Office of the High Commissioner for Human Rights and the New York State Office of the Attorney General.

Mitchell A. Kane is the Gerald L. Wallace Professor of Taxation at New York University School of Law. He clerked for the Honorable Karen LeCraft Henderson of the US Court of Appeals for the DC Circuit and practiced law with the firm of Covington & Burling before joining the faculty at the University of Virginia School of Law.

Tracy A. Kaye is a Professor of Law and Eric Byrne Research Fellow at Seton Hall Law School. She specializes in US federal income tax law and international, European Union, and comparative tax law. She has been the Fulbright Senior Research Scholar at the University of Luxembourg, PwC Visiting Professor at the Vienna University of Economics and Business, and Research Scholar at the Max Planck Institute for Intellectual Property, Competition, and Tax Law. Prior to beginning her academic career at Seton Hall Law School, Kaye earned a B.S. in Accountancy, *magna cum laude*, at the University of Illinois; an M.S. in Taxation at DePaul University; and her J.D., *cum laude*, at the Georgetown University Law Center.

Matti Kohonen is Principal Adviser on the Private Sector, at Christian Aid. He worked for over ten years on the impact of financial and tax policies on developing countries and populations, and is a founding member of the Tax Justice Network and co-editor of a volume entitled *Tax Justice: Putting Global Inequality on the Agenda*.

Kathleen A. Lahey is Professor and Queen's National Scholar, Faculty of Law, Queen's University, Canada, and specializes in tax law, fiscal policy, and human rights. She was a Visiting Professor in Fiscal Policy at Umeå University, Sweden, Visiting Scholar at the International Tax Program, Harvard Law School, and has multijurisdictional expertise in tax, economic laws, and fiscal policies.

Michael Lennard is Chief of International Tax Cooperation in the Financing for Development Office of the United Nations. He previously held posts at the Organisation for Economic Co-operation and Development (OECD), the Australian Tax Office, and the Australian Government's Office of International Law, where he worked on tax, trade, investment, and human rights issues.

Ewan Livingston is Head of Corporate Partnerships at ActionAid UK, an international charity that works with women and girls living in poverty. He leads ActionAid's engagement with the private sector on issues including tax and human rights.

Nicholas Lusiani is Senior Advisor at Oxfam, focused on tax and inequality. At the time of writing the article in this volume, he directed the Human Rights in Economic Policy Program at the Center for Economic and Social Rights. He previously worked in the fields of business and human rights, external debt, humanitarian relief, indigenous rights in the extractive industry, and criminal justice.

Ricardo Martner is Chief of the Fiscal Affairs Unit in the Economic Development Division of the UN Economic Commission for Latin America and the Caribbean (ECLAC), and has worked with ECLAC since 1986. He has written widely in the field of public finance.

Gianluca Mazzoni is an SJD candidate at the University of Michigan Law School, where he also completed his LLM degree in International Tax in 2016. He was previously a trainee tax lawyer in a leading Italian tax law firm. His research is focused on the interaction between the right to privacy and data protection and tax law.

Beverly Moran is Professor of Law and Professor of Sociology at Vanderbilt University Law School, where she has taught since 2001. In addition to her work on the Internal Revenue Code, her interdisciplinary and multidisciplinary work encompasses empirical legal studies, international and comparative tax law, Islamic law, labor law, law and development, legal education, legal philosophy, and politics.

Annet Wanyana Oguttu is a professor of tax law at the University of Pretoria. She has published extensively on international tax law and is a rated researcher under South Africa's National Research Foundation. In 2014, the President of South Africa appointed her as a Commissioner of the South African Law Reform Commission, and in 2013, she became a member of the Davis Tax Committee to assess South Africa's tax policy framework.

Nikki Reisch is the Legal Director of the Center for Human Rights and Global Justice and a supervising attorney in the Global Justice Clinic at New York University School of Law. She previously worked as an advocate challenging adverse impacts of international financial and development institutions on communities in the Global South, and clerked for the Second and Ninth Circuit Courts of Appeals.

Radhika Sarin is a private sector policy adviser at Oxfam. She has over a decade of experience in research, advocacy, and campaigning on environmental, social justice, and governance issues, with a focus on countries rich in natural resources, served for four years on the global Board of the Extractive Industries Transparency Initiative, and was international coordinator of the Publish What You Pay civil society coalition.

Daniel Shaviro is the Wayne Perry Professor of Taxation at New York University School of Law. He previously worked at Caplin & Drysdale, a leading tax specialty firm, and at the Joint Congressional Committee on Taxation, and taught at the University of Chicago Law School. His scholarly work examines tax policy, budget policy, and entitlements issues.

Andre L. Smith is currently a visiting associate professor at the Howard University School of Law. He is the author of numerous law review articles and book chapters on tax law, administrative law, and critical race tax theory, including *Black Tax: Tax Law and Racial Economic Justice* exploring the links between tax and racial subordination.

Carla Spivack is the Oxford Research Professor of Law and Director of the Certificate in Estate Planning, at Oklahoma City University School of Law. She has written several articles about the intersection of inheritance law with gender, race, and class, and is currently working on a book called *How American Property Law (Still) Cheats Women and What to Do About It*.

Miranda Stewart is Professor at the University of Melbourne Law School where she is director of taxation studies and the tax group. Miranda is also a fellow the Tax and Transfer Policy Institute, Crawford School of Public Policy at the Australian National University, where she was the inaugural director from 2014-2018. Miranda has more than twenty-five years' tax experience in academia, government, and the private sector and researches across a wide range of tax law and policy topics including tax and globalization, taxation of businesses, not-for-profits, gender equality, budgeting and tax reform.

Matti Ylönen has a PhD in World Politics and is a post-doctoral researcher in University of Helsinki. He has published extensively on tax havens, global governance, policy consultancies, development policy, and corporate power. In 2015, his article on the politics of intra-firm trade was awarded the Amartya Sen Prize at Yale University. Ylönen is currently on finalizing a book project that focuses on the intellectual history of corporate power.

INTRODUCTION

Fiscal Policy as Human Rights Policy

PHILIP ALSTON AND NIKKI REISCH

I. INTRODUCTION

Just over a century ago, in 1917, the Austrian sociologist Rudolf Goldscheid described the national budget as "the skeleton of the state stripped of all misleading ideologies" and coined the term "fiscal sociology" to describe the importance of adopting a multidisciplinary approach to the study of taxation and public finance.[1] One year later, Joseph Schumpeter famously used the same term and expressed a similar idea in observing that "[t]he spirit of a people, its cultural level, its social structure, the deeds its policy may prepare" are all "written in its fiscal history, stripped of all phrases."[2] Far from restricting this claim to any given society, he went further to argue that understanding fiscal policy is central to being able to discern "the thunder of world history."[3] In other words, fiscal policy[4] is not just a dry and dull set of statistics but rather holds the key to understanding the deepest values of a society, and potentially even the interactions among societies. Both Goldscheid and Schumpeter also sought to contrast what they considered to be the bare and incontestable facts reflected in the budget with the "misleading ideologies" and empty "phrases" used by politicians, bureaucrats, and others to describe or perhaps misrepresent the policies they were purporting to promote.

In his lecture, which addressed the crisis of what he termed "the tax state" in the aftermath of World War I and the focus on reparations payable to the victors, Schumpeter identified public finances as "one of the best starting points for an investigation of society, especially . . . its political life."[5] He distinguished between the "causal" and the "symptomatic" importance of fiscal policy,[6] which could either be the direct cause of change in society, or it could merely reflect changes that were brought about by other means.

The principal inquiry animating the present volume seeks to understand why, a century after these insights started to shape the work of scholars in many fields, the suggestion that fiscal policy, including taxation, might be determinative or reflective of key aspects of human rights policy is often met with puzzlement. The conventional wisdom, shared by most policymakers, professionals, and government officials in both fields, is that human rights and taxation have little to do with one another. They would, of course, acknowledge that there are indirect impacts and connections, but just as tax might be linked to domestic violence or migration policies or many other challenging issues, these limited interactions do not warrant an effort to try to bring the two fields into sustained conversation with one another. Various tax experts to whom we reached out in preparing the conference on which this book is based were skeptical of the proposition that tax policies and systems have significant implications for human rights policy and practice, let alone that human rights law has relevance for tax law. In part this may be because the field of "human rights" is considered by many unfamiliar with it to be synonymous with civil and political rights. Because tax laws are generally assumed not to overtly discriminate on the grounds of race, gender, sexual orientation, disability, or other impermissible classifications, the social policy consequences of tax policy are not the concern of tax specialists. Similarly, the intense bargaining and negotiation that goes into the making of tax policies is often seen as the epitome of democratic decision-making in practice, rather than as a process that might, by its opacity and propensity to be hijacked by special interests, pose a threat to the assumptions underlying the democratic state. It is thus not surprising that even a recent volume dedicated to promoting interdisciplinary approaches to tax, with the stated aim of covering "the aspects of legality, morality, and psychology of tax avoidance, and the challenges of measurement of economic effect of various tax avoidance activities," nevertheless contains no substantive discussion of human rights.[7]

The puzzlement is generally every bit as strong on the human rights side of the ledger. Most major human rights groups avoid engaging in issues that they characterize as involving redistribution, let alone becoming involved in debates over fiscal policy.[8] While a handful of scholars and several influential advocacy groups have focused on the intersections between human rights and fiscal policy,[9] most human rights advocates shy away from issues that they see as technical and opaque, that require expertise which they may not have or could not readily acquire, and that are not susceptible to the analytical techniques routinely used in relation to traditional human rights concerns to identify clear-cut violations, to name those responsible, and to prescribe the solution. Even Samuel Moyn, whose book *Not Enough* is relentlessly critical of the human rights movement for not having addressed issues of inequality in a meaningful way, undertakes no analysis at all of the relevance of tax policy in any such endeavor.[10]

None of this is to single out human rights and tax specialists as being exceptionally rigid or narrowly focused. Indeed, in historical terms, their lack of direct engagement is consistent with the observation that "[f]or much of the twentieth century, most historians, sociologists, legal scholars, and political scientists did not ask questions about the social or institutional roots or consequences of taxation" because public finance was a matter for economists, who in turn did not concern themselves with the broader social implications of taxation.[11] It may still be argued, however, that human rights scholars and practitioners have been a little slower than other disciplines in recent times to acknowledge the critically important linkages between the two fields.

In philosophy, for example, Liam Murphy and Thomas Nagel observed in 2002 that the theoretical debates on social and economic justice, provoked in part by John Rawls's book *A Theory of Justice*, had led to remarkably little engagement with tax policy, despite its centrality to most conceptions of justice.[12] But their analysis had a major impact and philosophers have subsequently become very actively involved in discussions around taxation and fiscal justice.[13] This does not mean, however, that the term human rights—let alone the body of rights specifically recognized in international law—has been a principal focus of attention. Thus, a recent volume in which a dozen different contributors reflect on the philosophical foundations of tax law, and which acknowledges the strong influence of Murphy and Nagel's *The Myth of Ownership*, contains many references to morality, justice, equality, and so on, but not a single reference to human rights or the attendant obligations assumed by all governments.[14]

Beyond the confines of philosophy, a range of other disciplines, including law, now engage systematically with the social and other implications of fiscal policy, leading some scholars to claim that this "new wave of multidisciplinary scholarship on taxation" signifies the emergence of a field which they call "the new fiscal sociology."[15] This nascent field synthesizes and transcends the three major streams of interdisciplinary work on tax that these authors identify as having dominated the period since World War II. These are: (1) modernization theory, which focused on the interactions between levels of development and fiscal policy; (2) elite theory, which sought to explain why people consent to pay taxes, despite the assumption of an underlying conflict of interest between rulers and the subjects they sought to tax; and (3) militarist theory, which viewed bellicosity as a prime motivation for developing more effective systems of tax collection. In both challenging and drawing upon each of these three approaches, the new fiscal sociology adopts a crosscutting approach that "points towards a new theory of taxation as a social contract."[16] While some of the writing in this burgeoning field, as well as the more longstanding critical tax literature,[17] addresses classic human rights issues such as racial inequality and gender discrimination,[18] for the most part the normative content and framework of international human rights law are rarely discussed.

It is of course not enough to merely point out either that the majority of human rights scholars and practitioners have been late in coming to the fiscal policy debate, or that most of those who are now engaged in multidisciplinary approaches to the consequences of fiscal policy pay scant, if any, regard to human rights norms. The burden of this book is to make the affirmative case as to why there are important synergies to be had if the fields of human rights and tax are brought into sustained conversation with one another.

This introduction seeks to respond to that challenge. Section II illustrates some of the linkages between tax and human rights. Section III outlines the content of the rich and diverse contributions made by the authors of the chapters that follow. Section IV argues that those who are concerned with growing income and wealth inequality, rapidly increasing economic insecurity among the middle class, the persistence of unconscionable levels of extreme poverty, and the rise of populist and illiberal regimes need to devote more attention to the fact that the dominant orthodox economic policies accord priority to the goal of fiscal consolidation, which has a range of extremely negative consequences. Finally, section V concludes by identifying some of the ways in which human rights norms should be brought to bear in future debates over fiscal policy.

II. ILLUSTRATING THE LINKAGES

Taxation affects which resources stay in private versus public hands, which activities are encouraged or discouraged, how much is available to the state, and who pays for and receives the public goods and services the state provides. Human rights, in turn, inform not only how tax policy should be made, but what policies are permissible, when, and why, setting parameters for the revenue-raising objectives and distributive effects of taxation, as well as the processes by which tax laws are adopted and implemented. In short, tax affects the realization of human rights in all countries, developed and developing alike, through its role in resource mobilization, redistribution, regulation, and representation.[19]

Resource mobilization: All rights cost money and require public policies to support them.[20] Taxes generate most of the revenue that states can use to protect and promote the rights of their populations. Because they largely determine the overall "size of the pie," fiscal policies are an indispensable part of the equation for determining, in accordance with the relevant international legal obligations, whether states have taken steps to the "maximum of available resources" to realize human rights.[21]

Redistribution: State budgets are fundamentally about redistribution of resources. Whether those policies are progressive or regressive depends on the nature of the government's tax policies along with its spending priorities. These in turn affect the types and degrees of inequality within the society. It is in large part because tax policy transfers resources from one part of society to another that it is both unpopular and contested. But it is also opaque. It is true that taxes imposed on the richest 20 percent in most countries will end up paying for the vast majority of social protection services.[22] Less frequently acknowledged but equally true, however, is the fact that, in many countries, the net transfers from the government budget to the wealthy will be far higher than any of the comparable amounts paid out in welfare or other public services to the poor. An analysis of winners and losers of US tax policy reached the following conclusion:

> Most tax expenditures redistribute from the rich and the upper-middle class to the middle and upper-middle classes. They help close the gap between the haves and the have-lots rather than between the have-nots and the have-lots. Normally we expect social programs to fight inequality and poverty. Tax expenditures address inequality in the upper half of the income distribution and generally do little to reduce poverty.[23]

Australian tax policies illustrate the same point. A 2018 report showed that the bottom 20 percent of Australians in terms of wealth received A$6.1 billion in tax concessions and exemptions, while the top 20 percent received over ten times that amount (A$68 billion).[24] And in Ghana, a 2017 study showed that very little fiscal redistribution takes place through the budget, and that were it not for in-kind benefits to the poor from health and education spending, the overall effect of government spending and taxation would actually increase poverty in Ghana.[25]

Tax policies also affect the distribution of resources among states. The differential tax treatment of domestic and foreign entities in a given country, and variations in tax law between jurisdictions, influence the global flow and distribution of assets.

Regulation: Tax policies incentivize or disincentivize a vast array of economic, social, cultural, political, religious, artistic, and other types of conduct. The list of tax-influenced decisions in any society is potentially infinite, including where children go to school, which media people watch or read, who gives money and for what causes, what forms of medical care will be accessible, and what environmentally friendly policies will be promoted. The issue of gender discrimination in taxation is a particularly good example in this regard. Taxes "affect patterns of marriage, childbearing, work, savings, education, charity, home ownership, and more."[26] While it is relatively uncommon today for tax laws to explicitly establish different rates or benefits for men and women, less overt forms of gender discrimination persist. For example, there is growing outrage over "pink taxes," involving higher prices charged for goods marketed to women and lower prices for comparable products marketed to men or sold as gender-neutral.[27] In addition, women are overrepresented among the poor and bear the brunt of cuts to public spending, whether through the direct loss of services on which they depend or the increase in unpaid care work they provide to make up for insufficient social support.[28]

Representation: The nature of the relationship between the government and the governed is reflected in and influenced by fiscal policy. In terms of design and implementation, taxes can either reinforce or undermine the state's accountability to the public and the robustness of democratic institutions.

One of the most important dimensions of the relationship between human rights and tax policies in the current era is the increasingly global nature of many of the challenges and thus of the needed solutions. More and more, both tax law and human rights law are called upon to address cross-border and multijurisdictional phenomena, such as the extraterritorial human rights impacts of state conduct and the global operations of companies, the tax consequences of which are not confined to a single territory. The sovereign territorial state is increasingly rivaled by the footloose transnational corporation, complicating efforts both to control corporate conduct (the human rights advocate's problem) and to capture corporate profit (the tax collector's problem). But the legal and regulatory frameworks for managing these impacts often remain rooted in one or other national jurisdiction. The growth of the global economy and the dominance of transnational enterprises today have eroded traditional notions of state sovereignty, enhancing the power and role of nonstate actors domestically and internationally. The displacement of the state as *the* central actor calls into question the continued relevance of international tax and human rights law and institutions insofar as they are designed around and rooted in the sovereign state. The shift poses a host of questions about how to effectively regulate conduct, implement, and enforce principles and norms in a world in which neither cause nor effect respects national borders.

Tax avoidance and evasion are by no means new phenomena. But the pervasiveness of the practices and the scale of the resultant revenue losses have garnered worldwide attention in the past several years, following unprecedented disclosures and sophisticated investigative reporting into the world of cross-border profit-shifting and offshore accounts. The leaking of the Paradise Papers in November 2017 is just the latest in a long and growing list of revelations about the widespread, systemic nature of officially sanctioned tax avoidance and evasion schemes that benefit corporations and rich individuals.[29] That list includes the 2014 LuxLeaks disclosures and the 2016 Panama Papers release, among others.[30]

Multinational corporations are especially well placed to exploit the climate of competition rather than cooperation between countries around tax matters by shifting their private profits between jurisdictions. Leaked information regarding multinational corporate tax deals has exposed how Ireland,[31] the Netherlands,[32] and Luxembourg[33] have facilitated tax avoidance by some of the world's largest companies, including Apple, Starbucks, Disney, IKEA, and Fiat. Similarly, a study released by the Australian tax office in December 2017 found that more than a third of "the largest public companies and multinational entities in Australia paid no tax in the most recent financial year on record."[34] Although facilitated by certain states' policies on financial secrecy and corporate reporting, corporations would not be able to minimize their tax burdens without the active involvement of various private actors, including lawyers and accountants.

The consequences of corporate tax dodging are by no means limited to financial secrecy states; losses affect both the host and home countries of the corporations involved. When wealthy entities avoid paying their fair share of taxes, the public suffers in multiple ways—and some populations disproportionately so. Nowhere does tax dodging take a larger toll than in developing countries, which depend more heavily than industrialized countries on corporate income tax as a source of public revenue and have far less cushion in their budgets to start.[35] Tax abuse, defined broadly as "practices contrary to the letter or spirit of global or national tax laws and policies,"[36] threatens rights, particularly in the Global South, for at least two reasons. First, because of overall resource scarcity, the consequences of lost revenues for the state's ability to combat poverty and fulfill its human rights obligations may be starker in many of the world's poorest countries than elsewhere. Second, many developing countries lack a broad tax base and suffer from weak tax administration, such that taxes paid by the corporate sector are among the few sources of public revenue.[37] The close interrelationship between tax havens in the North and tax avoidance in the South presents a potential opportunity to introduce the language of human rights into debates about fiscal policies in developed countries and to underscore the human rights obligations of those states not only to their own populations but also to persons abroad. It remains difficult, however, to connect the dots.

Although muted and far slower than many activists would like, official reactions to the tax scandals have been gathering steam. The European Commission has been at the forefront of attempts to curb tax abuse and the inter-state tax competition that fuels the practice, as exemplified by its pursuit of Ireland for providing a *de facto* tax haven to corporations like Apple. In December 2017, on the heels of the Paradise Papers exposé and following the conclusion of an EU inquiry into tax avoidance and evasion, the European Parliament adopted a recommendation calling on member states to implement public country-by-country reporting on corporate profits, subsidies, and taxes.[38] Transparency measures like this, long advocated by civil society organizations such as the Tax Justice Network, represent one way in which states can take back the reins and begin fulfilling their human rights obligations both to protect against third-party conduct that undermines human rights and to mobilize maximum available resources to realize human rights.

Other intergovernmental organizations have likewise increased their attention to global tax policies and problems, with discussions of taxation dominating G20 and Organisation for Economic Co-operation and Development (OECD) meetings in recent years,[39] as well as demands within the United Nations for the creation of a new international tax commission.[40]

III. CONTRIBUTIONS TO THIS VOLUME

The chapters in this volume demonstrate that there are many entry points into the broader debate about the relationship between human rights and taxation. The first part of the volume introduces fundamental points of intersection between the fields of tax and human rights, with scholars from both arenas discussing the promise and the limits of bringing the disciplines into dialogue with one another. This part includes an opening chapter that maps the evolving landscape of the tax and human rights debate, including its antecedents in discussions regarding public budgeting, critical tax theory, and development. The second set of chapters examines tax policy and problems in global perspective, focusing on the cross-border nature and human rights impacts of tax abuses and evaluating potential solutions. Part III looks at the role of states in facilitating or preventing harmful tax policies and practices, specifically through transparency regulations. The fourth part of the book includes chapters that look critically and creatively at the roles and responsibilities of private actors in shaping tax policy and practice, and prospects for holding tax wrongdoers accountable. Part IV brings together essays that examine various domestic tax laws and policies in light of the foundational human rights concepts of equality and nondiscrimination. The final part identifies synergies between the tax and human rights agendas around efforts to tackle economic, social, and political inequalities. It includes a chapter that highlights the redistributive potential of revenue-raising tools, and two chapters contrasting approaches to the feasibility and desirability of a universal basic income. The aim of this collection is to lay a foundation for a new, critical human rights discourse on tax policies and practices in an age of growing inequality. The contributions to this volume are not as geographically representative as the editors would have liked. The focus is primarily on tax policies and practices in the global North. This is in part because of the outsize influence exerted by US tax laws on those of many other countries, whether through a demonstration effect, influence on policy assumptions, or tax competition. Nonetheless, there is a need for future conversations on tax and human rights to better address diverse realities, and to bring in diverse voices, from across the globe.

In Part I the opening chapters grapple with the task of conceptualizing the relationship between tax and human rights, and identifying the fundamental changes required to bring the two fields into alignment. From the human rights perspective, there is a need for advocates to address the economic and fiscal challenges and trade-offs involved in implementing human rights obligations, rather than sticking to the familiar terrain of defining normative principles. This shift requires them to take account of issues of economic and social justice accompanied by a fairer societal distribution of resources.

With an eye toward the challenges of tackling implementation, Olivier De Schutter's chapter focuses on the application of human rights law to state tax policy, identifying normative principles by which UN human rights treaty supervisory bodies, like the Committee on Economic, Social and Cultural Rights, can assess whether a state's tax laws and practices comply with its human rights obligations. He identifies four key objectives toward which state tax policies must strive: widening the tax base, ensuring progressivity, plugging holes in the tax system, and strengthening participation and accountability around tax policy. De Schutter emphasizes that the progressivity of a state's fiscal policy depends on not only how tax revenues are *raised* but also how they are *spent*. He provides an overview of recent literature on the impacts of tax policy on investment decisions, and traces recent international efforts to curb illicit financial flows. Stemming the loss of state revenue to cross-border tax abuses, De Schutter argues, will require action on at least three fronts: to strengthen the capacity of domestic tax administrations, to increase recognition of states' extraterritorial human rights obligations, and to enhance the due diligence undertaken by corporations and financial institutions to minimize tax avoidance.

Sandra Fredman proposes a four-dimensional conception of substantive equality to evaluate the gendered impacts of taxation policies from a human rights perspective. She explores how patterns of persistent gender roles in work and migration interact with tax policy to produce asymmetrical fiscal outcomes, entrench gender stereotypes, and reinforce male-dominated institutions and structures in ways that violate the human right to equality. In particular, she examines the increased reliance on consumption taxes, such as the value-added tax (VAT), and continued joint filing requirements for married couples' personal income tax in many countries.

From the perspective of tax scholars, addressing the patently unsatisfactory situation in the international tax regime requires a fundamental rethinking of the premises on which global taxing powers are allocated. Several chapters in this volume reconceptualize fairness in international taxation in light of human rights principles, scrutinizing the foundations for and distribution of the rights to tax, as well as the structure and objectives of international tax policies and institutions.

Mitchell Kane questions the rightful claims of developed and developing countries to portions of the "international tax base." He identifies a common starting point for tax and human rights experts intent on reform: the inadequacy of tax revenues. Although Kane is skeptical about what human rights discourse can add to existing tax reform incentives, he explores several possible normative angles. He offers a radical rethink of the allocation of taxing rights across countries, recasting the traditional source-residence dichotomy in favor of a system for allocating gains from trade between nations, and examining the duties states hold vis-à-vis one another to explore whether these alternative approaches could achieve more just outcomes. He suggests that surplus gains from trade between states, which cannot be said to belong to either state, could be allocated globally to those most in need. Kane further posits that there may be human rights justifications for requiring states with greater income and capacity in their tax administrations to undertake against-interest downward adjustments to profits booked in a country other than where they were generated.

Allison Christians explores the prospects for bringing legal claims seeking accountability for human rights harms due to tax policies and practices, based on the relationship between an individual and her own state, between an individual and a foreign state, or between two or more states. She traces the shortcomings of past attempts to challenge states' failure to raise sufficient tax revenue and corporations' failure to pay sufficient taxes, as well as efforts to define minimum standards of conduct that states owe one another. Although she views tax law as a viable target of human rights advocacy and legal action, she expresses skepticism about the capacity of the law to disentangle the multiplicity of causal factors that contribute to tax shortfalls or to surmount the opacity of taxpayer behavior. She acknowledges that pursuing accountability for tax abuses will require addressing not only state but corporate conduct.

Part II examines the global dimensions of tax policies and abuses, and the efficacy of institutional responses to date. Alex Cobham tackles questions of accountability by focusing on the role of states in actively procuring profit shifting across borders. He emphasizes taxation as a social act, with the potential not only to build or poison the social contract domestically, but to strengthen or undermine inter-state relations in the global community and the capacities of other states to fulfill the rights of their people. After sketching the different perceptions of state responsibility for financial secrecy and tax avoidance globally, Cobham identifies several tools that can be used to challenge the state's role in profit shifting. These range from state-shaming through human rights instruments, to inter-state claims under World Trade Organization (WTO) procedures and unilateral or multilateral tax measures that would affect state behavior.

Nicholas Lusiani and Mary Cosgrove examine the challenges of attributing responsibility for the cross-border impacts of tax and financial secrecy policies through "spillover assessments." They highlight the consequences of the human rights community's neglect of tough issues regarding public financing: human rights experts have been sidelined in debates about the fiscal foundations of social progress, and remain largely ignorant of one of "the most fundamental ways through which power and equality are mediated in society and in the economy: taxation."[41] The authors identify ten principles, based on eight lessons from experience with other types of impact assessments, which can help enhance the human rights-compatibility of tax spillover assessments. But they also acknowledge the significant methodological and political hurdles that remain to ensure all countries assess and address the impacts of their tax policies beyond their borders.

Chapters by Michael Lennard, Annet Oguttu, and Monica Iyer provide critical reflections on the promise and limitations of international tax reform efforts. In particular, they consider how discussions of problems that are truly global in scope have been dominated by a limited number of powerful countries and have expressly left untouched the fundamental biases in the international tax regime in favor of residence countries over source countries. They interrogate the consistency of international reform proposals with human rights principles and imperatives, including self-determination, equal representation, and access to information.

Beginning from the premise that addressing losses of revenue due to tax abuses and improving the international tax system is critical to the realization of human rights globally, Lennard takes an in-depth look at the Organisation for Economic Co-operation and Development (OECD) Base Erosion and Profit Shifting (BEPS) Project, critically examining the rhetorical commitments of OECD members to treating developing countries on an "equal footing." He highlights the systematic exclusion of non-OECD member countries from norm-setting bodies, and concerns about biases toward developed, capital-exporting countries in provisions regarding mandatory arbitration. These observations lead him to suggest that many of the BEPS outcomes will be less universally beneficial than advertised.

Oguttu and Iyer assess whether key components of the international tax reforms agreed through the BEPS Project will ensure that African countries get their fair share of taxes from multinational corporations operating within their borders, thereby in principle enabling the relevant governments to deliver on their human rights obligations. They focus on several of the abusive tax practices that are most concerning to African countries, as net capital-importers— namely, improper deductions of intragroup interest payments, payments for services, and payments of royalties for the use of intellectual property.

Part III turns to the responsibilities of states for enhancing tax transparency, and the tensions that exist between transparency measures and competing conceptions of the human rights of taxpayers and the public at large. Reuven Avi-Yonah and Gianluca Mazzoni explore the appropriate balance between strengthening tax revenue collection tools to ensure states have adequate resources to meet their human rights obligations, and protecting taxpayer rights to privacy and data security. Some readers may find controversial the authors' characterization of "legitimate protection of trade secrets" as a human right, but all will appreciate their careful analysis of the compatibility of corporate reporting obligations and other tax transparency measures under OECD and US requirements with the framework on privacy and data protection under the European Convention on Human Rights. The authors contend that current automatic information exchange requirements are overbroad and thus risk infringing on privacy and information rights. They call for enhanced due diligence procedures. On the other hand, they argue that public country-by-country reporting requirements would not infringe on taxpayer rights, both because corporations already make much of this information available and because legal entities do not have privacy rights.

As Joshua Blank and Arthur Cockfield discuss in their respective chapters, the design and timing of tax transparency measures can influence their efficacy. While challenging the conventional defenses of corporate tax privacy, Blank argues that such privacy may actually help limit the pressure faced by corporations to pursue more aggressive tax strategies. Adopting an "intercorporate" perspective, Blank contends that if firms had access to increased information about their competitors' tax practices, they could engage in reverse engineering or benchmarking, which could ultimately drive more tax avoidance. Blank does not categorically oppose increased corporate tax transparency in light of these risks, but rather calls on policymakers and human rights advocates interested in public disclosure to consider these unexpected consequences and the strategic defenses of tax privacy when evaluating reform proposals.

Arthur Cockfield takes a close look at exchange of information (EOI) policies, which have developed in recent years with a speed uncharacteristic of the tax field. He proposes several ways to make EOI policies fairer and more efficient, so as to maximize their potential to reduce illicit financial flows and curb abusive tax practices that undermine human rights. Cockfield calls for a focus on the exchange of high-quality information that can be cross-indexed and is useful to and verifiable by governments, while recognizing the challenges posed by taxpayer privacy concerns and misaligned government incentives.

In her chapter, Tracy Kaye warns of the risks of allowing a country as influential as the United States to lag behind in the global movement for tax transparency, and highlights the human rights imperatives for the United States to use information laws to regulate corporate conduct. She contends that compliance with the UN Guiding Principles on Business and Human Rights (UNGP) and other international human rights obligations requires the United States to increase disclosure of information regarding companies' beneficial ownership, as a means of combatting tax avoidance and evasion. She encourages advocates in the human rights community who are pushing for increased tax transparency to train their sights on the United States, as one of the largest and most persistent tax haven jurisdictions, hiding in plain view.

Miranda Stewart takes a step back from the technical policy discussions of the preceding chapters and explores the evolution of calls for tax transparency from a more sociological perspective. She identifies tensions between concepts of transparency and human rights, querying whether increased disclosure of taxpayer information actually serves to hold governments, rather than the targeted taxpayers, accountable.

Part IV examines the role of private actors implicated in abusive tax practices, from corporations to their lawyers and accountants, asking tough ethical questions, calling for greater attention to the role corporate power plays in influencing tax policies, and examining the prospects for greater corporate accountability through voluntary measures, regulation, or legal action. Through a fictional discussion between a lawyer and an economist, Daniel Shaviro invites readers to reflect on where the ethical lines should be drawn around what constitutes "legally defensible tax planning," given social justice imperatives. Because tax minimization by wealthy individuals and profitable corporations does not involve blatant fraud, Shaviro contends, one cannot simply call for "good corporate tax behavior" and lambast the ethics of those tax professionals who aid and abet the fraud. The issue requires greater nuance. The entertaining fictional dialogue emphasizes how fluid the concept of "legality" is in the realm of US tax law, given *ex ante* uncertainties about tax auditing and the leniency of penalties.

In a critical review of trends in the tax justice movement, Matti Ylönen advocates a shift away from the current focus on state responsibility for the human rights impacts of tax policy and practice, toward a greater emphasis on corporate power over states—a focus that was largely eclipsed when the anticorruption agenda displaced earlier international efforts to regulate corporate conduct. Through a historical overview of the discourse surrounding corporate power and corruption, Ylönen provides context for current debates around responsibility for and the consequences of tax abuse.

In their coauthored chapter, Matti Kohonen, Radhika Sarin, Troels Boerrild, and Ewan Livingston identify several areas of convergence between the fields of tax policy and human rights, including: the concept of the corporation as a unitary entity; the notion of extraterritorial impacts and obligations; and the risks of corporate personhood. The authors distinguish between the state-mediated impacts of tax abuse on human rights, experienced through the effects of lost tax revenues on the public budget, and those human rights impacts that stem more directly from corporate conduct, such as decisions regarding the location and quality of employment, consumer prices, and the treatment of local shareholders. Drawing on a report entitled *Getting to Good: Toward Responsible Corporate Tax Behaviors*, and the UNGP, the authors suggest some regulatory changes and voluntary corporate measures that could help curb abusive practices, and call for the inclusion of a wider range of stakeholders in debates about responsible taxation.

Céline Braumann's chapter takes up the challenge framed in Christians's chapter, regarding the impediments to pursuing accountability for the adverse impacts of tax policy and practices on human rights, holding tax avoiders accountable, and applying the right to remedy in the tax arena. Braumann explores the prospects for challenging a tax exemption granted to a private company by invoking the prohibition on discrimination in the European Charter on Human Rights. Braumann traces how a hypothetical equal protection suit brought by a smaller fast food company that does not enjoy the same tax exemption as McDonald's subsidiary in Luxembourg might be analyzed under the jurisprudence of the European Court of Human Rights. Braumann acknowledges the challenge of proving the protected grounds on which the discrimination claim would be based, qualifying the nature of the harm suffered, and overcoming any legitimate state justification for the differential economic treatment of companies. But, she suggests, such litigation could help expose how some types of state-sanctioned tax avoidance violate human rights, and problematize the notion that tax avoidance is "perfectly legal" under all legal regimes.

Picking up on the themes introduced by De Schutter and Fredman in the first part of the book, the chapters in Part V examine tax regimes in light of the foundational principles of human rights: equality and nondiscrimination. Beverly Moran examines how the US tax code, like many OECD country tax codes, favors capital over labor, and thereby is at odds with fundamental tenets of human rights and policy principles regarding equity. She argues that this bias in favor of capital may not only be counterproductive in terms of its impacts on revenue generation and tax administration. It also entrenches inequalities and disregards the ways in which the human body, with its labor capacity, is the most essential "asset" on which most people rely. Labor, she contends, therefore should enjoy the preferences, such as the realization principle and depreciation, from which capital currently benefits.

The chapter coauthored by Bridget Crawford and Carla Spivack and that written by Andre Smith tackle taxation and group subordination, articulating the imperative for tax reform as a component of broader campaigns for gender and racial equality. Crawford and Spivack examine the gender biases embedded in facially neutral tax laws, focusing specifically on so-called "tampon taxes," levies exacted on menstrual hygiene products. They catalog the various human rights affected by tampon taxes, including the rights to be free from discrimination, to health, to education, to work, and to dignity, and contemplate potential venues and strategies for legal challenges in the European Union, the United States, and elsewhere. Strikingly, the European Court of Human Rights precedents they cite regarding gender discrimination involve suits brought by men complaining of disparate treatment (being denied benefits to which similarly situated women were entitled)—much as some of the earliest cases recognizing gender discrimination in the United States were brought by men.[42]

Andre Smith queries whether there is a national trend in the United States toward disproportionate imposition of regressive taxes on low-income communities of color, reflective of a deliberate effort to shift the tax burden from the wealthy and white to the poor and black. He examines the evidence, from places like Ferguson, Missouri, that policing for profit amounts to a form of regressive and racially subordinating taxation exacted disproportionately on African Americans, through fines, fees, and forfeiture driven by budget demands rather than safety needs.[43] Smith then looks at whether "sin" taxes, such as soda and cigarette taxes, may suffer from the same disconnect between their stated public health aims and their disparate impacts on low-income communities of color. Given the fluid definition of what constitutes a "tax" in the United States, Smith encourages readers to consider whether the various voter suppression tactics on the rise in recent years amount to twenty-first-century poll taxes.

Kathleen Lahey argues that the widespread and growing reliance on consumption taxes across the globe is at odds with fundamental human rights, particularly those of women in the most impoverished countries. Drawing on an extensive data set from one low-income country, Lahey exposes the inadequacy of current measures to mitigate the regressive impacts of value-added tax (VAT), particularly on female-headed households and female-owned businesses. She argues that the text of the Convention on the Elimination of All Forms of Discrimination Against Women (CEDAW), the CEDAW Committee's jurisprudence, and the Beijing Platform all mandate the use of more progressive tax strategies, such as graduated personal income taxes and broader VAT exemptions to cover all basic needs, as well as gender-impact analysis of taxation and correction of discriminatory policies.

The final part of the book looks at areas of synergy in the tax and human rights agendas around issues of economic inequality, with a particular focus on the relationship between fiscal policy and social protection. Although taxation has the capacity to alleviate inequality through redistribution, as Michael Hanni and Ricardo Martner argue, current tax policies and new tax proposals risk entrenching the divide. Loopholes, meanwhile, remain largely untouched. Based on their survey of inequality trends and the redistributive potential of fiscal policies in Latin America, the authors suggest that increased mobilization of tax revenues from the middle class, the segment of society with the highest "tax morale," could help rectify the frayed fiscal compact—the fragile agreement between the governed and the government about what sums the former owe as taxpayers and what services the latter provides in return. Hanni and Martner suggest that a new fiscal compact might be constructed around the Sustainable Development Goals, through a holistic approach focused on public tax revenues and spending priorities. They emphasize the need to: rely on direct taxation, which could help close the gap between the rich and the poor and improve the realization of human rights; maximize the potential redistributive impacts of taxes and transfers; and improve service delivery.

Daniel Hemel's chapter takes the form of a philosophical argument, positing what he describes as a human rights–based justification for national basic income schemes, which he contrasts with justifications based on welfarist principles or notions of entitlement to a share of the global commons. Starting from the premise that a state is a collective enterprise that generates a surplus—which he assumes to be an economic or financial surplus, readily monetizable—Hemel contends that any human being who is an "obedient" member of that state has a right to some share of the surplus, though not necessarily an equal share to others, nor a uniform share across countries. That right, which arises from the relationship between the individual and the state, and is independent of need, could justify the entitlement to a basic income. Hemel maintains such income should be provided in cash, not in kind, because the latter risks depriving the individual of the enjoyment of his share of the surplus—in effect, forcing him to forfeit or transfer it to others if he does not use the public goods or services provided by the state. He explores several potential counterarguments and leaves readers to ponder whether the theoretical justification offered for universal basic income would overcome the "infeasibility challenge," because it does not hold that every individual is entitled to the same absolute amount of income, but rather that he or she is entitled to some share, based on the size of the surplus generated in the state of which he or she is a law-abiding member.

Finally, Philip Alston examines the arguments for and against a universal basic income (UBI) in light of the provisions of international human rights law, and also takes issue with some of the arguments put forward in the preceding chapter by Hemel. Alston emphasizes the importance of more creative approaches to ensuring social protection throughout society and suggests that a UBI might be an important step forward in some societies but not in others. He notes that proponents of the scheme cite radically different arguments to support it, and that the potential of any such scheme will depend very largely on which of these diverse motivations is dominant in shaping the approach adopted.

IV. SHINING THE SPOTLIGHT ON FISCAL CONSOLIDATION

A key issue that underpins some of the phenomena examined in the chapters reviewed above is the policy of fiscal consolidation, strongly promoted by most international economic institutions and prized by financial markets. Because none of the other contributions to the volume examine it in any detail, this section explores the role that this particular fiscal policy has played and continues to play in relation to major challenges such as economic insecurity, radical inequality, extreme poverty, and particularly the rise of populist and illiberal regimes. The last of these problems has become particularly acute in the wake of the Brexit vote, Donald Trump's election, the global turn to populism, and the evolution of a range of nominally democratic regimes openly manifesting strong authoritarian tendencies.[44] More specifically, many governments "have repudiated liberal norms of tolerance and openness, restricted press freedom, attacked institutional checks that promote the rule of law, and catalyzed constitutional and statutory transformations that promise to entrench populist coalitions beyond fresh democratic defeat."[45] The result is that the "formal accoutrements of elections and partisan competition persist largely as tattered facades masking increasingly authoritarian political formations."[46] The key question for our purposes is how fiscal policies are relevant to these developments.

While scholars and commentators have offered many explanations for these trends, most have acknowledged the role played by the increasing economic insecurity experienced by the middle class and often linked to the consequences of globalization and the pursuit of neoliberal policies. Even Ben Bernanke, the former Chairman of the US Federal Reserve Bank, and a staunch defender of most aspects of the neoliberal world order, has described the main challenges to the US economy as stagnant median wages, limited upward mobility, social dysfunction, and political alienation. As an antidote, he has argued for the need to "refocus attention on both the moral necessity and practical benefits of helping people cope with the economic disruptions that accompany growth."[47] Fiscal policy is crucial to that endeavor, and if the moral dimensions are really going to be taken seriously, there is a strong argument that human rights norms such as the right to an adequate standard of living would be an appropriate starting point.

The starting point for understanding the linkages between human rights and fiscal policies in the era of rising nationalism, authoritarianism, and disillusionment with the traditional role of the state is to review the main characteristics of the fiscal policies that have been aggressively promoted by powerful actors at the international level in recent years and that have shaped or at least influenced economic policy in the vast majority of countries. In historical terms, it is possible to trace the evolution of mainstream fiscal orthodoxy starting with the "tax state" of the post–World War II era, which relied heavily on generating significant tax revenues in order to support a strong welfare role for the state. It was followed by the "debt state" of the 1980s and 1990s in which governments let expenditures outpace revenue, then borrowed heavily, and were ultimately forced to retrench. The current fiscal era has been termed that of the "consolidation state."[48] Underpinned by powerfully ascendant neoliberal economic theories, the emphasis is on the quest to achieve fiscal consolidation or sustainability, which translates into the reduction of deficits either by reducing expenditures or by raising taxes.[49]

"Consolidation" is a euphemism that, in the abstract, has neutral and even benign connotations. It contrasts with the term "austerity" that was widely used to describe the sort of "adjustment" policies that the International Monetary Fund and its allies energetically promoted around the globe with the emergence of the "Washington Consensus" in the 1980s. But the

Fund now shuns the use of words such as austerity and adjustment and talks instead about the need for fiscal consolidation and fiscal sustainability.[50] While it insists that its prescriptions are carefully tailored to the circumstances of each country, there is a sense that the basic advice is as predictable as the daily weather forecast in Ireland, which invariably foresees scattered showers and sunny spells. Advice proffered to Ghana in 2017 captures its essence:

> Restoring fiscal discipline and putting debt on a downward path will require credible and sustained fiscal consolidation, underpinned by strong structural fiscal reforms.[51]

In the eyes of the Fund, most countries need to reduce debt-to-GDP ratios, some dramatically, others less so. This requires a sustained period of fiscal tightening in terms of both revenues and expenditures. In particular, spending on healthcare, care for the aging, and entitlement programs should be cut to ensure long-term sustainability. A key role in achieving these measures should be accorded to fiscal institutions, through the adoption of strong fiscal rules.[52]

As the Fund, the World Bank, the OECD, and financial markets have relentlessly pushed states to adopt the values and techniques of the consolidation state over the past three decades, the economic and social underpinnings of communities around the world have thus been driven by fiscal policies, and not by the human rights commitments that might have been expected to provide at least part of the blueprint. Fiscal consolidation rather than the right to life or the right to healthcare has been the defining value in reshaping not just budgetary priorities but also the whole gamut of social policies and human rights policy more generally. As Streeck puts it, states have been pushed to devote "themselves to fiscal consolidation, in order to convince financial markets that they will consider their obligations as debtors sacrosanct and will give them unconditional priority over their political obligations to their citizens, doing 'whatever it takes' to remain fit for debt service."[53] From the perspective of international human rights law, one might also add that their legal obligations, both constitutional and international, have also been trumped by the priority given to fiscal consolidation.

As noted above, the new fiscal orthodoxy has a number of key ingredients, all of which have important implications for the human rights agenda. The analysis that follows identifies some of these elements and explores how they might have an impact on respect for human rights.

A. THE SIZE OF THE BUDGETARY ENVELOPE

In an analysis that sought to encapsulate the main requirements linked to fiscal consolidation, the OECD observed that the budget cuts required were likely to be between 4 percent and 10 percent of GDP "for most countries."[54] But, consistent with most such analyses, the report endeavored to soften the impact of such an enormous cut by suggesting that it might be compensated for through greater efficiency, the reduction of fiscal exemptions, and the expansion of environmental taxes. The reality, however is that greater efficiency rarely results in the maintenance of existing levels of service or assistance, fiscal exemptions are maintained because they benefit the elites, and the revenue gains from environmental taxes will not automatically be diverted back to sustain other budgetary items.

Significant reductions in budget expenditures thus require choices to be made and neither the IMF nor the OECD, nor other international actors promoting fiscal consolidation, have been prepared to address the issue of human rights, let alone to identify any specific budget items—beyond a nebulously defined "social protection"—that should be shielded in the process of consolidation. In one of the earliest efforts to link fiscal issues explicitly to rights protection, Holmes and Sunstein made the point that all rights cost money, and thus require public funding. They added that this applies to civil and political rights as much as to social rights. Thus, in the context of the United States, the fact that private liberties have public costs:

> . . . is true not only of rights to Social Security, Medicare, and food stamps, but also of rights to private property, freedom from speech, immunity from police abuse, contractual liberty, free exercise of religion, and indeed of the full panoply of rights characteristic of the American tradition.[55]

Although their analysis is compatible with the standards and content of international human rights law, their focus on the US situation led them to a more flexible and open-ended conception of how rights are recognized and protected. But precisely for that reason, their insights are directly applicable to what happens at the national level when a government is confronted with demands to undertake fiscal consolidation. As they put it, when legal rights are thought of in terms of public finance, they can clearly be seen "as politically created and collectively funded instruments designed to promote human welfare."[56] It follows, however, that major reductions in government expenditures provide the occasion to pick and choose which rights will be protected, to what extent, for whom, and how.

Rather than reflecting on what rights have been constricted in the process of fiscal consolidation, the point for present purposes is that the process itself is not a neutral one in terms of its impact on rights and that it can have a potentially major impact on rights-related aspects of the budget, as it does on the welfare and entitlement side. There are thus powerful reasons why human rights proponents need to engage with, and be vigilant during, the process of consolidation.

B. PRIVATIZATION

The central role of privatization within the context of fiscal consolidation is undoubted. The precise reasons for its centrality are less clear, however. The principal motivations include: the opportunity to generate a one-time injection of revenue into the budget by selling state assets; the assumption that the private sector is inevitably more efficient than the public sector; the likelihood that private enterprises will respond more effectively to market forces; the assumption that the entrepreneurial spirit makes private employers more open to technological and other forms of innovation; the assumption that privatized enterprises are less likely to be unionized and will thus not have to deal with unwanted demands from employees; and the pursuit of a libertarian ideological agenda that aims to "deconstruct the administrative state."[57] But it can also be done out of necessity, in the sense that the cutting of state budgets leaves governments with no choice but to either eliminate certain services or to contract them out to the private sector.

Much human rights–based analysis of privatization has focused on its impact on economic and social rights, such as the right to water in the context of the privatization of utilities. But civil and political rights are also directly threatened by diverse forms of privatization. Recent developments in the United States, especially at the state and local levels, provide a good illustration of the resulting risks. Several such phenomena have been identified in recent detailed reports published by human rights groups. They include the following.

Bail bonds: In the United States, some 11 million people are admitted to local jails annually. For various reasons, the amounts of bail being set by judges are on the rise, which means that nonwealthy defendants will remain in jail, with consequences such as job loss, disrupted childcare, and rent default. The principal way out, then, becomes to take a loan from a private "bail bond corporation," many of which charge very high loan rates and indulge in various practices that further penalize low-income clients. Studies have documented that these corporations, which now constitute a $2 billion-a-year industry and exist in only one other country in the world (the Philippines), distort the justice system by encouraging excessive and often unnecessary levels of bail. They also lobby in state legislatures to maintain the status quo despite significant pressure from human rights groups and others to implement a more equitable and just system.[58] They have become "the payday lenders of the criminal justice world, offering quick relief to desperate customers at high prices," but unlike other lenders, many states have given them the authority to arrest their clients for a wide range of reasons.[59] They epitomize the ugly face of the privatization of criminal justice in the United States of America.

Fines and fees: Draconian budget cuts (fiscal consolidation) at the state and local levels have encouraged the use of the criminal justice system in order to generate revenue, and often to fund expenditure that has nothing to do with justice. The role of the police and the local court system in explicitly setting out to cover revenue holes by more aggressive policing and the imposition of more demanding monetary punishments was documented in great detail in a 2015 report by the US Department of Justice, conducted in the aftermath of a highly publicized and racist police killing of a black man in Ferguson, Missouri.[60] The practice, which violates a wide range of human rights, is pervasive around the country and can be clearly linked back to fiscal policies that have shrunk budgets for law enforcement and much else to unsustainable levels, combined with the political unpalatability of raising taxes.[61]

Privatizing risk assessments: Partly in order to make the relevant processes more clearly evidence-based, algorithms are increasingly being used to identify "high-risk" individuals and areas, and to inform processes such as granting bail. The risk-assessment tools are developed by private corporations and invariably contain commercially valuable proprietary information that the owners of the software will refuse to divulge to courts or to legislative decision-makers. This raises serious concerns about transparency, accountability, and due process.[62]

Privatizing probation: Criminologists have long debated the respective merits of surveillance versus treatment models of supervised probation, and research continues to show the beneficial effects of a balanced approach in terms of improving offender outcomes.[63] But several states in the United States now make extensive use of private probation companies for people convicted of misdemeanors or traffic violations. The attraction is that the services cost the state nothing, since the person on probation pays the full cost to the company. The latter is authorized to charge fees, as well as to order drug and alcohol tests, all at the probationers' expense. Failure to pay can eventually lead to a custodial sentence. The result is that companies "have a direct financial interest in keeping their clients under probation as long as possible, and using every tool available to urge payment of fees, particularly those paid directly to the company."[64] The overall system thus involves a deeply problematic transfer of the sovereign power to restrict a person's liberty to private actors.

Public enforcement of private debts: In twenty-six states in the United States, judges issue arrest warrants for alleged debtors at the request of private debt collectors, thus violating both domestic law and international human rights standards. The practice generally affects only low-income individuals and subjects them "to court appearances, arrest warrants that appear on background checks, and jail time that interfere with their wages, their jobs, their ability to find housing, and more."[65]

The US criminal justice system has been ranked twenty-sixth out of 113 countries in terms of respect for fundamental rights.[66] While privatization of criminal justice functions in response to budgetary pressures is only one factor among many, the available evidence suggests a causal connection, or at least a strong correlation, between fiscal consolidation, privatized justice, and poor human rights outcomes.

The renewed push toward privatization in myriad realms, from criminal justice to public infrastructure such as water and sanitation systems and services such as healthcare and education, is both a reflection of and a contributor to waning faith in the state. The outsourcing of government functions to the private sector, whether driven by existing budgetary shortfalls or ideology, is poised to make the state's incapacity a self-fulfilling prophecy. The impoverishment of the state itself undermines the legitimacy of human rights and tax, alike, as both demand robust state action and citizen acceptance thereof. The eclipsing of the public sphere by the private sector also complicates the exercise of taxation and regulatory oversight— potentially making state functions less, not more, efficient. There are parallels between the debates around the VAT and those around privatization of social services: in theory, both could achieve positive "efficiencies." In reality, however, correcting the regressive impacts of consumption taxes like the VAT and of market-led allocation, to ensure fair (or at least not grossly unequal) distributive outcomes, requires active intervention by the regulatory state and the resources to support it. Far too often, however, the transfer programs or regulatory policies designed to mitigate regressive tax incidence or correct market failures are not implemented or are poorly designed, leaving the promise of VAT and privatization, as positive tools for the people, unfulfilled.

The concrete consequences of privatization for the respect, protection, and fulfillment of human rights confront human rights proponents with an existential question: can they continue to concentrate only on what is feasible within a system that is required to function with ever fewer public resources, or must they tackle broader issues of fiscal policy?

C. DECENTRALIZATION OF RESPONSIBILITY

Another of the direct consequences of policies of fiscal consolidation involving major tax cuts and expenditure reductions has been the transfer, either directly or indirectly, of responsibility for social programs to states or local authorities, and from them to local communities or individuals who must bear their own costs for public goods or services that were previously provided or subsidized by the state.

Many examples could be cited. In the United Kingdom, the national government has cut social spending dramatically since 2010. One of the techniques used to achieve these cuts has been to decentralize responsibility to local councils, but the latter have been given significantly less money to spend on essential services than was previously available. Because the councils have limited opportunities to increase revenue, they have tended to slash services, resulting in many instances in cuts of more than one-third since 2010.[67] In human rights terms, the consequences have been dramatic for minorities, disadvantaged groups, and women. For example, black households lost about 5 percent of their net income, more than double that for white households. Households with one or more disabled member were hit far harder than nondisabled families. Single parents lost far more from other family groups, and "women lose more than men from reforms at every income level." The combined effect of the welfare cuts and tax reforms has been to "boost the incomes of the top two deciles, while reducing incomes substantially for the bottom half of the income distribution."[68]

In the United States, cuts in federal spending and grants to states following the 2008 recession left many local governments unable to perform essential functions.[69] It is widely predicted that the major federal tax cuts enacted in December 2017 will not only "turbocharge" inequality in the United States but also lead to systematic and potentially draconian cuts in social spending, partly to pay for the tax cuts for the very wealthy and large corporations.[70]

In addition, many state governments in the United States have embraced a philosophy of small government combined with an aversion to social provision, leading them to cut taxes and social spending dramatically. Oklahoma provides an example of a state in which the right to education has been a principal victim of this combination. Many high schools are now open only four days a week, and teachers, who are in short supply and whose salaries have been frozen for ten years, often earn less than full-time workers at Walmart. Emergency certifications are routinely given to enable unqualified persons to work as teachers. According to *The Economist*, the explanation is that "deep tax cuts have wrecked the state's finances."[71] In addition to major cuts in income tax rates, the legislature slashed corporate taxes on oil production, thus depriving the state budget of almost half a billion dollars in one year. Over a decade, funding for K–12 education was cut by 28.2 percent. Raising taxes is extremely difficult, however, because a 1992 referendum requires tax increases to be approved by three-quarters of the legislature.[72]

Equally problematic to such cuts to the right to education, is the reliance on law enforcement and judicial authorities to raise general budget revenues. As noted above, many city and county authorities around the country have sought to overcome the effects of ever-shrinking tax revenues by encouraging an overzealous pursuit of people for minor or trumped-up traffic and conduct violations, combined with escalating fines and fees attached to nonimmediate payment.[73] As the Ferguson, Missouri, investigation has documented, the impact of such practices falls disproportionately on poor people of color, whose communities are surveilled and policed more heavily than others.[74]

Such problems also exist in emerging economies, as the example of Brazil illustrates. The constitutionally entrenched cap on social spending adopted in 2016, and discussed below, nominally applied only to the federal level, but the reality is that there are very significant flow-on effects experienced by states and municipalities within Brazil, which in turn reduce their own spending on health, education, and other forms of social protection. The impact on women's rights is reported to have been especially dramatic.[75]

V. LINKING HUMAN RIGHTS AND FISCAL POLICY

Based on all of the chapters in this volume and the preceding analysis, this concluding section identifies some of the key ways in which human rights norms should feature in future debates over fiscal policy.

A. GIVING CONTENT TO THE SOCIAL CONTRACT

Concepts of fairness and justice in taxation are not new.[76] There is a long-established, robust, and critical literature examining the distributive impacts of domestic tax policies, including vertical and horizontal equity, as well as intergenerational and intra- and inter-family equity. What is new is the place that human rights standards and obligations now occupy within the debate. In their pathbreaking work on tax and justice, Murphy and Nagel made the compelling point that tax cannot be looked at on its own: "What matters is not whether taxes—considered in themselves—are justly imposed, but rather whether the totality of a government's treatment

of its subjects, its expenditures along with its taxes, is just."[77] Their conclusion is that traditional considerations such as interest and efficiency will continue to dominate such debates
unless theories of distributive justice are introduced to combat the libertarian assumptions that
often prevail. But absent anchoring in an agreed, normative framework—such as that furnished
by human rights law—such theories will inevitably remain controversial, and the weight to be
accorded to any particular element in the theory will be hotly debated.

Similarly, the new fiscal sociology calls for tax to be seen as part of a social contract, but it
does not spell out how the contours of that contract are to be defined. More recent works have
started the process of introducing human rights norms as a standard against which to assess
the equity of international tax systems.[78] But the next stage needs to involve more explicit use
of states' voluntarily accepted, binding human rights obligations to give more precise content to
the social contract.

Both taxation and human rights law are, in their essence, about the relationship between
the individual and the state. The social contract sets forth the rights and responsibilities of citizens and the state. If human rights provide the content of that contract, taxation provides the
means of its implementation. The power to tax derives from the consent of the governed to
the government's collection and expenditure of revenues on behalf of the people as a whole.
Likewise, the duties and entitlements that make up human rights reflect a presumption that the
state exists by and for the people, and that the people likewise depend on the state for their welfare. The social contract so central to both taxation and human rights, however, is today frayed
and the state itself, in question.

Tax and human rights are at the heart of fundamental debates about the appropriate balance in society between the public and private sectors. Tax policy is, at base, a *social* tool. Thus
it cannot be divorced from principles regarding social priorities and entitlements, which are
human rights. Indeed, human rights law is, at core, a framework to guide social policy and resource distribution. Human rights are principles for distribution within society—there have
to be enough resources for a functioning judicial system, to achieve security for all, to realize
a nondiscrimination agenda, and to ensure equal access to these mechanisms of law and government. Taxes are tools for effectuating that distribution and supplying the state with the
funds needed to fulfill those purposes. What is needed is greater recognition that the fields
of tax and human rights are inherently intertwined and face a common challenge today: the
reconceptualization of what constitutes a just society and the social good.

Progress on the realization of human rights cannot be achieved without prioritizing social
policies—clarifying commitments to social welfare, social goods, and the entitlements to which
membership in a political community gives rise. Tax experts, in turn, must acknowledge that
what they are doing has human rights implications. The objective is not to turn human rights
proponents into accountants or tax lawyers into social workers, but to facilitate interlocution.
Both constituencies can start reaching out and transforming their practices. There is no easy formula, but experts in both domains must admit that to silo each discipline is not only artificial, in
that it distorts rather than reflects the way the world works; it is also a highly political act, which
deflects attention from common concerns about the social good.

B. BENCHMARKS FOR EVALUATING TAX POLICIES

In addition to defining the contours of the social contract, human rights standards provide important individual benchmarks against which to evaluate specific tax policies. The most obvious example is the use of nondiscrimination and substantive equality principles to assess the

justness and permissibility of proposed tax policies. But there is also a more proactive approach which seeks to introduce principles of altruism or solidarity that go beyond the assumptions of standard political economy, according to which "an individual's position in the income distribution determines her preferences for redistribution."[79] If, for example, debates over homelessness policy are to move beyond begrudging notions of charity, there needs to be acknowledgment of the principles underlying the right to housing and the right to an adequate standard of living. The human rights framework is by no means the only way to transcend arguments based on charity or self-interest, but it is the most widely accepted internationally and the best developed in terms of its normative implications.

C. REINFORCING DEMOCRACY

Rather than being viewed primarily in terms of its economic or financial implications, fiscal policy needs to be seen as integrally linked to human rights to participation and to the quality of democracy in any given society. Many of the great historical landmarks in Western human rights history—the Magna Carta, and the French and American Bills of Rights—have important origins in revolts over authoritarian fiscal policies, and the linkage is encapsulated in slogans such as "no taxation without representation."[80] And political scientists have long modeled the impact of different types of democratic institutions (parliamentary versus presidential, the influence of corporatist actors, the degree of voter turnout) on tax policy.[81]

A range of developments in political economy since the late twentieth century, however, threaten to undermine the links between taxation and democracy in general and the meaningful exercise of specific political human rights in particular. As noted below, rapidly growing income and wealth inequality in most societies disempower large segments of society. As Crouch has argued, even in the absence of "state capture" by political elites:

> powerful corporate interests can be expected to deploy political resources to ensure that [various forms of] regulation [are] shaped to favour their interests, there always being a steep inequality between their capacity and that of mass publics to exercise influence over rule-making and regulation.[82]

The experience of the United States is salutary in this regard. Less than two decades into this century, two major rounds of tax cuts have been legislated. In 2001, under President George W. Bush, "Democrats were almost nonplayers . . . Republicans used the powers of their congressional and White House leadership to control the language of the debate and the policy alternatives considered."[83] In 2017, under President Trump, even larger cuts were adopted with minimal public debate, no assessment of the fiscal impact, a closed negotiation exclusively among Republicans, and voting on a long and complex text which virtually no congressional members had had the time to read.[84]

More generally, large-scale privatization of formerly public goods has reduced the scope of many tax debates, and transferred key decisions to market players. The adoption of constitutional restrictions has constrained the options available to the democratic process, as in the examples of Oklahoma and Brazil noted above. Constraints imposed by international organizations such as the IMF or the European Union further reduce the role of democratic decision makers. And international trade agreements are generally negotiated in secrecy, with no genuine opportunity for the public to influence decisions on major matters of policy that might never be revisited in practice. In many respects, the result is to decouple economic management from democratic decision-making.[85]

Human rights proponents are thus confronted with a choice. They can either resign themselves to accepting that the space for advocating respect for rights and upholding democratic procedures has shrunk dramatically and will continue to shrink in the years ahead, or they can engage in debates over fiscal and related policies in ways that very few of them have been prepared to do to date.

D. RESHAPING CONSTITUTIONALISM

In the 1980s and 1990s, a wave of constitution-making swept many parts of the globe. The overwhelmingly dominant trend was to entrench forms of democracy and the rule of law, to codify a wide range of civil and political rights, and to recognize an important array of economic, social, and cultural rights. Human rights proponents have continued to celebrate the great achievements of this era. Today, there have been relatively few efforts to amend or roll back these constitutional guarantees, but what has passed largely unremarked is a potentially even more important trend of constitutional or entrenched legislative provisions designed to constrain the fiscal policy options that are open to democratic decision-making.

The trend has its origins in the United States and especially the adoption of Proposition 13 in California in 1978. "Prop 13," as it is known, amended the state constitution to reduce property taxes, cap future increases, and require a two-thirds vote of the legislature to increase state taxes, thereby marking the beginning of what has been benignly termed the "taxpayers' revolt" in the United States. It could also be seen as a revolt by the well-off against the payment of taxes to ensure governmental provision of schooling and other social services to the less well-off. Since that time, many states have adopted tax expenditure limitations (TEL) designed to lock "in the preferences of a set of political principals by constraining the future actions of potentially unknown and hostile agents,"[86] and these are often linked to balanced-budget rules and supermajority voting requirements. Cities and counties in most states have also adopted TEL-type mechanisms.[87] In addition, concerted efforts are currently being made in the United States to introduce a balanced-budget amendment to the federal Constitution, thus locking in strict limits on governmental expenditures. Legislatures in twenty-seven states have passed resolutions calling for a constitutional convention for this purpose, and some commentators have predicted that seven additional states might well join this group, thus reaching the threshold required for the convening of a convention under Article V of the Constitution.[88] An American Civil Liberties Union expert has expressed concern that such an initiative could result in a disastrous weakening of civil liberties.[89]

The European Union has also sought to lock in a form of fiscal consolidation, initially through its 1992 Maastricht treaty on economic and monetary union (Treaty on European Union) that established economic convergence criteria in relation to inflation rates, public finances, public debt, interest rates, and exchange rate stability. In 2012, the Fiscal Stability treaty (Treaty on Stability, Coordination and Governance in the Economic and Monetary Union) required states to have a balanced budget and to establish an independent monitoring institution to undertake fiscal surveillance. It is assumed, however, that these provisions will be implemented in ways that are consistent with respect for fundamental human rights.

In contrast, in December 2016, the Brazilian Senate approved a constitutional amendment capping public spending for twenty years, allowing it to rise no more than inflation, and suspending the Constitution's requirements regarding minimum funding for education, health, and social assistance. The *Washington Post* dubbed the measure "the mother of all austerity plans,"[90] while critics called it "unprecedented"[91] and "draconian."[92] The public expenditure ceiling was adopted without consideration of less regressive alternatives to address the country's budgetary crisis, such as reforming the tax system to increase government revenues from wealthier taxpayers and decrease the burden disproportionately borne by lower-income earners.

A recent analysis showed that from 2015 to 2017 social investments by the federal government in Brazil were reduced by 6 percent of the total budget. Subsequent to the entry into force of the constitutional amendment "expenditures specifically benefitting women were reduced by 58 per cent . . . , while the number of specialised services offered to women suffering from violence was also reduced by 15 per cent between 2014 and 2016, and are now frozen at this level."[93] At the same time, gender equality initiatives have been undermined through a diminished status given to the Secretariat for Women's Policies, no new shelters to protect women against violence were built in 2017, and public campaigns to prevent violence against women have been absent since 2014 due to budget cuts.[94]

There are good reasons to expect that attempts will be made in other countries to emulate the Brazilian initiative, which was strongly and publicly supported by the IMF.[95] Human rights and tax groups will need to work closely together to make the case against such approaches, which threaten to reverse the constitutional advances of previous years.

E. EXPANDING THE HUMAN RIGHTS AGENDA

One message emerging from this volume is that human rights proponents can no longer pursue the limited agenda that has been the bread and butter of human rights research and advocacy for the past half-century, focused on reiterating the normative principles enshrined in numerous international treaties, exposing transgressions, and assuming that change will come without any engagement with the structural issues that often shape and facilitate the violations they are criticizing. Fiscal policies and the broader economic, social, and political priorities they reflect must become an integral part of the overall debate, even if specific groups insist on pursuing more specialized agendas.

1. Designing Tax Regimes to Maximize Resource Availability

For all of its undoubted strengths, one of the enduring weaknesses of the international human rights regime has been its failure, or refusal, to come to grips with the underlying economic implications of rights policies. Despite the wishful thinking of many libertarian commentators and conservative politicians, there are virtually no rights without budgetary implications. All require resource expenditures. Human rights treaties, however, take the line that civil and political rights must be implemented without regard to resource implications, while economic, social, and cultural rights can only be implemented if resources are "available," and the standard used to make that assessment has generally been excessively deferential to the calculations offered by the state concerned.

If human rights proponents airbrush fiscal and broader resource issues out of the equation, it might not be surprising for economists to respond by arguing that human rights considerations are not theirs to worry about. Those concerned with civil and political rights must adopt a more realistic position that acknowledges that resource dimensions are almost always relevant, and that a nuanced policy along those lines is not tantamount to conceding that respect for those rights suddenly becomes entirely contingent upon resources being available. Recent pronouncements by the Committee on Economic, Social and Cultural Rights, along with scholarly and advocacy work on budget analysis and the concept of "maximum available resources," point to the need for more sustained and sophisticated reflection on the role of resource mobilization in relation to those rights.

Much of the recent writing on taxation and human rights has been undertaken from a "violations" perspective, in the sense that it has focused on abuses by corporations and wealthy individuals, and on governments that facilitate those entities in diverting revenues from the countries in which they operate or reside. This is in marked contrast to the approach taken by the proponents of the Social Protection Floor Initiative who have placed the resource challenge front and center by devoting major attention to demonstrating the affordability of such an approach in each country.

2. Extraterritorial Impacts and Obligations

Much has been written by scholars on the extraterritorial human rights obligations of states, but little attention has been given so far to the foreseeable effects of their tax regimes on other countries, and the impact of the activities of their corporate citizens abroad. Further reflection is needed to clarify how states should implement their duties to regulate the extraterritorial conduct of their citizens (whether corporate or natural persons) and assess the impacts of their fiscal policies and tax structures on the capacity of other states to mobilize the maximum available resources, as well as how those duties should be promoted and by whom. Although they do not address tax policies and practices explicitly, the UNGP[96] reflect an evolution in the normative framework regarding the extraterritorial obligations of state actors and endeavor to promote greater consensus around the principle that nonstate actors also have duties with respect to their impacts on human rights beyond the borders of their home states. The Maastricht Principles on Extraterritorial Obligations of States in the Area of Economic, Social and Cultural Rights,[97] and the UN Guidelines on Extreme Poverty and Human Rights, adopted in 2012,[98] put forward strong claims in this respect, but it remains unclear how these principles might be translated into concrete changes to tax structures and policies at the domestic and international levels. Nor is it clear what mechanisms exist to identify and assign liability for extraterritorial harms attributable to tax policies or to the absence of regulation in one jurisdiction. While the chapter in this volume by Lusiani and Cosgrove provides practical guidance for the conduct of human rights impact assessments of tax policies, human rights scholars in general have a way to go to catch up with the tax literature on externalities or "spillover effects" of national tax regimes.

3. Corporate Duties and Practices

Despite the importance of taxation to the human rights "footprint" of a corporation, there has been little effort to date to integrate taxation into the development of normative frameworks for business conduct. The UNGP, for example, do not explicitly address the issue, and discussions regarding the implementation of the corporate "due diligence" requirement have not yet articulated how a corporation's tax policies and practices should be factored into risk assessments and accountability measures. In the absence of more multilateral efforts to address corporate tax conduct as part of businesses' human rights responsibilities, some companies are taking it upon themselves to develop their own principles or codes of conduct—such as the B-Team initiative, described in chapter 1.[99] To the extent that self-regulation may fall short in this area, there is a need for deeper engagement by civil society actors, academics, and policymakers in defining the rules of the game to which corporations must adhere. Tax experts might help identify the areas in which corporate tax practices are most likely to have adverse consequences on public revenue collection or the ways in which tax policies create perverse incentives or loopholes. They could also work with human rights scholars to identify the types of measures corporations should undertake to ensure their operations respect human rights.

4. Enforcement and Accountability

Any discussion of taxation from a human rights perspective, as opposed to the perspective of fairness alone, necessarily raises questions of accountability and enforceability. In addition to theorizing with greater specificity the source of the duties borne by host states, home states, nonstate actors, and intergovernmental bodies with respect to preventing and remedying tax abuses or avoiding and justifying retrogressive effects, there is a need to conceptualize the avenues through which those actors could be held accountable. How, and in what venues might these duties be enforced? What does the right to a remedy mean with respect to taxation-related human rights harms?[100] Who has standing to hold transnational tax evaders accountable? Can private individuals or groups of individuals sue to vindicate their rights, or is state enforcement the only option? Could the WTO or other trade-related bodies provide a forum for state complaints against other state facilitators of tax abuse or against private actors receiving differential tax treatment? The state aid cases pursued by the European Commission, discussed above, offer some examples and insights into potential future claims. More work is needed to enhance the expertise and capacity of international, regional, and national human rights bodies to evaluate claims of harm based on tax and fiscal policies.

5. Inequality

Many economists, including Anthony Atkinson, Joseph Stiglitz, Nora Lustig, Branko Milanovic, and Thomas Piketty, have highlighted the negative consequences of extreme and growing wealth and income inequalities at the national level, and Oxfam International has taken the lead in promoting public awareness of the damaging consequences for development of such unbalanced economic distributions. But extreme inequality not only undermines balanced and sustainable economic growth; it also has a highly detrimental effect on the enjoyment of all human rights. While the impact on efforts to promote economic and social rights is obvious, there is less recognition of the fact that increased economic insecurity, and the domination of politics by economic elites, undermines support for, and ultimately the viability of, the democratic systems of governance upon which the human rights framework depends.[101]

Walter Scheidel has argued that there is little that can be done peacefully to stop the march of mass inequality and argues that history shows that it has only ever been reduced by violent means, and in particular as a result of mass mobilization warfare, transformative revolution, state failure, or lethal pandemics.[102] But this grim picture is far from that painted by economists dealing with inequality, to whom it seems clear that progressive fiscal policies and targeted redistribution can indeed reverse the march of inequality.[103] Yet despite some recognition of its importance,[104] most of those working in the fields of taxation and human rights have so far failed to give the question of extreme inequality the urgent attention that it demands. This needs to change.

The main message of the present volume is that fiscal policy and human rights policy are inextricably linked and that it is time to overcome the artificial barriers that have separated the two fields. There is no magic recipe or equation that captures the exact nature of the relationship. The interactions are manifold and often complex, but they are undeniable. Endless advocacy designed to perfect human rights policy can be undone with the addition or deletion of a single line item expropriation in a national budget. Those who seek to ensure that the policies of governments and other actors respect, promote, and fulfill human rights overlook the fiscal dimensions at their peril.

NOTES

1. R. Goldscheid, *Staatssozialismus oder Staatskapitalismzis* (1917). For a broad-brush history of fiscal sociology, see J. Backhaus, 'Fiscal Sociology: What For?', 61 *American Journal of Economics and Sociology* (2002), 55; and J. L. Campbell, 'The State and Fiscal Sociology', 19 *Annual Review of Sociology* (1993), 163.
2. J. A. Schumpeter, 'The Crisis of the Tax State', *in* R. Swedberg (ed.), *The Economics and Sociology of Capitalism* (1991), 99, at 100.
3. Ibid. ("In some historical periods the immediate formative influence of the fiscal needs and policy of the state on the development of the economy and with it on all forms of life and all aspects of culture explains practically all the major features of events. . . .").
4. The authors understand the term "fiscal policy" to encompass all government laws, regulations, and programs designed to raise revenue, alter the distribution of income or assets among the governed, or allocate public spending. "Fiscal policy" includes but is not limited to tax policy. In this introduction, the authors use tax and fiscal policy interchangeably to denote those measures adopted by the state that affect the public budget.
5. Schumpeter, *supra* note 2 at 101.
6. Ibid.
7. Y. Epifantseva and N. Hashimzade, 'Introduction', *in* N. Hashimzade and Y. Epifantseva (eds.), *The Routledge Companion to Tax Avoidance Research* (2018), 1.
8. K. Roth, 'Defending Economic, Social and Cultural Rights: Practical Issues Faced by an International Human Rights Organization', 26(1) *Human Rights Quarterly* (2004), 63–73.
9. See, for example, Diane Elson and Radhika Balakrishnan, *Economic Policy and Human Rights: Holding Governments to Account* (2011); Center for Economic and Social Rights, *Assessing Austerity: Monitoring the Human Rights Impacts of Fiscal Consolidation* (2018); and International Bar Association Human Rights Institute (IBAHRI), *Tax Abuses, Poverty and Human Rights* (2013).
10. S. Moyn, *Not Enough: Human Rights in an Unequal World* (2018). While the index to the book lists seventeen separate entries under the heading "taxation," all of them are fleeting mentions of tax policies advocated by various authors and political leaders (ranging from the Jacobins and Thomas Paine to the Nazis, Franklin Delano Roosevelt, Augusto Pinochet, Ronald Reagan, and Margaret Thatcher).
11. I. Martin, A. K. Mehrotra, and M. Prasad, 'The Thunder of History: The Origins and Development of the New Fiscal Sociology', in I. Martin, A. K. Mehrotra, and M. Prasad (eds.), *The New Fiscal Sociology: Taxation in Comparative and Historical Perspective* (2009), 6.
12. L. Murphy and T. Nagel, *The Myth of Ownership: Taxes and Justice* (2002), 4.
13. See, e.g., M. Bhandari (ed.), *Philosophical Foundations of Tax Law* (2017); Thomas Pogge and Krishen Mehta (eds.), *Global Tax Fairness* (2016).
14. Ibid.

15. See *The New Fiscal Sociology,* *supra* note 11.

16. Ibid. at 14.

17. Critical tax theory emerged in the 1990s as an attempt to inject antisubordination principles into tax analysis. Some of the earliest critical tax scholarship explored how tax policy contributes to social hierarchy and discrimination along gender and racial lines. See, e.g., B. I Moran and W. Whitford, 'A Black Critique of the Internal Revenue Code', 1 *Wisconsin Law Review* 751 (1996); K. B. Brown and M. L. Fellows (eds.), *Taxing America* (1997) (addressing topics such as the impact of the tax marriage bonus on gender and racial equality and the contribution of tax law to racial housing segregation); see also A. C. Infanti and B. Crawford, *Critical Tax Theory: An Introduction,* Legal Studies Research Paper Series Working Paper No. 2009-04 (2009), at 12 ("[A]ll critical tax scholarship shares one or more of the following goals: (1) to uncover bias in the tax laws; (2) to explore and expose how the tax laws both reflect and construct social meaning; and (3) to educate nontax scholars and lawyers about the interconnectedness of taxation, social justice, and progressive political movements."); K. B. Brown, M. L. Fellows, and B. J. Crawford, 'The Past, Present, and Future of Critical Tax Theory: A Conversation', 10 *Pittsburgh Tax Review* (2012), 59, 60–65.

18. See, e.g., Andre Smith, *Tax Law and Racial Economic Justice* (2015); I. W. Martin and K. Beck, 'Property Tax Limitation and Racial Inequality in Effective Tax Rates', 43(2) *Critical Sociology* (2017), 221–236; B. J. Crawford and A.C. Infanti, 'Introduction to the Feminist Judgments: Rewritten Tax Opinions Project' (10 Apr. 2017), *in* ibid. (eds.), *Feminist Judgments: Rewritten Tax Opinions* (2017), at 3–21.

19. Some tax justice advocates refer to the "Four R's" of taxation as revenue, redistribution, repricing, and representation. See Tax Justice Network, *The Four "Rs"* (9 July 2007), http://taxjustice.blogspot.com/2007/07/four-rs.html. The Center for Economic and Social Rights has described the relevance of taxation to human rights along three axes: revenue generation, resource redistribution, and accountability. See, e.g., I. Saiz, 'Resourcing Rights: Combating Tax Injustice from a Human Rights Perspective', *in* A. Nolan, R. O'Connell, and C. Harvey (eds.), *Public Finance and Human Rights: budgets and the promotion of economic and social rights* (2013), http://archive.cesr.org/downloads/resourcing.rights.ignacio.saiz.2013.pdf.

20. S. Holmes and C. R. Sunstein, *The Cost of Rights: Why Liberty Depends on Taxes* (1999).

21. Article 2 of the International Covenant on Economic, Social, and Cultural Rights (ICESCR) provides: "[E]ach State Party to the present Covenant undertakes to take steps . . . especially economic and technical, to the maximum of its available resources, with a view to achieving progressively the full realization of the rights recognized in the present Covenant. . . ."

22. C. R. Howard, 'Making Taxes the Life of the Party', *in The New Fiscal Sociology, supra* note 11, at 86, 93.

23. Ibid at 94.

24. E. Dawson and W. Smith, *The Cost of Privilege*, A Research Paper by Per Capita for Anglicare Australia (Mar. 2018).

25. S. D. Younger, E. Osei-Assibey, and F. Oppong, 'Fiscal Incidence in Ghana', 21 *Review of Development Economics* (2017), e47.

26. E. McCaffery, 'Where's the Sex in Fiscal Sociology?: Taxation and Gender in Comparative Perspective', *in The New Fiscal Sociology, supra* note 11, at 216.

27. See, e.g., U.S. Congress, Joint Economic Committee, *The Pink Tax: How Gender-Based Pricing Hurts Women's Buying Power* (Dec. 2016), https://www.jec.senate.gov/public/_cache/files/8a42df04-8b6d-4949-b20b-6f40a326db9e/the-pink-tax---how-gender-based-pricing-hurts-women-s-buying-power.pdf; A. Ngabirano, 'Pink Tax' forces women to pay more than men', *USA Today* (27 Mar. 2017), https://www.usatoday.com/story/money/business/2017/03/27/pink-tax-forces-women-pay-more-than-men/99462846/.

28. See K. Donald and R. Moussié, *Redistributing Unpaid Care Work—Why Tax Matters for Women's Rights*, Institute of Development Studies Policy Briefing, Issue 109 (Jan. 2016).

29. See 'Paradise Papers: Everything you need to know about the leak', *BBC* (10 Nov. 2017), available online at http://www.bbc.com/news/world-41880153; see also *About the Paradise Papers*

Investigation, International Consortium of Investigative Journalists, available online at https://www.icij.org/investigations/paradise-papers/about/ (last visited 10 Apr. 2018).

30. See generally, *All Our Investigations*, International Consortium of Investigative Journalists, https://www.icij.org/investigations/ (last visited 10 Apr. 2018).

31. See, e.g., P. Cohen and J. Kanter, 'Europeans Accuse Ireland of Giving Apple Illegal Tax Break', *New York Times* (30 Sept. 2014); V. Houlder, V. Boland, and J. Politi, 'Tax avoidance: The Irish inversion', *The Financial Times* (29 Apr. 2014), available online at http://www.ft.com/cms/s/2/d9b4fd34-ca3f-11e3-8a31-00144feabdc0.html#axzz3PBwSnjgW.

32. D. Hakim, 'Europe Takes Aim at Deals Created to Escape Taxes: The Tax Attraction Between Starbucks and the Netherlands', *New York Times* (14 Nov. 2014).

33. S. Bowers, 'Luxembourg Tax Files: How tiny state rubber-stamped tax avoidance on an industrial scale', *The Guardian* (5 Nov. 2014).

34. G. Hutchens, 'Australian tax office says 36% of big firms and multinationals paid no tax', *The Guardian* (7 Dec. 2017), https://www.theguardian.com/australia-news/2017/dec/07/australian-tax-office-says-36-of-big-firms-and-multinationals-paid-no-tax.

35. See, e.g., *Paradise Papers: the hidden costs of tax dodging*, Oxfam (8 Nov. 2017), https://www.oxfam.org/en/even-it/paradise-papers-hidden-costs-tax-dodging (estimating that poor countries lose more than $100 billion annually to corporate tax avoidance).

36. This is the definition used by the International Bar Association in its report *Tax Abuses, Poverty, and Human Rights* (hereafter IBAHRI Report), available online at http://www.ibanet.org/Article/Detail.aspx?ArticleUid=b2ca2f0d-2684-40b3-9222-a484841d6dbc. Tax abuse is not often discussed as a human rights issue in the developed world, although the sophisticated tax-planning and avoidance strategies used by corporations and wealthy individuals certainly limit the resources available to realize rights there too. (Then again, social problems in countries like the United States are rarely ever framed in terms of "human rights," as opposed to constitutional rights.) According to the report on fiscal policy issued by the former Special Rapporteur on extreme poverty and human rights, "globally, approximately $3 trillion of government revenue is lost to tax evasion every year," with the greatest losses in high-income countries. UN Doc. A/HRC/26/28 (22 May 2014), at 15, available online at http://www.ohchr.org/EN/HRBodies/HRC/RegularSessions/Session26/Documents/A_HRC_26_28_ENG.doc.

37. See, e.g., IMF Policy Paper, *Spillovers in International Corporate Taxation* (May 2014), 7, available online at http://www.imf.org/external/np/pp/eng/2014/050914.pdf; see also Oxfam, *Business Among Friends: Why corporate tax dodgers are not yet losing sleep over global tax reform* (May 2014), 6, available online at http://www.oxfam.org/sites/www.oxfam.org/files/bp185-business-among-friends-corporate-tax-reform-120514-en_0.pdf.

38. European Parliament recommendation of 13 December 2017 to the Council and the Commission following the inquiry into money laundering, tax avoidance and tax evasion, para. 40 (2016/3044(RSP)) (13 Dec. 2017).

39. See, e.g., OECD and the G20, OECD, https://www.oecd.org/g20/topics/taxation/ (last visited 10 Apr. 2017).

40. E. Anyangwe, 'Addis Ababa talks risk deadlock over UN agency for tax', *The Guardian* (15 July 2015), https://www.theguardian.com/global-development-professionals-network/2015/jul/15/addis-ababa-talks-risk-deadlock-over-un-agency-for-tax-ffd3-financing-for-development

41. See *infra* at 161–162.

42. See, for example, Craig v. Boren, 429 U.S. 190 (1976).

43. Discussed *infra* at 16, 18.

44. P. Alston, 'The Populist Challenge to Human Rights', 9 *Journal of Human Rights Practice* (2017), 1.

45. T. Ginsburg, A. Huq, and M. Versteeg, "The Coming Demise of Liberal Constitutionalism?', 85 *Chicago Law Review* (2018), 239, at 241.

46. Ibid at 242.

47. B. S. Bernanke, 'When Growth Is Not Enough', European Central Bank Forum on Central Banking at Sintra, June 26, 2017.

48. W. Streeck, 'A New Regime', *in* D. King and P. Le Galès (eds.), *Reconfiguring European States in Crisis* (2017), 139.

49. Ibid.

50. For a detailed analysis of the role of the IMF in terms of social protection, see Report of the Special Rapporteur on extreme poverty and human rights, UN Doc. A/HRC/38/33 (2018) (by Philip Alston).

51. Ghana, Staff Report for the 2017 Article IV consultation, fourth review under the extended credit facility arrangement, request for waiver for nonobservance of performance criteria, and request for extension and rephasing of the arrangement, IMF (1 Aug. 2017), at 1.

52. A. Kentikelenis, T. Stubbs, and L. King, 'IMF Conditionality and Development Policy Space, 1985–2014', 23 *Review of International Political Economy* (2016), 543; and S. Babb and A. Kentikelenis, 'International Financial Institutions as Agents of Neoliberalism', *in* D. Cahill, M. Cooper, M. Konings, and D. Primrose (eds.), *The SAGE Handbook of Neoliberalism* (2018), 16.

53. Streeck, *supra* note 48, at 150.

54. D. Sutherland, P. Hoeller, and R. Merola, Fiscal Consolidation: How Much, How Fast and by What Means? OECD Economic Policy Papers, No. 1, Apr. 2012, at 7.

55. Holmes and Sunstein, *supra* note 20, at 220.

56. Ibid. at 221.

57. P. Rucker and R. Costa, 'Bannon Vows a Daily Fight for "Deconstruction of the Administrative State"', *Washington Post*, 24 Feb. 2017.

58. Human Rights Watch, '"Set up to Fail", The Impact of Offender-Funded Private Probation on the Poor', 20 Feb. 2018, available at https://www.hrw.org/report/2018/02/20/set-fail/impact-offender-funded-private-probation-poor.

59. J. Silver-Greenberg and S. Dewan, 'When Bail Feels Less like Freedom, More like Extortion', *New York Times*, 31 Mar. 2018.

60. United States Department of Justice, Civil Rights Division, *Investigation of the Ferguson Police Department* (4 Mar. 2015). ("The City budgets for sizeable increases in municipal fines and fees each year, exhorts police and court staff to deliver those revenue increases, and closely monitors whether those increases are achieved." P. 3).

61. K. Henricks and D. C. Harvey, 'Not One but Many: Monetary Punishment and the Fergusons of America', 32 *Sociological Forum* (2017), 930.

62. Written submission to the Special Rapporteur from the AI Now Institute.

63. E. K. Drake, 'The Monetary Benefits and Costs of Community Supervision', 34 *Journal of Contemporary Criminal Justice* (2018), 47, at 59.

64. Human Rights Watch, *"Set Up to Fail": The Impact of Offender-Funded Private Probation on the Poor* (2018).

65. American Council for Civil Liberties, *A Pound of Flesh: The Criminalization of Private Debt* (2018).

66. World Justice Project, Rule of Law Index 2017–2018, available at http://data.worldjusticeproject.org/#/groups/USA

67. 'Britain's local councils face financial crisis: Amid a painful fiscal squeeze, some authorities may soon be unable to meet their statutory obligations', *The Economist* (28 Jan. 2017).

68. J. Portes and H. Reed, *Distributional results for the impact of tax and welfare reforms between 2010–17, modelled in the 2021/22 tax year: Interim findings*, Equality and Human Rights Commission, Research report, Nov. 2017, at 30, https://www.equalityhumanrights.com/sites/default/files/impact-of-tax-and-welfare-reforms-2010-2017-interim-report_0.pdf.

69. See, e.g., D. Klepper and B. Witte, 'States Raise Fees, Fines to Salvage Budgets and Avoid Tax Increases', *Associated Press* (24 July 2011).

70. See D. Leonhart, 'A Tax Plan to Turbocharge Inequality, in 3 Charts', Op-ed, *New York Times* (17 Dec. 2017), https://www.nytimes.com/2017/12/17/opinion/taxes-inequality-charts.html.

71. 'Education in America: What's the matter with Oklahoma?', *The Economist*, 30 Jan. 2018, available online at https://www.economist.com/news/united-states/21736102-low-teacher-pay-and-severe-budget-cuts-are-driving-schools-brink-whats-matter.

72. Ibid.

73. E. Shaw, *Where local governments are paying the bills with police fines* (26 Sept. 2016), https://sunlightfoundation.com/2016/09/26/where-local-governments-are-paying-the-bills-with-police-fines/.

74. Department of Justice report, *supra* note 60 ("The City's emphasis on revenue generation has a profound effect on FPD's approach to law enforcement.... Ferguson has allowed its focus on revenue generation to fundamentally compromise the role of Ferguson's municipal court.... The harms of Ferguson's police and court practices are borne disproportionately by African Americans, and there is evidence that this is due in part to intentional discrimination on the basis of race."). See also U.S. Commission on Civil Rights, Targeted Fines and Fees Against Communities of Color: Civil Rights & Constitutional Implications 23 (Sept. 2017), http://www.usccr.gov/pubs/Statutory_Enforcement_Report2017.pdf (explaining that Ferguson is not unique, and that "[a]mong the fifty cities with the highest proportion of revenues from fines, the median size of African American population ... is more than five times greater than the national median."); G. Lopez, *Study: Cities Rely More on Fines for Revenue If They Have More Black Residents*, Vox (7 July 2017), https://www.vox.com/identities/2017/7/7/15929196/police-fines-study-racism; National Center for State Courts, *Trends in State Courts 2017: Fines, Fees, and Bail Practices: Challenges and Opportunities* (2017), http://www.ncsc.org/~/media/Microsites/Files/Trends%202017/Eliminating-Racial-Impact-Trends-2017.ashx.

75. G. David, 'The Impacts of IMF-backed Austerity on Women's Rights in Brazil', *Bretton Woods Observer*, Spring 2018, available online at http://www.brettonwoodsproject.org/2018/03/impacts-imf-backed-austerity-womens-rights-brazil/.

76. See, e.g., A. Maslove (ed.), *Fairness in Taxation: Exploring the Principles* (1993); American Bar Association, *Tax Avoidance, Tax Evasion* (1987).

77. Murphy and Nagel, *supra* note 12, at 25.

78. T. Pogge and K. Mehta, 'The Moral Significance of Tax-Motivated Illicit Financial Outflows', *in* ibid. (eds.), *Global Tax Fairness* (2016), 4–5 ("[M]assive reductions in existing human rights deficits could be achieved by allowing poor countries to collect reasonable taxes from MNCs and from their own most affluent nationals, assuming the resulting revenues were appropriately spent.").

79. M. Dimick, D. Rueda, and D. Stegmueller, 'Models of Other-Regarding Preferences, Inequality, and Redistribution', 21 *Annual Review of Political Science* (2018), 2.

80. See generally A. C. Gould and P. J. Baker, 'Democracy and Taxation', 5 *Annual Review of Political Science* (2002), 87.

81. E. Kiser and S. M. Karceski, 'Political Economy of Taxation', 20 *Annual Review of Political Science* (2017), 75–92 [6.8–6.9].

82. C. Crouch, 'The Limitations of the Limited State', *in* King and Le Galès, *supra* note 48, at 239.

83. J. S. Hacker and P. Pierson, *Off Center: The Republican Revolution and the Erosion of American Democracy* (2005), 63–64.

84. Statement on Visit to the USA, by Professor Philip Alston, United Nations Special Rapporteur on extreme poverty and human rights, Washington, Dec. 15, 2017, para. 46.

85. See generally Streeck, *supra* note 48, at 154.

86. T. Kousser, M. D. McCubbins, and E. Moule, 'For Whom the TEL Tolls: Can State and Expenditure Limits Effectively Reduce Spending?', 8 *State Politics and Policy* (2008), 331

87. J. I. Stallmann et al., 'Surveying the Effects of Limitations on Taxes and Expenditures: What Do/Don't We Know?', 3 *Journal of Public and Nonprofit Affairs* (2017), 197; and J. M. Kulik and N. Ermasova, 'Tax Expenditure Limitations (TELs) and State Expenditure Structure in the USA', 18 *Public Organization Review* (2018), 53.

88. 'America Might See a New Constitutional Convention in a Few Years', *The Economist*, 30 Sept. 2017.

89. J. Stanley, 'Calls For a Constitutional Convention Heating Up in the States', *ACLU Blog*, 3 Feb. 2015, https://www.aclu.org/blog/free-future/calls-constitutional-convention-heating-states.

90. S. Sims, 'Brazil passes the mother of all austerity plans', *Washington Post*, 16 Dec. 2016.

91. Conectas, CESR, INESC, Oxfam Bresil, *Brazil's Constitutional Austerity Amendment: A leap into the darkness; With no prior human rights impact assessment, public expenditure cap proposal condemns Brazil to backsliding* (Dec. 2016), http://www.cesr.org/sites/default/files/downloads/pec55_eng_final.pdf (published in El País on 1 Dec. 2016).

92. Letter from members of U.S. Congress to Ambassador Sergio Silva Do Amaral (18 Jan. 2017), https://conyers.house.gov/media-center/press-releases/prominent-members-us-congress-call-brazil-protect-rights-political.

93. David, *supra* note 75.

94. Ibid.

95. International Monetary Fund, *Brazil: 2017 Article IV Consultation-Press Release; Staff Report; and Statement by the Executive Director for Brazil* (2017), available online at https://www.imf.org/en/Publications/CR/Issues/2017/07/13/Brazil-2017-Article-IV-Consultation-Press-Release-Staff-Report-and-Statement-by-the-45081. See ibid., Press Release, at 2 ("The government aims to restore fiscal sustainability by gradually bringing primary balances toward surplus territory, with the support of the constitutional expenditure ceiling and social security reform"); ibid. Staff Report, at 11 (noting that "Policy is Heading in the Right Direction" and citing to the constitutional expenditure cap).

96. UN Office of the High Comm'r for Human Rights, Guiding Principles on Business and Human Rights, UN Doc. HR/PUB/11/04 (2011), http://www.ohchr.org/Documents/Publications/GuidingPrinciplesBusinessHR_EN.pdf.

97. *See* Maastricht Principles on Extraterritorial Obligations of States in the Area of Economic, Social and Cultural Rights (2013), available online at http://www.etoconsortium.org/nc/en/main-navigation/library/maastricht-principles/?tx_drblob_pi1%5BdownloadUid%5D=23.

98. These Guidelines expressly address home state responsibility, under principles of international co-operation and assistance, for assessing extraterritorial risks and impacts of laws, policies, and practice. See http://www.ohchr.org/EN/Issues/Poverty/Pages/DGPIntroduction.aspx.

99. See *infra* at 44.

100. Most of the human rights consequences of taxation discussed in the literature implicate economic, social, and cultural rights. The right to an effective remedy is not expressly addressed in the ICESCR. However, the Committee on Economic, Social and Cultural Rights (CESCR) has found the right to remedy inherent in the Covenant. And the General Assembly has passed a resolution underscoring that the right pertains to all violations. See GA Resolution 60/147; see also CESR, *A Post-2015 Fiscal Revolution* (2014), at 11 & n.61.

101. Even the IMF acknowledges these risks: "While some inequality is inevitable in a market-based economic system as a result of differences in talent, effort, and luck, excessive inequality could erode social cohesion, lead to political polarization, and ultimately lower economic growth." *IMF Fiscal Monitor: Tackling Inequality*, Oct. 2017, at 1.

102. W. Scheidel, *The Great Leveler: Violence and the History of Inequality from the Stone Age to the Twenty-First Century* (2017).

103. R. S. Avi-Yonah and O. Avi-Yonah, *Be Careful What You Wish For?: Reducing Inequality in the 21st Century*, University of Michigan, Public Law and Legal Theory Research Paper Series, Paper No. 547, Apr. 2017, at http://ssrn.com/abstract=2958401.

104. M. Valencia, *Reducing Inequality in Latin America: The Role of Tax Policy* (2017).

PART 1

THE RELEVANCE OF HUMAN
RIGHTS TO TAX LAW,
POLICY, AND PRACTICE

CHAPTER 1

TAXATION AND HUMAN RIGHTS

Mapping the Landscape

NIKKI REISCH

I. HUMANIZING TAXATION

A decade ago, the phrases "tax policy" and "human rights" were rarely uttered in the same room, let alone in the same report. Today, the human impacts of tax laws and loopholes figure prominently in policy roundtables and press headlines. In January 2018, for example, Winnie Byanyima, Executive Director of Oxfam International, told business leaders and politicians at the World Economic Forum, "Tax avoidance isn't just about euros, yens and dollars: it's about human rights. [It's a]bout people who are denied services to help them lift themselves out of poverty because of tax avoidance."[1] In February 2018, an independent expert appointed by the UN Human Rights Council issued a report examining how the tax policies of a prominent financial secrecy jurisdiction, Switzerland, affect enjoyment of human rights within and outside the country.[2] Just months earlier, investigative reporting on the so-called "Paradise Papers"— the latest in a series of high-profile leaks revealing systemic tax avoidance by corporations and wealthy individuals—prompted European and UN officials to call for greater crackdown on tax dodgers, noting that lost revenues undermine the realization of human rights.[3]

To be sure, there is nothing new about the observation that taxation affects individuals and society in myriad ways, altering income and wealth distribution and shaping behaviors. The political economy of taxation and its social consequences have long piqued the interest of scholars and policymakers. Nor is it novel to recognize that the payment of taxes or their avoidance can make or break a government's ability to provide goods and services to the governed. The problem of tax dodging has been a persistent preoccupation for decades. In 1980, the International Bar Association convened a conference on tax avoidance and evasion, noting that the "game" between taxpayers and their advisers on the one hand, and governments' tax administrators on the other, was only likely to get more cutthroat.[4] And indeed it has: Studies released in 2017 show that the use of tax havens continues to rise, while fierce tax competition between countries has driven steady declines in corporate tax rates across the globe, threatening steep revenue losses in some jurisdictions.[5]

What is a relatively recent phenomenon, however, is the effort to analyze the implications of global tax "wrongs" for human rights and scrutinize the content of tax rules through the lens of human rights law. In the ten years since the 2008 financial crisis, the issue of taxation has taken center stage in global debates about poverty, inequality, and economic reform. Concerns over the growing wealth and income gap, the visible social and political impacts of economic downturn, and the costs of austerity measures adopted in response to the crisis, have focused attention on the role of tax as both part of the problem and part of the solution to these trends threatening human rights.

Civil society organizations have been at the forefront of efforts to situate tax in a human rights context, by explicitly using the language and law of human rights to address tax policy and practice. Although traditional human rights organizations, such as Amnesty International and Human Rights Watch, have largely neglected fiscal policies,[6] some groups, such as the Center for Economic and Social Rights (CESR), have long argued that tax and spending measures have profound effects on the realization of human rights.[7] National tax regimes have been the subject of considerable human rights analysis, particularly on the part of women's rights groups that have challenged gender bias in tax codes and exposed the discriminatory impacts of certain tax measures, like the value-added tax (VAT) and joint filing of income taxes. Long-standing advocacy around budgeting for rights in many countries has expanded the focus on public spending and austerity measures to encompass the rights-compatibility of resource generation through taxation. International tax matters and the cross-border impacts of tax policies, however, have only recently been recognized as a human rights issue, largely in the wake of the 2008 global financial crisis and high-profile scandals around multinational corporations skirting taxes. The linkages have come into focus through human rights publications such as the International Bar Association's 2013 report, *Tax Abuses, Poverty and Human Rights*,[8] and a 2014 report on fiscal policy by the UN Special Rapporteur on extreme poverty and human rights, as well as sustained efforts by groups like CESR to strengthen rights-based analysis of tax policy and build alliances between tax justice and human rights advocates.[9]

As part of a growing tax justice movement, major anti-poverty and development organizations have sharpened the focus on tax as a critical issue for development and for combating global inequality, and are increasingly framing the debate in human rights terms.[10] The Tax Justice Network (TJN) was ahead of the curve in calling attention to the impacts of tax policy on development when it was founded in 2003. Today it is one of the leading groups influencing international tax reform debates,[11] particularly through its Financial Secrecy Index,[12] a go-to authority for information on the ways that states are facilitating or combating tax evasion and avoidance. TJN has teamed up with CESR and other human rights groups, like New York University's Global Justice Clinic, to illustrate how complex financial secrecy regimes contribute to concrete human rights harms and to push human rights institutions to act.[13] Oxfam,[14] Action Aid,[15] and Christian Aid[16] have played a central role in highlighting how rich countries' tax policies and tax avoidance by their multinationals harm developing countries in dire need of public revenues.[17] These groups worked to make taxation a key issue in the post-2015 Sustainable Development Goals[18] and a key part of the ongoing push for corporate accountability. The 2015 Lima Declaration on Tax Justice and Human Rights, endorsed by over 150 organizations around the globe, and the subsequent 2017 Bogota Declaration on Tax and Women's Rights, coordinated by the Global Alliance for Tax Justice,[19] reflect the growing commitment of diverse civil society actors to treat tax policy as human rights policy, and to challenge the inadequacy and inequity of tax policies, domestically and internationally.[20]

Buoyed by the work of investigative journalists to expose the widespread and systemic nature of tax abuses,[21] this growing chorus of civil society voices has garnered the attention of
policymakers, including those in international human rights institutions. During the past five
years, UN independent human rights experts and treaty bodies have been outspoken about the
duties of states to consider the implications of their tax policies for human rights both within and
outside of their borders. When states report to human rights treaty bodies on their compliance
with their treaty obligations today, they are more likely to face questions regarding their tax laws
than they were in the past.[22] Other intergovernmental bodies, such as the European Union,[23] the
G20, and the Organisation for Economic Co-operation and Development (OECD),[24] as well as
international financial institutions, including the World Bank and International Monetary Fund
(IMF),[25] have elevated issues of tax reform and domestic resource mobilization on their respective policy agendas. While these bodies rarely address how human rights law bears on state tax
regimes and enforcement practices, the pressure to do so is mounting.

The pressure to apply human rights law in the tax realm is coming not only from public interest groups seeking to deploy it as a sword to achieve increased tax transparency, progressivity
and accountability. A growing number of private actors, including businesses and wealthy
individuals, are also using human rights law as a shield to defend themselves against more stringent tax rates and reporting rules.[26] What these dueling approaches have in common, at least,
is a recognition that the realms of tax and human rights intersect.[27] The navigation of those
intersections remains contested, however, as a number of the chapters in this volume discuss.

The academic literature is catching up to these rapidly evolving public debates. A sizable body of scholarship already exists on public finance, macroeconomic policy, and human
rights.[28] With limited exception,[29] however, it focuses primarily on the spending side of the
ledger and the domestic level. A robust literature likewise examines the social impacts of specific tax policies, such VAT, from distributive justice and critical tax theory perspectives.[30] But
few such pieces address international human rights or the international tax system explicitly.
This volume and several other recent works[31] seek to fill those gaps, encouraging more direct
dialogue between tax and human rights experts on international as well as domestic tax policies.

The purpose of this chapter is twofold. First, it identifies several arenas in which the growing
discourse on human rights and taxation is particularly salient and where there are important
antecedents on which to build. Those include the fields of public budget analysis, development
finance, and corporate accountability. Second, it highlights markers of progress toward treating
tax policy as human rights policy, documenting steps taken by international and regional human
rights bodies to address taxation from a human rights perspective. The chapter concludes with
some reflections on persistent gaps and potential future directions for research, scholarship and
advocacy in this area.

II. CONTEXT FOR THE DEBATE ON TAX
AND HUMAN RIGHTS

Taxation is critical to the realization of human rights in both developed and developing countries. While the potential linkages between taxation and human rights are manifold, they can be
grouped under three broad headings: resource mobilization, redistribution, and accountability.
First and foremost, taxes generate revenues that states may use to protect and promote the rights
of their populations. Because they influence the "size of the pie," tax laws and related fiscal policies

are essential to the principle in human rights law that states should take steps to the "maximum of available resources" to realize human rights.[32] Ensuring adequate public revenues from taxation is a necessary but insufficient condition to guarantee the fulfillment of human rights. The effect on rights depends not only on how (and how much) revenue is raised, but how it is used.

Second, beyond determining the amount of resources a state has at its disposal to deliver on its human rights obligations, tax policies affect the distribution of resources within and between states. The regressive or progressive nature of a state's tax structure shapes the allocation of income and assets across the population, and across borders, and thereby affects various types of inequality. Furthermore, tax policies designed to incentivize certain types of economic activities or social behaviors can have human rights consequences for the individuals whose conduct is regulated and those on whom the costs or benefits of the targeted activities fall.

Finally, fiscal policies, including taxation, are a central feature of the relationship between the government and the governed. When designed and implemented well, taxes can reinforce the state's accountability to the public and strengthen democracy. When designed and implemented poorly, taxes can undermine confidence in the state and in the democratic process.

These linkages, although strong, have not always received due attention in the academic literature and global policy forums. Their relative absence from past discussions reflects the chronic neglect of economic and financial policies by most human rights scholars and practitioners, and the reluctance of many economists to look beyond their data sets and the marketplace at the social impacts of economic choices. The emerging discourse on taxation and human rights is not, however, without antecedents. It builds upon a robust academic literature and myriad practitioner resources in the fields of public budgeting for human rights (especially women's rights) and critical tax theory, as well as policy discussions addressing sustainable development and corporate accountability. To be sure, the tax and human rights nexus is pertinent to a number of other areas of study as well, including political philosophy, sociology, and the anthropology of law, to name just a few. A review of the literature in those other areas, however, is outside the scope of this chapter.

A. BUDGET ANALYSIS AND ADVOCACY

Increased attention to the links between human rights and tax today strengthens existing work on budget transparency and rights-based public budgeting. Consideration of the compatibility of tax measures with human rights helps ensure that budget advocacy addresses the full fiscal cycle, from revenue-raising to spending. As a government's most important policy document, the public budget "is an essential means by which to assess government's efforts for the realization of human rights."[33] Well before taxation became a hot topic among human rights scholars and practitioners, participatory budget monitoring and fiscal transparency measures were understood as tools of social justice and human rights advocacy.[34] In an effort to popularize the use of such tools, various groups have produced practitioners' guides on budget advocacy that is "rights-thematic, group-based, or both,"[35] such as budgeting for children's rights,[36] women's rights,[37] and the rights to health[38] and to food.[39] For example, the International Budget Partnership,[40] one of the pioneering organizations working on budget transparency, produced a handbook applying Article 2 of the International Covenant on Economic, Social and Cultural Rights (ICESCR) to public budgets.[41]

Until recently, much of the human rights work on public finance and fiscal policy largely ignored taxation. That is beginning to change, however, and the human rights dimensions of tax policy and practice are increasingly reflected in budget-related advocacy. In 2017, the

Office of the United Nations High Commissioner for Human Rights (OHCHR) worked with International Budget Partnership (IBP) to publish a comprehensive guide to "Realizing Rights through Government Budgets."[42] In contrast to earlier publications on rights-compatible budgeting that scarcely mention taxation,[43] this new guide addresses both revenue-raising, through a variety of forms of taxation, and budget allocation. It considers the human rights constraints on and implications of decisions regarding the size of the fiscal envelope, as well as the design of specific tax policies.

The same trends toward inclusion of tax in budget advocacy work are visible among women's rights organizations, which have been at the forefront of using human rights for budget policy work in support of gender equality. UN Women and the Committee on the Elimination of Discrimination Against Women (CEDAW Committee) pioneered tools for gender-responsive budgeting (GBR). For example, *Budgeting for Women's Rights, Monitoring Government Budgets for Compliance with CEDAW: A Summary Guide for Policy Makers, Gender Equality and Human Rights Advocates*,[44] published in 2006, assists readers to evaluate budgets against state treaty obligations and identify equality-enhancing approaches to fiscal policy. Although GBR has tended to focus on public spending,[45] the 2006 guide has a section dedicated to analyzing the gender impacts of policies for generating public revenues—be that through taxation or other sources—and the framework is increasingly being applied to revenue policies. In 2018, Oxfam published *A Guide to Gender-Responsive Budgeting*, which focuses on how both revenue-raising and spending decisions "meet and respond to the different needs of everyone, including women and men, girls and boys."[46] In September 2018, the European Parliament issued a draft report on gender equality and taxation policies that calls on the European Commission and member states to take gender-responsive approaches to ensure "that all policies for mobilising resources and allocating expenditure promote gender equality."[47]

Scholars have helped to document the impacts of such gender justice strategies in action[48] and have sharpened analytical tools for evaluating macroeconomic policies and public expenditure against a range of human rights obligations under various international treaties, including the Convention on the Elimination of All Forms of Discrimination Against Women (CEDAW), the Convention on the Rights of the Child, and ICESCR.[49] *Applying an international human rights framework to state budget allocations: rights and resources* articulates a methodology grounded in the ICESCR for analyzing sectoral budget allocations, such as funding for mental health and housing.[50] A multidisciplinary collection edited by Aoife Nolan, Rory O'Connell, and Colin Harvey, *Human Rights and Public Finance*, addresses the role of legislative and executive branches in realizing economic and social rights, principally through fiscal policies.[51] While the majority of the chapters in the book focus on spending measures, Ignacio Saiz's contribution, "Resourcing Rights," looks specifically at taxation and tax avoidance as a human rights issue.[52]

Scholarship on public budgeting and human rights is part of a broader literature on economic policy and human rights, which has helped give shape to the principle of "maximum available resources"—derived from Article 2 of the ICESCR. The groundbreaking work by Diane Elson, Radhika Balakrishnan, and Raj Panel, *Rethinking Macroeconomic Strategies from a Human Rights Perspective*,[53] sought to bring human rights and economics into conversation and provided a foundation for subsequent research and writing focused more specifically on taxation and fiscal policies. That piece and later articles the authors wrote with others[54] challenge approaches to human rights advocacy that take the amount of resources available to deliver on rights as given. In a more recent work, *Rethinking Economic Policy for Social Justice: The Radical Potential of Human Rights*, Balakrishnan, Elson, and James Heintz discuss how central precepts of human rights should guide tax policy and efforts to improve tax collection, among other sources of state revenue.[55]

Since 2008, practitioners and scholars working at the intersection of economic policy and human rights have analyzed how the financial crisis and austerity measures adopted in response have exacerbated or mitigated impacts on the most vulnerable populations.[56] These studies have fueled further interest in taxation, as both part of the cause of fiscal crises and their social consequences, and as a potential tool to rectify global imbalances. CESR has spearheaded work examining the regressive effects of austerity measures in multiple countries,[57] and has contributed to the development of a methodology for assessing the human rights impacts of fiscal consolidation, including regressive tax changes which are among the hallmarks of austerity.[58] CESR's 2018 briefing, *Assessing Austerity: Monitoring the Human Rights Impacts of Fiscal Consolidation*,[59] helped lay the foundation for the Guiding Principles on Human Rights Impact Assessments of Economic Reforms, a draft of which was issued later that same year by the UN Independent Expert on Debt and Human Rights at the behest of the Human Rights Council.[60]

This work on austerity builds on a series of studies by UN experts and intergovernmental bodies, calling attention to the impacts of the global financial crisis on the rights of the poor, due in particular to precipitous job losses and rising food prices.[61] Beyond the consequences of the crisis itself, the consequences of *responses* to the crisis have likewise garnered increased UN attention, with various studies documenting the disparate effects of fiscal consolidation on the realization of economic, social, and cultural rights.[62] The former Special Rapporteur on extreme poverty and human rights, Magdalena Sepulveda, issued several reports addressing the human rights dimensions of the crisis and state responses to it.[63] The Human Rights Commissioner of the Council of Europe published a report in November 2013 entitled, *Safeguarding Human Rights in Times of Economic Crisis*, which concluded that austerity measures were exacerbating the adverse impacts of the crisis on human rights.[64] In December 2015, the Council's Steering Committee for Human Rights published a feasibility study on *The impact of the economic crisis and austerity measures on human rights in Europe*,[65] which surveys cases that have been brought in European courts challenging austerity measures and identifies several potential ways forward for exploring these issues.

In addition to calling attention to the costs of regressive tax and spending measures, the fallout from the financial crisis has prompted interest in progressive tax "solutions," such as a global financial transaction tax[66] and other measures to tamp down on banking speculation and make financial actors, rather than the public, pay when things go awry.[67] A coalition of economists, policymakers, scholars, and nongovernmental organization (NGO) representatives launched a campaign for a financial transaction tax in the United States, called the Robin Hood Tax.[68] CESR and other members of the Righting Finance[69] coalition have characterized the financial transaction tax as a "human rights imperative," arguing that it would: help governments mobilize maximum available resources to realize human rights in a progressive, equalizing manner; support governments' duty to protect against human rights abuses by discouraging risk-taking; and provide some redress for the deprivations of rights caused by the financial crisis.[70] In his bestselling book, *Capital in the Twenty-First Century*, Thomas Piketty called for a progressive global tax on capital—a proposal distinct from a financial transaction tax, but one that similarly requires global cooperation in the sharing of financial and tax information so as to enable accurate assessment of individuals' net wealth.[71] Even the IMF has suggested that financial transaction taxes or a global wealth tax could be a good idea.[72]

These publications highlight the gap between international human rights law standards on the one hand, and national and global policy responses to successive waves of financial and economic crises on the other. More broadly, increased attention to taxation as a crucial determinant of the size and shape of the fiscal pie encourages a greater role for human rights scholars and practitioners in upstream budget policy debates regarding revenue-raising, and a more realistic understanding of competing demands on the public purse.

B. TAXATION AND DEVELOPMENT

The emerging discourse on tax and human rights is particularly salient to long-standing discussions of the relationship between tax and development. Historically, much of that discussion has focused on how the design of domestic tax policies and tax holidays in developing countries could encourage foreign direct investment and facilitate tax administration. International development institutions have long faced criticism for their tax policy advice to developing countries, which has encouraged widespread adoption of consumption taxes like the VAT and lower corporate taxes, shifting the tax burden onto the poorest. More recently, attention has turned to the ways in which international tax policies and practices, including tax abuse, affect developing country budgets disproportionately. As scholars and practitioners connect the dots to the human rights consequences of these fiscal trends, they are encouraging policymakers to look to human rights law, as well as economic doctrine, when setting the parameters for tax measures and doling out policy advice aimed at spurring economic development.[73]

When the 2008 economic recession triggered reductions in the foreign aid provided by industrialized countries, conversations about financing for the Millennium Development Goals (MDGs) focused increasingly on domestic resource mobilization through taxation. Questions naturally arose not only about how much revenue developing countries could generate on their own but also how much they were losing through outflows due to tax evasion and avoidance or forgoing entirely through tax holidays granted to attract investors.[74] During the negotiation of the successor agreement to the MDGs, the Sustainable Development Goals (SDGs), the issue of financing was front and center. Concerns about domestic resource mobilization and reform of the international tax regime topped the agenda of the Financing for Development Conference, held in Addis Ababa in July 2015. The Addis outcome document emphasized the need to build the capacity of government tax administrations, combat tax avoidance, and strengthen the UN Committee of Experts on International Cooperation in Tax Matters.[75] The final version of the SDGs, adopted later that year, contains commitments to "significantly reduce" illicit financial flows by 2030,[76] to staunch fiscal losses, and "[s]trengthen domestic resource mobilization, including through international support to developing countries, to improve domestic capacity for tax and other revenue collection."[77]

The pressure to address taxation in the SDGs came largely from civil society groups and governments from the Global South.[78] For example, a 2014 report by CESR and Christian Aid, *A Post-2015 Fiscal Revolution: Human Rights Policy Brief*,[79] advocates that states fulfill certain tax policy obligations with a view toward realizing the Sustainable Development Goals. The report emphasizes transparency, tax retention, and measures designed to reduce income inequality. It includes an overview of various measures that could be implemented to boost public revenues, including policies to end tax evasion, the imposition of taxes on financial transactions and carbon emissions, and the cancellation of odious debt. It proposes six targets for the post-2015 development agenda, based on illustrative indicators and benchmarks: (1) raise resources to deliver essential services to all; (2) end tax evasion and illicit flows; (3) reduce inequality through progressive tax structures; (4) improve states' redistributive capacities to enhance equality of all socioeconomic groups; (5) ensure access to information and participation in fiscal policy design and implementation; and (6) guarantee public and judicial oversight.[80]

At the same time as groups pushed to put tax on the agenda, civil society mounted pressure to make the SDGs human rights–compatible. That effort met with mixed success; for example, critics have pointed out that there is no freestanding human rights goal in the final SDGs and no attempt to index the goals expressly to human rights law.[81] Nonetheless, the implicit integration of human rights principles, such as transparency, accountability, participation, equality, and nondiscrimination, across many of the goals[82] encourages the incorporation of human rights considerations in the design and evaluation of policies aimed at achieving targets regarding domestic resource mobilization and tax abuse.

The pressure to boost domestic resource mobilization and plug leakages of tax revenue from developing countries has prompted some experts at international development and finance institutions to question long-held assumptions about taxation and evaluate the impacts of their work in this area. For example, a joint report by the IMF, OECD, United Nations, and World Bank in 2011, "Supporting the Development of More Effective Tax Systems," made recommendations to the G20 regarding measures industrialized countries can take to boost developing country capacity to administer tax regimes and curb avoidance and abuses by multinational corporations.[83] Other IMF research addresses the challenges of tax design and enforcement in the post-crisis era of rising income inequality.[84] More critical reflection on the IMF's traditional tax policy advice emerged in 2016 with publications such as "Neoliberalism Oversold?,"[85] and in 2017 with the October issue of the IMF's Fiscal Monitor, entitled "Tackling Inequality." The latter describes an overall decline in the progressivity of income tax systems around the world, citing the regressive impacts of reforms to tax and transfer programs and low levels of taxation of capital income. The authors conclude that increasing marginal taxes on top-end earners would not negatively affect growth, that tackling tax avoidance is key, and that filling gaps in social safety nets or considering universal, rather than means-tested, programs, such as universal basic income (UBI) (explored in the final chapters in this volume), would help decrease inequality.[86]

During this same period, researchers at the IMF have also begun to address the extraterritorial impacts of a country's tax policies, begging questions about the obligations that flow therefrom, including under human rights law. In 2014, the IMF released a staff report entitled "Spillovers in International Corporate Taxation," which examined the effects of one country's rules and practices with regard to corporate taxation on other countries. It concluded that tax policies influence tax avoidance behavior extraterritorially and have particularly significant impacts on revenue in low-income countries.[87] Following the adoption of sweeping reforms to the corporate tax code in the United States, a 2018 IMF evaluation found that the changes would likely result in the loss of an average of 13 percent of corporate tax revenues across all countries, exacerbating resource scarcity particularly in developing countries.[88]

Although several of the Fund's recent research products may reflect a more progressive turn in the thinking of some of the institution's economists, its lending packages and policy advice to indebted countries remain focused on fiscal consolidation, as discussed in the introduction to this volume, and its attention to human rights impacts, negligible.[89] The same applies to much of the work done by the Fund's sister institution, the World Bank Group, in the area of taxation. A February 2017 internal evaluation of World Bank Group support for tax reform brought to light aspects of the institution's public and private financing and advisory activities previously unseen.[90] It found that the majority of the Bank's tax policy projects that aimed at raising government revenue and/or strengthening the investment climate were also coupled with fiscal consolidation measures, including requirements that governments eliminate tax exemptions, some of which are crucial for redistribution. Likewise there was a conspicuous lack of attention to the equity of tax systems, and insufficient effort by the institution to measure whether reforms designed to ease tax administration affected revenue collection or compliance.[91]

Although the human rights implications of taxation are not yet part of the regular dialogue across the International Financial Institutions, critical perspectives on tax policies are becoming more mainstream. The Inter-American Development Bank's flagship publication in 2013, "More than Revenue: Taxation as Development Tool," argues that taxes should be designed to promote development, not just raise revenues, and identifies some of the problems with tax systems in the region, including evasion, regressive structures, and the failure to use taxes to improve environmental and social welfare.[92] In February 2018, the first global conference of the Platform for Collaboration on Tax was held in New York, to discuss needed reforms in the areas of tax policy and administration to ensure implementation of the Sustainable Development Goals. A joint initiative of the IMF, OECD, United Nations, and the World Bank Group, the Platform seeks to bolster collaboration between the sponsor institutions, support capacity-building in the area of tax for developing countries, and facilitate the participation of the latter in multilateral dialogues regarding international tax policy.[93]

What's clear from the above is that development institutions and policymakers are increasingly discussing the social implications of fiscal policy, as well as the economic impacts of taxing and spending. Although the concept of "human rights" rarely surfaces in those discussions,[94] there are more opportunities to bring human rights concepts and laws to the table as tax policies are shaped, and—given the nature of current global crises—more reason to do so now than ever.

C. CORPORATE ACCOUNTABILITY

A third critical context for the emerging discourse on tax and human rights is the ongoing movement to define the scope of corporate responsibility under human rights law, and to hold corporations accountable for human rights harms. Since the Human Rights Council's endorsement of the UN Guiding Principles on Business and Human Rights in 2011, the number of "human rights policies" at corporations has multiplied, as have efforts to require corporations to conduct human rights due diligence and impact assessments.[95] While compliance with some host and home country laws regulating corporate conduct figures centrally in these efforts, the issue of tax compliance has been largely absent from the discussion about corporate human rights duties.[96] That is beginning to change, as investigative journalists, NGOs, and policymakers connect the dots between corporate tax behavior and the deprivation of rights in various countries where companies operate.

Between 2014 and 2017, a series of leaks and investigative reports exposed how various countries, banks, accountants, and law firms facilitate tax dodging by corporations and wealthy individuals. Some of the first disclosures revealed that Ireland,[97] the Netherlands,[98] and Luxembourg[99] have facilitated tax avoidance by some of the world's largest companies, including Apple, Starbucks, Disney, IKEA, and Fiat. In what has come to be known as the "LuxLeaks" scandal, documents uncovered by the International Consortium of Investigative Journalists (ICIJ) revealed how companies have used aggressive tax planning strategies and entered into secret deals with the government of Luxembourg to avoid paying billions in taxes.[100] The European Commission has launched investigations into the tax deals and whether the role played by EU member states constitutes illegal state aid.[101] In 2016, it concluded that Ireland had provided illegal state aid to Apple, through tax benefits that allowed the company to avoid paying 13 billion euros.[102] Following the threat of a suit before the European Court of Justice for noncompliance with the decision,[103] Ireland was set to begin recovering the unpaid revenues in 2018, to be held in escrow pending outcome of the appeal.[104]

In 2015, 2016, and 2017, revelations snowballed, from the Swiss Leaks scandal to the Panama Papers and Paradise Papers, fueling public outcry. The Paradise Papers, disclosed in November 2017, include 13.4 million leaked files that "expose offshore holdings of political leaders and their financiers as well as household-name companies that slash taxes through transactions conducted in secret."[105] This leak followed on the heels of the Panama Papers, a trove of over 11.5 million files leaked from a law firm in Panama that specialized in creating shell companies and other corporate vehicles designed to help businesses avoid tax payments.[106] In 2013, a far smaller number of documents leaked from the Swiss branch of HSBC bank (merely 60,000 files), caused an uproar when it exposed how the bank was profiting from dealings with criminals and tax dodgers from all over the world.[107]

Hard-hitting NGO reports and campaign materials by ActionAid, Christian Aid, Oxfam, and others, have detailed the harmful effects of the corporate tax evasion and avoidance exposed by these investigations, particularly in developing countries. In 2010, ActionAid was among the first organizations to issue a report on the costs of corporate tax abuse. Its publication, *Calling Time: Why SAB Miller Should Stop Dodging Taxes in Africa*,[108] helped build interest in the need for reform of the broken international tax system. The report's findings were debated in various fora, including the UN Tax Committee, the African Tax Administration Forum, and the OECD.[109] ActionAid built on this work with a series of reports published in 2013 that profile other corporate practices and government policies that deprive developing countries of needed revenues. For example, *Sweet Nothings: the human cost of a British sugar giant avoiding taxes in southern Africa*, profiles how much tax revenue Zambia lost as a result of the tax-planning practices of Associated British Foods group, and how that money could have been used to improve human rights conditions.[110] Another report estimates that tax breaks for corporations, offered by developing countries as "incentives" to lure investment, may cost African countries up to $138 billion per year.[111] In addition to profiling the human costs of such tax incentives (for example, by comparing lost revenues to healthcare services or teacher salaries that could have been paid for with those funds), ActionAid cites research showing that the inducements are neither necessary to attract investment nor a source of net benefits for the countries that offer them, in terms of overall levels of investment or economic growth.[112] ActionAid has since trained its sights on other structural and legal conditions that enable tax abuses or fail to prevent them, including the provisions of tax treaties. In 2016, ActionAid released *Mistreated: The tax treaties that are depriving the world's poorest countries of vital revenue*,[113] along with a publicly available data set of the bilateral tax treaties binding between countries.

Reports by Christian Aid have similarly helped document effects of tax policies on the poor, shaping the narrative and building public interest in an issue previously seen as too dry and technical to form the basis of a popular campaign. One such report, *Who Pays the Price: Hunger, the Hidden Cost of Tax Injustice*, examines the revenues lost in developing countries due to tax avoidance and corporate use of tax secrecy jurisdictions, like Switzerland, to funnel profits offshore and transact sales of resources extracted abroad.[114] The report juxtaposes the tax gap in developing countries with estimates of the cost of ending global hunger. A May 2014 report addressed the problem of opacity in the financial sector and discussed how the use of secrecy jurisdictions facilitates tax dodging and undermines countries' efforts to cope with the ongoing effects of the 2008 financial crisis.[115]

Although its publications rarely reference human rights explicitly, the leading global anti-poverty organization, Oxfam International, initiated a tax justice campaign several years ago and in short order has become one of the most vocal civil society groups advocating for international tax reform.[116] Oxfam has helped propel tax justice into the international spot-light, particularly in the context of its "Even it Up" campaign to end extreme inequality.[117] Its May 2014 report, *Business among friends: Why corporate tax dodgers are not yet losing sleep over global tax reform*, discusses the magnitude of unpaid corporate tax liability in developing countries, as well as giveaways in the form of tax holidays and other concessions.[118] It also critiques ongoing intergovernmental processes focused on taxation, highlighting their biases in favor of developed countries and corporations, and their inadequate attention to developing country needs. A 2016 report, *Tax Battles: The Dangerous Global Race to the Bottom on Corporate Tax*, profiles the world's fifteen worst corporate tax havens, and analyzes how the continued existence of tax havens and persistent competition between countries over corporate tax rates combines to harm poor states in particular.[119] The following year, Oxfam published *Making Tax Vanish*, which traces the abusive practices of one multinational consumer goods company to failures in the global tax regime.[120]

The Netherlands-based Center for Research on Multinational Corporations (SOMO) was among the first of the relatively few organizations to expressly address how tax abuse relates to the UN Guiding Principles on Business and Human Rights (UNGP).[121] *Private Gain—Public Loss*,[122] a report on mailbox companies, tax avoidance, and human rights, exposes the imbalance between the benefits reaped by several extractive industry companies that call the Netherlands home, and the costs borne by the developing countries in which they operate and from which they divert revenues. Eschewing highly technical terms, SOMO explains how international corporations avoid or minimize their tax liability by setting up holding companies or other conduit entities in the Netherlands.[123] Pointing to the principles of international cooperation and assistance, the state duty to protect, and various "soft law" instruments, such as the UN Guiding Principles on Business and Human Rights, the OECD Guidelines on Multinational Enterprises, and General Comments of the UN Committee on Economic, Social and Cultural Rights (CESCR), SOMO addresses the extraterritorial obligations that countries like the Netherlands bear both for the impacts of the overseas operations of their corporate "citizens," and for the effects of Dutch tax and fiscal policies on the capacity of other states to mobilize maximum available resources for the realization of human rights.[124] As discussed below and in chapter 7 of this volume, by Lusiani and Cosgrove, some international human rights bodies have taken up the notion that states are responsible for the effects of their tax policies outside their borders. Getting states to regulate the tax behavior of their corporate citizens abroad, however, remains a challenge.

As issues of taxation have become more prominent in the media and in NGO campaigns, businesses have become more sensitive to the reputational risks posed by their tax practices. In an effort to reach the business audience, in 2013, ActionAid published *Tax Responsibility: An Investor Guide*. Designed for use by (institutional) investors, the report discusses the reputational, financial, and regulatory risks of aggressive and secretive tax practices, not to developing countries but to the corporations in which investors may be placing their funds. The guide sets out criteria on tax responsibility and provides guidance on how to analyze and minimize tax-related risk. A 2015 publication entitled, *Getting to Good: Toward Responsible Corporate Tax Behavior*, co-authored by Oxfam, ActionAid, and Christian Aid,[125] puts the onus on corporations to change their practices. The discussion paper, which is expanded upon in chapter 17 in this volume, addresses "why and how approaching tax responsibility beyond legal compliance benefits companies and the developing countries in which they operate."[126] Like SOMO's report, *Getting to Good* expressly grounds the proposed approach to responsible tax behavior in the UNGP, with a particular emphasis on the due diligence and impact assessment prongs of the UNGP.[127]

In a move reminiscent of the corporate social responsibility boom of the early 2000s, and indicative of the level of concern the above-mentioned media and NGO campaigns have caused, some businesses are trying to get out ahead of potential binding regulations and legal reforms regarding tax compliance by adopting voluntary measures. In February 2018, a group of multinational companies joined together to form what they call "The B Team" and issued a set of principles regarding "good" corporate tax practice.[128] The seven principles outlined in the B Team's platform include a commitment to greater transparency regarding business tax structures and practices. The corporate signatories pledge to publish an explanation of their group structure and a list of all their business entities with ownership information; an explanation of why the corporation has entities operating in low tax jurisdictions; annual information regarding the company's overall effective tax rate and country-specific tax payments; and information regarding "financially material tax incentives" received.[129]

While such voluntary approaches may denote an important change in corporate culture regarding the acceptability of tax avoidance, many believe that regulatory changes are required to fix a fundamentally broken system. In 2015, at the urging of a civil society coalition comprising many of the NGOs active in this area, the Independent Commission for the Reform of Corporate Taxation (ICRICT) was formed with the mission of broadening the limited debates around the international corporate tax regime and generating specific proposals regarding taxation of multinational companies. The Commission, which considers that multinational corporations act as, and therefore should be taxed as, single entities doing business across borders, put forward a proposal in 2018 for a system of global formulary apportionment and a minimum corporate tax rate.[130] Although ICRICT refers to human rights in its founding declaration, its proposals rely on the language of fairness, rather than the text of human rights law. A deeper understanding of the linkages between human rights and tax laws could reinforce the foundations for radical reforms in the area of corporate regulation.

The above three areas are just some of the current debates in which discussion of the intersection between tax and human rights may be relevant. The following section provides a brief summary of recent publications and policy developments that illustrate the progress being made toward treating tax policy as human rights policy.

III. MARKERS OF PROGRESS ON HUMAN RIGHTS AND TAXATION

In 2013, the International Bar Association Human Rights Institute (IBAHRI) convened a Task Force on Illicit Financial Flows, Poverty, and Human Rights, to examine questions regarding the types of tax structures and transactions that affect revenues in developing and developed countries, the boundary between legal tax avoidance and illegal evasion, legal responsibility for tax abuses, and the measures needed to address the problem, including the duty of lawyers to assist in preventing and combating the negative impacts of tax abuse on human rights. The resulting report, entitled *Tax Abuses, Poverty, and Human Rights*,[131] addresses how human rights law relates to transfer pricing and other cross-border intragroup transactions; the negotiation of tax holidays and incentives;[132] the taxation of natural resources; and the use of offshore investment accounts. The report highlights the need for international human rights mechanisms to grapple with tax abuses, and urges UN bodies to conduct further research on the relationship between tax abuse, poverty, and human rights.[133] A number of UN institutions have taken up that call.

United Nations treaty bodies, charged with interpreting and monitoring the implementation of human rights conventions, have been instrumental in highlighting the human rights implications of tax policy and practice through their reviews of state party compliance and their general comments. Since 2015, the Committee on Economic, Social and Cultural Rights has issued recommendations to several states addressing tax policy and illicit financial flows. In 2016, for example, the Committee's Concluding Observations to the United Kingdom expressed concern that "financial secrecy legislation and permissive rules on corporate tax are affecting the ability of the State party, as well other States, to meet their obligation to mobilize the maximum available resources for the implementation of economic, social and cultural rights" and recommended that the government "take strict measures to combat tax abuse by high-net-worth individuals and corporations."[134] The Committee has also called on Honduras,[135] Paraguay,[136] Angola,[137] Burkina Faso,[138] and Lichtenstein[139] to take similar steps, including to tackle illicit financial flows, in the context of their state party reviews.

The CEDAW Committee has perhaps gone the furthest, introducing questions regarding domestic tax policies and their extraterritorial impacts into its state party reviews on numerous occasions since 2016. Prompted by the work of a coalition of civil society groups, including the Global Justice Clinic at NYU School of Law, the Center for Economic and Social Rights, and the Tax Justice Network,[140] the CEDAW Committee expressed concern about the impacts of Swiss corporate reporting and tax laws on the ability of other states to mobilize the maximum available resources for the realization of women's rights, and issued a strong recommendation to Switzerland in 2016: "undertake independent, participatory and periodic impact assessments of the extraterritorial effects of its financial secrecy and corporate tax policies on women's rights and substantive equality, and ensure that such assessments are conducted in an impartial manner with public disclosure of the methodology and findings."[141] In 2017 and 2018, the Committee posed similar questions and issued similar recommendations to Luxembourg,[142] Singapore,[143] and Barbados.[144] The Committee's concluding observations on Barbados's report not only addressed the extraterritorial, gendered impacts of its financial secrecy policies and rules on corporate reporting, but also highlighted the disproportionate adverse effect of its austerity policies and specific tax measures, such as VAT, on women domestically.[145]

Treaty bodies have also begun to address taxation more explicitly in their general comments and recommendations. In May 2016, the Committee on the Rights of the Child issued a General Comment on Public Budgeting that called on states to cooperate in eradicating abusive tax practices.[146] This General Comment built upon prior work by the Committee on Economic, Social and Cultural Rights and the CEDAW Committee concerning the human rights dimensions of budget policy, and particularly the principle of nonretrogression.[147] In 2017, the Committee on Economic, Social and Cultural Rights issued a General Comment on business and human rights that clearly identifies tax competition as "inconsistent with human rights," and urges states to "encourage business actors whose conduct they are in a position to influence to ensure that they do not undermine the efforts of the States in which they operate to fully realize the Covenant rights, for instance by resorting to tax evasion or tax avoidance strategies in the countries concerned."[148]

Independent experts appointed by the United Nations have likewise raised their voices in recent years about the relationship between tax policy and human rights. As noted above, Magdalena Sepúlveda Carmona, the former Special Rapporteur on extreme poverty and human rights, issued a report in 2014 detailing the human rights consequences of fiscal policy, including both revenue raising through taxation and spending measures.[149] The report followed closely on the heels of the IBAHRI study, but was broader in its consideration of the design of domestic tax laws, not just their avoidance. Her analysis suggests that a state's compliance with human rights obligations to meet the minimum core needs of its population may require the establishment of progressive taxation systems in order to redress discrimination and ensure equal access to economic, social, and cultural rights. That is, human rights law may demand certain approaches to revenue generation, even as it permits variations in policy design based on country-specific conditions. She also emphasized that the rights to participation, transparency, accountability, and access to information apply equally to the design and implementation of tax measures. Obligations of international assistance and cooperation likewise come into play, triggering the duties of states to prevent abuse, regulate tax planning, and support stronger tax administrations, particularly in developing countries. In accordance with their duties to refrain from conduct that would impair the ability of other states to fulfill their human rights obligations and to create an enabling environment for the realization of rights, states must not facilitate tax avoidance or constrain other states' ability to implement fiscal policies beneficial for their populations.[150] The Special Rapporteur underscored the inadequacy of the current rules governing cross-border financial flows and the interaction of different jurisdictions' tax regimes, calling for "[a] new multilateral tax regime based on the premise of tax cooperation over competition."[151] Her successor, Special Rapporteur Philip Alston, has continued the mandate's focus on fiscal policy as a crucial determinant of human rights. In reports on his visits to various countries, including Chile and the United States, as well as thematic reports, Alston has frequently examined the impacts of taxation on people living in poverty and on inequality.[152]

The pioneering work of the Special Rapporteur on extreme poverty and human rights fueled the Human Rights Council's interest in issues of fiscal policy, prompting resolutions mandating further research into related issues by other experts. In 2016, the Independent Expert on foreign debt and human rights issued a report on the relationship between illicit financial flows and human rights, which underscores many of the fundamental connections between public revenues lost through tax abuse and the deprivation of rights.[153] In early 2018, he issued a report on the effects of Swiss tax and financial secrecy policies on human rights within and outside of Switzerland. Following on the heels of the CEDAW recommendation to Switzerland mentioned above, the Independent Expert set out to "study Switzerland's policies and efforts, at national and international level, aiming at curbing illicit financial flows, tax abuse and corruption and their impact on the enjoyment of human rights within and outside Switzerland."[154] While he observed some progress, the Independent Expert highlighted the need to integrate human rights considerations more consistently across economic and financial policies, including, among other recommendations, through the conduct of a human rights impact assessment of then-proposed corporate tax reforms.[155] In 2016, the UN Independent Expert on the promotion of a democratic and equitable international order also addressed tax matters, calling on the new Secretary General of the United Nations to convene a world conference on the abolition of tax havens.[156]

Regional human rights bodies also have begun to enter the tax justice debate. In its first report on poverty and human rights in the Americas, published in December 2017, the Inter-American Commission on Human Rights emphasized the importance of examining fiscal policies, including taxation, when assessing the problem of poverty and measures to address it.[157] The Commission's report explicitly references two hearings held in 2015 and 2016, on fiscal policy and human rights in Latin America and the human rights impacts of austerity measures in the region.[158] Both hearings were sponsored by civil society organizations active in the field of tax justice, including the Center for Economic and Social Rights and the International Budget Partnership. In December 2017, the African Commission on Human and Peoples' Rights issued a "Statement on Illicit Financial Flight and other Concerns Arising from the Paradise Papers,"[159] expressing concern about corporate abuse of tax loopholes, tax havens, and shell companies that deprive African governments of billions of dollars annually. The statement, which was written by the Commission's Working Group on Extractive Industries, Environment and Human Rights, followed an earlier resolution from 2013 on illicit flight of capital from Africa.[160] The African Charter on Human and Peoples' Rights is noteworthy in that it includes among the duties of the individual the duty "to pay taxes imposed by law in the interest of the society."[161] This explicit reference in Africa's foundational human rights instrument to the fiscal obligations of individuals invites regional and national human rights institutions across the continent to deepen their engagement on issues of taxation.

The above survey of recent tax-related developments within international human rights institutions reflects the rapid rise in awareness regarding the human rights impacts and imperatives of tax policy. It also reflects the broad range of rights affected by fiscal policy. But other opportunities to integrate critical tax analysis in human rights reporting and enforcement procedures remain yet unexplored. For example, fiscal policy rarely surfaces in the Universal Periodic Review (UPR) process, through which each UN member state submits to peer review of its human rights record. Indeed, UPR debates and recommendations have tended to neglect economic and social rights,[162] and have all but ignored the impacts of fiscal policy on the protection of civil and political rights. The onus is on civil society actors, as well as member states, to ensure that discussions about human rights implementation do not occur in isolation from discussions about tax revenues and spending. The door to such dialogue has been opened, but there is a long way to go before tax matters are routinely addressed in human rights fora, and longer still before human rights experts get a seat at the table where tax policy is set.

IV. CONCLUSION

If today there is active debate on the connections between tax and human rights, it is due largely to the persistent and innovative efforts of civil society organizations and the willingness of some scholars to push disciplinary boundaries. The many civil society publications issued on fiscal policy and human rights in recent years have helped advance multiple objectives: (1) they sketch the magnitude of revenues not captured by existing tax collection processes or that are diverted from the public purse; (2) they attempt to draw lines of accountability between those losses and the "home states" of the actors avoiding tax payments or the tax jurisdictions that facilitate such avoidance; (3) they relate the emerging norms of conduct and the expectation that nonstate actors, such as the corporations committing tax abuses, respect human rights and the impact of corporate activity in the "host states" where they do business; (4) they provide guidance and examples of how to apply human rights principles to the analyses of government tax structures, budget processes, and spending; and (5) they reinforce the importance of promoting meaningful public participation, transparency, and accountability in the formulation, implementation, and review of taxation policies. Various websites serve as repositories of relevant publications.[163]

While still relatively limited, new scholarship addressing the human rights impacts of international tax policy and abusive corporate tax practices[164] as well as a growing body of critical tax literature at the domestic level, is also helping to establish a foundation for mainstreaming tax in human rights policy and human rights in tax policy. A 2016 book edited by Thomas Pogge and Krishen Mehta, *Global Tax Fairness*, confronts the implications of tax policies and practices for social and economic justice, examining specific policy proposals designed to enhance global financial transparency. While not a strictly legal analysis, a 2017 publication by Paul Beckett, *Tax Havens and International Human Rights*, delves into the definition and workings of tax havens and their relationship to international human rights law, with an emphasis on state obligations regarding the extraterritorial effects of their policies. Human rights concerns have long been implicit in critical tax scholarship addressing domestic tax laws from the perspective of social policy and distributive justice.[165] Books such as *Critical Tax Theory: An Introduction* and *Feminist Judgments: Rewritten Tax Opinions* examine the ways that tax regimes may discriminate on the basis of race, gender, sexual orientation, or economic status, but mostly do so without express reference to human rights instruments, institutions, or jurisprudence.[166] Although for the most part tax law is "still not 'contaminated' by human rights interrogations,"[167] that is changing, thanks to the urging of scholars, such as Allison Christians, who have been instrumental in introducing concepts of human rights into the tax law literature.[168]

As the consensus around the need for a major overhaul of the international tax system grows, critical thinking is needed to envision a new tax architecture, grounded in human rights principles rather than business priorities. Moreover, more work is needed to translate critical analysis into concrete avenues for holding duty-bearers responsible, to shift the focus of the conversation from tax accounting to accountable taxation. Scholars should assess whether the concept of taxpayer standing permits suits against taxing authorities not only for the improper allocation of tax funds, but for the inadequate generation of funds to satisfy the state's legal obligations under human rights law. And they should explore whether any analogous doctrines support transnational claims against companies that avoid taxes or the states that make such avoidance possible. The growing exposure of tax abuses has raised public ire, but there is a need for more creative thinking about where and how to right those tax wrongs.

A confluence of political and economic factors has laid the foundation for, and increased the interest in, scholarship exploring the intersections between human rights and taxation. Ample avenues exist to deepen our understanding of the ways that tax policy and practice enable or constrain the realization of human rights, and to investigate the potential of human rights law and principles to improve the design and implementation of tax policies domestically and internationally. The essays in this volume take some steps down these paths and invite others to follow.

NOTES

1. *Beyond the Paradise Papers*, World Economic Forum, 25 Jan. 2018, 08:49, available online at https://www.weforum.org/events/world-economic-forum-annual-meeting-2018/sessions/a0W0X00000AgoNmUAJ?tab=LiveBlogs&stream=day-3-2018&stream-item=coming-up-the-crypto-asset-bubble.
2. Report of the Independent Expert on the effects of foreign debt and other related financial obligations of States on the full enjoyment of all human rights, particularly economic, social and cultural rights, on his visit to Switzerland, UN Doc. A/HRC/37/54/Add.3, 23 Feb. 2018 (by Juan Pablo Bohoslavsky).
3. S. Alecci, *EU, UN Experts Push for Tax Dodging Crackdown after Paradise Papers*, International Consortium of Investigative Journalists, 16 Nov. 2017, available online at https://www.icij.org/investigations/paradise-papers/eu-un-experts-push-tax-dodging-crackdown-paradise-papers/
4. International Bar Association, *Tax Avoidance, Tax Evasion* (1987).
5. See, e.g., G. Zucman, 'The desperate inequality behind global tax dodging', *The Guardian*, 8 Nov. 2017, available online at https://www.theguardian.com/commentisfree/2017/nov/08/tax-havens-dodging-theft-multinationals-avoiding-tax; M. Keen, 'False Profits: Avoidance by multinationals and competition between governments are forcing a rethink of the international tax system', 54(3) *Finance & Development* (2017), 10–13.

6. There are of course, some exceptions. See, e.g., FIDH and Hellenic League for Human Rights, *Downgrading Rights: the cost of austerity in Greece* (2014).

7. See *History*, Center for Economic and Social Rights, http://cesr.org/history (last visited 10 Mar. 2018).

8. International Bar Association Human Rights Institute, *Tax Abuses, Poverty and Human Rights* (2013).

9. See generally *Challenging Fiscal Abuse and Promoting Human Rights–Aligned Tax Policies*, Center for Economic and Social Rights, http://www.cesr.org/human-rights-taxation (last visited 18 Sept. 2018).

10. For example, Oxfam published a blog in November 2017 entitled "Why tax dodging is a human rights issue," available online at https://blogs.oxfam.org/en/blogs/17-11-21-why-tax-dodging-human-rights-issue, 21 Nov. 2017.

11. See, for example, the June 2014 issue of Tax Justice Network's newsletter focused on human rights, including a feature on the Special Rapporteur's report on fiscal policy, 9(2) *Tax Justice Focus: The newsletter of the tax justice network: The Human Rights Issue* (2014), available online at https://www.taxjustice.net/wp-content/uploads/2013/04/TJF-June-2014-Human-Rights.pdf.

12. *Financial Secrecy Index*, Tax Justice Network, https://www.financialsecrecyindex.com/ (last visited 10 Mar. 2018).

13. See Alliance Sud, Center for Economic and Social Rights (CESR), Global Justice Clinic (GJC), Public Eye, Tax Justice Network (TJN), *Swiss Responsibility for the Extraterritorial Impacts of Tax Abuse on Women's Rights* (2016), available online at https://chrgj.org/wp-content/uploads/2016/12/FULL-SUBMISSION-to-CEDAW-Swiss-Responsibility-for-the-Extraterritorial-Impacts-of-Tax-Abuse-on-Women%E2%80%99s-Rights-.pdf; CESR, GJC, TJN, *UK Responsibility for the Impacts of Cross-Border Tax Abuse on Economic, Social and Cultural Rights* (2016), https://chrgj.org/wp-content/uploads/2016/12/SUBMISSION-to-CESCR-UK-Responsibility-for-the-Impacts-of-Crossborder-Tax-Abuse-on-Economic-Social-and-Cultural-Rights.pdf.

14. *Tax Justice*, Oxfam, https://www.oxfam.org/en/tags/tax-justice (last visited 10 Mar. 2018).

15. *Tax Power*, ActionAid, http://www.actionaid.org/tax-power (last visited 10 Mar. 2018).

16. *Tax Justice*, Christian Aid, https://www.christianaid.org.uk/campaigns/tax-justice-campaign (last visited 10 Mar. 2018).

17. See discussion on corporate accountability, *infra* at 41–44.

18. See Sustainable Development Goals, Goal 16, Target 16.4 (aiming to reduce illicit financial flows).

19. The Global Alliance for Tax Justice is a network of civil society organizations, individuals, and trade unions, "united in campaigning for greater transparency, democratic oversight and redistribution of wealth in national and global tax systems." See Global Alliance for Tax Justice, https://www.globaltaxjustice.org (last visited 20 Sept. 2018).

20. See Lima Declaration on Tax Justice (2015), http://www.cesr.org/sites/default/files/Lima_Declaration_Tax_Justice_Human_Rights.pdf; Bogota Declaration on Tax Justice for Women's Rights (2017), https://www.globaltaxjustice.org/sites/default/files/EN_Bogota-Declaration-Tax-Justice-for-Womens-Rights_0.pdf.

21. See, e.g., *Investigations*, International Consortium of Investigative Journalists, https://www.icij.org/investigations/ (last visited 10 Mar. 2018).

22. A search on the OHCHR's Universal Human Rights Index reveals that "tax" was mentioned as part of treaty bodies' "concluding observations" on state party reports over 100 times between June 2008 and June 2018, but fewer than a dozen times between 2001 and 2008. See https://uhri.ohchr.org/en [search for "tax" and filter for "concluding observations" and "treaty bodies."].

23. See, e.g., *The Fight against Tax Fraud and Tax Evasion*, European Commission, https://ec.europa.eu/taxation_customs/fight-against-tax-fraud-tax-evasion_en (last visited 10 Mar. 2018); *Corporate Tax Avoidance: Agreement Reached on Tax Intermediaries*, European Council, 13 Mar. 2018, http://www.consilium.europa.eu/en/press/press-releases/2018/03/13/corporate-tax-avoidance-agreement-reached-on-tax-intermediaries/; *Taxation: Council Publishes EU List of Non-Cooperative Jurisdictions*, European Council, 5 Dec. 2017, http://www.consilium.europa.eu/en/press/press-releases/2017/12/05/taxation-council-publishes-an-eu-list-of-non-cooperative-jurisdictions/.

24. See generally, *Base Erosion and Profit Shifting*, OECD, http://www.oecd.org/tax/beps/ (last visited 18 Sept. 2018).

25. The World Bank Group and the International Monetary Fund have ramped up their research and advisory work on taxation, and now coordinate a new global "Platform for Collaboration on Tax." *Platform for Collaboration on Tax*, The World Bank, http://www.worldbank.org/en/programs/platform-for-tax-collaboration (last visited 10 Mar. 2018).

26. See Robert Verkaik, 'The super-rich are trying to exploit human rights law to dodge tax', Opinion, *The Guardian*, 16 Nov. 2017, available online at https://www.theguardian.com/commentisfree/2017/nov/16/human-rights-act-tax-dodge-tax-isle-of-man-law ("A powerful alliance of big business and the super-wealthy have used lawyers and lobbyists to cynically exploit human rights laws to ensure tax havens keep secret the real identities of those who benefit from their low taxes.").

27. Although animated by different preoccupations from those that drive the tax justice movement, literature on taxpayer rights draws on human rights law to address the interests of individual taxpayers vis-à-vis the state. See, e.g., G. Kofler, M. Poiares Maduro, and P. Pistone (eds.), *Human Rights and Taxation in Europe and the World* (2011), at 115–119 & nn.9–15 (discussing which human rights taxpayers may invoke, particularly under the European Convention of Human Rights, and citing relevant literature).

28. See, e.g., A. Nolan, C. Harvey, and R. O'Connell (eds.), *Human Rights and Public Finance: Budgets and the Promotion of Economic and Social Rights* (2013).

29. Attiya Waris, a Kenyan legal scholar, has been a pioneer in combining a human rights law analysis with concepts of fiscal sociology, to propose new approaches to tax policy that can help re-legitimate the state and address the needs of its people. See, e.g., A. Warris, *Tax and Development: Solving Kenya's Fiscal Crisis through Human Rights: A Case Study of Kenya's Constituency Development Fund* (2013).

30. See, e.g., C. Grown and I. Valodia (eds.), *Taxation and Gender Equity: A comparative analysis of direct and indirect taxes in developing and developed countries* (2010) (presenting country studies that provide a gender analysis of the incidence of direct and indirect taxes, with a focus on gendered differences in employment, unpaid work and care, expenditure, and property rights, and attention to explicit and implicit biases in tax policy design); see also K. Brooks, et al. (eds.), *Challenging gender inequality in tax policy making: comparative perspectives* (2011) (exploring the "effects that gender norms and practices have had in shaping tax law and policy in different countries, and how taxation in turn impacts upon the possibilities for equality along gender, race, class, sexuality, and other lines"); E. J. Mcaffery, *Taxing Women* (2007) (detailing historic and persistent gender biases in the US tax system).

31. See, e.g., T. Pogge and K. Mehta (eds.), *Global Tax Fairness* (2016); P. Beckett, *Tax Havens and International Human Rights* (2017).

32. International Covenant on Economic, Social and Cultural Rights, UN Doc. A/Res/2200 (XXI), 6 Dec. 1966, 993 UNTS 3, at art. 2.

33. Office of the High Commissioner for Human Rights (OHCHR) and International Budget Partnership (IBP), *Realizing Human Rights through Government Budgets* (2017), at 7.

34. Strategies of participatory budgeting have been honed in some countries of the Global South. The Institute for Democracy in South Africa (IDASA), for example, undertook early work on budget analysis, including analyzing the alignment of expenditure and tax policies from the perspective of women and children in post-apartheid South Africa. See D. P. Moynihan, 'Citizen Participation in Budgeting: Prospects for Developing Countries', *in* A. Shah (ed.), *Participatory Budgeting* (2007), at 70–71 (discussing IDASA's examination of gender and revenues). See also T. Smith, Institute for Democracy in South Africa, *Women and Tax in South Africa* (2002); National Economic and Social Rights Initiative (NESRI), *Moving Toward Human Rights Budgeting: Examples from Around the World: Background briefing prepared by NESRI* (2011).

35. A. Nolan, 'Putting ESR-Based Budget Analysis into Practice: Addressing the Conceptual Challenges', *in Human Rights and Public Finance, supra* note 28, at 43–44.

36. See, e.g., Save the Children and Center for Children's Rights, *Budget for Children Analysis* (2010); A. Nolan, 'Economic and Social Rights, Budgets and the Convention on the Rights of the Child', 21 *International Journal of Children's Rights* (2013), 248.

37. See, e.g., D. Elson, *Budgeting for Women's Rights: Monitoring Government Budgets for Compliance with CEDAW* (2006).

38. H. Hofbauer, A. Blyberg, and W. Krafchik, Fundar, International Budget Project, FUNDAR, *Dignity Counts: A guide to using budget analysis to advance human rights* (2004).

39. See Food and Agriculture Organisation (FAO), *Budget Work to Advance the Right to Food: Many a Slip* (2009); FAO, *Advocacy on the right to food based on the analysis of government budgets* (2014).

40. See *Library*, International Budget Partnership, http://internationalbudget.org/library/ (last visited 18 Sept. 2018).

41. A. Blyberg and H. Hofbauer, International Budget Partnership, *Article 2 & Governments' Budgets* (2014). This handbook includes a section on retrogression due to tax reforms that reduce resources for economic and social rights, as well as case studies on inequality and the tax system. See also *Human Rights Budgeting*, NESRI, https://www.nesri.org/initiatives/human-rights-budgeting (last visited 18 Sept. 2018).

42. OHCHR and IBP, *supra* note 33.

43. See, e.g., *Dignity Counts, supra* note 38.

44. UNIFEM, J. Huckerby (ed.), *Budgeting for Women's Rights: Monitoring Government Budgets for Compliance with CEDAW* (2008) (based on a report by D. Elson).

45. D. Budlender and G. Hewitt, *Engendering Budgets: A Practitioners' Guide to Understanding and Implementing Gender-Responsive Budgets* (2003), at 102 ("Overall, gender budget work has tended to focus on the expenditure side of the budget rather than on revenue."); see also European Parliament, *Gender Responsive Budgeting: Innovative Approaches to Budgeting* (2015).

46. Oxfam, *A Guide to Gender-Responsive Budgeting* (2018).

47. Committee on Economic and Monetary Affairs; Committee on Women's Rights and Gender Equality, *Draft Report on gender equality and taxation policies in the EU* (2018/2095(INI)), 6 Sept. 2018.

48. See, e.g., Z. Khan and N. Burn (eds.), *Financing for Gender Equality Realising Women's Rights through Gender Responsive Budgeting* (2017).

49. See, e.g., R. O'Connell et al. (eds.), *Applying an International Human Rights Framework to State Budget Allocations: Rights and Resources* (2014).

50. Ibid.; see also C. Harvey and E. Rooney, 'Integrating Human Rights? Socio-Economic Rights and Budget Analysis', 14 *European Human Rights Law Review* (2010), 266–279.

51. *Human Rights and Public Finance, supra* note 28.

52. I. Saiz, 'Resourcing Rights: Combating Tax Injustice from a Human Rights Perspective', *in Human Rights and Public Finance, supra* note 28, at 78. See also Jaakko Kuosmanen, *Towards 'Human Rights Compatible' Public Budgets—an Account of Institutional Virtues*, 64(3) *Political Studies* (2016), 683–698 (discussing the role of institutional design in rights-compatible budgeting).

53. R. Balakrishnan, D. Elson, and R. Patel, *Rethinking Macro Economic Strategies from a Human Rights Perspective (Why MES with Human Rights II)* (2009).

54. R. Balakrishnan, D. Elson, J. Heitz, and N. Lusiani, Center for Women's Global Leadership, *Maximum Available Resources & Human Rights* (2011); see also R. Balakrishnan, D. Elson, and J. Heitz, 'Public Finance, Maximum Available Resources and Human Rights', *in Human Rights and Public Finance, supra* note 28, at 13–40.

55. R. Balakrishnan, J. Heitz, and D. Elson, *Rethinking Economic Policy for Social Justice: The radical potential of human rights* (2016), at 52–67.

56. M. Dowell-Jones, 'The Economics of the Austerity Crisis: Unpicking Some Human Rights Argument', 15(2) *Human Rights Law Review* (2015).

57. See *Rights in Crisis*, CESR, http://www.cesr.org/section.php?id=139 (last visited 12 Apr. 2018).

58. CESR, *Assessing Austerity: Monitoring the Human Rights Impacts of Fiscal Consolidation—A Briefing* (2018).

59. Ibid.; see also N. Lusiani, *Human Rights in an Age of Austerity: Casualty or Compass?*, 16 May 2018, available online at http://socialprotection-humanrights.org/expertcom/human-rights-in-an-age-of-austerity-casualty-or-compass/.

60. Independent Expert on the effects of foreign debt and other related international financial obligations of States on the full enjoyment of all human rights, particularly economic, social and cultural rights, Draft Guiding Principles on Human Rights Impact Assessments of Economic Reforms, Draft for Public Consultation (Aug. 2018) (by Juan Pablo Bohoslavsky), available online at https://www.ohchr.org/en/issues/development/iedebt/pages/debtandimpactassessments.aspx (citing Human Rights Council Resolutions 34/03 and 37/11).

61. See, e.g., Report of the independent expert on the question of human rights and extreme poverty on the impact of the current global financial crisis on people living in extreme poverty and the enjoyment of their human rights, UN Doc. A/HRC/64/279, 11 Aug. 2009 (by Magdalena Sepúlveda Carmona).

62. See OHCHR, *Report on Austerity Measures and Economic and Social Rights* (2013), at 12; see also UN OHCHR, *Open Letter to States Parties regarding the protection of rights in the context of economic crisis*, 16 May 2012, available online at http://www2.ohchr.org/english/bodies/cescr/docs/LetterCESCRtoSP16.05.12.pdf.

63. See Report of the Independent Expert on the question of human rights and extreme poverty, on a human rights–based approach to recovery, UN Doc. A/HRC/17/34, 17 Mar. 2011 (by Magdalena Sepúlveda Carmona); see also *supra* note 61.

64. Commissioner for Human Rights, Council of Europe, *Safeguarding human rights in times of economic crisis* (2013).

65. Steering Committee for Human Rights, Council of Europe, *The Impact of the economic crisis and austerity measures on human rights in Europe: Feasibility Study* (2015).

66. The European Commission proposed a financial transaction tax in 2013, see *Proposal for a Council Directive: implementing enhanced cooperation in the area of financial transaction tax*, European Commission 2013/0045 (CNS), 14 Feb. 2013, but it remains controversial. As of the end of 2014, only eleven EU member states had signed on, and among those states that endorse the idea, disagreements regarding the details persist. See I. Dendrinou and G. Steinhauser, 'EU Nations Remain Divided on Financial Transactions Tax: Differences Exist Between the 11 Nations That Agreed to the Tax', *The Wall Street Journal*, 6 Nov. 2014, available online at http://www.wsj.com/articles/eu-nations-remain-divided-on-financial-transactions-tax-1415306897. In January 2015, US Representative Van Hollen proposed a financial transactions tax in the United States, but it has not been taken up. See Rep. C. Van Hollen, *An Action Plan to Grow the Paychecks of All, Not Just the Wealth of a Few*, 12 Jan. 2015, available online at http://democrats.budget.house.gov/sites/democrats.budget.house.gov/files/documents/Action%20Plan%20-%20PDF.pdf; see also Press Release, Center for Economic and Policy Research, *Democrats' Plan for Financial Transactions Tax Would Bring Financial Markets into 21st Century*, 12 Jan. 2015, available online at http://www.cepr.net/index.php/press-releases/press-releases/baker-statement-on-ftt-and-democrat-proposal.

67. The Dodd-Frank Act, enacted in 2010, implemented a number of reforms intended to curb financial speculation and limit public exposure to the costs of risk-taking by financial institutions. Lobbyists for the financial industry have worked hard to roll back those regulations. In May 2018, Congress partially repealed the law's application to some banks. A. Rappeport and E. Flitter, 'Congress Approves First Big Dodd-Frank Rollback', *New York Times*, 22 May 2018, available online at https://www.nytimes.com/2018/05/22/business/congress-passes-dodd-frank-rollback-for-smaller-banks.html.

68. See Robin Hood Tax, http://www.robinhoodtax.org (last visited 18 Sept. 2018); *see also* Oxfam, *Robin Hood Tax Media Brief* (2014), available at online at http://www.oxfam.org/sites/www.oxfam.org/files/ftt_media_briefing_-_english.pdf.

69. See Righting Finance: A bottom up approach to righting financial regulation, http://www.rightingfinance.org (last visited 18 Sept. 2018).

70. CESR, *Financial Transactions Tax: A Human Rights Imperative, A Bottom-Up Approach to Righting Financial Regulation*, Issue No. 3 (2012), http://www.cesr.org/financial-transactions-tax-human-rights-imperative.

71. See generally Thomas Piketty, *Capital in the Twenty-First Century* (2014), at 515–539.

72. See, e.g., IMF, *Taxing Our Way out of—or into?—Trouble* (2013), at 34–38, 49; John D. Brondolo, IMF Working Paper, *Taxing Financial Transactions: Assessment of Administrative Feasibility*, WP/11/185 (2011), at 45.

73. Attiya Waris, professor at the Faculty of Law, Nairobi University, is one of the first scholars to make the case for using a human rights approach to taxation to improve tax collection and distribution, and to rehabilitate the fiscal state. See *supra* note 29.

74. Research suggests that corporate tax concessions offered by many developing countries to incentivize foreign direct investment result in a net loss of revenue, because forgone taxes outweigh investment gains. See, e.g., J. Chai and R. Goyal, IMF, *Tax Concessions and Foreign Direct Investment in the Eastern Caribbean Currency Union*, WP/08/257 (2008). According to the authors, "[a] broad cross-country analysis shows that FDI is not related to incentives," suggesting that countries are getting little in return for the substantial revenue losses caused by tax concessions.

75. *Addis Ababa Action Agenda*, Resolution adopted by the General Assembly on 27 July 2015, UN Doc. A/RES/69/313, 17 Aug. 2015.

76. *Transforming our world: the 2030 Agenda for Sustainable Development*, Resolution Adopted by the General Assembly on 25 Sept. 2015, UN Doc. A/RES/70/1, 21 Oct. 2015, at para. 16.4.

77. Ibid. at para. 17.1.

78. See, e.g., *Statement on Behalf of the Group of 77 and China by the H.E. Ambassador Kingsley J.N. Mamabolo, Permanent Representative of the Republic of South Africa, Chair of the Group of 77*, at the Roundtable on Ensuring Policy Coherence and an Enabling Environment at all levels for Sustainable Development and the Third International Conference on Financing for Development, 14 July 2015, available online at http://www.g77.org/statement/getstatement.php?id=150714b.

79. CESR, *A Post-2015 Fiscal Revolution: Human Rights Policy Brief* (2014).

80. Ibid. at 12–15; see also Christian Aid, *Tax and the post-2015 Agenda* (2013).

81. See I. T. Winkler and C. Williams, 'The Sustainable Development Goals and Human Rights: A Critical Early Review', 20(8) *International Journal of Human Rights* (2017); S. McInerney-Lankford, 'Human Rights and the SDGs: Progress or a Missed Opportunity?', *Oxford Human Rights Hub: A global perspective on human rights*, 6 Jan. 2017, available online at http://ohrh.law.ox.ac.uk/human-rights-and-the-sdgs-progress-or-a-missed-opportunity/; R. Kaufman, 'Localizing Human Rights in the United States Through the 2030 Sustainable Development Agenda', 49 *Columbia Human Rights Law Review* (2017), 99, 101–112; but see The Danish Institute for Human Rights, *Human Rights and the SDGs*, https://www.humanrights.dk/our-work/sustainable-development/human-rights-sdgs (last visited 18 Sept. 2018) (contending that "[m]ore than 90% of the Sustainable Development Goals (SDGs) targets are linked to international human rights and labour standards").

82. See, e.g., the Danish Institute for Human Rights, *The Human Rights Guide to the Sustainable Development Goals*, http://sdg.humanrights.dk/ (identifying the human rights law support for individual SDG goals and targets through an interactive online platform).

83. Supporting the Development of More Effective Tax Systems: A Report to the G-20 Development Working Group by the IMF, OECD, UN and World Bank (2011); see also ActionAid UK, *Approaches and Impacts: IFI tax policy in developing countries* (2011).

84. See IMF, *Taxing Our Way out of—or into?—Trouble* (2013).

85. J. D. Ostry, P. Loungani, and D. Furceri, 'Neoliberalism: Oversold?', 53(2) *Finance & Development* (2016), 38.

86. IMF, Fiscal Monitor: *Tackling Inequality* (Oct. 2017).

87. IMF, *Spillovers on International Corporate Taxation*, 9 May 2014.

88. S. Beer, A. D. Klemm, and T. Matheson, IMF, *Tax Spillovers from US Corporate Income Tax Reform* (2018); see also N. Lusiani, CESR, *Tax abuse leads to human rights abuse: IMF confirms U.S. corporate tax changes are likely to intensify public resource scarcity overseas*, 20 July 2018, available online at http://www.cesr.org/tax-abuse-leads-human-rights-abuse.

89. See generally Report of the Special Rapporteur on extreme poverty and human rights, UN Doc. A/HRC/38/33, 8 May 2018 (by Philip Alston) (focusing on the IMF and its impact on social protection).

90. Independent Evaluation Group, World Bank, *Tax Revenue Mobilization: Lessons from World Bank Group Support for Tax Reform* (2017).

91. Ibid. at viii–xiv.

92. Inter-American Development Bank, Executive Summary, *in More than Revenue: Taxation as a Development Tool* (2013).

93. See Platform for Collaboration on Tax, http://www.worldbank.org/en/programs/platform-for-tax-collaboration (last visited 11 Mar. 2018).

94. See Report of the Special Rapporteur on extreme poverty and human rights, UN Doc. A/70/274, 4 Aug. 2015 (on the human rights policy of the World Bank) (by Philip Alston).

95. For a discussion of corporate responses to the UNGP, see Shift, *Human Rights Reporting: Are companies telling investors what they need to know?* (2017). Definitions and tools regarding human rights impact assessments are collected on the Business and Human Rights Resource Center, at https://www.business-humanrights.org/en/tools-guidance-0.

96. There are some notable exceptions, as discussed in chapter 17. *See also* S. Darcy, ' "The Elephant in the Room": Corporate Tax Avoidance and Business and Human Rights', 2 *Business & Human Rights Journal* (2017), 1, 21–28 (assessing the potential for addressing corporate tax avoidance through the UNGP).

97. See, e.g., P. Cohen and J. Kanter, 'Europeans Accuse Ireland of Giving Apple Illegal Tax Break', *New York Times*, 30 Sept. 2014; V. Houlder, V. Boland, and J. Politi, 'Tax avoidance: The Irish inversion', *The Financial Times*, 29 Apr. 2014.

98. D. Hakim, 'Europe Takes Aim at Deals Created to Escape Taxes: The Tax Attraction Between Starbucks and the Netherlands', *New York Times*, 14 Nov. 2014.

99. S. Bowers, 'Luxembourg Tax Files: How tiny state rubber-stamped tax avoidance on an industrial scale', *The Guardian*, 5 Nov. 2014.

100. See International Consortium of Investigative Journalists, *Luxembourg Leaks: Global Companies' Secrets Exposed*, https://www.icij.org/investigations/luxembourg-leaks/ (last visited 18 Sept. 2018).

101. See, e.g., V. Houlder, C. Oliver, and V. Boland, 'EU probe shines spotlight on national tax authorities', *The Financial Times*, 11 June 2014.

102. Press Release, European Commission, *State aid: Ireland gave illegal tax benefits to Apple worth up to €13 billion*, 30 Aug. 2016, available online at http://europa.eu/rapid/press-release_IP-16-2923_en.htm.

103. Press Release, European Commission, *State aid: Commission refers Ireland to Court for failure to recover illegal tax benefits from Apple worth up to €13 billion*, 4 Oct. 2017, available online at http://europa.eu/rapid/press-release_IP-17-3702_en.htm.

104. 'Ireland expects Apple EU tax appeal to be heard in autumn: Timeframe confirmed for joint challenge against EU ruling for €13bn in disputed taxes', *The Guardian*, 24 Apr. 2018.

105. *About the Paradise Papers Investigation*, ICIJ, https://www.icij.org/investigations/paradise-papers/about/ (last visited 18 Sept. 2018).

106. *The Panama Papers, About the Investigation*, ICIJ, https://www.icij.org/investigations/panama-papers/pages/panama-papers-about-the-investigation/ (last visited 18 Sept. 2018).

107. *About this Project: Swiss Leaks*, ICIJ, https://www.icij.org/investigations/swiss-leaks/about-project-swiss-leaks/ (last visited 18 Sept. 2018).

108. ActionAid, *Calling Time: Why SAB Miller Should Stop Dodging Taxes in Africa* (2010), at 3.

109. Ibid.

110. ActionAid, *Sweet Nothings: the Human cost of a British sugar giant avoiding taxes in southern Africa* (2013).

111. This estimate was based on a sixteen-country average cost of statutory corporate income tax exemptions only, not discretionary incentives or other exemptions, calculated as a share of GDP and extrapolated to all developing countries. See ActionAid, *Give us a break: How big companies are getting tax-free deals* (2013), at 8.

112. Ibid. at 10.
113. ActionAid, *Mistreated: The tax treaties that are depriving the world's poorest countries of vital revenue* (2016).
114. Christian Aid, *Who Pays the Price: Hunger, the Hidden Cost of Tax Injustice* (2013).
115. See Christian Aid, *FTSEcrecy: the culture of concealment throughout the FTSE* (2014).
116. See *Tax Justice*, Oxfam, http://www.oxfam.org/en/tags/tax-justice.
117. See *Even it Up*, Oxfam, https://www.oxfam.org/en/campaigns/even-it-up.
118. See Oxfam, *Business among friends: Why corporate tax dodgers are not yet losing sleep over global tax reform*, 185 Oxfam Briefing Paper (2014).
119. Oxfam, *Tax Battles: The Dangerous Global Race to the Bottom on Corporate Tax*, Oxfam Policy Brief (2016).
120. Oliver Pearce, Oxfam, *Making Tax Vanish: How the practices of consumer goods MNC RB show that the international tax system is broken*, 13 July 2017, available online at https://www.oxfam.org/en/research/making-tax-vanish.
121. See also Steuergerechtigkeit, *Taxes and Human Rights: Policy Brief of the Tax Justice Network Germany* (2013) (discussing how tax abuse, by impeding a state's mobilization of maximum available resources, could constitute a violation of rights contrary to the business responsibility to respect under the UNGP).
122. SOMO, *Private Gain–Public Loss: Mailbox Companies, Tax Avoidance, and Human Rights* (2013).
123. See ibid. at 44–69.
124. See, e.g., ibid. at 23–36, 111–117 (discussing measures to increase accountability and provide access to remedy).
125. T. Boerrild, M. Kohonen, R. Sarin, K. Stares, and M. Lewis, *Getting to Good: Toward Responsible Corporate Tax Behavior* (2015).
126. Ibid.
127. See ibid. at 37, Annex A (How our approach corresponds to elements of the corporate responsibility to respect human rights (UNGP Pillar 2).
128. See The B Team, *New Bar for Responsible Tax: The B Team's Responsible Tax Principles* (2018), available online at http://www.bteam.org/announcements/responsibletax-2/.
129. Ibid. at 8.
130. Independent Commission for the Reform of International Corporate Taxation (ICRICT), *A Roadmap to improve Rules for Taxing Multinationals* (2018), available online at http://www.icrict.com/icrict-documents-a-fairer-future-for-global-taxation.
131. See IBAHRI, *supra* note 8.
132. In sub-Saharan Africa between 1980 and 2005, the proportion of countries providing incentives rose from 45 percent to 69 percent. Effective corporate tax rates have dropped close to or even below zero in many developing countries. See S. M. Ali Abbas and A. Klemm, *A Partial Race to the Bottom: Corporate Tax Developments in Emerging and Developing Economies*, IMF Working Paper (2012), at 9.
133. See IBAHRI, *supra* note 8, at 140–142.
134. Committee on Economic, Social and Cultural Rights (CESCR), *Concluding Observations: United Kingdom of Great Britain and Northern Ireland*, UN Doc. E/C.12/GBR/CO/6, 14 July 2016, at paras. 16–17.
135. CESCR, *Concluding Observations: Honduras*, UN Doc. E/C.12/HND/CO/2, 11 July 2016, at paras. 19–20.
136. CESCR, *Concluding Observations: Paraguay*, UN Doc. E/C.12/PRY/CO/4, 20 Mar. 2015, at paras. 10–11.
137. CESCR, *Concluding Observations: Angola*, UN Doc. E/C.12/AGO/CO/4-5, 15 July 2016, at para. 9.
138. CESCR, *Concluding Observations: Burkina Faso*, UN Doc. E/C.12/BFA/CO/1, 12 July 2016, at paras. 9–10.
139. CESCR, *Concluding Observations: Lichtenstein*, UN Doc. E/C.12/LIE/CO/2-3, 3 July 2017, at paras. 9–10.
140. See Alliance Sud et al., *supra* note 13.

141. Committee on the Elimination of Discrimination Against Women (CEDAW), *Concluding Observations on the Combined Fourth and Fifth Periodic Reports of Switzerland*, UN Doc. CEDAW/C/CHE/CO/4-5, 25 Nov. 2016, at para. 41(a).

142. CEDAW, *Concluding observations on the combined sixth and seventh periodic reports of Luxembourg*, UN Doc. CEDAW/C/LUX/CO/6-7, 14 Mar. 2018, at paras. 15, 16(c).

143. CEDAW, *Concluding Observations on the fifth periodic report of Singapore*, UN Doc. CEDAW/C/SGP/CO/5, 21 Nov. 2017, at paras. 32, 33.

144. CEDAW, *Concluding Observations on the combined fifth to eighth periodic reports of Barbados*, UN Doc. CEDAW/C/BRB/CO/5-8, 24 July 2017, at paras. 37, 38(b).

145. Ibid. at para. 37.

146. Committee on the Rights of the Child, *General Comment No. 19 on Public Budgeting for the Realisation of Children's Rights*, UN Doc. CRC/C/GC/19, 20 July 2016, at paras. 75–77.

147. See, e.g., CESCR, *General Comment 3: The nature of States parties' obligations*, UN Doc. E/1991/23, 1 Jan. 1991, at para. 9; CESCR, *General Comment 12: The right to adequate food (art. 11)*, UN Doc. E/C.12/1999/5, 12 May 1999, at para. 45; CESCR, *General Comment 14: The right to the highest attainable standard of health*, UN Doc. E/C.12/2000/4, 11 Aug. 2000, at para. 32; CESCR, *General Comment 15: The Right to Water*, UN Doc. E/C.12/2002/11, 20 Jan 2003, at para. 19.

148. CESCR, *General Comment No. 24 on State obligations under the International Covenant on Economic, Social and Cultural Rights in the context of business activities*, UN Doc. E/C.12/GC/24, 10 Aug. 2107, at para. 37.

149. See Report of the Special Rapporteur on extreme poverty and human rights, UN Doc. A/HRC/26/28, 22 May 2014 (by Magdalena Sepúlveda Carmona), at paras. 44–49.

150. Ibid. paras. 32, 75.

151. Ibid. para. 78.

152. See, e.g., Report of the Special Rapporteur on extreme poverty and human rights on his mission to the United States of America, UN Doc. A/HRC/38/33/Add.1, 4 May 2018 (by Philip Alston), at paras. 5, 79; Report of the Special Rapporteur on extreme poverty and human rights on his mission to Chile, UN Doc. A/HRC/32/31/Add.1, 8 Apr. 2016 (by Philip Alston), at paras. 13, 50; Report of the Special Rapporteur on extreme poverty and human rights, UN Doc. A/HRC/29/31, 27 May 2015 (by Philip Alston) (addressing extreme poverty and extreme inequality).

153. Final study on illicit financial flows, human rights and the 2030 Agenda for Sustainable Development of the Independent Expert on the effects of foreign debt and other related financial obligations of States on the full enjoyment of all human rights, particularly economic, social and cultural rights, UN Doc. A/HRC/31/61, 15 Jan. 2016 (by Juan Pablo Bohoslavsky).

154. Report of the Independent Expert on the effects of foreign debt and other related financial obligations of States on the full enjoyment of all human rights, particularly economic, social and cultural rights, on his visit to Switzerland, UN Doc. A/HRC/37/54/Add.3, 23 Feb. 2018 (by Juan Pablo Bohoslavsky).

155. Ibid., paras. 38, 92(i).

156. Press Release, OHCHR, *Convene world conference on abolition of tax havens, human rights expert urges the GA and next UN Secretary-General*, 13 Oct. 2016, available online at https://www.ohchr.org/en/NewsEvents/Pages/DisplayNews.aspx?NewsID=20672&LangID=E.

157. Inter-American Development Bank, *Report on Poverty and Human Rights in the Americas*, Doc. 147, OEA/Ser.L/V/II.164, 7 Sept. 2017, at paras. 495–502.

158. Ibid. at para. 494.

159. African Commission on Human and Peoples' Rights, *Statement of the African Commission on Human and Peoples' Rights on illicit financial flight and other concerns arising out of the Paradise Papers*, 12 Dec. 2017, available online at http://www.achpr.org/press/2017/12/d380/.

160. Ibid.

161. African Charter on Human and Peoples' Rights, art. 29(6), adopted in Nairobi 27 June 1981, entered into Force 21 Oct. 1986.

162. See, e.g., CESR, *The Universal Periodic Review: A Skewed Agenda; Trends analysis of the UPR's coverage of economic, social and cultural rights* (2016) (discussing neglect of ESC rights in the UPR process and noting that less than a fifth of the recommendations issued address ESC).

163. *Human Rights in Tax Policy*, CESR, http://www.cesr.org/human-rights-taxation (last visited 12 Apr. 2018).

164. See, e.g., J. L. Flanagan, 'Holding U.S. Corporations Accountable: Toward a Convergence of U.S. International Tax Policy and International Human Rights', 45 *Pepperdine Law Review* (2018), 685; S. Darcy, '"The Elephant in the Room": Corporate Tax Avoidance & Business and Human Rights', 2(1) *Business & Human Rights Journal* (2017), 1; A. West, 'Multinational Tax Avoidance: Virtue Ethics and the Role of Accountant', *Journal of Business Ethics* (2017); N. Mendis, 'A Comment on the Interface of Harmful Tax Practices, Human Rights and WTO Law, in Light of the Panama Papers Scandal and Argentina-Financial Services Case', 9 *Indian Journal of International Economic Law* (2018), 19; M. Greggi, 'Human rights, fundamental rights and international tax law', *European Tax Studies* (2014), No. 2, at 1–5.

165. Recent examples include B. J. Crawford and A. C. Infanti (eds.), *Feminist Judgments: Rewritten Tax Opinions* (2017) and A. Smith, *Tax Law and Racial Economic Justice: Black Tax* (2015). In the United States, various academic articles examine the gendered and racially disparate impacts of tax laws. See, e.g., Isaac William Martin and Kevin Beck, 'Property Tax Limitation and Racial Inequality in Effective Tax Rates', 43(2) *Critical Sociology* (2017), 221–236.

166. A. C. Infanti and B. J. Crawford (eds.), *Critical Tax Theory: An Introduction* (2009); B. J. Crawford and A. C. Infanti (eds.), Feminist Judgments: Rewritten Tax Opinions (2017).

167. *See* T. Georgopolous, *Tax Treaties and Human/Constitutional Rights: Bridging the Gap? Tax relief in a cosmopolitan context* (2004), available online at http://www.law.nyu.edu/sites/default/files/upload_documents/gffgeorgopoulospaper.pdf.

168. See, e.g., A. Christians, *Human Rights at the Borders of Tax Sovereignty*, 27 Feb. 2017, available online at https://ssrn.com/abstract=2924925 or http://dx.doi.org/10.2139/ssrn.2924925; A. Christians, *Taxpayer Rights in the United States* (14 Oct. 2016), *in* C. Jiménez (ed.), *Derecho Tributario Y Derechos Humanos/Tax Law and Human Rights* (2016), available online at https://ssrn.com/abstract=2809750; A. Christians, 'Fair Taxation as a Human Right', 9 *International Review of Constitutionalism* (2009), 211, 214.

CHAPTER 2

TAXING FOR THE REALIZATION OF ECONOMIC, SOCIAL, AND CULTURAL RIGHTS

OLIVIER DE SCHUTTER

I. INTRODUCTION

The International Covenant on Economic, Social and Cultural Rights commits the states parties to "take steps, individually and through international assistance and co-operation, especially economic and technical, *to the maximum of [their] available resources, with a view to achieving progressively the full realization of the rights recognized in the present Covenant by all appropriate means*, including particularly the adoption of legislative measures."[1] This "progressive realization" clause is typically seen as a weakness—as an indication that economic, social, and cultural rights are still undervalued in the international human rights regime in comparison to the more "classical" civil and political rights. But it can also be seen as a strength. With this provision, how states mobilize resources and how they define their spending priorities become human rights issues. Such decisions cannot be left to the arbitrary and capricious choices of states: they can and must be subject to a searching inquiry by courts and other bodies in charge of enforcing the Covenant on Economic, Social and Cultural Rights.

Taxation policies are human rights policies.[2] They are so for three reasons. First, taxation allows states to mobilize resources in order to invest in health, education, housing, social protection, electricity and water provision, or transport infrastructure, all of which are indispensable for the enjoyment of the rights of the Covenant, both because of the needs they respond to directly[3] and because these services alleviate the burden that women shoulder. If they did not have the ability to mobilize domestic revenues through taxation, states would have to cut down on the provision of these services, and women would be particularly affected since—in the current division of gender roles that remains dominant in most regions of the world—it is still they who take care of the infants, children, and the elderly, and fetch the firewood or water to meet the household needs.[4] Second, taxation allows states to redistribute wealth from the richest parts of the population to the poorest. The impacts on the reduction of inequalities and, therefore, on

Tax, Inequality, and Human Rights. Philip Alston and Nikki Reisch.
© Oxford University Press 2019. Published 2019 by Oxford University Press.

the effective enjoyment of human rights, can be significant. Third, and finally, the shaping of taxation policies are central to democratic self-determination. From the perspective of human rights, to which the principles of participation and accountability are central, *how* the decisions were reached in order to mobilize resources and in making spending decisions shall matter as much as *what* decisions were made.

Taxation, of course, is not the only tool at the disposal of states to finance public policies in support of the realization of economic, social, and cultural rights, and it is not the only tool through which inequality can be reduced. Indeed, other important sources of domestic revenues include trade tariffs (on imports and on exports), the royalty fees obtained from companies (both domestic and foreign) exploiting natural resources, as well as fees that may be imposed on the users of public services such as schools or hospitals. States may also borrow to finance their policies,[5] and they may obtain resources from the international community in the form of development assistance. The position that taxation occupies in this typology is nevertheless unique: more than any other source of public revenue, it embodies the civic contract between the people and the government, and, since the public pays, it constitutes a strong incentive for greater accountability.

This chapter is an attempt to define the normative framework that could guide the assessment by the Committee on Economic, Social and Cultural Rights of the tax policies of the states parties to the Covenant. It argues that four key norms could be taken into consideration in this regard. First, there is a need to expand the tax base in order to ensure that taxation, combined with other sources of public revenue, can fund public policies that support the realization of economic, social, and cultural rights—including access to healthcare, to education, and to housing, but also to social security. Second, there is a need to speed up the reduction of poverty, and thus ensure effective enjoyment of economic and social rights for each individual, by ensuring that tax policies are sufficiently progressive. Third, there is a need to step up efforts to combat tax evasion: increasing tax levels without also addressing tax evasion would be like pouring water into a leaking bucket. Fourth, the requirements of participation and of democratic accountability could be strengthened in the area of taxation. These components of a human rights–compliant tax policy are reviewed in turn.

II. WIDENING THE TAX BASE

In 2009, basing himself on data from 2000–2005, Martin Ravallion famously arrived at the conclusion that only by imposing "prohibitive" tax rates (of 60 percent and above, and often beyond 100 percent) on the relatively rich (that is, on those whose incomes exceed $13 per day in 2005, based on Purchasing Power Parity (PPP), which corresponds to the level of consumption defining the poverty line in rich countries) would it be possible for low-income countries to effectively end poverty. In other terms: although various other measures might be relied on to reduce poverty in these countries, poverty was considered to be so widespread, and wealth creation so woefully insufficient, that taxation was not a promising way to achieve this objective.[6] The implication was that, for these poor countries, redistribution of wealth was not a substitute for economic growth and international support: before wealth could be redistributed, there needed to be wealth to share.

Ten years have passed, however, during which economic growth has been strong for most of the countries of this group: more recent research, using a methodology very similar to that of Ravallion, has come to the conclusion that "most developing countries [now] have the financial scope to dramatically speed up the end of poverty based on national capacities at the global poverty lines of $1.90 or the $2.50 line."[7] That means an untapped potential. In many countries, particularly developing countries, the tax base is very low, and does not allow the states concerned to mobilize sufficient resources for the fulfillment of the rights in the Covenant.[8] Interregional differences are huge in this area: in developed countries, revenue from personal income tax is 8.4 percent of GDP, whereas in Latin American countries for instance, this tax generates only 1.4 percent of GDP.[9] It has been noted that "if all developing countries were able to raise 15 per cent of their national income in tax, a commonly accepted minimum figure (the OECD average is 37 per cent), they could realize at least an additional $198 billion per year, more than all foreign development assistance combined."[10]

A specific area in which action could be taken to widen the tax base in order to fund the realization of social rights is by reducing, or eliminating entirely, favorable fiscal treatment granted to foreign investors in order to attract capital. There is in fact ample evidence that such "tax holidays" or even, more generally, legal protections granted to investors, have little or no impact on the ability of the country to attract investment.[11] The major determinants of foreign direct investment (FDI) are economic factors such as market size and trade openness, as measured by exports and imports in relation to total GDP.[12] For other variables there is less consensus in the literature. In general, studies find that political and economic factors such as market size, skilled labor, and trade policies are more important for the locational decision of foreign investment than the legal structure for protection of investors' rights and the ability to avoid double taxation by double-taxation treaties.[13] In other terms, if there is one means through which revenues from taxation could increase rather painlessly (and at a relatively low administrative cost), it is by raising the taxes owed by foreign corporations operating in the country, or by closing loopholes, such as price transfer mechanisms, allowing such corporations to escape local taxes—if not entirely, at least to a very large extent.

III. IMPLEMENTING PROGRESSIVE TAX POLICIES

The former UN Special Rapporteur on extreme poverty and human rights argued that states should be encouraged to

> set up a progressive tax system with real redistributive capacity that preserves, and progressively increases, the income of poorer households. . . . [A]ffirmative action measures aimed at assisting the most disadvantaged individuals and groups that have suffered from historical or persistent discrimination, such as well-designed subsidies or tax exemptions, would not be discriminatory. In contrast, a flat tax whereby all people are required to pay an equal proportion of their income would not be conducive in achieving substantive equality, as it limits the redistributive function of taxation.[14]

Her successor in the mandate, Philip Alston, emphasized this point further, regretting that we are still far from "recognizing the fact that tax policy is, in many respects, human rights policy,"[15] despite the obvious contribution taxation makes to the fulfillment of human rights: "The regressive or progressive nature of a State's tax structure, and the groups and purposes for which it gives exemptions or deductions, shapes the allocation of income and assets across the population, and thereby affects levels of inequality and human rights enjoyment."[16] It is time that these calls be heeded.

A. PROGRESSIVITY OF TAXATION AS A HUMAN RIGHTS REQUIREMENT

Redistributive fiscal policies and social spending, particularly on social security, have had a major role to play to reduce the levels of inequality that would result from market incomes for different groups of the population. In Organisation for Economic Co-operation and Development (OECD) countries, public cash transfers, together with income taxes and social security contributions, were estimated to reduce inequality among the working-age population (measured by the Gini coefficient) by an average of about one-quarter across OECD countries during the period from the mid-1980s to the late 2000s.[17] Few graphs illustrate this contribution of redistributive public policies better than a graph presented by the OECD in 2011, which contrasts the levels of inequality resulting from market incomes alone with the levels of inequality resulting from net incomes, after taxation and redistribution are taken into account. Combining progressive taxation schemes with subsidies to various forms of social protection, it appears, reduced inequality within the working-age population by about one-quarter, on average, in OECD countries, and the impacts are even larger in Nordic countries, in Belgium and in Germany. Figure 2.1 illustrates this impact.

Both by reducing the weight of pretax income inequalities and by increasing the fiscal capacity of the state, a progressive tax system has an important role to play in the fulfillment of social rights. The Committee on Economic, Social and Cultural Rights has therefore regularly expressed its concern at reforms of the taxation system that would make it less progressive (for instance, by shifting the burden from corporations to families, or by increasing value-added tax (VAT) rates on essential items). For example, in Concluding Observations addressed to the United Kingdom, the Committee deplored

the adverse impact that recent changes to the fiscal policy in the State party, such as the increase in the threshold for the payment of inheritance tax and the increase of the value added tax, as well as

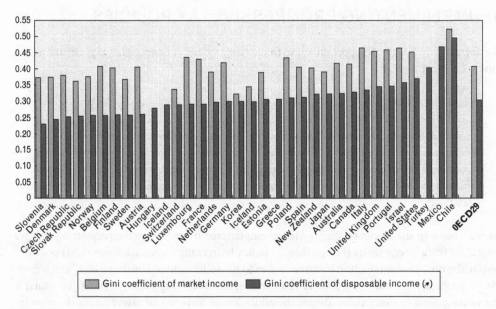

FIGURE 2.1: Impacts on inequality (measured as Gini coefficient) of the difference between market incomes and net (disposable) incomes following taxation and social security transfers, OECD countries, late 2000s (data from 2006 to 2009, depending on the data available for each country)

Source: OECD, Divided We Stand: Why Inequalities Keep Rising (2011), ch. 6, fig. 6.1.

the gradual reduction of the tax on corporate incomes, are having on the ability of the State party to address persistent social inequality and to collect sufficient resources to achieve the full realization of economic, social and cultural rights for the benefit of disadvantaged and marginalized individuals and groups.[18]

B. PROGRESSIVITY PROPERLY UNDERSTOOD

Three remarks are in order, however. First, it is important to relate progressivity in taxation schemes with the scope and content of the redistributive policies adopted within each country. A progressive tax system can have an impact on the reduction of inequalities only if the revenue from the taxes collected is redistributed through social policies that benefit the poor, rather than being spent on investments that only allow the rich to become richer. For the effective realization of economic, social, and cultural rights, it is the combination of revenue mobilization and of spending choices that matters, and neither of these two elements alone shall in itself suffice to assess whether the efforts of the state are sufficient: just like one can easily imagine a state with generous social policies addressed at tackling poverty, but in which such policies are essentially financed by the poor themselves,[19] it is possible to have a state tax the rich but not use the revenues collected in ways that have a significant impact on the reduction of inequalities.

Second, the ability for even a progressive tax system to reduce inequalities depends not only on the contribution of the richest part of the population to public revenue in *percentage* terms, but also on the *absolute* levels of such contributions: if, for example, the richest decile of the population pays 90 percent of the total income taxes collected in the country, the taxation system may be said to be progressive according to the most common measure of tax progressivity known as the Kakwani index. But if those richest 10 percent are taxed at very low rates, the redistributive capacity of the taxation system remains very limited: such a redistributive capacity is captured by another index, known as the Reynolds-Smolensky index, which measures the difference in income distribution before and after the tax is imposed.[20] One important consequence of this distinction is that a tax reform that may at first appear as regressive because the proportion of the total tax revenue paid by the richest part of the population will decrease (leading, in other terms, the effort to be spread across a larger part of the population), nevertheless may have progressive consequences if the overall tax rates and thus the revenue the state may mobilize are increased.

Third, the introduction of a progressive taxation scheme could have counterproductive impacts if it resulted in choking the economy and significantly slowing down economic activity, thus, in the medium to long term, destroying the very revenue base the state may be able to count on in order to finance its social policies. This, however, is an area in which the persistence of certain myths often has made a disservice to public debate. One assumption in particular, popularized as the "Kuznets curve," is that the growth of inequality is an inevitable price to pay for economic growth, so that the introduction of policies to combat inequalities, if it occurs too early, might damage the prospects for development.[21] However, quite apart from the fact that the original reasoning of Simon Kuznets, which applied to fast-growing nations going through rapid processes of industrialization and urbanization, could not be transposed to advanced industrial economies in which these processes are completed, the ideological uses made of his work does not correspond to the actual findings of Kuznets: whereas there may have been, historically, a correlation between the structural transformation linked to industrialization and the increase of inequality, it does not follow that such increase should be treated as a condition for industrialization—indeed, one may suspect that industrialization would have been far less damaging to social cohesion, and thus far more sustainable, with robust redistributive schemes compensating the losers by transferring resources from the gainers. Nor indeed, do such ideological uses have any (other) solid data to rely on. Quite to the contrary in fact, there is now a consensus that high levels of taxation, allowing the state to adopt robust redistributive policies and provide high-quality public services, far from being an obstacle to economic growth, are an indispensable ingredient thereof: the International Monetary Fund (IMF) found that "the combined direct and indirect effects of redistribution, including the growth effects of the resulting lower inequality, are on average pro-growth."[22] Indeed, more recent research has generalized findings initially focused on OECD countries, which concluded that the concentration of incomes at the top impeded growth, whereas growth in contrast was stimulated by increasing the portion of total wealth going to the lowest quintile of the population or to the middle class. Researchers from the IMF thus found "an inverse relationship between the income share accruing to the rich (top 20 percent) and economic growth":

> If the income share of the top 20 percent increases by 1 percentage point, GDP growth is actually 0.08 percentage point *lower* in the following five years, suggesting that the benefits do not trickle down. Instead, a similar increase in the income share of the bottom 20 percent (the poor) is associated with 0.38 percentage point *higher* growth. This positive relationship between disposable income shares and higher growth continues to hold for the second and third quintiles (the middle class).[23]

There is no trade-off, therefore, between the understandable desire of low-income countries to grow their economy and the reduction of inequality within these countries by progressive taxation and redistribution schemes.

There are therefore strong reasons to define the adoption of strongly progressive taxation schemes as a condition for the realization of economic, social, and cultural rights, and thus as a duty for the states parties to the Covenant on Economic, Social and Cultural Rights. Yet, for many governments, progressive taxation with powerful inequality-reducing impacts may be difficult to achieve. Indirect taxes (such as VAT) are easier to collect, and therefore, despite their regressive impacts (since poor households spend a higher proportion of their incomes on buying consumer goods[24]), they may be the preferred way for governments with a weak administrative capacity to collect revenue. Moreover, because capital is more mobile than labor and households, it is tempting to reduce the levels of taxation of capital, particularly by lowering the corporate tax and the personal income tax for the highest income earners,[25] and to compensate this by increasing the taxation of wage earners and households.

It has been demonstrated time and again that the level of taxes paid by corporations plays only a minor role in the decisions of investors concerning the location of their investment.[26] Yet, the myth persists that attracting investors by lowering the corporate tax rate is a sustainable strategy, as if the comparative advantage of countries could consist in maintaining them unable to educate a highly qualified workforce, to maintain well-functioning public services, or to improve the quality of life for those working under their jurisdiction. Fiscal competition persists. It is stimulated by indicators such as the *doing business* ranking of the World Bank,[27] which—contrary to findings of organizations such as the OECD or IMF—still suggests that the lowering of corporate taxes is a valid means to attract investment, because countries that reduce tax rates, or raise the threshold for taxable income, or provide for a larger set of exemptions, get approval.

Thus for instance, *Paying Taxes 2017: The Global Picture*, a background study to the doing business ranking jointly authored by the World Bank and by PwC, concludes from a review of 190 countries' tax regimes that the total tax rate (the cost of all taxes borne, as a percent of commercial profit) decreased by 0.1 percent in 2015, to reach 40.6 percent—a result of thirty-eight jurisdictions decreasing taxes, while forty-four raised taxes (but did so to a lesser extent).[28] The World Bank's commentary included in the study acknowledges that "[t]axes are important to the proper functioning of an economy. They are the main source of federal, state and local government revenues used to fund health care, education, public transport, unemployment benefits and pensions, among others."[29] Yet, the ranking at least implicitly sends the exact opposite message, as the better ranked countries are those where the costs of doing business go down: among the eleven factors according to which countries are ranked in the 2017 edition of the *Doing Business* report (the fourteenth of its kind) are "payments, time and total tax rate for a firm to comply with all tax regulations as well as post-filing processes."[30] Moreover, the report suggests that the shift from direct taxes (such as those, in particular, on corporate incomes) to indirect taxes are a rather positive trend: "Consumption taxes, primarily in the form of value-added tax, goods and services tax (GST) as well as sales and use tax (SUT), have grown to be a major source of tax revenues for governments across the globe as they begin to appreciate that taxing consumption provides a more certain tax revenue stream than taxing income or profit. Governments worldwide are looking to raise more of their taxes from indirect taxes, which from a business perspective should be more neutral than direct taxes."[31]

The result of such pressures is that we have fiscal policies that, instead of shifting more of the tax burden to the wealthiest corporations and the richest individuals, as both economic common sense and human rights would require, end up taxing wage earners and consumers through VAT and the imposition of users' fees in sectors such as health or education. According to calculations of the World Bank, the average total tax rate payable by businesses on their commercial profits decreased from 53.5 percent to 40.8 percent between 2005 and 2015.[32] Although some countries moved in the opposite direction (Argentina and Chile are examples in Latin America; Malaysia and Niger provide illustrations in Asia and in Africa), the trend downward is massive: for many countries, the reduction of corporate taxes is measured in double digits.[33] On average, the total tax rates in the euro area countries went from 51.0 percent to 43.6 percent, a trend corresponding roughly to the tendency in the European Union as a whole.[34] But the phenomenon is especially spectacular in the countries classified by the United Nations as least developed, where the rate went down on average from 75.4 percent to 44.7 percent; in heavily indebted poor countries alone, the decrease was from 81.2 percent to 52.7 percent.[35]

IV. EFFECTIVELY COMBATING TAX EVASION AND ILLICIT FINANCIAL FLOWS

The fight against tax evasion is the third channel through which tax policies can be made to contribute better to the realization of economic, social, and cultural rights. Tax evasion represents a huge loss to countries and is of particular consequence (as a percentage of their public budgets) in low- and middle-income countries.[36] In 2008, Global Financial Integrity estimated that, during the 2002–2006 period, illicit financial flows represented an average of between $859 billion and $1.06 trillion on a yearly basis.[37] For Africa alone, a conservative estimate is that illicit financial flows out of the region have amounted to a total of $854 billion for the period 1970–2008.[38] These outflows have been growing steadily throughout the period at an average rate of 12.1 percent per year (with peaks reached in oil-producing countries such as Nigeria and Sudan linked to increases in the price of oil). The impacts are considerable: by the end of 2008, the same study notes, the cumulative impact of these outflows meant that each African woman, man, and child lost $989 to illicit financial outflows.[39] In fact, the total financial flows for 1970–2008 represent a sum far in excess of the external debt of all African countries ($279 billion in 2008): in other terms, taking into account illicit financial flows, Africa is a net creditor to the world, and by tackling such illicit financial flows, about $600 billion could have been mobilized for the fight against poverty on the continent.[40] Sixty to 65 percent of the total illicit financial flows are due to commercial tax evasion, which results from overpricing imports and underpricing exports on customs documents, and thereby illegally transferring money abroad. Although the situation in Africa is particularly troubling, the continent is not alone in this regard. For instance, according to the Inter-American Development Bank, evasion rates of personal and corporate income taxes average 50 percent in ten representative Latin American countries, among which Guatemala tops the league with an evasion rate of 70 percent.[41]

Improving tax collection is now described as a priority in various international outcome documents. In the Addis Ababa Action Agenda, adopted at the Third International Conference on Financing for Development in July 2015, the Heads of State and Government and High Representatives "recognize[d] that significant additional domestic public resources, supplemented by international assistance as appropriate, will be critical to realizing sustainable development and achieving the sustainable development goals," and they committed to "enhancing revenue administration through modernized, progressive tax systems, improved tax policy and more efficient tax collection."[42] They pledged to "work to improve the fairness, transparency, efficiency and effectiveness of our tax systems, including by broadening the tax base and continuing efforts to integrate the informal sector into the formal economy in line with country circumstances."[43] Though not explicitly defined as a human rights requirement, these commitments should be seen as a component of the duty of progressive realization.

A. STRENGTHENING THE ABILITY TO COLLECT TAXES

Effectively combating tax evasion requires strengthening tax administrations (by dedicating sufficient personnel and resources to the task).[44] The High-Level Panel on Illicit Financial Flows from Africa established under the auspices of the African Union and the UN Economic Commission for Africa, recommended in this regard a particular focus on "developing the required capacities, establishing or strengthening necessary institutions including transfer pricing units, and providing resources for the effective functioning of these institutions," and "holding multinationals accountable for fraudulent practices by setting up requirements for their transfer of funds and business practices."[45] This should also be treated as a priority since the failure to effectively address tax evasion has regressive impacts, disproportionately affecting the poor:

> High net-worth individuals and large corporations . . . have a far greater ability to evade taxes as they are able to pay tax advisers, lawyers and accountants (who may sometimes provide inappropriate advice and assistance) and to open undeclared foreign bank accounts in low-tax jurisdictions. Tax abuse by corporations and high net-worth individuals forces Governments to raise revenue from other sources: often regressive taxes, the burden of which falls hardest on the poor. Therefore, if States do not tackle tax abuse, they are likely to be disproportionately benefiting wealthy individuals to the detriment of the most disadvantaged. Monitoring, preventing and

punishing abuse is therefore essential in order to comply with human rights principles and improve the distributive effects of tax systems.[46]

Combating illicit financial flows is therefore a human rights issue. Indeed, recognizing that "illicit capital flight undermines the capacity of State Parties to implement the African Charter on Human and Peoples' Rights and to attain the Millennium Development Goals," the African Commission on Human and Peoples' Rights has called upon states parties to the African Charter "to examine their national tax laws and policies towards preventing illicit capital flight in Africa."[47]

B. THE ROLE OF EXTRATERRITORIAL HUMAN RIGHTS OBLIGATIONS

Strengthening domestic institutions tasked with combating tax evasion will not suffice, however. This is one area in which such efforts shall only be fully effective if supported by international cooperation, requiring that all countries comply with their extraterritorial human rights obligations.[48] Though classic forms of international cooperation have a role to play in this regard, "aid for tax" strategies—by supporting local institutions in charge of tax collection[49]—will remain insufficient unless complemented by reforms in the countries which receive illicit financial flows from tax evasion or other forms of economic crime such as corruption. This concerns in particular the countries under whose jurisdiction tax havens are currently left unaddressed, or whose bank secrecy laws facilitate tax evasion. As noted by the Special Rapporteur on extreme poverty and human rights: "Individual countries, in particular low-income countries, are severely constrained in the measures that they alone can take against tax abuse. Illicit financial flows are international in nature and therefore beyond the capacity of any one State alone to tackle. The availability of offshore financial centres (tax havens) that offer low or no taxes and secrecy is a major factor."[50]

There are signs that governments are finally taking these issues more seriously. In 2010, the Convention on Mutual Administrative Assistance in Tax Matters, initially the result of a joint effort of the OECD and the Council of Europe in 1988, was amended in order to allow for the participation of developing countries.[51] The new text was opened for signature on June 1, 2011. It now covers 109 jurisdictions, including 15 jurisdictions covered by extension.[52] It provides for various forms of administrative cooperation between states in the assessment and collection of taxes, facilitating the exchange of information and the recovery of foreign tax claims with a view to supporting states' efforts to combat tax avoidance and evasion. At the same time, the G20 has identified Base Erosion and Profit Shifting (BEPS) as a major concern for tax justice worldwide: the ability of states to raise public revenue is undermined as multinational companies are taking advantage of differences between tax rates by artificially shifting profits across borders, rather than declaring such profits (and paying the corresponding taxes) where their productive activities take place. The OECD adopted a 15-point action plan in 2013 in order to address this, to be progressively implemented in the next few years.[53]

That these efforts are essential for the fulfillment of human rights is made increasingly explicit by UN human rights treaty bodies. The Committee on Economic, Social and Cultural Rights noted in Concluding Observations related to the United Kingdom that "financial secrecy legislation [allowing its Overseas Territories and Crown Dependencies to prosper as tax havens] and permissive rules on corporate tax are affecting the ability of the State party, as well other

States, to meet their obligation to mobilize the maximum available resources for the implementation of economic, social and cultural rights," and recommended that the state party "intensify its efforts, in coordination with its Overseas Territories and Crown Dependencies, to address global tax abuse."[54]

Nor is the Committee on Economic, Social and Cultural Rights isolated in this regard. A few months after the cited recommendation was addressed to the United Kingdom, the Committee on the Elimination of Discrimination Against Women recommended that Switzerland "[u]ndertake independent, participatory and periodic impact assessments of the extraterritorial effects of its financial secrecy and corporate tax policies on women's rights and substantive equality, and ensure that such assessments are conducted in an impartial manner with public disclosure of the methodology and finding."[55] The recommendation was prompted by a report[56] presented by a coalition of nongovernmental organizations and a human rights clinic, showing how cross-border tax abuse by corporations and individuals (in various forms including "controversial profit-shifting, fraudulent under-reporting of the value of taxable transactions, and the use of off-shore accounts to hide taxable income"[57]) have an impact on the ability of developing countries to protect and fulfill women's rights. As the report explained:

> The loss of revenues to cross-border tax abuse contributes to the underfunding of essential services, institutions, and infrastructure on which women depend, from health care and education to public courts and transportation systems, as well as programs designed specifically to protect and promote women's rights. Inadequate spending on social services often takes a heavy toll on women in particular, as they typically bear the burden of care-giving and performing unpaid work when public institutions fall short.[58]

In addition, development cooperation may support efforts at the domestic level to combat illicit financial flows. In 2011, development aid contributing to such efforts (by programs strengthening the judiciary or anticorruption authorities, for instance) represented 11 percent of total official development assistance (ODA) from OECD countries.[59] Such interventions can be highly effective: in Kenya, a $20,000 support program led to an increase of $33 million in increased tax revenue during a one-year period (2012–2013), which represents a rate of return of $1,650 for each dollar spent.[60] Here again, however, such efforts could go further. Staff within the relevant public sector authorities could be trained to facilitate investigations of economic crimes and asset recovery. Developing countries could be encouraged to make this a top political priority. Support to local civil society organizations acting as watchdogs to denounce corruption or tax evasion could be increased.[61]

C. THE ROLE OF THE PRIVATE SECTOR:
FINANCIAL INSTITUTIONS

Although the main responsibility in tacking illicit financial flows lies with governments, the private sector—banks and other financial institutions—also has a role to play in this regard. Indeed, it could be argued that a failure to discharge their responsibilities to prevent tax abuse is a violation, by these entities, of their commitments in the area of human rights. The Guiding Principles on Business and Human Rights[62] set out a requirement that business enterprises respect human rights, which includes an expectation that companies act with due diligence: corporations, the Guiding Principles state, should "act with due diligence to avoid infringing on the rights of others and to address adverse impacts with which they are involved."[63] This means that they should put in place "a human rights due-diligence process to identify, prevent, mitigate and account for how they address their impacts on human rights."[64] The OECD Guidelines for Multinational Enterprises, following their revision in 2011 to insert a human rights chapter (chapter IV), also include due diligence in the definition of the responsibility of business enterprises to respect human rights.[65]

Such due diligence obligations require companies to take measures to ensure that their clients do not evade their duties to pay taxes in the jurisdictions in which they reside. This interpretation is confirmed by Principle 17 of the Guiding Principles on Business and Human Rights, which provides that human rights due diligence should cover "adverse human rights impacts that the business enterprise may cause or contribute to through its own activities, or which may be directly linked to its operations, products or services by its business relationships."[66] Similarly, the OECD Guidelines for Multinational Enterprises provide that business enterprises domiciled in OECD countries should "seek ways to prevent or mitigate adverse human rights impacts that are directly linked to their business operations, products or services by a business relationship, even if they do not contribute to those impacts."[67] As explained in the Commentary to these Guidelines (in para. 43), this implies an expectation that

> an enterprise, acting alone or in co-operation with other entities, as appropriate, . . . use its leverage to influence the entity causing the adverse human rights impact to prevent or mitigate that impact. "Business relationships" include relationships with business partners, entities in its supply chain, and any other non-State or State entity directly linked to its business operations, products or services. Among the factors that will enter into the determination of the appropriate action in such situations are the enterprise's leverage over the entity concerned, how crucial the relationship is to the enterprise, the severity of the impact, and whether terminating the relationship with the entity itself would have adverse human rights impacts.[68]

The OECD Guidelines for Multinational Enterprises also provide that companies "encourage, where practicable, business partners, including suppliers and sub-contractors, to apply principles of responsible business conduct compatible with the Guidelines."[69]

The responsibilities of banks and other financial institutions to ensure that they support, rather than undermine, the efforts of governments to combat tax evasion, follows from the simple fact that without a mechanism to launder the money, economic actors will be less tempted to violate their tax obligations. Yet, Global Witness and others have warned that many regulations aimed at combating laundering were ignored or circumvented by financial actors.[70] This comes at a considerable price for developing countries: in 2015, the UN Office on Drugs and Crime estimated that the amount of the money laundered each year was the equivalent of 2–5 percent of total GDP, or $800 billion to $2 trillion.[71]

Some attempts have been made to make private financial actors aware of their responsibilities. The Financial Action Task Force (FATF), an independent intergovernmental body established in 1989 to support the fight against money laundering, adopted a set of recommendations addressed to its Member States. Known as the *International Standards on Combating Money Laundering and the Financing of Terrorism and Proliferation* (AML/CFT standards), the recommendations were initially drawn up in 1990; they were most recently updated in 2012, and have been endorsed by 180 countries.[72] While it is not possible here to describe in detail the full set of recommendations, it may be relevant to note that they include imposing on financial institutions that they undertake customer due diligence (CDD) upon establishing business relationships with new clients or for occasional transactions, whether because they reach a certain level or because there is a suspicion of money laundering or terrorist financing. CDD means: identifying the customer and verifying that customer's identity; identifying the "beneficial owner," and "taking reasonable measures to verify the identity of the beneficial owner, such that the financial institution is satisfied that it knows who the beneficial owner is" (where the client is a corporation, this means understanding the corporate structure sufficiently to see who is "behind" public-facing entities); "understanding and, . . . obtaining information on the purpose and intended nature of the business relationship"; and "conducting ongoing due diligence on the business relationship and scrutiny of transactions undertaken throughout the course of that relationship to ensure that the transactions being conducted are consistent with the institution's knowledge of the customer, their business and risk profile, including, where necessary, the source of funds."[73]

The FATF recommendations on the need to seek information about beneficial owners are of particular importance. Indeed, a major obstacle to the effective enforcement of money-laundering regulations is that the identity of the real owners of corporate structures may remain hidden, or can only be known to the authorities in country A (where the company is domiciled and regulated) by seeking information from country B (from where the company is administered). Noting that in many cases financial institutions did not seek to identify the beneficial owner when establishing a business relationship, the authors of a World Bank 2011 study on the laundering of the products of economic crime highlight the importance of imposing due diligence obligations on banks and other financial intermediaries such as trust and company service providers.[74] This, the study noted, would oblige service providers to "collect information and conduct due diligence on matters about which they might prefer to remain ignorant": "If a service provider is obligated to gather full due diligence information, it becomes impossible for the intermediary to legitimately plead ignorance regarding the background of a client or the source of his or her funds."[75] Moreover, the collection of such information by the financial intermediaries facilitates inquiries, providing investigators with an adequate source of information.

Even apart from the fact that they are not, by any means, fully implemented in the participating countries, the AML/CFT standards remain insufficient to effectively combat the widespread practice of tax evasion. Gaps remain, for instance, in enforcing the duty of financial institutions to ensure that they identify the beneficial owner. First, where investigators seek to have access to information retained by an attorney, the attorney-client privilege is invoked to oppose this and shield information from scrutiny. Such a barrier should be lifted where circumstances allow: the 2011 World Bank study referred to above notes that many jurisdictions have introduced exceptions to the legal professional privilege "in cases in which the attorney is acting as a financial intermediary or in some other strictly fiduciary or transactional capacity, rather than as a legal advocate."[76] Second, international cooperation is essential to the success of the provisions concerning the need to identify the beneficial owner: in order to save the considerable costs involved in having to seek information concerning the "real owners" of companies from authorities of another country than the country where the company is registered, countries should be encouraged to adopt regulations to ensure that information concerning beneficial ownership of any entity incorporated under its laws is available with a person who is *resident* in that country.[77]

In order for the AML/CFT standards to be truly effective, the incentives of bankers should be aligned with the legal duties imposed on the financial institutions themselves. This is not currently the case. Global Witness rightly notes that, as long as prosecuting authorities remain hesitant to impose sanctions on the bank executives themselves, as individuals, these executives will remain tempted to treat the risk of their institution being fined for lack of due diligence in dealing with funds of suspect origin as a mere "business risk," that may be worth taking as long as the benefits outweigh the potential costs to the institution. It is encouraging to note, however, that in recent years prosecuting authorities (particularly in the United States) have appeared more willing to impose sanctions not only on financial institutions but also on individuals working within such institutions—although more frequently on middle-level employees than on the "directing minds" such as CEOs and members of the board.[78]

V. PARTICIPATION AND ACCOUNTABILITY IN TAXATION POLICIES

After the Committee on Economic, Social and Cultural Rights expressed its concern about fiscal reforms introduced by the United Kingdom, such as increases in the threshold for the payment of inheritance tax and increases of the value-added tax or cuts to the tax rates of corporations, it recommended that the United Kingdom "conduct a human rights impact assessment, with broad public participation, of the recent changes introduced to its fiscal policy, including an analysis of the distributional consequences and the tax burden of different income sectors and marginalized and disadvantaged groups."[79] Similarly, the Special Procedures of the Human Rights Council that deplored the impacts on poor families of the Welfare Reform and Work Act enacted by the United Kingdom in 2016, criticized the lack of credibility of the impact assessments preceding the cuts to welfare benefits, noting that these cuts were based on often unproven assumptions and that the government had failed to explore the full range of alternative options to ensure the sustainability of the welfare system. They asked the government to indicate whether they had "consulted the individuals, groups and families most likely to be affected by the Act."[80] Thus, emerges a fourth requirement in the design of tax policies: that they be subject to effective democratic control.

Strengthening participation, transparency, and accountability in budgetary decision-making is a way to ensure that budgetary priorities take into account the interests of the most marginalized groups within society. The point barely requires elaboration: economic marginalization (the deprivation of social and economic rights) typically is paired with political disempowerment (violations of civil and political rights, in particular the right to take part in the conduct of public affairs), leading to a vicious cycle in which because the poor are unable to influence political processes, the policies adopted serve the elites rather than respond to the needs of the most disadvantaged.[81]

Strengthening the participation of the poor in shaping policies can help to break this cycle, leading in turn to the adoption of policies that will be more attentive to their needs.[82] It shall also strengthen the negotiating position of departments dealing with health, education, or social welfare, whose demands frequently compete with those from departments concerned with law and order—the Interior, National Defense, or Justice—particularly in relatively weakly governed countries in which controlling the population and law enforcement are seen are major challenges on which the very stability of the government may depend. If civil society organizations are involved in defining the budgetary priorities, it is likely that they will support the "human development" sectors within the state. Finally, in the competition between macroeconomic policies that keep the public debt under control and thus reassure the external creditors of the state, and meeting the needs of the population, strengthening participation improves the bargaining position of the government in its negotiation with its creditors and with international financial institutions in particular. While this makes it more difficult for the government to find an agreement with creditors in situations where it needs financial support, the creditors may take solace in the fact that transparency and accountability may improve the efficiency of public policies, and maximize the effectiveness of public investment in reducing poverty and placing the country on the track of sustainable human development.[83]

In the fulfillment by the Committee on Economic, Social and Cultural Rights of its monitoring role under the International Covenant on Economic, Social and Cultural Rights, the insistence on participation and accountability also presents a major advantage: it reduces the tension between supervision of compliance by an international body of independent experts and democratic self-determination. The Covenant, after all, relies on deliberately vague wording to evoke the duty to progressively realize the rights of the Covenant "to the maximum of its available resources," and any attempt to go beyond that wording to clarify the content of such duty shall be met with suspicion by the states parties. By emphasizing participation and accountability in the design and implementation of taxation policies, the Committee conveniently can retreat from substance to procedure—or, to borrow from the phrase of John Hart Ely, from a "representation-restricting" theory of rights adjudication to a "representation-reinforcing" approach, in which judicial review concerns itself more with "questions of participation" than with "the substantive merits of the political choice under attack."[84] This is not to say that the Committee abdicates its duty to assess taxation policies from the substantive point of view, asking in particular whether enough is done to widen the tax base, to ensure adequate redistribution from the riches to the poorest parts of the population, and to combat tax evasion. These substantive requirements, however, should be read in the light of the procedural requirements of participation and accountability: such procedural requirements are both an additional requirement imposed on states, and a means to ensure that the margin of discretion left to states in the design of their taxation policies is used in ways that truly benefit the poor.

VI. CONCLUSION

In theory, the Committee on Economic, Social and Cultural Rights has all the tools it requires to strengthen the role of the International Covenant on Economic, Social and Cultural Rights in the design and implementation of taxation policies. A consensus is emerging on the need to strengthen domestic resource mobilization, in order to make development less dependent on foreign support and to increase accountability of governments toward their populations. The fight against inequalities, and thus the need for robust redistributive taxation schemes, is broadly recognized as a priority. There is wide agreement, too, on the importance of reinforcing the ability of local tax administrations to combat tax evasion, and on the indispensable role both of international cooperation in this regard (by the clamping down on tax havens and the lifting of bank secrecy legislation that favor money laundering), and on the need to regulate the private financial sector. Finally, the role of participation and accountability in the design of taxation policies is increasingly acknowledged: reforming decision-making so that such choices are not the result of backdoor negotiations between politicians and technocrats, but rather the outcome of public deliberation involving large segments of society, is one key ingredient to ensure that taxation policies serve the needs of the poor.

Enforcing these four key requirements remains a challenge, however. In many countries, the economic elites exercise a disproportionate influence on political decision-making, and they resist any significant fiscal reform that could threaten their privileges.[85] The myth according to which low rates of corporate taxation are a condition for attracting foreign capital persists, despite the wealth of studies that have demonstrated the opposite—that investors care more about the quality of the workforce and of public service, the quality of governance, and economic factors such as market size and trade openness. Some governments still do not accept the idea that the efforts of poor countries in combating tax evasion should be supported by rich countries, not only by ODA going to improving governance but also by more structural measures concerning the removal of any loophole facilitating the practice of tax evasion. While tax evasion is criticized, at least rhetorically, tax optimization techniques and the widespread use of price transfer mechanisms by transnational corporations have only recently been evoked as a problem at the highest political level, leading to the adoption within the OECD of the action plan against base erosion and profit shifting. It shall be the responsibility of the Committee on Economic, Social and Cultural Rights to continue to insist on such obstacles being removed, on such myths being dissipated, and on such pledges being kept.

NOTES

1. Art. 2(1), International Covenant on Economic, Social and Cultural Rights 1966, 993 UNTS 3 (emphasis added).
2. Human Rights Council, Report of the Special Rapporteur on Extreme Poverty and Human Rights, Philip Alston, UN Doc. A/HRC/29/31, 26 May 2015, at para. 53.
3. It may be worth recalling that the "adequate house," in the view of the Committee on Economic, Social and Cultural Rights, is one that, in particular, ensures access to "safe drinking water, energy for cooking, heating and lighting, sanitation and washing facilities" and is "in a location which allows access to employment options, health-care services, schools, child-care centres and other social facilities [in particular since] the temporal and financial costs of getting to and from the place of work can place excessive demands upon the budgets of poor households" (Committee on Economic, Social and Cultural Rights, General Comment No. 4: The Right to Adequate Housing (Art. 11(1) of the Covenant), UN Doc. E/1992/23, 1 Jan. 1992, at paras. 8(b) and (f)).
4. See General Assembly, Report of the Special Rapporteur on Extreme Poverty and Human Rights, Magdalena Sepúlveda Carmona, UN Doc. A/68/293, 9 Aug. 2013.
5. Although this may come at the risk of increasing their annual public deficit and, ultimately, their public debt, it may be justified particularly in times of economic downturn and insofar as the debt finances policies that may be seen as investments rather than merely as a stopgap to meet current expenditures. R. Roy and A. Heuty (eds.), *Fiscal Space: Policy Options for Financing Human Development* (2009).
6. M. Ravallion, *Do Poorer Countries Have Less Capacity for Redistribution?* (World Bank Policy Research Working Paper 5046, 1 Sept. 2009), available online at https://openknowledge.worldbank.org/handle/10986/4238 (last visited 27 June 2017).
7. C. Hoy and A. Sumner, *Gasoline, Guns and Giveaways: Is There New Capacity for Redistribution to End Three Quarters of Global Poverty?* (Center for Global Development Working Paper 433, Aug. 2016), available online at https://www.cgdev.org/sites/default/files/gasoline-guns-and-giveaways-end-three-quarters-global-poverty-0.pdf, at 19 (last visited 27 June 2017).
8. See, for instance, Human Rights Council, Report of the Special Rapporteur on the Right to Food, Olivier De Schutter, on his Mission to Guatemala, UN Doc. A/13/33/Add.4, 26 Jan. 2010, at para. 87.
9. A. Corbacho, V. Frebes Cibils, and E. Lora (eds.), *More than Revenue: Taxation as a Development Tool* (2013), at 115. This discrepancy, as a measure of the degree of progressivity of the tax system (i.e., of its ability to reduce inequalities) is hardly attenuated by taking into account the proportion the personal income tax represented in the total tax burden: in OECD countries, the total tax

burden represents 34.8 percent of the GDP, and it is 23.4 percent in Latin America. Therefore, the personal income tax represents about one-quarter of the tax burden in OECD countries, but only 5.98 percent of the tax burden in Latin American countries.

10. Human Rights Council, Report of the Special Rapporteur on Extreme Poverty and Human Rights, Magdalena Sepúlveda Carmona, UN Doc. A/HRC/26/28, 22 May 2014, at para. 56 (citing ActionAid, *Accounting for Poverty: How International Tax Rules Keep People Poor* (2009), available online https://www.actionaid.org.uk/sites/default/files/doc_lib/accounting_for_poverty.pdf, at 5 (last visited 27 June 2017)).

11. For a more systematic treatment, see O. De Schutter, J. F. Swinnen, and J. Wouters, 'Introduction: Foreign Direct Investment and Human Development', *in* O. De Schutter et al. (eds.), *Foreign Direct Investment and Human Development: The Law and Economics of International Investment Agreements* (2012), 1. See also World Bank, Results of Investor Motivation Survey Conducted in the EAC (East African Community), presentation made to the Tax Compact in Lusaka, Zambia (2013), cited in OECD, *Development Co-Operation Report 2014: Mobilising Resources for Sustainable Development* (2014), available online at http://observ-ocd.org/sites/observ-ocd.org/files/publicacion/docs/informe_coop.desen_._2014_ocde.pdf, at 151 (according to which "[a] large majority of investors covered by investor motivation surveys of the World Bank's Investment Climate Advisory claim that in the majority of cases (for instance over 90% in Rwanda, Tanzania and Uganda) they would have invested even if incentives were not provided").

12. A greater emphasis has been placed in recent years on the latter determinant as a result of globalization and the development of global supply chains. Even in this regard, however, the relationship is by no means automatic, as illustrated by the situation of sub-Saharan African countries that are very open to trade but that nevertheless are generally not able to attract FDI.

13. The economic empirical literature confirms the suspicion expressed by some in the legal literature (M. Sornarajah, 'State Responsibility and Bilateral Investment Treaties', 20 *Journal of World Trade Law* (1986), 79; J. Webb Jackee, 'Do Bilateral Investment Treaties Promote Foreign Direct Investment? Some Hints from Alternative Evidence', 51 *Virginia Journal of International Law* (2011), 397): there is weak evidence that the conclusion of investment agreements guaranteeing extensive rights to investors has more than a marginal impact on FDI inflows, and where it does seem to have some effect, it is mostly as a substitute for poor institutional quality, particularly in sub-Saharan African countries or in transition economies swiftly moving toward open market policies.

14. Human Rights Council, *supra* note 10, at para. 16.

15. Human Rights Council, *supra* note 2, at para. 53.

16. Ibid.

17. OECD, *Divided We Stand: Why Inequality Keeps Rising* (2011).

18. Committee on Economic, Social and Cultural Rights, Concluding Observations on the Sixth Periodic Report of the United Kingdom of Great Britain and Northern Ireland, UN Doc. E/C.12/GBR/CO/6, 14 July 2016, at para. 16.

19. See, e.g., Human Rights Council, Report of the Special Rapporteur on the Right to Food, Olivier De Schutter, on his Mission to Brazil, UN Doc. A/HRC/13/33/Add.6, 19 Feb. 2009, at para. 36: "The tax structure in Brazil remains highly regressive. Tax rates are high for goods and services and low for income and property, bringing about very inequitable outcomes. [. . .] [W]hile the social programmes developed under the 'Zero Hunger' strategy are impressive in scope, they are essentially funded by the very persons whom they seek to benefit, as the regressive system of taxation seriously limits the redistributive impact of the programmes. Only by introducing a tax reform that would reverse the current situation could Brazil claim to be seeking to realize the right to adequate food by taking steps to the maximum of its available resources."

20. The Kakwani and the Reynolds-Smolensky indexes appeared simultaneously in the economic literature: see N. C. Kakwani, 'Measurement of Tax Progressivity: An International Comparison', 87(435) *The Economic Journal* (1977), 71; and M. O. Reynolds and E. Smolensky, *Public Expenditures, Taxes and the Distribution of Income: The United States, 1950, 1961, 1970* (1977). For a general presentation, see J. Haughton and S. Khandker, *Handbook on Inequality and Poverty* (2009) (Ch. 15: 'The

Effects of Taxation and Spending on Inequality and Poverty'). The reliance on these measures has been criticized on the ground that they fail to take into account the changes in revenue that may result from the introduction of tax reforms: see S. Díaz de Sarralde, C. Garcimartín, and J. Ruiz-Huerta, 'The Paradox of Progressivity in Low-Tax Countries: Income Tax in Guatemala', 102 *CEPAL Review* (Dec. 2010), 85.

21. See S. Kuznets, 'Economic Growth and Income Inequality', 45 *American Economic Review* (Mar. 1955), 1.

22. Human Rights Council, *supra* note 10, at para. 40, citing J. D. Ostry, A. Berg, and C. G. Tsangarides, *Redistribution, Inequality and Growth* (IMF Staff Discussion Note No. 14/02, 17 Feb. 2014), available online at https://www.imf.org/en/Publications/Staff-Discussion-Notes/Issues/2016/12/31/Redistribution-Inequality-and-Growth-41291 (last visited 27 June 2017). See also A. Berg and J. D. Ostry, *Inequality and Unsustainable Growth: Two Sides of the Same Coin?* (IMF Staff Discussion Note No. 11/08, 8 Apr. 2011), available online at https://www.imf.org/en/Publications/Staff-Discussion-Notes/Issues/2016/12/31/Inequality-and-Unsustainable-Growth-Two-Sides-of-the-Same-Coin-24686 (last visited 27 June 2017).

23. E. Dabla-Norris et al., *Causes and Consequences of Income Inequality* (IMF Staff Discussion Note No. 15/13, 15 June 2015), available online https://www.imf.org/en/Publications/Staff-Discussion-Notes/Issues/2016/12/31/Causes-and-Consequences-of-Income-Inequality-A-Global-Perspective-42986, at 7 (last visited 27 June 2017).

24. D. Elson, R. Balakrishnan, and J. Heintz, 'Public Finance, Maximum Available Resources and Human Rights', *in* A. Nolan, R. O'Connell, and C. Harvey (eds.), *Human Rights and Public Finance: Budgets and the Promotion of Economic and Social Rights* (2013), 13, at 28; and in the same volume, I. Saiz, 'Resourcing Rights: Combating Tax Injustice from a Human Rights Perspective', 77, at 84. It is important to note, however, that although VAT is regressive when calculations are made on income (the poorest households contribute more as a proportion of their income), this regressivity either disappears or is significantly attenuated when calculated on the basis of consumption (that is, the higher levels of consumption of the rich and the high VAT rates on luxury items that are only affordable to the rich, leads to a situation in which the rich contribute more to the revenues collected through VAT than the poor). See Corbacho et al., *supra* note 9, at 167–168.

25. IMF, *Fiscal Policy and Income Inequality* (Policy Paper, 23 Jan. 2014), available online at https://www.imf.org/external/np/pp/eng/2014/012314.pdf, at 37 (estimating that top personal income taxes were lowered by about 30 percent on average since 1980).

26. See the references cited *supra*, note 11.

27. See *Doing Business*, The World Bank, available online at http://www.doingbusiness.org/ (last visited 16 Jan. 2018).

28. World Bank and PwC, *Paying Taxes 2017: The Global Picture* (2017), available online at https://www.pwc.com/gx/en/paying-taxes/pdf/pwc-paying-taxes-2017.pdf (last visited 27 June 2017). Rather awkwardly, this total is obtained by including in the calculation of the total tax rate "the sum of all the different taxes and contributions payable after accounting for allowable deductions and exemptions," into which fall five categories: "profit or corporate income tax, social contributions and labour taxes paid by the employer (in respect of which all mandatory contributions are included, even if paid to a private entity such as a requited pension fund), property taxes, turnover taxes and other taxes (such as municipal fees and vehicle and fuel taxes)" (ibid. 91 (in Appendix 1 concerning the methodology)). [This deviates from standard practice. For instance, the IMF's Government Financial Statistics Manual recommends that levies for the collection of waste or environmental taxes to compensate for pollution, as well as employers' contributions to employees' health or pension funds be treated as distinct from general taxes: the methodology followed in *Paying Taxes 2017* results in a misleadingly high estimate of the tax burden, which increases the pressure on governments to reduce the costs for businesses in all the areas covered. See J. K. Sundaram and A. Chowdhury, *World Bank Must Stop Encouraging Harmful Tax Competition*, 26 Apr. 2017, available online at http://www.ipsnews.net/2017/04/world-bank-must-stop-encouraging-harmful-tax-competition/ (last visited 27 June 2017).

29. World Bank and PwC, *supra* note 28, at 20.

30. World Bank, *Doing Business 2017: Equal Opportunity for All* (2017), available online at http://documents.worldbank.org/curated/en/172361477516970361/Doing-business-2017-equal-opportunity-for-all, at 14 (table 2.1.) (last visited 27 June 2017).

31. World Bank and PwC, *supra* note 28, at 82.

32. This is a nonweighted average: small economies count as much as large ones in the calculation of the average. The total tax rate, for the purpose of this calculation, is the "amount of taxes and mandatory contributions payable by businesses after accounting for allowable deductions and exemptions as a share of commercial profits." For more details, see World Bank, *Total Tax Rate (% of Commercial Profits)*, available online at http://data.worldbank.org/indicator/IC.TAX.TOTL.CP.ZS ?end=2015&start=2005&view=chart (last visited 27 June 2017). Some countries have lowered corporate taxes faster than others: during this ten-year period, Albania lowered corporate taxes from 58.2 percent to 36.5 percent, Belarus from 137.3 percent to 51.8 percent, and Uzbekistan from 96.7 percent to 41.1 percent; Canada went from 47.5 percent to 21.1 percent, and Paraguay from 54.5 percent to 35.0 percent. Turkey moved from 52.8 percent to 40.9 percent.

33. Ibid.

34. Ibid.

35. Ibid.

36. For a useful assessment, see OECD, *Development Co-Operation Report 2014: Mobilising Resources for Sustainable Development, supra* note 11, Ch. II.13.

37. D. Kar and D. Cartwright-Smith, *Illicit Financial Flows from Developing Countries: 2002–2006*, 14 Dec. 2008, available online at http://www.gfintegrity.org/report/global-illicit-flows-report-2008/ (last visited 27 June 2017).

38. D. Kar and D. Cartwright-Smith, *Illicit Financial Flows from Africa: Hidden Resource for Development*, 26 Mar. 2010, available online at http://www.gfintegrity.org/report/briefing-paper-illicit-flows-from-africa/ (last visited 27 June 2017).

39. Ibid. at 12.

40. This was also the conclusion reached by L. Ndikumana and J. K. Boyce, *New Estimates of Capital Flight from Sub-Saharan African Countries: Linkages with External Borrowing and Policy Options* (Political Economy Research Institute/University of Massachusetts Amherst, Working Paper No. 166, Apr. 2008), available online at http://scholarworks.umass.edu/cgi/viewcontent. cgi?article=1137&context=peri_workingpapers (last visited 27 June 2017).

41. Corbacho et al., *supra* note 9, at 121 (fig. 7.4.). These estimates are based on data from the period 2003–2010, with different years for the different countries (for Guatemala for instance, the reference year is 2006). They should therefore be treated with caution as a source of cross-country comparisons. They do provide, however, an idea of the magnitude of the problem.

42. Addis Ababa Action Agenda of the Third International Conference on Financing for Development (Addis Ababa Action Agenda), endorsed by the General Assembly in GA Res. 69/313, 27 July 2015, at para. 22.

43. Ibid.

44. Human Rights Council, *supra* note 10, at para. 57.

45. High-Level Panel on Illicit Financial Flows from Africa, *Illicit Financial Flows* (2014), available online at http://www.uneca.org/sites/default/files/PublicationFiles/iff_main_report_26feb_en.pdf, at 66 (last visited 28 June 2017).

46. Human Rights Council, *supra* note 10, para. 60.

47. African Commission on Human and Peoples' Rights, Resolution 236 on Illicit Capital Flight from Africa, 23 Apr. 2013.

48. The Maastricht Principles on Extraterritorial Obligations of States in the Area of Economic, Social and Cultural Rights seek to bring together the rather disparate contributions from judicial and nonjudicial bodies to this fast-developing area of human rights law. They were endorsed on 28 September 2011 by a range of nongovernmental organizations and human rights experts, including mandate holders within the Special Procedures established by the Human Rights Council. See O. De Schutter et al., 'Commentary to the Maastricht Principles on Extraterritorial Obligations of States in the area of Economic, Social and Cultural Rights', 34 *Human Rights Quarterly* (2012), 1084.

49. See in this regard OECD, *Tax and Development: Aid Modalities for Strengthening Tax Systems* (2013).

50. Human Rights Council, *supra* note 10, at para. 61.

51. OECD and Council of Europe, *The Multilateral Convention on Mutual Administrative Assistance in Tax Matters: Amended by the 2010 Protocol* (2011), available online at http://www.keepeek. com/Digital-Asset-Management/oecd/taxation/the-multilateral-convention-on-mutual-administrative-assistance-in-tax-matters_9789264115606-en#.WW_Ix4qQyRs#page3 (last visited 19 July 2017).

52. Thus, Anguilla, Bermuda, the British Virgin Islands, the Cayman Islands, Gibraltar, Guernsey, the Isle of Man, Jersey, Montserrat, and the Turks and Caicos Islands are covered by extension from the United Kingdom; Aruba, Curaçao, and Sint Maarten, the latter two formerly part of the Netherlands Antilles, are covered by extension from the Netherlands; the Faroe Islands are covered by extension of Denmark.

53. OECD, *supra* note 11, at 167–176.

54. Committee on Economic, Social and Cultural Rights, *supra* note 18, at paras. 16–17.

55. Committee on the Elimination of Discrimination Against Women, Concluding Observations on the Combined Fourth and Fifth Reports of Switzerland, UN Doc. CEDAW/C/CHE/CO/4-5, 18 Nov. 2016, at para. 41.

56. Alliance Sud, Center for Economic and Social Rights, Global Justice Clinic of New York University School of Law, Public Eye and Tax Justice Network, *Swiss Responsibility for the Extraterritorial Impacts of Tax Abuse on Women's Rights*, 2 Nov. 2016, available online at http://chrgj.org/wp-content/uploads/2016/12/switzerland_cedaw_submission_2nov201628.pdf (last visited 28 June 2017).

57. Ibid. at 1.

58. Ibid. at 2.

59. OECD, *Illicit Financial Flows from Developing Countries: Measuring OECD Responses* (2014).

60. OECD, *supra* note 11, at 170.

61. Ibid. at 162–163.

62. Human Rights Council, Resolution 17/4: Human Rights and Transnational Corporations and other Business Enterprises, UN Doc. A/HRC/RES/17/4, 6 July 2011 (and, for the text of the Guiding Principles on Business and Human Rights, see Human Rights Council, Report of the Special Representative of the Secretary-General on the Issue of Human Rights and Transnational Corporations and other Business Enterprises, John Ruggie, UN Doc. A/HRC/17/31, 21 Mar. 2011). The Guiding Principles on Business and Human Rights were approved by the Human Rights Council at its seventeenth session on 16 June 2011. They clarify the content of the "Protect, Respect, Remedy" framework defining the respective obligations of States and corporations. On the Guiding Principles on Business and Human Rights, see, inter alia, S. Deva and D. Bilchitz (eds.), *Human Rights Obligations of Business: Beyond the Corporate Responsibility to Respect?* (2013); on the due diligence component of the responsibility to respect human rights, see O. De Schutter et al., *Human Rights Due Diligence: The Role of States* (2012).

63. Human Rights Council, *Guiding Principles on Business and Human Rights, supra* note 62, at para. 6.

64. See, for a more detailed description of what this entails, ibid. Principle 17.

65. OECD, *Guidelines for Multinational Enterprises* (2011 ed.), available online at https://www.oecd. org/corporate/mne/48004323.pdf, at 31 (last visited 19 July 2017).

66. Human Rights Council, *Guiding Principles on Business and Human Rights, supra* note 62, Principle 17.

67. OECD, *supra* note 65, at 31.

68. Ibid. at 33, para. 43.

69. Ibid. at II. General Policies, para. 13 (last visited 19 July 2017).

70. Global Witness, *Undue Diligence. How Banks Do Business with Corrupt Regimes* (2009), available online at http://www.u4.no/recommended-reading/undue-diligence-how-banks-do-business-with-corrupt-regimes/ (last visited 28 June 2017).

71. See United Nations Office on Drugs and Crime, *Money Laundering and Globalization*, available online at https://www.unodc.org/unodc/en/money-laundering/globalization.html (last visited 28 June 2017).

72. Text of the recommendations available online at http://www.fatf-gafi.org/media/fatf/documents/recommendations/pdfs/FATF_Recommendations.pdf (last visited 28 June 2017).

73. Ibid. Recommendation 10.

74. E. van der Does de Willebois et al., *The Puppet Masters. How the Corrupt Use Legal Structures to Hide Stolen Assets and What to Do About It* (2011), available online at https://star.worldbank.org/star/sites/star/files/puppetmastersv1.pdf (last visited 28 June 2017).

75. Ibid. at 5.

76. Ibid. at 6. The 2015 EU Anti-Money Laundering and Terrorist Financing Directive provides in this regard that, whereas "obliged entities" "know, suspect or have reasonable grounds to suspect" that funds result from criminal activity or are related to terrorist financing should report their suspicion to the authorities, this may not apply to "notaries, other independent legal professionals, auditors, external accountants and tax advisors *only to the strict extent that* such exemption relates to information that they receive from, or obtain on, one of their clients, in the course of ascertaining the legal position of their client, or performing their task of defending or representing that client in, or concerning, judicial proceedings, including providing advice on instituting or avoiding such proceedings, whether such information is received or obtained before, during or after such proceedings" (emphasis added): see Directive (EU) 2015/849 of the European Parliament and of the Council of 20 May 2015 on the Prevention of the Use of the Financial System for the Purposes of Money Laundering or Terrorist Financing, amending Regulation (EU) No. 648/2012 of the European Parliament and of the Council, and repealing Directive 2005/60/EC of the European Parliament and of the Council and Commission Directive 2006/70/EC, OJ L 141/73 [hereinafter the EU Anti-Money Laundering and Terrorist Financing Directive].

77. van der Does de Willebois et al., *supra* note 74, at 7. This is why the 2015 EU Anti-Money Laundering and Terrorist Financing Directive provides that the EU member states must ensure that "corporate and other legal entities incorporated within their territory are required to obtain and hold adequate, accurate and current information on their beneficial ownership, including the details of the beneficial interests held": EU Anti-Money Laundering and Terrorist Financing Directive, *supra* note 76, at art. 20(1).

78. For details, see Global Witness, *Banks and Dirty Money: How the Financial System Enables State Looting at a Devastating Human Cost* (2015), available online at https://www.globalwitness.org/en/campaigns/corruption-and-money-laundering/banks-and-dirty-money/ (last visited 28 June 2017). The recent EU Anti-Money Laundering and Terrorist Financing Directive again represents a promising step in this direction: it provides that where legal persons are found to have breached their obligations under the national law implementing the directive, "sanctions and measures can be applied to the members of the management body and to other natural persons who under national law are responsible for the breach": see EU Anti-Money Laundering and Terrorist Financing Directive, *supra* note 76, at art. 58(4).

79. Committee on Economic, Social and Cultural Rights, *supra* note 18, at para. 17.

80. See the Allegation Letter addressed to the United Kingdom by the Special Rapporteur on Adequate Housing, the Special Rapporteur on the Rights of Persons with Disabilities, the Special Rapporteur on Extreme Poverty and Human Rights, and the Special Rapporteur on the Right to Food (ref. AL GBR 1/2016, 8 April 2016, on file with author). See in particular questions 5 ("What evidence is available to demonstrate that the Employment Support Allowance for persons in the WRAG [Work Related Activity Group: people deemed unfit to work as result of health problems or a disability] has created a disincentive for them to take steps towards work? Further, what evidence is available to demonstrate that they would be incentivised to move towards work by reducing the Employment Support Allowance, in view of the fact that they have been assessed not fit for work?"), 7 ("What evidence is available to establish that your Excellency's Government has considered alternative options to the benefit cut, in the context of the full use of maximum available resources?"), 12 ("Please indicate whether there has been an independent review and assessment of the Act and

if so, provide details. Please also indicate whether the human rights of persons likely to be subject to the benefit cut have been considered in the review/assessment and what the findings were."), and 13 ("Could you please indicate what mechanism will be available to monitor negative effects of the Act?"). The response of the United Kingdom was sent on 14 July 2016 (Verbal Note of the UK Mission to the United Nations in Geneva, No. 231, on file with author). On these procedural dimensions, it states simply: "As per the usual Parliamentary process, the Public Bill Committee took 6 oral evidence sessions with a range of stakeholders representing interest groups, which are recorded in the parliamentary record. Furthermore, an open call for evidence was held with 86 pieces of evidence submitted and considered over the course of 8 months of Parliamentary scrutiny and 26 Parliamentary sessions." The scantiness of the response on the procedural questions raised is perhaps a good measure of how subversive these questions are.

81. See Human Rights Council, *supra* note 2, at para. 21 (citing United Nations Research Institute for Social Development, *Combating Poverty and Inequality: Structural Change, Social Policy and Politics* (2010), available online at http://www.unrisd.org/unrisd/website/document.nsf/ (httpAuxPages)/92B1D5057F43149CC125779600434441?OpenDocument&panel=additional, at 6 (last visited 28 June 2017)) ("Economic inequalities seem to encourage political capture and the unequal realization of civil and political rights. High levels of economic inequalities 'may create institutions that maintain the political, economic and social privileges of the elite and lock the poor into poverty traps from which it is difficult to escape'"). For instance, the governing elites may veto tax reforms that would lead to a more progressive system of taxation, and they may undermine efforts at combating the practices of tax evasion that they, more than the average citizen, may be able to rely on: see Corbacho et al., *supra* note 9, at 3 ("One of the rent-seeking mechanisms that the most affluent have imposed on the rest of society is the regressive design of the tax structure. Opportunities to evade taxes that vary greatly across income groups compound this perverse structure, shrinking the effective tax bases and resulting in low levels of revenue").

82. See, e.g., World Health Organization, *World Health Report 2010: Health Systems Financing: The Path to Universal Coverage* (2011), available online at http://www.who.int/whr/2010/en/, at 25 (last visited 28 June 2017) ("Dealing with universal health coverage also means dealing with the poor and the marginalized, people who are often politically disenfranchised and lack representation. This is why making health a key political issue is so important and why civil society, joined by eminent champions of universal coverage, can help persuade politicians to move health financing for universal coverage to the top of the political agenda"). For a powerful empirical study relating the diffusion of power in society (i.e., its degree of democratization) with the adoption of pro-poor policies, see M. S. Kimenyi, 'Economic Rights, Human Development Effort, and Institutions', *in* S. Hertel and L. Minkler (eds.), *Economic Rights: Conceptual, Measurement, and Policy Issues* (2007), 182, as well as the previous effort of this scholar finding a statistical correlation between indicators of power diffusion and progress along the Human Development Index: M. S. Kimenyi, *Institutions of Governance, Power Diffusion and Pro-Poor Growth and Policies* (2005).

83. World Health Organization, *supra* note 82, at 25 ("Improving efficiency and accountability may also convince ministries of finance, and increasingly donors, that more funding will be well used").

84. J. H. Ely, *Democracy and Distrust: A Theory of Judicial Review* (1980), at 181.

85. See, e.g., M. Gilens, *Affluence & Influence: Economic Inequality and Political Power in America* (2012); M. Gilens and B. Page, 'Testing Theories of American Politics: Elites, Interest Groups and Average Citizens', 12(3) *Perspectives on Politics* (2014), 564.

CHAPTER 3

TAXATION AS A HUMAN RIGHTS ISSUE

Gender and Substantive Equality

SANDRA FREDMAN

"Death, taxes and childbirth! There's never any convenient time for any of them."
—Margaret Mitchell, *Gone with the Wind*

I. INTRODUCTION

The persistence of deeply gendered roles in societies across the globe means that taxation systems have important gendered consequences. Most importantly, the continued ascription to women of primary child-caring roles has significant implications for their role in the paid workforce. While women are entering the paid workforce in increasing numbers, they continue to perform the bulk of unpaid domestic and childcare work, with the result that their participation in the paid workforce is often intermittent, precarious, and low-paid. In developing countries, where the formal workforce is still only a relatively small proportion of the total labor market, women form the majority of workers in the informal sector. Women also predominate among family and domestic workers, with the growing number of migrant domestic workers reflecting the globalization of female low-paid work. On the other hand, women are important beneficiaries of public spending, through their use of public services and as recipients of welfare benefits. In addition, many are employed in the public sector, and, as primary caregivers, are highly likely to pick up the slack where public services are contracted.

These patterns have close interactions with taxation systems. For example, the balance between income tax and consumer taxes has important implications. Although the fact that they tend to be low-paid means that women workers may pay less by way of personal income tax, as consumers of essential products they may pay more in consumer taxes. Similarly, the

Tax, Inequality, and Human Rights. Philip Alston and Nikki Reisch.
© Oxford University Press 2019. Published 2019 by Oxford University Press.

extent to which social security payments are linked to formal employment has ramifications for gender equality. As casual and precarious workers, many women may not have the benefit of employment-related social security contributions, affecting their social insurance rights and in particular their pensions. Equally importantly, systems that attach employment-related taxes to formal employment might encourage employers to reconfigure working relations in favor of casual, agency or self-employed relationships which might be cheaper for the employer. Indeed, the movement toward flexibilization of the paid workforce has been one of the primary sources of the increasing precariousness of women's employment.[1] The structure of personal allowances and taxation exemptions might similarly entrench gendered roles, although often in complex ways. Moreover, tax avoidance and evasion which reduce the revenue base and lead to cuts in public services clearly affect women, not only as workers and as service users but also because such cuts often increase their responsibility for unpaid caring and domestic work.

This chapter aims to explore the application of the right to equality to taxation systems and their administration. Diane Elson's work in 2006 was central in revealing the ways that taxation systems can violate the Convention on the Elimination of All Forms of Discrimination Against Women (CEDAW).[2] More recently, CEDAW was used as a critical framework to analyze taxation in developing and developed countries. In their enormously valuable detailed study of taxation and gender equity in eight countries, the Taxation and Gender Equity project edited by Grown and Valodia provides a rich source of empirical evidence on which to draw.[3] The importance of a human rights approach to taxation has been developed in pioneering work by the UN Special Rapporteur on extreme poverty, both previous and current. In her report of 2014, then Special Rapporteur Magdalena Sepúlveda outlined relevant human rights obligations to guide and inform state revenue-raising practices and made recommendations for fiscal and tax policies that are grounded in human rights.[4] Particularly innovative has been the 2016 submission to CEDAW by a group of civil society organizations demonstrating the ways that Swiss secrecy laws regarding taxation violate CEDAW, by allowing very large amounts of revenue to flow out of the countries in which it is earned.[5] This revenue outflow seriously depletes the resources available to signatory states to respect, protect, and fulfill their obligations to gender equality under CEDAW.

The right to equality is centrally implicated in taxation systems, both in the consequences of those systems for revenue raising and in their role in reinforcing or changing behaviors. A straightforward notion of equality as equal treatment, however, will not illuminate the complex ways in which gendered social relations are affected by taxation systems. Indeed, equal treatment in taxation might have regressive consequences, as the move toward value-added tax (VAT) and other indirect taxes to compensate for loss of trade taxes in the current global economy demonstrates. Instead, drawing on CEDAW and previous work of the author, this chapter develops and applies a multidimensional conception of substantive equality. Since taxation systems differ in their detail and conception in different countries, the aim is not to prescribe any particular solution. Instead, the chapter uses the framework of substantive equality in order to illuminate and address the ways in which taxation systems might breach the right to equality and how they should be modified to address such breaches. Examples will be drawn from different jurisdictions to illustrate how these principles might be used without attempting to be comprehensive.

This chapter differs from the concept of optimal taxation, currently preferred by economists, which takes the goals of a policymaker as given and aims to design a taxation system to achieve those goals. Instead, the chapter aims to determine when taxation systems or aspects of such systems can be regarded as breaching the human right to equality. The right to equality is found in all major human rights instruments, and particularly, in relation to women, in CEDAW. There is also now greater agreement that the right to equality takes a substantive form, as well as a procedural one, although the precise content is still contentious. The four-dimensional approach to the right to equality used in this chapter draws on the various conceptions of substantive equality to create an analytic framework according to which existing taxation systems can be evaluated to determine their compatibility with the human right to gender equality. While it does not prescribe specific solutions, which are necessarily context-based and rooted in individual systems, this approach does provide means to continually evaluate any solution attempted by a state to correct a violation.

The chapter focuses primarily on states' responsibility for respecting, protecting, and fulfilling the right to equality in relation to taxation. In this globalized world, there is a powerful argument for a strong duty of co-operation between states to prevent tax avoidance and evasion.

In addition, the duty to protect includes a duty on states to prevent third parties, such as multinationals from avoiding tax. The more challenging question as to the extent to which corporations and other nonstate actors should be responsible in their own right is not dealt with in this chapter.

II. THE RIGHT TO EQUALITY AND TAXATION

Equality in taxation systems is generally analyzed in terms of equity, which denotes a broad but ambiguous idea of "fairness."[6] Analysts distinguish horizontal from vertical equity. Horizontal equity means that taxpayers who are equally situated in economic terms should be treated equally for tax purposes, whereas vertical equity signifies that taxpayers who are differently situated should be treated appropriately differently. Progressive taxation, meaning that taxpayers should be treated appropriately differently according to their ability to pay, might therefore be a type of vertical equity.[7]

These conceptions map onto the Aristotelean conception familiar in human rights law, namely that likes should be treated alike, and differences should be treated appropriately to their level of difference (the equal treatment principle, or formal equality). They also raise the same problems as the Aristotelean equal treatment principle. Particularly difficult is the question of when circumstances are appropriately the same or appropriately different. Elson gives the example of two households with the same income. Should they be treated the same if one household has two earners and the other only one? Similarly, should two individuals with the same income be treated the same if one saves and earns interests on her savings and the other uses all her income and may later need to draw on state benefits?[8] A related problem concerns the appropriate unit of comparison. Should it be the individual, the family, or the household? The ongoing influence of gendered roles within the family mean that taxation based on households and families might replicate or reinforce gendered structures; but it is not necessarily the case that individual systems achieve horizontal equality.[9] Ultimately, although the equal treatment principle might appear neutral or mechanical, it embeds policy choices based on background ideologies which need to be uncovered. In taxation as in human rights law, it is therefore necessary to move beyond formal equality or the equal treatment principle, to more substantive conceptions of equality.[10]

There are several different understandings of substantive equality, some focusing on equality of opportunity, others on equality of results, or dignity. At first sight, equality of results is the more appropriate conception for taxation systems. Progressive tax systems are openly redistributive, moving the focus from equal treatment to reducing inequalities of outcome. Equality of outcome is not, however, sufficient. It does not, for example, resolve the question of the appropriate unit of comparison. Equalizing the outcome for households might disguise the gender effect of taxation systems on the gendered relationships within the household. A gendered perspective also requires sensitivity to gender stereotypes and stigma, to voice and participation, and to whether existing relationships are entrenched or transformed. I have therefore argued for a four-dimensional conception of equality, which includes the insights of equality of outcome, but also aims to address stereotypes and stigma, lack of voice, and structural obstacles. The four-dimensional framework of substantive equality in relation to gender regards the right to equality as aiming to (1) redress disadvantage (the redistributive dimension); (2) address stigma, stereotyping, prejudice, and hatred (the recognition dimension); (3) facilitate participation and voice (the participative dimension); and (4) accommodate difference and transform gendered structures in society (the transformative dimension).[11] The four dimensions are mutually supportive rather than falling into any lexical priority. Thus, the potential weakness of any one dimension applied on its own can be counteracted by a different dimension. Similarly, tensions between the dimensions can be resolved by considering them all together.

The multidimensional conception of substantive equality functions as a valuable tool in evaluating taxation systems for their impact on gender. Taxation systems vary widely, as do the social contexts in which they operate, making it impossible to provide a comprehensive assessment of the gendered implications of taxation or to generalize. Nevertheless, there are some foundational principles which apply in some form or another to different taxation systems. As Valodia put it, tax policy has "tended over particular periods to converge across countries around the same set of broad considerations, irrespective of national or political context."[12] Correspondingly, gendered social patterns, while differing in their detail, have clear common elements. The aim of this chapter is to sketch out some of the ways that a substantive equality approach might illuminate gendered implications of taxation, and point to possible policy solutions that could follow. There is, however, far more work to be done in elaborating this approach.

III. SUBSTANTIVE EQUALITY: A FOUR-DIMENSIONAL APPROACH

The four-dimensional framework of gender-related substantive equality introduced above is briefly elaborated below, together with some of the ways in which it might apply to evaluating tax systems to determine whether they are in breach of the human right to equality. In the subsequent parts, two particularly challenging aspects of taxation and gender are examined: the role of care work, and the role of VAT and other indirect taxes.

First, substantive equality should concentrate on *remedying disadvantage* (the redistributive dimension), rather than achieving gender neutrality. This dimension draws on the move from equality of treatment to equality of outcome, but it goes further in its express asymmetry. It is not sufficient to treat people equally badly, or to equalize outcomes at a lower level, since this would not remedy disadvantage. Only if the position of those who are worse off is raised to that of the better off can equality in this sense be satisfied. This means that while progressive tax measures may be regarded as breaching the equal treatment principle by treating people differently, they do not breach the right to substantive equality as long as their aim or effect is to redress discriminatory disadvantage.

This enables us to solve the conundrum as to why it might be acceptable to impose higher taxes on items such as alcohol and tobacco, which might be indirectly discriminatory against men who disproportionately consume these goods, while at the same time imposing lower rates of taxes on medical care, which again might be implicitly biased against men because they consume less of these goods than women.[13] Substantive equality does not outlaw all differential treatment: in fact it might require differential treatment to redress disadvantage. By disincentivizing the use of "demerit" goods, or goods which may have adverse effects on those who consume them and others, such differential treatment could indeed redress disadvantage. Women also have specifically different needs in relation to reproductive healthcare, justifying extra expenditure on healthcare.[14] Placing taxes on demerit goods as well as luxury items is therefore very different from taxing basic foodstuffs, sanitary towels, and children's goods. It is true that it is possible that by making such goods more expensive, men could transfer the cost to women by contributing less to the household income.[15] This is an empirical fact which needs to be established. On the other hand, it is also possible that taxation could change behavior, reducing violence and improving general health. It should be noted too that in some countries, such as the United Kingdom, tobacco taxes in practice impact particularly on poor female breadwinner households.[16] This, however, reflects a policy decision to use taxation to address the problem of high levels of smoking among young women in the United Kingdom. Whether or not taxation induces such behavioral changes is a matter for further empirical study. Such study needs to be undertaken to determine whether disadvantage is in fact reduced or aggravated. It is also possible that lower taxes for basic foodstuffs or sanitary towels may not reduce their costs, since the cost born by the producers or retailers of these goods might be passed on to consumers.[17] Again, this is a matter for empirical proof. The analytic framework does not resolve these issues, but requires any solution to meet the criterion of redressing gendered disadvantage, rather than requiring all to be treated alike.

A similar analysis can be applied to the provision of a higher exemption threshold for women in India, which deliberately discriminates in favor of women to encourage women to undertake paid employment.[18] This can be contrasted with explicitly discriminatory structures in favor of men. Thus in Morocco, dependents include the taxpayer's wife, but not the taxpayer's husband unless the latter can prove that her husband and children are financially dependent on her.[19] In assessing the equality implications of these two measures, the question is not whether there is express or implicit bias against women or men, but whether it genuinely addresses disadvantage. The Moroccan example clearly reinforces gendered stereotypes, entrenching disadvantage. The Indian exemption is more complex. Valodia argues that because this rule only affects the tiny minority of women who work in the formal sector in India, and because there is little evidence to show that it has in fact promoted gender equality, this is not a recommended approach.[20] Rather than assuming that this is not desirable because it explicitly favors women, however, the assumption should be that it benefits women, a presumption which might be rebutted by appropriate evidence. Indeed, CEDAW advocates "special temporary measures"[21] to redress gender-related disadvantage. It would clearly be important to find the evidence of the exemption policy's effect on women, but the fact that few benefit should not be a reason against it. It is only if it causes or exacerbates disadvantage that it should be rejected on equality grounds.

It is also important to interrogate the meaning of "disadvantage" for these purposes. To the extent that women are among the poorest in society, regressive tax measures will harm women. But it is not a coincidence that women predominate among those who are the least well off in society. Disadvantage in this context takes into account the ways in which gender structures that disadvantage. This requires the first dimension to be read together with the second (the recognition dimension), which aims *to redress stigma, stereotyping, prejudice, and violence.* Gendered stereotypes have a fundamental effect on women's role in society and their experience of poverty. As a start, there are still too many jurisdictions which maintain directly discriminatory laws.[22] Many of these laws seriously curtail the ability of women to access paid work or property rights, therefore being a direct cause of women's poverty. This is particularly true of laws on marriage, property, and inheritance. In many countries, women are still deprived of full legal status on marriage;[23] and it is commonplace for inheritance laws to discriminate against women.[24] Customary law, recognized as a source of personal law in a number of countries, frequently provides for patrilineal succession, excluding women from inheritance; and in a number of countries, such laws are exempt from constitutional equality guarantees.[25] Explicit legal discrimination against women in tax regimes can still be found in countries around the world.

Even where laws do not expressly discriminate against women, gender continues to shape women's experience of poverty. In almost every country, women are ascribed gendered roles which give them primary responsibility for childcare, eldercare, and housework. At the same time, women are increasingly contributing to household income through paid work. This double burden has serious implications for women. Constraints on time and mobility mean that their opportunities in the job market are often limited.[26] Women's market work is therefore dispro- portionately concentrated in part-time and precarious jobs. This has been exacerbated in recent years. With the growing movement toward "flexibilization" of labor markets throughout the world, many firms are increasingly making use of subcontracted women home workers at very low wages to replace core full-time workers.[27] Women also predominate in the informal sector. In sub-Saharan Africa, 84 percent of women nonagricultural workers are informally employed compared to 63 percent for men, and if informal agricultural work is included, these figures are even higher.[28] Moreover, the informal economy is segmented by employment status and by sex. The highest-paid segment, microentrepreneurs who hire others, is predominantly male, while women are overrepresented in the lowest-paid segment of the informal economy—as home workers or industrial outworkers.[29] Alternatively, many women are required to make a stark choice and leave their homes to work in other people's houses as domestic workers or even to migrate to other countries to find work. In the Philippines, one of the major sources of GDP takes the form of remittances from women working as domestic workers abroad.[30] Women's continuing primary responsibility for home work and childcare also affects the value attached to women's market work. Because domestic work and childcare are done for free at home, much of women's paid work of a similar type is seriously undervalued. This includes catering, cleaning, caring work, and agricultural work.[31]

The combination of the first two dimensions, namely, *the need to redress disadvantage which follows a pattern of stereotypical gendered roles*, has implications for the nature of the tax system. Clearly many women do not earn enough to be within the personal income tax net. Systems of allowances and exemptions will not benefit them. At the same time, women as consumers will be particularly burdened with indirect consumer taxes. Indeed, women whose gendered roles put them in the position of primary caregiver may have different consumption patterns from men, focusing more on consumption for the purposes of basic nutrition and childcare, than on luxury goods. Exemptions might therefore need to be targeted at these consumption patterns. In South Africa, for example, a women-led campaign resulted in exemptions from sales tax for paraffin, the fuel primarily used for cooking.[32] In the United Kingdom, there are exemptions for children's clothing and shoes. The constructive nature of these exemptions is that they are available to anyone who fulfills these roles, both men and women. Thus, they do not necessarily reinforce gendered roles while at the same time recognizing them. VAT and other indirect taxes are examined in more detail below.

In addition to stereotyping, the recognition dimension of substantive inequality also addresses stigma, humiliation, and violence on grounds of gender. This has purchase in relation to the question of whether redistribution should happen through the tax system or through the benefit system. There are still many societies in which those who receive benefits are subject to stigma and humiliation, labeled as scroungers or free-riders. Single mothers are particularly targeted by campaigns of this sort. Substantive equality might therefore require that, rather than collecting taxes and redistributing them through benefits, some of the redistributive work is done through the tax system. The system of tax credits in the United Kingdom, although in many ways identical to benefits, was designed at least in part to deflect neoliberal ideologies which stigmatized users of benefits.[33]

The third dimension of substantive equality aims to facilitate *participation and voice* (the participative dimension). The gendered implications of this dimension are felt both at the macropolitical level and at the microlevel of family and community. At the political level, the slogan of no taxation without representation should be taken seriously. As has been recognized in several jurisdictions, equality should specifically compensate for the absence of political power of groups "to whose needs and wishes elected officials have no apparent interest in attending."[34] Substantive equality requires decision makers to hear and respond to the voices of women, rather than imposing top-down decisions. But this is equally important at the level of the family and community. As Sweetman puts it, poverty is "as much about agency compromised by abuse, stress, fatigue and voicelessness as it is about lack of resources."[35] Although this lack of agency is also felt by poor men, gender continues to have a specific impact on women's ability to exercise power to access resources. For example, as Chant notes, household income may bear no relation to women's poverty because women may not be able to access it: "Feminist research has shown that inequitable resource allocation can often lead to 'secondary' poverty among women and children in male-headed households, and, as such, for many women the capacity to command and allocate resources may be more important than the actual resource base in their households."[36] This is also true for access to information and information technology.[37]

This differential access to the means of political participation has important implications for the design of taxation systems. Bird demonstrates that taxation systems are primarily a matter of politics, and often the loudest voices are those of elites, who need to be convinced that what they gain from a taxation system is worth what they pay into it. As more middle classes have come into the range of personal income taxation, politicians have had to respond more readily to their demands. Women are notoriously underrepresented in politics and public decision-making.

On the other hand, women who do exercise voice can make important gains. The campaign in South Africa for exemptions for paraffin is a good example: led by the South African Women's Budget Initiative, and supported by civil society and international agencies, the campaign achieved a zero rate of VAT for paraffin, which is the cooking fuel used by many households and a central household purchase for poor women.[38] Similarly, in the United Kingdom, the initial proposal to apply the Working Families Tax Credit through the pay packet to one earner was changed in response to feminist protest, allowing families to choose to whom the credit should be paid.[39] At the same time, participation and voice, too, crucially need to interact with the other dimensions, particularly redressing disadvantage and addressing stereotyping and stigma. Women's voices are not sufficient if they do not highlight and attempt to redress gendered disadvantage. Thus a woman prime minister in the United Kingdom, such as Margaret Thatcher or now Theresa May, may not fulfill this goal when they actively further policies, both in the taxation and the benefit system, which are detrimental to women and reinforce gendered roles.

This is a clear area in which human rights have an important role to play. Human rights can themselves give an avenue for advocacy and can strengthen women's voices. This can be seen powerfully in the recent pioneering submission made to the CEDAW Committee as part of the periodic process of review of Switzerland. In their groundbreaking submission to the CEDAW Committee, five nongovernmental organizations (NGOs) demonstrated convincingly how secrecy and lack of transparency in Swiss taxation rules permit corporations and private individuals to denude other countries of rightful revenue. This breaches Switzerland's duty not to impede the fulfillment of the equality rights of women in those countries. But it also demonstrates how important transparency and voice are to the furtherance of substantive equality. Without a human rights platform, these claims would not be heard. Magdalena Sepúlveda similarly highlights the crucial role of lack of participation of women and poor people in tax systems. Even where such claims do not eventually win the argument, as in Switzerland itself, there is still an intrinsic value in articulating claims for substantive equality.

The fourth dimension of substantive equality (the transformative dimension) entails recognition of the ways in which the structures of society entrench women's disadvantage. Instead of requiring women to conform to male norms, substantive equality requires *transformation of existing male-oriented institutions and social structures*. This reflects the requirement in CEDAW Article 5 that states parties should take all appropriate measures "[t]o modify the social and cultural patterns of conduct of men and women, with a view to achieving the elimination of prejudices and customary and all other practices which are based on the idea of the inferiority or the superiority of either of the sexes or on stereotyped roles for men and women." With this comes the imperative to transcend the public-private divide, recognizing the ways in which imbalances in power in the family can reinforce power imbalances in the public sphere and vice versa. In particular, childcare and parenting need to be recognized as a shared social responsibility, and working patterns need to be changed to accommodate this. Substantive equality also requires the accommodation of differences between women.

This is the most challenging of the dimensions. There are many aspects of taxation systems which reflect and reinforce gendered roles in society. At times this is obvious, but at times, it may be necessary to conduct empirical studies to discover whether they do so and how they can be changed to achieve the transformative dimension. While the redistributive consequences of tax systems have been studied rigorously and in detail, it is much more difficult to capture the behavioral consequences. Grown concludes that no personal income system can yet be classified as transforming gender relations.[40] Particularly challenging is how to capture the value of care work, without at the same time reinforcing gendered roles which regard care work as separate and subject to different rules to breadwinning work. This is explored in more detail below.

One of the key advantages of a multidimensional approach is that it provides a framework within which to address the interaction between dimensions. The idea of the four-dimensional structure is to draw explicit attention to all four dimensions in evaluating positions or programs. Rather than viewing one as a trump over the others, the dimensions should mediate each other, leading to a synthesis or more nuanced response. For example, measures aimed at redistribution can themselves cause recognition harms, such as the stigma experienced by welfare beneficiaries. The four-dimensional approach makes it possible to address these tensions. Given that equality aims to redress disadvantage as well as to address stigma, it is crucial to design both welfare and taxation measures in ways that advance dignity as well as redistribution. A good example is the system of taxation in Argentina, where all nonlabor income from jointly owned businesses or financial investments is allocated to the husband's tax return. This may well result in a lower tax burden for women in this situation.[41] However, the impact on redressing disadvantage needs to be weighed against the stigma and stereotyping signified by submerging the woman's identity into that of her husband. On the other hand, simply addressing stigmatic harms without paying serious attention to structural change is unlikely to achieve substantive equality. The participatory dimension also needs to be considered together with other dimensions. As mentioned above, while voice is important, it is not necessarily an end in itself, if those women who speak have the effect of worsening other women's disadvantage or perpetuating stigma, prejudice, or violence.

It is central to this approach that a breach of the principles of substantive equality would constitute a violation of the right to equality in CEDAW as elaborated by the CEDAW committee. Although tax is not mentioned in CEDAW as such, there are several key provisions which apply in the context of tax and its implications for benefit systems. Article 2 of CEDAW is a wide-ranging injunction to states to adopt appropriate legislative and other measures prohibiting all discrimination against women; to refrain from engaging in any act or practice of discrimination against women and to ensure that all public authorities and institutions do so too; to take all appropriate measures to eliminate discrimination against women by any person, organization, or enterprise; to take all appropriate measures, including legislation, to modify or abolish existing law, regulations, customs, and practices which constitute discrimination against women. Article 3 goes even further, and requires states parties to take all appropriate measure, including legislation, to ensure the full development and advancement of women to guarantee that they can exercise human rights on a basis of equality with men. Particularly important is the requirement in Article 3 that these steps be taken in the economic field, as well as the political, social, and cultural fields. Article 15 requires equality before the law. Article 13 states that men and women must enjoy the same rights to family benefits, and Article 16 requires states to eliminate discrimination against women in all matters relating to marriage and family relations. This is elaborated in General Recommendation 21 (Equality in Marriage and Family Relations), which states that women should have the right to enjoy financial independence. Most radically, Article 5 requires a modification of social and cultural patterns to eliminate sex role stereotyping.

In the next section, some of the recent trends in taxation are analyzed through the lens of substantive equality to illustrate their effect on gender and the extent to which they potentially violate the right to equality for women.

A. SHIFT TO CONSUMPTION TAXES

Recent trends in taxation systems worldwide show similar patterns. In the three decades after World War I, the accepted academic view of good tax policy, at least for developed countries, was grounded in broad-based personal income tax with progressive rates, which incorporated capital gains tax, corporate tax, and death duties or estate taxes. Indirect taxes, according to Bird, were considered a "necessary evil" and international aspects of taxation were ignored.[42] However, since the 1970s and 1980s, many countries have reformed personal income tax to reduce the highest marginal tax rates, while competition for inward investment has led to a lowering of corporate tax.[43] In the meanwhile, trade taxes have been sharply diminished to comply with the dictates of free trade through globalization. Many countries therefore increased their reliance on broad-based VAT to compensate for their loss of revenue through trade taxes. At the same time, the World Bank and the International Monetary Fund (IMF) have shifted their emphasis away from the objective of equity and progressivity, which had featured centrally in tax policies until the mid-1970s. Instead, they began to regard efficiency and ease of tax administration as the primary goal of a good taxation system.[44] This was partly a reaction to a perceived weakness in state capacity to collect taxes. But it also had an ideological component, namely, that equity and poverty reduction should not be the concern of taxation. Instead, it was argued that redistributive policies should be conducted through revenue expenditure on benefits and other programs. The focus of tax policy should therefore be on ease of administration and greater resource mobilization.[45] As Genschel and Seelkopf put it, "The new emphasis is on tax neutrality, simplicity and efficiency. Distributive issues are relegated to the spending side of the budget: even regressive taxation is now often considered socially desirable if it serves to efficiently fund progressive expenditure programmes."[46] Thus the Organisation for Economic Co-operation and Development (OECD) has taken the view since 1980 that the ideal form of VAT is a broad-based single-rate tax, which would enable significant revenues to be raised while decreasing administration and compliance costs. It is also maintained that VAT is not an appropriate tool for advancing equity considerations.[47]

The result is that international organizations, including the World Bank and the IMF, regularly advise non-Western countries to reduce trade taxes and develop broad-based taxes. This has led to a steep decline in trade taxes[48] and a marked shift toward VAT and consumption taxes. Moreover, statutory corporate taxes have fallen by approximately 20 percent since the 1980s.[49] There is also clear evidence that participation in IMF programs significantly increases the probability of VAT adoption.[50] While there may have been signs of change in the IMF and World Bank policy, their most recent advice to countries such as Thailand and Costa Rica included recommendations for raising VAT and lowering corporate income tax.[51] Similarly, it was reported in May 2016 that the World Bank had approved a large loan to Egypt conditional on its implementing a VAT law.[52]

A gendered analysis of this trend, through the lens of substantive equality, can shed some light on the problematic consequences of such policies for the fulfillment of the human right to equality. It could be argued that efficiency in tax collection is likely to increase the revenue available to governments for social spending, which would benefit women in all the respects mentioned above. Clearly, this might further the redistributive dimension, reducing disadvantage. Bringing in the other dimensions, however, reveals several potential problematic consequences. The first is the assumption that the extra revenue will in fact be spent on gender sensitive redistributive measures. This may well not be the case. The effect of efficient tax collection on redressing disadvantage is therefore contingent on the way in which the extra budget is used. The second is that redistribution through the benefit system instead of the taxation system can be highly stigmatic. This is particularly true of means-tested cash transfers, which, as we have seen, frequently casts beneficiaries not as rights holders but as scroungers or passive recipients. This is even more so for the IMF's and World Bank's particularly favored approach, conditional cash transfers, which require women to perform gendered roles as a condition for receiving cash transfers, without giving men equivalent responsibilities.[53] This breaches the recognition dimension of substantive equality—entrenching stigma and stereotypes. Instead, redistribution through reducing the tax burden on women in the first place might enhance their agency and autonomy. This brings in the third dimension, the participation dimension. Women do not have a say in determining how taxes are structured: these are a requirement from the IMF or World Bank. Moreover, aiming at redistribution through the benefit system might not effectively counter the regressive impact of indirect consumption taxes, because of the administrative difficulty, for example, in reaching all of those in fact entitled to such transfers.[54] This means that far from achieving structural change as required by the transformative dimension, inequality is perpetuated.

One way of addressing the regressive consequences of VAT and similar taxes, especially from a gendered perspective, is to provide for exemptions or zero-rated goods. If the exemptions match women's specific consumption patterns, this might change the effect of the tax substantially. Indeed, in the empirical research conducted by the Taxation and Gender Equity project, VAT was found to be mildly progressive if appropriate exemptions or zero ratings are placed on basic foodstuffs, children's clothes, and similar basic consumption items. Simulations aimed at making the system of indirect taxes more gender aware suggested that "there are grounds for specific and targeted use of the tax system to improve gender equality outcomes."[55] Particularly useful examples were zero-rating of children's clothing in the United Kingdom and of paraffin in South Africa.

However, such exemptions remain controversial. A recent report by Judge Dennis Davis in South Africa was critical of such exemptions, arguing that because they were available to all consumers, they tended to benefit far more middle-class consumers than poor ones.[56] The report acknowledges that VAT in South Africa would be regressive in the absence of zero-rated food items; and that, since VAT uses up a part of everyone's income, its effect is to increase poverty: that is 5 percent more people fall under the poverty line than would in the absence of VAT.[57] It also acknowledges that when zero ratings are taken into consideration, VAT is broadly neutral. This means households across the income distribution pay broadly the same proportion of their income in VAT.[58] Nevertheless, the report takes the view that benefits through the expenditure rather than revenue side of the budget could be much more precisely targeted.

This is borne out by a study by Jansen and Calitz, who maintain that because goods that are zero-rated are consumed by all consumers, whether rich or poor, rich taxpayers receive a greater monetary benefit. They conclude that "zero rating is not a very effective way of improving the position of the poor—it costs too much in terms of benefits that accrue to the rich."[59] Their statistical analysis shows that the poorest households in South Africa spend relatively more on zero-rated goods, in this case maize meal. At the same time, because high-income households spend a much larger absolute amount on these goods, they receive a higher benefit in terms of actual rands. The result is that of the revenue loss in 2011–2012 to the South African Treasury of R8,661 million through zero rating, the poorest 40 percent of households received a benefit of R3,396 million while the richer 60 percent received R5,265 million.[60] In other words, zero rating provides a larger proportional benefit to the poor, but a larger absolute benefit to the rich.[61] The argument is therefore that it would be much more effective to target the R8,661 million to pro-poverty redistribution.

The Davis report comes to a similar conclusion. According to the report, R41 billion in revenue was forgone in the 2011–2012 fiscal year due to zero rating (R19 billion of which was in relation to basic foodstuffs),[62] but the majority of the benefit went to more affluent sectors of the population. Davis therefore concludes that "the current zero-rating is equivalent to a generalized subsidy which mostly favors the richest sectors of the population, at a high cost for public finances. As such, zero rating is a very imprecise instrument for the pursuit of equity objectives. In trying to assist the poor, more of the benefit flows to the non-poor than the poor."[63] On the other hand, the Davis report acknowledges that removing zero rating would not be fully compensated for within the current benefit system in South Africa, which focuses on households with children, old-age pensioners, or disabled persons. Compensatory mechanisms for households with only unemployed or working-poor adults that do not receive cash transfers do not at present exist.[64] The report concludes, therefore, that it would be very difficult to eliminate current zero ratings. At best, it would be appropriate to consider only retaining items that more clearly benefit poor households, such as maize meal, brown bread, rice, and vegetables, while withdrawing those items most obviously consumed by the more affluent households, such as fruit and milk.

It can be seen that a gender analysis might yield a different result. It is notable that neither the Davis report nor the research by Jansen and Calitz mention the impact on women. This would require the empirical research to examine specifically the extent to which the combination of zero rating and other aspects of the revenue system, such as ease of administration, and the expenditure system, such as availability of social security benefits, would in reality redress gendered disadvantage without reinforcing stigma and gendered stereotyping. Certainly, Sepúlveda reports research which shows that the negative effects of indirect taxes on the income of people living in poverty can be greater than the positive effect of cash transfers.[65] In any event, withdrawing zero ratings on fruit and milk in South Africa would make it even more expensive for poor households to buy these products. The extent to which women participate in these decisions and the impact on their ability to participate should also be taken into account.

Finally, the question arises as to the need for structural change. Providing VAT exemptions might palliate the shift from trade and corporate taxes, but it will not change the underlying gendered structures whereby women remain primarily responsible for caring work. Instead, other, more transformative means should be found to widen the tax base. An obvious one is to close tax loopholes and prevent cross-border tax evasion. As the innovative complaint to the CEDAW Committee in relation to Switzerland emphasized, by depriving other countries of revenue from business based there, the Swiss policy of secrecy and lack of transparency is directly interfering with the ability of host states to fund basic rights and especially to ensure gender transformation as required by CEDAW.

B. UNPAID CARE WORK AND THE ROLE
OF PERSONAL ALLOWANCES

A second issue which is central to a gendered analysis of taxation is the way in which unpaid care work features. It is now well documented that women continue to carry the burden of the majority of unpaid work. The question is how this is reflected in taxation systems. Traditionally, many taxation systems assumed that the household comprised a male breadwinner and female homemaker. Any earnings by the wife were considered an optional extra, and therefore could be taxed at a higher rate. On the other hand, married men were given allowances for dependents and therefore in practice taxed at a lower rate.[66] For example, in the United Kingdom, for most of the twentieth century, income tax law aggregated the resources of both spouses and treated them as those of the husband. Married men received an allowance greater than that given to a single person in recognition of the "special legal and moral obligations he has to support his wife."[67] If the wife worked, the husband received an extra allowance, namely, the wife's earned income allowance. Because the husband's allowance was greater than that of a working wife, and because other allowances, such as mortgage interest relief, were set against his income and not hers, his take-home pay was necessarily higher than hers even if they were earning the same.[68] This was not reformed until 1990, when individual filing was introduced. Several developed countries still have joint taxation systems, including the Czech Republic, France, Germany, Luxembourg, Ireland, Poland, Switzerland, and the United States. Systems of joint filing might discourage women from working if their earnings are lower than that of their spouse: because a woman's income is added to that of her spouse for taxation purposes, women pay tax at the highest marginal rate of the higher-earning spouse. If their income were taken alone, women in this position would pay a lower marginal rate. This combined with the high cost of childcare can operate as strong disincentives to the lower-earning partner, who, given the worldwide gender pay gap, is most often the woman. Indeed, a recent report by the International Labour Organization (ILO) cites empirical studies showing that labor income tax affects labor force participation of women more than men.[69]

The ILO therefore recommends individual income taxation to increase women's labor force participation. Indeed, many systems have now turned from joint filing to individual filing, although the tax system still determines how exemptions or allowances are allocated. Generally speaking, if a woman earns less than her partner in a two-earner household, she benefits from individual filing since she has her own allowance. She can also keep her financial affairs private, an important issue.

One conundrum which this seems to raise is that separate taxation favors a household with two earners over a single-earner household with the same income. Where the household consists of a single breadwinner (usually male) and a partner performing all the unpaid work of the household, there is generally only one personal allowance. A dual-earner, dual household will benefit from two personal allowances. The result is that the former will invariably pay a higher rate of tax than the latter. Himmelweit argues that this is a step toward gender equality in employment because it favors a household with two earners over households with a single earner with the same income, thus discouraging households where the wife is dependent on the husband's earnings.[70] However, several analysts have argued that this fails to give proper value to the unpaid work provided by financially dependent partners or spouses to the household, and which should be factored into the tax treatment of the household.[71] Others argue that it is unfair to treat households with one homemaker and one earner better than one with two paid earners. Grown suggests, however, that if household services are counted as income, then the household with one earner and a stay-at-home partner will have a greater ability to pay than a two-earner household, which has to purchase the services otherwise provided. On the other hand, as Elson points out, taxes have to be paid in money, and unpaid work cannot be magically turned into cash to meet the bills.[72] This analysis should also factor in single-parent households. The Taxation and Gender Equity study found that in Argentina, Ghana, and Morocco, there is a deduction for a dependent spouse, with the result that single-parent households where the parent is in paid work bear a larger tax burden than male breadwinner households with financially dependent spouses.[73]

These conundrums arise because of the conceptions of vertical and horizontal tax equity cling too closely to the formal conception of equality which requires likes to be treated alike and differences according to their differences. The four-dimensional approach to substantive equality is helpful here in that it requires a much broader perspective than comparing different households without considering the underlying principles leading to these outcomes. Redressing gendered disadvantage; addressing stigma and stereotypes; facilitating participation; and promoting transformation of patriarchal social structures, point directly to the main goal, which is to redistribute unpaid care work away from women as the primary carers. As Magdalena Sepúlveda has powerfully argued, this requires not just the redistribution but also the reduction of unpaid care work.[74] To genuinely achieve substantive equality, especially the transformative dimension, tax systems should be designed to to promote gender-sensitive public services, water, sanitation, and public transport, which reduce the drudgery and intensity of unpaid care work. There is also a need to redistribute unpaid care work from women to men and from women to the state. This requires investment in paid care professionals, including teachers, nurses, child-minders, and others. As Sepúlveda puts it, "States should shift from a strategy of reliance on market and voluntary provision of care that is informal and exploitative to one that allows professional, decently paid and compassionate forms of care."[75] In addition, states should design tax systems to promote an equal sharing of both paid and unpaid work between women and men.[76] This approach stretches beyond the personal income tax regime, which, as we have seen, only covers a limited number of people, to include everyone who undertakes un-paid caring work. Thus it is obvious that women who are not paid for their caring work never-theless pay VAT on their consumption.

Within the personal income tax regime, it is clear, as argued above, that substantive equality is breached in all its dimensions if an allowance for a dependent spouse is payable only to male heads of household. But this is not sufficient. The transformative dimension of substantive equality would clearly indicate that the aim of the tax regime should be to incentivize households that share both paid and unpaid work. How this is achieved might require careful fine-tuning of tax allowances and exemptions within any particular tax system. More work is clearly needed to evaluate the impact of different regimes on behavioral change. For example, unpaid work needs to attract a monetary recognition from the state which goes directly to the person doing the work, almost invariably the woman, rather than to the partner in paid work. Family allowances and child benefits have traditionally performed this role, being paid to the mother herself. This, however, could be seen to entrench gender differences. Instead, the South African system gives child benefits to the primary caregiver. In the United Kingdom, the tax credit system could be used to achieve this sort of aim, rather than leaving it to the benefit system. A complementary solution is to use tax revenue to provide socialized solutions for unpaid caring work, through the availability of publicly funded childcare. Incentives to share unpaid work could also be built into the system, such as allowing each partner to regard unpaid work as a deductible expense against paid income, up to a nontransferable limit. The partner who does the work benefits, but there is an incentive effect on the household because of the nontransferable nature. Of course, evidence of unpaid work is more difficult to establish, but these are the principles along which this problem should be considered.

None of this has taken account of single parent families, among which female-headed household are in the vast majority. These households are least well-off under the system of per-sonal allowances because there is only one person who must do all the paid and unpaid work, with the availability of only one personal allowance. Here again, the tax and benefit system need to work together to raise the personal allowance for such a worker, giving her more pretax income and therefore more income overall. This means that the first dimension, redressing disadvantage, is fulfilled, but without breaching the second, namely generating stigma for the female-headed household. This system will also address what Chant calls the feminization of responsibility and recognize that time is a valuable asset which should be considered in any system.[77]

IV. CONCLUSION

The social consequences of taxation systems, particularly their relationship to benefits and other redistributive measures, are complex and at times controversial. This chapter has not attempted to design the optimal tax system or suggest how different goals should be weighed. However, the human right to substantive gender equality is a demanding one. It requires policy choices to be analyzed against the criteria of substantive equality and refashioned to avoid violation. Building on the rich contributions of other feminist authors, this chapter has sketched some of the ways in which this analysis could be conducted, based on a four-dimensional understanding of the aims of the right to equality. It is hoped that this takes forward the project in a meaningful way. But much work remains to be done.

NOTES

1. S. Fredman, 'Labour Law in Flux: The Changing Composition of the Workforce', 25 *Industrial Law Journal* (1997), 337.
2. D. Elson, *Budgeting for Women's Rights: Monitoring Government Budgets for Compliance with CEDAW* (2006).
3. C. Grown and I. Valodia (eds.), *Taxation and Gender Equity* (2010).
4. Human Rights Council, Report of the Special Rapporteur on Extreme Poverty and Human Rights, Magdalena Sepúlveda Carmona, UN Doc. A/HRC/26/28, 22 May 2014.
5. Berne Declaration et al., *Submission to the Committee on the Elimination of Discrimination Against Women—State Responsibility for the Impacts of Cross-Border Tax Abuse on Women's Rights and Gender Equality*, 22 Feb. 2016, available online at http://chrgj.org/wp-content/uploads/2016/12/switzerland_cedaw_submission_2nov201628.pdf.
6. C. Grown, 'Taxation and Gender Equality: A Conceptual Framework', *in* C. Grown and I. Valodia (eds.), *Taxation and Gender Equity* (2010), 1, at 7.
7. Ibid.; Elson, *supra* note 2, at 73.
8. Elson, *supra* note 2, at 74.
9. Grown, *supra* note 6, at 9.
10. Committee on the Elimination of Discrimination Against Women, General Recommendation No. 25: Article 4, Paragraph 1 of the Convention (Temporary Special Measures) (2004).
11. S. Fredman, *Discrimination Law* (2nd ed., 2011); S. Fredman, 'Substantive Equality Revisited', 14 (3) *I•CON* (2016), 712.
12. I. Valodia, 'Conclusion and Policy Recommendations', *in* C. Grown and I. Valodia (eds.), *Taxation and Gender Equity* (2010), 299.
13. Grown, *supra* note 6, at 15 (citing J. G. Stotsky, 'How Tax Systems Treat Men and Women Differently', 34(1) *Finance and Development* (1997), 30).
14. Ibid. at 16
15. Valodia, *supra* note 12, at 309.
16. J. De Henau, S. Himmelweit, and C. Santos, 'Gender Equality and Taxation: A UK Study', *in* C. Grown and I. Valodia (eds.), *Taxation and Gender Equity* (2010), 261, at 287.
17. See further Institute for Fiscal Studies, *Tax by Design*, 13 Sept. 2011, available online at https://www.ifs.org.uk/docs/taxbydesign.pdf, at 162–166 (last visited 30 May 2017).
18. P. Chakraborty et al., 'Gender Equality and Taxation in India', *in* C. Grown and I. Valodia, *Taxation and Gender Equity* (2010), 94, at 102.
19. Valodia, *supra* note 12, at 304.
20. Ibid. at 304–305.
21. Article 4, Convention on the Elimination of All Forms of Discrimination Against Women 1979, 1249 UNTS 13.
22. World Bank and International Financial Corporation, *Women, Business and the Law 2014: Removing Restrictions to Enhance Gender Equality* (2013), available online at http://wbl.worldbank.org/~/media/WBG/WBL/Documents/Reports/2014/Women-Business-and-the-Law-2014-FullReport.pdf?la=en, at 8 (last visited 23 May 2017).
23. Botswana, Burundi, Cameroon, Central African Republic, Chad, Comoros, Democratic Republic of Congo, Republic of Congo, Cote d'Ivoire, Gabon, Guinea, Guinea-Bissau, Madagascar, Mali, Mauritania, Niger, Rwanda, Senegal, Somalia, Sudan, Swaziland and Togo: ibid.
24. Ibid.
25. M. Hallward-Driemeier and T. Hasan, *Empowering Women: Legal Rights and Economic Opportunities in Africa* (2013), available online at http://documents.worldbank.org/curated/en/854741468007857028/pdf/730710PUB0EPI001200pub0date01004012.pdf (last visited 23 May 2017).
26. Human Rights Council, Report of the Special Rapporteur on the Right to Food, Olivier De Schutter—Women's Rights and the Right to Food, UN Doc. A/HRC/22/50, 24 Dec. 2012, at para. 2.

27. ILO, *Equality at Work: Tackling the Challenge—Global Report under the Follow-up to the ILO Declaration on Fundamental Principles and Rights at Work* (2007), available online at http://www.ilo.org/wcmsp5/groups/public/---dgreports/---dcomm/---webdev/documents/publication/wcms_082607.pdf (last visited 23 May 2017).

28. Women in Informal Employment Globalizing and Organizing, *Women and Men in Informal Employment: Key Facts and New MDG3 Indicator,* available online at http://wiego.org/sites/wiego.org/files/resources/files/Women-Men-in-Informal-Employment.pdf (last visited 23 May 2017).

29. Ibid.

30. See S. Fredman, 'Home from Home: Migrant Domestic Workers and the ILO Convention on Domestic Workers', *in* C. Costello and M. Freedland (eds.), *Migrants at Work: Immigration and Vulnerability in Labour Law* (2014), 399.

31. F. Bettio and A. Verashchagina, *Gender Segregation in the Labour Market: Root Causes, Implications and Policy Responses in the EU* (2009).

32. R. Hinds, *Increasing Financial Investment in Women and Girls through Gender Responsive Budgeting*, 12 Feb. 2014, available online at http://www.gsdrc.org/docs/open/hdq1081.pdf (last visited 23 May 2017).

33. De Henau, Himmelweit, and Santos, *supra* note 16, at 270.

34. J. H. Ely, *Democracy and Distrust: A Theory of Judicial Review* (1980), at 46.

35. C. Sweetman, 'Editorial', *in* C. Sweetman (ed.), *Gender and the Millennium Development Goals* (2005), 2, at 3.

36. S. Chant, 'Rethinking the Feminisation of Poverty', 7 *Journal of Development and Capabilities* (2006), 201, at 205.

37. L. Scott, *Thinking Critically About Women's Entrepreneurship in Developing Countries*, available online at http://www.sbs.ox.ac.uk/sites/default/files/Skoll_Centre/Docs/essay-scott.pdf (last visited 23 May 2017).

38. Hinds, *supra* note 32.

39. De Henau, Himmelweit, and Santos, *supra* note 16, at 270.

40. Grown, *supra* note 6, at 17.

41. Ibid. at 13.

42. R. Bird, *Taxation and Development: What Have We Leaned from Fifty Years of Research?* (July 2013), available online at http://www.ids.ac.uk/files/dmfile/Wp427.pdf, at 6 (last visited 23 May 2017).

43. Ibid. at 10–11; P. Genschel and L. Seelkopf, 'Did They Learn to Tax? Taxation Trends Outside the OECD', 12 *Review of International Political Economy* (2016), 316, at 323.

44. Valodia, *supra* note 12, at 300; Bird, *supra* note 42, at 10.

45. Valodia, *supra* note 12, at 301.

46. Genschel and Seelkopf, *supra* note 43, at 317.

47. The Davis Tax Committee, *First Interim Report on VAT to the Minister of Finance* (Dec. 2014), available online at http://www.taxcom.org.za/docs/20150707%20DTC%20VAT%20First%20Interim%20Report%20-%20website.pdf (last visited 23 May 2017).

48. Genschel and Seelkopf, *supra* note 43, at 323.

49. Ibid. at 326.

50. Ibid. at 335.

51. M. Kohonen, *World Bank and IMF: Where Do They Stand on Progressive and Responsible Taxation?* (Aug. 2016), available online at http://www.brettonwoodsproject.org/wp-content/uploads/2016/08/At-Issue-Tax-Platform-WB-IMF-1.pdf (last visited 23 May 2017).

52. Ibid.

53. S. Fredman, 'Engendering Social Welfare Rights', *in* B. Goldblatt and L. Lamarache (eds.), *Women's Rights to Social Security and Social Protection* (2015), 19.

54. I am grateful to the editors for suggesting this point.

55. Valodia, *supra* note 12, at 309.

56. The Davis Tax Committee, *supra* note 47.

57. Ibid.

58. Ibid. at 16–17.

59. A. Jansen and E. Calitz, *How Effective Is VAT Zero Rating as a Pro-Poor Policy?* (July 2015), available online at http://www.econ3x3.org/article/how-effective-vat-zero-rating-pro-poor-policy, at 2 (last visited 23 May 2017).

60. Ibid. at 3.

61. The Davis Tax Committee, *supra* note 47, at 2.

62. Ibid. at 20.

63. Ibid. at 26.

64. Ibid. at 27.

65. Report of the Special Rapporteur on Extreme Poverty and Human Rights, Magdalena Sepúlveda Carmona, *supra* note 4, at para. 47.

66. See, e.g., South Africa before the first democratic election: D. Budlender, D. Casale, and I. Valodia, 'Gender Equality and Taxation in South Africa', *in* C. Grown and I. Valodia (eds.), *Taxation and Gender Equity* (2010), 206, at 211; the United Kingdom prior to 1990: S. Fredman, *Women and the Law* (1997), 94; Argentina currently: C. Enriquez, N. Gherardi, and D. Rossignolol, 'Gender Equality and Taxation in Argentina', *in* C. Grown and I. Valodia (eds.), *Taxation and Gender Equity* (2010), 64.

67. Inland Revenue (now H.M Revenue and Customs), The Taxation of Husband and Wife, 1980, Cm. 8093 (UK).

68. Fredman, *supra* note 66, at 94.

69. ILO, *Women at Work: Trends 2016* (2016), available online at http://www.ilo.org/wcmsp5/groups/public/---dgreports/---dcomm/---publ/documents/publication/wcms_457317.pdf, at 92.

70. S. Himmelweit, 'Making Visible the Hidden Economy: The Case for Gender-Impact Analysis of Economic Policy', 8(1) *Feminist Economics* (2002), 49, at 61.

71. See discussion in Grown, *supra* note 6, at 10–11.

72. Elson, *supra* note 2, at 82.

73. Grown, *supra* note 6, at 10.

74. General Assembly, Report of the Special Rapporteur on Extreme Poverty and Human Rights, UN Doc. A/68/293, 9 Aug. 2013.

75. Ibid. at para. 100.

76. Ibid. at para. 85.

77. S. Chant, 'The "Feminisation of Poverty" and the "Feminisation" of Anti-Poverty Programmes: Room for Revision?', 43 *Journal of Development Studies* (2008), 165.

CHAPTER 4

TAX AND HUMAN RIGHTS

The Moral Valence of Entitlements to Tax, Sovereignty, and Collectives

MITCHELL A. KANE

I. INTRODUCTION

The general appeal of tying the discourse of human rights to the reform of the international tax system is not difficult to understand. Consider some key aspects of the case. First, coming from the domain of tax experts, it is so often stated that the current architecture of the international tax system has failed to adequately adapt to the globalization and digitization of the economy that such assertions have some time ago crossed into the land of platitude.[1] Further, it is clear that the grave concern of the moment is inadequate taxation rather than excessive taxation. Thus concerns about "double nontaxation" have taken center stage, pushing the long-standing worries about "double taxation" into a subordinate role, at least for now.[2] In other words, an operative assumption underlying much of the current reform efforts is that a better tax system would, in the aggregate, raise more revenue across the world, not less.

Second, coming from the domain of experts in human rights law, it would seem that a starting point in bridging the fields of human rights law and tax law is to focus on the revenue generation capacity of public finance and its relationship to redressing human rights shortfalls. The achievement of human rights is not always costly. But often monetary constraints do loom large, whether the issue is curtailment of extreme poverty, access to healthcare, provision of meaningful education opportunities, or a host of other costly services that underlie achievement of human rights.[3]

Third, the basic connection between the first two points is readily apparent. If the tax rules are in dire need of reform in ways that augment revenue and if incremental revenue is an important aspect of expanding enjoyment of human rights, then surely the reform of the tax system ought, at the very least, to be undertaken with an eye to the effects on the fulfillment of human rights. More ambitiously, perhaps these effects should be a central component of reform efforts. Further, the link here is deeper than the mere fact that there is pressure for increased revenue

Tax, Inequality, and Human Rights. Philip Alston and Nikki Reisch.
© Oxford University Press 2019. Published 2019 by Oxford University Press.

collection in one domain and a demand for increased revenue expenditure in another. There are, of course, many worthy uses for increased governmental revenue that could be brought onto the table. Some such uses would surely tie to the bolstering of support for human rights; others would not. Thus one would seem to face an initial justificatory hurdle. What is the tie between incremental revenue and a particular use for such revenue? And, why the focus on incremental revenue? If the claim is that satisfaction of human rights has some particular claim on incremental revenue from tax reform, then one would have to face the further problem that such satisfaction is also a more worthy claimant on inframarginal governmental revenue as well. So why the particular focus on current efforts to reform the international tax system? These are difficult questions, but there is a prima facie case to be made to connect the domain of tax and human rights—at least with respect to the relationship between developed and developing countries.

If one conceives of the "international tax base" as a resource, it does not function like most (or any) other resources in the world. I cannot think of another resource for which there is a universally accepted basis for developing countries having a claim to sovereign entitlement over the resource (that is, under a source theory of taxation with respect to the tax base "resource") but for which such right is frequently ceded to far wealthier countries. If the same dynamic were to arise, for example, with natural resources, such result would clearly be seen as a pernicious application of the principles of colonialism. The import of this observation for the inquiry here is that existing revenue in developed country coffers and incremental revenue from possible reform of the international tax system are not substitutes. There is a massive difference between developed countries redirecting a portion of existing revenue toward the redress of human rights shortfalls in developing countries on the one hand, and a restructuring of the basic understanding of international tax entitlements such that developing countries have a superior claim to revenues as their own in the first instance on the other.

I have just sketched what I take to be the basic, high-level prima facie case for a potential connection between tax and human rights, at least as applied to issues of international taxation. Casting the issue as one of human rights would serve to focus attention on the grave import of questions surrounding international allocation of tax base and tax and development, broadly construed. Such a role for human rights discourse is not particularly legal, as it stops far short of connecting particular violators of particular rights with the details of the typical sophisticated international tax planning transaction. For that reason my focus in these comments will be on the higher level, more abstract connection between tax and human rights and the way in which a focus on human rights might plausibly shape reform of the international tax system.

Now for a dose of pessimism. To date I have seen very little to convince me that international tax reform efforts currently underway will connect to the concerns of human rights in any meaningful way. That pessimism flows from an observation and assessment of the current state of affairs in both the real world of tax policymaking and in the academic world.

Regarding the world of tax policymakers, the obvious focal point at present is the Organisation for Economic Co-operation and Development (OECD) project on Base Erosion and Profit Shifting (BEPS). The project has been hailed by its participants and its proponents as remarkable. Upon issuance of the BEPS Final Reports the OECD Secretary-General referred to the proposals therein as representing "the most fundamental changes to international tax rules in a century."[4] With due acknowledgment for the immense time and effort that has been put into the package of BEPS Final Reports, the vast array of proposals fall into the category of what could be considered incremental, modest reform, rather than fundamental shifts in thinking that would be necessary to meaningfully revise the international tax system in a way that would have substantial effect on the problems of extreme poverty and the deprivation of human rights. The possible exception here is the large shift in the direction of transparency—a shift that really would have been almost unthinkable when the OECD first took up its work on harmful tax practices in the mid-1990s.[5] The move to transparency is all good and should be lauded, but it does not evidence any sort of fundamental consideration of how to divide the international tax base between developed and developing countries.

Regarding the academic world of tax scholarship, linking tax and human rights under the dominant public finance paradigm presents serious hurdles. There are two chief actors whose behavior we might seek to reform by connecting the demand for respect of human rights with taxation: governments and taxpayers, particularly multinational corporations. One might add lawyers as a third category, but if we take lawyers to be faithful agents of their principals, then one should rightly focus attention on the taxpayer rather than the adviser when describing underlying substantive duties to respect rights. The insurmountable challenge under the dominant paradigm regarding governments is that the analysis and evaluation of the tax function is a domestic affair. It thus does not take account of international distributional issues. The insurmountable challenge under the dominant paradigm regarding taxpayers (at least if they are corporations) is that corporations themselves are never viewed as relevant objects of analysis under a welfarist framework. This makes for an impossible fit with the basic view coming from the field of human rights, in which corporations can in themselves hold duties regarding rights.[6]

This pessimistic note is not to say that forging a connection between tax and human rights is impossible. It is to say that forging such a connection through incremental change to the existing policy framework and from within the dominant scholarly framework will be very difficult indeed. The basic thesis of this chapter, then, is that if it is right to draw such a connection, it will require disruptive shifts in the existing framework, not marginal ones.

The discussion below is broken down into two aspects. First, I will spell out in more detail some of the limitations of working within existing paradigms. Second, I will suggest some possible ways in which one might rethink tax policy in more radical ways. I will mention three possibilities, though they are lightly sketched and meant to be suggestive only. One possibility is a recasting of the basic source-residence dichotomy that deeply pervades the existing approach to international taxation. A second is to consider tax policy with an eye to duties that nations may hold with respect to one another. A third is to rethink the role of corporate incidence analysis in tax policy.

As should be clear from these initial comments, I intend to deal with only one aspect of the potential agenda regarding the possible connections between tax and human rights. In particular, I am concerned here with issues of international taxation as opposed to wholly domestic resource mobilization; issues of substantive law as opposed to issues of transparency and information exchange; and issues regarding corporate taxpayers as opposed to issues raised by individual taxpayers.

II. THE CHALLENGES OF INCREMENTAL REFORM WITHIN EXISTING PARADIGMS

In this section of the chapter, I discuss what I take to be some central hurdles to connecting the fields of tax and human rights within what I take broadly to be existing governmental and scholarly commitments—and potential incremental reforms in light of those commitments. Although somewhat artificial, I will divide the discussion into two parts. The first part will focus on the policymaking space at the level of national governments and international organizations such as the OECD and the United Nations. The second part will focus on academic analysis of tax policy. One reason to separate the discussion in this way is that the two domains connect differently with the potential duty holders under a human-rights-grounded analysis. Specifically, the first part will focus on the question whether human rights discourse could produce important imperatives for governments in setting their tax policy. The second part will address the question whether human rights discourse could produce important imperatives for taxpayers, here taken to be multinational corporations.

A. TAX POLICYMAKING—SEEING GOVERNMENT AS DUTY HOLDER

There is a common causal story leading to foment in the tax community and in the human rights community. Specifically, the ability of large multinational corporations to engage in creative tax planning has led to increasing outrage from both domains that these actors are not paying their "fair share" of taxes. Tax specialists are more likely to decry the simple breakdown of outdated rules in their ability to deal with global supply chains and the increasing share of the economy occupied by services and intangibles. Human rights specialists are more likely to decry the catastrophic loss of revenue from aggressive planning schemes which could provide a crucial component of development finance and underwrite poverty alleviation and the provision of a range of social services and goods. But the basic target would seem to be the same. One might imagine that such shared outrage might lead to common cause as well in determining an appropriate remedy. But here the story becomes more complicated and tendentious. We have seen the issuance of final reports from the OECD BEPS Project in 2015 and are now in the process of observing how various countries will implement different aspects of the recommendations flowing from the project. The interesting question is how and to what extent might the fact that human rights lawyers are party to the relevant discussions and reform efforts affect outcomes? At least within the bounds of what has been on the table in considerations at the OECD and in terms of what has come out of the OECD BEPS Project, there is little to suggest that the addition of a human rights angle would have much effect or impact at all. To elaborate, consider both a general and a more specific observation.

The general observation relates to basic governmental incentives and attitudes toward revenue collection at the moment. As the name itself suggests, BEPS is about counteracting the loss of tax base. That is, the fundamental underlying motive is to increase the collection of tax revenue as compared to a baseline with the use of current instruments.[7] Thus a human rights component would not seem to add much in a motivational sense. But nor could it be expected to add anything in a technical sense. Tax law is already replete with anti-abuse tools, such as doctrines that look to the economic substance of a transaction rather than its form and statutory general anti-avoidance rules. If the targeted transactions are ones that are technically legal (obviously we don't need additional tools for those that are not) but which are sufficiently out of step with legislative intent that it is thought claimed tax benefits should be denied, it is highly unlikely that challenges to the technical aspects of transactions sounding in human rights law could ever be sufficiently fine-tuned to shut down transactions that had survived the gauntlet of existing tools. In short, where governments are already seeking to target and shut down the very same transactions that human rights lawyers find problematic, it is difficult to see how human rights lawyers have much to add in the way of potential legal fixes—though of course they may add quite a bit by bringing greater attention to these issues in the first instance.

One might counter here that clearly not all governments are interested in raising more revenue in all cases. It is no small part of the problem that some jurisdictions may effectively be complicit in aggressive schemes. That is, jurisdictions may find it in their interest to use the tax system to nominally attract tax base from some other jurisdictions in cases where the base would not have naturally arisen there. Such a jurisdiction can be better off because some tax revenue is better than none, even though jurisdictions that have lost base may count losses higher than any gains to the jurisdiction that has raided its base. But whatever one thinks of such a dynamic, this too is not an obvious target for the tools of the human rights lawyer. The basic conceit of the BEPS Project is to tax income where it actually arises.[8] Supposing any income actually does arise in the jurisdiction perceived to be a base raider, then it would not seem problematic that the jurisdiction chooses to tax it at a low rate.[9] Or, at the very least, it is no more problematic than any instance in which a jurisdiction chooses not to tax domestic source income at a higher rate and then transfer incremental revenues for the use of international development. But that sort of argument would surely prove too much and would be almost entirely divorced from the central focus of the BEPS Project.

Suppose, alternatively, that the income really does arise in some other jurisdiction but the taxpayer has managed to report it in our base-raiding jurisdiction. That would seem to be the basic setup in the recent high-profile state aid cases in the European Union, in which the European Commission has found that certain US companies have received impermissible selective advantages through the grant of administrative tax rulings. For example, in the case involving Ireland's dealings with Apple Inc., the European Commission found that Ireland should now collect in excess of $14 billion from Apple, reflecting a combination of past taxes, interest, and penalties.[10] There would, however, seem to be no substantive argument supporting the idea that the profits associated with that massive tax bill actually arose in Ireland under any plausible theory of source taxation. Apple undertook some operations in Ireland, but nobody has advanced an argument explaining how the activities in Ireland could have possibly generated the associated profit.

That is what makes these unappealing cases from the standpoint of the human rights advocate. The central claim of the European Commission in the Apple investigation is that income derived from sales into EU member states has been taxed at a very low effective rate due in part to Ireland's complicity in blessing Apple's overall tax-planning structure. Although the bulk of Apple's profit on European sales should be understood to have arisen outside Ireland, the proposed solution according to the European Commission is for Ireland to collect more in tax. Coming from the perspective of the human rights advocate it would seem very much at odds with the basic link meant to be forged between taxation, human rights, and extreme poverty. That is, one would think the goals of the human rights project would more naturally align with preservation of and bolstering of source country taxing rights.

This brings me to the more specific observation. Perhaps the lesson to be learned from the EU state aid cases is simply that the fundamental problem lies with the vacuousness of the current manner in which profits are allocated in the first instance. The fact that a company like Apple can take the position that the bulk of its profits on European sales are earned in some offshore low-tax jurisdiction is based almost entirely on the intercompany pricing arrangements under which Apple holds its intellectual property and earns royalties in some low-tax jurisdiction. That result flows from the operation of the prevailing arm's-length standard, which in turn has already been targeted as a major potential source of reform by commentators considering the connections between tax and human rights.[11] In that respect it has been suggested that a shift to a unitary system with formulary apportionment would be an important advance.[12] Further, one of the important outputs of the BEPS Project has been a common template for country-by-country reporting.[13] It is widely understood that the requirement of country-by-country reporting could be an important foot in the door for advocates of formulary apportionment who seek to unseat the arm's-length standard.[14] Thus it would seem that here we have the most natural and strongest confluence of a key output coming from intergovernmental reform efforts in the tax policy world and a key point of focus of the human rights community.

But any such confluence is limited for a couple of reasons. First, the debates about the merits and demerits of an arm's-length standard versus formulary apportionment are very well rehearsed at this point.[15] There is little that human rights discourse could do to tip the balance of these arguments in a technical sense. To be clear, if one system were consistent with preservation of human rights and the other contrary to it, then surely this fact alone should carry the day if other factors are in equipoise. But although the fact of such closer alignment has been asserted, it has been neither argued nor proven. The promise that would seem to be held out by tying together tax and human rights is to affect a substantial shift in allocation of tax base in a way that would assist in addressing extreme poverty. Moving from the arm's-length standard to formulary apportionment is a very timid move in that direction, if it moves in that direction at all.

What one wants here is a substantive argument for rethinking allocation of the tax base. Formulary apportionment lacks such substance. A strong case here would suggest that there are sounder ways to think about where income arises in substance and that such allocations in fact favor historically less well-off countries. The distributional consequences of formulary apportionment are, of course, entirely indeterminate because everything depends on the allocation factors. To the extent that one thinks the allocations will favor developing countries this is merely by fiat—that is, by assumption that the chosen factors will point in this direction. But why would anyone assume the factors would play out that way? To the extent formulary apportionment is thought to offer redress to the sorts of complex tax-planning structures employed by multinational corporations, this is generally accomplished not by solving the problem of figuring out how and where to tax intangibles but rather by simply ignoring intangibles. Policymakers and governments that have some plausible claim to tax income from intangible income are likely to reject such approaches out of hand. For this reason, forging the connection between tax and human rights here is going to require more. It is going to require a substantive rethinking of the historic interaction between the source and residence entitlements.

B. SEEING THE TAXPAYER AS DUTY HOLDER

Presumably the bottom-line impact of bringing human rights discourse to bear on the behavior of taxpayers would be to have the decision makers in multinational corporations recognize the human rights impacts of their tax planning, leading to voluntary decisions to engage in less aggressive tax planning than would otherwise be the case. As a practical matter for corporate tax managers this seems a very tall order. It goes without saying that we must be talking about a class of cases that survive scrutiny under existing specific law, including anti-abuse doctrines. If the cases did not survive such scrutiny, then they do not have the blessing of law currently and adding a necessarily vague human rights connection on top of the charge of illegality would seem to be of minimal import. Although presumably there could be additional deterrence achieved from reputational harms, this would be a very bluntly tailored approach as compared to standard ways of achieving deterrence, such as monetary penalties.

The cases of much greater interest are the ones that are in fact legal under existing substantive tax law. Could a human rights connection appropriately affect the proper standard of conduct here? If so, it would mean that some number of positions that would be taken and that would survive scrutiny on audit or in litigation would nonetheless be denoted as positions that should nonetheless not have been taken. The tax manager will naturally ask what standard is to be applied here—that is, under what test should the corporation not take actions that otherwise satisfy the test of legality? It is very difficult to know how one could even begin to articulate such a standard, given that the basic human rights connection is drawn in terms of general revenue collection. But that connection is going to exist equally for every dollar raised from the corporation. Thus the human rights discourse would seem to give no substantive standard at all under which a tax manager could know which actions are permissible and which not.

Thus the hurdle from the practitioner's standpoint is that there is no obvious way to connect the supposed harm (that is, reduced revenue and inadequate financial resources for provision of human rights) with a workable legal standard. There is an analog problem from the standpoint of the general academic analysis of corporate tax policy. Under the prevailing public finance orthodoxy one would never care about corporations themselves under a welfarist analysis. Rather, welfare effects could only be determined by understanding the economic incidence of the corporate tax. From that perspective it would make no sense to charge corporations with certain duties deriving from human rights law based on the degree of aggressiveness of a transaction or position. All that would matter would be the welfare effects given determined tax incidence. After all, it is certainly possible as a matter of theory that the incidence of tax savings from the most aggressive (though ultimately legal) transactions imaginable could flow entirely to relatively poor individuals with highly salutary results for the welfarist. For example, it cannot be ruled out as a matter of theory that tax savings of a multinational might not be passed on to employees of the multinational in developing countries with high marginal welfare gains. More generally, one has absolutely no reason to think that the incidence effects from transactions that are thought to be the suspect ones (that is, the transactions that are close to the line on legality) correlate in any meaningful way with the problem that one is presumably attempting to work on.

To be sure, there may be many ills associated with aggressive tax planning. The resources devoted to planning, and the required counterresponses of governments, are deadweight costs to the system. More generally, the complexity surrounding the taxation of international transactions makes the sector a costly one for governments to tax, based on a comparison of costs of administration to revenue collected. But from within the dominant welfarist framework there is again no reason to think that these concerns link up with the human rights–based concerns about extreme poverty. If anything, the concerns about aggressive tax planning may simply bolster calls to eliminate corporate taxes altogether. But typically, concerns from the development sector run counter to this, arguing in favor of retaining corporate taxation because of the important positive revenue impacts on budgets of developing countries, which can often tax corporations more readily than other taxpayers.

The above discussion has been meant to show some of the substantial hurdles in identifying duties of either governments or taxpayers derived from within the framework of human rights discourse. But those hurdles arise from within the commitments of a well-trodden conceptual framework on the tax side, both in the governmental policymaking sector and in the academic sector. What if one were to think more radically about reform to the existing international tax framework? In the remainder of these comments I consider three avenues for further exploration, each of which calls into question a certain shibboleth of the existing regime.

III. RETHINKING THE SOURCE-RESIDENCE PARADIGM

The basic architecture of the international tax system has a fairly well understood structure. Countries have an authority to tax income either on the basis of source or residence. These entitlements often overlap. The function of unilateral abatements of tax as well as the bilateral tax treaty network historically was to ensure relief from double taxation. This obviously requires jurisdictions to cede taxing rights over income they could tax. The historical compromise was thought to be very roughly that source jurisdictions should tax active business income and residence jurisdictions should tax passive income owned by their tax residents.

The current breakdown of this basic arrangement is also well understood. To be stable, one requires agreed rules to locate income (that is, to source it) and agreed rules to tie taxpayers to a particular jurisdiction (that is to determine residence). But the location of income is highly malleable and not capable of ready agreement, particularly with respect to intangibles. The location of individuals is easier to determine, at least in a static sense. But the factors that plausibly feed into residence are not static, especially for corporate taxpayers.

Given these well-understood soft spots in the system, some of the basic calls for both incremental and supposed fundamental reform are not surprising. Thus a shift to formulary apportionment would seem to cut through the problem of location of income, by simply stipulating allocation keys to unitary enterprises. And recent calls for adoption of destination-based consumption taxes as a replacement revenue source for the standard corporate income tax rest on the observation that locational choices for consumption are less elastic than for income production factors or for location of owners of capital. These sorts of reform proposals have been evaluated in the literature.[16] I will not rehearse these arguments, but will rather only reiterate a point made above. I do not see that human rights law has much valence in pushing these debates one way or the other.

What I propose here instead is a more fundamental rethinking of the source-residence dichotomy that pervades thinking on international tax. Specifically, suppose that one conceived the international tax allocation problem purely on a transactional or contractual model involving buyers and sellers. This will call to mind a market analogy, but as will become clear, one should not assume the existence of a market, because one of the points I'd like to call into question is the very relevance of market evolution to the fundamental question about allocation of tax base.

One could begin by undertaking a thought exercise with an example that nobody really seems to question. Suppose some natural resource exists clearly within the territorial boundaries of some sovereign. Suppose further that the state retains a 100 percent ownership interest in the resource and that the state has such a large proportionate share of the world's supply of the resource that it is the global price setter. Indeed, to take the most extreme case, let's suppose the resource exists only within the boundaries of a single sovereign. The sovereign then sets prices like any monopolist. Further, the sovereign of course will retain 100 percent of the profit from selling this resource—that is, the difference between gross price net of costs of extraction and other transaction costs. Nobody would question this outcome. Nobody would suggest that some portion of the profit must be turned over to buyers of the resource.

What happens if the extraction and sale of the natural resource is privatized and distributed through a market mechanism? Bracketing complicated issues about the moment of privatization and the ability of the state to capture present value of future profits upon transfer of state ownership, one would expect that so long as there are no private monopolies, competition will drive prices down. Some amount of consumer surplus will be realized by buyers of the resource, which surplus was previously realized by the state seller of the resource. From a tax perspective, under existing norms the state may very well have a curtailed base. That is, the state will be able to tax the profits from the sale of the resource (on a residence basis if sold by home country taxpayers or likely on a source basis if not), but there is absolutely no mechanism under existing norms for the state to tax realized consumer surplus of foreign purchasers of the resource. Of course it is possible that the aggregate base may go up if, for example, the private sector is better at controlling costs. But whatever the views of proponents of markets on that question, there is no logical necessity here. Perhaps the sovereign in question is a particularly benign, efficient one, which has already realized any plausible cost savings.

This extreme example is meant to elicit the following basic point. Under existing norms, the allocation of tax base is contingently related to the amount of market evolution in an economy. The greater the degree of evolution in the market toward competition, the more sovereigns seem potentially to cede tax base that would have been nonproblematically viewed as theirs if resources were state-owned. Conversely, as the amount of market competition decreases, under prevailing norms a sovereign may become entitled to more base. For these purposes, note that decrease in competition need not mean state ownership of resources; it could also mean state-granted monopolies (including intellectual property–based property rights) to nonstate actors. Although this seems to be a plausible description of the relationship between market evolution and the allocation of international tax base, I am not aware of any scholarly attempt to justify this basic result. Why should the degree of market evolution dictate the allocation of base? If the basic goal is to locate income in some sense and we are convinced it is adequately located inside a sovereign with state ownership, what is the actual theoretical case for claiming that the income is no longer relevantly within the sovereign simply because price has come down? One could simply assert that the jurisdiction of the producer gets to tax or enjoy producer surplus and not consumer surplus. But why? What is the actual basis of such an assertion, particularly if it is in the power of the producer to convert consumer surplus to producer surplus through an action of nationalization?

In a recent paper I applied this basic observation to a much-disputed concrete problem in the current international tax space.[17] Specifically, a number of countries have attempted of late to argue that arm's-length transfer pricing ought to be applied with due acknowledgment of so-called location savings. Thus if a multinational firm earns profits by virtue of reducing costs, such cost reductions being uniquely available in a certain location, then that jurisdiction where such savings arise should be allocated a portion of this profit. A common alternative would be to compensate a locally owned subsidiary in the jurisdiction of cost savings on a routine cost-plus basis. That amount is likely to be much lower than an allocable share of profits. The current analysis to this problem offered by the OECD is very much grounded in existing commitments and norms—and not surprisingly shows the intense limits of operating in a world of incremental reform to existing agreements and documents that have begun to show their age.

That analysis would look something like this. An embodied premise in the arm's-length standard is that we ought to tax commonly controlled taxpayers and unrelated taxpayers the same. If one were to acquire low-cost inputs from an unrelated party in conditions where there is local market competition, then the provider of such inputs will be unable to bargain for any surplus. If it tries, then it will presumably be undersold and the buyer will look elsewhere. Thus the tax base in the jurisdiction of the factor input will see only compensation based on the low cost as part of the tax base. Now imagine that local production is done by a wholly owned subsidiary. Some jurisdictions claim that the subsidiary should be allocated some of the profit from the location savings. That is, the claim is to tax the controlled subsidiary in a more onerous fashion than the uncontrolled one. How could that possibly be justified under the current system, which is built with great attention to achieve parity between the related and unrelated cases?

The general conceptual flaw in that analysis is to take the treatment of the unrelated case as fixed and determined. Under existing norms in the unrelated case, a local production company would not be realizing the relevant profit from location savings and the purchaser of such input would be realizing profit but would have no taxable presence in the jurisdiction of supply of the input. But this result on taxable presence is contingent. One could, of course, rewrite the rules such that the purchaser did have a taxable presence. In the language of existing bilateral agreements we would say the purchaser has a permanent establishment, or PE, in virtue of this activity. There is no way to come even close to that result under existing treaty language. But that language too is contingent. The interesting question is what is the substantively sound answer to the question about allocation if we were writing on a completely blank slate. Here I come back to the point about market evolution. If the sovereign where the "location savings" are realized were to nationalize the relevant sector, then presumably it would then be able to capture the relevant profit (up to the point it could be undersold by some other jurisdiction). If the degree of market evolution is not normatively determinative to the question of allocation of tax base, then there is a case to be made that in the unrelated party case the purchaser should have a taxable presence, and in the related party case one could then allocate a portion of the profits from location savings to the controlled production subsidiary (while also achieving parity).

One can now generalize. It has been common in the critiques of arm's-length transfer pricing to suggest that components of a commonly controlled enterprise function as if in a bilateral monopoly relationship.[18] In particular, there is said to be some surplus from common control (that is, the synergistic gains of common ownership) which conceptually cannot be allocated to any particular member of the group because such gain does not belong to any particular member. Rather, it is a gain that arises only in virtue of the group, and it is indeterminate whom it belongs to, much like the indeterminacy of allocation of surplus in the bilateral monopoly case. As an aside, I should note that proponents of formulary apportionment take it as a virtue of that approach that it solves this allocation problem. But this is a subspecies of the broader problem of intangibles. Formulary apportionment solves this problem only be sweeping it under the rug. If the surplus exists and if it must be allocated in some fashion and if any method of allocation is arbitrary, then it is no solution to favor one arbitrary solution over another.

My approach here is rather different. Rather than sweeping the problem of surplus under the rug, what if we put it front and center? The international tax system is, of course, structured around state taxation of market actors. My central point here, though, is that the connection between international tax base allocation and market evolution has not been well developed. Firms and states (and families!) are just different forms of collectives. Thus one can replicate the bargaining problems that arise between one form of collective and another. If one conceives of states as the relevant bargaining actors and thinks about how this relates to surplus gains from trade, then one potentially has the seeds of an approach to allocation that could displace the source-residence dichotomy. Consider an extreme case: two and only two states, no private property or firms, trade between the states. This is bilateral monopoly. States have simply occupied the role of firms in the standard model. It seems plausible to say here that there is some amount each state could have earned even in the absence of trade.[19] That amount rightly belongs to that state. Then there is the surplus. We don't have any obvious way, it would seem, to allocate such amount in a way that clearly aligns with any particular surplus belonging to one state rather than the other. A series of observations are in order.

First, although much more would have to be said than I have space to argue here, I believe there is substantial normative appeal to conceiving the general problem of allocation of tax base as a justificatory problem with the states as the relevant primary actors. That is we should use as a normative baseline the case of states *qua* states trading with one another. This is not at all how we approach the problem as a practical matter, of course. We approach the problem through the legal relationship between state and taxpayer. Where taxpayers engage in activities throughout the world, the relationship between state and taxpayer necessarily has inter-nation allocation consequences. Although those consequences are of primary normative importance, almost the entire structure of the system is based on a different relationship—that between taxpayer and state. This too is contingent and path dependent. It reflects the simple fact that states generally interacted with their taxpayers in a domestic sense first. Trade expanded, and we had to make the old rules fit the new reality.

Second, the suggestion that we rethink the international tax system under a normative framework of allocating gains from trade across nations is crazily ambitious. To be sure, as a purely conceptual matter I can readily identify four components. Unitary sovereigns with no markets trading with one another would generate profits that could be divided among three aspects: (1) the profit the first sovereign would have earned absent trade; (2) the profit the second sovereign would have earned absent trade; and (3) the surplus from trade. A fourth component is any additional surplus generated by the existence of national markets. My basic normative stance is that the first and second components nonproblematically belong to the relevant sovereign who could have earned the profit in isolation; the third component is indeterminate and requires some further elaborated moral principle to allocate; and the fourth component is complicated and would require much work on my part (but I might initially say that if the gain can be tied to a particular national market, then this should be allocated to the state that created that market). Even assuming one accepts the normativity of this, the empirical task of putting concrete numbers on these categories is almost beyond imagination.

The current doctrinal framework is not structured in any way to match the components sketched above. For example, suppose a firm produces in its home country and sells some output abroad. Under current rules one can readily imagine a taxable presence based on the sales force abroad, with an allocable amount of profit based on those foreign sales. Under the framework sketched above, the international allocation would look very different because some of the profit from foreign sales may well have been earned even absent trade. Of course it may have been more profitable to sell the marginal widget abroad than at home, but that does not mean there would not have been any home country profit. The current framework really has no apparatus to separate these components.

Third, notwithstanding the difficulty of meshing existing doctrinal structures with the proposed normative framework, it might nonetheless be the case that the proposed normative frame could be used as a sort of heuristic to evaluate at least certain results under the existing system. It could, for example, justify at least some allocations under the existing rules that would not otherwise seem justifiable.

Fourth, probably the most substantial hurdle to connecting tax and human rights is that while cross-border funding commitments could well assist in the more expansive provision of human rights, taxation at present is thoroughly grounded in the nation state and domestic distributive commitments. Might the normative frame suggested above give a possible way out of that trap? The current system is based on the idea that all income belongs to the tax base of some state. Often it belongs to more than one state, in which case we need remedial efforts to relieve double taxation. If the income seems not to belong to the base of any state, then the prevailing dogma is that this is an extreme pathology, whether it goes by the label of "double nontaxation" or "stateless income."

I would like to make a bold statement here, which is that such cases may not be pathological at all. If there are surplus gains from trade between nations, then in the sense of international allocation of tax base it could rightly be said that the gains actually do not belong to any state. In a world where most or almost all states are trading simultaneously, then substantial gains from trade belong to nobody. But if they belong to nobody, we might as well say they belong to everybody. And if they belong to everybody, it is not such a long way to arguing that resources should be directed to those most in need in the world. Again, I don't mean to understate the very high empirical burden of figuring out what such a quantity might actually be. But I at least hope to have made space for a fairly radical way to connect a universalist ideal to an institution that remains for the time being almost entirely grounded in the nation state.

IV. ACTING OUTSIDE OF NATIONAL INTEREST

The discussion in section III was meant to address the issue of states as duty holders through a rethinking of the basic source-residence dichotomy. In this section, I discuss the issue of states as duty holders but from within the basic prevailing source-residence paradigm.

It has become a fairly standard position at least in US tax policy circles that in setting international tax policy the United States should think about its own interests.[20] How to define US interests is, not surprisingly, a difficult question. That's especially the case given the inevitable trade-offs between domestic winners and losers under any policy choice as well as the dynamic nature of who counts as a US person in the first place (whether corporate or individual). Notwithstanding these difficulties, the basic position that the United States should think about national rather than global interests is taken as almost self-evident.[21] Policy positions asserted in the past that are nominally premised on global standards, such as global efficiency, are thus explained away as either incoherent or as misnomers for policies that are really about furthering the national interest.[22] If one accepts the basic favoring of national interest, then there would, as noted, seem to be an immediate tension with the universalist aspirations of human rights discourse.

One can consider that point in somewhat more detail by thinking about allocation of tax base from within the basic existing paradigm. Suppose it is the case that there is some truth to the matter about where income arises, or at the very least that we could reach some general consensus about this in at least some important portion of cases.[23] Consider potential base allocation across a developed country and a developing country, with such categories roughly denoting the possibility that there are revenue constraints in the latter that are so severe as to curtail enjoyment of human rights but not so in the former.

If income is "really" appropriately sourced to the developed country, then there is no obvious link to the human rights issue. One could say that for such income this is no different than any other income sourced to such developed country. If the income is "really" appropriately sourced to the developing country and it is booked there by the taxpayer, then there would also seem to be no issue. The developing country would already have the right to tax the income in the first instance. It might not do so under some incentive-based scheme and it might be better policy to tax the amount (even if this were to drive some investment away), but it is difficult to see how casting this as a human rights issue changes much of anything. A third possibility is that the income is "really" appropriately sourced to the developing country but is booked to the developed country in the first instance. This case is more interesting.

One might say once again that casting this as a matter of human rights is not really helpful or important because if by assumption we could have agreement that the income "really" arises in the developing country, then the existing legal instruments would seem sufficient for the developing country to claim the tax base. But of course that simplistic argument ignores the resource constraints on the developing country that put it in the position such that human rights are relevant in the first place. Those constraints affect tax administration just as much as anything else.

For example, suppose profit is being booked under a preferential regime in a developed country even though there is some decent claim the income should actually be sourced in the developing country. For example, suppose a deductible royalty is paid out of the developing country at a price of $50x even though a sound administration of the arm's-length standard would suggest a royalty in the neighborhood of $10x. The taxpayer might like this if the effective rate achieved on the income inclusion is lower than the effective rate on the deduction. The developed country might like this if it means more revenue for it in the aggregate than would be the case if the price charged were arm's-length. The central problem is that the developing country may have no sufficient capacity to administer a system that will yield an appropriate adjustment. It may lack relevant databases of comparables, and it may lack technical expertise to apply the existing complex framework of the transfer pricing rules. Worse, those rules have essentially been put in place by the developed countries.

Under current arrangements there is likely to be little recourse. The developed country has no incentive to seek an adjustment pushing profit back to the true source country. And the developing country has the incentive but no resources.

Accordingly, one fairly radical modification to the existing framework would place on the developed country an obligation here to seek an adjustment. I say radical because that adjustment would be against interest, thus countering the basic idea that countries should set policy to advance national interest. Note that it seems something of a dead end to target the rate structure of the country where the profit is booked. It will be difficult to make that challenge while still respecting the basic idea of rate sovereignty. However, what I suggest here is that there may be some deeper basis for claiming an affirmative obligation to seek an against-interest downward adjustment. The basis of that claim is properly linked to the differential capacity of the two jurisdictions and the idea that the base really does belong to the developing country. From this standpoint the human rights based claim may be important as a justification for against-interest adjustments. Countries standing in a similar footing, by contrast, could quite plausibly take the position that there is no obligation to make affirmative downward adjustments.

V. CORPORATIONS AND DUTIES OF COLLECTIVES

Sections III and IV have dealt with different aspects of the relevance of the state to the problem under consideration. In this final section, I consider briefly the question of corporations. Some of the existing writing on the potential connection between tax and human rights seems to take it as a given that corporate taxpayers could be relevant duty holders under a rights-based analysis. Presumably, this would mean that the relevant taxpayers would be required, in light of their duties, not to take certain tax positions that they would have otherwise deemed legal (or at least sufficiently uncertain in their illegality to warrant taking a risky position).

I have already sketched above the way in which this approach seems in immediate tension with the prevailing public finance analysis of corporate taxpayers, which would insist that one always think of incidence effects on corporations in determining the welfare consequences of tax burdens. To repeat the example from above, what if a particular tax savings from a seemingly aggressive transaction would generate tax savings that are passed on to particularly deserving individuals? This basic point is only aggravated by the fact that the ultimate connection between tax (and spending) and the stated problem of central concern (extreme poverty) is indirect rather than direct. Corporate actors take many actions that may have far greater direct relevance to individuals living in poverty (e.g., what prices are to be charged for lifesaving drugs or what safety precautions will voluntarily be put in place in otherwise unregulated work environments). Overall firm cost structure (including tax cost) may have crucial bearing on these other interactions. Arguably, what one cares about is this whole package of the way in which the corporation interacts with individuals, rather than the question of legal incidence of tax in isolation.

There is much to be said for this prevailing view. Here, I want only to observe that the dominance of this approach in tax policy circles ought not to preclude the attempt to link affirmative duties of corporations from a human rights standpoint, irrespective of incidence effects. The view that takes corporations (or any collective for that matter) as not morally relevant in themselves is of course itself contingent on a very particular ethical view of the world. It is a truism that if what you care about is welfare of individuals (including the aggregation thereof into social welfare), then you ought not to care about the rights and duties of collectives in and of themselves, but rather only the welfare effects of such rights or duties on individuals. But not everybody accepts welfarism and the allied views on the connections between individuals and collectives. That has been true for a very long time with respect to the state. Consider, for example, the distance between Plato's ideal view of the state in *The Republic*, as compared to the view that collectives should be disaggregated into constituent members to undertake any ethical analysis. In modernity, consider the rise of calls for corporate social responsibility, which is understood not merely as a profit-maximizing instrumental phenomenon which benefits shareholders but rather as an independent moral obligation. So too in human rights discourse generally where it is well established that corporations, as opposed to individual actors within corporations, can hold duties in this respect.

I do not here offer further thoughts on how to operationalize the idea of corporation as duty holder in practice. For reasons mentioned above, there are substantial challenges to inducing the individual human actors that control and act on behalf of corporations to act in the right way, at least given the current lack of specificity on the content of any duties. Further, even if incidence effects should not in the end be wholly determinative of the ethical evaluation of certain rules and actions, surely such effects may often at least be relevant. Even accepting these complications, however, I do not see this as an impossible hurdle to connecting tax and human rights. The ethical position of placing first-order duties on corporations themselves would seem to have broad popular support and is in line with certain approaches to ethics. The challenges here are operational rather than ethical.

VI. CONCLUSION

Connecting the discourse of human rights law to reform of the international tax system is difficult but not impossible. Given the common focus across the domains on particular transactions and structures thought to be abusive and offensive, it would be natural to attempt to hitch the human rights legal apparatus to current international tax reform efforts. I have attempted to say here why that would be a mistake. Success will require a much bolder vision of reform. I have sketched here three such possible avenues: rethinking the source-residence dichotomy as the chief means of allocating the international tax base; rethinking the duties of the nation state as including certain against-sovereign-interest actions; and rethinking the ethical status of collective private entities in the tax system.

NOTES

1. For an early example in the literature calling for broad reconsideration of the international tax system on these grounds, see M. J. Graetz, 'Taxing International Income—Inadequate Principles, Outdated Concepts, and Unsatisfactory Policy', 54 *Tax Law Review* (2000), 261.

2. See OECD, *OECD/G20 Base Erosion and Profit Shifting Project Explanatory Statement*, 5 Oct. 2015, available online at https://www.oecd.org/ctp/beps-explanatory-statement-2015.pdf, at para. 7.

3. On the connection between taxation, poverty and human rights in particular, see International Bar Association, *Tax Abuses, Poverty and Human Rights: A Report of the International Bar Association's Human Rights Institute Task Force on Illicit Financial Flows, Poverty and Human Rights* (2013), available online at http://www.ibanet.org/Document/Default.aspx?DocumentUid=4977CB3D-4988-4C9C-84C7-9050A5CB2311 (last visited 30 May 2017).

4. OECD, Press Release to Accompany BEPS 2015 Final Reports, 5 Oct. 2015, available online at http://www.oecd.org/tax/oecd-presents-outputs-of-oecd-g20-beps-project-for-discussion-at-g20-finance-ministers-meeting.htm (last visited 22 May 2017).

5. For the chief provisions regarding disclosure see OECD, *Mandatory Disclosure Rules, Action 12—2015 Final Report*, 5 Oct. 2015, available online at http://www.oecd.org/tax/mandatory-disclosure-rules-action-12-2015-final-report-9789264241442-en.htm (last visited 30 May 2017); and OECD, *Transfer Pricing Documentation and Country-by-Country Reporting, Action 13—2015 Final Report*, 5 Oct. 2015, available online at http://www.oecd.org/tax/transfer-pricing-documentation-and-country-by-country-reporting-action-13-2015-final-report-9789264241480-en.htm (last visited 30 May 2017).

6. For background on corporate responsibilities, see N. Pillay, 'The Corporate Responsibility to Respect: A Human Rights Milestone', *International Labour and Social Policy Review* (2009).

7. OECD, *supra* note 2, at para. 2.

8. Ibid. at para. 1.

9. This, of course, begs the question whether the interjurisdictional tax competition at issue is somehow problematic in itself. It may be. But tax scholars and policymakers have struggled over the last several decades to provide a general normative framework that would allow one to distinguish permissible from impermissible tax competition. It is interesting here to contrast the BEPS Project with the OECD's original project on "harmful tax competition." The output of that project was a document, the first half of which was devoted to a systematic attempt to describe the characteristics of tax havens and harmful preferential tax regimes. See OECD, *Harmful Tax Competition: An Emerging Global Issue* (1998), available online at http://www.oecd.org/tax/transparency/44430243.pdf. By contrast, the BEPS Final Reports offer no such attempt to delineate harmful tax competition. The perceived evil, rather, is simply the divorce between the jurisdiction where income is reported and the jurisdiction where the income has actually arisen.

10. In addition to Ireland, state aid investigations have also involved the Netherlands and Luxembourg. See D. Shaviro, 'Friends Without Benefits?: The Treasury and EU State Aid', 83 *Tax Notes International* (2016), 1067.

11. International Bar Association, *supra* note 3, at 33.

12. Ibid. at 33–34.

13. See OECD, *Transfer Pricing Documentation and Country-by-Country Reporting, Action 13—2015 Final Report, supra* note 5.

14. See A. M. Parker, 'Country-by-Country Reporting: A Path to Transparency, Or a Prelude to a Formulary Apportionment Approach?', *Tax Management Transfer Pricing Report*, 12 Nov. 2013.
15. For an overview, see R. S. Avi-Yonah, 'The Rise and Fall of Arm's Length: A Study in the Evolution of U.S. International Taxation', 9 *Finance and Tax Law Review* (2006), 310.
16. See A. J. Auerbach, M. Devereux, and H. Simpson, 'Taxing Corporate Income', *in* J. Mirrlees (ed.), *Dimensions of Tax Design* (2010), 837.
17. M. Kane, 'Location Savings and Segmented Factor Input Markets: In Search of a Tax Treaty Solution', 41 *Brooklyn Journal of International Law* (2016), 1108.
18. For an extended discussion of this issue, see M. Kane, 'Transfer Pricing, Integration and Synergy Intangibles: A Consensus Approach to the Arm's Length Standard', 6 *World Tax Journal* (2014), 282, at 292–293.
19. The argument here echoes the argument made by Aaron James that the gains from trade in a global economy ought to be allocated with reference to what states would have had in conditions of autarky. A. James, *Fairness in Practice: A Social Contract for Global Economy* (2012). James does not discuss the implications of his argument for the tax system generally or for the issue of allocation of the international tax base specifically.
20. See, e.g., Graetz, *supra* note 1, at 280–281.
21. For a counterargument, see M. Kane, 'Considering "Reconsidering the Taxation of Foreign Income"', 62 *Tax Law Review* (2009), 299, at 304–305.
22. See D. Shaviro, 'Why Worldwide Welfare as a Normative Standard in U.S. Tax Policy', 60 *Tax Law Review* (2007), 155, at 157.
23. This is a controversial claim. For a defense, see M. Kane, 'A Defense of Source Rules in International Taxation', 32 *Yale Journal on Regulation* (2015), 311.

CHAPTER 5

THE SEARCH FOR HUMAN RIGHTS IN TAX

ALLISON CHRISTIANS

I. INTRODUCTION

The Latin phrase *Ubi Jus, Ubi Remedium* declares ambitiously that for every wrong, the law provides a remedy. Many observers of the modern international tax order observe great wrongs in a global system that perpetuates vast wealth disparities by consistently serving the interests of the world's richest people, companies, and countries, at a high cost to everyone else. Some scholars and advocates have turned to human rights law in search of remedy, but existing legal structures have so far proven inapposite to the task. Why is that, and is the campaign to find human rights in tax doomed to fail?

Using a case study to illustrate the scope and magnitude of issues involved, this chapter examines three conceivable approaches to raising claims about human rights in tax and analyzes why each is frustrated in practice owing to both domestic and international legal structures surrounding rights and remedies. Intergovernmental agreement has the potential to resolve the impasse, but practical and political barriers make such a resolution unlikely. Accordingly, the chapter concludes that advocates' goals of finding remedies for observed wrongs will continue to be frustrated unless societies begin to conceptualize rights attending to taxation.

There are a number of ways in which an individual may raise a claim that her rights have been violated in connection with taxation, each of which generally depends on some recognized relationship between the claimant and the person, entity, or institution being asked to remedy the perceived wrong. Since taxation typically involves an act by a state, it might seem to the casual observer that human rights claims in tax must be about the rights an individual holds in relation to her status as a taxpayer. That is a relevant relationship for exploring rights, but it is not the only one. Instead, there are at least three distinct kinds of relationships involving the state that could theoretically give rise to human rights claims in respect of tax.[1] As in all areas of law, there is a gulf between theory and reality; the span of that gulf differs in each case.

The three relationships I have in mind are those among (1) individuals and their own states; (2) individuals and foreign states; and (3) states among themselves as members of the

Tax, Inequality, and Human Rights. Philip Alston and Nikki Reisch.

international community. In each case, organizations may be formed to represent the interests of individuals, but at stake in all cases is the protection of individual rights.[2] Each relationship category presents difficult conceptualizations of human rights in taxation given contemporary systemic legal parameters. For that reason the categories are explored through a case study. The prospects for human rights claims within each relationship are discussed in turn.

II. INDIVIDUAL RIGHTS WITHIN THE SOVEREIGN STATE

A standard human rights approach to an inquiry about human rights begins with the state, the primary actor responsible for providing specified protections, as spelled out in law. Thinking about human rights in tax from the perspective of the individual in relation to the state is perhaps the most accessible route into the tax and human rights nexus, even if the framework this presents is ultimately insufficient to the task.

The framework is simply stated: an individual seeks to be treated fairly by the state, not to be abused by officials, not to be treated in a discriminatory manner, and so on, all in accordance with domestic rights laws and jurisprudence.[3] For example, Canada's Charter of Rights provides inter alia that "[e]veryone has the right to life, liberty and security of the person and the right not to be deprived thereof except in accordance with the principles of fundamental justice" and that "[e]veryone has the right to be secure against unreasonable search or seizure."[4] These kinds of rights, which are universally recognized and included in constitutional and legislative documents across the globe, must be reconciled with the state's exercise of its power to tax.[5]

The foundational challenge for any government therefore is determining how the state may require resources from individuals without trampling individual rights to life, property, and security. At the same time, it is virtually impossible to imagine how individuals could ensure the protection of any of these rights, unless they provide resources to the state to act on their behalf. Instead, natural rights attributed to each individual must be reconciled with what is institutionally necessary to enable their protection.[6] For this reason, we may conclude that states come to a decision to tax, rather than simply seizing any available resources, precisely because they understand that the need for revenue must be balanced with individual rights.[7]

A state might err in reconciling this balance with respect to its own polity in at least two distinct ways, with very different implications for the legal system.[8] The first way is by allowing the institutions of the state to be used in ways that harm individuals' substantive or procedural rights, such as by allowing officials to misuse taxpayer information for political or pecuniary gain. The second is to design a tax regime that systematically privileges certain groups or categories of individuals while systematically creating disadvantages or harms to others. The former type of harm is more directly addressed within the existing legal framework of statutory rights protections than the latter. Each is discussed below.

A. THE TAXPAYER AS RIGHTS HOLDER

When the state allows its officials to use the tax law in ways that interfere with individual rights, it is often conceptualized as a violation of the individual's rights as a taxpayer.[9] The idea is that individuals are compelled to enter into a relationship with the state that involves the latter laying a prior claim to some of the former's resources and, for certain kinds of tax systems and most benefits programs, having an intimate relationship with their personal and financial affairs.[10] But being compelled by necessity to enter into that relationship, taxpayers cannot be assumed to have abandoned all other rights. Rights against unreasonable interference, as well as the right to respect for family and private life, are enshrined in various domestic legal regimes and multinational agreements that are not supplanted by the tax system.[11]

A fairly rare topic within the scholarly literature until recently,[12] taxpayer rights now have been articulated in charters and similar statements in more than one hundred nations. These documents state the substantive and procedural rights of taxpayers in relation to the tax authority in its exercise of administration and compliance.[13] Typically, they reiterate basic rights, such as those respecting due process, appeal, and privacy, as well as against unreasonable search and seizure. The rights articulated are those a person has in relation to the agency enforcing the tax law. These rights are generally silent on the policies underlying the law and the political procedures involved in reforming the law to remedy injustices.

Limited to a narrowly defined relationship between the taxpayer and the tax authority, taxpayer rights do not represent the end of the state's obligation when it comes to taxation. The individual's claim to fair treatment by the tax authority is not a useful framework for understanding some of the other, more fundamental, ways that human rights may be harmed by the state's use of its power to tax. These other harms are much more difficult to perceive, and not always directly traced to a single source of harm, such as the actions of a tax compliance officer. Beyond her status as a taxpayer, the individual is a holder of rights more generally in her relationship with the state.

B. THE INDIVIDUAL AS RIGHTS HOLDER

Moving from the individual as taxpayer framework to one that views the individual more generally as a holder of rights the state may be bound to protect, a concrete case study becomes useful. As a note of caution, the use of a case to explore this domain risks implying that the rights and challenges at stake are applicable only within the context presented.[14] On the contrary, supporting examples from other contexts demonstrate that the rights of individuals vis-à-vis the state discussed in the following case are critically important to all societies. The case was chosen because it vividly demonstrates the range of rights at issue.

The case to be examined involves individuals resident in Zambia, a democratic republic in Southern Africa with a population of approximately 16 million, which is integrally connected to the global economy through extensive trade and investment.[15] Zambia's population provides a useful case study for the examination of human rights in tax because the country has been the subject of several tax-based human rights inquiries, reports, legal challenges, and even documentary filmmaking by nongovernmental organizations (NGOs).[16] Many of the main drivers in the search for human rights in tax have roots in the actions of tax justice campaigners in Zambia. Further, the efforts of these campaigners in Zambia are connected to related tax and human rights study and advocacy around the world, including in the United Kingdom and the United States.

Zambia has been a candidate for human rights campaigns because, despite its inevitable vulnerability to global forces, the overall economic picture suggests that the country's resources are abundant enough to fund the kinds of infrastructure and services necessary to protect human rights.[17] Zambia had one of the world's fastest growing economies during the past decade, with annual real GDP growth averaging roughly 6.7 percent, but hovering just over 3 percent in 2015 due to "falling copper prices, reduced power generation, and depreciation of the [national currency]."[18] Yet, about half of Zambia's population lives in conditions of poverty and almost a third of the population lives in what the UN Development Programme (UNDP) defines as "severe" poverty—indicating that they are lacking not only financial resources but are also deprived of education and health services.[19] While Zambia's GDP has been on an overall upward trend since 2001, its inequality is simultaneously rising; the country's Gini coefficient places it as one of the world's ten most unequal societies.[20]

The question thus raised is whether, given the overall resources available to the government through taxation and budgeting powers, the poorest among Zambia's population are entitled to some sort of protection against the deprivation they face. If they are so entitled, some legal structure is necessary to fulfill these rights, namely, by requiring the government to raise the necessary revenue in an appropriate manner, and then spend it on appropriate institutions and services. Potential litigants would thus need to design a legal strategy around a justiciable entitlement to services. It is less clear whether they would also need to establish that those services must be funded through taxation (if other forms of raising revenue, such as borrowing, would create other long-term pressures on state spending).

For example, a legal adviser searching for a claim in human rights might consider the possibility that the state has failed to collect sufficient revenue through taxation as a matter of political choice, out of incompetence or bad faith. Alternatively, the adviser might consider the possibility that the state has enacted laws that would raise enough revenue were they fully implemented, but implementation has been incomplete due to a lack of administrative capacity, bad faith, or a combination of the two. If administrative capacity seems to be the reason for insufficient revenue collection, the adviser might look to the reasons underlying implementation problems, which might lead back to an inquiry about political choices.

Finding an ultimate culprit in all probability will turn out to be an impossible quest. Human rights failures of the type potentially playing out for a large segment of the population of Zambia seem to occur not because of one reason or because of the actions of one actor or institution, but because of a multiplicity of such reasons and actions. Even so, sorting out who owes what to whom is the point and purpose of law. If the tax system is in some way at fault for the human rights situation in Zambia, it seems appropriate to search the law for some means to assign responsibility and seek redress.

1. Legislated Rights

In Zambia, as in most countries, the most relevant primary legal sources of taxpayer rights are legislated. The Constitution of 1996, as amended through 2016,[21] and the International Covenant on Economic, Social and Cultural Rights (ICESCR), to which Zambia is a party, are two main sources of rights in Zambia.[22] The Constitution includes a bill of rights, which sets out protections for civil and political rights and a judicial path for redress.[23] The 1996 Constitution also laid out a series of economic and social right undertakings, stating for instance that the state "shall endeavour to provide clear and safe water, adequate medical and health facilities and decent shelter for all persons."[24] These provisions were removed in their entirety from the 2016 Constitution, however, and a referendum to enact a new bill of rights is yet to be adopted.[25]

Explicit economic and social rights protections are thus notably absent in current Zambian law. The absence of undertakings with respect to education reappears in the context of the

ICESCR, to which Zambia has made a very specific reservation indicating its intention to post-pone any obligations with respect to primary education on resourcing grounds.[26]

All human rights undoubtedly depend on the deployment of resources for their protection, so all undertakings that a state might make with respect to human rights are implicit promises to ensure that adequate resources are gathered and deployed in the service of those rights. Magdalena Sepúlveda Carmona, in her capacity as the former UN Special Rapporteur on extreme poverty and human rights, stated in 2014, "States that claim resource constraints have the burden of proof to show that every effort has been made to move towards the full enjoyment of economic, social and cultural rights as a matter of priority, and that they are truly unable rather than unwilling to meet these obligations."[27] Though the principle is sound, without a justici-able path to judicial scrutiny, it is difficult to predict how the promises of this statement can be realized.

Further, it is clear that the Zambian government does not make its tax policy choices in isolation or immune from external forces; it is instead heavily affected by its interaction with global markets and with other nations. In formulating tax policy, Zambian lawmakers do not simply follow the logic of internal political struggle any more than any other country would. Instead, they must constantly contend with the fact that they are in competition with other countries for inbound investment in local industries. Lawmakers must accordingly examine the extent to which their tax system, as one regulatory factor in firms' locational decisions, impacts investment and subsequent economic outcomes in their country.[28] As Zambia is like other countries in this respect, it should be expected that private firms will seek to persuade lawmakers to adopt regimes that are favorable to the firms, whether or not such regimes are ever ultimately assessed for their impact.

2. Systemic Pressures

Like most governments, Zambia would like to raise tax revenue from its natural resources as they enrich the global economy; on the other hand, it also seeks to attract foreign investment capital from the global economy. These two goals are universally shared and put virtually all governments in a policy quandary. On one hand, it takes financial resources to build and maintain the kind of physical, social, and legal infrastructure necessary to enable market transactions, including direct and indirect investment in local trade and industry. That makes taxation of international trade and commerce attractive, if not vitally necessary to sustain the state as a going concern. On the other hand, governments often want to avoid imposing tax where doing so might reduce the volume of trade and investment, thus reducing local employment and economic outcomes while putting their personal political careers at risk.[29]

Lawmakers therefore rely heavily on tax incentives of various types as tools to balance their economic and political goals. Some tax incentives are designed to attract "real" investment—that is, in business operations that involve property, equipment, and labor.[30] Others are designed to attract financial or legal transactions or arrangements, to which global profits may be attributed.[31] In both cases, the goal is to relieve tax on certain taxpayers or types of investments in hopes of gaining spillover effects of local employment and consumption, which can then be taxed to replace the lost revenues. The difficulty for Zambia, as it is for governments around the world, is that its own attempts to attract investment are constantly pressured or even undermined by the efforts of other states to do likewise. Moreover, even as governments navigate this impossible terrain, they must contend with the perpetual gap between expectation and reality in terms of their preferred tax rules and outcomes, as taxpayers work within and across borders to achieve favorable tax results. Thus even as governments seek to facilitate some kinds of tax avoidance behavior by enticing taxpayers with tax incentives, they must devise strategies to protect themselves against strategic behavior by taxpayers and other foreign governments alike. All governments are thus engaged in a global competition for capital, with the result an unwinnable race to the bottom in terms of tax. This worry has been the impetus for global tax coordination efforts spearheaded by the Organisation for Economic Co-operation and Development (OECD), most notably its recent effort to counter certain tax practices it identifies as contributing to tax "base erosion and profit shifting."[32]

Accordingly, the search for rights in tax does not stop at the boundaries of the state. If it is possible that the actions of a foreign state may be to blame, even in part, for human rights violations resulting from the failure to raise adequate public revenues, the search for human rights in tax will be forced beyond the domestic legal realm of constitutions, laws, and charters. NGOs concerned with human rights have sought accountability across territorial borders, but it has been a long—and to date unsuccessful—struggle, as discussed in the following part.

III. BEYOND THE STATE: INDIVIDUALS VS. FOREIGN STATES

NGOs have approached the tax situation in Zambia as mainly a product of tax avoidance by taxpayers facilitated by foreign governments that enable diversion of profits out of the Zambian tax base and into their own. The avenues for pursuing foreign governments for this kind of impact are few and obscure. Again, the case of Zambia is instructive, as a group of local and foreign NGOs sought a means to challenge foreign states for contributing to human rights violations in the country.[33]

The NGOs turned for this purpose to a relatively obscure soft law code of conduct that includes various best practices for multinationals: the OECD's Guidelines for Multinational Enterprises.[34] These Guidelines call upon multinationals to (among other undertakings) adhere to the OECD's "arm's length transfer pricing standards" wherever they operate, and to structure transactions consistent with economic principles unless there are specific local laws allowing deviation from this general rule. The Guidelines are nonbinding standards, but they provide a process for dispute resolution in cases where multinationals are perceived to be violating their terms.

A. NEGOTIATED CONFLICT RESOLUTION

In brief, the Guidelines provide: "Governments adhering to the Guidelines will implement them and encourage their use. They will establish National Contact Points that promote the Guidelines and act as a forum for discussion . . . The adhering Governments will also participate in appropriate review and consultation procedures to address issues concerning interpretation of the Guidelines in a changing world."[35] Accordingly, even though the Guidelines are nonbinding in formal legal terms, states have agreed that certain procedures will be available to challenge actions (or inactions) by the states that have signed on to them.[36]

The dispute resolution regime allows any person to bring a complaint concerning perceived violations of the Guidelines by multinationals, by lodging a request to a designated government official (referred to as a "National Contact Point" (NCP)) in the multinational's home state.[37]

This offers a kind of third-party standing that is unusual in taxation regimes.[38] The mechanism itself appears rather ineffectual, but NGOs are persistent, and if they meet success, opportunities could be created for additional third-party standing suits.

The NCP's job is to "[r]espond to enquiries about the Guidelines from: a) other National Contact Points; b) the business community, worker organisations, other non-governmental organisations and the public; and c) governments of non-adhering countries."[39] Thus any person who thinks a multinational is engaged in behavior inconsistent with the Guidelines may make a complaint to the NCP in the country or countries where the target multinational is organized or operates. The Guidelines state that NCPs "will" respond to enquiries from the public and assess issues raised, and, if the National Contact Point decides that the issues merit further review, will consult with the complainant and with the multinational about the issue raised, facilitate mediation, come to a decision, and publish their results.[40]

In providing this assistance, the Guidelines state that the NCP will "[m]ake an initial assessment of whether the issues raised merit further examination and respond to the parties involved . . . consult with these parties . . . facilitate access to consensual and non-adversarial means, such as conciliation or mediation [and] make the results of the procedures publicly available."[41] All of these undertakings should be evident in the event any cases are brought to the NCP.

An independent organization, OECD Watch, catalogues NCP complaints made under the Guidelines.[42] A search of their collection of documents reveals that most of the complaints raising taxation as an issue seem to involve conflict minerals and corruption charges (including bribery and financing armed rebels), but the process is also being used to challenge international tax planning by multinationals, specifically with respect to transfer pricing. A case in point involves Glencore, a commodities broker based in Switzerland, with operations in Zambia.

B. CASE STUDY: GLENCORE

In 2011, four NGOs worked together to launch a complaint under the Guidelines—in OECD terms, a "Specific Instance"—against Glencore International AG and First Quantum Minerals Ltd., in respect of their 90 percent stake in Mopani Copper Mines Plc. in Zambia.[43] The NGOs were the Center for Trade Policy and Development (Zambia), the Berne Declaration (Switzerland), l'Entraide Missionnaire (Canada), and Mining Watch (Canada). The complaint was made before the Swiss and Canadian National Contact Points, because Switzerland and Canada are the home countries of Glencore International AG and First Quantum Minerals Ltd., respectively.

Glencore International AG is one of the world's largest suppliers of commodities and raw materials. First Quantum Minerals Ltd. is in the business of mineral extraction and development, and produces copper, gold, and sulfuric acid.[44] Together, Glencore and First Quantum directly or indirectly owned 90 percent of the shares in Mopani Copper Mines Plc., the largest mining corporation operating in Zambia and one of the country's largest producers of copper and cobalt.[45]

In their Specific Instance, the NGOs alleged that Glencore and First Quantum, through their controlling interest, caused Mopani Copper Mines to manipulate its financial accounts in order to avoid taxation in Zambia by defying the arm's-length transfer pricing standard required by the Guidelines.[46] An audit conducted by international accountants at the request of the Zambian authorities in 2008 concluded that Mopani employs various techniques in order to avoid paying taxes in Zambia, including overestimation of operating costs, underestimation of production volumes, transfer pricing manipulation, and breach of arm's-length transfer pricing standards.[47] The complainants argue that these actions were in breach of provisions in the OECD Guidelines concerning Taxation and General Policies.[48]

In their complaint, the NGOs asked the National Contact Points to do three things. First, they wanted the National Contact Points to formally recognize that Glencore International AG and First Quantum Minerals Ltd. had committed violations of the OECD Guidelines.[49] Second, they sought to have the NCPs ensure "by all necessary means" that Glencore International AG and First Quantum Minerals Ltd. refund the tax money the Mopani group should have paid to the Zambian Revenue Authority had the companies' transactions been lawfully conducted, and had transfer pricing not been manipulated.[50] Finally, they wanted the NCPs to require Glencore International AG and First Quantum Minerals Ltd. to commit themselves to "comply scrupulously" with the OECD Guidelines and with Zambian laws and regulations going forward.[51]

The Swiss and Canadian NCPs agreed among themselves that the Swiss NCP would take the lead in handling the complaint.[52] In October 2011, the Swiss NCP concluded its confidential initial assessment and accepted the complaint.[53] In July 2012, both parties (the NGOs and the two companies) accepted the Swiss NCP's offer to facilitate mediation.[54] The NCP convened a meeting of the parties, led by an external mediator. According to the complainants, the company rejected all of the complainants' allegations without providing any evidence in support of their position.[55]

The Swiss NCP concluded in November 2012, that, in the words of OECD Watch, "the parties agreed to disagree."[56] OECD Watch reported that "the complainants are disappointed that the agreement did not go further than an agreement to disagree. They feel that the result shows that there is little value in engaging in a dialogue with the companies on these issues. According to the complainants, the company has not complied with its commitment as part of the agreement to respond to a detailed set of questions regarding its tax payments."[57] The OECD procedure thus ended with no resolution, and no mechanism for appeal on procedural or substantive grounds. Even so, there do not seem to be any barriers (other than resource constraints of would-be complainants) to reopening the case by simply filing a new complaint.

Other NCP complaints on similar grounds have ended similarly. For instance, a complaint was lodged with the UK National Contact Point against National Grid Transco in 2003 in connection with its acquisition of Copperbelt Energy Co. (CEC) in Zambia, stating that "financial and tax incentives given to CEC are alleged to have resulted in an unstable macroeconomic environment by having increased the tax burden on the poor, having introduced discriminatory treatment and massive externalisation of funds."[58] The case was closed by the UK NCP in 2005 "for 'want of prosecution.' "[59] It is not clear what that means. Another case, NiZA et al. vs. Chemie Pharmacie Holland (CPH), a conflict minerals complaint opened in 2003, sought clarification of whether tax payments made by CPH subsidiaries in the Democratic Republic of the Congo were consistent with the Guidelines.[60] The case was first accepted but then quickly rejected by the Dutch NCP in 2004, for "lack of an investment nexus."[61]

Finally, a complaint brought by War on Want and Change to Win against Alliance Boots was opened in November 2013 and quickly rejected by the UK National Contact Point for offering only "unsubstantiated" allegations.[62] The NGOs had alleged that Alliance Boots violated the Guidelines' disclosure and tax provisions, by, *inter alia*, failing to act

> in accordance with the spirit of UK taxation laws by shifting profits to offshore tax havens using
> complex financial instruments, shell financial companies in Luxembourg, and payments from one

party to another to finance the purchase of company debt in a circular manner. The complainants sought mediation to bring concrete reforms of the company's governance, tax, and disclosure procedures so they are aligned with the Guidelines.[63]

This is a useful case for observers of the emerging links between tax justice and human rights, but further action requires the NGO to reopen the case with "substantiated" allegations, which seems all but impossible to do given the confidentiality that typically surrounds corporate tax planning.

C. CASE STUDY: AFRIMEX

At least one NGO seems to have had a modicum of success within the OECD parameters. Global Witness brought a complaint against Afrimex, a UK company operating in the Democratic Republic of the Congo, regarding tax payments made by Afrimex to an "armed rebel group with a well-documented record of carrying out grave human rights abuses."[64] The UK National Contact Point agreed with many of Global Witness' charges and concluded that "Afrimex failed to contribute to the sustainable development in the region; to respect human rights; or to influence business partners and suppliers to adhere to the Guidelines."[65]

Global Witness later followed up with Afrimex, and the company said that it had stopped trading in minerals. But Global Witness appeared skeptical:

> [T]he case illustrates the severe limitations of relying on voluntary guidelines to hold companies to account. The OECD Guidelines for Multinational Enterprises thus remain a weak, non-binding mechanism. The NCP does not have the legal powers to enforce decisions arising from its conclusions and there is no in-built mechanism for following up its recommendations. The UK government will have to take further action to ensure that the investigation and conclusions of the NCP are more than just a theoretical exercise.[66]

This suggests that the OECD process may not be a promising mechanism for those seeking to challenge the ways in which multinationals use international tax planning to avoid paying tax in poor countries. Alternatively, the cases to date may simply demonstrate that stronger cases or arguments are needed to test the limits of the OECD process. In any case, to date the OECD process appears to be the only readily available option for third parties to put legal pressure on what they view as systemic contributors to objectionable multinational tax avoidance.

Instead, individuals are likely limited to social activism, placing pressure on their own governments to act to protect the tax base. Using social pressure is perhaps not a very hopeful strategy to employ against the governments in poor countries, where officials cannot necessarily be expected to put resources into fighting battles of principle against their economically and politically stronger allies and trade partners. Protest has, however, become a successful strategy in some richer countries where activist groups have managed to put items on the global tax agenda. Their belief is that advancing their agenda may help poorer counties to raise more revenues from multinationals, which they hope will be spent on fulfilling human rights. Recent international developments in state-state relations on tax are a testament to the viability of activism in influencing political agenda setting; whether expected revenue gains and desired spending decisions follow remains to be seen.

IV. BY THE STATE: INTER-NATION PURSUIT OF RIGHTS

The Multinational Guidelines discussed above are one example of how the OECD coordinates global tax cooperation. It furthers this task through a model tax treaty, commentaries thereto, and numerous guidelines. Its most recent initiative seeks to counter certain forms of "Base Erosion and Profit Shifting" (BEPS). In response to past criticisms of its exclusive and insular grip on the development of the global tax policy norms that led to BEPS, the OECD invited selected nonmember states to participate in developing its initiative. It now invites all countries of the world to sign on to a new framework it is building for BEPS implementation.[67]

The BEPS Project should be seen as a culmination of many years of deliberation at the OECD regarding what types of tax competition are acceptable among sovereign states. While not explicitly stated, this deliberation emerged from an implicit notion that sovereign states have obligations to one another owing to their mutual sovereignty. A closer inspection of the OECD's efforts highlights the normative shortfalls that ultimately make OECD-led tax cooperation difficult to square with the search for human rights in tax.

A. DUTY TO COOPERATE

The OECD's work on defining what is "fair" in international taxation can be traced to its 1998 initiative on tax havens, during which the OECD advanced the idea that "countries may be forced by spillover effects to modify their tax bases, even though a more desirable result could have been achieved through intensifying international co-operation."[68] "Spillover effect" is an economics term that generally connotes the impact of one state's policy actions on the economic outcomes of other states.[69] The OECD's expressed fear was that one state could design tax policies that would undermine the policymaking autonomy of another, thus violating the latter's sovereignty.

The OECD accordingly argued that states might be obligated to refrain from actions that impede or adversely impact the tax efforts or economic outcomes of others.[70] By 2006, the OECD had concluded that "tax competition between countries [must be] based upon transparent and internationally accepted standards . . . to counter the increased cross-border opportunities to unlawfully avoid or evade national taxes enacted by democratically elected legislatures."[71] In a 2011 report to G20 countries, the International Monetary Fund (IMF), World Bank, OECD, and United Nations together encouraged G20 members to undertake spillover analyses "of any proposed changes to their tax systems that may have a significant impact on the fiscal circumstances of developing countries . . . in moving, for instance, from residence to territorial systems."[72] The BEPS Project reasserts and refines spillover analysis by first defining specified obligations among states and then measuring and monitoring the fulfillment or failure of these obligations via peer review.[73]

These events may be characterized as an effort of some states to protect their own sovereign prerogatives by forcing others to comply with a set of standards that the former states designed, implemented, and monitored.[74] In its 1998 report, in the series of successive reports it produced on Harmful Tax Practices through 2006, and in BEPS, the OECD offers no normative explanation for determining which states are entitled to curb the sovereignty of others. The earlier reports implied that since the sovereignty of some OECD member states appeared to be at risk from the actions of some nonmember states, the former had entitlements that the latter were duty-bound to respect.[75] But BEPS now justifies the OECD's development of international standards to be universally implemented on grounds that all states are at risk of having their sovereignty undermined by all others.[76] The global adherence to the minimum standards of BEPS, as monitored by peer review, could provide a laboratory for testing that theory.

B. SETTING STANDARDS AND MONITORING

The BEPS minimum standards signal the OECD's commitment to expanding international acceptance of the idea that states may owe certain obligations to each other with respect to taxation.[77] The minimum standards are laid out in four categories: country-by-country (CbC) reporting, tax treaty abuse, harmful tax practices, and cross-border tax dispute resolution. These minimum standards develop a framework for cross-border cooperation that could potentially be used to challenge the kinds of practices for which NGOs unsuccessfully sought redress in the National Contact Point process. However, this potential will depend very much on whether and how the OECD will defend its standards against noncompliance by states. To date, the contemplated compliance mechanism appears to be peer pressure. Depending on the item for which compliance is sought, peer pressure could be seen as a useful and viable tool to further human rights protections, or it could be viewed as antithetical to that end.

The first of these standards, CbC reporting, is most clearly the product of international tax justice advocacy groups, including those that sought to shed light on the mining sector in Zambia.[78] As such, this might be the most promising aspect of the BEPS work in terms of using peer pressure to protect that which law currently does not protect. The core idea of CbC reporting is that multinationals should disclose how much tax they pay in each country in which they operate, and that every country in which a multinational operates should have equal access to the information of the group. Tax justice advocacy groups have consistently called for CbC disclosure to be public on grounds that public scrutiny is a necessary check on an otherwise obscure global system in which governments accept and even facilitate tax avoidance by major multinationals.[79] In contrast, the OECD has so far indicated its intent to limit CbC reporting to governments, and attached strict use and confidentiality limitations on grounds that taxpayers must retain these rights.[80]

The OECD's proposed structure makes CbC a solely government-to-government exercise, and may leave the essential problem of protecting taxpayer rights unresolved because it stops short of building public accountability into the tax system. As originally conceived by tax justice advocates, CbC reporting was designed as an accounting disclosure regime, following the successful adoption of similar transparency norms in the extractive industries.[81] The purpose of disclosure was to compel companies to view the payment of tax, especially in poorer countries, as a component of good tax management. The OECD's version of confidential data sharing among BEPS associate governments eliminates this accountability mechanism for the time being, but many expect that some form of CbC reporting will eventually become public.

The OECD's other minimum standards may be less promising as potential bases upon which third parties could lodge future human rights claims against countries that appear to fall below a given international tax standard. Even so, the fact that these standards call for states to respond in a specified way makes them potential candidates. For example, the second minimum standard is a renewed effort to address harmful tax practices by adopting a specified nexus rule for tax incentives relating to intellectual property (IP).[82] This standard is articulated as a quest to develop a "level playing field" upon which countries may use their tax systems to attract inward investment, but only to the extent such efforts are aimed at real investment as opposed to paper profits.[83] Critics view the OECD's framework as tacit acceptance of a form of tax competition that happens to be favored by OECD countries. Certainly, regimes designed to attract IP-related investment are proliferating among OECD member states.[84] The current focus of policymakers and scholars seems to be on the means and methods for making these regimes compliant with the OECD standard rather than examining their effects on other countries, but ongoing peer monitoring and public pressure could alter that course in the future.

Similarly, the OECD's minimum standard addressing the problem of abuses of the bilateral tax treaty system is of potential value to those considering future tax-based human rights complaints. As defined by the OECD, abuse generally connotes planning by taxpayers that was in some fashion not intended (or is no longer accepted) by the parties to the affected treaties. The OECD proposes to counter these vulnerabilities by revising the terms of treaties going forward to exclude certain business formations or transactions from treaty coverage.[85] Peer monitoring of countries' progress in adopting these provisions could provide NGOs with additional information to pursue public campaigns against tax planning by multinationals in the name of human rights.

In the meantime, the attention to treaty-based tax minimization at the OECD has also renewed interest in and focused the applicability of spillover analysis on tax treaties between richer and poorer states. The Netherlands and Ireland undertook such analyses to investigate the effects of their tax systems, and specifically their treaty regimes, on the economies of developing countries. Each ultimately concluded that their domestic policies should not be considered overly detrimental, especially in comparison with the actions of other states, but each has resolved in various ways to bring equity issues into their future dealings with less affluent countries.[86] Similarly, in 2017 the UK Parliament considered but rejected the Double Taxation Treaties (Developing Countries) Bill, which would have required the government to assess and report on the impact of British tax treaties with developing countries, on grounds that the United Kingdom has a duty "to have regard to reducing poverty overseas in entering negotiations [and] to assess and report on reducing poverty before a treaty is signed."[87] These analyses and legislative proposals seem to be direct responses to the public pressure created by NGOs regarding the effects of the international tax regime on countries like Zambia. While little of substance has been achieved to date, the embedding of these principles in the OECD peer-monitoring process lays some groundwork for further public pressure and future legal reforms.[88]

C. RIGHT TO PARTICIPATE

Finally, the OECD has created an "Inclusive Framework" whereby all non-OECD countries that are willing to sign on to the BEPS Action Plans will become BEPS Associates and participate in implementing the BEPS standards and engage in peer monitoring and review.[89] This framework is subject to the criticism that BEPS Associates are invited to join an initiative with an agenda they were not invited to develop.[90] On the other hand, once created, the framework might facilitate the participation of stakeholders beyond member country government representatives and private sector tax professionals, namely, the nongovernmental sector.

Nongovernmental organizations such as the Tax Justice Network were instrumental in creating the sociopolitical conditions that led the OECD to develop the BEPS initiative, and they will have an interest in participating in tax governance going forward. At least some NGOs and independent researchers have called for an international tax organization that would bring together all countries to engage in cooperation and end tax competition.[91] The OECD's new Inclusive Framework may not be the one envisioned by these tax justice advocates, but it may ultimately prove to be adaptable to their purposes.

Despite the promise of a new inclusive framework, the OECD's planned measures to prevent BEPS will not necessarily result in reforms that will lead to more revenues for poor countries; moreover, the project currently says nothing about how revenues will be spent, whether in service of human rights or otherwise, but could theoretically contemplate such questions in the future. In keeping with the efforts of individuals to pursue human rights in tax, the efforts of states to navigate what is fair among themselves are similarly unsatisfactory. It seems that most of the avenues for finding human rights in tax either raise insurmountable legal difficulties or are unlikely to produce an adequate response to the identified problem.

V. CONCLUSION

The search for human rights in tax is a relatively recent phenomenon. The search for justice in tax, on the other hand, has been a perpetual subject of debate. With taxation a major means by which human obligations in community are expressed, we must expect continuous revisiting of core concepts, shared assumptions, and persistent failures to address ongoing harms. In contemporary discourse, the apparently increasing inability or unwillingness (or both) of states to tax the profits of the world's more profitable companies is in itself troubling. When this is combined with the observation that shortfalls in revenues have led to major failures in the support necessary to protect basic human rights, it is appropriate to question all of the regulatory regimes that might contribute to these conditions. Tax law is, as a result, a viable target for proponents of human rights, even if the solutions are far from obvious, the available institutions currently lacking in political and financial capacity, and the technical complexity overwhelming. Perhaps the only plausible conclusion that can be drawn about how taxation is, or could be, connected to human rights is that far more study is needed. Such study will inevitably look beyond the confines of the state and seek ways to incorporate multinationals into the picture more directly. NGOs have taken up this challenge in various ways, and are now actively pursuing alternatives to challenge ongoing human rights failures across the globe with taxation as a potential subject of interest.[92] It remains to be seen how the legal system will mediate this emerging area of inquiry.

NOTES

1. It is also possible to raise human rights issues with nonstate actors, that is, corporations. Litigants may raise private law actions against company practices, shareholders may launch actions in respect of fiduciary responsibilities of managers, or individuals may use nonlegal processes to pressure companies to adhere to corporate social responsibility norms. See, e.g., A. Christians, 'Tax Activism and the Global Movement for Development through Transparency', *in* M. Stewart and Y. Brauner (eds.), *Tax, Law and Development* (2013), 288.
2. As a result, for purposes of this discussion, I equate the actions of a nongovernmental group or organization in pursuing a given human rights claim on behalf of one or a number of individuals to a claim based on the relationship between the individual and the other party, be it a corporate entity or a government.

3. For discussion and case studies, see A. Christians, 'Taxpayer Rights in the United States', *in* C. A. Jiménez (ed.), *Tax Law and Human Rights* (2016), available online at https://papers.ssrn.com/sol3/papers.cfm?abstract_id=2809750 (last visited 15 January 2019); A. Christians, 'Taxpayer Rights in Canada', *in* C. A. Jiménez (ed.), *Tax Law and Human Rights* (2016), available online at https://papers.ssrn.com/sol3/papers.cfm?abstract_id=2797381 (last visited 15 January 2019).

4. Canadian Charter of Rights and Freedoms, Part I of the Constitution Act, 1982, being Schedule B to the Canada Act, 1982, c. 11 (UK), at arts. 7 and 8.

5. As discussed below, the provisions in the Charter will be familiar to scholars of international human rights law as they are laid out in the Universal Declaration of Human Rights, UN Doc. A/RES/217 (III), 10 Dec. 1948 [hereinafter UDHR].

6. One prominent book on the philosophy of taxation argues that the state has a justifiable claim of right to tax because it contributes to economic outcomes by providing the laws, institutions, and mechanisms necessary to enable market transactions. L. B. Murphy and T. Nagel, *The Myth of Ownership: Taxes and Justice* (2002).

7. See, e.g., Order in Council, PC 1962-1334, reprinted in Canada, Royal Commission on Taxation, Report (Ottawa: Queen's Printer, 1966) (Chair: Kenneth LeM Carter), vol. 1 at v (stating that "[t]axation is one method of transferring command over goods and services from individuals and families to the state. If equity were not of vital concern taxes would be unnecessary. The state could simply commandeer what it needed. The burden of a reduced private command over goods and services would then be borne by those individuals and families who happened to be within easy reach of the state.").

8. Harms to those beyond the polity are a distinct issue addressed in later parts of this chapter.

9. The definition of a taxpayer also typically includes legal entities including corporations, trusts, partnerships, and other business and investment organizations. For this reason, taxpayer rights are by definition not limited to individual rights.

10. For a discussion, see A. Cockfield, 'Protecting Taxpayer Privacy Rights Under Enhanced Cross Border Tax Information Exchange: Toward A Multilateral Taxpayer Bill of Rights', 42(2) *U.B.C. Law Review* (2010), 419, at 420: "tax information, which includes a taxpayer's income and an individual's personal circumstances (e.g. to support a claim for a disability tax credit), is a particularly sensitive form of personal information, and can be used to build a detailed profile of individual identity, including religious and political beliefs."

11. Including, for example, art. 8 ECHR (protecting the right to respect for private life, family life, home, and correspondence, and providing that "there shall be no interference by a public authority with the exercise of this right except such as is in accordance with the law and is necessary in a democratic society in the interests of national security, public safety, or the economic well-being of the country, for the prevention of disorder or crime, for the protection of health or morals, or for the protection of the rights and freedoms of others.").

12. The tax literature related to this topic, while still sparse, has recently expanded and revealed recurring issues across jurisdictions. The seminal work on the topic is D. Bentley, *Taxpayer Rights: Theory, Origin and Implementation* (2007). For a recent comparative study, see P. Baker and P. Pistone, *The Practical Protection of Taxpayers' Fundamental Rights* (International Fiscal Association, 2015), available online at http://www.cfe-eutax.org/sites/default/files/Session%20II_IFA%20General%20Report%202015%2C%20Baker%20Pistone%2C%20The%20practical%20protection%20of%20taxpayers%C2%B4%20fundamental%20rights.pdf.

13. See, e.g., Australian Tax Office, *Australian Taxpayers' Charter*, available online at https://www.ato.gov.au/About-ATO/Commitments-and-reporting/Taxpayers--charter/ (last visited 15 January 2019); Canada Revenue Agency, *Taxpayer Bill of Rights*, available online at http://www.cra-arc.gc.ca/rights/ (last visited 15 January 2019); HM Revenue and Customs, *Your Charter*, available online at https://www.gov.uk/government/publications/your-charter/your-charter (last visited 16 May 2017); IRS, *Your Rights as a Taxpayer*, available online at https://www.irs.gov/pub/irs-pdf/p1.pdf (last visited 15 January 2019). Most are administrative pronouncements rather than legislative acts. This is in keeping with the role of taxpayer charters, which are "concerned with tax administration and collection [and] aim to enhance the taxpayer/revenue authority relationship": D.

Bentley, *The Significance of Declarations of Taxpayers' Rights and Global Standards for the Delivery of Tax Services by Revenue Authorities* (2002), available online at http://epublications.bond.edu.au/cgi/viewcontent.cgi?article=1034&context=law_pubs, at 2. Bentley adds that "Declarations of Taxpayers' Rights are not intended to expand legal or administrative rights. They usually only restate existing rights and set out service standards [and they] usually reiterate strongly the obligations of taxpayers": at 3.

14. The purpose of undertaking a case study is to study "an instance of a class of events [which is] a phenomenon of scientific interest . . . with the aim of developing theory (or 'generic knowledge') regarding the causes of similarities or differences among instances (cases) of that class of events": A. L. George and A. Bennett, *Case Studies and Theory Development in the Social Sciences* (2005), 5. For a discussion of the use of case studies to develop theory in international tax, see A. Christians, 'Case Study Research and International Tax Theory', 55 *Saint Louis University Law Journal* (2011), 331.

15. Zambia is likely best known from the outside as a leading source of copper—a vital ingredient in every power grid and, more personally, every electronic device in use across the planet. Zambia exports several billion dollars' worth of copper every year: World Bank Group, *Powering the Zambian Economy* (6th Zambia Economic Brief, 2015), available online at http://documents.worldbank.org/curated/en/551761468197338422/pdf/101704-WP-P157243-PUBLIC-Box394818B-World-Bank-Zambia.pdf.

16. See War on Want, *Extracting Minerals, Extracting Wealth: How Zambia Is Losing $3 Billion a Year from Corporate Tax Dodging* (2015), available online at http://www.waronwant.org/sites/default/files/WarOnWant_ZambiaTaxReport_web.pdf; M. Hill, *Zambia Says Tax Avoidance Led by Miners Costs $2 Billion a Year*, 25 Nov. 2012, cited in ibid., at 6; *Zambia's Tax Losses*, 30 Apr. 2013, available online at http://www.ft.com/cms/s/0/93b47d9a-b196-11e2-b324-00144feabdc0.html (last visited 15 January 2019); ActionAid, *ActionAid Exposes Tax Avoidance by Associated British Food Group in Zambia*, 14 Feb. 2013, available online at https://www.actionaid.org.uk/latest-news/actionaid-exposes-tax-avoidance-by-associated-british-food-group-in-zambia (last visited 15 January 2019); *Tax Avoidance by Multinational Companies Still Rampant in Zambia—ActionAid*, 6 May 2013, available online at https://www.lusakatimes.com/2013/05/06/tax-avoidance-by-multinational-companies-still-rampant-in-zambia-action-aid/ (last visited 15 Janaury 2019); C. Guldbrandsen, *Stealing Africa—Why Poverty?* (2013), available online at http://www.youtube.com/watch?v=WNYemuiAOfU (lasted visited 15 Janaury 2019) (documenting the efforts of an NGO to challenge the low taxation of the Zambian copper mining industry); A. Odiot and A. Gallet, *Good Copper, Bad Copper* (2012), available online at http://www.youtube.com/watch?v=uamzirLswjk (last visited 15 January 2019) (outlining the environmental, health and economic impacts of copper mining in Zambia and tracing the international tax structure of Glencore, a major mining company operating in Zambia but headquartered in Switzerland).

17. World Bank, *Zambia*, available online at http://data.worldbank.org/country/Zambia (last visited 15 January 2019) (estimated per capita gross national income of US$1,300 in 2017).

18. CIA World Factbook, available online at https://www.cia.gov/library/publications/resources/the-world-factbook/geos/za.html (last visited 15 January 2019).

19. UNDP, *Human Development Report 2014—Sustaining Human Progress: Reducing Vulnerabilities and Building Resilience* (2012), available online at http://hdr.undp.org/sites/default/files/hdr14-report-en-1.pdf, at 181 (last visited 15 January 2019); UNDP Human Development Indicators: Zambia, at http://hdr.undp.org/en/countries/profiles/ZMB (last visited 15 January 2019). The primary school dropout rate is 44.5%, while 40% of the country's children suffer from malnutrition and 12 percent of adults (aged 15–49) suffer from HIV: ibid.

20. African Development Bank Group, *Annual Report 2014* (2014), available online at http://www.afdb.org/fileadmin/uploads/afdb/Documents/Generic-Documents/Annual_Report_2014_-Full.pdf, at 25 (last visited 15 January 2019); see also CIA World Factbook, https://www.cia.gov/library/publications/the-world-factbook/rankorder/2172rank.html (last visited 15 January 2019).

21. Constitution of Zambia 1996; Constitution of Zambia 2016.

22. 1966, 999 UNTS 3.

23. Constitution of Zambia of 1996, at art. III (unamended in the Constitution of 2016).
24. Constitution of 1996, at art. 112, repealed in the Constitution of 2016 at para. 8 ("The Constitution is amended by the repeal of Parts VI to XIV inclusive").
25. Referendum of 11 August 2016. As a result, under current law there appears to be no mechanism for legal challenges of failures by the Zambian government to provide certain fundamentally necessary resources.
26. United Nations Treaty Collection, *International Covenant on Economic, Social and Cultural Rights (New York, 16 December 1966), Declarations and Reservations*, available online at https://treaties.un.org/Pages/ViewDetails.aspx?src=IND&mtdsg_no=IV-3&chapter=4&lang=en#EndDec ("Zambia . . . reserves the right to postpone the application of article 13 (2) (a) of the Covenant, in so far as it relates to primary education; since . . . the problems of implementation, and particularly the financial implications, are such that full application of the principles in question cannot be guaranteed at this stage.").
27. Human Rights Council, Report of the Special Rapporteur on Extreme Poverty and Human Rights, Magdalena Sepúlveda Carmona, UN Doc. A/HRC/26/28, 22 May 2014, at para. 26.
28. The degree to which various tax factors influence firms' location decisions continues to be a matter of debate among economists. Tax policy seems clearly central to such decisions where other factors such as labor pool, property protections, and ease of business operations are more or less equal. For a recent discussion and overview of studies, see R. B. Davies and N. Killeen, *Location Decisions of Non-Bank Financial Foreign Direct Investment: Firm-Level Evidence from Europe* (UCD School of Economics, Working Paper 15/26, Nov. 2015), available online at http://www.ucd.ie/t4cms/WP15_26.pdf ("The probability of a country being chosen as the location for a new foreign affiliate is found to be negatively associated with higher corporate tax rates and geographic distance but increases with the size and financial development of the host country. The financial regulatory regime in the host country and gravity related controls such as the home and host country sharing a common legal system, language, border and currency are also found to impact the likelihood of non-bank financial FDI": at 1).
29. The literature on the impacts of taxation and tax incentives on FDI is inconclusive but suggests that taxation is not the only or even a main factor in locational decisions of multinational firms. See, e.g., B. A. Blonigen, 'A Review of the Empirical Literature on FDI Determinants', 33 *Atlantic Economic Journal* (2005), 383 (tax may be one determinant of location decisions, but other determinants such as infrastructure and talent pool are as or more important); M. M. Stack, G. Ravishankar, and E. J. Pentecost, 'FDI Performance: A Stochastic Frontier Analysis of Location and Variance Determinants', 47 *Applied Economics* (2015), 3229 (noting that firms make locational decisions based on, inter alia, economic strength, talent pool, and geographical factors); C. Bellak, M. Leibrecht, and J. P. Damijan, 'Infrastructure Endowment and Corporate Income Taxes as Determinants of Foreign Direct Investment in Central and Eastern European Countries', 32 *The World Economy* (2009), 267 (showing that higher taxes may not deter FDI where the host country boasts strong infrastructure). *Contra*, see J. Slemrod, 'Competitive Advantage and the Optimal Tax Treatment of the Foreign-Source Income of Multinationals: The Case of the United States and Japan', 91 *American Journal of Tax Policy* (1991), 113 ("It is nothing new to hear that taxes on business reduce the incentive to invest and innovate, and are therefore detrimental to a nation's economy"); M. A Desai and J. R. Hines Jr., 'Old Rules and New Realities: Corporate Tax Policy in a Global Setting', 57 *National Tax Journal* (2004), 937, at 957 (taxation of foreign income impedes productivity of US firms abroad as well as investment in the United States).
30. Free zones and tax holidays for manufacturing operations are common examples.
31. Incentives for insurance and financial services companies are common examples.
32. See A. Christians and S. Shay, 'Assessing BEPS: Origins, Standards, and Responses', 102A *Cahiers de droit fiscal international* (2017) (analyzing observations made by reporters from forty-eight countries regarding the origins of the BEPS Project).
33. The NGOs were the Center for Trade Policy and Development (Zambia), the Berne Declaration (Switzerland), l'Entraide Missionnaire (Canada), and Mining Watch (Canada). See OECD Watch, *Sherpa et al v Glencore & First Quantum Minerals*, available online at http://oecdwatch.org/cases/Case_209 (last visited 15 January 2019).

34. OECD, *OECD Guidelines for Multinational Enterprises* (2011 ed.), available online at http://www. oecd.org/daf/inv/mne/48004323.pdf. The Guidelines were updated in 2011 for the fifth time since they were first adopted in 1976.

35. Ibid. at 18.

36. Ibid. at 37, 71.

37. Ibid. at 71–75.

38. That is, while many states have so-called "whistleblower" laws that would allow (and sometimes reward) taxpayers to inform the authorities of suspected violations of the tax law by others, a taxpayer cannot typically sue the tax administration for its failure to pursue another taxpayer; it is typically seen as the administration's right to decide what cases to pursue and under what circumstances.

39. OECD, *supra* note 34, at 72.

40. Ibid. at 72: "The National Contact Point will contribute to the resolution of issues that arise relating to implementation of the Guidelines in specific instances in a manner that is impartial, predictable, equitable and compatible with the principles and standards of the Guidelines. The NCP will offer a forum for discussion and assist the business community, worker organizations, other nongovernmental organizations, and other interested parties concerned to deal with the issues raised in an efficient and timely manner and in accordance with applicable law."

41. Ibid. at 72–73.

42. OECD Watch, available online at http://oecdwatch.org/ (last visited 15 January 2019).

43. Sherpa et al., *Specific Instance Regarding Glencore International AG and First Quantum Minerals Ltd and their Alleged Violations of the OECD Guidelines for Multinational Enterprises via the Activities of Mopani Copper Mines Plc in Zambia*, 12 Apr. 2011, available online at https://www.oecdwatch. org/cases/Case_209 (last visited 15 January 2019).

44. First Quantum was the target of a prior Specific Instance in 2001, regarding the operating conditions of Mopani Copper Mines Plc. in Zambia. This was referred to in the 2011 Specific Instance Complaint. See ibid. at 3.2.

45. OECD Watch, *supra* note 33.

46. Specifically, the NGOs charged the companies with having violated the following provisions of the *Guidelines* (2000 ed.): Version 2000, Chapter II (General Policies) paras. 1, 5, 6; Chapter X (Taxation). See Sherpa et al., *supra* note 43, at 2.2.

47. European Investment Bank, *Mopani Copper Project: Summary of the Investigation of the Inspectorate General Fraud Investigation (IG/IN)*, 29 Jan. 2015, available online at http://www. eib.org/attachments/press/mopani_copper_mines_summary_of_the_main_findings_en.pdf, at 1 (last visited 15 January 2019): "At the end of 2008, an audit was commissioned by the Zambian Revenues Authority (the ZRA) on the Mining Industry in Zambia. This audit was conducted by Grant Thornton and Econ Poyry and took place from December 2008 to the end of 2009 and covered the tax years 2006/2007 and 2007/2008. On 9 February 2011, a draft version of the pilot audit report (the Leaked Draft Report), highlighting alleged irregularities concerning Mopani's operational costs, revenues, transfer pricing, employee expenses and overheads, was leaked to the press."

48. OECD, *supra* note 34, at Part II (General Policies) and Part X (Taxation).

49. Sherpa et al., *supra* note 43, at Part C: Plaintiffs' Demands (last visited 22 June 2017).

50. Ibid.

51. Ibid.

52. National Contact Point of Switzerland, *Final Statement: Specific Instance regarding Taxation Policy by Mopani Copper Mines Plc and Glencore International AG and First Quantum Minerals Ltd in Zambia*, 28 Nov. 2012, available online at https://www.oecdwatch.org/cases/Case_209, at para. 9 (last visited 15 January 2019).

53. Ibid. at para. 11.

54. Ibid. at paras. 12–16.

55. OECD Watch, *supra* note 33, see "Developments/Outcome."

56. Ibid.

57. Ibid.

58. OECD Watch, *CBE vs. National Grid Transco*, 25 July 2003, available online at http://oecdwatch. org/cases/Case_34 (last visited 15 January 2019).

59. Ibid. see "Developments/Outcome."

60. OECD Watch, *NiZA et al. vs. CPH*, 3 July 2003, available online at http://oecdwatch.org/cases/ Case_33 (last visited 15 January 2019).

61. Ministerie van Economische Zaken, *National Contact Point Statement*, at 1, 1 May 2004, available online at https://www.oecdwatch.org/cases/Case_33 (last visited 15 January 2019).

62. OECD Watch, *War on Want & Change to Win vs. Alliance Boots*, 28 Nov. 2013, available online at http://oecdwatch.org/cases/Case_314 (last visited 15 January 2019).

63. Ibid. See "Summary of the Case."

64. OECD Watch, *Global Witness vs. Afrimex*, 20 Feb. 2007, available online at http://oecdwatch.org/ cases/Case_114 (last visited 15 January 2019).

65. National Contact Point of the United Kingdom, *Final Statement by the UK National Contact Point for the OECD Guidelines for Multinational Enterprises: Afrimex (UK) Ltd*, available online at http:// oecdwatch.org/cases/Case_114, at 1 (last visited 15 January 2019).

66. Global Witness, *Faced with a Gun, What Can You Do? War and the Militarization of Mining in Eastern Congo*, at 69 (2009), available online at http://oecdwatch.org/cases-fr/Case_114/797/at_ download/file (last visited 15 January 2019).

67. OECD, *About BEPS and the Inclusive Framework*, available online at http://www.oecd.org/tax/ beps/beps-about.htm#membership (last visited 15 January 2019).

68. OECD, *Harmful Tax Competition: An Emerging Global Issue* (1998), available online at https:// www.oecd.org/tax/transparency/44430243.pdf, at 14 (last visited 15 January 2019).

69. However, it is also used more casually by noneconomists to connote the general impact of one state's policy choices on that of others.

70. All of these claims are explored in A. Christians, 'Sovereignty, Taxation and Social Contract', 18 *Minnesota Journal of International Law* 99 (2009), at 125 (discussing OECD claims that states should refrain from, inter alia, impeding a country's autonomy in the design of its tax system; adversely impacting the tax base in another country; creating externalities that allow the state to bear little of the cost of its own preferential tax regimes; allowing people to benefit from public goods without contributing to them; frustrating other country's audit procedures; distorting trade and investment with deliberately non-neutral tax regimes; causing a shift of targeted activities to economies outside the OECD area by employing an "unwarranted competitive advantage"; or limiting the effectiveness of the OECD's cooperative exercise (using "practices [that] are anti-competitive and can undercut the gains that tax competition generates").

71. OECD, *The OECD's Project on Harmful Tax Practices: 2006 Update on Progress in Member Countries* (2006), available online at http://www.oecd.org/ctp/harmful/37446434.pdf, at para. 3 (last visited 15 January 2019).

72. IMF, OECD, UN, and the World Bank, *Supporting the Development of More Effective Tax Systems: A Report to the G-20 Development Working Group* (2011), available online at http://www.oecd.org/ ctp/48993634.pdf.

73. For a discussion, see A. Christians, 'BEPS and the New International Tax Order', 6 *Brigham Young University Law Review* (2016), 1603 (outlining the process for peer review of the four "minimum standards" that were agreed to in BEPS, together with additional agreed monitoring areas).

74. OECD, *BEPS—Frequently Asked Questions*, available online at http://www.oecd.org/tax/beps/ beps-frequentlyaskedquestions.htm ("[The BEPS outputs] are soft law legal instruments. They are not legally binding but there is an expectation that they will be implemented accordingly by coun- tries that are part of the consensus. The past track record in the tax area is rather positive. . . . [A]ll OECD and G20 countries have committed to consistent implementation in the areas of preventing treaty shopping, Country-by-Country Reporting, fighting harmful tax practices and improving dispute resolution.") (last visited 15 January 2019).

75. I explored the failure of principled explanation of this logic in Christians, *supra* note 70.

76. OECD, *Action Plan on Base Erosion and Profit Shifting* (2013), available online at http://www.oecd.org/tax/beps/action-plan-on-base-erosion-and-profit-shifting-9789264202719-en.htm (last visited 15 January 2019).

77. Some of the Action items provide for actions to be executed by governments internally or in the future, while others do not directly call for governmental response with a minimum standard, recommendation, or best practice. The latter include Action 1 (addressing the tax challenges of the digital economy), Action 11 (Measuring and monitoring BEPS), Action 12 (Mandatory disclosure rules), Action 14 (Making dispute resolution mechanisms more effective), and Action 15 (Developing a multilateral instrument to modify bilateral tax treaties).

78. For an analysis of how these groups made their policy goals the subject of OECD attention, see Christians, *supra* note 1.

79. See Tax Justice Network, *Country by Country Reporting: Shedding Light onto Financial Statements* (2010), available online at http://www.taxresearch.org.uk/Documents/CBCDec2010.pdf (last visited 15 January 2019).

80. OECD, *Transfer Pricing Documentation and Country by Country Reporting, Action 13—2015 Final Report*, 5 Oct. 2015, available online at http://www.oecd.org/tax/transfer-pricing-documentation-and-country-by-country-reporting-action-13-2015-final-report-9789264241480-en.htm, at 5 (last visited 15 January 2019); OECD, *Action 13: Country-by-Country Reporting Implementation Package* (2015) [hereinafter, Action 13 Implementation Package], at 13 (including the above conditions in model legislation) and 19 (including the same conditions in a multilateral agreement to govern information exchange). In addition, the Action 13 Implementation Package contains a lengthy confidentiality and data safeguards questionnaire to "ensure the confidentiality of exchanged tax information and limit its use to appropriate purposes," ibid. at 23.

81. Task Force on Financial Integrity and Economic Development, *Country-by-Country Reporting: Holding Multinational Corporations to Account Wherever They Are* (June 2009), available online at https://financialtransparency.org/reports/country-by-country-reporting-holding-multinational-corporations-to-account-wherever-they-are/ (last visited 15 January 2019).

82. See OECD, *Countering Harmful Tax Practices More Effectively, Taking into Account Transparency and Substance, Action 5—2015 Final Report*, 5 Oct. 2015, available online at http://www.oecd.org/tax/countering-harmful-tax-practices-more-effectively-taking-into-account-transparency-and-substance-action-5-2015-final-report-9789264241190-en.htm (last visited 15 January 2019).

83. The minimum standard specifically calls for states to undertake two commitments. The first is to align domestic legal or administrative practices to a single standard, namely, the use of a "nexus" approach for allocating the income from intellectual property. See ibid. at 67.

84. Over the last fifteen years, sixteen countries have adopted intellectual property (IP) boxes; all are OECD member countries. In addition, India (a non-OECD member but a key BEPS associate country) released a budget in 2016 that proposed a patent box to be effective 1 April 2017. State, provincial, and national lawmakers in the United States and Canada have also considered adopting patent box regimes. For a discussion, see P. Merrill, 'Innovation Boxes: BEPS and Beyond', 69 *National Tax Journal* (2016), 4.

85. The minimum standard in this area involves an optional menu: it involves adopting in all new treaties (as well as the new OECD Model treaty and likely also the MLI) either: (1) a principle purpose test alone; (2) a principal purpose test combined with a limitation on benefits provision; or (3) a limitation on benefits provision combined with a specified anti-conduit rule. It is not yet clear what will happen if countries take inconsistent positions in their bilateral treaties. Nor is it clear how a multilateral treaty works with an array of options for the signatories.

86. See Netherlands Ministry of Foreign Affairs, *Evaluation Issues in Financing for Development: Analysing Effects of Dutch Corporate Tax Policy on Developing Countries* (IOB Study, Nov. 2013), available online at https://www.government.nl/documents/reports/2013/11/14/iob-study-evaluation-issues-in-financing-for-development-analysing-effects-of-dutch-corporate-tax-policy-on-developing-countries (last visited 15 January 2019); IBFD, *IBFD Spillover Analysis: Possible Effects of the Irish Tax System on Developing Economies* (July 2015), available online at http://www.budget.gov.ie/Budgets/2016/Documents/IBFD_Irish_Spillover_Analysis_Report_pub.pdf.

87. Double Taxation Treaties (Developing Countries) Bill 2016-17, HC Bill [16] cl. 1.

88. The final category of OECD minimum standards involves treaty-based dispute resolution. OECD, *Making Dispute Resolution Mechanisms More Effective, Action 14—2015 Final Report*, 5 Oct. 2015, available online at http://www.oecd.org/ctp/making-dispute-resolution-mechanisms-more-effective-action-14-2015-final-report-9789264241633-en.htm (last visited 15 January 2019). The OECD's goal is to implement streamlined procedures to respond to the increase in double taxation that is expected to occur as countries adopt anti-BEPS measures. It is not clear whether this minimum standard will benefit poorer states; the opposite is possibly the case. See, e.g., A. Christians, 'How Nations Share', 87 *Indiana Law Journal* (2012), 1407.

89. OECD, *supra* note 67.

90. Allison Christians and Laurens van Apeldoorn, The OECD Inclusive Framework, 72:4 Bulletin for Int'l Tax. 226 (2018).

91. See, e.g., Global Alliance for Tax Justice, *The world needs a United Nations Global Tax Body now: The most equitable way to create a fairer global tax system* (18 Apr. 2016), available online at http://www.taxjustice.net/wp-content/uploads/2013/04/GATJ-statement-GlobalTaxBodyPanamaPapers_18Apr2016.pdf; Oxfam, *An Economy for the 1%: How privilege and power in the economy drive extreme inequality and how this can be stopped*, 18 Jan. 2016, available online at https://www.oxfam.org/sites/www.oxfam.org/files/file_attachments/bp210-economy-one-percent-tax-havens-180116-summ-en_0.pdf, at 10 (calling on governments to create a global tax body).

92. See, e.g., Center for Economic and Social Rights, *Advancing Fiscal Justice Through Human Rights: An Overview of CESR's Publications* (2015), available online at http://www.cesr.org/sites/default/files/CESR.fiscal.justice.publications.pdf; International Bar Association, *Tax Abuses, Poverty and Human Rights: A Report of the International Bar Association's Human Rights Institute Task Force on Illicit Financial Flows, Poverty and Human Rights* (2013), available online at http://www.ibanet.org/Document/Default.aspx?DocumentUid=4977CB3D-4988-4C9C-84C7-9050A5CB2311 (last visited 15 January 2019); see also Report of the Special Rapporteur on extreme poverty and human rights, UN Doc. A/HRC/26/28, 22 May 2014 (by Magdalena Sepúlveda), available online at http://www.ohchr.org/EN/HRBodies/HRC/RegularSessions/Session26/Documents/A_HRC_26_28_ENG.doc.

PART 2

TAX ABUSE IN GLOBAL PERSPECTIVE

Cross-Border Dimensions and International Responses

CHAPTER 6

PROCURING PROFIT SHIFTING

The State Role in Tax Avoidance

ALEX COBHAM

I. INTRODUCTION

The most obvious frame for considering tax behavior is one which focuses on the behavior of taxpayers, both individuals and companies. But such a frame detracts and distracts from the ultimately more important role of the state—not least, as a procurer of profit shifting from other jurisdictions where companies' real economic activity takes place. This chapter focuses on the state role within the wider range of international tax injustices, before setting out a number of potential responses.

Tax is fundamental to the emergence of a state which is both able and willing to support the progressive realization of human rights—and the relationships here go far beyond revenue. The 4Rs of tax[1] provide a simple framework to consider these. Revenue is clearly crucial to states' ability to provide public services from effective administration and the rule of law to health, education, and infrastructure; as redistribution is crucial to contain or eradicate both horizontal and vertical inequalities. Less obvious may be the role of taxation in repricing—ensuring that the true public costs and benefits of social goods (like education) and ills (such as tobacco consumption and carbon dioxide emission) are reflected in market prices.

Perhaps the most important result of tax, however, is also often overlooked: political representation. Prolonged reliance on revenues from natural resources or foreign aid tends to undermine channels of responsive government, giving rise to corruption and broader failures of accountability.[2] The act of paying tax, especially direct taxes (those on income, profit, and capital gains) rather than indirect (e.g., consumption) taxes, leads taxpayers to see government as spending their money—and therefore to seek accountability for how that spending is made.

Short-term political pressures often militate against direct taxation, since indirect taxes like value-added tax (VAT) are less salient to voters. The potential longer-term benefits of direct taxes, in terms both of lower inequality and stronger representation, may be sacrificed to political expediency. Such a dynamic poses risks to countries with strong, long-established institutions of political representation; it also can present a major obstacle to development in countries with less well-established institutions.

A particular risk for the latter is that for decades the major multilateral and bilateral aid donors, led by the International Monetary Fund (IMF), promoted an entirely inappropriate "tax consensus" composed of the elimination of trade taxes (a major revenue source in lower-income countries); the introduction and expansion of VAT (even after the IMF's own research,[3] showed this to be revenue-negative for low-income countries already struggling with the lowest tax-GDP ratios); and the neglect and/or active erosion of direct taxes on income, profits, and capital gains.[4] The latter component aligned with the lobbying of multinationals and their "Big Four" accounting and professional services firms, adding to the pressure on governments not to pursue more effective and progressive tax policies.

This overall pressure creates a potentially vicious circle in which governments take short-term actions reflecting political calculations and external pressures, but which ultimately undermine their own legitimacy. The circle may be exacerbated by the growing inequality associated with promoting indirect taxes such as VAT at the expense of progressive, direct taxation. Higher inequality tends to be correlated with lower social trust, and lower trust with higher corruption/weaker governance.[5] The tax channel implies that policies giving rise to higher inequality will also tend to weaken governance.

Paying tax is a social act, reflecting common feeling and trust in others' compliance. And on the state side, levying taxes is also a social act—with the potential to build the social contract, or to poison it. Tax is therefore central to the progressive realization of human rights, through its influence on the *ability* of the state (through available revenues); on the *will* of the state (through the long-term emergence and sustenance of effective and accountable political representation); and on the *drivers* of state action (through expressed public sentiment).

But states also play a critical role in relation to one another's tax systems, through two main channels of extraterritorial impact. By the provision of financial secrecy to other states' citizens and taxpayers, a state can thwart those others' ability to pursue effective taxation and the progressive achievement of human rights that can follow (as well as key aspects of the rule of law). And through the procuring of profit shifting, on which this chapter focuses, a state may not only erode the revenue-raising ability of other states but also the latter's ability to pursue effective tax and industrial development policies more broadly, again undermining the progressive achievement of human rights.

This chapter begins with a brief history of the changing narratives of the state during the recent history of tax justice. An underlying issue is the importance of data. Here, as elsewhere, there is a direct and mutual relationship between inequalities of power and decisions over what is counted. For this reason, the tax justice policy agenda has included from the outset a strong focus on tax transparency measures. The most compelling evidence on the state role in procuring profit shifting is then laid out, with discussion of the scale of the more immediate human rights impacts. Finally, the scope for challenges to this state role is explored, and a variety of opportunities identified.

II. THE CHANGING PROFILE OF THE STATE IN TAX JUSTICE

The modern history of the international tax justice movement can usefully be seen as beginning in the late 1990s. Thematically, there are two main strands to consider: financial secrecy and corporate tax avoidance. While financial secrecy often features in avoidance strategies, it is more typically thought of as providing cover for the outright hiding of ownership of assets— whether to facilitate individual tax evasion, bribery, corrupt political conflicts of interest, abuses of antimonopoly and other market regulation, or the laundering of the proceeds of crime. Systematic tax avoidance, on the other hand, is the province of multinational companies, typically with the services of the "Big Four" accounting and audit firms.

Given this difference, it is perhaps not surprising that the role of the state has been conceived of quite differently in the two strands. Analysis of the provision of financial secrecy and its instruments, such as anonymous companies or numbered bank accounts, has tended to emphasize state responsibility for the resulting forms of corruption. Responsibility for avoidance, meanwhile, has largely been seen to lie with the tax (non)payers themselves.

In reality, there are state and tax payer/criminal roles in both areas. While financial secrecy is indeed provided directly, and only, by state actions, the role of international banks and professional services firms including the "Big Four" is well documented in the development of and active lobbying for specific secrecy instruments and weakening of financial regulation. Palan details the "commercialisation of sovereignty" in smaller financial centers.[6] Shaxson identifies a ratchet effect through which lobbyists use their success in one jurisdiction to push for change in others—not least egregiously, the role of PwC in manipulating Jersey law as a tool to achieve a new corporate form in the United Kingdom, uniquely combining both limited liability and limited transparency.[7]

The role of professional enablers in promoting financial secrecy finds a parallel of sorts in the role of the state in avoidance. While avoidance may be carried out by companies, using advice and structures marketed by their professional advisers, the central role of states in creating the conditions for successful avoidance should not be overlooked.

A. FINANCIAL SECRECY

Within the two areas, the perception of the state role—and therefore the aims and expectations of policymakers—have varied substantially over time. In the late 1990s, only financial secrecy was the focus of international concern. More specifically, secrecy had become a concern for rich countries, not least due to their mounting worries over tax evasion, and so it was the Organisation for Economic Co-operation and Development (OECD) that led a reform process.

That process, perhaps inevitably, focused overwhelmingly on non-OECD financial centers. In common with the work of the International Monetary Fund, pressure on "tax havens" reflected lists of jurisdictions that were drawn up without reference to any objectively verifiable criteria. Inevitably, this led to lists in which smaller, politically less influential jurisdictions were overrepresented; while major financial centers including many OECD members were simply absent.

This had significant consequences. First, independent experts and civil society actors viewed the approach as illegitimate, ineffective, and/or unjust; and second, smaller financial centers united politically around the argument for a "level playing field."[8] The immediate impact was that when the new George W. Bush administration in the United States withdrew support, the OECD process was quietly shelved with little external resistance.

The episode had longer-term consequences too. Among smaller centers, a degree of unity against external interference has persisted. Both the rhetoric of, and genuine commitment to, a level playing field, appear strong;[9] while the OECD itself fully adopted the same rhetoric.[10] At the same time, an increasingly engaged global tax justice movement has driven a meaningful focus on objectively verifiable indicators of secrecy.

The flagship publication of the Tax Justice Network (TJN), which had been formally established in 2003, is the Financial Secrecy Index (FSI). From the first discussions of the index in Nairobi in January 2007, it was envisaged as a direct challenge to the politically charged "tax haven" lists devised by international organizations including the OECD. The aim, instead, was to develop a set of indicators reflecting a standard to which all jurisdictions—including major OECD members themselves—could be held fairly accountable.[11]

Published every two years since 2009, with major media coverage and increasing use in both policy circles and academic research, the FSI has established itself as *the* global "tax haven" ranking. This put the state at the center of financial secrecy debates: no longer in terms of those jurisdictions too weak or ill-connected to escape being listed, but now on the basis of specific state actions and omissions.

In addition to setting a demonstrably level playing field for all assessed jurisdictions, the FSI has also played a role in shifting the tenor of discussions around corruption and financial secrecy. While major secrecy jurisdictions such as Switzerland and Singapore had long featured among the best performers on Transparency International's Corruption Perceptions Index, with poorer countries and those in sub-Saharan Africa overwhelmingly overrepresented among the worst performers, the FSI reflected instead the importance of high-income financial centers in driving and incentivizing corrupt behavior.

More generally, the rise of the FSI and the narrative of the level playing field coincided with the global financial crisis—which in turn precipitated a need for genuine, revenue-enhancing progress among OECD member states. This convergence led to the first international "tax haven" list based on objectively verifiable criteria, produced as the basis for the London G20's claim to be ending bank secrecy in 2009. And while the criterion chosen was extremely weak, this reflected primarily a lack of technical understanding from policymakers rather than a lack of political will[12]—and so marked an important turning point in the evolution of "list" approaches.

The necessary development of more meaningful jurisdiction assessments by the OECD has not solved the problem of the organization's apparent inability to call out the failures of its own members—but it has laid bare the necessary gymnastics. When the OECD heralded the leak of the Panama Papers in 2016 by labeling Panama as the last major financial center not to have signed up to its multilateral financial transparency process, there could be no hiding that the biggest OECD member—the United States—had not itself done so.

While the headline stories of the Panama Papers focused on individuals, many of them politicians from around the world, the policy response addressed the behavior of jurisdictions. The London anticorruption summit that followed, for example, saw the biggest commitment to date of countries outside the European Union to end the existence of anonymous company structures in their jurisdictions. In other words, notwithstanding the scrutiny of individuals that followed the leak, the Panama Papers clearly emphasized state responsibilities in creating the necessary conditions.

In the realm of financial secrecy, it seems likely that high-income countries will continue not to apply standards equally to themselves as to others. But this will be increasingly obvious, and embarrassing, with the emergence of a broad consensus on the key, objectively verifiable standards to be met.

B. CORPORATE TAX AVOIDANCE

The area of corporate tax avoidance has also seen significant change over time. News stories on egregious cases concerning individual multinationals are so commonplace today that it is easy to forget that the first major story was just ten years ago. On November 6, 2007, *The Guardian* ran a front-page story, resulting from a six-month investigation of the international banana trade supported by the Tax Justice Network, under the headline: "Revealed: how multinational companies avoid the taxman."[13] The "dog bites man" feel of the headline reflects just how little prior coverage of this issue there had been.

The headline also reflects the main narrative, which has persisted since: that tax avoidance is perpetrated *by* multinationals and *against* the state. Subsequent exposés—for example of Apple, SAB Miller, and Starbucks—were typically met with two responses: (1) companies have a duty to shareholders to minimize their tax, and (2) each multinational group abides by the law (and taxation) in each country where it operates. By implication, and sometimes explicitly, this response throws the onus back onto states: if you don't like the outcome of your rules, change them.

In general, such responses have been met with public skepticism. The shareholder duty element has largely fallen away. First, legal advice obtained by the Tax Justice Network from a top law firm provides a direct challenge to the claim.[14] Second, academic evidence has shown that shareholders do not benefit from lower effective tax rates—in fact, they face higher risks but no higher return.[15] Third, public awareness of the costs of tax avoidance has risen sharply, so that rather than seeing it as "smart" business, it is increasingly seen as antisocial business practice.

Recent developments have, however, for the first time, put a closer focus on the role of the state in avoidance: the LuxLeaks revelations showed how Luxembourg had approved hundreds of secret low- or zero-tax deals proposed by the "Big Four" accounting firms of major multinationals, led by PwC; and the European Commission's state aid investigations showed the Belgian and Irish states as directing substantial efforts to procure profit shifting from fellow EU member states. The Irish case, in which the Commission followed up on revelations by a US Senate committee investigation that a large share of Apple's profits are recorded in an Ireland-based entity without tax jurisdiction, was pivotal to this ongoing shift.

Finally, as the following section sets out, the phenomenon of profit shifting had itself changed over the period—from a marginal activity in the early 1990s, to a globally significant one by the late 2000s. By 2013, therefore, when fiscal pressures on high-income countries due to the financial crisis led the G20 to mandate the OECD to overhaul international tax rules, the emphasis was not on disciplining multinationals but on eliminating from state arrangements the deliberately created loopholes and the scope for abuse.

The single, agreed aim of the OECD Base Erosion and Profit Shifting initiative (BEPS) was to reduce the misalignment between the profits of multinationals and the location of their real economic activity. In practice, however, this aim was defeated by two factors. First, important countries ended up seeking to protect their "competitive" measures instead of collaborating—so, for example, the United Kingdom's defense of a mechanism to attract profit shifting using intangible assets led to the OECD codifying rather than eliminating the "patent box," with the inevitable effect of its adoption in many more countries.

Second, the entire BEPS approach was hamstrung by the insistence on maintaining, rhetorically at least, the commitment to "separate accounting." This is the treatment of individual entities within a multinational group as separate for tax purposes, so that the appropriate allocation of taxable profit between entities—and therefore the appropriate overall tax treatment—relies upon establishing appropriate prices for intragroup transactions. This process of establishing transfer prices aims to reflect prices between unrelated market participants—i.e., "arm's-length pricing"—and *does not* have any necessary relation to the degree of profit misalignment. As such, the scope for progress on the agreed aim was limited by design, from the outset.

It remains the case that the state role is more prominent in the sphere of financial secrecy than in that of corporate tax avoidance; but it is also true that the state role has become more clearly the focus in both areas, not least due to the efforts of the tax justice civil society movement to drive progress. An interesting development here is the European Union's process to establish a common list of noncooperative jurisdictions.[16] This list is to be based on a wide range of—at least in part, objectively verifiable—criteria that reflect taxation of multinationals and seek to identify state attempts to attract misalignment. The criteria have largely been developed transparently, including with requests for input from those jurisdictions under consideration.

The European Union has been unable to consider its own member states in this assessment. Final agreement on, and application of, objectively verifiable criteria would at least allow any observer to apply these equally to member states. As with OECD standards in respect of financial secrecy, the double standard will at least become clearly visible.

C. UNCOUNTED, AND THE ABC OF TAX TRANSPARENCY

State responsibilities in respect of tax justice are manifold, but transparency measures are of particular importance because of the role of opacity in one state, in allowing abuses in others to go unchecked. Such deliberately engineered opacity forms a significant component of the phenomenon of the "uncounted":

> The term "uncounted" is used to describe a politically motivated failure to count. This takes two main forms. First, there may be people and groups at the bottom of distributions (e.g., income) whose "uncounting" adds another level to their marginalization, for example, where they are absent from statistics that inform policy prioritization. Second, there may be people and groups at the top of distributions who are further empowered by being able to go uncounted—not least by hiding income and wealth from taxation and regulation.
>
> In either case, the phenomenon is not a random or arbitrary one. Being uncounted is not generally a matter of coincidence, but reflects power: the lack of it, or its excess.[17]

Following the formal establishment of the Tax Justice Network in 2003, internationally engaged experts from law, accounting, economics, and other fields contributed to the development of a policy platform to challenge the problems of tax havenry and associated evasion and avoidance—not least by addressing the power and inequality associated with the uncounted at the top.

The core of this policy platform is the ABC of tax transparency:

- Automatic, multilateral exchange of tax information
- Beneficial ownership (public registries for companies, trusts, and foundations); and
- Country-by-country reporting by multinational companies, in public.

The A and B relate primarily to the financial secrecy sphere. Automatic exchange of tax information was intended as a direct challenge to the then OECD standard of information exchange "upon request." This required requesting authorities to lay out substantial detail of the individual they were examining, and whose bank account information they sought. This in turn allowed secrecy jurisdictions multiple opportunities to stall and to reject requests on spurious grounds.

In contrast, automatic exchange provides for regular multilateral exchange of data about all relevant accountholders—literally, the end of banking secrecy. The first multilateral exchanges under what has now become the OECD standard took place in late 2017. Despite important loopholes and significant challenges to ensure the inclusion of lower-income countries, this represents a major step forward.

Public registries of beneficial ownership are intended to eliminate secret ownership of assets. This can occur through anonymously held vehicles, including companies, trusts, and foundations, or other legal structures that can play the equivalent role of separating a warm-blooded individual from that which they control and/or which benefits them financially. Gradually, including through revisions to the EU anti–money laundering directive, public registers are emerging as the international standard.

Offshore centers with some specialization in anonymous ownership, including a number of British overseas territories and crown dependencies, argue that their systems are superior to public registers. Most rely on information being held by company or trust formation agents, in theory available on request to law enforcement or other agencies upon their having accepted a request from counterparts in other jurisdictions. In practice, this system has continually limited the supply of useful information.

The Panama Papers revealed the inner workings of one Panamanian law firm supplying anonymous ownership services, mainly in British jurisdictions, to a range of international banks and the "Big Four" accounting firms. The revelations provided absolute confirmation that the response to requests, when data is held by such third parties, is typically circumvention—through the changing of ownership (real or apparent), or the explicit reporting of false information, which of course cannot be verified by authorities since no true records are available. As such, this leak—and others before and since—have significantly strengthened the momentum for public registers. This dynamic has also shown the extent to which certain jurisdictions, having sold their sovereignty to the anonymous ownership sector, are forced to defend the status quo.

The C of tax transparency refers to public country-by-country reporting by multinational companies. The sphere of financial and nonfinancial disclosure by companies operating internationally has long been a battlefield between states and companies. The G77—the group of lower-income countries which felt most explicitly the power of OECD countries' multinationals operating in their jurisdictions—expended significant efforts in the 1970s and 1980s on raising the level of disclosure, as the basis for greater accountability for the development impact of those corporate operations. These efforts included a concerted attempt to create new reporting standards within the UN system. The UN Centre on Transnational Corporations (UNCTC) was established in 1975 and abolished in 1992, during which time the G77 came close but ultimately failed in achieving any new disclosure regime.[18]

The emergence of the Tax Justice Network in the early 2000s marked the beginning of a new phase in the battle for disclosure, with the publication of the first draft accounting standard for country-by-country reporting.[19] The standard identified key variables on multinationals' economic activity, declared profits, and tax paid, along with the requirement for information on the names and line of business for each entity of a multinational operating in each country. While initially written off as unrealistic, the standard rapidly became a central point in discussions over multinational tax avoidance.

Traction was achieved first with respect to the extractives sector, in part due to a supporting narrative that emphasized the importance of lower-income country citizens benefiting from their own resource wealth. At the same time, however, that narrative was easily bent by corporate lobbyists to suggest the emphasis should be on government corruption rather than private sector responsibilities. The capture of the Extractive Industries Transparency Initiative (EITI) followed this pattern, with the initial transparency measures providing denominators only useful for government accountability (e.g., to compare declared receipts and actual spending with companies' declared payments). Only much later did the default disclosure scheme come to include denominators that would support corporate accountability (e.g., to compare tax and royalty payments with measures of the total value of extracted resources and total profit made).

Nonetheless, campaigning nongovernmental organizations (NGOs) such as Publish What You Pay, with the support of major investors including George Soros, were able to push the demand for a country-by-country standard for the sector onto the agenda of the International Accounting Standards Board (IASB). The IASB went as far as to produce a draft standard in the late 2000s before the process was closed down, due to the combined resistance of companies and the "Big Four" accounting firms that have long dominated the IASB. Ongoing pressure has, however, led the EITI to adopt a much more serious set of core transparency positions, and the European Union and United States to legislate requirements for country-by-country reporting in the extractive sector (albeit the latter has been struck down by President Donald Trump after years of legal challenge from US extractive industry companies).

The European Union has also passed a form of country-by-country reporting requirement for financial institutions, under the fourth Capital Requirements Directive (CRD IV), as public and policymaker understanding of the importance of this type of disclosure has grown. While none of the measures for public reporting to date have fully met the TJN proposals in terms of either the range of variables, or the consistency and comparability of the data to be reported,[20] they reflect a gradual shift in the public expectations that underpin the ongoing disclosure battle.

The most important step so far has been the OECD's creation of a standard for *private* country-by-country reporting to tax authorities. This standard closely reflects the original TJN proposals, and was developed at the behest of the G20 and G8 countries as part of the major effort to curtail multinational tax avoidance that ran from 2013 to 2015. The Base Erosion and Profit Shifting (BEPS) Action Plan is widely seen to have failed, patching the existing system rather than making the kind of more radical change necessary. However, the BEPS plan did deliver a significant step forward: consensus on a single goal, to reduce the misalignment between the location of multinationals' real economic activity, and where their profits are declared. Importantly, despite the weakness of the actual changes to tax rules put in place, this commitment was backed by a commitment to counting.

BEPS Action 11 committed the OECD to measuring and monitoring misalignment over time, in other words to providing accountability for the entire effort by ensuring that the consensus target of misalignment did not go uncounted. BEPS Action 13 (out of 15) saw the creation of the country-by-country reporting standard, but with limited access. Intense lobbying around BEPS Action 13 secured successive dilutions of the original proposal. This began with a powerful pushback against the data being public, but has continued since. First, it was agreed that data would only be provided to tax authorities. Next, this was limited to *home country* tax authorities only. Complex arrangements have been put in place for the "exchange" of data with host countries, i.e., the provision of data by largely OECD countries to largely lower-income countries, with various criteria that the latter must meet and conditions they must commit to before being deemed worthy.

As such, the position remains far from the original intention of ensuring public accountability for the profit shifting behavior of both multinational companies and their advisers, and of tax authorities. Now that the compliance costs are sunk, it seems likely that publication will follow. The European Parliament is fully supportive, and "trialogue" with the European Commission and member states is likely to give rise to an EU decision within the coming year. The United Kingdom has already legislated to allow public reporting, but is yet to enact it.

In the meantime, the delivery of BEPS 11 will represent the most powerful progress ever seen in terms of revealing some of the contours of the biggest economic actors on the planet: the "gorillas in the mist" that are multinational companies. BEPS 11's delivery will take the form of annual publication of partially aggregated country-by-country reporting statistics and analysis of patterns of misalignment. While suppressing details of company-level misalignment, this data will show clearly for the first time, the global pattern of profit shifting by the largest multinationals (from any host country).

The following section reviews the current state of knowledge on profit shifting, which is necessarily based on more partial data because of the power of corporate lobbying to maintain—for now—their opacity in this respect. Our focus is on the state role, however, and here the findings emerge more clearly. Some indicative estimates of the scale of impact are also explored.

III. PROFIT SHIFTING: UNCOUNTED HUMAN RIGHTS IMPACTS AND THE STATE ROLE

A. THE SCALE OF PROCURED PROFIT SHIFTING

Table 6.1 summarizes the best estimates of the scale of profit shifting currently available, in terms of robustness and global coverage of countries. The main studies are those of IMF researchers.[21] These studies have been influential in the policy debate, and each offers an answer to the question of the scale of profit shifting worldwide and how much tax revenue governments lose, in most cases providing estimates for many countries worldwide. The studies are listed in an approximate order of perceived credibility and relevance of their estimates.

Crivelli et al. estimate global revenue losses of up to $650 billion a year due to profit shifting related to "tax havens," by estimating the spillover from other countries' tax rates to each countries' revenues, and evaluating a counterfactual in which tax havens' tax rates are not lower than elsewhere.[22] Cobham and Janský use alternative revenue data to revisit this result, finding losses of around $500 billion a year—but consistent with Crivelli et al., that a disproportionate share of the losses (around $200 billion) arise in lower-income countries.[23]

The UN Conference on Trade and Development (UNCTAD) estimates revenue losses due to tax avoidance schemes that exploit a particular channel: the use of offshore hubs (tax havens) as conduits for direct investment, which is seen to depress the reported rate of return on investment in lower-income countries.[24] This channel is estimated to cause revenue losses of around $100 billion a year, i.e., half of the IMF researchers' total estimate. While of interest and broadly supportive, this partial approach does not necessarily give rise to jurisdiction-level findings that should be expected to be consistent with the overall pattern.

OECD combines estimates of revenue losses due to both profit shifting related to tax rate differentials (differences in tax rates across countries) and differences in average effective tax rates for large affiliates of multinational enterprises (MNEs) and domestic companies, and finds

Table 6.1: Summary of studies estimating global profit shifting
(and associated tax revenue losses)

Reference	Scale of profit shifting	Annual corporate income tax revenue loss estimates	International corporate tax avoidance estimated	More details on methodology	Published in an academic journal	Country-level estimates
Crivelli et al. (2016)		Long-run approximate estimates are $400 billion for OECD countries (1% of their GDP) and $200 billion for developing countries (1.3%) of their GDP.	BEPS related to "tax havens."	BEPS related to tax havens by looking at a counterfactual if the tax havens' tax rates were not lower than for other countries.	Yes	Yes (by a later study of Cobham & Janský (2018) which found overall losses near USD 500 billion)
UNCTAD (2015)		Around 8% of CIT, USD 200 billion in 2012 globally and USD 90 billion for developing countries.	BEPS through tax avoidance schemes that exploit a direct investment relationship via "tax haven" conduits.	Tax revenue losses due to tax avoidance schemes that exploit a direct investment relationship on the basis of lower reported rate of return for investment from offshore hubs.	No	Yes (by a later study of Janský & Palanský (2017))
OECD (2015)		USD 100–240 billion, or anywhere from 4%–10% of global corporate income tax (CIT) revenues in 2014. It ranges from 7.5% to 14% of developing countries' CIT revenue.	BEPS due to tax rate differentials and differences in average effective tax rates for large affiliates due to mismatches between tax systems and tax preferences.	BEPS related to tax rate differentials and differences in average effective tax rates for large affiliates of MNEs and domestic companies.	No	No
Clausing (2016)		US losses of USD 77–111 billion by 2012 due to US multinationals; other countries without low tax rates also suffering substantial losses.	BEPS by US-headquartered multinationals.	Misalignment between profits and location of real economic activity.	Yes	Yes

Table 6.1: Continued

Reference	Scale of profit shifting	Annual corporate income tax revenue loss estimates	International corporate tax avoidance estimated	More details on methodology	Published in an academic journal	Country-level estimates
Cobham & Janský (2017)		Global losses of USD 80–160 billion by 2012 due to US multinationals (25%–30% of global profits are shifted).	BEPS by US-headquartered multinationals.	Misalignment between profits and location of real economic activity.	Yes	Yes

Source: Based on analysis by Petr Janský.

a lower global total (up to $240 billion a year)—but relies on company balance sheet data, which is known to under represent both lower-income countries and financial secrecy jurisdictions ("tax havens"), both of which are expected to bias the revenue loss estimate strongly downward.[25] Cobham and Loretz use the same balance sheet database (Orbis) to identify patterns of profit misalignment at country level, and highlight the weaknesses in coverage—including the overrepresentation of EU company accounts.[26]

An alternative approach has been to use data that are stronger—in terms of comprehensive coverage within their sample, but weaker in terms of overall coverage. Here, both Clausing, and Cobham and Janský use data for US-headquartered multinationals only—but which do cover all such multinationals (in aggregate), and even after data suppression show a broader range of country-level findings.[27] While Clausing estimates profit shifting scale from derived semi-elasticities,[28] Cobham and Janský quantify the extent of misalignment between reported profits and indicators of economic activity, and find broadly similar results which are also in keeping with the rough order of global losses estimated by Crivelli et al.[29]

Overall, three conclusions about the scale of multinational profit shifting can be drawn from these collected studies. First, in terms of the contours of the problem, the findings indicate that only a small number of jurisdictions are consistently the recipients of disproportionate volumes of profit related to economic activity elsewhere. Second, the scale of shifted profits and revenue losses are widely distributed across other jurisdictions, with the highest values in high-income countries but the most intense losses in relation to GDP and especially to tax revenues, in lower-income countries. Third, the overall scale of multinationals' profit shifting may reach the level of being a material distortion to global economic accounts; and the worldwide revenue losses may lie between $500 billion and $650 billion annually.

An important weakness in the approach underlying the leading global scale estimates is the reliance on differences in statutory tax rates (due to the lack of consistent data on real effective tax rates paid by multinationals). This may not influence the overall scale, but has clear implications for jurisdiction-level findings. In particular, profit-shifting hubs that maintain high statutory rates but offer near-zero effective rates will not be identified. For this reason, country-level estimates of the revenue "winners" may be more reliable where based on company-level data, partially aggregated or otherwise.

Figures 6.1 and 6.2 show the country-level measures of profit misalignment that emerge from the studies focusing specifically on this question. Figure 6.1 shows the results of Cobham and Loretz, who use company balance sheet data, in which EU companies are overrepresented;[30] while Figure 6.2 shows the results of Cobham and Janský, using data for US-headquartered multinationals only.[31] In each case, the figures show the shares of current taxable profit which would be lost or gained by individual jurisdictions, if they were to move to a share of profit in proportion to their share of real economic activity (i.e., the goal of the G20 and OECD BEPS process). This is shown for individual activity measures (employment, sales, and assets), as well as for the combined measure proposed by the European Commission for use with its Common Consolidated Corporate Tax Base (CCCTB).

Together, the two figures identify the key jurisdictions that benefit in revenue terms from the losses imposed on all other jurisdictions by multinationals' tax abuses—that is, the states which are consistent procurers of profit shifting. The strongest findings in terms of the underlying data are those for US multinationals, summarized in Figure 6.3. The extent to which *inward* profit shifting is concentrated in just a handful of jurisdictions; and the near-zero effective tax rate in each case; point strongly toward the true nature of the process. Multinational companies and their advisers may be quick to exploit opportunities and will lobby aggressively to create, defend, and hide these opportunities and this behavior. But the shifting of profit is ultimately procured, quite deliberately, by jurisdictions that seek a small share of the tax base that should rightly arise in the jurisdictions of real economic activity.

Only fully public country-by-country reporting by multinationals will lay bare the full scale and distribution of the problem. The estimates and analysis summarized here, however, should leave no doubt of the nature of the problem. Partially aggregated data to be published in fulfillment of OECD BEPS Action 11 will go significantly further in confirming the procurers. Before considering possible countermeasures in the next section, we survey briefly some findings on the impact of losses due to profit shifting.

B. IMPACTS OF PROCURED PROFIT SHIFTING

The UN Sustainable Development Goals (SDGs), which set global targets for the period to 2030, break with the predecessor framework of the Millennium Development Goals (MDGs) in a number of ways, of which three are especially relevant here. First, while tax was invisible in the MDGs and aid to the fore, tax takes pride of place as the first means of implementation in the SDGs (target 17.1). Second, and relatedly, there is a separate target (16.4) to reduce illicit financial flows—including cross-border tax abuses by individuals and multinationals. Third, inequalities are at the core of the SDGs (having been largely peripheral in the MDGs). The redistributive role of tax and its revenue-raising character are both crucial to the delivery of the SDGs—to say nothing of the underlying importance of tax to strengthen political representation and governance over time.

A range of recent studies highlight the relationship with inequality. Alstadsæter, Johannesen, and Zucman use leaked data to show how strongly tax evasion in Scandinavia is concentrated in the top 0.01 percent of the wealth distribution; and hence how understated inequality will be if estimates rest on household surveys and tax-reporting data alone.[32] Cobham, Davis, Ibrahim, and Sumner use estimates of illicit flows to reach a similar conclusion for a range of lower-income countries.[33] The ability of elites to opt out of direct taxation—whether as individuals

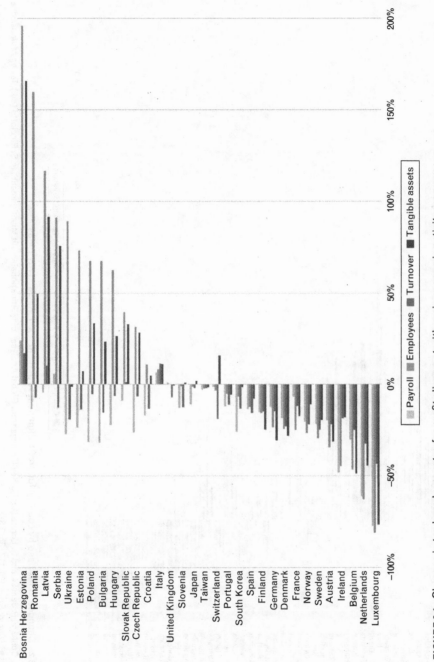

FIGURE 6.1: Changes in tax base by country, for profit alignment with main economic activity measures

Source: A. Cobham, P. Janský, and S. Loretz (2017), 'Key Findings from Global Analyses of Multinational Profit Misalignment', in S. Picciotto (ed.), *Taxing Multinational Enterprises as Unitary Firms* 100, 108 (fig. 7.1).

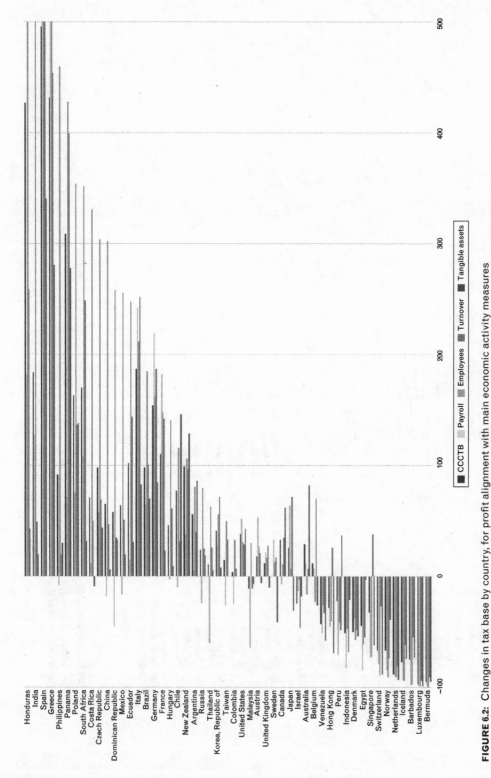

FIGURE 6.2: Changes in tax base by country, for profit alignment with main economic activity measures

Source: A. Cobham, P. Janský, and S. Loretz (2017), 'Key Findings from Global Analyses of Multinational Profit Misalignment', in S. Picciotto (ed.), *Taxing Multinational Enterprises as Unitary Firms* 100, 112 (fig. 7.3).

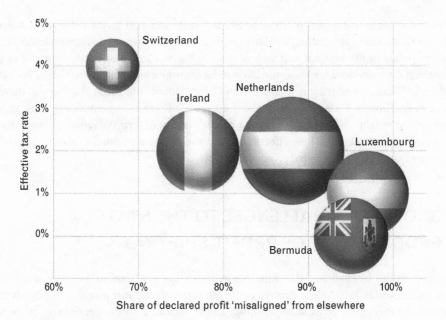

FIGURE 6.3: Major misalignment jurisdictions for US-headquartered multinationals, 2012

Source: A. Cobham and P. Janský, 'Measuring Misalignment: The Location of US Multinationals' Economic Activity versus the Location of Their Profits', *Development Policy Review* (2017). Size of bubbles is proportionate to total misaligned profits declared in each jurisdiction.

or as major companies—not only undermines the redistribution possible through given tax policies but also contributes with lobbying to reduce the attractiveness of pursuing redistribution. In the case of corporate taxation, multinational profit shifting creates an artificial disadvantage for smaller, national businesses—which are typically responsible for the majority of employment in a country.

The most direct estimates of impact relate to the costs of forgone public expenditure. Of these, the damage done by lost health spending has received the greatest attention. Christian Aid began the current wave of tax justice campaigning by international development NGOs with an estimate that revenue losses due to trade-based tax abuse could result in the needless deaths of nearly 1,000 children each day.[34] More recently, O'Hare et al. use illicit flow estimates with GDP elasticities of mortality to show that of thirty-four sub-Saharan African countries, a curtailment of illicit flows could see substantial mortality reductions—such that sixteen countries rather than six would have reached their MDG target by 2015.[35]

Reeves et al. explore the underlying relationship and find that "tax revenue was a major statistical determinant of progress towards universal health coverage" in lower-income countries, and that this is overwhelmingly driven by direct taxes on profits, income, and capital gains.[36] Using alternative revenue data, and a more robust regression approach, Carter and Cobham confirm the importance of tax generally, while adding some caveats and more detailed findings.[37] In particular, they find a larger statistical association between direct taxes and public health expenditure than between indirect taxes and health spending; and that countries making greater use of direct taxes tend in general to exhibit higher public health spending and broader coverage of and access to public health systems.

While further research continues to be needed, it is clear that forgone direct tax revenues due to multinational profit shifting will have disproportionately strong impacts on lower income countries' public health systems and their human rights outcomes. Since the estimates of scale indicate that the associated tax losses are likely to be disproportionately intense in lower-income countries as a share of existing revenue, there will be a double hit. Profit shifting will drive the greatest proportionate losses in exactly those countries where the revenues are most lacking, and where the benefit of (direct) tax revenues can be greatest in terms of reducing mortality and improving living standards. These effects can, and should, be attributed to those jurisdictions that procure the majority of global profit shifting.

IV. SCOPE FOR CHALLENGES TO THE STATE PROCUREMENT OF PROFIT SHIFTING

The opportunities to challenge the state role in procuring profit shifting can be divided into four main categories. International instruments can variously support progress through broader norm-setting; through specific state-shaming; and by allowing a direct economic threat to be made. A fourth set of options are available to jurisdictions in the form of unilateral and/or multilateral defensive measures against procuring states. We explore each in turn.

First, international instruments set norms for state behavior. Existing and envisaged instruments have the potential to provide explicit accountability for state procuring of profit shifting. Within the Sustainable Development Goals, the indicators for target 16.4 (to reduce illicit financial flows, including multinational tax abuses) are yet to be set. If indicators are limited to estimates of overall (out)flows at the country level, they will provide no accountability for the implicit underlying commitment to curtail attempts to procure profit shifting. Powerful indicators could be easily developed, however, such as the ratio for each jurisdiction of their share of the global profits of multinationals, to their share of the global economic activity of multinationals (say, of employment and sales). Ratios in excess of 100 percent would indicate inward profit shifting; sustained, high ratios would indicate a commitment to procuring profit shifting. For comparison, the ratios of Luxembourg, Bermuda, and the Netherlands for US multinationals per Cobham and Janský would exceed 400 percent.[38]

The UN system is currently debating appropriate indicators, and will review decisions in 2019 (after the OECD has begun to publish partially disaggregated data which would allow such measures to be constructed for all jurisdictions)—so this option is currently open, and appealing. However, there is a concerted effort to exclude multinational tax abuse retrospectively from the illicit flows target. If this opportunity is denied, then alternatives would include the possibility of a new international convention, designed to ensure equivalent jurisdiction-level accountability in respect of financial secrecy (e.g., commitments to automatic information exchange and beneficial ownership transparency), as well as in respect of profit shifting.

Existing instruments also provide for powerful state-shaming actions. Most obviously, Switzerland has been challenged for the impact of its policies on gender equality around the world. Following a submission from the Center for Economic and Social Rights and others in 2016,[39] the Committee on the Elimination of Discrimination Against Women criticized "the State party's financial secrecy policies and rules on corporate reporting and taxation [which] have a potentially negative impact on the ability of other States, particularly those already short of revenue, to mobilise the maximum available resources for the fulfilment of women's rights";

and urged Switzerland to honor its international human rights obligations by "undertaking in-dependent, participatory and periodic impact assessments of the extraterritorial effects of its financial secrecy and corporate tax policies on women's rights and substantive equality, and ensuring that such assessments are conducted in an impartial manner with public disclosure of the methodology and finding."[40] There is substantial scope to use human rights instruments in particular to shame both the state providers of financial secrecy and the state procurers of profit shifting, through consistent use of ongoing review processes.

International trade instruments provide a compelling alternative opportunity, namely, to bring a meaningful economic threat to bear. In the case of the World Trade Organization (WTO) and the General Agreement on Trade in Services (GATS), it is possible to envisage a state party bringing a case against a state procurer of profit shifting, on the basis that this behavior undermined the benefits to the first state of participating in economic trade under the relevant agreement. While the evidentiary threshold is high, the disciplining effect—on the named procurer and by demonstration on others—is potentially much greater than that of human rights instruments.

As discussed above, a great deal of profit shifting rests on the fact that international tax rules give multinationals scope to set transfer prices for intragroup trades, which can be manipulated to determine where taxable profits arise. Bastin assesses the scope for a challenge to transfer pricing at the state rather than multinational level, under the rules of the WTO, and identifies two abusive transfer pricing scenarios in which it might be possible to raise a complaint.[41] One falls under the terms of the Customs Valuation Agreement; the other, perhaps more interesting for a wider challenge, relates to the "non-violation nullification or impairment" provision of WTO agreements, which allows, in exceptional circumstances, for challenge on the grounds that the benefits which a member derives under certain WTO Agreements can be wrongly nullified or impaired as a result of the conduct of another member, *even if that conduct does not necessarily violate the relevant WTO Agreement.*

In the case of the GATT (General Agreement on Tariffs and Trade 1994), Bastin identifies this provision as Article XXIII(1)(b):

1. *If any contracting party should consider that any benefit accruing to it directly or indirectly under this Agreement is being nullified or impaired or that the attainment of any objective of the Agreement is being impeded as the result of*

   . . .

   (b) *the application by another contracting party of any measure, whether or not it conflicts with the provisions of this Agreement*

   . . .

   the contracting party may, with a view to the satisfactory adjustment of the matter, make written representations or proposals to the other contracting party or parties which it considers to be concerned. Any contracting party thus approached shall give sympathetic consideration to the representations or proposals made to it.

A dispute on this basis may be referred by the complainant to the WTO dispute settlement system, per Article XXIII(2), if no satisfactory agreement is effected between the two parties within a reasonable time.

While highlighting a 1950 GATT Panel that supported the Chilean complaint that Australia's removal of subsidies for imported nitrate of soda (a measure which did not otherwise breach the GATT) constituted a nullification and impairment of the benefit which Chile had derived from a previously negotiated tariff concession, Bastin emphasizes that appeal to XXIII(1)(b) has been exceptional only.[42] He sets out the four criteria for its use:

1. The WTO member must have applied a "measure" (which is current and does not pre-date the entry into force of the GATT).
2. The complainant member must have reasonably expected to receive a "benefit" due to GATT; as this historically referred to a reduction of tariffs, it would be novel to argue that the nullified benefit is something else (e.g., tax revenues).
3. Application of the measure must be shown to lead the expected benefit to the complainant to be nullified or impaired (a test of causation, in which the burden of proof lies with the complainant state).
4. The nullification or impairment of the benefit must contradict legitimate expectations of the complainant at the time of the agreement—i.e., the criterion will not be satisfied if the result could have reasonably been anticipated.

On this basis, Bastin finds it arguable that a WTO member which allows abusively transfer priced products to be exported "has nullified or impaired a benefit which the importing State legitimately expected to receive when it entered into the GATT, namely, that it would be free to calculate the 'actual value' of imports, as Article VII of the GATT mandates, on the basis of the 'transaction value' methodology set out in Article 1 of the CVA and without interference in or subversion of that exercise by the production of evidence of an alternative (transfer mispriced) valuation."[43]

Should such a case be brought and be supported, the remedies open to the dispute settlement board include the modification or withdrawal of the measure in question.

If we move beyond the specific trade pricing cases that Bastin considers, it is possible to envisage a wider class of measures. An obvious example might be the Luxembourg tax rulings that were exposed in the LuxLeaks, showing the systematic creation by the government—working hand in hand with "Big Four" accounting firms—of secret measures that created a massive incentive to shift into the jurisdiction profits arising from economic activity elsewhere.

To the extent that this particular case was characterized largely by manipulation of prices on intragroup debt, it might be necessary to appeal to the equivalent provision in the General Agreement on Trade in Services (GATS), where we find Article XXIII:

3. If any Member considers that any benefit it could reasonably have expected to accrue to it under a specific commitment of another Member under Part III of this Agreement is being nullified or impaired as a result of the application of any measure which does not conflict with the provisions of this Agreement, it may have recourse to the DSU. If the measure is determined by the DSB to have nullified or impaired such a benefit, the Member affected shall be entitled to a mutually satisfactory adjustment on the basis of paragraph 2 of Article XXI, which may include the modification or withdrawal of the measure . . .

Legislation around Dutch trust structures that are also attractive for profit shifting could also form the basis for evaluating a case, along with a range of measures apparently designed to attract profit shifting into each of the multiple jurisdictions identified in Figures 6.1–6.3 of this chapter. While a significant investment of resources would be required to research the validity of general cases and specific claims under this approach, this seems well justified by the potential payoff in terms of reshaping the incentives entirely for the small number of states dedicated to procuring profit shifting as a central element of their business model.

Finally, we briefly consider defensive (tax) measures that could be taken unilaterally or multilaterally. Most comprehensively, a state or regional bloc could simply break with the OECD arm's-length principle and instead adopt the logically superior approach of taxing at the unit of the multinational group itself, rather than that of individual subsidiaries within the group (superior because profit is maximized at the group level, so to avoid distortion tax should be levied at this level also). For lower-income countries, there is considerable political pressure from OECD governments and from multinationals and their advisers not to break with the OECD rules; so an alternative is to maintain nominal allegiance, but to introduce an alternative minimum corporate tax based on a unitary approach. For example, under this approach a tax authority could apportion to itself in taxable profit the proportion of a multinational's global profit equal to the proportion of its sales and employment taking place in the jurisdiction in question; and then levy tax at a smaller share of the statutory rate, say 80 percent, if and only if the multinational had through its transfer pricing and other arrangements achieved a lower level of taxable profit to declare under the arm's-length principle.

Such a formulary alternative minimum corporate tax (or FAMICT) would allow the country or bloc to maintain the OECD rules in principle at least, while also drawing a line on the extent of profit shifting that would be tolerated. For multinationals, it would offer the appeal of certainty and the chance to save on all transfer pricing (manipulation) costs. If adopted more widely, as success in revenue raising would likely encourage, this could be the evolutionary approach to a revolution in tax rules.

The European Union's move to a Common Consolidated Corporate Tax Base, and the application of formulary apportionment within the bloc, would put it alongside Canada, Switzerland, and the United States as major economies using a formulary approach to apportion taxable profits within their borders. But in the EU cases, the sub-bloc administrations are national governments rather than provinces, cantons, or states within a national federation—and so the EU move would more obviously set the path to take a worldwide formulary approach. In fact, without doing so, the CCCTB would address internal profit shifting but open the bloc even more to profit shifting out of the European Union; and so a worldwide approach may quickly become necessary even if it is not implemented from the outset.

Most gentle, but supporting the same eventual outcomes, is the policy decision to require publication of country-by-country reporting. The ongoing, annual accountability this would ensure for profit misalignment at the level of multinational companies, their Big Four advisers, and of jurisdictions, would lock in a policy dynamic that seems highly likely to eventually lead to widespread adoption of unitary tax approaches. But of course, for that reason, and the dramatic diminution in global revenue losses that would follow, there will continue to be very powerful resistance to this basic transparency measure. And for that reason in turn, there continues to be a need for greater use of human rights instruments to shame states procuring profit shifting, and for greater investment in researching the potential for high value challenges under WTO rules.

V. CONCLUSIONS

The continuing lack of transparency of multinationals' country-by-country reporting on economic activity, profits, and tax paid means that our knowledge of both the scale and the impacts of global profit shifting continues to rely on estimates rather than measurement. But those estimates are sufficiently robust for a number of important conclusions to be reached.

First, it is clear that forgone direct tax revenues due to multinational profit shifting are of the order of hundreds of billions of dollars annually. Second, the distribution of those losses is weighted toward high-income economies in absolute terms, but is most intense—in terms of the proportion of current revenues that are foregone—in lower-income countries. Third, those losses have disproportionately strong impacts on lower-income countries' public health systems and their human outcomes, including a range of mortality rates. Profit shifting therefore drives the greatest proportionate losses in exactly those countries where revenues are most lacking, and where the benefit of (direct) tax revenues can be greatest in terms of reducing mortality.

These effects can, and should, be attributed to those jurisdictions that procure the majority of global profit shifting. Those state procurers of profit shifting can already be identified—and prominent among them are the Netherlands, Luxembourg, Bermuda, Ireland, Switzerland, Singapore; and perhaps to a lesser extent, Belgium, Austria, and Barbados. This handful of jurisdictions is estimated to be responsible for the vast majority of global profit shifting, and the associated revenue losses suffered by countries at every income level.

Measures against these state procurers of profit shifting can take a number of forms. First, human rights instruments can be used to highlight the extraterritorial damage being done, and to drive political salience and responses by shaming. Second, indicators of profit shifting can and should be established in international mechanisms such as the reporting of the Sustainable Development Goals, to ensure continuing accountability for the state procurers. The ongoing OECD BEPS 11 Action of collating and publishing partially aggregated country-by-country reporting from multinationals will provide powerful data to ensure this accountability channel can operate. Third, the WTO rules open the possibility of raising disputes on the basis that the measures taken by state procurers to maintain their business models are likely unexpectedly to nullify and/or to impair the benefits of trade for other members. Such approaches should be vigorously pursued, given the potential to change dramatically the calculation made by state procurers.

Finally, individual jurisdictions and regional blocs should consider unilateral defensive measures to eliminate the impact of profit shifting. These measures can include the introduction of formulary alternative minimum corporate taxation or the outright replacement of the OECD arm's-length approach with unitary taxation using formulary apportionment. Minimally, governments should urgently consider requiring multinationals operating in their jurisdiction and benefiting from access to their markets, to publish their country-by-country reporting as a matter of course.

NOTES

1. A. Cobham, *Taxation policy and development*, Oxford Council on Good Governance, Economy Analysis 2 (2005), available online at http://www.taxjustice.net/cms/upload/pdf/OCGG_-_Alex_Cobham_-_Taxation_Policy_and_Development.pdf; A. Cobham, *The tax consensus has failed: Recommendation to policymakers and donors, researchers and civil society*, Oxford Council on Good Governance, Economy Recommendation 8 (2007), available online at http://www.taxjustice.net/cms/upload/pdf/Cobham_Tax_Consensus_Failed_08.pdf.
2. See generally W. Prichard, P. Salardi, and P. Segal, 'Taxation, non-tax revenue and democracy: New evidence using new cross-country data', *International Centre for Tax and Development*

Working Paper 23 (2015), available online at http://www.ictd.ac/publication/2-working-papers/16-taxation-non-tax-revenue-and-democracy-new-evidence-using-new-cross-country-data.

3. T. Baunsgaard and M. Keen, 'Tax revenue and (or?) trade liberalization', *IMF Working Paper* 05/112 (2005).

4. See C. Heady, 'Taxation policy in low-income countries', *in* T. Addison and A. Roe (eds.), *Fiscal Policy for Development* (2004); C. Adam and D. Bevan, 'Fiscal policy design in low-income countries', *in Fiscal Policy for Development* (T. Addison and A. Roe eds., 2004); A. Cobham, *The tax consensus has failed*, Oxford Council on Good Governance, Economy Recommendation 8 (2007), available online at http://www.taxjustice.net/cms/upload/pdf/Cobham_Tax_Consensus_Failed_08.pdf; J. Marshall, 'One size fits all? IMF tax policy in sub-Saharan Africa', *Christian Aid Occasional Paper* 2 (2009), available online at http://www.christianaid.org.uk/images/imfoccpaper.pdf.

5. E. Uslaner, *Corruption, Inequality and the Rule of Law* (2008).

6. R. Palan, 'Tax havens and the commercialization of state sovereignty', 56(1) *International Organization* (2002), 151.

7. N. Shaxson, *Treasure Islands: Tax havens and the men who stole the world* (2011).

8. See, e.g., S. Elliott, *Towards a Level Playing Field: Regulating Corporate Vehicles in Cross-border Transactions* (2002), available online at https://www.step.org/sites/default/files/Comms/Towards_A_Level_Playing_Field2ndEdition.pdf.

9. See, e.g., Cayman Finance, 'Transparency cooperation requires a level playing field', *Cayman Journal* (2013), available online at https://www.cayman.finance/2013/07/transparency-cooperation-requires-a-level-playing-field/; Guernsey Finance, 'Guernsey responds to Queen's Speech: Seeks level playing field on beneficial ownership', *We Are Guernsey* (2014), available online at https://www.weareguernsey.com/news/2014/guernsey-responds-to-queens-speech-seeks-level-playing-field-on-beneficial-ownership/.

10. See OECD, *Tax Cooperation: Towards a Level Playing Field—2006 Assessment by the Global Forum on Taxation* (2006); OECD *Tax Cooperation: Towards a Level Playing Field—2007 Assessment by the Global Forum on Taxation* (2007); OECD, *Tax Cooperation: Towards a Level Playing Field—2008 Assessment by the Global Forum on Taxation* (2008); OECD, *Tax Cooperation: Towards a Level Playing Field 2009—Assessment by the Global Forum on Transparency and Exchange of Information for Tax Purposes* (2009); OECD, *Tax Cooperation: Towards a Level Playing Field—2010 Assessment by the Global Forum on Transparency and Exchange of Information for Tax Purposes* (2010).

11. A. Cobham, 'Tax havens and illicit flows', *in* World Bank, *Draining Development: Controlling flows of illicit funds from developing countries*, 337–372 (P. Reuter ed., 2012); A. Cobham, P. Janský, and M. Meinzer, 'The Financial Secrecy Index: Shedding new light on the geography of secrecy', *Economic Geography* 91(3) (2015), 281–303, available online at https://doi:10.1111/ecge.12094.

12. This reflects both personal involvement in discussions with senior UK government figures in advance of the summit and subsequently; and personal exchanges with a range of other participants in pre-summit briefings with various G20 governments.

13. F. Lawrence and I. Griffiths, 'Revealed: how multinational companies avoid the taxman', *The Guardian*, 6 Nov. 2007, available online at https://www.theguardian.com/business/2007/nov/06/19.

14. Farrer & Co., 'Fiduciary duties and tax avoidance', *Opinion* (2013), available online at http://www.taxjustice.net/cms/upload/pdf/Farrer_and_Co_Opinion_on_Fiduciary_Duties_and_Tax_Avoidance.pdf.

15. C. Brooks et al., 'Do investors care about corporate taxes?', 38 *Journal of Corporate Finance* (2016), 218.

16. The EU list of non-cooperative jurisdictions for tax purposes", Dec. 5, 2017, at https://www.consilium.europa.eu/media/31945/st15429en17.pdf

17. A. Cobham, 'Uncounted: Power, inequalities and the post-2015 data revolution', 57(3–4) *Development* (2014), 321, available online at https://doi.org/10.1057/dev.2015.28.

18. S. Rahman, 'International accounting regulation by the United Nations: A power perspective', 11(5) *Accounting Auditing and Accountability Journal* (1998), 593; K. Hamdani and L. Ruffing,

United Nations Centre on Transnational Corporations: Corporate conduct and the public interest (2015).

19. R. Murphy, *A Proposed International Accounting Standard: Reporting Turnover and Tax by Location*, Association for Accountancy and Business Affairs: Essex (2003), available online at http://visar.csustan.edu/aaba/ProposedAccstd.pdf.

20. A. Cobham, J. Gray, and R. Murphy, 'What do they pay? Towards a public database to account for the economic activities and tax contributions of multinational corporations', *CITYPERC Working Paper* 2017-01, available online at https://www.city.ac.uk/__data/assets/pdf_file/0004/345469/CITYPERC-WPS-201701.pdf.

21. E. Crivelli, R. de Mooij, and M. Keen, 'Base erosion, profit shifting and developing countries', 72(3) *FinanzArchiv: Public Finance Analysis* (2016), 268, available online at https://doi.org/10.1628/001522116X14646834385460; UNCTAD, *World Investment Report 2015: Reforming International Investment Governance* (2015); OECD, *Measuring and Monitoring BEPS, Action 11—2015 Final Report* (2015), available online at http://www.oecd-ilibrary.org/content/book/9789264241343-en; K. Clausing, 'The effect of profit shifting on the corporate tax base in the United States and beyond', 69(4) *National Tax Journal* (2016), 905, available online at https://doi.org/10.17310/ntj.2016.4.09; A. Cobham and P. Janský, 'Global distribution of revenue loss from corporate tax avoidance— Re-estimation and country results', 30 *Journal of International Development* (2018) 206–232; International Monetary Fund, 'Spillovers in international corporate taxation', *IMF Policy Paper*, International Monetary Fund (2014), available online at https://www.imf.org/external/np/pp/eng/2014/050914.pdf.

22. E. Crivelli, R. de Mooij, and M. Keen, 2016, 'Base erosion, profit shifting and developing countries', 72(3) *FinanzArchiv: Public Finance Analysis* (2016), 268, available online at https://doi.org/10.1628/001522116X14646834385460.

23. A. Cobham and P. Janský, 'Global distribution of revenue loss from corporate tax avoidance— Re-estimation and country results', 30 *Journal of International Development* (2018), 206–232.

24. UNCTAD, *World Investment Report 2015: Reforming International Investment Governance* (2015).

25. OECD, *Measuring and Monitoring BEPS, Action 11—2015 Final Report* (2015), available online at http://www.oecd-ilibrary.org/content/book/9789264241343-en.

26. A. Cobham and S. Loretz, 'International distribution of the corporate tax base: Implications of different apportionment factors under unitary taxation', *International Centre for Tax and Development Working Paper 27* (2014).

27. K. Clausing, 'The effect of profit shifting on the corporate tax base in the United States and beyond', 69(4) *National Tax Journal* (2016), 905, available online at https://doi.org/10.17310/ntj.2016.4.09; A. Cobham and P. Janský, 'Measuring misalignment: The location of US multinationals' economic activity versus the location of their profits', Development Policy Review (2017), available online at https://doi.org/10.1111/dpr.12315.

28. K. Clausing, 'The effect of profit shifting on the corporate tax base in the United States and beyond', 69(4) *National Tax Journal* (2016), 905, available online at https://doi.org/10.17310/ntj.2016.4.09.

29. A. Cobham and P. Janský, 'Measuring misalignment: The location of US multinationals' economic activity versus the location of their profits', *Development Policy Review* (2017), available online at https://doi.org/10.1111/dpr.12315; see also Crivelli et al., 'Base erosion, profit shifting and developing countries', 72(3) *FinanzArchiv: Public Finance Analysis* (2016), 268, available online at https://doi.org/10.1628/001522116X14646834385460.

30. A. Cobham and S. Loretz, 'International distribution of the corporate tax base: Implications of different apportionment factors under unitary taxation', *International Centre for Tax and Development Working Paper 27* (2014).

31. A. Cobham and P. Janský, 'Measuring misalignment: The location of US multinationals' economic activity versus the location of their profits', *Development Policy Review* (2017), available online at https://doi.org/10.1111/dpr.12315.

32. A. Alstadsæter, N. Johannesen, and G. Zucman, 'Tax evasion and inequality', *NBER Working Paper* 23772 (2017).

33. A. Cobham, W. Davis, G. Ibrahim, and A. Sumner, 'Hidden inequality: How much difference would adjustment for illicit financial flows make to national income distributions?', 7(2) *Journal of Globalization and Development* (2016).

34. Christian Aid, *Death and Taxes: The true toll of tax dodging* (2008), available online at http://www.christianaid.org.uk/images/deathandtaxes.pdf.

35. B. O'Hare, I. Makuta, N. Bar-Zeev, L. Chiwaula, and A. Cobham, 'The effect of illicit financial flows on time to reach the fourth Millennium Development Goal in Sub-Saharan Africa: a quantitative analysis', 107(4) *Journal of the Royal Society of Medicine* (2014), 148.

36. A. Reeves, Y. Gourtsoyannis, S. Basu, D. McCoy, M. McKee, and D. Stuckler, 'Financing universal health coverage. effects of alternative tax structures on public health systems: cross-national modelling in 89 low-income and middle-income countries', 386(9990) *The Lancet* (2015), 274–280.

37. P. Carter and A. Cobham, 'Are taxes good for your health?', *UNU-WIDER Working Paper* 171 (2016).

38. A. Cobham and P. Janský, 'Measuring misalignment: The location of US multinationals' economic activity versus the location of their profits', *Development Policy Review* (2017), available online at https://doi.org/10.1111/dpr.12315.

39. Alliance Sud, Center for Economic and Social Rights, Public Eye, Global Justice Clinic of the NYU School of Law, & the Tax Justice Network, *Swiss Responsibility for the Extraterritorial Impacts of Tax Abuse on Women's Rights* (2016), available online at http://www.cesr.org/sites/default/files/downloads/switzerland_cedaw_submission_2nov2016.pdf.

40. Statement cited at http://www.taxjustice.net/2016/12/01/un-criticises-switzerland-pressure-mounts-human-rights-impacts-tax-havens/.

41. L. Bastin, 'Transfer Pricing and the WTO', 48(1) *Journal of World Trade* (2014), 59–80.

42. Ibid.

43. Ibid. at 78.

CHAPTER 7

A STRANGE ALCHEMY

Embedding Human Rights in Tax Policy Spillover Assessments

NICHOLAS LUSIANI AND MARY COSGROVE[1]

"When the happiness or misery of others depends in any respect upon our conduct, we dare not . . . prefer the interest of one to that of many . . . we value ourselves too much and other people too little, and that, by doing so, we render ourselves the proper object of the contempt and indignation of our brethren."

Adam Smith, *Theory of Moral Sentiments*, 1759

I. INTRODUCTION

One of the most striking paradoxes of the modern human rights movement has been its historic ambivalence toward addressing the material and economic requirements for realizing its vision. Seventy years have passed since the adoption of the Universal Declaration of Human Rights, yet it is only in the past decade or so that human rights advocates have begun interrogating the ways governments generate and allocate public monies.[2] A perfect storm of climate change, fiscal austerity, and economic inequality have come together most recently to expose the shallow foundations of the old, idealist assumptions that human rights could be realized without a financial cost. It is becoming increasingly obvious that every human right costs money.[3] While the social rights to education and healthcare generally require significant budgetary outlays, the police and military forces required to protect the rights to life, bodily integrity, and property are also significant drains on public budgets, as is an independent judiciary to ensure access to justice for all. Even the most "negative" of rights, such as the freedom from torture, freedom of speech, and freedom from discrimination, require positive measures, including well-funded oversight mechanisms to monitor progress and punish abuse. By avoiding tough debates about public financing, human rights advocates have not only limited their relevance to decisions about the fiscal foundations of social progress, they have also inadvertently neglected one of the

Tax, Inequality, and Human Rights. Philip Alston and Nikki Reisch.
© Oxford University Press 2019. Published 2019 by Oxford University Press.

most fundamental ways through which power and equality are mediated in society and in the economy: taxation.[4]

Today, human rights advocates can no longer afford to stay silent about how states raise, spend, and govern public money. Indeed, more and more civil society organizations,[5] UN human rights experts,[6] legal organizations,[7] and treaty bodies[8] are rapidly making up for decades of neglect of tax policy. These actors are increasingly highlighting the degree to which insufficient, inequitable, and unaccountable tax policy threatens governments' abilities to realize human rights. Innovative efforts are being made to apply the existing set of human rights norms and mechanisms to address the various challenges observed—one of the most ubiquitous of which is the phenomenon of cross-border tax abuse,[9] and in particular tax avoidance by multinational enterprises (MNEs).

The losses in public revenue stemming from various corporate tax-planning practices which exploit gaps in tax rules between countries to decrease a company's overall tax costs out of line with its economic substance (so-called "Base Erosion and Profit Shifting," or BEPS) are significant. While data unavailability and inconsistency prevent perfect tabulations, an estimated 4–10 percent of corporate income tax revenue worldwide is lost to corporate tax avoidance—a significant sum across countries North and South. Developing countries are disproportionately affected, losing between 7.5 percent and 14 percent of their corporate income tax revenue to MNE tax avoidance.[10] Alongside the substantial losses to public revenue that could have been used to protect and fulfill underfunded human rights, corporate tax avoidance has two other deleterious economic and political impacts.[11] First, avenues for corporate tax avoidance produce distributional impacts within societies. Restricting the ability of governments to tax some of the wealthiest sectors of the population, including multinational companies, their executives and shareholders, by obstructing the collection of capital and corporate tax revenue, increases pressure on fiscal policymakers and underresourced tax authorities to strike the unenviable Faustian bargain: slash spending on public services, hike more regressive and discriminatory forms of taxation, e.g., value-added tax (VAT) to offset the losses, or go further into public debt.[12] Either way, inequality deepens within and between countries.[13] A second knock-on effect of corporate tax avoidance is more directly political. Perceptions of high levels of corporate tax avoidance can undermine public trust, tax morale, and ultimately the accountability of government institutions.[14]

In the face of these growing concerns over the fiscal, distributive, and governance consequences of cross-border tax avoidance, international financial institutions, UN experts, development practitioners, tax justice advocates, human rights practitioners, and some governments have loosely converged around the need for countries to analyze the impact of their corporate tax systems overseas. The typical tool championed is the tax "spillover" assessment, with "spillovers" being defined here as the cross-border impact that one jurisdiction's tax rules or practices has on others. The difficulty of attributing causation for the falling tax revenues in one state to the particular tax policy of another state in the complex world of global trade, finance, and tax should not be underestimated. Nevertheless, two governments—Ireland[15] and the Netherlands[16]—have carried out such an exercise. The International Monetary Fund (IMF) has provided its own methodology,[17] and also commissioned a light spillover assessment of possible corporate tax reforms in the United States.[18]

In practice, what has been the effect of such assessments in uncovering the adverse impacts of tax policy? What lessons are applicable from decades of implementing other forms of environmental and social impact assessments? And how might embedding human rights principles into the purposes, processes, and methods of tax spillover impact assessments better recognize governments' respective responsibilities, engender responsiveness, and instill a measure of accountability over the unequally distributed power of states to tax the global economy?

Section II of this chapter sketches the history of tax spillover assessments, mapping out some of the rationales and institutional interests of the organizations proposing this measure. Section III presents findings as to the limitations—both technical and political—of those spillover studies carried out to date, placing these within the known limitations of other types of impact assessments. In light of these deficiencies, section IV explores the potential normative, technical, political, and practical added value of embedding human rights principles into tax spillover assessments, to more effectively assess and address the specific adverse overseas impacts of specific countries' tax policies. Section V concludes by identifying remaining challenges, and sketching out various gaps for future research.

II. GENEALOGY OF TAX SPILLOVER ASSESSMENTS: BIRTH OF AN IDEA, RATIONALES, AND INSTITUTIONAL INTERESTS

In 2010, the G20 asked the Organisation for Economic Co-operation and Development (OECD), the United Nations, the International Monetary Fund, and the World Bank to recommend ways in which G20 countries could assist in overcoming the capacity restraints of the tax systems of developing countries.[19] The resulting 2011 report, "Supporting the Development of More Effective Tax Systems" declared that:

> The G-20 countries' lead role in the debate on international tax system creates an obligation on them to ensure its smooth functioning. It would be appropriate for G-20 countries to undertake "spillover analyses" of any proposed changes to their tax systems that may have a significant impact on the fiscal circumstances of developing countries.[20]

The term "spillover" was not entirely new. It was used in tax policy discourse in the past, for example, in academic research,[21] as well as the OECD's 1998 Harmful Tax Competition report,[22] and early 2006 IMF research exploring the extraterritorial effects of a change in the US tax regime from a worldwide to a territorial system.[23] But this was the first time that these seminal international bodies recognized the special obligation of the governments of the world's major economic powers to monitor the impacts of their tax policies on poorer countries.

Many civil society groups hailed this as a positive development, having already incorporated to some degree this policy recommendation in their broader tax advocacy agenda. The UK nongovernmental organizations (NGOs) ActionAid, Christian Aid, and partners, for example, urged the UK government to carry out a spillover assessment of the potential impacts on developing countries of changes to UK Controlled Foreign Companies (CFCs) rules.[24] The Dutch think tank SOMO argued for its government to investigate the spillover impacts of its tax treaty network.[25] Christian Aid Ireland likewise called on the Irish government to conduct such an impact assessment.

As a result of this advocacy, a few governments embraced the idea. While it has not yet carried out such an impact study, the International Development Committee of the UK Parliament recommended that the government "assess new primary and secondary U.K. tax legislation against its likely impact on poverty reduction and revenue-raising in developing countries."[26] Two non-G20 governments—the Netherlands and Ireland—conducted tax spill-over assessments in 2014 and 2015, respectively.[27]

The IMF also contributed a 2014 Policy Paper on Spillovers in International Corporate Taxation.[28] The paper proposed a framework for assessing tax spillovers, and concluded that "spillover effects on corporate tax bases and rates are significant and sizable . . . especially marked and important for developing countries."[29] The Fund subsequently commissioned a paper which considered the spillover effects of a proposed US corporate tax reform,[30] including some of the findings in its 2016 Article IV consultation process with the country.[31]

Acknowledging that sporadic, individual national efforts alone would not work, civil society and some UN member states[32] went on to advocate for all developed countries to commit to conducting tax spillover assessments as part of the Sustainable Development Goals (SDGs) adopted by UN member states in 2015, and the commitments arising from the UN Financing for Development conference. While tax spillover assessment is not specifically mentioned in the SDGs, the 2015 Addis Ababa Accord did include an agreement by member states "to assess the impact of their policies on sustainable development," at least implicitly expressing support for a broader set of countries conducting such studies.[33]

In light of these advances, how effective have these spillover assessments been? Before evaluating them individually, it is useful to understand the various rationales buttressing the surprisingly wide-reaching support for this tool to begin with.

The initial policy rationale suggested by various proponents is straightforward. The tax laws, policies, and practices of particularly powerful economies are likely affecting the ability of tax administrations in other, less powerful, countries to raise revenue needed for sustainable development. Many of the arguments presented assert that certain benefits accruing to one country come at the direct expense of another county's ability to raise revenue—a sort of distribution of public revenue from one country to another. Many further argue that these tax spillovers are detrimental to all countries in fact, representing a collective action problem whereby national decisions create a collective inefficiency across countries.[34] Rather than a zero-sum game, all countries lose out as a result of the currently dysfunctional international tax rules. Competition over tax rates, for example, or profit shifting by multinational companies, reduces total tax paid across countries below what would otherwise be the case—ultimately resulting in the problem of stateless or untaxed income which no country benefits from. The problem according to this argument is not so much a transfer between countries, but a transfer from the public sector to multinational enterprises, their executives, their financial intermediaries, and ultimately their shareholders.

As an analytical due diligence tool, a tax spillover impact assessment has the potential to inject rationality into the overtly political tax policymaking process. Such assessments bring objective evidence to decision makers in ways that can counter interest-based logic with evidence-based policymaking, and enhance cooperation between relevant government departments as well as between the country of residence of an MNE and the source country where the company's activities take place. Spillover assessments can also provide essential information for tax policy-learning, informing policymakers in key decision points in the tax policymaking cycle, and allowing for more responsiveness to the inherently dynamic process of tax policy implementation. The 2011 report to the G20 referenced above gives further rationale for the proposal:

> While such (spillover) analyses will *of course* not always alter the course adopted, they may point to remedial measures to be incorporated into the reform and should be published for the international community to reflect upon—at a minimum, to enable developing countries to respond with parallel changes to their own systems if that would be helpful in protecting their revenue bases.[35]

For the IMF—arguably the most active proponent of the project—assessing tax spillovers is essential because these affect overall macroeconomic performance and possibly overall fiscal stability, which is the prime institutional objective of the Fund. Further, a broader uptake of tax spillover assessments by governments would allow the Fund to deploy its technical capacity in this area more broadly and more profoundly, consistently expressing its concern that these corporate tax spillovers disproportionately affect low- and middle-income countries.

For the OECD, meanwhile, governments' commitments to policy coherence for development are at stake in the debate over tax cooperation. Keen on seeking to retain its relevance in the debates over the international tax regime, the OECD has included elements of the proposal implicitly in its BEPS Action Plan, namely in Action Point 11.[36] Yet, observers have openly questioned to what degree the OECD would be willing to set up due diligence mechanisms which would effectively hold its own member states (including several financial secrecy jurisdictions) to account for undermining revenue generation in non-OECD countries.[37] For the Dutch[38] and Irish[39] governments, meanwhile, the tax spillover assessment provided an opportunity to better understand just how their tax policies do, and do not, affect poorer countries, in line with their commitments to policy coherence for sustainable development.

Finally, for many NGOs, rhetorical support for tax spillover assessments from the most prominent international organizations represented an unmissable strategic opportunity. If designed with the right safeguards in place, they argue, the spillover assessment could be an effective tool to provide reliable evidence on the role of rich countries and companies in effectively stripping the public revenue available for governments in the global South to invest in health, education, climate change mitigation, and other basic services.

In light of this institutional background, the following section identifies key lessons learned from decades of practice in the broader field of impact assessment to help frame our evaluation of the effectiveness of the tax spillover assessments carried out to date.

III. EVALUATING EXISTING TAX SPILLOVER ASSESSMENT METHODOLOGIES AGAINST RELEVANT PRACTICE

As international organizations and governments consider implementing tax spillover analyses stemming out of the Addis Ababa Action Accord commitments,[40] it is critical to take a step back to more objectively evaluate the effectiveness of the existing tax spillover assessments carried out by Ireland, the Netherlands, and partly the United States. As a benchmark for success, we draw on a literature review of decades of best (and worst practice) in the broader field of impact assessments (IAs), especially those used to assess social, environmental, and human rights impacts. Eight lessons can be learned from these experiences, each of which helps frame our evaluation of the effectiveness of the tax spillover analyses done to date.

A. LESSON ONE: FLEXIBLE METHODOLOGY

Experience from IA practice shows that an impact assessment cannot rely on a one-size-fits-all methodology. Flexibility and adaptability in both design and implementation are critical to ensure the tool adequately assesses the economic and political context in different countries, the differing policy levers of relevance, relevant political constituencies and audiences, etc.[41] Nevertheless, the flexibility of methods for impact assessments cannot be limitless. Impact assessments carried out over the past decades are often partial, and arbitrary in method design, with differing basic definitions and frameworks for assessment.[42] Without a broader *framework and common set of principles as an orienting structure*, IAs on the same subject cannot practically speaking be compared to one another, defeating the purpose of assessing one government's policy choices against another's. Without common methods and a common baseline against which to evaluate performance, it is particularly trying to understand an individual government's responsibilities for a global collective problem, such as corporate tax avoidance.

In this context, how have the tax spillover assessments under review compared? There is little practical consensus on a common framework of evaluation. The 2011 G20 report did not define what was meant by a "tax spillover," and provided no guidance on how a spillover analysis should be conducted. In practice, there have been deep differences in the *policy avenues or pathways assessed*, as well as the precise impacts monitored. The Dutch studies in 2013 focus almost exclusively on the impact of the country's network of double tax agreements (DTAs).[43] The 2015 Irish study is marginally more comprehensive, looking into various aspects of the taxation of corporate entities in Ireland. Yet neither considers the full range of policies that can lead to tax spillovers, many of which were identified in the 2014 IMF paper (see Table 7.1 below). Low tax rates or particular incentives can not only result in profit shifting (categorized as base spillovers in the Fund paper) arising from artificial ("paper") or substantial ("real") activities, but can force the other country to lower their tax rates ("strategic" spillovers). Neither the Irish nor the Dutch studies considered strategic spillovers, and both only addressed certain aspects of the base spillovers. While the Dutch reports were published before the IMF paper and thus did not have the benefit of its definitions and methodology, the Irish report was completed after the IMF paper and still used narrow definitions to assess the spillover effects of Irish policies.

Like the policy pathways chosen, the *type of impacts* addressed in each study are also quite different. The second Dutch study not only explores how the country's corporate tax policy is materially worsening the levels of investment and revenue uptake in developing countries but also explores the inequality and governance impacts. The first Dutch study and the Irish study meanwhile are focused exclusively on revenue effects.

Further, the *benchmark* against which the studies assessed the impacts of the countries' policies was problematic. In both the Dutch and Irish studies, the provisions of the DTAs between that country and developing countries were compared with the DTAs between those same developing countries and selected high-income or fast-growing economies—a questionable benchmark given the well-documented power imbalances in the negotiation of such DTAs between richer and poorer countries.[44] A more symmetrical yardstick of the "spillover" impact of the treaties would compare, for example, the withholding tax rates which would apply in the absence of the treaty to those allowed under the treaty.

It is entirely reasonable that the policy channels and scope of impacts assessed diverge somewhat across the studies, given differing national economies and roles in the international tax system. Yet, interviews conducted by the authors[45] suggest that the different focuses and scopes of the studies were not so much driven by differing objective circumstances as much as more practical concerns of data availability, time constraints, particular capacities of the research teams, and the differing political interests of the commissioning agencies.

Table 7.1: (Dis)Similarities in policy pathways and impacts of different tax spillover assessments

	IMF General	Ireland	Netherlands I	Netherlands II	IMF on US
Spillover pathway					
Corporate tax transparency/opacity rules (e.g., beneficial ownership, country-by-country reporting standards)					
Statutory rates' impact on tax competition race to the bottom					
Network of bilateral double taxation agreements (e.g., "treaty shopping")					
Preferential regimes (e.g., IP boxes)					
Hybrid mismatches					
Controlled Foreign Corporation (CFC) rules					
Type of impact					
Real and financial flows (e.g., FDI)					
Revenue loss through base spillovers					
Revenue loss through strategic spillovers and tax competition					
Repricing effects (e.g., interest rates)					
Inequality					
Governance					

Caption: ▬ = addressed in depth; ▬ = mentioned but not addressed in depth; ▬ = not addressed at all

B. LESSON TWO: POLITICAL CONSIDERATIONS

This leads us to a second perennial problem encountered in impact assessment practice over the decades: *political preconditioning*. The framing of the study, and in particular of the screening phase to decide on the policy channels and scope of impacts, is very often restricted to those areas that benefit the government, rather than objectively chosen to determine the actual impacts. After an extensive review of impact assessments done for the European Commission, for example, an expert group found that:

> in the practice of impact assessment there is evidence of *posthoc* rationalisation and legitimation of outcomes that are pre-determined by the premises of the techniques employed.[46]

Rather than an open, deliberative process to objectively comprehend policy impacts, observers point out that a priori political judgments, disguised as technical rationality, often implicitly bias many social, environmental and human rights impact assessments (HRIAs), predisposing them to the prerogatives of power to the point of undermining the validity of the findings. The biggest risk here is that the IAs could be used to justify fait accompli decisions, with the ultimate performative effect of pacifying, or eliminating the need for, further public debate[47]—precisely the opposite effect of what was intended.

How did the tax spillover assessments conducted perform with regard to political preconditioning? There is some evidence that the choices regarding the policy pathways to evaluate were less than purely objective and proactive, but instead were influenced by a desire to head off reputational risks. Arguably, both governments wanted a "good news" tax story. Before the first Dutch report, the role of the Netherlands' tax treaties had been the subject of a number of civil society reports, and Malawi had taken the unusual step of canceling its DTA with the country,[48] showing the extent to which Dutch tax policies were being questioned. Similarly, the Irish analysis was undertaken at a time when the country was in need of some good press on its tax policies. Still stung by being branded a "tax haven" during the US Senate inquiry into Apple,[49] Ireland was seeking to rehabilitate its image. The commissioning of the Irish spillover analysis coincided with the closing of the much publicized "double Irish" structure to new entrants from January 2015,[50] the country was heralding its commitment to the OECD BEPS Project, and the DTA with Zambia—a focus of a critical report by ActionAid[51]—was in the process of renegotiation. With this backdrop, the purpose of the analysis, for at least some within government, was arguably to strengthen the narrative that Ireland was a respectable member of the international tax community rather than to highlight existing problems in the current tax laws.

The most salient example of these politically preconditioned choices was the Irish study's decision to exclude an evaluation of "real substantive activities,"[52] focusing only on paper or artificial transactions. Restricting the scope of the report in this manner prevented any official questioning of Ireland's very low, and politically non-negotiable, 12.5 percent corporate tax rate.[53] Excluding these policy pathways of spillovers ran counter to the 2014 IMF paper described above, which concluded that strategic spillovers, like the effect of one country dropping its corporate income rate below standard, are a significant obstacle for developing countries in mobilizing sufficient revenue across countries. While Ireland's low corporate income tax rate may not directly drive developing country governments to decrease their rates, the indirect, global impacts of tax competition have run adverse to the revenue potential of all countries—rich and poor alike. What's more, the official response to any criticism of Ireland's tax policies since the completion of the Irish report invariably includes a reference to the fact that Ireland is one of only two countries to have carried out a tax spillover analysis[54]—suggesting it has been used to defend existing policies rather than to rethink them.

C. LESSON THREE: NEUTRALITY

A third related concern is often voiced about the *independence and objectivity* of impact assessments more broadly, particularly relevant where the IA is undertaken by the government itself. Despite the basic premise that conflicts of interest must be avoided and the powers of evaluation kept separate from the powers of policymaking, many impact assessments have suffered from poor institutional design which prevented, rather than protected, independence.[55] In the case of the Irish and Dutch tax spillover assessments, which government body commissioned the study seemed to be one important determinant in the reports' different scope and findings. Neither of the Dutch reports was commissioned by the Ministry of Finance, the department most involved in negotiating DTAs; instead, the first was commissioned by the Ministry of Foreign Affairs, while the second was conducted by an Independent Evaluation Office within the Ministry of Foreign Affairs. Both concluded that the DTAs in place were problematic for developing countries' tax administrations.

By contrast, the Irish report was commissioned by its Department of Finance. While it received extensive input from the Department of Foreign Affairs and Trade, the Irish report's conclusions were "broadly positive." Despite the revelation that over half of outward foreign direct investment (FDI) from Ireland goes to Bermuda, Jersey, Luxembourg, the Netherlands, and Switzerland, the government report concluded that there was no evidence that Ireland is used as a conduit in international tax avoidance. In a number of sections, positive conclusions were drawn even though there was acknowledged lack of available information,[56] for example on special purpose entities (SPEs) in Ireland. It is conceivable that negative tax spillovers would have been detected had the Department of Foreign Affairs, or an independent body, led the study. The Department of Foreign Affairs has a long history of prioritizing development cooperation assistance, an interest inevitably different from the Department of Finance whose key priority has been to increase FDI. Ultimately, the governance of the design and implementation of impact assessments is critical to ensuring an objective and independent assessment, unfettered by the passing political exigencies of the agency commissioning it.

D. LESSON FOUR: TIMELINESS

If IA practice is any guide, the *timing and frequency of the impact assessment within the policy cycle* is equally crucial in setting an impact assessment up for success. Ex post facto evaluations can be useful for assessing—and to some degree ameliorating—the effects of policy on the ground. Yet they cannot prevent these impacts altogether as they are not factored into the design of the policy in the first place.

As ex post facto studies, the Dutch and Irish tax spillover assessments suffer from these weaknesses. While partly conceptualized as baseline studies in line with the 2011 recommendations to the G20, there do not seem to be any plans at present to conduct a follow-up tax spillover assessment in Ireland nor in the Netherlands, posing significant constraints on the ongoing effectiveness of the tool. While ex ante assessments may be more methodologically demanding, especially when addressing the foreseeability of future impacts,[57] they are essential to ensuring proper information is available in time to actually influence public discussion on the issue in key moments in the policy cycle. Rather than being seen as a one-time exercise giving a snapshot of short-term, easily quantifiable impacts, best practices in the IA field suggest that assessments should be seen as policy-learning tools, conducted in a cyclical, iterative manner with ongoing monitoring and review over time.[58]

E. LESSON FIVE: TRANSPARENCY

A fifth common concern in IA practice relates to *transparency* about how impact assessments are undertaken. Many impact assessments are designed and implemented by a small group of technical experts. The steps taken, and the assumptions, data, and judgments on which the experts rely are not made public. Consequently, the study's accuracy, objectivity, and even legitimacy are left unquestioned.[59] When the authors are freed from the need to justify their actions externally, groupthink can be a very powerful driver of conformity in the methodologies chosen and the conclusions drawn.[60] In view of these transparency concerns, the Irish and Dutch governments did share basic information about the methodology, process, and important trade and investment data. Yet, data access was far from complete. Important layers of macroeconomic data held by the government were not made available to the teams conducting the spillover analyses, and key microdata of company transactions and tax returns were even less available.

F. LESSON SIX: INCLUSION

Apprehensions are commonly shared about the lack inclusivity and *participation* of key actors in the IA process.[61] By restricting the debate to a small cadre of policymakers and technical experts, it is argued, these processes often conceal, rather than reveal, the inherent value judgments, political pre-positions and uncertainties among the evaluation team. Rather than a process to simply legitimize projects,[62] best practices in IA engage a wide range of perspectives and affected actors for a more objective identification of where these assumptions, uncertainties, and divergent value judgments lie.[63] In this sense, the Dutch studies received very little if any public input. The Irish Department of Finance did, to its credit, organize a public consultation to inform its spillover assessment.[64] A cross-section of civil society advocates, academics, and tax experts participated. Yet, little effort was made to proactively seek input from key stakeholders such as tax administrations in low-income countries, tax academics, or civil society experts. This participation deficit may explain some of the gaps in the findings.

G. LESSON SEVEN: ADEQUATE RESOURCES

Many well-intentioned IAs have languished as a result of *a lack of time, financial, and human resources* allotted.[65] Tight timelines, meager budgets, poor quality control are common critiques in IA practice. Too often, the makeup of the assessment team itself fails to include relevant disciplines and perspectives, with real impacts on the findings. Teams dominated by economists have tended to concentrate more on economic impacts, while marginalizing social impacts. IA teams with less economic expertise, meanwhile, have tended to underexplore causality and underpredict future consequences inherent to the policy.[66] From interviews with those involved in the tax spillover assessments, it is clear that tight timelines, limited budgetary allocations, and an exclusive reliance on the tax expertise of the research teams conditioned the outcomes, in particular the comprehensiveness of the policy pathways explored. This is evidenced in the Irish report, which was prepared without the involvement of any Irish tax experts or any low-income countries' tax administrators. The decision to exclude consideration of Ireland's low corporate tax rate was justified on the basis that the rate applies only to "real substantive activity."[67] Yet, local tax knowledge would have highlighted the publicly available rulings that have granted this low rate to group financing and leasing activities with as few as one Irish-based employee.[68] Potential artificial profit shifting to take advantage of the 12.5 percent corporate income tax rate was therefore not investigated, to the detriment of arriving at a more objective assessment.

H. LESSON EIGHT: IMPACT

Finally, and perhaps most significantly, widespread concerns have arisen from IA practice about the ultimate effectiveness of IAs in actually *altering the policy choices* they conclude to be harmful. Evidence suggests that policy learning, and the ultimate utilization of knowledge developed by IAs, is relatively scarce. In many cases, IAs only inform policy design "at the margins."[69] These conclusions may be unduly pessimistic given the methodological difficulties of drawing causal inferences between policy change and impact assessments. Decision-making is not linear, and "the positivist information provision model" underlying many IAs (i.e., more and better information must inevitably lead to better decisions) is clearly overly simplistic.[70] Without an empowered accountability mechanism and built-in trigger to ensure policy action when an IA reveals harmful impact, the ultimate effectiveness of IAs in shaping better outcomes is dubious.

Have the Dutch and Irish tax spillover assessments actually affected the laws and policies under review? Unsurprisingly, perhaps, the main change resulting from both studies concerned the main subject of the impact assessments: DTAs. Both countries have renegotiated certain bilateral tax treaties which were determined to be out of step with current OECD standards. The newer DTAs between the Netherlands and developing countries now include anti-abuse provisions to deter "treaty shopping," for example, as well as increased withholding taxes. Some observers have also made the case that the Dutch spillover report catalyzed broader multilateral action, in particular through the BEPS action points 6 (on treaty abuse) and 15 (multilateral instrument). Ireland, for its part, has renegotiated its DTAs with Zambia and Pakistan to allow for greater withholding taxes in the source country.[71] Neither of these new treaties contain anti-abuse clauses (a recommendation of the G20 report), and the new treaty with Zambia would still allow for some of the tax avoidance to continue through the payment of "management service" fees.[72] Given the adverse publicity surrounding the old Ireland–Zambia DTA where tax was avoided by paying management fees to a shell Irish company (and which was referenced in the Ireland's spillover analysis), it would be expected that both countries would have an interest in ensuring Zambia retained taxing rights over such payments. In contrast, the new treaty with Pakistan, which was being negotiated simultaneously, allows for withholding taxes of up to 10 percent in payments for management services. This highlights the inconsistent approach in Irish tax diplomacy despite the spillover analysis exercise.[73] Even more importantly, the Irish spillover analysis has not affected any of the most significant tax policy spillovers, in particular the 12.5 percent corporate income tax rate and the use of special purpose entity structures where Irish companies with little or no substance are used as conduits to facilitate the transfer of profits to jurisdictions with little or no tax.

As this section has shown, lessons learned from decades of IA practice point to the need for tax spillover assessments to combine technical rigor with participatory vigor. While technical experts are critical to ensure objective and compelling findings, their discretion and overall influence (especially in the formative screening phase) must be conditioned by transparency, participation, and accountability in the policymaking process—a strange alchemy indeed.[74] In seeking to strike the right balance, how can human rights principles and criteria help to overcome the normative, conceptual, and methodological gaps seen in IAs to date? This is the subject of the next section.

IV. FROM "SPILLOVERS" TO INTEGRATED IMPACT ASSESSMENTS: HUMAN RIGHTS AS GUIDING PRINCIPLES FOR MORE EFFECTIVE TAX SPILLOVER ASSESSMENTS

The G20 report on spillovers noted the role of taxation in relieving poverty and delivering public services in developing countries.[75] Yet, none of the tax spillover analyses done to date assess the human rights impacts of tax policies. In fact, the words "human rights" do not even appear in any of the relevant reports. This was a mistake. Drawing on recent efforts to implement policy-oriented HRIAs in various national contexts[76] and relevant normative guidance,[77] this section explores to what degree a common series of human rights guiding principles might help to overcome some of the common deficiencies encountered in recent tax spillover assessments.[78] Inserting human rights principles into tax spillover assessments will not be a silver bullet, certainly. Yet, basing these tax spillover assessments more consciously on human rights norms can help address some of their most critical shortcomings.

To ground the analysis, what normative guidance can international law (in particular international human rights law) provide on cross-border tax abuses? Drawing on various provisions in the UN Charter,[79] the Universal Declaration of Human Rights,[80] and other international human rights treaties,[81] such as the International Covenant on Economic, Social and Cultural Rights,[82] as well as jurisprudence from regional and international bodies,[83] a growing number of legal experts argue that countries have a duty under international law to assess, and address, the impacts of their tax policies overseas. Countries whose conduct (actions or omissions) effectively erode another state's capacity to exercise its sovereignty in taxing legal and natural persons in its jurisdiction, stand in breach of their legal obligations to provide international cooperation and assistance. Any "reasonably foreseeable" impacts of a country's tax policy upon another—if left unassessed—may breach governments' obligations to respect the realization of human rights abroad.[84] This obligation to respect other countries' policy space is particularly incumbent on EU countries, which are bound by Article 208(1) of the Lisbon Treaty, which states unambiguously: "The Union shall take account of the objectives of development cooperation in the policies that it implements which are likely to affect developing countries."[85]

While a country clearly cannot be held responsible under international law for all the unknowable, remote consequences of its conduct overseas, state responsibility may be triggered when its policies or practices result in harmful human rights impacts which it knows or should have known about.[86] By mandating tax spillover assessments, governments can be seen to take one step toward acknowledging the foreseeable adverse impacts of their policies on human rights abroad.[87] One state's capacity to mobilize resources is dependent to some degree on another state's tax behavior. In this view, a tax spillover impact assessment is not only an important tool for evidence-based tax cooperation but also an instrument for pinpointing respective states' responsibilities for the collective problem of corporate tax avoidance. That is, the tool is a critical due diligence mechanism to bolster accountability and help institutionalize public oversight of tax policy by shifting the onus onto governments to show and prove their policies are not undermining the tax sovereignty and human rights realization overseas. On this reasoning, one UN human rights treaty body has already requested that Switzerland "undertake independent, participatory and periodic impact assessments of the extraterritorial effects of its financial secrecy and corporate tax policies" on human rights.[88] But what would this look like? We outline ten key principles for a human rights-framed tax spillover assessment.

A. FLEXIBILITY OF METHODS, BASED ON A COMMON NORMATIVE FRAMEWORK

A first added value of embedding human rights into tax spillover studies is that it allows state practice to be measured against a shared set of existing obligations entrenched in international legal instruments common to virtually all countries. While there would necessarily still be a margin of discretion in determining the precise methods chosen, the common international standards of human rights provide a useful yardstick in assessing the delineated responsibilities of different governments, putting an emphasis on cooperation over competition. Rather than measuring governments' tax conduct against the lowest common denominator of standard tax competition practice, as was the case in assessing Ireland and the Netherlands' DTAs, tax policy would be assessed for the degree to which it is effectively meeting the higher-order principle of tax cooperation to mobilize sufficient resources for human rights. While at first glance this norm of tax cooperation may seem overly ambiguous and therefore useless as a clear benchmark, various human rights bodies and institutions quoted in this chapter have provided much more clarity as to the respective obligations of states in fixing the broken international tax regime.[89] In particular, this shared normative framework based on existing international legal instruments codified by most states provides, in effect, a common grounding for analyzing *what* impacts by *what* policies of *which* actors (public duty bearers and other responsible private parties) should be assessed. This framework also clarifies *how* the assessments are to be carried out: with transparency and participation of all affected stakeholders. A human rights–framed tax spillover prioritizes the principles of equality and nondiscrimination, in particular by focusing its inquiry on those groups most gravely affected by the policy under question, rather than on an aggregated analysis of impact.[90] Furthermore, the human rights imperative of accountability for harms implies that these impact assessments should be designed in a way which actually triggers policy change.

B. COMPREHENSIVE ASSESSMENT OF SPILLOVER PATHWAYS

Human rights duties, furthermore, are relevant to public policies across the board, giving an impetus to a more comprehensive assessment of the tax policy pathways which affect the ability of governments to raise revenue for human rights overseas. Rather than an indiscriminate (or worse, prearranged) choice of the particular policy areas to be assessed, a human rights approach would start with a common set of plausible pathways, which each government would need to factor into its screening phase, the aim of which would be to identify which policies to analyze in depth. The rationale for choosing to focus on any particular subset of these pathways would be shared and justified openly for debate at the formative stage to encourage a broader group of affected stakeholders to engage in the design of the study. Starting more comprehensively in this way would help prevent the type of reductionism and political preconditioning which has plagued many IAs to date. The more comprehensive set of spillover pathways which the IMF 2014 paper explores is a good starting point, but should arguably be expanded to include other key ways in which spillovers occur, such as lax corporate reporting requirements (e.g., lack of information on ultimate beneficial ownership), CFC rules, preferential regimes (e.g., IP boxes), or other key pathways which emerge in the future.

C. INTEGRATED SCOPE OF IMPACT AREAS

Rather than a patchy, arbitrary, or even biased selection of the scope of impacts to be evaluated, an HRIA of tax policies would allow for a more integrated substantive focus on multiple impacts.[91] While existing impact assessments focus on revenues, investment flows, or other economic outcomes as "aims" themselves, human rights–centered spillover analyses would understand these economic variables as a "means" to a different end: realizing human rights. This does not mean that a human rights–informed tax spillover assessment would necessarily aim to evaluate how tax policy is directly affecting the realization of all human rights abroad. Such an endeavor would be tenuous—both methodologically and politically—as the process of assessing impacts is mediated through the other domestic government's primary duty to realize these human rights. Nonetheless, the spillover assessment could take the revenue, inequality, repricing, and governance effects of tax policy—impacts that the second Dutch study helpfully charts out—as proxies for an enabling environment for human rights. Rather than reducing the scope of impact to measuring revenue or FDI flows alone, this more holistic understanding of relevant impact areas would allow for more attention to the repercussions of one country's tax policy on another country's political economy—a key aspect of human rights fulfillment in practice.

D. INDEPENDENCE AND OBJECTIVITY

While designed with the aim of driving policy choices which realize rather than undermine human rights, human rights–informed tax spillovers must remain independent and objective so as not to undermine their empirical effectiveness.[92] As seen in past IA practice, conflicts of interest arise when these studies are commissioned and overseen by the same government whose policies the study attempts to evaluate. The principle of independence should be respected in future tax spillover assessments by creating a firewall between the policymakers and the assessors. To avoid conflicts, it would be wise for an independent body to carry out such assessments. One proposal might be to house these assessments with an international institution (some argue the IMF, or a global tax body under the auspices of the United Nations) less prone to domestic political influence, with the legitimacy and capacity to lead the design and implementation of tax spillovers to ensure objectivity and independence. Likewise, independent bodies at the national level, such as national human rights institutions, might be well placed to lead or participate in this task. Country-level data, such as company tax returns, would arguably still need to come from the government, but the methodology for evaluating the data and the conclusions drawn from it should ultimately be left to more independent analysis. In countries where the recommendations of the national human rights institution are routinely ignored by the government, the benefits of increased independence may be negated by the low political priority afforded to the outcomes. In such jurisdictions, the inclusion of the national human rights institution as a partner in the process might be a suitable compromise.

E. PERIODIC, CYCLICAL, AND ITERATIVE PROCESS TO INDUCE POLICY LEARNING AND CHANGE

If it is to actually induce policy learning and help decision makers adapt to an inherently dynamic process, a human rights–informed tax spillover process would also be prepared to track changes over time, assessing the shorter-term, and the longer-term impacts, of tax policy. More of a process than a product in line with human rights standards on participation in the design of public policies, a HRIA of tax policy would be organized as an ongoing, iterative method plugged into the ebbs and flows of the national tax policy cycle in ways which allow the findings to inform, shape, and even disrupt decision-making. A first baseline study could be conducted (as the 2011 report to the G20 suggests),[93] followed by periodic reassessments. As a corollary to the kinds of ex ante cost-benefit analyses some countries require for proposed legislation and regulations, ex ante spillover assessments could be mandated any time a relevant policy change is proposed to ensure findings and recommendations inform policymakers. Ex post facto studies would also monitor impacts over time.[94] If begun soon, this iterative process could provide a very helpful evaluation of the effectiveness of the ongoing implementation of the BEPS Action Plan. Those leading the BEPS process portray the current implementation stage as "inclusive" following criticism of the initial phase.[95] Yet, the impact of such a spillover analysis will be limited if the benchmark is the status quo. In a system where poorer countries are already disadvantaged, analysis aimed at not making matters worse, rather than seeking to make matters better, is insufficient.

F. PROPORTIONALITY AND RISK ASSESSMENT APPROACH

A robust ex ante impact assessment would require accurate predictive capacities,[96] which may not be possible given the large number of dynamic variables involved in the revenue impacts of corporate tax policy overseas. The attribution of responsibility is equally challenging. This is especially the case when considering the adverse impacts of bilateral tax treaties. If a company takes advantage of meager withholding rules provided for in a tax treaty, which one of the two state parties are to blame? Rather than imagining that the tax spillover tool can predict with quantifiable precision all the possible overseas impacts of a particular country's tax policy now and into the future, a *risk assessment approach* would be useful. As has been proposed in HRIAs of trade and investment treaties,[97] a human rights–informed tax spillover assessment should apply the *precautionary principle*, recognizing from the outset the various ways that tax policy could reasonably affect harm in other countries. Even where these impacts are not yet fully demonstrated and quantified, the burden of proof would rest with the government to show that its tax policy is doing no harm, identifying the existence and degree of risk on the budget of particular countries of particular tax policies, then monitoring these risks overtime. Such an approach would be closest to that used in the second Dutch report where, in the absence of economic data, the author used case studies to identify risks.[98]

In tandem with the precautionary principle, a *proportionality rule* could be used in this context to develop a decision tree of sorts. If the risk of overseas spillover is considered low, but the domestic benefits high, the policy could be considered safe to go ahead as planned. If the overseas risks are high, but the domestic benefits low, the policy should clearly be ceased. If both the overseas risks and domestic benefits are high, a negotiation could proceed between relevant parties to develop a framework for mitigation and compensation. If risks are truly un-certain, governments should commit to freeze activities until the impacts are clearer over time, in cooperation with other tax administrations. In any event, a real premium should be placed on tracking and monitoring impacts overtime, as tax flows change significantly from year to year. The proportionality rule would also be helpful in determining which countries should be obliged to carry out spillover assessments—arguably those with the most systemic influence on the workings of the international tax system.

G. TRANSPARENCY OF PROCESS AND OF POLICIES IN QUESTION

Transparency is a hallmark of human rights. Applying the principle of transparency more in-tentionally to the tax spillover assessment process could have several benefits. First, framing ac-cess to information about the overseas impact of tax policy as a fundamental right guaranteed under international law[99] could help support researchers, and the general public, to access rel-evant tax and trade data, a commonly observed obstacle. Beyond providing an avenue to drive tax transparency, the assessment itself would seek to answer the question of whether or not the government is respecting the best practices in international tax transparency (e.g., auto-matic exchange of corporate tax-related information, public registries of beneficial ownership of companies, trusts, etc.) as this has a demonstrable effect on the ability of other countries to raise revenue.[100] Framing these spillover assessments within human rights also allows the use of freedom of information laws to access data relevant to assessing the impact of a country's tax policies.

H. PARTICIPATION AND INCLUSION OF AFFECTED ACTORS

Contrary to recent learnings in IA practice, tax spillover assessments to date have been quite closed affairs, dominated by a handful of technical tax experts, a limited set of methods, and prone to a restricted framings and therefore constrained findings. Best practices in the IA field dovetail interestingly with the human right of people to participate in public decision-making affecting them,[101] as tax policy surely does. Including a wide range of perspectives, values and policy objectives is considered productive in all stages, especially in the preliminary screening and scoping exercise, when the overall framing can still be redirected and expanded.[102] The goal is to engender a process of inclusion that clarifies, rather than conceals, important polit-ical choices (not only by those consulted but also of the team conducting the IA), and to avoid the crowd-pleasing effect of mono-disciplinary and uni-perspective discussions. A broader and more inclusive group of involved parties (for example, tax administrations and tax advocates in affected countries) can also provide a better understanding of the differentiated impacts of tax policy on different population groups or countries, provide information to analyze the differing needs and interests of the various stakeholders, and widen the feeling of ownership over the ul-timate recommendations of the study—a key objective if the assessment seeks to affect the real political economy of tax policy.

Designing a more participatory tax spillover assessment will inevitably require more time and financial resources. But it need not overly obstruct efficiency. Various cases exist of IAs that combine an open, participatory process with a robust and efficient research study. For example, setting up expert and multistakeholder committees with representatives from all relevant sectors to evaluate the key decision points along the way from the screening through to the scoping, research, and conclusion phases has worked in other settings. Rather than being conceived as a one-off technical assessment of discrete, quantifiable impacts of a constricted layer of tax policies, the participatory tax impact assessment would instead be designed to assess foreseeable risks, and insert public debate and critical reflection into the disorderly, and thoroughly political, reality of tax policymaking.[103] According to one evaluation of the state of the art of IAs, "instead of being characterized as objective analysis leading to better decisions, assessment should be regarded as a way of bringing diverse perspectives to bear on complex issues, and as a set of formal and informal procedures in which learning can take place, both within and between the different interest groups involved. This view of the role of assessment has interesting implications, because it emphasizes the importance of open and deliberative approaches, especially when the issues under investigation are complex ones on which there is little or no consensus."[104]

I. QUALITY CONTROL, WITH INTERDISCIPLINARY AND PROPERLY RESOURCED EVALUATION TEAMS

Another key consideration in setting up an effective tax spillover assessment involves resourcing, namely, in time, budget, and the depth and breadth of expertise on the assessing team. Allowing for a more comprehensive framing and more informed findings requires time, money, and an interdisciplinary team with complementary knowledge and skills including human rights and tax law, economics, and public finance expertise, as well as social science expertise to assist in the design of participatory research methodologies.[105] Experience also shows that it is useful to ensure that the person(s) commissioning the paper are knowledgeable about the issues at hand to ensure overall quality control.

J. ACCOUNTABILITY AND STATUS OF FINDINGS IN TRIGGERING POLICY CHANGE

Finally, and perhaps most importantly to uphold the normative objectives of tax spillover assessments, the findings and conclusions of the study should factor into the tax policy decision-making process itself. These assessments should be designed in ways which trigger policy and legislative action to address the adverse impacts, identify responsible parties, and include recommendations and clear timelines for remedy. This principle of accountability is essential to ensure that the ultimate effect of a tax spillover assessment is to sharpen rather than dull state responsibilities for tax abuse, and to uncover rather than to cover up instances in which one government raises public revenue at the expense of another. The purpose of the tax spillover assessment, in this sense, should be to enhance state accountability for the impacts of its policies overseas.

V. REMAINING CHALLENGES AND GAPS IN RESEARCH

Tax spillover analysis is still in its infancy. Though it has the nominal support of many influential international bodies and civil society actors, it has yet to be embraced by G20 governments. The failure of larger economies to adopt this measure is likely due to the political implications of such reports. While carrying out such a review can support policy coherence and assist states in fulfilling their international obligations, the centrality of tax policy to state sovereignty makes governments reluctant to undertake unilateral actions which may limit their tax policy space. The former Special Rapporteur on extreme poverty acknowledged the difficulty in obtaining international agreement in relation to taxation due in part to the "reluctance of states to cede any sovereignty."[106]

Integrating human rights guiding principles into the practice of tax spillover assessments, this chapter has found, can provide value. Yet a number of tough methodological and political obstacles remain, many of which are inherent to the act of policy impact evaluation more generally. Together, these remaining challenges provide for a fertile future research agenda.

Methodologically, the empirical accuracy of tax·spillover assessments continues to be thwarted by the failure of governments to ensure access to relevant data, made more complex by the right to privacy concerns of many companies in accessing the microdata which would be so useful in determining the impact of changes in tax policy.[107] Quantifiably measuring the scale of a problem thoroughly veiled behind complex group structures and various layers of data opacity is next to impossible without accepting relatively wide margins of error. This lack of data results in a self-censoring of sorts, as it prevents many governments and international institutions from even engaging in the attempt to monitor spillovers. Innovative techniques are emerging to use the data to be released under the various BEPS-related tax transparency initiatives, but much more can and should be done. Linked to the question of access to information is the pervasive problem of causation. With what degree of certainty can we conclude that a particular dimension of one country's corporate tax policy, say a reduction of the corporate income tax rate or the existence of a preferential tax regime, necessarily induced a second country to lose out in its tax base? The problem of causation also reinforces the problem of attribution. The normative effectiveness of the tool is challenged as it relies in part in the possibility to attribute one state's capacity to mobilize resources to another state's tax behavior.

Alongside these tough methodological challenges, various political question marks continue to frustrate effective tax spillover assessments. First, the freedom from discrimination is a fundamental principle of human rights which in impact assessments puts a premium on identifying those individual and groups most affected by a particular project or policy, and prioritizing remedy of any harms they face over others in a more advantaged position. While it is possible to some degree to disaggregate the adverse impact of domestic tax policy, how might this be done when debating the right of sovereign governments to tax multinational economic activity? Might the "ability to pay" principle, used to justify progressive taxation domestically, provide a normative value to justify increased rights to tax multinational business to those countries that are both disproportionately affected by corporate tax abuse, and simultaneously in greater need of public revenue?[108]

Further, tax spillover analysis will not, necessarily, reveal clear villains and victims. The legal and regulatory regimes enabling multinational tax avoidance, starting with bilateral tax treaties, have been put in place by both source and residence countries. Both developed and developing countries are in some way complicit. While source countries face disproportionate burdens, they are rarely passive victims. Tax spillover impact assessments—if done right—could be powerful processes to identify the respective responsibilities of particular countries for corporate tax avoidance. As tax avoidance undermines the ability of states to finance human rights, governments who are found to facilitate, enable, or permit tax avoidance which foreseeably strip revenues from other states, may well be in breach the legal duty to international cooperation and assistance in the universal realization of human rights. Yet, more research is needed on how to do so in ways which also recognizing the concurrent duties of affected countries.

Third, recent practice of IAs illustrates that many are plagued by a certain indeterminacy which prevents their effectiveness. That is, the assessing teams of various IAs have rather inconclusively concluded that it is not possible to make a determinative judgment about the impacts which occurred.[109] In those cases, does this mean that the project or policy should uncritically continue as originally planned? Given the methodological challenges of tax spillover assessments described above, there is a real risk that the very exercise of assessing the impact of tax policy overseas could unintentionally justify an unjust policy, pacifying, normalizing, or eliminating further public debate, and reaffirming the current distribution of taxing powers. More thinking is needed on how to prevent these unintended and perverse consequences.

Fourth, tax spillover assessments stand on an underlying assumption that if each individual country assessed and addressed the impacts of its tax policies overseas then the system overall would tend to restrict cross-border tax abuses. Yet, it is very possible that these individual actions would not by themselves challenge the foundations of the international tax system based on an antiquated division of source and residence countries with multinational companies treated as multiple entities rather than the single economic and political entity they are in practice. In this perspective, impact assessments can better point out deficiencies in international tax governance, but will not, on their own, provide proactive proposals to overhaul the system as such.

A fifth political challenge is perhaps the most basic. As many longtime experts have found, tax policy—perhaps more than any other policy area besides national security—today is thoroughly driven by national interest, over and above almost all other considerations. Whether in high-stake negotiations over bilateral tax treaties, or within international bodies such as the OECD and the United Nations set up with the express objective of tax cooperation, the center of political gravity of international tax debates is thoroughly domestic. There are still very few governments which are willing to reform the rules of the international tax regime in ways which favor their fellow countries, especially those facing the worst impacts of corporate tax avoidance. As economic growth is projected to remain languid in North and South over the next decade,[110] perceptions that the international tax field is a fundamentally zero-sum game are strong and growing, with more and more governments arguing that any improvements in the taxing rights of a neighboring country come at their expense. In the context of resurgent economic nationalism in many countries, especially the United States, the political appetite to conduct human rights–informed tax spillover assessments is uncertain to say the least. In fact, these types of impact assessments may be misused politically in the sense that a finding of negative spillovers may be precisely what some nationalistic tax policymakers would benefit most from, as policies that poach tax revenues from another jurisdiction could be pitched as a "win" in the global tax wars to come.

If that is the case, those countries most responsible for the human rights impacts of multinational corporate tax avoidance, in Adam Smith's memorable words, may remain "the proper object of the contempt and indignation," leading to deepening tax competition and deteriorating fiscal positions across countries. In contrast, embedding human rights norms into the substance and process of international tax policymaking could have profound impacts in widening fiscal space, solidifying cooperation, and more effectively holding to account those who benefit from contemptuous tax practices.

NOTES

1. This paper was drafted in the summer of 2017. The authors express their deep appreciation to the following people for the time offered for interviews: Mr. Joe Stead, OECD Tax and Development Unit; Mr. Francis Weyzig, Oxfam Novib; Mr. Martin Hearson, London School of Economics; Ms. Victoria Perry, International Monetary Fund; Mr. Sorley McCaughey, Christian Aid Ireland; and Mr. Brendan Crowley, Department of Finance, Ireland. Thanks also to Ignacio Saiz, Allison Corkery, and Sergio Chaparro from the Center for Economic and Social Rights (CESR) for their valuable comments, as well as Portia Karegreya for her research assistance. The views expressed are not necessarily those of CESR nor Oxfam. Any mistakes or errors are the authors' alone. In full disclosure, one of the authors has been actively involved in recent advocacy within national and United Nations fora for the widespread implementation of tax spillover assessments.
2. See, for example, I. Saiz, 'Resourcing Rights: Combating Tax Injustice from a Human Rights Perspective', *in* A. Nolan, R. O'Connell, and C. Harvey (eds.), *Human Rights and Public Finance: Budgets and the Promotion of Economic and Social Rights* (2013), 78; A. Nolan, 'Economic and Social Rights, Budgets and the Convention on the Rights of the Child', 21 *The International Journal of Children's Rights* (2013), 248; International Bar Association, *Tax Abuses, Poverty and Human Rights: A Report of the International Bar Association's Human Rights Institute Task Force on Illicit Financial Flows, Poverty and Human Rights* (2013), available online at http://www.ibanet. org/Document/Default.aspx?DocumentUid=4977CB3D-4988-4C9C-84C7-9050A5CB2311 (last visited 6 June 2017).
3. S. Holmes and C. Sunstein, *The Cost of Rights: Why Liberty Depends on Taxes* (1999).
4. See, for example, J. Schumpeter, *The Crisis of the Tax State* (1919); I. W. Martin et al. (eds.), *The New Fiscal Sociology: Taxation in Comparative and Historical Perspective* (2009).
5. See, for example, *Lima Declaration on Tax Justice and Human Rights* (2014), available online at http://cesr.org/endorse-lima-declaration-tax-justice-and-human-rights (last visited 6 June 2017); Center for Economic and Social Rights, *A Post-2015 Fiscal Revolution: Human Rights Policy Brief* (2014), available online at http://cesr.org/sites/default/files/fiscal.revolution.pdf; ActionAid, *Taxing Solutions: How Tighter Tax Rules for Big Business Could Help End Poverty* (2008), available online at https://www.actionaid.org.uk/sites/default/files/doc_lib/taxing_solutions_report.pdf; Christian Aid, *Who Pays the Price? Hunger: The Hidden Cost of Tax Injustice* (2013), available online at http://www.christianaid.org.uk/images/Who-pays-the-price-Hunger-the-hidden-cost-of-tax-injustice-May-2013.pdf.
6. See, for example, Human Rights Council, Report of the Special Rapporteur on Extreme Poverty and Human Rights, Magdalena Sepúlveda Carmona, UN Doc. A/HRC/26/28, 22 May 2014, at paras. 44–49; Human Rights Council, Final Study on Illicit Financial Flows, Human Rights and the 2030 Agenda for Sustainable Development, UN. Doc. A/HRC/31/61, 15 Jan. 2016, at para. 43; Council of Europe Commissioner for Human Rights, *Safeguarding Human Rights in Times of Economic Crisis* (2013), available online at https://wcd.coe.int/ViewDoc.jsp?id=2130915 (last visited 6 June 2017).
7. International Bar Association, *supra* note 2.
8. See, for example, Committee on Economic, Social and Cultural Rights, Concluding Observations on the Third Periodic Report of Ireland, UN Doc. E/C.12/IRL/CO/3, 8 July 2015, at para. 11 (recommending the State to "consider reviewing its tax regime, with a view to increasing its revenues to restore the pre-crisis levels of public services and social benefits, in a transparent and participatory manner"); Committee on Economic, Social and Cultural Rights, Report on the Twenty-Second, Twenty-Third and Twenty-Fourth Sessions, UN Doc. E/2001/22; E/C.12/ 2000/21, at paras. 82 (expressing concern about the negative effect of Georgia's taxation system

on poverty) and 370 (praising Australia's progressive tax reforms to reduce income tax for most working Australians); Committee on the Rights of the Child, Consideration of Reports Submitted by States Parties Under Article 44 of the Convention—Concluding Observations: Georgia, UN Doc. CRC/C/15/Add.124, 28 June 2000, at paras. 18–19; Committee on the Rights of the Child, General Comment No. 19 on Public Budgeting for the Realization of Children's Rights (Art. 4), UN Doc. CRC/C/GC/19, 20 July 2016, at paras. 74–77.

9. In this chapter, cross-border tax abuse refers to the exploitation of interstate transactions by individuals or corporations to evade, avoid, or minimize due payment of taxes in ways which are harmful to the public purse. This definition includes losses due to tax-related illicit financial flows (in particular trade mis-invoicing), the offshoring of personal income, as well as corporate tax avoidance. The last dimension—tax avoidance by multinational enterprise—is the focus of this particular chapter.

10. For a comprehensive literature review on the subject, see OECD, *Measuring and Monitoring BEPS, Action 11—2015 Final Report*, 5 Oct. 2015, available online at http://dx.doi.org/10.1787/9789264241343-en (last visited 6 June 2017); see also E. Crivelli, R. De Mooji, and M. Keen, *Base Erosion, Profit Shifting, and Developing Countries: IMF Working Paper* (2015), available online at https://www.imf.org/external/pubs/ft/wp/2015/wp15118.pdf.

11. N. Lusiani, '"Only the Little People Pay Taxes": Tax Evasion and Switzerland's Extraterritorial Obligations to Economic, Social and Cultural Rights in Zambia', *in* M. Gibney and W. Vandenhole (eds.), *Litigating Transnational Human Rights Obligations: Alternative Judgments* (2014), 116.

12. See Norwegian Ministry of Foreign Affairs, *Tax Havens and Development: Status, Analyses and Measures: Report from the Norwegian Government Commission on Capital Flight from Poor Countries* (2009), available online at https://www.regjeringen.no/contentassets/0a903cdd09fc423 ab21f43c3504f466a/en-gb/pdfs/nou200920090019000en_pdfs.pdf, at 67.

13. See, for example, Center for Economic and Social Rights, *From Disparity to Dignity: Tackling Economic Inequality through the Sustainable Development Goals* (2016), available online at http://cesr.org/sites/default/files/disparity_to_dignity_SDG10.pdf.

14. See, for example, M. Moore, *How Does Taxation Affect the Quality of Governance?* (Institute of Development Studies Working Paper, 2007), available online at http://www2.ids.ac.uk/gdr/cfs/pdfs/Wp280.pdf.

15. Irish Department of Finance, *IBFD Spillover Analysis: Possible Effects of the Irish Tax System on Developing Economies* (2015)

16. The Netherlands commissioned two reports, the First Report being: Ministry of Foreign Affairs, the Netherlands, *Onderzoek belastingverdragen met ontwikkelingslanden* (2013), available online at https://www.rijksoverheid.nl/documenten/brieven/2013/08/30/onderzoek-belastingverdragen (last visited 6 June 2017); the Second Report is: Ministry of Foreign Affairs, the Netherlands, *Evaluation Issues in Financing for Development: Analysing Effects of Dutch Corporate Tax Policy on Developing Countries* (2013), available online at https://www.government.nl/binaries/government/documents/reports/2013/11/14/iob-study-evaluation-issues-in-financing-for-development-analysing-effects-of-dutch-corporate-tax-policy-on-developing-countries/iob-study-evaluation-issues-in-financing-for-development.pdf.

17. IMF, *Policy Paper: Spillovers in International Corporate Taxation*, 9 May 2014, available online at https://www.imf.org/external/np/pp/eng/2014/050914.pdf.

18. This paper was drafted before the enactment of the 2017 Tax Cuts and Jobs Act in the US. E. Kleinbard, K. Clausing, and T. Matheson, *U.S. Corporate Income Tax Reform and its Spillovers*, 5 July 2016, available online at https://www.imf.org/external/pubs/cat/longres.aspx?sk=44050.0 (last visited 6 June 2017).

19. IMF, OECD, UN, and the World Bank, *Supporting the Development of More Effective Tax Systems: A Report to the G-20 Development Working Group* (2011), available online at http://www.oecd.org/ctp/48993634.pdf, at 9.

20. Ibid.

21. P. Thalmann, L. H. Goulder, and F. Delorme, *Assessing the International Spillover Effects of Capital Income Taxation: IHS Research Memorandum No. 341* (1994), available online at http://irihs.ihs.ac.at/730/1/fo341.pdf.

22. "If the spillover effects of particular tax practices are so substantial that they are concluded to be poaching other countries' tax bases, such practices would be doubtlessly labelled 'harmful tax competition.'" OECD, *Harmful Tax Competition: An Emerging Global Issue* (1998), available online at http://www.oecd-ilibrary.org/taxation/harmful-tax-competition_9789264162945-en, at 16 (last visited 21 Mar. 2017).

23. P. Mullins, *Moving to Territoriality? Implications for the United States and the Rest of the World* (2006), available online at https://www.imf.org/external/pubs/ft/wp/2006/wp06161.pdf.

24. A. Goodall, 'CFC Reform: UK Resists Calls for Assessment of Impact on Developing Countries', *Tax Journal*, 3 Feb. 2012, available online at https://www.taxjournal.com/articles/cfc-reform-uk-resists-calls-assessment-impact-developing-countries-40061 (last visited 6 June 2017).

25. Centre for Research on Multination Corporations (SOMO), *Should The Netherlands Sign Tax Treaties with Developing Countries?* (2013), available online at https://www.somo.nl/should-the-netherlands-sign-tax-treaties-with-developing-countries/ (last visited 6 June 2017).

26. United Kingdom International Development Committee, *Fourth Report—Tax in Developing Countries: Increasing Resources for Development* (2012), available online at http://www.publications.parliament.uk/pa/cm201213/cmselect/cmintdev/130/13006.htm#a8, at para. 55 (last visited 6 June 2017).

27. Irish Spillover Report, *supra* note 15, Dutch Reports, *supra* note 16.

28. IMF, *supra* note 17.

29. Ibid.

30. Kleinbard, Clausing, and Matheson, *supra* note 18.

31. IMF, *United States: 2016 Article IV Consultation Staff Report*, available online at https://www.imf.org/external/pubs/cat/longres.aspx?sk=44079.0 (last visited 6 June 2017).

32. See Irish Spillover Report, *supra* note 15, at i, where the Irish Finance Minister Michael Noonan expressed his view that 'in order to show full commitment and foster a trusting relationship between the developed and developing world, all developed countries should undertake such a spillover analysis. The combined efforts of many countries will be required to form a full picture of how developing economies are affected by other domestic tax regimes.'

33. Addis Ababa Action Agenda of the Third International Conference on Financing for Development (Addis Ababa Action Agenda), endorsed by the General Assembly in GA Res. 69/313, 27 July 2015, at para. 103.

34. IMF, *supra* note 17.

35. Emphasis added by authors. G20 Report, *supra* note 19.

36. OECD, *supra* note 10.

37. Gleaned from interviews conducted for this paper, on file with authors.

38. Dutch Reports, *supra* note 16.

39. Irish Report, *supra* note 15.

40. Addis Ababa Action Agenda, *supra* note 33.

41. World Bank, *Human Rights Impact Assessments: A Review of the Literature, Differences with other forms of Assessments and Relevance for Development* (2013), available online at http://siteresources.worldbank.org/PROJECTS/Resources/40940-1331068268558/HRIA_Web.pdf).

42. A. Bond and J. Pope, 'The State of the Art of Impact Assessment in 2012', 30 *Impact Assessment and Project Appraisal* (2012), 1, at 3.

43. The two Dutch reports, while both under the auspices of the Ministry for Foreign Affairs, were commissioned by different departments within the ministry. The terms of reference for the First Report limited that study to potential unintentional treaty shopping arising from the Netherlands DTAs with developing countries. The Second Report considered how the Dutch tax regime for multinationals, including tax treaties, impacts or could impact on developing countries.

44. See, for example, K. Brooks, 'Tax Treaty Treatment of Royalty Payments from Low-Income Countries: A Comparison of Canada and Australia's Policies', 5(2) *eJournal of Tax Research* (2007), 169.

45. Gleaned from interviews conducted for this chapter, on file with authors.

46. See Network of European Environment and Sustainable Development Advisory Councils (NEESDAC), *Impact Assessment of European Commission Policies: Achievements and Prospects* (2006), at 7.

47. See C. M. Radaelli, 'Regulating Rule-Making via Impact Assessment', 23 *Governance: An International Journal of Policy, Administration, and Institutions* (2010), 89.

48. This followed on from the earlier cancellation by Mongolia of its DTA with the Netherlands.

49. See, for example, S. Carswell, S. Lynch, and A. Beesley, 'Ireland Labelled a "Tax Haven" as US Senate Investigates Apple's Offshore Strategies', *Irish Times*, 22 May 2013, available online at http://www.irishtimes.com/business/technology/ireland-labelled-a-tax-haven-as-us-senate-investigates-apple-s-offshore-strategies-1.1402008 (last visited 13 June 2017).

50. Those already utilizing this scheme continue to benefit until 2021.

51. ActionAid, *Sweet Nothings: The Human Cost of a British Sugar Giant Avoiding Taxes in Southern Africa* (2013), available online at https://www.actionaid.org.uk/sites/default/files/doc_lib/sweet_nothings.pdf.

52. See Irish Report, *supra* note 15, at 66.

53. See, e.g., E. English, 'Enda Kenny Vows No Change to Corporate Tax Rate', *Irish Examiner*, 24 Sept. 2016, available online at http://www.irishexaminer.com/ireland/enda-kenny-vows-no-change-to-corporate-tax-rate-422585.html (last visited 6 June 2017).

54. See, e.g., the Government response (Deputy Simon Harris) to a parliamentary debate on Ireland's corporation tax policies, available online at http://oireachtasdebates.oireachtas.ie/debates%20authoring/debateswebpack.nsf/takes/dail2015100600048 (last visited 31 July 2017); the speech of the Minister for Finance when seeking parliamentary permission to appeal the Apple State Aid decision, available online at http://oireachtasdebates.oireachtas.ie/debates%20authoring/debateswebpack.nsf/takes/dail2016090700008?opendocument (last visited 31 July 2017), and the speech of the Minister for Finance to a forum on corporate tax fairness, available online at http://www.finance.gov.ie/news-centre/speeches/current-minister/minister-noonan-corporate-tax-fairness-responsibility-and (31 July 2017).

55. Bond and Pope, *supra* note 42, at 3.

56. For example, in relation to trade in services and in respect of conduit locations.

57. World Bank, *supra* note 41; Columbia Center on Sustainable Investment, Sciences Po Law School Clinic, and the Columbia Law School Human Rights Institute, *Human Rights Impact Assessments of Large-Scale Foreign Investments: A Collaborative Reflection Roundtable Outcome Document* (2014), available online at http://www.sciencespo.fr/ecole-de-droit/sites/sciencespo.fr.ecole-de-droit/files/Human%20Rights%20Impact%20Assessments%20-%20A%20Collaborative%20Reflection.pdf.

58. J. Harrison, *Human Rights Impact Assessments of Free Trade Agreements: What Is the State of the Art?*, 5 Nov. 2010, available online at http://www.oefse.at/fileadmin/content/Downloads/Veranstaltungen/Tagungsdokus/James_Harrison_Trade_HRIA_paper_5_11_2013.pdf.

59. World Bank, *supra* note 41, at 17–18.

60. NEESDAC, *supra* note 46; World Bank, *supra* note 41.

61. Bond and Pope, *supra* note 42, at 3.

62. A. M. Esteves, D. Franks, and F. Vanclay, 'Social Impact Assessment: The State of the Art', 30 *Impact Assessment and Project Appraisal* (2012), 34, at 37.

63. NEESDAC, *supra* note 46, at 8; F. Baxewanos and W. Raza, *Human Rights Impact Assessments as a New Tool for Development Policy?* (2013), available online at http://www.oefse.at/fileadmin/content/Downloads/Publikationen/Workingpaper/WP37_Human_Rights.pdf.

64. Irish Report, *supra* note 15.

65. Bond and Pope, *supra* note 42, at 4; Esteves, Franks, and Vanclay, *supra* note 62, at 36.

66. Harrison, *supra* note 58.

67. Irish Report, *supra* note 15, at 66.

68. These precedents are available online at http://www.revenue.ie/en/about/publications/classification-trading-activity/index.html (last visited 31 July 2017).

69. J. Hertin et al., 'Rationalising the Policy Mess? *Ex Ante* Assessment and the Utilisation of Knowledge in the Policy Process', 41 *Environment and Planning A.* (2009), 1185, at 1196; see also

C. M. Radaelli, 'Measuring Policy Learning: Regulatory Impact Assessment in Europe', 16 *Journal of European Public Policy* (2009), 1145.

70. Bond and Pope, *supra* note 42, at 3.

71. *Convention between Ireland and the Republic of Zambia for the Avoidance of Double Taxation and the Prevention of Fiscal Evasion with Respect to Taxes on Income and Capital Gains*, 31 Mar. 2015, available online at http://www.revenue.ie/en/tax-professionals/tax-agreements/double-taxation-treaties/z/zambia-2015.pdf [hereinafter Ireland–Zambia DTA]; *Convention between the Government of Ireland and the Government of the Islamic Republic of Pakistan for the Avoidance of Double Taxation and the Prevention of Fiscal Evasion with Respect to Taxes on Income*, 16 Apr. 2015, available online at http://www.revenue.ie/en/tax-professionals/tax-agreements/double-taxation-treaties/p/pakistan-2015.pdf [hereinafter Ireland–Pakistan DTA].

72. Ireland–Zambia DTA, *supra* note 71, the definition in Article 12 of "royalties" does not encompass technical services or management fees and so such payments are taxable only in the county of residence under Article 22.

73. Ireland–Pakistan DTA, *supra* note 71, Article 12 includes management fees in the definition of royalties which may be subject to tax at up to 10 percent in the country of source.

74. D. Kennedy, *A World of Struggle: How Power, Law and Expertise Shape the Global Political Economy* (2016).

75. G20 Report, *supra* note 19, at 8.

76. See, for example, Thai National Human Rights Commission, *Ex Ante Assessment of the Thai-US Bilateral Free Trade Agreement* (NB: While the original report has since been removed from the Commission's website, details of its contents were published by Bilaterals.org, *Thai Human Rights Commission Criticises FTA with US*, 26 Jan. 2007, available online at http://www.bilaterals.org/?thai-human-rights-commission&lang=es (last visited 13 June 2017)); European Commission, *Trade Sustainability Impact Assessment in Support of Negotiations of a DCFTA between the EU and Egypt*, 3 Nov. 2014, available online at http://trade.ec.europa.eu/doclib/docs/2015/february/tradoc_153139.pdf; S. Walker, *The Future of Human Rights Impact Assessments of Trade Agreements* (2009); A. Paasch, F. Garbers, and T. Hirsch, *Trade Policies and Hunger: The Impact of Trade Liberalisation on the Right to Food of Rice Farming Communities in Ghana, Honduras and Indonesia* (2007), available online at http://www.e-alliance.ch/typo3conf/ext/naw_securedl/secure9eca.pdf?u=0&file=fileadmin/user_upload/docs/EAA_TradePoliciesHungerRiceResearch_FullStudy_A4_EN.pdf&t=1433841564&hash=6f1a602a4fdac44e55b9f5827382d315 (last visited 6 June 2017).

77. In particular, lessons are drawn from P. Hunt and G. MacNaughton, *Impact Assessments, Poverty and Human Rights: A Case Study Using the Right to the Highest Attainable Standard of Health* (2006), available online at http://www.who.int/hhr/Series_6_Impact%20Assessments_Hunt_MacNaughton1.pdf; and more recently the Report of the former UN Special Rapporteur on the right to food, Olivier De Schutter, Guiding Principles on Human Rights Impact Assessments of Trade and Investment Agreements, UN Doc. A/HRC/19/59/Add.5, 19 Dec. 2011; see also L. Forman and G. MacNaughton, 'Lessons Learned: A Framework Methodology for Human Rights Impact Assessment of Intellectual Property Protections in Trade Agreements', 34(1) *Impact Assessment and Project Appraisal* (2016), 55.

78. For reference, see Human Rights Council, Final Study on Illicit Financial Flows, Human Rights and the 2030 Agenda for Sustainable Development of the Independent Expert on the Effects of Foreign Debt and other Related International Financial Obligations of States on the Full Enjoyment of all Human Rights, Particularly Economic, Social and Cultural Rights, UN Doc. A/HRC/31/61, 15 Jan. 2016, at para. 83: "States should conduct human rights impact assessments of their tax policies, to ensure that they do not have negative impacts abroad. These should be periodic and independently verified, with public participation in defining the risks and potential extraterritorial impacts. Impact assessments should analyse not only the implications for revenue streams, but also the distributive and governance spillover effects of a country's tax regime abroad. If and when negative spillovers are found, impact assessments should trigger policy action including explicit recommendations for responsible parties and clear deadlines for remedies and redress."

79. Specifically, Article 55 states, "With a view to the creation of conditions of stability and well-being . . . the United Nations shall promote: . . . (3) Universal respect for, and observance of, human rights and fundamental freedoms for all without distinction as to race, sex, language, or religion," as well as, "higher standards of living, full employment, and conditions of economic and social progress and development; solutions of international economic, social, health, and related problems, and international cultural and educational cooperation. . . ." Article 56 further states, "All Members pledge themselves to take joint and separate action in co-operation with the Organization for the achievement of the purposes set forth in Article 55," Charter of the United Nations, UNCIO XV, 335; amendments by General Assembly Resolution in UNTS 557, 143/638, 308/892, 119.

80. Article 28 stipulates that "[e]veryone is entitled to a social and international order in which the rights and freedoms in this Declaration can be fully realized." Universal Declaration of Human Rights, GA Res. 217 (III) A, 10 Dec. 1948 [hereinafter UDHR].

81. The duty of international cooperation and assistance in the full realization of economic, social, and cultural rights is included in Article 32 of the Convention on the Rights of Persons with Disabilities 2006 (2515 UNTS 3) and Articles 4, 24(4) and 28(3) of the Convention on the Rights of the Child 1989 (1577 UNTS 3), as well as in Articles 2(1) and 11(1) of the International Covenant on Economic, Social and Cultural Rights 1966 (993 UNTS 3).

82. Specifically, Articles 2(1) states, "Each State Party to the present Covenant undertakes to take steps, individually *and through international assistance and co-operation*, especially economic and technical, to the maximum of its available resources, with a view to achieving progressively the full realization of the rights recognized in the present Covenant by all appropriate means," International Covenant on Economic, Social and Cultural Rights 1966, 993 UNTS 3 (emphasis added).

83. See, e.g., Human Rights Committee, Communication No. 1539/2006, *Munaf v. Romania*, UN Doc. CCPR/C/96/D/1539/2006, 21 Aug. 2009, at para. 14.2; ECtHR, *Al-Skeini and Others v. the United Kingdom*, Appl. No. 55721/07, Judgment of 7 July 2011, at para. 133, decision available online at http://hudoc.echr.coe.int/; Inter-American Commission on Human Rights, *Saldano v. Argentina*, Report No. 38/99, Inter-Am. C.H.R., OEA/Ser.L/V/II.95 Doc. 7 rev., at para. 17. The General Assembly has affirmed that "all States should make all efforts to ensure that their international policies of a political and economic nature, including international trade agreements, do not have a negative impact on the right to food in other countries," GA Res. 59/202, 31 Mar. 2005, at paras. 20, 32.

84. See *Maastricht Principles on Extraterritorial Obligation of States in the Area of Economic, Social and Cultural Rights* (2012), available online at http://www.icj.org/wp-content/uploads/2012/12/HRQMaastricht-Maastricht-Principles-on-ETO.pdf, Principle 14; for further analysis, see Center for Economic and Social Rights, New York University School of Law Global Justice Clinic, Tax Justice Network, *UK Responsibility for the Impacts of Cross-border Tax Abuse on Economic, Social and Cultural Rights: Submission to the Committee on Economic Social and Cultural Rights* (2016).

85. Treaty of Lisbon Amending the Treaty on European Union and the Treaty Establishing the European Community, 13 Dec. 2007, OJ 2007 C 306/1, Article 208(1).

86. See *Maastricht Principles on Extraterritorial Obligation of States in the area of Economic, Social and Cultural Rights, supra* note 84; see also the UN Guiding Principles on Extreme Poverty and Human Rights which state unambiguously that "States have an obligation to avoid conduct that would create a foreseeable risk of impairing the enjoyment of human rights by persons living in poverty beyond their borders and to conduct assessments of the extraterritorial impacts of laws, policies and practices," Human Rights Council, Final Draft of the Guiding Principles on Extreme Poverty and Human Rights, submitted by the Special Rapporteur on Extreme Poverty and Human Rights, Magdalena Sepúlveda Carmona, UN Doc. A/HRC/21/39, 18 July 2012, at para. 92.

87. See, for example, *Report of the Special Rapporteur on Extreme Poverty and Human Rights, supra* note 6, at paras. 30–33.

88. Committee on the Elimination of Discrimination Against Women, Concluding Observations on the Combined Fourth and Fifth Periodic Reports of Switzerland, UN Doc. CEDAW/C/CHE/CO/4-5, 18 Nov. 2016, at para. 41.

89. See the observations of the Committee on Economic, Social and Cultural Rights, *supra* note 8; the Committee on the Elimination of Discrimination Against Women, *supra* note 88; the reports of the Special Procedures to the Human Rights Council, *supra* note 6. Committee on Economic, Social and Cultural Rights, Concluding Observations on the Sixth Periodic Report of the United Kingdom of Great Britain and Northern Ireland, UN Doc. E/C.12/GBR/CO/6, 14 July 2016, at paras. 16–17. See also A. Christians, 'Human Rights at the Borders of Tax Sovereignty' (2017), available online at https://papers.ssrn.com/sol3/papers.cfm?abstract_id=2924925 (last visited 28 July 2017).

90. Harrison, *supra* note 58.

91. Ibid.

92. Baxewanos and Raza, *supra* note 63.

93. G20 Report *supra* note 19.

94. World Bank, *supra* note 41.

95. See, e.g., OECD, *First Meeting of the New Inclusive Framework to Tackle Base Erosion and Profit Shifting Marks a New Era in International Tax Co-operation*, 30 June 2016, available online at http://www.oecd.org/tax/beps/first-meeting-of-the-new-inclusive-framework-to-tackle-base-erosion-and-profit-shifting-marks-a-new-era-in-international-tax-co-operation.htm (last visited 13 June 2017).

96. Columbia Center on Sustainable Investment et al., *supra* note 57.

97. See De Schutter, *supra* note 77, para. 3.2

98. Second Dutch Report, *supra* note 16. See in particular chapter 4 where tax avoidance pathways are illustrated with examples from around the world and chapter 5 where the impact of Dutch special purpose entities are explained using case studies.

99. Art. 19, UDHR; Art. 19, International Covenant on Civil and Political Rights 1966, 999 UNTS 171 [hereinafter ICCPR].

100. See OECD, *Action 11, supra* note 10.

101. According to the UN Human Rights Committee, the right to participation in the conduct of public affairs covers "all aspects of public administration, including the formulation and implementation of policy at international, national, regional and local levels": General Comment 25, UN Doc. CCPR/C/21/Rev.1/Add.7, 27 Aug. 1996, at para. 5. This right is protected under, inter alia, Arts. 21 and 27 of the UDHR, Art. 25 of the ICCPR, Arts. 13.1 and 15.1 of the International Covenant on Economic, Social and Cultural Rights 1966, 993 UNTS 3, Arts. 7, 8, 13(c) and 14.2 of the Convention on the Elimination of All Forms of Discrimination Against Women 1979, 1249 UNTS 13, Art. 5(e)(vi) of the International Convention on Elimination of All Forms of Racial Discrimination 1966, 660 UNTS 195, Arts. 12 and 31 of the Convention on the Rights of the Child 1989, 1577 UNTS 3, Arts. 3(c), 4.3, 9, 29 and 30 of, the Convention on the Rights of Persons with Disabilities 2006, 2515 UNTS 3, Arts. 41 and 42.2 of the International Convention on the Rights of All Migrant Workers and Members of their Families 1990, 2220 UNTS 3, Arts. 1.1, 2 and 8.2 of the United Nations Declaration on the Right to Development, A/RES/41/128, 4 Dec. 1986, and Arts. 5, 18, 19 and 41 of the United Nations Declaration on the Rights of Indigenous Peoples, GA Res. 61/295, 13 Sept. 2007.

102. NEESDAC, *supra* note 46.

103. See C. Adelle and S. Weiland, 'Policy Assessment: The State of the Art', 30 *Impact Assessment and Project Appraisal* (2012), 25.

104. NEESDAC, *supra* note 46, at 7; see also S. Owens, T. Rayner, and O. Bina. 'New Agendas for Appraisal: Reflections on Theory, Practice and Research', 36(11) *Environment and Planning A.* (2004), 1943; see also C. M. Radaelli, 'Diffusion Without Convergence: How Political Context Shapes the Adoption of Regulatory Impact Assessment', 12 *Journal of European Public Policy* (2005), 924.

105. Harrison, *supra* note 58.

106. *Report of the Special Rapporteur on Extreme Poverty and Human Rights, supra* note 6, at para. 34.

107. See R. S. Avi-Yonah and G. Mazzoni, "Taxation and Human Rights: A Delicate Balance," Chapter 11 in this volume.

108. For more on rethinking the normative foundations of the international tax regime, see Christians, *supra* note 89; I. Benshalom, 'The New Poor at Our Gates: Global Justice Implications for International Trade and Tax Law', 85 *New York University Law Review* (2010), 1.
109. See, for example, the recent HRIA of the Marlin mining project in Guatemala, in World Bank, *supra* note 41.
110. See, for example, IMF, 'Growth Conundrum', 54(1) *Finance & Development* (2017).

CHAPTER 8

TAX ABUSE AND IMPLICATIONS FOR HUMAN RIGHTS IN AFRICA

ANNET WANYANA OGUTTU AND MONICA IYER

I. INTRODUCTION

As in other parts of the world, economic development in Africa depends primarily on the efforts of African countries themselves and their ability to mobilize revenue domestically.[1] Corporate taxes from multinational enterprises (MNEs) are one of the most important sources of domestic revenue in Africa. However, MNE tax-avoidance schemes that erode tax bases and shift profits to low-tax and tax haven jurisdictions hamper the ability of African states to effectively derive revenue from corporate taxes.

Unlike illegal tax evasion, tax avoidance involves exploiting loopholes in tax laws within technically legal parameters.[2] Over time, however, courts have moved from holding that a taxpayer was not legally or morally prevented from engaging in tax-avoiding transactions[3] to a condemnation of tax avoidance and its limitation of a government's ability to pursue its objectives.[4] Consequently, some countries,[5] such as South Africa, have introduced the notion of "impermissible tax avoidance" to refer to tax-avoidance practices that extend beyond what is legally acceptable[6]—practices that often involve taxpayers adhering to the letter of the law but actually not following the intention behind it, when they keep their assets and income in low-tax and tax haven jurisdictions.[7]

The ideal way of funding government expenditure is by generating income through taxes.[8] Modern society condemns tax avoidance because of the impact that it can have on the state purse, on development, and on the ability of the state to achieve one of its central objectives: satisfying the needs and protecting the interests of all its citizens and fulfilling their human rights. Recognizing the problems engendered by tax avoidance, the international community has recently taken measures to ensure that taxpayers involved in cross-border trade pay their fair share of taxes. In 2013, the Organisation for Economic Co-operation and Development (OECD) instituted its Action Plan on Base Erosion and Profit Shifting (BEPS),[9] which aims to ensure that profits are taxed where the profit-generating economic activities are performed and where value is created.[10] This chapter analyzes whether the international tax reform measures instituted under the OECD's BEPS Project are effective in ensuring African countries get a fair share of taxes from MNEs transacting within their borders, so that they can finance their development goals and promote the human rights of their citizens.

II. REVENUE MOBILIZATION, CORPORATE TAXES, AND HUMAN RIGHTS IN AFRICA

With an increase in global capital flows to markets across Africa,[11] as investors have begun to recognize that "Africa is the new frontier of the global economy,"[12] African countries have seen growing investment from MNEs[13] eager to exploit their resource bases.[14] However as MNEs invest globally and into African markets, many employ tax-avoidance strategies to lessen their global tax exposure and maximize profits.[15] With the varying tax rates among countries, MNEs often find it advantageous to situate their capital or proceeds in jurisdictions where the yield will attract the least possible tax,[16] and to shift profits to low-tax and no-tax jurisdictions. While concerns about these practices are common throughout the world, they are compounded in many African countries by the lack of proper laws to counter such strategies. Faced with the rise of globalization, the cross-border tax planning strategies of MNEs, and the resultant effects of capital mobility on the fiscal integrity of their economies, African countries suffer great losses in an inefficient international corporate tax system. They must ensure that their international tax laws and administrative structures appropriately cope with the changing global business models of MNEs.[17]

For many developed countries, corporate taxes are not a large contributor to total public revenue. In these countries, corporate income taxes raise, on average, revenue equivalent to around 3 percent of GDP or about 10 percent of total tax revenue.[18] In developing countries, however, corporate taxes generally exceed 25 percent of total revenue, since there are fewer realistic alternative sources of revenue.[19] In African countries, corporate taxes contribute on average 29 percent of total revenue,[20] and a significant portion of this revenue is derived from MNEs. For example, in 2014, Rwanda reported that 70 percent of its tax base comes from MNEs; Nigeria reported that MNEs represent 88 percent of the country's tax base; and in Burundi, one MNE alone contributed nearly 20 percent of the country's total tax collection.[21]

Tax avoidance deprives governments of revenue that is necessary for, and that could be spent on, economic development and the fulfillment of human rights obligations. Article 2(1) of the International Covenant on Economic, Social and Cultural Rights (ICESCR) requires a commitment by each state party to devote the "maximum of its available resources, with a view to achieving progressively the full realization of the rights recognized" in the Covenant.[22] This requirement has been incorporated in the laws of many African states.[23]

Much of the discussion of resources in the context of human rights rightly focuses on allocation and distribution of the resources available to governments. "Often a narrow interpretation is adopted, assuming that available resources have been fixed by previous policy choices and that the government's main duty lies in efficient administration of these resources."[24] However, the collection of those resources, including through taxation, "is one of the key policy instruments states have to shape the conditions in which all human rights . . . can be fulfilled."[25]

Human rights treaties are law and give rise to legal obligations. The international human rights law regime also imposes responsibilities on other actors, including individuals and corporations, to, at a minimum, respect the human rights of others.[26] Accordingly when states fail to collect adequate revenues that should be allocated to the fulfillment of human rights, in-cluding by enabling tax-avoidance practices or allowing them to persist, they are failing to meet their international obligations.[27] Similarly, when corporate taxpayers engage in tax-avoidance practices, they are failing in their responsibility to respect human rights.[28]

Further, tax avoidance has human rights impacts beyond lost revenues. It has important effects on equality and nondiscrimination. As a global nongovernmental organization (NGO) coalition declared in 2015, "Taxation . . . plays a fundamental role in redistributing resources in ways that can prevent and redress gender, economic and other inequalities and reduce the disparities in human rights enjoyment that flow from them."[29] Corporate tax avoidance shifts tax responsibility onto those most in need, further exacerbating economic inequalities.[30] Important human rights principles like transparency, accountability, and participation also suffer as a result of tax avoidance. A fair and effective tax system encourages citizen confidence in government and sense of shared interest in government action. By contrast, when a tax system is seen as easily evaded by the largest taxpayers, ordinary citizens are likely to lose that sense of fairness and accountability.[31]

Preserving the corporate tax base by addressing BEPS issues is crucial for African countries[32] not only in fostering sustainable development and ensuring that governments can fund public goods and services and protect human rights but also in building more equitable economies and societies and in strengthening democratic governance. As discussed in the following sections, however, the fundamental design of the international taxation system has long undermined the ability of developing nations, particularly in Africa, to fairly tax MNEs operating within their borders—and recent tax reform efforts do not go far enough to dismantle the flawed foundation of the current regime.

III. HISTORY OF ENSURING TAXPAYERS PAY THEIR FAIR SHARE OF CROSS-BORDER TAXES

A. HISTORICAL EVOLUTION OF THE INTERNATIONAL TAX SYSTEM

The story of international tax cooperation is in large part a story of the struggle to achieve a bal-ance between the taxation rights of source and residence countries. It is a story of the struggle to ensure international tax equity by striking a reasonable compromise between the interests of net capital-exporting and net capital-importing nations. The former derive revenues from taxing value added at the production stage while the latter derive revenues from taxing the in-come generated by sales activities.[33] Sharing of tax revenues provides an incentive for residence and source countries to cooperate in reducing international double taxation, hence promoting international trade.

In the era following World War I,[34] concerns arose that companies involved in international commerce were evading and avoiding taxes, and this capital flight proved an obstacle to recon-struction efforts.[35] In 1928, the League of Nations published its first international Model Tax Convention (MTC), recognizing the importance of sharing taxing rights between source and residence countries.[36] Under this original MTC, where double taxation arose, the rights of the source country to tax were permitted to prevail since the income arose within that country.[37] However, the 1928 MTC adopted the "permanent establishment" (PE) concept,[38] which curtailed source taxation in that source states could only tax business activities of a foreign enterprise if the enterprise had a substantial economic presence in that state.[39] The PE concept is currently defined in Article 5(1) of the OECD MTC (see below),[40] as a fixed place of business through which the business of an enterprise is wholly or partly carried out.

The next two draft MTCs exemplified the struggle between source and residence countries to arrive at a fair allocation of taxing rights. In 1940 and in 1943, the Fiscal Committee of the League of Nations met in Mexico City and revised the 1928 MTC, issuing a new draft convention (the Mexico Draft).[41] The Mexico Draft allocated primary jurisdiction to tax to the source state—a position favoring developing countries, including most African countries. It also asserted that all business profits derived in a country would be taxable there unless the activities were "isolated and occasional" and even if the enterprise did not have a PE in the country.[42] The Mexico Draft further allowed source countries to tax investment income[43] by, for example, providing that the proceeds from the right to use a patent or secret process would be taxable where the right is exploited.[44] However, in 1945 the Fiscal Committee of the League of Nations met in London and promulgated the London Draft,[45] which, unlike the Mexico Draft, required an enterprise resident in one state to have a PE in another state for that other state to tax any of its business profits. The London Draft also imposed limitations on taxation of investment income by source states, and it reserved the right to tax royalties to residence states.[46]

When the League of Nations was replaced by the United Nations in 1945, the work of developing the MTC eventually passed to the OECD.[47] In 1963, the OECD published its first Draft MTC,[48] which was finalized in 1977 (OECD MTC). This OECD MTC favored capital-exporting countries rather than capital-importing countries, and resulted in barriers to source taxation which opened up opportunities for tax-minimizing strategies.[49] Although it has been revised repeatedly over the years, the OECD MTC has remained consistent on this fundamental point. Thus for years, with the lone exception of the short-lived Mexico Draft, the international tax framework has privileged the interests of developed countries, both in its substance and in who participates in its development.

In order to counter the dominance of the OECD, developing countries have attempted to initiate parallel processes in more inclusive bodies.[50] In 1967, the UN Economic and Social Council created an ad hoc working group (UN Experts) to formulate guidelines for tax treaties between developed and developing countries.[51] In 1980, the UN Experts published the UN Model Double Taxation Convention between Developed and Developing Countries (UN MTC).[52] Since the core of the UN MTC was derived from the OECD MTC, it has loopholes that allow foreign investors to limit their tax exposure in source countries.[53] The UN MTC does depart, however, from the OECD MTC in some respects. For example, with respect to the PE concept it allows for additional taxation for source countries, including through taxation of royalties with limits to be determined through bilateral negotiations, and it gives taxing rights over any other income not specified in the MTC to the source state.[54]

The work of the UN Experts has been hampered, however, due to underfunding. In November 2004, the UN elevated the UN Experts to the status of a permanent UN Committee, in hopes of increasing the voice of developing countries in international forums dealing with tax issues.[55] In the outcome document of the United Nations' Third International Conference on Financing for Development held in Addis Ababa in 2015,[56] world leaders decided to enhance the Committee's resources in order to strengthen its effectiveness and operational capacity. However, proposals at that Conference by developing countries to upgrade the UN Committee to a global intergovernmental tax body were vehemently rejected by developed countries.[57]

The OECD has tried to involve developing countries in its deliberations on tax treaties and international taxation in certain ways described below, but without allowing developing countries to influence core decisions.[58] In the face of serious administrative challenges and the lack of funding of the UN Committee, developing countries appear to have given up on the fight and developed countries have largely taken the upper hand in international tax issues. The UN Committee itself has many representatives from developed countries, and this has been a factor in the body becoming less and less influential in developing international tax reforms.[59]

In promulgating a system that strongly favors their interests at the expense of source countries, residence countries are contributing to shortfalls in the resources available to respect, protect, and fulfill the human rights of source country citizens. Signatories to the ICESCR pledged to take steps "individually *and through international cooperation*" to ensure the realization of Covenant rights.[60] The Maastricht Principles on Extraterritorial Obligations of States in the area of Economic, Social, and Cultural Rights, a highly influential set of expert opinions on international human rights law, explain that countries are required to "desist from acts and omissions that create a real risk of nullifying or impairing the enjoyment of economic, social and cultural rights extraterritorially,"[61] and to take steps to ensure that the MNEs that they are in a position to regulate do not violate or impair these rights.[62] Accordingly, in dictating an international tax regime that impairs the realization of the human rights of people living in the developing world, developed countries may be violating their own human rights treaty obligations, as well as making it more difficult for developing countries to fulfil theirs.

B. RECENT REFORM EFFORTS

With the rise of globalization and the increase in sophisticated MNE tax-avoidance schemes, the focus of international tax policy has been on enforcement of existing anti-tax-avoidance legislation rather than revising international tax principles relating to equitable allocation of taxing rights. In 1998, the OECD issued a Report on Harmful Tax Competition,[63] which targeted the harmful tax practices of tax haven jurisdictions and preferential tax regimes.[64] At that time, however, there was little political will among the governments of rich economies to deal with their own harmful tax practices and preferential tax regimes.[65] OECD member states such as Switzerland and Luxembourg which today are widely recognized as tax havens were not included in a 2000 OECD list of tax havens.[66] Thus, the OECD was criticized for wielding its power against smaller nations that are designated as tax havens while ignoring the practices of its member states.[67]

In the aftermath of the 2007–2008 global financial crisis, concerns about MNEs not paying their fair share of taxes were again brought to the forefront, in part through the advocacy of NGOs like Christian Aid[68] and the Tax Justice Network.[69] These concerns grew more relevant as budget shortfalls prompted many countries to take austerity measures, cutting social programs to the detriment of those already suffering most in the global economic slowdown.[70] As a result, at the 2012 G20 summit, national leaders explicitly referred to the need to prevent base erosion and profit shifting,[71] and in February 2013 the OECD released its BEPS Report,[72] following which political will to address BEPS increased.[73] But as the next section discusses, the BEPS agenda may not get to the heart of the problem of tax avoidance in Africa.

IV. THE OECD BEPS AGENDA: DOES IT ADDRESS THE FUNDAMENTAL INTERNATIONAL TAX REFORM ISSUES MOST PERTINENT TO AFRICAN COUNTRIES?

Concerns about BEPS are not new in Africa. For decades, African countries have struggled with residents shifting money to developed countries and tax haven jurisdictions.[74] In May 2016, Tax Justice Network estimated that more $12 trillion from developing countries is held offshore.[75] The OECD notes abundant circumstantial evidence that BEPS behaviors are widespread, but there are no solid conclusions about how much BEPS actually occurs.[76] Some NGOs have developed estimates to provide a proxy for BEPS behavior. Global Financial Integrity estimates that over a thirty-nine-year period, Africa lost a staggering $854 billion in cumulative capital flight.[77] It must be noted, however, that the notion of capital flight includes both licit and illicit capital flows,[78] and it is BEPS, not illicit financial flows, that are the focus of this chapter.

While the resultant tax losses may be smaller in absolute numbers, estimates of the impact of BEPS on developing countries are higher as a percentage of tax revenues than they are in developed countries, given developing countries' greater reliance on corporate tax revenues.[79] This is confirmed by a 2015 International Monetary Fund (IMF) Working Paper, which suggests that spillover effects—the impact of one country's tax policies on the tax bases of other countries[80]— are substantially larger in developing countries than in developed countries, implying a similar global distribution of the costs of BEPS.[81]

When the OECD issued its BEPS Action Plan in 2013, it noted that ensuring international consensus in addressing BEPS would require incorporating the perspectives of developing countries.[82] However, a number of NGOs and actors in developing countries argued that the initial drafting of the BEPS Action Plan was driven exclusively by the interests of developed countries, which are, again, mostly resident countries for purposes of international taxing rights. These actors criticized the BEPS Action Plan for reinforcing a system that exacerbates global inequality,[83] and the OECD's initial regional consultations with developing countries for only serving as orientation to a preexisting plan, falling short of global equal participation in the formulation of reforms. Critics have asserted[84] that the OECD's BEPS Action Plan was a reactionary approach to meet revenue demands by European countries to cover their budgetary deficits.[85]

Since then, however, the OECD has made some effort to ensure the BEPS agenda takes into perspective the interest of developing countries.[86] The OECD and G20 have also made commitments to support developing country revenue authorities and tax systems.[87] During their participation in the BEPS Project, developing countries expressed their strong interest in sustaining their engagement through the establishment of a more inclusive framework, including other international organizations and regional tax organizations.[88] Thus, in 2016, the OECD designed a more inclusive framework for monitoring BEPS implementation with all interested countries participating on an equal footing.[89]

Even though BEPS is a global concern, the nature of BEPS concerns is not uniform for all countries. Certain BEPS schemes that undermine the European or American tax base do not coincide with the African paradigm. The BEPS challenges that African countries face, as mainly capital-importing countries,[90] may be different in nature and scale from those faced by developed countries, as mainly capital-exporting countries.[91] For most African countries, most of the

BEPS Action Plans will bring benefits only in the long term, as and when their economies and administrative capacities advance.

The OECD notes that the BEPS Project is intended to ensure that profits are taxed where economic activities generating the profits are performed and where value is created.[92] While it would seem to follow from this stated intent that the Project necessarily addresses the question of fair allocation of taxing rights, the OECD has made it clear that fundamental issues which divide predominantly capital-exporting and capital-importing countries were beyond the scope of the BEPS Project.[93] By not addressing the fundamental issue that is at the center of diverging interests of developed and developing countries when it comes to international taxation, the BEPS Project could be viewed as a "window-dressing" exercise. The OECD chose to focus on curtailing sophisticated tax-avoidance schemes by strengthening existing anti-avoidance provisions. MNEs have abused these existing laws, however, making them largely ineffective. Given that MNEs are always a step ahead in devising new tax-avoidance strategies, one wonders whether emphasis on strengthening anti-avoidance laws will achieve much. The OECD seems to have missed an opportunity to evaluate the whole tax system and deal with the very root of the problems inherent in international taxation.

Further, some BEPS action items that started off strong were significantly watered down when the taxing rights of certain OECD members were threatened. For example, some matters relevant to developing countries which were raised in the Public Discussion Draft on Action 5 (which with deals with preventing artificial avoidance of PE status) are not in the final report.[94] While these developed countries were busy ensuring that their interests were protected in the new international tax regime, the historical fundamental interests of developing countries were excluded. This is in part because developing countries were excluded from the discussion. Such exclusion is itself antithetical to the tenets of the human rights regime.

Participation is a key human rights principle, enshrined in many human rights treaties.[95] Although most discussion of participation in human rights concerns the rights of the individual with respect to their own national government, equal participation of states in international governance matters is also key to advancing human rights. This is implicit in Article 28 of the Universal Declaration of Human Rights (UDHR), which holds that "[e]veryone is entitled to a social and international order in which the rights and freedoms set forth in this Declaration can be fully realized." The discussion below illustrates how—by failing to give developing countries a seat at the table, and thus failing to address fundamental issues of the allocation of taxing rights for certain income types—international tax reform efforts still disadvantage developing countries and subsequently impair their ability to realize human rights.

V. HOW EFFECTIVE IS THE BEPS PROJECT IN ENSURING TAXATION OF SOME BASE-ERODING PAYMENTS TO MNES?

African countries are particularly concerned about three corporate practices that minimize MNE tax liability: (1) base-eroding payments by MNEs transacting within their borders, including excessive interest deductions claimed from taxable income by MNEs for funding investments based in these countries; (2) excessive service fee payments claimed from taxable income by MNEs for administrative services offered to related entities in these countries; and (3) excessive royalty payments to MNEs for their intellectual property that is exploited in an

African country. Often these payments are shrouded in the obscurity that surrounds corporate structures, beneficial ownership, and intragroup transactions, resulting in erosion of the source tax base of African countries. These practices not only reduce the amount of revenue that governments retain and thus have available to finance human rights but also shift the tax burden onto local businesses and individuals.

A. IMPACT OF BASE-ERODING INTEREST PAYMENTS ON AFRICAN COUNTRIES

The OECD's BEPS Report notes that "the use of interest (in particular related party interest) is perhaps one of the most simple of the profit-shifting techniques utilised in international tax planning."[96] Interest on a loan is generally considered a deductible expense in computing the taxable income of MNE subsidiary companies, whereas dividend distributions as a result of share capital are considered profit and therefore are not deductible.[97] Thus, MNEs find loan financing more advantageous in reducing source country tax and devise "thin capitalization" schemes to ensure that their subsidiary companies are financed with more debt than equity capital.[98] The IMF notes that debt shifting through intragroup loans is of significant concern in developing countries,[99] which often lack effective provisions to guard against the use of debt to shift profits to lower tax jurisdictions.[100] Where loans are granted among related entities and the lender is located outside the country of the interest payer, the interest payments can be a major risk for base erosion. To prevent the erosion of tax bases, countries often enact various measures to curtail excessive interest deductions, including the arm's-length principle (ALP),[101] the fixed ratio approach,[102] targeted anti-avoidance rules,[103] and withholding taxes.

1. OECD Recommendations to Address Base-Eroding Interest Payments

In Action 4 of its BEPS Report, the OECD evaluated the various methods that countries apply to curtail excessive interest deductions and recommended that countries enact legislation that applies a fixed ratio rule, which limits an entity's net interest deductions to debt/earnings before interest, taxes, depreciation, and amortization (EBITDA) to a fixed ratio of between 10 percent and 30 percent.[104] This fixed ratio may be supplemented with a worldwide group ratio rule to offer relief to companies in groups that are more highly leveraged for reasons other than tax and with other provisions that reduce the impact of the rules on entities which pose less BEPS risk.[105]

2. Critique of OECD Recommendations to Address Base-Eroding Interest Payments

The OECD emphasizes enacting legislation to curtail excessive interest deductions, but bilateral tax treaties may ultimately override the effectiveness of these provisions. Even though countries may have such legislation in place, tax treaty income allocation rules (which normally override domestic rules) will limit the amount of interest that a source country can tax. For treaties based on the OECD MTC, Article 11(1) gives the primary taxing right for interest arising in a source country to the state of residence of the interest recipient. Article 11(2) grants the source country a right to tax interest at a limit of 10 percent, if the beneficial owner thereof is a resident of the residence state. Article 11(3) gives exclusive taxing rights to the source state if the beneficial owner of the interest carries on business in the source state through a PE and the debt claim in respect of which the interest is paid is effectively connected with such PE. Any double taxation that arises is usually addressed in terms of Article 23A of the OECD MTC where the resident state has to give a tax credit to the recipient of the interest.

Thus for the source state to tax interest, it has to first prove beneficial ownership by the recipient. According to the OECD MTC, a nominee or agent who is a treaty country resident may not claim benefits if the person who has all the economic interest in, and all the control over, property (the beneficial owner) is not also a resident. Furthermore, a conduit company cannot be regarded as a beneficial owner if it has, as a practical matter, very narrow powers which render it a mere fiduciary or administrator acting on account of the interested parties.[106] The OECD further explains that "beneficial ownership" means "the right to use and enjoy" the amount "unconstrained by a contractual or legal obligation to pass on the payment received to another person."[107] Proving beneficial ownership, however, is a deeply complex matter internationally, and one made more difficult in light of unfavorable international legal precedents.[108]

The concealment of beneficial ownership information can impede the realization of a key human right, that of access to information. A right of access to public information, such as company registries, is included in Article 19 of the International Covenant on Civil and Political Rights (ICCPR).[109] Despite this, advocates have highlighted the difficulty of using this right to access information on beneficial ownership.[110] When companies conceal beneficial ownership information, they are interfering with this right and thus violating their duty to respect human rights—not to mention impeding the ability of the taxing state to fulfill its human rights obligations.

Even though the OECD MTC states that the taxable amount for interest shall not exceed 10 percent, it also permits the competent authorities to settle the application of the limitation.[111] Thus in practice the interest rate in most African countries' tax treaties is often reduced below 10 percent (sometimes to zero—for example Article 11(3)of Uganda's treaty with Netherlands exempts Uganda from taxing interest on a loan guaranteed by a bank if the repayment period is three years or more). Tax officials from developing countries often find that withholding tax rates are one of the key areas on which they must fight when negotiating double taxation agreements.[112] These low rates open treaties to abuse—a major BEPS concern.[113]

Such low or zero withholding taxes on not only interest payments but also dividends are one of the reasons why in June 2013 Malawi terminated its 1969 colonial treaty with the United Kingdom, Northern Ireland, and the Netherlands.[114] The new 2014 treaty which Malawi signed only with the Netherlands contains an anti-treaty abuse provision and higher withholding tax rates.[115] The Netherlands also has renegotiated tax treaties with twenty-three other developing countries, including Ethiopia, Ghana, Kenya, and Zambia, each with an anti-abuse provision and increased withholding tax rates.[116] Thus, curtailing base-eroding interest payments is not only about enacting anti-avoidance provisions, as emphasized by the OECD BEPS Project, it is also about ensuring that the taxation rates in the treaties are not so low that they encourage treaty abuse. Much as tax treaty rules provide a higher limit above which tax must not be levied, there should also be a lower limit in the MTCs below which the tax rate must not fall. MTCs could for instance set a range of between 5 percent and 10 percent, within which countries can negotiate. If the Netherlands has realized that its treaty policy with developing countries was abusive, this is a matter that should have been addressed in the OECD BEPS Project.

B. IMPACT OF BASE-ERODING ROYALTY PAYMENTS
ON AFRICAN COUNTRIES

In most jurisdictions, royalties derived from the use of intellectual property (IP) are included in the gross income of the recipient and taxed.[117] For the payer of the royalties, expenses incurred in the exploitation of IP are a deductible expense in the calculation of taxable income.[118] Where an MNE invests IP in a subsidiary based in another country, expenses incurred for exploiting the IP paid by the subsidiary company to the MNE may be claimed as a deductible expense. MNEs are able to manipulate the level of these expenses in order to minimize the source country's ability to tax.

Even though African countries are largely importers of IP developed by MNEs based in developed countries,[119] there are a few cases of IP that has been developed in Africa such that the royalty income should be taxed in the African country where the recipient of the royalties has residence. However, due to the mobility of IP, the "residence" of the IP can be easily migrated offshore to a low-tax jurisdiction with a subsequent loss of revenue for the jurisdiction where the owner of the IP resides.[120] For example, ActionAid explains that many of SABMiller's local beer brands were invented in African countries,[121] but these brands were sold by the London-based beer company to its subsidiary in the Netherlands to take advantage of tax rules which permit companies to pay low taxes on royalties.[122] Control over and ability to benefit from the IP developed in a country is an element of the right to self-determination, which is so important in international human rights law that it is provided in the common first article of the two major international human rights covenants, the ICESCR[123] and the ICCPR.[124] This article states in its second paragraph that "[a]ll peoples may, for their own ends, freely dispose of their natural wealth and resources without prejudice to any obligations arising out of international economic co-operation, based upon the principle of mutual benefit, and international law." Thus the natural wealth and resources of a state, including the IP generated by the labor of its people, should be used for the social benefit of the people of that state.[125]

1. OECD Recommendations to Address Base-Eroding Royalty Payments

In its BEPS Reports, the OECD only addressed the BEPS concerns pertaining to royalties from a transfer pricing perspective. The term transfer pricing describes the process by which related entities, such as affiliates or subsidiaries of the same corporation, set prices at which they transfer goods or services between each other. It can entail the systematic manipulation of prices in order to reduce profits or increase profits artificially or cause losses and avoid taxes in a specific country.[126] To curb such transfer pricing abuses, Article 9(1) of the OECD MTC recommends the use of the ALP.

In its BEPS Project, the OECD acknowledged that transfer pricing issues pertaining to intangibles, including IP, are a key concern to governments and taxpayers, due to insufficient international guidance on the definition, identification, and valuation of intangibles.[127] Applying the ALP to intangibles is also particularly challenging due to their unique nature, which makes it difficult to find market benchmarks against which to conduct an objective comparability analysis. In Action 8 of the BEPS Project, the OECD revised Chapter VI of its Transfer Pricing Guidelines to provide a clear definition of "intangibles,"[128] as well as examples.[129] Action 8 explains that legal ownership alone does not necessarily entail a right to all (or any) of the return from exploiting the intangible. The entities performing value-creating functions related to the development, enhancement, maintenance, protection, and exploitation (DEMPE) of the intangibles should be entitled to an appropriate remuneration reflecting the value of their contributions.[130] If these guidelines are followed, and an African-based subsidiary to an MNE performs any of the DEMPE functions, such value-creating functions can be taxable in the source country—i.e., in the African country in which the value is created.

2. Critique of OECD Recommendations to Address Base-Eroding Royalty Payments

While sound on paper, in practice, applying the OECD Transfer Pricing Guidelines is quite challenging for African countries. It is difficult to find African comparables (meaning market-rate benchmarks with which to establish pricing), as there are very few organized companies in any given sector and there are hardly any African benchmarking databases. When assessing the arm's-length criteria of related-party transactions, African countries tend to accept European comparables, which often require adjustment to fit emerging market businesses. There is also a general lack of administrative capacity and technical expertise among African tax authorities to process the data. Moreover, addressing transfer pricing of intangibles is not the priority concern for African countries, which continue to suffer from treaties that unfairly allocate taxing rights for royalties between source and residence states.

Unlike the UN MTC, which permits source countries to tax royalties subject to a maximum percentage that is mutually agreed upon,[131] Article 12(1) of the OECD MTC provides that royalties arising in a contracting state and beneficially owned by a resident of the other contracting state shall be taxable only in that other state. In effect, it is only the resident state of the beneficial owner of the royalties that may tax. Under Article 12(3), the source state may tax the royalties if the beneficial owner of the royalties carries on business in the source state through a PE situated therein, and the right or property in respect of which the royalties are paid is effectively connected with such PE.[132] The challenges of proving beneficial ownership, as discussed above, also apply with respect to taxing royalties. Even where beneficial ownership of royalties can be proved, the next hurdle is for the source country to establish that the beneficial owner carries on business in the source state through a PE situated therein.[133] But the PE concept as set out in Article 5 of the OECD MTC (discussed in section III above) excludes many activities that are key to the creation of real value in the modern economy. Under the current rules, a MNE could claim its research and development activities (from which royalties could be derived) in a source country are preparatory or auxiliary in nature, and thus its activities would not qualify as a PE and the source state would not be able to tax the royalties derived from these activities.[134]

In Action 7 of its BEPS Project, the OECD acknowledges that the true value of a MNE's profits cannot be determined without considering the value contributed through research and development or the creation of products in source countries. It notes that depending on the circumstances, business activities that were previously considered to be merely preparatory or auxiliary in nature may nowadays be core business activities of an enterprise.[135] Thus the OECD will modify Article 5(4) in its next update to the MTC to ensure that each of the exceptions to the PE concept is restricted to activities that are of a preparatory or auxiliary character.[136] The OECD clarifies that a preparatory or auxiliary activity is one which precedes the main activity, is carried out for a short period of time,[137] or is "supportive" in nature and is not vital to the main activity being carried out. Thus, where conducting an activity requires a significant amount of assets or employees, such activity cannot be considered to be auxiliary in nature. Apart from this important clarification—the implementation of which remains to be seen—the OECD has not addressed the allocation of taxing rights issues that are pertinent to source countries.

C. IMPACT OF BASE-ERODING SERVICE FEE PAYMENTS ON AFRICAN COUNTRIES

MNEs normally arrange for a wide range of administrative, technical, financial, commercial, and other services for group members. The cost of providing such services may be borne by the parent or by a specially designated group member. Since it is not in the interests of an MNE group to incur costs unnecessarily, they often come up with measures to provide intragroup services efficiently.[138] The concern for source countries, including many in Africa, is that often MNEs claim excessive deductions for head office expenses on management, technical, and service fees, while paying little or no taxes in source countries.[139] To protect their tax bases against excessive deductions for such fees, developing countries like Uganda, Ghana, and South Africa often levy withholding taxes.[140]

1. OECD Recommendations to Address Base-Eroding Service Fee Payments

Under Action 10 of the BEPS Project, the OECD proposed revisions to Chapter VII of their Transfer Pricing Guidelines on how to benchmark cross-border services so as protect against BEPS. The guidance promotes a simplified method for determining arm's-length charges for services that are: supportive in nature; not part of the core business of the MNE; do not require the use or creation of unique and valuable intangibles; and do not involve the assumption or control of significant risk.[141] The OECD suggests that where excessive charges for intragroup management services are viewed as being a major BEPS challenge, a threshold can be applied whereby, for services that exceed the threshold, a full transfer pricing analysis is performed.[142] The OECD notes for the approach to work, many countries need to agree on adopting it before 2018. The OECD would then design the structure of the threshold and other implementation issues.[143] Although this simplified approach may address some of the challenges that African countries face in applying transfer pricing provisions to low value-adding intragroup services, it is not a solution to their concerns regarding the allocation of taxing rights for service income, as it does not solve the fact that the OECD MTC does not have an article that specifically deals with service income, as discussed below.

2. Critique of OECD Recommendations to Address Base-Eroding Service Fee Payments

The OECD addresses taxation of service fees under Articles 5 and 7 of the OECD MTC, providing that a source country may only tax services fees of a foreign service provider if that foreign provider has a PE in the source country for more than six months in a year. Under Article 7, only profits attributable to the PE are taxable in the source state, using the ALP according to the OECD Transfer Pricing Guidelines, which, as explained above, are challenging for African countries to apply. The OECD's approach in Article 7(2) of attributing profits to a PE that may be taxed by source countries is also problematic, because it recognizes the internal dealings of a PE and its head office and prices them on an arm's-length basis without regard to the actual profits of the enterprise of which the PE is a part. This implies that nonactual service/management fees (including notional interest and royalties) from the head office may be charged to the PE. This approach differs from the approach in the UN MTC and in the 2008 version of the OECD MTC (upon which many of African countries' treaties are still based), whereby only the actual, and not notional, income and expenses of the PE are allocated.[144] To preserve their tax bases, a number of developing countries have reserved the right to use Article 7 in the 2008 version of the OECD MTC.[145] Many African countries have also signed treaties with articles on services, management, and technical fees, deviating from the OECD and the UN MTC.[146] To address these concerns, in 2012, the United Nations started working on a technical services article which is now included in its 2017 MTC. This article will allow developing countries to levy a tax on payments made to the overseas providers of "technical services" even when there is no physical presence in their country. Developing countries are optimistic that this service fee article will help them deal with the tax abuses that impact on human rights.

VI. CONCLUSION

International tax reform needs to address issues relating to the allocation of taxing rights between source and residence countries. Attempts to apply piecemeal solutions to individual issues while ignoring this underlying fundamental issue will not curb the possibilities for BEPS. Efforts to ensure MNEs pay their fair share of taxes in the countries where they transact business need to acknowledge that the interests of source countries and those of residence countries differ in many respects. For an international tax system to ensure fair allocation of taxing rights from global income of MNEs it should not be skewed toward protecting only the interests of residence countries. International cooperation in tax matters, and calls for a more inclusive approach that takes into consideration the interests of developing countries on an equal footing, must be reflected in the policies and decisions made.

An international tax reform agenda that is one-sided will only result in international tax anarchy as developing countries in which the MNEs invest may choose to devise their own approaches to protect their tax bases, with harmful impacts on international trade. Ignoring the concerns of developing countries will not make them go away. Resolving issues pertaining to taxation of service income, for example, is very important to developing countries but the OECD did not address it in the BEPS Project. African countries are concerned that the OECD seems to be suggesting that the ALP is the panacea for most international tax problems, despite the fact that developing countries have challenges applying this principle due to the lack of comparable transactions in many instances.

Article 28 of the UDHR holds that "[e]veryone is entitled to a social and international order in which the rights and freedoms set forth in this Declaration can be fully realized." The current international tax system, even if it fully incorporates the OECD BEPS Action Plan, fails to live up to this ideal, by depriving African states and other developing countries of the power, policy space, and resources necessary to fulfill their development objectives and their human rights obligations. In order to fulfill our collective goals and achieve human rights for all, the global community must incorporate the voices and priorities of developing countries into international tax reform efforts.

NOTES

1. United Nations Conference on Trade and Development, *Economic Development in Africa* (2007), available online at http://unctad.org/en/Docs/aldcafrica2007_en.pdf, at ch. 1.

2. D. Meyerowitz, *Meyerowitz on Income Tax* (2009), at para. 29.1; A. Rapakko, *Base Company Taxation* (1989), at 39.

3. See, e.g., *Levene v. IRC* [1928] AC 21 (United Kingdom House of Lords); *Ayrshire Pullman Motors Services and DM Ritchie v. IRC* 14 TC 754 (United Kingdom House of Lords); *ICR v. Duke of Westminster* 51 TIR 467 (United Kingdom House of Lords).

4. M. Brooks and J. Head, 'Tax Avoidance: In Economics, Law and Public Choice', *in* G. S. Cooper (ed.), *Tax Avoidance and the Rule of Law* (1997), 53. The morality of tax avoidance was questioned in cases such as *Re Weston's Settlements* [1968] All ER 338 at 342 (United Kingdom Court of Appeal); *CIR v. McGuckian* [1997] 3 All ER 817 (United Kingdom House of Lords); *IRC v. Burmah Oil Co Ltd* [1982] STC 30 at 32 (United Kingdom House of Lords).

5. See Australian Government, *Final Report of the Review of Business Taxation: A System Redesigned* (1999), available online at http://rbt.treasury.gov.au/publications/paper4/, at 6.2(c) (last visited 12 July 2017).

6. South African Revenue Service, *Discussion Paper on Tax Avoidance and Section 103 of the Income Tax Act, 1962 (Act No. 58 of 1962)* (2005), available online at http://www.sars.gov.za/AllDocs/LegalDoclib/DiscPapers/LAPD-LPrep-DP-2005-01%20-%20Discussion%20Paper%20Tax%20Avoidance%20Section%20103%20of%20Income%20Tax%20Act%201962.pdf. See also the general anti-avoidance provisions in Section 80A-L of South Africa's Income Tax Act 58 of 1962, as amended.

7. The OECD defines a tax haven as a jurisdiction that actively makes itself available for the avoidance of tax that would have been paid in high-tax countries. See OECD, *International Tax Avoidance and Evasion: Four Related Studies* (1987), at 1.

8. African Development Bank, *African Economic Outlook* (2014), available online at https://www.afdb.org/en/knowledge/publications/african-economic-outlook/african-economic-outlook-2014/, at 48 (last visited 12 July 2017).

9. OECD, *Action Plan on Base Erosion and Profit Shifting* (2013), available online at https://www.oecd.org/ctp/BEPSActionPlan.pdf, at 25.

10. OECD, *Base Erosion and Profit Shifting Project Explanatory Statement* (2015), available online at https://www.oecd.org/ctp/beps-explanatory-statement-2015.pdf, at para. 11.

11. D. Rodrik, *Global Capital Heads for the Frontier*, 10 Mar. 2015, available online at https://www.project-syndicate.org/commentary/frontier-market-economy-fad-by-dani-rodrik-2015-03?barrier=accessreg#gF68rVbSm1yo1JIC.32 (last visited 12 July 2017).

12. Ibid.

13. C. W. Corey, *Africa: Continent Is the New Frontier of Global Economy*, 10 Oct. 2008, available online at http://allafrica.com/stories/200810130097.html (last visited 14 Aug. 2017) (quoting J. A. Simon, US ambassador to the African Union).

14. Report of the High Level Panel on Illicit Financial Flows from Africa, *Track It, Stop It, Get It: Illicit Financial Flows* (2015), available online at https://www.uneca.org/sites/default/files/PublicationFiles/iff_main_report_26feb_en.pdf, at 53.

15. See, e.g., ibid.

16. L. U. Cavelti, C. Jaag, and T. F. Rohner, *Why Corporate Taxation Means Source Taxation: A Response to the OECD's Actions Against Base Erosion and Profit Shifting* (Swiss Economics Working Paper 0054, Apr. 2016), available online at http://ssrn.com/abstract=2773614 (last visited 12 July 2017).

17. OECD, *supra* note 9, at 25.

18. R. S. Avi-Yonah, *Hanging Together: A Multilateral Approach to Taxing Multinationals* (University of Michigan Public Law Research Paper No. 364, University of Michigan Law and Economics Research Paper No. 15-012, 4 Aug. 2015), available online at http://ssrn.com/abstract=2344760 (last visited 12 July 2017).

19. E. Crivelli, R. De Mooij, and M. Keen, *Base Erosion, Profit Shifting and Developing Countries* (IMF Working Paper WP/15/118, May 2015), available online at https://www.imf.org/external/pubs/ft/wp/2015/wp15118.pdf, at 3.

20. Avi-Yonah, *supra* note 18.

21. African Tax Administration Forum, *African Tax Outlook* (2016), at 57.

22. Article 21, International Covenant on Economic, Social and Cultural Rights 1966, 993 UNTS 3.

23. See, e.g., Sections 25(5), 26, and 27 of the Constitution of the Republic of South Africa 1996.

24. R. Balakrishnan et al., *Maximum Available Resources & Human Rights* (Rutgers University Center for Women's Global Leadership Analytical Report, 2011), available online at http://www.cwgl.rutgers.edu/docman/economic-and-social-rights-publications/362-maximumavailableresources-pdf/file, at 2.

25. I. Saiz, 'Resourcing Rights: Combating Tax Injustice from a Human Rights Perspective', *in* A. Nolan, R. O'Connell, and C. Harvey (eds.), *Human Rights and Public Finance: Budgets and the Promotion of Economic and Social Rights* (2013), 77, at 80.

26. See, e.g., Human Rights Council, Report of the Special Representative of the Secretary-General on the issue of Human Rights and Transnational Corporations and Other Business Enterprises, John Ruggie, *Guiding Principles on Business and Human Rights: Implementing the United Nations Protect, Respect and Remedy Framework*, UN Doc. A/HRC/17/31, 21 Mar. 2011.

27. See International Bar Association, *Tax Abuses, Poverty and Human Rights: A Report of the International Bar Association's Human Rights Institute Task Force on Illicit Financial Flows, Poverty and Human Rights* (2013), available online at http://www.ibanet.org/Document/Default.aspx?DocumentUid=4977CB3D-4988-4C9C-84C7-9050A5CB2311, at 105–116 (last visited 12 July 2017).

28. Ibid. at 117–125.

29. Center for Economic and Social Rights, *Lima Declaration on Tax Justice and Human Rights*, 24 July 2015, available online at http://www.cesr.org/endorse-lima-declaration-tax-justice-and-human-rights (last visited 12 July 2017).

30. Saiz, *supra* note 25.

31. See, e.g., International Bar Association, *supra* note 27, at 92–93.

32. N. Nene, South African Minister of Finance, Speech at the African Tax Administration Forum Conference on Cross Border Taxation in Africa (21 Apr. 2015), available online at http://www.gov.za/speeches/page-1-11-speech-minister-finance-mr-nhlanhla-nene-ataf-conference-cross-border-taxation (last visited 12 July 2015).

33. A. A. Skaar, *Permanent Establishment: Erosion of a Tax Treaty Principle* (1991), at 88–95.

34. R. S. Avi-Yonah, *Advanced Introduction to International Tax Law* (2015), at 3.

35. M. J. McIntyre, *Developing Countries and International Cooperation on Income Tax Matters: A Historical View* (2015), at 1.

36. Ibid. at 3.

37. Avi-Yonah, *supra* note 18, at 3.

38. Skaar, *supra* note 33, at 75–77.

39. K. Vogel, *Double Tax Conventions* (1997), at 280.

40. OECD, *Model Tax Convention on Income and on Capital 2014 (Full Version)* (2015), available online at http://www.oecd.org/tax/treaties/model-tax-convention-on-income-and-on-capital-2015-full-version-9789264239081-en.htm, at art. 5(1) (last visited 26 July 2017).

41. J. A. Becerra, *Interpretation and Application of Tax Treaties* (2007), at ch. 2, para. 2.1.

42. McIntyre, *supra* note 35, at 4.

43. Becerra, *supra* note 41, at ch. 2, para. 2.3.

44. McIntyre, *supra* note 35, at 4.

45. League of Nations Fiscal Committee, *Report on the Work of the 10th Session of the Fiscal Committee* (1946), available online at http://biblio-archive.unog.ch/Dateien/CouncilMSD/C-37-M-37-1946-II-A_EN.pdf, at 8.

46. McIntyre, *supra* note 35, at 4.

47. The OECD is an international organization that was established in 1961 to contribute to economic development and growth in its member countries. Though the primary focus of the OECD is on member countries, its additional goals of contributing to the expansion of world trade and the development of the world economy affect nonmembers as well. See OECD, *History*, available online at http://www.oecd.org/about/history/ (last visited 12 July 2017).

48. OECD, *Draft Double Taxation Convention on Income and on Capital: Report of the OECD Fiscal committee* (1963).

49. McIntyre, *supra* note 35, at 5.

50. Ibid. at 6.

51. Ibid.

52. See UN Department of Economic and Social Affairs, *Model Double Taxation Convention between Developed and Developing Countries* (2011), available online at http://www.un.org/esa/ffd/tax/unmodel.htm, at para. 8 of the Introduction (last visited 14 Aug. 2017).

53. McIntyre, *supra* note 35, at 6.

54. Ibid.

55. Ibid. at 23.

56. Addis Ababa Action Agenda of the Third International Conference on Financing for Development (Addis Ababa Action Agenda), endorsed by the General Assembly in GA Res. 69/313, 27 July 2015, at para. 23.

57. B. Muchhala and R. Sengupta, *Third Conference on Financing for Development: Outcome Document Adopted without Intergovernmental Tax Body or New Financial Commitments*, 16 July 2015, available online at http://www.twn.my/title2/wto.info/2015/ti150711.htm (last visited 12 July 2017).

58. McIntyre, *supra* note 35, at 6.

59. In 1980, the membership of the UN ad hoc group of experts was increased to twenty-five members: ten from developed countries and fifteen from developing countries. See ibid.

60. ICESCR, *supra* note 22, Article 2(1) (emphasis added).

61. ETO Consortium, *Maastricht Principles on Extraterritorial Obligations of States in the Area of Economic, Social and Cultural Rights* (2011), available online at http://www.etoconsortium.org/en/main-navigation/library/maastricht-principles/, at para. 13 (last visited 13 July 2017).

62. Ibid. at para. 24.

63. OECD, *Harmful Tax Competition* (1998), at para. 74.

64. A harmful preferential tax regime can occur in both tax haven and high-tax jurisdictions. Harmful tax regimes are characterized by having no or low effective tax rates on income; the regimes are ring-fenced, and there is a general lack of transparency and effective exchange of information with other countries. See ibid. at para. 75.

65. *United States Senate Permanent Subcommittee on Investigations: Hearing on Offshore Transactions*, 1 Aug. 2006 (prepared testimony of Reuven S. Avi-Yonah, Irwin I. Cohen Professor of Law, University of Michigan Law School).

66. OECD, *List of Unco-operative Tax Havens*, available online at http://www.oecd.org/countries/monaco/listofunco-operativetaxhavens.htm (last visited 13 July 2017).

67. P. Gumbel, 'The Storm Over Tax Havens: Corporate Scandals Have Boosted the Pressure on Offshore Havens to Open Their Books. Some Have Done So—But Global Crackdown Has A Long Way to Go', *Time Magazine*, 16 Feb. 2004, at 42–43.

68. Christian Aid, *Death and Taxes: The True Toll of Tax Dodging* (2008), available online at http://www.christianaid.org.uk/images/deathandtaxes.pdf, at 21–23.

69. Tax Justice Network, *Tax Havens & Financial Crisis*, available online at http://www.taxjustice.net/topics/finance-sector/tax-havens-financial-crisis/ (last visited 13 July 2017).

70. Center for Strategic and International Studies, *Paying for Development: Domestic Resource Mobilization*, 5 May 2014, available online at http://csis.org/publication/paying-development-domestic-resource-mobilization (last visited 13 July 2017).

71. *G20 Leaders' Declaration* (Los Cabos Mexico, 2012), available online at http://www.g20.utoronto.ca/2012/2012-0619-loscabos.pdf.

72. OECD, *supra* note 9, at 7, 47.

73. Crivelli, De Mooij, and Keen, *supra* note 19, at 3.
74. A. Ginsberg, *International Tax Havens* (2nd ed., 1997), at 5–6; S. Shane, 'Panama Papers Reveal Wide Use of Shell Companies by African Officials', *New York Times*, 25 July 2016, available online at https://www.nytimes.com/2016/07/25/world/americas/panama-papers-reveal-wide-use-of-shell-companies-by-african-officials.html (last visited 13 July 2017).
75. Tax Justice Network, *Size of the Problems*, available online at http://www.taxjustice.net/topics/more/size-of-the-problem/ (last visited 13 July 2017).
76. OECD, *supra* note 9, at 18.
77. Global Financial Integrity, *Illicit Financial Flows from Africa: Hidden Resource for Development* (2010), available online at http://www.gfintegrity.org/storage/gfip/documents/reports/gfi_africareport_web.pdf, at 1.
78. Licit capital flight is often recorded and can be tracked, significantly lowering the probability that it has a corrupt or criminal source. In contrast, illicit financial flows are by nature unrecorded. See Global Financial Integrity, *Illicit Financial Flows from Developing Countries: 2003–2012*, Dec. 2014, available online at http://www.gfintegrity.org/wp-content/uploads/2014/12/Illicit-Financial-Flows-from-Developing-Countries-2003-2012.pdf.
79. OECD, *supra* note 10, at para. 2.
80. Crivelli, De Mooij, and Keen, *supra* note 19, at 4.
81. Ibid.
82. OECD, *supra* note 9, at 25.
83. Press Note, Francophone LIC Finance Ministers Network, LIC Ministers Demand Their Fair Share of Global Tax Revenues, 9 Oct. 2014, available online at https://www.francophonie.org/IMG/pdf/minmeet_washington_oct2014_press_note_en.pdf.
84. A. W. Oguttu, *Tax Base Erosion and Profit Shifting in Africa—Part 1: Africa's Response to the OECD BEPS Action Plan* (International Centre for Tax and Development, Working Paper 54, June 2016), available online at http://www.ictd.ac/publication/2-working-papers/127-tax-base-erosion-and-profit-shifting-in-africa-part-1-africa-s-response-to-the-oecd-beps-action-plan, at 20 (last visited 13 July 2017).
85. OECD, *Budget Deficits: What Governments Are Doing*, available online at http://www.oecd.org/southafrica/budgetdeficitswhatgovernmentsaredoing.htm (last visited 13 July 2017).
86. See, e.g., OECD, *Aligning Transfer Pricing Outcomes with Value Creation, Actions 8–10—2015 Final Reports*, 5 Oct. 2015, available online at http://www.oecd.org/ctp/aligning-transfer-pricing-outcomes-with-value-creation-actions-8-10-2015-final-reports-9789264241244-en.htm, at 67 (incorporating developing country concerns pertaining to transfer pricing of commodities) (last visited 13 July 2017).
87. OECD, *Strategy for Deepening Developing Country Engagement in the BEPS Project* (2014), available online at http://www.oecd.org/tax/strategy-deepening-developing-country-engagement.pdf; see also OECD, *Tax Inspectors Without Borders*, available online at http://www.oecd.org/tax/taxinspectors.htm (last visited 13 July 2017); G20 Development Working Group Domestic Resource Mobilisation, *G20 Response to 2014 Reports on Base Erosion and Profit Shifting and Automatic Exchange of Tax Information for Developing Economies* (2014), available online at http://www.g20.utoronto.ca/2014/16%20G20%20response%20to%202014%20reports%20on%20BEPS%20and%20AEOI%20for%20developing%20economies.pdf, at 6.
88. OECD, *supra* note 10, at para. 30.
89. OECD, *Inclusive Framework on BEPS: A Global Answer to a Global Issue* (Mar. 2017), available online at https://www.oecd.org/tax/flyer-implementing-the-beps-package-building-an-inclusive-framework.pdf. The first meeting of the Inclusive Framework, which took place in Kyoto in 2016, brought together representatives from eighty-two countries, including countries in Africa. OECD, *First Meeting of the New Inclusive Framework to Tackle Base Erosion and Profit Shifting Marks a New Era in International Tax Co-operation*, 30 June 2016, available online at http://www.oecd.org/tax/beps/first-meeting-of-the-new-inclusive-framework-to-tackle-base-erosion-and-profit-shifting-marks-a-new-era-in-international-tax-co-operation.htm (last visited 13 July 2017).

90. See UN Committee of Experts on International Cooperation in Tax Matters, Responses to Questionnaire for Developing Countries from the UN Subcommittee on Base Erosion and Profit Shifting, 30 Sept. 2014, UN Doc. E/C.18/2014/CRP.12, at 3.

91. OECD, *Addressing the Tax Challenges of the Digital Economy, Action 1—2015 Final Report*, 5 Oct. 2015, available online at http://www.oecd.org/tax/addressing-the-tax-challenges-of-the-digital-economy-action-1-2015-final-report-9789264241046-en.htm, at 3 (last visited 13 July 2017).

92. OECD, *supra* note 10, at para. 11.

93. OECD, *supra* note 9, at 25.

94. For example, PE issues pertaining to insurance companies and subsidiary company "entity isolation" schemes, see OECD, *BEPS Action 7: Preventing the Artificial Avoidance of PE Status* (Public Discussion Draft, 31 Oct. 2014–9 Jan. 2015), available online at http://www.oecd.org/ctp/treaties/discussion-draft-action-7-prevent-artificial-avoidance-pe-status.htm, at paras. 31–42 (last visited 14 Aug. 2017). See also M. Cadesky, R. Rinninsland, and K. Lobo, Presentation to the Asia-Oceania Tax Consultants' Association 2014 Conference: The U.S. View on BEPS (Oct. 2014), available online at http://publications.ruchelaw.com/pdfs/2014-10/US_View_On_BEPS_AOTCA.pdf.

95. See Office of the High Commissioner for Human Rights, *Equal Participation in Political and Public Affairs*, available online at http://www.ohchr.org/EN/Issues/Pages/EqualParticipation.aspx (last visited 13 July 2017).

96. OECD, *supra* note 9, at 25.

97. B. Arnold and M. J. McIntyre, *International Tax Primer* (2002), at 72–73; L. Olivier and M. Honiball, *International Tax: A South African Perspective* (2011), at 649.

98. G. Richardson, D. Hanlon, and L. Nethercott, 'Thin Capitalization: An Anglo-American Comparison', 24(2) *The International Tax Journal* (1998), 36.

99. IMF, *Spillovers in International Corporate Taxation* (2014), at 30.

100. Ibid. at 24.

101. The arm's-length principle as set out in Article 9(1) of the OECD MTC provides that when conditions are made or imposed between two associated enterprises which differ from those which would have been made between independent enterprises, then any profits which would, but for those conditions, have accrued to one of the enterprises, may be included in the profits of that enterprise and taxed accordingly. In South Africa for instance, Section 31 of the Income Tax Act 58 of 1962, as amended by the Taxation Laws Amendment Act 24 of 2011, provides that the ALP has to be applied to financial assistance in cross border transactions.

102. Under this approach a fixed debt/equity ratio is used as a "safe harbor" in setting the parameters within which the ALP applies, and the interest relating to the debt above the fixed ratio is not deductible. Uganda and Ghana both employ a fixed ratio approach. See KPMG, *Uganda Fiscal Guide* (2012–2013), at 13; Section 33(1), Ghana's Income Tax Act 896 of 2015.

103. See, e.g., South Africa's Income Tax Act 58 of 1962.

104. See OECD, *BEPS Action 4: Interest Deductions and Other Financial Payments* (Public Discussion Draft, 18 Dec. 2014–6 Feb. 2015), available online at http://www.oecd.org/ctp/aggressive/discussion-draft-action-4-interest-deductions.pdf, at paras. 15–25, 147–163.

105. See OECD, *Limiting Base Erosion Involving Interest Deductions and Other Financial Payments, Action 4—2015 Final Report*, 5 Oct. 2015, available online at http://www.oecd-ilibrary.org/docserver/download/2315311e.pdf?expires=1499959474&id=id&accname=guest&checksum=CD8862E85A06A0F1B2B44F6303A671D2, at paras. 23, 78, and 99 (last visited 13 July 2017).

106. OECD, *Report on the Use of Base Companies* (1987), at para. 14(b).

107. OECD, *OECD Model Tax Convention: Revised Proposals Concerning the Meaning of "Beneficial Owner" in Articles 10, 11, and 12* (Revised Public Discussion Draft, 19 Oct.–15 Dec. 2012), available online at https://www.oecd.org/ctp/treaties/Beneficialownership.pdf, see para, 12.1 of the Commentary on Article 10, para. 9.1 of the Commentary on Article 11, and para. 4 of the Commentary on Article 12.

108. See, e.g., *Velcro Canada Inc. v. The Queen*, 2012 TCC 57 (Tax Court of Canada); *Prevost Car Inc. v. Her Majesty the Queen*, 2008 TCC 231 (Tax Court of Canada).

109. See, e.g., Human Rights Committee, General Comment No. 34, Article 19: Freedoms of Opinion and Expression, 12 Sept. 2011, UN Doc. CCPR/C/GC/34, at paras. 18–19.
110. See Access Info Europe and Organized Crime and Corruption Reporting Project, *"It's None of Your Business!" 10 Obstacles to Accessing Company Register Data Using the Right to Information*, 7 Apr. 2016, available online at https://www.access-info.org/wp-content/uploads/CompanyRegisters_Report_7April2016.pdf.
111. OECD, *Model Tax Convention on Income and on Capital 2014 (Full Version)* (2015), available online at http://www.oecd.org/tax/treaties/model-tax-convention-on-income-and-on-capital-2015-full-version-9789264239081-en.htm, at art. 11(2) (last visited 26 July 2017).
112. ActionAid, *Calling Time: Why SABMiller Should Stop Dodging Taxes in Africa* (2012), available online at https://www.actionaid.org.uk/sites/default/files/doc_lib/calling_time_on_tax_avoidance.pdf, at 24.
113. OECD, *supra* note 111, at para. 13.
114. Multinational Tax and Transfer Pricing News, *Netherlands Renegotiates Tax Treaties with Developing Nations to Add Antiabuse Clause*, 23 June 2015, available online at http://mnetax.com/netherlands-renegotiates-tax-treaties-ethiopia-ghana-kenya-zambia-to-add-antiabuse-clause-hopes-add-clause-23-treaties-9530 (last visited 13 July 2017).
115. Multinational Tax and Transfer Pricing News, *The Netherlands' Renegotiated Tax Treaty with Malawi Includes Antiabuse Provisions*, 23 Apr. 2015, available online at http://mnetax.com/netherlands-renegotiated-tax-treaty-malawi-includes-antiabuse-provisions-8213 (last visited 26 July 2017).
116. Multinational Tax and Transfer Pricing News, *supra* note 114.
117. See, e.g., South Africa, paras. *(g)*(ii)*bis, (g)*(iii), and *(g*A), respectively, of the definition of gross income in Section 1 of the Income Tax Act 58 of 1962.
118. See, e.g., Section 11D of South Africa's Income Tax 58 of 1962.
119. K. Holmes, 'International Tax Aspects of Income Derived from the Supply of Intellectual Property: Royalties vs. Business Profits', *in* A. Lymer and J. Hasseldine (eds.), *The International Taxation System* (2002), 181, at 190.
120. E. L. Guruli, 'International Taxation: Application of Source Rules to Income from Intangible Property', 5 *Houston Business and Tax Law Journal* (2005), 204, at 206.
121. ActionAid, *supra* note 112, at 6.
122. Ibid.
123. ICESCR, *supra* note 22, Article 1.
124. Article 1, International Covenant on Civil and Political Rights 1966, 999 UNTS 171.
125. R. C. Dreyfuss and C. Rodríguez-Garavito, *Balancing Wealth and Health: The Battle over Intellectual Property and Access to Medicines in Latin America* (2014), at 316; M. Lemma, 'Ethiopia: Intellectual Property for Generating Wealth, Fostering Development', *The Ethiopian Herald*, available online at http://allafrica.com/stories/201509030417.html (last visited 13 July 2017).
126. A. W. Oguttu, 'Transfer Pricing and Tax Avoidance: Is the Arm's Length Principle Still Relevant in the e-Commerce Era?', 18(2) *South African Mercantile Law Journal* (2006), 138, at 139.
127. OECD, *Revised Discussion Draft on Transfer Pricing Aspects of Intangibles* (Public Consultation, 30 July 2013), available online at https://www.oecd.org/tax/revised-discussion-draft-intangibles.pdf, at para. 35.
128. OECD, *Aligning Transfer Pricing Outcomes with Value Creation, Actions 8–10—2015 Final Reports*, 5 Oct. 2015, available online at http://www.oecd.org/ctp/aligning-transfer-pricing-outcomes-with-value-creation-actions-8-10-2015-final-reports-9789264241244-en.htm, at 67 (last visited 13 July 2017).
129. Ibid. at 70–73.
130. Ibid. at 74.
131. Article 12 of the UN MTC.
132. OECD, *Model Tax Convention on Income and on Capital 2014 (Full Version)* (2015), available online at http://www.oecd.org/tax/treaties/model-tax-convention-on-income-and-on-capital-2015-full-version-9789264239081-en.htm, at art. 12(3) (last visited 26 July 2017).

133. Holmes, *supra* note 119, at 190.
134. F. Akunobera, 'Uganda', *in* M. Lang, P. Pistone, J. Schuch, and C. Staringer (eds.), *The Impact of the OECD and UN Model Tax Conventions on Bilateral Tax Treaties* (2012), 1083.
135. OECD, *Preventing the Artificial Avoidance of Permanent Establishment Status, Action 7—2015 Final Report*, 5 Oct. 2015, available online at http://www.oecd.org/ctp/preventing-the-artificial-avoidance-of-permanent-establishment-status-action-7-2015-final-report-9789264241220-en.htm (last visited 13 July 2017).
136. Ibid. at 10.
137. Ibid. at 17.
138. OECD/G20, Final Report on Actions 8-10 (2015), at 143.
139. Ibid.
140. Uganda Income Tax Act, Chapter 340, Section 83(1); Ghana Internal Revenue Act 592 of 2000; Sections 51A–51H, in Chapter II of South Africa's Income Tax Act 58 of 1962.
141. Ibid. at 153–543.
142. Ibid. at 159.
143. Ibid. at 142.
144. Deloitte Australia, *ATO Paper on Profit Allocation to Bank Branches* (2011), available online at http://newsletters.usdbriefs.com/2011/Tax/ALS/a111010_6.pdf.
145. Examples are Chile, Greece, Mexico, and Turkey. See reservations to Article 7(2) of the OECD MTC.
146. See, e.g., Article 12, DTA between Ghana and Germany, entered into force 14 December 2007. Article 12, DTA between The Netherlands and Ghana, entered into force 10 March 2008; Article 13, DTA between South Africa and Uganda, entered into force 9 April 2001.

CHAPTER 9

SOME ASPECTS OF THE ARCHITECTURE OF INTERNATIONAL TAX REFORM (AND THEIR HUMAN RIGHTS–RELATED CONSEQUENCES)

MICHAEL LENNARD

I. A CATHEDRAL IS BUILT

A. INTRODUCTION

At the Third International Conference on Financing for Development in Addis Ababa on July 16, 2015, Mr. Zeid Ra'ad Al Hussein, UN High Commissioner for Human Rights, addressed the relationship between the UN Financing for Development approach and Human Rights issues. He noted that:

> Financing for development must satisfy the demands of all persons to have their most basic needs met in a world that does not lack the means, but has failed to demonstrate the will, to make human rights a reality for all.[1]

He further recognized that:

> Commitments have been made to combat tax evasion, prevent illicit financial flows, improve transparency, promote tax cooperation at all levels, and ensure that businesses pay their fair share of taxes.[2]

So what is the connection between international tax cooperation, including efforts to combat tax avoidance and evasion, which sits in the United Nations under the head of Financing for

Development, and human rights? The High Commissioner elaborated this important connection by noting, among other things that:

> [U]nder core human rights treaties, States are obligated to mobilize and allocate the maximum available resources for the progressive realization of economic, social and cultural rights, as well as to advance civil and political rights and the right to development . . . [Such mobilization includes] progressive tax systems that are equitable and that benefit the poorest and the most vulnerable while ensuring that those with the most means pay their fair share. [. . .]
>
> [. . .] More must be done to ensure coherence, including full respect by current international legal regimes for trade, finance, and investment for norms and standards for labour, the environment, human rights, equality and sustainability. When States act in these arenas, including as members of multilateral institutions, appropriate environmental, social and human rights safeguards must be applied.
>
> [. . .]
>
> Financing development the right way requires States to establish appropriate regulations and accountability mechanisms for all actors in the development and economic spheres. It further requires all actors to respect human rights and to do no harm to their realization.[3]

All these, and perhaps other aspects of human rights–related obligations, have a resonance in the tax world, something explored further in other chapters of this book. This chapter explores how international tax norms are generated, because without sufficient involvement of developing countries, including the least developed, in the discussion and establishment of norms (while allowing legitimate policy space for developing countries to reflect their realities), maximum resources for development may not be mobilized and allocated. The result is a limitation on the opportunities for tax systems to advance labor,[4] environment,[5] and human rights[6] standards in ways that are progressive not regressive, and to ensure accountability of taxpayers in meeting their tax obligations in the developing world.

With that background it is important to recognize that there is a great deal of concern expressed by many developing countries about their lack of real participation in the development of what are being promoted as global tax norms or standards.[7] The Organisation for Economic Co-operation and Development (OECD)/G20 Base Erosion and Profit Shifting (BEPS) Project has brought some of these issues to the forefront. Because the BEPS Project has been such a high-level political one, few country officials, especially lower-level bureaucrats, raise their heads above the parapet singly to express these concerns overtly. Nonetheless, they often emerge in other public fora, or in the views projected by regional or other types of country groupings.

The G77 and China, a group of 134 developing countries, frequently assert the need for the United Nations to be afforded a greater role in the formation of international taxation norms.[8] This refrain is in some respects a proxy for the very practical concerns of many tax policymakers and administrators in many countries about the cementing into place of an architecture of international tax reform—and just as importantly nonreform—that will not sufficiently reflect developing country realities and priorities, and may already be out of date. An even greater cause for concern: the dominance of the OECD-led tax architecture may seriously limit the chances for achieving more modern, universal, and truly cooperative structures.

The worry is that, at a time when a modern cathedral of transparent glass and flexible configuration might be built, adapted to modern needs, a contemporary recreation of Notre Dame de Paris is instead rising up. This is a technical achievement to be sure, but it is employing the architects and builders of the past, not the future. In so doing, it is exhausting the budget and political capital for a more forward-looking tax architecture over the coming years, and remains grounded in a lost world of mandatory veneration rather than voluntary attachment based on justice and relevance.

The rest of this chapter examines, against this background, how the international tax norm-setting mechanisms, especially those emerging as a result of recent OECD/G20 initiatives, may positively or negatively affect attainment of the Sustainable Development Goals and the achievement of human rights.

B. TAX AND SUSTAINABLE DEVELOPMENT

Tax represents an avenue to more modern sustainable development-focused economies, responsive to modern challenges. The importance of this relationship was illustrated by the centrality of tax issues at the Addis Ababa Financing for Development Conference in 2015, which was very surprising to most development practitioners. The major and last unresolved issue at that Conference was the upgrading to intergovernmental status of the UN Committee of Experts on International Cooperation in Tax Matters[9]—a move sought by the G77 and China. Although the state participants at the conference ostensibly rejected the upgrade after strong positioning and lobbying, the outcome document of the Conference effectively left the issue unresolved in the longer term, as a continuing point of discord between the developed and developing worlds.

The importance which tax assumes in the 2017 Inter-Agency Task Force Report on *Financing for Development: Progress and Prospects* is also striking, with 267 references to "tax."[10] The Report notes, for example, the relevance of tax to sustainable development when it states, "[i]nternational tax norms have important distributional implications, both between the private sector and governments as well as among governments, and thus impact sustainable development and investment."[11] The outpouring of official calls from countries at the April 2017 UN Economic and Social Council Annual Meeting on International Tax Cooperation in Tax Matters[12] for an upgrading of the UN Tax Committee included the following call from the G77 and China Group, a recognized UN country grouping:

> The Group of 77 and China highlights the situation that there is still no single global inclusive forum for international tax cooperation at the intergovernmental level. While it may be indicated that a certain level of dialogue and initiative actions are taking place at the international level regarding cooperation on tax matters, the Group underscores that the United Nations is the only universal forum where these issues can be discussed in an open, transparent, and inclusive manner, considering that other processes might be outlined from a perspective that safeguards the interests of constituents from developed countries.
>
> The Group of 77 and China urge Member States to consider the upgrading of the Committee of Experts on International Cooperation in Tax Matters, by transforming it from experts acting in their own capacity, to an inter-governmental subsidiary body of the Economic and Social Council (ECOSOC), with experts representing their respective governments. This upgrading is necessary and important to allow all Member States to participate in a mechanism that is inclusive and participatory.[13]

To recognize this concern among developing countries is not to lack admiration for some of the OECD/G20 BEPS achievements and architecture. There is much that is useful to developing countries in the BEPS outcomes, especially in combating what is commonly regarded by both developing and developed countries as tax avoidance or evasion, such as through international profit shifting (transfer mispricing).

C. BEPS AS A COMMON CHALLENGE

BEPS is an issue for countries generally, and one that has become increasingly urgent in recent years, for the reasons noted by Kimberley Clausing:

> Corporate tax base erosion due to profit shifting is a large and consequential problem. Reduced revenues from one source must be compensated for by higher tax revenues from other sources, or lower government spending, or increased budget deficits; none of these possibilities is particularly attractive.
>
> Beyond revenue consequences, corporate tax base erosion and profit shifting also affects the larger integrity of the tax system. [. . .]
>
> Further, corporate tax base erosion has consequences for the distributional burden of the tax system as a whole, consequences that are noteworthy due to the large documented increases in income inequality in recent decades. [. . .] [T]he corporate tax has an essential role in taxing capital income, which is far more concentrated than labor income.[14]

For many developing countries, BEPS activities of multinational enterprises (MNEs) (whether addressed by the BEPS Project or not) are especially problematic for several reasons, including: (1) the fragility of their revenue systems (especially in the many developing countries where there is heavy reliance on extractive industries taxation[15]); (2) the difficulty of addressing in informational, legislative and administrative terms, often very complex BEPS schemes; (3) the greater proportional importance of corporate income tax in many developing country tax systems;[16] and (4) the need for personal taxpayers to see that MNEs will be held to account in meeting their tax obligations.

D. THE COMMONALITY OF THE RESPONSE?

While BEPS *is* in many respects a common problem, the Action Plan[17] was essentially developed without non-OECD and G20-country input. Moreover, it was developed within a swift time frame and with an architecture that inherently limited active input to change its direction in any substantial way. Even with the best will in the world, a general relevance to the realities of countries, including the least developed, is not "baked-in" to the development process of that Action Plan and cannot be tested until the policy and administrative approaches at country level are more fully unrolled. That process is still in its early days, and in the author's view, based on contact with country officials and taxpayers, is likely to involve significant differences of approach and interpretation at policy, administrative, and court decision level, even among countries purporting to follow the tax rules.

Some issues of great practical relevance to developing countries in combatting BEPS, such as use of withholding tax regimes, were not part of the Project. The OECD likewise overtly avoided responding to the call to re-examine the allocation by treaty of taxing rights between the "source state" (where profit-making engagement in a country's economy occurs) and the "residence state" of the profit maker.[18] The OECD Model Tax Convention[19] tends to favor the latter, the capital-exporting state, while the UN Model Tax Convention[20] tends to favor the former, the capital-importing state. Finally, the halting BEPS work on the impact of the digitalized economy on tax may be the slowest part of the BEPS Project to evolve and conclude, precisely because it appears to carry within it an inevitably increased push for greater source state taxation of services[21] and other transactions more broadly (including basedon market access without a physical presence).[22]

The BEPS outcomes on preventing the granting of treaty benefits inappropriate circumstances (Action 6) countering avoidance of permanent establishments (Action 7), and transfer pricing (Actions 8–10) also clearly in practice give more armory to countries enforcing source state taxation.

The UN Tax Committee decided at its recent sessions, including in April 2017, to adopt many of the BEPS provisions tightening up the UN Model Tax Convention against tax avoidance and evasion—such as by manipulation of the "permanent establishment" concept, which generally governs whether an entity is sufficiently engaged in an economy for that source country to tax profits made, under tax treaties. The BEPS Project's attempt to address the substance of arrangements, rather than form alone,[23] is particularly useful for preserving developing country tax bases, even if not always easy to administer.

Addressing abuses that offend the common perspectives of developed and developing countries therefore represents a welcome step, but there are differences that broadly reflect developed and developing country divides, such as to whether provision of technical services into a country should be taxable even if the company does not have a physical presence in a country—an advance agreed for inclusion in the 2017 UN Model Tax Convention and based on developing country treaties. The BEPS Project, in contrast, kept the OECD country preference for requiring physical presence for a period of months. On issues such as whether unresolved tax disputes between countries should be subject to binding mandatory arbitration, or should be resolved only if and when both countries agree, the developing countries' skepticism of mandatory binding arbitration[24] was echoed by similar skepticism among some OECD countries, and by some of the economically stronger non-OECD but G20 member countries, such as India and China, during the BEPS Project negotiations.

Even so, the BEPS Final Report on the dispute resolution issue and the Multilateral Legal Instrument—designed to quickly implement the BEPS tax treaty outcomes[25]—reflects some sort of a rearguard action to try to establish mandatory binding arbitration as the "gold standard" going forward. The current OECD/G20 work on tax certainty for businesses, discussed below,[26] can perhaps also be seen as an aspect of this rearguard action.

Although it does not specifically address the question of arbitration as a way of unblocking stalled mutual agreement procedure (MAP) discussions, the introduction into the process of peer review and monitoring of the implementation of the BEPS Action 14 minimum standard for dispute resolution, as well as the introduction of a questionnaire for taxpayers[27] about the conduct by governments of MAPs (such as the reasons why a MAP request by a taxpayer was denied by the revenue authority), can be viewed as another such rearguard action. This questionnaire is especially interesting, as the MAP has until now been guarded, in the OECD (and UN) Model Tax Conventions, as essentially a matter between countries. That is, even where arbitration is included, it is included not as concluding the MAP itself, but rather as something that needs to be implemented by those who direct the MAP—the "Competent Authorities" of the countries—unless the taxpayer does not accept it, or (in the case of the UN arbitration option) where both competent authorities reject the arbitral decision.

E. THE BEPS PROJECT—AN "EQUAL FOOTING" OR "SHAKY GROUND"?

The OECD literature suggests that the BEPS outcomes are the work of a highly collaborative process, and that the large number of countries involved are acting "on an equal footing" as between developed and developing country.[28] The term "on an equal footing" has never been well defined and in fact seems to derive from US constitutional law, with additional states being admitted to the Union as full members with the same rights as the original states and with the phrase "on an equal footing" used in relevant State Accession Acts to reflect that equality.[29] In the current context, the phrase seems to have been kept deliberately vague, but appears to be used to denote that even if non-OECD countries are not members of a key decision body such as the OECD Committee on Fiscal Affairs, they will in effect be listened to as though they are.[30]

Opinions differ among participants as to whether this concept of an equal footing has been achieved, and therefore whether the OECD/G20's BEPS Project responses to tax avoidance and evasion challenges have emerged by global acclamation or by the impossibility of effective resistance. However, in the author's experience, the differing opinions often correlate to whether those expressing views are from governments or MNEs, or from OECD/G20 countries or non-OECD/G20 countries.

Because of the elevated political environment of the OECD/G20 BEPS process, overt public criticism of the process by lower level operatives required to deal with its intricacies is far less common than behind-the-scenes hair-pulling. The fact that different countries attend meetings and sign on to fora and instruments is currently being used as an indicator of globally harmonious international tax policy development. There has been a very vigorous attempt by the OECD to maximize the numbers of participants in the quest for global legitimacy (though much more in implementing bodies than in policy setting bodies), but country involvement in such a process does not necessarily reflect a real "hearts and minds" commitment to the processes and outcomes as they have emerged from the OECD/G20 processes. Rather, that participation may reflect pressure put on the political operators, such as country finance ministers, and the need to be seen as acceding to OECD/G20 standards and avoiding retaliation. The concerns of lower level tax experts are powerless in halting this sort of political momentum, but those who do not feel they have sufficient ownership over the standards, or that those standards are not relevant to their country's situation, may seek a terrible, and uncertain, revenge in the areas where their powers lie: namely, the interpretation and implementation of the uncertain parts of the standards, and the ability to point to similar "outbreaks" among policymakers and administrators of larger developing and developed countries.

The unrolling of the BEPS outcomes in practice may indeed shine light on the lack of better alternatives and the need to develop them, or on the level of pressure that ministers feel to quickly sign on to something about which they and (often especially) their technical advisers may have reservations, but as to which they feel little room to move. If that happens, the unrolling of BEPS standards at country level may be a messy and uncertain process, but may play its part in developing better standards in future, including ones that better reflect the linkages with human rights obligations of countries. Both the norm development and implementation processes in the area of tax would better reflect larger realities if subject to more interdisciplinary scrutiny—including by human rights experts with tax experience, a small but hopefully growing band. Tax cooperation is ultimately too important systemically to be left entirely to experts purely in tax, as nongovernmental organizations (NGOs) are increasingly recognizing.

At the 14th Session of the UN Conference on Trade and Development in Nairobi in July 2016, an interesting attempt was made to introduce the concept of "equal footing" more generally into the architecture of international tax norm setting. As one nongovernmental representative noted:

> During the conference, the rich countries deleted references to the rights of developing countries to participate on an equal footing in the work on international tax matters. This was a sad replay

of last year's summit on financing for development in Addis Ababa, where developing countries fought hard, but lost their battle for a new intergovernmental UN tax body, which would have given them the right to a seat at the table when global tax standards are negotiated.[31]

Most OECD countries seem to be supporting *intergovernmental* fora at the OECD level, including those involving developing countries, but not at the UN level, where the Tax Committee members formally act in a personal capacity. In fact, all government nominees to the Committee (and therefore all Committee members, as the UN Secretary-General can only choose from country nominees) recently have actually been government officials. The reality is probably that they de facto, though not de jure, reflect their governments' views, which they may have had a part in designing and at least are likely to project in any international fora.

There is also a widespread perception that the OECD fora where developing country membership (as compared to a lesser form of engagement) is encouraged tend inevitably to be bodies that essentially implement already determined standards, rather than setting them. The Global Forum for Transparency and Information Exchange for Tax Purposes and the Inclusive Framework, discussed below, are examples of such bodies.

II. SOME SPECIFIC BEPS OUTCOMES

Beyond the BEPS process, it is worth analyzing some of the substantive elements of the OECD/BEPS system for developing global norms to address how far such an "equal footing" is possible and is being achieved under the structures and modalities used. Alternatively, is the concept of an equal footing more akin to the modern-sounding but very old concept of "virtual representation,"[32] with representatives holding the real decision-making power said to be looking after not just their interests, but also your own, not necessarily aligned, ones? As one author has noted: "Stated in its most simple form, the doctrine held that although non-electors were not *actually* represented in the British legislature, they were represented *virtually*; that is, they were not represented just in contemplation of constitutional law, but were in fact, not fiction, represented."[33]

A. THE DIGITALIZED ECONOMY

The OECD/BEPS work on the implications of the digital economy has not progressed with the speed of other actions. This is widely attributed to the likelihood that the expected direction of any comprehensive work in this area would be along the lines of further retention of taxing rights of countries where there is an engagement in the digital economy. Even some traditional capital-exporting developed countries, such as France, are concerned at the inability to tax, under often antiquated treaty rules only allowing taxation by the state of such engagement where there is physical presence in the state for a few months. The UN work is in some respects more advanced in its new optional UN Model Tax Convention Fees for Technical Services provision,[34] which recognizes that (often very high) profits can quickly occur in the digital economy without such a geographical presence over time. The UN provision therefore permits taxation of profits made without a geographical or time requirement. The provision of technical services to a local is seen as itself showing sufficient economic engagement in the economy. There are unresolved differences about what constitutes "sufficient economic engagement" more generally, and as is clear from the development of the UN Fees for Technical Services provision itself, developing countries tend to take a wider view of this concept, often seeking greater source-country taxation under tax treaties than developed countries wish to accept. This reflects the greater concern in key parts of the UN Model Tax Convention for preserving source taxing rights of countries. These provisions stand in contrast to the OECD Model Tax Convention, which often restricts such taxation rights to the state of residence of the corporation.

The BEPS Project did not in any substantive way address withholding taxes. This is a key, easily administrable way of ensuring at least some profits are taxed where economic engagement occurs, despite the (easily manipulated) residence of the profit maker. Further work on the digital economy needs to bear in mind the importance of withholding taxes in combatting avoidance and evasion of taxation on digital profits. Solutions that are somewhat "blunt-edged" but fair may be necessary to ensure sufficient certainty but also administrability by tax authorities in most developing countries, which so often have very limited resources in terms of personnel, information, and even legislation.

B. THE MULTILATERAL INSTRUMENT

1. The Language of the MLI

The commendable idea of the OECD-developed Multilateral Instrument (MLI)[35] is that it is an accelerated way of operationalizing decisions by countries to sign up to BEPS "minimum standards" as they become part of the OECD "inclusive framework." It amends existing treaties to conform to the outcomes of the following BEPS action points: Action 2 (Hybrid Mismatches), Action 6 (Treaty Abuse), Action 7 (Artificial Avoidance of Permanent Establishment (PE) Status), and Action 14 (Improving Dispute Resolution). The progress of the MLI is important because: there is clearly (based on anecdotal evidence from countries) pressure being placed—especially at the political level—on developing countries to speedily sign up to the MLI;[36] it is a complex task for countries to work out the effect of it on their existing treaties with particular countries, especially with all the options available to countries; it may make it harder to argue for non-MLI wording in bilateral treaties that are not covered by the MLI itself; and there will be pressure to have some developing countries agree to mandatory binding arbitration under the MLI framework, with tax competition then encouraging "competing" developing countries to follow.

The MLI gives countries the flexibility to specify which existing treaties are covered, how they will meet certain aspects of the minimum standards, and to opt out of all or part of provisions which extend beyond the minimum standard where both parties agree to amend their treaties in the same way for that particular article (i.e., there is a "match") that a treaty article will be amended.[37]

There will no doubt be interpretative issues about what particular words and phrases in the MLI mean, and with an unwieldy process of calling for a Conference of the Parties on issues of the MLI,[38] most matters will probably be regarded as issues of interpretation under the covered (and modified) bilateral agreements themselves. Such interpretation matters will be left to the mechanisms in those agreements—the MAP procedure.[39] This will give an extra responsibility to panels in cases where mandatory binding arbitration is included, so any limitation on such an interpretative role would need to be clearly identified in the rules of procedure for conduct of such arbitration.

The Explanatory Statement for the MLI[40] has been clearly identified as an important document for interpretative purposes, following the Vienna Convention on the Law of Treaties (VCLT).[41] The VCLT sets forth interpretation rules which both the UN[42] and OECD[43] Model Tax Conventions recognize as relevant for countries generally, whether party to the treaty or not—in which case they are regarded as representing a codification of customary international law. The Explanatory Statement addresses its own status at paragraph 11:

> The text of this explanatory statement to accompany the Convention ("Explanatory Statement") was prepared by the participants in the *ad hoc* Group, and in the Sub-Group on Arbitration, to provide clarification of the approach taken in the Convention and how each provision is intended to affect tax agreements covered by the Convention ("Covered Tax Agreements"). It therefore reflects the agreed understanding of the negotiators with respect to the Convention. It includes descriptions of the types of treaty provisions which are intended to be covered and the ways in which they are intended to be modified. The members of the *ad hoc* group adopted this Explanatory Statement on 24 November 2016 at the same time as adopting the text of the Convention.[44]

There will be further *travaux préparatoires* of the MLI in the hands of the OECD Secretariat, though they would probably not properly be usable in court or administrative proceedings unless they become public. As noted by the WTO Panel in the *European Communities—Chicken Cuts* case, when considering the meaning of "salted":

> In support, we note that Ian Sinclair has stated that: ". . . recourse to *travaux préparatoires* does not depend on the participation in the drafting of the text of the State against whom the travaux are invoked. To hold otherwise would disrupt the unity of a multilateral treaty, since it would imply that two different methods of interpretation should be employed, the one for States which participated in the *travaux prèparatoires* and the other for States which did not so participate. One qualification should, however, be made. The *travaux préparatoires* should be in the public domain so that States which have not participated in the drafting of the text should have the possibility of consulting them. *Travaux préparatoires* which are kept secret by negotiating States should not be capable of being invoked against subsequently acceding States." We see no reason why these comments would not be equally applicable with respect to "circumstances of conclusion" under Article 32 of the *Vienna Convention*.[45]

Paragraph 12 of the MLI Explanatory Statement explicitly also brings in the BEPS Final Reports as relevant interpretative material.

Finally, on the point of interpretation, the MLI gives preference to English or French language text versions even where a covered agreement might make, for example, the Malaysian language text equally authentic. As the Explanatory Statement notes at paragraph 317:

> The final clause of the Convention provides the authentic languages of the Convention are English and French. Accordingly, where questions of interpretation arise in relation to Covered Tax Agreements concluded in other languages or in relation to translations of the Convention into other languages, it may be necessary to refer back to the English or French authentic texts of the Convention.[46]

Already stretched developing countries therefore need a good understanding of English language texts, including the MLI and its Explanatory Statement.

2. The MLI and the UN Model Tax Convention

The MLI is already having another effect. Wording in the MLI is being used to argue in UN Tax Committee sessions that the 2017 UN Model Tax Convention should follow that wording as an expression of what developing countries will have to agree to in their bilateral treaties, either because they are parties to the MLI or because developed countries will insist on the MLI wording in bilateral negotiations. This argument is a dangerous one in many respects for the formation of international tax norms. First, while the OECD made much of the fact that over one hundred jurisdictions were in some sense involved in the negotiations for the MLI there were as yet no parties bound by it—adoption alone did not result in that, and as at 29 January 2019, only 19 countries were parties.[47].

Second, and even when countries have joined up to the MLI, it is explicitly only intended to operationalize BEPS changes for existing treaties, rather than to mandate what new treaties will say. Countries may agree, for whatever reasons, and with varying degrees of "true belief" join up to the MLI as a whole, as part of the "package deal" with some things they like and some things they do not, but may prefer different wordings of particular clauses in new treaties ungoverned by the MLI.

3. The MLI and Mandatory Binding Arbitration

As outlined in a UN Secretariat paper in 2015,[48] there have been concerns expressed by many developing countries about bringing in mandatory arbitration dispute settlement processes under treaties. The chief concerns raised include, among others: what is often referred to as a "loss of sovereignty" in an agreement to abide by a third party's decision; the potential resource costs of arbitration; and whether the arbitral process, which is essentially not subject to appeal, would be used to expand panel jurisdiction, since panelists benefit financially from jurisdiction being found (by themselves).

Further issues relate to unfamiliarity in many countries with arbitration, which might prevent them from putting their best case forward, or might mean they lack the expertise needed to determine what further skills and experts need to be brought in, and who is available to meet those needs. There is also a legitimate concern as to whether the sorts of people who would be qualified and available for arbitral panels would be more often than not on the pro-investment/pro-business side of the "encouraging investment vs. ensuring taxation for development" spectrum. This preoccupation is animated by the fact that government officials would be either ineligible, or would not have decisive votes in a panel, and there are only very limited numbers of independent academicians in most developing countries on issues such as transfer pricing (the likely most arbitrated issue).

The MLI does not address these concerns. Ultimately, dealing with them may involve institutional structures that are seen as focused on assisting developing countries in gaining expertise and in the conduct of particular cases, as happens in the World Trade Organization.[49] What is of more concern is that the MLI seems poised to try to re-establish mandatory binding arbitration as the "gold standard" for dispute settlement under the MAP. No doubt those preferring mandatory binding arbitration will seek to have key developing countries in Africa, Asia, and the Americas adopt it and then let the competition between investment-seeking states do its best to further spread the practice so that it may become the norm in treaties, rather than the exception. The emphasis on certainty noted above, including in the OECD tax certainty work referenced, is mostly addressing uncertainty from the perspective of taxpayers. This appears to be largely as a response to (often legitimate) business concerns at the uncertainties created by changes as a result of the BEPS Project. There is unfortunately less focus on improving developing country certainty that revenue based on taxing profits made in that country can be used for development.

One MLI possibility should be at least considered by many developing countries—that of adopting Article 16 of the MLI but *not* the rule allowing a case to be presented to either competent authority. To allow presentation to either competent authority means that instead of being required to present a case to the state of residence or nationality (as is required under both the existing UN and OECD Model Tax Conventions) such as Tanzania, the Tanzanian MNE group company may take its case to either country party to a treaty, such as the United States, if it is, for example, transacting with the head office in that country. While Tanzania may regard the case put by the MNE subsidiary resident in its country as unjustified,[50] the other treaty party (the United States) may not. Allowing the latter to make the decision on whether the case is justified as a MAP case may not reflect the proper interpretation of the treaty and can yet have serious consequences. This approach of wider taxpayer choice, taken (unsurprisingly) from US treaty practice, as so much of BEPS is, would allow a taxpayer to avoid the possibility that Tanzania will conclude the claim is unjustified and that the matter therefore does not enter into the MAP dispute resolution process.

The OECD discussion paper on Action 14 makes the intention clear:

> As interpretations of treaty provisions may vary between treaty partners, circumstances may arise in which one competent authority does not find the objection presented by the taxpayer under paragraph 1 of Article 25 to be justified, whilst the other competent authority would find the objection to be justified. For example, some competent authorities may be hesitant or find it difficult to overturn assessments made by their own tax administrations and, consequently, may unilaterally determine, under paragraph 2 of Article 25, that the taxpayer's objection is not justified and therefore refuse to discuss the case with the competent authority of the other State (which may consider the objection to be justified). Given this dynamic, a process in which a competent authority can unilaterally determine, under paragraph 2 of Article 25, that the taxpayer's objection is not justified—and thereby prevent the case from being addressed bilaterally through the second stage of the MAP—raises legitimate issues as to the bilateral nature of treaty application and implementation.[51]

It is true that some claims may be inappropriately left out of MAP, but this change may mean that matters which were *appropriately* left out of MAP (for example, because the taxpayer's objection is legitimately regarded by the developing country as not covered by the treaty) are brought into it (because the developed country incorrectly takes a contrary view). Under a traditional MAP, without mandatory binding arbitration, that preference for the investor position as compared with the country of investment position may not be of much practical importance as that country is not forced into a solution.

Another real impact of the taxpayer-oriented approach in the OECD approach to mandatory binding arbitration, has to do with the venue of the arbitration. Venue can be very important as to the convenience of attending, the familiarity or unfamiliarity of the developing country representatives with the forum (such as the local arbitration forum) and connections or otherwise with the personnel.

As the UN secretariat paper noted on this point:

> The venue of ITDRP [the international tax dispute resolution procedure] can be very important in creating confidence in the system for all affected stakeholders. There would need to be rules as to

where the proceedings should take place. A default option could be developed, allowing the CAs ["Competent Authorities"] to choose an alternative on a case by case basis or on a more systemic basis by advance agreement. If there was an institution set up as part of the agreement, it could be the default venue. The interplay between ITDRP in MAP proceedings and the venue for that ITDRP perhaps needs further discussion. The ability of the taxpayer in a MAP to choose which CA to take its request to, as proposed in the OECD Final Report on Action 1481 may, for example, have implications for venue, since paragraphs 12 of both the OECD and UN model agreements provide that:

> Unless agreed otherwise by the competent authorities, the competent authority to which the case giving rise to the arbitration was initially presented will be responsible for the logistical arrangements for the meetings of the arbitral panel and will provide the administrative personnel necessary for the conduct of the arbitration process. The administrative personnel so provided will report only to the Chair of the arbitration panel concerning any matter related to that process.[52]

Obviously the dispute would be heard in that country in most or all cases. Of course, where a group has members within two countries, the same choice of venue would be made depending upon which member sought a MAP, even without the changes proposed by the OECD. The change to allow a single taxpayer to choose the forum and the administering authority facilitates this choice, however, and may prove significant in practice.

The tax authorities of some, especially developed, countries do have close relations with arbitration providers that a "visiting" tax authority may feel puts it at a disadvantage in an arbitral forum, at least on procedural issues, which can be very important in arbitral proceedings. The Internal Revenue Service, for example has an established relationship with the International Centre for Dispute Resolution in New York and the American Arbitration Association.[53] Few developing country tax authorities can boast the same, and they might have concerns that the developed country relationships with arbitration centers may lend a de facto advantage on the important procedural aspects of arbitration, especially if the venue provisions for a dispute allow the taxpayer to in effect choose where the arbitration is held.

C. THE INCLUSIVE FRAMEWORK

1. The Nature of the Framework

The Inclusive Framework is essentially an implementing framework for the BEPS outcomes, as its promotional brochure notes:

> Members of the framework work on an equal footing to tackle tax avoidance, to improve the coherence of international tax rules, and to ensure a more transparent tax environment. In particular, the framework:—develops standards in respect of remaining BEPS issues;—will review the implementation of agreed minimum standards through an effective monitoring system;—monitors BEPS issues, including tax challenges raised by the digital economy; and—facilitates the implementation processes of the Members by providing further guidance and by supporting development of toolkits to support low-capacity developing countries.[54]

Membership is through invitation, rather than as of right for non-G20 or OECD countries, with the position being as follows:

For countries and jurisdictions that have not been formally invited yet, a decision on formal invitation as BEPS Associate will be taken by the Inclusive Framework on BEPS and the OECD Council. Invited countries and jurisdictions will become BEPS Associates upon receipt of a positive response to the formal invitation from the OECD Secretary-General.[55]

It is evidence of how deeply embedded in the OECD the Inclusive Framework is that the Council, which apparently must approve invitations, is composed only of OECD members. Moreover, the Council Secretariat is the OECD's Secretariat, generally only open to citizens of OECD member countries. Even if the exceptional example is taken of the Global Forum on Transparency and Information Exchange for Tax Purposes, where nonmembers may be part of the Secretariat, OECD countries are as likely to be overrepresented as they are in that secretariat. Although the head of the Global Forum is from India, the heads of all three units are from OECD countries, as is the other main position of head of Communications.[56] There are very few citizens of only non-OECD countries, and several dual citizens of both OECD and non-OECD countries.

Although the Global Forum Secretariat is stated by the OECD as being "a self-standing dedicated Secretariat, based in the OECD Centre for Tax Policy and Administration,"[57] in fact, the normal staff reporting lines and duties to the OECD as an institution apply.[58] Likewise, "normal" OECD recruitment requirements apply, including for "excellent written and oral command of one of the two official languages of the OECD (English and French)."[59] Such characteristics seem to reflect the Secretariat's placement in the Centre for Tax Policy and Administration (CTPA).

Global Forum decisions are consensus-based, which is much more possible in an implementing body than a standard-setting one, although it is always possible to have a consensus decision with options (a "differentiated consensus"). The same issues seem to arise with the Inclusive Framework and the MLI secretarial support.

The Inclusive Framework also requires payment of an annual fee,[60] as well as commitment to four BEPS minimum standards:[61]

1. Model provisions to prevent treaty abuse (including treaty shopping) by impeding the use of conduit companies to channel investments through countries and jurisdictions with favourable tax treaties in order to obtain reduced rates of taxation;
2. Standardised Country-by-Country (CbC) Reporting that will give tax administrations a global picture of where MNEs' profits, tax and economic activities are reported, and the ability to use this information to assess transfer pricing and other BEPS risks, so they can focus audit resources where they will be most effective;
3. A revitalised peer review process to address harmful tax practices, including patent boxes where they include harmful features, as well as a commitment to transparency through the mandatory spontaneous exchange of relevant information on taxpayer-specific rulings which, in the absence of such information exchange, could give rise to BEPS concerns; and
4. An agreement to secure progress on dispute resolution, with the strong political commitment to the effective and timely resolution of disputes through the mutual agreement procedure (MAP).

Some emphasis has been put, including in OECD speeches,[62] on some standard-setting functions among the Inclusive Framework's raft of implementing roles. This is particularly the case with respect to profit splits—a method for analyzing transfer pricing—and is reflected in the promotional brochure:

Standard setting in respect of remaining BEPS issues

The Members of the framework set standards on remaining BEPS issues, for example, in the area of tax treaties and transfer pricing. This includes the work on the development of guidance on transfer pricing, on the application of profit split methods and on financial transactions.[63]

The OECD revised Guidance on Profit Splits,[64] released after the formation and first meeting of the Inclusive Framework, did not suggest a significant role for the Inclusive Framework in the development of norms regarding profit splitting (which in any case would only be following the tracks set down by the BEPS outcomes). Instead, the Guidance reverts to the traditional OECD member bodies for norm development:

This draft sets out the text of proposed revised guidance on the application of the transactional profit split method, together with a number of questions. The questions are intended to elicit responses which will then be taken into account by Working Party No. 6 in considering revisions to the relevant guidance in Chapter II of the Transfer Pricing Guidelines.[65]

This is especially important as it seems that developing countries, even within the G20, appear to see a greater role for profit splits in the future as reflecting value creation in global value chains (especially in the absence of comparable data). Traditional OECD powers, in contrast, seem more likely to take the view that profit splits are no more important that they were before.[66]

These aspects of the Inclusive Framework should be seen in the context of how the OECD decision-making apparatus operates. As the OECD notes in its "Background Briefing on the Inclusive Framework":

The OECD's work programme on tax is carried out by the CFA [Committee on Fiscal Affairs] through groups of national experts, organised by technical area in Working Parties and other bodies. These working groups develop international tax standards and guidance, as well as all the technical work [. . .]. The working groups, being subsidiary bodies of the CFA, meet regularly, and discuss draft documents prepared by the OECD Secretariat, with input received by members of the related groups. During these meetings, where technicalities are discussed and standards are developed, delegates reach agreements by consensus. The working groups report to the CFA where senior officials of member countries can: i) decide, on a consensus-based approach, on the working groups' outcomes; ii) hold further discussions on issues working groups could not reach consensus on; or iii) require the working groups to carry out further work.[67]

In practice, this means that the OECD's decision-making process for tax purposes has a two-layer structure. At the first level, countries' technical experts participate in the decision-making at the level of the working groups and work closely with their respective CFA delegates in order to make them fully aware of the technicalities discussed at the subsidiary levels. On the second level, countries' senior officials participate in the CFA decision process to ensure a political commitment to the CFA outcomes. Embodied in the CFA, the Inclusive Framework on BEPS makes use of this consensus-based mechanism whereby all members participate on an equal footing.[68]

It is reported that the Director of the OECD CTPA, Pascal Saint-Amans, has contemplated that the Inclusive Framework may eventually go beyond BEPS-related mandates.[69] The challenge for the OECD, however, is whether (1) it would be willing to cede organizing control over such a body on the one hand, so that it truly became an independent forum with its policy direction set by members on a one-country, one-vote basis, and risk results that OECD members might not wish to be swept away on; or (2) it is possible, on the other hand, to credibly appear as a global tax policy deliberating body, while it is kept under a tight decision-making rein—as to the key decisions—by some members only. Whether, structurally, a body in which developing countries must pay to participate is a proper one for any broader aspirations, remains another serious question.

D. TAX CERTAINTY

1. The OECD/IMF Tax Certainty Report

The OECD has commenced work, with the support of the G20, on tax certainty, including a questionnaire for business designed as part of a project: "to work on solutions to support certainty in the tax system with the aim to promote investment, trade and balanced growth."[70] An important manifestation of this work is the 2017 OECD/IMF report to the G20, now with a 2018 update.[71] The report "explores the nature of tax uncertainty, its main sources and effects on business decisions and outlines a set of concrete and practical approaches to help policymakers and tax administrations shape a more certain tax environment."[72] It addresses the risks to investment caused by uncertainty,[73] and suggests legislative and administrative options to bring greater certainty, including in dispute settlement.[74]

2. The Follow-up Work

The Tax Certainty Report is a welcome one, including the work proposed to engage more with developing country-related issues on this complex matter, to complement the learnings from capacity building.[75] That follow-up work will need to be cognizant, however, of:

1. the perception among many countries that certainty on tax issues is often sought by MNEs when it favors their tax position, but that *un*certainty is often sought when it similarly favors their tax positions;
2. the need for information flows under the BEPS Project and other initiatives to function effectively, so that the information gaps between developing country tax administrations on the one hand and developed country tax administrations and MNEs on the other are reduced;
3. the need to recognize that "certainty" should not be seen as contrary to the "substance over form" approach that permeates the BEPS Project outcome and the UN tax cooperation work. (For example, black letter law approaches to corporate residency and asset ownership have been abused to avoid taxes where economic activity occurs and profits are truly made, often under the pretext of legal certainty.);
4. the continuing debate (and differences of approach) as to whether a more "substance over form" approach to transfer pricing aspects of the BEPS Project, are more "pragmatic" expressions of the existing arm's-length standard or a departure from it justified as an anti-abuse rule;[76]
5. the need to recognize that differentiated approaches and timelines, which are at times necessary to reflect developing country realities, support rather than detract from certainty; and
6. the reality that active involvement of developing countries in key norm-developing fora and decisions is key to ensuring greater "ownership" of those norms, greater consistency

in them, greater transparency, and greater certainty for administrations, as well as business and advisers.

The Tax Justice Network has noted (not without justification) that calls for greater certainty tend really to be calls for lower taxes.[77] It might be observed that where MNEs can leverage uncertainty, such as over what is an arm's-length price, to their benefit, they will embrace it as an inferior alternative to certainty that they *need not* pay taxes, but a superior alternative to certainty that they *must* pay taxes.

E. COUNTRY-BY-COUNTRY REPORTING

There is a real concern among many MNEs and their advisers about the possibility that aspects not just of the Country-by-Country Report, but also of the Master File, which gives a broad picture of an MNE's operations, may become public—meaning, get into the hands of NGOs and the press. This concern is often expressed in terms of the need to protect legitimate commercial confidentiality. The new emphasis on Master File issues, however, might also be at least in some cases due to a concern about wider public scrutiny, particularly by those with technical expertise and a powerful communication channel to the way the MNE does business. There is particular sensitivity around scrutiny of the way MNEs do business with developing countries, and especially whether the same approach is taken in dealing with the developing country tax authorities as with the US or German authorities, for example.

This new front in the defense against public disclosure of transfer pricing information probably is related to the similar fight against public country reporting of the type proposed by the European Commission.[78] The author's view is that public disclosure of Country-by-Country Reports, Master Files, and Local Files is an inevitability; it is merely a question of when. Furthermore, MNEs making their positions public before they are forced to, as a way of telling their "story," may potentially yield a great deal of good will, especially among younger, more socially conscious shareholders and consumers, as well as pension funds.

Of course goodwill could quickly dissipate if the natural suspicion by many developing country tax authorities of MNEs "coming clean" is shown to be justified in the case of such MNEs, by reports that appear to provide a great deal of information but avoid providing the full story of a MNEs engagement in the developing country's economy. In order to minimize this risk, MNEs should be ready to explain their reports and how they relate to their tax returns in developing countries. They should do so in a way that not only speaks to tax officials in those countries but also explains their case to the common man, the NGOs, and the media. It is in the interest of MNEs that their reports not appear to be overly legalistic, composed of "alternative facts" or be economical with the truth.

III. STRESS-TESTING THE CATHEDRAL

A. THE GOOD, THE BAD, THE UGLY?

The BEPS process has a great deal of potential to address some of the gaps that exist between developing and developed countries. It has potential to help provide developing countries with the information they need to properly defend their tax bases, though that will not happen by magic; there is a great deal of information technology, information interpretation, and handling capacity needed to unlock these benefits with sufficient speed to protect the tax base.

There is also an abiding feeling among many developing countries, especially those not yet able to be part of automatic exchange, that their information needs, which involve some cost to the partner countries, may not be given the same attention by some developed countries as the provision of information to fellow OECD members, especially if responding to their information needs would prejudice OECD-resident MNEs that may be perceived in those OECD countries as major employers and "national champions." In this respect, it is useful to remember that OECD members providing information about their resident MNEs may, under bilateral tax treaties, end up having to give tax credits or exemptions for taxation levied on the MNE in the developing countries. In other words, there could be a clear monetary disincentive toward sharing such information, especially with countries with which they do not have close and regular relations.

Such a reluctance on the part of OECD members to provide information that might make life difficult for their MNEs abroad, should not be assumed, but the situation needs to be carefully monitored. This is all the more the case in an increasingly nationalist context, where the misquotation attributed to former CEO of General Motors that "what is good for GM is good for America" risks becoming a policy approach followed not just in America but in other countries also.

Another key gap is the capability gap between countries. There has been an increase in provision of capacity to developing countries, even if it sometimes may be more focused on BEPS capability than on other non-BEPS issues that may be of more immediate concern to developing countries. The legal gaps in many developing countries in terms of combatting tax avoidance and the BEPS Project may assist this, although some of the hesitancies and difficulties in passing legislation and keeping it updated may result in resistance. The judiciary will, in many countries, play a decisive role in implementing BEPS, especially through the interpretation of the "substance over form" spirit that imbues much of BEPS work,[79] such as on transfer pricing. BEPS implementation and capacity building don't really speak to that key issue.

B. NORM SETTING

There is, however, one dimension of the inequality between developing and developing countries for which the BEPS Project has an uncomfortable, and in some perspectives, perhaps even an inverse, relationship: the gap between them with respect to the power to influence norm setting. This is a gap that many developed countries have little interest in narrowing. The long-running issue of whether the UN Tax Committee should become an intergovernmental body (rather than a body of experts acting in their own capacity) is a proxy for this bigger battle over the control room of international tax norm setting. In the run up to the Addis Ababa Financing for Development Conference in 2015, OECD country representatives expressed their main arguments against this upgrading of the Committee (which is widely expected to give more profile to the work of the Committee as a reflection of governmental views)—in the following ways:

1. There is no room for new or upgraded tax bodies (usually followed by the establishment of a new OECD body reaching out for developing country participation, such an expanded OECD Committee on Fiscal Affairs, or the Inclusive Framework that followed Addis);

2.   Newer OECD bodies such as the Global Forum on Information Exchange (or more lat-
     terly the Inclusive Framework) with their wide country participation fulfill the functions
     that an upgraded UN Tax Committee would have (neglecting the fact that those bodies
     where non-OECD country membership is actively sought are, when one looks at their
     mandates,[80] fundamentally not norm-deliberating or norm-creating bodies, but bodies
     mandated to implement received standards);
3.   Taxation issues should be addressed by experts, rather than government officials (perhaps
     something of an insult to government experts, and a little hard to reconcile with all the
     OECD tax norm deliberations or its implementation bodies being intergovernmental).

The G20 mandates to the OECD seem careful not to upset the current balance on norm
setting. For example, the OECD has requested the Global Forum "to monitor and review the
implementation of the OECD Standard on AEOI; and to help developing countries identify
their need for technical assistance and capacity building in order to participate in and benefit
from AEOI."[81]

C. REASONS FOR BEPS CONCESSIONS

As noted above, however, some concessions have been made to source country taxation (such as
on emphasising substance over form). The author's view is that there are at least three reasons.
The first is that some traditional capital exporters—among developing countries—see themselves as "importers" of new technologies in the more digitalized global economy. The flashpoint
is an increasingly "source country" orientation toward taxing the profits of companies that interface with one's residents, where they profit from that interaction through selling products to that
resident and/or monetizing the data provided by the resident, even without physical presence of
the profit maker in the country where the activity occurs.

The United Kingdom Diverted Profits Tax[82] (whereby a 25 percent tax is charged on profits
said to be artificially diverted from the United Kingdom) might be seen as an example of a traditional residence taxation country (the United Kingdom) exercising source-country taxing rights,
under what might be described as the pretense that the profits had been diverted from having a
UK source. In other words, the United Kingdom is effectively exercising source-country taxing
rights as if there was engagement in the UK economy through a permanent establishment while
not seeking to open the floodgates to the application of broader source-country identifications
and taxing rights in the digitalized economy by broadening the definition of what constitutes a
permanent establishment. Australia has also adopted a similar tax.[83]

A second explanation for the concessions may be the quest for ongoing OECD relevance—
the recognition that to maintain credibility going forward, the OECD tax effort had to include
the G20 countries which were not OECD members, especially China, India, and Brazil. As those
countries have mixed interests as capital-exporters and capital-importers, drawing them into
the process has given greater resonance to the OECD work globally, but has also introduced
elements of more aggressive source country assertions of norm-setting power. For example,
such assertion of source-country power can be seen in the assessments of how much value
is added in the developing world for transfer-pricing purposes, but also in the resistance to
alien concepts for those countries such as mandatory binding arbitration of tax disputes. That
resistance may not only have dented the hopes of business for that seismic change in global tax
relations but also may have emboldened some OECD countries to resist such arbitration. The

presence of China, Brazil, and India at the "high table" may in some ways make them more like traditional OECD countries, but may make some OECD countries more like them—a systemic risk for OECD cohesiveness.

A third major reason why concessions have been made, even to NGO calls such as for country-by-country reporting, is the very spotlight that NGOs and the media, including social media, have put on the tax abuses conducted by some MNEs. As adverted to by the Ecuadoran Foreign Minister early in 2017,[84] the increasing concerns by citizens about loss of revenue through tax avoidance and evasion is changing the dynamic and encouraging countries other than the usual suspects, to take higher profile positions on these matters. The role of NGOs and the investigative press in spurring this development was noted.

The above-mentioned BEPS concessions have occurred at a time when governments have the common interest of seeking additional revenue, and this commonality of the enterprise has encouraged a more ambitious program than would otherwise be possible. Governments are concerned about losing control of the tax debate, and personal taxpayers are losing their appetite for meeting their own tax obligations because of their perceptions about how poorly some MNEs meet their tax responsibilities.

IV. THE NEXT GREAT EDIFICE?

If the top table on development of global tax norms has been enlarged, it still remains a top table—perhaps more inclusive than in the past but also far more exclusive than it is inclusive. One concession in particular has not been made to developing countries: the creation of a truly inclusive and universal deliberating body on tax norms. The perceived risk to capital-exporting countries and their companies of such a broad-based body giving greater voice and power to capital-importing states has so far held sway. The opportunities that such a body offers have not yet been fully appreciated—the chance of widely accepted standards that carry a general sense of ownership and reinforce the importance of reasonable compromise, and are more likely to be consistently applied at practical level. Nor, in the author's view has the ultimate inevitability of such a body emerging been sufficiently recognized, with a consequent risk that when the body does emerge, it will unnecessarily carry the deep scars of a long drawn out resistance by many developed countries to the legitimate aspirations of other countries.

The current division in country positions, unfortunately along largely developed/developing country lines, calls for a greater appreciation of benefits to all stakeholders in tax systems, including MNEs, of a credible system that balances the investment climate needed for sustainable development with the necessity for revenues that can provide the schools, hospitals, and other infrastructure needed for development. Such a balance will be sufficiently respectful of taxpayer rights but also the meeting of their legal obligations to pay tax. Such an approach best respects the need for reasonable levels of certainty by taxpayers as to their tax responsibilities but also the need for some reasonable certainty that taxpayers will meet their legal obligations to pay taxes on profits from their engagement in an economy.

This approach will also help lift citizens out of poverty, degradation, and strife and will fulfill, at ground level, the promise that taxes are indeed the price we pay for a civilized society,[85] as well as the necessary cost of development and the attainment of human rights for the poorest and weakest.

Much more remains to be done if we wish to put developing country realities and priorities at the heart of the voyage, as opposed to merely inviting them onto the bus (and asking for the fare, as the Global Forum and Inclusive Framework require payment for participation also). They need to be actively involved in destination and route planning, choosing the appropriate vehicle, equipping and driving it. Only then will they feel they are more than tourists in a previously constructed BEPSland.

Many developed countries will resist such an outcome, as a perceived loss of global norm-setting influence on their part and as carrying risks of greater source country taxation of their MNEs. Moving to a more truly global tax cooperation system, embracing human rights obligations and other wider aspects of the UN system, will therefore require concerted interdisciplinary efforts, patience, and persistence. It will require an ability to focus all, including the resisters, on the unsustainability for all stakeholders in tax systems of any more narrowly "owned" system. Augmentation is required, in terms of country participation and also integration with more practical understandings of government obligations to their citizenry, to citizens of other countries, and to other nations.

Such developments would represent a great change for international tax norm setting, but a necessary one, and the healthy process of disruption currently underway, lends a unique opportunity for that process to begin.

NOTES

1. *Third International Conference on Financing for Development Statement on behalf of Mr. Zeid Ra'ad Al Hussein, United Nations High Commissioner for Human Rights, delivered by Mr. Idrissa Kane, Regional Representative, UNOHCHR-Eastern Africa Office*, Addis Ababa, 16 July 2015, available online at http://www.ohchr.org/EN/NewsEvents/Pages/DisplayNews.aspx?NewsID=16246 (last visited 31 Jan. 2019).
2. Ibid.
3. Ibid.
4. Such as the important distinction in tax and labor rights terms between "employees" and "independent contractors."
5. Such as in supporting environmental improvements for the benefits of the citizenry and ensuring, for example, that the tax system operates during the life of an oil, gas, or mining project to ensure environmental cleanup is funded after the project is no longer productive. Both are important aspects of current UN tax cooperation work.
6. The role of tax systems in directly promoting human rights compliance is an emerging issue, but an obvious area of connection is that international cooperation to support direct taxation (such as income taxes, and their payments by multinationals) reduces the need to rely on regressive indirect taxes.
7. See, for example, P. Saint-Amans, *Global Tax and Transparency: We Have the Tools, Now We Must Make Them Work* (2016), available online at http://www.oecd.org/tax/global-tax-transparency-we-have-the-tools.htm (last visited 31 Jan. 2019).
8. See, for example, T. Deen, *Ecuador Revives Campaign for UN Tax Body*, 27 Jan. 2017, available online at http://www.ipsnews.net/2017/01/ecuador-revives-campaign-for-un-tax-body/ (last visited 31 Jan. 2019).
9. See for example E. Anyangwe, 'Glee, Relief and Regret: Addis Ababa Outcome Receives Mixed Reception', *The Guardian*, 16 July 2015, available online at https://www.theguardian.com/global-development/2015/jul/16/outcome-document-addis-ababa-ffd3-financing-for-development (last visited 31 Jan. 2019); R. Greenhill, *From Addis to New York: What Does the FFD Summit Imply for the SDGs?*, 23 July 2015, available online at https://www.devex.com/news/from-addis-to-new-york-what-does-the-ffd-summit-imply-for-the-sdgs-86581 (last visited 31 Jan. 2019).

10. UN Inter-Agency Task Force Report on Financing for Development, *Financing for Development: Progress and Prospects, 2017* (2017), available online at https://developmentfinance. un.org/financing-development-progress-and-prospects-2017 (last visited 31 Jan. 2019).

11. Ibid. at 34.

12. UN Web TV, *Special Meeting on International Cooperation in Tax Matters—Economic and Social Council, 2017 Session,* 7 Apr. 2017, available online at http://webtv.un.org/meetings-events/watch/ 17th-meeting-special-meeting-on-international-cooperation-in-tax-matters-economic-and- social-council-2017-session/5390306774001 (last visited 31 Jan. 2019).

13. G77, *Statement on behalf of the Group of 77 and China by Carola Iñiguez, Undersecretary of International Organizations of Ecuador, at the ECOSOC Special Meeting on International Cooperation in Tax Matters,* 7 Apr. 2017, available online at http://www.g77.org/statement/ getstatement.php?id=170407b (last visited 31 Jan. 2019).

14. K. Clausing, *The Effect of Profit Shifting on the Corporate Tax Base in the United States and Beyond,* 17 June 2016, available online at https://papers.ssrn.com/sol3/papers.cfm?abstract_id=2685442, at 1 (last visited 31 Jan. 2019).

15. IMF, *Macroeconomic Policy Frameworks for Resource-Rich Developing Countries* (2012), available online at http://www.imf.org/external/np/pp/eng/2012/082412.pdf, at 14; D. Wilde, *Key Issues in Natural Resource Taxation and Revenue Management in the Commonwealth* (2016), at 25.

16. UNCTAD, *World Investment Report 2015: Reforming International Investment Governance* (2015), available online at http://unctad.org/en/pages/PublicationWebflyer.aspx?publicationid=1245, at 182 (last visited 31 Jan. 2019); Tax Justice Network, *Key Issues in Natural Resource Taxation and Revenue Management in the Commonwealth* (2016), available online at http://www.taxjustice.net/ 2015/03/18/new-report-ten-reasons-to-defend-the-corporate-income-tax/, at 5 (last visited 31 Jan. 2019).

17. OECD, *Action Plan on Base Erosion and Profit Shifting* (2013), available online at https://www. oecd.org/ctp/BEPSActionPlan.pdf [hereinafter BEPS Action Plan].

18. Ibid. at 11.

19. OECD, *Model Convention with Respect to Taxes on Income and on Capital* (2017), available online at http://www.oecd.org/ctp/treaties/model-tax-convention-on-income-and-on-capital-condensed- version-20745419.htm.

20. United Nations Department of Economic and Social Affairs, *United Nations Model Double Taxation Convention between Developed and Developing Countries* (2017), available online at https://www. un.org/esa/ffd/wp-content/uploads/2018/05/MDT_2017.pdf.

21. Such as the new Optional Article 12A on Taxation of Fees for Technical Services in the UN Model Double Taxation Convention between Developed and Developing Countries (see Economic and Social Council, Committee of Experts on International Cooperation in Tax Matters—Report on the Fourteenth Session, UN Doc. E/2017/45-E/C.18/2017/3, 2017), based on developing country practice. See also A. Báez Moreno, 'The Taxation of Technical Services under the United Nations Model Double Taxation Convention: A Rushed—Yet Appropriate—Proposal for (Developing) Countries?', 7(3) *World Tax Journal* (2015). See further, on the injection of Indian "source country" perspectives into the discussion, R. Nayak (Taxsutra), *Addressing the Tax Challenges of the Digital Economy: OECD's Action Plan on Base Erosion and Profit Shifting (BEPS),* 23 July 2013, avail- able online at http://www.ey.com/Publication/vwLUAssets/EY_Tax_Alert_-_BEPS_ActionPlan_ Digital_Economy_RN/$File/EY-BEPS-ActionPlan-Digital-Economy-RN.pdf.

22. See, for example, L. Cavelti, C. Jaag, and T. Rohner, *Why Corporate Taxation Means Source Taxation: A Response to the OECD's Actions Against Base Erosion and Profit Shifting* (2016), avail- able online at https://papers.ssrn.com/sol3/papers.cfm?abstract_id=2773614. See also M. Lennard, 'Act of Creation: the OECD/G20 test of "value creation" as a basis for taxing rights and its relevance to developing countries' (2018) 25(3) *Transnational Corporations* 55, available online at https:// unctad.org/en/PublicationChapters/diaeia2018d5a4_en.pdf

23. Most obviously in the transfer pricing outcomes, where the wording of the contract need not be followed if the actual business conduct and the attendant circumstances do not support its terms as reflecting economic realities.

24. This skepticism is seen in the "warier" approach to mandatory binding arbitration in the UN Model Tax Convention as compared to the OECD Model Tax Convention, as well as in the lack of developing country take-up of such arbitration under the Multilateral Convention to Implement Tax Treaty Related Measures to Prevent Base Erosion and Profit Shifting. See OECD, *Signatories and Parties to the Multilateral Convention to Implement Tax Treaty Related Measures to Prevent Base Erosion and Profit Shifting*, as regularly updated, available online at http://www.oecd.org/tax/treaties/beps-mli-signatories-and-parties.pdf. See also, for some of the basis of the developing country skepticism: M. Lennard, 'Transfer Pricing Arbitration as an Option for Developing Countries' (2014) 42(3) *Intertax* 179.

25. OECD, *Multilateral Convention to Implement Tax Treaty Related Measures to Prevent Base Erosion and Profit Shifting*, 24 Nov. 2016, available online at http://www.oecd.org/tax/treaties/multilateral-convention-to-implement-tax-treaty-related-measures-to-prevent-BEPS.pdf (last visited 31 Jan. 2019).

26. OECD, *OECD Launches Business Survey on Tax Certainty to Support G20 Tax Agenda*, 18 Oct. 2016, available online at http://www.oecd.org/ctp/tax-policy/oecd-launches-business-survey-on-tax-certainty-to-support-g20-tax-agenda.htm (last visited 31 Jan. 2019). An OECD/IMF report followed in 2017: *IMF/OECD Report for the G20 Finance Ministers*, 18 Mar. 2017, available at: https://www.oecd.org/tax/tax-policy/tax-certainty-report-oecd-imf-report-g20-finance-ministers-march-2017.pdf.

27. Forum on Tax Administration MAP Forum, *BEPS Action 14—Making Dispute Resolution Mechanisms More Effective: Questionnaire for Taxpayers*, available online at https://www.oecd.org/tax/beps/beps-action-14-peer-review-taxpayer-questionnaire.docx (last visited 31 Jan. 2019).

28. See, for example, OECD, *Inclusive Framework on BEPS: A Global Answer to a Global Issue*, Mar. 2017, available online at http://www.oecd.org/tax/beps/beps-about.htm, at 1 (last visited 31 Jan. 2019).

29. See, for example, Family Guardian, *Equal Footing*, available online at http://famguardian.org/publications/propertyrights/eqlfoot.html (last visited 11 Apr. 2017); J. Huston, *The Northwest Ordinance of 1787* (1987); W. Ellis, *The Ordinance of 1787: The Nation Begins* (1987).

30. See, for example, OECD, *Background Brief: Inclusive Framework on BEPS*, Jan. 2017, available online at https://www.oecd.org/ctp/background-brief-inclusive-framework-for-beps-implementation.pdf, where the closest thing to a definition is at footnote 2: "The new countries and jurisdictions to the Inclusive Framework participate in the CFA as 'BEPS Associates.' Also the G20 countries that are non-OECD members have participated as BEPS Associates in the CFA since the establishment of the BEPS Project, whereas OECD members were automatically Member of the BEPS Project. As all countries and jurisdictions participating in the Inclusive Framework collaborate on an equal footing, this text will refer—for the matter of clarity—to all participating countries and jurisdictions as Members of the Inclusive Framework on BEPS."

31. T. M. Ryding, 'On Debt and Taxation, Rich and Poor Countries Are Worlds Apart', *The Guardian*, 26 July 2016, available online at https://www.theguardian.com/global-development/2016/jul/26/debt-taxation-rich-poor-countries-worlds-apart-un-trade-conference-kenya (last visited 31 Jan. 2019).

32. J. Reid, *The Concept of Representation in the Age of the American Revolution* (1989).

33. Ibid. at 50.

34. See *supra* note 21. The provision will be part of the 2017 UN Model Tax Convention, to be released in October 2017.

35. OECD, *Multilateral Convention to Implement Tax Treaty Related Measures to Prevent Base Erosion and Profit Shifting*, *supra* note 25.

36. See, for example, D. Ring, 'Developing Countries in an Age of Transparency and Disclosure', 2016(6) *Brigham Young University Law Review* (2017), 1767, at 1810.

37. BDO United Kingdom, *Multilateral Instrument to Implement BEPS Actions and the UK Treasury's Response*, 16 Jan. 2017, available online at https://www.bdo.co.uk/en-gb/insights/business-edge/business-edge-2017/multilateral-instrument-to-implement-beps-actions (last visited 31 Jan. 2019).

38. OECD, *Multilateral Convention to Implement Tax Treaty Related Measures to Prevent Base Erosion and Profit Shifting, supra* note 25, Article 32(2). Article 31 deals with the requirements for this; one-third of the members must support convening such a Conference of the Parties.

39. Ibid. at Article 32(1).

40. OECD, *Explanatory Statement to the Multilateral Convention to Implement Tax Treaty Related Measures to Prevent Base Erosion and Profit Shifting,* available online at https://www.oecd.org/tax/treaties/explanatory-statement-multilateral-convention-to-implement-tax-treaty-related-measures-to-prevent-BEPS.pdf.

41. Vienna Convention on the Law of Treaties 1969, 1155 UNTS 331.

42. See, for example, *United Nations Model Double Taxation Convention between Developed and Developing Countries, supra* note 20, at para. 30 of the Commentary on Article 1.

43. See, for example, OECD, *Multilateral Convention to Implement Tax Treaty Related Measures to Prevent Base Erosion and Profit Shifting, supra* note 25, at para. 79 of the Commentary on Article 24.

44. *Supra* note 40 at para. 11.

45. WTO, *European Communities—Customs Classification of Frozen Boneless Chicken Cuts—Complaint by Brazil—Report of the Panel,* 30 May 2005, WT/DS/269/R, at note 574 (internal citations omitted).

46. OECD Explanatory Statement, *supra* note 44, at para. 317.

47. OECD, *Multilateral Convention to Implement Tax Treaty Related Measures to Prevent Base Erosion and Profit Shifting, supra* note 25. The OECD updated list of signatories and parties to the MLI is available online at http://www.oecd.org/tax/treaties/beps-mli-signatories-and-parties.pdf

48. UN Committee of Experts on International Cooperation in Tax Matters, Secretariat Paper on Alternative Dispute Resolution in Taxation, UN Doc. E/C.18/2015/CRP.8, 8 Oct. 2015. See also M. Lennard, 'Transfer Pricing Arbitration as an Option for Developing Countries', 42(3) *Intertax* (2014), 179.

49. See, for example, WTO, *Developing Countries in WTO Dispute Settlement,* available online at https://www.wto.org/english/tratop_e/dispu_e/disp_settlement_cbt_e/c11s1p1_e.htm (last visited 31 Jan. 2019).

50. Article 25(2) of the UN Model Tax Convention, following the wording of the OECD Model Tax Convention provides that (emphasis added): "The competent authority shall endeavour, *if the objection appears to it to be justified* and if it is not itself able to arrive at a satisfactory solution, to resolve the case by mutual agreement with the competent authority of the other Contracting State, with a view to the avoidance of taxation which is not in accordance with this Convention."

51. OECD, *BEPS Action 14: Make Dispute Resolution Mechanisms More Effective* (Public Discussion Draft, 18 Dec. 2014), available online at https://www.oecd.org/ctp/dispute/discussion-draft-action-14-make-dispute-resolution-mechanisms-more-effective.pdf.

52. Committee of Experts on International Cooperation in Tax Matters, *supra* note 48, at para. 157.

53. See, for example, IRS, *Mandatory Tax Treaty Arbitration,* available online at https://www.irs.gov/businesses/international-businesses/mandatory-tax-treaty-arbitration (last visited 31 Jan. 2019); ICDR, *ICDR Selected by IRS to Arbitrate International Tax Cases,* 4 Nov. 2010.

54. OECD, *supra* note 30, at 7.

55. Ibid. at 14.

56. OECD Global Forum on Transparency and Exchange of Information for Tax Purposes, *Global Forum Secretariat's Organisational Structure,* available online at http://www.oecd.org/tax/transparency/about-the-global-forum/global-forum-secretariat.pdf.

57. OECD Global Forum on Transparency and Exchange of Information for Tax Purposes, *About the Global Forum,* available online at http://www.oecd.org/tax/transparency/about-the-global-forum/ (last visited 31 Jan. 2019).

58. As the OECD Staff Rules (which apply to the Global Forum staff), for example, state at Regulation 2: "a) . . . Officials are subject to the authority of the Secretary General, to whom they are responsible for the discharge of their duties; b) Officials shall carry out their duties and regulate their conduct always bearing in mind the interests of the Organisation and the international character of their

duties." OECD, *Staff Regulations, Rules and Instructions Applicable to Officials of the Organisation*, Jan. 2019, available online at https://www.oecd.org/careers/Staff_Rules_en.pdf.

59. See, for example, UN Jobs, *Tax Policy Analysts—Transparency and Exchange of Information for Tax Purposes, Paris*, available online at https://unjobs.org/vacancies/1414004111317 (last visited 31 Jan. 2019).

60. € 15,000 per country plus a further GNP-based amount. See OECD, *Summary of Outcomes of the Meeting of the Global Forum on Transparency and Exchange of Information for Tax Purposes Held in Mexico on 1–2 September 2009*, available online at http://www.oecd.org/ctp/exchange-of-tax-information/43610626.pdf.

61. OECD, *supra* note 30, at 20.

62. See, for example, presentation of P. Saint-Amans, Director of the OECD Centre for Tax Policy and Administration in S. L. Goundar, 'U.K. was "Difficult Friend" to BEPS Process, OECD Official Says', 82 *Tax Notes International*, 20 June 2016, 1158, at 1159.

63. OECD, *supra* note 30, at 13, para. 3.1.

64. OECD, *BEPS Actions 8–10: Revised Guidance on Profit Splits* (Public Discussion Draft, 4 July–5 Sept. 2016), available online at https://www.oecd.org/tax/transfer-pricing/BEPS-discussion-draft-on-the-revised-guidance-on-profit-splits.pdf, at 1.

65. Ibid. at 1.

66. M. Herzfeld, 'The Year in Review: Whither the International Tax System?', 85 *Tax Notes International*, 2 Jan. 2017, 22.

67. OECD, *supra* note 30, at 11.

68. Ibid. at 11–12.

69. A. Lewis, 'G-20 to Have Larger Role in Tax Policy', 84 *Tax Notes International*, 3 Oct. 2016, 41, at 42.

70. OECD, *OECD Launches Business Survey on Tax Certainty to Support G20 Tax Agenda*, 18 Oct. 2016, available online at http://www.oecd.org/ctp/tax-policy/oecd-launches-business-survey-on-tax-certainty-to-support-g20-tax-agenda.htm (last visited 31 Jan. 2019).

71. IMF and OECD, *Tax Certainty: Report for the G20 Finance Ministers*, Mar. 2017, available online at http://www.oecd.org/tax/tax-policy/tax-certainty-report-oecd-imf-report-g20-finance-ministers-march-2017.pdf. The 2018 update is available online at http://www.oecd.org/ctp/tax-policy/tax-certainty-update-oecd-imf-report-g20-finance-ministers-july-2018.pdf.

72. Ibid. at 5.

73. Ibid. at 6.

74. Ibid. at 7.

75. Ibid. at 8.

76. See, e.g., M. Herzfeld, 'Will the OECD's 'Pragmatic Fudge' Save Transfer Pricing?', 83 *Tax Notes International*, 1 Aug. 2016, 360.

77. Tax Justice Network, *Beware the Siren Song of "Tax Certainty"*, 4 Oct. 2016, available online at http://www.taxjustice.net/2016/10/04/dont-fall-siren-song-tax-certainty/ (last visited 31 Jan. 2019).

78. As to European developments, see for example, R. McWilliams, 'Multinationals: Ready Your Public CbC Explanations', 85 *Tax Notes International*, 9 Jan. 2017, 132.

79. See, for example, PricewaterhouseCoopers, *"Anti-abuse" Themes in the OECD's Final BEPS Reports*, 4 Oct. 2016, https://www.pwc.com/gx/en/tax/newsletters/tax-controversy-dispute-resolution/assets/pwc-TCDR-OECD-BEPS-anti-abuse-themes.pdf.

80. As to the Global Forum, see OECD Global Forum on Transparency and Exchange of Information for Tax Purposes, *supra* note 57. As to the Inclusive Framework, see OECD, *About the Inclusive Framework on BEPS*, available online at http://www.oecd.org/tax/beps/beps-about.htm (last visited 31 Jan. 2019).

81. OECD Global Forum on Transparency and Exchange of Information for Tax Purposes, *supra* note 56.

82. J. Silbering-Meyer and R. Sledz, *HMRC Issues New Guidance on UK's Diverted Profits Tax*, 6 Apr. 2016, http://taxexecutive.org/hmrc-issues-new-guidance-on-uks-diverted-profits-tax/ (last visited 31 Jan. 2019); BBC News, *Diageo Told to Pay £107m in Extra Tax in Profits Row*, 10 May 2017, available online at, http://www.bbc.com/news/business-39871218 (last visited 31 Jan. 2019).

83. Australian Taxation Office, *Diverted Profits Tax*, 2017, available online at https://www.ato.gov.au/
General/New-legislation/In-detail/Direct-taxes/Income-tax-for-businesses/Diverted-profits-tax/
(last visited 31 Jan. 2019).

84. T. Sprackland, 'Minister Stresses Preference for Multilateralism', 85 *Tax Notes International*, 23 Jan.
2017, 333.

85. *Compania General De Tabacos De Filipinas v. Collector of Internal Revenue*, 275 U.S. 87, 100 (1927)
(Wendell Holmes Jr., J, dissenting).

THE RESPONSIBILITIES OF GOVERNMENTS

The Case of Transparency

CHAPTER 10

TRANSPARENCY, TAX, AND HUMAN RIGHTS

MIRANDA STEWART

"What in fact was the Rousseauist dream that motivated many of the revolutionaries? It was the dream of a transparent society, visible and legible in each of its parts, the dream of there no longer existing any zones of darkness, zones established by the privileges of royal power or the prerogatives of some corporation . . ."[1]

"[T]he more strictly we are watched, the better we behave."[2]

I. INTRODUCTION

Transparency has attracted unprecedented attention in national and global debates about taxation in recent years. It has been adopted as a slogan and a goal by international organizations, governments, nongovernmental organizations (NGOs), academic commentators, media, and citizens across the political spectrum. There has been a particular focus on transparency as a mechanism to enforce taxation of large multinational enterprises (MNEs) and to ensure tax compliance by high-wealth individuals, with a specific goal of addressing tax avoidance and evasion especially through the hiding by such taxpayers of income and assets in tax havens.

The pursuit of transparency in taxation is consistent with broader trends, indicated by the observation of John Braithwaite and Peter Drahos nearly two decades ago that transparency was "the most striking emergent principle" in regulatory approaches to globalization,[3] and by recent observations that transparency is a "buzzword" to solve global governance[4] and a "strong international norm."[5] In addition to the promotion of transparency as a key strategy for global tax enforcement, transparency has also been aimed variously at ending corruption and abuse of power by private and public agents or entities; disciplining the fiscal actions and processes of governments by constraining spending or reducing taxes; strengthening financial and other markets; building participatory democracy; protecting human rights; supporting economic

Tax, Inequality, and Human Rights. Philip Alston and Nikki Reisch.
© Oxford University Press 2019. Published 2019 by Oxford University Press.

development and good governance in general; and ensuring compliance with environmental and other global policies.

This chapter explores tax transparency in the context of some of the previous governmental, private, and civil society initiatives about transparency of the last thirty years. The goal is to better understand what meanings are assumed in, or ascribed to, the concept of transparency in taxation in contemporary debates and in particular, to understand how transparency may connect to a human rights agenda in taxation. The chapter also explores potential contradictions and limits of tax transparency in a human rights context. Finally, this chapter considers what transparency in taxation can and should achieve in the current era.

II. MEANINGS AND USES OF "TRANSPARENCY"

In general, calls for "transparency" seek the communication or accessibility of data, decision-making, and outcomes by an actor, institution, or agency, about a particular activity or process, for surveillance, scrutiny, testing and evaluation by others. However, *who* is transparent, concerning *what* data, process, or outcomes, for what *purpose* transparency is advocated, *how* transparency is achieved, and how it is *intended to achieve* the stated purpose, differ depending on the context. The basic definition of "transparency" refers to transparency of information, but the discourse of transparency also implies a holding to account of the powerful. It is assumed that knowledge is power and so calls for transparency more or less explicitly have implications for the circulation, concentration, and legitimacy of power in society. On the other hand, transparency may be needed to ensure compliance with a regulatory regime, such as tax law. This is the disciplinary or policing mode of transparency about those being regulated by a powerful institution or regulator. This mode is particularly pertinent in today's era of surveillance and big data analytics.[6]

The recent discourse about tax transparency concerns the transparency of corporations or citizens as taxpayers to governments (and, possibly, to the public by some form of media or broad disclosure), rather than of governments to the people.[7] As explained by Winnie Byanyima (in the foreword to this volume), the call for transparency of taxpayers about their income, profits, and assets responds to a widespread perception that wealthy companies and individuals are sidestepping their duties to pay tax, and in this way, themselves contributing to the abuse of human rights, such that the social contract on which both tax and human rights are based, is undermined. This approach to tax transparency, which could be called a human rights approach, views effective taxation to fund government as necessary for the delivery of human rights and tax transparency as instrumental in achieving that goal.

The increased weight of transparency in contemporary discourse does not concern only the political realm. Transparency is also an ideal in the context of economic transactions in the market.[8] Many, perhaps most, modern regulatory regimes concerning transparency have as their main goal removing information asymmetries in markets so as to ensure better, faster, and more accurate flows of information between private actors, including businesses, to their managers, shareholders, investors, lenders, consumers, and employees.[9] Transparency is seen as key to improved corporate governance, as well as political governance; indeed, it is suggested that "transparency is becoming the most important business rule."[10] The call for increased transparency to support the market has overlapped with calls for transparency in taxation. The resonance of transparency with both economic and human rights discourses may seem a fortunate alignment; however, it should also lead us to be cautious about the meanings and uses of transparency, and whether we prefer to support a human-centered, social, or nonmarket meaning of the concept.

III. TRANSPARENCY OF GOVERNMENTS

In contrast to the current meaning of tax transparency—of *companies and individuals to governments*—the primary meaning of transparency since the 1980s focused on the transparency of *governments to the people*. Transparency has been seen as essential to better governance and government.[11] The Encyclopedia of American Politics defines transparency as "government's obligation to share information with citizens . . . at the heart of how citizens hold their public officials accountable."[12] Dominique Bessire observes that the Russian word "Glasnost," popularized during the 1980s by Mikhail Gorbachev, means "transparency"; and in adopting this slogan as descriptive of his political and economic reforms, Gorbachev "was in tune with a phenomenon" of society at that time.[13] The goal of transparency was adopted by the Organisation for Economic Co-operation and Development (OECD), which defined "transparency" as "meaning that reliable, relevant and timely information about the activities of government is available to the public."[14] A narrower definition, also focused on governmental transparency, is "the release of information that is relevant for evaluating institutions."[15]

During the 1990s, most international activism and policy development on transparency was aimed at holding governments to account either to the public directly; to the public's elected representatives; to independent institutions such as national audit agencies; or to external institutions, investors or lenders.[16] It has been suggested that this kind of transparency of governments to the people could even amount to a human right, or at least, is instrumental in ensuring human rights are delivered by holding governments to account.[17]

A. FISCAL TRANSPARENCY

In 1996, the International Monetary Fund (IMF) called for more fiscal transparency of governments to creditors and especially to the IMF itself as a lender of last resort.[18] This quickly extended to the surveillance and imposition of conditions by the IMF on budgeting, taxing, and spending activities of borrower governments. Similar pressure for transparency, albeit not as extreme, was felt in developed countries, as the OECD called for increased transparency of member state government budgets to enforce fiscal discipline, for example, by credit rating agencies.[19]

A series of economic crises in the 1990s pushed the focus toward government fiscal transparency. In particular, the Asian financial crisis of 1997 led to increased scrutiny of both government policy in the affected Southeast Asian countries and the speculators and currency traders whose actions caused a disastrous outflow of financial investment from those countries. The first IMF Code of Good Practices on Fiscal Transparency was approved in April 1998, and several revisions of the Code have been published since then.[20] The IMF Code is a widely dispersed "soft law" standard for fiscal transparency. For countries that sought to borrow from the IMF, implementation of the Code was examined through a surveillance process in a detailed fiscal Review of Observance of Standards and Codes.[21] At the same time as the IMF developed these processes, the World Bank was developing highly detailed poverty reduction accountability mechanisms and public financial management processes for developing country clients.[22]

At first glance, fiscal transparency seems undoubtedly good, but it also has costs and unintended consequences. Lisa Philipps and I have argued that, while fiscal transparency "is generally discussed as a neutral procedural norm that will produce better or more predictable fiscal policy . . . transparency standards have more normative content than their usual treatment suggests and may serve different constituencies and substantive policy ends depending on the types of disclosure and processes they require."[23] The focus of the IMF and OECD was to promote fiscal discipline of governments and improve credibility with investors, lenders, and donors. The high levels of conditionality and the political and economic constraints on developing country governments in these processes have been widely studied.[24] The IMF continually expressed concern about "excessive public indebtedness" of governments (suggested as producing negative consequences for growth as well as "upwards pressure . . . on global real interest rates").[25] The IMF was explicit about the purpose of transparency being accountability *to the market* of governments:

> Timely publication of a clearly presented budget document makes it easier for the market to evaluate the government's intentions and allows the market itself to impose a constructive discipline on the government. Transparency increases the political risk of unsustainable policies, whereas the lack thereof means that fiscal profligacy can go undetected longer than it otherwise would.[26]

The OECD Best Practices for Budget Transparency sought to promote soft norms of fiscal transparency and, later, independent fiscal institutions which became widely adopted in OECD member states and throughout the European Union.[27] These "soft law" and institutional approaches were a move away from "hard" fiscal rules or deficit constraints,[28] but were aimed at the same goal of fiscal discipline. Initially, this was a response to concerns about the longer-term fiscal sustainability of governments:

> Though many OECD countries reduced their large deficits during the 1990s, budget balances are clearly at risk in the current financial crisis as well as because of the longer term spending pressures associated with demographic aging, such as health care and pension. The OECD has predicted that the fiscal consequences of aging populations will be "severe" in virtually all its member countries. From its perspective, the main purpose of transparency measures is to encourage spending restraint by revealing "the true cost of government activities."[29]

In the aftermath of the Global Financial Crisis (GFC), fiscal discipline and even austerity was intended to severely contain spending so as to repair fiscal deficits. Yet it is not clear that transparency can produce the positive effects on fiscal sustainability and good government that it is supposed to deliver. Widely disseminated and much-lauded transparent budget processes, such as the Medium-Term Expenditure Framework have made little noticeable difference to the accountability of government budgeting (if current deficits are any indication),[30] while better budget estimates and more effective revenue forecasting has proven difficult to achieve even for a rich country government such as Australia. For example, Australian forecasting formulas have consistently underpredicted tax revenues during boom times and overpredicted them during the current economic slowdown.[31]

Transparency of government budgets also may have only limited influence in producing tax reform to enhance efficiency or increase revenues. For example, developing countries established numerous tax incentives for foreign direct investment in the last few decades and these continue to be widespread in many countries.[32] Many have criticized developing countries' use of such "tax expenditures," pointing to negative effects on corporate tax revenue and on the efficiency and fairness of tax systems.[33] Transparent reporting of these incentives would render them more visible to the public and less susceptible, potentially, to corruption. However, such reporting has not generally led to elimination of tax incentives. This is likely because governments are subject to political and market pressures to compete for foreign direct investment in the global economy, so tax incentives remain widely used.[34]

Constraint of public expenditure and keeping taxes down in rich countries (while, somehow, efficiently raising taxes in poor countries) was the primary focus of fiscal transparency norms of the 1990s and early 2000s. The fear of future "unsustainable" costs of government has become stronger and more embedded since fiscal transparency became accepted as a norm. Neil Buchanan has warned that "generational" accounting in the United States tends to raise false fears that social programs are unaffordable over the long term or will be excessively burdensome to future generations.[35] Requiring such a report directs treasury officials to gather and analyze particular data focused on the longer term which in itself, may overemphasize the values of fiscal prudence and discipline. For example, the Australian Intergenerational Report of 2015 (required by the Australian Charter of Budget Honesty) predicts an ever-upward trending fiscal deficit because of assumptions about the fiscal cost of the old-age pension.[36] This has led to policy proposals to cap age pensions: if this was done, long-term fiscal balance would be achieved at the expense of the elderly with low income and assets, who would be rendered poorer and poorer relative to wage earners.[37]

Another development in fiscal transparency under consideration in the European Union, New Zealand, and Australia, is the so-called "social investment approach" to the welfare state.[38] The Australian government has just "costed" welfare spending for the whole population and come up with the terrifyingly large number of A\$4.8 trillion.[39] However, it is very unclear what this number means for the well-being of either the current population including welfare recipients and taxpayers, or the future population. These examples indicate how transparency norms are harnessed in the service of austerity, rather than a neutral goal of informing the public about fiscal decision-making, or to support *raising* taxes to fund public goods and services. Long-term budgeting seems like a good idea, but it may be misleading and it obscures the distributional impacts of budgets on the *current* population both within and between nations.

A positive effect of these developments was the increased transparency of the international financial organizations themselves. Scrutiny of the economic policies and conditions proposed by the IMF and the World Bank increased and many of their reports and documentation were made available for the first time. In the space of a couple of years from 1997 to 1999, the IMF went from a closed organization to publishing most of its country surveillance reports on the world wide web where anybody could download and read them. This required consent of governments, which was sometimes withheld, but it seems in most cases publication occurred and remains the norm today. This was part of a larger turn toward transparency as an element of good global governance and a means by which international organizations sought greater legitimacy for their own regimes.[40]

B. TRANSPARENCY AND ANTICORRUPTION ACTIVISM

The budget transparency measures of the 1990s developed alongside an important transparency movement aimed at corruption, money laundering, and similar practices involving both business and governments. The German-based NGO, Transparency International, was established in 1993 with the aim of exposing corruption that was not criminalized in many countries.[41] In this context, transparency was seen as potentially useful in the growing fight against corruption and money laundering.[42] The transparency focus on anticorruption also turned attention toward corporate governance and transparency of businesses.

In the last fifteen years, especially since 9/11, there has been significantly increased attention paid to tracing financial transactions, money laundering, and the illegal financing of global terrorism. The work around corruption involving private actors and governments led to a greater focus in on the financial and tax affairs of individuals and legal entities such as companies and trusts. This revealed the relationship between criminal or terrorist elements and "legal" aspects of the international financial system, which often took place in offshore financial centers or tax havens. Not surprisingly, it was found that those engaged in money laundering or dealings to finance illegal activities were also involved in tax evasion. Jason Sharman traced the origins of the tax transparency movement in the anticorruption and financial crime processes in *Havens in a Storm*.[43]

Civil society organizations also built on the work of the IMF and the OECD concerning fiscal transparency, with the aim of opening budgets to public scrutiny so as to support democratic processes and improve citizen participation in budgeting.[44] For example, the Centre on Budget and Policy Priorities (Washington, D.C.) and its International Budget Partnership (IBP) launched an Open Budget Initiative (OBI) in 2006 establishing an index with the goal of scrutinizing fiscal transparency practices and establishing minimum benchmarks in countries around the world.[45] The OBI continues today, now with 115 countries evaluated in the 2017 budget transparency index.[46]

A key goal of these NGOs was to support inclusive economic development, through better budgeting and reduced corruption. One author engaged in setting up the IBP explained:

> [I]n the context of widespread poverty in the developing world, citizens and civil society organizations are increasingly focusing on the budget and its effects on the distribution of resources, leading them to demand more and better budget information.[47]

The NGOs—and, latterly, the international financial institutions—were keen from the beginning to demonstrate common interest and consensus across both market and democracy or justice actors:

> [T]he idea of promoting open budgets is one that can gather support from a wide range of actors, leading to a coalition not available on other issues. Business interests often favor open budgets because they provide a better understood context in which to invest. International organizations support them because they feel open budgets are essential to good governance. Civil society organizations favor open budgets reflecting their general support of more open and democratic societies. Governments find them hard to oppose.[48]

An important collaboration between governments, business and civil society was the Extractive Industries Transparency Initiative (EITI),[49] launched in 2002 to achieve transparency of resource payments and revenues. This followed a prior civil society initiative, *Publish What You Pay*.[50] Today, forty-eight member states have joined the EITI and are undergoing the commitment and implementation process, while thirty-one states are allegedly compliant.[51] Recent empirical evidence suggests that use of the EITI may have helped to prevent or minimize corruption in resource revenue collection and management.[52]

The OECD, with the peak aid body, the Development Assistance Committee, the World Bank, and key donor states, meanwhile increased scrutiny of aid in its Public Expenditure and Financial Accountability program that assesses public financial management of recipient countries.[53] These processes were intended to ensure that recipients and donors, as well as those actually delivering aid on the ground, were more transparent and therefore accountable to all stakeholders, so as to ensure poverty relief and development goals were achieved.[54]

To summarise all of these transparency developments in the context of human rights: Government, and institutional, transparency accountability is seen as one tool to ensure accountability in the delivery of public goods and services, which are necessary to ensure social, economic, and civil rights are achieved.[55] However, the new transparency frameworks also had costs. They generated highly detailed surveillance of developing country budgets and substantial pressure to report on processes. There was sometimes a tension between external accountability of governments with respect to aid and debt and internal accountability to their own citizens.[56]

In spite of the significant consensus and cross-fertilization about the value and uses of fiscal transparency across all stakeholder groups, the dominant purpose of "transparency" in the 1990s and 2000s was focused on fiscal austerity, expenditure constraint, and market discipline of governments. Other approaches to fiscal data and measurement that might have made governments and markets more transparent in their effects—by placing emphasis on distributional aspects of the budget, changing the definition of Gross Domestic Product (GDP), and/or rendering visible the household, informal, and "care" economy in a feminist approach of gender budgeting—gained far less traction in the discourse of transparency at this time.

IV. TRANSPARENCY OF TAXPAYERS

Let us now turn now to consider transparency of taxpayers' tax and financial information. This requires us to investigate three aspects: first, the transparency of tax information from the taxpayer to his or her own government; second, whether tax transparency should extend *beyond* the boundaries of the taxpayer's own government to include sharing of taxpayer information with *other* governments in jurisdictions in which a taxpayer may have carried out activity or have income; and third, whether public transparency of a taxpayer's information, profits, or tax paid is warranted.

The idea that transparency of taxpayers to their own government will increase compliance has deep roots, as indicated by the quote from Jeremy Bentham at the beginning of this chapter. Bentham proposed constant surveillance of prisoner populations as a more efficient (and more humane) approach to prison management, in his famous Panopticon. Today, financial transparency of individuals and companies has been defined as a "dominant principle," and the prevailing view is that "where secrecy lies, roguery is not far behind."[57] A key element of the definition of a "tax haven" promulgated by the OECD was that a tax haven was a "secrecy" jurisdiction.[58] Tax haven jurisdictions until very recently held onto their status as secrecy jurisdictions with significant financial expertise, but this status has been overturned through the OECD Global Forum process for implementation of tax transparency.

A. TRANSPARENCY OF TAXPAYERS TO THEIR
OWN GOVERNMENT

Governments that raise substantial taxes, which have been called successful "tax states," have long had strong information gathering and investigative powers under which their revenue agencies can demand information from taxpayers.[59] This coercive power to gather information in order to collect taxes seems always to be constrained in successful tax states by a set of rules that can be called the "fiscal constitution," which ensures that taxes, and information-gathering powers, are legitimate.[60] The need for information about taxpayers has increased commensurately with the dramatic increase in numbers of taxpayers, types of tax, and levels of taxation. At the same time, technological and bureaucratic capacity to administer complex tax systems has increased. To enforce taxation of individuals, information is also required from legal entities, or intermediaries, as governments have only succeeded in collecting substantial taxes through harnessing capabilities of corporate actors, withholding agents, banks and other governments to support the bureaucratic processes of taxation. Governmental systems for accessing and managing taxpayer information and collecting tax developed hand in hand with corporate enterprise in the last century.[61] At the same time, individuals have themselves harnessed legal entities such as companies and trusts for private benefit, to disguise their income and assets and reduce their tax.

The argument for transparency of taxpayer information to governments has encountered an opposite discourse of the right of taxpayers to the protection of confidentiality of their information, which may also be grounded in a human right to privacy. The ability of governments to obtain information from taxpayers (and people they deal with) has required the implicit or explicit consent of those taxpayers and this has led to strict confidentiality requirements and limits on the ability of governments to use taxpayer information.[62] It has taken an extraordinary combination of events, triggered only a decade ago by the GFC and the G20 and OECD response to it, to overcome these deep-rooted legal and normative assumptions about taxpayer confidentiality.[63]

B. TRANSPARENCY OF TAX INFORMATION
BETWEEN GOVERNMENTS

Serious action to increase transparency in sharing taxpayer information *between* governments is very recent. The political leadership of the G20 and OECD, combined with new technological platforms and transnational bureaucratic and legal networks of trust and cooperation between tax agencies, has made the sharing of taxpayer information between governments feasible. It is, increasingly, a normal part of bureaucratic tax enforcement to enable governments to collect their own national taxes primarily from their own resident taxpayers, who may hold income or assets offshore.

The G20 Leaders Communiqué of 2009 set out to achieve financial stabilization in the context of the GFC which it called "the greatest challenge to the world economy in modern times."[64] The G20 countries expressed concern about the sustainability of public finances and the risks posed by offshore tax avoidance and committed to take action against tax havens so as to prevent individuals and corporations hiding assets and income offshore. From 2012, the G20 authorized the OECD to proceed with its Base Erosion and Profit Shifting (BEPS) Project, asserting that "the era of bank secrecy is over."[65]

These developments had their origins in the OECD Harmful Tax Competition project of the 1990s, which aimed to shut down or control tax havens.[66] The Harmful Tax Competition project failed to establish basic norms and processes of tax information sharing. National tax administrations were slow, secretive, and reluctant to cooperate with each other and Switzerland and Luxembourg refused to cooperate.[67] More generally, governments were outflanked in the global economy by the agility, flexibility, and "monocentric complexity" of MNEs.[68]

A decade later the G20-OECD action against tax havens gained momentum following several scandals about tax evasion around the world.[69] In February 2008, the German tax authorities launched a highly public investigation into a former chief executive of Deutsch Post, who was alleged to have evaded more than €1 million in German taxes through hiding funds in Liechtenstein accounts.[70] The German authorities used a stolen CD-ROM sold to them by a former employee of a Liechtenstein investment company, which also contained information about investors from the United States, Britain, Sweden, France, Australia, Canada, and other countries.[71] The revenue agencies of many of those countries acquired the information for their own tax enforcement.[72] The US Federal Bureau of Investigation made a formal request to Switzerland for information regarding a tax-evasion case, prompted by inside information from whistle-blower and former UBS private banker Bradley Birkenfeld.[73] The information concerned secret Swiss bank accounts being sold to US taxpayers to evade taxes. A year later, the US Internal Revenue Service forced Swiss investment bank UBS to hand over the names of 4,450 American clients who had allegedly hidden more than US$18 billion in offshore accounts.[74] The Australian Taxation Office established Project Wickenby in 2006, a cross-agency investigation aimed at countering tax evasion.[75] Actor Paul Hogan, of *Crocodile Dundee* fame, was caught in the net and details of his offshore accounts were made public through court proceedings.[76]

Around this time, the public and development community also began to take notice of tax evasion in developing countries. In 2008, think tank Global Financial Integrity issued a report that estimated illicit financial flows from developing countries at as much as US$1 trillion, including billions from India to Swiss bank accounts.[77] Tax haven secrecy was further undermined by essentially uncontrolled leaks by the International Consortium of Investigative Journalists (ICIL). This new wave of publicity has been driven partly by a new technological capacity to obtain, store, analyze, and publish "big data." The disclosure of lists of names on a CD-ROM in the Liechtenstein leaks, which seemed so shocking in 2011, has since been swamped by LuxLeaks and again by the Panama Papers.[78]

Since 2012, the new wave of government-to-government tax transparency is based on automatic digital sharing of data. While this cooperation is still subject to numerous caveats and limitations, these processes have rapidly expanded. In 2013, the G20 and G8 endorsed automatic exchange as the new global standard.[79] At the Brisbane Summit, G20 leaders confirmed their commitment to implement the automatic exchange of information on individual financial bank accounts before 2018.[80]

While familiar global players including the OECD and European Union remain key actors in the BEPS Project, the G20 has been an active and visible leader.[81] The G20 gave the drive to tax transparency a broader legitimacy across Brazil, Russia, India, China, and South Africa (BRICS) and observer countries. A second important political player is the Global Forum on Transparency and Tax Information Exchange.[82] The so-called Inclusive Framework on BEPS[83] of the OECD/G20 now includes 115 countries supposedly on an equal footing, seeking to work together to deal with corporate tax avoidance.

Today, 126 countries or territories are covered by the Multilateral Convention on tax administrative cooperation.[84] Under its auspices, sixty-one revenue agencies have signed the Multilateral Competent Authority Agreement on Automatic Exchange of Financial Information.[85] China has signed up and is seeking to lead in tax diplomacy. To that end, it hosted the 105th Forum on Tax Administration, including forty-six countries in Beijing in May 2016.

There is not space to address the BEPS Project in detail here, and it is discussed more fully in other chapters in this volume. It is not clear that the BEPS Project—even including its transparency norms—will achieve the aspirational goal of reforming the international tax system. Indeed, it may be that the BEPS project cannot stop the process of global tax competition between countries seeking investment by MNEs, and it may not even achieve transparency of beneficial ownership or genuine compliance with information sharing between countries. Governments remain keenly aware of competition for international investment. Corporate tax rates have trended down since the 1980s, and offshore financial centers have increased their role, even as they have acquiesced in tax information sharing platforms.

The most lasting legacy of the BEPS Project may be country-by-country (CbC) reporting for MNEs,[86] which has been made possible through new automatic data-sharing platforms. The first exchanges of CbC Reports of MNE revenues, profits, and taxes by jurisdiction took place in mid-2018.[87] Australia, like many other countries, has implemented CbC reporting effective January 1, 2016.[88] The OECD claims there are over 2000 bilateral "activated" exchange relationships for CbC reporting and seventy-five jurisdictions committed to sharing CbC Reports.[89] However, there are strict taxpayer confidentiality and usage restrictions on CbC Reports: they are not public.[90] The strict conditions and technological demands of CbC reporting mean that developing country tax agencies are less likely to satisfy the conditions for obtaining access to CbC Reports in the short term. The lack of publicity restricts the ability of NGOs and the public to survey and criticize the tax paid (or unpaid) by MNEs.

C. PUBLIC REPORTING OF TAXPAYER DATA

Today, the public reporting of taxes paid, or not paid, and of what would otherwise be private financial and tax transactions is on the political agenda, including publicity of CbC Reports. This would be a dramatic shift away from the current law in most countries around the world. In only a few countries (Finland, Norway and Japan being examples), there was historically, or remains today, a tradition of public tax transparency.[91] In other countries, the disclosure of tax returns of those in high office, such as in the US presidential election (honored by most candidates, except for President Donald Trump), has been a tradition. However, as discussed above, in most countries, taxpayer secrecy is a strong legal requirement that is carefully observed by the revenue agency.

This chapter does not explore the right to privacy of taxpayers in detail; however, two observations may be made. First, the UN Declaration of Human Rights provides protection from "arbitrary interference" with privacy, not a right to privacy in all circumstances.[92] Second, the transparency of different "private" actors such as individuals or corporate entities (especially large MNEs) is frequently conflated in debates about privacy; however, a quite different analysis of the right of privacy in taxation may arise in each case.

Calls for increased financial transparency from taxpayers to the government may be perceived as an extension of coercive government power that is inimical to human rights in certain contexts. This may be the case, for example, if the tax law is complex or uncertain, but taxpayers are nonetheless required to provide full information and are subjected to detailed surveillance of their financial and economic activities—that is, transparency does not go both ways.[93] A larger question, which cannot be addressed in this chapter, is what is the moral or rights-based approach to tax transparency for a government that abuses or breaches human rights, is corrupt or predatory, or is just bad at delivering public goods and services for the people?

The early history of transparency in the context of the corporate tax in the United States is informative for current debates. The publicity of corporate tax returns was part of the original argument for enacting a US corporate tax in 1909.[94] Publicity was one element in a complicated debate about federal regulation of corporations, with particular attention being paid to the "trusts" or large, monopoly corporations—the equivalent of MNEs today.[95] Marjorie Kornhauser explains that "publicity of information about corporations was an important facet of both the Roosevelt and Taft" efforts at federal regulation and taxation of corporations.[96] There was a debate about the meaning of transparency at the time: in its broadest sense, "publicity" meant giving the general populace access to information about corporations, but in a narrower sense, "publicity" was limited to providing the government with information.[97] The information in which the public was particularly interested was not, primarily, about tax paid by corporations. It was about the profits, income, and activities of corporations, which were not reported through other regulatory systems to investors or lenders. Corporations opposed "publicity" (or transparency) both to government and to the public.

The US corporate tax of 1909 included a requirement that corporate tax returns were required to be filed with the Office of the Commissioner of Inland Revenue and thereby became public records "open to inspection as such."[98] In initial regulations, the Secretary of the Treasury stated that the requirement of publicity was clear and the revenue authority had "no discretion whatsoever."[99] Yet within six months, the Treasury was reviewing the "extent of the publicity of such returns," and it then backtracked on this commitment.[100] Ultimately, it was determined that the tax returns of publicly held corporations would be made public (as part of financial regulation of those companies), but not those of privately held corporations. These tax publicity rules were the "forerunner of Securities and Exchange Commission reporting."[101] We can see some clear parallels between the challenge of regulation and publicity concerning modern MNE taxation and profits, and those debates of more than a century ago.

Most countries do not yet propose to enact public reporting of corporate taxes or profits, although the issue is being hotly debated in Europe and other jurisdictions.[102] In this context, it is interesting to examine a law enacted in Australia in 2014 that mandates public reporting by the Commissioner of Taxation of total income, taxable income, and tax paid by large companies.[103] In the first report, the Commissioner stated that this "forms part of a wider domestic and global push for improved corporate transparency. It is intended to inform public debate about tax policy, particularly in relation to the corporate tax system."[104] The fourth report under this measure was released in December 2018.[105] Like previous reports, it reveals that about one-third of Australian multinationals paid no tax in that fiscal year, and some paid only a low amount of tax relative to reported gross income.[106] Some consistent patterns of non-payment of tax have emerged for some companies.

The Australian Treasury has also established a Voluntary Tax Transparency Code for Australian companies.[107] After a slow start, more than one hundred corporations have now signed up to the voluntary disclosure regime.[108] Those corporations include major banks, the Australian groups in MNEs such as Unilever, Shell, and Rio Tinto, some infrastructure and advising firms, and telecommunications corporations such as Vodafone (Vodafone is almost unique in voluntarily disclosing its tax and profit globally).[109] This is only a small proportion of several thousand companies that would fit the conditions for voluntary disclosure.

The Voluntary Code requires a minimum disclosure of information, including a reconciliation of accounting profit to tax expense and income tax paid; identification of material temporary and nontemporary differences; an accounting effective company tax rate; and a statement of the company's approach to tax strategy and compliance, among other things.[110] Target audiences of the report are stated to include "interested users" (such as social justice groups, media, analysts, and shareholders) and general users (the "person in the street").[111]

It seems that Australia is on a pathway toward requiring public disclosure of taxes by corporations with gross annual income of A$100 million or more, as a normal part of the tax and regulatory landscape for large corporations. Other countries may follow. This raises an important question: What is the function of *public* disclosure of taxpayer information?

Public reporting does not directly increase the ability of the revenue agency to collect tax: the revenue agency already has all of the information that is now publicly reported—and sometimes much more—available to it. Public reporting may increase the motivation of the revenue agency to collect revenue. Public reporting may also, or alternatively, lead to better compliance behavior by taxpayers. Public disclosure of taxes (un)paid may lead to pressure on corporations from consumers or investors, to change their taxpaying behavior as an element of corporate social responsibility—reducing their use of tax havens, making them responsive to their clients and consumers, and building a social license to operate. Whether this is the case is the subject of ongoing research by scholars, with mixed results to date.[112]

A third reason for public tax transparency may be to educate the public about corporate tax compliance including why some companies might legitimately pay no tax in a particular year.[113] For example, the carry forward of company losses permitted in most company tax regimes can lead to nil or low tax in one or several tax years, but this is not likely to be well understood by the public. Australia's tax system, like that in many other countries, exempts foreign business income from company tax, and companies get credits against tax in relation to dividends paid from other companies that have paid tax. If companies choose to disclose their tax affairs voluntarily, they can explain these features of their tax and business activities, which may result in lower tax paid, with more detail than is possible for the Commissioner of Taxation in the compulsory public report. The value of this educative function is unclear. One might be skeptical about how much the public will really understand, or care, about the specifics of corporate tax profiles for any particular company.

I suggest that if public disclosure has any role to play in revenue collection, it essentially operates as an indirect accountability check on the *government* not the taxpayer. Public reporting puts political pressure on governments to achieve better tax collection and stronger tax laws. The revenue agency must be able to justify its own enforcement operations with respect to large corporate taxpayers which, perhaps continually over time, report nil or low tax paid. This may well be a useful function of public tax transparency.

Therefore, the main function of public tax transparency for corporations is to be an instrument of governmental, rather than corporate, accountability. Taking this analysis further, we could consider large corporations, especially MNEs, as having a quasi-regulatory or state-like character. This means that corporate transparency is linked to governmental transparency, and both are necessary to support the public good. A strong case can be made for this, once it is recalled (as discussed above) that companies and other legal intermediaries are crucial vehicles for collection of all taxes that fund government—including pay-as-you-go wage taxes and social security taxes from employees and value-added taxes on sales to consumers—as well as corporate tax. As MNEs now operate globally, so too can governments cooperate across borders. In the global, digital era, where technology makes disclosure feasible, it makes sense for the public to demand accountability and transparency on taxation from MNEs, and governments.

We might take a different view of tax transparency for individuals. As noted above, a few countries have a tradition of personal tax transparency, but in most countries taxpayer privacy remains closely protected, sometimes preventing sharing of information even between different departments within a government. This is frequently justified as important in ensuring trust and compliance with tax laws.[114]

Ken Devos and Marcus Zackrisson undertake a detailed discussion of the pros and cons of publicity of individual taxpayer information.[115] They explain how the Norwegian tradition of publishing tax returns exists in a broader culture of publicity in government administration, and in a small, homogeneous country with a strong communitarian culture, this has been unquestioned.[116] Should this kind of public disclosure be mandated for individuals in a country such as Australia, or the United States, without that communitarian cultural history? It seems wrong to allow leaks to journalists to reveal to the public on an essentially random basis, the income, assets, or activities of individuals, even if they have income or assets in low-tax jurisdictions, rather than addressing the issue in a more systematic way. Devos and Zackrisson, like Kornhauser, suggest that a form of limited public transparency of taxpayer information could improve compliance and trust. However, they also observe recent pressure in Norway to *increase* taxpayer privacy in the face of globalization and digitization that would expose taxpayers to scrutiny (or unscrupulous access), not just from their own, trusted population, but from all over the world.[117]

It may be possible to justify a position that those who directly engage in and benefit from globalization—by earning income and holding assets abroad—should be subject to public tax transparency. These may often (though not always) be high-wealth individuals. On the other hand, the risk of disclosure may be even greater for those who invest or do business offshore.

The current hot issue for individual tax disclosure concerns the public disclosure of beneficial ownership of companies and trusts that are located in jurisdictions around the world (and particularly in tax havens).[118] The disclosure of beneficial ownership may logically be seen to be an extension of information sharing and tax cooperation between governments in support of their own national taxes. Some MNEs have supported enhanced individual tax disclosure of beneficial ownership, while still opposing public CbC reporting of their own profits.[119] It seems likely that a national, or global, register of beneficial ownership of these entities and an end to anonymous entity ownership would be a valuable contribution to support revenue collection; however, it is less clear that this register should be public. To date, agreement and enforcement of beneficial ownership disclosure has proved difficult to achieve, and so far, even a confidential register of beneficial ownership has not yet been established in many countries.

V. HOW CAN TAX TRANSPARENCY SERVE HUMAN RIGHTS?

Since the 1990s, we have seen significant moves toward increased transparency, both of governments and of taxpayers. These moves were given impetus by international economic and fiscal crises and have led to the embedding of new transparency norms for governments, companies, and, potentially, individual citizens.

Budget transparency aims to make government taxing and spending—fiscal decision-making—more transparent to citizens. This may help in fighting corruption, broadening democratic contestability of taxes, and making government spending more accountable. As a budget management tool, transparency has probably facilitated governmental access to other revenue sources, especially financial credit, helping in a diffuse way to maintain trust across governments and markets. Frequently, however, budget transparency has served to enforce fiscal "discipline" of governments, especially of developing countries, to external lenders and donors rather than to their own citizens. It is widely accepted that many externally driven policies of fiscal constraint and structural adjustment have produced negative outcomes for many people in developing countries.

Shifting our focus to the transparency of taxpayers, including individuals and companies, *to* governments, *between* governments, and *to the public*, implicitly accepts that governmental taxing power should be strengthened. It is important to remember that levying taxes is a coercive exercise of government power and increased tax transparency will augment that power. A human rights argument in favor of tax transparency posits that funding governments with adequate taxation is the best way to deliver public goods and services and there is a significant economic development case for increased taxes to support social and economic rights. However, we should remember the relationship between taxpayer rights and secrecy which underpins the fiscal bargain in many countries.

The corporate tax remains a crucial mechanism for tax collection in most countries and here, the argument for public transparency is stronger, at least for large companies.[120] As explained above, governments need tax information from companies and governments should (and increasingly do) share this information with other governments to collect company tax. Large companies, especially MNEs that operate globally, have quasi-governmental characteristics and control enormous resources. This justifies increased tax transparency to and between governments, and even to the public, by these taxpayers.

From a tax collection perspective, transparency of tax information is only one step toward the ultimate goal of collection of adequate tax revenues by governments. The new expansion of tax transparency norms essentially recognizes the role of companies as intermediaries in a wider regulatory system of transparency obligations on both taxpayers *and* governments.

For individuals who have bank accounts, trusts, and companies in tax havens, disclosure of beneficial ownership, and obtaining tax information from these intermediaries about their underlying owners is essential for tax enforcement. This supports a call for enhanced transparency of taxpayer information to their own governments, and through intergovernmental cooperation, to other governments seeking to assess tax on the income, assets, and profits of individual taxpayers. It is less clear, however, that *public* disclosure of such individuals or their tax information is required. Calls for public disclosure of individual tax information reveal a lack of trust, not only of the high-wealth individuals who are suspected of engaging in tax evasion or avoidance, but also of governments themselves, as complicit or otherwise failing to act in the best interests of their citizens.

This lack of trust in governmental ability or willingness to enforce tax laws against high-wealth individuals or corporations may be justified. The spate of leaks and tax scandals publicized through ICIL suggests that in spite of fiscal crises, governments may be unwilling, or unable, to take needed steps to enforce taxation or to obtain information about the offshore holdings of high-wealth individuals. This may be because of corruption or political vested interests, or it may result from a desire by governments not to impede the business or investment activities of their own citizens in a competitive global economy. Governments made the policies and laws that until very recently have permitted MNEs and high-wealth individuals to shift capital globally, to rely on legal entities and on secrecy laws and—famously—to permit MNEs to accumulate capital offshore in tax havens so as to avoid home country taxation, while also minimizing taxation abroad. Seen in this light, the key role for advocates of tax transparency is to maintain pressure to hold governments accountable in administering fair and effective tax systems.

Politicians frequently blame MNEs or high-wealth individuals for tax avoidance and failing to pay their "fair share," while themselves failing to take politically responsible steps to ensure tax collection, or to reform the domestic tax base of their own country. In focusing on tax transparency of individuals and corporations, we should not lose sight of the need to hold governments to account in achieving taxing and spending decisions that would support economic development, redistribution, and the social state so as to actually achieve human rights. We also need to demand accountability of governments for decisions that embed fiscal austerity; recklessly argue that taxes should be cut; or highlight supposed future "costs" of social welfare while failing to fully address current inequities and failures of policy.

Globally, governments should continue to develop a more transparent global fiscal framework of automated data sharing. Transparency of corporate tax information to the public may be useful for tax enforcement, most importantly if it achieves the indirect aim of holding governments to account and taxpayers to their lawful obligations, or if it reinforces the necessary compact of trust between taxpayers and governments. Transparency of individual tax information to the public is less likely to assist in this goal, and it is not clear that the benefits outweigh the opposing concern to limit coercive or arbitrary action by governments.

Foucault's observation, quoted at the beginning of this chapter, reminds us that the "dream" of transparency, like the revolutionary dream, is both valuable and unattainable, and that increased transparency inevitably brings with it increased surveillance and discipline, as well as contributing to compliance with tax law. The biggest win from establishing a global tax transparency regime will be the support it provides to maintain compliance and legitimacy of national tax systems in a global context. The fight for fair revenue raising and resource distribution around the globe will continue.

NOTES

1. M. Foucault, 'The Eye of Power', *in* C. Gordon (ed.), *Power/Knowledge: Selected Interviews and Other Writings 1972–1977* (1980), 146–165, at 152.
2. J. Bentham, *Writings on the Poor Laws* (M. Quinn ed., 2001), at 277.
3. J. Braithwaite and P. Drahos, *Global Business Regulation* (2000), at 508.
4. T. N Hale, 'Transparency, Accountability and Global Governance', 14 *Global Governance* (2008), 73.
5. M. Bauhr and N. Nasiritousi, 'Resisting Transparency: Corruption, Legitimacy, and the Quality of Global Environmental Policies', 12(4) *Global Environmental Politics* (2012), 9.
6. The linking of power, transparency, and knowledge dates to the Enlightenment and finds revolutionary expression in Rousseau and organizational expression with Bentham's *Panopticon*, as discussed by M. Foucault, *supra* note 1.
7. See, e.g., J. D. Blank, 'Should Corporate Tax Returns Be Public?', 11(1) *New York University Journal of Law and Business* (2014), 159.
8. D. Bessire, 'Transparency: A Two-Way Mirror?', 32(5)B *International Journal of Social Economics* (2005), 424.

9. C. Hood, 'Transparency in Historical Perspective', in C. Hood and D. Heald (eds.), *Transparency: The Key to Better Governance?* (2006), 3, at 16–17.

10. M. V. Halter, M. C. C. de Arruda, and R. B. Halter, 'Transparency to Reduce Corruption? Dropping Hints for Private Organizations in Brazil', 84 *Journal of Business Ethics* (2009), 373, at 377.

11. C. Hood and D. Heald (eds.), *Transparency: The Key to Better Governance?* (2006).

12. Ballotpedia, *Government Transparency*, available online at https://ballotpedia.org/Government_transparency (last visited 23 May 2017).

13. Bessire, *supra* note 8, at 425.

14. OECD, *Public Sector Transparency and Accountability: Making It Happen* (2002), at 3.

15. Bauhr and Nasirtousi, *supra* note 5, at 11; see also M. Bauhr and M. Grimes, *What Is Government Transparency?* (2012), available online at http://qog.pol.gu.se/digitalAssets/1418/1418047_2012_16_bauhr_grimes.pdf; A. Bellver and D. Kaufmann, *Transparenting Transparency: Initial Empirics and Policy Applications* (World Bank Policy Research Working Paper, 2005), available online at https://papers.ssrn.com/sol3/papers.cfm?abstract_id=808664 (last visited 30 May 2017).

16. Hood, *supra* note 9.

17. P. Birkinshaw, 'Transparency as a Human Right', in C. Hood and D. Heald (eds.), *Transparency: The Key to Better Governance?* (2006), 47.

18. See, e.g., M. Petrie, *The IMF Fiscal Transparency Code: A Potentially Powerful New Anti-Corruption Tool* (1999), available online at http://iacconference.org.s3-website.eu-central-1.amazonaws.com/documents/9th_iacc_workshop_The_IMF_Fiscal_Transparency_Code.doc, at 4–5 (describing the IMF's new focus on quality of member state governance in 1996, which culminated in adoption of the Code of Good Practices on Fiscal Transparency in 1998); M. Petrie, The World Bank PREM Notes, *The Current State of Fiscal Transparency: Norms, Assessment, and Country Practices* (2013), available online at http://siteresources.worldbank.org/PUBLICSECTORANDGOVERNANCE/Resources/285741-1361973400317/GPSMSpecialSeries4.pdf, at 1.

19. See, e.g., OECD, *Best Practices for Budget Transparency* (2002), available online at https://www.oecd.org/governance/budgeting/Best%20Practices%20Budget%20Transparency%20-%20complete%20with%20cover%20page.pdf.

20. IMF, *The Fiscal Transparency Code* (2014), available online at http://blog-pfm.imf.org/files/ft-code.pdf.

21. See IMF, *Reports on the Observance of Standards and Codes (ROSCs)*, last updated 4 Jan. 2017, available online at http://www.imf.org/external/NP/rosc/rosc.aspx (last visited 18 Aug. 2017).

22. See the detailed discussion in L. Philipps and M. Stewart, 'Fiscal Transparency: Global Norms, Domestic Laws and the Politics of Budgets', 34 *Brooklyn Journal of International Law* (2009), 797.

23. Ibid. at 829.

24. In the tax area, see M. Stewart, 'Global Trajectories of Tax Reform: The Discourse of Tax Reform in Developing and Transition Countries', 44 *Harvard International Law Journal* (2003), 139; M. Stewart and S. Jogarajan, 'The International Monetary Fund and Tax Reform', 2 *British Tax Review* (2004), 146. NGOs have produced numerous reports, for example, Eurodad, *World Bank and IMF Conditionality: A Development Injustice* (2006), available online at http://www.eurodad.org (last visited 13 Aug. 2017).

25. Press Release, IMF, Communiqué of the Interim Committee of the Board of Governors of the International Monetary Fund, 29 Sept. 1996, available online at http://www.imf.org/external/np/sec/pr/1996/pr9649.htm (last visited 13 Aug. 2017). This concern of the 1990s is somewhat ironic given the extremely low, or negative, interest rates today.

26. G. Kopits and J. Craig, *Transparency in Government Operations* (IMF Occasional Paper No. 158, Dec. 1998), available online at https://www.imf.org/external/pubs/ft/op/158/op158.pdf.

27. OECD, *Best Practices for Budget Transparency* (2002), available online at https://www.oecd.org/gov/budgeting/Best%20Practices%20Budget%20Transparency%20-%20complete%20with%20cover%20page.pdf.

28. See, e.g., X. Debrun and M. S. Kumar, 'The Discipline Enhancing Role of Fiscal Institutions: Theory and Empirical Evidence', Working Paper WP/07/171 (2007); C. Wyplosz, 'Fiscal Policy: Institutions

vs. Rules', Working Paper No 03/2002, HEI: Report prepared for the Swedish Government's Committee on Stabilization Policy in the EMU (2002).

29. Philipps and Stewart, *supra* note 22, at 814; OECD, 'Enhancing the Cost Effectiveness of Public Spending: Experience in OECD Countries', 37 *OECD Journal: Economic Studies* (2004), 109, at 117–118, 120–123 (quoting I. Joumard et al.).

30. Australia is in its tenth year of budget deficit. See Australian Treasury, *Budget 2017–18, Budget Paper 1*, Statement 3, Chart 5, p. 3–20, available online at http://www.budget.gov.au.

31. See, e.g., L. Fisher and G. Kingston, *Is Treasury Still Too Optimistic About Revenue?*, Austaxpolicy: Tax and Transfer Policy Blog, 27 Mar. 2017, available online at http://www.austaxpolicy.com/treasury-still-optimistic-revenue/ (based on L. A. Fisher and G. Kingston, 'Improved Forecasts of Tax Revenue via the Permanent Income Hypothesis', 50(1) *The Australian Economic Review* (2017), 21–31).

32. Tax Justice Network Africa and ActionAid International, *Tax Competition in East Africa: A Race to the Bottom?* (Apr. 2012), available online at http://www.taxjusticeafrica.net/?page_id=1435&lang=en (last visited 21 Aug. 2017); Tax Justice Network Africa and ActionAid International, *Still Racing Toward the Bottom? Corporate Tax Incentives in East Africa* (June 2016), available online at http://www.taxjusticeafrica.net/?page_id=1435&lang=en (last visited 21 Aug. 2017).

33. M. Keen and A. Simone, 'Tax Policy in Developing Countries: Some Lessons from the 1990s and Some Challenges Ahead', *in* S. Gupta, B. Clements, and G. Inchauste (eds.), *Helping Countries Develop: The Role of Fiscal Policy* (2004), 302; Cf. K. Brown, 'Harmful Tax Competition: The OECD View', 32 *George Washington Journal of International Law and Economics* (1999), 311 (book review).

34. See further M. Burton and M. Stewart, *Tax Expenditure Reporting: A Guide for Civil Society Advocates* (2011).

35. N. H. Buchanan, 'Social Security, Generational Justice and Long-Term Deficits', 58 *Tax Law Review* (2005), 275, at 312.

36. Australian Treasury, *2015 Intergenerational Report: Australia in 2055*, Mar. 2015, available online at http://www.treasury.gov.au/~/media/Treasury/Publications%20and%20Media/Publications/2015/2015%20Intergenerational%20Report/Downloads/PDF/2015_IGR.ashx, at 65–70 (last visited 21 Aug. 2017).

37. Ibid. at 69.

38. K. Van Kersbergen and A. Hemerijck, 'Two Decades of Change in Europe: The Emergence of the Social Investment State', 41 *Journal of Social Policy* (2012), 475.

39. P. Whiteford, *The $4.8 Trillion Dollar Question: Will an "Investment Approach" to Welfare Help the Most Disadvantaged?*, 20 Sept. 2016, available online at http://theconversation.com/the-4-8-trillion-dollar-question-will-an-investment-approach-to-welfare-help-the-most-disadvantaged-65628 (last visited 24 May 2017).

40. See, e.g., Hale, *supra* note 4; D. Curtin and A. J. Meijer, 'Does Transparency Strengthen Legitimacy? A Critical Analysis of European Union Policy Documents', 11 *Information Polity* (2006), 109.

41. See Transparency International, *Our History*, available online at https://www.transparency.org/whoweare/history/ (last visited 24 May 2017). Among a lot of other goals and consequences of TI's work, the OECD was persuaded to establish a convention requiring countries to outlaw deductions for bribes—leading to domestic tax law amendments in many countries during the late 1990s.

42. M. Petrie, Paper presented at the 9th International Anti-Corruption Conference: The IMF Fiscal Transparency Code—A Potentially Powerful New Anti-Corruption Tool (10–15 Oct. 1999), at 4.

43. J. Sharman, *Havens in a Storm* (2006).

44. See discussion in Philipps and Stewart, *supra* note 22.

45. International Budget Partnership, *About the Open Budget Initiative*, available online at http://www.internationalbudget.org/opening-budgets/open-budget-initiative/ (last visited 24 May 2017); International Budget Partnership, *Transparency and Participation in the Budget Process: Why Focus on Budget Transparency and Participation*, available online at http://www.internationalbudget.org/themes/BudTrans/index.htm (last visited 24 May 2017).

46. International Budget Partnership, *Open Budget Survey 2017 Report* (2018), available online at https://www.internationalbudget.org/open-budget-survey/ (last visited 12 Apr. 2018).
47. A. Fölscher et al., *Transparency and Participation in the Budget Process—South Africa: A Country Report* (2000).
48. Ibid. at 6, note 4.
49. See The Extractive Industries Transparency Initiative, available online at http://www.eiti.org (last visited 24 May 2017).
50. The history is on the EITI website, ibid.; see also M. Longhorn, M. Rahim, and K. Sadiq, 'Country-by-Country Reporting: An Assessment of Its Objective and Scope', 14(1) *eJournal of Tax Research* (2016), 4.
51. EITI, *Country Status Against the EITI Rules (2007–2016)*, available online at https://eiti.org/countries-archive (last visited 21 Aug. 2017).
52. E. Papyrakis, M. Rieger, and E. Gilberthorpe, 'Corruption and the Extractive Industries Transparency Initiative', 53(2) *Journal of Development Studies* (2017), 295.
53. OECD, *Paris Declaration on Aid Effectiveness: Ownership, Harmonization, Alignment, Results and Mutual Accountability*, 2 Mar. 2005, available online at http://www.oecd.org/dac/effectiveness/34428351.pdf; Public Expenditure and Financial Accountability, *About PEFA*, available online at https://pefa.org/what-pefa (last visited 24 May 2017).
54. Public Expenditure and Financial Accountability, *PEFA 2016 FAQs*, available online at https://pefa.org/content/pefa-2016-faqs (last visited 24 May 2017).
55. See, e.g., A. J. Ody, C. C. Griffin, D. Ferranti, J. Jacinto, and N. Warren, *Enhancing Development through Better Use of Public Resources: How Independent Watchdog Groups Can Help* (2006), available online at https://www.brookings.edu/research/enhancing-development-through-better-use-of-public-resources-how-independent-watchdog-groups-can-help/ (last visited 31 Jan. 2018).
56. See Philipps and Stewart, *supra* note 22.
57. J. Sharman, 'Privacy as Roguery: Personal Financial Information in an Age of Transparency', 87(4) *Public Administration* (2009), 717.
58. OECD, *Tax Co-operation 2009: Towards a Level Playing Field* argues that the era of "bank secrecy as a shield for tax evaders" in "unco-operative jurisdictions" was coming to an end, available online at http://www.oecd.org/ctp/harmful/oecdassessmentshowsbanksecrecyasashieldfortaxevaderscomingtoanend.htm (last visited 13 Aug. 2017).
59. C. Hood, 'The "Tax State" in the Information Age', in T. V. Paul, G. Ikenberry, and J. Hall (eds.), *The Nation-State in Question* (2003) 213; J. Schumpeter, *The Crisis of the Tax State* (1918); M. Stewart, 'The Tax State, Benefit and Legitimacy', in P. Harris (ed.), *History of Tax Law*, Vol. 7 (2015), 483.
60. See, e.g., G. Wolfram, 'Taxpayer Rights and the Fiscal Constitution', in D. Racheter and R. Wagner (eds.), *Politics, taxation, and the rule of law: the power to tax in constitutional perspective* (2002).
61. For example, pay-as-you-go withholding of wage and social security taxes depends on formal employment and payroll systems of large corporate employers. See also Braithwaite and Drahos, *supra* note 3.
62. As shown in the detailed country studies of confidentiality rules in tax laws, E. Kristoffersson, M. Lang, P. Pistone, J. Schuch, C. Staringer, and A. Storck (eds.), *Tax Secrecy and Tax Transparency: The Relevance of Confidentiality in Tax Law* (2013).
63. Ibid.
64. Ibid.
65. G20 Research Group, *G20 Action Plan for Recovery and Reform*, 2 Apr. 2009, available online at http://www.g20.utoronto.ca/2009/2009communique0402.pdf.
66. OECD, *Harmful Tax Competition: An Emerging Global Issue* (1998), available online at http://www.oecd-ilibrary.org/taxation/harmful-tax-competition_9789264162945-en (last visited 21 Aug. 2017).
67. M. Stewart, 'Transnational Tax Information Exchange Networks: Steps Towards a Globalized, Legitimate Tax Administration', 4(2) *World Tax Journal* (2012), 152.
68. Braithwaite and Drahos, *supra* note 3; S. Picciotto, *International Business Taxation as a Study in the Internationalization of Business Regulation* (1992).

69. See, e.g., T. A. Van Kampen and L. J. de Rijke, 'The Kreditetbank Luxembourg and the Liechtenstein Tax Affairs: Notes on the Balance Between the Exchange of Information Between States and the Protection of Fundamental Rights', 2008-5 *EC Tax Review* (2009), 221; B. J. Bondi, 'Don't Tread on Me: Has the United States Government's Quest for Customer Records from UBS Sounded the Death Knell for Swiss Bank Secrecy Laws?', 30 *Northwestern Journal of International Law and Business* (2010), 1.

70. B. Schmid, *Authorities Investigating Deutsche Post CEO for Tax Evasion*, 14 Feb. 2008, available online at http://www.spiegel.de/international/business/raid-on-zumwinkel-s-home-and-office-authorities-investigating-deutsche-post-ceo-for-tax-evasion-a-535230.html (last visited 21 Aug. 2017).

71. Ibid.

72. Van Kampen and de Rijke, *supra* note 69.

73. D. Kocieniewski, 'Whistle-Blower Awarded $104 Million by I.R.S.', *New York Times*, 11 Sept. 2012, available online at http://www.nytimes.com/2012/09/12/business/whistle-blower-awarded-104-million-by-irs.html (last visited 21 Aug. 2017).

74. D. Marsan, 'FATCA: The Global Financial System Must Now Implement a New U.S. Reporting and Withholding System for Foreign Account Tax Compliance, Which Will Create Significant New Exposures—Managing this Risk (Part I)', *Taxes* (2010), 27, at 37.

75. Australian Tax Office, *Project Wickenby Has Delivered*, available online at https://www.ato.gov.au/general/the-fight-against-tax-crime/news-and-results/project-wickenby-has-delivered/ (last visited 21 Aug. 2017).

76. B. Malkin, *Crocodile Dundee Paul Hogan's Off-Shore Tax Accounts to be Published*, 16 June 2010, available online at http://www.telegraph.co.uk/news/worldnews/australiaandthepacific/australia/7832537/Crocodile-Dundee-Paul-Hogans-off-shore-tax-accounts-to-be-published.html (last visited 24 May 2017).

77. Global Financial Integrity, *Illicit Financial Flows from Developing Countries 2002–2006* (Dec. 2008), available online at http://www.gfintegrity.org/storage/gfip/executive%20-%20final%20version%201-5-09.pdf.

78. See *Investigations*, International Consortium of Investigative Journalists, https://www.icij.org/investigations/; *Offshore Leaks Database*, available online at https://offshoreleaks.icij.org/ (last viewed 31 Jan. 2018) (detailing the Panama Papers, Luxembourg Leaks, and Paradise Papers scandals, among others).

79. OECD, *A Step Change in Tax Transparency: Delivering a Standardised, Secure and Cost Effective Model of Bilateral Automatic Exchange for the Multilateral Context* (June 2013), available online at https://www.oecd.org/ctp/exchange-of-tax-information/taxtransparency_G8report.pdf.

80. G20, *G20 Brisbane Summit 2014: Leader's Communiqué* (Nov. 2014), available online at http://www.g20australia.org/sites/default/files/g20_resources/library/brisbane_g20_leaders_summit_communique.pdf.

81. G20, *G20 London Summit 2009: Leaders' Statement*, 2 Apr. 2009, available online at http://www.g20.utoronto.ca/summits/2009london.html (last visited 21 Aug. 2017).

82. OECD, *Global Forum on Transparency and Exchange of Information for Tax Purposes*, available online at http://www.oecd.org/tax/transparency/ (last visited 21 Aug. 2017).

83. OECD, *First Meeting of the New Inclusive Framework to Tackle Base Erosion and Profit Shifting Marks a New Era in International Tax Cooperation*, 30 June 2016, available online at http://www.oecd.org/ctp/first-meeting-of-the-new-inclusive-framework-to-tackle-base-erosion-and-profit-shifting-marks-a-new-era-in-international-tax-co-operation.htm (last visited 24 May 2017).

84. Australian Tax Office, *Automatic Exchange of Information Guidance—CRS and FATCA*, 21 Apr. 2017, available online at https://www.ato.gov.au/General/International-tax-agreements/In-detail/International-arrangements/Automatic-exchange-of-information---guidance-material/ (last visited 24 May 2017).

85. Authorized under Article 6 of the Multilateral Convention. OECD, *Multilateral Competent Authority Agreement on Automatic Exchange of Financial Account Information*, available online

at http://www.oecd.org/ctp/exchange-of-tax-information/multilateral-competent-authority-agreement.pdf.

86. OECD, *Country-by-Country Reporting*, available online at http://www.oecd.org/tax/beps/country-by-country-reporting.htm (last visited 21 Aug. 2017).

87. OECD, *Country-by-country reporting*, available online at http://www.oecd.org/tax/beps/country-by-country-reporting.htm (last visited 1 Jan. 2018); OECD, *BEPS Action 13: Jurisdictions implement final regulations for first filings of CbC reports, with over 1400 bilateral relationships now in place for the automatic exchange of CbC information* (21 Dec. 2017), available online at http://www.oecd.org/tax/beps/beps-action13-jurisdictions-implement-final-regulations-for-first-filings-of-cbc-reports.htm (last visited 31 Jan. 2018).

88. Australian Tax Office, *Country-by-Country Reporting*, 12 Apr. 2017, available online at https://www.ato.gov.au/Business/International-tax-for-business/In-detail/Transfer-pricing/Country-by-Country-reporting/ (last visited 24 May 2017). See Longhorn et al., *supra* note 50 for a history.

89. OECD, *Signatories of the Multilateral Competent Authority Agreement on the Exchange of Country-by-Country Reports (CbC MCAA) and Signing Dates*, status as of 22 June 2017, available online at http://www.oecd.org/tax/beps/country-by-country-reporting.htm (last visited 21 Aug. 2017).

90. *Multilateral Competent Authority Agreement on Automatic Exchange of Financial Account Information*, Section 5, available online at http://www.oecd.org/ctp/exchange-of-tax-information/multilateral-competent-authority-agreement.pdf.

91. See discussion in E. E. Bo, J. Slemrod, and T. O. Thoresen, 'Taxes on the Internet: Deterrence Effects of Public Disclosure', 7(1) *American Economic Journal: Economic Policy* (2015), 36–62.

92. General Assembly, Universal Declaration of Human Rights, UN Doc. A/Res/217(III), 10 Dec. 1948, Article 12: "No person shall be subject to arbitrary interference with his privacy, family, home or correspondence, nor to attacks upon his honour and reputation. Everyone has the right to the protection of the law against such interference or attacks."

93. See, e.g., C. A. Kettler, 'Mirror, Mirror on the Wall, What's Transparency After All?', 9 *DePaul Business & Commercial Law Journal* (2011), 321, discussing US Inland Revenue Commissioner's powers to demand information from taxpayers about uncertain tax positions, including from the boards of directors of large companies.

94. M. Kornhauser, 'Corporate Regulation and the Origins of the Corporate Income Tax', 66 *Indiana Law Journal* (1990), 53, at 66; R. S. Avi-Yonah, 'Corporations, Society, and the State: A Defense of the Corporate Tax', 90 *Vanderbilt Law Review* (2004), 1193, especially at 1221–1229.

95. Other countries did not face the same challenges that the United States did in regulating their corporations. In Australia, the Constitution which took effect in 1901 explicitly gave the federal government power to regulate (and tax) corporations, perhaps after observation of the late nineteenth-century issues concerning federal regulation in the United States.

96. Kornhauser, *supra* note 94, at 72.

97. Ibid. at 81.

98. Ibid. at 119.

99. Ibid. at 125.

100. Ibid. at 126–127.

101. Ibid. at 131.

102. See, e.g., European Parliament recommendation of 13 December 2017 to the Council and the Commission following the inquiry into money laundering, tax avoidance, and tax evasion (2016/3044(RSP)).

103. Taxation Administration Act 1953 (Cth), Section 3C.

104. Australian Tax Office, *Corporate Tax Transparency Report for the 2013–14 Income Year*, 22 Mar. 2016, available online at https://www.ato.gov.au/Business/Large-business/In-detail/Tax-transparency/Corporate-tax-transparency-report-for-the-2013-14-income-year/ (last visited 24 May 2017).

105. Australian Tax Office, *Corporate tax transparency report for 2015–16*, available online at https://www.ato.gov.au/Media-centre/Media-releases/Corporate-tax-transparency-report-for-2015-16/ (last viewed 16 Jan. 2019). The report lists the total income, taxable income and tax paid for the

2015–2016 tax year for listed companies with gross income of A$100 million or more, private companies with gross income of A$200 million or more, and resource companies.

106. Ibid.

107. Australian Treasury, Board of Taxation, *A Tax Transparency Code: A Report to the Treasurer*, Feb. 2016, available online at http://taxboard.gov.au/files/2016/05/BoT_TransparencyCode_Final-report.pdf.

108. The register of companies is available online at http://taxboard.gov.au/current-activities/transparency-code-register/ (last visited 13 Aug. 2017). On Vodafone, see https://www.vodafone.com/content/index/about/sustainability/operating-responsibly/tax-and-our-contribution-to-economies.html (last visited 16 Jan. 2019).

109. Ibid.

110. Australia Board of Taxation, *supra* note 107, at ch. 8.

111. Ibid. at 13.

112. See, e.g., F. Huseynov and B. K. Klamm, 'Tax avoidance, tax management and corporate social responsibility', 18(4) *Journal of Corporate Finance* (2012), 804–827; L. Watson, 'Corporate Social Responsibility, Tax Avoidance, and Earnings Performance', 37(2) *Journal of the American Taxation Association* (2015), 1–21; J. L. Hoopes, L. A. Robinson, and J. B. Slemrod, 'Public Tax-Return Disclosure', *Tuck School of Business Working Paper No. 2888385* (last revised 14 Dec. 2017) (discussing the Australian regime), available online at SSRN, https://papers.ssrn.com/sol3/papers.cfm?abstract_id=2888385. Hoopes et al. conclude that there may be a small consumer backlash to public disclosure by large private companies, and some investor backlash, but the latter being most likely due to anticipated policy change rather than consumer backlash.

113. Board of Taxation, *Corporate Tax Transparency Code and Register*, available online at http://taxboard.gov.au/current-activities/transparency-code-register/ (last visited 31 Jan. 2018).

114. See Kristoffersson et al., *supra* note 62; K. Devos and M. Zackrisson, 'Tax Compliance and the Public Disclosure of Tax Information: An Australia/Norway Comparison', 13(1) *eJournal of Tax Research* (2015), 108, available online at http://www.austlii.edu.au/au/journals/eJTR/2015/4.pdf.

115. Devos and Zackrisson, ibid.

116. Ibid. at 120–123.

117. Ibid. at 122.

118. This is the addressed by the Financial Action Task Force (FATF); see FATF, *Transparency and Beneficial Ownership* (2014), available online at http://www.fatf-gafi.org/media/fatf/documents/reports/Guidance-transparency-beneficial-ownership.pdf. Australia has begun consulting on a beneficial ownership register for companies: Australian Government—The Treasury, *Increasing Transparency of the Beneficial Ownership of Companies* (Consultation Paper, 13 Feb. 2017), available online at http://www.treasury.gov.au/ConsultationsandReviews/Consultations/2017/Beneficial-ownership-of-companies (last visited 14 Aug. 2017).

119. See, e.g., BHP Billiton, *Economic Contribution and Payments to Governments Report 2016* (2016), available online at https://www.bhp.com/-/media/bhp/documents/investors/annual-reports/2016/bhpbillitoneconomiccontributionandpaymentstogovernments2016.pdf?la=en, at 1.

120. For a recent discussion, see L. Abramovsky, A. Klemm, and D. Phillips, 'Corporate Tax in Developing Countries: Current Trends and Design Issues', 35 *Fiscal Studies* (2014), 559–588. doi:10.1111/j.1475-5890.2014.12042.x.

CHAPTER 11

TAXATION AND HUMAN RIGHTS

A Delicate Balance

REUVEN S. AVI-YONAH AND GIANLUCA MAZZONI

I. INTRODUCTION

The intersection of tax law and human rights can be viewed from two opposing perspectives. On the one hand, the ability of rich residents of developing countries and multinational corporations operating in those countries to evade or avoid taxation is directly linked to violations of human rights in those countries, especially from the perspective of social and economic rights like health and education. Providing such countries with the means to fight back and collect adequate revenues is essential in advancing such rights. On the other hand, some of the techniques used to achieve adequate revenue collection, like automatic exchange of information (AEoI) and country-by-country reporting (CbCR), risk violating other human rights like privacy and the legitimate protection of trade secrets. This chapter seeks to discuss both aspects and the need to find a reasonable balance between them.

The first part will be dedicated to the compatibility of reporting obligations under the US Foreign Account Tax Compliance Act (FATCA) and the Organisation for Economic Co-operation and Development (OECD) Common Reporting Standard (CRS) with the EU harmonized framework on privacy and data protection as enshrined in the European Convention on Human Rights (ECHR), the Charter of Fundamental Rights of the European Union (CFREU), and Directive 95/46/EC. It will be argued that AEoI under FATCA and CRS go beyond what is strictly necessary to achieve the goal of fighting offshore tax evasion. For example, reporting obligations apply even to persons for whom there is no evidence capable of suggesting that their conduct might have a link, even an indirect or remote one, with tax evasion. In the authors' opinion, low-risk accounts should be exempted from reporting. The question is how to identify those financial institutions and accounts that present a low risk of being used to evade taxes in order to exclude them from the scope of reporting obligations. To this extent, the authors suggest an enhancement of due diligence procedures through the elaboration of a list of subjective and objective "red flag indicators" as provided under the anti–money laundering legislation (AML). That list would facilitate not only the detection of those accounts that present a high risk of tax evasion but also of a reasonable balance between the AEoI and the right to privacy and to the protection of personal data.

If any legal uncertainty arising from any conflict between the AEoI and the right to respect for private life and to data protection is not rapidly removed, there is a great risk that large parts of the edifice erected for AEoI might be struck down by the Court of Justice of the European Union with the undesirable consequence that national tax authorities will not have, at their disposal, the necessary measures to provide their residents the above-mentioned social and economic rights of health and education.

II. FATCA, CRS, AND HUMAN RIGHTS

A. THE INTERACTION BETWEEN CROSS-BORDER EXCHANGE OF INFORMATION AND THE RIGHT TO PRIVACY

The right to privacy does not share the same scope of protection between the tax and nontax context. The notion of privacy in tax law is not as broad as in tort law or in constitutional law. Taxpayers cannot claim the right to be let alone or be free from unwarranted governmental intrusion. The reason is that, at stake, there is also the country's economic well-being to be protected. As Justice Roberts argued in *Bull v. U.S.*, taxes are the "lifeblood" of government.[1] Therefore, an appropriate balance is required between societal and individual interest.

This tax exceptionalism can be seen in *Yeong Yae Yun v. U.S.*, a case involving cross-border exchange of information between the Internal Revenue Service (IRS) and Korean taxing authorities, where it was held that "[p]etitioners have no legitimate expectation of privacy in their bank accounts."[2] In addition, since the IRS International Examiner also sent copies of the summons to the Korean taxpayers, the court ruled that all administrative steps necessary for the issuance of a proper summons were fulfilled.[3]

Such view has also been shared by the European Court of Human Rights (ECtHR). Article 8 (right to respect for private and family life) of the ECHR has been recently raised in *G.S.B. v. Switzerland*, which concerned the transmission to US tax authorities of the applicant's bank account details in connection with the mutual assistance agreement signed between Switzerland and the United States after the UBS scandal.[4] The ECtHR held that there has been no violation of Article 8, since "only his bank account details, that is to say purely financial information, had been disclosed. No private details or data closely linked to his identity, which would have deserved enhanced protection, had been transmitted."[5] Moreover, the applicant had benefited from several effective and genuine procedural guarantees against the transfer of his data to the US tax authorities.

For these reasons, the authors believe that in the context of taxation and, in particular, within the process of international exchange of information, individuals are only entitled to procedural safeguards, not a substantive right to privacy. These procedural rights are: (1) the right to be informed of the information request; (2) the right to participate in the investigations in the requested state; and (3) the right to challenge the assessment decision in the requesting state.[6] The absence of a procedural right (notification, consultation, or intervention) might constitute an infringement of the substantive right, i.e., the right to privacy.[7] In other words, taxpayers will not be in the position to effectively protect this substantive right without any basic procedural right.[8] The results of a survey conducted by Philip Baker and Pasquale Pistone indicate that only

22 percent of the countries examined provide a taxpayer the right to be informed before information is sought from third parties in response to a specific request for exchange of information, and only 17 percent provide a taxpayer the right to be heard by the tax authorities before information related to him is exchanged with another country.[9]

The importance of procedural safeguards has also been highlighted by two recent judgments of the ECtHR, e.g., *M.N. & Others v. San Marino*[10] and *Brito Ferrinho Bexiga Villa-Nova v. Portugal*.[11] The first case concerns the complaint of four Italian nationals about a decision by the San Marino judicial authorities ordering the seizure of banking documents pertaining to them and their lack to access to court to challenge that decision. The second case concerns access to the bank accounts of a lawyer charged with tax fraud. Each is discussed in turn.

In the context of criminal proceedings instituted in Italy against several individuals (not including the applicants) who were charged, inter alia, of a number of offences, the Italian prosecutors asked the San Marino authorities for assistance. Following that, the San Marino first-instance tribunal ordered an investigation in respect of all banks, fiduciary institutes, and trust companies in San Marino. The applicants lodged a complaint before the judge of criminal appeals against the decision concerning the seizure of banking documents related to them. They noted the absence of the *fumus delicti* and of any link between the crimes at issue and their position. In February and June 2011, complaints were declared inadmissible because of the lack of juridical interest of the appellants.[12] The judge of criminal appeals further noted that any breach of the rights of a person who may only have an eventual interest in the effects of the *exequatur decision* had to be raised in the ambit of the Italian jurisdictions.[13] The third-instance criminal judge confirmed the appeal decision.

Based on ECHR Article 6(1), the applicants complained that they did not have effective access to court to complain about the *exequatur* decision. They further complained under Article 8 that the measure had interfered with their private life and correspondence and it had failed to provide relevant procedural safeguards. Last, they complained that they had been denied an effective remedy for the purposes of their Article 8 complaint, in breach of Article 13.

The ECtHR first concluded that the seizure of banking data amounted to interference for the purposes of Article 8.[14] However, the interference was prescribed by law[15] and pursued various legitimate aims, namely, the prevention of crime, etc.[16] Therefore, the ECtHR had to determine whether the measure was necessary in a democratic society and, in particular, whether it was accompanied by the relevant procedural safeguards.[17] In this regard, the ECtHR found that the applicants did not have the "effective control" to which citizens are entitled under the rule of law and which would have been capable of restricting the interference in question to what was "necessary in a democratic society."[18] Accordingly, there had been a violation of the right to privacy.

Similar conclusions were reached by the ECtHR in the case of *Brito Ferrinho Bexiga Villa-Nova v. Portugal*.[19] While inspecting the accounts of Ms. de Brito Ferrinho Bexiga Villa-Nova's law firm, the tax authorities noted that she had not remitted value-added tax on professional fees which had been deposited into her personal bank account. Accordingly, tax authorities asked for details of that account. She refused on grounds of professional confidentiality and bank secrecy.

Under a domestic law provision, however, the prosecuting authorities may require the Court of Appeal to authorize the lifting of professional confidentiality and bank secrecy. The investigating judge requested it here and on January 12, 2010, the Court of Appeal ordered the lifting on the grounds that the principles of administration of justice and ascertainment of the material truth should prevail over private interests. Ms. Brito Ferrinho Bexiga Villa-Nova's appeal before the Supreme Court was declared inadmissible. Therefore, she complained of a breach of Articles 6, 8, and 13 of the ECHR.

The ECtHR held that the consultation of her personal bank statements had constituted an interference with her right to respect for professional confidentiality, which fell within the scope of private life. That interference was in accordance with the law and pursued a legitimate aim. However, as argued by Baker,[20] it could not be regarded as necessary in a democratic society since the lack of procedural guarantees and effective judicial control meant that there was not a fair balance between the demands of the general interest and the requirements of the protection of the applicant's right to respect for her private life. As observed by the ECtHR, she had not been involved in the proceedings at any time and had thus been unable to submit her arguments.

B. AUTOMATIC EXCHANGE OF INFORMATION AND THE RIGHT TO DATA PROTECTION

On the other hand, as discussed by Baker and Pistone, in the case of AEoI, the issues of taxpayer protection are different. Here, another fundamental right, separate and distinct from the right to privacy, comes into play: the right to data protection.

The protection of personal data is enshrined in several EU legal sources, including the treaties establishing the European Union.[21] However, the central piece of legislation protecting the right to data protection is Directive 95/46/EC,[22] which will be replaced by a General Data Protection Regulation.

In particular, according to Article 6(1) of the Directive 95/46/EC, personal data must be: (1) processed fairly and lawfully (legal basis); (2) collected for specified, explicit, and legitimate purposes and not further processed in a way incompatible with those purposes (purpose limitation); (3) adequate, relevant, and not excessive in relation to the purposes for which they are collected and/or further processed (necessity and proportionality); (4) accurate and, where necessary, kept up to date; (5) kept in a form which permits identification of data subjects for no longer than is necessary for the purposes for which the data were collected or for which they are further processed (data retention).[23]

In addition, personal data may be processed only if the data subject has unambiguously given his consent, which means "any freely given specific and informed indication of his wishes by which the data subject signifies his agreement to personal data relating to him being processed."[24] Moreover, the data subject has the right of access to their own data and to have the data rectified, erased, or blocked when the processing does not comply with the provisions of the Directive, especially because of the incomplete or inaccurate nature of the data.[25]

Additional safeguards are included in Article 11 (right to be informed about the data processing and the transfer of data), Article 23 (right to receive compensation for the damage suffered as a result of an unlawful processing operation), and Article 25 ("transfer to a third country of personal data . . . may only take place if . . . the third country in question ensures an adequate level of protection"[26]).

Based on the concerns expressed by the Working Party set up under Article 29 of Directive 95/46/EC and on the recent judgments of the Court of Justice of the European Union (CJEU), namely, *Digital Rights Ireland* (Joined Cases C-293/12 and C-594/12)[27] and *Smaranda Bara* (Case C-201/14),[28] neither FATCA nor OECD CRS or DAC2 are fully compliant with the right to data protection.

In particular, under FATCA, foreign financial institutions (FFIs) are required to report to the IRS, directly or through their home government, the following information: (1) the name, address, and Taxpayer Identification Number (TIN) of each account holder which is a specified

US person and, in the case of any account holder which is a US-owned foreign entity, the name, address, and TIN of each substantial US owner of such entity; (2) the account number; (3) the account balance; (4) the gross receipts and gross withdrawals or payments from the account.[29] In a letter of June 21, 2012, the Working Party stated: ". . . FATCA must be mutually recognized as necessary from an EU perspective. This requires . . . [a] careful assessment of how FATCA's goals balance with that of . . . the right to a private and family life, i.e. *by demonstrating necessity by proving that the required data are the minimum necessary in relation to the purpose. A bulk transfer and the screening of all these data is not the best way to achieve such a goal.*"[30]

Similarly, in a letter of September 18, 2014 on CRS, the Working Party underlined that "*it is necessary to demonstrably prove the necessity of the foreseen processing and that the required data are the minimum necessary for attaining the stated purpose.*"[31] It also observed: "The practical roll-out of CRS in Europe based on existing FATCA IT solutions currently lacks adequate data protection safeguards, notwithstanding the EU proposed to amend the Directive 2011/16/EU regarding mandatory automatic exchange of information in the field of taxation. *This Directive*—which could be considered as transposition of the US FATCA and CRS in EU law—*so far falls short of data protection safeguards.*"[32]

As a consequence of these concerns, Article 25 of Directive 2011/16/EU was amended in December 2014 through Article 1(5) of Council Directive 2014/107/EU.[33] The original text of Article 25 became paragraph 1 and three new paragraphs were added:[34]

2. Reporting Financial Institutions and the competent authorities of each Member State shall be considered to be data controllers for the purposes of Directive 95/46/EC.

3. Notwithstanding paragraph 1, each Member State shall ensure that each Reporting Financial Institution under its jurisdiction informs each individual Reportable Person concerned that the information relating to him referred to in Article 8(3a) will be collected and transferred in accordance with this Directive and shall ensure that the Reporting Financial Institution provides to that individual all information that he is entitled to under its domestic legislation implementing Directive 95/46/EC in sufficient time for the individual to exercise his data protection rights and, in any case, before the Reporting Financial Institution concerned reports the information referred to in Article 8(3a) to the competent authority of its Member State of residence.

4. Information processed in accordance with this Directive shall be retained for no longer than necessary to achieve the purposes of this Directive, and in any case in accordance with each data controller's domestic rules on statute of limitations.

As argued by Baker,[35] this was a critical change for EU member states since it clarified the scope of the taxpayer's right to be informed. Under the new wording, each Reporting Financial Institution (RFI) is required to inform the taxpayer that information will be collected and transferred and to do so in sufficient time for the individual to exercise his data-protection rights (including: the right to be *informed* of the identity of the controller, the purposes of the processing, the recipients or categories of recipients of the data; the right of *access* to data and the right to have data *rectified* in case of inaccuracies).

The right to be *informed* has been recently discussed by the CJEU in *Smaranda Bara and Others*.[36] The case concerned the transfer of income data between two public bodies, including the tax administration, of a member state. The CJEU held that the transfer of data from the national tax authority to the National Health Insurance Fund, without first informing[37] the individuals concerned, was a breach of Article 10, 11, and 13 of the Data Protection Directive.[38] According to Baker,[39] this clearly has significant ramifications for the systems currently being put in place for automatic exchange of financial information in tax matters between reporting institutions and tax authorities and between tax authorities of different states.

It should be noted that the modification of December 2014 was not exempt from criticism, especially the new paragraph 4, which refers to the retention of data. According to Maryte Somare and Viktoria Wöhrer,[40] due to the lack of clear deadlines this provision does not substantially enhance data protection and is most certainly not enough to ensure the proportionality of data retention. Indeed, Article 25(4) is formulated in a way which does not allow one to objectively determine the data-retention period as required by the CJEU in *Digital Rights Ireland*[41] and the Working Party's Guidelines.[42]

However, in the authors' opinion, the most critical aspect is that all these forms of AEoI do not request the existence of indicia of unlawful behavior of taxpayers. Borrowing the words of CJEU in *Digital Rights Ireland*, AEoI applies even to persons for whom there is no evidence capable of suggesting that their conduct might have a link, even indirect or remote, with tax evasion. Thus, AEoI could be considered disproportionate since it fails to narrow down the reporting obligations to individuals suspected of tax evasion. What can be done?

The European Data Protection Supervisor (EDPS) in its opinion on the EU-Switzerland agreement on AEoI argued that:

> [T]he Agreement should have included provisions and criteria that explicitly link the reporting of personal data concerning financial accounts to possible tax evasion and that exempt low-risk accounts from reporting. In this respect, such criteria should be applicable *ex ante* to determine which accounts (and which information) would need to be reported. Only at that stage—once the relevance (or irrelevance) of the reporting for the purpose of countering tax evasion has been established—the electronic search might help determining the residence of the account holder.[43]

In this regard, the authors suggest an enhancement of due diligence procedures through the elaboration of a list of subjective and objective "*red flag indicators*" as provided under the AML. That list would facilitate the detection of those accounts that present a high risk of tax evasion. Only once the likelihood of tax evasion has been assessed, would FFIs be required to report those accounts.

III. COUNTRY-BY-COUNTRY REPORTING
AND CORPORATE TAX PRIVACY

A. PUBLIC DISCLOSURE OF COUNTRY-BY-COUNTRY REPORTING: A MATTER OF PRIVACY OR COMPETITIVE DISADVANTAGES?

This second part is dedicated to the interaction between country-by-country reporting (CbCR) and corporate tax privacy. The first author has argued elsewhere that the question whether the results of CbCR should be made public has nothing to do with privacy.[44]

Corporations are legal entities, and the concept of privacy does not apply to them.[45] As argued by Cockfield and MacArthur,[46] corporate taxpayer privacy concerns are more concrete in relation to the tax information of small closely held private corporations. The argument is that small privately held corporations merely serve as the alter egos of their owners.[47] Their business matters are inextricably intermingled with the individual shareholder's personal financial affairs.[48] Therefore, revealing the taxes paid by a small, "mom-and-pop" closely held corporation might be viewed as violating legitimate expectations of privacy by its shareholders.[49] But this is not the case here, since multinational enterprise (MNE) groups with annual consolidated group revenue less than EUR 750 million will be exempted from the general filing requirement.[50]

B. THREE (UN)ANSWERED QUESTIONS ON CBCR

Instead, whether or not large multinationals should be required to publish CbCR depends on the following questions:

1. Does CbCR include information that could reasonably be regarded as confidential, in that revealing it will lead competitors to discover future business plans (like the APAs[51])?
2. Do these costs overcome the advantage of making CbCR public, which is to increase pressure on companies to align their reported profits with the location in which they pay taxes?
3. For US-based multinationals, some of the information included in CbCR is already public (e.g., profits reported by subsidiaries in tax havens). Would making CbCR public change significantly the information that is already publicly available?

With regard to the first question, it should be noted that, under the current EU Commission proposal,[52] MNEs will be required to disclose to the public significant financial information, including: (1) the nature of the activities, (2) the number of employees, (3) the total net turnover made, which includes the turnover made with third parties as well as between companies within a group, (4) the profit made before tax, (5) the amount of income tax due in the country as a reason of the profits made in the current year in that country, (6) the amount of tax actually paid during that year, and (7) the accumulated earnings.[53] As has already been argued,[54] none of the financial information mandated by CbCR, in either the maximalist or the minimalist version, would constitute a trade, business, or other secret as defined by the OECD in the commentary on the model treaty. In the authors' opinion, the information that could reasonably constitute a commercial or trade secret and put the corporation at a competitive disadvantage are included in the *Master*[55] or *Local File*.[56] For example, MNEs will be required to generally describe in the master file their overall strategy for development, ownership, and exploitation of intangibles, including location of principal R&D facilities and location of R&D management, as well as important drivers of business profit and important business restructuring transactions, acquisitions, and divestitures occurring during the fiscal year.[57] However, neither the OECD Action 13 report nor the EU Commission proposal makes such information publicly accessible.[58] Nonetheless, the master file will be available to all relevant tax administrations of the countries where the MNE had operations, but on a confidential basis.[59] Thus, concerns raised over public disclosure of the data reported in the CbCR template seem to be exaggerated and are based more on fear than on reality.

With regard to the second question, do the costs outweigh the benefits of making CbCR public? Evers, Meier, and Spengel argued that CbCR is associated with several direct and implicit costs.[60] According to their opinion, direct costs would arise for adjusting the existing financial reporting systems to the requirements of CbCR.[61] On the other hand, implicit costs of CbCR would primarily stem from disclosing the information to the public.[62] Publishing commercially sensitive information could harm firm competitiveness. Finally, they argued that CbCR could be potentially associated with the danger of double taxation.[63] Tax authorities of source jurisdictions might use the newly disclosed data to support their own claims towards MNEs[64] or adopt anti-abuse provisions.[65]

The authors believe that CbCR requirements would not impose any significant additional burdens on MNEs. As argued by Richard Murphy, attribution of profits to countries already has to take place for tax purposes and, under existing financial reporting standards, the reporting of geographically delineated data is already permitted.[66] One major company suggested that the additional costs incurred by MNEs to prepare data for CbCR would be very small.[67]

In relation to implicit costs, the authors do not believe that public disclosure of CbCR will harm competitiveness. As noted by the All-Party Parliamentary Group (APPG) on Responsible Tax, this argument is unproven.[68] In July 2013, Directive 2013/36/EU, the so-called Capital Requirements Directive IV (CRD IV) was adopted. Its Article 89 introduces a new country-by-country public reporting obligation for banks and investment firms. From January 1, 2015, these institutions will have to report annually, for each country in which they have an establishment, data on: (1) name(s), activities, geographical location; (2) turnover; (3) number of employees on a full-time equivalent basis; (4) profit or loss before tax; (5) tax on profit or loss and; (6) public subsidies received. It also requires the Commission to conduct a general assessment as regards potential negative economic consequences of the public disclosure of country-by-country data, including the impact on competitiveness, investment, and credit availability and the stability of the financial system. Therefore, the Commission awarded a study to PwC on the potential positive and negative consequences of CbCR, including a stakeholder survey and an econometric analysis of the impact of disclosure quality on capital markets outcomes. The majority of respondents (53 percent) felt that Article 89 would have *no impact on the competitiveness of EU institutions.*[69]

In conclusion, as argued by Pomp, opponents of public disclosure have never been able to illustrate how knowing the amount of tax paid or credit claimed reveals anything of competitive value.[70] Moreover, in those situations, timing is also very important.[71]

In contrast to these potential costs, someone argued that CbCR might solve the key issue of general lack of information and, most importantly, have a deterrent effect.[72] In particular, in his comments on OECD Discussion Draft of January 2014, Antony Ting stated: "[I]f a MNE knows that it will have to disclose the detailed country-by-country information to tax administrations, *it may have less incentive to undertake aggressive BEPS transactions.*"[73] Proponents of public disclosure of corporate tax returns have made a similar argument. They argue that disclosure will promote increased tax compliance, either by discouraging outright evasion or because companies *might become less inclined to take aggressive tax positions such as tax shelters that are arguably within the rules.*[74] In this regard, a study by Joel Slemrod, Thor O. Thoresen, and Erlend E. Bø, found an approximately 3 percent average increase in reported income among business owners when Norway made its returns searchable online in 2001.[75] On the other hand, Hasegawa et al. argue that in the Japanese case, companies' taxable income did not decline after the end of the public disclosure system in 2004.[76]

CbCR could also be a very effective tool in increasing MNEs' accountability. Customers could put pressure on multinationals to increase tax payments in different consumer markets.[77] Despite what Evers et al. argued,[78] MNEs publicly accused of having engaged in aggressive tax planning suffer from damage to their reputation.[79] This is what happened with the Starbucks saga in the United Kingdom. Thousands of customers were angry over revelations[80] that it has paid only £8.6 million in tax in fifteen years of trading in the United Kingdom on revenue of more than £3.4 billion.[81] Starbucks reduced its taxable profit through:[82] (1) an intercompany loan between the US Starbucks business and the UK Starbucks with the interest rate set at a higher rate than any similar loan; (2) a 4.7 percent payment for intellectual property (which was 6 percent until recently) that the UK company paid to the Netherlands-based company, and (3) a 20 percent markup that the Netherlands-based company paid to the Swiss-based company on its coffee-buying operations. Within a few days of the publication of the parliamentary investigative committee report,[83] Starbucks announced that it would voluntarily pay £20 million in UK corporate tax over 2013 and 2014.[84] Finally, as argued by Christiana HJI Panayi, yielding to international pressure, Amazon changed its business structure so that from May 1, 2015, it would record sales made to customers in the United Kingdom and some other jurisdictions in those jurisdictions rather than in Luxembourg.[85]

With regard to the third and last question, as noted above for US-based multinationals, some of the information included in CbCR is already public, e.g., profits reported by subsidiaries in tax havens.[86] Citizens for Tax Justice recently stated that the majority of US offshore subsidiary profits were earned in ten low-tax jurisdictions, namely, Netherlands, Ireland, Bermuda, Luxembourg, Cayman Islands, Switzerland, Bahamas, Singapore, Hong Kong, and British Virgin Islands.[87] Using data from World Bank, CTJ estimates that US affiliate corporate profits were 1,884 percent of Bermuda's GDP and 1,313 percent of Cayman Islands' GDP in 2012.[88] In the same vein, a study by Keightley and Stupak, based on data from the US Bureau of Economic Analysis (BEA), estimates that seven tax-preferred jurisdictions (Netherlands, Ireland, Luxembourg, Bermuda, Switzerland, Singapore, and UK Caribbean Islands) accounted for 50.1 percent of all profits reported as being earned outside the United States, in comparison to the 14.6 percent being reported in the three non-tax-preferred jurisdictions (United Kingdom, Canada, and Norway).[89] Interestingly, they argue that there is no connection or, in other words, there is a large discrepancy between the location where US MNEs report profits with that of their physical presence (where their employees and tangible capital are located).[90] This may be an indication of profit shifting by US MNEs. The authors believe that public CbCR will increase pressure on companies to align their reported profits with the location in which they are truly and economically active. Therefore, it is likely that a reduction in the share of profits reported by subsidiaries in low-tax jurisdictions might occur.

IV. CONCLUSION

Tax law has always been considered somehow deeply different from other areas of law, mainly because of the public nature of the relationship between the taxpayer and the tax authority. This exceptional attitude toward tax has also had unfortunate effects on the applicability of basic procedural guarantees to tax proceedings, such as the right to be heard before any individual measure which adversely affects a person is taken. *"Taxes are the lifeblood of government and their prompt and certain availability an imperious need,"* ruled the Supreme Court in *Bull v. U.S.*[91] Thus,

> the usual procedure for the recovery of debts is reversed in the field of taxation. Payment precedes defense, and the burden of proof, normally on the claimant, is shifted to the taxpayer. The assessment supersedes the pleading, proof, and judgment necessary in an action at law, and has the force of such a judgment. The ordinary defendant stands in judgment only after a hearing. *The taxpayer*

often is afforded his hearing after judgment and after payment, and his only redress for unjust admin-
istrative action is the right to claim restitution.[92]

This exceptional view of tax is also reflected in EoIR and AEoI. States are compelled to re-strict taxpayers' rights to the extent required in order safeguard their important financial interest. However, in the authors' opinion, recent judgments of the European Courts have eroded this ob-ligation by striking down those measures that did not provide a *proportionate balance* between the legitimate interest of the state and the conflicting rights of individuals. Legal challenges might arise from the current different versions of AEoI mainly because of the massive and in-discriminate collection of data. Absent any indicia of unlawful behavior, AEoI goes *beyond what is strictly necessary* to achieve the goal of fighting against offshore tax evasion.

On the other hand, the second part of this chapter was dedicated to the intersection of corporate privacy and public disclosure of CbCR. The US Supreme Court made it clear that corporations cannot claim equality with individuals regarding right to privacy. Therefore, whether the results of CbCR should be made public has nothing to do with privacy but rather turns on three (un)answered questions. First, the information disclosed under CbCR does not appear to be commercially confidential. Second, numerous existing financial reporting systems are already technically able to provide country-specific data. Third, there will be no negative impact on the competitiveness of reporting institutions. Therefore, no significant additional burden would be imposed on MNEs by making CbCR public. Finally, as the first author argued elsewhere,[93] the threat of revealing corporate tax information could be a very effective in curbing corporate tax shelters and other abusive arrangements designed to eliminate corporate tax. The mere threat of public disclosure is likely to do more than an audit to keep large corporations from crossing the line that differentiates between reasonable tax planning and unduly aggressive tax minimization. That is a line that is hard to define precisely. The potential for public disclo-sure would help keep corporations on the safe side of that line. Sunshine is, as Justice Brandeis once said, the best disinfectant.

NOTES

1. *Bull v. United States*, 295 U.S. 247, 259 (1935).
2. *Yeong Yae Yun v. United States*, No. CV 00-06975 MMM BQRx, 2000 U.S. Dist. LEXIS 20188, at *12.
3. Ibid. at *4.
4. ECtHR, *G.S.B. v. Switzerland*, Appl. no. 28601/11, Judgment of 22 Dec. 2015. All ECtHR decisions are available online at http://hudoc.echr.coe.int/. The UBS scandal arose after the United States sought to investigate a multibillion dollar tax evasion scheme involving the Swiss bank.
5. Ibid. at para. 93.
6. X. Oberson, *International Exchange of Information in Tax Matters, Towards Global Transparency* (2015), at 238; J. M. Calderón Carrero and A. Quintas Seara, 'The Taxpayer's Right of Defence in Cross-Border Exchange-of-Information Procedures', 68 *Bulletin for International Taxation* (2014), 9, at 504: "Those 'participation rights' include: the notification of the request for information to the taxpayer; the right to be heard before transmitting the information to the requesting state; and the right to challenge the decision of the requested state concerning the transmission of the informa-tion gathered."
7. P. Baker, 'Taxation and the European Convention on Human Rights', 40 *European Taxation* (2000), 8, at 326: "The only point one might make with respect to the exchange of information relates to the question of whether there is adequate judicial supervision of exchange under the EC Directive

or under a tax treaty. Though practice varies from country to country, in most countries a tax-payer is not informed that information which has been gathered by one revenue authority is being exchanged with the authorities of another country. *In the absence of notification, the taxpayer is in no position to challenge the exchange of information.* Bearing in mind the decision in *Funke* with respect to the importance of judicial safeguards on infringements of the right of privacy, *one won-ders whether the absence of any opportunity to challenge an exchange of information might constitute a breach of the Convention.*" (emphasis added).

8. Oberson, *supra* note 6, at 238–242: "... absent rights of defense in the requested State, based for instance on the 'fact gathering' doctrine, the taxpayer will in our view not enjoy an effective right of protection."

9. P. Baker and P. Pistone, 'The Practical Protection Of Taxpayers' Fundamental Rights', *in* International Fiscal Association, 100B *Cahiers De Droit Fiscal International* (2015), at 60, notes 220–221.

10. ECtHR, *M.N. And Others v. San Marino*, Appl. no. 28005/12, Judgment of 7 Oct. 2015.

11. ECtHR, *Brito Ferrinho Bexiga Villa-Nova v. Portugal*, Appl. no. 69436/10, Judgment of 1 Mar. 2016; see Press Release, Registrar of the Court, Tax Authorities' Consultation of Lawyer's Bank Accounts Amounted to an Interference With Her Right to Respect for Private Life (1 Dec. 2015), available online at http://hudoc.echr.coe.int/eng-press#%20 (last visited 26 May 2017). For a comment on these two cases, see P. Baker, 'Some Recent Decisions of the European Court of Human Rights on Tax Matters (and Related Decisions of the European Court of Justice)', 56 *European Taxation* (2016), 8, at 342–351.

12. ECtHR, *M.N. And Others v. San Marino*, Appl. no. 28005/12, Judgment of 7 Oct. 2015, at para. 13: "... an *exequatur* decision may only be challenged by a person who is involved in the investi-gation being carried out by the requested authority, or by a third party who is not investigated but who was been subjected to the measure."

13. Ibid. at para. 27: "... the applicants were indirectly involved by the effects that the evidence col-lected through the enforcement of the *exequatur* decision could possibly have within the legal system of the Italian state."

14. Ibid. at para. 55.

15. Ibid. at para. 74.

16. Ibid. para. 75.

17. Ibid. at para. 76.

18. Ibid. at para. 83. See also para. 79: "... the applicant ... only became officially aware of the exe-quatur decision and its implementation ... more than a year after the measure was ordered"; para. 80: "... there is no immediate reason why term 'interested persons' in Article 30.3 of Law no. 104/2009 should be interpreted as referring solely to persons affected by the order such as the charged and the owners or possessors of the banking and fiduciary institutes/establishments but not to the applicant, who was also affected by the measure"; para. 81: "... the Government have not shown, by means of examples or effective and substantiated argumentation, that [an ordinary civil remedy] could have examined the applicant's challenges to the exequatur decision in a timely procedure, or that it could have, if necessary, annulled the said order or its consequences in respect of the applicant."

19. ECtHR, *Brito Ferrinho Bexiga Villa-Nova v. Portugal*, Appl. no. 69436/10, Judgment of 1 Dec. 2015.

20. Baker, *supra* note 7, at 349.

21. Art. 16, Treaty on the Functioning of the European Union (TFEU): "1. Everyone has the right to the protection of personal data concerning them. 2. The European Parliament and the Council, acting in accordance with the ordinary legislative procedure, shall lay down the rules relating to the pro-tection of individuals with regard to the processing of personal data by Union institutions, bodies, offices and agencies, and by the Member States when carrying out activities which fall within the scope of Union law, and the rules relating to the free movement of such data. Compliance with these rules shall be subject to the control of independent authorities. The rules adopted on the basis of this Article shall be without prejudice to the specific rules laid down in Article 39 of the Treaty on European Union"; Art. 8, Charter of Fundamental Rights of the European Union: "1. Everyone has the right to the protection of personal data concerning him or her. 2. Such data must

be processed fairly for specified purposes and on the basis of the consent of the person concerned or some other legitimate basis laid down by law. Everyone has the right of access to data which has been collected concerning him or her, and the right to have it rectified. 3. Compliance with these rules shall be subject to control by an independent authority."

22. Directive 95/46/EC of the European Parliament and of the Council of 24 October 1995 on the protection of individuals with regard to the processing of personal data and on the free movement of such data, OJ 1995 L 281/31.

23. Ibid.

24. Ibid. Art 2(h).

25. Ibid. Art 12(b).

26. Ibid. Art 25(1).

27. European Court of Justice, Joined Cases (C-293/12 and C-594/12), *Digital Rights Ireland Ltd* and *Kärntner Landesregierung and others* (Grand Chamber), 8 Apr. 2014.

28. European Court of Justice, Case C-201/14, *Smaranda Bara and Others v. Presidentele Casei Nationale de Asigurari de Sanatate and Others*, Judgment of the Court (Third Chamber), 1 Oct. 2015.

29. I.R.C §1471(c)(1).

30. Letter from Jacob Kohnstamm, Chairman of the Article 29 Data Protection Working Party, to Heinz Zourek, Director General of Taxation and Customs Union, European Commission, 21 June 2016, available online at http://ec.europa.eu/justice/data-protection/article-29/documentation/other-document/files/2012/20120621_letter_to_taxud_fatca_en.pdf, at para. 8.3 (emphasis added) (last visited 13 Sept. 2017).

31. Annex to letter from Isabelle Falque-Pierrotin, Chairwoman of the Article 29 Data Protection Working Party, to OECD, G20, European Commission, European Parliament, Council of the European Union, 18 Sept. 2014, available online at http://ec.europa.eu/justice/data-protection/article-29/documentation/other-document/index_en.htm#maincontentSec4 (emphasis added) (last visited 13 Sept. 2017).

32. Letter from Isabelle Falque-Pierrotin, Chairwoman of the Article 29 Data Protection Working Party, to OECD, G20, European Commission, European Parliament, Council of the European Union, 18 Sept. 2014, available online at http://ec.europa.eu/justice/data-protection/article-29/documentation/other-document/index_en.htm#maincontentSec4 (emphasis added) (last visited 13 Sept. 2017).

33. Council Directive 2014/107/EU of 9 December 2014 amending Directive 2011/16/EU as regards mandatory exchange of information in the field of taxation, OJ 2014 L 359/1.

34. Ibid. Art 1(5).

35. P. Baker, 'Privacy Rights in an Age of Transparency: A European Perspective', *Tax Notes International* (9 May 2016), at 586.

36. Case C-201/14, *Smaranda Bara and Others v. Presidentele Casei Nationale de Asigurari de Sanatate and Others*, Judgment of the Court (Third Chamber), 1 Oct. 2015.

37. Ibid. at para. 74: ". . . the requirement to inform the data subjects about the processing of their personal data, which guarantees transparency of all processing, is all the more important since it affects the exercise by the data subjects of their right of access to the data being processed, referred to in Article 12 of Directive 95/46, and their right to object to the processing of those data, set out in Article 14 of that directive."

38. Ibid. at para. 34: "It follows that the requirement of fair processing of personal data laid down in Article 6 of Directive 95/46 requires a public administrative body to inform the data subjects of the transfer of those data to another public administrative body for the purpose of their processing by the latter in its capacity as recipient of those data."

39. Baker, *supra* note 7, at 351.

40. M. Somare and V. Wöhrer, 'Automatic Exchange of Financial Information under the Directive on Administrative Cooperation in the Light of the Global Movement towards Transparency', 43 *Intertax* (2015), 12, at 812; S. Moreno González, 'The Automatic Exchange of Tax Information and the Protection of Personal Data in the European Union: Reflections on the Latest Jurisprudential and Normative Advances', 25(3) *EC Tax Review* (2016), 146, at 153: ". . . in our opinion, the absence

of clear time frames does not substantially improve the protection of data and, in light of the Digital Rights Ireland case . . . could be insufficient to guarantee the principle of proportionality."

41. Joined Cases C-293/12 and C-594/12 *Digital Rights Ireland and Others v. Minister for Communications, Marine and Natural Resources and Others*, Judgment of the Court (Grand Chamber), 8 Apr. 2014, at paras. 63 and 64: ". . . Article 6 of Directive 2006/24 requires that those data be retained for a period of at least six months, *without any distinction* being made between the categories of data set out in Article 5 of that directive on the basis of their possible usefulness for the purposes of the objective pursued or according to the persons concerned. Furthermore, that period is set at between a minimum of 6 months and a maximum of 24 months, *but it is not stated that the determination of the period of retention must be based on objective criteria in order to ensure that is limited to what is strictly necessary.*" (emphasis added).

42. Article 29 Data Protection Working Party, *Guidelines For Member States On The Criteria To Ensure Compliance With Data Protection Requirements In The Context Of The Automatic Exchange Of Personal Data For Tax Purposes*, 16 Dec. 2015, available online at http://ec.europa.eu/justice/data-protection/article-29/documentation/opinion-recommendation/files/2015/wp234_en.pdf, at 7 (last visited 19 May 2017).

43. European Data Protection Supervisor, *Opinion Of The EDPS On The EU-Switzerland Agreement On The Automatic Exchange Of Tax Information*, 8 July 2015, available online at https://edps.europa.eu/sites/edp/files/publication/15-07-08_eu_switzerland_en.pdf, at 5 (last visited 26 May 2017).

44. See, e.g., R. S. Avi-Yonah, 'Country by Country Reporting and Corporate Privacy: Some Unanswered Questions', 8(1) *Columbia Journal of Tax Law—Tax Matters* (2016), 1.

45. See *Hale v. Henkel*, 201 U.S. 43, 74–75 (1906): "Conceding that the witness was an officer of the corporation under investigation, and that he was entitled to assert the rights of the corporation with respect to the production of its books and papers, we are of the opinion that *there is a clear distinction in this particular between an individual and a corporation, and that the latter has no right to refuse to submit its books and papers for an examination at the suit of the State.* The individual may stand upon his constitutional rights as a citizen . . . Upon the other hand, the corporation is a creature of the State. It is presumed to be incorporated for the benefit of the public. It receives certain special privileges and franchises, and holds them subject to the laws of the State and the limitations of its charter . . . It would be a strange anomaly to hold that a State, having chartered a corporation to make use of certain franchises, could not in the exercise of its sovereignty inquire how these franchises had been employed, and whether they had been abused, and demand the production of the corporate books and papers for that purpose"; *California Bankers Ass'n v. Shultz*, 416 U.S. 21, 65–66 (U.S. Cal. 1974): "While they may and should have protection from unlawful demands made in the name of public investigation, *corporations can claim no equality with individuals in the enjoyment of a right to privacy.* They are endowed with public attributes. They have a collective impact upon society, from which they derive the privilege of acting as artificial entities. The Federal Government allows them the privilege of engaging in interstate commerce. Favors from government often carry with them an enhanced measure of regulation. Even if one were to regard the request for information in this case as caused by nothing more than official curiosity, nevertheless law-enforcing agencies have a legitimate right to satisfy themselves that corporate behavior is consistent with the law and the public interest" (emphasis added); A. Cockfield and C. MacArthur, 'Country-by-Country Reporting and Commercial Confidentiality', 63(3) *Canadian Tax Journal/Revue Fiscale Canadienne* (2015), 627, at 650–651: "At the outset, it is important to note that, in Canada and elsewhere, there are often different legal conceptions of the right to privacy for individuals (natural persons) and for business entities such as corporations that are legal persons (albeit of the artificial variety). As discussed in the legal academic literature, taxpayer privacy rights tend to focus on individual rights." For a (different) European perspective, see J. Kokott and C. Sobotta, 'The Distinction Between Privacy and Data Protection in the Jurisprudence of the CJEU and the ECtHR', 3(4) *International Data Privacy Law* (2013), 222, at 225: "However, as regards the personal scope, the European Court of Justice has excluded legal persons from data protection, *though they can rely on the right to privacy.* It is difficult to base this exclusion on the wording of the Charter, as both privacy and data protection are granted to 'everyone.' However,

the definition adopted by the Luxembourg Court results from Article 2(a) and Recital 2 of the Data Protection Directive, which limit data protection to natural persons. The Convention on Data Protection seems to be more ambiguous in this regard, as it refers to 'individuals' in Article 2(a). But the similarly binding French version of the Convention uses the clearer term '*personne physique*' that also excludes legal persons." In this sense, see Joined Cases C-92/09 and C-93/09, *Volker und Markus Schecke and Eifert* [2010] ECR I-11063, at para. 53: ". . . legal persons can claim the protection of Articles 7 and 8 of the Charter in relation to such identification only in so far as the official title of the legal person identifies one or more natural persons"; para. 87: ". . . The seriousness of the breach of the right to protection of personal data manifests itself in different ways for, on the one hand, legal persons and, on the other, natural persons. It is necessary to point out in this regard that legal persons are already subject to a more onerous obligation in respect of the publication of data relating to them"; ECtHR, *Bernh Larsen Holding AS and Others v. Norway*, Appl. no. 24117/08, Final Judgment of 8 July 2013, at para. 159: "One factor that militates in favor of strict scrutiny in the present case is that the backup copy comprised all existing documents on the server, regardless of their relevance for tax assessment purposes . . . On the other hand, the fact that the measure was aimed at legal persons meant that a wider margin of appreciation could be applied than would have been the case had it concerned an individual."

46. Cockfield and MacArthur, *supra* note 45, at 654.

47. R. Pomp, 'The Disclosure of State Corporate Income Tax Data: Turning the Clock Back to the Future', 22 *Capital University Law Review* (1993), 373, at 451.

48. Ibid. at 451.

49. Ibid. at 437.

50. OECD, *Transfer Pricing Documentation and Country-by-Country Reporting, Action 13—Final Report* (2015), available online at http://dx.doi.org/10.1787/9789264241480-en, at 21 (last visited 19 May 2017): "It is believed that the exemption [. . .] which provides a threshold of EUR 750 million, will exclude approximately 85 to 90 percent of MNE groups from the requirement to file the Country-by-Country Report, but that the Country-by-Country Report will nevertheless be filed by MNE groups controlling approximately 90 percent of corporate revenues. The prescribed exemption threshold therefore represents an appropriate balancing of reporting burden and benefit to tax administrations"; see also Commission Proposal for a Directive of the European Parliament and of the Council amending Directive 2013/34/EU as Regards Disclosure of Income Tax Information by Certain Undertakings and Branches, COM (2016) 198 final (12 Apr. 2016), at 2: "This proposal focusses on corporate groups with a worldwide consolidated net turnover of more than EUR 750 million, in line with the scope of global OECD initiatives on tax transparency. The proposal does not impose any obligations on small and medium-sized companies." For these reasons, the authors believe there are similarities between the campaign against public CbCR and that against the "pink slip" provision inserted in the Revenue Act of May 10, 1934; see M. Kornhauser, 'More Historical Perspective on Publication of Corporate Returns', 96 *Tax Notes* (2002), 745, at 746: ". . . The key to the campaign's success was the same one used more than 60 years later to secure the repeal of the estate tax. *Although in both instances fewer than 10 percent of the population were affected, opponents gained support by focusing on the damage done to the 'common man' and the small businessman* . . . The campaign urged people to send [. . .] protest pink slip plus other antipublicity letters and telegrams to their congressmen. *Thousands of ordinary people who would never be touched by the publicity did so*, often using form letters and/or sending in the mock pink slip emblazoned with the refusal to pay. They protested that publicity of income tax returns would, invade their privacy, reveal business secrets, create harassing sales pitches, and increase crimes targeted at the wealthy, especially kidnapping . . ."; see also D. Lenter, D. Shackelford, and J. Slemrod, 'Public Disclosure of Corporate Tax Return Information: Accounting, Economics and Legal Issues', 56(4) *National Tax Journal* (2003), 803, at 809–810 (emphasis added).

51. K. E. Hickman, 'Should Advance Pricing Agreements be Published?', 19 *Northwestern Journal of International Law and Business* (1998–1999), 171, at 191: "Entities contemplating the advance pricing agreement process have already expressed concern over confidentiality with respect to the extensive disclosures required. To reach agreement with the IRS on the appropriate transfer pricing

methodology, a multinational corporation is required to provide *sensitive financial and proprietary technical data concerning business organization and cost structures, relationships with controlled entities, divisions of responsibility, and research and production activities.* Required publication of advance pricing agreements, even in redacted form, could result in a decrease in the number of such agreements sought and corresponding increase in audits and litigation over transfer pricing issues"; M. McIntyre, 'The Case for Public Disclosure of Advance Rulings on Transfer Pricing Methodologies', 2 *Tax Notes International* (1990), 1127.

52. Proposal for a Directive of the European Parliament and of the Council amending Directive 2013/34/EU as regards disclosure of income tax information by certain undertakings and branches, COM/2016/0198 final—2016/0107 (COD).

53. Ibid., Art. 48(c).

54. Cockfield and MacArthur, *supra* note 45, at 656.

55. OECD, *supra* note 50, at 15: "The information required in the master file provides a 'blueprint' of the MNE group and contains relevant information that can be grouped in five categories: a) the MNE group's organizational structure; b) a description of the MNE's business or businesses; c) the MNE's intangibles; d) the MNE's intercompany financial activities; and (e) the MNE's financial and tax positions."

Douglas Holtz-Eakin, former director of the Congressional Budget Office, defined the master file as the *multinational's "playbook"* since it provides: "an overview of the company's business, the global allocation of its activities and income, and its overall transfer pricing policies—a complete picture of its global operations, profit drivers, supply chains, intangibles and financing"; see D. Holtz-Eakin, 'Subsidiaries in Europe? Playbook, Please', *Wall Street Journal*, 27 Dec. 2015, available online at http://www.wsj.com/articles/subsidiaries-in-europe-playbook-please-1451259515 (last visited 23 June 2017). In the same vein, see letter from Orrin G. Hatch, Chairman, Senate Finance Committee, and Paul D. Ryan, Chairman, House Ways and Means Committee, to Jacob Lew, Secretary of the Treasury, 9 June 2015, available online at http://www.finance.senate.gov/imo/media/doc/Hatch,%20Ryan%20Call%20on%20Treasury%20to%20Engage%20Congress%20on%20OECD%20International%20Tax%20Project.pdf, at 1 (last visited 23 June 2017): "[W]e are concerned about the country-by-country (CbC) reporting standards that will contain sensitive information related to a U.S. multinational's group operations. We are also concerned that Treasury has appeared to agree that foreign governments will be able to collect the so-called 'master file' information directly from U.S. multinationals without any assurances of confidentiality or that the information collection is needed. *The master file contains information well beyond what could be obtained in public filings and that is even more sensitive for privately-held multinational companies.*" For a comment on the letter sent by Sen. Hatch and Rep. Ryan to the Secretary of the Treasury, see M. Levey, I. Gerdes, and A. Mansfield, 'The Key BEPS Action Items Causing Discussion in the United States', 44 *Intertax* (2016), 5, at 404–405. Finally, in less alarming tones, Joshua D. Blank argued that "access to the BEPS master file of multinational corporations should be restricted to participating taxing authorities rather than provided to the general public"; see J. D. Blank, 'Reconsidering Corporate Tax Privacy', 11(1) *New York University Journal of Law & Business* (2014), 31, at 105–109. Cf. Y. Brauner (arguing that CbCR must be publicly available), 'What the BEPS?', 16 *Florida Tax Review* (2014), 55, at 106; R. S. Avi-Yonah and H. Xu, 'Evaluating BEPS: A Reconsideration of the Benefits Principle and Proposal for UN Oversight', 6(2) *Harvard Business Law Review* (2016), 185 (arguing that the relevant stakeholders and the public need to have access to the MNEs' transfer pricing documentation).

56. OECD, *supra* note 50, at 15: ". . . The local file focuses on information relevant to the transfer pricing analysis related to transactions taking place between a local country affiliate and associated enterprises in different countries and which are material in the context of the local country's tax system. Such information would include relevant financial information regarding those specific transactions, a comparability analysis, and the selection and application of the most appropriate transfer pricing method. . . ."

57. Ibid. at 25.

58. Press Release, European Commission, Fact Sheet—Introducing Public Country-by-Country Reporting for Multinational Enterprises—Question & Answers, 12 Apr. 2016, available online at http://europa.eu/rapid/press-release_MEMO-16-1351_en.htm?locale=en (last visited 23 June 2017): "Public reporting does not serve the same purpose as information sharing and reporting between tax authorities. There are some types of information that are required to be shared between tax authorities, but that are not part of this latest proposal for public CbCR. EU tax authorities will receive 12 pieces of information, whereas public CbCR will consist of just seven pieces of information. EU tax authorities will receive more granular data for all third countries in which an EU company is active. They will also get from companies more complex data relating to the breakdown of a group's turnover between that made with external parties and that made solely between group entities, as well as figures for stated capital and a company's tangible assets. When it comes to public disclosure, it is important that EU citizens get information about where in the EU companies are paying taxes. Citizens also have a legitimate interest in knowing whether companies active in the EU are also active in so-called tax havens. However, demanding publicly disaggregated data for all third countries could affect companies' competitiveness and divulge information on key strategic investments in a given country. Similarly, the disclosure of turnover and purchases within a group poses a threat to multinationals in that it could divulge key information to competitors."

59. OECD, *supra* note 50, at 19: "Tax administrations should take all reasonable steps to ensure that there is no public disclosure of confidential information (trade secrets, scientific secrets, etc.) and other commercially sensitive information contained in the documentation package (master file, local file and Country-by-Country Report). Tax administrations should also assure taxpayers that the information presented in transfer pricing documentation will remain confidential. In cases where disclosure is required in public court proceedings or judicial decisions, every effort should be made to ensure that confidentiality is maintained and that information is disclosed only to the extent needed."

60. M. T. Evers, I. Meier, and C. Spengel, 'Transparency in Financial Reporting: Is Country-by-Country Reporting Suitable to Combat International Profit Shifting?', 68(6/7) *Bulletin for International Taxation* (2014), 295, at 301.

61. Ibid.

62. Ibid.

63. Ibid.

64. J. Blouin, 'Transparency and Financial Accounting', 68(6/7) *Bulletin for International Taxation* (2014), 304, at 307: "Frankly, Action 13 sounds as though it is a request for apportionment information. Unless an apportionment regime is approved, *this proposal could result in countries choosing to pursue tax claims using this information when it suits a particular country*. Countries that would not benefit from apportionment would most likely continue to pursue some arm's length principle measure of activity. Country-by-country reporting without coordination rules could simply exacerbate existing cross-jurisdictional transfer pricing conflicts." (emphasis added).

65. M. Sala, 'Country-by-Country Reporting: Potential Audit and Legislative Risks For MNEs', 73 *Tax Notes International* (2014), 1127, at 1129: "Consider, for example, an auditor's review of the manufacturing subsidiary of an MNE. The entity has typically collected nominal margins on the production of merchandise for distribution to sales affiliates in other jurisdictions. Under the arm's length standard, this was supportable; development of intellectual property occurred elsewhere in the organization, and no strategic or other high-value functions were performed at this location. Despite a supportable transfer price, a local country auditor will now receive a CbC template showing: • a high proportion of total headcount and/or payroll located in the manufacturing jurisdiction; • a high proportion of total enterprise tangible asset balances; and • a tax return reflecting relatively low allocation of the total enterprise's profit. Will the manufacturing country auditor, armed with apportionment like data notionally supporting greater profit allocation to the manufacturer, use these data in support of a deficiency notice? In the longer term, will these jurisdictions adopt antiabuse provisions using these data to bring taxable income in line with 'economic activity'?"

66. R. Murphy, *Country-by-Country Reporting—Holding Multinational Corporations to Account Wherever They Are*, Task Force on Financial Integrity and Economic Development (2009), available online at http://www.financialtransparency.org/wp-content/uploads/2015/04/Final_CbyC_Report_Published.pdf, at 21 (last visited 19 May 2017); Cockfield and MacArthur, *supra* note 45, at 646: "MNEs already need to calculate taxable profits in most countries where they operate in order to comply with local tax laws. Hence, they already keep records and disclose taxable profits and taxes paid to the relevant tax authorities. In addition, certain countries mandate the public disclosure of such information by public corporations."

67. Murphy, *supra* note 66, at 28; Transparency International et al., *Why Public Country-by-Country Reporting for Large Multinationals Is a Must*, 24 Feb. 2016, available online at http://www.transparencyinternational.eu/wp-content/uploads/2016/03/Joint_Civil_Society_QA_pCBCR-2016.pdf, at 6–7 (last visited 19 May 2017): "Her Majesty's Revenues & Customs (HMRC) in the United Kingdom did an assessment of the implementation costs for businesses of CbCR and found that 'one-off costs are estimated as negligible, with annual costs to businesses affected by the measure of £0.2 million'. These are not significant costs for most transnational enterprises and rate as insignificant when compared to the likely benefits of increased transparency."

68. The All-Party Parliamentary Group: Responsible Tax, *A More Responsible Global Tax System or a 'Sticking Plaster'? An Examination of the OECD's Base Erosion and Profit Shifting (BEPS) Process and Recommendations* (2016), available online at https://www.appgresponsibletax.org.uk/publications/, at 9 (last visited 19 May 2017).

69. European Commission, *General Assessment Of Potential Economic Consequences of Country-by-Country Reporting Under CRD IV* (2014), available online at: https://www.pwc.com/gx/en/eu-institutions-services/pdf/pwc-cbcr-report-en.pdf, at 9 (last visited 19 May 2017): "The fact that three of the fourteen GSIBs have published their Article 89 disclosures in full in 2014 would suggest that they are not overly concerned that there will be a detrimental effect on their competitiveness. While many stakeholders recognized that there is a compliance cost for firms in complying with Article 89, it was generally felt not to be significant when compared to the overall cost of the wider regulatory compliance burdens faced by the reporting institutions. The compliance cost associated with Article 89 therefore seems unlikely to disadvantage reporting institutions significantly compared to non-reporting institutions."

70. Pomp, *supra* note 47.

71. Ibid. at 439: ". . . even if this information were relevant in the abstract, it is unlikely to be available in a timely-enough fashion to be very useful. For information to be valuable, a business needs to know yesterday what a competitor is going to do tomorrow . . . Yesterday's information obtained tomorrow is worthless to a competitor."

72. M. A. Grau Ruiz, 'Country-by-Country Reporting: The Primary Concerns Raised by a Dynamic Approach', 68(10) *Bulletin for International Taxation* (2014), 557, at 559; OECD, *Public Comments Received Volume I: Letters to A to C—Discussion Draft on Transfer Pricing Documentation and CbC Reporting*, 23 Feb. 2014, available online at http://www.oecd.org/ctp/transfer-pricing/volume1.pdf, at 65–66 (last visited 19 May 2017).

73. OECD, *supra* note 72, at 66.

74. Lenter, Shackelford, and Slemrod, *supra* note 50, at 820.

75. J. Slemrod, T. Thoresen, and E. Bø, 'Taxes on the Internet: Deterrence Effects of Public Disclosure', 7(1) *American Economic Journal: Economic Policy* (2015), 36.

76. M. Hasegawa et al., *The Effect of Public Disclosure on Reported Taxable Income: Evidence from Individuals and Corporations in Japan*, 12 Mar. 2012, available online at http://ssrn.com/abstract=1653948, at 29 (last visited 19 May 2017). Nonetheless as the first author argued elsewhere: "this does not mean that US payments would remain the same if disclosure were adopted. There are good reasons to suspect that Japanese corporations are less aggressive (with or without disclosure) vis a vis the Japanese National Tax Administration than US corporations are toward the IRS; Japan did not have a corporate tax shelter phenomenon like the US did"; R. S. Avi-Yonah and A. Siman, 'The One Percent Solution: Corporate Tax Returns Should be Public (and How to Get There)', 73 *Tax Notes International* (2014), 627, at 627–628.

77. Evers, Meier, and Spengel, *supra* note 60, at 301.

78. Ibid. at 302.

79. A. Christians, 'How Starbucks Lost Its Social License—And Paid £20 Million to Get It Back', 71 *Tax Notes International* (2013), 637, at 639 (". . . But the message from the OECD in its base erosion and profit shifting project and the response from professionals in the U.S. tax community are that *reputational risk is a very real phenomenon facing multinationals if the public judges them to be too successful in reducing their tax bills.* Starbucks's experience overseas demonstrates that *ignoring reputational risk carries a potentially high cost: acquiescence to the unpredictable and uncontrollable terms of a social license to operate*.") (emphasis added).

80. T. Bergin, *Special Report: How Starbucks Avoids U.K. Taxes*, 15 Oct. 2012, available online at http://uk.reuters.com/article/uk-britain-starbucks-tax-idUKBRE89E0EW20121015 (last visited 19 May 2017)

81. J. Thompson and V. Houlder, *Starbucks Faces Boycott Calls Over Tax Affairs*, 17 Oct. 2012, available online at http://www.ft.com/cms/s/0/5cd14dcc-187f-11e2-8705-00144feabdc0.html #axzz4IMnXYSkw (last visited 23 June 2017).

82. E. Kleinbard, 'Through a Latte Darkly: Starbucks's Stateless Income Planning', 139 *Tax Notes* (2013), 1515.

83. H. M. Revenue and Customs, *Public Accounts Committee—Nineteenth Report*, 28 Nov. 2012, available online at http://www.publications.parliament.uk/pa/cm201213/cmselect/cmpubacc/716/71602.htm (last visited 23 June 2017).

84. V. Houlder, J. Pickard, L. Lucas, and B. Jopson, *Starbucks to Pay £20m U.K. Corporate Tax*, 7 Dec. 2012, available online at https://www.ft.com/content/ac97bb1e-3fa5-11e2-b0ce-00144feabdc0 (last visited 23 June 2017).

85. C. Panayi, *Advanced Issues in International and European Tax Law* (2015); L. Fleisher and S. Schechner, *Amazon Changes Tax Practices in Europe Amid Investigations*, 24 May 2015, available online at http://www.wsj.com/articles/amazon-changes-tax-practices-in-europe-amid-investigations-1432480170 (last visited 19 May 2017).

86. United States Internal Revenue Service, *SOI Tax Stats—Controlled Foreign Corporations*, available online at https://www.irs.gov/uac/soi-tax-stats-controlled-foreign-corporations (last visited 23 June 2017). Data taken from Form 5471, Schedule C.

87. Citizens for Tax Justice, *American Corporations Tell IRS the Majority of Their Offshore Profits Are in 10 Tax Havens*, 7 Apr. 2016, available online at http://ctj.org/pdf/corpoffshore0416.pdf, at 1 (last visited 19 May 2017): "Recently released data from the Internal Revenue Service show that U.S. corporations claim that 59 percent of their foreign subsidiaries' pretax worldwide income is being earned in ten tiny tax havens."

88. Ibid: "Amazingly, American corporations reported to the IRS that the profits their subsidiaries earned in 2012 (the latest year for which data are available) in Bermuda, the Cayman Islands, the Bahamas and Luxembourg were greater than the entire gross domestic product (GDP) of those nations in that year. For example, in Bermuda, U.S. corporations claimed they earned more than $18 for each $1 of actual GDP."

89. M. P. Keightley and J. M. Stupak, Congressional Research Service, R44013, Corporate Tax Base Erosion and Profit Shifting (BEPS): An Examination of the Data (30 Apr. 2015), at 4–5.

90. Ibid. at 6: "While accounting for 50% of reported profits reported worldwide, 5% of employees and 11% of property can be attributed to the tax-preferred country group. In contrast, the three non-tax-preferred countries of Canada, Norway, and the United Kingdom account for 20% of employees and 29% of property held by American MNCs worldwide"; K. A. Clausing, *The Effect of Profit Shifting on the Corporate Tax Base in the United States and Beyond*, 17 June 2016, available online at http://ssrn.com/abstract=2685442, at 7–8 (last visited 19 May 2017): "The U.S. Bureau of Economic Analysis (BEA) does annual surveys of U.S. based multinational firms and their affiliated firms abroad. These data indicate a large discrepancy between the physical operations of U.S. multinational firm affiliates abroad and the locations in which they report their income. For example, Figure 1 shows the top locations of U.S. multinational firm affiliate gross profits in 2012; gross profits are net income with foreign income tax payments added. Of the top nine locations, seven of them

are tax havens with effective tax rates less than 5%: Netherlands, Ireland, Luxembourg, Bermuda, Switzerland, Singapore, and the UK Caribbean Islands (including the Caymans) . . . These countries alone account for 50% of all foreign income earned by affiliates of U.S. multinational firms, but they only account for 5% of all foreign employment of such firms. Further, the economic size of these countries is quite small relative to this disproportionate profit; their combined population is less than that of Spain, or California"; G. Zucman, 'Taxing Across Borders: Tracking Personal Wealth and Corporate Profits', 28 *Journal of Economic Perspectives* (2014), 4, at 128: "So 31 percent (650/2,100) of US corporate profits were made abroad in 2013. Where do the $650 billion of foreign profits come from? The balance of payments provides a country-by-country decomposition of this total, indicating that 55 percent are made in six tax havens: The Netherlands, Bermuda, Luxembourg, Ireland, Singapore, and Switzerland."

91. 295 U.S. 247, 259 (1935).
92. Ibid. at 260.
93. Avi-Yonah and Siman, *supra* note 76, at 627–628.

CHAPTER 12

CORPORATE TAX PRIVACY AND HUMAN RIGHTS

JOSHUA D. BLANK*

I. INTRODUCTION

As one of its core missions, Google strives to empower its users to navigate vast quantities of information, whether web pages, family photos, or alternative driving routes, as quickly and as easily as possible.[1] An emphasis on achieving creative and efficient solutions pervades Google's business operations[2]—including its own tax planning. For example, during the past decade, while Google earned billions of dollars in online advertising revenue in the United States and abroad, it also minimized its global tax liabilities by deploying labyrinthine legal structures such as the "Double Irish Dutch Sandwich," in which the company's earnings in Europe, the Middle East, and Africa were distributed from an Irish subsidiary to a Dutch subsidiary to the Bermuda branch of another Irish subsidiary, where the tax rate on corporate income was zero.[3] Google is by no means alone in pursuit of lower taxes, as many other household name corporations, including Apple,[4] Starbucks,[5] and Amazon,[6] among others,[7] have deployed similar tax strategies. But because the tax returns of corporations are protected by broad tax privacy rules in the United States and other jurisdictions,[8] the surprisingly low tax burdens and specific tax-avoidance techniques of Google and a handful of other multinational corporations have entered the public consciousness not as a result of voluntary disclosures by the corporations themselves, but rather, through a combination of legislative hearings, whistleblower reports, and investigative journalism.[9]

Policymakers in the United States and around the globe have intensified their focus on corporate tax-avoidance strategies in recent years. In 2013 and 2014, for example, the US Senate Permanent Subcommittee on Investigations held high-profile hearings on profit shifting from high-tax to low-tax jurisdictions by multinational corporations,[10] estimated to cost the United States at least $90 billion in lost tax revenue annually,[11] as well as the reporting of earnings of US multinational corporations outside of the reach of the US tax system, estimated at as much as $2 trillion.[12] Internationally, in September 2015, the Organisation for Economic Co-operation and Development (OECD) issued a comprehensive package of measures to combat strategies

Tax, Inequality, and Human Rights. Philip Alston and Nikki Reisch.
© Oxford University Press 2019. Published 2019 by Oxford University Press.

that have allowed multinational corporations to artificially shift their profits to jurisdictions that impose little or even no tax liability ("Base Erosion and Profit Shifting" or BEPS).[13] In 2016, the European Commission concluded that, over a period of years, Ireland provided illegal state aid to Apple worth over $14 billion by issuing favorable advance tax rulings to the corporation.[14]

The international effort to address corporate tax avoidance is not motivated solely by a desire to ensure that corporations comply with legislative intent underlying statutory tax provisions or with judicial doctrine. Increasingly, the global focus on combating corporate tax avoidance occurs as part of the broader campaign to protect human rights.[15] As a special task force of tax and human rights experts concluded in 2013, aggressive corporate tax-avoidance strategies "have considerable negative impacts on the enjoyment of human rights"[16] by depriving governments of the resources necessary to protect "economic, social and cultural rights, and to create and strengthen the institutions that uphold civil and political rights."[17]

Proponents of this view claim that the current climate surrounding corporate tax avoidance threatens human rights for two primary reasons. First, some human rights advocates argue that by depriving governments of tax revenue that could be used for redistribution, corporate tax avoidance may increase poverty and economic inequality.[18] These results may ultimately lead to violations of human rights, ranging from the loss of adequate housing[19] to deprivation of life and physical integrity.[20] Second, because most governments, including that of the United States, do not disclose corporate tax return information publicly, human rights advocates argue that current law threatens individuals' right to access information regarding matters of public concern.[21] Without corporate tax return information, they argue, the public may not possess the information needed to understand how corporations apply the tax law in practice and to hold the government that enacted and enforces these laws accountable.[22]

In the midst of this global examination of corporate tax planning, policymakers, human rights advocates, and scholars have increasingly issued calls for greater "tax transparency" by multinational corporations and by governments. Many have posed a familiar question: should the tax returns of corporations be publicly accessible?[23]

The arguments for and against public disclosure of corporate tax returns have remained remarkably consistent throughout the past century. In the United States, while the Corporate Excise Tax of 1909 required corporate tax returns to be open to public inspection,[24] under current law, the Internal Revenue Service (IRS) is prohibited from releasing any return information of a corporation publicly.[25]

Proponents of public disclosure, ranging from President William Howard Taft[26] to present-day scholars such as Reuven Avi-Yonah,[27] Richard Pomp,[28] Joseph Thorndike,[29] and Marjorie Kornhauser,[30] assert that mandated public disclosure of corporate tax returns would increase the detection capabilities of the IRS, introduce shaming as a powerful abuse deterrent, and enhance public education and debate regarding corporate tax issues. A number of advocacy groups, such as Tax Justice Network, have argued that increased tax transparency through the public disclosure of corporate tax returns could lessen the potential for human rights abuses by discouraging the use of tax havens and other tax strategies that may exacerbate poverty and economic inequality.[31] Others, such as ActionAid, further contend that increased corporate tax transparency is essential to democratic governance.[32]

In response, opponents of corporate tax return disclosure measures typically argue that such proposals would violate equity principles by rescinding tax privacy protections from corporate taxpayers without doing the same to individual taxpayers, result in information overload rather than understandable explanations of a corporation's tax obligations to the United States and other countries, and expose trade secrets and other proprietary information, which could diminish corporations' willingness to cooperate with the taxing authority.[33] As I will argue, several of these defenses are not convincing justifications for corporate tax privacy as a result of their questionable theoretical and empirical foundations.

Throughout this debate, participants have focused exclusively on the potential reactions of a corporation's managers, shareholders, and consumers to a corporation's disclosure of its own tax return information. They have questioned, for instance, whether managers would be hesitant to deliver information to the taxing authority or decline to participate in tax-avoidance strategies if they knew others—shareholders, advocacy groups, consumers, non-US governments—could also observe these actions. There is, however, another perspective, which neither policymakers nor scholars have considered thus far: how would the ability of a corporation's stakeholders and agents to observe *other* corporations' tax return information affect the corporation's compliance with the tax law?

This chapter examines the relationship of corporate tax privacy and tax compliance from this new vantage point, which it terms the "intercorporate perspective." While policymakers, human rights advocates, and tax scholars often characterize mandatory public disclosure of corporate tax return information as an unalloyed good, this chapter reveals a different side to corporate tax privacy. As it argues, an unappreciated value of corporate tax privacy is that it can limit the pressure to pursue aggressive tax planning and reporting that corporate tax directors often face from significant shareholders, nontax managers, and even themselves. Corporate tax privacy provides the government with valuable strategic defenses by restraining the ability of a corporation's stakeholders and agents to engage in "benchmarking" and "reverse engineering," behaviors that would likely cause some tax directors to pursue more aggressive tax planning and reporting. Yet, at the same time, increased public access to certain corporate tax return information could enable the public to participate in informed debate and discussion of the corporate tax law and to question whether the government is applying the tax law to corporate taxpayers effectively and fairly.

While mandatory public disclosure measures could have the counterintuitive effect of encouraging rather than deterring corporate tax aggressiveness, a result in conflict with the objectives of many tax reform and human rights proponents, this chapter does not conclude that all corporate tax return information should receive tax privacy protections. Rather, it offers a set of guidelines, including consideration of the strategic defenses of corporate tax privacy, which will better equip policymakers, scholars, and human rights advocates to evaluate specific proposals to make corporate tax return information public.

II. WHY CORPORATE TAX PRIVACY?

Since the birth of the corporate income tax in the United States, policymakers have debated whether the tax returns of corporations should be accessible by the public. This section describes US corporate tax information that is observable from public sources today and considers the traditional arguments for and against public disclosure of corporate tax return information.

A. CORPORATE TAX RETURN INFORMATION
OBSERVABLE TODAY

Extracting information about the tax liabilities, payments and strategies of US corporations from publicly available sources is no easy task.[34] Even though publicly traded corporations are required to disclose voluminous nontax financial information in a variety of public fora, tax privacy shields nearly all tax return information from public view.

The primary sources of corporate tax return information observable today are documents filed by publicly traded corporations with the US Securities and Exchange Commission (SEC). A corporation's annual Form 10-K includes financial statements, which are governed by generally accepted accounting principles (GAAP), as interpreted by the Financial Accounting Standards Board (FASB).[35] A description of tax information that publicly traded corporations disclose in their SEC filings is presented below.

Global Effective Tax Rate. Publicly traded corporations are required to disclose their "effective tax rate" each year in their Form 10-K.[36] For example, in its 2011 Form 10-K, Google disclosed an effective tax rate of 21 percent.[37] This tax rate, however, is highly ambiguous. The figure is calculated using Google's GAAP income, not its US taxable income, and using a GAAP measure of tax expense, not a cash tax measure.[38] GAAP accounting treats certain significant items, such as municipal bond interest, goodwill, and depreciation of tangible property, differently from income tax accounting.[39] In addition, Google reports its effective tax rate on an aggregate *global*, rather than US, basis.[40]

Cash Taxes Paid. It is extraordinarily difficult for nonexpert observers, including journalists, to discern from a corporation's public filings the amount of cash taxes the corporation actually pays to any government. As the vast majority of corporations report on the "indirect method" of cash flow statements, the specific amount of cash taxes paid to the US or other governments is not apparent from SEC disclosure documents.[41]

Uncertain Tax Positions. In 2006, FASB issued Interpretation 48 of Financial Accounting Standard 109,[42] which prevents corporations from recognizing tax benefits for financial accounting purposes unless they are "more likely than not" to be upheld if audited by the IRS and subject to review by a court of competent jurisdiction.[43] Corporations must disclose their aggregate tax reserves established for uncertain tax positions in their Form 10-K, along with certain other information, but generally are not required to report on specific tax uncertainties.[44]

Net Operating Loss Carryforwards. When a corporation's allowable tax deductions exceed its taxable income, a "net operating loss"[45] results. US corporations are required to disclose in SEC filings the amount of their net operating losses.[46]

Permanently Reinvested Earnings. Large US multinational corporations defer US tax liability on their non-US earnings by keeping them offshore in non-US subsidiaries. Under normal rules of accounting, a corporation would have to anticipate the ultimate distribution of untaxed foreign subsidiary earnings and thus account for the future US tax consequences today by reporting a "deferred tax liability."[47] If a corporation makes an election, however, it is not required to establish a deferred tax liability for the US tax that would result upon repatriation of the offshore earnings as long as these earnings are "permanently reinvested earnings."[48]

B. THE CORPORATE TAX PRIVACY DEBATE

Current US tax privacy rules conceal most corporate tax return information from public view. Securities and accounting regulations in the United States do little to bring corporate tax return information to light, even for publicly traded corporations. This subpart outlines the primary arguments offered by proponents and opponents of mandated public disclosure of corporate tax returns over the course of the past century and considers the merits of each of them.

1. Arguments for Public Disclosure

Proponents of mandated public disclosure have argued that providing the public with access to corporations' tax returns would enhance the ability of the government to detect questionable tax positions, deter the managers of a corporation from pursuing aggressive tax strategies as a result of the threat of public shaming, and educate the public regarding corporate tax law.

(a) Increased Detection

Public disclosure proponents assert that by exposing a corporation's tax returns to "[m]illions of eyes," the government would enlist the assistance of the public as a "watchdog," which would aid its tax enforcement efforts.[49] Some tax scholars have argued that mandated public disclosure would serve as an "automatic enforcement device"[50] by "increas[ing] the chance of getting caught" due to public scrutiny.[51] Others have argued that enhanced detection is especially likely as a result of the IRS's ability to provide whistleblower rewards to informants.[52] Under current law, the IRS pays informants rewards of up to 30 percent of the proceeds that it collects using information they have provided to the IRS.[53] By addressing corporate tax avoidance through mandatory public disclosure measures, the government, both in the United States and in other countries, could use increased tax collections to address poverty and economic inequality, among other social issues.

This rationale for mandated public disclosure depends on questionable assumptions, at least with respect to the United States. The argument assumes that the IRS would have the audit capacity to investigate the large volume of tips from citizens and reporters that could result from a public access regime, even though many of them may not lead to the discovery of tax noncompliance. A review of the IRS's historic resource weaknesses should cast significant doubt on this assumption.[54] Further, while the IRS has paid rewards to informants, the individuals who are most capable of reporting the most valuable information to the IRS are those who are already working inside the corporation, often in the tax department.[55] It is unlikely that the participation of the general public in reviewing corporate tax returns would strengthen the IRS's ability to obtain valuable information from informants.

(b) Public Shaming

Another frequent argument in favor of mandated public disclosure is that it would introduce the threat of public shaming as a deterrent against aggressive corporate tax planning.[56] Several proponents of this view have argued that in a public disclosure regime, managers "might be leery of paying only nominal amounts of tax"[57] out of fear of backlash from shareholders, business partners, and consumers.[58]

In contrast to these claims, as I have argued elsewhere, public shaming is not a compelling rationale for mandated public disclosure.[59] There is little evidence to support the assertion that publicity of a corporation's use of aggressive, or even abusive, tax planning would result in communal ostracism of the corporation. When the press has reported on the tax-avoidance strategies of large US multinational corporations, the corporations involved have not suffered significant drops in stock price, widespread boycotts of their products or calls from shareholders for management reform. Michelle Hanlon and Joel Slemrod have found that publicity of a corporation's use of tax shelters does not result in drops in stock price as significant as the types of drops that occur following public reports of financial accounting fraud.[60] Another recent study found that consumer-facing corporations, those that sell at least one highly rated brand, are no less likely than other corporations to operate in a tax haven jurisdiction.[61]

Corporate managers appear to consider potential public reaction when pursuing transactions that implicate patriotism by requiring their corporations to relocate outside the United States. Following the "corporate inversion wave" of 2014 and 2015, where many US corporations pursued transactions that caused them to merge with non-US target corporations, enabling them to escape US taxation,[62] several politicians, including then President Barack Obama and then presidential candidate Donald J. Trump, decried the transactions as "unpatriotic"[63] and "job-killing."[64] Nevertheless, numerous consumer-focused public corporations continued to pursue the strategy.[65]

(c) Public Education and Debate

A final argument in favor of public disclosure of corporate tax returns is that it could serve an educational function by enhancing the public's understanding of the corporate tax law. Proponents of this view have characterized public disclosure of corporate tax returns as a "powerful tool for analysts who follow companies and industries"[66] and as a way to educate the public about "how much corporations actually pay in taxes."[67] The public education rationale is consistent with the public's right of information, which is protected by the International Covenant on Civil and Political Rights[68] and other international human rights treaties.[69] As some commentators have argued, greater tax transparency may enable the public to question aspects of the corporate tax law that give rise to abusive tax planning, confront corporations that engage in abusive tax planning, and hold the taxing authority accountable for enforcing the tax law, both in letter and spirit.[70]

With the aid of the news media, public disclosure of corporate tax return information would enable the public to learn about the corporate tax system through vivid specific examples of named corporations. Compared to anonymous statistical information or arcane statutory language, these specific examples would likely stimulate public debate, which could ultimately motivate legislative action. As section IV will argue, as a matter of human rights, including public access to information on matters of public concern and citizen participation in public affairs, the goal of enhancing public awareness and debate of the corporate tax law should serve as the primary objective of measures that would mandate public disclosure of corporate tax return information.

2. Arguments against Public Disclosure

In response to these arguments, public disclosure opponents offer consistent defenses of corporate tax privacy. These include assertions that public disclosure would cause corporate taxpayers to be treated differently from individual taxpayers, result in information overload, and expose corporations' proprietary information to competitors. Several of these defenses rest on shaky grounds.

(a) Equity with Individuals

Opponents of proposals to require publicly traded corporations to disclose tax return information often object to these measures on equity grounds, claiming that they rescind tax privacy protections for corporate taxpayers, but not for individuals. Other responses from opponents of public disclosure contend that tax privacy is a "core American value"[71] that should be offered to "individuals *and* corporations."[72]

But corporate and individual taxpayers are different in ways that are relevant to the tax privacy debate. Unlike individuals, corporations are owned by investors that have an interest in comparing a corporation's income reported for tax purposes against that reported for financial accounting purposes. Indeed, one reason that legislators sought the publicity provision in 1909 was to prevent stock watering and abusive promoter schemes.[73] Further, public disclosure of certain corporate tax return information, such as US tax liability, would not pose the threats to physical safety and risk of theft that individuals might face if this information were public.[74] Finally, due to the unfamiliar nature of the substantive corporate tax law to most people, public awareness of basic elements of the tax law is lacking more in the corporate rather than individual context.

(b) Information Overload

Opponents often argue that mandated public disclosure would result in information overload rather than the delivery of information relevant to investors, policymakers, or the general public. For example, the Tax Executives Institute frequently argues that in a public disclosure regime, "investors may not be able to discern meaning from what would be truckloads of tax return information."[75] Opponents use this concern to conclude that all corporate tax return information should remain private.

This defense of corporate tax privacy is not persuasive as a response to all corporate tax return public disclosure measures. It presumes that if a corporation's tax returns were publicly accessible, individual investors and members of the general public would attempt to interpret corporate tax return information directly. A more plausible characterization is that if corporations' tax returns were public, sophisticated intermediaries, such as journalists, financial advisers, and empirical scholars, would comb through the documents and report relevant information.[76]

(c) Proprietary Information

Last, opponents consistently argue that public disclosure of corporate tax return information would expose a corporation's sensitive proprietary information to the public, including to competitors. For instance, the Tax Executives Institute has asserted that public disclosure measures would reveal "confidential and proprietary data not currently contained in consolidated financial statements . . . to the world."[77] Opponents of public disclosure often argue that public disclosure of proprietary information would threaten tax privacy's function as a "cornerstone of voluntary compliance"[78] by corporate taxpayers. Just as then Treasury Secretary Andrew Mellon argued in the 1930s, present-day opponents argue that corporations will provide proprietary information to the IRS only if it "stops with the government."[79]

Advocates of public disclosure often reject this concern for several reasons. First, public disclosure opponents have failed to present concrete examples of the types of corporate tax return documents that, if publicly disclosed, would expose proprietary information. Second, public disclosure opponents present this concern in response to nearly all public disclosure measures.[80] Finally, opponents of public disclosure have not addressed *how* corporate taxpayers would reduce cooperation with the IRS in response to the threat of public disclosure of proprietary information. Despite these weaknesses, however, as section IV will discuss, concern regarding exposure of proprietary information is the only compelling argument presented by opponents of public disclosure thus far.

III. CORPORATE TAX PRIVACY AND CORPORATE TAX AGGRESSIVENESS

Participants in the corporate tax privacy debate have focused almost exclusively on the potential reactions of a corporation's managers, shareholders, and consumers to a requirement that the corporation publicly disclose its own tax return information. In contrast to that approach, this section examines public disclosure of corporate tax return information from the intercorporate perspective: how would the ability of a corporation's stakeholders and agents to observe *other* corporations' tax return information affect how the corporation complies with the tax law? As this section argues, by keeping certain return information from public view, corporate tax privacy can limit the pressure to engage in more aggressive tax planning and reporting that corporate tax directors face from significant shareholders and nontax managers, and even from themselves.

A. STRATEGIC DEFENSES AGAINST CORPORATE TAX AGGRESSIVENESS

1. Benchmarking

Tax privacy provides the government with a valuable strategic defense against increased corporate tax aggressiveness. Public disclosure of complete corporate tax returns, a position proposed by several public access advocates, would reveal significant information otherwise unobservable today about a corporation's tax planning and reporting practices. Complete tax returns of multinational corporations include IRS Form 1120, an annual return that describes the corporation's gross income, deductions, taxable income, and taxes owed, and also include dozens of attached forms, schedules, and explanatory documents that may, in total, amount to tens of thousands of pages.[81] By keeping certain corporate tax return information from public view, corporate tax privacy prevents interested parties from establishing "benchmarks of aggressiveness" in several critical tax compliance areas and from pressuring tax directors to pursue more aggressive strategies to keep pace with their competitors.

Influential shareholder groups, particularly activist investment funds, are among the most likely parties to use publicly available corporate tax return information to apply such pressure. Activist investment funds regularly synthesize information about a corporation's operations and recommend specific actions.[82] In recent years, these funds have delivered detailed proposals related to tax planning, concerning actions such as tax-free spin-off transactions[83] and corporate inversion mergers.[84] With public disclosure, these funds could evaluate their own corporation's relative tax aggressiveness in areas such as transfer pricing, participation in potentially abusive tax strategies and methods of disclosure of specific questionable transactions to the IRS, among others. Access to certain return information, thus, would provide these funds with newfound ability to compare their corporations' tax reporting practices in specific areas to that of other corporations and to utilize the information to urge corporations in which they invest to pursue specific aggressive tax strategies.

Similarly, nontax managers frequently consider tax-avoidance strategies that they believe other corporations are pursuing; public access to corporate tax return information would only increase this comparative analysis. Upon hearing the news that a major competitor has engaged in aggressive tax planning to cut its corporate tax bill, some members of a corporation's board of directors and nontax management exhibit a reaction that has been described as "structure envy,"[85] meaning that they "demand to know why they don't have the same tax savings."[86] With public disclosure, nontax managers could analyze tax strategies of competitors, such as by reviewing specific documents that corporations are required to file with the IRS to enhance its ability to identify potentially abusive tax strategies—such as IRS Form 8886 (Reportable Transaction Statement), Schedule UTP (Uncertain Tax Positions), and others. Public disclosure of certain corporate tax return information, thus, could lead nontax managers to question why their own tax director has not pursued more aggressive tax planning.

In addition, without the curtain of corporate tax privacy, advisers, and other third-party groups could use publicly available corporate tax return data to aid nontax corporate managers and tax directors in establishing and meeting benchmarks for tax aggressiveness in specific areas of tax planning and compliance. Each of the "Big Four" accounting firms—KPMG, PricewaterhouseCoopers, Deloitte, and Ernst & Young—houses a "benchmarking" department.[87] These groups assist corporate clients in measuring their "performance against best-in-class companies to identify improvement"[88] in a variety of areas, such as executive compensation, inventory, and staffing costs. Notably, the Big Four do not include "tax planning" among the areas in which they currently deliver benchmarking services, even though they often advise large public corporations.[89] One explanation for this omission is that in their engagement letters, these firms explicitly agree not to disclose any information about their clients' tax planning or interactions with the IRS to other clients.[90] Public disclosure of corporate tax return information could enable the accounting firms to overcome this contractual obstacle. Other private firms, such as Audit Analytics, already analyze large quantities of data in regulatory filings and deliver "peer reports" to clients.[91] With publicly available corporate tax return information, these data analysts could easily deliver similar services to encourage overly conservative corporate tax directors to consider alternative tax strategies utilized by their more aggressive competitors.

Increased pressure from nontax management and, indirectly, from influential shareholders and third-party advisers would likely affect the tax reporting and compliance decisions of corporate tax directors. Faced with detailed information about the transfer pricing structures of their more aggressive competitor corporations, for example, some tax directors would likely explore the use of specific jurisdictions, including tax havens, or cost-sharing structures that lower their own corporation's tax burden. As another example, with public access, corporate tax directors may point to benchmarking reports from accounting firms or information from other corporations' returns to pressure their outside tax lawyers to deliver written opinions regarding aggressive transactions and strategies, which the law firms had previously declined to issue. Public disclosure of corporate tax return information, consequently, could threaten the gatekeeping function that tax lawyers have traditionally played in advising clients that the most aggressive tax strategies are not consistent with the tax law.[92]

A vivid illustration of the benchmarking effect of publicity of corporate tax-avoidance strategies can be observed in the inversion wave of 2013 through 2015. In these types of transactions, a US corporation would merge with a non-US company located in a low-tax jurisdiction, such as Ireland, where following the merger, the US corporation's shareholders retained up to 79.9 percent of the combined entity's stock in the merger.[93] After the dust settled, the original shareholders of the US corporation would retain control of the merged entity, which would then pay a lower tax rate. As many high-profile consumer-focused public corporations pursued this strategy, influential shareholder groups met with the board of directors and management of their own corporations to argue that they should embrace the strategy as well.[94] In meetings with legislators, corporate executives reported that they "might be forced to [invert]" in order to match similar moves by competitors.[95] Several major US corporations, including those with high-profile consumer brands, such as Medtronic,[96] Mylan,[97] Johnson Controls,[98] Civeo Corp.,[99] and ARRIS Group, Inc.,[100] among others, engaged in inversion transactions through 2016.[101] By contrast, when the board of directors of Walgreens declined to relocate its corporate headquarters to the United Kingdom as part of its merger with British-based Alliance Boots in 2014—a decision which caused Walgreens to continue to be subject to US corporate income tax on its worldwide income—the corporation's stock price immediately dropped over 14 percent in value.[102]

Unlike nearly all other corporate tax-avoidance techniques that take place behind the curtain of corporate tax privacy, the corporate inversion strategy occurred in the public eye. The technique involved a significant business combination and required corporations to obtain shareholder approval and disclose the event publicly under securities regulation.[103] As one corporate manager commented, when corporate executives learned of the inversion technique, it began to "snowball."[104] This reaction is consistent with the characterization of the inversion wave by Ed Kleinbard, a tax law scholar and former law firm partner, as illustrating "herd behavior,"[105] where "CEOs find it difficult to be the only gazelle on the veldt that remains in place when all the others madly gallop off in one direction or another."[106] If all corporate tax returns were publicly accessible, the same types of shareholder groups involved in inversion campaigns could scour this information in order to determine whether their own corporations are pursuing some of the aggressive tax strategies utilized by their competitors.

In 2014 and 2015, the Treasury Department issued proposed regulations that contain a number of provisions designed to limit the economic benefits of tax-motivated inversion transactions.[107] This regulatory response illustrates the difficulty that the taxing authority faces in responding to increased use of new tax-avoidance strategies.

First, the Treasury's proposed regulations described in the notice were not retroactive. The lack of retroactivity helps explain why certain tax-avoidance strategies "snowball." As corporations expect that the government may attempt to counteract the new strategy, many rush to engage in the strategy before the announcement of preventative rules.

Second, the ability of the government to stem the flourishing avoidance strategy is constrained as a result of the Treasury's limited legal authority. The proposed regulations, for instance, lacked rules regarding tax-deductible interest payments from US corporations to foreign parents following the inversion merger, causing some commentators to describe the regulations as "modest."[108] (In 2016, the Treasury issued enhanced anti-inversion regulations, including rules that addressed the use of corporate debt to reduce US tax liability.[109])

Finally, by addressing aggressive tax strategies through regulatory, as opposed to statutory, actions, the government's remedies may be short-lived. For example, immediately following the inauguration of President Donald J. Trump in January 2017, the White House imposed a "regulatory freeze," which halted the implementation of some of the anti-inversion regulations proposed by the Obama administration.[110] Further, in April 2017, President Trump signed an executive order directing the Secretary of the Treasury to review all "significant tax regulations" issued in 2016.[111] Despite then candidate Donald J. Trump's criticism of corporate inversions throughout the 2016 presidential campaign,[112] his 2017 executive actions placed the viability of some of the most comprehensive anti-inversion measures in doubt.[113]

2. Reverse Engineering

Corporate tax privacy also restricts the ability of sophisticated advisers and, ultimately, tax directors to observe documents that would allow them to better predict the likelihood of certain IRS enforcement actions. The IRS engages in cat-and-mouse dynamics with corporate taxpayers that have the upper hand in designing and concealing tax-avoidance strategies.[114] When viewed in large quantities over extended periods of time, certain publicly available corporate tax return information would enable sophisticated analysts to identify the types of tax positions that have the greatest probability of resulting in challenges from the IRS. Corporate tax directors would likely respond to this analysis by adjusting their own corporation's tax reporting and planning behavior.

With complete public access, tax advisers and corporate tax directors could observe documents that would reveal the responses of the IRS to the reported tax positions of their competitors, information not otherwise observable today, absent the rare case of litigation. Certain corporate tax return documents, especially those that describe the IRS's settlements with corporate taxpayers and assertion of tax penalties, would allow for reverse engineering. Such information could lead some corporate tax directors to avoid certain strategies that are likely to draw IRS attention, while other information could encourage some corporate tax directors to adopt the more aggressive actions of their competitor corporations that do not appear to have resulted in challenges from the IRS.

More importantly, with complete public access, tax advisory and data analysis firms would have the ability to conduct empirical analysis, which would reveal, using quantitative rather than anecdotal methods, the types of tax positions and filing actions that are most statistically likely to result in detection and challenge by the IRS.[115] The major accounting firms and other advisory firms that conduct quantitative analysis would have strong economic incentives to use publicly available corporate tax return data to create statistical models that could predict whether certain tax reporting and filing actions in different circumstances would result in the government's use of audits, deficiency assertions, and tax penalties. Currently, the major accounting firms do not advertise their use of such statistical models to clients.[116] One plausible reason for this absence is that these firms are reluctant to advertise that they have developed models that enable clients to avoid detection and challenge by the IRS.[117] Public disclosure of complete corporate tax return information would provide these firms with the ability to advertise statistical modeling openly. And the Big Four would likely face market pressure to develop such models, given that public disclosure would invite competition from data analysis groups, such as Audit Analytics, which do not offer tax advisory services currently.[118]

IV. WHAT CORPORATE TAX RETURN INFORMATION
SHOULD BE PUBLIC

As section III demonstrated, excessive public disclosure of corporate tax return information could encourage, rather than deter, aggressive corporate tax planning. Is the implication of this analysis that all corporate tax return information should remain hidden from public view? As this section argues, the answer is no. The strategic defenses of corporate tax privacy are not the only factors that policymakers should take into account. This section offers three guiding principles that policymakers should consider when evaluating proposals to make all or part of corporate tax return information public.

A. GUIDING PRINCIPLES

Rather than engage in sweeping "public versus private" debates over disclosure of corporate tax return information,[119] policymakers should consider several factors when deciding whether to support proposals to make corporations' tax return information publicly accessible. As section II argued, policymakers should disregard as unpersuasive two traditional arguments in favor of public disclosure, that it would increase the IRS's detection capabilities and achieve deterrence with the threat of public shaming, and two common objections to public disclosure, that it would violate equity principles and result in information overload. In contrast, I argue that policymakers should consider how each proposal is likely to affect the strategic defenses of corporate tax privacy, exposure of proprietary information, and the quality of public awareness and debate of corporate tax issues.

1. Would Public Disclosure Diminish Strategic Defenses of Corporate Tax Privacy?

Policymakers should consider on a case-by-case basis the potential effects of each corporate tax return public disclosure measure on the strategic defenses of corporate tax privacy. Mandatory public disclosure of certain tax forms could exacerbate corporate tax aggressiveness by enabling a corporation's stakeholders and agents to engage in benchmarking and reverse engineering. For example, if US corporations were required to publicly disclose their complete tax returns, including all schedules and forms,[120] significant shareholders, nontax managers, and corporate tax directors could establish, and then attempt to meet, benchmarks of aggressiveness in several tax compliance areas. With access to complete corporate tax returns, a corporation's stakeholders could view other corporations' IRS forms that describe related party transactions, including loans, services, and transfers of goods, such as IRS Form 5471 (filed by US corporations with non-US subsidiaries)[121] and IRS Form 5472 (filed by US corporations with non-US parent corporations).[122] This information would reveal whether a corporation engages in tax planning involving specific jurisdictions.[123]

Access to complete corporate tax returns would also arm tax advisers and corporate tax directors with otherwise unobservable information about the actions of the IRS in corporate tax enforcement. At the end of an audit, if the taxpayer owes additional tax liability or tax penalties, the IRS prepares IRS Form 5701 (Notice of Proposed Adjustment)[124] and IRS Form 870 (Waiver of Restrictions on Assessment).[125] Public access to complete corporate tax returns, including these forms, would reveal IRS challenges and settlements that occur in controversies related to transfer pricing and reportable transactions, among many others. Similar effects could occur under measures that would require public disclosure of forms that reveal when corporations have paid an "economic substance" tax penalty[126] to the IRS,[127] or the base erosion and profit shifting "master file" (including complete corporate structure charts and the location of intangible assets) and proposed by the OECD.[128]

By contrast, mandatory public disclosure of more limited corporate tax return information may not present risks to the strategic defenses of corporate tax privacy discussed above. For example, IRS Form 1120, the annual US corporate income tax return, absent any accompanying schedules, forms or attachments, is one single-sided page.[129] The first page of IRS Form 1120 reveals a corporation's ultimate annual taxable income and tax liability, among other items, but does not reveal the specific tax-planning techniques, such as transfer pricing structures involving tax haven jurisdictions, that the corporation used to achieve these results.[130] As this form would not reveal the results of IRS audits, imposition of tax penalties or IRS guidance issued directly to the taxpayer, corporate tax directors and their advisers would have little ability to use it to reverse engineer the IRS's approach to corporate tax enforcement. Other possibilities of more limited forms of publicly accessible corporate tax return information that pose little risk to the strategic defenses of corporate tax privacy include IRS Schedule M-3 (a three-page document that large corporations file with the IRS, which requires them to reconcile the differences between their book and US taxable income on a consolidated basis)[131] and a corporate "pink slip" (an abbreviated list of certain corporate tax information).[132]

Some human rights advocates may object that any limitation on public access to documents that describe the tax strategies used by specific corporate taxpayers or specific enforcement actions of the IRS disregards the public's right of access to information on matters of public concern.[133] There are several responses to this concern.

First, the government can still preserve transparency by releasing statistical data regarding its corporate tax enforcement practices without providing enough detail about specific named corporations to enable benchmarking and reverse engineering. As an example, the IRS annually publishes its "Data Book," which provides aggregate statistics regarding corporate taxpayers' audit rates, tax penalties, and taxes paid.[134] The IRS could increase the specificity of its published aggregate tax enforcement statistics without revealing details that would enable analysts to reverse engineer the IRS's audit and related enforcement strategies.[135] For instance, in 2017, the IRS reported that it assessed $499,190,000 in "accuracy penalties" against individual taxpayers in the 2016 fiscal year.[136] Instead of reporting this one aggregate figure, it could distill it into the multiple tax penalties that fall into this broad category, such as tax penalties for substantial understatement of income tax, substantial valuation misstatement, substantial overstatement of pension liabilities, substantial estate or gift tax valuation understatement, understatement of reportable transactions, among others.[137]

Second, policymakers should provide a direct explanation for retaining tax privacy protections for corporate tax return information, whether it relates to tax enforcement or some other concern. For example, to preempt objections that the government is not acting transparently, the Treasury Department could describe such a rationale in the preamble to regulations that address the type of corporate tax return information that is subject to mandatory public disclosure.

Finally, the government should maintain institutions that oversee the operation of the IRS and report their findings to the public. Under current law, this oversight is provided by several bodies, including the Treasury Inspector General for Tax Administration,[138] the IRS Oversight Board,[139] and Congress itself.[140]

2. Would Public Disclosure Expose Proprietary Information?

Policymakers should also consider the potential exposure of a corporation's proprietary information when evaluating public disclosure measures. As this subpart argues, if policymakers embrace a public disclosure measure without considering the possibility that it would expose proprietary information, they may overlook potential adverse effects on voluntary compliance by taxpayers.

Before proceeding, a definition of "proprietary" information is necessary. One possibility is that it is information that is (1) economically valuable, (2) subject to reasonable measures by the corporation to keep it secret, and (3) not readily obtainable from public sources. This definition is derived from employment law.[141] Regardless of its source, the key point is that proprietary information in the corporate tax context is that which has economic value because its disclosure could harm the corporation or benefit a competitor.[142] Some corporate tax return documents indeed contain sensitive information about the inner workings of a corporation that is not otherwise publicly available. Certain tax forms, for example, reveal a corporation's business structure,[143] trading strategy,[144] compensation of high-level employees,[145] and research expenditures. At the same time, other tax return information, such as the aggregate amount of tax paid to the US government in a particular tax year, does not reveal proprietary information.

An adverse consequence that could result from public disclosure of a corporation's proprietary information is that some tax directors may reduce the quality and quantity of disclosure they make to the IRS regarding specific expenses and transactions if they perceive that competitors would benefit from viewing this information. Corporate tax directors regularly use their discretion in revealing information to the IRS regarding certain tax positions and transactions, through submissions such as reportable transaction forms,[146] Schedule UTP,[147] and dozens of other forms. In addition, tax directors often voluntarily provide written explanations of certain deductions and other items.[148] In these cases, where tax directors can apply their own judgment regarding the amount of detail to provide to the IRS, a public disclosure regime could cause some corporations to withhold details regarding transactions and expenses that would benefit competitors if exposed. The resulting harm is that reduced voluntary disclosure would further strain tax enforcement resources, as IRS agents would now need to seek information that corporations would otherwise offer to them.

3. Would Public Disclosure Enhance Public Awareness and Debate?

Finally, policymakers should consider the potential effects of each measure on public awareness and debate of corporate tax issues. International human rights documents protect individuals' right to access information on matters of public concern.[149] In protecting this right, these documents embrace the concept that an informed public is an essential element of democracy.[150] Without access to information that explains how individuals and businesses apply the law in practice, citizens may be unable to question and debate whether the government should change the law or enact new law.[151] One of the rationales for making corporate tax return information public, therefore, should be that this disclosure would result in a better informed public, which in turn, could have the positive effect of encouraging legislators to debate and seek legislative change.

As behavioral research has long shown, specific examples can have a more profound effect on individuals' perceptions than anonymous statistics.[152] Specific examples include a description of the identifying traits of a person or thing, which may include a name, occupation, or physical features.[153] The name "Apple," for instance, is more likely to trigger a memorable image than the term "consumer electronics corporation." Cognitive psychologists have demonstrated that specific examples cause individuals to create mental images, which, in turn, can help them understand concepts or arguments.[154] Neuroscientists have even shown that brain activity is affected by the vividness of a specific example of a person or thing.[155]

Similarly, past tax reform experiences in the United States illustrate that tax issues can attract significant public interest and lead to legislative change when the public learns about them through the vehicle of specific examples of named corporations. The 1980s are a storied period in American tax history, when Congress generated enough bipartisan legislative support to enact multiple major pieces of tax legislation, including the landmark Tax Reform Act of 1986.[156] During this period, Congress enacted major changes to the corporate tax law, including the repeal of *General Utilities*[157] and a number of significant base-broadening measures.[158]

Commentators have cited public awareness of specific examples of corporate tax avoidance as having a significant impact on Congress's decision to act on tax legislation during this period.[159] In the years immediately preceding the Tax Reform Act of 1986, Citizens for Tax Justice, an advocacy group, published a list of major corporations that had paid no income tax as a result of safe harbor leasing and other tax-planning techniques.[160] As one scholar has characterized it, this revelation had a "profound effect on educating the public and on shaping public opinion."[161]

Targeted public disclosure proposals, such as mandatory public disclosure of IRS Form 1120 only, IRS Schedule M-3, or a corporate "pink slip,"[162] could enable the public to learn fundamental information about a corporation's tax affairs that is otherwise unobservable today. Specifically, these measures would enable the media to publicize a large multinational US corporation's federal tax liability (for tax, not GAAP purposes) each year, the amount of cash taxes it paid to the US government and the amount of tax it owed and paid to governments other than the US federal government.[163] In addition, public access would enable the public to learn about the extent to which the US government subsidized the corporation's payment of taxes to non-US governments through the foreign tax credit.[164]

Public access could also enable the media to raise public awareness of corporate "tax expenditures," where Congress essentially embeds spending programs in the tax law, by describing named corporations that have used these tax provisions to reduce their US tax liability. In 2011, for example, US corporations utilized tax expenditure provisions that cost the US government over $180 billion.[165] Some of these tax expenditures account for a large portion of the forgone revenue, namely, accelerated depreciation and deferral of income from controlled foreign corporations.[166] Others involve much more obscure tax issues such as the tax credit that certain corporations receive when they produce barrels of nonconventional fuel sources or when they produce agri-biodiesel fuel.[167] Public access to certain corporate tax return information could raise public awareness of these expenditures and encourage members of Congress to review their performance more regularly.

Reporters, politicians, and advocacy groups often attempt to utilize the little corporate tax information that is publicly available to reveal the tax affairs of well-known US corporations. These attempts frequently result in inaccurate statements about a corporation's tax positions.[168] In addition, the limited data available today causes the public to pay attention to corporations that are reported to pay no, or nearly no, annual tax to the US government[169] rather than on other corporations that have engaged in aggressive tax planning to reduce an otherwise high global effective tax rate.[170]

Public access to certain corporate tax return information could enable both nonpartisan research institutions and tax advocacy groups[171] to conduct more sophisticated empirical analysis of specific corporations' tax affairs, such as their use of tax expenditure provisions and international tax treaty provisions to avoid US taxation. If properly designed, public access to corporate tax return information could result in greater clarity in public discussions of corporate tax issues and thus achieve the objective of a more informed citizenry.

How should policymakers take these three guiding principles into account when evaluating specific public disclosure measures? Cost-benefit analysis is a tool that the US government has utilized when analyzing health, environmental, and safety regulations. Yet, it is unlikely to be useful in this context. Some of the costs, such as lost tax revenue due to increased use of certain aggressive tax strategies, may be measurable over time. Other costs, such as advantages to business competitors or harm to the IRS's enforcement efforts, and benefits, such as increased public debate, may not be quantifiable even with simplifying assumptions.

Instead, policymakers should start with a baseline of transparency that as much corporate tax return information as possible should be publicly accessible. They should then analyze the specific documents that would be subject to a public disclosure requirement under the proposed measure and exempt items that would (1) encourage benchmarking and reverse engineering, (2) expose proprietary information of corporations to competitors, or (3) result in confusion rather than clarity regarding corporate tax issues. As an added safeguard of transparency, policymakers could also explain publicly the rationale for exemptions for any corporate tax return information from public access requirements. Rather than assigning weights to each individual principle or attempting to put a number on the unquantifiable, this approach would enable policymakers to enhance public awareness and debate of the corporate tax law without generating the potential adverse consequences discussed above.

V. CONCLUSION

By examining the relationship of corporate tax privacy and tax compliance from a new perspective, this chapter has offered two contributions to the growing dialogue between the corporate tax and human rights communities.

First, while some human rights advocates have suggested that requiring corporations to publish their tax return information could alleviate poverty and economic inequality and bolster individuals' right to access information regarding matters of public concern, this chapter has presented reasons to approach such public disclosure efforts with caution. As it has shown, a previously unnoticed benefit of corporate tax privacy is that it can limit the pressure to engage in more aggressive tax planning and reporting practices that corporate tax directors face from external sources, such as significant shareholders and nontax managers, and even from themselves. Specifically, corporate tax privacy provides the government with valuable strategic defenses by restraining the ability of a corporation's stakeholders and agents to engage in benchmarking and reverse engineering, behaviors that would likely cause some tax directors to engage in more aggressive tax planning and reporting.

Second, this chapter has offered guiding principles that policymakers should consider when evaluating proposals to make all or part of corporate tax return information publicly accessible. As this chapter has argued, policymakers should assess each corporate tax return public disclosure proposal separately by considering its potential effects on: (1) the strategic defenses of corporate tax privacy; (2) exposure of proprietary information of corporate taxpayers; and (3) public awareness and debate of corporate tax issues.

The answer to the question of whether the public's "right to know" should outweigh corporations' tax privacy interests is neither simple nor universal. The more nuanced analysis of corporate tax privacy presented in this chapter should have important implications for legislators, government officials, human rights activists, and empirical and legal scholars.

NOTES

* Portions of this chapter were originally published in J. D. Blank, 'Reconsidering Corporate Tax Privacy', 11 *New York University Journal of Law & Business* (2014), 31.

1. *Google: Ten Things We Know to be True*, available online at http://www.1000manifestos.com/ google-ten-things-know-be-true/ (last visited 7 June 2017).

2. See, e.g., S. Levy, *In the Plex: How Google Thinks, Works and Shapes Our Lives* (2011), at 9–69.

3. See J. Drucker, *Google 2.4% Rate Shows How $60 Billion Is Lost to Tax Loopholes*, 21 Oct. 2010, available online at http://www.bloomberg.com/news/2010-10-21/google-2-4-rate-shows-how-60-billion-u- s-revenue-lost-to-tax-loopholes.html (last visited 7 June 2017). J. Chew, *7 Corporate Giants Accused of Evading Billions in Taxes*, 11 Mar. 2016, available online at http://fortune.com/2016/03/11/apple-google- taxes-eu/ (describing accusations of Google's tax avoidance in Europe) (last visited 1 July 2017). For de- tailed discussion, see E. Kleinbard, 'Stateless Income', 11 *Florida Tax Review* (2011), 699, at 701–714.

4. See Memorandum from Senators Carl Levin and John McCain on Offshore Profit Shifting and the United States Tax Code—Part 2 (Apple Inc.) to the Members of the Permanent Subcommittee on Investigations (21 May 2013).

5. See, e.g., E. Kleinbard, 'Through a Latte, Darkly: Starbucks's Stateless Income Planning', 139 *Tax Notes* (2013), 1515, at 1516–1535.

6. T. Bergin, *Insight: In Europe's Tax Race, It's the Base, Not the Rate, That Counts*, 18 Feb. 2013, available online at http://www.reuters.com/article/2013/02/18/us-tax-contest-europe- idUSBRE91H07B20130218 (last visited 7 June 2017).

7. See, e.g., J. Drucker, *U.S. Companies Dodge $60 Billion in Taxes Even Tea Party Condemns*, Bloomberg (May 13, 2010, 3:00 PM), http://www. bloomberg.com/news/2010-05-13/american- companies-dodge-60-billion-in-taxes-even-tea-party-would-condemn.html.

8. I.R.C. § 6103 (2012).

9. See, e.g., Drucker, *supra* note 3; House of Commons Committee of Public Accounts (U.K.), *Tax Avoidance-Google: Ninth Report of Session 2013–14*, 13 June 2013, available online at https://www. publications.parliament.uk/pa/cm201314/cmselect/cmpubacc/112/112.pdf.

10. See, e.g., Levin and McCain, *supra* note 4; Caterpillar's Offshore Tax Strategy: Hearing Before the Permanent Subcommittee on Investigations of the Senate Committee on Homeland Security and Governmental Affairs, 113th Congress 408 (2014).

11. See K. Clausing, 'The Revenue Effects of Multinational Firm Income Shifting', 130 *Tax Notes* (2011), 1580, at 1585.

12. See Testimony of Edward D. Kleinbard, *in* Tax Reform: Tax Havens, Base Erosion and Profit- Shifting: Hearing Before the House Committee On Ways and Means, 113th Congress 6 (2013).

13. OECD, *Final BEPS Package for Reform of the International Tax System to Tackle Tax Avoidance*, available online at http://www.oecd.org/tax/beps-2015-final-reports.htm (last visited 20 July 2017).

14. Press Release, European Commission, State Aid: Ireland Gave Illegal Tax Benefits to Apple Worth up to €13 Billion, 30 Aug. 2016, available online at http://europa.eu/rapid/press-release_IP-16- 2923_en.htm (last visited 2 July 2017). The European Commission has reached similar prelim- inary decisions in cases involving Starbucks, Fiat, and Amazon. See United States Department of the Treasury, *The European Commission's Recent State Aid Investigations of Transfer Pricing Rulings* (2016), available online at https://www.treasury.gov/resource-center/tax-policy/treaties/ Documents/White-Paper-State-Aid.pdf.

15. See, e.g., International Bar Association, *Tax Abuses, Poverty and Human Rights: A Report of the International Bar Association's Human Rights Institute Task Force on Illicit Financial Flows, Poverty and Human Rights* (2013), available online at http://www.ibanet.org/Document/Default. aspx?DocumentUid=4977CB3D-4988-4C9C-84C7-9050A5CB2311 (last visited 12 June 2017); Tax Justice Network, *Ten Reasons to Defend the Corporation Tax* (2015), available online at http:// www.taxjustice.net/2015/03/18/new-report-ten-reasons-to-defend-the-corporate-income-tax/, at 6 ("the corporate tax curbs inequality and protects democracy") (last visited 20 July 2017); Tax

Justice Network, *Human Rights,* available online at http://www.taxjustice.net/topics/inequality-democracy/human-rights/ (last visited 20 July 2017); Y. Brauner and M. Stewart, *Tax, Law and Development* (2013), at 292–294 (summarizing advocacy groups' arguments regarding links between corporate tax avoidance and human rights abuses).

16. International Bar Association, *supra* note 15, at 2.

17. Ibid.

18. International Bar Association, *supra* note 15, at 93–102 (citing the Human Rights Council, Final Draft of the Guiding Principles on Extreme Poverty and Human Rights, submitted by the Special Rapporteur on Extreme Poverty and Human Rights, Magdalena Sepúlveda Carmona, UN Doc. A/HRC/21/39, 18 July 2012).

19. Art. 25, Universal Declaration of Human Rights, GA Res. 217 (III) A, 10 Dec. 1948.

20. Art. 3, UDHR, *supra* note 19.

21. See Art. 19 and Art. 25, International Covenant on Civil and Political Rights 1966, 999 UNTS 171; International Bar Association, *supra* note 15, at 102; Brauner and Stewart, *supra* note 15, at 292.

22. See International Bar Association, *supra* note 15, at 102–104; O. Huitson, *Time for Tax Transparency in the UK,* 21 Dec. 2011, available online at https://www.opendemocracy.net/ourkingdom/oliver-huitson/time-for-tax-transparency-in-uk (last visited 20 July 2017).

23. See, e.g., B. Bartlett, *Can Publicity Curb Corporate Tax Avoidance?,* 31 Jan. 2013, available online at http://blogs.ft.com/the-a-list/2013/01/31/can-publicity-curb-corporate-tax-avoidance/ (last visited 7 June 2017); A. Christians, 'Do We Need to Know More About Our Public Companies?', 66 *Tax Notes International* (2012), 843; F. Salmon, *Why Public Companies Should Have Public Tax Returns,* 21 May 2013, available online at http://blogs.reuters.com/felix-salmon/2013/05/21/why-public-companies-should-have-public-tax-returns/ (last visited 8 June 2017); Editorial Board of Bloomberg View, *On Corporate Taxes, Put the Public in Publicly Traded: View,* 5 Oct. 2011, available online at http://www.bloomberg.com/news/2011-10-06/on-corporate-taxes-put-the-public-in-publicly-traded-view.html (last visited 7 June 2017); C. Rampell, 'Shareholders, Public Deserve Tax Transparency', *Washington Post,* 21 Aug. 2014, available online at http://www.washingtonpost.com/opinions/catherine-rampell-shareholders-public-deserve-tax-transparen-cy/2014/08/21/f547d980-296d-11e4-8593-da634b334390_story.html (last visited 7 June 2017).

24. Act of Aug. 5, 1909, ch. 6, § 38, 36 Stat. 11, 112 (repealed).

25. I.R.C. §§ 6103(a), (b)(2), (c) (2012).

26. 44 Cong. Rec. 3344–45 (1909). For discussion, see M. Kornhauser, 'Corporate Regulation and the Origin of the Corporate Income Tax', 66 *Indiana Law Journal* (1990), 55, at 96.

27. R. Avi-Yonah and A. Siman, 'The One Percent Solution: Corporate Tax Returns Should Be Public (And How to Get There)', 74 *Tax Notes International* (2014), 627.

28. R. Pomp, 'The Disclosure of State Corporate Income Tax Data: Turning the Clock Back to the Future', 22 *Capital University Law Review* (1993), 373.

29. J. Thorndike, 'Promoting Honesty by Releasing Corporate Tax Returns', 96 *Tax Notes* (2002), 324.

30. See, e.g., M. Kornhauser, 'Doing the Full Monty: Will Publicizing Tax Information Increase Compliance?', 18 *Canadian Journal of Law & Jurisprudence* (2005), 95, at 113; see also M. Everson, 'A Reform Tool: Tax Returns', *Washington Post,* 18 Oct. 2008.

31. See Tax Justice Network, *Human Rights, supra* note 15.

32. ActionAid, *Achieving Tax Justice,* available online at https://www.actionaid.org.uk/about-us/policy-and-research/tax-justice (last visited 20 July 2017). For further discussion of ActionAid's arguments, see Brauner and Stewart, *supra* note 15 at 292.

33. See, e.g., Tax Executives Institute, 'Comments on Massachusetts Initiative to Require Disclosure of Corporate Tax Returns', 44(4) *Tax Executive* (1992), 300; Tax Executives Institute, 'TEI Opposes Public Disclosure of Corporate Tax Returns', 58(3) *Tax Executive* (2006), 241.

34. See, e.g., M. Hanlon, 'What Can We Infer About a Firm's Taxable Income from its Financial Statements?', 56 *National Tax Journal* (2003), 831.

35. *SEC Form 10-K,* available online at http://www.sec.gov/answers/form10k.htm (last visited 8 June 2017).

36. Financial Accounting Standards Board, *Income Taxes: Accounting Standards Codification* (2009), §
740-10-30.
37. Google Inc., *Annual Report (Form 10-K)* (2011), at 36.
38. Ibid.
39. For discussion, see D. Shaviro, 'The Optimal Relationship Between Taxable Income and Financial
Accounting Income: Analysis and a Proposal', 97 *Georgetown Law Journal* (2009), 423; Kleinbard,
supra note 5, at 741 note 96.
40. *Income Taxes: Accounting Standards Codification, supra* note 38, at §§ 740-270-35-3, 740-270-30-19.
41. See, e.g., C. Horngren et al., *Introduction to Financial Accounting* (11th ed., 2013), at 193.
42. *Accounting for Uncertainty in Income Taxes, Statement of Financial Accounting Standards No. 48*
(2006) (codified at *Income Taxes: Accounting Standards Codification, supra* note 38, § 740-10-25-6-
7, at 13).
43. *Income Taxes: Accounting Standards Codification, supra* note 38, § 740-10-55-3.
44. Ibid. § 740-10-25-6-7.
45. I.R.C. § 172 (2012).
46. *Income Taxes: Accounting Standards Codification, supra* note 38, § 740-10-50-3(a).
47. Financial Accounting Standards Board, *Foreign Currency Matters, Accounting Standards
Codification* (2009), § 830-30-45-21.
48. *Income Taxes: Accounting Standards Codification, supra* note 38, § 740-10-55-209.
49. See, e.g., J. Thorndike, 'The Thorndike Challenge', 122 *Tax Notes* (2009), 691, at 691–692.
50. A. Bernasek, 'Should Tax Bills Be Public Information?', *New York Times*, 14 Feb. 2010, at BU11.
51. Kornhauser, *supra* note 31.
52. See, e.g., D. Ventry Jr., 'Whistleblowers and Qui Tam for Tax', 61 *Tax Law.* (2008), 357, at 385.
53. I.R.C. § 7623(b)(1) (2012).
54. See IRS Oversight Board, *FY2011 IRS Budget Recommendation Special Report* (2010), available online at http://www.foreffectivegov.org/files/budget/IRSOBFY11BUDGETREPORT.pdf, at 9–11.
55. See L. Browning, 'The Perks of Being a Whistle-blower', *Newsweek*, 30 Jan. 2014, available online at
http://www.newsweek.com/how-would-you-spend-30-1-trillion-227390 (last visited 7 June 2017).
56. See, e.g., Kornhauser, *supra* note 31, at 104; J. Soled and D. Ventry Jr., 'A Little Shame Might Just
Deter Tax Cheaters', *USA Today*, 10 Apr. 2008, at 12A.
57. Pomp, *supra* note 29, at 444.
58. See, e.g., Soled and Ventry Jr., *supra* note 60.
59. See J. Blank, 'What's Wrong with Shaming Corporate Tax Abuse', 62 *Tax Law Review* (2009), 539,
at 581.
60. M. Hanlon and J. Slemrod, 'What Does Tax Aggressiveness Signal? Evidence from Stock Price
Reactions to News About Tax Shelter Involvement', 93 *Journal of Public Economics* (2009), 126,
at 128.
61. C. Austin and R. Wilson, *Are Reputational Costs a Determinant of Tax Avoidance?* (2013), available online at http://papers.ssrn.com/sol3/papers.cfm?abstract_id=2216879## (last visited 7
June 2017).
62. For discussion, see S. Raice, 'How Tax Inversions Became the Hottest Trend in M&A', *Wall Street
Journal*, 5 Aug. 2014, available online at http://online.wsj.com/articles/how-tax-inversions-
became-the-hottest-trend-in-m-a-1407240175 (last visited 7 June 2017).
63. See, e.g., K. Zezima, 'Obama: Tax Loophole that Allows Companies to Leave the U.S. Is
"Unpatriotic"', *Washington Post*, 24 July 2014, available online at http://www.washingtonpost.com/
blogs/post-politics/wp/2014/07/24/obama-tax-loophole-that-allows-companies-to-leave-the-u-s-
is-unpatriotic/ (last visited 7 June 2017).
64. S. Donnan, B. Jopson, and S. Fleming, 'Trump Pledges "Tax Revolution" for US Business', *Financial
Times*, 8 Aug. 2016 (quoting Trump as promising, once elected, to attack "job-killing corporate
inversions.").
65. For list of corporate inversions from 1982 through 2016, see *Tracking Tax Runaways*, 1 Mar. 2017,
available online at https://www.bloomberg.com/graphics/tax-inversion-tracker/ (last visited 20
July 2017).

66. Everson, *supra* note 31.
67. See Bartlett, *supra* note 24.
68. Art. 19 and Art. 25, ICCPR, *supra* note 21.
69. See, e.g., Art. 13, American Convention on Human Rights 1969, OAS Treaty Series No. 36.
70. See, e.g., International Bar Association, *supra* note 15.
71. Ibid.
72. Ibid. (emphasis added).
73. For discussion, see Kornhauser, *supra* note 27.
74. See, e.g., 'Income Publicity Called Kidnap Aid', *New York Times*, 25 Feb. 1935, at 2.
75. P. Mohr et al., 'Tax Scholars Discuss Corporate Disclosure, Book-Tax Reporting', 99 *Tax Notes* (2003), 617.
76. See, e.g., J. Graham, J. Raedy, and D. Shackleford, 'Research Accounting for Income Taxes', 53 *Journal of Accounting and Economics* (2012), 412.
77. Tax Executives Institute, 'TEI Opposes Public Disclosure of Corporate Tax Returns', *supra* note 33.
78. Nick Greenia, U.S. Internal Revenue Service, *A New External Research Program at the U.S. Tax Agency's Statistical Office: Background, Challenges, Possibilities with Federal Tax Data* (2009), at 3 ("IRS is obsessed with protecting taxpayer confidentiality primarily for one reason. It is viewed as the cornerstone of voluntary compliance, which is considered the backbone of the tax system itself. Anything which threatens, or is perceived to threaten, the protection of taxpayer confidentiality—including statistical use—is unacceptable and will not be tolerated."); see also Tax Executives Institute, 'TEI Opposes Public Disclosure of Corporate Tax Returns', *supra* note 33.
79. Office of Tax Policy, Department of the Treasury, *Report to Congress on Scope and Use of Taxpayer Confidentiality and Disclosure* (2000), at 19.
80. See, e.g., Tax Executives Institute, 'TEI Opposes Public Disclosure of Corporate Tax Returns', *supra* note 34.
81. See J. McCormack, *GE Filed 57,000-Page Tax Return, Paid No Taxes on $14 Billion in Profits*, 17 Nov. 2011, available online at http://www.weeklystandard.com/ge-filed-57000-page-tax-return-paid-no-taxes-on-14-billion-in-profits/article/609137 (last visited 3 July 2017).
82. See, e.g., Valeant Pharmaceuticals International, Inc., *Prospectus (Form 425)*, 23 Apr. 2014.
83. See, e.g., M. De La Merced, 'Hedge Fund Presses Case for Breakup of Darden Restaurants', *New York Times*, 17 Dec. 2013, available online at http://dealbook.nytimes.com/2013/12/17/hedge-fund-presses-case-for-breakup-of-darden-restaurants/?php=true&_type=blogs&_r=0 (last visited 7 June 2017); J. Polson, 'Hess Files for Tax-Free Spinoff of Gas-Station Network', 8 Jan. 2014, available online at http://www.bloomberg.com/news/2014-01-08/hess-files-papers-for-tax-free-spinoff-of-gas-station-network.html (last visited 7 June 2017); P. Whitfield, *BHP Shares Surge on Elliott Management Call to Spin Off Oil Business*, 10 Apr. 2017, available online at https://www.thestreet.com/story/14079463/1/bhp-shares-surge-on-elliott-management-call-to-spin-off-oil-business.html (last visited 3 July 2017).
84. See, e.g., K. Jefford, *IHG Shareholder Pushes for Tax Inversion Bid*, 5 Aug. 2014, available online at http://www.cityam.com/1407198172/ihg-shareholder-pushes-tax-inversion-bid (last visited 7 June 2017).
85. See Ernst & Young, *Media Interaction and Reputational Risk: Issues and Strategies* (2013).
86. Ibid.
87. See Deloitte, *Global Benchmarking Center*, available online at http://www.deloitte.com/view/en_US/us/Services/consulting/Strategy-Operations/8fc7dc4733997210VgnVCM200000bb42f00aRCRD.htm (8 June 2017); Ernst & Young, *EY's Benchmarking Capability*, available online at http://www.ey.com/Publication/vwLUAssets/EY-benchmarking-capability/$FILE/EY-benchmarking-capability.pdf; KPMG, *Benchmarking*, available online at https://home.kpmg.com/gr/en/home/services/advisory/management-consulting/people-services/compensation-benefits-surveys/benefits-benchmarking.html (8 June 2017); PricewaterhouseCoopers, *PwC Benchmarking*, http://www.pwc.com/us/en/benchmarking-services/index.jhtml (8 June 2017).
88. PricewaterhouseCoopers, *supra* note 98.
89. See, e.g., ibid.

90. See, e.g., KPMG, *General Terms and Conditions—KPMG Accountants* (2016), available online at https://home.kpmg.com/be/en/home/insights/2016/04/general-terms-conditions-accountants.html (last visited 8 June 2017).

91. Audit Analytics, *Audit Analytics Peer Reporter*, available online at http://www.auditanalytics.com/0002/peer-reporter.php (last visited 7 June 2017).

92. For discussion, see R. Holmes Perkins, 'The Tax Lawyer as Gatekeeper', 49 *University of Louisville Law Review* (2010), 185, at 192–199.

93. See I.R.C. § 7874(b) (2012). For a description of inversions, see E. Kleinbard, ' "Competitiveness" Has Nothing to Do with It', 144 *Tax Notes* (2014), 1055.

94. See, e.g., E. Hammond, 'Walgreens Urged to Leave U.S. for Tax Cut', *Financial Times*, 13 Apr. 2014, available online at https://www.ft.com/content/55a76778-c294-11e3-9370-00144feabdc0 (last visited 8 June 2017).

95. L. Montgomery, 'U.S. Policymakers Gird for Rash of Corporate Expatriations', *Washington Post*, 6 Aug. 2014, available online at http://www.washingtonpost.com/business/economy/us-policymakers-gird-for-rash-of-corporate-expatriations/2014/08/05/4898ca5e-18d9-11e4-9349-84d4a85be981_story.html (last visited 7 June 2017).

96. See D. Cimilluca, D. Mattioli, and J. Walker, 'Medical Merger Part of "Tax Inversion" Wave', *Wall Street Journal*, 15 June 2014, available online at http://online.wsj.com/articles/medical-merger-part-of-tax-inversion-wave-1402876390 (last visited 7 June 2017); Press Release, Medtronic, Medtronic Completes Acquisition of Covidien, 26 January 2015, available online at http://newsroom.medtronic.com/phoenix.zhtml?c=251324&p=irol-newsArticle&ID=2010595 (last visited 20 July 2017).

97. See N. Grover, *Mylan Presses on with Tax-Inversion Abbott Deal*, 7 Aug. 2014, available online at http://www.reuters.com/article/2014/08/07/mylan-results-idUSL4N0QD46G20140807 (last visited 7 June 2017).

98. Press Release, Johnson Controls, Johnson Controls and Tyco Complete Merger, 6 Sept. 2016, available online at http://www.johnsoncontrols.com/media-center/news/press-releases/2016/09/06/johnson-controls-and-tyco-complete-merger (last visited 3 July 2017).

99. Press Release, Civeo Corporation, Civeo Corporation Announces the Completion of the Redomiciling of the Company to Canada, 7 July 2015, available online at http://ir.civeo.com/releasedetail.cfm?releaseid=922598 (last visited 3 July 2017).

100. Press Release, ARRIS, ARRIS Completes Pace Acquisition, 4 Jan. 2016, available online at http://ir.arris.com/phoenix.zhtml?c=87823&p=irol-newsArticle&ID=2126035 (last visited 2 July 2017).

101. See Bloomberg, *supra* note 76.

102. See K. Hjelmgaard and K. McCoy, 'Walgreens Stock Smacked after Tax Inversion Out', *USA Today*, 6 Aug. 2014, available online at http://www.usatoday.com/story/money/business/2014/08/06/walgreens-alliance-boots-chicago/13659809/ (last visited 7 June 2017).

103. See, e.g., Press Release, Chiquita Brands International, Inc., Chiquita Brands International, Inc. and Fyffes PLC to Combine to Create Leading Global Produce Company, 10 Mar. 2014.

104. D. Gelles, 'Health Care Deal Is Latest to Seek Corporate Tax Shelter Abroad', *New York Times*, 6 Nov. 2013, available online at http://dealbook.nytimes.com/2013/11/06/health-care-deal-is-latest-to-seek-corporate-tax-shelter-abroad/ (last visited 7 June 2017).

105. Kleinbard, *supra* note 104.

106. Ibid.

107. See IRS Notice 2014-52 and IRS Notice 2015-79.

108. See, e.g., V. Fleischer, 'Treasury Takes a Modest Step on Inversions', *New York Times*, 23 Sept. 2014.

109. See Treas. Reg. § 1.7874-8T (2016) (enhancing Section 7874 anti-inversion statute); T.D. 9790 (Oct. 21, 2016) (treatment of certain interests in corporations as stock or indebtedness).

110. The White House Office of the Press Secretary, *Memorandum for the Heads of Executive Departments and Agencies*, 20 Jan. 2017, available online at https://www.whitehouse.gov/the-press-office/2017/01/20/memorandum-heads-executive-departments-and-agencies (last visited 20 July 2017). See A. Versprille, *Trump's Regulatory Freeze: How Broad and for How Long?*, 26 Jan. 2017, available online at https://www.bna.com/trumps-regulatory-freeze-n73014450305/ (last visited 20 July 2017).

111. Executive Order 13789 (Apr. 21, 2017).
112. See, e.g., Donnan et al. at note 70 and accompanying text.
113. See A. Velarde and E. Foster, 'Trump Order Will Require Review of Significant 2016 Tax Regs', 155 *Tax Notes* (1 May 2017), 585; R. Schroeder, *Corporate-Inversion Rules Under Trump Microscope in Move to Lighten Tax Burdens*, 21 Apr. 2017, available online at http://www.marketwatch.com/story/corporate-inversion-rules-to-be-reviewed-under-trump-order-mnuchin-says-2017-04-21 (last visited 20 July 2017).
114. For discussion, see M. Chirelstein and L. Zelenak, 'Tax Shelters and the Search for a Silver Bullet', 105 *Columbia Law Review* (2005), 1939, 1950.
115. See ibid.
116. See PricewaterhouseCoopers, *supra* note 98.
117. See, e.g., L. Browning, 'KPMG Developed New Version of Tax Shelter I.R.S. Had Disallowed', *New York Times*, 26 Aug. 2004, available online at http://www.nytimes.com/2004/08/26/business/kpmg-developed-new-version-of-tax-shelter-irs-had-disallowed.html (last visited 7 June 2017).
118. See Audit Analytics Peer Reporter, *supra* note 102.
119. See, e.g., Salmon, *supra* note 24; Editorial Board of Bloomberg View, *supra* note 24; A. Sloan, 'Hey Corporate America: Show Us Your Tax Returns', *Fortune*, 17 Nov. 2011, available online at http://fortune.com/2011/11/17/hey-corporate-america-show-us-your-tax-returns/ (last visited 7 June 2017).
120. See IRS, *Instructions for Form 1120* (2013), available online at http://www.irs.gov/pub/irs-pdf/i1120.pdf.
121. IRS, *Form 5471* (Rev. Dec. 2012), available online at http://www.irs.gov/pub/irs-pdf/f5471.pdf.
122. IRS, *Form 5472* (Rev. Dec. 2012), available online at http://www.irs.gov/pub/irs-pdf/f5472.pdf.
123. See Treas. Reg. § 1.482-7(k)(4)(ii)(C) (2014).
124. IRS, *Form 5701* (Rev. Dec. 2006).
125. IRS, *Form 870* (Rev. Mar. 1992), available online at http://www.irs.gov/pub/irs-utl/form870.pdf.
126. I.R.C. § 6662(b)(6) (2012).
127. See, e.g., Press Release, Senator Charles Grassley, Grassley Highlights Corporate Loophole Closers in New Tax Bill, 14 Oct. 2004, available online at http://www.finance.senate.gov/newsroom/chairman/release/?id=0226539a-1c0d-4b69-96e3-5094c8923f32 (last visited 20 July 2017).
128. See OECD, *Transfer Pricing Documentation and Country-by-Country Reporting, Action 13—2015 Final Report*, 5 Oct. 2015, available online at http://www.oecd.org/ctp/transfer-pricing-documentation-and-country-by-country-reporting-action-13-2015-final-report-9789264241480-en.htm (last visited 20 July 2017).
129. IRS, *Form 1120* (2013), available online at http://www.irs.gov/pub/irs-pdf/f1120.pdf.
130. Ibid.
131. IRS, *Schedule M-3* (Form 1120) (2016), available online at https://www.irs.gov/pub/irs-access/f1120sm3_accessible.pdf.
132. Such a proposal was proposed in the United States in 1934, but was not implemented. Revenue Act of May 10, 1934, ch. 277, § 55(b), 48 Stat. 680, 698.
133. See Art. 19, ICCPR, *supra* note 21. See International Bar Association, *supra* note 15, at 146.
134. See IRS, *Data Book* (2017), available online at https://www.irs.gov/pub/irs-soi/16databk.pdf.
135. For discussion, see J. D. Blank, *The Timing of Tax Transparency*, 90 *Southern California Law Review* (2017), 449.
136. IRS, *supra* note 134 at 42.
137. See ibid. at 42, note 4.
138. See Treasury Inspector General for Tax Administration, *About TIGTA*, http://www.treasury.gov/tigta/about.shtml#2 (last visited 8 June 2017).
139. See United States Department of Treasury, *IRS Oversight Board*, available online at http://www.treasury.gov/irsob/Pages/default.aspx (last visited 8 June 2017).
140. See I.R.C. § 6103(f) (2012).
141. See Restatement (Third) of Employment Law § 8.02 (Tentative Draft No. 4, 2011); see also Uniform Trade Secrets Act, 14 U.L.A. 433 (1985).

142. For further discussion, see Restatement (Third) of Employment Law 69 (Tentative Draft No. 4, 2011).
143. See, e.g., IRS, *Schedule N (Form 1120)* (2013), available online at http://www.irs.gov/pub/irs-access/f1120sn_accessible.pdf (revealing non-US jurisdictions in which a US corporation owns subsidiaries); IRS, *Schedule G (Form 1120)* (Rev. Dec. 2011), available online at http://www.irs.gov/pub/irs-access/f1120sg_accessible.pdf; IRS, *Form 5472* (Rev. Dec. 2012), available online at http://www.irs.gov/pub/irs-access/f5472_accessible.pdf (identifying 25 percent non-US owners).
144. IRS, *Schedule D (Form 1120)* (2013), available online at https://www.irs.gov/pub/irs-pdf/f1120sd.pdf.
145. IRS, *Form 1125-E* (Rev. Dec. 2013), available online at http://www.irs.gov/pub/irs-pdf/f1125e.pdf.
146. IRS, *Instructions for Form 8886* (Rev. Mar. 2011), available online at http://www.irs.gov/pub/irs-pdf/i8886.pdf.
147. IRS, *Schedule UTP (Form 1120)* (2013), available online at http://www.irs.gov/pub/irs-prior/f1120utp--2013.pdf.
148. See, e.g., IRS, *Instructions for Form 1120* (2013), available online at http://www.irs.gov/pub/irs-pdf/i1120.pdf, at 3.
149. Art. 19 and Art. 25, ICCPR, *supra* note 21.
150. See M. McDonagh, 'The Right to Information in International Human Rights Law', 13 *Human Rights Law Review* (2013), 25, at 29–37.
151. See Art. 25, ICCPR, *supra* note 21. See also J. Rawls, *A Theory of Justice* (rev. ed. 1999), at 14–15.
152. See generally S. Kosslyn et al., *The Case for Mental Imagery* (2006), at 3–23; S. Kosslyn and W. Thompson, 'When Is Early Visual Cortex Activated During Visual Mental Imagery?', 129 *Psychological Bulletin* (2003), 723.
153. See P. Mazzocco and T. Brock, 'Understanding the Role of Mental Imagery in Persuasion: A Cognitive Resources Model Analysis', *in* L. Kahle and C. Kim (eds.), *Creating Images and the Psychology of Marketing Communication* (2006), 65.
154. See, e.g., N. Ellis, 'Word Meaning and the Links Between the Verbal System and Modalities of Perception and Imagery', *in* R. H. Logie and M. Denis (eds.), *Mental Images in Human Condition* (1991), 313.
155. See K. M. O'Craven and N. Kanwisher, 'Mental Imagery of Faces and Places Activates Corresponding Stimulus-Specific Brain Regions', 126 *Journal of Cognitive Neuroscience* (2000), 1013, at 1013–1023.
156. Tax Reform Act of 1986, Pub. L. No. 99-514, 100 Stat. 2085; Tax Equity and Fiscal Responsibility Act of 1982, Pub. L. No. 97-248, 96 Stat. 324; Economic Recovery Tax Act of 1981, Pub. L. No. 97-34, 95 Stat. 172; Deficit Reduction Act of 1984, Pub. L. No. 98-369, 98 Stat. 494.
157. *Gen. Utilities & Operating Co. v. Helvering*, 296 U.S. 200 (1935), overruled by I.R.C. § 311(b) (2012).
158. Tax Reform Act of 1986, Pub. L. No. 99-514, 100 Stat. 2085.
159. See, e.g., R. Pomp, 'State Tax Expenditure Budgets—And Beyond', *in* S. Gold (ed.), *The Unfinished Agenda for State Tax Reform* (1988), 65, at 74.
160. Citizens for Tax Justice, *Corporate Income Taxes in the Reagan Years* (1984); Citizens for Tax Justice, *Corporate Taxpayers & Corporate Freeloaders* (1985).
161. Pomp, *supra* note 29, at 375.
162. *See supra* notes 129–132 and accompanying text.
163. See IRS, *Form 1120*, *supra* note 141, at ll. 30–36.
164. See IRS, *Form 1118* (Rev. Dec. 2013).
165. United States Government Accountability Office, *Corporate Tax Expenditures: Information on Estimated Revenue Losses and Related Federal Spending Programs* (2013).
166. Ibid. at 11.
167. Ibid. at 30.
168. See, e.g., T. Worstall, 'Bloomberg's Getting in a Mess with This Apple Taxes Story', *Forbes*, 30 May 2013, available online at http://www.forbes.com/sites/timworstall/2013/05/30/bloombergs-getting-in-a-mess-with-this-apple-taxes-story/ (last visited 7 June 2017); E. MacDonald, *NY Times Gets Apple's Effective Tax Rate Wrong*, Fox Business, 20 Apr. 2012, available online at

http://www.foxbusiness.com/technology/2012/04/30/did-new-york-times-get-apples-effective-tax-rate-wrong/ (last visited 7 June 2017).

169. See, e.g., Citizens for Tax Justice, *The Sorry State of Corporate Taxes* (2014).
170. See D. Shaviro, 'Beyond Public Choice and Public Interest: A Study of the Legislative Process by Tax Legislation in the 1980s', 139 *University of Pennsylvania Law Review* (1990), 1, at 60
171. See, e.g., Citizens for Tax Justice, *Background and History*, available online at http://ctj.org/about/background.php (last visited 7 June 2017).

CHAPTER 13

HOW COUNTRIES SHOULD SHARE TAX INFORMATION

ARTHUR J. COCKFIELD

I. INTRODUCTION

Civil war has raged in South Sudan since 2013. Since the beginning of this war, corrupt elites and war profiteers have illegally diverted and hidden hundreds of millions of dollars through anonymous investments in tax havens.[1] At the same time, roughly five out of ten million citizens remain and subsist in near-starvation circumstances.[2] As long as elites can profit from war and hide the monies offshore, they may not have incentives to end the conflict. International tax and finance laws allow for these secret offshore accounts and hence contribute to international human rights violations in South Sudan and elsewhere.[3]

In fact, in a 2014 report the UN Special Rapporteur on extreme poverty and human rights identified international tax policy as a significant contributor to global poverty and income inequality.[4] In support, analysis of the first major tax haven data leak shows how elites in low- and middle-income countries move and hide money offshore and how special tax incentives allow firms to greatly reduce their global tax liabilities.[5] Capital flight from some low-income countries exceeds the amount of inward foreign aid, reducing available public resources and leading to devastating consequences, including starvation, disease, and human rights violations.[6]

In addition, multinational firms, which are often based in wealthier countries, operate and exploit natural resources in developing countries, at times without paying any significant tax. This leads to the so-called resource curse where resource-rich countries in the developing world frequently do not benefit from economic growth or tax revenues as a result of resource exploitation.[7] At times, this is attributable to corruption that occurs within some developing countries where bribes or gifts are provided by nonresident multinational firms to local government officials in exchange for tax concessions (see section II.B).

The main policy response thus far to all these challenges is to encourage countries to exchange tax and financial information so that home countries can better enforce their tax laws to inhibit undesired activities. Accordingly, designing optimal exchange of information (EOI) laws and policies for cross-border tax purposes is one of the main challenges for contemporary international tax law and policy. While the roots of EOI go back to the post–World War I environment, the process began to gather real policy steam with the 1998 Organisation for Economic Co-operation and Development (OECD) report on Harmful Tax Competition that threatened to blacklist any noncooperative tax haven.[8] In particular, governments now seek to encourage more and better EOI to inhibit a host of revenue-depleting activities, including aggressive international tax avoidance, offshore tax evasion, and international money laundering.[9]

Since the OECD's opening shot in the late 1990s, there have been series of ambitious EOI reforms, a somewhat stunning development in the normally glacially paced world of international tax law. Recent reforms include US unilateral action via the Foreign Account Tax Compliance Act (FATCA),[10] bilateral tax information exchange agreements (TIEAs), and multilateral efforts to share bulk cross-border tax information on an automatic basis called the Common Reporting Standard (CRS) and country-by-country reporting (CbCR).

Given the important relationship among fair taxation, revenue collection, and the preservation of human rights, this chapter discusses EOI initiatives with an eye toward optimal law and policy. By providing a transaction cost perspective, it shows how governments can reduce taxpayer and government costs by focusing on (1) the exchange of high-quality tax and non-tax data; (2) the provision of training and resources to low- and middle-income countries to facilitate international tax administration; (3) the application of data analytics to exchanged and domestic sources of tax and nontax information; and (4) the development of taxpayer privacy safeguards.

The chapter is organized as follows. Section II provides context by reviewing how taxpayers and tax authorities have mixed views on the need for global financial transparency, and how the recent and varied EOI reforms reflect this state of affairs. Section III reviews the central policy challenges involved in efficient and fair EOI: (1) the need to transfer high-quality information (that is, information that is available, useful, and verifiable for tax authorities); (2) how to protect taxpayer privacy interests while ensuring that tax systems can collect tax revenues from elites and multinational firms; and (3) how to ensure meaningful enforcement of EOI by countries that have strong financial secrecy laws and/or lack tax administration resources. A final section concludes.

II. TRANSACTION COSTS AND CROSS-BORDER TAX INFORMATION EXCHANGE REFORMS

This section provides context by, first, setting out the main information and incentive problems facing tax authorities when they seek information concerning international investment income and, second, by discussing the main US and international law and policy responses to these problems.

A. HIGH TRANSACTION COSTS AND EOI REFORMS

This section outlines the main transaction cost[11] challenges confronting EOI reforms, and calls for legal and policy solutions that reduce transaction costs facing taxpayers and tax authorities. Depending on the context, laws and policies (and accompanying bureaucracies) can either reduce or increase these transaction costs, promoting or discouraging efficiencies. Unlike the private sector, there are no competitive markets for most goods and services supplied by the public sector. As a result, "high transaction costs gravitate to the polity."[12] As subsequently discussed, this is certainly the case with respect to EOI initiatives within the international tax regime.

1. Taxpayers' Preference for Global Financial Opacity

Under the current international tax regime, governments generally do not know anything about a resident taxpayer's global activities beyond taxpayer self-disclosure. Enhanced EOI would seek to change this state of affairs by providing governments with more and better sources of tax information about their resident taxpayers' global activities. Taxpayers engaged in offshore tax evasion and international money laundering clearly prefer the status quo that makes it difficult or impossible for authorities to investigate and track their criminal activities. Less obviously, many taxpayers engaged in legitimate cross-border economic transactions and investments also prefer the current regime with its high transaction costs and lack of global financial transparency.

Information asymmetries raise transaction costs facing taxpayers engaged in cross-border transactions and investments.[13] A taxpayer does not know what sort of assessment will take place after a tax return is filed. In particular, multinational firms pay a hedge price to guard against risks that they will be overtaxed by domestic and foreign tax authorities on their sources of cross-border income (including the risk that a public revelation of any tax plan may harm the firm's reputation and reduce the value of intangible assets like brand or goodwill).[14]

All of this hedging takes place in an environment of highly complex technical rules, making it difficult for taxpayers to predict how domestic tax laws and tax treaties will mesh with foreign tax laws. In particular, many governments now deploy increasingly technical rules—specific anti-avoidance rules (SAARs), general anti-avoidance rules (GAARs), judicially promoted anti-avoidance rules, and so on—to thwart aggressive tax avoidance strategies. This technical complexity contributes to high taxpayer transaction costs due to resources deployed to assess how the rules interact as well as how they will be enforced. Many taxpayers with the resources to engage in cross-border tax planning are actually financially better off under this regime as long as their transaction costs are outweighed by global tax savings.[15]

Moreover, under the current approach taxpayers have an informational advantage over tax authorities as the latter "ex ante lacks information about the true facts and circumstances on the taxable case, whereas the taxpayer has strong incentives not to disclose all available information."[16]

As revealed by writings by accounting academics in this area, taxpayers involved in legitimate businesses at times prefer less financial transparency when it comes to the disclosure of tax and financial information concerning their international activities.[17] First, enhanced EOI may trigger a higher risk of audit, forcing the taxpayer to deploy resources to guard against this risk. Second, taxpayers may desire to hide "sensitive" forms of financial information that could be discerned through EOI reforms (e.g., reporting on taxes paid in every country where a firm operates could reveal profit margins for a global supply chain).

Third, taxpayers may wish to guard against the risk that trade secrets or commercially confidential information will be improperly revealed by governments to foreign competitors, harming their ability to compete. Finally, managers may prefer less transparency to hide their suboptimal allocation of global resources from their own shareholders; greater global financial transparency would let analysts discover and reveal this poor performance.

2. Tax Authorities and Mixed Incentives

While taxpayers generally prefer less global financial transparency, many governments throughout the world have mixed incentives regarding EOI initiatives. These governments are confronted with different and at times conflicting political incentives as they pursue distinct national socioeconomic agendas through their tax systems.

On the one hand, governments want a fair and efficient tax system to promote compliance and revenue collection. More and better cross-border tax information will allow governments to pursue criminal investigations into offshore tax evasion and international money laundering in circumstances where taxpayers use business entities to mask criminal activities.

In addition, enhanced EOI would help tax authorities audit aggressive international tax planning. As noted above, taxpayers have knowledge of their specific facts and circumstances while tax authorities must find and assess noncompliant tax returns without such knowledge. Accordingly, the information battle often takes place between insiders (taxpayers) and outsiders (tax authorities). These endlessly varied fact patterns combined with tax complexity noted previously significantly raise enforcement costs for tax authorities.[18]

From an inter-nation equity perspective, global financial transparency via EOI may also encourage good governance in low-income countries where foreign multinational firms exploit natural resources without paying any significant tax. This failure to pay tax is part of the so-called resource curse where, paradoxically, countries with abundant natural resources sometimes suffer from a lack of economic growth and/or democratic institutions compared to countries with fewer natural resources. In addition, governments may wish to inhibit the ability of tax systems to distort economic decision-making, which reduces economic growth as firms deploy resources for tax reasons and not out of economic rationales (hence resources do not get deployed to their most productive uses). Greater global financial transparency also works against the agency problem noted above where the agent (that is, the manager) hides suboptimal performance from its principal (that is, the shareholder). Finally, EOI could help law enforcement officials detect and disrupt cross-border terrorist financing, promoting national security objectives.

On the other hand, governments often assert the need for "tax competitive" rules to support their domestic industries' efforts to engage in cross-border activities.[19] For this reason, governments around the world pass tax laws to effectively subsidize the international operations of their resident taxpayers who, it is thought, will be in a better position to compete with foreign firms.[20] Similarly, governments may heed taxpayers who advocate that enhanced EOI will unduly raise compliance and other costs, and harm firm competitiveness.

In addition to offering special tax breaks for multinational firms, some governments subvert global financial transparency through their financial secrecy laws to encourage more inward foreign direct and portfolio investments. These governments face a moral hazard as EOI initiatives may make their countries less attractive to nonresident investors who wish to maintain anonymity (out of fear of sanctions from the home country). For instance, US state corporate laws at times allow taxpayers to mask the identity of the beneficial owner of shares of business entities (e.g., Delaware limited liability companies). China has also taken steps to ensure that financial secrecy laws mask true ownership identities in jurisdictions such as Hong Kong and Macau. Under this view, governments are purposely undermining global financial transparency initiatives by raising transaction costs for other governments, making it difficult or impossible for them to enforce their domestic tax laws over income generated abroad (see also section III.C, below).

In summary, governments around the world face different and often conflicting incentives surrounding possible EOI reforms. These mixed incentives have contributed to a mishmash of complex recent EOI reforms.

B. OVERVIEW OF RECENT REFORMS

The modern EOI system was initiated by the League of Nations in the post–World War I environment. A report by the famed "group of four" tax economists laid the foundation for the modern international tax regime by setting out which country should be entitled to tax cross-border transactions and hence enjoy the resulting tax revenues.[21] In addition, the report recommended the adoption of bilateral tax treaty provisions that would contemplate sharing tax information to inhibit "fiscal evasion" (now generally referred to as "offshore tax evasion"). Earlier League of Nations model tax treaties eventually evolved into the OECD model tax treaty, first put into place in 1963.[22] There are now over 3,000 bilateral tax treaties in the world that contain an EOI provision similar to Article 26 of the OECD model.[23]

The following discussion provides an overview of four recent key EOI developments: a unilateral effort by the United States commonly known as the Foreign Account Tax Compliance Act (FATCA); the promotion of bilateral TIEAs; a multilateral effort to share taxpayer information called the Common Reporting Standard; and another multilateral reform advocating cross-border sharing of multinational firm tax and financial information called country-by-country reporting.

1. Unilateralism via US FATCA

FATCA was passed by Congress in 2010 and came into general effect in 2013.[24] Under FATCA, foreign banks must provide financial information concerning all "U.S. persons" (including citizens and residents living abroad) directly to the Internal Revenue Service (IRS). If the foreign banks do not cooperate, provisions under FATCA would impose a punitive withholding tax on cross-border bank transactions from foreign countries.

As a result of this risk to their banking sectors, foreign governments agreed to enter into intergovernmental agreements (IGAs) with the US government.[25] For instance, Canada signed an IGA with the United States whereby Canadian banks must collect specified financial information concerning any identified US persons and send this first to the Canadian tax authorities for subsequent transfer to the IRS. By the end of 2015, 110 countries had agreed to an IGA.

2. Bilateralism through Tax Information Exchange Agreements

As mentioned in the introduction to this chapter, the more recent push for enhanced EOI began with the OECD Harmful Tax Competition Project in 1998 (which was later named the Forum on Harmful Tax Practices).[26] The report encouraged the adoption of agreements between OECD countries and low or nil tax jurisdictions (commonly referred to as tax havens, although sometimes termed "international financial centers"). In 2002, the OECD developed a model TIEA to serve as a template for these new treaties. By January 1, 2016, over 700 bilateral TIEAs had been signed.

A major drawback of TIEAs is that they operate on the basis of "information on request." For instance, if the UK government wanted to find out about the dealings of a UK resident taxpayer with a Singaporean bank, then the UK authorities would need to identify the relevant bank and specify the name of the taxpayer and the nature of the information they need. This places governments in a catch-22 position because offshore monies are typically held in anonymous accounts and the tax authorities do not have sufficient information to request the relevant taxpayer information in the first place. The most comprehensive analysis of TIEAs to date suggests that, while TIEAs helpfully established international norms surrounding EOI and global financial transparency, they largely failed to reduce offshore tax evasion or aggressive international tax planning.[27]

3. Multilateralism via the Common Reporting Standard

The OECD reforms were later joined by the G20 to more broadly represent countries that would be subject to EOI obligations. The OECD and the G20 supervise the Global Forum on Transparency and Exchange of Information for Tax Purposes, which as of this writing, has 135 participating countries. Both the OECD and the G20 came to view the TIEA approach as deficient, especially with respect to the "information on request" approach noted above.

Accordingly, in 2013 with the G20 Summit at St. Petersburg, the G20 and OECD endorsed the Common Reporting Standard as the global standard. A related multilateral agreement contemplates the automatic sharing of bulk taxpayer information across borders.[28] Under this approach, a participating country such as Singapore is supposed to pass laws that mandate the automatic collection by banks of foreign investor tax information then transfer this information to other participating countries such as the United Kingdom. Through a peer review processes, the Global Forum tries to ensure that its members implement and comply with promised EOI standards and obligations.

As of this writing, over ninety countries, including Canada, have agreed to implement the Common Reporting Standard. The United States so far has refused to sign on, preferring to focus on its domestic initiatives such as FATCA.

4. Multilateralism and Tracking Multinational Firm Tax Payments

The policy push for the next EOI reform—called country-by-country reporting (CbCR)—began in 2002 with a related effort by the Extractive Industries Transparency Initiative (EITI).[29] EITI encourages governments and extractive industries (that is, companies involved with mining and other resource extraction) to provide more financial disclosures to the public. The purpose behind this initiative is to inhibit the "resource curse," mentioned in the introduction to this chapter, whereby developing countries often collect little to no tax revenues when multinational firms exploit their natural resources. If revenues are in fact collected, the focus on transparency of natural resource revenues is meant to allow citizens to judge whether resource revenues are being spent well and to prevent their leaders from using the cover of secrecy to embezzle public resources. Participating companies and national governments can voluntarily adopt EITI transparency measures that include country-by-country reporting whereby taxpayers disclose where, and how much, tax is paid.

In 2013, the OECD also began an ambitious plan to counter "Base Erosion and Profit Shifting" (BEPS) by multinational firms. BEPS refers to the many international tax avoidance plans that firms adopt to legally reduce their global tax liabilities, often by shifting paper profits to tax havens. After three years of reform efforts, the OECD produced its final recommendations, including for all participating countries to adopt CbCR.[30] Under CbCR, multinational firms for the first time would need to disclose to home and foreign tax authorities their tax and other payments in every country where they operate. Currently, most countries do not require such information disclosures. CbCR also only applies to very large multinational firms with annual consolidated group revenues that exceed €750 million (or roughly $850 million).

CbCR is mainly directed at helping governments audit aggressive international tax avoidance to reduce revenue losses in high-tax countries. Under the proposed approach, a parent corporation files a CbCR report following an OECD template; the report will then be shared with other countries that are participating in automatic information exchanges. It is hoped tax authorities will be able to identify important indicators such as their country's relative share of global tax revenues. As of May 2016, thirty-nine countries had signed a related multilateral agreement, which commits them to implementing CbCR.[31]

C. SUMMARY

As things currently stand, the global financial system can be characterized as opaque as tax authorities generally know little to nothing beyond taxpayer self-disclosure. Accordingly, a tax authority finds itself at a distinct informational disadvantage, especially regarding purposeful nondisclosures relating to offshore tax evasion. While there appears increasing policy and academic support for EOI initiatives that promote global financial transparency, the current international tax regime, with its high transaction costs for taxpayers and tax authorities, does not seem particularly amenable to producing optimal outcomes.

In particular, governments have imperfect information to discern whether their international tax laws and policies promote sought-after national interest objectives (these governments are "boundedly rational" in transaction cost terms). On the one hand, they want to promote firm competitiveness via preferential tax treatment of foreign income. In addition, many countries maintain financial secrecy laws to encourage inward investments. On the other, governments want a fair tax system that maximizes revenue collection and promotes human rights (see section II.A). These mixed political incentives reduce the potential for welfare-maximizing cooperative moves among governments.

Nevertheless, in recent years worries about revenue losses from offshore evasion and aggressive international tax planning have brought governments to the bargaining table. The complex network of tax treaties, TIEAs, and IGAs, as well as larger multilateral reforms focusing on CRS and CbCR reflect this state of affairs, raising transaction costs for all parties.

All of these efforts seek to provide governments with more and better tax information, and reduce costs through agreement on underlying EOI rules and principles. The reforms, however, largely do not address how financial secrecy laws subvert global financial transparency initiatives. Nor do they address legal technical complexity that raises transaction costs, and makes it even harder for low- and middle-income countries to implement and enforce EOI. While the EOI reforms are positive steps, given an environment of high transaction costs, it may be difficult to make progress in addressing key policy challenges, a topic to which we now turn.

III. ASSESSING THE CENTRAL LEGAL AND POLICY CHALLENGES

This section emphasizes how, to promote enforceability, the ideal EOI system delivers high-quality tax information while providing needed legal protections for taxpayer privacy.

A. INFORMATION QUALITY

A key issue in cross-border tax information exchanges involves the quality of exchanged tax-payer information. The Common Reporting Standard and other initiatives emphasize the automatic exchange of so-called bulk taxpayer information. According to the OECD, for example, automatic exchanges of bulk taxpayer information is the most effective way to help assist tax authorities with enforcing their cross-border tax laws.[32] As suggested by tax compliance writings, however, more information is not necessarily better.[33] Tax authorities may be overwhelmed with data and may not have the resources to parse through it to identify helpful leads. As subsequently explored, high-quality information is tax and nontax data that is available, useful, and verifiable.

1. Available Information

Available information is tax and nontax information that is potentially accessible by governments for EOI purposes. A tax authority must first identify a taxpayer and related offshore income before it can conduct risk analysis that accounts for factors such as the size of the taxpayer and the industry in which the taxpayer works. Writings on tax compliance emphasize how tax authorities can tap into existing information streams to bolster and confirm a taxpayer's disclosed income.[34] In particular, third-party reporting and tax-withholding disclosures can provide information to tax authorities to allow them to better gauge risks of offshore tax evasion and aggressive international tax planning.

Third-party reporting of tax and financial information can be cross-matched with transferred tax information to support information quality. Empirical studies generally suggest that third-party reporting (that is, information provided by someone other than the taxpayer, such as a bank reporting interest income) goes a long way to addressing the "tax gap."[35] Even self-assessment systems, such as ones deployed in the United States and Canada, are broadly supported by third-party reporting efforts.

In addition to third-party reporting, *effective tax withholding* is an important element of tax administration. For instance, different types of withholding account for roughly 75 percent of personal income tax revenues for OECD countries.[36] Value-added taxes (VATs) are sometimes thought to be superior to income taxes from a tax-enforcement perspective in part because VATs provide rebates to taxpayers (other than final consumers) and hence operate in a similar fashion to a creditable withholding tax: under this approach, taxpayers have an incentive to report taxable transactions so they can collect the VAT rebates and thus do not technically pay any taxes, as only the final consumers do so. Similarly, "traditional" withholding taxes on cross-border passive income (that is, rents, royalties, dividends, and interest) help to enforce tax laws by imposing the disclosure and withholding obligations on the payor.

The most prominent example of information exchange and withholding for cross-border purposes is the European Union's Savings Directive where members automatically exchange information about portfolio nonresident interest payments (alternatively, if an exchange of information does not occur then the country where the investment takes place will tax the interest and send the bulk of the resulting tax revenues to the residence country).[37] Accordingly, this EOI measure ensures tax payment via withholding or provides the government with another source of information to contrast against the taxpayer's tax filings. The Directive was repealed in 2015 in favor of pursuing automatic cross-border tax information exchanges under the OECD's Common Reporting Standard outlined in section II.B.3.[38]

A similar measure to the older Savings Directive may be needed to promote effective EOI at the global level. As Reuven Avi-Yonah has explained, as long as there is one nonparticipating country, then undisclosed investment monies can flow to this outlier.[39] His proposed solution resembles the EU Savings Directive as it would impose a withholding tax on these monies whenever they flow to a noncooperative country. Building on these views, I previously outlined how online technologies—an extranet among participating countries—could be used to impose such a withholding tax.[40]

Another major barrier to effective EOI is that many countries simply do not track these tax information sources so that they are unable to exchange this information when called upon to do so. As subsequently discussed, many low- and middle-income countries also lack the administrative resources to collect and transfer this information (see section III.C).

2. Useful Information

Not all tax information is created equal. From a tax administration perspective, some sources of information, or relationships among different sources, are superior to others. Governments should hence focus on ensuring that available information is useful for tax authorities.

To start, the information exchanged needs to be *relatable* to other recipient country taxpayer information. The most frequently touted solution is for countries to agree on a *common taxpayer identification number*. This number could be matched against the unique one provided by each government; a software program could readily identify whether the taxpayer had disclosed all of his or her sources of foreign income.

Another need is for transferred information to identify *the beneficial owner* of an offshore asset (that is, the ultimate human being who owns the asset). One of the main barriers to effective EOI is the lack of information in this area as a result of financial secrecy laws that mask the identities of beneficial owners.[41]

In addition, the ability of tax authorities to engage in taxpayer segmentation (that is, separating taxpayers into different risk groups) is increasingly seen as a necessary step to better identify risks. Hence *transferred information that enables taxpayer segmentation* promotes information quality. For example, many OECD governments have created audit groups that focus on high-net-worth individuals, which seem appropriate given their larger share of resources and potential contribution of tax revenues.[42] High-net-worth individuals also tend to be more mobile internationally, and engage in more aggressive tax planning structured by tax advisors. Governments have also expanded information reporting for entities owned by these individuals along with broader disclosure of foreign assets and transactions.

Another way tax authorities are looking to bolster the quality of transferred information is by *cross-indexing it against nontax data*. For an example of an initiative to reduce tax cheating, Greek auditors took satellite photos from Google Earth as well as aerial photos from helicopters to collect images of pools, luxury cars, and villas to help sustain audits against taxpayers who disclosed few assets or little income: one such audit revealed that Athenian suburbs did not have 324 swimming pools, as had been disclosed by taxpayers, but rather 16,974.[43]

The transferred information should have sufficient "volume, variety and velocity" to constitute *big data so that it can be subjected to data analytics*.[44] The collection of big data and use of data analytics enhances information quality and has the potential to reduce transaction costs by better identifying risks for audit and enforcement purposes. Data analytics is the computer analysis of big data to reveal patterns or other information that is useful to governments, businesses, or other analysts. The basic idea is that, while different data points from different sources may appear unrelated, data analytics can potentially provide insights by combining all of the data points to reveal new information and connections that had been previously undetected, helping to target tax audits.

Finally, promoting *disclosures by smaller offshore financial intermediaries* (e.g., trust, finance and other offshore service providers) will also promote information quality and help tax authorities understand the nature and amount of offshore investments held by their residents. Current reform efforts, including by the Financial Action Tax Force (FATF), focus on enhancing disclosure obligations for financial intermediaries to report on offshore assets maintained by foreigners.

As revealed by an analysis of tax haven data leaks, a major vulnerability in these efforts is the lack of reporting by hundreds of offshore service providers such as trust, finance, or other financial service providers based in tax havens. In many cases, these offshore service providers at times did not report accurate tax and financial information on cross-border investments as required by FATF recommendations. Noncompliance resulted from a lack of due diligence, willful neglect, and legal insulation through indemnification agreements between the offshore service provider and the nonresident investor.[45]

Yet even these smaller players often have funds transferred to larger financial institutions, which generally strive to comply with FATF disclosure requirements (or, more technically, the domestic legislation that implements these requirements). Reporting obligations can be cross-referenced against amounts transferred to and from the larger institutions to smaller banks with help from offshore service providers. Moreover, offshore service providers often manage monies on behalf of individuals and organizations engaged in offshore tax evasion (by, for instance, forming a corporate trustee for a nonresident trust that holds legal title to the illicitly earned monies).

Tracking the offshore service providers name along with any prior compliance problems would provide another important piece of information for tax and law enforcement authorities.

3. Verifiable Information

There are several related issues surrounding data verifiability. Governments need to feel confident that the transferred information has so-called data integrity. First, tax authorities need to know who owned the transferred data that had been collected. Some countries have laws that provide governments with direct access to a taxpayer's database while others do not.

Second, governments need assurances that the transferred information accurately represents the underlying information (e.g., sales receipts) that gave rise to the data. Evidence should be collected to show the data was not tampered with by the taxpayer or some third party. As touched on below, data integrity is related to the issue of data security in that outside hackers may illegally access, change, or delete taxpayer information.

B. TAXPAYER PRIVACY

As I explored in another work, there are two discrete but related elements surrounding effective EOI.[46] First, the cross-border tax exchange should be efficient in that it should promote low enforcement and administrative costs for tax authorities and low compliance costs for taxpayers. Second, the exchange must be fair in that any transferred information will attract a requisite level of legal protection for taxpayer privacy and other rights. The two issues are related in that a tax authority will be reluctant to engage in EOI if it worries that its taxpayers' privacy and other rights will be harmed. This section touches on how taxpayer privacy concerns serve as an ongoing barrier to effective EOI, as well as how reforms can address this challenge.

1. Taxpayer Privacy as a Human Right

Privacy can be portrayed as a critical human right in a free and just society. This human right protects an individual's right to freedom of expression, freedom of mobility, freedom to engage in political dissent, and so on. Similarly, Article 12 of the UN Universal Declaration of Human Rights maintains, "No one shall be subjected to arbitrary interference with his privacy, family, home or correspondence, nor to attacks upon his honor and reputation. Everyone has the right to the protection of the law against such interference or attacks."

In privacy law writings, financial information privacy, including taxpayer information, is typically cited as one of the most sensitive forms of privacy because it can provide a detailed profile of an individual's identity and behavior (e.g., an individual's tax return includes information on donations, health matters, income levels, disability status, names and ages of any dependents, and so on).[47] Historically, taxpayer privacy has been protected for reasons that include personal security as criminals might be tempted to kidnap the children of individuals whose wealth was revealed by tax disclosures. In addition, individuals may wish to conceal their financial dealings to protect against envy or political reprisals.

National financial privacy rights and laws vary around the world in part because certain cultures are more sensitive to perceived incursions into financial privacy, potentially as a result of historical developments. For instance, historical taxpayer privacy concerns—where a home could be searched, assets seized, and taxpayers improperly imprisoned without due process protections—served as a catalyst for the earliest Western laws, including the Charter of Liberties of 1100 and the Magna Carta of 1215, that sought to bind the power of the king.[48] In certain countries such as Canada and the United States, privacy interests are additionally protected by constitutional guarantees that cannot generally be violated by state action (e.g., the right to be free from an improper search and seizure).

All of this has led to serious government concerns that transferred tax information will not be protected to the extent provided by the law of the transferring country. Relatedly, governments worry about the possible misuse of transferred information where countries sanction taxpayers for political reasons, potentially violating human rights. Another area of concern is the possible triggering of so-called false positives that target innocent taxpayers based on flawed data.

In addition, there have been ongoing apprehensions surrounding the interaction between technology and taxpayer privacy for some time, from concerns surrounding the usage of electronic records in the 1970s, the movement from analog to digital storage in the 1980s, online return filing and software audits in the 1990s, and, more recently, collecting taxpayer information to tax global digital goods and services in the 2000s.[49] A major barrier to enhanced EOI is the worry that new technologies, which enable the mass storage and transmission of detailed taxpayer information, will violate privacy laws, policies, and interests.

These worries have gained credence as a result of data leaks such as WikiLeaks that show governments, including the United States and Canada, conduct surveillance efforts to collect "economic intelligence" by stealing corporate secrets from overseas competitors.[50] The related tax worry is that governments will misuse transferred tax and financial information to help domestic companies and undermine foreign ones.

Finally, the data security of transferred information remains a significant concern. For instance, the IRS experiences one million attempts every week to hack its information technology systems.[51] If countries do not adopt appropriate network security safeguards and protocols, then transferred information is at risk of illegal collection, use, and disclosure.

For all of these reasons, privacy researchers tend to emphasize theories and analytical frameworks that broadly protect privacy interests. Accordingly, privacy researchers, including tax law academics, tend to argue for an expansive definition of privacy to reduce the chance that privacy rights and interests will be eroded. The outcome is broad protections for taxpayer privacy rights in the domestic and international context, which can serve as a barrier to EOI reforms.

2. Addressing Privacy Challenges

While this matter has been understudied since the push for enhanced EOI began in the late 1990s, more recent reform efforts have tried to more explicitly engage with taxpayer privacy concerns. For example, under the CbCR reforms noted in section II.B, governments must agree to provide and enforce legal protections to maintain the confidentiality of reported information equivalent to the protection under an income tax treaty or other EOI agreement. Further, the automatic transmission of CbCR information is limited to those countries that satisfy these requirements. The OECD plans additional reforms to monitor compliance with the taxpayer privacy commitments.

In another work, I suggested these EOI efforts could be bolstered via a multilateral taxpayer bill of rights to provide assurances that transferred tax and financial information will attract a minimal level of legal and policy protection.[52] In particular, this bill of rights could incorporate widely accepted fair information practices (FIPs) (e.g., accountability, notice, choice, access and security) that serve as the basis for domestic privacy laws (e.g., Canada's federal privacy law[53]), international privacy laws (e.g., the European Union's General Data Protection Regulation[54]), and administrative guidelines (e.g., the US Federal Trade Commission's data privacy guidelines[55]).

These FIPs are used to smooth over conflicts caused by different national privacy laws. FIPs also strive to promote data integrity and data security. A recent example of their usage is the 2016 European Union–United States Privacy Shield that is designed to protect individuals' privacy rights when personal data is transferred from European companies to US ones.[56]

Beyond these pragmatic policy responses, researchers need to do a better job at addressing conceptual questions surrounding the use of privacy law as a barrier to EOI reforms. Consider, for instance, the distributive justice implications of the current regime: the main beneficiaries of a lack of global financial transparency are multinational corporations and high-net-worth individuals (along with criminals).[57] The main bearers of the cost of the regime are average taxpayers and citizens as a result of the revenue losses associated with offshore tax evasion and aggressive international tax planning. Most distressingly, global financial opacity allows corrupt elites to move and hide stolen monies offshore and encourages devastating consequences for some low income countries, including starvation and other human rights violations (see section I).

Privacy researchers have examined distributive concerns of privacy laws through different theoretical lenses.[58] Some of these writings claim that privacy researchers should be wary of conceptual tools that lead to privacy law being used as a weapon to promote unbalanced outcomes that protect the interests of the more powerful at the expense of the least powerful. The analysis seems particularly relevant for EOI reforms as a key purpose of tax systems is to enhance the overall welfare of citizens and residents, including the promotion of human rights. Under the International Covenant on Economic, Social and Cultural Rights (ICESCR), a multilateral treaty adopted by the UN General Assembly, participating countries promise to encourage the adoption of economic, social, and cultural rights, including the right to education and to an adequate standard of living.[59] To pursue these goals, governments need to adopt a fair tax system that collects revenues from wealthy taxpayers, including multinational firms, and prevents elites from hiding their monies in offshore tax havens.

In particular, broader conceptions of the "social value" of privacy consider the overall impact of privacy laws and policies on privacy rights of both individuals and communities.[60] These views call for more nuanced analysis in situations where privacy rights protect powerful taxpayers with foreign investments (along with criminals) at the expense of the interests of average taxpayers.

C. ENFORCEMENT

As discussed throughout this chapter, governments are currently trying to fight two main international tax battles against offshore tax evasion and aggressive international tax avoidance. Success within these battles will result in more tax revenues. As Walter Hellerstein notes, however, success will only be achieved if governments are able to link their enforcement jurisdiction with their existing legal jurisdiction.[61]

1. Reducing the Underground Economy

With respect to the first battle, much of offshore tax evasion is related to a country's underground economy (for instance, an off-grid cash-only restaurant where the owner squirrels away undisclosed income in an anonymous offshore account). A variety of incentives have been discussed to inhibit the underground economy, including the greater usage of value-added taxes, electronic fiscal devices (e.g., electronic cash registers that are certified by the government), lotteries where consumers can turn in receipts, tax reductions for proof of payment, and tax rebates for the use of credit/debit card (to reduce cash transactions).[62] According to the International Monetary Fund, these efforts have led to mixed results, at best.[63]

More recently, works have recognized the importance of less tangible cultural forces in promoting taxpayer compliance (the cultural forces and social norms are sometimes collectively termed "taxpayer morale").[64] These factors influence compliance behavior, including whether a resident taxpayer feels patriotic toward her country and whether she thinks she is getting a roughly fair return on a tax payment. Accordingly, it may be difficult for tax law and enforcement reforms alone to change taxpayer compliance conduct in a significant way.

Nevertheless, in the international sphere whistleblowing initiatives appear to offer hope to uncover global financial crimes such as the UBS bank scandal. There is emerging evidence that whistleblowing programs can have a material impact on revenue collection: as a result of the UBS whistleblower, the US government forced the Swiss government to transfer information concerning over 2,000 anonymous accounts maintained by Americans. In the United States, whistleblowing rewards have been steadily growing to roughly $501 million in 2015.[65]

2. Financial Secrecy Laws and Misaligned Incentives

Countries have historically jealously guarded their rights to develop tax and financial privacy laws as they wish. Accordingly, tax havens and many other countries passed financial secrecy laws to anonymize the identity of the ultimate owner of investments. The end result has been the traditional near-anonymity offered by global capital markets for private financial and, in many cases, nonfinancial wealth (e.g., a Manhattan condo). Up to roughly fifteen years ago, an investor who placed his or her money in an offshore bank account could be reasonably confident that nobody would learn of its existence. This state of affairs greatly increases transaction costs facing tax authorities that seek information regarding offshore transactions.

Tax authorities also face significant bargaining costs if their audit involves the international criminal aspects of a taxpayer's activities: investigations and prosecutions can take years to complete with potentially weak sanctions if the taxpayer is ever convicted. For this reason, taxpayers engaged in offshore tax evasion are sometimes offered different forms of relief through voluntary disclosure programs, including amnesty from criminal prosecutions, should they disclose their offshore assets and income in a timely fashion.

The main enforcement challenge is a lack of international cooperation due to misaligned political incentives.[66] Elites within low- and middle-income (often nondemocratic) countries use international financial secrecy as an exit strategy that allows them to move and hide monies offshore (to preserve their family wealth and security). Tax havens, even if they are forced into binding agreements such as TIEAs, have incentives to subvert the system (e.g., by developing new business and legal entities that may fall outside of current FATF disclosure obligations) and shirk (e.g., by not meaningfully enforcing EOI agreements by ensuring they do not maintain necessary records subject to a transfer request).

Low-income countries additionally may not have the human resources and physical infrastructure to enforce their own domestic tax laws, let alone engage in effective EOI.[67] Foreign aid and other resources need to be directed at bolstering the tax administration efforts for these low-income countries. This effort would promote global financial transparency, and reduce transaction costs faced by the tax authorities in high-income countries as they would be in a better position to track the cross-border investments of their own citizens and residents.

Wealthier OECD countries benefit from this state of affairs because they are net recipients of trillions of dollars in capital flight leaving other countries.[68] For instance, the three largest OECD economies—the United States, Germany, and Japan—are ranked by Tax Justice Network in the world's top twelve financial secrecy jurisdictions along with tax havens such as Switzerland and Luxembourg.[69]

As a result of these misaligned incentives, countries cannot agree, for instance, on a binding supranational agreement that would abolish all financial secrecy laws. Notably, taxpayer privacy concerns serve as perhaps the main plausible rationale for refusing to enter into such an agreement, highlighting the need to protect privacy interests to encourage enforcement (see section III.B).

D. SUMMARY

Many governments now have over two decades' worth of experience with automatic tax information exchange. Most recently, governments have signed onto the Common Reporting Standard to promote automatic bulk exchanges. While automatic bulk EOI is a worthy goal, improving the quality of the exchanged information is the next area of obvious focus.

Data availability, usefulness, and verifiability are three components of high-quality information that can help governments pursue their cross-border investigations and audits. In particular, transferred information should be relatable to domestic tax identification measures, and checked against third-party reporting, and withholding tax disclosures. Once this is done, governments can conduct analysis to determine audit risk by focusing on issues such as taxpayer segmentation, dealings between the taxpayer and offshore service providers, and cross-indexing tax and financial information against nontax data (e.g., insurance policy disclosures).

Against this desire for high-quality tax information stands (shrugs?) taxpayer privacy concerns. The apprehensions arise from the varied levels of domestic legal protection afforded to privacy rights, along with the risk of abuse or misuse of transferred information. Accordingly, broader multilateral agreement on privacy protections is likely a prerequisite to effective EOI. This hoped-for cooperation is hindered by the fact that many countries refuse to abolish their financial secrecy laws, which stands as one of the main barriers to optimal reform.

IV. CONCLUSION

A lack of global financial transparency permits corrupt elites and others to drain their countries of financial resources then hide these monies offshore. In some cases, such as the South Sudanese example in the introduction to this chapter, much of the remaining population suffers from starvation and other human rights violations. In other situations, developing countries provide multinational firms with tax breaks that allow these firms to exploit resources and reap significant profits—while paying little to no taxes. In addition, complex cross-border tax planning structures can subvert the intent of tax laws by lowering global financial tax liabilities for wealthy taxpayers. All of these forms of underpayment or nonpayment of taxes to governments deprive the state of monies needed to deliver on its human rights obligations through the provision of public goods and services, from a functioning judiciary to healthcare, education, environmental regulation, housing, and an adequate standard of living.

To fight against offshore tax evasion and aggressive international tax avoidance, governments increasingly turn to cross-border exchanges of (tax) information (EOI). More and better information could promote global financial transparency and address information asymmetry problems that bedevil enforcement efforts. The last ten years has witnessed a number of related reforms, including a US unilateral effort known as the Foreign Account Tax Compliance Act, an OECD initiative to promote bilateral tax information exchange agreements and multilateral agreements regarding the Common Reporting Standard and country-by-country reporting.

As countries build on these initiatives and deploy new ones, they are increasingly studying optimal EOI laws and policies. While ongoing reforms emphasize exchanges of "bulk" or mass taxpayer data, less attention has been paid to promoting high-quality tax information exchanges to support government audits and investigations. High-quality information is information that: (1) can be accessed and cross-indexed by governments against other information sources; (2) is useful for tax administration purposes; and (3) is verifiable to ensure data integrity. The exchange and usage of high-quality tax information would reduce transaction costs for tax authorities as they could more readily identify taxpayers engaged in offshore tax evasion and aggressive international tax planning.

Yet there are ongoing barriers that inhibit the exchange of high-quality tax information. Taxpayer privacy remains a concern, given the varied national and international rules that protect taxpayer privacy interests, along with disagreement on appropriate safeguards. Tax havens and other countries asometimes maintain financial secrecy laws that make it difficult or impossible to determine the ultimate owner of cross-border investments. Moreover, many low-income countries lack the human and physical resources to engage in automatic EOI, let alone ensure the transferred information is of high quality. Foreign aid and other resources should be directed at bolstering the tax administration of these countries, which would promote global financial transparency and help other countries enforce their own tax laws over international investments.

NOTES

1. A revised and expanded version of this chapter appeared in 50 *Vanderbilt Journal of Transnational Law* (2017), 1091. The Sentry, *War Crimes Shouldn't Pay: Stopping the Looting and Destruction in South Sudan* (2016), available online at https://cdn.thesentry.org/wp-content/uploads/2016/09/Sentry_WCSP_Finalx.pdf, at 11 (citing a speech from the president of South Sudan: "An estimated $4 billion are unaccounted for or, simply put, stolen by former and current officials, as well as corrupt individuals with close ties to government officials").
2. Ibid. at 5 (noting roughly 5 out of 10 million citizens receive food aid to stave off starvation).
3. The Office of the United Nations High Commissioner for Human Rights has called South Sudan "one of the most horrendous human rights situations in the world." Ibid. at 13.
4. Human Rights Council, Report of the Special Rapporteur on Extreme Poverty and Human Rights, Ms. Maria Magdalena Sepúlveda Carmona, UN Doc. A/HRC/26/28, 22 May 2014. See also International Bar Association, *Tax Abuses, Poverty and Human Rights: A Report of the International Bar Association's Human Rights Institute Task Force on Illicit Financial Flows, Poverty and Human Rights* (2013), available online at http://www.ibanet.org/Document/Default.aspx?DocumentUid=4977CB3D-4988-4C9C-84C7-9050A5CB2311, at 18–19 (last visited 8 June 2017).
5. The data leak, obtained by the International Consortium for Investigative Journalists in 2012, included over 2.5 million documents. The leak revealed, among other things, over 20,000 offshore accounts maintained by Chinese individuals. A. J. Cockfield, 'Big Data and Tax Haven Secrecy', 12 *Florida Tax Review* (2016), 483, at 510–517.
6. L. Ndikumana and J. Boyce, *New Estimates of Capital Flight from Sub-Saharan African Countries: Linkages with External Borrowing and Policy Options* (2008), available online at http://scholarworks.umass.edu/cgi/viewcontent.cgi?article=1137&context=peri_workingpapers, at 27–30 (concluding that a "narrow, relatively wealthy stratum" of the populations of the countries under study maintained assets in foreign countries that exceeded the national public debts of their own countries) (last visited 8 June 2017).
7. See A. Christians, 'Putting the Reign Back in Sovereign', 40 *Pepperdine Law Review* (2013), 1373.
8. OECD, *Harmful Tax Competition: An Emerging Global Issue* (1998).
9. For background policy pressures, see S. A. Dean, 'The Incomplete Global Market for Tax Information', 49 *Boston College Law Review* (2008), 605.
10. The initial legislation, entitled the Foreign Account Tax Compliance Act (FATCA), was not enacted. See H.R. 3933, 111th Cong. (1st Sess. 2009). The legislation was subsequently passed within a large omnibus legislative package that was mainly directed at job creation. See Hiring Incentives to Restore Employment Act, Pub. L. No. 111-147, para. 501, 124 Stat. 71 (2010). The provisions to implement FATCA are now contained in Sections 1471 to 1474 of the Internal Revenue Code (Sup. 2011).
11. Transaction costs are the costs associated with discerning a price on a given exchange. While transaction costs are normally discussed in the context of private sector exchanges, transaction cost economics and transaction cost politics extend the analysis to the public sphere. Under these approaches, government institutions (that is, informal and formal rules) along with government

institutional arrangements (that is, organizations) determine the level of transaction costs facing private sector and government actors, which in turn influences economic activities. O. E. Williamson, 'Public and Private Bureaucracies: A Transaction Cost Economics Perspective', 15 *The Journal of Law, Economics, & Organization* (1999), 306.

12. See D. North, 'A Transaction Cost Theory of Politics', 2 *Journal of Theoretical Politics* (1990), 355, at 362.

13. For discussion, see A. J. Cockfield, 'The Limits of the International Tax Regime as a Commitment Projector', 33 *Virginia Tax Review* (2013), 59 (describing the international tax regime as a legal and political system that enables credible government commitments to actors such as taxpayers in order to reduce transaction costs).

14. See A. J. Cockfield and C. MacArthur, 'Country-by-Country Reporting and Commercial Confidentiality', 63 *Canadian Tax Journal* (2015), 627, at 644–645.

15. See V. Fleischer, 'Regulatory Arbitrage', 89 *Texas Law Review* (2010), 227 (discussing how transaction costs affect tax-planning incentives).

16. M. Brem and T. Tucha, 'Globalization, Multinationals, and Tax Base Allocation: Advance Pricing Agreements as Shifts in International Taxation?', *in* C. Read and G. Gregoriou (eds.), *International Taxation Handbook: Policy, Practice, Standards, and Regulation* (2007), 111, at 141.

17. We reviewed empirical studies within the accounting field that show mixed results concerning the relationship between reporting geographic earnings and protecting commercial secrets: some studies conclude that geographic earnings disclosures harm the competitiveness of firms, while others suggest that such disclosures do not promote these harmful outcomes. Cockfield and MacArthur, *supra* note 14, at 647–650.

18. In transaction cost terminology, each taxpayer has its own relationship-specific investment (e.g., its own unique intellectual property to exploit). For a discussion of relationship-specific investments, see O. E. Williamson, 'The New Institutional Economics: Taking Stock, Looking Ahead', 38(3) *Journal of Economic Literature* (2000), 595, at 596–600.

19. Critics of the tax competitiveness criterion state that it is not grounded in any substantive tax policy and should not serve as a guide to international tax policy. See P. R. McDaniel, 'Territorial vs Worldwide International Tax Systems: Which Is Better for the U.S.?', 8 *Florida Tax Review* (2007), 283, at 301.

20. As of January 2018, the United States adopted a new approach whereby most active business income earned in foreign countries is no longer subject to residence-based taxation.

21. See Professors Bruins, Einaudi, Seligman, and Sir Josiah Stamp, *Report on Double Taxation Submitted to the Financial Committee* (1923).

22. See OECD, *Model Tax Convention on Income and on Capital* (Condensed Version, 2010), at 26–27. For background discussion, see M. J. Graetz and M. M. O'Hear, 'The "Original Intent" of U.S. International Taxation', 46 *Duke Law Journal* (1997), 1027.

23. V. Thuronyi, 'Tax Cooperation and a Multilateral Tax Treaty', 26 *Brooklyn Journal of International Law* (2001), 1641, at 1641 (discussing the influence of the OECD model tax treaty on the global network of bilateral tax treaties).

24. The legislation now comprises Sections 1471 to 1474 of the Internal Revenue Code, along with over 500 pages of related regulations.

25. For discussion and critique of FATCA, see S. D. Michel and H. D. Rosenbloom, 'FATCA and Foreign Bank Accounts: Has the U.S. Overreached?', 62 *Tax Notes International* (2011), 709, at 712; A. Christians and A. J. Cockfield, *Submissions to Finance Department on Implementation of FATCA in Canada*, 10 Mar. 2014, available online at https://papers.ssrn.com/sol3/papers.cfm?abstract_id=2407264 (last visited 8 June 2017).

26. For discussion, see R. T. Kudrle, 'The OECD and the International Tax Regime: Persistence Pays Off', 16 *Journal of Comparative Politics* (2014), 201 (claiming OECD institutional processes effectively promoted EOI reforms via horizontal diffusion of policy).

27. See D. Kerzner and D. Chodikoff, *International Tax Evasion in the Global Information Age* (2016), at 344.

28. OECD, *CRS Multilateral Competent Authority Agreement* (2014), available online at http://www.oecd.org/tax/automatic-exchange/international-framework-for-the-crs/multilateral-competent-authority-agreement.pdf. This agreement in turn is based on Article 6 of an earlier multilateral agreement. See OECD, *Convention on Mutual Administrative Assistance in Tax Matters* (1998), available online at http://www.oecd.org/ctp/exchange-of-tax-information/theconventiononmutualadministrativeassistanceintaxmatters-background.htm (last visited 8 June 2017). We discuss the arguments for and against CbCR along with possible extension to limited public disclosures. See Cockfield and MacArthur, *supra* note 14, at 640–644, 657–660.

29. Information concerning this program is set out at the Extractive Industries Transparency Initiative website at https://eiti.org/.

30. CbCR falls under Action 13 of the OECD BEPS Action Plan. See OECD, *Action Plan on Base Erosion and Profit Shifting* (2013), available online at https://www.oecd.org/ctp/BEPSActionPlan.pdf, Action 13, 'Re-Examine Transfer Pricing Documentation' (last visited 8 June 2017).

31. OECD, *Multilateral Competent Authority Agreement for the Automatic Exchange of Country-by-Country Reports* (2014), available online at http://www.oecd.org/tax/automatic-exchange/about-automatic-exchange/cbc-mcaa.pdf.

32. OECD, *Manual on the Implementation of Exchange of Information Provisions for Tax Purposes: Module 3 on Automatic (or Routine) Exchange of Information* (2006), at 3.

33. For discussion, see W. Cui, 'Information Reporting and State Capacity' (draft, 2016) (questioning the link between information reporting and tax compliance).

34. See, e.g., L. Lederman, 'Reducing Information Gaps to Reduce the Tax Gap: When Is Information Reporting Warranted?', 78 *Fordham Law Review* (2010), 1733 (discussing six factors to evaluate whether information reporting is likely to be efficient).

35. The tax gap is the amount of revenue loss between the amount of tax required to be paid under tax law and the amount that is actually paid by taxpayers. See IRS, *The Tax Gap*, available online at https://www.irs.gov/uac/the-tax-gap (discussing how third-party reporting can assist with tax enforcement) (last visited 21 July 2017).

36. International Monetary Fund, *Current Challenges in Revenue Mobilization: Improving Tax Compliance* (2015), available online at https://www.imf.org/external/np/pp/eng/2015/020215a.pdf, at 18.

37. See European Union, Council Directive 2003/48/EC of 3 June 2003 on Taxation of Savings Income in the Form of Interest Payments, OJ 2003 L 157/38.

38. See European Union, Council Directive 2014/107/EU, OJ 2014 L 359/1. This Directive entered into force on Jan. 1, 2016.

39. R. Avi-Yonah, 'Globalization, Tax Competition, and the Fiscal Crisis of the Welfare State', 113 *Harvard Law Review* (2000), 1573, at 1667–1669.

40. A. J. Cockfield, 'Transforming the Internet into a Taxable Forum: A Case Study in E-Commerce Taxation', 85 *Minnesota Law Review* (2001), 1171, at 1235–1263.

41. See Human Rights Council, *supra* note 4, at paras. 20–21.

42. Countries with such audit groups include Canada, the United States, France, Ireland, the United Kingdom, New Zealand, South Africa, and Japan. See IMF, *supra* note 36, at 27. The top 1 percent in the United Kingdom and the United States now account for approximately one-quarter and one-third, respectively, of personal income tax revenues. Ibid. at 26.

43. See D. Steinvorth, 'Finding Swimming Pools with Google Earth: Greek Government Hauls in Billions in Back Taxes', *Der Spiegel*, 2 Aug. 2011, available online at http://www.spiegel.de/international/europe/finding-swimming-pools-with-google-earth-greek-government-hauls-in-billions-in-back-taxes-a-709703.html (last visited 7 June 2017).

44. See M. Alles and G. Gray, *A Framework for Analyzing the Potential Role of Big Data in Auditing: A Synthesis of the Literature* (Working Paper, 2014).

45. See Cockfield, *supra* note 5, at 519–522.

46. See Cockfield, *infra* note 52, at 454.

47. P. Baker and A. Groenhagen, *The Protection of Taxpayers Rights—An International Codification* (2001). See also A. J. Sawyer, 'A Comparison of New Zealand Taxpayers' Rights with Selected Civil Law and Common Law Countries - Have New Zealand Taxpayers Been "Short-Changed"?', 32 *Vanderbilt Journal of Transnational Law* (1999), 1345.

48. See A. J. Cockfield and J. Mayles, 'The Influence of Historical Tax Law Developments on Anglo-American Law and Politics', 3 *Columbia Journal of Tax Law* (2013), 40.

49. For discussion, see A. J. Cockfield et al., *Taxing Global Digital Commerce* (2013), at 515–518.

50. WikiLeaks not only revealed the NSA information collection practices but also provided evidence that Canadian spies, including the Communications Security Establishment of Canada (CSEC), were (bizarrely) spying on the Brazilian mining ministry. See C. Freeze and S. Nolen, 'Charges that Canada Spied on Brazil Unveil CSEC's Inner Workings', *Globe and Mail*, 7 Oct. 2013, available online at https://www.theglobeandmail.com/news/world/brazil-spying-report-spotlights-canadas-electronic-eavesdroppers/article14720003/ (last visited 8 June 2017).

51. S. R. Johnson, 'The Future of American Tax Administration: Conceptual Alternatives and Political Realities', 7 *Columbia Journal of Tax Law* (2016), 17.

52. A. J. Cockfield, 'Protecting Taxpayer Privacy under Enhanced Cross-border Tax Information Exchange: Toward a Multilateral Taxpayer Bill of Rights', 42 *University of British Columbia Law Review* (2010), 420.

53. Personal Information Protection and Electronic Documents Act (S.C. 2000, c. 5, as amended) (Can.).

54. European Union, Regulation 2016/679 of the European Parliament and of the Council of 27 April 2016 on the protection of natural persons with regard to the processing of personal data and on the free movement of such data, and repealing Directive 95/46/EC.

55. United Stated Federal Trade Commission, *Privacy Online: Fair Information Practices in the Electronic Marketplace, A Report to Congress* (May 2000), available online at https://www.ftc.gov/reports/privacy-online-fair-information-practices-electronic-marketplace-federal-trade-commission, at 18 (last visited 21 July 2017).

56. See European Commission, *Guide to the E.U.-U.S. Privacy Shield* (2016), available online at http://ec.europa.eu/justice/data-protection/files/eu-us_privacy_shield_guide_en.pdf, at 9–19.

57. The state of affairs actually incentivizes taxpayers to engage in offshore tax evasion by lowering the transaction costs they face. See L. Benham, 'Licit and Illicit Responses to Regulation', *in* C. Ménard and M. Shirley (eds.), *Handbook of New Institutional Economics* 591, at 605 (describing how regulatory solutions can incentivize illegal activities).

58. J. Bailey, 'Towards an Equality-Enhancing Conception of Privacy', 31(2) *Dalhousie Law Journal* (2008), 267; A. Allen, *Why Privacy Isn't Everything: Feminist Reflections on Personal Accountability* (2003).

59. International Covenant on Economic, Social and Cultural Rights 1996, 993 UNTS 3.

60. These conceptions typically rely on an extension of Westin's famed discussion of information privacy. A. Westin, *Privacy and Freedom* (1967), at 7; P. Regan, *Legislating Privacy: Technology, Social Values and Public Policy* (1995); A. J. Cockfield 'Protecting the Social Value of Privacy in the Context of State Investigations Using New Technologies', 40 *University of British Columbia Law Review* (2007), 421.

61. W. Hellerstein, 'Jurisdiction to Tax Income and Consumption in the New Economy: A Theoretical and Comparative Perspective', 38 *Georgia Law Review* (2003), 1.

62. For discussion, see J. Bankman, 'Eight Truths about Collecting Taxes from the Cash Economy', 117 *Tax Notes* (2007), 506.

63. IMF, *supra* note 36, at 30.

64. Ibid. at 21.

65. See IRS Whistleblower Office, *Fiscal Year 2015 Report to Congress* (2016), available online at https://www.irs.gov/pub/whistleblower/WB_Annual_Report_FY_15_Final%20Ready%20for%20Commissioner%20Feb%208.pdf.

66. See Cockfield, *supra* note 5, at 535–538.

67. See A. Easson and D. Holland, *Taxation and Foreign Direct Investment: The Experience of the Economies in Transition* (OECD, 1995); T. Besley and T. Persson, 'Why Do Developing Countries Tax So Little?', 28 *Journal of Economic Perspectives* (2014), 99; Human Rights Council, *supra* note 4, at para. 79 (recommending the provision of resources and technical assistance to support low-income countries' tax administrations).

68. The first major tax haven data leak revealed over 20,000 offshore accounts maintained by Chinese individuals, primarily for purposes of cross-border investments. Over US$1 trillion in capital is estimated to have fled China in the last ten years. See M. Walker Guevara et al., 'Leaked Records Reveal Offshore Holdings of China's Elite', *International Consortium of Investigative Journalists*, 21 Jan. 2013.

69. See Tax Justice Network, *Financial Secrecy Index 2015: Methodology* (2015), at 75–79.

CHAPTER 14

UNITED STATES' RESPONSIBILITY TO PROMOTE FINANCIAL TRANSPARENCY

TRACY A. KAYE*

I. INTRODUCTION

A 2013 report by the International Bar Association's Human Rights Institute on tax abuses, poverty, and human rights concludes that "[a]ctions of states that encourage or facilitate tax abuses" could violate international human rights.[1] Facilitating offshore investment can be such a tax abuse, contributing to the tax gap in developing countries by allowing wealthy individuals and companies to evade taxes on monies held offshore.[2] The negative effect of the resulting revenue losses on the ability of countries to meet their human rights commitments is becoming increasingly apparent.[3] The Boston Consulting Group calculates that roughly 25 percent of private wealth in the Middle East, Africa, and Latin America is booked offshore, totaling approximately $3.1 trillion.[4] A report by the Tax Justice Network estimates between $21 trillion to $32 trillion of unreported private financial wealth was held offshore by wealthy individuals at the end of 2010.[5] Gabriel Zucman disagrees, estimating that only 8 percent of household global financial wealth (equivalent to $7.6 trillion) can be found in tax havens—a sum that nevertheless deprives governments of $200 billion in annual revenue.[6] Tax administrations have a responsibility to tackle this serious taxpayer compliance problem and make extraordinary efforts to improve taxpayer compliance in the interest of fairness. What is perhaps most troublesome, however, is that as other governments improve their financial transparency, the share of offshore wealth destined for the United States increases.[7] "That 'giant sucking sound' you hear? It is the sound of money rushing to the USA to avoid" global account tax compliance activities (GATCA) reporting required by the OECD.[8]

It is generally understood that the automatic exchange of taxpayer information among tax administrations is an effective way to fight offshore tax evasion. Thus, the global financial transparency movement encourages jurisdictions to commit to implementing the Common Reporting Standard for Automatic Exchange of Information (CRS) developed by the Organisation for

Tax, Inequality, and Human Rights. Philip Alston and Nikki Reisch.

Economic Co-operation and Development (OECD).[9] The international standards that are being developed to promote greater transparency and ensure effective exchanges of tax information should aid tax authorities in combating tax evasion. Over one hundred jurisdictions have committed to implementing CRS in 2017 or 2018, but the United States is not one of them.[10] This is despite the fact that as a member of the G20, the United States joined in reaffirming its commitment to international tax cooperation and financial transparency at the July 2017 summit in Hamburg, Germany.[11]

The global movement toward financial transparency is marching on, but the United States is falling behind its peers due to legislative and regulatory inaction caused by political gridlock. The US Foreign Account Tax Compliance Act (FATCA) requires foreign financial institutions (FFIs) to report certain information about financial accounts held by US taxpayers or by foreign entities in which US taxpayers hold a substantial ownership interest.[12] As of January 25, 2018, over 287,000 FFIs have registered with the Internal Revenue Service (IRS).[13] In return, the United States has committed to reciprocal information sharing in its intergovernmental agreements with more than fifty jurisdictions.[14] However, pursuant to the Bank Deposit Interest Reporting regulations finalized in 2012, the United States is only able to share the amount of interest paid to foreign individuals who are residents of forty-five specified countries instead of the more detailed information required by FATCA.[15] In contrast to the FFIs that report to the United States, the US banks are only reporting on the individual accounts of foreign residents. Thus, the information exchange rules for banks in the United States with respect to foreign residents are easily avoided if the bank account is held in the name of a shell corporation.[16]

This chapter will discuss the legislative and regulatory changes that are necessary for the United States to fully participate in the global financial transparency movement. This includes the collection of beneficial ownership information for any legal entities formed in the United States. The Global Forum on Transparency and Exchange of Information for Tax Purposes (Global Forum), which monitors the OECD work being done on tax transparency and exchange of information,[17] found the United States to be only "Largely Compliant" concerning ownership information and reliable accounting records for entities during its peer review of the US tax system.[18] Information exchange partners had complained about the unavailability of beneficial ownership information of limited liability companies (LLCs) in several states, including Delaware.[19] These omissions have been heavily criticized by the international community and have led to the United States being labeled a tax haven.[20] This is serious because "[t]ax havens are at the heart of financial, budgetary, and democratic crises."[21]

The United Nations' Guiding Principles on Business and Human Rights (GPBHR) implement the United Nations' "Protect, Respect, and Remedy Framework," which deals with human rights and business enterprises.[22] The Commentary to the GPBHR reiterates the obligations of states under international human rights law to protect the human rights of their citizens, which includes protecting them against human rights abuses by third parties.[23] This means the state must take "appropriate steps to prevent, investigate, punish, and redress" such abuses through effective "policies, legislation, regulations and adjudication."[24] Failure to prevent tax abuses by private actors can be considered a breach of the United States' international human rights obligations.[25] This chapter concludes that the United States must participate in the global financial transparency movement if it is to properly implement the Guiding Principles.

II. AUTOMATIC EXCHANGE OF INFORMATION

A. FATCA AND THE RIGHT TO PRIVACY

Although offshore tax evasion is a global problem, the United States initially chose a unilateral legislative response: FATCA.[26] Enacted in 2010,[27] FATCA essentially enlists FFIs to report directly to the IRS certain information about financial accounts held by US taxpayers or by foreign entities in which US taxpayers hold a substantial ownership interest.[28] FFIs began reporting financial information on their US account holders in 2015 with respect to 2014 tax information.[29]

Such financial reporting has exposed tensions between the right to privacy and tax transparency. The Universal Declaration of Human Rights articulates a right to privacy specifying that, "[n]o one shall be subjected to arbitrary interference with his privacy . . . Everyone has the right to the protection of the law against such interference or attacks."[30] Therefore, some argue "every person has the right to minimize the amount of data flowing to others, including to the government, provided doing so does not violate any laws."[31] For example, Senator Rand Paul filed a lawsuit with members of Republican Overseas Action[32] in the US District Court for the Southern District of Ohio on July 14, 2015, challenging the constitutionality of FATCA.[33] One of their arguments is that "FATCA eschews the privacy rights enshrined in the Bill of Rights in favor of efficiency and compliance by requiring institutions to report citizens' account information to the IRS even when the IRS has no reason to suspect that a particular taxpayer is violating the tax laws."[34]

The US District Court for the Southern District of Ohio denied the FATCA plaintiffs' motion for preliminary injunctive relief based on a lack of standing, and the Sixth Circuit affirmed the judgment of the district court.[35] Furthermore, the district court held that the FATCA statute is rationally related to the legitimate state interest of addressing offshore tax evasion.[36] US citizens and residents who are banking within the United States have their payments of interest reported by the US payor to the IRS.[37] US taxpayers tolerate this loss of financial privacy because it is imperative to the efficient functioning of the tax system and because of the limitations on the access by others to such financial information.[38]

Although many scholars have stressed the importance of tax transparency in making the US tax system work properly,[39] there has been a vigorous debate about the public disclosure of tax returns since the enactment of the income tax.[40] Since 1976, however, tax return data is confidential and cannot be disclosed by the IRS except under specific circumstances outlined in the Internal Revenue Code.[41] But there is no financial privacy for US citizens and residents regarding disclosure of information *to the IRS* with respect to US bank accounts, and there is no reason for disparate treatment just because a bank account is held offshore. The proof that FATCA was needed to enforce parity, is that over $10 billion has been collected from the 55,800 taxpayers who have participated in the IRS's Offshore Voluntary Disclosure Programs and the additional 48,000 taxpayers who have used the streamlined procedures. Those programs have been in place since 2009 to allow US taxpayers to disclose overseas assets and limit exposure to civil penalties and criminal prosecution for nondisclosure.[42]

B. FATCA AND BILATERAL AGREEMENTS

The United States chose to resolve the many issues that arose in the implementation of FATCA through bilateral agreements known as Intergovernmental Agreements (IGAs). Many of the

FFIs are governed by these IGAs, which have been negotiated by the FFIs' governments with the United States to facilitate the effective implementation of the FATCA requirements found in the Internal Revenue Code and corresponding regulations.[43] The US Treasury published two versions (a reciprocal version and a nonreciprocal version) of a Model IGA to Improve Tax Compliance and to Implement FATCA (Treasury Model I) in 2012.[44] Bank secrecy legislation in certain jurisdictions as well as other domestic legal impediments regarding data protection and privacy laws necessitated the use of such agreements.[45] The Treasury Models allow the financial institutions of these countries to report the required FATCA information to their own governments, which then transmit the data to the IRS.[46] The United States has more than 110 IGAs with various jurisdictions.[47] This number includes nonreciprocal IGAs as well as the reciprocal IGAs previously discussed.

For purposes of ascertaining which financial accounts held by foreign entities are affected, the FATCA statute defines substantial ownership by a US taxpayer as direct or indirect ownership of more than 10 percent of such foreign entity.[48] This rule is instrumental in precluding US taxpayers from avoiding FATCA by holding their accounts through foreign entities.[49] However, the IGAs substitute the concept of "controlling persons"[50] for the statutory definition of "substantial U.S. owner." Critics argue that this modification severely weakens the rule by raising the substantial ownership threshold for all banks located in an IGA jurisdiction to 25 percent and assert that the 25 percent threshold is easily avoided.[51] One positive ramification of the IGAs is that the United States realized that in order to undertake these bilateral arrangements, it would also have to be willing to provide these same foreign countries with information.[52] Many of the IGAs are reciprocal agreements with the FATCA partner jurisdictions. This means that the United States has committed to "pursuing equivalent levels of exchange" with respect to the collection and reporting of financial information to the respective authorities on the US financial accounts of residents of that jurisdiction.[53] Furthermore, Treasury Model 1A IGAs commit the United States to "pursuing the adoption of regulations and advocating and supporting relevant legislation to achieve such equivalent levels of reciprocal automatic information exchange."[54]

C. THE COMMON REPORTING STANDARD

In 2013, the G20 finance ministers unanimously endorsed the OECD's proposal for a global model for multilateral automatic exchange of tax information known as CRS[55] and committed "to automatic exchange of information as the new, global standard."[56] Forty-nine countries pledged to exchange information on financial accounts beginning in 2017, and another fifty-three jurisdictions will begin this exchange in 2018.[57] The United States is not one of these countries. The OECD notes that the United States will be undertaking automatic information exchanges from 2015 onward in accordance with FATCA and pursuant to its IGAs with other jurisdictions.[58] In its 2016 economic survey of the United States, the OECD recommends that the United States also commit to implementing the CRS by 2017 or 2018.[59]

The Convention on Mutual Administrative Assistance in Tax Matters (the Convention), signed in 1988, has always provided for automatic exchange of information.[60] Accordingly, adopters of CRS have been encouraged to sign the Convention rather than negotiate new bilateral agreements.[61] The number of signatories to the Convention exceeds one hundred.[62] The Multilateral Competent Authority Agreement on Automatic Exchange of Financial Account Information will be used to implement the CRS.[63] As of January 2018, the United States was not participating.[64]

The United States' position with respect to the global automatic exchange of information is that it is pursuing automatic information exchanges beginning in 2015 through FATCA.[65] The first deadline for the exchange of information for IGA jurisdictions was September 30, 2015. Details of over 30,000 financial accounts worth over $5 billion were provided to the IRS by the Australian Tax Office.[66] The Canadian Revenue Agency confirmed that it completed its first exchange with the IRS of approximately 155,000 pieces of banking information for US persons with accounts in Canada.[67] On October 2, 2015, the IRS announced its exchange of financial account information with certain foreign tax administrations with no details.[68]

The IRS will only engage in reciprocal information exchanges with foreign jurisdictions that meet stringent privacy and technical standards.[69] According to the disclosure report filed in 2014, automatic exchange of information with foreign governments was suspended in 2013 in order to update the processes the IRS used "to assess whether U.S. exchange partners have the appropriate legal framework and infrastructure to safeguard the information exchanged."[70] The disclosure report required to be filed by the IRS with respect to 2015, the first year of automatic exchange with certain foreign governments, does not show any significant increase in the exchange of information despite FATCA reciprocity requirements.[71] However, there was improvement in 2016. Over 4.1 million disclosures with respect to reportable accounts held by residents of foreign jurisdictions were made to the foreign jurisdiction tax administrations (authorized by the revenue procedure) in accordance with Article 2(2)(b) of the respective IGAs.[72]

Despite its pledge of reciprocal information sharing in its IGAs with more than fifty jurisdictions,[73] the United States is legally able to share only the amount of interest paid to foreign recipients who are residents of the forty-five countries listed in Rev. Proc. 2017-46 (having been determined to meet stringent privacy and technical standards).[74] As noted above, FATCA requires more detailed information, such as account balances, and obligates foreign financial institutions to ascertain the substantial US owners of certain legal entities while the US banks only report on the individual accounts of foreign residents.[75] Thus, the US Bank Deposit Interest regulations with respect to foreign accountholders are easily avoided.[76] The CRS, on the other hand, ensures transparency by requiring "institutions to look through and determine controlling persons for both passive nonfinancial entities and investment entities in nonparticipating jurisdictions."[77] Critics have remarked that US resistance to the global disclosure standards of CRS is effectively making the United States "the biggest tax haven in the world."[78]

III. THE UNITED STATES IS A TAX HAVEN?

"Less obvious than the risks of active abuse ... but cumulatively as harmful to society, are the acts of omission that secrecy makes possible—such as the failure of many to carry their part of the collective tax burden whenever they can conceal some of their income."[79]

During the 1990s, the United States declared war on foreign tax havens ignoring the fact that, according to many commentators, the United States itself serves as a tax haven to many.[80] According to Nicholas Shaxson, the world comprises "approximately sixty secrecy jurisdictions that are divided into four groups," one of which includes "a United States zone of influence."[81] As of 2010, the United States had negotiated tax treaties or tax information exchange agreements with over eighty-five countries,[82] but until 2014 had meaningful information exchange only with Canada.[83] Banks were not required to automatically report the interest payments made to foreign persons unless the US bank deposit interest was paid to Canadian residents.[84] This information had not been collected or made available for any other jurisdiction.[85] Thus, the US government had no information to exchange with its other treaty partners, resulting in de facto bank secrecy.[86]

A. BANK DEPOSIT INTEREST REPORTING REGULATIONS

The Bill Clinton administration grew concerned that US taxpayers were avoiding the information reporting system by falsely claiming foreign status.[87] A regulation proposed in 2001,[88] which would have required the reporting of US bank deposit interest paid to foreign persons, met with such intense opposition that the George W. Bush administration withdrew it.[89] A decade later, in 2011, new proposed regulations extended "the information reporting requirement to include bank deposit interest paid to nonresident alien individuals who are residents of any foreign country."[90] The preamble to these proposed regulations noted the "growing global consensus regarding the importance of cooperative information exchange for tax purposes."[91]

However, there has been a long history in the United States of affording financial privacy to foreign persons for many reasons, including the encouragement of the use of US banks.[92] Proposed regulations mandating automatic reporting to the IRS of interest paid to foreign persons were met with vociferous opposition for years until a compromise was finally adopted in 2012.[93] The Florida banking industry predicted a massive outflow of capital to other countries, perhaps as much as $100 billion in deposits.[94] Florida's Commissioner for Financial Regulation's survey found that 41 percent of deposits in south Florida state-chartered commercial banks are nonresident alien (NRA) deposits, of which 26 percent are individual deposits. Furthermore, 90 percent of deposits in foreign banks in south Florida are NRA deposits, of which 31 percent are individual deposits.[95]

Clearly, certain members of Congress are concerned about foreign capital flight if the United States no longer provides banking secrecy to foreign persons. This is because once the IRS is in possession of the bank deposit information, Internal Revenue Code Section 6103(k)(4) allows disclosure to the tax authorities of the foreign person's residence.[96] The privacy argument used on behalf of foreign persons was to posit the dire consequences should that resident country's government be "oppressive, corrupt, unstable, or otherwise irresponsible" leading to "expropriation or persecution."[97] Other concerns include inappropriate safeguards with respect to confidentiality, which might lead to criminal use of the information resulting in robberies or kidnappings.[98] Professor Julie Roin, however, has argued that "bank secrecy laws and tax haven entities encourage corrupt administration and corrupt administrators."[99]

In 2012, a compromise was reached and regulations regarding the reporting of interest paid to foreign individuals were finalized with some changes.[100] Starting with payments of interest made in 2013, both US and certain nonresident accounts are uniformly disclosed to the IRS.[101] This should facilitate "the ability of the United States to offer cooperative, reciprocal tax information exchange arrangements" with designated foreign tax administrations.[102] The preamble to the finalized bank deposit interest regulations stressed that information will only be exchanged where the United States is satisfied that the "foreign jurisdiction's legal framework" guarantees the confidentiality of the taxpayer information.[103] Thus, the finalized bank deposit interest regulations only require reporting of interest paid to a foreign individual resident in a country with which the United States has deemed that there is an appropriate information exchange agreement in force.[104]

As previously discussed, there was no automatic exchange of information with foreign governments in 2013[105] while the procedure was suspended to assess the US exchange partners' legal framework and infrastructure for safeguarding the information exchanged.[106] As of January 2018, forty-five countries are eligible for the automatic exchange of the information being collected under these regulations.[107] The only countries in the Americas on the list are Brazil, Colombia, Mexico, and Panama.[108]

Senator Levin, former Chairman of the Permanent Subcommittee on Investigations, had strongly recommended that the bank deposit interest regulations also be made applicable to accounts opened by corporations, trusts, or other entities that are beneficially owned by individuals.[109] However, this recommendation was unfortunately not followed. Thus, the bank deposit interest reporting rules only apply to the nonbusiness interest on directly held bank deposits of certain nonresident individuals.[110] This loophole was highlighted in critiques of the previous versions of this regulation. Scholars explained that by treating a foreign corporation as the beneficial owner of the income, the effectiveness of this regulation was severely limited.[111]

FATCA, on the other hand, requires FFIs to report on accounts held by an entity where more than 10 percent is owned by a US person, although the threshold is raised to 25 percent where the FFI is in a jurisdiction with an IGA.[112] FFIs are also required to report account balances and any dividends, interest, and gross proceeds paid to the account. As the United States is expecting global compliance from foreign financial institutions, US financial institutions should be collecting the same information as our FATCA partners and FFIs.[113] A former UBS employee commented: "How ironic—no, how *perverse*—that the USA, which has been so sanctimonious in its condemnation of Swiss banks, has become the banking secrecy jurisdiction *du jour*."[114]

B. RECIPROCITY IN THE EXCHANGE OF INFORMATION

The Barack Obama administration acknowledged the importance of the information received from the FATCA partners to IRS enforcement efforts against offshore tax evasion.[115] As detailed in the IGAs, these jurisdictions expect US cooperation and reciprocity in information exchange.[116] Following the enactment of FATCA, the Obama administration repeatedly proposed that US financial institutions should be required to report to the IRS the same information currently required of the FFIs, such as account balances and gross proceeds.[117] It is concerning that the current breakdown of the US legislative process has not allowed the United States to participate fully in the global movement toward transparency after having been the leading proponent of this movement.[118] In a letter to Congress in 2016, then Treasury Secretary Lew urged Congress to "enact legislation approving pending tax treaties and granting reciprocal Foreign Account Tax Compliance Act (FATCA) information sharing."[119] As of January 2018, no such action has been taken.

In 2016, an article in *Bloomberg Businessweek* noted that "[b]y resisting new global disclosure standards, the U.S. is . . . becoming the go-to place to stash foreign wealth. Everyone from London lawyers to Swiss trust companies is . . . helping the world's rich move accounts from places like the Bahamas and the British Virgin Islands to Nevada, Wyoming, and South Dakota."[120] A report by the Tax Justice Network (TJN) severely criticizes the United States' unwillingness to participate in transparency initiatives such as the CRS and the creation of public registers of beneficial ownership. The latest TJN report moves the United States up from third place to second place on its financial secrecy index in 2018, due to its growing share of the offshore financial services industry (up from 19.6 percent in 2015 to 22.3 percent in 2018).[121] Commentators are suspicious that congressional reluctance to enact any legislative reforms is about "giving America's financial centres an edge."[122]

C. BENEFICIAL OWNERSHIP LEGISLATION
IN THE UNITED STATES

On April 4, 2016, the International Consortium of Investigative Journalists announced their access to the "Panama Papers," 11.5 million documents comprising forty years of emails, bank accounts, and client records from the Panamanian law firm Mossack Fonseca.[123] This latest public disclosure reveals the offshore accounts of individuals and corporations from over 200 countries as well as the prevalent use of anonymous offshore shell companies. That the offshoring of wealth affects nearly all countries demonstrates that the movement toward global transparency is inevitable. The Panama Papers are also a powerful reminder that transparency matters greatly in the war on tax evasion and highlighted the damaging use of shell corporations to enable such tax evasion.

The global reaction to the Panama Papers was swift.[124] "The recent leaks exposed loopholes that still allow tax evaders to hide funds offshore," said Moscovici, EU Commissioner for Economic and Financial Affairs, Taxation, and Customs. "These loopholes must be closed and our measures to stamp out tax abuse must be intensified."[125] The ranking member of the US Senate Finance Committee has requested "information about the Treasury Department's efforts to combat tax abuse by anonymous shell companies."[126] Senator Ron Wyden is also advocating for a registry of corporations' beneficial owners to aid in law enforcement.[127] Wyden sent a letter to the Nevada Secretary of State expressing "concern about the use of anonymous shell companies as vehicles for terrorist financing, tax evasion, and fraud,"[128] and noting that Mossack Fonseca has ties to more than 1,000 shell companies in Nevada.[129]

The G20 had previously announced the need for improvements in the implementation of international standards on transparency and the availability of beneficial ownership information.[130] Citing the disclosure of the "Panama Papers" as having brought the issues of illicit financial activity and tax evasion into the public spotlight, the Obama administration set forth various regulatory and legislative initiatives designed "to combat money laundering, corruption, and tax evasion."[131] The Treasury Department finalized a Customer Due Diligence (CDD) Final Rule, proposed Beneficial Ownership legislation, and proposed regulations requiring foreign-owned entities to obtain an employer identification number (EIN) from the IRS.[132] Then Treasury Secretary Jack Lew said that these actions "mark[ed] a significant step forward to increase transparency and to prevent abusive conduct within the financial system."[133]

Covered financial institutions were not "required to know the identity of the individuals who own or control their legal entity customers (also known as beneficial owners),"[134] which allowed anonymous access to the financial system. The CDD final rule's beneficial ownership requirement attempts to address this weakness and will bring the United States into compliance with international standards and commitments.[135] The CDD final rule requires among other actions, the identification and verification of the identity of the beneficial owners of companies opening accounts.[136] The Final Rule sets forth a two-pronged definition of beneficial owner: (1) "each individual, if any, who directly or indirectly owned 25 percent of the equity" of the legal entity (the ownership prong); and (2) an "individual with significant responsibility to control, manage, or direct" the legal entity (control prong).[137]

Various nongovernmental organizations have voiced a concern with the 25 percent threshold, arguing that it is too easily avoided.[138] Global Financial Integrity criticizes the CDD Final Rule because where there is no individual with a 25 percent interest, "the only person named will be the manager."[139] Transparency International notes that the Panama Papers demonstrated that officials named in leadership positions in anonymous companies are often merely figureheads while the legal entity is controlled through other means.[140] Financial institutions must instead direct their efforts toward securing information about the individuals who actually exercise control of a legal entity.

The second piece of the Obama administration financial transparency package asked Congress to pass legislation that would require companies to report accurate beneficial ownership information to the Treasury Department at the time of a company's incorporation, noting that the ability to use anonymous shell companies to hide beneficial ownership is a "significant weakness in the U.S. anti-money laundering . . . regime that can only be resolved by Congressional action."[141] However, for years Senators Carl Levin and Chuck Grassley had been advocating legislation that would have required states to document the beneficial owners of the corporations, to no avail.[142] Similar legislation, the True Incorporation Transparency for Law Enforcement Act, was introduced in the 115th Congress on June 28, 2017.[143]

The third piece of the financial transparency package comprises final regulations issued in December 2016, which require a foreign-owned single-member LLC to obtain an employer identification number and satisfy the reporting and associated compliance requirements that apply to 25 percent foreign-owned domestic corporations under Section 6038A.[144] The Treasury took this regulatory action in order to specifically address one of the weaknesses in the availability of ownership information that was identified by the Global Forum as part of the United States' Peer Review.[145] However, the Financial Accountability and Corporate Transparency (FACT) Coalition had criticized the regulations[146] because the form to obtain an EIN only requires that the company provide the name of the "responsible party" who controls, manages, or directs the company.[147] This person is not necessarily the beneficial owner but could be a director or officer of the company.

Policies regarding financial and tax transparency are not just issues that concern bureaucrats in Washington. They touch on the heart of how corporations and individuals operate in society, how the government regulates them, and what resources are available to serve the public interest. The next section explores how the obligations of the United States under international human rights law and norms may require it to take more robust action than it has to date, to increase transparency and curb abusive tax practices.

IV. TAX TRANSPARENCY AND HUMAN RIGHTS

The General Assembly of the United Nations tasked the Office of the High Commissioner for Human Rights (OHCHR) with "ensur[ing] that the protection and enjoyment of human rights is a reality in the lives of all people."[148] OHCHR supports the various human rights monitoring mechanisms in the UN system such as the Human Rights Council (HRC). The HRC was created in 2006 and is responsible for promoting and protecting human rights around the world.[149] One of its functions is to undertake a Universal Periodic Review (UPR) of the status of each State's compliance with its human rights obligations and commitments.[150]

The UPR is a unique process that "provides the opportunity for each State to declare what actions they have taken to improve the human rights situations in their countries and to fulfill their human rights obligations."[151] Reviews consist of a national report submitted by the State itself, a summary prepared by the OHCHR of stakeholders' submissions,[152] and a compilation of various reports from other sources.[153] The United States submitted its latest National Report on February 13, 2015.[154] Unfortunately, there was no discussion of any financial transparency issues in the National Report or the OHCHR compilation report.[155] However, in the stakeholders report, Accountability Counsel[156] commented that "in order to fulfill its obligations under the UN Guiding Principles on Business and Human Rights, the US should . . . increase transparency with a view to providing remedies for business-related abuses at home and abroad."[157] Accountability Counsel also urged that the United States fully implement the UN Guiding Principles on Business and Human Rights (GPBHR).[158]

The Guiding Principles implement the United Nations' "Protect, Respect, and Remedy Framework" that deals with human rights and business enterprises.[159] These principles were unanimously endorsed by HRC resolution in 2011.[160] The GPBHR set forth three general principles, including the State's duty to protect human rights.[161] With respect to this duty, the "Guiding Principles are grounded in recognition of . . . [the] States' existing obligations to respect, protect and fulfill human rights and fundamental freedoms."[162] The second principle speaks to "[t]he role of business enterprises as specialized organs of society" and their "require[ment] to comply with all applicable laws and to respect human rights."[163] Arguably, this principle encompasses businesses' duty to pay their fair share of taxes and thereby not undermine the ability of the State to fulfill its human rights obligations. The Commentary to the GPBHR reiterates a State's international human rights law obligation to protect against human rights abuses by third parties, including businesses.[164] This means the State must take "appropriate steps to prevent, investigate, punish, and redress such abuses through effective policies, legislation, regulations, and adjudication."[165] Furthermore, a State must promote the rule of law, ensure the fairness of its application, and inter alia provide for procedural and legal transparency.[166]

Thus, I posit that facilitating or enabling offshore tax evasion foreseeably contributes to the violation of human rights. Given the obligations of the United States under human rights treaties that it has ratified, including the International Covenant on Civil and Political Rights (ICCPR), and in view of the US government's stated support for human rights, the United States must enact whatever legislation is necessary to enable the appropriate exchange of information with treaty partners to aid them in their respective wars on tax evasion. This would also fulfill the obligation of reciprocity promised by many of the FATCA IGAs. The United States must also acknowledge its duty of international cooperation, as reflected in the UN Charter, which includes facilitating an environment for the fulfillment of human rights.[167]

This duty to protect and support human rights also requires the passage of effective beneficial ownership legislation. The Panama Papers have demonstrated that the use of anonymous shell corporations is facilitating tax evasion. The Commentary to the GPBHR notes that a State might "breach its international human rights obligations where such abuse can be attributed to [it]." I posit that the intentional attraction of foreign money to US banks by having restrictive information exchange policies may constitute such an abuse. The Commentary goes on to note that it may also be a violation of international human rights obligations when the State fails to take any action to prevent the private actor's abuse. The US Congress is fully aware that anonymous shell corporations are being formed in states like Nevada, Wyoming, and Delaware and has not passed legislation to require the beneficial ownership information that would stop this practice. At meetings in Washington and Delaware in March 2017, the European Parliament's special Panama Papers investigative committee (PANA) appealed to US lawmakers to close these loopholes by introducing beneficial ownership registers. The PANA delegation was told that it was too early in the Donald Trump administration to discern policy direction as key high-level positions need to be filled.[168] Unfortunately, as a prominent whistleblower noted, "[t]ax evasion cannot possibly be fixed while elected officials are pleading for money from the very elites who have the strongest incentives to avoid taxes relative to any other segment of the population."[169]

Given the political nature of this situation, "naming and shaming" is required to obtain the desired result. As previously discussed, the OECD has explicitly acknowledged that the information supplied by the United States pursuant to its FATCA IGAs is not identical to the information required to be supplied under the CRS and has called on the United States to adopt the CRS by 2017 or 2018.[170] The OECD noted in its report for the G20 meeting in April 2016, that "jurisdictions that seek to profit from a lack of transparency can no longer be tolerated."[171] The report points out that tax evasion "deprives governments of the resources" needed to fund public services and causes "unacceptable inequality among citizens."[172] The United States will be subject to a second round of peer reviews by the Global Forum, which will also assess the new strengthened standard on the availability of beneficial ownership as set out by the FATF.[173] This may incentivize the United States to take the required legislative action but given the current political climate may yield nothing more than a weak compromise.

Unfortunately, the OECD's objective criteria that were used to identify noncooperative jurisdictions with respect to the implementation of the tax transparency standards were so weak that only Trinidad and Tobago made it on the list.[174] The criteria include: "implementation of the Exchange of Information on Request (EOIR) standard, the implementation of the Automatic Exchange of Information (AEOI) standard and joining the multilateral Convention on Mutual Administrative Assistance in Tax Matters (multilateral Convention)."[175] All that is needed to be considered cooperative is satisfaction of two out of the three following benchmarks: "i) a 'Largely Compliant' rating with respect to the EOIR standard; ii) a commitment to implement the AEOI standard . . . ;" and iii) "participation in the multilateral Convention or a sufficiently broad exchange network."[176] Thus, the United States, which received a rating of "Compliant" with respect to the EOIR standard[177] and has ratified the multilateral Convention (although not the 2010 Protocol), is not on the OECD list of noncooperative jurisdictions.

The Tax Justice Network, however, has ranked the United States in second place after Switzerland on its financial secrecy index because of its unwillingness to participate in transparency initiatives such as the CRS and the creation of public registers of beneficial ownership.[178] Furthermore, the study commissioned by the Greens/European Free Alliance group in the European Parliament has recommended that the European Union consider including the United States on its common European blacklist of tax havens "unless it effectively ensures registration of beneficial ownership information for companies and commits to equal levels of automatic exchange of information with European countries."[179] Although the United States was one of ninety-two jurisdictions investigated for potential inclusion on the EU tax haven blacklist, it was not included on the final list of seventeen countries.[180]

V. CONCLUSION

Efforts to include financial transparency in the human rights agenda should aim to increase the pressure on the United States to join the global movement for tax transparency. The former US Treasury Secretary admitted in a 2016 letter to Congress that "gaps remain in our laws that allow bad actors to deliberately use U.S. companies to hide money laundering, tax evasion, and other illicit financial activities."[181] Neither the US National Report nor the Office of the High Commissioner's report on the Universal Periodic Review of the United States makes any reference to tax evasion, offshore banking, or even the Guiding Principles on Business and Human Rights. More civil society groups must demand financial transparency legislation from the US Congress. The public must be made aware of the consequences of the United States enabling tax evasion. This issue is even more urgent as the 115th Congress appears to be rolling back previous transparency initiatives.[182]

There is a need for more in depth reporting of studies such as *Global Shell Games: Testing Money Launderers' and Terrorist Financiers' Access to Shell Companies*, which found that "obtaining an anonymous shell company is . . . easier in the U.S. than in the rest of the world."[183] Coverage such as the *60 Minutes* report chronicling the Global Witness' undercover interviews of New York attorneys asked to bring questionably sourced funds into the United States, will make this topic more concrete for the American citizen.[184] The connection between human rights and enabling tax evasion must be illustrated. The US government must be called upon to report on its financial transparency status in its next UPR report. The United States needs to truly commit to financial transparency. There is not yet enough domestic public outcry, however, to convince the United States to report on tax evasion as a human rights violation.

Likewise, more outcry is needed at the international level. The United States needs a serious push from the global community so that sufficient pressure is exerted on Congress to enact the legislative changes necessary for the United States to be a true participant in the global movement for financial transparency. The Human Rights Council needs to bring tax evasion to the forefront of their human rights discussions and Universal Periodic Review reports—not just for the United States, but for all countries. In 2011, the Human Rights Council created a Working Group to help implement the GPBHR.[185] This Working Group holds an annual Forum on Business and Human Rights. At the forum, the Working Group is tasked with "discuss[ing] trends and challenges in the implementation of the Guiding Principles [on Business and Human Rights] and promot[ing] dialogue and cooperation on issues linked to business and human rights, as well as identifying good practices."[186] To date, however, tax abuse and financial transparency have not been emphasized enough at the annual forums, which attract thousands of participants.[187] Inducing the United States to act requires increasing public scrutiny of the ways in which enabling tax evasion threatens human rights. Discussing these linkages at high-profile public events like the UN Forum would be a credible first step.

NOTES

* I would like to gratefully acknowledge discussions with and comments from Kristen Boon and Maggie Lewis, the research assistance of Wesley Buirkle and Lindsay Weibel, and the financial support provided by the Seton Hall University School of Law Dean's Research Fellowship program.

1. International Bar Association, *Tax Abuses, Poverty and Human Rights: A Report of the International Bar Association's Human Rights Institute Task Force on Illicit Financial Flows, Poverty and Human Rights* (2013), available online at http://www.ibanet.org/Document/Default. aspx?DocumentUid=4977CB3D-4988-4C9C-84C7-9050A5CB2311, at 148 (last visited 12 June 2017) [hereinafter *IBA Human Rights Task Force Report*].
2. Ibid. at 2–3. ("[T]ax abuses deprive governments of the resources required to respect, promote and fulfil human rights"; ibid. at 103).
3. See T. Pogge and K. Mehta (eds.), *Global Tax Fairness* (2016). See also S. Darcy, '"The Elephant in the Room"': Corporate Tax Avoidance & Business and Human Rights', 2 *Business and Human Rights*

Journal (2017), available online at https://papers.ssrn.com/sol3/papers.cfm?abstract_id=2797219, at 11 (last visited 12 June 2017). The Committee on the Rights of the Child has reprimanded those countries "where tax evasion, alongside corruption, have negatively impacted on the level of resources available for the implementation of the Convention." Ibid. at 9.

4. Boston Consulting Group, *Global Wealth 2016: Navigating the New Client Landscape* (2016), available online at https://www.bcgperspectives.com/content/articles/financial-institutions-consumer-insight-global-wealth-2016/?chapter=2#chapter2_section3 (last visited 12 June 2017).

5. See Tax Justice Network, *The Price of Offshore Revisited* (2012), available online at http://www.taxjustice.net/cms/upload/pdf/Price_of_Offshore_Revisited_120722.pdf, at 5.

6. G. Zucman, T. Fagan, and T. Piketty, *The Hidden Wealth of Nations: The Scourge of Tax Havens* (2015), at 35, 40–43, 47, 52. Three-fourths of such wealth goes unrecorded. G. Zucman, 'The Missing Wealth of Nations: Are Europe and the U.S. Net Debtors or Net Creditors?', 128 *Quarterly Journal of Economics* (2013), 1321, at 1321–1322, 1343.

7. The Economist, *The Biggest Loophole of All*, 20 Feb. 2016, available online at http://www.economist.com/news/international/21693219-having-launched-and-led-battle-against-offshore-tax-evasion-america-now-part (last visited 12 June 2017). The United States is listed as one of the top ten tax havens where money is hidden. L. Clarke-Billings, *Panama Papers: Top Ten Tax Havens—Where the Money Is Hidden*, 6 Apr. 2016, available online at http://www.newsweek.com/panama-papers-top-ten-tax-havens-where-money-hidden-444512 (last visited 12 June 2017).

8. P. A. Cotorceanu, 'Hiding in Plain Sight: How Non-US Persons Can *Legally* Avoid Reporting Under Both FATCA and GATCA', 21(10) *Trusts & Trustees* (2015), 1050. The author uses GATCA to refer to the OECD's Standard for Automatic Exchange of Financial Account Information in Tax Matters or global account tax compliance activities. Ibid. at note 3.

9. See OECD, *Standard for Automatic Exchange of Financial Account Information in Tax Matters: Second Edition* (2017) 15–16, available online at http://www.oecd-ilibrary.org/docserver/download/2316531e.pdf?expires=1499389130&id=id&accname=guest&checksum=7D5D8E9303FD6A06158D6D08A6BAD147 (last visited 6 July 2017) [hereinafter OECD, *Standard for Automatic Exchange*].

10. See *infra* section II.C.

11. G20, *G20 Leaders' Declaration*, 7–8 July 2017, available online at http://www.g20.org/gipfeldokumente/G20-leaders-declaration.pdf.

12. Hiring Incentives to Restore Employment Act, Pub. L. No. 111-147, § 501–35, 124 Stat. 71, 97–115 (2010). The Foreign Account Tax Compliance Act (FATCA) added Sections 1471 to 1474 to the Internal Revenue Code (IRC).

13. IRS, *FATCA Foreign Financial Institution (FFI) List Search and Download Tool* (2017), available online at http://apps.irs.gov/app/fatcaFfiList/flu.jsf (last visited 4 Feb. 2018).

14. See United States Department of the Treasury, *Resource Center: Foreign Account Tax Compliance Act (FATCA)*, 19 Dec. 2017, available online at http://www.treasury.gov/resource-center/tax-policy/treaties/Pages/FATCA.aspx (last visited 4 Feb. 2018).

15. T.D. 9584, 77 Fed. Reg. 23391-01 (2012) [hereinafter Bank Deposit Interest regulations]. Revenue procedures list the countries and territories eligible for the automatic exchange of the information being collected under these regulations. See Rev. Proc. 2014-64, 2014-53 I.R.B. 1022 at § 4. This list has been increased from a single country, Canada, to a list of forty-five countries. See Rev. Proc. 2015-50, 2015-42 I.R.B. 583, Rev. Proc. 2016-18, 2016-17 I.R.B. 635, Rev. Proc. 2016-56, 2016-52 I.R.B. 920-921, Rev. Proc. 2017-31, 2017-16 I.R.B. 1104, and Rev. Proc. 2017-46, 2017-43 I.R.B. 372.

16. See *infra* section III.A.

17. OECD, *The Global Forum of Transparency and Exchange of Information for Tax Purposes: Information Brief* (2013), available online at http://www.oecd.org/tax/transparency/global_forum_background%20brief.pdf, at 2.

18. OECD, *Global Forum on Transparency and Exchange of Information for Tax Purposes, Phase 1 and Phase 2 Reviews* (Nov. 2016), available online at http://www.oecd.org/tax/transparency/GFratings.pdf, at 24; see also OECD, *Global Forum on Transparency and Exchange of*

Information for Tax Purposes (Nov. 2017), available online at http://www.oecd.org/tax/trans-parency/exchange-of-information-on-request/ratings/#d.en.342263 [hereinafter OECD, Phase 1 and Phase 2 Reviews].

19. OECD, *Global Forum on Transparency and Exchange of Information for Tax Purposes Peer Reviews: United States 2011*, 7 June 2011, available online at http://dx.doi.org/10.1787/9789264115064-en, at 38–39, 87 (last visited 13 June 2017) [hereinafter OECD, United States 2011 Review].

20. See Tax Justice Network, *Financial Secrecy Index: Narrative Report on USA* (2015), available online at http://www.financialsecrecyindex.com/PDF/USA.pdf.

21. Zucman, *supra* note 6, at 1.

22. *IBA Human Rights Task Force Report, supra* note 1, at 118.

23. OHCHR, *Guiding Principles on Business and Human Rights: Implementing the United Nations 'Protect, Respect and Remedy' Framework* (2011), available online at http://www.ohchr.org/Documents/Publications/GuidingPrinciplesBusinessHR_EN.pdf, at 3 [hereinafter Guiding Principles].

24. Ibid.

25. Ibid.

26. T. Kaye, 'Innovations in the War on Tax Evasion', *BYU Law Review* (2014), 363, at 364.

27. Hiring Incentives to Restore Employment Act, Pub. L. No. 111-147, § 501–35, 124 Stat. 71, 97–115 (2010).

28. 26 U.S.C. § 1471(b)(1), (d)(1) (2017).

29. Treas. Reg. § 1.1471-5(a)(2) and § 1.1471-4(d)(3)(v); see also 26 U.S.C. § 1471(c) (2017).

30. Art. 12, Universal Declaration of Human Rights, GA Res. 217 (III) A, 10 Dec. 1948.

31. Cotorceanu, *supra* note 8, at 1.

32. W. R. Davis and A. Velarde, 'Sen. Paul Files Lawsuit Challenging FATCA', 79 *Tax Notes International* (2015), 226.

33. Verified Complaint for Declaratory and Injunctive Relief at 2, *Crawford v. U.S. Dep't of the Treasury*, No. 3:15-cv-250, 2015 WL 5697552 (S.D. Ohio Sept. 29, 2015).

34. Ibid. at 1.

35. *Crawford v. U.S. Dep't of the Treasury*, No. 3:15-cv-250, 2015 WL 5697552, at *11, *16 (S.D. Ohio Sept. 29, 2015). See also *Crawford v. U.S. Dep't of the Treasury*, 868 F.3d 438 (6th Cir. 2017).

36. The United States District Court also dismissed the complaint for lack of jurisdiction on Apr. 25, 2016. See *Crawford v. U.S. Dep't of the Treasury*, No. 3:15-cv-250, 2015 WL 5697552 (S.D. Ohio Sept. 29, 2015), reproduced in 'U.S. District Court Dismisses FATCA Challenge on Jurisdictional Grounds', *Worldwide Tax Daily*, 28 Apr. 2016, 82–84.

37. 26 U.S.C. § 6049 (2017).

38. C. Blum, 'Sharing Bank Deposit Information with Other Countries: Should Tax Compliance or Privacy Claims Prevail?', 6 *Florida Tax Review* (2004), 579, at 609–611. See also L. Burman and J. Slemrod, *Taxes in America: What Everyone Needs to Know* (2013), at 179 (Tax evasion is much less prevalent when income is subject to information reporting.).

39. See, e.g., J. Roin, 'Competition and Evasion: Another Perspective on International Competition', 80 *Georgetown Law Journal* (2001), 543, at 599–600.

40. See, e.g., J. D. Blank, 'USA', *in* E. Kristoffersson et al. (eds.), *Tax Secrecy and Tax Transparency* (2013), 1163.

41. 26 U.S.C. § 6103 (2017).

42. IRS, *Offshore Voluntary Compliance Efforts Top $10 Billion; More than 100,000 Taxpayers Come Back into Compliance*, News Release IR-2016-137, 21 Oct. 2016, available online at https://www.irs.gov/uac/newsroom/offshore-voluntary-compliance-efforts-top-10-billion-more-than-100000-taxpayers-come-back-into-compliance (last visited 13 June 2017).

43. See United States Department of the Treasury, *Treasury Releases Model Intergovernmental Agreement for Implementing the Foreign Account Tax Compliance Act to Improve Offshore Tax Compliance and Reduce Burden*, 26 July 2012, http://www.treasury.gov/press-center/press-releases/Pages/tg1653.aspx (last visited 13 June 2017).

44. See United States Department of the Treasury, *Model Intergovernmental Agreement to Improve Tax Compliance and to Implement FATCA*, available online at http://www.treasury.gov/press-center/press-releases/Documents/reciprocal.pdf [hereinafter Treasury Model I]; see also United States Department of the Treasury, *Model Intergovernmental Agreement to Improve Tax Compliance and to Implement FATCA [Nonreciprocal Version]*, available online at http://www.treasury.gov/press-center/press-releases/Documents/nonreciprocal.pdf [hereinafter Treasury Model I Nonreciprocal Version].

45. In a speech before the New York State Bar Association, Acting Assistant Treasury Secretary Emily McMahon acknowledged that some countries faced legal impediments to complying with the requirement to report accountholder information directly to the IRS. United States Department of the Treasury, *Remarks by Acting Assistant Secretary Emily McMahon at the NY State Bar Association Annual Meeting*, 25 Jan. 2012, available online at http://www.treasury.gov/press-center/press-releases/Pages/tg1399.aspx (last visited 13 June 2017) [hereinafter McMahon Remarks].

46. See United States Department of the Treasury, *Agreement Between the Government of the United States of America and the Government of [FATCA Partner] to Improve International Tax Compliance and to Implement FATCA*, 30 Nov. 2016, available online at http://www.treasury.gov/resource-center/tax-policy/treaties/Documents/FATCA-Reciprocal-Model-1A-Agreement-Preexisting-TIEA-or-DTC-11-30-14.pdf, at 1, 16 [hereinafter Treasury Model IA].

47. See *Resource Center: Foreign Account Tax Compliance Act (FATCA), supra* note 14.

48. 26 U.S.C. §§ 1471(d), 1473(2)(A)(i) (2017).

49. Interest earned on certain deposits is exempt from tax even though treated as US-source income in order to encourage foreign persons to use US banks. 26 U.S.C. § 871(i)(2)(A) (2017). Wealthy Americans took advantage of this tax exemption by pretending to be foreigners through the creation of offshore entities.

50. Treasury Model I, *supra* note 44, at art. 1(1)(nn); see also Treasury Model I Nonreciprocal Version, *supra* note 44, at art. 1(1)(ii). ("The term 'Controlling Persons' shall be interpreted in a manner consistent with the Recommendations of the Financial Action Task Force.").

51. See A. E. Lorenzo and A. Bennett, *Wyden Opening Tax Evasion Inquiry Based on Panama Leak*, 11 Apr. 2016, available online at http://law.wayne.edu/pdfs/bloomberg_bna_article_2_for_levin_center_website.pdf; see also C. Kentouris, *New US AML Rules: Tough Enough to Catch the Bad Guys?*, 15 May 2016, available online at http://finops.co/investors/new-us-aml-rules-tough-enough-to-catch-the-bad-guys/ (last visited 13 June 2017).

52. See McMahon Remarks, *supra* note 45. ("[B]ilateral solutions require reciprocity. . . . [W]e see no principled basis on which to require that financial institutions based in other countries collect and provide us with information on U.S. taxpayers, if we take the position that our own institutions should be exempt from similar requirements. . . . it will be critical to the success of our efforts to implement FATCA that we are able to reciprocate."). Ibid.

53. See, e.g., Agreement Between the Government of the United States of America and the Government of the Grand Duchy of Luxembourg to Improve International Tax Compliance and with Respect to The U.S. Information Reporting Provisions Commonly Known as the Foreign Account Tax Compliance Act, U.S.-Lux, 28 March 2014, T.I.A.S. No. 15-729.1, available online at https://www.treasury.gov/resource-center/tax-policy/treaties/Documents/FATCA-Agreement-Luxembourg-3-28-2014.pdf.

54. Treasury Model IA, *supra* note 46, at art. 6(1).

55. See OECD, *Standard for Automatic Exchange, supra* note 9, at 9–10.

56. G20, *Communiqué Meeting of Finance Ministers and Central Bank Governors Moscow*, 19–20 July 2013, available online at http://www.mof.go.jp/english/international_policy/convention/g20/130720.htm, at point 19 (last visited 13 June 2017).

57. For the complete list of countries, see OECD, *AEOI: Status of Commitments* (Nov. 2017), available online at http://www.oecd.org/tax/transparency/AEOI-commitments.pdf.

58. OECD, *OECD Secretary-General Report to G20 Finance Ministers*, 23–24 July 2016, available online at https://www.oecd.org/ctp/oecd-secretary-general-tax-report-g20-finance-ministers-july-2016.pdf, at 21 [hereinafter 2016 Report to G20].

59. OECD, *OECD Economic Surveys: United States* 37, (2016), available online at http://www.oecd.org/eco/surveys/United-States-2016-overview.pdf [hereinafter OECD Economic Surveys].

60. See OECD, *Convention on Mutual Administrative Assistance in Tax Matters and Amending Protocols* (2011), available online at https://www.oecd.org/ctp/exchange-of-tax-information/ENG-Amended-Convention.pdf, at Chapter III-Forms of Assistance, Section I-Exchange of Information, Arts. 4–7 (last visited 13 June 2017).

61. The G20 Finance Ministers Communiqué of April 15, 2016, called on all relevant countries to sign the Convention. Ministry of Finance of the People's Republic of China, *Communiqué: G20 Finance Ministers and Central Bank Governors Meeting* (2016), available online at http://wjb.mof.gov.cn/pindaoliebiao/gongzuodongtai/201604/t20160416_1952794.html (last visited 13 June 2017).

62. See OECD, *Jurisdictions Participating in the Convention on Mutual Administrative Assistance in Tax Matters Status*, 15 Dec. 2017, available online at http://www.oecd.org/tax/exchange-of-tax-information/Status_of_convention.pdf.

63. See OECD, *The CRS Multilateral Competent Authority Agreement (MCAA)* (2014), available online at http://www.oecd.org/tax/automatic-exchange/international-framework-for-the-crs/ (last visited 13 June 2017).

64. See generally OECD, *Signatories of the Multilateral Competent Authority Agreement on Automatic Exchange of Financial Account Information and Intended First Information Exchange Date*, 19 August 2016, available online at https://www.oecd.org/ctp/exchange-of-tax-information/MCAA-Signatories.pdf.

65. 2016 Report to G20, *supra* note 58.

66. Australian Taxation Office, *A Major Step in Global Transparency*, 23 Sept. 2015, available online at https://www.ato.gov.au/Media-centre/Media-releases/A-major-step-in-global-transparency/ (last visited 13 June 2017).

67. P. Menyasz, *Canada Completes First FATCA Data Exchange with IRS*, 2 Oct. 2015, available online at http://news.bna.com/dtln/DTLNWB/split_display.adp?fedfid=76698052&vname=dtrnot&jd=a0h3m3q8e7&split=0 (last visited 3 Jan. 2017).

68. IRS, *IRS Announces Key Milestone in FATCA Implementation; U.S. Begins Reciprocal Automatic Exchange of Tax Information under Intergovernmental Agreements*, News Release IR-2015-111, 2 Oct. 2015, available online at https://www.irs.gov/uac/newsroom/irs-announces-key-milestone-in-fatca-implementation-u-s-begins-reciprocal-automatic-exchange-of-tax-information-under-intergovernmental-agreements (last visited 13 June 2017).

69. See R. W. Wood, *U.S. Ranks as Top Tax Haven, Refusing to Share Tax Data Despite FATCA*, 3 Nov. 2015, available online at http://www.forbes.com/sites/robertwood/2015/11/03/u-s-ranks-as-top-tax-haven-refusing-to-share-tax-data-despite-fatca/#1b5b5ddd5928 (last visited 3 Jan. 2017). See also Tax Justice Network, *Financial Secrecy Index 2015 Reveals Improving Global Financial Transparency, But USA Threatens Progress*, 2 Nov. 2015, available online at http://www.taxjustice.net/wp-content/uploads/2013/04/FSI-2015-Presser.pdf.

70. United States Congress Joint Committee on Taxation, *Disclosure Report for Public Inspection Pursuant to Internal Revenue Code Section 6103(p)(3)(C) for Calendar Year 2013*, 22 May 2014, available online at https://www.jct.gov/publications.html?func=download&id=4602&chk=4602&no_html=1 (last visited 13 June 2017).

71. United States Congress Joint Committee on Taxation, *Disclosure Report for Public Inspection Pursuant to Internal Revenue Code Section 6103(p)(3)(C) for Calendar Year 2015*, 18 Apr. 2016, available online at https://www.jct.gov/publications.html?func=startdown&id=4899 (last visited 13 June 2017). The 2.6 million exchanges in 2015 fall short of the 2.8 million exchanges that took place in 2009, before FATCA was enacted. United States Congress Joint Committee on Taxation, *Disclosure Report for Public Inspection Pursuant to Internal Revenue Code Section 6103(p)(3) (C) for Calendar Year 2009*, 15 Apr. 2010, available online at https://www.jct.gov/publications.html?func=startdown&id=3680 (last visited 8 July 2017). Data for 2009 has been adjusted pursuant to a conversation by author with an IRS staff member.

72. United States Congress Joint Committee on Taxation, *Disclosure Report for Public Inspection Pursuant to Internal Revenue Code Section 6103(p)(3)(C) for Calendar Year 2016* 5, 3 May 2017,

available online at https://www.jct.gov/publications.html?func=startdown&id=4991 (last visited 8 July 2017).

73. *Resource Center: Foreign Account Tax Compliance Act (FATCA), supra* note 14.

74. Rev. Proc. 2017-46, 2017-43 I.R.B. 372.

75. See *infra* section III.A.

76. See J. Zarroli, *Want to Set Up a Shell Corporation to Hide Your Millions? No Problem*, 13 Apr. 2016, available online at http://www.npr.org/2016/04/13/474101127/want-to-set-up-a-shell-corporation-to-hide-your-millions-no-problem (last visited 13 June 2017).

77. A. Velarde, 'Official Questions Treatment of U.S. on OECD Reporting Standard', 147 *Tax Notes* (2015), 1008, at 1008.

78. J. Drucker, *The World's Favorite New Tax Haven Is the United States*, 27 Jan. 2016, available online at http://www.bloomberg.com/news/articles/2016-01-27/the-world-s-favorite-new-tax-haven-is-the-united-states (last visited 13 June 2017).

79. S. Bok, *Secrets: On the Ethics of Concealment and Revelation* (1983), at 106.

80. L. A. Sheppard, 'FATCA Is a Drone: What to Do about Compliance', 64 *Tax Notes International* (2011), 10, at 11. ("[An] expensive . . . war . . . , Vietnam, prompted the United States to set itself up as a tax haven for foreign investors wanting the safety of Treasury securities. . . . [Now] [t]he United States is a tax haven for Latin Americans."); see also C. Gnaedinger, 'U.S. Ranks First in Financial Secrecy', 56 *Tax Notes International* (2009), 407, at 407.

81. N. Shaxson, *Treasure Islands: Tax Havens and the Men Who Stole the World* (2011), at 14.

82. See *supra* note 15 for the revenue procedures that list the countries.

83. R. Goulder, 'How the U.S. Is a Tax Haven for Mexico's Wealthy', 55 *Tax Notes International* (2009), 695, at 695.

84. Ibid. See also Treas. Reg. §§ 1.6049-4(b)(5), 1.6049-6(e)(4) (prior to amendment in 2012).

85. Under US international tax law, foreign persons are not subject to tax in the United States on portfolio interest income. 26 U.S.C. §§ 871(h), 881(c) (2017).

86. D. Spencer, 'New U.S. Regs. on Reporting Nonresident Alien Bank Deposit Interest', 22(6) *Journal of International Taxation* (2011), 30, at 32.

87. Blum, *supra* note 38, at 581–582.

88. Guidance on Reporting of Deposit Interest Paid to Nonresident Aliens, 66 Fed. Reg. 3925 (proposed 17 Jan. 2001).

89. Blum, *supra* note 38, at 581–582.

90. See Guidance on Reporting Interest Paid to Nonresident Aliens, 76 Fed. Reg. 1105, 1105–1106 (IRS Proposed 7 Jan. 2011).

91. Ibid. at 1106. The preamble also noted that this change would "further strengthen the United States exchange of information program, consistent with adequate provisions for reciprocity, usability, and confidentiality."

92. See *supra* notes 80–86 and accompanying text.

93. See, e.g., U.S. Department of the Treasury, Internal Revenue Service, Public Hearing on Proposed Regulations 26 C.F.R. Part 31 'Guidance on Reporting Interest Paid to Nonresident Aliens', 18 May 2011, (statement by Francisca Mordi, Vice President and Sr. Tax Counsel, American Bankers Association), available online at http://www.gfintegrity.org/storage/gfip/documents/Capitol_Hill/2011-10811-1-irs-hearingtranscript.pdf, at 15.

94. Ibid. at 5 (statement by Alex Sanchez, President, and CEO, Florida Bankers Association).

95. Ibid. at 8 (statement by Thomas Cardwell, Commissioner, State of Florida Office of Financial Regulation).

96. 26 U.S.C. § 6103(k)(4) (2017).

97. Blum, *supra* note 38, at 624–625.

98. Ibid. at 625.

99. Roin, *supra* note 39, at 598–599.

100. Bank Deposit Interest regulations, *supra* note 15.

101. Treas. Reg. §§ 1.6049-4, 1.6049-5, 1.6049-6 (as amended in 2012).

102. *Proposed Regulations to Require Reporting of Nonresident Alien Deposit Interest Income: Hearing Before the House Subcommittee on Financial Institutions and Consumer Credit of the House*

Committee on Financial Services, 112th Cong. 96 (2011) (letter from Sen. Carl Levin to Commissioner Douglas H. Shulman) [hereinafter Hearing on Interest Reporting Regulations].

103. Bank Deposit Interest regulations, *supra* note 15, at 23392.
104. Ibid. at 23393 (noting that these countries must be willing and able to reciprocate as well as have effective confidentiality laws and practices).
105. *Disclosure Report for Public Inspection Pursuant to Internal Revenue Code Section 6103(p)(3)(C) for Calendar Year 2013, supra* note 70, at 3.
106. United States Congress Joint Committee on Taxation, *Disclosure Report for Public Inspection Pursuant to Internal Revenue Code Section 6103(p)(3)(C) for Calendar Year 2014*, 5 June 2015, available online at https://www.jct.gov/publications.html?func=download&id=4787&chk=4787&no_html=1, at 4 (last visited 13 June 2017).
107. See Rev. Proc. 2017-46, 2017-43 I.R.B. 372 at §3 for a list of the countries.
108. Ibid.
109. See Hearing on Interest Reporting Regulations, *supra* note 102, at 99 ("[I]f a financial institution knows that the beneficial owner of an account is a non-U.S. individual, the financial institution should disclose the account . . . even if . . . nominally held in the name of a foreign entity."). Senators Levin and Grassley were also advocating legislation that would require states to document the beneficial owners of the corporations. See S. 1483, 112th Cong. (2011).
110. See L. A. Sheppard, 'Will U.S. Hypocrisy on Information Sharing Continue?', 138 *Tax Notes* (2013), 253, at 256. ("[I]n other words, the stupid rich. Because the sophisticated rich use corporations and Delaware LLCs, they would not be affected.").
111. See S. E. Shay, J. C. Fleming, and R. J. Peroni, 'What's Source Got to Do with it? Source Rules and U.S. International Taxation', 56 *Tax Law Review* (2002), 81, at 125–126.
112. See 26 U.S.C. §§1471(d), 1473(2)(A)(i) (2017).
113. See Kaye, *supra* note 26, at 390.
114. Cotorceanu, *supra* note 8, at 5.
115. United States Department of the Treasury, *General Explanations of the Administration's Fiscal Year 2017 Revenue Proposals* (2016), available online at https://www.treasury.gov/resource-center/tax-policy/Documents/General-Explanations-FY2017.pdf, at 202 [hereinafter 2017 Greenbook].
116. Treasury Model IA, *supra* note 46, (includes 'a political commitment to pursue the adoption of regulations and to advocate and support relevant legislation to achieve such equivalent levels of reciprocal automatic exchange.').
117. 2017 Greenbook, *supra* note 115, at 203. See also United States Department of the Treasury, *General Explanations of the Administration's Fiscal Year 2016 Revenue Proposals* (2015), available online at https://www.treasury.gov/resource-center/tax-policy/Documents/General-Explanations-FY2016.pdf.
118. T. Kaye, 'Tax Transparency: A Tale of Two Countries', 39 *Fordham International Law Journal* (2016), 1153, at 1199.
119. Letter from Jacob J. Lew, Secretary, United States Department of the Treasury, to Paul D. Ryan, Speaker, US House of Representatives (5 May 2016) [hereinafter Lew Letter], at 2.
120. Drucker, *supra* note 78 (noting how Rothschild, a European financial institution, is moving the wealth of foreign clients out of tax havens such as Bermuda into trusts set up in Nevada, "one of several states promoting low taxes and confidentiality in their trust laws.").
121. Tax Justice Network, *Financial Secrecy Index—2018 Results*, available online at https://www.financialsecrecyindex.com/introduction/fsi-2018-results [hereinafter FSI-2018].
122. The Economist, *supra* note 7.
123. International Consortium of Investigative Journalists, *Giant Leak of Offshore Financial Records Exposes Global Array of Crime and Corruption*, 3 Apr. 2016, available online at https://panamapapers.icij.org/20160403-panama-papers-global-overview.html (last visited 13 June 2017).
124. The connections between several world leaders and offshore shell companies has resulted in global investigations of these alleged schemes to evade taxes. See W. Hoke, 'HSBC Receives Worldwide Information Requests Following Panama Papers', *Worldwide Tax Daily*, 4 Aug. 2016, 150–155.

125. European Commission, *Fair Taxation: The Commission Sets Out Next Steps to Increase Tax Transparency and Tackle Tax Abuse*, 5 July 2016, available online at http://europa.eu/rapid/press-release_IP-16-2354_en.htm (last visited 13 June 2017).

126. Letter from Ron Wyden, Ranking Member, United States Senate Committee on Finance, to Jacob Lew, Secretary, United States Department of the Treasury (19 Oct. 2016).

127. Lorenzo and Bennett, *supra* note 51.

128. M. Kish, *In Wake of Panama Papers Report, Wyden Expands Probe into Anonymous Companies*, 10 May 2016, available online at http://www.bizjournals.com/portland/blog/2016/05/in-wake-of-panama-papers-report-wyden-expands.html (last visited 13 June 2017).

129. Letter from Ron Wyden, Ranking Member, United States Senate Committee on Finance, to Barbara K. Cegavske, Secretary of State, Nevada (10 May 2016).

130. G20, *Communiqué, G20 Finance Ministers and Central Bank Governors Meeting Washington D.C.*, 16–17 Apr. 2015, available online at http://g20.org.tr/wp-content/uploads/2015/04/April-G20-FMCBG-Communique-Final.pdf, at 3.

131. Press Release, United States Department of the Treasury, *Treasury Announces Key Regulations and Legislation to Counter Money Laundering and Corruption, Combat Tax Evasion*, 5 May 2016, available online at https://www.treasury.gov/press-center/press-releases/Pages/jl0451.aspx (last visited 13 June 2017) [hereinafter Treasury Press Release].

132. Lew Letter, *supra* note 119, at 2.

133. Treasury Press Release, *supra* note 131.

134. The term "covered financial institution" refers to: (1) banks; (2) brokers or dealers in securities; (3) mutual funds; and (4) futures commission merchants and introducing brokers in commodities. 31 C.F.R. §§1020.220, 1023.220, 1024.220, 1026.220 (2017). Ibid.

135. Customer Due Diligence Requirements for Financial Institutions; Final Rule, 81 Fed. Reg. 29398 (11 May 2016).

136. Ibid.

137. 31 C.F.R. §1010.230(d) (2017).

138. Financial Accountability and Corporate Transparency (FACT) Coalition, *Anti-Money Laundering Experts Deeply Concerned by Administration's Flawed 'Panama Papers' Response*, 6 May 2016, available online at https://thefactcoalition.org/anti-money-laundering-experts-deeply-concerned-by-administrations-flawed-panama-papers-response/ (last visited 13 June 2017).

139. Global Financial Integrity, *New Treasury Rule on Beneficial Ownership Fails to Ensure that Beneficial Owners are Identified*, 9 May 2016, available online http://www.gfintegrity.org/press-release/new-treasury-rule-on-beneficial-ownership-fails-to-ensure-that-beneficial-owners-are-identified/ (last visited 13 June 2017).

140. Transparency International, *US Treasury Issues New Rules on Customer Due Diligence, but Gaps Remain and More Action Needed*, 6 May 2016, available online at http://www.transparency.org/news/pressrelease/us_treasury_issues_new_rules_on_customer_due_diligence_but_gaps_remain_and (last visited 13 June 2017).

141. Treasury Press Release, *supra* note 131.

142. See Incorporation Transparency and Law Enforcement Assistance Act, S. 1483, 112th Cong. (2011). This legislation was introduced in the 114th Congress as S. 2489 by Senator Whitehouse. S. 2489, 114th Cong. (2016). It was also introduced in the House of Representatives as H.R. 4450. Incorporation Transparency and Law Enforcement Assistance Act, H.R. 4450, 114th Cong. (2016).

143. This legislation was introduced by Senators Grassley, Feinstein, and Whitehouse. S. 1454, 115th Cong. (2017). It was also introduced in the House of Representatives as the Corporate Transparency Act. H.R. 3089, 115th Cong. (2017).

144. Treatment of Certain Domestic Entities Disregarded as Separate From Their Owners as Corporations For Purposes of Section 6038A; Final Regulations, 81 Fed. Reg. 89849 (13 Dec. 2016); see also 26 C.F.R. §§ 1.6038A-1, 1.6038A-2, 301.7701-2.

145. OECD, United States 2011 Review, *supra* note 19, at 38–39, 87.

146. See FACT Coalition, *Incorporation Transparency and Law Enforcement Assistance Act, S. 1465: Frequently Asked Questions* (2016), available online at http://thefactcoalition.org/

incorporation-transparency/incorporation-transparency-and-law-enforcement-assistance-act-s-1465-frequently-asked-questions/ (last visited 13 June 2017). The FACT Coalition is a "nonpartisan alliance of more than 100 state, national, and international organizations." See FACT website at https://thefactcoalition.org/wp-content/uploads/2016/08/About-FACT-July-2016-PRINT-FINAL.pdf.

147. See IRS, *Specific Instructions for Form SS-4* (2016), available online at https://www.irs.gov/instructions/iss4/ch02.html (last visited 13 June 2017).

148. OHCHR, *Who We Are* (2016), available online at http://www.ohchr.org/EN/AboutUs/Pages/WhoWeAre.aspx (last visited 13 June 2017).

149. GA Res. 60/251, 3 Apr. 2006.

150. OHCHR, *Universal Periodic Review* (2016), available online at http://www.ohchr.org/EN/HRBodies/UPR/Pages/UPRMain.aspx (last visited 13 June 2017).

151. Ibid.

152. HRC Res. 16/21, 12 Apr. 2011.

153. HRC Res. 5/1, 18 June 2007.

154. HRC, National Report Submitted in Accordance with Paragraph 5 of the Annex to Human Rights Council Resolution 16/21: United States of America, UN Doc. A/HRC/WG.6/22/USA/1, 13 Feb. 2015.

155. HRC, Compilation Prepared by the Office of the United Nations High Commissioner for Human Rights in Accordance with Paragraph 15(b) of the Annex to Human Rights Council Resolution 5/1 and Paragraph 5 of the Annex to Council Resolution 16/21: United States of America, UN Doc. A/HRC/WG.6/22/USA/2, 2 Mar. 2015.

156. The Accountability Counsel is a nonprofit that advocates for "independent, fair, transparent, accessible and effective accountability . . .". The Accountability Counsel, *Policy* (2016), available online at http://www.accountabilitycounsel.org/policy/ (last visited 13 June 2017).

157. HRC, Summary Prepared by the Office of the United Nations High Commissioner for Human Rights in Accordance with Paragraph 15(c) of the Annex to Human Rights Council Resolution 5/1 and Paragraph 5 of the Annex to Council Resolution 16/21: United States of America, UN Doc. A/HRC/WG.6/22/USA/3, 16 Feb. 2015, at 3.

158. Ibid.

159. See Guiding Principles, *supra* note 23.

160. GA Res. 17/4, 6 July 2011.

161. Guiding Principles, *supra* note 23.

162. Ibid.

163. Ibid.

164. Guiding Principles, *supra* note 23, at 3.

165. Ibid.

166. Ibid.

167. Arts. 55–56, Charter of the United Nations, UNCIO XV, 335; amendments by General Assembly Resolution in UNTS 557, 143/638, 308/892, 119.

168. J. Kirwin, *EU Panama Papers Probe Head: U.S. Tax Loopholes Must Be Closed*, 27 Mar. 2017, available online at http://www.bna.com/dtln/DTLNWB/split display.adp?fedfid=107930712&vname=dtrnot&wsn=499256000&searchid=30192434&doctypeid=1&type=date&mode=doc&split=0&scm=DTLNWB&pg=0 (last visited 13 July 2017).

169. *John Doe's Manifesto* (2016), available online at http://panamapapers.sueddeutsche.de/articles/572c897a5632a39742ed34ef/ (last visited 13 June 2017).

170. OECD Economic Surveys, *supra* note 59. "Congress has yet to enact the required proposed legislation" to establish parity with the CRS as to the specific types of information exchanged. Ibid.

171. OECD, *OECD Secretary-General Report to G20 Finance Ministers*, April 2016, available online at https://www.oecd.org/g20/topics/taxation/oecd-secretary-general-tax-report-g20-finance-ministers-april-2016.pdf, at 6.

172. Ibid.

173. OECD Economic Surveys, *supra* note 59.

174. OECD, *OECD Secretary-General Report to G20 Leaders*, July 2017, available online at https://www. oecd.org/tax/oecd-secretary-general-tax-report-g20-leaders-july-2017.pdf, at 9; see also S. S. Johnston, 'OECD Hails Tax Transparency Progress, Much to NGO Disappointment', 87 *Tax Notes International* (2017), 34, at 34.

175. 2016 Report to G20, *supra* note 58, at 11.

176. Ibid.

177. OECD, Phase 1 and Phase 2 Reviews, *supra* note 18.

178. FSI-2018, *supra* note 121.

179. A. Knobel, *The Role of the U.S. as a Tax Haven: New Greens/EFA Research Looks at Implications for Europe*, 11 May 2016, available online at http://www.greens-efa.eu/the-role-of-the-united-states-as-a-tax-haven-15525.html (last visited 13 June 2017).

180. J. Kirwin, 'U.S. Among 92 Nations Screened by EU for Tax Havens', 249 DTR I-1 *Daily Tax Report* (2016); see also European Council, *Criteria and Process Leading to the Establishment of the EU List of Non-Cooperative Jurisdictions for Tax Purposes—Council Conclusions*, Doc. 14166/16, 8 Nov. 2016; Council of the European Union, *Council Conclusions on the EU list of non-cooperative jurisdictions for tax purposes* (5 Dec. 2017), available online at http://www.consilium.europa.eu/media/31945/st15429en17.pdf.

181. Lew Letter, *supra* note 119.

182. See, e.g., Act of Feb. 14, 2017, Pub. L. No. 115-4, 131 Stat. 9 (providing for congressional disapproval of a rule submitted by the Securities and Exchange Commission relating to "Disclosure of Payments by Resource Extraction Issuers").

183. M. Findley, D. Nielson, and J. Sharman, *Global Shell Games: Testing Money Launderers' and Terrorist Financiers' Access to Shell Companies* (2012), available online at https://www.griffith.edu.au/business-government/centre-governance-public-policy/research-publications/?a=454625 (last visited 13 June 2017).

184. Global Witness, *Undercover in New York: Our Hidden Camera Investigation Reveals How Suspect Money Can Enter the U.S.*, 31 Jan. 2016, available online at https://www.globalwitness.org/shadyinc/ (last visited 13 June 2017).

185. OHCHR, *Working Group on the Issue of Human Rights and Transnational Corporations and Enterprises* (2016), available online at http://www.ohchr.org/EN/Issues/Business/Pages/WGHRandtransnationalcorporationsandotherbusiness.aspx (last visited 13 June 2017).

186. OHCHR, *United Nations Forum on Business and Human Right* (2016), available online at http://www.ohchr.org/EN/Issues/Business/Forum/Pages/ForumonBusinessandHumanRights.aspx (last visited 13 June 2017).

187. The Sixth annual forum was held in Geneva 27–29 November 2017 with participants representing governments, national human rights institutions, businesses, civil society, trade unions, human rights defenders, lawyers, and academia. In his closing remarks, Mr. Surya Deva notes that tax evasion and tax avoidance undermine the States' ability to "have much-needed resources to realise human rights." See S. Deva, Chairperson of the UN Working Group on Business and Human Rights, closing remarks at 2017 UN Forum on Business and Human Rights, 29 Nov. 2017, available online at http://www.ohchr.org/Documents/Issues/Business/ForumSession6/ClosingSuryaDeva.pdf, at 2, 3.

PART 4

PRIVATE ACTORS
AND THE PUBLIC PURSE

*The Roles of Corporations, Lawyers, and Accountants
in Tax Abuse*

CHAPTER 15

INTERROGATING THE RELATIONSHIP BETWEEN "LEGALLY DEFENSIBLE" TAX PLANNING AND SOCIAL JUSTICE

DANIEL SHAVIRO

I. INTRODUCTION

A. UNDERLYING AMBIGUITIES

Suppose that straight-out tax fraud, such as the use of offshore bank accounts to get paid without leaving a paper trail for the US tax authorities, was playing a major role in the rise of high-end inequality. That is, suppose such behavior, rather than being concentrated among the owners of cash businesses who generally are not super-rich, was mainly the province of billionaires, along with—begging the question, for now, of how this relates to inequality between *people*—highly profitable corporations. Then there would obviously be a need to focus on corporate social responsibility with regard to tax-planning behavior, and on the ethics of any tax professionals who aided or knew about the cheating.

In practice, however, outright fraud generally is not a prominent feature of such taxpayers' planning. This reflects their interests and incentives, not just the influence of any ethical considerations. Given both the level of scrutiny that such taxpayers may expect and the availability of other mechanisms for reducing their tax burdens, fraud for them, to paraphrase Prince Talleyrand, would not just be a crime—it would be a mistake. Thus, it should come as no surprise that the tax-reducing strategies of super-rich individuals and highly profitable corporations commonly qualify as what I will call "legally defensible."[1] This term, however, covers tax planning that may vary across a range in at least three important dimensions:

Tax, Inequality, and Human Rights. Philip Alston and Nikki Reisch.
© Oxford University Press 2019. Published 2019 by Oxford University Press.

Likelihood of legal correctness. Some tax-reporting positions are clearly legally correct, whether on their face or because the Internal Revenue Service (IRS) has agreed to them in advance. At the limit, a clearly correct position is one that would be 100 percent certain of being upheld ex post, even in the face of close IRS scrutiny that reflected adequate resources, an accurate understanding of all pertinent facts, and a willingness to litigate if necessary.

In other cases, however, the ex ante likelihood of correctness, as judged by the taxpayer's advisers,[2] may be considerably less than 100 percent. Consider Table 15.1—submitted to the IRS by the American Institute of Certified Public Accountants (AICPA)—which gives a common version of the standards that tax professionals use when writing opinion letters to taxpayers regarding the merits of a particular tax-reporting position.

Suppose we define a legally defensible position as one that has at least a "reasonable basis"— the relevant legal threshold, under certain circumstances, for avoiding tax penalties.[3] (The intuitive reason for setting it so low might be that surely taxpayers are entitled to take "reasonable" positions in their own favor, even if the likelihood of success is below 50 percent.) At this level— but indeed, even if taxpayers are taking multiple "will" positions, each with a separate 90 percent probability of success—they may be expected to pay too little tax, relative to the case where all relevant legal issues were fully scrutinized, and thus (by definition) resolved ex post "correctly." Ex ante legal uncertainty also, in the absence of sufficient "strict liability" penalties, gives taxpayers an incentive to play the "audit lottery"—that is, to count on (and perhaps attempt to enhance) the unlikelihood of full review of their tax positions, even if these are always legally defensible.[4]

Consistency with legislative or regulatory intent. Tax planning that is legally defensible sometimes can have results that are clearly ridiculous, in the sense that they cannot logically be defended. For example, various convoluted financial transactions that were prevalent in the 1990s took advantage of peculiar interactions between distinct tax provisions to permit taxpayers to claim that, simply by reason of causing cash to travel around in a circle, they were entitled to deduct huge losses. In such cases, even if the transactions initially are sustained upon challenge, one may expect that the government will respond by changing the rules, so that they will cease to work.[5] The tax shelter industry therefore works hard at searching for new transactions that

Table 15.1: Opinion "quality"*

Will	At least 90% probability of success if challenged by IRS
Should	At least 70% probability of success if challenged by IRS
More likely than not	Greater than 50% probability of success if challenged by IRS
Substantial authority	At least 40% probability of success; weight of authorities in support is "substantial" relative to that of authorities opposing the position
Realistic possibility of success	At least 1 in 3 probability of success if challenged by IRS
Reasonable basis	Significantly higher than "not frivolous," but lower than one-third
Not frivolous	Not patently improper; some merit to position
Frivolous	Patently improper

*It is telling, perhaps, that the term opinion "quality," in tax practice, refers to how high a level of confidence the opinion-writer is willing to express—not how convincing, thorough, or fair the analysis is. A "will" opinion thus has the highest possible "quality."

Source: American Institute of Certified Public Accountants (AICPA), Statements on Standards for Tax Services (2010), available online at https://www.irs.gov/pub/irs-utl/statements_on_standards_for_tax_services.pdf.

can be sold to first-generation taxpayers, before being detected by the government and promptly (but only prospectively) shut down—at which point the promoters may roll out the next items on their "product lines."[6]

By contrast, other tax benefits clearly *were* intended by Congress or the Treasury (when devising regulations within its discretionary powers), with the consequences that (1) detection is not an issue, and (2) the benefits may be expected to remain in place indefinitely, unless there is a new political decision to change policy. Thus, consider the exclusion of municipal bond interest from taxable income,[7] or the allowance of accelerated depreciation (in excess of economic depreciation) for various assets.[8] These rules offer deliberate tax benefits that are meant to encourage particular types of investments—potentially with the effect, in practice, of driving down the after-tax returns from such investments so that they are no greater than those available from fully taxed alternatives.

There is also a middle range, in which taxpayers discover new tax-planning opportunities that may not have been anticipated by Congress or the Treasury, and that might never have been deliberately adopted, but that prove resilient once discovered. Such reliance may reflect one or more of the burden of legislative inertia, status quo bias, and broader reliance claims by taxpayers. Thus, consider the so-called "Wall Street Rule," under which, as Lee Sheppard has noted, taxpayers "take aggressive positions, and they figure if enough of them . . . [do so], and there's billions of dollars at stake, then the IRS is kind of estopped from arguing with them because so much would blow up."[9] In effect, aggressive taxpayers become collectively "too big to fail."

Ordinary course of business versus carefully contrived. Candidates for public office who release their tax returns, and who are criticized for having paid too little tax, typically defend themselves by saying that they paid everything they owed, and not a penny more. This may give the impression that all they did, in effect, was passively tote things up and decline to overpay (in the sense of making a voluntary contribution on top of one's legally mandated liability). Such an impression may be misleading, however, insofar as careful tax planning yielded the result that one sees—and especially if it involved taking advantage of the audit lottery, and/or of arguably unintended tax-planning opportunities.

B. SETTING THE STAGE FOR AN EXPLORATORY DIALOGUE

Again, if tax minimization by super-rich individuals and highly profitable corporations mainly involved straight-out fraud, there would be a simple and straightforward case for demanding "good corporate tax behavior," and for focusing on the ethics of any tax professionals who aid and abet the fraud. Things become more complicated, however, when one looks instead at legally defensible tax planning. To be sure, legal defensibility does not support the conclusion: "Move on—nothing to see here"—indeed, far from it. However, it may cause the associated normative and empirical issues to be both two-sided and hard to resolve.

To help illustrate this point, while also locating some of the main fault lines raised by social justice challenges to legally defensible high-end tax planning, I have chosen here to employ an unusual format: that of a dialogue between two wholly fictitious individuals. This dialogue is not meant to be Socratic. That is, neither discussant leads the other on a journey from ignorance to wisdom. Instead, each has good points to make, and they do not reach full consensus. In addition, neither discussant speaks entirely for me, nor is either based on any particular individual whom I have ever known or heard about. They are simply vehicles for me to set forth competing points of view, in each case more crisply and decisively than I could if speaking directly for (and as) myself, given my belief, in many instances, that opposing arguments may each have some merit.

I will call my two discussants Megan and Russell. Megan is a tenured tax law professor, while Russell is an economist at an accounting firm who works closely with both lawyers and accountants, on both tax planning and lobbying matters. Megan and Russell are old friends who used to work together at the Treasury Department. During their Treasury days, they both thought of themselves as idealistically pro-government, which they would have defined as favoring increases in the extent to which high-income individuals and corporations faced effective tax rates that were closer to, though not above, their statutory rates.

Nowadays, both Megan and (more strongly) Russell feel that their thinking in those days was a bit simplistic. While Megan still generally favors increasing high-end effective tax rates, she is now more keenly aware than she used to be of the associated efficiency costs and practical difficulties, especially when this can only be attempted via second-best (or ninety-ninth best) means. Russell does not think well of all the transactions, or support all of the client positions, on which he works in connection with his job. However, he now has greater understanding of, and sympathy for, the competitive pressures and compliance burdens that businesses (and tax advisers!) face than he had during his government days. In addition, he has grown highly skeptical regarding the policy merits of convoluted pro-government rules that, as his experience teaches him, often just create tedious and resource-wasting mazes through which he must (or at least can and does) help his clients to navigate.

Megan and Russell agree to conduct a dialogue regarding the relationship between social justice and legally defensible tax planning. They leave open the question for discussion the question of what "social justice" might mean in this setting, although presumably it might relate both to the bottom line (in the sense of how much tax wealthy individuals and large corporations do and should pay) and to the process by which they determine their self-reported tax liabilities. Megan's and Russell's mutual aim is to seek common ground, or at least a specification of their differences through reasoned discussion—not to try to win a debate. The discussion is organized around four distinct propositions, two advanced by each of them. The propositions are as follows:

1. MEGAN: Large-scale tax avoidance by wealthy individuals and large companies that is legally defensible can nonetheless harm social justice and public morale.
2. RUSSELL: Taxpayers have a right to pay as little tax as they legally can. If you don't like the results, change the rules!
3. MEGAN: Tax advisers' professional and personal ethical obligations require them to do more than just minimize expected tax liability.
4. RUSSELL: It's a tactical error for social justice advocates to focus on "corporate social responsibility" and tax professionals' ethics, rather than exclusively focusing on the existing rules and resulting incentives.[10]

II. DISCUSSION OF THE FIRST PROPOSITION

MEGAN: You picked "rock," and I picked "paper," so I get to go first.

RUSSELL: I should have known that you would pick "paper." How many do you write in a year, anyway?

MEGAN: Never mind that. As you know, because we coordinated our topics in advance, my first proposition holds: *Large-scale tax avoidance by wealthy individuals and large companies that is legally defensible can nonetheless harm social justice and public morale*. I am hoping that you will quickly agree with me on this one, and we can move on.

RUSSELL: I'll need to hear more from you first. Granted, large-scale tax avoidance by wealthy individuals can increase high-end wealth concentration, which I join you in disliking. At least, that would seem to be its direct effect, but don't we also need to think about the indirect effects? As for large companies, obviously I'm going to ask you to address who bears the corporate tax. What if the incidence increasingly falls on labor, not on management or shareholders or holders of capital generally?

MEGAN: Can I start answering you now?

RUSSELL: I also have questions about social justice and public morale.

MEGAN: All in good time. I'll start with wealthy individuals. Is this a Republican thing? Job creators and "I built that"?

RUSSELL: Not at all. Or at least it doesn't have to be. As you would probably have guessed, I give campaign donations to both parties. But let's look at a business founder who creates a new billion-dollar company. The salary that he or she gets is deductible by the company anyway, so why do we even care about that—leaving aside the spread between the top individual rate and the corporate rate. Meanwhile, people get upset if the founder's capital gains are taxed at just 20 percent. But even apart from state and local taxes, and the Medicare tax on investment income, and for that matter the estate tax, there's also the entity-level corporate tax. Capital gains just reflect changes in the present value of the company's future expected profits, which generally are taxable, at least in theory.

MEGAN: Key words there, "at least in theory."

RUSSELL: Granted. But when you're talking about an income tax, as well as an estate tax, you are affecting incentives not just to work but also to save and invest. Now admittedly, there isn't strong econometric evidence that savings rates are highly tax-responsive. But still, there's clearly a tax-incidence question. You could raise tax rates on saving by high-income US individuals, or on investment by anyone in the United States, and the effect could be to lower labor productivity and wages further down the income spectrum. I'm not saying it would be—but don't you need to know?

MEGAN: Fair enough. But suppose we're taxing rents that these people earn from having high ability, or first-mover advantages, or special opportunities, or monopoly power, or whatever else it is. Then there's actually an element of free money, in efficiency terms, from taxing people at the top, and they will bear the incidence.

RUSSELL: Okay, enough about that. I don't really disagree with you about taxing rich people more, so long as it's done intelligently, which is probably unlikely. But cracking down on tax shelters is often a great thing, as it certainly was in the early 2000s, when people had to be scared out of doing sleazy transactions that didn't even work. Some people in my line of work went to jail—and they deserved it. But we're talking about "legally permissible" tax planning, in an environment where the IRS has fortunately made it clear that it is very serious about anti–tax shelter doctrines, such as requiring economic substance and business purpose.

MEGAN: You mentioned companies, and the incidence of the corporate tax. Obviously, there are complicated efficiency issues if Apple can use tax haven subsidiaries to avoid paying much tax anywhere, while purely domestic US companies may be paying much closer to a 35 percent effective rate, even leaving aside the shareholder-level tax. But on the other hand, I agree that we also have to think about Apple versus other multinationals, including non-US companies. Let's leave all that aside, because it's about efficiency, not directly about inequality. But still, if Steve Jobs' salary was $1 per year because he was getting stock appreciation, and Apple isn't paying much entity-level tax because of its international tax planning, and then he gets tax-free basis step-up at death for all the appreciated shares, that only leaves the estate tax, which is notoriously porous in its own right.

RUSSELL: Fair enough. I may disagree with you more later in our colloquy than on Proposition One. And, if we're parsing your exact words, it's certainly true that legally defensible tax avoidance, especially when it's allowed to be large-scale, can harm social justice and public morale and probably has at times done so. But let's interrogate those two terms a bit more. By "social justice," do you also mean the safety net and treatment of the poor?

MEGAN: Potentially. One point about rising high-end wealth concentration is that it distorts the political system. We saw this at work in 2008, after the financial crisis. Austerity on both sides of the Atlantic, and the amazingly tepid response to sustained high unemployment, reflected where money and power are concentrated these days. And whether legally defensible high-end tax avoidance had a large indirect impact on this or a small one—probably the latter—surely its direction is clear.

RUSSELL: Once again, we risk being boringly in agreement. But I don't agree that legally defensible tax planning, as defined by existing rules, has made anti-poverty or entitlements programs in the United States budgetarily unaffordable. If those things are underfunded, that's a political choice, and we don't seem to have trouble spending money on things— say, national defense or homeland security, not to mention the Iraq War back when that happened—that have sufficient backing.

MEGAN: Maybe. I'll let that pass. What's your point on morale?

RUSSELL: Just that those who dislike aggressive tax planning by rich people and big corporations—maybe for good reasons—often like to throw in the extra argument that general public morale and compliance are suffering. That could be so, but I'd like to see more proof.

MEGAN: Other people in the biz tend to rely on that argument more than I do.

RUSSELL: Maybe it's an American thing. Look at how people in England got angry about Starbucks reporting UK tax losses. But we're an anti-tax country. People don't care. No one's refusing to buy Apple products because of their tax planning.

MEGAN: Or maybe it's a United States versus Europe thing. Maybe what they don't like in Europe is US companies not paying enough tax to them.

RUSSELL: Either way, if Americans are still buying Apple products, I doubt that their tax-paying morale is being seriously affected either.

MEGAN: I'll demur on this, because people have become so cynical about politics on so many fronts and for so many reasons. But I'm not relying heavily on the tax compliance issue, nor do I think I need to.

III. DISCUSSION OF THE SECOND PROPOSITION

RUSSELL: My turn. Given how agreeable I just was, for the most part, I am hoping that you will endorse the following proposition: *Taxpayers have a right to pay as little tax as they legally can. If you don't like the results, change the rules!*

MEGAN: Let me open with a low blow: lobbying.

RUSSELL: Wait a second, we agreed we wouldn't discuss that.

MEGAN: Because you agreed you couldn't defend it.

RUSSELL: No, because I agreed that our political system is so screwed up that of course there's lobbying that distorts the law. But that's a political problem, not a compliance problem.

MEGAN: So you guys might as well join the crowd at the trough.

RUSSELL: Ouch. Low blow there. But please keep in mind, in general I only lobby for things that I can reasonably defend.

MEGAN: In general?

RUSSELL: Yes. No one's a saint, least of all me, but I can't be an effective advocate if the things I'm saying don't make sense to me.

MEGAN: Very noble of you.

RUSSELL: Plus, there's such a thing as specialization, for lobbying like everything else. The firm would be devaluing me as an asset if they asked me to lobby for crass and stupid things.

MEGAN: Besides, they have other folks for that.

RUSSELL: Or the clients can go to other firms. And anyway we're not the political muscle, so generally we're only going to be hired if there's a reasonable argument and they want someone to explain it to the staff people.

MEGAN: You realize that not even trying to defend lobbying is a pretty big concession on your part regarding whether we should just change the rules. It's like: "Other than that, Mrs. Lincoln, how did you like the play?"

RUSSELL: Not at all. It's about keeping a clear distinction in our minds between our system's political defects, on the one hand, and the relevance of legally defensible tax planning on the other hand. They're separate things. The problems with the one don't tell us straightaway whether it helps or not to focus on the other—which is the exact thing we're arguing about.

MEGAN: Fair enough. That's why I agreed to leave out lobbying.

RUSSELL: Okay, back to Proposition Two: *Taxpayers have a right to pay as little tax as they legally can. If you don't like the results, change the rules!* Which I realize could be tough.

MEGAN: I'm going to give you a yes and no here. Or rather, make that two yeses and two noes. I think you have two distinct propositions.

RUSSELL: One for each sentence? I could have used a semicolon and made it all one sentence. But I suppose that wouldn't have helped.

MEGAN: That's right. But let me refine my yeses and noes. The first sentence is true, but irrelevant if you are trying to draw the broader implications that I suspect you are. The second one I also agree with, but I wonder if you are trying to make the best into the enemy of the good, so far as reform efforts are concerned. Also, we can change penalty rules that affect tax planning—not just substantive rules that affect the pre-penalty tax consequences of a given fact pattern.

RUSSELL: Okay, let's slow down here a bit. I'll do as you like and defend one sentence at a time. So let's start with the first one: "Taxpayers have a right to pay as little tax as they legally can." You seem to be assuming that I mean this as a normative statement: if they have a right to do something, then there can't be any complaint about the end result of what they're doing. I agree that people often argue that way about tax planning. But I mean something much simpler, which tends to unify my two sentences into a single proposition: because they have this right, legally speaking and in terms of the consequences that they will face, it's not going to be helpful to gripe about morality. Instead, we need to change the rules—potentially including the penalty rules.

MEGAN: I suppose we have no choice here but to bring up that old Learned Hand chestnut, from *Gregory v. Helvering*.[11] Lawyer or not, by now you must know it as well as I do.

RUSSELL: Okay, I'll do the honors. [He punches a few buttons on his phone.] You can see I was ready for this. "Any one may so arrange his affairs that his taxes shall be as low as possible; he is not bound to choose that pattern which will best pay the Treasury; there is not even a patriotic duty to increase one's taxes." But of course Justice Hand—

MEGAN: Judge Hand. He wasn't on the Supreme Court.

RUSSELL: Fine. But of course Learned Hand—I've always loved that name—goes on to hold for the government, and more or less to invent the modern economic substance doctrine.[12]

MEGAN: Then, to show what he means by rejecting literalism in tax statutory interpretation when it leads to what he calls unintended results, he says something about how "a melody is more than the notes." That is definitely not the most pellucid guidance ever given by a court in a tax opinion.

RUSSELL: I always call in my lawyer colleagues when we have an economic substance issue. Luckily, they've never quoted that sentence to me—if they did, and expected me to think it helped, I'd probably punch someone in the face.

MEGAN: But you probably have heard the line: "I know it when I see it."

RUSSELL: Is that from *Gregory*?

MEGAN: No, but it's lawyer talk or judge talk of the same kind.

RUSSELL: I didn't think it was *Gregory*. But anyway, I'm not complaining about vague, touchy-feely doctrines. I know from experience that the tax system needs them. In terms of the proposition, my point is simply this. Taxpayers will do what they have a current legal right to do. It doesn't mean that they shouldn't feel bad about it—we'll get to that issue later. And it doesn't mean that the rules shouldn't be changed. But if you give particular incentives to economic actors—and here, a "right" to pay as little tax as they can merely refers to the set of consequences they'll face in alternative scenarios—you can't be too surprised if they act on those incentives.

MEGAN: In other words, mere exhortation isn't likely to help much.

RUSSELL: At least, it won't help unless it's tied to greater consequences than seem likely here. Again, Apple's right to pay fewer taxes, rather than more, will not prevent the managers from voluntarily "overpaying"—in scare quotes—if they believe that doing so is in the shareholders' best interest—whether for consumer goodwill reasons or any other.

MEGAN: Let's hear it for managers who only care about shareholder welfare.

RUSSELL: In fairness, there are some well-governed companies out there, and not all of them are closely held. But yes, managerial incentives matter plenty as well. And indeed, companies sometimes "shirk"—again in scare quotes—on minimizing tax as much as they should, from the shareholders' standpoint, because of the reputational or other downside risks that the managers would face in cases where a reasonable ploy ex ante didn't work out ex post.

MEGAN: Okay, with those clarifications I am willing to accept your first sentence, "Taxpayers have a right to pay as little tax as they legally can." Only, as explained, it's pretty much circular and doesn't add anything.

RUSSELL: What it adds is a dose of realism. But let's move onto the second sentence. "If you don't like the results, change the rules!" You seem to think I meant just the substantive rules. But I also definitely meant to include the penalty rules.

MEGAN: So let's talk about those now. Today, tax penalty rules generally require some kind of fault, such as negligence, from the lack of a reasonable basis for your position, or from failing to comply with disclosure rules.

RUSSELL: I assume you wouldn't send people to jail without fault.

MEGAN: Sure, but that's criminal tax fraud, so you need mens rea. But civil tax penalties are just monetary sanctions—say, 20 or 30 percent of a given underpayment, depending on which rule you have in mind.

RUSSELL: You're saying they should be higher?

MEGAN: Maybe, but first let's look at fault. If we had no-fault, strict liability penalties for a tax underpayment, and we set the penalties at the right level, that would be one thing. But we don't. So, I'm sorry to say this, but we need to go back to your first sentence again and add in legal uncertainty.

RUSSELL: Okay. "Taxpayers have a right to pay as little tax as they legally can."

MEGAN: Suppose there was complete legal certainty about the correct tax-reporting position in all cases. Then, everyone would know exactly what they should pay—at least, they would know if they hired your firm. But let's make it even simpler—suppose they didn't need to hire your firm, because all of the answers were facially obvious, like not hiding cash from the IRS. So now they have a right to pay what they owe, not a penny more unless they feel like it, and we throw them in jail if they deliberately get it wrong.

RUSSELL: Leaving aside mistake and all that.

MEGAN: Sure. But now let's go the real world, where there's pervasive legal uncertainty. And it's not just ex post in a planning sense: "Here's what I did. How much do I owe?" It's also ex ante: "Should I do X? How much would I owe then?" In this world, when I am filing a tax return under uncertainty, what's the amount that I have to pay?

RUSSELL: Now you should definitely use my firm.

MEGAN: I couldn't afford it.

RUSSELL: That's okay, the work wouldn't be interesting anyway. But that's a compliment, not an insult.

MEGAN: Thank you. But suppose I were your type of client. You tell me, if I do X, more likely than not I can report it like so. But say there's a 49 percent chance the position you're telling me that I can take is wrong. If I take a hundred such positions, then presumably on average about forty-nine of them are wrong.

RUSSELL: Or at least they would be so held on average, if our analysis is exactly right.

MEGAN: But probably none of them will ever be audited. And even if a few are, I won't owe penalties on any that I lose.

RUSSELL: I think I see where you're going.

MEGAN: Well-advised taxpayers—rich people and big corporations—often have complicated returns and good advisers. Even if they're acting in complete good faith, and even if they never take any position unless it's more likely than not to be correct, they're paying too little tax, relative to what they would pay if everything were decided correctly.

RUSSELL: It's even worse than that. First of all, even among the taxpayers who hire us—and they're generally a compliant bunch—reasonable basis is often plenty good enough. Even if they need to disclose, sometimes they overdisclose, so the IRS doesn't know what to look for.

MEGAN: Including Fortune 500 companies?

RUSSELL: Well, a lot of the big public companies require "more likely than not," because otherwise they don't get the accounting benefit. But then, second of all, clients can opinion-shop, and they also can pressure the adviser over opinion quality.

MEGAN: Nice.

RUSSELL: Well, it's not all bad. When they're still planning a transaction, we can say: "Do X and we'll get to 'more likely than not.'" But the other side of the coin is, *they* can say: "Joe Smith at the Such-and-So firm will give us 'more likely than not.' So what's *your* problem?"

MEGAN: So you either give in or lose the opinion letter.

RUSSELL: No one really wants to sign the opinion letter anyway. Or at least that's what the lawyers tell me—luckily, I don't have to sign anything. But if you don't give in, you lose the transaction work, or in our case, maybe the auditing work that goes with the opinion letter.

MEGAN: So, is there a lot of pressure to give in?

RUSSELL: Well, the other side of the coin for the lawyer is his reputation. Plus, hopefully, the firm cares about his reputation. But people can kill their careers by being too cautious, as well as too eager.

MEGAN: Okay, back to uncertainty and the right to pay as little tax as you owe. Once we have uncertainty, people are systematically underpaying, due to the audit lottery and the lack of no-fault penalties, even if they are acting in what we would call complete good faith. And this is mainly an issue for rich people and big corporations. So we are back to my distributional story from Proposition 1.

RUSSELL: And you'd fix this through no-fault penalties? How would you set the penalties?

MEGAN: In theory, it should depend purely on the probability of detection—that is, on the audit lottery odds. If there's a 20 percent chance that the IRS will vet your position, a 5-to-1 penalty, in the case where you lose, makes you indifferent between more uncertain and less uncertain positions. But don't ask me how to determine the odds in practice—I'm just giving you a benchmark.

RUSSELL: And this applies even if you had a good-faith "Will" opinion, based on a 95 percent likelihood of correctness, but then you just happened to lose?

MEGAN: Right. But of course you won't lose very often and face the penalty, in that set of cases.

RUSSELL: The clients I know would just love this. But mind you, it isn't my problem.

MEGAN: So what if they're risk-averse. They can get insurance.

RUSSELL: Tax insurance? You know what happened to that. A couple of start-ups tried to offer it about ten years ago, but it failed.

MEGAN: If the penalty rules were set properly, there'd be more demand for it.

RUSSELL: It didn't fail because there wasn't demand—it failed because they didn't know how to price it. Apparently, they were calling lawyers on the deals and asking them what the likelihood of correctness was.

MEGAN: Wow, that's like the car insurance company asking me how good a driver I am, so they can set the rate.

RUSSELL: Exactly.

MEGAN: But that makes the legal uncertainty problem even worse. Who's to say that a "more likely than not" opinion is even truly 51 out of 100?

RUSSELL: Agreed. And it's probably a subjectivist claim anyway, not a frequentist one. But let's get back to my proposition. Second sentence: "If you don't like the results, change the rules." I don't need to decide whether or not I like no-fault penalties, or how to set the odds, or how to deal with taxpayers' risk aversion, or how it would actually work in practice. You've noted a problem, from the effects of legal uncertainty on how much tax rich people and corporations actually pay, compared to what they would pay if all issues were resolved "correctly"—with big scare quotes, this time. I agree that you have a point.

MEGAN: It also goes to the incentive effects of legal uncertainty, along with the polluting and corruption of the market for legal advice.

RUSSELL: Okay, I still agree. But the thing is, we're now debating what the rules should be. So I win.

MEGAN: You win? That's very male of you. Thanks.

RUSSELL: Any time.

MEGAN: But the thing is, you actually don't win. Given that we don't have legal certainty, or rules that avoid rewarding taxpayers that deliberately seek out uncertain positions, so that they can pay less tax than otherwise in expected value, I'm back to your first sentence. I don't know what it means to "have a right to pay as little tax as you legally can." You have an entire industry that's founded on legal uncertainty, not to mention a grossly underfunded IRS that lacks the resources for a proper audit rate.

RUSSELL: Not to mention that taxpayers who are audited may complain to Congress—at least, if they are worth auditing.

MEGAN: So unless you make the first sentence completely meaningless and circular—which I guess you've already agreed to—all that's left from your entire proposition is the fairly banal point that it's desirable, all else equal, to set taxpayers' incentives properly, whatever that might mean in practice.

RUSSELL: You call it banal, but that's only because you agree with me that incentives are important. In the real world out there, it's actually worth emphasizing.

MEGAN: Compared to blaming people like you. Well, at least you're well paid.

RUSSELL: No complaints there, although you should see some of our clients. Or try the other families in my kids' private schools.

MEGAN: But just because I'd like to get the rules right, too, doesn't mean I'm letting you off the hook. So let's go to Proposition Three, which addresses your sort's ethical obligations.

RUSSELL: "Your sort." I like that.

IV. DISCUSSION OF THE THIRD PROPOSITION

MEGAN: As you'll recall, my next proposition goes: *Tax advisers' professional and personal ethical obligations require them to do more than just minimize expected tax liability.*

RUSSELL: Well, that's certainly true. Minimizing tax liability is not even exactly what the client wants.

MEGAN: You mean, if you're also a business adviser?

RUSSELL: Even if you just do tax. You want to be able to describe the choices and trade-offs, and how they would affect the tax analysis. But the final choice is the client's. And not everyone wants to minimize expected tax liability. There are risk issues, confidence intervals, financial accounting considerations, and reputational or other trade-offs. A good tax adviser is a team player and just offers inputs to the broader analysis.

MEGAN: Plus, of course, the goal isn't minimizing tax liability. To do that, all you need tell the client is to go ahead and lose money. Tax liability zero, perhaps even refunds for a company's past year's taxes. So what I meant was, maximizing after-tax income, which implies minimizing expected tax liability, adjusting for risk and all else equal.

RUSSELL: Fair enough. But what are you getting at? This isn't still about uncertainty, or is it?

MEGAN: There's one piece that is about uncertainty, but I'm looking at something bigger.

RUSSELL: As the saying goes, "Proceed, governor."

MEGAN: Okay, first here's one thing it's not about. The tax adviser says, if you do X, which you disvalue at $10 million, there's a 51 percent chance that your correctly measured tax liability declines by $15 million. The other 49 percent, your tax liability stays the same. The taxpayer wouldn't do X if review of the position were certain, because it scores out as a negative. But given the low probability of serious IRS review, the actual expected tax saving from the reporting position is close to the full $15 million. So the client does X.

RUSSELL: You're saying your point is not about that?

MEGAN: I have a hard time blaming the tax adviser for performing the analysis and correctly, let's assume, analyzing the tax consequences of X. Now, as I was just saying, I don't like the incentive here, and I think it might have broader social justice effects when we observe who gets these tax-planning opportunities, and I think it undermines your observation about paying just the tax you owe, but we've been through that, and I don't blame the tax adviser for anything—yet.

RUSSELL: So where do you start having a problem?

MEGAN: A few things. First, telling the taxpayer to do it because the audit risk is low.

RUSSELL: The opinion letters can't address the audit risk, of course. They just assess the probabilities if the IRS does review an issue. But agreed, this is a ticklish area. It's hard not to answer the question about audit probabilities, when you're asked.

MEGAN: Second, helping the taxpayer to structure it so the audit risk will be lower.

RUSSELL: Another gray area. People certainly counsel disclosing absolutely everything, knowing that it will tend to divert attention from the things that really need to be disclosed. But I would think they're careful about how they say this.

MEGAN: Third, change my hypothetical in a couple of ways. First, while I tend to think about probability in continuous terms—51 percent versus 49 percent probability of correctness doesn't make all that much difference to me—let's start driving down the probability of correctness. Say the tax adviser is pointing out all sorts of things that are just reasonable basis. Does that mean, say, a 20 percent chance of being correct?

RUSSELL: Thereabouts.

MEGAN: Again, it's not the threshold I care about, but getting closer to zero. But also, let's suppose that the adviser isn't just passively answering questions, like: "What are the merits of this position? What about that one?" Suppose the adviser is combing the Tax Code and looking through the regulations, trying to find long-shot tax-planning tricks that might just be good enough to use without commission of tax fraud.

RUSSELL: That's definitely a market niche.

MEGAN: I also have in mind an example where the chance of legal correctness is very high—we can even say 100 percent, for argument's sake—and yet there are ethical issues. But let's deal with the probabilistic cases first.

RUSSELL: You rightly point to a fraught area. But even leaving aside the penalty rules and whether they should do something different, it's inherent to the agency problem. Start with taxpayers versus the IRS. From an aggregate social welfare standpoint, the taxpayers have the wrong objective. They are trying to maximize personal utility, not social utility. Socially, the taxes they pay are a transfer; personally, they're a cost. But we accept this. They are expected, and even entitled, to try to maximize after-tax income, all else equal, subject to observing the criminal laws.

MEGAN: And using penalties, among other rules, to shape their incentives.

RUSSELL: Yes, but not to optimize their incentives, from a social standpoint, at every margin. We accept that people might work less due to the marginal incentive effects of the income tax, and while that affects the optimal marginal rate structure, it doesn't mean they're immoral for working less—unless we're asking them to be saints.

MEGAN: I assume you'll be bringing up the tax advisers any moment now.

RUSSELL: Bear with me. People can't do everything for themselves—they need agents. And those agents have fiduciary duties toward them. Some of those agents are tax advisers.

MEGAN: Others are, say, criminal defense lawyers.

RUSSELL: Yes. And defense lawyers owe their clients their best efforts at defending them.

MEGAN: Speak of fraught ethical relationships. You can't knowingly put on false testimony. On the other hand, you can't refuse to give your client the best possible defense, just because you have your doubts. The easy way out is not to take the case, but someone has to take it. And if the defendant has money, it will be someone who's good.

RUSSELL: I wouldn't want that job. But again, it's inherent in the agency relationship.

MEGAN: Criminal defense lawyers are also officers of the court.

RUSSELL: What about tax lawyers?

MEGAN: They're not literally officers of the court unless they're appearing in court. But they are members of the bar, and that involves ethical responsibilities.

RUSSELL: Aren't those at least partly just about being a faithful agent?

MEGAN: Yes, and some would say also about protecting lawyers' monopoly in the legal services market—although, in tax, that's weakened by the role of accountants. But there are also ethical obligations toward improving the legal system.

RUSSELL: Of course. But where do you cash them out, in terms of tax advice about minimizing tax liability? Taking as given, of course, that fraud and other crimes are impermissible, and that there are gray areas as you move from avoiding needless audit red flags toward counseling concealment.

MEGAN: Let's take my case with 100 percent certainty of being legally correct. It can still be unethical. Maybe not in terms of violating the code of professional responsibility for lawyers, or in any legally enforceable sense—but in how we judge people, and how we urge them to act.

RUSSELL: So you're saying, we tell a client, if you do X, you will pay $10 million less tax, with 100 percent certainty of being correct, and it might be unethical? Given the agency relationship, wouldn't it be unethical *not* to tell the client, if the delegation is broad enough?

MEGAN: Let me give you two cases. Both involve the so-called high-basis, low-value tax shelter, which Joseph Bankman wrote about some years ago.[13] This was a silly accounting manipulation, involving the tax-free incorporation rules, which in theory permitted unlimited loss creation by corporate taxpayers. It seemingly worked as a matter of black letter law, but was vulnerable, to say the least, under a variety of common law doctrines such as the economic substance requirement. But Joe says—I put this on my phone, just like you had the Learned Hand quote: "It is easy to see that if this shelter were respected (say, approved in a Revenue Ruling), it would reduce corporate taxable income to near zero."[14]

RUSSELL: We looked at high-basis, low-value shelters, and decided to pass.

MEGAN: Good for you.

RUSSELL: I can't speak for everyone in my firm, however.

MEGAN: Suppose, although it's absurd, that things happened just like Joe said. The IRS and Treasury expressly approve the deal, and corporate tax revenues are headed to zero.

RUSSELL: Do they seek legislation to eliminate it prospectively?

MEGAN: The scenario is too ridiculous for me to need to answer that question. But Case One, out of my two cases, is the one where all that has actually happened, and you are the tax adviser for a firm that is considering doing it.

RUSSELL: I take it you can say, go ahead.

MEGAN: Yes. Even if you think the government was wrong in its legal analysis, I don't think that, as an ethical matter, you or your client need to be the lone holdout. Of course, it would be laudable if you supported reform efforts to get rid of the loophole, and unethical to oppose the reform efforts on bogus grounds.

RUSSELL: What about not so bogus grounds, such as that the corporate tax is inefficient, and this at least gets rid of it?

MEGAN: Well now, we're starting to get into academic ethics and values, which would be a further conversation. But certainly, if that's what you believe, you should say so. Others will judge whether they think it's a good argument. And if you're paid for saying it, they'll judge that, too.

RUSSELL: So what is Case Two?

MEGAN: That is where you are the one who came up with the shelter. And now let's forget about the Treasury approving it, which was just to make a hypothetical point. Suppose you are combing the Internal Revenue Code, looking for unexpected and unintended interactions between distinct provisions, which will turn into loss generators. Assume that they work, in cases where you can gin up enough economic substance, but that Congress or the Treasury will eliminate them as soon as word leaks out. And when that happens, no problem. You've already sold those deals enough times, people are starting to do their own knockoffs anyway, and it's time for the next generation of deals.

RUSSELL: Say you're an early adopter, but not the inventor. Is that better, or worse?

MEGAN: Well, now we're into matters of degree. The point I want to make is that not just lawyers, but people generally, should do better than this. It's not something to be proud of. I'd be ashamed of myself if I were doing it. And I would aspirationally urge people—my students, for example—to do different and better things with their lives.

RUSSELL: Two comments in response. First, I agree with you up to a point. But if people have incentives to do things, they are going to do them. It's like an ecological niche for nasty things like mosquitoes. At a certain point it's just hand-waving to say you don't like those people or those things. And shouldn't you be focusing your attention on law reform?

MEGAN: It isn't either/or. Besides, there are always going to be holes in the system, of one kind or another. And maybe inciting people to be more thoughtful about what they do with their lives can have an influence at the margin.

RUSSELL: Okay, I'm not opposed to that—although maybe I'm more skeptical than you are about the payoff. We'll return to that for my next proposition. But here's my second comment. How far do you take it, and where do you draw the line?

MEGAN: There may not be entirely clear lines. That's why it's a general aspirational point, not an enforceable legal rule.

RUSSELL: Well, let me press you further. On the high-basis, low-value shelter, in Case Two that we agree is more realistic than Case One, I take it that the key is that the government would eliminate it ASAP. So it amounts to exploiting a temporary glitch. But what about some more durable tax-planning examples? The "Double Irish Dutch Sandwich" got a lot of media play several years ago. It was a highly structured and artificial set of arrangements, navigating through the tax laws of multiple countries, that US multinationals used to create "stateless income." But a bunch of press articles revealed it, and life just went on.

MEGAN: Isn't it dead now?

RUSSELL: Ireland eventually changed its rules so it would no longer work, but that was only after it had been around for decades—admittedly, not all of them spent in public.

MEGAN: That's a more complicated example in some ways, due to the international element. The companies weren't just avoiding US taxes but also foreign taxes, so we as Americans have to decide what to think about that.

RUSSELL: Check your ethics at the national border?

MEGAN: Either way, that's a further conversation. A purely domestic example, where US companies were avoiding US taxes on what was purely US-source income, and exclusively using the tax rules, might not have lasted so long.

RUSSELL: But someone invented the Double Irish Dutch Sandwich—possibly a tax adviser for Apple, back in the 1980s.[15] Was that unethical?

MEGAN: I bet it was lucrative. But let's put it this way. All else equal, I wouldn't feel proud about it, if doing things like that was my life's work.

RUSSELL: Someone else would have done it anyway.

MEGAN: Great, so let them.

RUSSELL: But you wouldn't do it yourself?

MEGAN: I didn't say that. It isn't murder.

RUSSELL: Does it get back to what I said before about not asking people to be saints? We can't build a system on altruism.

MEGAN: It's all a matter of context. Obviously I agree that, even if I should happen to write a tax policy piece that's based on a utilitarian social welfare function, I am not going to go home and give away all my money to people who are poorer than me. Even leaving aside the case of special duties toward one's children.

RUSSELL: But at least you don't do what I do professionally, so that's in the plus column for you.

MEGAN: I didn't say that either. You keep putting words in my mouth. And besides, there are people who do far more altruistic things with their lives than I do with mine. I'm kind of an art for art's sake type of gal academically, more than a do-gooder.

RUSSELL: But would you say, you turned down the big law firm money because you strongly believed—well, I'll let you finish the sentence.

MEGAN: I did what I thought I'd enjoy the most, and also what I thought I'd be best at.

RUSSELL: As an economist, I didn't have the same academic prospects as you did in law. Maybe teaching oversubscribed Econ 101 classes in the Midwest somewhere, then trying to crack the top journals so I'd get tenure. And I don't really have the patience to be elite with either data or econometrics.

MEGAN: Like me, you prefer the big picture, but academics in your field aren't as friendly to it as in mine.

RUSSELL: So I'm also doing what I'm good at, and I even enjoy it most of the time. Only, it does frequently involve helping high-net-worth individuals and big corporations pay less tax than they would otherwise—which may sometimes even be good policy. And it also can be interesting, like solving a puzzle.

MEGAN: Okay.

RUSSELL: But you wouldn't feel good about doing it yourself.

MEGAN: No, but admittedly I might have done it if I just happened to like different things, and to have a different skill set. So in that sense, it's not about ethics at all.

RUSSELL: And anyway, we're just haggling over the price.

MEGAN: Absolutely.

RUSSELL: Where does that leave us on Proposition Three?

MEGAN: Still saying, at least for my part, that tax adviser can be an honorable profession, but it's important to do it as honorably as possible. That means keeping some focus on the long-term quality of the system. And not doing everything that might "work."

RUSSELL: And I'm still saying, for my part, that we should all do our best, but no one has to be a saint. And an agent's job is to help the principal, albeit within ethical limits that would apply to the principal itself.

MEGAN: Nice gender-neutral term there, "itself."

RUSSELL: I was thinking about my corporate clients.

MEGAN: But also, experts face some ethical considerations that don't apply to the principal. Criminal defense again—no one blames the defendant as much for lying, as we would rightly blame a defense lawyer who went over the line.

RUSSELL: So now you're minimizing corporate social responsibility, in favor of blaming the advisers?

MEGAN: I haven't actually said "corporate social responsibility," until just now. But I'd be happy to use moral suasion to influence them both.

RUSSELL: That's a perfect lead-in for our final proposition.

MEGAN: Go ahead.

V. DISCUSSION OF THE FOURTH PROPOSITION

RUSSELL: Last up for the day: *It's a tactical error for social justice advocates to focus on "corporate social responsibility" and tax professionals' ethics, rather than exclusively focusing on the existing rules and resulting incentives.*

MEGAN: So now we're just talking tactics.

RUSSELL: Exactly.

MEGAN: So you're offering friendly advice from across the aisle. But doesn't it follow automatically from Proposition Two, once you interpreted it as saying that only incentives matter? So what's the new angle here?

RUSSELL: Well, here I'm talking about distraction and wasted effort. Exhorting companies to be good corporate citizens, when there's no evidence that consumers care, is just people having fun, preaching to the choir at academic conferences. Or else, it's really silly things that cheapen public dialogue—like saying that a US corporation, which is an intangible web of contracts, is "unpatriotic" if the managers seek to increase shareholder value.

MEGAN: By inverting, if that's what it takes.

RUSSELL: Yes, if the rules make that feasible and advantageous. Which is not to judge what the rules should be.

MEGAN: I'll check, not raise, your bid on management just serving the shareholders. There's also the stakeholder view, but it's not my area. So let me make two other points instead. The first is about behavior, and the second is about politics.

RUSSELL: Whose behavior?

MEGAN: Corporate tax directors and their bosses and tax advisers. You've been talking about incentives, but what about fashions, and trends, and follow-the-leader? Take corporate tax shelters back in the day. It became a thing. And it wasn't just incentives. A lot of what people were doing was really stupid. But if everyone else you knew was doing it, you'd feel pressure to do it, too.

RUSSELL: Or else your boss would ask you why you weren't doing it.

MEGAN: Similar point about aggressive corporate tax planning that's legally defensible or better. As I understand it—although you'd know better than I—there are all these comparative pressures on the tax directors at big companies, focused on the effective tax rate. The point isn't to pay 10 percent instead of 20 percent, at least for its own sake. It's that, if the other guys are all paying 20 percent, that's good enough, but if they're down to 10 percent, then you'd better get there too. So it's not actually, at least directly, about shareholder welfare.

RUSSELL: I agree that people think that way. And it might even be part of how they get to shareholder welfare, given agency costs.

MEGAN: But you don't need to have a stakeholder view of how companies ought to be managed in order to say, since we consider taxes paid a transfer, rather than a social cost, we want to discourage companies from tax planning too aggressively. If that involves relying on agency costs and managerial shirking of shareholder welfare promotion, so be it.

RUSSELL: But how does this relate back to a corporate social responsibility agenda?

MEGAN: It could be part of an effort to change the social pressures people follow, as opposed to just incentives or shareholder welfare in tax planning.

RUSSELL: Like Take Your Kid to Work Day?

MEGAN: In effect.

RUSSELL: I don't see it. Talk from the outside about corporate social responsibility only matters if it affects something that they care about on the inside, like consumer goodwill. Again, I don't see that happening in the United States, like with Apple and iPhone sales. And if they embrace it from the inside, it's either trivial, like Take Your Kid to Work Day, or else it's marketing.

MEGAN: So how would you respond to follow-the-leader behavior in aggressive tax planning?

RUSSELL: For corporate tax shelters, it was enforcement. People went to jail, institutions got embarrassed, and the whole thing calmed down a bit. And by the way, we should distinguish the individual side—people buying son-of-BOSS shelters was all about believing it might actually work, and then finding out that it didn't. So there it was a more rational process, without the same agency costs.

MEGAN: What about legally defensible tax planning that we don't like?

RUSSELL: There I really can't see exhortation or the corporate social responsibility agenda making a major difference, given that the consumers don't care.

MEGAN: Okay, suppose I take your point that, even though behavior matters and it's not just rationality and incentives, social justice advocates may not have access to the right set of tools to change corporate culture from the outside. So let me turn to my point about politics.

RUSSELL: I figured that was your main one.

MEGAN: Let's talk about inversions being called unpatriotic. You seemed to be offended by that. And it's true I wouldn't discuss them that way if I were writing an academic article. But say you're advising the White House about how to build public support for new anti-inversion rules. Should they talk about repatriation taxes and subpart F? Hopscotch loans and earnings-stripping? Or should they use concepts that people can understand?

RUSSELL: Like, that a company with personnel around the world, traded on global stock markets, and not even made of flesh and blood, is a "Benedict Arnold" if it merges with a foreign company based partly on US tax considerations.

MEGAN: Why not, if that's what it takes?

RUSSELL: It's not elevating discourse or improving public understanding. It's finding villains for complicated problems. It's blaming people within the companies who are rationally following their incentives.

MEGAN: Welcome to politics. The world is complicated, and people are busy. They like simple narratives. And no one's being strung up on a lamppost. I should be as hard-pressed as the Pfizer CEO, with his $20 million annual compensation.[16]

RUSSELL: Whatever happened to art for art's sake?

MEGAN: Different roles for different folks. But I thought you were talking about tactical errors, and I'm arguing that, if people who think US corporate inversions are bad for social justice hear it being discussed in terms that they might not themselves use analytically, they might figure that the political experts who are on their side must know what they are doing. So it's not a tactical error; it's the way the public political game is played.

RUSSELL: Of course, we're taking it for granted here that the rhetoric will only be deployed when the legislation is in fact good. It can just as easily be deployed to support bad legislation.

MEGAN: Well, what about competitiveness talk in support of US companies? A lot of people say that's nonsense, too. But it's salient, and you have to fight fire with fire—at least if you're in politics, which I'm not.

RUSSELL: But anyway, that example may be too easy for you. Say there's a concrete proposal to do X, Y, and Z about inversions. So it goes to the political marketing team, and they talk about how unpatriotic it is. But a lot of the time, isn't it just "Apple is bad,"—"No, Apple is smart," or maybe it's Google or Facebook, and the whole thing just devolves into namechecking.

MEGAN: What do you propose instead?

RUSSELL: I like the journalism—investigative reporting—that's been done on these companies. It's been enormously helpful, although obviously not to them. But Washington policymaking is a private dialogue, for the most part, anyway. So do the analysis, make proposals, and keep it concrete.

MEGAN: Again, I don't see why it's either/or.

RUSSELL: You think you're making additional allies. But what if you're also putting some people off, or else just losing your focus?

MEGAN: Well, at this point maybe *we're* losing our focus. I think we've both said what we had to say.

RUSSELL: Until next time, then. But it's been fun. Should I buy the first round?

MEGAN: I wish. But I'd better get to Union Station, or the Acela line will be halfway down the concourse.

NOTES

1. At times, this feature of high-end tax planning weakens a bit. For example, in the late 1990s and early 2000s, there was a vogue of investing in abusive tax shelters, such as the so-called "Son-of-BOSS"

transaction, which the government repeatedly successfully challenged in court and made the basis for imposing tax penalties. There were also criminal convictions of such transactions' promoters. See, e.g., T. Rostain and M. C. Regan Jr., *Confidence Games: Lawyers, Accountants, and the Tax Shelter Industry* (2014). Even these tax shelter transactions, however, were not so clearly fraudulent as hiding income. Thus, the taxpayers who used them generally only faced civil penalties.

2. What the ex ante likelihood of correctness actually means here is open to question. Suppose a taxpayer has a unique set of facts and takes a particular position in reporting its tax consequences. Its treatment either will be questioned by the IRS or not, and if ultimately litigated will either be sustained or not. A tax professional who concludes that the likelihood of its being sustained is, say, 70 percent, is not making a testable frequentist claim about a particular group of items, but might be viewed as expressing her subjective view of the odds at which she would be indifferent, as between taking one side or the other of a bet on the outcome, if she were risk-neutral.

3. See I.R.C. § 6662. Unless otherwise indicated, all statutory references are to the Internal Revenue Code of 1986, as amended. Under this provision, disclosure may be required to permit invocation of the "reasonable basis" defense against the imposition of a penalty.

4. See D. Shaviro, 'Disclosure and Civil Penalty Rules in the U.S. Legal Response to Corporate Tax Shelters', *in* W. Schön (ed.), *Tax and Corporate Governance* (2008), 229.

5. See, e.g., J. Bankman, 'The Tax Shelter Problem', 57 *National Tax Journal* (2004), 925, 927.

6. See ibid. at 930.

7. See I.R.C. § 103.

8. See I.R.C. § 168.

9. Quoted in B. T. Borden and D. Reiss, *Wall Street Rules Applied to REMIC Classification* (Sept. 2012), available at http://brooklynworks.brooklaw.edu/cgi/viewcontent.cgi?article=1018&context=faculty, at 1 (last visited 30 May 2017).

10. The reader will note that Megan and Russell never use the term "human rights," as distinct from "social justice." This reflects common habits of mind and rhetoric in the American tax policy community, which (in my experience) tends to think of "human rights" as pertaining to protecting vulnerable individuals against abuse, and not as an apt frame for expressing concepts of broader social responsibility. This limitation in usage may be just semantic, or if interpreted as having substantive content it might be debatable, but I view applying it here as sociologically realistic.

11. 69 F.2d 809 (2d Cir. 1934), *aff'd*, 293 U.S. 465 (1935).

12. While Russell does not bother to define modern economic substance doctrine, as he and Megan are both very familiar with it, it is "a judicial doctrine . . . [recently codified in] Internal Revenue Code Section 7701(o)(5)(A) . . . that disallows [income] tax benefits . . . if the transaction that produces those benefits lacks economic substance or a business purpose." IRS Notice 2014-58, 2014-2 C.B. 746.

13. Megan is thinking of J. Bankman, 'The New Market in Corporate Tax Shelters', 83 *Tax Notes* (1999), 1775.

14. Ibid. at 1777.

15. Unless he is relying on personal or industry knowledge, Russell may have read about Apple's early tax innovations—not limited to the Double Irish Dutch Sandwich—in C. Duhigg and D. Kocieniewski, 'How Apple Sidesteps Billions in Taxes', *New York Times*, 28 Apr. 2012, available at http://www.nytimes.com/2012/04/29/business/apples-tax-strategy-aims-at-low-tax-states-and-nations.html (last visited 30 May 2017).

16. Megan may have seen something like FiercePharma's online estimate, at http://www.fiercepharma.com/special-report/ian-read-pfizer (last visited 24 May 2017), that Pfizer CEO Ian Read (who presided over the failed Allergan merger/inversion) received total 2014 compensation worth $23.28 million.

CHAPTER 16

WHO'S TO BLAME FOR THE MONEY DRAIN? CORPORATE POWER AND CORRUPTION AS COMPETING NARRATIVES FOR LOST RESOURCES

MATTI YLÖNEN

I. INTRODUCTION

Fighting corruption has been one of the most prominent goals of development policy since the late 1990s. The emergence of an anticorruption agenda was not the result of a particular increase in corruption at that time, however, but rather was the result of a multitude of political forces and a shift in the development policy thinking. One important factor that enabled the rise of the anticorruption agenda was the demise of the analytical and policy framework focusing on corporate power over states, which was championed by the UN Centre for Transnational Corporations (UNCTC) in the 1970s. The UNCTC was an independent research center that operated from 1975 to 1993 with a mandate to study the role of large corporations in developing countries. Its project faced severe hardships in the 1980s amid the changing political and intellectual climate, resulting in the destruction of its epistemic community and ultimately the dissolution of the UNCTC in 1993. I maintain that the resulting intellectual vacuum created an environment that supported analyses and policy frameworks focused on the role of public sector corruption in developing countries.

One result of these dynamics was that the development policy community largely ignored the role of the "pinstripe infrastructure"[1] of financial intermediaries, professionals, and tax havens in corruption for more than two decades. It was only with the rise of the tax justice agenda in the 2000s that corruption watchdogs began to recognize these drivers of corruption. However, this awakening has remained half-hearted, as most of the discussions on corruption still focus solely

Tax, Inequality, and Human Rights. Philip Alston and Nikki Reisch.

on public officials and politicians. I argue that understanding these broader ideological shifts is highly relevant also for the human rights agenda. Explaining why and how developing countries are losing vital tax income can help to shape the policy responses needed to support the fulfillment of human rights. In particular, it is not enough to demand that states construct well-functioning tax systems in order to fulfill their human rights obligations. Rather, equal attention should be paid to the international structures that sustain the corporate power that enables international tax flight. Our current conceptions of business and human rights, however, do not put enough emphasis on the structural powers of large corporations over developing countries. This issue needs more attention.

The rest of this chapter progresses as follows. In the next section, I discuss the role of narratives behind national development policies, and introduce the aforementioned two paradigms. Section III discusses in more detail the evolution and contributions of the corporate power and corporate planning frameworks that the UNCTC developed, especially in the 1970s.[2] In the fourth section, I analyze the emergence and evolution of the anticorruption development agenda, especially from the 1990s onward. The penultimate section discusses the reasons behind the demise of the UNCTC's corporate power agenda and how its oblivion created political space for the emergence of the anticorruption agenda and narrative. In addition, this section focuses on the challenges that the tax justice movement and the emerging tax justice policy agenda have managed to pose to the prevailing anticorruption framework. Finally, the last section discusses the implications for further research.

II. TWO NARRATIVES ABOUT LOST RESOURCES

We need narratives to explain how certain societal problems have arisen and why they persist, and to offer hope by indicating what could be done to solve the perceived problems. In reality, societal problems are typically multifaceted and any attempt to explain them using a single narrative is likely doomed to fail. At any given point in time, however, only one or at best a few narratives can reach paradigmatic status[3] and act as a beacon for policymakers. What is more, these paradigmatic policy narratives often inspire researchers, resulting in a body of research that comments on or draws from the currently dominant narratives. This can create a self-enforcing cycle where attention begets more attention. In this process, competing theories and historical precedents may be forgotten.

Depending on one's individual perspective, the role of narratives in development can be an extremely broad topic. In order to tackle this challenge, my particular focus is on narratives that center on misuse of resources that should have been directed to people in need. Therefore, I will not focus very much on questions that ask if the international trade system is just or unjust, what should be done regarding the debt problems of developing countries, or what cultural or social factors may be at work in developing countries. Rather, I focus first on the narrative that identifies corporate malpractice as one reason for the domestic resource drain, and second on the narrative that puts the blame on corrupted civil servants and politicians of developing countries. I will argue that the triumph of the latter narrative is closely connected with the emergence of the human rights agenda as the underlying framework of the anticorruption efforts.

Balakrishnan Rajagopal has noted how "human rights and corruption discourses constitute, as it were, the two sides of the legitimacy coin, and that both have the same intellectual pedigree."[4] Citing examples from Transparency International and other anticorruption organizations, Rajagopal argues that according to the "view of the corruption–human rights dialectic, both are seen as external to each other in some way, having quite autonomous existences, in a relationship of a sort of inverse proportion: as corruption goes up, human rights comes down."[5] The corruption discourse "performs the crucial task of restoring faith in the western ideals of liberal democracy, rule of law, and development."[6] Should the corruption problem be solved, "the belief goes, development would benefit all, everyone would enjoy rights, rule of law would flourish, and democracy would actually constrain power."[7] While this may be a provocative conclusion, it does contain a significant seed of truth.

I will argue that the anticorruption narrative must be reinvented in order for it to remain relevant, and that understanding these dynamics are also important for the efforts to establish the linkage between taxes and human rights. Despite decades of relentless anticorruption work by development agencies, the underlying problems have not been solved. Even more importantly, the anticorruption paradigm has failed to tackle the issues of revenue loss and tax flight. Tax justice advocates have argued that the cost of "traditional" domestic corruption, attributable to public sector actors, pales in comparison to the resources lost due to tax avoidance and profit shifting by large international enterprises when illicit financial flows from developing countries are considered.[8] Moreover, tax justice campaigners have also argued that this state of affairs is fueled by tax rules imposed by rich countries and enabled by financial intermediaries and secrecy jurisdictions that often operate with tacit or explicit support from many of the world's richest countries.[9] Partly as a result of these developments, researchers have pointed out that sub-Saharan African countries may actually be seen as net creditors to the rest of the world, when capital flight is taken into account.[10]

Tax justice campaigns have at least to some extent reinstated the focus on corporate power over states in tax matters. This has forced anticorruption campaigners to recognize that the tax planning power of large corporations is a serious issue, which affects the international anticorruption agenda. After this realization, it is difficult to imagine how the anticorruption agenda can survive in the form that James Wolfensohn, then the President of the World Bank Group, defined it in his iconic 1996 and 1997 addresses to the Bank's annual meetings. In 1996, Wolfensohn set the agenda by stating, "[L]et's not mince words: we need to deal with the cancer of corruption," and continued by portraying corruption as "a major barrier to sound and equitable development."[11] In Wolfensohn's vision, anticorruption efforts were to be part of the "new compact" for development focusing on poverty reduction. In the following year's address, Wolfensohn continued, emphasizing that "corruption, by definition, is exclusive: it promotes the interests of the few over the many. We must fight it wherever we find it," and arguing that the World Bank's support to countries should be conditioned on their efforts to address corruption.[12]

I discuss the rise of the anticorruption narrative over the past twenty to thirty years by comparing it to the earlier paradigmatic narrative of corporate regulation championed by the UNCTC. I will argue that the UNCTC agenda was surprisingly farsighted in its analysis of the power of large corporations to plan their internal wealth chains as they wished using secrecy jurisdictions and other conduit countries. The UNCTC approach also stressed the empowerment of governments to regulate the operations of large corporations, with a particular focus on developing countries and transitional economies. In other words, the UNCTC saw corporations as entities that needed to be regulated and states as the legitimate actors for enforcing said regulation, with appropriate support from international agencies.

The anticorruption agenda provides an interesting contrast to the UNCTC's corporate power agenda, as well as an explanatory framework for the nearly complete devastation of the UNCTC's narrative. While the concept of corruption is old, the anticorruption agenda only started to take shape around the same time as the UNCTC's decline began—that is, in the late 1970s and early 1980s (even though the issue had been discussed in earlier decades as well).[13]

Correlation does not necessarily imply causation, but it is evident that the anticorruption agenda helped both in exposing the weakest points in the UNCTC's corporate planning framework, and in serving as an ideologically convenient vehicle for shifting the blame of global and local economic injustices from the shoulders of large corporations to developing countries. The anticorruption agenda resonated well with the aims and tools of the structural adjustment programs that the International Monetary Fund (IMF) championed in the 1980s,[14] as well as with efforts to deregulate world trade by reducing state control of trade and institutionalizing the new trade regime in supranational law.[15] After the focus of the development policy community shifted increasingly from corporate wrongdoings to state failures, it became more natural to focus on states both in attempts to tackle corruption and to promote human rights.

III. THE CORPORATE POWER FRAMEWORK

The international development policy agenda started to take shape after the Second World War. The earliest efforts were targeted toward rebuilding war-torn Europe. It was decolonization that turned attention toward how to provide ladders of development to a large group of newly independent countries in the Cold War context. This era also saw the re-emergence of international corporate taxation as a major policy issue.[16] The backbone for these discussions was the international tax regime created in the 1910s, based on background work by the International Chamber of Commerce and enforced by the League of Nations.[17] This early tax regime aimed at removing double taxation and was based on the separate entity principle. The principle treats all companies belonging to a single enterprise as separate entities, and deems that they should use arm's-length prices in their intrafirm transactions.[18] Arm's-length pricing dictates that prices used in intrafirm trade should be the same as independent companies would use in their transactions. Only after the issue of double taxation had been addressed did the issue of undertaxation, which the separate entity principle facilitated, become relevant.[19]

After the Second World War, the work to abolish double taxation continued first as an Organisation for Economic Development and Co-operation (OECD)-led initiative.[20] The Paris-based organization advocated a generally more hands-off approach to economic affairs compared to the more Keynesian mainstream ideas of the time.[21] The work on double taxation reached a major milestone in 1956 when the OECD's Fiscal Committee began elaborating a draft convention to address this concern. The outcome was a document titled *Draft Double Taxation Convention on Income and Capital*, adopted in July 1963. To a lesser extent, this convention also addressed the problem of international tax avoidance, proposing that tax administrations should exchange more information on tax matters.[22]

In addition to this, the OECD also discussed tax and development issues in a report titled *Fiscal Incentives for Private Investment in Developing Countries*.[23] The report noted that it "is of major importance for a capital importing country to adopt provisions which would keep it from becoming a tax shelter for investors from industrialized countries."[24] It also pointed to the problems created by "round-tripping," i.e., capital leaving and re-entering countries in the hope of gaining tax benefits.[25] These issues were also discussed in the United States in Senate hearings and within the John Kennedy administration.[26]

Many of the early development theorists saw corruption as a necessary phenomenon that was needed to circumvent bureaucratic regulations in newly independent countries.[27] This school of thought drew partly from the economic history of the United States, where the gilded era of giant railroad and utility enterprises in the 1870s and 1880s was characterized by large-scale corruption *and* economic growth.[28] Things began to change at the start of the 1970s, as the corrupting influence of large multinational enterprises (MNEs) began to generate discussion in developing countries and in the United Nations.[29] The newly independent countries secured a solid majority within the United Nations after the World War II, and these former colonies were eager to put forward an agenda for changing the terms of the world economy into ones more favorable for them. At the same time, several scandals involving large MNEs emerged in developing countries.[30]

It was the United Nations, however, that eventually took the initiative in analyzing and tackling international corporate tax avoidance. The first strand of this work by the United Nations originated from resolution 1273 (XLIII) of the Economic and Social Council (ECOSOC), passed on August 1967, which requested that the Secretary-General "set up an *ad hoc* working group consisting of experts and tax administrators to explore ways and means for facilitating the conclusion of tax treaties between developed and developing countries."[31] The working group consisted of representatives nominated by governments, and it published several reports in the 1970s. The work resulted in the draft model double taxation treaty accompanied by a manual for implementation, first published in 1980.[32] The UN Secretariat then produced a model convention that reproduced the Group's work, which itself was built partially on the double tax convention that the OECD had produced.[33] Ultimately in 2004, the group was renamed the "Committee of Experts on International Cooperation in Tax Matters"—commonly known as the UN Tax Committee.[34] Since its inception, the Group stressed many concerns that are familiar from contemporary debates.[35] In addition to its focus on tax information exchange, the Group addressed many other issues from tax havens to transfer pricing, which was the special focus of the 1975 report.[36]

The second strand arose from the "UN efforts to regulate the operations of transnational corporations and was in part directed to address accounting issues."[37] This process fed into the UN Code of Conduct on Transnational Corporations, which was negotiated over several years but finally abandoned in the early 1990s.[38] This work began at the 1972 meeting of the ECOSOC, where the Chilean representative called for the United Nations to appoint a high-ranking expert commission to study the role of multinational corporations in developing countries.[39] The appointment of this commission was impulsed by the biggest corporate exposé of the time, namely, the US Senate subcommittee report in 1971 that confirmed the involvement of the International Telegraph and Telephone Corporation (ITT) in destabilizing the government of Salvador Allende in Chile.[40] In 1972, the ECOSOC appointed a twenty-member Group of Eminent Persons (GEP), with nine members from the public sector, six from academia, and five from private and public enterprises.[41] The GEP was mandated to investigate the role of transnational corporations and their impact on the process of development.[42] In its final report, the GEP recommended establishing a Commission for Transnational Corporations and an Information and Research Center on Transnational Corporations under the ECOSOC.[43] One year later, the UNCTC began its work as an autonomous center of the UN Secretariat in New York, where it continued to operate until 1993.[44]

Several subgroups were then established under the UNCTC, covering many policy areas. One of the key groups was the UN group of accounting experts (GEISAR) that convened in 1976.[45] The group made several recommendations in terms of widening corporate financial transparency, and the GEP also made several important policy contributions.[46] Its 1974 report noted how "advances in communications technology allow many multinational corporations to pursue global strategies which, rather than maximizing the profits or growth of individual affiliates, seek to advance the interest of the enterprise as a whole," helped by a "lack of harmonization of policies among countries, in monetary or tax fields for example," which allows transnationally mobile multinational corporations to "circumvent national policies or render them ineffective."[47] These developments were facilitated "by corporate planning mechanisms situated in a few industrial countries,"[48] resulting in a situation where "the 'invisible hand' of the market is far from the only force guiding economic decisions."[49]

Moreover, the GEP report noted that large corporations have various opportunities for price discrimination and (abusive) transfer pricing.[50] As a result, "a policy framework which may be adequate for dealing with national corporations needs to be modified when dealing with multinational ones,"[51] as state-level attempts to raise taxes "can be negated by vertically or horizontally integrated multinational corporations through transfer pricing and the use of tax havens."[52]

A year before the GEP report, the *Multinational Corporations in World Development* report of the UNCTC also addressed these issues in detail. It noted that the "large incidence of inter-affiliate transactions and attendant transfer pricing can distort the real picture, as can other practices involving capitalization, accounting procedures, and control of local resources." The report argued that this distortion takes place by charging prices for imports that are "far above prevailing 'world' prices, and conversely those for exports have been below world prices."[53] As a result, "their prices are not determined by the market mechanism but by the corporations themselves."[54] Several other UNCTC reports put forward similar and surprisingly farsighted analyses.[55]

Based on the aforementioned analyses, the UNCTC groups made several policy proposals that resemble many of the key initiatives that have been discussed in the OECD, United Nations, and elsewhere since the 2007–2009 financial crisis. These initiatives included a proposal for increasing mandatory country- and segment-level reporting of key financial figures or large corporations, developing automatic forms of information exchange between tax authorities, discussing unitary taxation, and increasing South-South cooperation on these themes. Due to pressure from the UNCTC and the urge to compete with its proposals, even the often-conservative OECD found itself endorsing quite ambitious reporting recommendations for large corporations, including: the structure of the enterprise, the geographical areas where the company operates, sales by geographic area and by major lines of business, significant new capital investments, the sources and uses of funds of the company as a whole, the average number of employees and the R&D expenditures in each geographical area, the policies followed for intragroup pricing, and the accounting policies.[56]

This history was largely forgotten, however, as the epistemic community around the UNCTC was shattered and the narrative of global development and global economy underwent an overhaul after the Latin American debt crisis began in 1982 and political tides changed. Meanwhile, the United States and other powerful countries had never genuinely embraced the UNCTC, as they preferred continuing work on these themes in the OECD and other agencies where they were in control. I will now turn to a discussion of the anticorruption narrative that to some extent supplanted the earlier corporate planning paradigm, as well as how these two compare.

IV. THE EVOLUTION OF THE ANTICORRUPTION NARRATIVE

"Oil companies involved in Angola should ensure that, in Angola and in other countries with similar problems of lack of transparency and government accountability, a policy of 'full transparency' is adopted."

A Crude Awakening, *Global Witness 1999*

"Illicit financial flows should not be a human rights concern for States only. While States have the primary duty to respect, protect and fulfil human rights, business enterprises are also required to 'avoid causing or contributing to adverse human rights impacts through their own activities, and address such impacts when they occur' as set out in the Guiding Principles on Business and Human Rights (guiding principle 13)."

Illicit financial flows, human rights and the post-2015 development agenda,
UN General Assembly 2015

In the early 1990s, the international development policy agenda was in disarray. The Cold War was ending, taking with it the ideological competition for the hearts and minds of developing countries' leaders between the Eastern and Western blocs. The Latin American debt crisis and subsequent debt crises had shattered development optimism for much of the Southern world. In industrial policy, import substitution had lost much of its appeal and many countries began to see foreign direct investment as a tool for development. This was accelerated by changes in the world economy, as large companies began to outsource an increasing number of their activities to international value chains and subcontractors, which challenged the prevailing conceptions of the core and the periphery in the world economy. Finally, all of this was enforced and cemented by the aggressive structural adjustment policies that came with the debt crises and changes in world politics and within the professional economic policy circles. During this intellectual turmoil, the UNCTC and the ideas it had developed lost their appeal and were subsequently largely forgotten.[57] As a result, the time was ripe in the early 1990s for novel explanations about why people in many developing countries remained in poverty when the economic theories that had undergirded the trade deregulation and structural adjustment programs promised them prosperity.

The anticorruption agenda was in many ways a perfect remedy for this situation. First, there was undeniable factual evidence that during the post-colonial decades many newly independent countries had transformed into dictatorships or kleptocratic states where high-ranking officials and politicians reaped the highest benefits. Second, while it was not easy to combine the political factors of corruption with econometric models, this agenda provided a convenient explanation for why the hands-off models of economic governance did not deliver the promised benefits. Finally, given that corporate power had become an unfashionable topic, there was simply a vacuum in the international development policy thinking that the anticorruption agenda filled, at least partially.

There are multiple ways to define corruption, and the subtle—or sometimes overt—differences between them reveal a great deal about the sensitivity and normative nature of this concept. The most classic definition comes from Colin Nye, who maintained that corruption is "behaviour which deviates from the formal duties of a public role because of private-regarding (personal, close family, private clique) pecuniary or status gains; or violates rules against the exercise of certain types of private-regarding influence."[58] In his paradigm-defining 1988 book on corruption, Robert Klitgaard argued that, "corruption exists when an individual illicitly puts personal interests above those of the people and ideals he or she is pledged to serve."[59] While Klitgaard noted that corruption could occur either in private or public sectors, in practice the agenda he was setting shifted the blame for societal problems from private wrongdoings to public failures and embezzlements. In a manner typical of many accounts on corruption, Klitgaard also noted how "what is corrupt in one society may not be in another."[60] This underlines the normative aspects of any definition given to this term. In the words of Arvind Jain, "how corruption is defined actually ends up determining what gets modeled and measured."[61]

In some cases, corruption is even determined in ways that exclude the role and responsibility of the private sector entirely. For example, Toke Aidt defines corruption as the "sale of government property for private gain."[62] It is for good reason, therefore, that Inge Amundsen states that "corruption is understood as everything from the paying of bribes to civil servants in return for some favor and the theft of public purses, to a wide range of dubious economic and political practices in which politicians and bureaucrats enrich themselves," or ultimately as "any abusive use of public power to a personal end."[63] There is no doubt that part of the pervasiveness and strength of the anticorruption agenda has arisen at least partly from this vagueness of definition. As a general catch-all category, it is often easy to identify some aspects of corruption in many societal maladies.

Given the prominence of anticorruption efforts in today's development agenda, it is easy to forget how recently this theme reached its present standing. While corruption-related problems have received a substantial amount of theorizing and empirical research at least since the 1950s, it took a long time before these issues came to international attention.[64] After Klitgaard tellingly noted in his classic 1988 work, *Controlling Corruption*, that the literature on international development is "surprisingly silent" about problems caused by corruption, things evolved rapidly.[65] We need to go back to the history of the Foreign Corrupt Practices Act of the United States in order to understand the evolution of the anticorruption agenda.

In the late 1970s, there was a growing awareness in the United States that US corporations were engaged in giving bribes to foreign government officials in exchange for procurement contracts or sales commissions.[66] Driven partly by the attention created by the Watergate scandal, a Special Presidential Task Force began to study the problem in March 1976. The Securities and Exchange Commission (SEC) also conducted a special study on this issue, suggesting that corrupt payments erode public confidence in American business and advocated requirements for more transparent internal auditing. Bills were proposed to tackle the problem and several congressional hearings took place in 1976.[67]

The real breakthrough of anticorruption efforts into the international agenda took place in the 1990s. The structural adjustment programs of the 1980s had paved way to the "good governance" agenda, and were based on a notion that failures of the public sector lay in the heart of the development failures in Africa.[68] The initial focus on macroeconomics and privatization was gradually extended to cover anticorruption efforts as well. This development was driven by the World Bank, as the IMF was initially reluctant to embrace the broader good governance agenda, which it deemed as too political and outside its mandate. This changed in mid-1990s, when the IMF Board of Governors adopted a Declaration on Partnership for Sustainable Global Growth.[69]

A definite milestone were the two speeches given by Wolfensohn, then President of the World Bank, in his addresses to the organization's annual meetings in 1996 and 1997, quoted in the introduction to this chapter. By the mid-1990s, anticorruption had become a major theme in many other forums as well. As often happens, the interest of political scientists and economists followed policy developments. Thus, in 2001, Jain was able to state in his review of corruption literature that the study of corruption had come to an age, "driven by a realisation among international development experts that development requires, above all, good governance."[70]

The change of attitude was significant, given the World Bank's hesitancy to address the issue before the emergence of the good governance agenda.[71] The paradigm shift in the World Bank and the IMF reflected a broader international development at that time. The year 1995 marked an important milestone as the non-governmental organization Transparency International (TI) unveiled the first edition of its Corruption Perception Index (CPI), together with the Internet Centre for Corruption Research at the University of Passau.[72] Soon, the CPI reached definitive status in the corruption measurement business, and it has been a highly influential and much publicized ranking ever since. De Maria has noted that for a long time, CPI has been "un-questionably accepted as a valid and reliable indicator of "corruption" by African governments, donors, media and academia."[73] After TI and the World Bank had made their headways into anticorruption field, the OECD's Anti-Bribery Convention was adopted in 1999, with the UN Convention against Corruption created four years later.

Despite the lip service paid to the role of the private sector in corruption, the great majority of the key analyses and policy initiatives around this subject have focused explicitly on public sector corruption. This can be seen, for example, in Jain's terminology of "bureaucratic corrup-tion" and "legislative corruption."[74] An even more telling example of this phenomenon can be found in the work of Klitgaard. After defining corruption in a way that leaves open the relative importance of the public and private sectors in sustaining corruption, Klitgaard goes on to de-velop his argument using case studies, devoting most space to discussion of the Philippines. Together with some other countries he discusses more briefly (Mexico, Ghana), this would have offered sufficient material to discuss extensive private sector wrongdoings had Klitgaard chosen to do so, but his focus was elsewhere.

Following the example of these and other scholars, the anticorruption agenda started to tackle perceived public sector failures. In 2001, this agenda had reached a point where a re-view of relevant literature could state with confidence that "we now believe that corruption is inimical" to an environment that "stimulates self-sustaining growth and development," and that unsuitable policies are a result of "decision-makers distorting economic policies for their own interest."[75] The result has been "a rapidly growing anti-corruption movement, or 'industry,' spreading under close western supervision across Africa," which is sometimes detached from the everyday realities of these countries.[76]

Why did the corruption discourse emerge in the 1990s from relative obscurity to rise to prominence in mainstream global development and economic thinking? In 1998, Vito Tanzi noted seven possible explanations. All of them point to the answer that "corruption is simply attracting more attention now than in the past," not that there was any significant growth in cor-ruption in quantitative or qualitative terms.[77]

First, Tanzi pointed to the end of the Cold War and the "end of political hypocrisy that had made the decision makers in some industrial countries ignore the political corruption that existed in particular countries."[78] Another aspect of this same phenomenon was highlighted by Baker, Shaxson, and Christensen, who noted that it "was considered impolite, as well as un-helpful to certain parochial institutional interests, to delve too deeply into untoward behavior by the elites of newly sovereign and proud countries."[79]

Second, according to Tanzi, there had been a reluctance to talk about corruption "by those familiar with these countries, [and] there was also a tendency not to focus on corruption in the centrally planned economies." It is also worth noting, however, that in the current world economy characterized by tax competition or tax wars[80] between nations, there also can be incentives not to focus on corporate malpractices in order to please investors and large foreign corporations. Or, to take an even broader view, political considerations always steer the imposi-tion of dominant development narratives. Third, Tanzi argued that "the increase in recent years in the number of countries with democratic governments and free and active media has created an environment in which discussion of corruption is no longer a taboo."[81]

Fourth, Tanzi noted that, "globalization has brought individuals from countries with little corruption into frequent contact with those from countries where corruption is endemic." Fifth, "a growing role has been played by nongovernmental organizations (NGOs), such as Transparency International, in publicizing the problems of corruption and in trying to create anticorruption movements," and additionally, a "greater reliance on the market for economic decisions and the increased need to be competitive have created an environment in which the pursuit of efficiency has acquired greater importance." These two factors can be equally helpful in understanding the rise of the corporate tax-avoidance agenda. Finally, Tanzi argues that "American policymakers have argued that American exporters have lost out in foreign deals because they have not been allowed by law to pay bribes to foreign officials."[82] In addition to these explanations, the broader ideological changes occurring at the time, discussed above, were also undoubtedly a major factor. However, seen from a more historical view, one key explanation was the neglect of any analysis of the role of large corporations in producing development failures.

V. THE TAX JUSTICE MOVEMENT AND THE (RE)EMERGENCE OF THE CORPORATE POWER AGENDA

Today, we have already moved a few steps forward from the situation in the early 2000s when unsuitable policies were seen as a result of "decision-makers distorting economic policies for their own interest."[83] One important—though not very widely known—rupture in this narrative was the 2012 article *Hidden Trillions: Secrecy, Corruption, and the Offshore Interface* by John Christensen, the director of the Tax Justice Network. In his article, Christensen aptly noted that even though corruption discourse had so far "focused predominantly on bribery, or more accurately on bribe-taking by public officials in developing countries and transition economies," corruption also has a supply-side that is "backed by a large infrastructure of financial and legal intermediaries," the majority of which reside in secrecy jurisdictions, more commonly known as tax havens. It is these operators "who provide an interface between illicit activities and the mainstream financial markets."[84]

In another article written by Nicholas Shaxson together with Raymond Baker and Christensen, the authors attributed the relative lack of attention to corruption prior to the 1990s to the separation of political economy "into political science and an economics profession, which was driven toward macro approaches in an effort to 'harden' itself methodologically" in the post–World War II decades.[85] According to these authors, the "result was a sharp positivist, quantitative bias that by definition ruled out serious consideration of factors that could not be readily measured—corruption being, almost by definition, such a factor."[86] While there is probably a significant amount of truth in this, there is another reason for why the anticorruption agenda emerged in the mid-1990s besides the one put forward by Baker et al. and Tanzi— namely, the obfuscation of earlier narratives that focused on corporate power over states.

The critique put forward by Christensen's Tax Justice Network, Global Witness, and other actors has had an impact on Transparency International. Transparency International defines corruption as "the abuse of entrusted power for private gain,"[87] and lately it has started to see that this power can be private as well. In late 2007, the new head of TI, Cobus de Swardt, told the *Financial Times* that London and other global financial centers were to expect "much greater pressure" from Swardt's organization, and that "corruption 'facilitated by bankers and financial centers' had received too little attention by the global pressure group," but that this was about to change.[88] Since then, this "second wave" in the fight against corruption has resulted in various new initiatives. For example, TI has been monitoring the country-by-country level of transparency of large corporations, working on the role of tax systems in facilitating corruption,[89] and reporting on lobbying in Europe.[90] Despite these laudable initiatives, however, the Corruption

Perception Index continues to be the best-known concept of TI, and the definition TI gives corruption on its website is still tilted toward public sector corruption.[91]

The 1990s and early 2000s saw the development of initiatives demanding greater transparency of the tax and other payments made by the extractive industry companies.[92] One important milestone was achieved in 1999, when an NGO, Global Witness, published a report entitled *A Crude Awakening*. The report exposed the complicity of the oil and banking industries in the plundering of state assets during Angola's thirty-year civil war. It claimed that the "international oil companies are paying vast sums (the future development potential of Angola) into a black hole" and that "the international oil companies must accept that they are playing with the politics and lives of Angola's people."[93] The report concluded that companies operating in Angola should "publish what they pay" to the government. This led to the establishment of an NGO coalition, Publish What You Pay (PWYP), which called on companies to publish what they paid and governments to publish what they earned as "a necessary first step towards a more accountable system for the management of natural resource revenues."[94] Today, the coalition includes more than 800 NGOs around the world.[95]

The public attention generated pressure on intergovernmental organizations. The Extractive Industries Transparency Initiative (EITI) was created by the initiative of the UK government in 2002–2003 to foster voluntary reporting on tax payments in the extractive industries. There were mixed motives behind this move. Haufler argued that then UK Prime Minister Tony Blair "shifted the focus of the EITI away from company reporting, which is the target of PWYP activism, to reporting and membership by governments."[96] The anticorruption agenda provided a convenient subtext for this resolution. After this decision was made, an EITI secretariat was set up in Oslo as an organization describing itself as "a multi-stakeholder coalition of governments, companies, investors, civil society organisations, and partner organisations."[97] The EITI requires participating governments to produce "comprehensive EITI Reports that include full government disclosure of extractive industry revenues, and disclosure of all material payments to government by oil, gas and mining companies."[98] The EITI encourages companies to support the initiative and "to promote the Standard internationally and in countries where it operates."[99] Despite its limited scope, PWYP and many other NGOs have been partially supportive of the EITI while continuing to criticize its perceived flaws.[100] At the same time, PWYP continues to campaign for the disclosure of information not covered by the EITI (e.g., mandatory disclosure of the project-level payments).

Wójcik noted the importance of the "initiatives calling for improved transparency in the extractive industries, particularly with regard to payments between corporations and host governments," behind the calls for that the tax justice movement started to advocate in this millennium, in particular the call for broad country-by-country reporting.[101] This rising awareness of the problems contributed to the increasing interest in good governance and transparency in the donor community, as demonstrated by the EITI initiative. This concurrent interest in more transparent management and increasing awareness of the problems caused by the resource curse created grounds for demands for increased transparency of the extractive industry revenues.

Today's proposals for broadening corporate transparency go much further than the EITI's recommendations. After years of intensive civil society campaigning, in 2015 the OECD agreed on a full country-level disclosure of the key financial items of large corporations. This was a major step forward, even though information will be reported only for tax authorities and not for the wider public, and there are other limiting preconditions as well.[102] In contrast to the earlier focus on prevention of corruption, today's proposals put more emphasis on enhancing tax compliance and reducing risks associated with nontransparent corporate structures in all industries. The reporting models that tax justice campaigners have been promoting in this millennium would allow informed outside spectators to assess a company's tax aggressiveness and different kinds of risks, among other things, whereas the information provided in the EITI reports does not allow this kind of analysis. Today, PWYP also endorses broad country-by-country reporting while continuing to campaign for its original demands.[103]

To recap, the demands for financial transparency were first fueled by the anticorruption and transparency agenda. Much less attention was paid to the problems created by profit shifting.[104] This was a natural result in an intellectual environment where corporate power had become an unfashionable topic and there was a vacuum in the international development policy thinking that the more corporate-friendly anticorruption agenda helped fill. However, when the corporate power narrative returned with the emergence of tax justice campaigning in the early 2000s, this had an impact on the anticorruption paradigm as well. Consequently, the state-centric initiatives began to look increasingly outdated, and slowly the agenda started to shift in order to accommodate a broader range of concerns. Most importantly, these concerns included the crucial question of how to address the vast powers that large corporations have over developing countries.

VI. CONCLUSION

"Taxation is the new frontier for those concerned with state-building in developing countries," Deborah A. Bräutigam argued in the opening words of the book *Taxation and State Building in Developing Countries* in 2008. Tax issues had just started to gather broader attention within the development community, followed by the scholarly interest. Bräutigam went on to argue that "taxation may play the central role in building and sustaining the power of states, and shaping their ties to society."[105] In addition to the three "Rs" of taxation—namely, revenue, redistribution, and repricing—an important aspect of tax systems is the "fourth R," namely, representation, given that well-functioning tax systems also foster state building, the human rights agenda. and the sustainability of democratic societies.[106]

However, reducing political corruption in developing countries is not a sufficient condition for creating these kinds of public goods. Rather, many of the same concerns on corporate power and tax flight that were noted in the United Nations in the 1970s remain unsolved. Any viable agenda on human rights—especially social rights—needs to take seriously the problems created by corporate power over developing countries. In addition to the already discussed problems of tax avoidance and tax evasion, the bargaining power of large corporations over smaller states is also an outcome of structural problems that discourage developing countries from collecting taxes needed for human development. Here, a key problem is international tax competition, or more accurately tax wars[107] between nations. This international pressure pushes decision makers in developing countries to turn a blind eye to corporate wrongdoings and to offer tax breaks and other sweeteners to large enterprises in exchange for investments. The contrast with the 1970s when developing countries were pushing for major international reforms could hardly be clearer.

What is needed are more comprehensive frameworks for analyzing the reasons behind the obstacles to domestic resource mobilization, which pay close attention to both public and private factors that prevent the fulfillment of social rights and development goals. This would be crucial not only for focusing on the best mix of policy responses to tackle the perceived ills but also as a guidance for further research on particular topics. To give an example, in hindsight the destruction of the UNCTC was truly a misfortune for the whole international community, even though the majority of policymakers probably did not see it that way back then. Whenever the policy efforts of the international development community become tilted toward one paradigm over all others, there is a real danger that important viewpoints are neglected completely.

Even though the human rights impacts of large corporations have received increasing attention in the past years, both practical and theoretical discussions on human rights still largely center on states. As a symptom of this tendency, problems in fulfilling human rights obligations are often discussed in the context of state failures and corrupt regimes. This state-centered approach is also supported by the fact that, apart from a few poorly enforced initiatives, there is a lack of binding human rights obligations for large enterprises. This problem is even more nuanced in the field of corporate taxation, where the OECD's Code of Conduct for Multinational Enterprises is the only guideline that explicitly discusses issues such as transfer pricing.[108] These guidelines were originally developed as a response to the UNCTC's work on the Code of Conduct for transnational corporations, and the OECD's Code of Conduct has suffered from very weak enforcement even regarding the more traditional environmental and labor concerns.[109]

Even well-intentioned developing country governments may find themselves unable to increase their tax revenues, however, without more stringent international regulation of large enterprises and especially their internal tax and financing arrangements. In order to remedy this situation, there is an urgent need for advances in topical policy proposals such as public country-by-country reporting and unitary taxation.[110] It would also be very helpful, however, to reignite policy and theoretical discussion on establishing an ambitious, binding code of conduct for multinational enterprises, not unlike the one that the UNCTC was working on decades ago.

NOTES

1. M. Hampton and J. Christensen, 'Competing Industries in Islands: A New Tourism Approach', 34(4), *Annals of Tourism Research* (2007).
2. This part of the chapter relies in many ways on the background work I conducted in my earlier article, see M. Ylönen, 'Back from Oblivion? The Rise and Fall of the Early Initiatives Against Corporate Tax Avoidance from the 1960s to the 1980s' 23 Transnational Corporations (2017), at 33.
3. T. S. Kuhn, *The Structure of Scientific Revolutions* (1962).
4. B. Rajagopal, 'Corruption, Legitimacy and Human Rights: The Dialectic of the Relationship', 14 *Connecticut Journal of International Law* (1999), 495, at 498.
5. Ibid. at 498–499.
6. Ibid. at 503.
7. Ibid. at 503.
8. P. Chowla and T. Falcao, *Illicit Financial Flows: Concepts and Scope* (United Nations Financing for Development Working Paper, 5 Dec. 2016).
9. B. Schuman, *Usual Suspects? Co-Conspirators in the Business of Tax Dodging* (A Study Commissioned by the Greens/FPA Group in the European Parliament, 23 Jan. 2017).
10. L. Ndikumana and J. K. Boyce, *New Estimates of Capital Flight from Sub-Saharan African Countries: Linkages with External Borrowing and Policy Options* "Political Economy Research Institute, University of Massachusetts, Amherst, Working Paper 166 (2008).
11. J. D. Wolfensohn, President, World Bank Group, Annual Meeting Address (1 Oct. 1996).
12. J. D. Wolfensohn, President, World Bank Group, 'The Challenge of Inclusion', Annual Meeting Address (23 Sept. 1997).
13. Ylönen, *supra* note 2.
14. R. Rowden, *The Deadly Ideas of Neoliberalism: How the IMF Has Undermined Public Health and the Fight Against AIDS* (2009).

15. S. Gill, *Power and Resistance in the New World Order* (2nd ed., 2008).
16. R. S. Avi-Yonah, 'All of a Piece Throughout: The Four Ages of U.S. International Taxation', 25(2) *Virginia Tax Review* (2005–2006), 313.
17. T. Rixen, *The Political Economy of International Tax Governance* (2008), at 88; T. Rixen, 'From Double Tax Avoidance to Tax Competition: Explaining the Institutional Trajectory of International Tax Governance', 18(2) *Review of International Political Economy* (2010), 197.
18. L. Eden, 'The Arm's Length Standard: Making It Work in a 21st-Century World of Multinationals and Nations States', *in* T. Pogge and K. Mehta (eds.), *Global Tax Fairness* (2016), 153.
19. Rixen, 'From Double Tax Avoidance to Tax Competition', *supra* note 17.
20. Rixen, *The Political Economy of International Tax Governance, supra* note 17, at 48–51; S. Picciotto, *International Business Taxation: A Study in the Internationalization of Business Regulation* (1992), at 48–51.
21. R. A. Williams, 'The OECD and Foreign Investment Rules: The Global Promotion of Liberalization', *in* R. Mahon and S. McBride (eds.), *The OECD and Transnational Governance* (2008), 117, at 118.
22. S. S. Surrey, 'United Nations Group of Experts and the Guidelines for Tax Treaties between Developed and Developing Countries', 19(1) *Harvard International Law Journal* (1978), 1; Rixen, *The Political Economy of International Tax Governance, supra* note 17.
23. OECD, *Fiscal Incentives for Private Investment in Developing Countries* (1964).
24. Ibid.
25. Ibid. at 55.
26. Rixen, 'From Double Tax Avoidance to Tax Competition', *supra* note 17, at 17; G. D. Webster, 'Current Developments in Federal Income Taxation', 29(3) *Tennessee Law Review* (1962), 419.
27. N. H. Leff, 'Economic Development Through Bureaucratic Corruption', 8(3) *American Behavioral Scientist* (1964), 8, 8–14; J. S. Nye, 'Corruption and Political Development: A Cost-Benefit Analysis', 61(2) *American Political Science Review* (1967), 417, 419–420; S. P. Huntington, *Political Order in Changing Societies* (1968), at 69.
28. J. T. Gathii, 'Defining the Relationship between Human Rights and Corruption', 31(1) *University of Pennsylvania Journal of International Law* (2009), 125, at 136.
29. Ibid. at 127.
30. Ibid. at 138.
31. Ylönen, *supra* note 2.
32. For a historical review, see B. Kosters, 'The United Nations Model Tax Convention and Its Recent Developments', *Asia-Pacific Tax Bulletin* (Jan.–Feb. 2004).
33. Ylönen, *supra* note 2; Surrey, *supra* note 22.
34. T. Rixen, *The Political Economy of International Tax Governance, supra* note 17, at 147–148; Ylönen, *supra* note 2.
35. United Nations, *Tax Treaties Between Developed and Developing Countries* (1969); United Nations, *Tax Treaties Between Developed and Developing Countries: Second Report* (1970); United Nations, *Tax Treaties Between Developed and Developing Countries: Third Report* (1972); United Nations, *Tax Treaties Between Developed and Developing Countries: Fourth Report* (1973); United Nations, *The Impact of Multinational Corporations on Development and on International Relations* (1974); United Nations, *Tax Treaties Between Developed and Developing Countries: Fifth Report* (1975); United Nations, *Tax Treaties Between Developed and Developing Countries: Sixth Report* (1976); United Nations, *Tax Treaties Between Developed and Developing Countries: Seventh Report* (1978); United Nations, *Manual for the negotiation of bilateral tax treaties between developed and developing countries* (1979); Ylönen, *supra* note 2.
36. United Nations, *Tax Treaties Between Developed and Developing Countries: Fifth Report, supra* note 35.
37. Ylönen, *supra* note 2.
38. Ibid.
39. S. F. Rahman, 'International Accounting Regulation by the United Nations: A Power Perspective', 11(5) *Accounting, Auditing & Accountability Journal* (1998), 593; T. Sagafi-Nejad, J. H. Dunning,

and H. V. Perlmutter, *The UN and Transnational Corporations: From Code of Conduct to Global Compact* (2008); Ylönen, *supra* note 2.

40. K. Hamdani and L. Ruffing, *United Nations Centre on Transnational Corporations: Corporate Conduct and the Public Interest* (2015); Rahman, *supra* note 39, at 595; Sagafi-Nejad et al., *supra* note 39, at 42–43.

41. Sagafi-Nejad et al., *supra* note 39, at 57.

42. ECOSOC, Resolutions: Supplement No. 1, UN Doc. E/5209, 3–28 July 1972, at 4.

43. The UN Department of Economic and Social Affairs prepared a background report titled 'Multinational Corporations in Development' in 1973 for the GEP. Many of the recommendations and analyses of the GEP group drew heavily from this 1973 report. See Hamdani and Ruffing, *supra* note 40; Rahman, *supra* note 39, at 599; Sagafi-Nejad et al., *supra* note 39, at 59.

44. Sagafi-Nejad et al., *supra* note 39, at 6; K. P. Sauvant, 'The Negotiations of the United Nations Code of Conduct on Transnational Corporations: Experience and Lessons Learned', 16(1) *The Journal of World Investment and Trade* (2015), 11.

45. In addition, a Working Group on the Code of Conduct was created under the UNCTC. See Rahman, *supra* note 39; Sauvant, *supra* note 44, at 20.

46. Ylönen, *supra* note 2.

47. UN (1974), *supra* note 35, at 30.

48. Ibid. at 30.

49. Ibid. at 41.

50. Ibid. at 30.

51. Ibid. at 31.

52. Ibid. at 35.

53. Ibid. at 32.

54. Ibid. at 33.

55. Ylönen, *supra* note 2.

56. S. S. Surrey, 'Reflections on the Allocation of Income and Expenses among National Tax Jurisdictions', 10 *Law & Policy in International Business* (1978), 409, at 434–435.

57. Ylönen, *supra* note 2.

58. Quoted in I. Amundsen, *Political Corruption: Introduction to the Issues* (1999), at 2.

59. R. Klitgaard, *Controlling Corruption* (1991), at xi.

60. Ibid.

61. A. K. Jain, 'Corruption: A Review', 15(1) *Journal of Economic Surveys* (2001), 71, at 73.

62. T. S. Aidt, 'Corruption, Institutions, and Economic Development', 25(2) *Oxford Review of Economic Policy* (2008), 271.

63. Amundsen, *supra* note 58, at 1.

64. Ibid. at 1.

65. Klitgaard, *supra* note 59, at 6.

66. Gathii, *supra* note 28, at 141.

67. Ibid. at 142.

68. Rowden, *supra* note 14, at 75.

69. Gathii, *supra* note 28, at 145.

70. Jain, *supra* note 61, at 71.

71. R. Baker, N. Shaxson, and J. Christensen, 'Catching Up with Corruption', 4(1) *The American Interest* (2008), 65.

72. J. G. Labsdorff, *Measuring the Dark Side of Human Nature: The Birth of the Corruption Perceptions Index*, available online at http://www.icgg.org/corruption.cpi_childhooddays.html (last visited 24 July 2017).

73. W. De Maria, 'Measurements and Markets: Deconstructing the Corruption Perception Index', 21(7) *International Journal of Public Sector Management* (2008), 777, at 778.

74. Jain, *supra* note 61.

75. Ibid. at 71.

76. De Maria, *supra* note 73, at 778.

77. V. Tanzi, 'Corruption Around the World: Causes, Consequences, Scope, and Cures', 45(4) *IMF Staff Papers* (1998), 559, at 560.
78. Ibid. at 560
79. Baker et al., *supra* note 71.
80. J. Christensen and N. Shaxson, 'Tax Competitiveness—A Dangerous Obsession', *in* T. Pogge and K. Mehta (eds.), *Global Tax Fairness* (2016), 265.
81. Tanzi, *supra* note 77, at 560.
82. Ibid. at 561.
83. Jain, *supra* note 61, at 71
84. J. Christensen, 'The Hidden Trillions: Secrecy, Corruption, and the Offshore Interface', 57(3) *Crime, Law & Social Change* (2012), 325, at 326.
85. Baker et al., *supra* note 71.
86. Ibid.
87. Transparency International, *What Is Corruption?* (2017), available online at https://www.transparency.org/what-is-corruption/ (last visited 10 July 2017).
88. H. Williamson, 'Anti-Graft Watchdog to Step Up Pressure on West', *Financial Times*, 15 Nov. 2007.
89. M. Hearson, *Tax Systems: A Channel for Corruption or a Way to Fight It?* (Transparency International Working Paper No. 3, 2015).
90. S. Mulcahy, *Lobbying in Europe: Hidden Influence, Privileged Access* (2015), available online at https://www.transparency.org/whatwedo/publication/lobbying_in_europe (last visited 12 June 2017).
91. Interestingly, the rationale of Transparency International could be used verbatim to describe the agenda put forward by the UNCTC as well: "Corruption is one of the greatest challenges of the contemporary world. It undermines good government, fundamentally distorts public policy, leads to the misallocation of resources, harms the private sector and private sector development and particularly hurts the poor. Controlling it is only possible with the cooperation of a wide range of stakeholders in the integrity system, including most importantly the state, civil society, and the private sector. There is also a crucial role to be played by international institutions" (Transparency International, *Mission Statement*, available online at http://transparency.org.au/index.php/about-us/mission-statement/ (last visited 12 June 2017)). This speaks volumes about the paradigmatic nature of both the corruption narrative and the narrative of corporate planning. Neither narrative alone can explain the great challenges the states and the international community have been facing and still continue to face in modern times, but one thing is for certain: neglect of either state or corporate failures will lead into tilted policies and unsatisfactory outcomes.
92. A. Christians, 'Tax Activists and the Global Movement for Development Through Transparency' (2012), available online at http://papers.ssrn.com/abstract=2029055, at 3 (last visited 12 June 2017).
93. Global Witness, *A Crude Awakening: The Role of the Oil and Banking Industries in Angola's Civil War and the Plunder of State Assets* (1999), available online at https://www.globalwitness.org/sites/default/files/pdfs/A%20Crude%20Awakening.pdf, at 2.
94. Publish What You Pay, *History*, available online at http://www.publishwhatyoupay.no/en/about-pwyp-norway/history/history (last visited 10 July 2017).
95. Publish What You Pay, *About Us*, available online at http://www.publishwhatyoupay.org/about (last visited 12 June 2017).
96. V. Haufler, 'Disclosure as Governance: The Extractive Industries Transparency Initiative and Resource Management in the Developing World', 10(3) *Global Environmental Politics* (2009), 53, at 65.
97. Extractive Industries Transparency Initiative (EITI), *Stakeholders*, available online at https://eiti.org/supporters (last visited 12 June 2017).
98. EITI, *EITI Factsheet 2017* (2017), available online at https://eiti.org/document/factsheet (last visited 24 July 2017).
99. Ibid.

100. S. Gallhofer and J. Haslam, 'Exploring Social, Political and Economic Dimensions of Accounting in the Global Context: The International Accounting Standards Board and Accounting Disaggregation', 5(4) *Socio-Economic Review* (2007), 633, at 649; Haufler, *supra* note 96, at 66.

101. D. Wójcik, 'Shining Light on Globalization: The Political Economy of Country-by-Country Reporting' (2012), available online at https://papers.ssrn.com/sol3/papers.cfm?abstract_id= 2163449, at 6 (last visited 12 June 2017).

102. Financial Transparency Coalition, *OECD Country-by-Country Reporting: Only for the Strong?*, 17 Sept. 2015, available online at https://financialtransparency.org/oecd-country-by-country-reporting-only-for-the-strong/ (last visited 12 June 2017).

103. Publish What You Pay, *Extended Country-by-Country Reporting. The 3-Minute Version*, available online at http://www.publishwhatyoupay.org/pwyp-resources/extended-country-by-country-reporting-the-3-minute-version/ (last visited 10 July 2017).

104. Haufler, *supra* note 96, at 54.

105. D. Bräutigam, 'Introduction: Taxation and State-Building in Developing Countries', *in* D. Bräutigam, O. H. Fjeldstad, and M. Moore (eds.), *Taxation and State Building in Developing Countries* (2008)

106. Tax Justice Network, *The Four "Rs"*, 9 July 2007, available online at http://taxjustice.blogspot.com/ 2007/07/four-rs.html (last visited 11 July 2017).

107. Christensen and Shaxson, *supra* note 80 at 265.

108. International Bar Association, *Tax Abuses, Poverty and Human Rights: A Report of the International Bar Association's Human Rights Institute Task Force on Illicit Financial Flows, Poverty and Human Rights* (2013), available online at http://www.ibanet.org/Document/Default. aspx?DocumentUid=4977CB3D-4988-4C9C-84C7-9050A5CB2311 (last visited 24 July 2017).

109. OECD Watch, *Remedy Remains Rare: An Analysis of 15 Years of NCP Cases and Their Contribution to Improve Access to Remedy for Victims of Corporate Misconduct* (June 2015).

110. S. Picciotto, 'Towards Unitary Taxation', *in* T. Pogge and K. Mehta (eds.), *Global Tax Fairness* (2016), 221; R. Murphy, 'Country-by-Country Reporting', *in* T. Pogge and K. Mehta (eds.), *Global Tax Fairness* (2016), 96.

CHAPTER 17

CREATING A HUMAN RIGHTS FRAMEWORK FOR MAPPING AND ADDRESSING CORPORATE TAX ABUSES

MATTI KOHONEN, RADHIKA SARIN, TROELS BOERRILD, AND EWAN LIVINGSTON

I. INTRODUCTION

The fields of international tax policy and business and human rights each have emerged as important areas of study in recent years, receiving ever greater attention in public debates and policy circles. In large part, their development has occurred in isolation. Closer inspection, however, reveals a growing similarity between the key concepts and critical debates in both the fields.

Human rights arguments are playing an increasingly prominent role in tax policy debates. They have provided a useful counterpoint to extreme interpretations of the notion of tax sovereignty, which have made it more difficult to effectively clamp down on cross-border tax competition, tax avoidance, and tax evasion.[1] Human rights advocates have also successfully argued that tax revenue is essential for states to realize human rights obligations, such as the rights to health and education, or indeed to finance the public infrastructure needed to raise living standards, increase equality, and build well-functioning economies and societies.[2] While much recent work, including this chapter, focuses on corporate taxation,[3] there is growing attention to all aspects of domestic resource mobilization and fiscal policy. This heightened awareness of tax policies is necessary to ensure that adequate revenues exist in the context of the UN Financing for Development process, which links to funding for the Sustainable Development Goals.[4]

From a wider sustainable development perspective, tax systems serve many purposes including: (1) *raising revenue*: generating funds to deliver essential services; (2) *redistribution*: addressing poverty and inequality; (3) *representation*: building accountability of governments to citizens and reclaiming policy space, as exemplified by campaigns to eliminate taxes on sanitary pads or to end other discriminatory tax policies;[5] and (4) *repricing*: limiting public "bads" while encouraging public goods,[6] such as tobacco control efforts focused on increasing cigarette taxes and in some cases earmarking revenues for health financing.[7] A human rights lens adds further dimensions to the analysis of fiscal systems, enabling us to examine fiscal policies based on principles such as equity and nondiscrimination. Indeed, it is argued that "human rights discourse provides a context for explaining what goals should drive state tax policy decisions."[8]

On the national level, Attiya Waris has argued that "human rights may solve the legitimacy issue for tax and simultaneously tax may solve the realisation dilemma in human rights."[9] She considers that taxation is a key aspect for states in realizing international human rights obligations under both the international covenants, the International Covenant on Economic, Social and Cultural Rights (ICESCR) and the International Covenant on Civil and Political Rights (ICCPR).[10] Aldo Caliari argues that human rights principles such as "[e]quality and non-discrimination also have implications for assessing the real impacts of social-spending programmes, setting the income tax threshold, and setting adequate processes for assessing differential impacts of tax policy."[11] In terms of international human rights discussions, states have committed to the principle that tax policies of one country should not undermine the capacity of other countries to raise revenue.[12] Despite the normative acceptance of this principle in international treaties, Allison Christians argues that "tax policy experts assume for the most part that no such responsibility exists. Policy tradeoffs are therefore made within a paradigm limited by unexamined assumptions about whose interests matter."[13]

There is an extensive commentary on key human rights treaties that link taxation to core human rights. For example, Principle 17 of the Maastricht Principles on Extraterritorial Obligations of States in the Area of Economic, Social and Cultural Rights, provides:

> States must elaborate, interpret and apply relevant international agreements and standards in a manner consistent with their human rights obligations. Such obligations include those pertaining to international trade, investment, finance, taxation, environmental protection, development cooperation, and security.[14]

Furthermore, Maastricht Principle 29 states that there should additionally be an *international enabling environment* for the enjoyment of economic, social, and cultural rights, including tax matters.[15] Meanwhile the former UN Special Rapporteur on extreme poverty and human rights, Magdalena Sepúlveda Carmona, links corporate tax and human rights via Principle 13 of the UN Guiding Principles on Business and Human Rights (UNGPs):

> Business practices that avoid taxation may breach their responsibility to respect insofar as such actions have a negative human rights impact (principle 13) . . . In addition, business enterprises that knowingly avoid paying tax are purposefully depriving countries of the resources they need to fulfil their human rights obligations.[16]

According to Principle 13(a) of the UNGPs, the responsibility to respect human rights requires that business enterprises avoid causing or contributing to adverse human rights impacts through their own activities and address such impacts when they occur. The UNGPs are also clear about the scope of responsibility for potentially abusive practices extending to all business relationships, which may prove to be illustrative also in resolving the separate entity versus unitary (or consolidated) view of a company for tax assessment purposes (explored in more detail below). Principle 13(b) of the UNGPs states that the responsibility to respect human rights requires that business enterprises "[s]eek to prevent or mitigate adverse human rights impacts that are directly linked to their operations, products or services by their business relationships, even if they have not contributed to those impacts."[17] Many commentators have examined the connection between these general principles and corporate tax behavior. David Scheffer, for instance, states that it is "entirely plausible that refraining from tax avoidance schemes could fit within the Ruggie framework."[18] Susan Ariel Aaronson and Ian Higham agree, noting that "corporate responsibility to pay taxes, which essentially are investments in public goods, is a key, albeit missing, element"[19] of the UNGPs, as taxes are, in both direct and indirect ways, vital in supporting the realization of human rights. Finally, the International Bar Association (IBA) states:

> The recently developed UN Guiding Principles on Business and Human Rights clarify the obligations of states to ensure coherence among corporate law, tax policy and human rights. Furthermore, they set out the responsibilities of business enterprises to avoid any negative impacts on human rights throughout their operations and business relationships. Indeed, the UN Guiding Principles—and other international standards related to corporate social responsibility—can assist in the articulation of new due diligence requirements related to the tax practices of multinational enterprises in different economic sectors (including financial, accounting and legal services).[20]

Against this backdrop, this chapter proceeds in three sections. The first section following this introduction identifies areas of interest common to the fields of tax and human rights—namely, in relation to: (1) the concept of the multinational enterprise as a unitary firm, rather than a collection of separate entities; (2) the concept of the extraterritorial impacts and obligations of states and corporations; and (3) the risk of conceiving of corporations as rights holders (which we later discuss as the "risk of corporate personhood"), with the capacity to assert rights in forums including investor-state arbitration. The second section of the chapter addresses the human rights impacts of abusive tax practices, distinguishing between state-mediated impacts (i.e., effects on the public purse) and more direct impacts of corporate conduct on human welfare (i.e., effects on the availability and quality of jobs, impacts on shareholders, etc.). The final section, which draws on an earlier nongovernmental organization (NGO) report titled *Getting to Good: Towards Responsible Corporate Tax Behaviour*,[21] discusses what kinds of changes in tax rules and regulations, and/or voluntary approaches to corporate reform, are needed to eradicate abusive tax practices.

II. CONVERGENCE OF INTERNATIONAL TAX NORMS AND HUMAN RIGHTS FRAMEWORKS

Should corporate tax abuses be considered human rights abuses, and thus also be addressed through human rights frameworks? Many tax experts are likely to question the link, while human rights experts for the most part have yet to consider the combination of issues. If we compare the two fields carefully, the following principles arise both in the literature on international corporate taxation and that on business and human rights:

1. the principle of a company being a single entity;
2. the principle of extraterritoriality;
3. the risks of corporate personhood.

These principles are all highly relevant to corporations' human rights due diligence and risk assessment of their tax policies. Applying a business and human rights perspective to international tax law can clarify responsibilities of companies toward their other stakeholders as well as their relationship with subsidiaries and business partners in terms of responsible tax conduct. The following subsections discuss the relevance of these principles to the fields of tax and human rights, and explore how they should influence rights-based assessments and reforms of corporate tax policies and practices.

A. CORPORATION AS SINGLE—NOT SEPARATE—ENTITY

Up to now, human rights frameworks have had little impact on the way tax structures or tax filings are made, especially by multinational enterprises (MNEs).[22] When tax is seen purely as an area of legal compliance, human rights impact on business tax practices is not considered an issue. This is due to a failure to recognize grey areas of practices and impacts on third parties, or to an overly narrow definition of human rights impacts. Unlike tax rules, human rights principles do not treat corporations as separate entities. UNGP Principle 23 states that "all business enterprises have the same responsibility to respect human rights wherever they operate."[23] This responsibility also extends to business relationships involving—for instance—financing, supply chains, and joint ventures, while recognizing that companies may have different levels of leverage in such situations.

There is still no consensus, however, on whether corporations comprised of multiple affiliates and subsidiaries should be treated as a single entity in tax terms. David Spencer disagrees with the unitary definition of a company because "the problem is . . . also determining if the MNE is operating more than one unitary business."[24] This problem is illustrated in the case of conglomerates that have weaker bonds between business units limited to intragroup financing and brokering relationships. Spencer views financial and asset ownership linkages as weaker than operational linkages for tax purposes. Sol Picciotto, on the other hand, argues that "[u]nitary taxation should be applied to all legal entities (companies, partnerships, trusts, etc.) which are (i) under common control or direction, and (ii) engaged in same or related business activities."[25] Civil society organizations that belong to the Global Alliance for Tax Justice (GATJ) also tend to view financial ties as group ties, and are critical of the limited scope and ambition of the Organisation for Economic Co-operation and Development's (OECD's) announced Base Erosion and Profit Shifting (BEPS) Action Plan: "True progress towards fair taxation of multinational corporations . . . requires the abandonment of the separate entity concept and the adoption of a different principle which clearly states that multinationals should be treated as unitary firms."[26]

The OECD still utilizes the so-called "arm's-length principle" of taxing MNEs on a separate entity basis, where tax law applies to each legal entity in a business group as if they were separate businesses. The OECD Transfer Pricing Guidelines[27] outline five broad methods for calculating an intragroup transfer price based either on finding comparable transactions in unrelated firms, or establishing profit margins in transactions. The OECD BEPS Project does not significantly change these transfer pricing guidelines. The UN Practical Manual on Transfer Pricing for Developing Countries recognizes divergent practices where the arm's-length principle is not considered to work in several emerging economies, including South Africa, India, Brazil, and China.[28] The recent OECD BEPS Project implicitly accepted the assumption that a company is a single unitary entity when it identified the concern that there is an "increased segregation between the location where actual business activities and investment take place and the location where profits are reported for tax purposes."[29] Nonetheless, the OECD BEPS Action Plan does not make any important changes to the separate entity taxation principle, as it keeps the taxing rights largely unchanged. The Action Plan states: "Countries have long worked and are strongly committed to eliminate such double taxation in order to minimise trade distortions and impediments to sustainable economic growth, while affirming their sovereign right to establish their own tax rules."[30]

The OECD's legalistically reductionist view of the problem of international taxation sits in tension with the normative principle expressed in a G20 ministerial statement, which instructs the OECD that its Action Plan "should provide countries with domestic and international instruments that will better align rights to tax with economic activity."[31] This directive has been seen by some to contradict the OECD's arm's-length principle as there is an increasing reference to global value chains in understanding the operation of an MNE, while not providing tools for shifting taxation to such value chains.[32] The circular logic of the arm's-length principle makes it a poor principle of international soft law. A clearer emphasis on the notion of a global value chain is found in the UN Practical Manual on Transfer Pricing, which states that "MNEs create organizational structures and develop strategies to arrange the cross-border production of goods and services in locations around the world and to determine the level of intra-entity or intra-group integration . . . The key feature of MNEs is that they are integrated (global) businesses."[33]

These guidelines can be utilized and interpreted in an abusive way by business enterprises as they allow for businesses to structure cross-charging group functions in low-tax jurisdictions, and benefit from unintended consequences of incompatible and incoherent tax systems. Indeed, several studies indicate that individual executives play a significant role in determining the level of tax avoidance that firms undertake.[34] One study argues that a "CEO can affect tax avoidance by setting the 'tone at the top' with regard to the firm's tax activities,"[35] and another study considers that while "the direct effect of tax avoidance is to increase the after-tax value of the firm, these effects are potentially offset, particularly in poorly governed firms, by the increased opportunities for managerial rent diversion."[36] In the second case, not only do members of the public lose out in terms of tax revenue but shareholders also see diminished returns due to rent diversion as part of aggressive tax-planning structures.

The political commitment of the G20 to align international tax norms with economic reality has brought in some measures that begin to have features common with the business and human rights approach. The implementation of this normative principle of aligning tax norms with economic reality is taking place via a greater focus on transfer pricing documentation, including reporting on intrafirm transactions on a country-by-country basis (BEPS Action 13) that treats a corporate group as a single entity. Sol Picciotto argues that the country-by-country reporting (CbCR) requirement in BEPS Action 13 creates a foundation for addressing a company on a consolidated basis, but considers that "there is surely scope for much more work here by the OECD, notably in developing a template for tax accounts as a basis for consolidated accounts, especially in view of the increased use of the profit-split method."[37]

B. EXTRATERRITORIAL IMPACTS AND OBLIGATIONS

Another innovation in the BEPS Action 13 is the possibility of an extraterritorial application of CbCR tax-reporting requirements even when the country or territory where a subsidiary is located does not require the production of annual accounts, or when the country in question does not agree to exchange CbCR information with tax authorities in third countries.[38] In practice, the proposed OECD Transfer Pricing Documentation and CbCR Documentation[39] include, first, the CbCR template containing key financial information about taxes and other financial operations in each country where the company operates and, second, a CbCR Masterfile, which includes explanation of the company operations per jurisdiction and other functional analysis to better interpret some of the quantitative figures in the template. The new guidance proposes a level of centralization of the tax function in companies that may provide a basis for behavior change if a responsible tax strategy is chosen. Indeed, as Rasmus Christensen states: "[Country-by-country reporting] is one of the more inauspicious regulatory innovations that provides the best illustration of the BEPS challenge to the separate entity principle: *reporting mechanisms*."[40] Reporting mechanisms can shape the way authorities and other stakeholders who have access to such data view the local company as a part of a unitary group rather than as a separate entity.

BEPS Action 13 additionally provides three conditions that trigger what the OECD calls a "safety valve" or what one might call an *extraterritorial* application of the CbCR requirement:

1. the parent is not required to file in its home country;
2. international information exchange or treaty-sharing agreements are insufficient for the report to be exchanged from the parent company's home country; or
3. there has been a "systemic failure" by the home country as regards the report.

This *safety valve* is, in effect, an extraterritorial obligation, leading Rasmus Christensen to observe that "we are, after all, requiring purely local managers to provide information beyond the geographic boundaries of their authority, no?"[41] This extraterritorial reporting element creates responsibilities beyond the separate entity, and demonstrates that a local entity can be responsible for wider group activities.

C. THE RISK OF CORPORATE PERSONHOOD

The unitary form of a company can also come with certain risks, including granting companies and investors rights beyond what they would otherwise have as separate entities. Corporate personhood as a concept is problematic, because human rights as such should not apply to a legal entity which can be dissolved, go bankrupt, be sold, and be divided up—issues that are not options for physical persons who have inalienable rights due to their very humanity and indivisible personhood. However, companies have already been recognized to enjoy certain human rights. For example, Article 6 of the European Convention on Human Rights (ECHR),[42] has been interpreted to protect corporations against excessive penalties for failing to pay taxes or levies—a protection normally discussed in terms of individual citizens.[43] Other cases such as the one concerning the tax investigation of the Swiss-based bank UBS by French authorities have been rejected by the European Court of Human Rights (ECtHR).[44] The UBS case took place in Switzerland with more stringent banking secrecy laws and practices than France, but the Court rejected UBS's arguments that its fair trial rights were violated. Reuven Avi-Yonah and Gianluca Mazzoni note that in the case of corporate entities, the US Supreme Court has "made it clear that corporations cannot claim equality with individuals regarding right to privacy."[45] Indeed, similar cases have not been seen in other global or regional human rights forums.

Another risk relating to corporate personhood arises in the context of BEPS Action 14,[46] which proposes the establishment of a mechanism to settle corporate tax disputes. While it is the dispute settlement process that poses a problem, it can be justified on the basis of the company having certain rights against arbitrary or unjust treatment in the host country's court. On commercial grounds, the argument in support such dispute settlement procedures is that favorable investor treatment leads to greater inward investment. This may involve a developing country agreeing, under the mutual agreement procedure (MAP), with a foreign company or investor to designate an arbitration or commercial court outside of its territory to act as a location for settling disputes. The BEPS Action 14 may mean that many more tax disputes over a government's efforts to seek tax payments from a company are settled in courts outside of the country in question. The key concern of civil society is that, unlike normal court procedures, MAPs tend to be secretive, and thus cannot fulfill the objectives set out in BEPS Action 14 of achieving principled, fair, and objective settlements.[47]

Human rights principles could, however, also be used to counter the inclusion of BEPS Action 14 as it could be seen to go against the principle of a fair trial if such a trial is held behind closed doors. Fair trial rights also require access to justice, and in this case the Independent Commission on the Reform of International Corporate Taxation (ICRICT) has argued that "arbitration often finds developing countries at a disadvantage because they lack the financing for such fees as well as legal teams of tax experts."[48] This is already the case with the increase in MAP cases, which have risen in number from 2,352 in 2006 to 5,423 in 2014.[49] There is no clear data about these cases and their regional breakdown, but the rise in the number of cases in some regions demonstrates an increased demand for dispute settlement processes either requested by governments or companies themselves. For instance, there is little evidence of the increased use of MAP cases in African countries. Arbitration clauses in tax treaties have triggered opposition from China and India, which do not agree that mandatory and binding arbitration is an appropriate tool to resolve issues under MAP.[50] The OECD—in pushing for the mandatory dispute settlement process—had to back down and only seek commitments from countries toward more effective, but not necessarily mandatory or binding, dispute settlement in the BEPS process.[51] The risk of corporate personhood should be recognized as potentially undermining the duty of states to collect revenue, and subsequently the way in which revenue collection supports the progressive realization of various human rights enjoyed by individual citizens through public expenditure.

D. TAX AS A COMPONENT OF HUMAN RIGHTS DUE DILIGENCE

Despite the areas of convergence between the fields of tax and human rights, discussed above, current debate on the implementation of the human rights responsibilities of business tends to exclude tax as a specific area of human rights impact assessment.[52] Indeed, Principle 19 of the UNGPs states that a company is expected to address any adverse human rights impacts directly linked to its business by using its "leverage." "Leverage is considered to exist where the enterprise has the ability to effect change in the wrongful practices of an entity that causes a harm . . . If the business enterprise has leverage to prevent or mitigate the adverse impact, it should exercise it. And if it lacks leverage there may be ways for the enterprise to increase it."[53] The concept of leverage reinforces the view that a conglomerate can be treated as a single entity under the UNGP framework. The use of such leverage can be a basis for resolving abusive business practices, including tax abuses, from a business and human rights perspective.

In both fields, recent developments do not yet provide a basis for changing the law regarding the separate entity principle, but the added layer of responsibility introduced by the UNGP is complementary in making a risk assessment and in conducting impact assessments. It is only when either internal or external accountability mechanisms (variously based on human rights frameworks) are employed that a company begins to respond to views by stakeholders through impact assessment. Examples of internal accountability mechanisms include creating, publishing, and implementing a tax strategy or an internally developed human rights policy which includes tax issues; and examples of external accountability measures include public country-by-country reporting in the European Union[54] as well as demands by NGOs to investigate corporate tax abuses through human rights processes.[55]

One of the first steps for many in the corporate social responsibility and responsible investment fields has been to develop ways of identifying red flags such as the "difference between the effective tax rate on a company's income statement and the weighted average of statutory rates based on the firm's geographic sales mix."[56] To further investigate these and other red flags, a responsible investor may look at whether tax is formally a part of the risk oversight mandate of the company's board, and how tax-planning policies are managed, from board down to the line-manager level.

Many companies now conduct tax-related due diligence to assess risks related to their tax positions, and some, including Vodafone[57] and BHP Billiton,[58] have made their approach to tax public. Specifically, they present evidence of how they live according to their principles, pay taxes in different jurisdictions, and conduct risk analysis of their tax positions. These tax-impact assessments consider the entire group. While they are not directly motivated by the UNGPs, nor framed as "human rights impact assessments," these processes are compatible with many of the principles in UNGPs.

If an MNE adopts a risk-based approach to taxation at the group level, it means that an MNE addresses a group-level tax strategy, which is approved by the company board and appropriate risk committees. However, a group subsidiary may feel that it is managing its own tax practices according to its legal duties toward the host state in which it operates rather than a group structure strategy. If a local tax manager were to take a different view based on legal interpretation of the subsidiary as a separate legal entity, the subsidiary could potentially deviate from, and thereby undermine, the company's group tax strategy. Equally, there is also the risk of the group imposing financing arrangements on subsidiaries (for instance, thin capitalization[59]) to reduce the net tax liability of the group, thus potentially involving the subsidiary in tax avoidance charges.

CbCR is currently considered a feature of companies' "risk assessment" activities, rather than the basis for tax assessments, which are still done on a separate entity level. Nonetheless, the technical design and practices of putting together country-by-country reports will lead to new ways of understanding and visualizing MNEs, which is likely to have tax implications. What the CbCR does is to allow tax authorities to locate the subsidiary in their country as part of a global value chain and have a second level of risk assessment of a company's tax practices that already comply with legal provisions in all countries where the company operates. If the risk assessment triggers a tax inspection, the exercise may lead to a tax adjustment. CbCR would facilitate the move away from a separate entity principle and toward taxing companies in the unitary form based on their global value chains—a notion around which there is convergence in both the tax and human rights fields. Public CbCR would allow wider tax stakeholders (civil society, parliamentarians, media) to be part of this process, and provide more comprehensive and timely information for developing country authorities.

III. THE HUMAN RIGHTS IMPACTS OF ABUSIVE CORPORATE TAX BEHAVIOR

A. INTRODUCTION

This section explores two dimensions of the human rights impacts of tax-related corporate decisions: (1) impacts mediated by the state; and (2) impacts not mediated by the state. Impacts mediated by the state result from corporate tax behavior that affects the level of government income and subsequent decisions by the government on spending. These fiscal effects can have human rights impacts by way of depriving governments of the funds they need to realize the fundamental rights of their citizens. Other state-mediated impacts can arise from tax-related legal and regulatory processes that are checked by the judiciary or other dispute resolution processes and access to information mechanisms provided by the state, such as access to information concerning beneficial owners or company directors or beneficiaries of a trust.

Human rights impacts not mediated by the state arise from tax-motivated corporate decision-making that affects the human rights of employees, customers, and citizens in the countries where the company operates. Human rights impacts may concern women's access to equal employment and the quality of jobs more generally; the transfer of technology and skills to developing economies; and investment and prices of goods and services.

Bringing the tax justice and human rights discourses together requires some initial consideration of the terminology and classification of tax practices. The former UN Special Rapporteur on extreme poverty and human rights, Magdalena Sepúlveda Carmona, conceptualizes *tax abuse* in the narrow context of illegality, while recognizing the role of facilitators in tax abuses: "Tax abuse includes tax evasion, fraud and other illegal practices, including the tax losses resulting from other illicit financial flows, such as bribery and money laundering."[60] In her 2014 report to the UN Human Rights Council, the Special Rapporteur mainly addressed the responsibility of states in tackling tax abuses, noting: "High-income States that enable or fail to tackle tax abuse and illicit financial flows must shoulder some responsibility for the shortcomings of the tax and public finance systems in developing countries and related poverty rates, lack of enjoyment of human rights and economic inequalities."[61]

However, the debate by international organizations and human rights institutions has only just started with respect to how tax abuses are considered in human rights terms, and the understanding of what is considered *abusive* is evolving so as to include wider issues of tax avoidance. For instance, the IBA outlines a broader set of practices that it considers abusive:

> The tax abuses of greatest concern of the Task Force included: transfer pricing and other cross-border intra-group transactions; the negotiation of tax holidays and incentives; the taxation of natural resources; and the use of offshore investment accounts. Secrecy jurisdictions are also a concern because of their role in facilitating tax abuses.[62]

The definition of a tax abuse in the IBA report includes many areas in tax law that are ordinarily considered *legal* tax avoidance—including aggressive use of transfer pricing. The broader definition is also shared by the International Monetary Fund (IMF), which has identified its own short list of potentially abusive tax practices, based on its technical advice to developing country governments. The list includes, among other practices:

1. **Abusive transfer pricing**—exploiting weaknesses in the arm's-length principle, ranging from potential mispricing of natural resources to the transfer of intellectual property rights to low-tax jurisdictions early in their development, when they are hard to value;

2. **Thin capitalization**—taking deductions in high-tax countries by, for example, borrowing there to lend to affiliates in lower-tax jurisdictions;

3. **Risk transfer**—conducting operations in high-tax jurisdictions on a contractual basis, so limiting the profits that arise there;

4. **Exploiting mismatches**—tax arbitrage opportunities can arise if different countries classify the same entity, transaction, or financial instrument differently;

5. **Treaty shopping**—treaty networks can be used to route income so as to reduce taxes;

6. **Locating asset sales in low-tax jurisdictions**—to avoid capital gains taxes—a particular concern in the context of recent resource discoveries in some low-tax countries;

7. **Deferral**—companies resident in countries operating worldwide systems can defer home taxation of business income earned abroad by delaying paying it to the parent;

8. **Inversion**—companies may be able to escape repatriation charges or Controlled Foreign Corporation (CFC) rules by changing their residence.[63]

Many forms of tax avoidance are increasingly perceived as abusive, and raise concerns with tax authorities precisely because they constitute a purposeful reduction of taxes paid. We consider that it is useful to define tax avoidance as a purposeful arrangement of corporate affairs designed to minimize the amount of tax that the company claims to owe. This should be distinguished from ordinary tax compliance, which involves some level of planning and which yields uncontroversial tax savings, such as claiming tax exemptions and credits where they conform to both the letter and the spirit of the law.

B. EXAMPLES OF STATE-MEDIATED IMPACTS OF CORPORATE TAX PRACTICES

Tax planning practices have been at the center of tax scandals and public concerns over responsible tax management. An example is locating a company's support functions, such as expatriate managers running day-to-day manufacturing operations, in various countries, while formally employing them under an offshore management or other intragroup services company registered in a low-tax jurisdiction. Such offshore management functions are relatively typical examples of the provision of intragroup services that tend to be priced at headquarter price levels, which, when compared with subsidiary country price levels in developing countries, are likely to seem inflated.

Another tax abuse relates to "treaty shopping," whereby a company may, for tax purposes, structure a profit-yielding transaction indirectly through a third and unrelated jurisdiction, which offers, for example, lower taxes on dividends, interest, and royalty payments.

Avoidance of capital gains taxes is another form of tax abuse that raises human rights concerns. If the aim is to protect human rights, the objective in terms of capital gains taxes should be to help to prevent tax-free indirect transfers of interest—a major problem especially in the extractives industries. The IMF has estimated that such indirect transfers have made it

CASE STUDY 1: How Treaty Shopping Deprives Countries of Revenue

Over a period of six years (2009–2014), Paladin, an Australian mining company operating in Malawi, managed to avoid paying over $27.5 million in withholding taxes through treaty shopping.[64]

Treaty shopping is a common practice of companies routing investments through third countries purely in order to take advantage of tax breaks enshrined in those third countries' treaties. Paladin did this by routing intracompany interest and management fee payments from its Malawian subsidiary to the Australian parent company via a subsidiary in the Netherlands.

The Malawi–Netherlands tax treaty in force at the time did not allow Malawi to apply withholding taxes on interest payments and management fees paid from Malawi to the Netherlands. Had the Malawian subsidiary sent the money straight to the Australian parent without the money passing through the Dutch subsidiary—which had no employees and effectively just acted as a conduit for the payments—Malawi would have been able to apply a 15 percent statutory withholding tax to those payments, because Malawi and Australia do not have a tax treaty.[65]

impossible, for example, for Mauritania to tax a $4 billion gain that a company made on the sale of its Mauritanian gold mine via a Bahamas subsidiary.[66]

Another case study of capital gains tax abuse in Uganda generated a lengthy court battle for over $300 million in a capital gains tax dispute between two oil companies[67]—an amount nearly equivalent to the country's health budget, which stood at $420 million in 2013.[68] Furthermore, there are cases of civil society pressure being important for ensuring that the government seeks to recover lost tax revenues from companies, advocating for more accountability concerning tax incentives. Individual companies cannot be held solely responsible for government tax policies. But companies do influence tax incentive regimes, and sometimes negotiate directly with finance ministries and investment promotion agencies to create and exploit company-specific tax incentives and relief.

C. EXAMPLES OF NONSTATE MEDIATED TAX PRACTICES

In addition to the impacts that abusive tax practices have on state budgets, and thereby on the human rights of the residents of that state, tax-motivated company decisions can have direct impacts on the rights of employees, consumers, shareholders, and those communities affected by corporate operations. For example, a company hopping from jurisdiction to jurisdiction to chase a string of discretionary tax holidays is not likely to invest in local infrastructure and economies and is less likely to create good-quality, highly skilled jobs, as its investment decisions depend on tax incentives and it will move elsewhere once the incentive runs out or is matched in another jurisdiction. This is the case in Brazil where the presence of the Ford Motor Company plant led to competitive "fiscal wars" of bidding between different Brazilian states with the

CASE STUDY 2: Advocating for Greater Scrutiny of Tax Incentives in East Africa

In April 2012, ActionAid and Tax Justice Network–Africa published a report that examined the impact of tax incentives on four countries—Kenya, Uganda, Tanzania, and Rwanda, all of which are members of the East African Community (EAC). The report offered recommendations to those countries on how to end a *race to the bottom* in corporate tax rates in the region.[69]

A follow-up report published in June 2016 found the region was still losing around $1.5 billion and possibly up to $2 billion of revenue each year by granting tax incentives to foreign companies. This second report found that EAC governments have taken some positive steps to reduce tax incentives, especially those related to value-added tax (VAT), which are increasing tax collection and providing vital additional revenue that could be spent on providing critical services. However, they are still failing to eliminate all unnecessary tax incentives. Countries are still providing generous tax breaks in the form of tax holidays, capital-gains tax allowances, and royalty exemptions and, as a result, continue to lose colossal amounts of revenue.[70]

Despite increased questioning of the value of these exemptions, it is unclear how these tax incentives will be revised, costed, and phased out in practice, or what resources and expertise governments have to carry out this work. The report also critiques the continued confidentiality of the agreements in which such tax exemptions are granted.

incentives offered to attract investment amounting to an estimated total cost per employee of $172,000.[71]

Abusive tax behavior can also increase the prevalence of corruption, which can deny citizens their civil and political rights. Global Witness—a London-based NGO—has argued that the commodities giant Glencore made secret loans to offshore companies operating in the Democratic Republic of Congo owned by unrelated parties and knowingly entered into loss-making deals with them from 2007 to 2010.[72] The use of secretive offshore companies can directly facilitate corruption by both public and private actors, for example, by hindering the use of provisions that prevent politicians from owning mining rights when there is a conflict of interest. The danger of such a situation is clear: corrupt decision makers could transfer lucrative assets to companies with which they are involved, while turning a blind eye to tax abuse and granting tax exemptions to companies.[73]

Tax-related due diligence can help identify external impacts of tax-motivated transactions in areas other than government revenue. For instance, a company's decision to use tax-motivated debt financing to artificially depress the profits of a particular subsidiary could result in reduced wages or job losses—and adversely affect local minority shareholders as a result of reduced distributable reserves. Another example could involve moving the employment of a factory's managers for tax purposes from the local subsidiary to a management hub in a low-tax jurisdiction, which may dis-incentivize the company from employing local managers, thereby hindering the availability of higher-skilled, better-paid employment within that country. The tax-motivated reasons may affect a corporate group's tax liabilities and tax payments across several jurisdictions, including where the group's brick-and-mortar operations are located.

Other nonstate mediated or direct impacts of tax abuses relate to women's rights. Kate Donald and Rachel Moussié argue that "[c]orporations . . . rely on women's cheap labor within global supply chains to increase their profits, while avoiding taxes and social security benefits that could pay for public services and support unpaid care work."[74] Similarly tax incentives to large companies established in Special Economic Zones (SEZs) in India have been found to have negative impacts on the quality of women's employment, working conditions, and social protection,[75] while SEZs more generally have been found to limit the action of trade unions and contribute to clamping down on the freedom of association.[76] The Panama Papers scandal was also found to have gender-differentiated impacts in at least two ways: first, as the majority of the beneficiaries of offshored wealth are men; and second, women's greater reliance on fiscal and budget spending due to their greater role in terms of unpaid care work, means that women suffer more acutely when public budgets are limited due in part to tax avoidance by those who hide their wealth offshore.[77]

The relationship between tax abuses and labor practices has also drawn attention. During a recent visit to Chile, the UN Special Rapporteur on extreme poverty and human rights expressed concern over local laws which permitted "firms to splinter by using multiple tax identities, thereby avoiding the thresholds that would require them to permit collective bargaining at the company level."[78] This practice enables the company to undermine key International Labour Organization (ILO) treaties that protect the right to union organization and collective bargaining due to splitting the company into two separate entities.[79]

D. WIDER UNDERSTANDING OF ABUSIVE TAX BEHAVIOR

Which practices constitute tax abuse is still a matter of debate, but a growing number of examples are starting to make at least a public case against certain tax practices such as treaty shopping and questionable methods to obtain tax incentives. Case-study evidence is helpful in this regard to consider if a corporate practice should be considered as abusive.

The focus of the tax and human rights debate so far has been on state-mediated human rights impacts that take place via loss of tax revenue through corporate tax abuses, while nonstate mediated human rights impacts resulting directly from a tax-motivated corporate transactions have received somewhat less attention. Such direct impacts may be of equal importance to stakeholders, however, as the impacts of revenue loss on financing government expenditure. Direct job losses, increased likelihood of corruption, violations of women's rights, or reduction in shareholder value for local investment partners can lead to cases being brought against the company in both commercial and labor tribunals, in addition to tax charges by revenue authorities.

While the authors are unaware of any cases to date of companies being taken to court over the human rights impacts of corporate tax behavior, further investigation of such cases would provide an avenue for considering claims against some companies where direct human rights impacts can be attributed to their actions. Importantly, the judicial system is not the only forum in which human rights remedies can be pursued; complaints to national human rights institutions, such as ombudsmen, human rights commissions, and equality bodies, as well as international human rights bodies, merits further exploration.

IV. INTERFACE BETWEEN BEHAVIOR CHANGE AND RULE CHANGE

A. INTRODUCTION

In most cases, there will be a role for both states and companies to play in preventing and addressing adverse human rights impacts linked to corporate tax behavior. In many cases the human rights impact of corporate tax practices can be addressed by a variety of actors—by the government, tax authorities, courts, labor tribunals, and national human rights structures (and at times by nonstate institutions, in the case of accounting standard setting bodies, arbitration courts, or designated arbitrators).

To explore the scope of responsible corporate tax behavior that may address the potential human rights impacts of tax practices, in 2015, ActionAid reviewed forty-five sources of recommendations for responsible corporate tax behavior[80] and concluded that "[n]one of the frameworks [] reviewed yet provide any detailed guidance on how this [human rights impact assessment of tax-related corporate behavior] could or should be done—the challenge for responsible business will be to work out what impact assessment of tax behavior looks like in practice."[81]

B. VOLUNTARY METHODS OF ADDRESSING HUMAN RIGHTS IMPACTS OF CORPORATE TAX BEHAVIOR

Based on the findings of the mapping study, a joint NGO discussion paper titled *Getting to Good: Towards Responsible Corporate Tax Behaviors*[82] was published in 2015 to address the central question of how responsible tax behavior could address the human rights impacts of corporate tax practices. The paper suggests three basic principles and identifies eight key issue areas of relevant tax-related corporate behavior. This framework draws on the elements of the corporate responsibility to respect human rights, outlined in the second pillar of the UNGPs (see Table 17.1).

In an effort to work around the polarizing problem of defining tax *evasion* versus tax *avoidance*, this framework proposes impact assessment as a method of determining abusive behavior. In order to encourage behavior change—as far as possible—the proposals largely focused on positive behaviors. The value of this framework lies in its presentation of a scheme for *improving impact* and *reducing harm*, by setting out a series of tax practices that could have potential harmful human rights impacts and identifying more positive alternative behaviors.

For instance, a tax-responsible company or group will make incremental changes to its structures and tax-related transactions in booking less of its income, profits, and gains through legal entities in jurisdictions where they attract low or no tax, and in which related assets and activities are not located.[83] There have been cases of MNEs closing down subsidiaries in inactive low-tax jurisdictions, including the announcement by Unilever CEO Paul Polman in 2014 that the company was closing the few remaining nonoperating subsidiaries in tax havens and HSBC Chairman Douglas Flint confirming a 30 percent reduction in the number of nonoperating subsidiaries in tax havens.[84] These moves were probably motivated by the intent to reduce the overall number of tax haven subsidiaries in publicly available company information databases,

Table 17.1: A framework for responsible tax behavior

Key principles	Corresponding elements of the Corporate Responsibility to Respect Human Rights (UNGPs Pillar 2)	Key issue areas of tax-related corporate behavior
A tax responsible company:		
Transparency Is radically and proactively transparent about its business structure and operations, its tax affairs, and its tax decision-making;	• Having a publicly available human rights policy approved at the most senior level of the business enterprise (UNGP 16 a) • Communicating how human rights impacts are addressed (UNGP 17)	1. Tax-planning practices 2. Public transparency and reporting 3. Nonpublic disclosure 4. Relationships with tax authorities 5. Tax function management and governance 6. Impact evaluation of tax policy and practice 7. Tax lobbying/advocacy 8. Tax incentives
Assessment Assesses and publicly reports the fiscal, economic, and social impacts (positive and negative) of its tax-related decisions and practices in a manner that is accessible and comprehensive;	• Assessing actual and potential human rights impacts (UNGP 17)	
Progressive and measurable improvement Takes steps—progressively, measurably and in dialogue with its stakeholders—to improve the impact of its tax behavior on sustainable development and on the human rights of employees, customers, and citizens in the places where it does business.*	• Avoid infringing on the human rights of others (UNGP 11) • Addressing adverse human rights impacts with which the business is involved (UNGP 11) • Integrating and acting upon findings of human rights impacts and tracking responses (UNGP 17) • Engaging in remediation (UNGP 22) • Provide for or cooperate in remediation through legitimate processes	

* Oxfam, Getting to Good, Annex A, at 37.

thus reducing the risk of being seen to abusively utilize low-tax jurisdictions to reduce overall tax payments to governments.

To take another example, a positive alternative to offshoring management services in low-tax jurisdictions would be for a corporate group to ensure that all of the income from its day-to-day management functions is booked in places where operations relating to those functions take place; perhaps by making the operational companies the legal employers of the managers, rather than a separate offshore entity. This type of change will also help to reduce the risk of a company being accused by tax authorities of contributing to base erosion through management fees, service payments, royalties, and commission payments to low-tax jurisdictions.[85]

One positive, voluntary corporate behavior change that could help counter treaty shopping would involve making payments for goods, services, equity, and loans directly to the entities—both related and unrelated—that actually provide those goods, services, and financing. Where payments are made to related parties, it ensures that those payments are made to entities tax-resident in the countries where the goods, services, and financing are actually generated or provided. By ensuring that business relationships correspond to economic activities, companies also reduce their risk of being exposed and thus suffering reputational losses.

In response to concern about avoidance of capital gains tax, a corporate group could restructure its ownership and holding structures to ensure that when the group sells significant assets, the capital gains generated by the sale are taxable in the country where the asset is located (in the case of a physical asset or corporate entity) or where it has been created and developed (in the case of an intangible asset).

Most companies appreciate that they can—and in some areas already do—go beyond strict legal compliance on tax, not least when dealing with revenue authorities in developing countries. For example, SAB Miller (now part of ABInBev) publishes a list of the key tax incentives it receives.[86]

C. LIMITS TO THE EFFECTIVENESS OF VOLUNTARY MEASURES

Companies indicate that they can only take very modest steps beyond legal compliance on tax due to concerns about commercial confidentiality (in relation to tax transparency) and potential loss of competitiveness, or the perception that such steps would increase their overall tax bill and potentially be seen as being contrary to their (fiduciary) obligations to shareholders. Such an interpretation depends on the understanding of fiduciary obligations, and the role of risk and impact assessment in determining it. Therefore, when discussing tax as an issue of corporate responsibility with companies, we generally hear a clear preference for relying on mandatory measures to influence corporate tax behavior.

Nonetheless, when faced with proposed rule changes that would apply equally to all companies (in an industry), businesses—often through their industry associations—routinely argue against additional mandatory measures to regulate corporate tax behavior. Resistance to rule change may be cultural, or due to rule changes being unilateral or affecting only a small number of countries or companies. Where competitors are not obliged to take similar steps, most companies express reluctance to go too far beyond legal compliance in fear of suffering a loss of competitiveness.

Voluntary behavior change by companies is, therefore, not a substitute for binding regulations through which companies can be held accountable by governments. The basis for a fairer, better-functioning tax system is reform of tax laws and standards, both domestic and international, and their effective implementation. Tax justice advocates have argued for government-led reforms and binding rules and accordingly have actively advocated for governments to engage in inclusive global discussions (involving developing countries) on a host of issues, such as those listed below (see Table 17.2).

The systemic weaknesses in the current tax system clearly demonstrate that the solution to corporate tax avoidance in a globalized economy requires fundamental reform of corporate tax rules on an equally global scale. For the foreseeable future, however, companies will continue to face an international tax environment of inconsistent and incomplete regulation, which offers huge scope for arbitrage and the minimization of tax payments, to the continuing detriment of those who depend on tax-funded public goods. Both rule change and behavior change will depend largely on the active participation of different stakeholders, many of whom have traditionally been excluded from tax policymaking either formally or through lack of capacity to meaningfully engage in dialogue. A stakeholder mapping of rights holders and duty bearers is helpful in order to determine the respective rights and responsibilities of different actors.

Table 17.2: Changes proposed by civil society groups to tax rules

Generally, civil society groups call on governments to:*

a) put an end to the race to the bottom caused by competitive granting of tax incentives and lowering of tax rates;
b) end the use of "tax havens" for tax avoidance purposes;
c) reallocate tax rights between countries;
d) address avoidance of capital gains tax;
e) undertake work to prevent manipulation of internal transfer prices.

Specifically, we are calling for governments and institutions to:

a) ensure the participation of developing countries in all global tax reform processes on an equal footing, under the auspices of the UN;
b) ensure that taxes are paid where the economic activity to which they relate takes place;
c) review tax treaties, revise them where they are harmful to developing countries, and negotiate them so that they are coherent with public policies;
d) review tax rules and revise them where they are harmful to developing countries;
e) adopt a common, binding and ambitious definition of what a tax haven is, and provide blacklists and sanctions to deter their use for tax avoidance purposes;
f) ensure that anti-tax-haven (controlled foreign company) rules are effective;
g) support national, regional and global efforts to promote tax transparency at all levels, including:
   i. mandatory public country-by-country reporting for companies;
   ii. transparency of who really owns the companies, trusts and foundations (through disclosure of beneficial ownership);
   iii. transparent corporate structures;
h) a multilateral system for exchanging tax information on an automatic basis, including developing countries from the start with non-reciprocal commitments;
i) measure and review tax incentives;
j) increase penalties for tax avoiders.

* ActionAid, Christian Aid, and Oxfam, *supra* note 21, at 10.

D. UNDERSTANDING THE ROLES AND RESPONSIBILITIES
OF RELEVANT STAKEHOLDERS

The scope for rule and regulatory change is often limited due to the compliance-focused mindset, rather than human rights culture yet taking root in the tax profession. The compliance mindset also narrows down the participation of stakeholders. When tax is discussed from a purely legal perspective, we mostly see the interests of the investor group and revenue authorities being catered for in tax law and accounting standards. According to the Scottish Human Rights Council:

> A human rights complaint fiscal framework requires accountability mechanisms that are both proactive and reactive. Proactive mechanisms allow participation at the point of design and reactive measure enables aggrieved parties to raise their concerns regarding tax law and policy. Accountability also means judicial and non-judicial remedies and these are only useful if people know they can use them, and have effective access to them.[87]

However, in the current situation the legitimate concerns of various stakeholders to assess the impact of a company's activities on the enjoyment of all human rights by different rights holders, ranging from local communities to employees and creditors, are largely ignored. As an example, the International Financial Reporting Standards (IFRS) framework developed by the International Accounting Standards Board, identifies the following actors as relevant stakeholders: "The primary users of general purpose financial reporting are present and potential investors, lenders and other creditors, who use that information to make decisions about buying, selling or holding equity or debt instruments and providing or settling loans or other forms of credit."[88]

As tax becomes discussed increasingly in a human rights context, it is important to broaden the circle of stakeholders included in the tax debate. Richard Murphy[89] points out that a much broader range of potentially affected stakeholders would include employees, suppliers, citizens, and civil society, as reflected in the Corporate Report issued by the Accounting Standards Steering Committee in 1975.[90] The UN Conference on Trade and Development also issued guidelines in 2008,[91] which included multiple stakeholders (see Table 17.3.)

It will vary by case and context which of these stakeholders are among the affected rights holders, because an economic impact does not automatically lead to an adverse human rights impact. Citizens and employees are evidently rights holders who could become the victims of adverse human rights impacts linked to corporate tax behavior, whereas investors would not enjoy human rights protection as corporate entities. Meanwhile, the government, judiciary, and legislators are duty bearers under the human rights framework—and they therefore have a role in remedying indirect impacts of corporate tax abuses.

V. CONCLUSION AND AREAS FOR FUTURE INQUIRY

We proposed in this chapter that there are broad areas of convergence between international tax norms and the human rights framework for corporate responsibility, as reflected in the UNGPs. In exploring this convergence, it is helpful to think about tax responsibility as an ongoing process of transparency, assessment, and progressive and measureable improvement in dialogue with a broad range of stakeholders, rather than considering tax policy and practice as an area

Table 17.3: Tax stakeholders

Stakeholder	Broader Category
a. Investors	i. The investor group
b. Loan creditors	
c. Investment advisers	
d. Pension funds	
e. Employees	ii. The employee group
f. Trade unions	
g. Other trading partners, whether as suppliers or customers	iii. The trading group
h. Governments, local authorities, and their institutions	iv. The political group
i. Legislators	
j. Regulators	v. The legal and regulatory group
k. The judiciary and those engaged in legal disputes	
l. The public and civil society, including local communities	vi. Civil society

of concern merely for revenue authorities and legal experts, addressed behind closed doors. The shift in the debate has already taken place in our view as companies and governments alike are increasingly engaged in the initial steps of this process by providing greater transparency either through voluntary disclosure and explicit statements of tax policies, or via government-regulated disclosure mechanisms.

The study of the convergence between tax and human rights remains, however, in its infancy, and there are still many gaps in the current understanding of tax abuses as human rights abuses. For example, the human rights abuses committed by facilitators and their role in reform remains relatively unexplored. In light of the Panama Papers scandal, there might be more interest among some facilitators to voluntarily become more responsible. The role of investors likewise requires further attention. Investors hold considerable leverage over potential tax abuses and themselves use financial conduits and intermediaries in low-tax jurisdictions.

A greater convergence between tax norms and human rights frameworks and sustainable development principles can help to move the debate away from simply looking at the impact of double taxation or the division of taxing rights. All stakeholders mentioned above can be considered as relevant under the UNGPs, and their roles should be discussed as the normative frameworks around responsible taxation are further developed. In all areas, as the debate advances toward examining the impact of tax policies and practices on the enjoyment of human rights both at home and abroad, addressing areas of convergence between the different stakeholders discussed here can lead to more equitable and progressive tax systems that support the realization of human rights.

NOTES

1. A. Christians, *Fair Taxation as a Basic Human Right* (University of Wisconsin Legal Studies Research Paper No. 1066, 2009), available online at https://papers.ssrn.com/sol3/papers.cfm?abstract_id=1272446&rec=1&srcabs=1400624&alg=1&pos=8, at 6 (last visited 7 Aug. 2017).

2. I. Saiz, 'Resourcing Rights: Combatting Tax Injustice from a Rights Perspective', *in* A. Nolan, R. O'Connell, and C. Harvey (eds.), *Human Rights and Public Finance: Budgets and the Promotion of Economic and Social Rights* (2013), 77.

3. Companies are just one of a number of different types of taxpayer. However corporate income taxes are relatively more important in developing countries making up 16 percent of government revenues compared to just over 8 percent in high-income countries. See IMF, *Spillovers in International Corporate Taxation* (2014), at 7.

4. Centre for Economic and Social Rights and Christian Aid, *A Post-2015 Fiscal Revolution—Human Rights Policy Brief* (2014), available online at http://www.cesr.org/sites/default/files/fiscal.revolution.pdf; ActionAid, *The Elephant in the Room: How to Finance Our Future* (2014), available online at http://www.actionaid.org/sites/files/actionaid/the_elephant_in_the_room_-_how_to_finance_our_future.pdf; Oxfam, *Making It Happen: Oxfam's Proposals for the Post-2015 Framework* (2014), available online at http://oxfamilibrary.openrepository.com/oxfam/bitstream/10546/317610/19/bp187-making-happen-proposals-post-2015-framework-170614-en.pdf.

5. A. Rogers, *What a Kenyan Community Can Teach Us About Menstrual Hygiene and Human Rights*, available online at https://www.one.org/us/2016/09/23/what-a-kenyan-community-can-teach-us-about-menstrual-hygiene-and-human-rights/ (last visited 10 June 2017).

6. Christian Aid and SOMO, *Tax Justice Advocacy: A Toolkit for Civil Society* (2011), at 2.

7. A. Jerret, *What the Philippines Can Teach Us About Tobacco Taxation*, 10 July 2015, available online at: https://www.weforum.org/agenda/2015/07/what-the-philippines-can-teach-us-about-tobacco-taxation/ (last visited 7 Aug. 2017).

8. Christians, *supra* note 1.

9. A. Waris, *Tax & Development: Solving Kenya's Fiscal Crisis through Human Rights: A Case Study of Kenya's Constituency Development Fund* (2013), at 124.

10. Ibid. at 131.

11. A. Caliari, *Equality, Non-Discrimination and Tax Policy: Asking the Right Questions*, 6 Apr. 2016, available online at http://www.rightingfinance.org/?p=1535 (last visited 12 June 2017).

12. United Nations Follow-up International Conference on Financing for Development to Review the Implementation of the Monetary Consensus, Outcome Document, UN Doc. A/CONF.212/L.1/Rev.1, 9 Dec. 2008, at para. 16.

13. A. Christians, *Fair Taxation as a Basic Human Right*, 27 Feb. 2014, available online at https://tax.network/achristians/fair-taxation-basic-human-right/ (last visited 9 June 2017).

14. O. De Schutter et al., 'Commentary to the Maastricht Principles on Extraterritorial Obligations of States in the Area of Economic, Social and Cultural Rights', 34 *Human Rights Quarterly* (2012), 1084.

15. W. Oberland, *Taxes and Human Rights* (Tax Justice Germany Network, Policy Brief No. 8, 2013), available online at http://www.l4bb.org/reports/taxes_human_rights.pdf.

16. Human Rights Council, Report of the Special Rapporteur on Extreme Poverty and Human Rights, Ms. Magdalena Sepúlveda Carmona, UN Doc. A/HRC/26/28, 22 May 2014, at para. 7.

17. United Nations Office of the High Commissioner, *Guiding Principles on Business and Human Rights: Implementing the United Nations "Protect, Respect and Remedy" Framework* (2011), available online at http://www.ohchr.org/Documents/Publications/GuidingPrinciplesBusinessHR_EN.pdf, at 15.

18. D. Scheffer, 'The Ethical Imperative of Curbing Corporate Tax Avoidance', 27(4) *Ethics and International Affairs* (2013), 361, at 365.

19. S. A. Aaronson and I. Higham, 'Re-righting Business: John Ruggie and the Struggle to Develop International Human Rights Standards for Transnational Firms', 35(2) *Human Rights Quarterly* (2012), 333, at 362.

20. International Bar Association, *Tax Abuses, Poverty and Human Rights: A Report of the International Bar Association's Human Rights Institute Task Force on Illicit Financial Flows, Poverty and Human Rights* (2013), at 105 available at http://www.ibanet.org/Document/Default.aspx?DocumentUid=4977CB3D-4988-4C9C-84C7-9050A5CB2311 (last visited 12 June 2017).

21. ActionAid, Christian Aid, and Oxfam, *Getting to Good—Towards Responsible Corporate Tax Behaviour* (2015), available at http://www.christianaid.org.uk/images/Getting-to-good-corporate-tax-November2015.pdf.

22. The terms "MNE" and "TNC" (used interchangeably here) not only cover large corporate groups but also smaller groups with one or more subsidiaries or permanent establishments (PEs) in countries other than those where the parent company or head office is located. See United Nations Conference on Trade and Development, Division on Investment and Enterprise, *UNCTAD Training Manual on Statistics for FDI and the Operations of TNCs: Volume II—Statistics on the Operations of Transnational Corporations* (2009), available online at http://unctad.org/en/docs/diaeia20092_en.pdf, at 15 (last accessed 7 Aug. 2017).

23. OHCHR, *supra* note 17, at 25.

24. D. Spencer, 'Picciotto's Dilemma: What Is Unitary Taxation?', 83 *Tax Notes International* (2016), 411, at 413.

25. S. Picciotto, *Towards Unitary Taxation of Transnational Corporations* (2012), available online at https://www.taxjustice.net/cms/upload/pdf/Towards_Unitary_Taxation_1-1.pdf.

26. Global Alliance for Tax Justice, *The OECD BEPS Project Tax Policies Not Fit for the 21st Century* (2014), available online at http://www.taxjustice.net/wp-content/uploads/2013/04/GATJ-beps.pdf.

27. OECD, *Transfer Pricing Guidelines for Multinational Enterprises and Tax Administrations* (2010).

28. United Nations, *United Nations Practical Manual on Transfer Pricing for Developing Countries* (2017), available online at http://www.un.org/esa/ffd/publications/united-nations-practical-manual-on-transfer-pricing-for-developing-countries-2017.html, ch. 10 (last visited 7 Aug. 2017).

29. OECD, *Action Plan on Base Erosion and Profit Shifting* (2013), available online at https://www.oecd.org/ctp/BEPSActionPlan.pdf, at 15.

30. Ibid. at 9.

31. Ibid. at 11.

32. D. Ernick, 'Integration, Fragmentation and Global Value Chains', 44 *Tax Management International Journal* (2015), 167.

33. United Nations, *Practical Manual, supra* note 28, at 41.

34. S. Dyreng, M. Hanlon, and E. L. Maydew, *The Effects of Executives on Corporate Tax Avoidance*, 9 Sept. 2009, available online at https://ssrn.com/abstract=1158060 (last visited 10 June 2017); M. A. Desai and D. Dharmapala, 'Corporate Tax Avoidance and High-Powered Incentives', 79 *Journal of Financial Economics* (2006), 145.

35. Dyreng et al., *supra* note 34, at 2.

36. Desai and Dharmapala, *supra* note 34, at 2.

37. S. Picciotto, 'Can the OECD Mend the International Tax System?', *Tax Analysts* (2013), 1105, at 1112.

38. OECD, *Action 13: Country-by-Country Reporting Implementation Package* (2015), available online at https://www.oecd.org/ctp/transfer-pricing/beps-action-13-country-by-country-reporting-implementation-package.pdf.

39. OECD, *Transfer Pricing Documentation and Country-by-Country Reporting, Action 13—2015 Final Report*, 5 Oct. 2015, available online at http://www.oecd.org/ctp/transfer-pricing-documentation-and-country-by-country-reporting-action-13-2015-final-report-9789264241480-en.htm (last visited 7 Aug. 2017).

40. R. C. Christensen, *The Quiet BEPS Revolution: Moving Away from the Separate Entity Principle*, 3 Aug. 2016, available online at https://phdskat.org/2016/08/03/beps-moving-away-from-separate-entity/ (last visited 7 Aug. 2017).

41. Ibid.

42. C. A. Ruiz Jimenez, 'Fair Trial on Taxation: The European and Inter-American Experience', *in* G. Kofler, M. P. Maduro, and P. Pistone (eds.), *Human Rights and Taxation in Europe and the World* (2011), 521, at 531.

43. P. Baker, *Some Recent Decisions of the European Court of Human Rights on Tax Matters* (June 2012), available online at http://www.fieldtax.com/wp-content/uploads/2014/12/2012-June.pdf, at 308.

44. J. Letzing, 'UBS Loses Human-Rights Appeal in French Tax-Evasion Case', *Wall Street Journal*, 12 Jan. 2017, available online at https://www.wsj.com/articles/ubs-loses-human-rights-appeal-in-french-tax-evasion-case-1484224332 (last visited 10 June 2017).

45. R. Avi-Yonah and G. Mazzoni, *Taxation and Human Rights: A Delicate Balance* (University of Michigan Public Law Research Paper No. 520, 2016), available online at https://ssrn.com/abstract=2834883 (last visited 7 Aug. 2017).

46. OECD, *Making Dispute Resolution Mechanisms More Effective, Action 14—2015 Final Report*, 5 Oct. 2015, available online at http://www.oecd.org/tax/making-dispute-resolution-mechanisms-more-effective-action-14-2015-final-report-9789264241633-en.htm (last visited 26 July 2017).

47. BEPS Monitoring Group, *Comments on BEPS Action 14: Make Dispute Settlement Process More Effective* (2015), available online at https://bepsmonitoringgroup.files.wordpress.com/2015/01/ap-14-dispute-resolution.pdf.

48. Independent Commission for Reform of International Corporate Taxation, *Evaluation of the Independent Commission for the Reform of International Corporate Taxation for the Base Erosion and Profit-Shifting Project of the G20 and OECD* (2016), available online at http://www.icrict.org/wp-content/uploads/2015/10/ICRICT_BEPS-Briefing_EN_web-version-1.pdf, at 2.

49. OECD, *Mutual Agreement Procedure Statistics for 2014*, available online at http://www.oecd.org/ctp/dispute/map-statistics-2014.htm (last visited 7 Aug. 2017).

50. Deloitte, *BEPS Action 14: Make Dispute Resolution Mechanisms More Effective* (2015), available online at https://www2.deloitte.com/content/dam/Deloitte/ie/Documents/Tax/Deloitte%20OECD%20BEPS%20Action%2014%20-%20Make%20dispute%20resolution%20mechanisms%20more%20effective%20December%202014.pdf.

51. OECD, *Action 14: Making Dispute Resolution Mechanism More Effective* (Public Discussion Draft, 18 Dec. 2014–16 Jan. 2015), available online at http://www.oecd.org/ctp/dispute/discussion-draft-action-14-make-dispute-resolution-mechanisms-more-effective.pdf.

52. S. Darcy, '"The Elephant in the Room": Corporate Tax Avoidance & Business and Human Rights', 2(1) *Business and Human Rights Journal* (2017), 1.

53. OHCHR, *supra* note 17, at 22.

54. K. Szeniawska, *Why Does a 4 Letter Tax Acronym—CBCR—Matter for Me and My Fellow Zambians?*, 28 June 2016, available online at http://www.actionaid.org/2016/06/why-does-4-letter-tax-acronym-cbcr-matter-me-and-my-fellow-zambians (last visited 27 July 2017).

55. S. Jespersen, R. Bejarano, and C. Poulsen-Hansen, *Corporate Responsibility, Fiscal Policy and Human Rights*, 4 May 2015, available online at http://oxfamibis.org/articles/corporate-responsibility-fiscal-policy-and-human-rights/ (last visited 27 July 2017).

56. Principles for Responsible Investment, *Engagement Guidance on Corporate Tax Responsibility: Why and How to Engage with Your Investee Companies* (2015), available at online https://www.unpri.org/download_report/8531 (last visited 7 Aug. 2017).

57. In the case of Vodafone, there is an impact assessment of its operations in Luxembourg (a commonly known tax haven jurisdiction) and voluntary public country-by-country reporting on taxes paid in all jurisdictions where it operates. Vodafone Group Plc, *Tax and Our Total Contribution to Public Finances 2015–16*, available online at http://www.vodafone.com/content/dam/sustainability/pdfs/vodafone_2016_tax.pdf#page=11 (last visited 7 Aug. 2017).

58. BHP Billiton assesses the tax and nontax reasons why it locates its operations in low-tax jurisdictions such as Singapore (in the case of marketing operations) and Guernsey (in the case of insurance operations). BHP Billiton, *Economic Contribution and Payments to Governments Report 2016* (2017), available online at http://www.bhp.com/media-and-insights/news-releases/2016/09/bhp-billiton-releases-economic-contribution-and-payments-to-governments-report-2016 (last visited 7 Aug. 2017).

59. Thin capitalization rules are not harmonized across countries, which means that such debt shifting and tax abuses related to financial structures remain commonplace. See J. Blouin, H. Huizinga, L. Laeven, and G. Nicodème, *Thin Capitalization Rules and Multinational Firm Capital Structure* (IMF Working Paper WP/14/12, 24 Jan. 2014), available online at https://www.imf.org/en/Publications/WP/Issues/2016/12/31/Thin-Capitalization-Rules-and-Multinational-Firm-Capital-Structure-41275 (last visited 7 Aug. 2017).

60. Human Rights Council, Report of the Special Rapporteur on Extreme Poverty and Human Rights, Ms. Magdalena Sepúlveda Carmona—Corrigendum, UN Doc. A/HRC/26/28/Corr.1, 21 July 2014, at para. 10.

61. Human Rights Council, *supra* note 16, at para. 75.

62. International Bar Association, *supra* note 20, at 2.

63. IMF, *supra* note 3, at 7.

64. ActionAid, *An Extractive Affair: How One Australian Mining Company's Tax Dealings Are Costing the World's Poorest Country Millions* (2015), available online at http://www.actionaid.org/sites/files/actionaid/malawi_tax_report_updated_table_16_june.pdf.

65. Ibid.

66. IMF, *supra* note 3, at 70.

67. T. Lay, *Tullow Sues Heritage—Uganda Pays the Price; Court Papers Published for $300m Oil Trial*, 28 Nov. 2011, available online at http://platformlondon.org/2011/11/28/tullow-sues-heritage-uganda-pays-the-price-court-papers-published-for-300m-oil-trial/ (last visited 12 June 2017).

68. Government Spending Watch, *Spending on Health in Uganda 2013* (2017), available online at http://www.governmentspendingwatch.org/spending-data/data?countries[0]=Uganda&sector[0]=health&exptype=plac&strail=total&units=DollarCurrent&year=2013&uid=0&view=data (last visited 12 June 2017).

69. ActionAid and Tax Justice Network—Africa, *Still Racing Toward The Bottom? Corporate Tax Incentives in East Africa* (2016), available online at http://www.actionaid.org/sites/files/actionaid/corporate_tax_incentives_in_east_africa_to_print.pdf.

70. Ibid.

71. World Bank, *World Development Report: Reshaping Economic Geography* (2009), available online at https://openknowledge.worldbank.org/handle/10986/5991, at 257 (last visited 7 Aug. 2017).

72. Global Witness, *Glencore and the Gatekeeper: How the World's Largest Commodities Trader Made a Friend of Congo's President $67 Million Richer* (2014), available online at https://www.globalwitness.org/documents/17897/glencore_and_the_gatekeeper_may_2014.pdf.

73. Global Witness, *Out of Africa: British Offshore Secrecy and Congo's Missing $1.5 billion* (2016), available online at https://www.globalwitness.org/documents/18357/Out_Of_Africa_final_EN.pdf.

74. K. Donald, and R. Moussié, 'Redistributing Unpaid Care Work—Why Tax Matters for Women's Rights', 109 *IDS Policy Briefing* (2016), at 3.

75. N. Hui, *Gender Implications of Tax Policies* (2013).

76. Christian Aid, *Taxing Men and Women: Why Gender Is Crucial for a Fair Tax System* (2014), available online at http://www.christianaid.org.uk/images/taxing-men-and-women-gender-analysis-report-july-2014.pdf, at 13.

77. C. Capraro, and F. Rhodes, *Why the Panama Papers Are a Feminist Issue*, 7 April 2016, available online at https://www.opendemocracy.net/5050/chiara-capraro-francesca-rhodes/why-panama-papers-are-feminist-issue (last visited 12 June 2017).

78. Human Rights Council, Report Of the Special Rapporteur On Extreme Poverty and Human Rights on his Mission To Chile, UN Doc. A/HRC/32/31/Add.1, 8 Apr. 2016, at para. 50.

79. See, e.g., ILO Convention 98, Right to Organise and Collective Bargaining Convention 1949; ILO Convention 98, Right to Organise and Collective Bargaining Convention, 1949; and ILO Convention 154, Collective Bargaining Convention, 1981.

80. These sources included recommendations by MNEs themselves, business federations and organizations, NGOs, corporate responsibility specialists, investor groups, tax advisers, legal professional bodies, governments, courts, intergovernmental organizations, and multistakeholder initiatives that bring together business, professional associations, and civil society.

81. ActionAid, *Responsible Tax Practices by Companies: A Mapping and Review of Current Proposals* (2015), available online at https://www.actionaid.org.uk/sites/default/files/publications/responsible_tax_practice.pdf.

82. ActionAid, Christian Aid and Oxfam, *supra* note 21, at 10.

83. The term low-tax jurisdiction is used in this chapter to mean a jurisdiction where preferential tax rules (of whatever nature) or secrecy provisions may lead to a substantial reduction in the overall amount of corporation tax paid.

84. ShareAction and Christian Aid, *Taxing Questions: Assessing Risk from Changes to International Tax Rules*, Oct. 2014, available online at http://www.christianaid.org.uk/Images/Tax-report-Taxing-Questions-Investor-Briefing-October2014_tcm15-80576.pdf, at 3.
85. Ibid. at 17.
86. SAB Miller Plc, *Our Approach to Tax 2016,* available online at http://www.ab-inbev.com/content/dam/universaltemplate/ab-inbev/investors/sabmiller/reports/our-approach-to-tax-reports/tax-report-2016.pdf.
87. Scottish Human Rights Council, *Submission to the Scottish Parliament's Call for Evidence on a Scottish Approach to Taxation* (2016), available online at http://www.scottishhumanrights.com/media/1339/shrc-submission-to-finance-committee-sep2016.docx, at 3 (last visited 12 June 2017).
88. Deloitte, *Conceptual Framework for Financial Reporting 2010* (2017), available online at https://www.iasplus.com/en/standards/other/framework (last visited 7 Aug. 2017).
89. Tax Research, *Who Are the Users of Accounts?* (2010), available online at http://www.taxresearch.org.uk/Documents/Accountsusers.pdf.
90. Accounting Standards Steering Committee of the Institute of Chartered Accountants in England and Wales, *The Corporate Report* (1975), available online at http://www.icaew.com/-/media/corporate/files/library/subjects/corporate-governance/corporate-report.ashx?la=en, at 15–27 (last visited 12 June 2017).
91. United Nations Conference on Trade and Development, *Guidance on Corporate Responsibility Indicators in Annual Reports* (2008), available online at http://unctad.org/en/docs/iteteb20076_en.pdf.

CHAPTER 18

ECHR LITIGATION AS A TOOL FOR TAX JUSTICE IN EUROPE

CÉLINE BRAUMANN

I. INTRODUCTION

The central claim of the tax justice movement echoes growing popular discontent with an economic system that seems to be rigged against the poor: the opaque landscape of international taxation was built to benefit elites. This structural bias undermines social welfare, exacerbates inequality, and deprives countries of resources that the less privileged, who cannot afford to dodge taxes, then have to replenish.[1] This understanding has prompted civil society and human rights lawyers to speak out against the injustice of current international tax policy.[2] Yet, there seems to be a lack of clarity about what exactly it is that upsets us about abusive tax practices. After all, many of the tax practices that have prompted public outrage in recent years are considered legal under international tax law; some are in a grey zone because no court or administration has yet ruled on their legality, while others are illegal but hard to detect and prosecute. One framework discussed as a yardstick for the legality of tax practices and consequently as an indicator of their justice or injustice is human rights law. Could human rights help to pin down the specific wrong associated with many tax "optimization" schemes? In other words, is there a human rights case for just taxation?

This chapter offers a tentative answer to this question, to add to the growing literature on the relationship between human rights and taxation. While evaluating these two disciplines together might seem like an artificial liaison, they are inherently connected: taxation is one of states' most crucial tools for fulfilling their human rights obligations.[3] Moreover, just like human rights, tax law is about the bond between individuals and the state.

To illustrate this liaison, this chapter examines a specific case of tax exemption, allegedly granted to a subsidiary of McDonald's by Luxembourg, under a specific provision of human rights law to determine whether the exemption constitutes "tax injustice." In the context of this chapter, tax injustice is narrowly defined as a tax practice or tax law that violates human

Tax, Inequality, and Human Rights. Philip Alston and Nikki Reisch.
© Oxford University Press 2019. Published 2019 by Oxford University Press.

rights law. The evaluation aims to demonstrate that even common practices considered natural consequences of international tax competition are not legal in every form; even if they
comply with international tax law, they could still violate other fields of law, like human
rights law.

The human rights norm against which the Luxembourg tax exemption will be measured is
the prohibition on discrimination in the European Convention on Human Rights (ECHR). The
question animating this chapter is: Does offering a tax exemption to one person but not to another constitute illegal discrimination? This approach might seem curious as the usual remedy
following a finding of discrimination is equal treatment, which in this case would mean the
applicant (complaining party before the European Court of Human Rights) claims a right to
receive the same discriminatory tax treatment (i.e., a tax exemption). The aim of this chapter is
not to promote such a result, as granting *more* tax exemptions would clearly not strengthen the
welfare state or decrease social and economic inequality. However, as will be discussed in more
detail in the final part of this chapter, the more likely reaction of Luxembourg would be to ab-
stain from future discriminatory tax treatment.

The analysis uses a corporate applicant, rather than a natural person. This decision is
entirely pragmatic, as the novel and admittedly contentious argument of this chapter is
more likely to prevail with a corporation.[4] Furthermore, by using a small corporation as
the applicant claiming discriminatory treatment in relation to McDonald's, a multinational
powerhouse, the test case still demonstrates the inequality between common and super-rich
taxpayers. There are people behind every fully taxed enterprise who ultimately shoulder
higher tax burdens than the tax-exempted multinational against which they have to compete. Raising awareness of the potential illegality—as opposed to mere immorality—of certain tax-avoidance schemes might show that a re-evaluation of international tax policy is
required as a matter of law, not just as a matter of charity. Proving this through human
rights litigation is a bottom-up approach through which non-privileged taxpayers could reclaim some ownership over international tax policy. This could shape the dialogue to better
serve the interests of the tax-paying masses, who have traditionally not had a seat at the tax
policy table.

However, one should not overstate the prospect of success of this test case. There are indeed some stumbling blocks the Court could deem too significant to find a human rights
violation. Accordingly, these stumbling blocks receive particular attention and critical evaluation in the discussion below. Although not free of challenges, a case such as the hypothetical
one discussed here could prove fruitful for various reasons, whether or not it results in the
finding of a violation. For the first time, a state would have to justify selective tax rulings at
least to a minimum extent, and disclose certain otherwise secret information. This would
help the public to better understand certain opaque tax practices. The case could also ignite
a dialogue about the human rights implications of international taxation which many consider long overdue. In short, the mere litigation of this case, regardless of its outcome, could
empower civil society by enforcing the role of human rights law as a system of checks and
balances on a state's exercise of power, and as a set of rules that requires the elites and the rest
to be treated as equals.

Section II explains the law and application of the ECHR's nondiscrimination provisions.
Section III describes the facts of the particular case examined in this chapter. Section IV applies
the nondiscrimination provisions to explore whether the assessed tax ruling would result in a
violation of the ECHR. The last section concludes by discussing possible implications of the
findings.

II. THE NONDISCRIMINATION FRAMEWORK
OF THE ECHR

Two provisions in the ECHR system govern the right to nondiscrimination: Article 14 of the Convention itself[5] and Article 1 of Protocol No. 12 to the ECHR (12th Protocol).

While the language of the two provisions is fairly similar, there are two major differences: Article 14 applies as an accessory prohibition—that is, it provides only that the enjoyment of the rights and freedoms set forth in the ECHR may not be applied in a discriminatory manner. Article 1 of the 12th Protocol, on the other hand, is a general prohibition on discrimination: no one may be discriminated against in the enjoyment of any right set forth by any law. Additionally, no discrimination by any public authority in the exercise of discretionary power (for example, granting certain subsidies)[6] may occur under Article 1 of the 12th Protocol. Thus, Article 1 of the 12th Protocol not only prohibits discriminatory denial of rights established by law, but also discrimination through behavior or conduct of the state in the exercise of its discretion.[7]

The second major difference is the number of ratifications. While the ECHR, and with it Article 14, has been ratified by forty-seven European states,[8] including all major European tax havens,[9] the 12th Protocol has only been ratified by nineteen states.[10] Although Luxembourg, the Netherlands, and Ireland are among those nineteen ratifying states, other important tax havens, like Switzerland and the United Kingdom, have not ratified the 12th Protocol. Consequently, the European Court of Human Rights (ECtHR) has only decided a few cases under Article 1 of the 12th Protocol,[11] while there is a plethora of case law regarding Article 14. However, the Court established in its *Sejdić* case on Article 1 of the 12th Protocol that the analysis of this provision is identical to the analysis under Article 14.[12] Accordingly, the following analysis is only based on Article 14, as a case that prevails under Article 14 would probably also prevail under Article 1 of the 12th Protocol.

The first step in the Article 14 analysis is to determine whether the application is admissible under Articles 34 and 35. Article 34 of the ECHR specifies standing before the Court, while Article 35 lays out the admissibility criteria for ECHR applications. The only potentially contentious requirements in this case are the exhaustion of domestic remedies and the classification of the applicant as an identifiable and actual victim of an ECHR violation, which will be discussed in more detail below.

The scope of the Court's jurisdiction is fairly broad: it extends to all citizens and noncitizens within the jurisdiction of an ECHR member state.[13] Even persons (whether individuals or legal entities) not within an ECHR member state's territory, but in a territory under a member state's effective control, can bring claims.[14]

Although the Court has identified rights that apply only to natural persons,[15] corporations can generally bring claims under the ECHR.[16] The right to property under Article 1 of Protocol No. 1 to the ECHR (1st Protocol), the relevant substantive right for this Article 14 analysis, explicitly covers "every natural or legal person."[17] The Court has already applied Article 14 to corporations in combination with the right to property.[18]

After having established admissibility, the applicant must prove the claim on the merits. First, it must be shown that he or she has been treated differentially in comparison to someone else. The ECtHR has established a distinction between direct and indirect discrimination. For direct discrimination, there must be "difference in the treatment of persons in analogous, or relevantly similar, situations" which is "based on an identifiable characteristic."[19] Thus, direct discrimination occurs when persons in similar situations are treated differently based on a protected characteristic, without a legitimate justification. The discrimination occurs on the basis of a protected ground if the comparator would have been treated less favorably as a member of the protected group to which the applicant belongs.[20] The discriminatory rule or practice does not have to refer to the protected ground explicitly; it suffices that the reason for discrimination is inseparable from the protected ground.[21]

The list of protected grounds under the ECHR is nonexhaustive.[22] Both Article 14 ECHR and Article 1 of the 12th Protocol enumerate "sex, race, colour, language, religion, political or other opinion, national or social origin, association with a national minority, property, birth or other status." "Other status" leaves the list open to additional protected grounds. The ECtHR has already made extensive use of the "other status" ground to include classifications not expressly mentioned in Article 14.[23]

Differential treatment on the basis of a protected ground is not a violation of the ECHR if the state can show a legitimate justification. Through this last part of the analysis, the Court leaves the states a margin of appreciation to allow for some degree of cultural, societal, or other differences in domestic law.[24]

The Court applies a system of shared burden of proof in its nondiscrimination cases.[25] The applicable, and often criticized,[26] evidentiary standard established by the Court in its case law is proof beyond a reasonable doubt.[27] However, the Court clarified in *Nachova* that this standard does not derive from domestic law, but follows a

> free evaluation of all evidence [. . .] [P]roof may follow from the coexistence of sufficiently strong, clear and concordant inferences or of similar unrebutted presumptions of fact. Moreover, the level of persuasion necessary [. . .] and [. . .] the distribution of the burden of proof are intrinsically linked to the specificity of the facts, the nature of the allegation made and the Convention right at stake.[28]

As Article 14 is an accessory provision, it is only applicable if the discrimination interferes with the enjoyment of one of the substantive ECHR rights. According to the Court, no actual violation of the substantive right is required to find an Article 14 violation; the discrimination must only be broadly related to the substantive right.[29] In the hypothetical case examined in this chapter, the substantive right affected by the allegedly discriminatory tax treatment is the right to property. Article 1 of the 1st Protocol stipulates that

> [e]very natural or legal person is entitled to the peaceful enjoyment of his possessions. No one shall be deprived of his possessions except in the public interest and subject to the conditions provided for by law and by the general principles of international law.
>
> The preceding provisions shall not, however, in any way impair the right of a State to enforce such laws as it deems necessary to control the use of property in accordance with the general interest or to secure the payment of taxes or other contributions or penalties.

The Court has repeatedly ruled that taxation interferes with the right to property so as to bring it within the scope of an Article 14 claim.[30] States have a wide margin of appreciation in relation to the right to property, which allows them to implement suitable economic and social policies.[31]

III. THE TEST CASE: SELECTIVE TAX RULINGS FOR MULTINATIONAL CORPORATIONS (MNCS)

In October 2015, the EU Commission ruled that selective tax advantages for Fiat in Luxembourg and Starbucks in the Netherlands constitute illegal state aid under EU antitrust law.[32] The EU press release stressed such tax rulings are considered "perfectly legal" under relevant tax laws.[33] This decision is special because tax incentives granted to corporations were scrutinized in a field other than international tax law, where they are commonly held to be lawful, and were found to be illegal. In 2016, the EU Commission made headlines with another decision on illegal state aid: Apple had allegedly cut its tax bill in Ireland by billions since 1991 through tax benefits granted by the government. The Commission ordered the recovery of the €13 billion Apple should have paid in taxes between 2003 and 2014.[34]

EU antitrust law makes it impermissible for EU states to engage in conduct that restricts or distorts competition in the EU single market. Agreements between states and corporations are considered anticompetitive if they give the corporation an unfair competitive advantage.[35] The EU Commission has declared certain tax advantages to be comparable to subsidies.[36]

In December 2015, the EU Commission revealed that it had started investigating tax rulings Luxembourg had allegedly granted to a subsidiary of McDonald's.[37] These rulings allowed McDonald's to effectively pay no corporate tax on its profits from royalties paid to it by European, Ukrainian and Russian franchises since 2009, either in Luxembourg or in the United States.[38] In December 2016, McDonald's announced its plans to move its non-US tax base from Luxembourg to the United Kingdom.[39] While McDonald's claims this decision is neither related to Brexit nor the EU Commission's investigations, it is noteworthy that the United Kingdom is considered a major tax haven.[40]

This analysis uses McDonald's tax exemption in Luxembourg as the test case. In the context of this paper, "McDonald's" refers to the subsidiary called McDonald's Europe Franchising SARL,[41] incorporated in Luxembourg. "McDonald's MNC" will refer to the controlling parent company McDonald's Corporation, incorporated in the United States. Until 2014, tax rulings in Luxembourg were based on an internal unpublished note issued in 1989.[42] This practice has changed post-LuxLeaks, which revealed detailed information about many of Luxembourg's secret and selective tax deals[43] and the EU Commission's related investigations. Since January 1, 2015, every taxpayer has the right to request an advance tax ruling by the authorities through Article 29a of the Luxembourgian *Abgabenordnung*, which formalized the tax-ruling procedure.[44] These tax rulings are an official confirmation of the future tax burden. They are not supposed to create an individualized, selective tax exemption or reduction;[45] they simply state what the applicant will have to pay under Luxembourgian tax law. This procedure is subject to a fee, which ranges between €3,000 and €10,000. It is not possible to appeal these tax rulings.[46]

The EU Commission's 2015 press release states the Commission's preliminary view "that a tax ruling granted by Luxembourg may have granted McDonald's an advantageous tax treatment in breach of EU State aid rules."[47] Luxembourg allegedly derogated from the provisions of national law and its double taxation agreement (DTA) with the United States, thereby giving McDonald's tax advantages not available to other companies in comparable factual and legal situations. McDonald's Europe Franchising SARL is headquartered in Luxembourg, where it allegedly employs thirteen people.[48] Under two Luxembourgian tax rulings from 2009, the corporation has not paid any corporate tax in Luxembourg, despite its large profits, which allegedly amount to more than €250 million in 2013 alone.[49] The first tax ruling from March 2009 provided that McDonald's did not owe any corporate tax in Luxembourg because the profits were taxed in the United States.[50] This ruling required McDonald's to submit proof every year that the royalties that were transferred to the US branch of McDonald's Europe Franchising were declared and subject to US taxation. Yet, McDonald's Europe Franchising did not have a taxable presence in the United States, as the corporation was not a permanent establishment under US law for the lack of sufficient business or trade undertaken in the United States. When McDonald's declared that it could not submit any proof of its taxation in the United States to the Luxembourgian authorities, it requested a second tax ruling. This second tax ruling exempted the company from providing evidence of its taxation in the United States, thereby effectively exempting the corporation from paying any corporate tax.[51]

While the proposed hypothetical case could have a similar outcome based on the Netherlands' or Ireland's conduct, Luxembourg seems more suitable for this litigation. First, Luxembourg is renowned for its tax rulings. In the Tax Justice Network's (TJN) 2015 Financial Secrecy Index, Luxembourg was ranked sixth.[52] Luxembourg has also suffered a major leak, the "LuxLeaks," in 2014, which revealed detailed information about many of Luxembourg's secret and selective tax deals.[53] Therefore, there is a relatively large amount of evidence of Luxembourg's practices, which might facilitate satisfying the burden of proof. Second, Luxembourg has ratified the 12th Protocol. While this chapter argues that selective tax incentives are illegal under both Article 14 ECHR and Article 1 of the 12th Protocol, the latter provision makes the argument more straightforward, as it is not accessory to a Convention right.

One may ask what McDonald's move to the United Kingdom means for this test case. This chapter was drafted before McDonald's announcement, and it is impossible to predict what the corporation's taxation will look like in the United Kingdom. However, the multinational giant only serves as a comparator in this case. The data about McDonald's tax exemption is required to prove differential treatment between the applicant, classifiable by a protected ground, and corporations like McDonald's, lacking this protected ground. McDonald's is not a party to the litigation, its presence is not required for the case's success. Furthermore, as of now, the United Kingdom remains a member state of the ECHR. Thus, a case under Article 14 could in theory be brought should the United Kingdom single out McDonald's for selective tax rulings.

IV. APPLICATION—DISCRIMINATION THROUGH TAX INCENTIVES

This part applies the framework of Article 14 to the differential treatment another Luxembourgian corporation faces in comparison to McDonald's. Notably, this analysis applies a reverse approach when creating a case hypothesis about nondiscrimination. That is, the starting point is not a particular person who feels discriminated against by the state and requires a comparator to prove illegal differential treatment; the starting point is a person (in this case, a legal person, McDonald's) who receives preferential treatment by the state, which constitutes discrimination against other unidentified persons.

Various entities could invoke Article 14 and petition the ECtHR on the grounds that McDonald's tax treatment is discriminatory, in that it denies them equal enjoyment of the right to property. As discussed in section II, both natural and legal persons can bring claims to the ECtHR.[54] The strongest claim would come from corporate taxpayers incorporated and with a source of income in Luxembourg that cannot benefit from the same tax ruling as McDonald's.

The following analysis calls the applicant corporation "X." X is a limited liability corporation, incorporated in Luxembourg and founded under Luxembourgian corporate law. X earns most of its profits from royalties paid by franchises. Most of the franchises are located in Luxembourg, but X expanded its operations to other states three years ago. The profits are taxed according to the Luxembourgian corporate tax rate.

As stated above, Article 14 is an accessory provision. Thus, it can only be invoked in relation to an interference with another Convention right. This prerequisite would be fulfilled in the hypothetical case: there is ample case law showing that the Court considers tax matters to fall under the right to property.[55] In *Burden*, the Court held that "taxation is in principle an interference with the right guaranteed by the first paragraph of Article 1 of Protocol No. 1, since it deprives the person concerned of a possession, namely the amount of money which must be paid."[56] Article 1 of the 1st Protocol even mentions taxes explicitly in its second paragraph, where it clarifies that the right to property shall not limit states in their power to "enforce such laws as it deems necessary [. . .] to secure the payment of taxes." As the Court explicitly stated in *Darby*, this second paragraph "establishes that the duty to pay tax falls within [Article 1's] field of application."[57] Article 14 does not require an actual violation of the substantive right to be applicable, an interference with the right in a broad sense is sufficient. While taxation in itself does usually not violate Article 1 of the 1st Protocol, "the issue is nonetheless within the Court's control [under Article 14], since the correct application of Article 1 of Protocol No. 1 is subject to its supervision."[58] Consequently, an interference with the comparator's equal enjoyment of the right to property occurred in the test case, which renders Article 14 applicable.

A. ADMISSIBILITY

According to Article 34, a case is admissible if the applicant has been "directly affected" by a Convention violation.[59] Fulfilling this requirement is unproblematic. X is directly affected by the differential treatment because McDonald's pays no corporate tax at all, while X must pay its full tax burden. Thus, the treatment has a direct financial effect on X.

Under Article 35, the Court can only exercise jurisdiction over a case after the exhaustion of all feasible, domestic remedies. There are two possible ways in which X could satisfy Article 35. X could either request an advance tax ruling under Article 29a of the *Abgabenordnung*, which would require X to pay a fee of €3,000 to €10,000 for an outcome that is relatively certain—the Luxembourgian authorities would probably apply the same tax rules and arrive at the same outcome as in previous years when determining X's tax burden. If the ruling does not grant the same advantages to X as Luxembourg granted McDonald's—effectively an exemption from any corporate tax—the corporation would certainly be "directly affected" in that it was discriminated against. Moreover, X would have exhausted all feasible domestic remedies under Luxembourgian law, as advance tax rulings under Article 29a are not subject to appeal.[60]

The second approach is more straightforward, faster, and less costly. The Court has carved out a number of exceptions to the exhaustion of domestic remedies requirement. As the Court put it, the exhaustion requirement should be applied with "some degree of flexibility and without excessive formalism."[61] To qualify as remedy, the domestic remedy must be "available and effective."[62] The decree that provides more detail on the Luxembourgian advance tax ruling procedure, dated December 24, 2014, is only one page long and fairly bare bones.[63] With the information that is publicly available, it is questionable whether the procedure would fall under the definition of a domestic remedy. The advance tax ruling procedure could not address the issue in a way that offers the desired relief, namely, a tax exemption. After all, an advance tax ruling only gives notice of the future tax burden according to the tax code. X has no right to a tax exemption under Luxembourgian law, as the authorities award them on a purely discretionary basis. The EU Commission's finding that McDonald's tax rulings did not violate the applicable tax laws (see footnote 37) does not change that X cannot attain the same effect, namely tax exemption, through a domestic remedy.

Yet, an advance tax ruling could theoretically render X exempt from paying tax if the authorities granted it. The Court has held that the domestic remedy must have a reasonable prospect of success to be considered effective.[64] The existence of such effective remedies "must be sufficiently certain not only in theory but also in practice."[65] The burden of proof of the effectiveness of a domestic remedy falls to the state pleading nonexhaustion.[66] Whether Luxembourg would be able to prove that X would have had a reasonable prospect of success in applying for an Article 29a ruling is questionable, also because Article 29a only offers a nonjudicial remedy, which makes its outcome even more uncertain and opaque. As Article 29a is not intended to result in a tax exemption, it is unlikely that Luxembourg could prove effectiveness. Finally, the Court has held domestic remedies ineffective if they do not have a precise time limit for the decision and thereby create uncertainty.[67] Article 29a and the 2014 decree do not stipulate a time limit for a tax ruling.

Article 35 does not require the applicant to make use of every single potentially effective remedy. Thus, resorting to one of them is sufficient if other remedies exist but have essentially the same purpose.[68] This chapter cannot offer a full analysis of the test case's litigation at the domestic level. Nevertheless, it must be noted that other local remedies might exist. For example, X could file an appeal, not against the Article 29a ruling but against the tax liability assessment, at the administrative division of Luxembourg's legal system.[69] An appeal of the administrative division's final decision to the Constitutional Court of Luxembourg would also be possible. However, the Constitutional Court is only competent for questions on the compatibility of laws with the Constitution of Luxembourg, which provides for the principle of equality for Luxembourgian nationals, including in tax matters.[70] As X does not claim that the tax code is unconstitutional, but that the tax officials have applied their discretion in a discriminatory manner, a constitutional appeal would not be an effective domestic remedy under the ECHR.[71]

Especially in light of the EU Commission's recent finding that the McDonald's tax rulings were not illegal per se (see footnote 37), it is advisable for X to go through the procedure of Article 29a or to contest its tax liability assessment. This would not only secure X's standing but could also produce evidence for the following steps of the analysis.

B. THE DIFFERENTIAL TREATMENT

As mentioned in section II, direct discrimination under Article 14 occurs when persons in relevantly similar situations do not receive similar treatment.[72] The applicant carries the burden of proof for this element and must establish a prima facie case of discrimination.[73]

In the case at hand, the legal person in a relevantly similar situation as X is McDonald's. As an insufficiently similar situation often leads the Court to conclude that the differential treatment was justified in a single analytical step,[74] this part of the analysis is crucial. Both McDonald's and X have profits that would be equally taxable. In the test case, practically any corporation with a full corporate tax burden in Luxembourg could theoretically be used as X. However, the aim is to find a corporation as similar as possible to McDonald's. Thus, the profits should derive from the same kind of economic activity. The ECtHR has already accepted comparators as relevantly similar if they fall under the same tax regime but receive differential treatment under that regime.[75] McDonald's falling under the Luxembourg-US Double Taxation Treaty (DTT) does not change that X is factually in a relevantly similar situation.

In *National & Provincial Building Society*,[76] the Court held that the compared corporations were not sufficiently similar because only the comparator, who had allegedly received preferential treatment, had engaged in litigation and had thereby secured the victories that led to the differential treatment. The applicant had forgone the benefits by failing to litigate. In light of this decision the success of the test case might depend on X's actual efforts to obtain a tax ruling like McDonald's.

McDonald's and X are the same kind of taxpayer under the same tax regime. Only the Luxembourgian interpretation of the Luxembourg-US DTT alters McDonald's tax treatment. The Luxembourgian tax code itself would treat them the same and would require both to pay the same tax rate. Thus, McDonald's and X are factually in relevantly similar situations and should therefore be treated the same legally as well.

The second element of this part of the analysis is also fulfilled: Luxembourg's selective tax incentives for only some companies constitute differential treatment. Some corporations must pay the full amount of taxes as stipulated by the tax codes, while other corporations are taxed significantly less due to selective tax rulings. The Court has declared this kind of treatment differential in its jurisprudence on tax matters.[77] Evidence to establish the presumption of differential treatment is easily accessible by comparing the findings of the EU Commission's McDonald's case and the amount of corporate taxes paid by X.

Because the similarity of X's and McDonald's situations is acknowledged by Luxembourgian law itself and because the differential treatment is relatively easy to prove, this phase of the test case should be unproblematic.

C. THE PROTECTED GROUNDS

The applicant carries the burden of proof to show prima facie discrimination in this part of the analysis.[78] If X succeeds in showing that differential treatment on the basis of a protected ground has occurred, the Court will review the rest of the case under the presumption of direct discrimination. The contentious question of this subsection is whether a protected ground covers X and whether the discriminatory treatment was based on this ground.

What is the real difference between McDonald's and X which led Luxembourg to offer a tax exemption to the one but not the other? The Court does not always distinguish neatly between the protected grounds in its assessments.[79] However, the classification can be relevant, as the case law indicates that categories of protected grounds enjoy varying degrees of protection.[80] With some grounds, differential treatment seems to be unacceptable as a matter of principle.[81] Other grounds, such as nationality, only allow differential treatment if the state can explain it with "very weighty reasons."[82] The protected ground of property does not require a heightened burden to justify differential treatment; it even entails a wide margin of appreciation.[83]

A real-life difference between corporations like McDonald's Europe Franchising and X is the former's connection to a multinational corporation (its global parent McDonald's MNC) and the difference in size and wealth that comes with this. McDonald's Europe Franchising is a subsidiary of the world's largest chain of fast food restaurants with accordingly massive profits and power. McDonald's MNC's status as an immensely rich and internationally successful MNC is one of the few things it has in common with other recipients of tax incentives, like Fiat, Starbucks, or Apple. While McDonald's Europe Franchising itself might not be as wealthy and powerful as its parent, it would be artificial to ignore the subsidiary's connection to the MNC as a major difference between the comparator and X. Evidence for this factual difference is easily accessible, as the connection between the parent and McDonald's Europe Franchising is publicly known.

While X does not have to prove any intent to discriminate on this basis,[84] it still has to establish a causal link between the protected ground and the differential treatment. As there is no law that provides that only corporations of a particular size may receive tax exemptions, demonstrating this causal link might be difficult. The best proof X could find is a record of tax exemptions granted in the past that clearly shows what kind of corporations have received preferential treatment. "[S]ufficiently strong, clear and concordant inferences or [. . .] similar unrebutted presumptions of fact" can satisfy the burden of proof.[85] Public information from leaks or the EU Commission's investigations could be the basis for such strong inferences. Furthermore, the Court has previously accepted statistical data as proof for the causal link between a protected ground and differential treatment.[86] If statistics show a practice is disproportionately unfavorable to a specific group, the presumption of discrimination is established.[87] Even without statistical data the ECtHR has already accepted proof of disproportionate effects of state behavior on a particular group. In *Opuz*,[88] the Court relied on assessments of Amnesty International, a national nongovernmental organization (NGO) and the UN Committee on the Elimination of Discrimination Against Women to come to the conclusion that women are victims of domestic violence more often than men.[89] There is no clear guidance in the Court's case law that allows predicting the type and amount of evidence required in the present case. In light of past decisions, assessments of the TJN in its Financial Secrecy Index or other data that shows the pattern of Luxembourg's practice of granting tax incentives could suffice to meet the burden of proof.

To succeed in this claim, the Court also has to accept that a corporation's connection or lack of connection to an MNC like McDonald's parent company falls under a protected ground. The relevant category of protected grounds could either be property or other status. Moreover, if Luxembourg contended that McDonald's received the tax exemption due to falling under the Luxembourg-US DTT, X could build its case on the protected ground of nationality. This would require the state to prove "very weighty reasons" for the differentiation in the justification phase. The Court's most relevant case of discrimination on the basis of property is *Chassagnou*.[90] In *Chassagnou*, the Court found a violation of Article 14 in combination with Article 1 of the 1st Protocol because a French law only forced small landowners to tolerate hunting on their property, while allowing large landowners to forbid it.[91] It could be argued that the differential treatment between McDonald's and X is likewise based on differences in property. In this case, the decisive difference in property comprises a number of elements: the fact that McDonald's Europe Franchising is owned by an MNC; the fact that this MNC is more flexible regarding the location of the subsidiary, which also gives the MNC more leverage in negotiations with Luxembourg; and the fact that the MNC is one of the wealthiest in the world, which explains Luxembourg's great interest in having the subsidiary's headquarters in Luxembourg. As the Court indicated in *Chassagnou*, it does not accept differential treatment because of proprietary differences unless the state shows a legitimate justification.[92]

The distinctions in wealth, size, and MNC-affiliation could also demonstrate differentiation based on "other grounds." In an effort to define what "other status" entails, the Court held that the difference in treatment must be based on "a personal characteristic ('status') by which persons or groups of persons are distinguishable from each other."[93] However, the Court has not applied this definition consistently, and it remains unclear what can and cannot fall under "other status."[94]

Lithgow helps to predict whether the Court would consider X to fall under a protected ground, be it property or other status.[95] In *Lithgow*, the Court scrutinized an alleged violation of Article 14 in combination with Article 1 of the 1st Protocol. The importance of *Lithgow* for X's case lies in the protected ground that the Court accepted for its analysis of some of the applicants: the nature of the corporations as either growing or declining companies.[96] This indicates that the Court is open to looking at differences in size and profitability of corporations as a protected ground. Moreover, the Court has already found the different legal status of corporations[97] or a differentiation between small and large unions[98] to be protected grounds. Thus the size and/or economic strength of a corporation might qualify as an impermissible basis on which to treat it differently from otherwise similar corporations.

Concluding this subsection, it is evident that the protected ground is a potential vulnerability of the test case. X could easily show that it is not owned by a MNC, let alone by one of McDonald's MNC's caliber and that it is also clearly not as wealthy or powerful as McDonald's MNC. However, it remains unclear whether the Court would accept this ground as a protected ground under Article 14. Furthermore, it is hard to predict whether X would be able to establish the causal link between this ground and the differential treatment. Nevertheless, nothing in the Court's case law suggests that X does not have a chance of success with its claim.

D. JUSTIFICATION FOR DIFFERENTIAL TREATMENT

The last part of the discrimination analysis is the most contentious and the least predictable. While the identification of a protected ground already gives rise to significant difficulties, the potential justification for the differential treatment is the Achilles' heel of the argument.

Assuming that the Court agrees with X in the preceding steps of the evaluation, Luxembourg can prevent the finding of discrimination under Article 14 or Article 1 of the 12th Protocol if it shows an adequate justification for the differential treatment. "[A] difference in the treatment of persons in relevantly similar situations [. . .] is discriminatory if it has no objective and reasonable justification; in other words, if it does not pursue a legitimate aim or if there is no reasonable relationship of proportionality between the means employed and the aim sought to be realized."[99] In this part of the analysis, Luxembourg carries the burden of proof,[100] which is a significant advantage for X.

The Court's approach to the proportionality principle under Article 14 is highly casuistic. In *Belgian Linguistics*, the Court required "a fair balance between the protection of the interests of the community and respect for the rights and freedoms safeguarded by the Convention."[101] This definition of a justification must be analyzed with due regard to the margin of appreciation granted to states under the Court's jurisprudence. The margin's main purpose is to grant sovereign states sufficient leeway to take national and local specificities and preferences into consideration while implementing the ECHR. According to Article 14 case law, "the scope of this margin will vary according to the circumstances, the subject-matter and its background."[102]

The Court has continuously granted a wide margin of appreciation in cases under Article 1 of the 1st Protocol for "general measures of economic and social strategies."[103] More specifically, the case law suggests that the margin of appreciation allows differential treatment concerning welfare or pensions unless it is "manifestly without reasonable foundation."[104] It must be noted that social welfare and pensions cannot be equated with tax exemptions. In relation to welfare payments and pensions, applicants claim that their income was not *increased* (through receipt of a state payment) by as much as would be required. In relation to tax exemptions, applicants claim their income was *diminished* (through payment of a tax to the state) by a greater amount than permissible. In the first case, which allows differentiation unless manifestly without reasonable foundation, applicants receive money from the welfare state. In the second case, applicants lose money they have worked for in order to fund that welfare state. Whether or not tax exemptions permit the same margin of appreciation as social welfare and pensions, Luxembourg must still prove the "fair balance" between the general interest and individual property rights.[105] Thus, the state has to show an objective and reasonable justification for differential treatment, "even taking into account the margin of appreciation" concerning economic and social policies.[106] The Court assesses the justification phase of cases involving the wide margin of appreciation for property rights in great detail.[107] A wide margin of appreciation does not absolve the state from proving justification.

Moreover, the justification needed to levy taxes is not necessarily the same justification needed to treat differentially when levying taxes. In *Darby*,[108] the Court did not mention a wider margin of appreciation, even though the case was about differential treatment under Sweden's tax code. The Court found a violation of Article 14 in combination with Article 1 of the 1st Protocol because Sweden had not shown a legitimate aim to justify that the nonresident Darby could not receive the same tax exemption as Swedish residents.[109]

In *Hentrich*, the Court held that preventing tax evasion may be a legitimate aim to justify interferences with Article 1 of the 1st Protocol by automatically suspecting certain types of transactions to constitute tax evasion.[110] Yet, the Court came to the conclusion that France had not struck the proper balance between the state's interest in curbing tax evasion and the individual's property rights; the means were declared disproportionate because of their lack of protection against arbitrariness in the relevant proceedings.[111] This goes to show that a state's margin of appreciation is in any case not wide enough to allow arbitrariness.[112]

There are a number of issues Luxembourg will face when trying to prove a justification. First, Luxembourg has to show that having McDonald's as a resident in Luxembourg actually serves a legitimate aim; i.e., that it has an overall positive effect on the state's economy and welfare. McDonald's allegedly employs only thirteen people in Luxembourg and derives its profits from royalties paid by franchises in other countries. McDonald's Europe Franchising does not operate factories in Luxembourg, nor does it produce anything else. Thus, Luxembourg might struggle to claim positive effects of McDonald's incorporation in the country. To be in the general interest, whatever additional investment or positive effects Luxembourg proffers must be weighed against the amount of taxes lost due to the exemption. The EU Commission stated during its investigation that McDonald's Europe Franchising received profits of €250 million in 2013 alone. This leads to the question whether the positive effects of McDonald's presence can in fact outweigh the loss in tax revenues since 2009. Luxembourg would need to prove all of this to show it pursued a legitimate aim.

Furthermore, Luxembourg has to show that the means employed to achieve this aim are proportionate and necessary. Thus, another difficulty could be the necessity of the tax exemption: would McDonald's not have established a subsidiary in Luxembourg without the tax ruling? There could be many other reasons for McDonald's decision to choose Luxembourg for its operations. And if a full exemption was necessary, was it also proportionate? In other words, was the differential treatment proportionate considering the lost revenues and potential anticompetitive effects if weighed against the exemption's intended positive effects? Was there enough protection from arbitrariness in the means employed when granting preferential tax rulings, as the Court required in *Hentrich*? And as the Court has already held that the prevention of tax evasion could be a legitimate state aim in interfering with property rights, should a means that looks a lot like the facilitation of tax avoidance be considered proportionate? Moreover, as the Court requires a "fair balance between the protection of the interests of the community and respect for the rights and freedoms safeguarded by the Convention,"[113] what are the interests of the community in this case? Are potential additional revenues due to investments, but a definite loss in revenues due to tax exemptions in the general interest, in light of the fact that granting exemptions is discretionary and not democratically legitimized through a law passed by the legislator? Is it in the interest of the community that only the rich get to avoid paying their taxes, which might foster anger of the masses against the elites?

To rebut the presumption of discrimination, Luxembourg would have to answer these questions. A more in-depth analysis of the potential justification of the differential treatment is futile for the purpose of this chapter, as the Court's case-by-case analysis makes a more conclusive answer speculative. At this point, it suffices to say that one could reasonably doubt that a legitimate justification for the differential treatment at hand exists.

V. CONCLUSION

The preceding analysis aimed to delineate the connection between taxation and human rights law on the basis of a concrete example. Should the Court hold that certain selective tax rulings are a violation of the prohibition of discrimination under the ECHR, this finding would set a powerful precedent to rebut the claim that tax avoidance is "perfectly legal." Accordingly, the hands-off treatment the international community has afforded tax-avoidance strategies might give rise to legal liability. Winning—or even losing—an ECHR case like the one presented would force states to assess and justify practices that have historically gone unnoticed and unaccounted for. A corresponding judgment might also incentivize states to re-evaluate whom their tax policies should ultimately serve—foreign MNCs or the national community.

To reform international tax policies, it is crucial to understand past practices and whether and why these practices should be considered broken and unjust. Through strategic litigation, civil society could finally obtain something it has not had for too long—a seat at the table with the architects of international taxation. This would increase civil society's role as a new lobby to counterweigh the traditional stakeholders in international tax, namely, states and corporations.

The test case chosen for this analysis entails a number of oddities. First, the applicant is a corporation—the very type of entity that allegedly already has a disproportionate and unjustified influence on international tax policy. Yet, as this analysis tries to demonstrate, there are inherent differences between certain corporations. Unfair tax practices can harm smaller corporations, and the individuals who own and operate them, in the same way as they harm individuals outside the corporate sphere. The underlying injustice is based on wealth, not on the taxpayer's status as natural or legal person. Accordingly, the interests of individuals and corporations can in fact align.

Second, what the applicant is trying to enforce is a right to the same treatment as the subsidiary of a powerful MNC. Consequently, the requested remedy is a tax exemption. This, of course, is not the aim of this hypothetical strategic litigation; the actual goal is to deter Luxembourg from granting tax exemptions in the first place. If X actually succeeded with its claim, Luxembourg would have two options to implement the Court's decision and prevent similar lawsuits. It could either grant tax exemptions to all corporate taxpayers or it could not grant any tax exemptions at all. Whatever Luxembourg's choice, all corporate taxpayers would have to be treated equally to be in line with the ECHR. Exempting all corporations from a corporate tax would probably be unaffordable for Luxembourg. Even more importantly, it would be unfair to all other types of income taxpayers. Consequently, it is more probable that Luxembourg would choose to not grant any corporate tax exemptions anymore and thereby bring about the desired effect of the proposed litigation.

McDonald's move to the United Kingdom after the Brexit referendum, which will render the United Kingdom outside the reach of the EU Commission, illustrates the problematic dynamics of current international tax policy. Critics of the tax justice movement often stress that MNCs can just move to another tax haven as soon as their last one has closed shop. However, why should potential double standards of states that are claiming to operate under a maxim of solidarity and equality remain unchallenged?

A perfect scenario would look somewhat like this: after *X v. Luxembourg*, the other ECHR member states re-evaluate their practices to prevent similar litigation. As some notorious tax havens have ratified the ECHR—e.g., Switzerland, the United Kingdom, the Netherlands, Ireland—this could have a significant impact on international tax competition. The European countries would probably not want to accept this disadvantage when competing with non-European countries. Consequently, European countries might want to employ some leverage to make other countries follow their lead in the direction of fairer tax policies.

Of course, perfect scenarios are inherently unlikely. Nevertheless, holding states accountable for their ECHR obligations is not a pipe dream, even if the result may seem impossible considering the current realities of international tax policy. The human rights case for tax justice might have its roots in a principle that is not that novel or unorthodox after all: the principle of equality. It is an existing means for rights holders to reclaim control over government policymaking and a means for the taxpaying majority to insist on their equality with the privileged minority. The proposed litigation could generate an ECtHR-approved label that classifies some tax-avoidance schemes as human rights violations. Suddenly, it would be a little more contentious to claim that state-approved tax exemptions are "perfectly legal." At the very least, it would be another nudge in the direction of greater tax justice.

NOTES

1. N. Shaxson, *Treasure Islands: Tax Havens and the Men Who Stole the World* (2012).
2. NYU Center for Human Rights and Global Justice, *CEDAW Calls Switzerland to Account for Effects of its Tax Policies on Women's Rights*, 28 Nov. 2016, available online at http://chrgj.org/cedaw-calls-switzerland-to-account-for-effects-of-its-tax-policies-on-womens-rights/ (last visited 13 July 2017); Open Society Foundations, *The Message of the Panama Papers*, 6 Apr. 2016, available online at https://www.opensocietyfoundations.org/voices/message-panama-papers (last visited 13 July 2017).
3. Center for Economic and Social Rights, *Human Rights in Tax Policy*, available online at http://www.cesr.org/human-rights-taxation (last visited 13 July 2017).
4. As McDonald's is a corporation, the applicant should also be a corporation to avoid Luxembourg from prevailing by justifying the differential treatment with differences between corporate and natural person taxpayers.
5. Council of Europe, European Convention for the Protection of Human Rights and Fundamental Freedoms 1950, ETS 5.
6. Council of Europe, Explanatory Report to the Protocol No. 12 to the Convention for the Protection of Human Rights and Fundamental Freedoms, European Treaty Series No. 177 (2000), at para. 22(iii).
7. Ibid. at para. 22.
8. Council of Europe, *Simplified Chart of Signatures and Ratifications* (status as of 15 Feb. 2017), available online at http://www.coe.int/en/web/conventions/search-on-treaties/-/conventions/chartSignature/3 (last visited 15 Feb. 2017).

9. Tax Justice Network, *Financial Secrecy Index*, 2 Nov. 2015, available online at http://www. financialsecrecyindex.com (last visited 13 July 2017).

10. Council of Europe, *supra* note 8.

11. All cases in this chapter refer to judgments of the ECtHR unless stated otherwise. See *Sejdić and Finci v. Bosnia and Herzegovina*, Appl. nos. 27996/06 and 34836/06, Judgment of 22 Dec. 2009; *Savez Crkava 'Rijec Zivota' and Others v. Croatia*, Appl. no. 7798/08, Judgment of 9 Dec. 2010; *Zornić v. Bosnia and Herzegovina*, Appl. no. 3681/06, Judgment of 15 July 2014; *Pilav v. Bosnia and Herzegovina*, Appl. no. 41939/07, Judgment of 9 June 2016; *Ramaer and Van Willigen v. the Netherlands*, Appl. no. 34880/12, Judgment of 23 Oct. 2012. All ECtHR decisions are available on-line at http://hudoc.echr.coe.int/.

12. *Sejdic, supra* note 11, at para. 55.

13. Art. 1 ECHR.

14. *Loizidou v. Turkey*, Appl. no. 15318/89, Judgment of 18 Dec. 1996.

15. W. H. Van den Muijsenbergh and S. Rezai, 'Corporations and the European Convention on Human Rights', 25 *Pacific McGeorge Global Business & Development Law Journal* (2012), 43, at 50–51.

16. See Art. 34 ECHR; A. Dignam, 'Companies and the Human Rights Act 1998', 26 *The Comparative Law Yearbook of International Business* (2004) 473, 487.

17. Art. 1 Prot. No. 1 ECHR (emphasis added); see also M. Addo, 'The Corporation as a Victim of Human Rights Violations', *in* M. Addo (ed.), *Human Rights Standards and the Responsibility of Transnational Corporations* (1999), 187, 192–195.

18. See, e.g., *Lithgow and Others v. United Kingdom*, Appl. nos. 9006/80, 9262/81, 9263/81, 9265/81, 9266/81, 9313/81, 9405/81, Judgment of 8 July 1986.

19. *Carson and Others v. United Kingdom*, Appl. no. 42184/05, Judgment of 16 Mar. 2010, at para. 61; *D.H. and Others v. Czech Republic*, Appl. no. 57325/00, Judgment of 13 Nov. 2007, at para. 175; *Burden v. United Kingdom*, Appl. no. 13378/05, Judgment of 29 Apr. 2008, at para. 60.

20. EU Agency for Fundamental Rights, *Handbook on European Non-Discrimination Law* (2010), at 26.

21. *Aziz v. Cyprus*, Appl. no. 69949/01, Judgment of 22 June 2004.

22. *Engel and Others v. Netherlands*, Appl. nos. 5101/71, 5354/72, 5102/71, 5370/72, 5100/71, Judgment of 8 June 1976, at para. 72.

23. Marital status in *Petrov v. Bulgaria*, Appl. no. 15197/02, Judgment of 22 May 2008; membership of an organization (e.g., a trade union) in *Danilenkov and Others v. Russia*, Appl. no. 67336/01, Judgment of 30 July 2009; parenthood of a child born out of wedlock in *Sommerfeld v. Germany*, Appl. no. 31871/96, Judgment of 8 July 2003; place of residence in *Carson, supra* note 19.

24. See, e.g., *Burden, supra* note 19, at para. 60, where the Court explains its interpretation of a legitimate justification.

25. O. M. Arnardóttir, 'Non-discrimination Under Article 14 ECHR: The Certain Aspects of the Laws of Proof', 51 *Scandinavian Studies in Law* (2007), 13, at 20.

26. Ibid. at 37–39.

27. Ibid. at 18.

28. *Nachova and Others v. Bulgaria*, Appl. nos. 43577/98, 43579/98, Judgment of 6 July 2005, at para. 147.

29. Case *"Relating to certain aspects of the laws on the use of languages in education in Belgium" v. Belgium*, Appl. nos. 1474/62, 1677/62, 1691/62, 1769/63, 1994/63, 2126/64, Judgment of 23 July 1968, at para. I.B.8-9 [hereinafter *Belgian Linguistics*].

30. Most recently, *Guberina v. Croatia*, Appl. no. 23682/13, Judgment of 22 Mar. 2016; *Arnaud and Others v. France*, Appl. nos. 36918/11, 36963/11, 36967/11, Judgment of 15 Jan. 2015; *Darby v. Sweden*, Appl. no. 11581/85, Judgment of 23 Oct. 1990.

31. *James v. United Kingdom*, Appl. no. 8793/79, Judgment of 21 Feb. 1986, at para. 46.

32. Press Release, European Commission, Commission Decides Selective Tax Advantages for Fiat in Luxembourg and Starbucks in The Netherlands are Illegal Under EU State Aid Rules, 21 Oct. 2015, available online at http://europa.eu/rapid/press-release_IP-15-5880_en.htm (last visited 13 July 2017).

33. Ibid.

34. Press Release, European Commission, State Aid: Ireland Gave Illegal Tax Benefits to Apple Worth up to €13 Billion, 30 Aug. 2016, available online at http://europa.eu/rapid/press-release_IP-16-2923_en.htm (last visited 13 July 2017); the decision is currently under appeal.

35. For an introduction to the basic principles of EU antitrust law, see EU Commission, *State Aid Control*, 21 Nov. 2014, available online at http://ec.europa.eu/competition/state_aid/overview/index_en.html (last visited 9 Aug. 2017).

36. See, e.g., Press Release, European Commission, State Aid: Commission Concludes Belgian "Excess Profit" Tax Scheme Illegal; Around €700 Million to be Recovered from 35 Multinational Companies, 11 Jan. 2016, available online at http://europa.eu/rapid/press-release_IP-16-42_en.htm (last visited 9 Aug. 2017): "It gives multinationals who were able to obtain such a tax ruling a preferential, selective subsidy compared with other companies."

37. However, on 19 September 2018, after the final draft of this chapter, the EU Commission declared in a press release that it had not found illegal state aid in its investigation of McDonald's, as the tax rulings did neither violate Luxembourg's tax law nor the applicable Luxembourg-US Double Taxation Treaty. Lacking a misapplication of the relevant tax law through a misinterpretation by Luxembourg, there was no case of illegal state aid. As this chapter merely uses the facts established by the EU Commission's investigation, which remain unchanged even after the 2018 press release, and scrutinizes them under human rights law, as opposed to EU competition law, this new development does not change the premise of the following analysis. See Press Release, European Commission, State aid: Commission investigation did not find that Luxembourg gave selective tax treatment to McDonald's, 19 Sept. 2018, available online at http://europa.eu/rapid/press-release_IP-18-5831_en.htm (last visited 19 January 2019).

38. Press Release, European Commission, State Aid: Commission Opens Formal Investigation into Luxembourg's Tax treatment of McDonald's, 3 Dec. 2015, available online at http://europa.eu/rapid/press-release_IP-15-6221_en.htm (last visited 13 July 2017).

39. T. Espiner, *McDonald's to Move Non-US Tax Base to UK*, 8 Dec. 2016, available online at http://www.bbc.com/news/business-38252802 (last visited 13 July 2017).

40. *Financial Secrecy Index, supra* note 9.

41. SARL stands for Société à Responsabilité Limitée, a corporate entity with limited liability for shareholders.

42. A. Maliy and C. Greeven, *Recent Developments in the Advance Tax Ruling Practices in Luxembourg and the Netherlands*, 27 Nov. 2015, available online at http://www.ibanet.org/Article/Detail.aspx?ArticleUid=eadb48e0-4cc0-4591-afac-4e7614278ad8 (last visited 13 July 2017).

43. The International Consortium of Investigative Journalists, *Explore the Documents: Luxembourg Leaks Database*, 9 Dec. 2014, available online at https://www.icij.org/project/luxembourg-leaks/explore-documents-luxembourg-leaks-database.

44. Art. 29a of Luxembourg's Abgabenordnung; Memorial Journal Officiel du Grand-Duché de Luxembourg, A No. 261.

45. Ernst & Young, *Luxembourg Establishes Framework for New Tax Ruling Practice*, 30 Jan. 2015, available online at http://www.ey.com/GL/en/Services/Tax/International-Tax/Alert--Luxembourg-establishes-framework-for-new-tax-ruling-practice.

46. Ibid; Art. 29a Abgabenordnung.

47. European Commission, *supra* note 38.

48. S. Bowers, *McDonald's to Be Investigated over Suspected Sweetheart Tax Arrangements, The Guardian*, 2 Dec. 2015, available online at https://www.theguardian.com/business/2015/dec/02/mcdonalds-suspected-sweetheart-tax-arrangements-luxembourg.

49. European Commission, *supra* note 38.

50. Ibid.

51. Ibid.

52. *Financial Secrecy Index, supra* note 9.

53. See *supra* note 45.

54. Van den Muijsenbergh and Rezai, *supra* note 15, at 49, 64.

55. *Darby, supra* note 30, at para. 30; *Hentrich v. France,* Appl. no. 13616/88, Judgment of 22 Sept. 1994; *Gasus Dosier- und Fördertechnik GmbH v. the Netherlands,* Appl. no. 15375/89, Judgment of 23 Feb. 1995; *National & Provincial Building Society, Leeds Permanent Building Society and Yorkshire Building Society v. United Kingdom,* Appl. nos. 21319/93, 21449/93, 21675/93, Judgment of 23 Oct. 1997; *S.A. Dangeville v. France,* Appl. no. 36677/97, Judgment of 16 Apr. 2002.

56. *Burden, supra* note 19, at para. 59.

57. *Darby, supra* note 30, at para. 30.

58. *Burden, supra* note 19, at para. 59.

59. *Ireland v. United Kingdom,* Appl. no. 5310/71, Judgement of 18 Jan. 1978, at paras. 239–240; *Klass and Others v. Germany,* Appl. no. 5029/71, Judgment of 6 Sept. 1978, at para. 33.

60. Ernst & Young, *supra* note 45; Art. 29a Abgabenordnung.

61. *Ringeisen v. Austria,* Appl. no. 2614/65, Judgment of 16 July 1971, at para.89.

62. *Akdivar and Others v. Turkey,* Appl. no. 21893/93, Judgment of 16 Sept. 1996, at paras. 65–66.

63. Memorial de Luxembourg, *supra* note 44.

64. *Scoppola v. Italy,* Appl. no. 10249/03, Judgment of 17 Sept. 2009, at para. 71.

65. *McFarlane v. Ireland,* Appl. no. 31333/06, Judgment of 10 Sept. 2010, at para. 107.

66. Ibid.

67. *Williams v. United Kingdom,* Appl. no. 32567/06, Judgment of 17 Feb. 2009.

68. *Moreira Barbosa v. Portugal,* Appl. no. 65681/01, Judgment of 21 Dec. 2004.

69. D. Richter and J. P. Winandy, 'National Report: Luxembourg', *in* L. Hinnekens (ed.), *Non Discrimination at the Crossroads of International Taxation* (2008), at 374–375.

70. EU Agency for Fundamental Rights, *Country Thematic Studies on Access to Justice: Luxembourg* (2011), available online at http://fra.europa.eu/en/country-report/2012/country-thematic-studies-access-justice (last visited 8 Aug. 2017).

71. *Sergey Smirnov v. Russia,* Appl. no. 14085/04, Decision on Admissibility of 6 July 2006.

72. *Fredin v. Sweden,* Appl. no. 12033/86, Judgment of 19 Feb. 1991, at para. 60.

73. O. M. Arnardottir, 'The Differences that Make a Difference: Recent Developments on the Discrimination Grounds and the Margin of Appreciation under Article 14 of the European Convention on Human Rights', 14 *Human Rights Law Review* (2014), 647, at 656–657.

74. Ibid. at 657–658; see, e.g., *Carson, supra* note 19, at paras. 78–79.

75. *Darby, supra* note 30; *Glor v. Switzerland,* Appl. no. 13444/04, Judgment of 30 Apr. 2009, at paras. 77–80.

76. *National & Provincial Building Society, supra* note 55.

77. *Darby, supra* note 30; *Glor, supra* note 75.

78. Arnardóttir, *supra* note 25, at 36; *Thlimmenos v. Greece,* Appl. no. 34369/97, Judgment of 6 Apr. 2000.

79. Arnardóttir, *supra* note 73, at 648.

80. *Chabauty v. France,* Appl. no. 57412/08, Judgment of 4 Oct. 2012, at para. 50.

81. Ibid., for example race or ethnicity.

82. *Gaygusuz v. Austria,* Appl. no. 17371/90, Judgment of 16 Sept. 1996.

83. *Chabauty, supra* note 80.

84. *D.H., supra* note 19, at paras. 184 and 194.

85. *Nachova, supra* note 28, at para. 147.

86. C. Danisi, 'How far can the European Court of Human Rights go in the fight against discrimination? Defining new standards in its nondiscrimination jurisprudence', 9 *International Journal of Constitutional Law* (2011), 793, at 797, 801.

87. EU Agency for Fundamental Rights, *supra* note 20, at 129; *Hoogendijk v. the Netherlands,* Appl. no. 58641/00, Judgment of 6 Jan. 2005; *D.H., supra* note 19, at para. 18 and paras. 193–195.

88. *Opuz v. Turkey,* Appl. no. 33401/02, Judgment of 9 June 2009.

89. Ibid. at paras. 192–193.

90. *Chassagnou and Others v. France,* Appl. no. 25088/94, 28331/95, 28443/95, Judgment of 29 Apr. 1999.

91. Ibid. at paras. 86–95.
92. Ibid. at para. 91.
93. *Kjeldsen, Busk Madsen and Pedersen v. Denmark*, Appl. no. 5926/72, 5095/71, 5920/72, Judgment of 7 Dec. 1976, at para. 56.
94. Arnardóttir, *supra* note 73, at 659–660; see, e.g., *Granos Organicos Nationales S.A. v. Germany*, Appl. no. 19508/07, Judgment of 22 Mar. 2012.
95. *Lithgow, supra* note 18.
96. Ibid. at para. 183.
97. *National & Provincial Building Society, supra* note 55.
98. *Swedish Engine Driver's Union v. Sweden*, Appl. no. 5614/72, Judgment of 6 Feb. 1976, at para. 46; *National Union of Belgian Police v. Belgium*, Appl. no. 4464/70, Judgment of 27 Oct. 1975.
99. *Burden, supra* note 19, at para. 60.
100. Arnardóttir, *supra* note 73, at 656.
101. *Belgian Linguistics, supra* note 29, at para. II.7.
102. *Lithgow, supra* note 18, at para. 177; *Chassagnou, supra* note 90, at para. 91.
103. *Carson, supra* note 19, at para. 61; *Case of British Gurkha Welfare Society and Others v. United Kingdom*, Appl. no. 44818/11, Judgment of 15 Sept. 2016, at paras. 62, 81.
104. *Stec and Others v. UK*, Appl. nos. 65731/01, 65900/01, Judgment of 12 Apr. 2006, at 52; *Carson, supra* note 19, at para. 61.
105. *Chassagnou, supra* note 90, at para. 75; *Hermann v. Germany*, Appl. no. 9300/07, Judgment of 26 June 2012, at para. 74.
106. *Fábián v. Hungary*, Appl. no. 78117/13, Judgment of 15 Dec. 2015, at para. 33; case currently before the Grand Chamber.
107. *Chabauty, supra* note 80, at paras. 41–55; *Andrle v. Czech Republic*, Appl. no. 6268/08, Judgment of 17 Feb. 2011, at paras. 52–61.
108. *Darby, supra* note 30.
109. Ibid. at paras. 33–34.
110. *Hentrich, supra* note 55, at para. 39.
111. Ibid. at para. 49.
112. The Court has reiterated that economic policies may not be arbitrary; see, e.g., most recently, *Gurkha Welfare Society, supra* note 103, at para. 84.
113. *Belgian Linguistics, supra* note 29, at para. II.7.

PART 5

TAXING EQUALITY

National Debates

CHAPTER 19

"TAXING FOR GROWTH" VS. "TAXING FOR EQUALITY"—USING HUMAN RIGHTS TO COMBAT GENDER INEQUALITIES, POVERTY, AND INCOME INEQUALITIES IN FISCAL LAWS

KATHLEEN A. LAHEY

I. TAXING FOR ECONOMIC GROWTH VS. TAXING FOR GENDER EQUALITY

Taxation practices are constitutive not just of states, but of societies. "Taxation" encompasses the range of normative standards designed by groups to meet their needs in sustainable ways.[1] It is significant for human rights perspectives on fiscal issues that in 2015, the global community adopted the UN Sustainable Development Goals, which evaluate policy outcomes in terms of state support for sustainable economic and gender equality, social protection regimes while working within the limits of planetary biosphere capacities, human rights to the "minimal conditions for a dignified life,"[2] and human sustainability.

Against this interdisciplinary view of governance principles and human rights, the history of taxation in most regions reveals preoccupation by powerful groups with accumulating capital and wealth by all available means—including by demanding special treatment in tax and spending laws. Debates over the use of corporations and households as tax units forms part of that history as they continue to be conceptualized as re/productive associations that exist to serve as conduits that channel ownership and taxation of incomes and capital into private hands and out of the hands of governments and public institutions.[3]

Tax, Inequality, and Human Rights. Philip Alston and Nikki Reisch.
© Oxford University Press 2019. Published 2019 by Oxford University Press.

A. THE "TAXING FOR GROWTH" AGENDA

It has long been agreed that taxes should be proportionate to ability to pay.[4] However, even those advocating the use of tax systems to mitigate inequalities in incomes and wealth have agreed that the search for equality should not allow high progressive income tax rates on capital or labor incomes to "impair motivation" to work and accumulate capital.[5] Thus efforts to bring capital gains into the tax bases of rich countries failed until the mid-1900s, when such taxes were introduced, but on terms that continue to encourage governments to tax both capital gains and corporate profits ever more lightly.

During the second half of the twentieth century, any balance that may have originally existed between principles of equality and ability to pay taxes versus a focus on capital accumulation and productivity discernibly shifted toward emphasis on "taxing for growth" in high-income countries. The original concept of equality in taxation had already been displaced by appeals to "equity" in 1920,[6] almost completely erasing the use of the term "equality" in tax policy discourses.[7] As part of that process, treating corporations as separate legal persons for purposes of taxation while eliminating the "double taxation" of corporations and shareholders gave rise to systems of corporate integration or imputation of corporate pretax profits to shareholders on the basis that they are more equitable. These systems effectively reduce corporate income taxes to the role of temporary withholding taxes and further erode capital gains taxation. At the same time, the separate legal personality of women has been increasingly ignored through reliance on the married couple as the personal income tax unit to reduce main earner spouse tax loads, which increases second earner (mainly female) tax loads.

As a result, fiscal policy debates increasingly have been framed around taxing for growth. The Thatcher government in the United Kingdom accelerated the shift from progressive taxation of personal and corporate incomes to increasing reliance on high-rate consumption taxes, and then used the fact that total tax revenues had fallen to justify reducing income security and social development spending. The Reagan government in the United States and then growing numbers of countries have since reframed tax systems this way, broadly under the guise of increasing economic efficiency and growth, but really as a response to popular demand for tax cuts. By 2005, the Organisation for Economic Co-operation and Development (OECD) began structural surveillance of the GDP growth of all its members each year[8] and, by 2007, had identified a set of tax and expenditure policies that it and like-minded international and regional financial institutions recommended for use in accelerating annual growth everywhere.

This "taxing for growth" formula calls for these changes, in descending order of priority: (1) reduce high personal and corporate income tax rates, employer social security contributions, and tax benefits and expenditures; (2) shift the revenue burden to other tax bases such as the value-added tax (VAT) or other consumption taxes; reduce health, social benefit, pension, disability, unemployment, and seasonal employment benefit spending (quantum and duration); and (3) increase women's paid work time by reducing tax barriers to second spouse paid work and making care resources more accessible.[9] The OECD has continued to apply this approach in every annual edition of *Going for Growth*.[10] This approach is also increasingly applied in the European Union and regionally, and by international development and financial institutions.

B. THE "TAXING FOR GENDER EQUALITY" AGENDA

In the midst of the "taxing for growth" movement, ratification of the Convention on the Elimination of All Forms of Discrimination Against Women (CEDAW)[11] in the early 1980s and then the adoption of the Beijing Platform for Action in 1995[12] resulted in recognition of gender equality as a fundamental human right. The Beijing Platform in particular has been important for the detailed guidance it provides on how all laws, policies, and practices are to be evaluated for gender impact—including those pertaining to taxation. In addition, the Platform requires states to provide evidence of full-scale gender mainstreaming and gender budgeting in the periodic implementation reviews called for by CEDAW. Since 2002, CEDAW has provided an optional protocol for the filing and adjudication of complaints brought against state parties under the Convention.[13]

In short, CEDAW and the Beijing Platform form a comprehensive global implementation framework designed to actively secure both formal and substantive equality in all laws, policies, and practices in all member countries, as well as in regional and global governance organizations.[14] However, even as these new gender-equality principles began to take hold, programmatic "taxing for growth" values took hold even faster, leading to some of the lowest tax-to-GDP ratios in decades in the period 1995–2015, and to actual deterioration in the levels of gender equality already established in many high-income tax-cutting countries.

The call for "taxing for gender equality" did not really begin to concretize in international human rights discourse until the early 2000s as the connection between ongoing structural tax-cutting and reversals in gender equality began to become apparent. Although domestic litigation over gender discrimination in tax laws had been initiated in the early 1970s, it was not until the 2007–2008 global financial crisis and resulting austerity policies that demands for gender equality in both tax and expenditure policies became urgent. At that point, the OECD and the European Commission began to take note of the relationship between fiscal policies and economic inequality, at least so far as they were concerned to activate women's paid work as a source of economic growth.[15] Beginning in 2010, the OECD and International Monetary Fund (IMF) began publishing reports on taxation and gender equality, searching for synergistic tax and fiscal policies to promote both equality and economic growth. As the Occupy movement protesting concentration of wealth in the hands of the rich accelerated in 2011, these international organizations also began publishing high-profile reports on both income inequalities and gender income inequalities.[16]

"Taxing for equality" strategies include reducing taxes on low earned incomes, particularly those of second earners and the self-employed, and increasing income security, pension, and training supports for low-income and low-skilled workers, single parents, and middle-income workers. These strategies are to be funded by increasing graduated personal and corporate income tax rates, and should be accompanied by increasing care resources to equalize unpaid workloads associated with low-paid work levels, as well as wealth and inheritance taxes. The use of tax expenditures and joint fiscal measures that have income- and gender-regressive effects are to be reduced. "Tackling inequalities" also calls for increased regulation of labor markets, livable wages, affordable education, and increased taxation of capital incomes. Tackling inequality studies have identified both tax and regulatory methods to reduce the exclusive focus on growth, and have also pinpointed new tax and transfer policies that can counteract poverty and reduce overall income inequalities, which are increasingly recognized as impediments to durable economic growth.[17]

In 2015, taxing for gender equality became an acknowledged global policy priority as new transnational normative standards were adopted in relation to poverty reduction, gender equality, economic durability, and environmental sustainability goals,[18] as well as in relation to revenue issues and financing for development.[19] The documents which articulated these standards contain express commitments to mainstream gender-equality and poverty-reduction policies on a systemic basis, including specifically in relation to all revenue issues.[20] These commitments apply to states in relation to all their domestic laws, policies, and practices, as well as to all government acts and nongovernmental actors affecting transnational and international relations.

At the same time, the UN system produced three important practical advances in "taxing for equality." The first was a 2014 report of the UN Special Rapporteur on extreme poverty and human rights detailing how the prevailing features of corporate and personal income, value-added, excise, sales, and property taxes, as well as fees, charges, and social benefit and economic development laws, systemically intensify women's economic disadvantages, perpetuate gender inequalities and poverty, and thus violate international human rights laws.[21] The Special Rapporteur's report identifies lack of progressivity, lack of appropriate exemptions, and failure to individualize tax laws as the most discriminatory features of personal income tax systems.[22] In corporate income taxation, the Special Rapporteur found that the growing numbers of low tax rates, special allowances, tax exemptions, and tax incentives impair state revenues and favor owners of investment capital.[23] Since men own disproportionately large shares of private capital and have greater social and financial ability to form incorporated businesses under conditions not equally available to women in countries at all levels of development, corporate tax benefits in particular exacerbate economic gender inequalities.

The Special Rapporteur singled out consumption taxes, the most important of which are value-added, sales, and other flat-rate taxes, for particular concern. She found that the growing use of the VAT to replace progressive income tax structures, without careful design, risks pushing those with low incomes more deeply into poverty, and has impaired development on a structural basis.[24]

To counter the many negative effects of existing tax and other fiscal policies on women, those living in poverty, and other vulnerable groups, the Special Rapporteur made detailed recommendations on practical fiscal changes that should be made to support gender equality. In sum, these recommendations are conceptually simple—use broad-based income tax systems with graduated rates built around actual ability to pay taxes to raise adequate and redistributive levels of revenues, and make minimal use of flat-rated consumption taxes, particularly when they render the basic necessities of living unaffordable to the poorest members of society.

The second development was two groundbreaking decisions issued by the UN Committee on the Elimination of Discrimination Against Women (CEDAW Committee) that held national governments accountable for failing to uphold their commitments to gender equality, poverty reduction, and fiscal equality in tax/expenditure policies. In these two decisions, discussed in more detail below, the CEDAW Committee recommended that the countries in question take detailed curative steps as well as make financial restitution to those injured. In other words, the CEDAW Committee established that tax and other fiscal policies alone or in the aggregate can provide the basis for rulings that such laws and policies violate international human rights.

In the 2014 *Blok* decision, the Netherlands was found to have violated women's maternity leave rights,[25] a point that had been mentioned repeatedly in CEDAW reviews of that country's periodic treaty implementation reports. In 2015, the *Canada Inquiry* decision held all levels of Canadian government accountable for a long and detailed list of violations of international rights regarding poverty reduction and gender equality, resulting from its persistent failure to take effective steps to lift indigenous women and communities from the depths of long-standing poverty.[26] In both decisions, the CEDAW Committee found that signing and ratifying the Convention bound states to implement it, and ordered restorative payments and policy change through formal programming.

The third development arose out of the periodic country review process under CEDAW. In its Concluding Observations regarding Switzerland, the Committee expressed concern that the country's financial secrecy, corporate reporting, and tax policies caused developing country budgetary shortfalls, and impaired their ability to mobilize the maximum available resources to fulfill women's human rights, and recommended transparent gender impact analysis of all such effects going forward.[27] In the Concluding Observations regarding Canada, the Committee expressed concern for the physical and socioeconomic damage done to women by mining companies in host countries.[28] Both Switzerland and Canada were advised to strengthen their trade and investment agreements and regulations governing the extraterritorial conduct of their corporate citizens, to recognize the primacy of women's and all human rights.

Clearly, a wide array of tax provisions negatively affect people disadvantaged by poverty, gender, and other personal characteristics. For purposes of examining the role of human rights laws in remedying fiscal discrimination, the remainder of this chapter examines the factual contexts and the growing use of consumption taxes—especially the VAT—to raise substantial shares of total revenues from those who do not have the ability to pay those taxes. Unlike direct taxes, which can be rendered somewhat progressive in impact through the use of graduated tax rates and broadly inclusive tax bases, consumption taxes are regressive in impact because those with low or no incomes are not necessarily exempt from paying the same rates as those with higher incomes. As such, the broad-based "upside down" incidence of consumption taxes has discriminatory effects on the basis of gender and/or poverty status that are widely recognized but tolerated in most countries, and are factually complex to quantify and describe. While many important tax/transfer laws also benefit those with higher incomes more than those with low incomes, the incidence of consumption taxes is particularly important because it has such predictable impact in the lowest-income countries in the world, and there is no sign of change in the use of this tax in the near future.

II. CONSUMPTION TAXES AND "ABILITY TO PAY" ENGAGE HUMAN RIGHTS

In the aftermath of the 2008 global financial crisis, taxing for growth advocates singled out increases in consumption tax rates (VAT, Goods and Services Tax (GST), and environmental taxes) and cuts to both personal income tax (PIT) and corporate income tax (CIT) rates as the best way to maintain adequate government revenues. Usually justified as a "tax shift" designed to accelerate the rate of economic growth,[29] the regressive impact of obtaining increased shares of revenue from the VAT or other flat-rated consumption taxes is not always denied in these policy documents. But the regressive impact of the VAT is often treated as being less important than the claim that the VAT is more administratively efficient than more complex forms of taxation like corporate or personal income taxes, and/or is seen as a necessary step along the way to accelerating economic growth, which is suggested will then enable governments to meet the needs of those living in poverty more fully.[30]

Inequalities in after-tax/transfer income have increased in most countries as the result of following recommendations to shift revenue production more heavily toward consumption taxes.[31] The VAT is popular with governments because with a broader tax base consisting of both goods and services, the VAT produces significantly more revenue than do sales taxes. This is described as a "business-friendly" tax because the economic incidence of the VAT is designed to fall only on final private consumers, not on businesses, although both unrecoverable or "trapped VAT" and high administrative costs do burden business profits. In addition, VAT rates have traditionally been significantly higher than sales taxes. These two features combined do indeed produce increased revenues.

But, because the VAT, like traditional services or excise taxes, is charged at the point of final sale, it must be paid by anyone who engages in consumption. Unlike income taxes, which look at total net taxable income at the end of the taxation period and which apply low-income exemptions to the total, the VAT and other consumption taxes are imposed as part of each sale occurring in the course of the taxation period, and there is no "final" accounting in which low- or no-income individuals can secure adjustment of their total VAT liabilities in the form of tax refunds. Proactive exemptions can be used, and, when used, do minimize these effects to some degree. However, they are usually quite limited in scope, and often fail to substantively ward off negative poverty and/or gender effects.

In high-income countries with adequate social welfare systems, the cost of the VAT may be factored into income maintenance amounts, or may be offset with VAT compensation costs for those with the lowest incomes. In such contexts, ability to pay the VAT is not seen as a particular concern, although governments have been known to reduce VAT or GST tax rates simply because it is not a popular tax with consumers, or have offered large VAT allowances to soften opposition to increases in consumer prices caused by shifting to the VAT. Overall, however, high VAT rates have become so routine in high-income countries that it is often assumed to be a reasonable type of tax for use in low-income and developing countries as well.

The policy and research literature on the use of consumption taxes in low-income, fragile, and developing country contexts has from time to time been highly critical of the VAT, and has (rightly) insisted, as has the Special Rapporteur on extreme poverty in her report, that the main revenue instrument in such contexts must be broad-based progressive personal and corporate income taxes that raise proportionately more revenue from those with the highest incomes. For example, in 2011, an Asian Development Bank evaluation of the Philippines plan to replace its corporate income tax with a new VAT advised the government not to take this step. The main reason given for this advice is that it would have made the total tax mix regressive in incidence. Instead, the ADB recommended that the government concentrate on improving its tax administration procedures to bring in revenues due and owing but not collectable due to weak procedures, and enact new high excise taxes on specific types of goods purchasable only by those with high incomes.[32]

In fact, the points made in this ADB report and reinforced in the Special Rapporteur's 2014 report are well known. Unfortunately, they just do not seem to matter when it comes down to the core question of how low-income, fragile, and developing countries should go about increasing their tax revenues. Paradoxically, the pressure to move forward with new and high VAT taxes in contexts like that of the Philippines has increased since member states agreed that the SDGs and the Addis Ababa Agenda for Action should stress the importance of developing country mobilization of domestic revenues to reduce reliance on overseas development assistance (ODA). Although numerous small and developing countries still have tax ratios in the single digits, governments that want to make the revenue shift from even moderate PIT and CIT rates to the VAT contend that the SDGs "require" them to do so because they have found that they just cannot raise enough revenue with income-based taxes.

Many low-income, fragile, and developing country governments have created various mechanisms to reduce the negative poverty and gender effects of their new VAT laws. However, these tend to be partial solutions that actually increase the administrative complexities and costs of the VAT in the internal economy, without solving the core problem of widespread lack of taxpayer ability to pay the tax. While most countries in this situation do make an effort to maintain appropriate PIT and CIT tax rates and system, there are many that do not.

In low PIT/CIT rate countries, the desire to keep income tax rates low or even to abolish them completely is usually justified by claiming that the VAT is more administratively and even more economically efficient, or by pointing out that because income taxes have failed to produce significant revenues in the past, they will also fail in the future. Often the reason for low income tax revenues can be traced to liberal and ongoing use of investment tax exemption certificates for considerable amounts of foreign source investment, or to the lack of adequate compliance capacity. On the other hand, it has also been suggested that "the economic and political power of rich taxpayers often allows them to prevent fiscal reforms that would increase their tax burdens," and "explains in part why many developing countries have not fully exploited personal income and property taxes and why their tax systems rarely achieve satisfactory progressivity (in other words, where the rich pay proportionately more taxes)."[33]

A. ABILITY TO PAY CONSUMPTION TAXES

Regardless of whether a government is committed to maintaining the overall progressivity of its total tax system or not, the principle of ability to pay taxes is a fundamental principle of tax fairness. Often associated with the canons of tax policy proclaimed by Adam Smith in 1700s England, the doctrine of "ability to pay" had in fact been central to discussions about the design of tax systems since the 1400s in Europe, and is today enshrined as a constitutional principle in Brazil and actively litigated in the European Union.[34]

In contemporary tax policy research, the "ability to pay" principle is often considered in the context of designing tax administration and compliance rules. In that context, the principle recognizes that governments should not spend time and resources attempting to collect taxes from those who have no money to pay them, and that simply exempting such persons from taxation will increase the administrative efficiency of the tax collection department.

At the income threshold of long-term or extreme poverty, however, imposition of taxes on those who do not have the ability to pay them can impair human survival and development. Factual lack of ability to pay a tax is qualitatively different from the administrative concept of "ability to pay" as used to determine compliance expectations. Factual inability to pay exists when the person receiving income, goods, or services either cannot actually pay the tax in question on such consumption at all, or is unlikely to be able to maintain human functionality on a sustainable basis if the tax is imposed in such circumstances on an ongoing basis.[35]

Most income tax systems do not attempt to collect the PIT from those with low or no incomes, and ensure this either by defining amounts of income that will be tax exempt or by offering low income tax credits to erase theoretical PIT liability.[36] Thus PIT systems tend to recognize ability to pay by defining liability thresholds. So long as PIT exemptions are high enough to enable taxpayers to pay for all basic consumption necessities out of untaxed income, those who do have taxable incomes are less likely to be unable to pay income taxes on that income. However, when personal income tax exemptions are too small to shelter income needed to pay for all basic necessities, factual ability to pay income taxes should be called into question.

As a tax on consumption, the VAT is qualitatively different from taxes on incomes. Depending on what specific exemptions are actually offered in VAT laws, the VAT is theoretically designed to tax most forms of human consumption. And the VAT taxes human consumption more or less as that consumption takes place, not when the income used to pay for consumption is received.[37] Thus the VAT and other consumption taxes present quite immediate and inescapable problems regarding ability to pay. It does not matter whether the individual needing those goods or services has enough funds to pay the VAT on them at the time of purchase. Inability to pay the VAT on consumption goods and services essential to human well-being means that individuals or households that must pay the VAT on essential consumption will then be forced to survive on something less than the necessities.[38]

The effect of the VAT on prices is sometimes trivialized as being "just a one-time price increase." But if incomes do not rise when a VAT is enacted—and normally they do not—then that one-time price increase becomes an "every time" price increase that will affect people's ability to pay for consumption goods and services for all time going forward. In other words, these increased costs of consumption due to the VAT are "just" one-time price increases—but they are permanent price increases.

In short, there is a very direct connection between liability for VAT taxes on current consumption and consequent lack of current cash to pay for VAT-bearing consumption. When sufficient detail on individual and household incomes and expenditures is available, the clearest picture of the tax incidence of the VAT is obtained by expressing the total cost of the VAT as a percentage of total actual income. When factual ability to pay a tax is the issue, government transfers and all other sources of cash incomes should be brought into the identification of total actual income.

However, when substantial numbers of those who consume VAT-taxed goods and services have no incomes, or when it is difficult to obtain accurate detailed data on incomes and expenditures, the need for some quantitative measure of incidence has led many researchers to use consumption expenditure instead of total income as the welfare measure. In that approach, the cost of VAT payments is expressed as a percentage of consumption expenditure, and not as a percentage of income.[39] While this approach tends to make the costs of the VAT appear less regressive than when income is used as the base, even studies that measure VAT costs as a share of consumption expenditure still clearly demonstrate that VAT taxes reduce actual financial capacity for consumption.[40] Those studies also demonstrate that unless basic necessities are exempt from VAT, the incidence of VAT usually falls more heavily on female-led households than on male-led households. This is because, on average, female-led households tend to have lower incomes and thus smaller budgets than male-headed households, with the result that male-led households spend more in general, including on VAT-taxed items, while women spend more of their funds on necessities, particularly on food.[41]

B. PIT VS. VAT: POVERTY AND GENDER INCIDENCE

This section illustrates the differential impacts of increasing reliance on flat-rated consumption taxes instead of on graduated PIT taxes to raise domestic revenues in low-income countries that have high poverty rates. This demonstration is important, because as a result of the Addis Ababa Agenda for Action resolutions and SDG 17.1, small, low-income, and developing countries are under increasing pressure to focus on mobilizing domestic revenues to meet their own SDG targets.[42] Under this shift in focus away from development and toward revenue mobilization, the use of the VAT in such contexts has been viewed favorably despite its known regressive distributional effects.

The illustration in this section uses 2011 income and expenditure survey data from a country with extremely high poverty, malnourishment, and maternal and infant mortality rates (Country X[43]) to show concretely how flat-rated consumption taxes versus graduated rate income taxes differentially affect those living with economic gender inequalities and poverty in such countries. Country X previously had PIT and CIT rates ranging up to 30 percent, but, in consultation with international financial development partners in previous decades, had reduced all income tax rates to some of the lowest in the region, and had also implemented very large PIT exemptions.

In response to the increased focus on fiscal issues and particularly on domestic revenue mobilization, the policy focus in Country X is now on the recommendation that it enact the VAT to increase domestic revenues as rapidly as possible. Some increases in PIT and CIT rates applicable to high incomes are also proposed to accompany the enactment of the VAT, along with steps to improve institutional capacity for more effective tax administration and compliance actions.

Table 19.1 shows how the tax burden from the addition of a 15 percent bracket to the PIT and the enactment of a 10 percent VAT would be allocated across households by income deciles and the gender of the head of the household. The proposed VAT exempts unprepared food, medical, and education costs for all. Small amounts of additional revenue are collected via CIT and excise increases not reflected in this table. Even with the proposed exemptions, however, 86 percent of all new revenues will be raised by the VAT.

The allocation of the new VAT and PIT tax burdens taken together can be described as being distributionally inverted or "upside down." This demonstrates that the "tax shift" from reliance on PIT to VAT will take proportionately very little from those with the highest incomes but proportionately very large shares from those with the lowest incomes. (Female-headed households are on average smaller than male-headed households and have lower incomes, but account for two-thirds of the households in the lowest income deciles.)

Table 19.1: New 10% VAT (with exemptions) and new 15% PIT as percentage of total household income, by decile and gender of head of household, 2011 USD

Income decile	PIT Male	PIT Female	PIT All	VAT Male	VAT Female	VAT All
1	—	—	—	30%	18%	27%
2	—	—	—	16%	13%	16%
3	—	—	—	14%	11%	13%
4	—	—	—	12%	11%	12%
5	—	—	—	10%	10%	10%
6	—	—	—	10%	7%	9%
7	—	—	—	9%	8%	9%
8	—	—		8%	8%	8%
9	0.02%	—	0.01%	9%	9%	9%
10	1.5%	0.78%	1.4%	10%	8%	9%
Total $51.6 million new revenues	$6.9 million	$0.3 million	$7.2 million	$40.5 million	$3.9 million	$44.4 million
100%			14%			86%

Source: On file with author. The VAT rate is 10% and the new 15% PIT rate applies to incomes over $40,000; the median income is less than $2,000; overall, only 25% of all women have incomes, and in 2011, women's average peak earning year incomes were no more than 30% of men's.

This distribution by itself does not necessarily mean that those in the lowest income deciles in every country will no longer have the ability to pay the VAT and still have enough cash to pay for all their essential needs. But it does mean that in those countries in which the majority of the population cannot afford to continue purchasing all the same basic necessities of living when the cost of the VAT is added to those purchases, imposing a new VAT on all consumption will make it more difficult or even financially impossible to maintain existing levels of minimal necessary consumption, regardless of whether they are currently adequate or inadequate.

Table 19.2 demonstrates that heavier reliance on new graduated PIT rates and a low 1 percent VAT rate can reduce the upside-down distribution shown in Table 19.1. Even without taking the effect of revenues from higher corporate income and excise tax rates into consideration, the balance of VAT revenues as compared with new PIT revenues in Table 19.2 is significantly different than in Table 19.1. In Table 19.2, there is still a risk that those with low incomes will not be able to maintain adequate levels of consumption, but the degree of risk is much lower. At the same time, because the new PIT revenues only affect those with the highest 50 percent of incomes, and at graduated rates, this also reduces the risks of intensified poverty for those in the middle income deciles.

From a distributional perspective, the allocation of new tax liabilities in Table 19.2 is still upside down in the lowest income deciles. Those in the lowest income deciles are still taxed regressively by the VAT, because the shares of income taken by VAT payments decline as incomes rise. However, the overall distribution begins to look more "right side up" in the top five deciles, where those in the top 40 percent are taxed progressively by the PIT. In this scenario, the new

Table 19.2: Allocation of new 1% VAT (with proposed exemptions) and new 5–30% PIT at household level, by annual household income decile, 2011 USD

Average annual household income in decile	Average annual VAT paid by household	VAT paid as % of household income	Average new 5–30% PIT paid by household	New 5–30% PIT paid as % of household income
1: $ 560	$ 9.50	2.7%	—	—
2: $ 920	$12.10	1.6%	—	—
3: $ 1,210	$13.60	1.3%	—	—
4: $ 1,500	$15.50	1.2%	—	—
5: $ 1,840	$16.20	1.0%	—	—
6: $ 2,290	$17.70	0.9%	$ 1	0.0%
7: $ 2,860	$22.00	0.9%	$ 6	0.20%
8: $ 3,720	$24.30	0.8%	$ 21	0.6%
9: $ 5,578	$36.30	0.9%	$ 62	1.2%
10: $14,454	$74.00	0.9%	$1,525	6.3%
All payors	$24.10	1.2%	$ 161	0.8%
Total $34.2 million new revenues	$4.4 million		$29.8 million	
100%	13%		87%	

Source: Copy on file with author. The 1% VAT estimates reflect exemptions for unprepared food, medical, and educational costs, and are calculated on actual household incomes, not on average household incomes; the PIT estimates reflect total additional PIT revenues from replacing one low PIT rate with graduated individual tax rates of $0–2,000: 0%; $2,000–4,000: 5%; $4,000–6,000: 10%; $6,000–8,000: 15%; $8,000–12,000: 20%; $12,000–14,000: 25%; over $14,000: 30%, and are expressed as a percentage of actual household incomes, not of average household incomes; additional new CIT and excise revenues are not included in this table.

PIT accounts for 87 percent of all new tax revenues, and the VAT accounts for just 13 percent of new revenues. This approach lifts 90 percent of the burden of the VAT off of those with the lowest incomes, and replaces it with new PIT taxes paid by the 40 percent with the highest incomes; no PIT is paid by the 60 percent with the lowest incomes, but they do still pay the 1 percent VAT on nonexempt consumption.

In this situation, it is still possible that those with the lowest incomes will not have the ability to pay the VAT and also maintain adequate levels of essential consumption. But the problem that remains to be solved is smaller in scale, and easier for low-income countries to redress through transfer programs. Thus payment of the VAT at such low rates is likely to cause less damage to those living on the lowest incomes than would a VAT charged at much higher rates.

C. DO VAT EXEMPTIONS FOR BASIC NECESSITIES GO FAR ENOUGH?

Despite the negative impact that the VAT can have on those living on low or no incomes, advocates of the VAT contend that it is inefficient to provide exemptions or reduced tax rates in VAT laws.[44] This contention carries considerable weight in contexts in which the main motivation for enacting VAT laws is that it is an efficient type of tax, once it has been implemented. Despite this advice, however, most developing countries and growing numbers of high-income countries do provide at least some types of exemptions, often for food, medical, and education expenses.[45] But can exemption of just some types of consumption for those with low incomes solve the problem? As Table 19.3 demonstrates, although it is important to provide VAT exemptions for the basic necessities of living, including not just food but also clothing, household equipment,

Table 19.3: 10% VAT on non-exempt basic necessities as percentage of average individual monthly income, by decile and gender, 2011 USD

Income deciles (individuals)	Average monthly incomes of individuals in decile	VAT on nonexempt basic needs ($1.98) as % of monthly income	Men in decile (%)	Women in decile (%)
1	—	($43.20)*	34%	66%
2	$9.63	20.6%	34%	66%
3	$16.67	11.9%	41%	59%
4	$23.33	8.5%	52%	48%
5	$30.77	6.4%	59%	41%
6	$40.00	5.0%	65%	35%
7	$51.67	3.8%	74%	26%
8	$65.00	3.0%	80%	20%
9	$84.67	2.3%	74%	26%
10	$131.67	1.5%	80%	20%
Median	$40.00	5.0%	60%	40%

Source: On file with author. Total cost of average minimum individual monthly basic needs per household survey data: $41.22; total cost of monthly basic necessities exempt from VAT: $21.47; total cost of monthly basic needs not exempt from VAT: $19.75; VAT payable on nonexempt items: $1.98; total cost of basic monthly needs plus VAT on nonexempt items: $41.22 plus VAT of $1.98 = $43.20;

* indicates that in the zero-income decile, in which women are heavily concentrated, the total income shortfall each month will be $43.20.

and transportation, those exemptions alone may not be sufficient in countries with high poverty rates and large numbers of people living on the margins of survival.

Table 19.3 shows in detail how failure to exempt all basic necessities from the VAT or other consumption taxes in a low-income country can substantially impair the ability to pay for essential consumption items. The data in Table 19.3 from Country X treats the cost of the average basic market basket of goods and services essential for human survival at the individual level as being equivalent to that reported by the average of all individuals in the sixth decile—$41.22.

Using $41.22 as the monthly cost of the average basic market basket for everyone in all ten deciles, Table 19.3 shows what percentage of monthly income in each decile will have to be paid for the cost of the VAT on basic needs that are not exempt from the VAT. With a 10 percent VAT, in the particular circumstances of Country X, this means that every individual will need $1.98 in extra income to pay the VAT on nonexempt basic needs consumption. The question examined in Table 19.3 is whether everyone in each decile will have the ability to pay the VAT on this nonexempt part of average minimum monthly consumption.

Table 19.3 demonstrates that only those individuals with incomes in the top of the sixth decile or higher will be able to afford to pay the full cost of all average basic necessities of living, plus the VAT on those basic necessities, if not all those basic necessities are exempt from the VAT.

What is important about Table 19.3 is that even individuals with an average monthly income of $40 (sixth decile) will still fall short of being able to afford the full cost of the average basic market basket of necessities. That $40 will not pay for the entire $41.22 monthly basic needs. If an individual with monthly income of $40 purchases $21.47 of VAT-exempt necessities, then only $16.84 will be left to pay for nonexempt necessities, because the balance must also cover the cost of the 10 percent VAT on that $16.84 in nonexempt goods or services, which would be $1.69. That $1.69 VAT is material in this situation, because that leaves the individual who needs at least $43.20 to pay for all basic needs ($41.22 plus $1.98 VAT on nonexempt basic needs) $3.20 short of being able to meet those needs. Such individuals thus have to make even more difficult choices as to what basic necessities can be obtained.

Governments that provide VAT exemptions for essential goods and services are definitely headed in a more constructive policy direction than are governments that provide no exemptions for essentials (for example, New Zealand, 15 percent VAT; Singapore, 7 percent VAT). However, none of the low- or middle-income countries at present maintain exemptions that will ensure that everyone living on low incomes will be able to pay a 10 percent VAT and still maintain sustainable living standards. In virtually all countries that have significantly low incomes, deep poverty levels, and/or high levels of poverty, what may appear to be relatively small amounts of nonexempt VAT liability will still reduce already inadequate consumption budgets to even lower levels than exist now.

The prevalence of economic gender discrimination makes the impact of nonexempt VAT liabilities even more serious for women in low-income countries. Country X is not unusual in having twice as many women as men in the lowest income deciles, as illustrated in Table 19.3. The predominance of women in the lowest income deciles means that women face larger VAT penalties on essential consumption needs than men. There are more than twice as many men than women in the seventh through tenth deciles in Table 19.3, with income levels at which the 10 percent VAT would not, on average, make it impossible to afford both the basic basket of consumption needs and the VAT payable on nonexempt basic items. Accordingly, men face substantially fewer and lower VAT penalties on essential consumption.

In sum, women as a class have much less ability to pay the VAT, while men as a class have substantially greater ability to pay the VAT. To say it differently, on average, VAT will reduce women's ability to meet their essential needs by a greater margin than it will impair men's ability to meet their essential needs.

III. VAT EXEMPTION OF ALL BASIC NEEDS IS A FUNDAMENTAL HUMAN RIGHT

A. MITIGATING THE REGRESSIVE IMPACTS OF VAT

Given the serious problems with food security, health, sanitation, water, housing, transportation, and personal care needs faced by the largest majority of those living in low-income countries, it would be far better to exempt the whole range of basic household and food items from the VAT than to assign piecemeal exemptions or special VAT rates. The right to meet basic minimum consumption needs without incurring the cost of the VAT on top of the costs of those needs should be seen as the basis for extending VAT exemptions not only to unprepared foods, medical, and education costs, but also to: all prepared foods; care resources; all items that form part of an adequate basic budget for personal care items; transportation; footwear, children's clothing; basic household implements; and, for those in subsistence conditions, seed, supplies, livestock, and tools essential to maintaining stable levels of subsistence output.

Expanding VAT exemptions to this extent would increase the cost to governments of providing these VAT exemptions to those at all income levels, even for those with the highest incomes. But, in reality, even in low-income countries, very few individuals are actually wealthy. In some low-income countries, for example, Fiji, only the top 1 percent of all incomes rise significantly above those of the other 99 percent, all of whom live on very low to quite modest incomes. And the value of VAT exemptions enjoyed by the wealthiest can easily be recaptured with effective graduated PIT rates, as has been done in Fiji.

Moreover, of course, there are other policy tools available. VAT allowances obviously should be added to all low-income social protection payments. In addition, those who can show that they do not have the ability to pay the VAT on items outside exemptions for unprepared foods, medical, and education costs could be granted basic needs VAT allowances or advance VAT refunds that are calculated to protect their ability to pay the VAT based on their estimated incomes. Careful costing of these policy options for low-income protection should be carried out using full details of the most recent income and expenditure results for each country contemplating these measures. There are many legislative precedents for both wide basic necessities exemptions and scaled VAT allowances.

Determining what policy tools can best minimize the negative financial effects of the VAT associated with gender, poverty, malnutrition, health risks, lack of education, language, culture, race, or infancy, however, is not the most pressing issue at this time. The core problem posed by the VAT is that it is increasingly viewed not as the risky revenue instrument that it is, when used in low-income countries, but rather as a real solution to the need for more tax revenue. The perceived ease of generating revenues through VAT has eclipsed concerns about the regressive nature and adverse human rights impacts of such indirect consumption taxes.

The motivation for seeking increased domestic revenue mobilization through VAT should not matter. It may be that some governments think that reducing income taxes and increasing consumption taxes will provide incentives for economic investment and accelerate growth. Others may have experienced difficulties in PIT and CIT tax compliance, or face political resistance to higher income tax rates. Some countries plan to use VAT revenues to fund new social protection programs to meet the subsistence needs of their lowest-income residents. Some countries may already need to replace ODA or other revenues with new tax revenues, and see the VAT as an effective route to doing so. All developing countries are under affirmative obligations to mobilize domestic revenues, and donor countries are now being asked to direct ODA toward financing for enhancing revenue mobilization.[46]

None of these policy objectives provides a compelling reason for pursuing increased domestic revenues via the VAT, when other types of taxes that allocate tax burdens more fairly can be implemented. The justifications are even less compelling in countries that have voluntarily reduced their PIT, CIT, excise, and/or trade taxes in order to attract more wealthy investors or residents.

B. CHALLENGING VAT UNDER DOMESTIC AND INTERNATIONAL LAW

From the perspective of potential human rights interventions, the 2003 VAT decision of the Colombian Constitutional Court provides important judicial authority for the proposition that ability to pay and meet the basic necessities of living must be respected in the design of all fiscal instruments.[47] This case challenged the constitutionality of removing long-standing VAT exemptions for basic necessities as a means of obtaining a "quick fix" to raise short-term revenues in the face of fiscal shortfalls. At the time the executive branch proposed to remove the exemptions, the VAT was already the country's biggest source of revenue. The executive's move was supported by international financial institutions that had given the government standby loans.[48] The Constitutional Court invalidated the elimination of the basic necessities exemptions on two grounds. It found that the Parliament had not openly considered the "implication for equity and progressiveness," which it was obligated to do. And it found that removing VAT exemptions for basic necessities was an "indiscriminate" expansion of the tax base that was invalid in light of the constitutional right to life, especially considering falling welfare spending, low tax burdens on the rich, and nonwelfare uses of the new revenues.[49]

In countries where there is no opportunity to challenge VAT-related human rights impacts comparable to the case before the Colombia constitutional court, or in situations where all other avenues of litigation have been exhausted domestically, the CEDAW Optional Protocol may provide an avenue for redress, as it did in the *Blok* and *Canadian Inquiry* complaints.[50] The provisions of the CEDAW and the Beijing Platform for Action provide detailed grounds not only for individual complaints before that treaty body but also for civil society submissions during a state's periodic review.

In the text of the CEDAW itself, the Preamble provides that a law will violate women's "equality of rights" whenever it creates "an obstacle to the participation of women, on equal terms with men" or "makes more difficult the full development of the potentialities of women." Undercutting women's ability to secure access to basic necessities by adding a VAT to the cost of the basic necessities of living would unquestionably meet those criteria, particularly when it can be shown that the government could have raised much-needed new revenues by restoring low PIT and CIT rates to their earlier higher levels. And for women and men with children who would risk becoming more malnourished due to government imposition of the VAT on household necessities, it could be shown that such a tax would also violate the general principle in the Preamble that "the upbringing of children requires a sharing of responsibility between men and women and society as a whole." In this context, the VAT would represent reduction of shared social responsibility for the upbringing of children, not positive sharing.

The general clauses in the CEDAW also offer grounds for such human rights challenges. Articles 1, 2(d) and (f), 3, 4, and 5(a) and (b) (general articles) all call for equality in policy formation, allocation of resources, decision-making authority, legal and substantive equality, and promotion of women's equality. Tax provisions that make it more difficult for women to secure, for themselves and for their families, enough basic necessities to ensure human survival and development facially violate these provisions. There is extensive research on how lack of adequate nutrition, water, sanitation, housing, education, medical, transportation, and housing facilities place women's equal chances of survival at risk. In particular, lack of adequate nutrition in most low-income countries increases the risk of maternal mortality, infant mortality, early childhood malnutrition leading to stunting and wasting, and reduced life changes of healthy development.[51] Recent studies suggest that subsequent nutritional improvements can help counter the effects of maternal and childhood poverty and malnourishment, but the decision to forgo early and ongoing intervention in favor of future restorative interventions would itself violate the fundamental human rights addressed in these provisions.[52]

Specific provisions of the CEDAW also speak to the effects of the VAT in low-income conditions. Articles 7 (political and public life, policy formation); 11(1)(d), (e) (employment, remuneration, benefits, and social security); 11(2)(b), (c), (d) (public life, paid work, maternity leave, job protection rights, and childcare resources); 13(a), (b), (c) (economic and social benefits); and 15(1), (2) (women in unpaid or subsistence areas) all prohibit policies, practices, and laws that discriminate against women on the basis of sex and call for "all appropriate action" to eliminate them. Given that the enactment of a VAT tends to deepen poverty and malnourishment, creating circumstances that reduce the chances of women, men, and children being able to afford the basic necessities of human development and functioning, there are ample grounds to demand more appropriate methods of producing government revenues.

In addition, the differential negative impact of the VAT on women-owned businesses creates separate grounds for complaints based on Articles 7, 11, 13, and 15. Women own fewer businesses than men, and these businesses are on average smaller, have fewer employees, are less profitable than men's, and have less access to capital from family, friends, or financial institutions. Thus women-owned businesses are more likely to end up with "trapped" VAT costs when they are too small to become registered VAT collectors, or cannot afford the costs of the level of formalization involved in becoming registered VAT collectors. With no way to recover or deduct the costs of VAT paid for supplies or services, women's smaller and less profitable businesses are further disadvantaged relative to men's businesses by implementation of the VAT, because "trapped" VAT either forces business owners to increase their prices (and thus lose customers), or to simply absorb the extra costs of the VAT to their businesses.[53]

The CEDAW Committee periodic state review reports have also placed increasing importance on the fiscal provisions of the Beijing Platform for Action. These include the importance of attaining gender equality in relation to fiscal and economic priorities regarding women and poverty (paras. 58(a)–(d)); equality for women in all economic relations, including the application of equality principles to fiscal instruments and the importance of gender budgeting (paras. 150, 155, 165(f), (i), 179(f)); the importance of maintaining effective institutional machinery responsible for gender mainstreaming (para. 205(c)); and active implementation of gender-equality reforms and impact analysis on all fiscal issues (paras. 345–353).

Of the Platform for Action provisions, paragraph 58 most directly calls for gender impact analysis and correction of discriminatory tax and transfer provisions like the issues posed by the use of the VAT in low-income countries:

(a) Review and modify, with the full and equal participation of women, macroeconomic and social policies with a view to achieving the objectives of the Platform for Action;

(b) Analyse, from a gender perspective, policies and programmes—including those related to . . . taxation . . . with respect to their impact on poverty, on inequality and particularly on women; assess their impact on family well-being and conditions and adjust them, as appropriate, to promote more equitable distribution of productive assets, wealth, opportunities, income and services;

(c) Pursue and implement sound and stable macroeconomic and sectoral policies that are designed and monitored with the full and equal participation of women, encourage broadbased sustained economic growth, address the structural causes of poverty and are aimed at eradicating poverty and reducing gender-based inequality within the overall framework of achieving people-centred development;

(d) Restructure and target the allocation of public expenditures to promote wo   men's economic opportunities and equal access productive resources and to address the basic social, educational and health needs of women, particularly those living in poverty.[54]

IV. CONCLUSION

The Beijing Platform and the CEDAW have been repeatedly confirmed, validated, and cross-linked to all components of the international human rights treaty system. Low-income countries may contend that they have to enact a VAT to meet their SDG domestic revenue mobilization targets and their CEDAW obligations to use "all available means" to mobilize domestic revenues and to fund poverty reduction policies. However, the Agreed Conclusions of the Commission on the Status of Women 60th session regarding the links between women's equality and empowerment and the SDGs explicitly affirm that while governments have obligations to fund gender-equality programs and ensure their durability, they must do this by means of tax measures that themselves are structurally consistent with the above principles set out paragraph 58 of the Platform.

Thus the UNCSW Agreed Conclusions state quite clearly that funding for gender-equality programs must itself be generated in a manner consistent with gender equality and that states remain under affirmative obligations to take action to "close resource gaps . . . including through the mobilization of financial resources from all sources . . . by enhancing revenue administration through modernized, progressive tax systems."[55]

The proliferation of tax-cut regimes combined with systemic reductions in government public expenditures has produced a growing need for government revenues. Widespread use of VAT rates, which are sometimes even higher than domestic PIT and CIT rates, to mobilize domestic revenues is not progressive taxation. To the contrary, it is one of the most extreme forms of regressive taxation. It is neither progressive policy nor a sustainable method of development to raise the revenues needed for poverty alleviation by disproportionately taxing those most in need of relief from poverty.

NOTES

1. See, e.g., R. L. Trosper, 'Northwest Coast Indigenous Institutions that Supported Resilience and Sustainability', 41 *Ecological Economics* (2002), 329, at 332–333.
2. See, e.g., J. Spangenberg, 'Institutional Change for Strong Sustainable Consumption: Sustainable Consumption and the Degrowth Economy', 10(1) *Sustainability: Science, Practice, and Policy* (2014), 62, at 62; see also UN Women, *Progress of the World's Women 2015–2016: Transforming Economies, Realizing Rights* (2016), available online at http://progress.unwomen.org/en/2015/pdf/ UNW_progressreport.pdf, at 209, figure 4.6.
3. The recognition of corporate structures and households as governance units dates back to Roman law. In the modern era, corporations definitively gained legal recognition as entities separate from their shareholders in the House of Lords decision in *Salomon v. A. Salomon and Company Ltd.* [1897] AC 22, [1895-9] All ER 33 ("The company is at law a different person altogether from the subscribers to the memorandum," per Macnaghten L.). Earlier in the 1800s, married women had gained property rights separate from their husbands, but were still considered to live within their husbands' fiscal space for tax and social spending purposes.
4. A. Smith, *The Wealth of Nations* (Methuen, 1904; orig. pub. 1776), Book V, Ch. II, Part II, paras. 25–28.
5. J. S. Mill, *Principles of Political Economy* (George Routledge, 1848), at 510.
6. *Report of the Royal Commission on Taxation* (1920) (UK), at 2, para. 6.
7. The 1966 Report of the Royal Commission on Taxation in Canada was strongly pressured to select economic growth as the top priority for fiscal policy. In the end, the Commission named "equity" as the most important priority on the basis that "a social and political system cannot be strong and enduring when a people becomes convinced that its tax structure does not distribute the tax burden fairly among all citizens." *Carter Commission, Report: Vol. 2* (1966), at 17. In terms of political justifications for budgetary choices, however, growth has been treated as being of greater practical importance in Canada since then, with, however, frequent references to the importance of equity.
8. OECD, *Economic Policy Reforms 2005: Going for Growth* (2005), available online at http://www. oecd.org/eco/labour/economicpolicyreformsgoingforgrowth2005.htm (last visited 9 June 2017).
9. OECD, *Economic Policy Reforms 2007: Going for Growth* (2007), available online at http://www. oecd.org/eco/growth/economicpolicyreformsgoingforgrowth2007.htm, at 17–19 (last visited 9 June 2017).
10. See, for example, OECD, *Economic Policy Reforms 2017: Going for Growth* (2017), available online at http://www.mzv.cz/public/d2/97/35/2331690_1692715_GfG_2017.pdf.
11. Convention on the Elimination of All Forms of Discrimination Against Women 1979, 1249 UNTS 13 [hereinafter CEDAW].
12. UN Women Watch, *Report of the Fourth World Conference on Women* (1995), available online at http://www.un.org/womenwatch/confer/beijing/reports/plateng.htm (last visited 9 June 2017).
13. Optional Protocol to the Convention on the Elimination of all forms of Discrimination Against Women, UN Doc. A/RES/54/4 (15 Oct. 1999), available online at http://www.ohchr.org/ Documents/HRBodies/CEDAW/OP_CEDAW_en.pdf.
14. See, for example, S. Fredman and B. Goldblatt, *Gender Equality and Human Rights* (2015), which brings Supreme Court of Canada jurisprudence on substantive equality directly into analysis of how gender equality is to be construed in applying CEDAW and the Beijing Platform.
15. See OECD, *Growing Unequal? Income Distribution and Poverty in OECD Countries* (2008).
16. OECD, *Gender and Taxation: Why Care about Taxation and Gender Equality?* (2010); OECD, *Divided We Stand: Why Inequality Keeps Rising* (2011); I. Joumard, M. Pisu, and D. Bloch, *Less Income Inequality and More Growth—Are They Compatible? Part 3. Income Redistribution via Taxes and Transfers across OECD Countries* (OECD Economics Department Working Papers, No. 926, 2012), available online at http://dx.doi.org/10.1787/5k9h296b1zjf-en (last visited 9 June 2017).

17. An influential report raising these points is M. Förster, A. Llena-Nozal, and V. Nafilyan, *Trends in Top Incomes and Their Taxation in OECD Countries* (OECD SEM Working Paper No. 59, 2014), available online at http://www.oecd.org/els/workingpapers (last visited 9 June 2017).

18. See General Assembly, Critical Milestones Toward Coherent, Efficient and Inclusive Follow-Up and Review at the Global Level, Report of the Secretary General, UN Doc. A/70/684, 15 Jan. 2016. The SDGs came into effect on 1 January 2016. Also see Paris Agreement (Framework Convention on Climate Change) 2015, CN.63.2016, CN.92.2016.

19. Addis Ababa Action Agenda of the Third International Conference on Financing for Development (Addis Ababa Action Agenda), endorsed by the General Assembly in GA Res. 69/313, 27 July 2015.

20. UN ECOSOC Commission on the Status of Women, Review and Appraisal of the Implementation of the Beijing Declaration, UN Doc. E/CN.6/2015/3, esp. at 65, para. 247, which explicitly commits to gender-based analysis of all fiscal measures in their linkages to gender and their impact on women.

21. Human Rights Council, Report of the Special Rapporteur on Extreme Poverty and Human Rights, Magdalena Sepúlveda Carmona on Mission to Mozambique, UN Doc. A/HRC/26/28/Add.1, 4 June 2014, esp. Sections I and II.

22. Ibid. 12–13.

23. Ibid. 16–17.

24. Ibid. 12–13.

25. Committee on the Elimination of Discrimination Against Women, Communication No. 36/2012, *Blok v. Netherlands*, UN Doc. CEDAW/C/57/D/36/2012, 24 Mar. 2014.

26. Committee on the Elimination of Discrimination Against Women, Report of the Inquiry Concerning Canada under Article 8 of the Optional Protocol to the Convention on the Elimination of All Forms of Discrimination Against Women, UN Doc. CEDAW/C/OP.8/CAN/1, 30 Mar. 2015.

27. Committee on the Elimination of Discrimination Against Women, Concluding Observations on the Combined Fourth and Fifth Periodic Reports of Switzerland, UN Doc. CEDAW/C/CHE/CO/4-5, 18 Nov. 2016, at paras. 40–41.

28. Committee on the Elimination of Discrimination Against Women, Concluding Observations on the Combined Eighth and Ninth Periodic Reports of Canada, UN Doc. CEDAW/C/CAN/CO/8-9, 25 Nov. 2016, at paras. 18–19.

29. OECD, *Tax Policy Reform and Economic Growth* (2010), available online at http://www.oecd.org/ctp/tax-policy/tax-policy-reform-and-economic-growth-9789264091085-en.htm (last visited 9 June 2017).

30. See, e.g., L. Ebrill et al., *The Modern VAT* (2001), at 28–38.

31. As measured by changes in market income and after-tax/transfer Gini coefficients; see OECD.Stat, *Income Distribution and Poverty*, available online at http://stats.oecd.org/Index.aspx?DataSetCode=IDD (last visited 9 June 2017).

32. N. Usui, *Tax Reforms Toward Fiscal Consolidation* (2011). The consultant used simulation methods to evaluate the impact of this proposed revenue shift on the allocation of the total after-tax load.

33. V. Tanzi and H. Zee, *Tax Policy for Developing Countries* (IMF Economic Issues No. 27, 2001).

34. See Smith, *supra* note 4, Book V, Ch. II, Part II; Brazil Constitution 1946, Article 202; Brazil Constitution 1988, Article 145 ("economic capacity of the taxpayer"), discussed in L. Cesarino Pessôa, 'The Historical Evolution of the Ability to Pay Principle in Brazil' ['Evoluzione storica del principio della capacità contributiva in Brasile'], 12(2) *Diritto e Pratica Tributaria Internazionale* (2015), 15 (unpublished translation provided by Dr. Pessôa); F. Vanistendael, 'Ability to Pay in European Community Law', 3 *EC Tax Review* (2014), 121, at 124 ("the ability to pay tax may . . . be regarded as forming part of the personal situation" in treaty law).

35. The principle of ability to pay taxes is one of the oldest and most universally accepted, but is most frequently used to justify the use to tax incomes at progressively higher rates on some version of the sacrifice theory. See, for example, M. Slade Kendrick, 'The Ability-to-Pay Theory of Taxation', 29(1) *American Economic Review* (1939), 92, at 92. The use of ability to pay to justify exempting those with low or no incomes from taxation has, however, emerged in human rights decisions,

and is impliedly recognized in studies demonstrating that spending tax compliance budgets on collecting taxes from those with low or no incomes is administratively inefficient.

36. Notable exceptions to this statement do exist. The Russian flat rated income tax provides no exemptions. Close examination of the size of personal income exemptions even in high-income countries reveals that many countries place ability to pay at risk by setting exemption levels lower than actual poverty levels or market basket measures of minimum necessary incomes.

37. Where credit facilities are available, the use of credit can unlink consumption from immediate payment.

38. In the past, some governments have collected taxes in the form of a portion of crops or as corvée labor. But in present practices, suppliers of goods or services are not permitted to "withhold" part of the goods or services being purchased in order to send them to the government, although that might be an informal practice.

39. This measure also has its limitations, especially when consumption expenditure may in fact be incurred by third parties or donors.

40. For a discussion of the advantages and disadvantages of using income versus expenditure as the welfare measure in VAT incidence studies, see C. Grown and H. Komatsu, 'Methodology and Comparative Analysis', *in* C. Grown and I. Valodia, *Taxation and Gender Equity* (2010), 23, at 33.

41. Ibid. each of the eight country studies; and see D. M. Casale, 'Indirect Taxation and Gender Equity: Evidence from South Africa', 18(3) *Feminist Economics* (2012), 25.

42. The United Nations has estimated that overall, developing country tax ratios (total tax revenues as a percentage of GDP) are just 17 percent, while ratios of at least 20 percent are needed to meet their SDG targets. See OECD, *Development Co-operation Report 2014: Mobilising Resources for Sustainable Development* (2014), available online at http://dx.doi.org/10.1787/dcr-2014-en, at 92 (last visited 17 July 2017).

43. See generally, Kathleen A. Lahey, Gender, Taxation and Equality in Developing Countries: Issues and Policy Recommendations, UN Women, April 2018, at https://www.globaltaxjustice.org/sites/default/files/Geder-Tax-Report-Fin-WEB.pdf.

44. See, e.g., R. Bird and P. Gendron, *VAT Revisited: A New Look at the Value Added Tax in Developing and Transitional Countries* (2005), at 89–98, for detailed discussion of VAT exemptions and zero-rating.

45. Ibid. Bird and Gendron provide several detailed examples of these types of special rules.

46. *Addis Ababa Action Agenda, supra* note 19, at para. 22.

47. Colombia Constitutional Court (2003). *Constitutional Review Judgment C-776-03*, per Espinosa, J., paras. 4.5.6 and 4.5.3.2.1, available online at http://www.corteconstitucional.gov.co/relatoria/2003/C-776-03.htm (last visited 9 June 2017) [Colombia, *Judgment C-776-03*].

48. For details of the revenue and political processes leading to this constitutional review, see M. Olivera, M. Pachón, and G. E. Perry, *The Political Economy of Fiscal Reform: The Case of Colombia, 1986–2006* (2010), at 20–24.

49. Colombia, *Judgment C-776-03*, paras. 4.5.6 and 4.5.3.2.1. For the details of the decision, see D. Landau and J. D. López Murcia, *Political Institutions and Judicial Role: An Approach in Context, the Case of the Colombian Constitutional Court* (2009), available online at http://www.scielo.org.co/scielo.php?script=sci_arttext&pid=S0041-90602009000200009, at 55–92 (last visited 9 June 2017).

50. *Blok v. Netherlands, supra* note 25; Committee on the Elimination of Discrimination Against Women, *supra* note 25, discussed in section I of this chapter.

51. See International Food Policy Research Institute, *Global Nutrition Report 2016: From Promise to Impact: Ending Malnutrition by 2030* (2016), especially table A3.2, at 120, table A3.3, at 121. Intergenerational transmission of such effects have also been found; e.g., S. P. Walker et al., 'Early Childhood Stunting Is Associated with Lower Developmental Levels in the Subsequent Generation of Children', 145(4) *Journal of Nutrition* (2015), 823.

52. S. Cueto et al., 'Postinfancy Growth, Schooling, and Cognitive Achievement: Young Lives', 98(6) *American Journal of Clinical Nutrition* (2013),1555.

53. See, e.g., P. Lehohla, *The Contribution of Small and Micro Enterprises to the Economy of the Country: A Survey of Non-VAT-registered Businesses in South Africa* (Statistics South Africa, 2002); A. Haroon Akram-Lodhi and I. van Staveren, *A Gender Analysis of the Impact of Indirect Taxes on*

Small and Medium Enterprises in Vietnam (2003), available online at http://www.genderbudgets. org/index.php (last visited 9 June 2017).

54. Beijing Platform for Action, UN Doc. A/CONF. 177/20 (1995), available online at http://www. un.org/womenwatch/daw/beijing/pdf/BDPfA%20E.pdf, at para. 58(a)–(d).

55. ECOSOC Commission on the Status of Women, Report on the Sixtieth Session, UN Doc. E/2016/ 27-E/CN.6/2016/22, 20 Mar. 2015 and 14–24 Mar. 2016, at 16; Women's Empowerment and the Link to Sustainable Development: 2016 Commission on the Status of Women Agreed Conclusions, available online at http://www.unwomen.org/-/media/headquarters/attachments/sections/csw/60/ csw60%20agreed%20conclusions%20conclusions%20en.pdf?la=en&vs=4409, at paras. 18 & bb.

CHAPTER 20

HUMAN RIGHTS AND THE TAXATION OF MENSTRUAL HYGIENE PRODUCTS IN AN UNEQUAL WORLD

BRIDGET J. CRAWFORD AND CARLA SPIVACK

I. INTRODUCTION

In much of the Western world, laws no longer contain sex-based classifications. In the United States, for example, women can serve on juries.[1] Women can obtain credit cards in their own names.[2] Women have an equal right to be appointed as an administrator of a decedent's intestate estate.[3] The tax laws—in the United States and elsewhere—however, contain numerous examples of hidden gender bias. Consider, for example, the fact that in the United States, employers who are sued for gender discrimination can deduct their payouts as business expenses, but women (and men) who suffer from employment discrimination on the basis of their gender must include the award in their gross income.[4] Careful scrutiny reveals that gender is deeply embedded in what seem to be facially neutral tax laws. One example of this is the "tampon tax"—an umbrella term that refers to sales, value-added taxes (VAT), and similar taxes imposed on menstrual hygiene products, whether tampons or not. That these products are subject to taxation—when there are no comparable products used by men, and the closest analogues avoid taxation—illustrates that tax reform is an essential component of a larger effort to achieve gender equality. Because gender equality is an integral part of a robust human rights agenda, tax reform also must be understood as key to realizing more meaningful human rights.

This chapter provides a snapshot overview of the current sales tax and VAT on menstrual hygiene products throughout the world. In most of the states in the United States, these items are subject to sales tax.[5] In much of the European Union, these products are treated as luxuries and are subject to the highest rate of VAT.[6] Access to affordable menstrual hygiene products implicates the human rights to be free from discrimination, to sanitation, to education, to dignity, and to work.[7] The discussion refers to examples from India and Kenya to illustrate the importance of access to both affordable menstrual hygiene products and private, hygienic sanitation facilities. Some state and local governments in the United States have taken actions to

Tax, Inequality, and Human Rights. Philip Alston and Nikki Reisch.

facilitate access to menstrual hygiene products, including elimination of all sales taxes and the provision of free products in public schools, jails, and homeless shelters.[8] Under the First Step Act, enacted in December, 2018, the US federal Bureau of Prisons must provide federal prisoners with sanitary napkins and tampons without charge.[9] In several of the United States, private plaintiffs have brought state class action law suits challenging the sales tax on menstrual hygiene products.[10] Although no similar case has come before the European Court of Human Rights or the European Court of Justice, both of those courts have recognized the link between taxation and human rights.[11] Several European cases might be helpful precedents for a future legal challenge. Public attention to this issue remains important, and the tampon tax is part of much needed gender-focused tax reform.

II. AN OVERVIEW OF SALES TAX AND VAT ON MENSTRUAL HYGIENE PRODUCTS

A. GENERAL THEORY OF SALES AND VAT TAX EXEMPTIONS

In the United States, each of the fifty states decides whether to implement a state sales tax system (there is no national sales tax in the United States). Five states—Alaska, Delaware, Oregon, Montana, and New Hampshire—have decided not to impose a sales tax.[12] The remaining forty-five states do impose and collect sales tax. The fiscal importance of the sales tax cannot be overstated. Aggregate sales tax collected by the states far exceeds state income tax revenue. In 2015, for example, states collected over $430 billion in sales taxes, but just over $338 billion in income taxes.[13] The sales tax is a meaningful source of revenue for the states that impose it.

In the forty-five states that have a sales tax, the system generally works as follows: the state imposes a tax on the sale of tangible property.[14] The retail seller collects the tax from the customer and then pays the tax to the state. By statutory definition, most sales get swept into the "taxable" net, unless they are specifically excluded from taxation.[15] Commonly excluded from the sales tax are food, medical supplies and necessities. And in thirty-five of the United States, as of January 1, 2019, menstrual hygiene products are subject to sales tax, typically because they are classified as nonmedical items or non-necessities (although many states are considering changing their tax laws).[16]

In many other countries, a national VAT system is the norm. Under a VAT system, tax is imposed at each stage in the production and distribution process, with the final stage coming when the product is sold to the retail customer.[17] In the European Union, to give just one example, the VAT allows for four categories of taxation: (1) exempt; (2) zero tax (meaning technically subject to taxation but not taxed); (3) "reduced rate" of not less than 5 percent for items deemed "necessities" (listed on a particular schedule); and (4) the "standard rate" of 15 percent or more for "luxuries".[18] Individual countries cannot change or eliminate VAT on their own; tax rates are strictly controlled.[19] Any reduction in VAT rates in EU countries must be approved by the EU Parliament.[20]

Items in the exempt category include healthcare services, sports activities, and education-related expenses such as university fees and supplies.[21] The exempt classification seems to have a fairly rational basis: items required for basic living or with an agreed-upon social utility—i.e., supplies for children, many cultural activities, charitable giving—are tax exempt. Included in the "zero rating" (or no tax) category are those items that are seeming "necessities."[22] Items in this category include children's clothing and footwear, medical supplies, and basic foodstuffs (like bread, flour, cheese, cereals, milk, fruit, vegetables, pasta, sugar).[23] Items eligible for the reduced rate are the supply of water and electricity for residential use, movie tickets, and hairdressing services.[24] Items taxed at the standard rate, in contrast, include prepared and catered foods, alcoholic beverages and adult clothing.[25]

To a certain extent, the system of value-added taxation is based on a rubric of "human flourishing."[26] That is, the theory underlying the VAT is that certain items that humans need to reach their full potential—not just physical necessities, like food and shelter, but also education and culture—should be accessible, without tax, to individuals in all member states.

Note further that even though there is a union-wide VAT and four categories of taxation, the European Union sets the minimum rate in each of the two taxable categories.[27] Individual national rates within the two taxable categories may vary from country to country.[28] In most states in the European Union, menstrual hygiene products are subject to taxation as nonessential luxury items, and as such, are taxed at the highest permissible rate.[29] The tax on menstrual hygiene products is 25 percent in Denmark and 19 percent in Germany, for example.[30] In the United Kingdom, the tampon tax rate is only 5 percent.[31] If one accepts the human flourishing rubric for the VAT classifications, the tampon tax seems like even more of an anomaly in the European Union than in the United States: while some states seem to provide tax exemptions with a similar rationale—Massachusetts does not tax food and clothing, for example[32]—many other states in the United States seemingly impose taxes wherever political expediency dictates.[33]

B. TAMPON TAXES IN THE UNITED STATES

In the United States, the existence, structure, and administration of the state sales tax is left to each state. In the thirty-five states that impose a tax on menstrual hygiene products, the decision does not seem to be universally deliberate. Some states have actively decided to tax these products, while others seem not to have considered the issue explicitly, yet do not fit menstrual hygiene products into any of the categories that the state recognizes as tax exempt. This has resulted in certain anomalies.

In Florida, for example, products that are tax exempt include medical products and supplies, medicinal drugs, and "common household remedies recommended and generally sold for internal and external use in the cure, mitigation, treatment, or prevention of illness or disease in human beings, but not including cosmetics or toilet articles, notwithstanding the presence of medicinal ingredients therein."[34] Up until January 18, 2018, when a new law took effect Florida, menstrual hygiene products were subject to taxation, even though they prevent infection and disease.

Up until September 1, 2016, New York imposed a sales tax on menstrual hygiene products.[35] But it designated as exempt condoms,[36] "incontinence liners,"[37] and "products that are intended as a hair regrowth treatment for use by human beings who experience hair loss or gradually thinning hair."[38] Prior to the change in law, "feminine hygiene products" were considered to be "generally used to control a normal bodily function and to maintain personal cleanliness" and thus subject to sales tax.[39]

C. TAMPON TAXES IN THE EUROPEAN UNION

The essential legal instrument regulating VAT application across the European Union, the EU VAT Directive, includes a minimum standard rate of 15 percent (at Point 29).[40] The Directive contains three provisions relevant to the imposition of VAT on menstrual hygiene products.

Article 98 states that member states may apply a discretionary reduced rate of 5 percent to goods and services listed in Annex III.[41] Annex III lists "contraception and sanitary products" as candidates for the reduced rate.[42] Menstrual hygiene products were charged at the standard rate in the United Kingdom until the 2000 Budget, for example. Then the VAT rate on menstrual hygiene products was lowered to 5 percent.[43]

Further support for reclassification of menstrual hygiene products as VAT-exempt exists in Article 132 of the VAT Directive, which permits VAT exemptions that are in the "public interest," including, for example, "medical care."[44] In addition, Articles 2 and 3(3) of the Treaty of the European Union make reference to ensuring equality between men and women.[45] Making menstrual hygiene products VAT-exempt would be a symbolic step to uphold these values, but the European Parliament would have to approve the changes. And it is unclear how post-Brexit Britain plans to address the issue of the tampon tax along with many other issues.

In general, EU tax law and its stated underlying principles seem to offer some avenues for challenging the tax on menstrual hygiene products.[46] Whether these will be more productive than challenges in the United States remains to be seen. While US law provides for equal protection challenges, which might require a showing that similar products used by men are not taxed, European law calls for EU-wide measures that advance equality between the sexes.[47] The latter, as a more general and aspirational directive, may provide more fertile ground for such challenges, as it seems to take into account such issues as the stigmatization of one sex to which discrepant taxation arguably contributes.

III. THE TAMPON TAX AND HUMAN RIGHTS

The tampon tax is a human rights issue because menstrual hygiene and affordable access to menstrual hygiene products are inextricably linked to rights to health, sanitation, education, dignity, and work, among other rights. Eliminating taxes on menstrual hygiene products is consistent with the human right to be free from discrimination and other rights that flow therefrom.[48] To be sure, sales tax and VAT are largely matters of domestic law for each nation or for a subdivision (such as a state, in the United States) in each nation. Even the European Union, which prescribes an overall VAT regime, does not prescribe specific rates (within the various categories). If anything, the VAT Directive limits national leeway in reducing or increasing the VAT. So the solution lies not with international treaties that deal with taxation, but rather actions brought in courts and other appropriate venues to draw the connection between affordable menstrual hygiene products and women's equal participation in society.

A. RIGHT TO BE FREE FROM DISCRIMINATION

Human rights law derives from a variety of sources, including international, regional and specialized treaties. The Universal Declaration of Human Rights (UDHR),[49] adopted by the UN General Assembly in 1948, is the foundational document that delineates the human rights that should be recognized by all member states. These include the right to equality and the right to be free from discrimination: "All are equal before the law and are entitled without any discrimination to equal protection of the law. All are entitled to equal protection against any discrimination in violation of this Declaration and against any incitement to such discrimination."[50] Because this document is a General Assembly Resolution, not a treaty, the principles of the UDHR are implemented through treaties such as the International Covenant on Civil and Political Rights (ICCPR),[51] the International Covenant on Economic, Social and Cultural Rights (ICESCR),[52] and regional agreements such as the European Convention for the Protection of Human Rights and Fundamental Freedoms (ECHR), the American Convention on Human Rights,[53] and the African Charter on Human and Peoples' Rights.[54]

Each of the implementing treaties contains specific provisions that prohibit discrimination and serve as the basis for the application of a variety of human rights, including the right of women to be free from discrimination and to equal protection under the law. Consider, for example, Article 14 of the ECHR:

> The enjoyment of the rights and freedoms set forth in this Convention shall be set forth without discrimination on any ground such as sex, race, color, language, religion, political or other opinion, national or social origin, association with a national minority, property, birth or other status.

Article 14 complaints must be brought in conjunction with one of the other articles which address substantive rights; the applicant must show discrimination in a substantive area.[55] Cases alleging violations of Article 14 in tax matters, for example, are brought under Article 1, Protection of Property, which states:

> Every natural or legal person is entitled to the peaceful enjoyment of his possessions. No one shall be deprived of his possessions except in the public interest and subject to the conditions provided by the law and by the general principles of international law.
>
> The preceding provision shall not, however, in any way impair the right of a State to enforce such laws as it seems necessary to control the use of property in accordance with the general interest or to secure the payment of taxes or other contributions or penalties.[56]

Consider also the antidiscrimination provisions of Article 26 of the ICCPR:

> All persons are equal before the law and are entitled without discrimination to the equal protection of the law. In this respect, the law shall prohibit any discrimination and guarantee to all persons equal and effective protection against discrimination on any ground such as race, color, sex, language, religion.[57]

This broad antidiscrimination language elaborates on the Universal Declaration's commitment to equality and freedom from discrimination.[58]

Another rich source for international human rights for women in particular is the Convention on the Elimination of All Forms of Discrimination Against Women (CEDAW), adopted by the UN General Assembly in 1979.[59] CEDAW consists of a preamble and thirty specific articles that many refer to as "an international bill of rights for women."[60] CEDAW Article 1 takes an expansive view of discrimination, defining it as "any distinction, exclusion or restriction made on the basis of sex which has the effect or purpose of impairing or nullifying the recognition, enjoyment or exercise by women, irrespective of their marital status, on a basis of equality of men and women, of human rights and fundamental freedoms in the political, economic, social, cultural, civil or any other field." The treaty was signed initially by sixty-four countries; as of January 1, 2019, over 188 countries are parties to CEDAW.[61] The party states agree to "take all appropriate measures, including legislation, to modify or abolish existing laws, regulations, customs and practices which constitute discrimination against women."[62] CEDAW was signed in 1980 by US

President Jimmy Carter, who sent the treaty to the Senate for advice and consent. The Senate Committee on Foreign Relations has never brought the treaty to a floor vote.[63]

A woman's right to be free from discrimination is violated when menstrual hygiene products are subject to sales tax when there are no similar products that men must use because of an involuntary, biological monthly occurrence, and when the closest analogous products used primarily by men are not subject to taxation. Taxing products used primarily, or even exclusively, by women is to tax them on the basis of their sex, something which is prohibited by international human rights norms.

B. RIGHT TO HEALTH

According to a recent study by Nielsen and Plan India, just 12 percent of India's estimated 355 million menstruating girls and women use sanitary napkins.[64] If these products were more affordable, more girls and women might prefer them over their current practices, which might include hand-washed cloth, grass, or other sustainable substances fashioned into absorbent pads, or no menstrual products at all.[65] Any tax on tampons or pads makes it more difficult for women, especially poor women, to practice good menstrual hygiene. (India repealed its tampon tax in July, 2018.) Poor hygiene may cause adverse physical health consequences, such as an increase in urogenital infections[66] like bacterial vaginal infections and vulva vaginal candidiasis.[67] But even if disposable tampons or sanitary napkins were more widely available, the lack of access to sanitation facilities would still be an obstacle to women's flourishing in many parts of the world.

Article 12 of the ICESCR recognizes "the right of everyone to the enjoyment of the highest attainable standard of physical and mental health."[68] That right has been interpreted to include access to "facilities, goods, services and conditions necessary for the realization of the highest attainable standard of health."[69] Health facilities, goods, and services must be "accessible to all, especially the most vulnerable or marginalized sections of the population in law and in fact, without discrimination."[70] The right to health includes not only the right to healthcare but also access to "the underlying determinants of health, such as access to safe and potable water and adequate sanitation."[71]

In 2015, the UN General Assembly passed and adopted by consensus a resolution acknowledging human rights to water and sanitation. All member states thus recognize that "the human right to safe drinking water entitles everyone, without discrimination, to have access to sufficient, safe, acceptable, physically accessible and affordable water for personal and domestic use," and also that "the human right to sanitation entitles everyone, without discrimination, to have physical and affordable access to sanitation, in all spheres of life, that is safe, hygienic, secure, socially and culturally acceptable and that provides privacy and ensures dignity."[72]

Access to water is especially important for women for a variety of reasons, including menstrual hygiene management. Menstrual hygiene management is an umbrella term given to a series of "best practices" for menstruating girls and women recommended by international humanitarian organizations like UNICEF and international health working groups like the Water Supply and Sanitation Collaborative Council.[73] These best practices include changing clothing and underwear regularly, changing hygienic pads several times a day, showering daily, washing the genitals after each trip to the bathroom, maintaining a normal school or work schedule, and eating a balanced diet.[74]

There is reason to believe that good menstrual hygiene management is elusive in much of the world. In one study of 160 adolescent girls in West Bengal in 2008, only 48.75 percent of girls knew that sanitary pads were used during menstruation, and only 11.25 percent of girls used them.[75] A 2015 report by UNICEF and the World Health Organization found that at least 500 million women and girls lack access to basic sanitation facilities, which makes menstrual hygiene management difficult or impossible.[76]

C. RIGHT TO EDUCATION

Lack of access to adequate menstrual hygiene facilities may lead girls or women to stay home from school and to fail to participate fully in public life. In November 1989, the UN General Assembly adopted the Convention on the Rights of the Child,[77] which derived from the UDHR and both the international covenants on human rights. As of June 20, 2016, 196 states are parties to this convention.[78] (The United States has signed the treaty, but the Senate has not yet given its advice and consent.[79]) It requires states to "ensure that all segments of society, in particular parents and children, are informed, have access to education and are supported in the use of basic knowledge of child health."[80]

In India, for example, 20 percent of girls reportedly drop out of school when they reach the age of menstruation.[81] In Kenya, government officials distribute approximately US$3 million worth of free sanitary pads at schools in poor communities so that girls will be more likely to stay in school.[82] The government supply is supplemented by private charities like the ZanaAfrica Foundation, which delivers free menstrual hygiene products to girls so that they are less likely to miss classes when they are menstruating for fear of staining their clothes, for example.[83] In 2004, the Kenyan government eliminated the sales tax on menstrual hygiene products in an effort to make them more affordable to girls and women.[84] In a country where over half the population lives on less than US$1 per day, the elimination of a twenty-cent tax on the $1.20 charged for an eight-pack of sanitary napkins can make a substantial difference in menstrual hygiene management.[85]

D. RIGHT TO WORK

Inadequate menstrual hygiene also impairs women's right to work, another human right. Article 23(1) of the UDHR states that "[e]veryone has the right to work, to free choice of employment, to just and favourable conditions of work and to protection against unemployment."[86] Yet a study in Bangladesh by HERProject, a global nonprofit that organizes women's empowerment programs in factories, found that 73 percent of female Bangladeshi garment workers said they missed an average of six days of work—and pay—a month due to vaginal infections, often caused by lack of menstrual sanitation.[87] Other studies confirm the finding that lack of menstrual hygiene products causes women to miss work.[88]

E. RIGHT TO DIGNITY

The 1948 UDHR enshrined the right to dignity in its preamble, which states that "recognition of the inherent dignity and of the equal and inalienable rights of all members of the human family is the foundation of freedom, justice and peace in the world."[89] Impairing access to hygiene, specifically menstrual hygiene, clearly undermines this right for women by making it difficult to maintain the cleanliness of their bodies and then subjecting them to ridicule and stigma for that very lack of cleanliness. As the Human Rights Initiative at the Central European University explains on its webpage:

> All human rights stem from the fundamental right to human dignity. When people who are bleeding every month are forced into seclusion, must use damp and soiled materials, are treated as second class citizens, dignity is difficult to maintain.[90]

The UN Human Rights Office has recognized this connection as well. In March 2014, it organized a conference called Inspiring Change to Promote Women's Rights and Dignity, which explored women's advances in securing their rights and dignity in areas like access to water, sanitation, and hygiene.[91] Jyoti Sanghera, Chief of the Human Rights Office Economic and Social Issues Section, explained that "the stigma around menstruation and menstrual hygiene is a violation of several human rights, most importantly of the right to human dignity."[92] Increasing the cost of menstrual sanitation and treating it as a luxury rather than a necessity clearly implicate women's right to dignity.

F. HUMAN RIGHTS CHALLENGES TO TAMPON TAX

1. Venues

Framing women's affordable access to menstrual hygiene products as a human rights issue opens the door to the possibility of appealing to international or regional bodies to address a complaint brought by an individual who alleges that the tax on menstrual hygiene products violates her right to be free from discrimination. In the case of the International Court of Justice, however, only states can submit a dispute to the court,[93] and it is difficult to see how one state would challenge another's domestic sales tax regime. But individuals may bring complaints against a state party under certain human rights treaties. Possible international venues might include the Human Rights Committee (for alleged violations of the ICCPR), the Committee on Elimination of Discrimination Against Women (for alleged violations of CEDAW), the Committee on Economic, Social and Cultural Rights (for alleged violations of the ICESCR), and the Committee on the Rights of the Child (for alleged violations the Convention on the Rights of the Child).[94] Possible regional venues include the European Court of Human Rights (ECtHR), the African Court of Human and Peoples' Rights, the African Commission on Human Rights, the Inter-American Court of Human Rights, and the Inter-American Commission on Human Rights.[95] The ECtHR is an especially promising venue, in light of some precedents in that court that suggest a connection between gender-differentiated tax treatment and human rights violations.

2. Precedents in ECtHR

So far, no cases have come before the ECtHR or the European Court of Justice challenging the tax on menstrual hygiene products. But both courts have decided cases that recognize a connection between taxation and human rights.[96] Generally speaking, other successful tax challenges have rested on a differential treatment of men and women under the tax laws. These cases implicate either Article 14 of the ECHR (the right to freedom from discrimination) and an alleged violation of Article 1's protection of property provisions, or Article 26 of the ICCPR (the right to freedom from discrimination).

One illustrative case is *Van Raalte v. The Netherlands*.[97] In that case, the Court evaluated a provision of Dutch law that exempted unmarried childless women forty-five years of age and older from paying taxes under the General Childcare Benefits Act, but did not exempt similarly situated men.[98] The petitioner, a sixty-three-year-old unmarried man with no children, was assessed a tax and objected on the grounds of sex discrimination under both Article 1 of the Netherlands Constitution (banning discrimination on the basis of sex) and Article 1 of Protocol 1 of the ECHR (the right to freedom from discrimination). After exhausting local remedies, the petitioner filed a claim with the ECtHR. The court found that no compelling reasons existed for the differing treatment. It rejected the Dutch government's claim that imposing the tax on older, childless women would cause them emotional harm, and that women should be exempt from the tax but similarly situated men should have to pay the tax.[99]

Another case similarly addresses gender-based tax laws. In *Case of Hobbs, Richard, Walsh and Geen v. The United Kingdom*, the petitioners were widowers who had applied for the so-called "Widow's Bereavement Allowance" (WBA), a particular tax benefit available to widows but not to widowers.[100] Inland Revenue denied all of the claims because of the sex of the applicants, i.e., they were widowers, not widows.[101] The law authorizing the WBA had been abolished prospectively for deaths occurring after April 6, 2000, but the petitioners' claims had all arisen between 1997 and 1999, before the date of abolition.[102] The petitioners claimed that Inland Revenue's refusal to grant them the WBA because of their sex was a violation of ECHR Article 14, read in conjunction with Article 1 of Protocol 1.[103]

In deciding for the petitioners, the Court began by acknowledging that "Article 14 does not prevent a member state from treating groups differently in order to correct 'factual inequalities' between them."[104] Indeed, the court went on, "in certain circumstances a failure to address inequality through different treatment may in itself give rise to a breach of the article."[105] Nonetheless, different treatment is discriminatory if it fails to "pursue a legitimate aim or if there is not a reasonable relationship of proportionality between the means employed and the aim sought to be realized."[106] In this context, the Court noted that the WBA had been introduced at a time when Great Britain charged married couples as single entities, allowing a man to claim a tax allowance for the wife's earnings. For the man, this allowance continued for a year after the wife's death, whereas a widow did not receive such a benefit. Thus the WBA had been a remedial measure when adopted, meant to cure a gendered discrepancy. The Court observed, however, that the government had introduced separate taxation of married men and women in 1990–1991, and that therefore the WBA became obsolete at that point.[107] For the tax law to continue to offer a tax benefit to women that it did not offer to men constituted a violation of Article 14 in conjunction with Article 1 of Protocol 1.[108]

In a similar case, *Willis v. United Kingdom*,[109] the Court found that another set of differing tax benefits for men and women violated Article 14 and Article 1 of Protocol 1. In *Willis*, the petitioner's wife had been the family breadwinner until she died of cancer at age thirty-nine. The widower-petitioner applied for the benefits to which a widow would have been entitled in the same circumstances, namely, a Widow's Payment and Widowed Mother's Allowance (the couple had two minor children at the time of the wife's death).[110] The government rejected both claims.[111] Petitioner then brought a claim alleging violations of Article 14 and Article 1 of Protocol 1, as well as a violation of Article 8, which guarantees the right to "respect for private and family life."[112] The court found that the disparate treatment of men and women in regard to the two benefits was "not based on any objective and reasonable justification" and that it therefore violated the ECHR.[113]

The ECtHR reached a similar conclusion in the *Case of Zeman v. Austria*.[114] In *Zeman*, the petitioner's retirement pension from the state had been adjusted downward due to his receipt of a portion of his deceased wife's pension as well as his own, a law that applied to widowers and not to widows.[115] In fact, the government had added a provision to the pension plan in 1994, which further differentiated men and women. This, the court found, was unjustifiable and a violation of the Article 14 and Article 1 of Protocol 1.[116]

Taken together, these cases suggest that the ECtHR is willing to hear cases that allege gender-based tax discrimination as a human rights issue. *Raalte* offers perhaps the most promising analogy, in that it invalidated a tax burden placed on only one sex without apparent justification. The Court's reasoning in *Raalte*, however, stressed that the discrepant tax treatment had no factual basis because it did not reflect reality: it noted that women forty-five years of age or older may well become eligible for benefits under the Act by marrying a man with children, or, with advances in technology, having her own biological children, or adopting, and that men under the age of forty-five may be unable to procreate.[117] Thus, the Court invalidated the law by undercutting the biologically based assumptions which the government used to justify it. In the case of the tax on menstrual hygiene products, there is an undeniable biological difference between men and women that makes women and girls the primary consumers of these products. But there is a strong argument that women are disproportionately paying these taxes because there are no products that men use solely because of an involuntary, biological monthly occurrence. Indeed, the most analogous products that address men's biological needs, such as condoms, are taxed at the reduced rate under the VAT.

An important issue implicated by any case that might be brought in the ECtHR or any other court or committee is the question of remedy. Pecuniary remedies are available, although losses may be awarded on an equitable basis, instead of actual financial loss suffered.[118] But because the tax on menstrual hygiene products has been so lucrative to governments, the Court might be reluctant to award more than symbolic pecuniary damages. Indeed, the enormity of the tax revenue from the sale of menstrual hygiene products is one of the main reasons that efforts of the French legislature, for example, to repeal the tax failed in the first place.[119] For administrative and political reasons, then, it seems unlikely that the ECtHR would be willing to order a large-scale payment of refunds to all consumers. It declined to award even individual damages in *Hobbs*[120] and *Raalte*,[121] for example, even though the court found that the tax laws were discriminatory.

In *Hobbs*, the petitioners argued that they should be compensated for the amount they would have received had they been eligible for the WBA, based on the principle of *restitutio in integrum*, i.e., the right to be made whole.[122] They also argued that compensation would provide an incentive for states not to engage in discrimination.[123] They correctly pointed out that the European Court of Justice had on many occasions used compensation as a way of "levelling up"—giving the complainant the same benefits as the favored group—rather than "levelling down"—denying compensation because neither group should have received the benefit.[124] But the ECtHR declined to award damages in *Hobbs*, calling the WBA an "anachronistic relic" that the government had abandoned in 1994. Justice did not require, said the Court, that "an anomaly should be further extended."[125] The rationale seems to be that the benefit the complainants were denied had never been justifiable, and therefore there was nothing for which to compensate them. The WBA had "unduly favored widows" over all other taxpayers. Unjustified at the time, and since abandoned, the anomalous benefit did not give rise to compensation.

The Court similarly declined to award damages in *Raalte*, even though it found that tax payments had been made under a law that violated the ECHR.[126] The Court noted that the finding of a violation of Article 1 of Protocol 1 does not "entitle the applicant to retrospective exemption from contributions under the scheme in question."[127] These cases suggest that the ECtHR would be unwilling to award any damages at all in a case challenging the tax on menstrual hygiene products.

Arguably the tampon tax is different because it is more visible than the taxes in the cases cited, and it is ongoing. While *Hobbs*, for example, involved a tax scheme which had been abolished, thus eliminating the need for the deterrent effect of a damages award, the tampon tax scheme is alive and well. In the case of menstrual hygiene products, members of one sex pay a discriminatory tax that benefits society at large, but the tax causes hardship to many girls and women. For that reason, the tampon tax may present a clear case for a class-based damages award. Politically, however, it might present more difficulty, unless substantial public opinion is brought to bear.

Because of a variety of legal traditions in the United States, direct appeals to state or local government or to domestic courts are more likely than international human rights bodies to be a plaintiff's first line of recourse against the tampon tax. The next part discusses how legislators, activists, and plaintiffs have attempted to remedy the financial inequities of the tampon tax in the United States.

IV. THE TAMPON TAX AND INEQUALITY

A. DIRECT GOVERNMENT ACTION: THE NEW YORK EXAMPLE

In June 2016, the New York City Council unanimously passed a law that makes tampons and pads available for free in all New York City public schools, homeless shelters, and jails.[128] Approximately 300,000 girls and women are expected to benefit from this reform.[129] In a press release that accompanied his signing the bill into law, New York City Mayor Bill de Blasio said, "There should be no stigma around something as fundamental as menstruation. These laws recognize that feminine hygiene products are a necessity—not a luxury."[130] Mayor de Blasio specifically recognized the connection between good menstrual hygiene and school attendance, saying, "No young person should miss class or be embarrassed at school because she needs a tampon or pad."[131] The legislation is especially significant given that an estimated 79 percent of all New York City public school students come from low-income families.[132] Significantly, the New York City law received national and international press in outlets including the *Huffington Post*,[133] *Slate*,[134] *US News & World Report*,[135] *Glamour*,[136] and the BBC.[137]

Legislation similar to New York's is under consideration in Sydney, Australia.[138] Free menstrual hygiene products would be available not only in homeless shelters but also in libraries and sporting venues.[139] Sydney City Councillor Edward Mandla has explained that he hopes that the government example would have a ripple effect in the private sector: in Sydney, he says, "There's money for everyone and lots of talk about equality. But there's little in practical leadership solutions. Providing free sanitary products is a low cost solution that ought to inspire corporations around Australia to follow suit."[140] In Sydney, as in the United States, there are already a variety of private efforts to supply menstrual hygiene products in homeless shelters,[141] so municipal legislation might lessen the need for private intervention. (Australia repealed its GST on menstrual hygiene products effective January 1, 2019.)

Regardless of the outcome of the Sydney legislation, the New York legislation already has spurred activists in other locations to begin to pressure their governments to provide free menstrual hygiene products. For example, women in Scotland have called on the national government for intervention.[142] In the United States, there is a "Free the Tampons" movement based in Ohio that seeks to "drive demand for freely accessible tampons and pads in restrooms outside the home."[143] In Dane County, Wisconsin, free menstrual hygiene products are available in some public buildings.[144] Whether local or state governments will respond to or expand existing programs, however, may depend in large part on a debate about the role of government in providing basic necessities to its citizenry.

In countries with less developed economies or established wealth, there is no realistic possibility that the government will provide free menstrual hygiene products. Schools are unlikely to have the financial resources to do so either. It is important (and more realistic) to focus on improving access to basic sanitation and toileting facilities in schools and workplaces. In schools in developing nations, it is important that girls have access to private toileting facilities where they can change their menstrual hygiene products. An estimated half of schools in developing nations do not have toilets at all, so this is an urgent priority.[145]

Intuitively one understands that there are substantial economic losses associated with menstruating girls and women who absent themselves from the public sphere, but there is limited data available.[146] A 2006 study funded by the David and Lucile Packard Foundation identifies hygiene as "fundamental" to health of female workers, citing as evidence of the need for better hygiene the fact that some female factory workers in India, for example, use cloth scraps from the factory floor to absorb their menstrual flow.[147]

It is not realistic for all governments to provide free menstrual hygiene products for girls and women. But in order to fulfill a commitment to human rights for girls and women, governments must improve access to basic sanitation facilities. Governments also should eliminate any sales tax on menstrual hygiene products as a crucial step in improving women's health and access to education.

B. CHALLENGES TO THE TAMPON TAX IN THE UNITED STATES

In the United States, there is no national sales tax, so the taxation of menstrual hygiene products is a matter left to each of the fifty states. As of January 1, 2019, fifteen states exempt menstrual hygiene products from sales tax. Five states—Alaska, Delaware, Oregon, Montana, and New Hampshire—impose no sales tax on any products at all.[148] Five states—Maryland, Massachusetts, Pennsylvania, Minnesota, and New Jersey—had repealed their sales tax on menstrual hygiene products prior to 2016.[149] Five states—New York, Connecticut, Illinois, Florida and Nevada—lifted their sales tax on menstrual hygiene products relatively recently.[150] The District of Columbia did so beginning in October 2017.[151] Several other states saw some legislation or debate on the tampon tax in recent legislative sessions, but still have a tax in effect.[152] The majority of US states treat menstrual hygiene products as taxable.[153] The efforts to change this are proceeding in both legislatures and courts.[154]

Simultaneously with these legislative reform efforts, several women recently have brought class action litigation to challenge the sales tax imposed on menstrual hygiene products. Five women in New York filed a class action law suit seeking to invalidate New York's sales tax, permanently enjoining the state of New York from collecting sales tax on tampons and sanitary napkins, seeking a refund of an estimated $14 million in sales tax collected in each of the last three years, and seeking attorneys' fees.[155] After the suit was filed, New York changed its law prospectively, so the injunctive claims became moot, and the plaintiffs voluntarily withdrew their claim. Other class actions challenging the state sales tax on menstrual hygiene products have been filed in Ohio (and that case is ongoing),[156] California (where the case was dismissed on procedural grounds),[157] and Florida (where the case was dismissed after the state prospectively repealed its tampon tax).[158]

V. CONCLUSION

The issue of the tampon tax has gained traction relatively quickly across national borders. A discriminatory sales tax on menstrual hygiene products might seem to be an unlikely rallying cry for legal reform and activism. But the "tampon tax" has attracted maximum attention. In one compact, alliterative phrase, activists have been able to communicate the crux of the issue: there is a tax on a product used mainly or exclusively by women, but there are no products that men must use (and pay tax on) because of an involuntary biological process. The closest analogous products that are used by men are not subject to taxation.

Gendered tax policies breed in a culture of silence and secrecy. Meaningful tax reform and gender justice will occur only when accurate information is visible to all citizens and when legislators commit to nondiscrimination in fiscal policies. For many years, the sales tax on menstrual hygiene products was a nonissue because no one was aware of it or paid attention to it. Change only came about when female consumers started to question why they were being taxed on a product that is essential for their health, when other elective items or products relating primarily to men's health escape taxation. It is not that this tax was imposed in secrecy, but rather that historic and contemporary cultural attitudes about women's menstruation contributed to either disengagement or silence about the tax. Reform in various US states has come only after legislative reform and pressure, and a similar pressure has been felt in countries around the world.[159]

One way of bringing more clarity to the issue of gender equity in taxation would be to require all local and national governments to engage in gender-based budgeting, or at least issue a statement to accompany any new legislation that evaluates any expected gender differential impact of the law.[160] Understanding how a fiscal policy might impact men and women differently is a precondition for creating nondiscriminatory tax laws. This type of systemic change may garner less public support—and generate fewer catchy slogans—than the tampon tax, but it is vitally important.

NOTES

1. Civil Rights Act, Pub. L. No. 85-315, § 152, 71 Stat. 634, 638 (codified as amended at 28 U.S.C. § 1861 (1988)).
2. See Equal Credit Opportunity Act, and amendments, 15 U.S.C. §§ 1691–1691f (1976).
3. See Reed v. Reed, 404 U.S. 71 (1971) (declaring unconstitutional an Idaho statute that preferred males over females as an administrator of a decedent's estate).
4. See K. Brown, 'Not Color- or Gender-Neutral: New Tax Treatment of Employment Discrimination Damages', 7 *Southern California Review of Law and Women's Studies* (1998), 223.
5. See *infra* section II.
6. Ibid.
7. See *infra* section III.
8. Ibid.
9. See, e.g., Formerly Incarcerated Reenter Society Transformed Safely Transitioning Every Person Act, Pub. L. No. 117-391 (2018).
10. Ibid.
11. See *infra* section II.F.2.

12. See T. Hillin, *These Are the U.S. States That Tax Women for Having Periods*, 3 June 2015, available online at http://fusion.net/story/142965/states-that-tax-tampons-period-tax/ (last visited 24 May 2017).

13. See United States Census Bureau, 2015 State Government Tax Collections, available online at https://factfinder.census.gov/faces/tableservices/jsf/pages/productview.xhtml?src=bkmk(last visited 24 May 2017).

14. See, e.g., T. Hurley, 'Curing the Structural Defect in State Tax Systems: Expanding the Tax Base to Include Services', 61 *Mercer Law Review* (2010), 491, at 497.

15. Ibid.

16. Ibid.

17. See, e.g., R. Alexander and L. Luna, 'Value-Added Taxes: An Ingredient in Corporate Tax Reform', 21 *Kansas Journal of Law and Public Policy* (2012), 409, at 412–414 (describing basic structure of VAT).

18. Council Directive 2006/112/EC, OJ L 347/1, Art. 99 ("The reduced rates shall be fixed as a percentage of the taxable amount, which may not be less than 5%"). The difference between the categories of exempt and zero tax is significant insofar as an item in the "zero" category can be moved up to one of the higher tax categories (but cannot return to the zero category). Annex III lists the goods eligible for taxation at the reduced rate. See ibid. at Annex III.

19. Ibid.

20. See ibid. at Preamble, para. 29.

21. Value Added Tax Act 1994, c. 23, sch. 9 (UK).

22. See, e.g., Value Added Tax Act,1994, c. 23, sch. 8 (UK).

23. See, e.g., H.M. Revenue and Customs, *VAT Rates on Different Goods and Services*, 4 Feb. 2014, available online at https://www.gov.uk/guidance/rates-of-vat-on-different-goods-and-services (listing various goods and services and applicable VAT rates) (last visited 24 May 2017).

24. Council Directive 2006/112, *supra* note 18, at Annex III (list of all items eligible for reduced rate).

25. See, e.g., H.M. Revenue and Customs, *supra* note 23 (describing tax rates applicable to adult clothing) and H.M. Revenue and Customs, *VAT Notice 709/1: Catering and Take-Away Food*, 7 Oct. 2013, available online at https://www.gov.uk/government/publications/vat-notice-7091-catering-and-take-away-food/vat-notice-7091-catering-and-take-away-food (describing tax rates applicable to catered foods) (last visited 24 May 2017).

26. See, e.g., T. Dagan, 'The Currency of Taxation', 84 *Fordham Law Review* (2016), 2537 (describing general relationship between and among tax systems, communities, and human flourishing).

27. See *supra* note 18 and accompanying text.

28. See European Commission, *VAT Rates Applied in the Member States of the European Union: Situation at 1st January 2017*, available online at http://ec.europa.eu/taxation_customs/sites/taxation/files/resources/documents/taxation/vat/how_vat_works/rates/vat_rates_en.pdf (listing VAT rates in member states).

29. J. Phelan, *Tampon Tax Is Real. Women Everywhere Pay Their Governments Extra to Have Periods*, 15 Aug. 2015, available online at http://www.globalpost.com/article/6630542/2015/08/13/what-tampon-tax-and-where-do-women-have-pay-it (detailing VAT rates in many European countries) (last visited 24 May 2017).

30. European Commission, *supra* note 28, at 3 (listing rates in each country). See also ibid (explaining that Denmark, Sweden, and Norway impose a standard VAT rate of 25 percent; Italy imposes a tax of 22 percent; Germany imposes a tax of 19 percent).

31. See H. Ellis-Petersen, 'Tampon Tax: £15m Raised to Be Spent on Women's Charities', *The Guardian UK*, 25 Nov. 2015, available online at https://www.theguardian.com/uk-news/2015/nov/25/tampon-tax-15m-womens-charities-george-osborne-spending-review (referring to efforts to end the 5 percent VAT on menstrual hygiene products) (last visited 24 May 2017).

32. See Massachusetts Department of Revenue, *A Guide to Sales and Use Tax*, available online at http://www.mass.gov/dor/individuals/taxpayer-help-and-resources/tax-guides/salesuse-tax-guide.html (listing tax-exempt items as 'apparel and fabric goods' and 'food and meals') (last visited 24 May 2017).

33. See *infra* section II.A.
34. Fla. Stat. § 212.08 (2015) and Fla. Admin. Code Ann. r. 12A-1.020 (2015) (exempting drugs, medicinal drugs, common household remedies from taxation).
35. Act of May 19, 2016, N.Y. Tax Law § 1115, N.Y. S07838 and Act of May 19, 2015, N.Y. Tax Law § 1115, N.Y. A07555A (same). The repeal took effect on 1 Sept. 2016.
36. New York States Department of Taxation and Finances, *Publication 840: A Guide to Sales Tax for Drugstores and Pharmacies*, Aug. 1998, available online at https://www.tax.ny.gov/pdf/publications/sales/pub840.pdf, at 12.
37. Ibid.
38. Ibid. at 8.
39. Ibid. at 9.
40. Council Directive, *supra* note 18, at Preamble, para. 29.
41. Ibid. at Art. 98 (providing that "Member States may apply either one or two reduced rates.").
42. Ibid. at Annex III.
43. M. Randall, *The 'Tampon Tax': A UK and EU Standstill*, 28 Oct. 2015, available online at http://eulawanalysis.blogspot.com/2015/10/the-tampon-tax-uk-and-eu-standstill.html (last visited 30 May 2017).
44. Council Directive, *supra* note 18, at Art. 132.
45. Treaty of Amsterdam Amending the Treaty on European Union, the Treaties Establishing the European Communities and Certain Related Acts, OJ 1997 C 340/1, at Arts. 2 and 3(3).
46. See *infra* section IV.
47. See *infra* section III. See also B. Crawford & E. Waldman, 'The Unconstitutional Tampon Tax,' *University of Richmond Law Review* (forthcoming 2019) (arguing tampon tax is type of unconstitutional sex discrimination).
48. In December 2016, the group called "Género y Justicia Económica" (Gender and Economic Justice) launched a campaign against the "tampon tax" in Colombia. See Inició Campaña, 'Menstruación Libre de Impuestos', *El Espectador*, 7 Dec. 2016, available online at http://www.elespectador.com/noticias/economia/inicio-campana-menstruacion-libre-de-impuestos-articulo-669254 (last visited 14 Aug. 2017). In June 2017, the same group filed a complaint with the Colombian Constitutional Court alleging that the VAT on menstrual hygiene products violates specific articles of the Colombia Political Constitution as well as a variety of human rights. See Grupo Género y Justicia Económica, de la Red Justicia Tributaria, demandará IVA a productos femeninos ante la Corte Constitucional, 13 June 2017, available online at http://justiciatributaria.co/blog/2017/06/13/grupo-genero-justicia-economica-la-red-justicia-tributaria-demandara-iva-productos-femeninos-ante-la-corte-constitucional/ (last visited 14 Aug. 2017).
49. General Assembly, Universal Declaration of Human Rights, 10 Dec. 1948, UN Doc. A/RES/217(III).
50. Ibid. at Art. 7.
51. International Covenant on Civil and Political Rights 1966, 999 UNTS 171.
52. International Covenant on Economic, Social and Cultural Rights 1966, 993 UNTS 3.
53. American Convention on Human Rights 1969, OASTS No. 36, 1144 UNTS 123.
54. African Charter on Human and Peoples' Rights 1981, 21 ILM 58.
55. ECtHR, *Van Raalte v. The Netherlands*, Appl. no. 20060/92, Judgment of 21 Feb. 1997, at 1. All ECtHR decisions are available online at http://hudoc.echr/coe/int/.
56. Protocol 1, Art. 1 ECHR.
57. ICCPR, *supra* note 51, at Art. 26.
58. See *supra* note 49.
59. Convention on the Elimination of All Forms of Discrimination Against Women 1979, 1249 UNTS 13.
60. See, e.g., M. Sunder, 'Piercing the Veil', 112(6) *Yale Law Journal* (2003), 1399, at n.124.
61. See United Nations Treaty Collection, Convention on the Elimination of All Forms of Discrimination Against Women, available online at https://treaties.un.org/Pages/ViewDetails.aspx?src=TREATY&mtdsg_no=IV-8&chapter=4&lang=en (last visited 30 June 2017).
62. CEDAW, *supra* note 59, at Art. 2(f).

63. See *supra* note 61.

64. A. Jones, *The Fight to End Period Shaming Is Going Mainstream*, 20 Apr. 2016, available online at http://www.newsweek.com/2016/04/29/womens-periods-menstruation-tampons-pads-449833.html (last visited 24 May 2017).

65. See, e.g., D. Gilson, *India's Menstruation Man*, available online at http://interactive.aljazeera.com/aje/shorts/india-menstruation-man/ (stating that 300 million women in India do not have access to safe menstrual hygiene products, describing cloth as one woman's preferred method of absorption of menstrual blood) (last visited 24 May 2017).

66. P. Das et al., *Menstrual Hygiene Practices, WASH Access and the Risk of Urogenital Infection in Women from Odisha, India*, 30 June 2015, available online at http://journals.plos.org/plosone/article?id=10.1371/journal.pone.0130777 (last visited 24 May 2017).

67. C. Sumpter and B. Torondel, *A Systematic Review of the Health and Social Effects of Menstrual Hygiene Management*, 23 Apr. 2013, available online at http://journals.plos.org/plosone/article?id=10.1371/journal.pone.0062004 (last visited 24 May 2017).

68. ICESCR, *supra* note 52, at Art. 12.

69. Committee on Economic, Social and Cultural Rights, General Comment No. 14: The Right to the Highest Attainable Standard of Health, UN Doc. E/C.12/2000/4, 11 Aug. 2000, at para. 9.

70. Ibid. at para. 12(b).

71. Ibid. at para. 9.

72. GA Res. 70/169, 22 Feb. 2016, at para. 2.

73. See, e.g., M. Sommer, *Utilizing Participatory and Quantitative Methods for Effective Menstrual-Hygiene Management Related Policy and Planning* (2010), on file with authors.

74. UNICEF, *Sharing Simple Facts: Useful Information about Menstrual Health and Hygiene*, 15 Jan. 2008, available online at http://www.unicefiec.org/document/sharing-simple-facts-useful-information-about-menstrual-health-and-hygiene-booklet-english (last visited 25 May 2017).

75. A. Dasgupta and M. Sargar, 'Menstrual Hygiene: How Hygienic Is the Adolescent Girl?', 33 *Indian Journal of Community Medicine* (2008), 77.

76. UNICEF and World Health Organization, *Progress on Sanitation and Drinking Water: 2015 Update and MDG Assessment* (2015), available online at http://files.unicef.org/publications/files/Progress_on_Sanitation_and_Drinking_Water_2015_Update_.pdf, at 45.

77. Convention on the Rights of the Child 1989, 1577 UNTS 3.

78. United Nations Human Rights Office of the High Commissioner, *Convention on the Rights of the Child*, 20 June 2016, available online at http://www.ohchr.org/Documents/HRBodies/CRC/OHCHR_Map_CRC.pdf.

79. Ibid.

80. Convention on the Rights of the Child, *supra* note 77, at Art. 24(2)(e).

81. Jones, *supra* note 64.

82. V. Hallet, *What Kenya Can Teach the U.S. About Menstrual Pads*, 10 May 2016, available online at http://www.npr.org/sections/goatsandsoda/2016/05/10/476741805/what-kenya-can-teach-the-u-s-about-menstrual-pads (last visited 25 May 2017).

83. Ibid.

84. Ibid. (giving credit for Kenya's progressive menstrual policies to female leaders in the country and some men who have championed the cause).

85. Ibid.

86. UDHR, *supra* note 49.

87. A. Klasing, *Menstrual Hygiene Day Links Periods and Human Rights*, 28 May 2014, available online at https://www.hrw.org/news/2014/05/28/menstrual-hygiene-day-links-periods-and-human-rights (last visited 25 May 2017).

88. See, e.g., K. Sinhal, *70% Can't Afford Sanitary Napkins, Reveals Study*, 23 Jan. 2011, available online at http://timesofindia.indiatimes.com/india/70-cant-afford-sanitary-napkins-reveals-study/articleshow/7344998.cms (reporting that a survey conducted in nine of India's largest cities showed that 31 percent of women reported missing an average of 2.2 days of work for this reason) (last visited 25 May 2017).

89. Ibid.

90. Central European University Human Rights Initiative, *Menstrual Hygiene Day*, 27 Oct. 2015, available online at https://hrsi.ceu.edu/news/2015-10-27/menstrual-hygiene-day (last visited 25 May 2017).

91. OHCHR, *Every Woman's Right to Water, Sanitation and Hygiene*, 14 Mar. 2014, available online at http://www.ohchr.org/EN/NewsEvents/Pages/Everywomansrighttowatersanitationandhygiene.aspx (last visited 25 May 2017).

92. Ibid.

93. International Court of Justice, *How the Court Works*, available online at http://www.icj-cij.org/court/index.php?p1=1&p2=6 (last visited 25 May 2017).

94. OHCHR, *Human Rights Treaty Bodies—Individual Communications*, available online at http://www.ohchr.org/EN/HRBodies/TBPetitions/Pages/IndividualCommunications.aspx#overviewprocedure (last visited 25 May 2017).

95. See generally R. J. Cook, 'International Human Rights Law Concerning Women: Case Notes and Comments', 23 *Vanderbilt Journal of Transnational Law* (1990), 779 (describing international and regional treaties as sources for challenging discrimination against women).

96. In 1996, the European Commission of Human Rights rejected a challenge to the United Kingdom's tax law that treated married couples differently than unmarried couples. See *Lindsay v. United Kingdom* (1986) 9 EHRR 355. The European Commission on Human Rights was abolished in 1998.

97. *Van Raalte v. The Netherlands, supra* note 55.

98. Ibid. After the challenged assessment, but before the case reached the European Court of Human Rights, this sex-based distinction was abandoned. Ibid. at paras. 12 and 28.

99. Ibid. at para. 43.

100. ECtHR, *Hobbs, Richard, Walsh and Geen v. The United Kingdom*, Appl. nos. 63684/00, 63475/00, 63484/00 and 63468/00, Judgment of 14 Nov. 2006.

101. Ibid. at paras. 8–19.

102. Ibid. at para. 25.

103. Ibid. at para. 41.

104. Ibid. at para. 52.

105. Ibid.

106. Ibid.

107. Ibid. at para. 53.

108. Ibid. at para. 54.

109. ECtHR, *Willis v. The United Kingdom*, Appl. no. 36042/97, Judgment of 11 June 2002.

110. Ibid. at para. 10.

111. Ibid. at para. 11.

112. Ibid. at para. 27.

113. Ibid. at para. 42. The Court declined to find a violation with respect to a third benefit applied for, the "Widow's Pension," because it found that the petitioner would not have been eligible for that benefit even if he had been a widow, at the time he applied for it. Ibid. at para. 50.

114. ECtHR, *Zeman v. Austria*, Appl. no. 23960/02, Judgment of 29 June 2006.

115. Ibid. at para. 15.

116. Ibid. at para. 41.

117. *Van Raalte v. The Netherlands*, note 54, at para. 43.

118. See, e.g., F. Nicola and I. Nifosi-Sutton, 'Assessing Regional Cooperation: New Trends Before the European Court of Human Rights and the European Court of Justice', 15 *Human Rights Brief* (2007), 11 ("Until recently, the ECHR's attitude toward reparations has been quite conservative, because it regards its power to afford reparations as discretionary. It has limited itself to stating that a violation of the Convention has occurred and awarding pecuniary or non-pecuniary compensation together with legal costs and expenses."); Council of Bars and Law Societies of Europe, *The European Court of Human Rights: Questions and Answers for Lawyers* (2014), available online at http://www.echr.coe.int/documents/guide_echr_lawyers_eng.pdf, at 12–13 (explaining that "just satisfaction" may be awarded for pecuniary damage but 'the Court may decide on an equitable basis not to award the full loss suffered').

119. See Randall, *supra* note 43.

120. *Hobbs, Richard, Walsh and Green v. The United Kingdom, supra* note 100.

121. *Van Raalte v. The Netherlands, supra* note 55.

122. *Hobbs, Richard, Walsh and Geen v. The United Kingdom, supra* note 100, at para. 61.

123. Ibid.

124. Ibid. at para. 62.

125. Ibid. at para. 65.

126. *Van Raalte v. The Netherlands, supra* note 55, at para. 50.

127. Ibid.

128. See, e.g., S. Grossman, 'NYC Mayor Signs Free Tampons for Schools, Jails, Shelters into Law', *Huffington Post*, 14 July 2016, available online at http://www.huffingtonpost.com/entry/new-york-city-mayor-bill-de-blasio-signs-tampons-free-law_us_5787bc57e4b08608d3336b27 (last visited 25 May 2017).

129. *Women's Groups Call on SNP to Offer Free Tampons to Scots Women*, 16 Aug. 2016, available online at http://www.eveningtimes.co.uk/news/14684951.Woman_s_groups_call_on_SNP_to_offer_free_tampons_to_Scots_women/ (estimating number of girls and women reached by New York City's distribution of free feminine hygiene products) (last visited 25 May 2017).

130. NYC Office of the Mayor, *Mayor de Blasio Signs Legislation Increasing Access to Feminine Hygiene Products for Students, Shelter Residents and Inmates*, 13 July 2016, available online at http://www1.nyc.gov/office-of-the-mayor/news/611-16/mayor-de-blasio-signs-legislation-increasing-access-feminine-hygiene-products-students- (last visited 25 May 2017).

131. Ibid. (adding that, "As a father, husband and feminist, I am proud to sign these bills into law.").

132. M. Mallon, 'New York City Is About to Give Free Tampons to People Who Need Them Most', *Glamour*, 22 June 2016, available online at http://www.glamour.com/story/new-york-city-is-about-to-give-free-tampons-to-people-who-need-them-most (last visited 25 May 2017).

133. Grossman, *supra* note 128.

134. C. Cauterucci, 'New York City Council Approves Free Tampons and Pads in Schools, Prisons and Shelters', *Slate*, 22 June 2016, available online at http://www.slate.com/blogs/xx_factor/2016/06/22/new_york_city_council_votes_to_give_free_tampons_and_pads_to_women_in_schools.html (last visited 25 May 2017).

135. *Free Tampons in NYC*, 21 June 2016, available online at https://www.usnews.com/news/news/articles/2016-06-21/nyc-weighs-novel-law-on-free-tampons-in-schools-elsewhere (last visited 25 May 2017).

136. Mallon, *supra* note 132.

137. *'Menstrual Equity': Free Tampons for New York City Schools and Jails*, 22 June 2016, available online at http://www.bbc.com/news/world-us-canada-36597949 (last visited 25 May 2017).

138. D. Nield, *Sydney Is Planning to Become the Second City to Offer Free Tampons to Women*, 22 July 2016, available online at http://www.sciencealert.com/sydney-joins-new-york-in-offering-free-tampons-for-women (last visited 25 May 2017).

139. Ibid.

140. L. Charleston, 'Sydney May Be the First City to Provide Free Sanitary Items', *Huffington Post*, 21 July 2016, available online at http://www.huffingtonpost.com.au/2016/07/20/sydney-may-be-the-first-city-to-provide-free-sanitary-items/ (last visited 25 May 2017).

141. See K. Amiet, 'Sanitary Products Could Soon Be Free for Sydney Women', *Elle*, 22 July 2016, available online at http://www.elle.com.au/news/free-sanitary-products-sydney-6603 (describing work of Share the Dignity in Queensland and the Melbourne Period Project in Victoria) (last visited 25 May 2017).

142. See, e.g., *Women's Groups Call on SNP to Offer Free Tampons to Scots Women, supra* note 129.

143. Free the Tampons, *About*, available online at http://www.freethetampons.org/about.html (last visited 25 May 2017).

144. See *Free Tampons in NYC, supra* note 135 (describing Wisconsin legislation).

145. Mailman School of Public Health at Columbia University, *Touch the Pickle: Demystifying Menstruation Around the World*, 4 Nov. 2015, available online at https://www.mailman.columbia.edu/public-health-now/news/touch-pickle-demystifying-menstruation-around-world ("UNICEF

estimates that about half of schools in the developing world do not have toilets, and among those that do, many facilities are not specific for girls, who may find it shameful and embarrassing to navigate menstruation in unisex toilets and latrines.") (last visited 25 May 2017).

146. See, e.g., M. Sommer, *World Bankers: Please Study Menstruation Costs*, 16 Aug. 2015, available online at http://womensenews.org/2015/04/world-bankers-please-study-menstruation-costs/ (last visited 25 May 2017).

147. Business for Social Responsibility—Her Project, *Women's General and Reproductive Health in Global Supply Chains*, Oct. 2006, available online at https://herproject.org/downloads/BSR-Womens-Health-Report-2006.pdf, at 20 and 42.

148. Hillin, *supra* note 12.

149. Ibid.

150. See, e.g., A. Jones, *New York Terminates the Tampon Tax*, 21 July 2016, available online at http://www.newsweek.com/new-york-tampon-tax-cuomo-periods-tampons-menstruation-donald-trump-482918 (reporting on New York's repeal of the tax on feminine hygiene products) (last visited 25 May 2017).

151. See the Feminine Hygiene and Diapers Sales Tax Exemption Amendment Act of 2016, B21-0696/A21-0557, Council of the District of Columbia, available online at http://lims.dccouncil.us/_layouts/15/uploader/AdminProxy.aspx?LegislationId=B21-0696 (last visited 30 May 2017). See also F. Nirappil, *D.C. to Lift Sales Tax on Diapers, Tampons*, 17 Nov. 2016, available online at https://www.washingtonpost.com/local/dc-politics/dc-to-lift-sales-tax-on-diapers-tampons/2016/11/17/5cc5f634-aceb-11e6-8b45-f8e493f06fcd_story.html?utm_term=.bf3824b1329c (last visited 25 May 2017).

152. Jones, *supra* note 150.

153. See *supra* section II.A.

154. 2015 NY A.B. 5216 (NS) § 2.

155. B. Crawford, 'Interview with Laura Strausfeld, New York Attorney Challenging the "Tampon Tax"', *Feminist Law Professors*, 15 Nov. 2016, available online at https://www.feministlawprofessors.com/2016/11/interview-laura-strausfeld-new-york-attorney-challenging-tampon-tax/ (last visited 30 May 2017).

156. See Complaint, *Rowitz v. Ohio Dep't of Taxation*, 2016-00197 (Ohio Ct. Claims, filed Mar. 14, 2016), dismissed without prejudice. Refiled as Rowitz v. State of Ohio et al., 2016-CV-003518 (Franklin Co. Ct. Common Pleas, filed Apr. 11, 2016). The suit is still pending.

157. B. Crawford, 'Interview with Zoe Salzman, New York Attorney Challenging the "Tampon Tax"', *Feminist Law Professors*, 28 July 2016, available online at https://www.feministlawprofessors.com/2016/07/interview-zoe-salzman-new-york-attorney-challenging-tampon-tax/ (last visited 30 May 2017).

158. See Order Denying Plaintiffs' Amended Motion for Partial Summary Judgment and Granting Florida Department of Revenue's Motion to Dismiss Second Amended Complaint and Granting Defendants' Florida Department of Revenue and Leon M. Biegalski Motion for Summary Judgment, *Carlee Wendell v. Florida Department of Revenue*, Case No. 2016 CA1526 (Circuit Court of the Second Judicial Circuit in and for Leon County, Florida). On Florida's prospective repeal of the tax on menstrual hygiene products, see 'Florida Joins Other States in Ending "Tampon Tax"', 25 May 2017, available online at https://www.usnews.com/news/best-states/florida/articles/2017-05-25/florida-gov-to-sign-tax-cut-bill-that-ends-tampon-tax (last visited June 30, 2017).

159. Drawing attention to the gender inequity of the tampon tax has not necessarily caused all governments to take the issue seriously. One news outlet reports that when a member of the Malaysian Parliament raised the issue, his remarks drew laughter. See *GST on Sanitary Napkins Gets Chuckles in Parliament*, 19 Mar. 2015, available online at http://www.freemalaysiatoday.com/category/nation/2015/03/19/gst-on-sanitary-napkins-provokes-laughter-in-parliament/ (last visited 25 May 2017).

160. For a discussion of gender-based budgeting generally, see, e.g., D. Budlender, R. Sharp, and K. Allen, *How to Do a Gender-Sensitive Budget Analysis: Contemporary Research and Practice* (1998); D. Budlender, *Gender Budgets Make Cents: Understanding Gender Responsive Budgets* (2002).

CHAPTER 21

RECENT CASES OF REGRESSIVE AND RACIALLY DISPARATE TAXATION IN THE UNITED STATES

ANDRE L. SMITH

I. OF RACE AND FAIR TAXATION

To most scholars, fair taxation in the United States means that taxes should, to the extent possible or practicable, be levied similarly upon similarly situated persons (horizontal equity), be administrable by the taxpayer and the revenue service (micro efficiency), minimally impede on free market transactions (macro efficiency), and, most importantly for purposes of this discussion, be levied on persons according to their ability to pay (vertical equity).[1]

Vertical equity means that those with wealth or high incomes should not just pay a greater amount but also a higher percentage of their incomes.[2] Based on the notion that all things—including money—have a diminishing marginal utility, the imposition of higher tax rates as income increases is designed to inflict equal harm across the taxpaying population. This is progressive taxation.

A regressive tax system places a higher burden on those with lower income or wealth.[3] State and local sales and consumption taxes tend to be regressive because poor people by definition cannot avoid the tax through increased saving. The Institute on Taxation and Economic Policy reports on the growing trend toward regressive sales taxes across the country.[4]

At the same time as state and local governments increase their reliance on sales and excise taxes, these governments are reducing property and income taxes.[5] Federal income taxes have been decreasing for some time, and the current administration is likely to cut them even further.[6] The estate tax is probably the most progressive tax there is, and its repeal is on the table (again).[7] Internationally, critics describe a race to the bottom in which nations across the globe are lowering corporate taxes and reducing social services for those in need, in order to retain wealthy individuals and companies as residents.[8]

Any discussion of fairness also raises the question of how taxation relates to group subordination.[9] Critical race tax theorists insist that taxation, while individually determined, can

Tax, Inequality, and Human Rights. Philip Alston and Nikki Reisch.

also be and has been, both intentionally and unintentionally, an agent of group subordination in terms of race, gender, sexual orientation, and other protected classes.[10] Scholars such as Beverly Moran, Bridget Crawford, and Anthony Infanti have demonstrated how provisions of the Internal Revenue Code can have an asymmetrical or disparate impact upon black people (or women, or . . .).[11] In *Craft v. United States*, even noted textualist Justice Scalia chastised the US Supreme Court's majority for interpreting the Code in a way that would be harmful to divorced women.[12]

In *Black Tax: Tax Law and Racial Economic Justice*, I attempted to show that the relationship between taxes and race is deep, indeed.[13] United States history is replete with instances of racist taxation, from slavery itself as a nearly 100 percent tax on black labor, to discriminatory taxes on free blacks, to poll taxes keeping blacks from voting in the Deep South, to the Federal Tariff transferring perhaps more than half of the profits from slavery to the North, to tax exemptions for racially discriminatory schools in communities seeking to avoid *Brown v. Board of Education*, among others.[14]

Today we ask whether racially neutral tax laws being implemented in cities and other jurisdictions with majority minority populations are not only unfairly regressive but also have disparate impacts upon people of color—i.e., are they racist?

Many of these taxes, like cigarette and soda taxes, are sold as efficient "sin" taxes, which raise revenue while also addressing another societal problem, like public health. Except, these sin taxes are not designed well if the goal is a meaningful effect on public health. They are easily avoidable by people with means who can shop (or choose to live) in low- or no-tax jurisdictions, while those who have no savings for vacations and such cannot avoid tax increases on the only luxuries they can afford.

Local communities are also using their law enforcement systems to raise revenue instead of concentrating on what's best for public safety. To the extent fines, fees, and civil asset forfeitures do not advance public safety goals, they represent regressive taxation. These trends lead one to wonder whether we are experiencing "class warfare" where conservative forces design regressive tax policies promoted under the guise of socially progressive paternalism.[15]

It also seems that such regressive taxes are being levied in communities with the least political capital, i.e., poor communities of color.[16] It is in this sense that they have disparate impacts or are asymmetrically distributed.[17]

If so, this phenomenon is not new. There is a history of communities that are facing financial exigencies correcting their budget deficits by levying formal and informal taxes on black people.[18] In *Tax and Slavery in the Ante-Bellum South*, George Ruble Woolfolk found that, during slavery, southern legislatures relied on taxes levied directly or indirectly on black people for over half of the state's budget.[19] Today, southern states are still more likely to finance state government through regressive sales taxes than through progressive income taxes.[20]

After Reconstruction, southern legislatures employed more sophisticated methods for keeping the incidence of taxation regressive and racially asymmetrical, relying primarily on informal taxes disguised as civil fines and court fees.[21] If they were unable to pay, blacks were re-enslaved by the state and leased to private companies.[22] Today, as documented in Department of Justice reports and elsewhere, jurisdictions across the United States are "policing for profit," or designing law enforcement strategies around the production of revenue for the state instead of toward greater domestic tranquility.[23]

The collateral consequence of formal and informal taxes levied disproportionately on black people includes more potentially violent confrontations with police and responses like the Black Lives Matter Movement. Eric Garner was killed by officers of the New York Police Department who thought he was selling contraband (nontaxed) cigarettes, or "loosies."[24]

Borrowing a term from Imani Perry, the following roughly details the mechanisms by which taxes are becoming "post-intentionally" racist.[25] In each instance, we will not find any expressed or stated desire from any official to subordinate black people or to purposefully take advantage of their relative lack of capital. Yet, here we are. Inability to avoid taxes is, as the Founders experienced, simply the consequence of being an "other" with less political power and representation.

There is a blueprint available for those who favor racial subordination, a means for balancing state and local budgets that places as much of the incidence on "others" as possible. As Derrick Bell pointed out in *Faces at the Bottom of the Well*, fair-minded people will excuse, accommodate, or even participate in racially subordinating behavior if it is in their interests to do so.[26] This is the essence of his Racial Realism. Here, we ponder whether well-intentioned white folks have lent their support to racist taxation, perhaps unwittingly, because the stated purposes of increased taxes satisfy their social desires while it squares with their financial interests to ignore the disparate racial ramifications.

II. POLICING FOR PROFIT AS REGRESSIVE AND RACIALLY DISPARATE INFORMAL TAXATION

A. DEPARTMENT OF JUSTICE REPORT ON FERGUSON, MISSOURI

Tickets, citations, and court fees in Ferguson, Missouri, should be considered informal taxes because they are issued and enforced primarily for the purpose of raising revenue, having little or nothing to do with protecting public safety.[27]

Once a majority-white "sundown town,"[28] Ferguson has become a predominately black community over the last thirty years. Although two-thirds of the population is black,[29] Ferguson only had four black police officers out of fifty-four during the period in question.[30] In a four-year span, between 2010 and 2014, the Ferguson Police Department (FPD) issued more than 90,000 citations for municipal code violations. Increasing in volume each year, they issued 50 percent more in 2014 than in 2010.[31]

The Department of Justice (DOJ) reports that the Ferguson Municipal Court fined residents as much as "$302 for a single Manner of Walking violation; $427 for a single Peace Disturbance violation; $531 for High Grass and Weeds; $777 for Resisting Arrest; and $792 for Failure to Obey, and $527 for Failure to Comply, which officers appear to use interchangeably."[32]

"Failure to Comply" is a favorite of FPD officers, with citations levied, despite the First Amendment, on seemingly anyone who says anything that displeases the officer. Complaining about an unreasonable search or seizure against the Fourth Amendment often resulted in a fine. FPD also levies tickets and citations for disorderly conduct in an overbroad, unconstitutional manner.[33]

The Ferguson Municipal Court is the collection arm of the FPD.[34] The chief of police supervises court personnel, who often adjudicate cases without the municipal judge. The court levies fines and fees, and issues warrants for imprisonment. Then, court personnel use incarceration as the typical means to coerce payment. In the words of the DOJ: "The municipal court does not act as a neutral arbiter of the law or a check on unlawful police conduct. Instead, the court primarily uses its judicial authority as the means to compel the payment of fines and fees that advance the City's financial interests."[35]

Ferguson's law enforcement practices are shaped by the city's focus on revenue rather than by public safety needs. This emphasis on revenue has compromised the institutional character of Ferguson's police department, contributing to a pattern of unconstitutional policing, and also has shaped its municipal court, leading to procedures that raise due process concerns and inflict unnecessary harm on members of the Ferguson community.[36]

City officials and the chief of police routinely discuss revenue targets that increase each year. To cite just one example, the city manager reportedly pushed for a 10 percent increase in 2013.[37] FPD officers are made well aware of revenue-seeking goals. The number of citations issued by each officer and squad is posted.[38] They are admonished and sometimes disciplined for not meeting those goals. The DOJ found that unconstitutional stops by Ferguson police officers, of both drivers and pedestrians, tended to be motivated by a desire to produce revenue either via citations or by enforcing warrants.[39]

The chief of police once set up speed traps on I-270 at the request of the city finance director, who identified revenue projections for the operation.[40]

On top of levying exorbitant fines, the municipal court routinely issues arrest warrants for unpaid fines and citations that result in further fines and fees as well as an automatic driver's license suspension. Unlike some other jurisdictions, Ferguson does not lift the license suspension until fines are paid in full.[41] Citizens complain that they cannot work and make money to pay their fines without their driver's license. Because of poor public transportation in Ferguson, the lack of a driver's license often leads to a further missed court date, which in turn results in another fine, more fees, and another warrant.[42]

Up until the DOJ investigation, the Ferguson Municipal Court also charged a $50 fee on top of the payment of fines in order to clear a warrant.[43] Another fee was assessed each time a defendant failed to appear, which could increase for multiple absences or repeat offenders. The assessed amount was almost completely discretionary and disproportionately applied against African Americans.[44]

The Ferguson Municipal Court issues these fees and fines without any regard for financial incapacity.[45] They offer no alternatives for those without the means to pay, such as community service. By adding its own charges to the original citation, plus interest, Ferguson residents often end up paying absurd amounts to settle minor offenses:

> [DOJ investigators] spoke, for example, with an African-American woman who has a still-pending case stemming from 2007, when, on a single occasion, she parked her car illegally. She received two citations and a $151 fine, plus fees. The woman, who experienced financial difficulties and periods of homelessness over several years, was charged with seven Failure to Appear offenses for missing court dates or fine payments on her parking tickets between 2007 and 2010. For each Failure to Appear, the court issued an arrest warrant and imposed new fines and fees. From 2007 to 2014, the woman was arrested twice, spent six days in jail, and paid $550 to the court for the events stemming from this single instance of illegal parking. Court records show that she twice attempted to make partial payments of $25 and $50, but the court returned those payments, refusing to accept anything less than payment in full. One of those payments was later accepted, but only after the court's letter rejecting payment by money order was returned as undeliverable. This woman is now making regular payments on the fine. As of December 2014, over seven years later, despite initially owing a $151 fine and having already paid $550, she still owed $541.[46]

The municipal court tends to find ways to prolong cases and exact more money from those least able to pay.[47] Because of interest and arcane court procedures, simple citations turn into fines, multiple arrests, more fees and fines, jail time, more fees and fines, which ultimately leads to people routinely paying several times more to the court than the amount of the original citation.[48]

Residents who do not have the means to pay a citation on the date of their hearing fear they will be jailed by the Court—so they often fail to appear, which, as explained above, has its own steep financial consequences. Data reveals one Failure to Appear charge for every citation issued. Failure to Appear fines accounted for 24 percent of revenue collected by the Court.[49]

Consider also that St. Louis County residents often owe several debts to numerous municipalities.[50]

Ferguson also devised ways for the municipal court to keep bond payments by instituting procedures designed to frustrate those who paid and satisfied their requirements. The DOJ found "substantial deficiencies in the way Ferguson police and court officials set, accept, refund, and forfeit bond payments."[51] When bonds are forfeited, the city does not apply any of it to the defendant's debt, keeping all of the money and the case open for potential future revenue. Even when the city is required to refund a defendant's bond, the city finance director mandated that they be sent by mail since a not-insignificant number will be returned as undeliverable and then claimed by the city.[52]

Ferguson requires in-court appearances for mundane violations, the nonattendance of which leads to a warrant, more fines, a suspended license, and fees—and arrest if you are black.[53] Over 200 independent minor violations require a court appearance in Ferguson, including for "Dog Creating Nuisance" as well as for "Overgrown Vegetation" and "Failure to Remove Leaf Debris." Second, bonds in Ferguson are higher than surrounding jurisdictions. Then, court procedures were designed to keep residents uninformed about the process and their own standing. Ordinarily in Ferguson, rules of practice and procedure are promulgated by the municipal judge and announced orally and ad hoc.[54] Without proper information on how to resolve their cases, Ferguson residents, especially the unsophisticated, often forfeit their bonds even when they have in fact complied with their terms.

Even the citations themselves lack pertinent information.[55] A reasonable person could receive a citation for "Failure to Remove Leaf Debris" and not know that the citation requires an in-court appearance. As a consequence, the individual may miss the court date and receive another citation, more fees, and a possible license suspension.[56]

The DOJ reports that due to the massive number of cases, which increase in volume each year, defendants must often wait outside for hours in inclement weather. Such delays are particularly burdensome on those with children. But while city officials offer no slack to impoverished residents, records indicate that the police chief and the collector of revenue received special treatment in dealing with their own citations.[57]

Having been reconfigured entirely toward revenue generation, the Ferguson Municipal Court is reminiscent of court systems in the Jim Crow South described by Douglas Blackmon in his Pulitzer Prize–winning book, *Slavery by Another Name*.[58]

Court officials admitted to DOJ investigators that the number of offenses requiring an appearance relates to revenue production and has nothing to do with public safety.[59]

This is a taxing scheme.

B. DISPARATE IMPACT AND DISCRIMINATORY INTENT

Comprising two-thirds of the Ferguson population, black residents accounted for 90 percent of the citations and 93 percent of the arrests.[60] Almost every citation for "Manner of Walking" or "Failure to Comply" was issued to an African American.[61] "African Americans account for 95% of Manner of Walking charges; 94% of all Fail to Comply charges; 92% of all Resisting Arrest charges; 92% of all Peace Disturbance charges; and 89% of all Failure to Obey charges. African Americans are 68% less likely than others to have their cases dismissed by the Municipal Judge, and in 2013 African-Americans accounted for 92% of cases in which an arrest warrant was issued."[62]

Black drivers in Ferguson are likewise stopped at disproportionate rates and are also searched during traffic stops more than any others. This, despite contraband being found in 30 percent of searches involving whites, but only 24 percent of searches involving blacks.[63] Regardless of the context, the DOJ statistics show African Americans were treated more harshly in every observable way. The DOJ report even included an anecdote relating to a bar brawl involving forty to fifty white males that resulted in only two arrests. By contrast, blacks were the defendants in all fourteen cases in which the only charge at a traffic stop was "resisting arrest."[64]

Half of all African Americans who received a citation got more than one for a single encounter. The same only happened to a quarter of non–African Americans.[65] FPD officers issued four or more citations to a single person during a single incident seventy-three times with respect to an African American resident, but only four times with respect to a non–African American.[66] No white person was ever issued five or more citations in one encounter, yet five or more citations were given to an African American at least thirty-five times. The "record" is fourteen citations in one encounter.[67] This was not by chance. This was not designed to increase public safety. This was informal taxation disproportionately levied upon black people.

The municipal court also discriminates against African Americans. Black defendants face longer sentences and longer delays, and are much more likely to be issued a warrant for failure to comply with rules and regulations. The municipal court is 50 percent more likely to issue an arrest warrant for a black resident. And despite Ferguson's diversity, 96 percent of those actually arrested by the FPD for outstanding warrants were black. Twenty-seven of the twenty-eight people arrested for outstanding warrants and held from more than two days were black.[68] Regardless of the offense, the court gave African Americans higher average fines.[69]

More than simply a neutral law causing a disparate impact, the DOJ found evidence of discriminatory intent:

> [The DOJ] investigation indicates that this disproportionate burden on African-Americans cannot
> be explained by any difference in the rate at which people of different races violate the law . . . We
> have uncovered significant evidence showing that racial bias has impermissibly played a role
> in shaping the actions of police and court officials in Ferguson. That evidence, detailed below,
> includes: 1) the consistency and magnitude of the racial disparities found throughout police and
> court enforcement actions; 2) direct communications by police supervisors and court officials that
> exhibit racial bias, particularly against African Americans; 3) a number of other communications
> by police and court officials that reflect harmful racial stereotypes; 4) the background and historic
> context surrounding FPD's racially disparate enforcement practices; 5) the fact that City, police,
> and court officials failed to take any meaningful steps to evaluate or address the race based impact
> of its law enforcement practices despite longstanding and widely reported racial disparities.[70]

C. DEFINITION OF TAX

The definition of "tax" is actually quite elusive. One need look no further than *NHIB v. Sebelius* (the Obamacare case) to see the US Supreme Court struggling with it.[71] Without providing a precise standard, the Court held that the penalty portion of the Affordable Care Act *could* be construed as a tax. Similarly, a court struck down a voter identification law because obtaining the identification required a fee, which the court held was an unconstitutional poll tax.[72] Therefore, a financial exaction can be a tax even if it is not labeled such.

Furthermore, to the extent the public policy goals have been subverted, policing for profit in terms of fines, forfeitures, and fees represents taxation. To the extent the levies are concentrated on those without wealth, they are regressive. And to the extent they are discriminatorily or asymmetrically applied, they represent racial subordination.

On the other hand, increased burdens on the voting franchise, like the closing of polling centers and other voter suppression tactics, have avoided the label of "poll tax" even if the incidental costs prevent scores of people from voting.[73] We have barely discussed the DOJ's assessment of excessive force used disproportionately against African Americans. Regardless of the legal standard, that is its own type of tax.[74] While it is important that the public understand the redistributive aspects of policing for profit, we should never forget that such schemes erode public trust and cooperation to the point that Mike Browns all over the country eventually refuse to surrender to it and suffer the ultimate penalty.[75] Similarly, we have not engaged in any meaningful discussion of sexual violence, whether investigated or perpetrated by the police.[76] The DOJ report on the Baltimore Police Department revealed outstanding hostility toward victims of sexual abuse.[77]

D. NATIONAL TREND

1. Fines

Policing for profit as regressive and racist taxation is a national trend, with many manifestations.[78] Municipalities throughout St. Louis County used similar tactics. While Ferguson gathered between 12 percent and 18 percent of the city's budget, one nearby town gathered 38 percent of its revenue from fines and court fees.[79]

Since then, reports have identified aspects of policing for profit all around the country, and the racial impact has been obvious. Dan Kopf of *Priceonomics* found that race was the dominant factor in determining whether a municipality resorted to raising revenue through law enforcement.[80] Researchers Michael Sances and Hye Yong You confirm Kopf's results and provide more detail: "We show that the use of fines as revenue is both commonplace and robustly connected to the proportion of residents who are black."[81] Whether the city is big or small, "cities with the largest share of black residents collect between $12 and $19 more per person than cities with the smallest black share of residents."[82]

Sances and You also find that the presence of a black member of city council influences (but does not prevent) the levying of such informal taxes. "[T]he relationship between race and fines is 50% less in cities with at least one black representative."[83] This sheds a new light on twenty-first-century poll taxes, or costs relating to voting, designed to reduce the number of black voters.[84]

2. Civil Asset Forfeiture

Policing for profit as racist taxation also includes giving law enforcement the authority to seize property they believe was linked to a crime, even if such a link is never proven.[85] Billions have been taken from people who were never charged with a crime, even though at least one study suggests that about half of all seizures are for less than $200.[86]

Because it is not considered a criminal seizure, various constitutional protections are unavailable to the victims, including the inability to hire a public defender to help recover wrongly taken sums. "Police often preempt this process by offering not to charge the underlying crime or initiate civil sanctions (such as taking away the property owner's children) if the property owner promises not to contest the seizure."[87] There are numerous law review articles that have explored the racially discriminatory implementation of civil asset forfeiture.[88]

3. Court and Incarceration Fees

Despite a Supreme Court case holding that citizens cannot be incarcerated simply for not paying a municipal fine, local courts routinely lock up poor people for nonpayment by holding them in "contempt of court."[89] As detailed by the DOJ Report on Ferguson, the practice is widespread, vicious, and often racially discriminatory.[90] The practice goes far beyond Missouri.

Fees are charged for contempt of court, warrants are served and arrests made for missed payments, fees are charged for serving the warrants, indigent defendants are charged for using a public defender regardless whether they are convicted, those who are not incarcerated are charged the full cost of probation services, and those who are incarcerated for nonpayment are charged a "pay for stay" fee for their jail cell.[91] "According to one study, the average, post-incarceration debt amounts to more than $13,000, and eats up around 60 percent of a formerly incarcerated person's income. Researchers found that more than 60 percent of formerly incarcerated individuals relied on family members to help them make payments, with more than 20 percent taking out loans to cover the cost. Nearly 10 percent of survey respondents indicated that family members' wages or tax refunds were garnished to make payments. For people of color, the consequences are even more acute."[92] Studies show that black people are incarcerated more often and for longer, thereby demonstrating a greater transfer of the burden to fund government from wealthy and white to poor and black.[93]

Studies confirm that these neutrally worded fees and fines and rules and regulations are applied in a discriminatory manner.[94] Moreover, the disparities extend to the juvenile justice system, where black children are held for longer periods, and therefore charged more, than white kids.[95] For those kids, the racial wealth gap is highly personal.

Incarceration debts cannot be discharged in bankruptcy.[96] And even though some states prohibit asking whether a job applicant has a criminal record, incarceration debts are included on the applicant's credit report.[97] Such a negative report can also affect one's application for housing. "Wide swaths of low-income communities' resources are being stripped away due to their inability to overcome the daunting financial burdened placed on them by state and local governments . . . Policy makers can limit the use of fines and fees that directly contribute to burdensome debt, can create barriers to housing and unemployment, and result in imprisonment and recidivism."[98]

Alexandra Bastien offers a menu of reforms designed to reduce the "taxing" nature of law enforcement: "Ability to Pay" hearings for all defendants; set guidelines for determining "ability to pay;" offer flexible penalty free payment plans; enact amnesty periods; cease warrant issuance for unpaid debt; divert indigent defendants into alternative programs; place caps on allowable revenue from fines and fees; eliminate application fees for juvenile record sealing; connect indigent defendants to workforce development programs; prohibit warrants and jail time for unpaid fees; provide free public defender services for debt hearings; eliminate private collection services of court debt; offer accessible payment plan options; eliminate bail for minor crimes; and so forth.[99]

Between racially discriminatory fines, fees, and forfeitures, there can be little doubt about a national trend toward using law enforcement to shift the burden of funding government from wealthy and white onto poor and black. This is more than arbitrary and capricious law enforcement policy. It is regressive and racist taxation. Regardless whether this trend is structural or intentional, it is hard to imagine a better way to surreptitiously maintain or widen the racial wealth gap.

III. IS THE PHILADELPHIA SODA TAX RACIST?

We may conclude that policing for profit represents regressive and racist taxation because (1) it disproportionately extracts funds from black people and people of color; (2) the extractions have a marginal impact on its stated purpose (public safety, public health); and (3) empirical studies show that not only is race a significant factor in determining whether a municipality is likely to use law enforcement to tax, but the extent also depends on whether there is any black presence on city council.[100]

Here we ask whether this trend of surreptitiously shifting the burden of funding local government onto people of color includes the disproportionate use of neutrally worded "sin" taxes on urban communities, the racist intent behind which, like policing for profit, may be inferred, from a marginal benefit to a stated public policy versus a significant shift of tax incidence from wealthy and white to poor and black?

The Philadelphia soda tax fails the first two "elements" of our standard. It causes a significant transfer of tax incidence by race, while having a marginal effect on public health. Still, empirical studies like those performed with respect to policing for profit are needed to determine whether the transfer of tax incidence along with the capricious justifications can be explained away by other factors.

In June 2016, the Philadelphia City Council voted 13–4 to pass a tax on sugary drinks and diet sodas. It did so at the behest of Mayor James Kenney and despite an intense lobbying effort by the American Beverage Association.[101] The city collects 1.5 cents per ounce of soda sold. On top of Philadelphia's 8 percent sales tax, purchasers of a 20-ounce soda pay an extra $0.30 per bottle. A two-liter bottle that often sells for 99 cents will cost an additional $1 tax, plus the sales tax.[102]

Public health advocates, including the American Heart Association, seek to reduce sugar consumption, hopefully thereby reducing the looming financial consequences of a national diabetes epidemic.[103] Sugary drinks contribute to a global obesity problem, and Philadelphia has one of the highest obesity rates in the United States.[104]

In addition, some of the proceeds from the soda tax will be dedicated to pre-K education for 6,500 students, the benefits of which inure to employers, children, and working parents.[105] Some funds will also go to restoring public parks, Philadelphia Community College, as well as other projects.

However, the public was not informed until days before the Philadelphia City Council voted that $41 million of the projected $91 millon to be raised through the tax was being diverted from education and earmarked for the city's bank accounts.[106] Such tactics lend support to the hypothesis that the local excise taxes on things like soda or cigarettes are part of a broader effort to shift the burden of local government from wealthy and white to poor and black.

But how could such a noble idea be racist, especially when quite a few black people support the soda tax? Former Mayor Michael Nutter, an African American, tried to implement this same tax, but was defeated by Philadelphia's City Council.[107]

The Philadelphia soda tax provides a useful illustration of how racism can work without racists.[108] That is, it illustrates institutional or structural racism, a phenomenon that tends to exacerbate racial wealth inequality but which is maintained by "well-meaning" people, whites and blacks alike. White folks who support the tax are not racists in the "popular" sense, neither are the black politicians who voted for it "sellouts" or "Uncle Toms."[109] They are simply trying to solve an immediate short-term problem for a specific locale.

But, while Philadelphians should be concerned with Philadelphia, critical race tax theorists take responsibility for pointing out the long-term, racial implications of legal rules, including taxes.[110] When we apply closer scrutiny to the soda tax, it looks suspicious.

First, the Philadelphia soda tax is far easier to avoid if you are white and wealthy than if you are poor and black. Levied only within the city limits, predominately white jurisdictions around Philadelphia are not subject to the soda tax. Plus, white people within the city of Philadelphia are disproportionately wealthier and are more able, therefore, to avoid the tax by shopping outside the jurisdiction.[111]

Second, the soda tax is poorly designed if a significant reduction of diabetes is the goal. Because diabetes is a national problem, not a Philadelphia one, a sugar or soda tax needs to be national (at least regional) to have a meaningful effect on public health. So long as people are mobile—and becoming more so every day, thanks to technology—a sugary drinks tax in Philly will not have a long-term health impact.

Proponents who acknowledge these issues contend that at a minimum the tax will get people talking and thinking about sugar consumption. They hope that the tax will encourage a much broader shift in priorities beyond their beverage choices. Opponents criticize the fact that sugary foods are not subject to the Philadelphia soda tax, lending to the argument that public health is but an ancillary goal—the real purpose behind the tax is simply to raise revenue without taxing wealthier people who may flee the jurisdiction.

The regressive and perhaps even the racist nature of the tax might be countered by "revenue recycling," returning the proceeds of sin taxes back to the neighborhoods from which they were extracted in the form of social services or programs.[112] Such social services and programs could include, for example, public pre-K education in low-income neighborhoods. Unfortunately, however, the soda tax is not designed to fund universal pre-K education—so there will be a question of which neighborhoods receive this benefit. Moreover, the value of providing pre-K education is discounted somewhat by the fact that the state of Pennsylvania and Philadelphia do not properly fund K–12 education. The systematic underfunding of education in low-income neighborhoods and the perpetuation of the inner-city school-to-prison pipeline are but further manifestations of institutionalized racism.[113]

The Philadelphia soda tax seems inefficiently designed if public health is the aim, unfairly regressive to the extent the incidence of taxation falls disproportionately on those with lesser means, and an example of asymmetrical market imperfections relating to race because from a national perspective the soda tax can be linked with myriad informal and formal taxes nationwide designed to reduce the incidence of taxation on the wealthy and increase the burden on poor people, particularly in communities that have the least relative political capital, i.e., poor black neighborhoods.

A. NATIONAL TREND?

Beyond Philadelphia, there is a trend toward more regressive tax systems, internationally, federally, and locally.

More and more states, cities, towns, and counties are either reducing state income tax rates or eliminating income taxes entirely.[114] Meanwhile, all types of sales taxes are being increased or newly introduced.[115] The legalization of marijuana provides another opportunity to tax the sale of goods.[116] Similarly, large cities like Chicago and Washington, D.C., have introduced "grocery bag" or "plastic bag" taxes.[117] A few jurisdictions regularly tax the provision of services. Others are seriously considering taxing a wider variety of transactions.[118]

Even the Black Lives Matters movement has adopted tax reform as part of its platform:

> As with most injustices in our economic and political systems, regressive taxation has hit Black people, low-income people, and people of color the hardest.
>
> Many municipalities have increasingly decreased the use of progressive taxation and instead resorted to privatization and new fees and higher sales taxes in order to maintain bare-boned public infrastructure with minimal social support. As a result, residents are being forced to pay more for public services like trash collection, access to water, sewage, public property maintenance, and parking meters.
>
> Across the country, low-income people, disproportionately Black and other people of color, pay proportionally more in state and local taxes than the wealthy: In the ten states with the most regressive tax structures, the poorest fifth pay up to seven times as much in state and local taxes and fees as the wealthiest residents, as a percentage of their income.[119]

Their prescription is to reduce sales and gross receipts taxes and shift these toward luxury taxes and taxes on extractive and polluting industries. "Tax policy is so regressive that these solutions will particularly benefit the lowest income families, which are disproportionately single Black women with children, both in terms of increased income and improved access to public services."[120]

Sales taxes can be designed to be less regressive. Pennsylvania and some other states exempt "necessaries" and "medicinals" from sales taxes.[121] However, we are just as likely to see states grant huge tax credits and the like for purchases only the wealthy can afford, like solar panels and energy-efficient cars.[122]

Increasingly regressive taxation represents a trend toward a more plutocratic society and governance structure. Less divisive justifications are offered, but they fail under closer inspection. For example, the West Virginia Center on Budget and Policy found that switching from income taxes to sales taxes does not appreciably grow the economy, countering the governor's pledge to support the economy by moving from income to sales taxes.[123]

It seems proposing regressive "sin" taxes is the most effective way nowadays to "market" tax increases. They are supposed to counter painful exactions from the poor with benefits to those taxed and the rest of society.[124] By taxing cigarettes, for example, and making them more expensive, the idea is that fewer people will smoke and develop cancer, heart disease, and other diseases related to smoking.[125] Because cigarettes produce very little positively for the consumer, there seems to be no loss to those who change their behavior by switching to a healthier, nontaxable substitute. Similarly, estimates suggest that a 20 percent reduction in sugar consumption could save catastrophic future healthcare costs, which is almost like getting paid a couple hundred dollars a year simply to live better.[126]

Except, things like cigarettes and soda are sometimes the only "luxury" poor people can afford.[127] First, consider that poor people smoke cigarettes a lot more than wealthy people do, and consume sugary beverages twice as much as those at the top of the income distribution.[128] Those better off financially can invest in other forms of pleasure or distraction—dangerous ones like skiing if they so choose. Those better off also have the means to avoid paying cigarette and soda taxes by purchasing their goods in no- or low-tax jurisdictions.

Second, increasing taxes on sugary beverages, like increasing taxes on cigarettes, is akin to "pimping" other people's addictions, because studies on cigarette taxes show that higher taxes discourage nonsmokers from trying tobacco but have little effect on those already addicted.[129] After all, cigarette and soda taxes are designed to close budget deficits. In Philadelphia, a portion of the proceeds were dedicated to preschool education.[130] The soda tax could not accomplish this purpose if its primary function were to get people to stop buying sugary drinks entirely. From the outset, most sin taxes are not designed to eliminate the "evil," but to profit from it.

According to Lockwood and Taubinsky:

> Our generally-applicable, quantifiable formulas show that it is not only how biased people are "on average" that matters; it matters who is biased. Whether the mistake is being made by low income or high-income consumers, whether the mistake is being made by those more or less elastic to the tax instrument, and whether the low income consumers are relatively more or less elastic to the tax instrument are critical questions for generating robust policy recommendations.[131]

Public health advocates need be mindful that these regressive sin taxes reduce poor people's liberty and property when life is already harder for them than for those who can avoid the levies and who can engage in their preferred dangerous activities free of special taxes.

Isolated sin taxes in a particular area create also job losses in those areas, as consumers with means take their business elsewhere.[132] In addition to official numbers, inner-city grocery stores and other shops also hire undocumented employees and pay them "cash under the table." Fewer profits from sodas and cigarettes likely means fewer opportunities in the underground economy as well.[133]

It should not be forgotten that taxation involves the power of the state to exact violence on the noncompliant, as well as those merely suspected of noncompliance. Increased taxation of goods encourages a black market in nontaxed contraband. The joke in Philadelphia is that those living close to the city limits can buy sodas in the suburbs and "hustle" them across municipal lines. Far from a joking matter, Eric Garner was killed by New York City police officers because they mistakenly thought he was selling "loosies," or nontaxed single cigarettes.[134]

B. EMPIRICAL QUESTIONS

More research is needed before we declare a "trend" toward regressive and racist taxation. Philadelphia's soda tax as one example of a racially suspicious tax does not prove a latent national conspiracy. Researchers interested in the question might ask, how many cities versus suburban and rural communities have increased consumption taxes? In other words, are cities more likely to enact consumption taxes than suburban and/or rural communities? Are cities with large black populations more likely than other cities to enact consumption taxes? Are states with large black rural populations more likely to enact sales tax schemes than states without large black rural populations? Is there any evidence that taxes in urban communities relate to African American consumption patterns?

As discussed above, Dan Kopf of *Priceonomics* has crunched the numbers and found that the single greatest factor influencing whether a community will commit to so-called "policing for profit" is the presence of a large, black population.[135] Sances and You confirm Kopf's study and add that the presence of black city council members tends to reduce the extent which cities use policing as taxation.[136] Similar studies are needed to determine whether other forms of regressive taxes are being disproportionately levied in black communities nationally.

IV. CONCLUSION

Since *Ferguson's Fault Lines: The Race Quake that Rocked a Nation*,[137] and the ensuing DOJ report on Ferguson, Missouri, there has been greater recognition of the surreptitious ways local governments are using law enforcement to shift the burden of funding government onto low-income citizens, and people of color most perniciously. To the extent these exactions do not accomplish public policy objectives, civil and criminal fines, civil asset forfeiture, and court and incarceration fees represent regressive and racist taxes. This chapter has queried whether this racially subordinating phenomenon, intentional or structural, includes the disproportionate levying of sin taxes on urban communities.

I do not suggest necessarily for African Americans to join the "Starve the Beast" movement, members of which suggest that all taxes are unfair and unjust.[138] Benjamin Lockwood and Dmitry Taubinsky show that some "sin" taxes can have a positive effect on public health while reducing wealth inequality.[139] However, they also show that taxes on addictive behavior and goods for which there are few reasonable alternatives are most likely worsen wealth inequality. Therefore, I would insist that public health advocates consider not only the regressive nature of taxes that penalize addictive behavior, like tobacco and sugar, but also the racial ramifications. Progressive-minded advocacy groups should be mindful when tax proposals aligned with their interests are likely to produce marginal gains to public health at the same time it switches the burden of funding local government from wealthy and white to poor and black.

Last, we note the effect of racially motivated poll taxes on the prevalence of formal and informal regressive and racially disparate taxes: studies show government is less responsive to black people, and even less when there is no black representation on city councils.[140] Voter suppression tactics that amount to twenty-first-century poll taxes reduce the influence black people have on the governments under which they live.

NOTES

1. R. Wood, 'Supreme Court Jurisprudence of Tax Fairness', 36 *Seton Hall Law Journal* (2006), 421. "Efficiency" is a loaded term as it relates to taxation, explored by many including Daniel Shaviro in *The Economics of Tax Law*, criticized by James Repetti in *What Is the Appropriate Role for Economic Efficiency in Formulating Tax Policy?*, and placed in the context of overall reasonableness by Thomas Nagel and Liam Murphy in *The Myth of Ownership*. See D. Shaviro, *The Economics of Tax Law* (2014); J. R. Repetti, Boston College Law School, Presentation to the Loyola University

Law School Colloquium: *The Role of Efficiency in Formulating Tax Policy* (2014); T. Nagel and L. Murphy, The *Myth of Ownership: Taxes and Justice* (2004).

2. L. E. Burman, *Taxes and Inequality* (2014), available online at http://www.taxpolicycenter.org/publications/taxes-and-inequality/full (last visited 14 July 2017).

3. Ibid.

4. Institute on Taxation and Economic Policy, *Fairness Matters: A Chart Book on Who Pays State and Local Taxes*, 26 Jan. 2017, available online at http://itep.org/itep_reports/2017/01/fairness-matters-a-chart-book-on-who-pays-state-and-local-taxes.php#.WMAuen_u2-c (last visited 14 July 2017).

5. Ibid.

6. T. Nitti, 'Trump's "Massive" Middle-Class Tax Cuts are Tiny Compared to Those Promised to the Rich', *Forbes*, 1 Mar. 2017, available online at https://www.forbes.com/sites/anthonynitti/2017/03/01/president-trump-promises-massive-middle-class-tax-cuts-but-will-he-deliver/#9542c736b9e6 (last visited 14 July 2017).

7. M. C. Mirow and B. A. McGovern, 'An Obituary of the Federal Estate Tax', 43 *Arizona Law Review* (2010), 625.

8. A. Gresham Bullock, 'The Tax Code, the Tax Gap, and Income Inequality: The Middle-Class Squeeze', 53 *Howard Law Journal* (2009), 249; D. Shaviro, 'Reckless Disregard: The Bush Administration's Policy of Cutting Taxes in the Face of an Enormous Fiscal Gap', 45 *Boston College Law Review* (2004), 1285.

9. N. Knauer, 'Critical Tax Policy: A Pathway to Reform?', 9 *Northwestern Journal of Law and Social Policy* (2014), 206.

10. Ibid.

11. D. Brown, 'Race and Class Matters in Tax Policy', 107 *Columbia Law Review* (2007), 790; B. Moran, 'Capitalism and the Tax System: A Search for Social Justice', 61 *Southern Methodist University Law Review* (2008), 337; K. B. Brown and M. L. Fellows (eds.), *Taxing America* (1997).

12. United States v. Craft, 535 U.S. 274 (2002).

13. A. Smith, *Tax Law and Racial Economic Justice: Black Tax* (2015).

14. Ibid. See also G. R. Woolfolk, 'Taxes and Slavery in the Ante Bellum South', 26 *Journal of Southern History* (1960), 180; C. J. Bryant, 'Without Representation, No Taxation: Free Blacks, Taxes, and Tax Exemptions Between the Revolutionary and Civil Wars', 21 *Michigan Journal of Race and Law* (2015), 91.

15. Gresham Bullock, *supra* note 8.

16. A. Rudiger, C. Albisa, and K. Kumodzi, 'A Progressive Restructuring of All Tax Codes at the Local, State, and Federal Levels to Ensure a Radical and Sustainable Redistribution of Wealth', part of The Movement for Black Lives' *A Vision for Black Lives: Policy Demands for Black Power, Freedom and Justice* initiative (2017), available online at https://policy.m4bl.org/downloads/ (last visited 6 Sept. 2017); M. W. Sances and H. Y. You, 'Who Pays for Government? Descriptive Representation and Exploitative Revenue Sources', 79(3) *Journal of Politics* (2017), 1090, at 1093.

17. A. Smith, 'Race, Law, and the Free Market: A Critical Law and Economics Conception of Racism as Asymmetrical Market Failure', 4 *Georgetown Journal of Modern Critical Race Perspectives* (2012), 39.

18. Smith, *supra* note 13. See also Woolfolk, *supra* note 14; Bryant, *supra* note 14.

19. See also Woolfolk, *supra* note 14; Bryant, *supra* note 14.

20. Institute on Taxation and Economic Policy, *supra* note 4.

21. D. A. Blackmon, *Slavery by Another Name: The Re-Enslavement of African Americans from Reconstruction to World War II* (2009), at n.20; A. Freeman, 'Racism in the Credit Card Industry', 95(4) *North Carolina Law Review* (2017), 1071.

22. Blackmon, *supra* note 21.

23. 'Policing and Profit', 128 *Harvard Law Review* (2015), 1723.

24. M. L. Hill, *Nobody: Casualties of America's War on the Vulnerable, from Ferguson to Flint* (2016).

25. I. Perry, *More Beautiful and More Terrible: The Embrace and Transcendence of Racial Inequality in the United States* (2011).

26. D. Bell, *Faces At the Bottom of the Well: The Permanence of Racism* (1992); D. Bell, 'Brown v. Board of Education and the Interest Converge Dilemma', 93 *Harvard Law Review* (1979), 518.

27. United States Department of Justice Civil Rights Division, *The Ferguson Report: Department of Justice Investigation of the Ferguson Police Department* (2015), at 2 [hereinafter DOJ Ferguson Report].
28. Ibid. at 76; J. W. Loewen, *Sundown Towns* (2005); K. Norwood, *Ferguson's Fault Lines: The Race Quake that Rocked a Nation* (2015).
29. DOJ Ferguson Report, *supra* note 27.
30. Ibid.
31. Ibid.
32. Ibid. at 52.
33. Ibid.
34. Ibid. at 3–4, 8, 9–15, 55.
35. Ibid. at 3.
36. Ibid. at 2.
37. Ibid.
38. Ibid.
39. Ibid. at 15–41.
40. Ibid. at 13.
41. Ibid. at 50–51.
42. Ibid. at 54–58.
43. Ibid. at 54–58.
44. Ibid. at 4–5, 56, 62–79.
45. Ibid. at 52–54.
46. Ibid. at 4.
47. Ibid. at 42 ("[The Department of Justice] investigation has uncovered substantial evidence that the court's procedures are constitutionally deficient and function to impede a person's ability to challenge or resolve a municipal charge, resulting in unnecessarily prolonged cases and an increased likelihood of running afoul of court requirements. At the same time, the court imposes severe penalties when a defendant fails to meet court requirements, including added fines and fees and arrest warrants that are unnecessary and run counter to public safety.").
48. Ibid.
49. Ibid. at 43.
50. Ibid. at 43, n.21.
51. Ibid. at 58.
52. Ibid. at 61–62.
53. Ibid. at 62.
54. Ibid. at 45.
55. Ibid. at 45–48.
56. Ibid. at 47–48.
57. Ibid. at 54.
58. Blackmon, *supra* note 21.
59. DOJ Ferguson Report, *supra* note 27, at 48–50.
60. Ibid. at 62–63.
61. Ibid.
62. Ibid. at 62–63.
63. Ibid. at 65.
64. Ibid.
65. Ibid. at 65–66.
66. Ibid.
67. Ibid. at 11.
68. Ibid.
69. Ibid. at 69.
70. Ibid. at 70–71.
71. National Federation of Independent Businesses v. Sebelius, 567 U.S. 519 (2012).

72. A. Ellis, 'The Cost of the Vote: Poll Taxes, Voter Identification Laws, and the Price of Democracy', 86 *Denver University Law Review* (2009), 1023; A. Smith, 'After Sebelius, When Does the Cost of Voting Become and Illegal Poll Tax?', 17 *Berkeley Journal of African-American Law & Policy* (2015), 230; R. Krotoszynski Jr., 'A Poll Tax by Another Name', *New York Times*, 14 Nov. 2016, available online at https://www.nytimes.com/2016/11/14/opinion/a-poll-tax-by-another-name.html?mcubz=1 (last visited 6 Sept. 2017).

73. Crawford v. Marion County Election Board, 553 U.S. 181 (2008).

74. J. Armour, *Negrophobia and Reasonable Racism: The Hidden Costs of Being Black in America* (2000).

75. Norwood, *supra* note 28.

76. D. Carbado, 'Predatory Policing', 85 *University of Missouri Kansas City Law Review* (2017), 545.

77. DOJ Ferguson Report, *supra* note 27, at 14.

78. 'Policing and Profit', *supra* note 23.

79. Sances and You, *supra* note 16.

80. D. Kopf, 'The Fining of Black America', *Priceonomics.com*, available online at https://priceonomics.com/the-fining-of-black-america/ (last visited 6 Sept. 2017).

81. Sances and You, *supra* note 16.

82. Ibid.

83. Ibid.

84. Ellis, *supra* note 72; Smith, *supra* note 72; Krotoszynski Jr., *supra* note 72.

85. D. Carbado, 'Predatory Policing', 85 *University of Missouri Kansas City Law Review* (2017), 545.

86. Ibid; 'Policing and Profit', *supra* note 23.

87. 'Policing and Profit', *supra* note 23.

88. See, e.g., M. Murphy, 'Race and Civil Asset Forfeiture: A Disparate Impact Hypothesis', 16 *Texas Journal of Civil Liberties & Civil Rights* (2011), 77, 80–83.

89. A. Bastien, *Ending the Debt Trap: Strategies to Stop the Abuse of Court-Imposed Fines and Fees* (Mar. 2017), available online at http://www.policylink.org/sites/default/files/ending-the-debt-trap-03-28-17.pdf.

90. DOJ Ferguson Report, *supra* note 27.

91. Bastien, *supra* note 89.

92. Ibid.

93. Ibid.

94. Ibid.

95. Ibid.

96. Ibid.

97. Ibid.

98. Ibid.

99. Ibid.

100. Sances and You, *supra* note 16.

101. K. Close, *A Steep Soda Tax Is About to Pass in Philadelphia*, 9 June 2016, available online at http://time.com/money/4362437/soda-tax-philadelphia-committee-vote/ (last visited 6 Sept. 2017); L. Cohen, *Philadelphia Passes Soda Tax After Mayor Rewrites Playbook*, 16 June 2016, available online at http://www.reuters.com/article/us-beverages-philadelphia-sodatax-idUSKCN0Z22G3 (last visited 6 Sept. 2017); J. Rawlins and C. Ileto, *Amended Version of Soda Tax Moves Forward in Philadelphia City Council*, 9 June 2016, available online at http://6abc.com/news/soda-tax-moves-forward-in-philadelphia-city-council-/1376785/ (last visited 6 Sept. 2017); C. Shupert and S. Drenkard, *Soda Tax Experiment Failing in Philadelphia Amid Consumer Angst and Revenue Shortfalls*, available online at https://taxfoundation.org/philadelphia-soda-tax-failing/?utm_source=Tax+Foundation+Newsletters&utm_campaign=0c4a9c5dd4-RSS_EMAIL_CAMPAIGN&utm_medium=email&utm_term=0_8387957ec9-0c4a9c5dd4-427664765&mc_cid=0c4a9c5dd4&mc_eid=577539e974#_ftn7, at 2 ("One highly notable feature of Philadelphia's soda tax compared to those adopted in other localities is that the soda tax was passed as a revenue-raising measure, as opposed to a health initiative designed at reducing obesity. Philadelphia Mayor Jim Kenney noted on PBS NewsHour in May of 2016: 'The ancillary benefit to this will be healthy choices, but it's not the purpose. The purpose of

imposing this 3-cents-an-ounce sugar-sweetened beverage tax is to allow people to get their kids educated and move them out of poverty into taxpaying citizens.'") (last visited 6 Sept. 2017); B. Tuttle, *People Really, REALLY Hate Philadelphia's Soda Tax*, 9 Jan. 2017, available online at http://time.com/money/4628832/philadelphia-soda-tax-gatorade-energy-drinks (last visited 6 Sept. 2017).

102. Close, *supra* note 101.

103. American Heart Association, *Decreasing Sugar-Sweetened Beverage Consumption: Policy Approaches to Obesity*, available online at https://www.heart.org/idc/groups/heart-public/@wcm/@adv/documents/downloadable/ucm_474846.pdf.

104. M. C. Borges et al., *Artificially Sweetened Beverages and the Response to the Global Obesity Crisis*, 3 Jan. 2017, available online at http://journals.plos.org/plosmedicine/article?id=10.1371/journal.pmed.1002195 (last visited 14 July 2017); Governing States and Localities, *America Watches as Philadelphia Battles Obesity* (Aug. 2013), available online at http://www.governing.com/topics/health-human-services/gov-america-watches-as-philly-battles-obesity.html (last visited 14 July 2017).

105. E. Ponsot, *Philadelphia Approves Tax on Sugar-Sweetened and Diet Beverages*, 16 June 2016, available online at http://www.pbs.org/newshour/rundown/philadelphia-becomes-first-major-u-s-city-to-pass-soda-tax/ (last visited 14 July 2017); L. Cohen, *Philadelphia Passes Soda Tax After Mayor Rewrites Playbook* (2017), available online at https://www.scientificamerican.com/article/philadelphia-passes-soda-tax-after-mayor-rewrites-playbook/ (last visited 14 July 2017); M. E. Hill and C. Davis, *The Short and Sweet on Taxing Soda* (Nov. 2016), available online at http://www.itep.org/pdf/sodatax111616.pdf.

106. Rawlins and Ileto, *supra* note 101 ("And now we're being told the need for the additional revenue is to support the fund balance," said City Council President Darrell Clark. "That should have been talked about early on in this process." "All along it was about pre-K and the kids, and you heard it as well as I did. It's not about that. Paying off debt service," said Daniel Grace, Teamsters Local 830. "He ought to be ashamed of himself.").

107. J. Brey and H. Otterbein, *The Soda Tax Battle's Biggest Winners and Losers*, 16 June 2016, available online at http://www.phillymag.com/citified/2016/06/16/soda-tax-passes-winners-and-losers/ (last visited 14 July 2017).

108. E. B. Silva, *Racism Without Racists* (4th ed. 2013).

109. See B. S. Starkey, *In Defense of Uncle Tom: Why Blacks Must Police Racial Loyalty* (2015).

110. A. C. Infanti and B. Crawford, *Critical Tax Theory: An Introduction* (2009); K. Brown and M. L. Fellows (eds.), *Taxing America* (1997); A. Smith, *Black Tax: Tax Law and Racial Economic Justice* (2015); D. Brown, 'Tales from a Tax Crit', 10 *Pittsburgh Tax Review* (2013), 47.

111. M. D. Layser, 'How Federal Tax Law Rewards Segregation', 93 *Indiana Law Journal* (forthcoming 2018).

112. D. B. Marron and A. C. Morris, *How Should Governments Use Revenue from Corrective Taxes?* (Jan. 2016), available online at https://www.brookings.edu/wp-content/uploads/2016/07/How-Should-Governments-Use-Revenue-from-Corrective-Taxes-Marron-Morris-1.pdf, at 4 ("Recycling corrective tax revenue into offsetting tax cuts can assuage concern that such taxes are a ploy to grow government. But revenue neutrality has downsides as well. Revenue neutrality may be difficult to accomplish given uncertainties in future revenues from a corrective tax and any offsetting tax cuts. In addition, it may be easier to achieve some distributional goals through spending than tax reductions. People who generally oppose wholesale revenue increases from corrective taxes should thus be open to modest deviations from revenue neutrality when they offer a more effective way to accomplish policy goals.").

113. M. Alexander, *The New Jim Crow* (2014), at 224; *Ending the School-to-Prison Pipeline: Hearing Before the Senate Judiciary Subcommittee on the Constitution, Civil Rights and Human Rights*, 112th Congress (2012) (written statement of the American Civil Liberties Union).

114. Institute on Taxation and Economic Policy, *supra* note 4.

115. Ibid.

116. R. Phillips, *Issues with Taxing Marijuana at the State Level* (May 2015), available online at https://itep.org/wp-content/uploads/marijuanaissuesreport.pdf.

117. Ibid.
118. M. E. Hill, *What to Watch in the States: Modernizing Sales Taxes for a 21st Century Economy*, 15 Feb. 2017, available online at http://www.taxjusticeblog.org/archive/2017/02/what_to_watch_in_the_states_mo.php#.WMA213_u2-c (discussing trend toward and expressing support for application of sales taxes to a wide array of services) (last visited 14 July 2017).
119. Rudiger, Albisa, and Kumodzi, *supra* note 16.
120. Ibid.
121. 72 Pennsylvania State Code, Section 7204.
122. B. B. Lockwood and D. Taubinsky, *Regressive Sin Taxes*, 6 Mar. 2017, available online at https://www.dropbox.com/s/jl3ct27103ktoy4/Lockwood_Taubinsky_sin_taxes.pdf?dl=0, at 4 ("[A] common objection to sin taxes is that they are regressive. Cigarettes and sugary drinks are consumed disproportionately by the poor, and energy efficiency subsidies are taken up disproportionately by the rich. This has lead to forceful opposition to the taxes on the grounds of fairness and equality" (citations omitted)).
123. T. Boettner, *Income Tax Cuts and Shifting to Sales Tax a Poor Strategy for Growing West Virginia's Economy* (Feb. 2017), available online at http://www.wvpolicy.org/wp-content/uploads/2017/03/WVCBP-Policy-Brief-F-pdf-1.pdf.
124. Lockwood and Taubinsky, *supra* note 122, at 4.
125. Hill and Davis, *supra* note 105.
126. *Knowledge@Wharton: Do Sin Taxes Really Change Consumer Behavior?*, 10 Feb. 2017, available online at http://knowledge.wharton.upenn.edu/article/do-sin-taxes-really-change-consumer-behavior/ (last visited 14 July 2017).
127. Hill and Davis, *supra* note 105.
128. *Do Sin Taxes Really Change Consumer Behavior?*, *supra* note 126.
129. Lockwood and Taubinsky, *supra* note 105.
130. Ibid.; Ponsot, *supra* note 105; Cohen, *supra* note 105.
131. Lockwood and Taubinsky, *supra* note 105.
132. J. Gunlock, *Philly's Drink Tax Is Hurting Consumers, Businesses, and the Poor*, 2 Feb. 2017, available online at http://www.nationalreview.com/article/444491/philadelphia-soda-tax-consumers-businesses-poor-hit-hardest-jim-kenney (last visited 14 July 2017).
133. S. Gonzales, *Regulation Madness: Philly "Soda Tax" Causes Massive Job Losses, Democrat Finger-Pointing*, 23 Feb. 2017, available online at http://www.theblaze.com/news/2017/02/23/regulation-madness-philly-soda-tax-causes-massive-job-losses-democrat-finger-pointing/ (last visited 6 Sept. 2017); *Jobs Gained and Lost from Philadelphia's Soda Tax*, 17 May 2017, available online at http://politicalcalculations.blogspot.com/2017/05/jobs-gained-and-lost-from-philadelphias.html# (last visited 6 Sept. 2017).
134. Hill, *supra* note 24.
135. Kopf, *supra* note 80.
136. Sances and You, *supra* note 16.
137. Norwood, *supra* note 28.
138. See, e.g., A. Hageman, V. Arnold, and S. Sutton, *Starving the Beast: Using Tax Policy and Governmental Budgeting to Drive Social Policy* (June 2007), available online at https://papers.ssrn.com/sol3/papers.cfm?abstract_id=997637 (last visited 7 Sept. 2017).
139. Lockwood and Taubinsky, *supra* note 105, at 3 ("The price elasticity of demand determines the relative importance of corrective benefits versus regressivity costs. When the elasticity is low, the tax has little effect on behavior and thus little corrective benefit—and so its regressivity costs dominate. Conversely, corrective benefits dominate when the elasticity is high.").
140. Sances and You, *supra* note 16 (showing that one black council member reduces the extent to which cities exploit their poor black citizens through exploitative policing).

CHAPTER 22

LABOR, CAPITAL, AND HUMAN RIGHTS

BEVERLY MORAN

I. INTRODUCTION

Until recently, academics were unaware of an association between taxation and human rights.[1] Now, scholars connect fiscal policy and human rights by demonstrating how "first world" countries use domestic and international tax systems to extract tax-free wealth and labor from the "developing world," thereby leaving local governments weakened and impoverished.[2] This chapter takes a different approach. Instead of "first world" exploiting "developing world" as a lens into human rights, this chapter asks how the United States' domestic federal tax system advances or impinges on human rights at home.

Section II uses the US Constitution and the Universal Declaration of Human Rights (UDHR) to illustrate links between taxation and human rights in a domestic setting. After establishing that protection of the human body and the ability to invest in human capital stand above property rights in the human rights pantheon, section II concludes that the human rights values expressed in the US Constitution and the UDHR call for a human rights–centered tax system that supports the social safety net and investment in human capital.

Section III shows how the US federal tax system, and the tax systems in nineteen other Organisation for Economic Co-operation and Development (OECD) nations, subsidize property through preferences for capital gains.[3] The capital gains preference is important because it violates economic neutrality.[4] Economic neutrality is a tax policy ideal meant to prevent taxes from distorting the economic system by driving dollars to low-tax investments.[5] Sales of investment property produce capital gains.[6] Rents, royalties, wages, and sales of inventory do not.[7] Very few people and companies can earn capital gains.[8] Thus, the low tax rate for capital gains violates economic neutrality and depletes government revenues that could support the social safety net rather than benefit high net worth taxpayers.

Section IV debunks justifications for the capital gains preference concluding that they are weak at best. In light of their fragile foundation, apologies favoring preferences for property over support for the social safety net and investment in human capital should fall in favor of greater human rights concerns.

In order to compare tax preferences for property to tax preferences for human capital, section V focuses on preferences for health and education in the Internal Revenue Code (IRC); section VI looks at Social Security; and section VII asks what the world would look like if the rules were flipped and labor received the vast portion of tax benefits.

The chapter concludes that examining investment in social safety and human capital is an appropriate lens through which to investigate how tax systems support domestic human rights, and identifies additional avenues of inquiry based on available data as well as information that is yet to be gathered.

II. HUMAN RIGHTS AND TAXATION

A. THE US CONSTITUTION AND THE UN UNIVERSAL DECLARATION OF HUMAN RIGHTS

This chapter uses the US Constitution and the UDHR to investigate connections between human rights and taxation. The US Constitution is one of the Enlightenment's greatest achievements.[9] As the first modern written constitution, it serves as a model across the globe.[10] The UDHR is also a pioneering text that the United Nations describes as ". . . a milestone document in the history of human rights . . . [that] sets out, for the first time, fundamental human rights to be universally protected."[11] Together, the US Constitution and the UDHR reveal connections between human rights and taxation through a shared intellectual history that includes such human rights concepts as taxation tied to representation, protections against confiscation of property through taxation, taxation as social control, taxation in support of a social safety net, and taxation to fund human capital.

1. US Constitution

The US Constitution's tax provisions with the most human rights effects call for no taxation without representation, no confiscatory taxation, and taxation as a means of social control. A discussion of each of these concepts follows below.

(a) Taxation Tied to Representation

The US Constitution gives Congress the right to raise taxes and requires that all federal tax legislation begin in the House of Representatives, i.e., the only popularly elected federal body at the time that the US Constitution became effective.[12] By placing taxation in the hands of an elected legislature, the US Constitution supports a widely acknowledged connection between human rights and taxation: no taxation without representation.[13]

(b) No Confiscatory Taxation

Although the US Constitution is the model for protecting private property in a capitalist framework, it did not originally protect all US citizens' property.[14] Instead, the US Constitution's body used tax law to protect wealth and slavery[15] while the Third, Fourth, and Fifth Amendments later protected property more generally.[16] The body of the US Constitution has other provisions that supported slavery.[17] This chapter does not discuss those provisions further.

(c) Taxation as an Instrument of Social Control

Although the US Constitution recognizes taxation as an instrument of social control, its tax rules are inconsistent in their support of human rights.[18] On the positive side is a special tax contained in Article I, Section 9 that penalized slave traders[19] and the Twenty-fourth Amendment's prohibition against a poll tax.[20] On the pro-property and anti–human rights side of the ledger is the much more powerful (and still extant) apportionment clause that immunized southern slavers and planters from federal taxes and that continues to protect property from federal taxation to this day.[21] The US Constitution's tax provisions demonstrate that for good and for ill, taxation is a powerful instrument of social control.

2. The Universal Declaration of Human Rights

As heir to US President Franklin Roosevelt's four freedoms,[22] the UDHR adds to the intellectual history of human rights and taxation by, for example, recognizing economic rights and the right to improve human capital as fundamental human rights.[23] In fact, status as a property owner is irrelevant under the UDHR.[24] Instead, as the recent movement to connect human rights and taxation echoes, the UDHR links human rights to taxation through the revenues governments need to address human rights concerns. In contrast, the US Constitution does not provide economic rights and once limited its benefits to property owners.[25]

B. SUPPORTING HUMAN RIGHTS THROUGH CAPITAL OR LABOR?

For most of human history, rulers raised revenues through trade and conquest.[26] Even today, some governments fill their coffers through sales of natural resources instead of taxes.[27] Taxes, like trade and conquest, raise government revenues; but taxes do more. Taxes fuel revolutionary fervor. The American Revolution is just one of many tax revolts.[28] Taxes help set political boundaries, like the ancient Abyssinian toll roads that announced the Ethiopian Empire.[29] Taxes expose who holds power and what the powerful value. Taxes make statements about social and cultural values, as in the exemption for churches found in every US jurisdiction.[30] This chapter looks at the value domestic federal taxes place on human rights.

Human rights fall on a spectrum. Some people have no rights to their bodies, their children, or their heritage that anyone (or any law) is bound to recognize.[31] Some people have nominally recognized legal rights without the social or economic power to enforce them.[32] At its creation, the US Constitution did not speak to the rights of slaves, conquered peoples, or the poor. Rather, the eighteenth-century US Constitution centered human rights in property protections and political freedoms such as "just compensation" and habeas corpus.[33]

In the midst of the Great Depression, President Roosevelt urged Congress to add "freedom from want" and "freedom from fear" to the eighteenth-century American freedoms. Roosevelt failed. At his death, poll taxes and poverty removed large swaths of the population from political power while the post-reconstruction Nadir denied even people of means access to political participation.[34] After the end of World War II, as newly liberated European colonies in Africa, the Americas, and Asia, received political freedom, the UDHR successfully expanded the definition of human rights to include economic and social protections. Now, under the UDHR, property rights are clearly a subset of a wider array of human rights.

For political, religious, social, and practical reasons, governments cannot simply choose what to tax. For example, a government might wish to tax all alcohol production but find itself unable to tax production that ends in personal consumption because that production is too hard to find (practical restrictions) and because the local culture supports tax-free local production to the point of rebellion.[35] If a government could reach every type of income with equal administrative effort, that government might favor an economically neutral tax system that reached income from property and labor equally.[36] An economically neutral tax system favors the capitalist ideal of government as an impartial referee in a mostly market-driven economy.

A government that favored an income tax system that encouraged the production and protection of human rights would have to decide what income to favor in support of its human rights aim. This protection could come in the form of: (1) not taxing certain types of income; (2) taxing certain types of income at lower rates than ordinary income; (3) allowing deductions or credits that support certain types of income. In terms of protecting income, the government has essentially two choices: income from property and income from labor. Selecting between income from property and income from labor forces a choice between different subsets of human rights. This chapter argues that although the Magna Carta and the US Constitution reach out to protect property owners, those owners had already achieved freedom from want and freedom from fear.[37] It was exactly because the Lords who negotiated the Magna Carta and the United States' Founding Fathers were free from want and fear that they were able to pursue higher level political and property rights. Freedom from want and freedom from fear are foundational human rights. Once government achieves a state where people can avoid want and fear, other human rights allow them to accumulate property in safety.[38]

Want and fear are more often associated with poverty than with wealth.[39] People who rely exclusively on income from their labor have significantly less wealth to rely on than people whose income comes solely from capital.[40] A reduced tax on labor—in other words, replacing the preference for capital gains with a lower rate on labor—increases after-tax returns for lower income people. A high capital gains rate on property would then subsidize a tax preference on labor, and could thereby help advance the rights to be free from want and fear. As discussed in section III below, the OECD nations have not chosen economically neutral income tax systems. Nor do their tax systems favor labor over capital. Instead of treating labor and capital equally, or providing a preference for labor, the OECD countries discussed in section III (including the United States) provide a preference for capital gains so that a higher tax on labor subsidizes a lower tax on property.

III. TAX PREFERENCES FOR PROPERTY

Section II suggests that there is a connection between human rights and taxation and that using capital to subsidize labor within a tax system enhances human rights. Taxation reaches labor and property. Human rights and property rights are not in conflict. Indeed, one Enlightenment insight is that human rights encompass property rights.[41] Nevertheless, the justification for preferring income from labor to income from capital starts with the observation that human rights protect human beings and that property rights are only a subset of the wider array of human rights. Certainly, in a human rights–driven tax system, rights associated with social welfare and investment in human capital are preferred to rights exclusively associated with property because freedom from want and from fear are foundational prerequisites to exercising property and political rights.

This section illustrates how the US tax system, like the systems of nineteen other OECD nations, does the opposite. Instead of protecting income from labor, each system uses labor to subsidize capital.

A. UNITED STATES

In the United States, capital receives better tax treatment than labor in at least three ways: (1) lower tax rates;[42] (2) the ability to time tax liability in order to take advantage of other items on the return[43] and of the time value of money, no matter what else appears on the return;[44] and (3) the opportunity to escape tax completely by passing property at death.[45]

1. Lower Capital Gains Rates

The amount of tax owed is a function of the tax rate multiplied by the tax base. If two people have the same tax base, but different tax rates, each will owe a different tax. So for example, a person who earns $100,000 from salary and pays a flat 40 percent rate will owe $40,000 in tax, while a person who earns $100,000 in capital gains will most likely pay $20,000. In the United States, the impact on labor is even greater when the separate wage tax is considered. A self-employed person earning $100,000 owes almost an additional 16 percent in Social Security and Medicare taxes for a total tax liability of more than $50,000 compared to the property owner's $20,000 tax bill.[46] As discussed in greater length in section III.B. below, most OECD countries provide a lower capital gains rate than the rate on income from wages. In the United States, the capital gains rate is approximately half of the tax rate on income from labor.[47]

2. Deferring Tax through the Realization Requirement

The realization requirement delays taxing property until the owner sells.[48] In contrast, most income tax systems reach income from labor when earned even if the taxpayer saves the income for decades. If holding onto property for investment is the same as holding onto earnings from labor, then the two types of income receive the same tax. Instead, the realization requirement allows property owners to time their tax liability until the year of sale while forcing the laborer to pay tax in the year the labor was performed and remunerated.

The ability to select which year income is included in the tax base sweetens the low capital gains rate in two ways. First, because property owners can select years with the best tax rates, tax revenues rise in years that the capital gains rate falls.[49] However, even if rates remained stable, which they certainly do not, the right to time tax payments also includes the ability to time offsetting deductions, losses, and credits, making tax liability disappear.[50] Second, an independent virtue of the capacity to time income—even in an era of stable flat rates—is that the longer a tax is delayed, the smaller its cost in today's dollars (the time value of money).[51]

3. Escaping Tax through Inheritance

Finally, if the taxpayer holds onto the property until death, his heirs will most likely escape tax completely.[52] This combination of lower rates, the ability to defer tax, the ability to time tax liability to coincide with the best rates and/or tax outcomes, and to avoid tax completely, is not available to labor. Instead, the US federal tax reaches labor immediately in the form of income tax and other taxes levied on wages. Further, the taxes on those wages are at high rates with virtually no opportunity to time the taxing event or take advantage of delay.[53]

B. OTHER OECD COUNTRIES

1. Lower Rate on Capital Gains

In 2006, the OECD released a report on capital gains (Capital Gains Report).[54] The report centered on twenty OECD members (OECD participants) that responded to an OECD questionnaire regarding how each participant country treated its individual taxpayers' capital gains.[55] The Report describes how each OECD participant taxed capital gains at a lower rate than labor even though they all also wanted simple tax systems and each reported that its own lower capital gains rate increased its tax system's complexity by creating incentives to transform ordinary income into capital gains.[56]

2. Benefit of Realization

Nineteen out of the twenty OECD questionnaire participants use a realization-based approach to capital gains.[57] As discussed above in regard to the United States, the realization requirement gives property owners (1) the ability to time tax results for the best rates, matching income to losses, deductions, and credits; and (2) the ability to exploit the time value of money by deferring taxation.[58]

3. Inheritance Tax

In the United States, yet another benefit that flows to property but not labor is the rule that allows heirs to avoid their decedents' untaxed gains.[59] As discussed in section III.A.2 above, the realization requirement defers tax on the appreciation of property until the owner sells the property. In some OECD countries like the United States, a taxpayer's death reduces or erases tax liability for any previously unrealized gains that flow through to heirs tax free.

The OECD participants took four different approaches to taxing unrealized income embedded in property at the taxpayer's death. Some OECD participants treat death as a realization event and recognize any previously untaxed gain at that time.[60] Others roll accrued gains over to inheritors and then tax the heirs when they dispose of the asset.[61] A few completely waive the capital gains tax but subject the fair market value of the estate to an estate tax.[62] The fourth approach is to tax both the fair market value of the estate and the previously untaxed capital gains in the inherited properties.[63]

IV. JUSTIFICATIONS FOR THE CAPITAL GAIN PREFERENCE

Beyond human rights, there are other interests that a capital gains preference in tax policy might (or might not) advance. One established pillar of US tax policy is horizontal equity.[64] Horizontal equity calls for taxpayers with the same amount of income to pay the same amount of tax. A special capital gains rate flouts that requirement by treating income from labor differently than income from capital, even when the two are identical in quantity and timing. Another foundational US tax principle is simplicity.[65] Yet, as noted above, exempting capital gains from tax, or providing a lower capital gains rate, creates greater system-wide complexity as taxpayers try to convert high-taxed ordinary income into low-taxed capital gains.

As discussed in section II.B. above, human rights considerations and economic neutrality argue against taxing capital more favorably than labor. Labor provides the foundational income required for freedom from want and freedom from need. Economic neutrality argues for taxing labor and capital equally, as do such other tax principles such as simplicity, transparency, and horizontal equity. Supporting the human rights values of freedom from want and freedom from fear, argues for using capital to subsidize labor. None of these values supports a lower capital gains tax rate. Given its damage to so many enduring tax virtues, what justifies a lower capital gains rate?

From its inception, the US income tax system has provided preferences for capital gains.[66] Nevertheless, in the United States, "special capital gains treatment appears to be supported more by a visceral belief that such income is special and should be segregated in treatment from other types of income, rather than by hard analysis justifying the preferential aspects of the system."[67]

The theories that support the capital gains preference are the product of shifting ideas and beliefs about economic growth, risk, and wealth.[68] Justifications for a lower capital gains rate should begin with the question: how does the lower rate serve the public?[69] Public good is sorely lacking from the most common justifications for the lower capital gains rate, several of which this chapter examines below.

A. ARGUMENT ONE: CAPITAL GAINS ARE NOT INCOME

One argument against taxing capital gains is that these gains are not income. Given that the wealthiest people in society earn capital gains and that income from capital gains is more able (and likely) to purchase luxuries than is labor income, it is difficult to imagine how capital gains are not income. One attempt to fire the imagination in that direction is the claim that capital gains are not income because capital transactions are not recurring. Under this argument, a dealer in fine art has ordinary income on every sale because his sales recur; but a taxpayer has no tax liability from the sale of a single painting held in a family for years.

This argument fails because:

> many other types of income may not have a repetitive nature, such as a year-end bonus, a taxable award or prize, or a one-time contractual fee. No one suggests that such income should be excluded because it occurs only once in a person's lifetime; a conceptual difference between non-repetitive ordinary income and isolated capital gains, justifying different treatment on a "recurrence" basis, is difficult to discern.[70]

Moreover, capital gains can come from oft-repeated transactions (like sales of stock holdings/ financial assets) without losing the lower capital gains rate so long as the taxpayer does not become a dealer in property.[71]

B. ARGUMENT TWO: ABSENT A LOW CAPITAL GAINS RATE, THE WEALTHY WILL FREEZE THEIR ASSETS

The argument holds that taxing capital gains at ordinary income rates would discourage "taxpayers from realizing capital gains . . . [thereby resulting in] fewer capital gains and losses, diminished taxes, and general rigidity in the capital market"[72]—hence, the freeze. One of the charms of the freeze argument is that it uses the fact that property receives two large tax advantages over labor in order to argue that property should receive a third, equally large, additional benefit.

As discussed above in section III, the first tax benefit to capital is the realization requirement that allows property owners to completely control when a tax occurs. With the realization requirement, a taxpayer can sell an asset in a low tax year or hold onto the asset in a high tax year thereby effectively selecting the best tax rate. The property owner can also time income for years that contain credits, losses, and deductions that further eliminate his tax liability. Even simply holding property generates time-value-of-money advantages through tax deferral.

The second tax benefit involved in the freeze argument is an adjustment to properties held in an estate that effectively eliminates any untaxed gain and thus also eliminates tax liability for beneficiaries.[73] For example, an artist might create a beautiful sculpture that would easily sell for $2 million. However, if the artist sells his sculpture, he now owes tax on that $2 million. On the other hand, should the artist die still holding the sculpture, his heirs will pay no tax when they sell it for the same $2 million. This benefit, sometimes called the step-up in basis at death, provides a powerful incentive to "freeze" assets.[74]

The freeze argument claims that a third tax benefit in the form of a preferential tax rate for long-term capital gains encourages property owners to break the ice and sell their properties rather than holding onto them until death.[75] In other words, a taxpayer who is inclined to keep property until he dies—when he knows that his heirs will pay no tax whatsoever—might be encouraged to sell the property if he will only pay half or less of the tax he would pay on wages. Thus, the freeze argument rests on the government's ability to predict how taxpayers will respond to a lower rate. Yet, there is no clear answer as to how taxpayers respond to capital gains tax rates.[76] Further, how can any tax due now ever be low enough now to compete with a zero rate in the future? In a realization-based tax system, the lock-in effect that supposedly forces taxpayers to freeze their assets is an argument for no capital gains tax at all. After all, if there is no tax at death, why punish the taxpayer for living? Why ever tax capital gains at all?

A counterargument accepts that freezes result from a combination of the realization requirement and the step-up in basis at death. However, the cure is not layering yet another tax benefit on top of the first two. Rather, the better course is to require accrual taxation of capital gains. By taxing the rise and fall in a property's value each year, estates pass a fair market value basis to heirs at death so that the property leaves the estate with no tax liability.[77] Further, merely including different rates for different types of income in a tax system increases complexity, decreases transparency, and encourages tax avoidance. The twenty OECD participants in the Capital Gains Report all taxed some capital gains in order to increase revenue and decrease the complications that no tax on capital gains invites.[78]

C. ARGUMENT THREE: BUNCHING

Another justification for taxing capital gains differently contends that, under a progressive rate structure, realizing a number of years' gains in a single tax period unfairly pushes the taxpayer into higher-than-usual tax rates.[79] For example, the taxpayer earns $100 a year appreciation in value over three years. This is his only income. If the taxpayer paid tax on the $100 a year, he would be in the 10 percent bracket and owe $30 total over the three years. Instead, the taxpayer sells on the first day of year four, earning $300 all in that year. The rate on the second $100 is 20 percent, and the rate on the third $100 is 40 percent. Now, instead of paying a $10 tax per year, or $30 total, the bill is $70 total. This is bunching. Bunching flows from the realization requirement and progressive rates. Although tax liability accumulates over many years, the tax system captures payment in only one year and taxes the larger amount at higher rates. If the rate remained the same across tax years, then the taxpayer still keeps the time value of money and losses nothing from the rates.

Bunching cannot hurt taxpayers who routinely pay at the highest rate, as do the taxpayers who typically earn capital gains. These taxpayers will always pay the highest rates on their income no matter how it is earned so that they essentially pay flat rates.[80] Thus, bunching gives these taxpayers the benefit of the time value of money combined with a flat rate. Using the example above, if the top rate is 40 percent, and the taxpayer always earns enough to pay some tax at the 40 percent rate, then whether the taxpayer earns $1 more or $1 million more, all will be taxed at the 40 percent rate. Further, as high-income individuals, "many taxpayers enjoy capital gains every year and therefore their income is not 'bunched up' in any one particular year on account of capital gains."[81]

In addition, to the extent that the taxpayer can take advantage of lower rates in a progressive rate structure,[82] bunching also occurs to ordinary income, but ordinary income gets no relief from bunching.

> For instance, a musician may labor a lifetime on a musical masterpiece; the copyright, if sold in a single year, results in a greater tax than if he had produced several lesser pieces over the years. The same tax outcome occurs for persons such as artists, writers, and tax lawyers who render opinions after years of research. Capital gains are not treated unfairly when compared to the many other cases of a theoretical grouping or bunching of income which occurs in a single year.[83]

Just as it circumvents freezes, an annual accrual method cures bunching.[84]

D. ARGUMENT FOUR: CAPITAL GAINS REFLECT INFLATION RATHER THAN TRUE APPRECIATION

The fourth argument supposes that inflation only affects capital and not labor.[85] Apparently, inflation increases the value of all property to the same extent so that all price increases reflect inflation and there is no real appreciation left to tax. At the same time, the inflation that forces up wages does not call for a decrease in rates.[86]

In fact, not all property values rise at the same rate. The increase in value above inflation is certainly income. Further, the taxpayer continues to enjoy the time value of money from the delay in tax caused by the realization requirement. That deferral compensates taxpayers for any tax on inflation.

Once again, accrual accounting is the cure for the fear that the system is taxing inflation rather than true economic gain.

E. ARGUMENT FIVE: ENCOURAGE SAVINGS AND PROMOTE ENTERPRISE

To understand the capital gains preference as a savings promotion device is to understand savings as primarily focused on capital assets.[87] In fact, many taxpayers place savings in ordinary income-producing assets such as bank accounts.[88] The capital gains preference undercuts the concept of tax neutrality as between investments. It steers savings away from investments that produce ordinary income (interest, rents, sales of inventory) and toward appreciating assets that produce capital gains, such as stocks, bonds, art work, and other capital assets.[89]

F. ARGUMENT SIX: RISK-TAKING

Some scholars argue that the capital gains preference reduces risk-taking, while other studies find that a capital gains tax actually increases risk-taking in search of lower tax rates.[90] If the capital gains preference is meant to subsidize risk-taking, then it forces the general public to bear part of the cost of the accumulation of private capital. The societal benefit that the public receives in return for this cost is unclear. In fact, a capital gains preference places additional tax costs on labor that create disincentives to work.[91]

G. HORIZONTAL AND VERTICAL EQUITY

Tax policy calls for horizontal equity to ensure that all income is taxed equally. Vertical equity is meant to guarantee that people with higher incomes pay a larger portion of their income in tax. Therefore, if the comparison is between a lower capital gains rate and no capital gains tax at all, then a capital gains preference contributes to both horizontal and vertical equity.[92] However, when compared to a system that taxes capital and ordinary income equally, the capital gains preference undercuts both horizontal and vertical equity. Capital gains violate horizontal equity by ensuring that two people with the same amount of income will not pay the same amount of tax. Low rates on capital gains go to people with high incomes, thereby violating vertical equity by allowing richer people to pay lower taxes.[93]

V. INVESTMENT IN HUMAN CAPITAL

The UDHR identifies health and education as foundation stones of human rights. The federal tax system subsidizes education and health.[94] With the idea that investments in the human body and human capital stand above property rights, this section asks if the federal tax provisions that subsidize health and education counterbalance the capital gains preferences so that, taken together, the benefits match. In this analysis, tax subsidies for health and education are proxies for direct investment in the social safety net and investment in human capital.

Each year, the Congressional Budget Office (CBO) produces a list of "tax expenditures."[95] Section V uses the tax expenditure budget estimates for 2016 to compare the value of capital gain preferences against the value of other provisions within the tax system that support education and health.

Tax expenditures are "revenue losses attributable to provisions of the Federal tax laws which allow a special exclusion, exemption, or deduction from gross income or which provide a special credit, a preferential rate of tax, or a deferral of tax liability."[96] Tax expenditure estimates draw on a comprehensive income tax, which defines income as the sum of consumption and change in net worth in a given period.[97]

Remarkably, the tax expenditure budget does not include the value of deferred taxes created by the realization requirement.[98] Nevertheless, although the lost value from the realization requirement is beyond the scope of this chapter, taxpayers and Congress recognize the value of deferral in everything from stock bonuses to pension plans.[99]

A. TAX SUPPORT FOR EDUCATION

Under US federal tax law, the cost of education falls into one of three categories: (1) Personal, in which case, IRC § 262 prohibits a tax benefit;[100] (2) Business, where IRC § 162 allows a deduction;[101] and (3) Capital, which prohibits tax benefits under IRC § 263.[102] Despite these general categories and limitations, Congress provides tax benefits for education within the IRC in the form of exclusions,[103] deductions,[104] savings plans,[105] and credits.[106] Not all benefits go directly to students. For example, the tax expenditure budget includes charitable contribution deductions for gifts to educational institutions.[107]

Exclusions are items that the federal government could tax as income but that Congress specifically decides to exempt.[108] Credits reduce tax liability, usually dollar for dollar.[109] A credit helps finance the cost of education by reducing the amount of tax owed and (perhaps) providing a refund over and above tax liability.[110] A deduction reduces the amount of income that is subject to tax, thus usually reducing the amount of tax owed.[111] Savings plans allow taxpayers to grow their capital tax free, and sometimes withdraw the income untaxed as well.[112]

According to the tax expenditure budget, in 2016 the federal tax system subsidized education by more than $40 billion.[113] By their nature, the tax benefits for education tend to provide greater economic support to the rich than to the poor. First, because people who earn below the median income of a family of four in the United States, rarely file a Schedule A on their tax return.[114] The Form 1040, Schedule A is required for many education-oriented tax benefits. Second, because the value of deductions rise as a taxpayer's marginal tax rate increases.[115] Accordingly, even if two taxpayers receive exactly the same deduction, the deduction's value is greater to the higher income individual. Finally, one of the richest tax preferences is for charitable contributions of appreciated capital gains property.[116] Donations to schools and hospitals receive greater tax benefits than contributions to other types of exempt organizations.[117] The greater tax benefits for charitable contributions of appreciated capital assets to schools, allows a taxpayer to completely avoid tax on any unrealized gain in the gift while deducting the full fair market value of the gift including the unrealized and untaxed capital appreciation.[118]

B. TAX SUPPORT FOR HEALTH

Medical expense deductions are severely limited by floors that prevent taxpayers from deducting costs until the medical expenses exceed 10 percent of adjusted gross income and by restrictions that place medical expense deductions "below the line" on the taxpayer's Schedule A.[119] As noted above, low-income taxpayers rarely use a Schedule A as part of their tax filings. Accordingly, low-income taxpayers rarely receive medical expense deductions and, even if they do, their low effective tax rates make the deductions less valuable for them than for high-income individuals. Nonetheless, the medical expense deduction, which alone cost the government over $7 billion in 2016, benefits high-income taxpayers almost exclusively.[120] The entire tax expenditures budget for health was over $262 billion in 2016.[121] The amount of the healthcare expenditures as compared to education expenses also favors the rich. For example, one significant element in the size difference between the two comes from the charitable gifts to hospitals as opposed to schools. As discussed above, the charitable gift deduction is almost exclusively a tax benefit for the rich because less than half of individual returns use Schedule A, and less than half of those returns make donations of appreciated capital gain property to exempt organizations.[122] Even within this rarefied group, those with the highest tax rate will benefit the most. Accordingly, the benefit flows toward upper-income groups.

C. CAPITAL GAINS AND OTHER BENEFITS FOR PROPERTY

The more than $250 billion for healthcare plus the $40 billion for education described in the tax expenditure budget dwarfs the $41 billion annual cost for the capital gains preference.[123] However, without information on the realization requirement's value—an omission in the CBO's expenditure report noted above—the comparison is lacking. Further, as discussed above, the benefits of the capital gains preference flows almost exclusively to wealthy people, as does the tax benefit for education and health. Those in the highest tax bracket have enough disposable income to invest in capital assets. Some people believe that, because many pension funds and individual retirement accounts hold stocks, their owners benefit from capital gains tax preferences. They do not. Monies from pensions and individual retirement accounts are taxed at the higher rates applied to ordinary income.[124] Finally, property receives many other benefits under the IRC that are absent from the tax expenditure budget and from this discussion.[125] For example, many costs associated with property ownership are deducted "above the line," as opposed to costs associated with labor, which are generally deducted "below the line." "Above the line" deductions are more valuable. The time value of money, and the ability to time gains to losses, are two additional benefits of property ownership that the tax expenditure budget does not calculate.

VI. SOCIAL SECURITY

Outside the income tax, the Social Security system purports to provide a safety net for disabled and retired workers.[126] The lived experience of the ill and the aged in the United States exposes some of the flaws in the Social Security system. First, as originally conceived, the Social Security old-age pension was set to pay out at an age significantly older than the average age at death.[127] In fact, the extension of human mortality in the second half of the twentieth century is a major cause for pressures on the pension portion of the system today.[128] Setting the benefit age so high that most people will never receive a benefit has human rights implications. Poor people, sick people, and ethnic minorities are all more likely to die before they receive benefits than are upper-middle-class whites.[129]

To this point, other than probable mortality, the United States has not used barriers to access old-age pension payments as a way of balancing the Social Security budget. In other words, those who survive to reach retirement age actually receive their pension benefit without onerous additional obstacles. Social Security old-age pension payments are relatively easy to apply for, and there are limited barriers to receiving payments. On the other hand, the disability benefits available under the Social Security system are extremely difficult to procure.[130] Obtaining Social Security disability payments is harder on every level than, for example, qualifying for the capital gains preference. The significance of the comparison is that the greater a person's wealth, the longer that person's projected life.[131] Conversely, the poorer a person, the more likely that person is to be sick or disabled, and the less likely she is to live long enough to earn Social Security. Further, poverty often correlates with minority status, gender, and age. The tax expenditure budget shows that the old-age pension benefit ($28,300,000,000) outpaces the cost of Social Security disability payments ($8,580,000,000), which then exceeds support for spouses, dependents, and survivors ($4,530,000,000).[132]

Tax policy calls for horizontal equity, i.e., tax people with equal incomes equally. On the surface, the Social Security tax appears to satisfy horizontal equity if people have the same income because the Social Security tax applies the same rate to all wages up to a maximum cutoff.[133] Yet, people do not pay the same tax if they each pay in the same amount but some people consistently receive back more than they paid in, while other poorer people have to work very hard to obtain disability benefit eligibility and often never receive any payments for either disability or old age.

What do human rights values contribute to a system that makes benefits easily obtainable for healthy people with resources and makes benefits flowing from the same sources difficult for sick people who are also less well-off? These concerns call for more investigation.

VII. HUMAN BODIES AND TAX BENEFITS

This chapter highlights some of the many benefits that flow to property, the social safety net, and human capital under US federal tax laws. Although the long history of support for the capital gains preference combined with an equally long history of silence on any connection between human rights and taxation might indicate otherwise, the tax expenditure budget, as currently calculated, displays as much support for human rights as for capital. Unfortunately, the apparent parity may be illusory because so many fundamental benefits to property are not included in the tax expenditure budget precisely because they are so fundamental.[134]

This section asks how the IRC might look if human beings, rather than capital, benefited from fundamental provisions like depreciation and realization.

A. ACCRUAL ACCOUNTING IN LIEU OF DEPRECIATION
AND REALIZATION

When depreciation and realization entered into accounting, they supported sound fiscal practices like: don't count your chickens before they hatch (realization) and put money away for a rainy day (depreciation). Even today, businesses use depreciation to keep track of their need to replace machinery, or realization to avoid fooling themselves or their bankers by overinflating the value of inventory.

Nevertheless, with the advent of international markets and microsecond multimillion-dollar transactions, realization and depreciation do not accurately reflect income in the way that placing property on accrual accounting achieves.[135] Placing property on accrual accounting directly addresses the concerns that led to the capital gains preference and makes the preference unnecessary. If property has actually declined in value in later years, then the taxpayer gets a deduction equal to the portion of the decline associated with a decline in function. Declines in value due to markets are capital losses, not depreciation. If property increases in value, then prior depreciation deductions are recaptured without the need to wait for the taxpayer to sell.

B. LIFE DECLINING WITH REASONABLE CERTAINTY

The present tax system provides realization and depreciation to property even though these rules make it more difficult to ascertain true income and value. Ironically, the system also completely denies depreciation and realization to human beings, even though the identical mathematical sophistication now makes valuation of human beings possible. As the UDHR recognizes, many people have only their bodies to support themselves throughout their entire lives, which is why, for example, the UDHR does not tie human rights to property ownership.[136] Yet people receive no tax recognition of their physical decline through a depreciation deduction. With a depreciation deduction, and the ability to use loss carry forwards, a student could reduce his tax liability now and in the future by deducting past depreciation on the decline in his body during his student years against the current income his studies helped generate. Realization might come into play to allow the government to reconcile the person's tax costs against their government benefits on the final return just as a sale reconciles depreciation for property. For example, if a person beat the odds and outlived his or her life expectancy by thirty years, that person might start to reflect depreciation recapture on his or her return during those last thirty years.

Applying depreciation and realization to human bodies strengthens the connection between human rights and taxation as well as the independent goal that taxes and the tax system clearly reflect income that undergirds so much of tax policy.

VIII. CONCLUSION

Scholars in the international arena use the US Constitution and the UDHR to make connections between human rights and taxation, which they describe primarily as "first world" countries extracting resources and labor from host countries tax-free leaving the lesser developed world less able to serve their populations. This chapter starts a conversation on what an investigation of domestic tax looks like from a human rights perspective and begins a domestic discussion of US federal tax laws by comparing support for education, old-age pensions, disability, and health to capital gains preferences. Capital gains preferences stand as a proxy for other tax benefits to property not included in the tax expenditure budget. Unfortunately, more research is required because the Congressional Budget Office's Tax Expenditure Budget does not account for tax benefits for property like time value of money and the realization requirement. Nor does it fully disaggregate beneficiaries of benefits across the population.

The chapter outlines a course of investigation for further study, including contrasting Social Security old-age pension and disability benefits, and exploring the consequences of shifting property to accrual accounting while providing the human body with generous depreciation deductions and tax deferral through realization.

NOTES

1. See, e.g., W. Hoke, 'Panel Explores Role of Human Rights Considerations in Tax Policy', 153 *Tax Notes* (3 Oct. 2016), 37; R. Jackson, 'Tax Abuse and Human Rights: Is There a Connection?', 72 *Tax Notes International* (4 Nov. 2013), 384; E. Avery, 'International Taxation and Human Rights', 46 *Tax Notes International* (18 June 2007), 1247.

2. W. Hoke, 'Consider Human Rights in Tax Avoidance Discussions, Oxfam Director Says', 83 *Tax Notes International* (26 Sept. 2016), 1124; P. Alston, Keynote Address at Christian Aid Conference on the Human Rights Impact of Tax and Fiscal Policy, Tax Policy Is Human Rights Policy: The Irish Debate (12 Feb. 2015).

3. The OECD comprises the governments of thirty-four member economies and more than seventy nonmember economies that produce internationally comparable statistical, economic, and social data. OECD member countries account for 63 percent of world GDP, three-quarters of world trade, 95 percent of world official development assistance, over half of the world's energy consumption, and 18 percent of the world's population. U.S. Mission to the Organization for Economic Cooperation and Development, *What Is the OECD?*, available online at https://usoecd.usmission.gov/our-relationship/about-the-oecd/what-is-the-oecd/ (last visited 28 June 2017).

4. J. G. Gravelle, *The Economic Effects of Taxing Capital Income* (1994); L. E. Burman, H. J. Aaron, and C. E. Steuerle (eds.), *Taxing Capital Income* (2007); E. S. Phelps, *Fiscal Neutrality Toward Economic Growth: Analysis of a Taxation Principle* (1965).

5. T. J. Cranstron, 'Economic Neutrality and the Compensating Use Tax', 16(4) *Stanford Law Review* (1964), 1016, 1022.

6. Y. Yuen and M. Racusin, 'Tax Benefits of Multi-Family Real Estate and Oil and Gas Investments', 99(1) *Practical Tax Strategies* (2017), 25, at 25.

7. L. E. Burman and P. D. Ricoy, 'Capital Gains and the People Who Realize Them', 50(3) *National Tax Journal* (1997), 427, at 438.

8. Ibid.

9. A. R. Amar, *America's Constitution: A Biography* (2006) (the US Constitution is exemplary); R. L. Lerner, 'Enlightenment Economics and the Framing of the U.S. Constitution', 35 *Harvard Journal of Law and Public Policy* (2012), 37, at 46 (the US Constitution is one of the great achievements of the Enlightenment).

10. D. S. Law and M. Versteeg, 'The Declining Influence of the United States Constitution', 87 *New York University Law Review* (2012), 762 (the US Constitution is the first modern written constitution); S. Gardbaum, 'The New Commonwealth Model of Constitutionalism', 49 *American Journal of Comparative Law* (2001), 707, at 711, note 11 (the US Constitution serves as a model for other constitutions).

11. Since its adoption in 1948, the UDHR has been translated into more than 360 languages—the most translated document in the world—and has inspired the constitutions of many newly independent states and many new democracies. United Nations, *Universal Declaration of Human Rights*, available online at http://www.un.org/en/universal-declaration-human-rights/index.html (last visited 28 June 2017).

12. US Constitution, Art. I, § 7, Cl. 1 ("All Bills for raising Revenue shall originate in the House of Representatives"). Direct election of Senators does not occur until the Seventeenth Amendment ("The Senate of the United States shall be composed of two Senators from each State, elected by the people thereof . . ."). US Constitution, Art. I, § 8, Cl. 1 ("The Congress shall have Power to lay and collect Taxes, Duties, Imposts and Excises").

13. S. Dowell, *History of Taxation and Taxes in England*, Vol. 1 (2013). H. M. Gladney, *No Taxation without Representation: 1768 Petition, Memorial, and Remonstrance* (2014) (the most eloquent and effective colonial taxation protest was a 1768 missive from Virginia to the British government.).

14. B. Moran, 'Capitalism and the Tax System: A Search for Social Justice', 61 *Southern Methodist University Law Review* (2008), 337 (capitalism protects private property). R. A. Epstein and M. J. Rizzo, 'The Ends of Capitalism: An Introduction', 23(1) *Supreme Court Economic Review* (2016), 1 (the US Constitution is a model for creating a capitalist nation).

15. US Constitution, Art. I, § 2, Cl. 3, first sentence requires that direct taxes be apportioned among the states. This provision was placed in the Constitution in order to prevent the federal government from imposing taxes on property, such as land and slaves. The southern states insisted on the provision because they were afraid that the northern states with their larger number of Representatives based on population would use taxes on slaves and land as a way of breaking up the plantation system. See R. L. Einhorn, *American Taxation, American Slavery* (2008).

16. Provisions in the US Bill of Rights that protect property include:

> Third Amendment ("No Soldier shall, in time of peace be quartered in any house, without the consent of the Owner, nor in time of war, but in a manner to be prescribed by law");
>
> Fourth Amendment ("The right of the people to be secure in their persons, houses, papers, and effects, against unreasonable searches and seizures");
>
> Fifth Amendment ("[N]or shall private property be taken for public use, without just compensation").

17. See, Article I, Section 2. That counts slaves as three-fifths of a human for purposes of representation and taxation. It reads:

> Representatives and direct Taxes shall be apportioned among the several States which may be included within this Union, according to their respective Numbers, which shall be determined by adding to the whole Number of free Persons, including those bound to Service for a term of years, and excluding Indians not taxed, three-fifths of all other Persons.

Article I, Section 9. Which taxes the slave trade and promises to end importation by 1808. It reads:

> The Migration and Importation of such Persons as any of the States now existing shall think proper to admit, shall not be prohibited by the Congress prior to the Year one thousand eight hundred and eight, but a Tax or duty may be imposed on such Importation, not exceeding ten dollars for each Person.

Article IV, Section 2. The fugitive-slave clause reads:

> No Person held to Service or Labour in one State, under the Laws thereof, escaping into another, shall, in Consequence of any Law or Regulation therein, be discharged from such Service or Labour, but shall be delivered up on Claim of the Party to whom Service or Labour may be due.

P. Finkelman, 'The Founders and Slavery: Little Ventured, Little Gained', 13(2) *Yale Journal of Law and the Humanities* (2001), 413, at 445.

18. Adam Smith in *Wealth of Nations* discusses taxation both as a source of revenue and as a source of social control. See, e.g., Moran, *supra* note 14. Provisions that support social control through taxation in the US Constitution include Art. I, § 2, Cl. 3, which prohibits federal taxes on lands and slaves (along with other wealth) and counts the slave population toward the number of representatives and the apportionment of taxes. The same provision differentiates between Native Americans who are subject to federal taxes and those who are not under federal control for tax purposes.

19. US Constitution, Art. I, § 9, Cl. 1 (penalty tax on the slave trade): "The Migration or Importation of such Persons as any of the States now existing shall think proper to admit, shall not be prohibited by the Congress prior to the Year one thousand eight hundred and eight, but a Tax or duty may be imposed on such Importation, not exceeding ten dollars for each Person."

20. US Constitution, Amendment XXIV, § 1:

> The right of citizens of the United States to vote in any primary or other election
> for President or Vice President for electors for President or Vice President, or for
> Senator or Representative in Congress, shall not be denied or abridged by the
> United States or any State by reason of failure to pay any poll tax or other tax.

21. Provisions in the body of the US Constitution that protected wealth and slavery include Art. I, § 2, Cl. 3 (" [D]irect Taxes shall be apportioned among the several States which may be included within this Union, according to their respective Numbers . . . ."). See Einhorn, *supra* note 15. Today, the apportionment clause still operates to prevent Congress from taxing land and other forms of wealth. Only the states may tax wealth under the US Constitution. Moran, *supra* note 14. See also Einhorn, *supra* note 15.

22. On 6 January 1941, President Franklin Roosevelt addressed the 77th Congress in what is now known as his "Four Freedoms" speech, referring to his declaration that:

> In the future days, which we seek to make secure, we look forward to a world
> founded upon four essential human freedoms.
>   The first is freedom of speech and expression—everywhere in the world.
>   The second is freedom of every person to worship God in his own way—
> everywhere in the world.
>   The third is freedom from want, which, translated into world terms, means
> economic understandings which will secure to every nation a healthy peacetime
> life for its inhabitants—everywhere in the world.
>   The fourth is freedom from fear, which, translated into world terms, means
> a world-wide reduction of armaments to such a point and in such a thorough
> fashion that no nation will be in a position to commit an act of physical aggression
> against any neighbor—anywhere in the world.

Full text of the speech available online at http://www.americanrhetoric.com/speeches/fdrthefourfreedoms.htm (last visited 28 June 2017).

23. For example:

> Art. 22: "social security and economic . . . rights indispensable for . . . dignity and
> the free development of . . . personality"
>   Art. 23: right to work, to free choice of employment, just and favorable
> remuneration, and equal pay for equal work
>   Art. 25: a standard of living adequate for health and well-being
>   Art. 26: free compulsory elementary education. Technical and professional
> education made generally available and higher education equally accessible to all
> based on merit.

24. UDHR declares that everyone is entitled to all the rights and freedoms set forth in the Declaration ". . . without distinction . . . [based on] . . . . . property" (Art. 2, Universal Declaration of Human Rights, GA Res. 217 (III) A, 10 Dec. 1948). See also Art. 17:

> (1) Everyone has the right to own property alone as well as in association with others.
> (2) No one shall be arbitrarily deprived of his property.

Contrast the United States at the adoption of the US Constitution when voting rights were limited to white men who held property. See, e.g., A. Keyssar, *The Right to Vote: The Contested History of Democracy in the United States* (2009), at XXI (the standard narrative is that franchise was sharply restricted at the nation's founding with landless white men mostly franchised by Civil War).

25. C. R. Sunstein, 'Why Does the American Constitution Lack Social and Economic Guarantees?', 56 *Syracuse Law Review* (2005), 1; C. Williamson, *American Suffrage: From Property to Democracy, 1760–1860* (1960), at 3–19 (suffrage limited to property owners in early United States).

26. P. M. Muhammad, 'The Trans-Atlantic Slave Trade: A Forgotten Crime Against Humanity as Defined by International Law', 19(4) *American University International Law Review* (2004), 883.

27. R. W. Corbisier, 'The Artic National Wildlife Refuge, Correlative Rights, and Sourdough: Not Just for Bread Anymore', 19 *Alaska Law Review* (2002), 393, at 404; S. Hertog, *Princes, Brokers, and Bureaucrats: Oil and the State in Saudi Arabia* (2010), at 132.

28. W. Hogeland, *The Whiskey Rebellion: George Washington, Alexander Hamilton, and the Frontier Rebels who Challenged America's Newfound Sovereignty* (2010) (attempt to tax home whiskey production caused secession movement); E. Aryeetey, J. Harrigan, and M. Nissanke (eds.), *Economic Reforms in Ghana: The Miracle and the Mirage* (2000) (Ghana revolt against the value-added tax imposed by the International Monetary Fund).

29. R. Pankhurst, *A Social History of Ethiopia: The Northern and Central Highlands from Early Medieval Times to the Rise of Emperor Téwodros II* (1992) (empire supported by extensive toll roads); B. Moran, 'Homogenized Law: Can the U.S. Learn from African Mistakes?', 25 *Fordham Journal of International Law* (2001), 361.

30. For a full review of the taxation of exempt organizations, see D. K. Jones, S. J. Willis, D. A. Brennan, and B. I. Moran, *The Tax Law of Charities and Other Exempt Organizations* (3rd ed. 2014).

31. M. A. Graber, *Dred Scott and the Problem of Constitutional Evil* (2006) (Supreme Court decision in *Dred Scott* declared that no black person had rights that any white person need recognize).

32. L. Graham, 'Reparations and the Indian Child Welfare Act', 25 *Legal Studies Forum* (2001), 619 (in the last century, Native Americans lost a significant percentage of their children to the federal government's adoption-out programs that placed Native American children in white homes). Today, South Asian Indians who sell their body parts to wealthy Westerners fall into this category. See, e.g., Col. Y Udaya Chandar, *The Ailing India* (2016).

33. Sunstein, *supra* note 25.

34. R. W. Logan, *The Negro in American Life and Thought: The Nadir, 1877–1901* (1954) (the Nadir is a term used to describe the terrible conditions in the southern United States after the withdrawal of federal troops following the Civil War). Poll taxes were allowed in the United States until passage of the Twenty-Fourth Amendment to the US Constitution.

35. This was a problem that the US government faced in the Whiskey Rebellion. See, e.g., T. P. Slaughter, *The Whiskey Rebellion: Frontier Epilogue to the American Revolution* (1988).

36. See discussion of economic neutrality in Cranston, *supra* note 5.

37. Sir I. Jennings, *Magna Carta and Its Influence in the World Today* (1965); D. B. Magraw, A. Martinez, and R. E. Brownell II (eds.), *Magna Carta and the Rule of Law* (2014).

38. A. Smith, *The Wealth of Nations* (E. Cannan ed., 1937).

39. E. Stillwaggon, *Stunted Lives, Stagnant Economies: Poverty, Disease, and Underdevelopment* (Rutgers University 1998); OECD and the World Health Organisation, *Poverty and Health* (2003), available online at http://www.who.int/tobacco/research/economics/publications/oecd_dac_pov_ health.pdf (last visited 19 Sept. 2017).

40. Burman, Aaron, and Steuerle, *supra* note 4, at 438.

41. See Lerner, *supra* note 9.

42. Congress generally sets the capital gains tax rate at 50 percent or less of its highest tax rate on labor. IRC § 1 (h) (lower tax rate on capital gains). Compare IRC § 1(a), (b), (c), (d) (highest rate on human labor is 39.6 percent) and § 1 (h) (highest capital gains rate is 25 percent but the more common rate is 20 percent).

43. Known as the realization requirement, the rule allows taxpayers to accumulate gains in property for years and not pay tax until the property is sold. For a discussion of the realization requirement see, M. E. Kornhauser, 'The Story of *Eisner v Macomber*: The Continuing Legacy of "Realization" in Tax Law and Policy', in P. Caron (ed.), *Tax Stories* (2nd ed., 2009), 95.

44. L. E. Burman and M. Phaup, 'Tax Expenditures, the Size and Efficiency of Government, and Implications for Budget Reform', 26 *Tax Policy and Economics* (2012), 93, at 103; OECD, *Taxation of Capital Gains of Individuals: Policy Considerations and Approaches* (Tax Policy Studies No. 14, 24 Nov. 2006), available online at http://www.oecd-ilibrary.org/taxation/taxation-of-capital-gains-of-individuals_9789264029507-en;jsessionid=2krgt4otxddrc.x-oecd-live-02, at 55 (last visited 29 June 2017) (identifies Canada, New Zealand, and Denmark as countries that treat death as a realization event for the heirs).

45. The exemptions under the estate tax are so large that most estates escape with no tax and all property within the estate adjusted to a fair market value basis. With an exemption of the first $5.49 million per individual—and nearly $11 million per couple—the Urban-Brookings Tax Policy Center calculated that the average size of estates paying the tax that year was $22.7 million, and that they paid an effective rate of 16.6 percent. B. J. O'Connor, 'Once Again, the Estate Tax May Die', *New York Times*, 18 Feb. 2017, available online at https://www.nytimes.com/2017/02/18/your-money/taxes/once-again-the-estate-tax-may-die.html.

46. The calculations are based on the highest tax rate applied to all $100,000 in each person's tax base. In fact, the progressive income tax rates would lower each taxpayer's final tax bill but the relationship between the two remains.

47. IRC § 1 (h).

48. D. H. Schenk, 'A Positive Account of the Realization Rule', 57 *Tax Law Review* (2003), 355.

49. See, e.g., A. Auerbach, 'Capital Gains Taxation in the United States: Realizations, Revenue and Rhetoric', 2 *Brookings Papers on Economic Activity* (1988), 595; S. Moore, 'Five Myths About Capital Gains Taxes', *Forbes*, 4 Aug. 2015, available online at http://www.forbes.com/sites/stevemoore/2015/08/04/five-myths-about-capital-gains-taxes/2/#6f5bcaae66a7 (last visited 28 June 2017). The paper explains that, after the capital gains tax hike in 1986 from 20 percent to 28 percent, capital gains revenues actually fell from $44 billion a year to $27 billion a year by 1991. After Bill Clinton cut the capital gains tax down to 20 percent again, capital gains revenues surged from $54 billion in 1996 to $99 billion in 1999. Lower rates, more revenues.

50. From 1998 to 2016, the capital gains rate has changed from 20 percent, to 15 percent, and then back to 20 percent again.

51. For a summary of the concept of the time value of money and rules adopted in the 1986 IRC to cope with the time value of money, see L. Lokken, 'The Time Value of Money Rules', 42 *Tax Law Review* (1986), 1.

52. IRC § 1014 provides for inherited property to take a fair market value basis at the time of the decedent's death. This new basis often works to erase any untaxed appreciation from the property so that the new owner may sell with no income tax consequences. N. M. Annick, 'Plugging the "Gaping Loophole" of the Step-Up in Basis at Death: A Proposal to Apply Carryover Basis to Excess Property', 8(2) *Pittsburg Tax Review* (2011), 75.

53. For a discussion of the timing of income from labor, see C. W. Sanchirico, 'A Critical Look at the Economic Argument for Taxing Only Labor Income', 63 *Tax Law Review* (2010), 867.

54. OECD, *supra* note 44.

55. The twenty OECD countries that responded to the capital gains questionnaire were: Australia, Canada, Czech Republic, Denmark, Finland, Germany, Iceland, Ireland, Italy, Luxembourg,

Mexico, the Netherlands, New Zealand, Norway, Portugal, Slovak Republic, Spain, Sweden, the United Kingdom, and the United States (participating countries). Ibid. at 7.

56. Ibid. at 9. See also V. Mayhall, 'Capital Gains Taxation—The First One Hundred Years', 41 *Louisiana Law Review* (1980–1981), 81. Separate and preferential taxation of capital transactions is a principle unique among most industrialized nations. Indeed, the presence of this principle in the income tax laws of the United States is largely responsible for the complexity of those laws. Ibid. The components of ordinary income are usually income from labor, rents, interest, dividends, and sales of inventory.

57. The exception is New Zealand, which uses accrual taxation of expected gains from corporate bonds. OECD, *supra* note 44, at 23.

58. See *supra* section III.A.

59. For a more in depth explanation of this benefit, see *infra* section IV.

60. B. Menking, 'Comment—Making Sense of Capital Gains Taxation', 39(1) *University of Kansas Law Review* (1990), 175 (Unlike the American system, Canadian law deems previously unrealized capital gains to be constructively realized when the taxpayer dies. Under constructive realization, death is treated as a sale for fair market value, and all gain is taxed to the decedent before the asset passes to the beneficiary at the increased basis).

61. OECD, *supra* note 44, at 55 (identifies the Netherlands, Australia, Spain, and Sweden as some of the OECD nations that roll over accrued capital gains at death and only force a tax when the beneficiaries sell).

62. This is the US estate tax system with the addition of a large exemption. The large exemption in the US estate tax that prevents the wealth tax from producing tax liability.

63. OECD, *supra* note 44, at 54–55.

64. L. Kaplow, 'Horizontal Equity: Measures in Search of a Principle', 42(2) *National Tax Journal* (1989), 139; P. Miller, 'The "Capital Asset" Concept: A Critique of Capital Gains Taxation', 59 *Yale Law Journal* (1950), 837.

65. S. A. Donaldson, 'The Easy Case Against Tax Simplification', 22(4) *Virginia Tax Review* (2003), 645.

66. A. K. Mehrotra, 'The Curious Beginnings of the Capital Gain Preference', 84(6) *Fordham Law Review* (2016), 2517.

67. Mayhall, *supra* note 56.

68. Mehrotra, *supra* note 66.

69. Kaplow, *supra* note 64, at 838.

70. Mayhall, *supra* note 56.

71. Although land sales often produce long-term capital gains, land is not always a capital asset that gives rise to a capital gain when sold. Land held for sale to customers in the ordinary course of business produces ordinary income. IRC § 1221 (1).

72. Ibid.

73. IRC § 1014 (the basis of property held in an estate is adjusted to fair market value on the date of the decedent's death).

74. Ibid.

75. G. R. Zodrow, 'Economic Analysis of Capital Gains Taxation: Realizations, Revenue, Efficiency and Equity', 48 *Tax Law Review* (1993), 419; Menking, *supra* note 60, at 183.

76. Ibid.

77. See the discussion *supra* note 57 (New Zealand uses accrual taxation of expected gains from corporate bonds).

78. OECD, *supra* note 44, at 8–9.

79. Ibid.

80. M. A. Cecil, 'Toward Adding Further Complexity to the Internal Revenue Code: A New Paradigm for the Deductibility of Capital Losses', 99 *University of Illinois Law Review* (1999), 1083, at 1087.

81. D. Q. Posin and D. B Tobin, *Principles of Federal Income Taxation* (7th ed. 2005), at 320.

82. J. W. Lee, 'Critique of Current Congressional Capital Gains Contentions', 15 *Virginia Tax Review* (1995), 1, at 4–5.

83. Van Mayhall, "Capital Gains Taxation", 41 Louisiana Law Review (1980), 81, at 94.

84. M. L. Fellows, 'A Comprehensive Attack on Tax Deferral', 88(4) *Michigan Law Review* (1990), 722.

85. "This rationale suggests that a capital gain is merely a current gauge of the value of money. Thus, a taxpayer who bought vacant land in 1970 for $10,000 and finds that he can sell it unimproved and unchanged in 1980 for $30,000, discovers that the dollar is worth one-third in 1980 of its 1970 value": Mayhall, *supra* note 56, at 94.

86. Ibid.

87. OECD, *supra* note 44, at 14–15.

88. B. Moran and W. Whitford, 'A Black Critique of the Internal Revenue Code', 4 *Wisconsin Law Review* (1996), 751, at 766.

89. For an in-depth discussion of savings and the capital gains preference, see L. Burman, *The Labyrinth of Capital Gains Tax Policy* (1999).

90. OECD, *supra* note 44, at 16–20.

91. Mayhall, *supra* note 56 (a reasonable conclusion is that the maintenance of preferential capital gains taxation results in increased rates of taxation on ordinary income to sustain the same revenue level and a resulting disincentive to work to produce more ordinary income).

92. OECD, *supra* note 44, at 14.

93. J. W. Lee III, 'The Capital Gains "Sieve" and the "Farce" of Progressivity 1921–1986', 1 *Hastings Business Law Journal* (2005), 1 (the capital gains preference reduces the effective income tax rate of high income individuals and thus undercuts the progressive rate structure and destroys horizontal equity).

94. S. S. Surrey, *Pathways to Tax Reform: The Concept of Tax Expenditures* (1973) (deductions, credits, and low tax rates are all the economic equivalent of a direct government investment).

95. The Congressional Budget Act of 1974 (Public Law 93-344).

96. 2 USC § 622 (3)—Definitions

97. E. G. Keith et al., 'Income Taxation', *in Encyclopedia Britannica* (discussion of Haig Simons model of income).

98. United States Department of the Treasury, Office of Tax Analysis, *Tax Expenditures FY2016*, available online at https://www.treasury.gov/resource-center/tax-policy/Documents/Tax-Expenditures-FY2016.pdf, at 2 (the deferral of tax on unrealized capital gains is not regarded as a tax expenditure).

99. C. H. Hanna, 'The Real Value of Tax Deferral', 61 *Florida Law Review* (2009), 203 (tax deferral is not as valuable to corporations as taxpayers imagine); D. Halperin, '2009 Erwin N. Griswold Lecture Before the American College of Tax Counsel: Rethinking the Advantage of Tax Deferral', 62(3) *The Tax Lawyer* (2009), 535; C. H. Hanna, 'Demystifying Tax Deferral', 52 *Southern Methodist University Law Review* (1999), 383 (why tax deferral is important). See also IRC § 83 (defers tax on property received in exchange for services) and IRC § 401 (qualified pensions receive deferral).

100. IRC § 262—Personal, living, and family expenses

   (a) **General rule**
   Except as otherwise expressly provided in this chapter, no deduction shall be allowed for personal, living, or family expenses.

101. 26 CFR 1.162-5—Expenses for education

   (a) **General rule.** Expenditures made by an individual for education (including research undertaken as part of his educational program) which are not expenditures of a type described in paragraph (b) (2) or (3) of this section are deductible as ordinary and necessary business expenses (even though the education may lead to a degree) if the education—
   (1) Maintains or improves skills required by the individual in his employment or other trade or business, or

(2) Meets the express requirements of the individual's employer, or the requirements of applicable law or regulations, imposed as a condition to the retention by the individual of an established employment relationship, status, or rate of compensation.

102. IRC § 263—Capital expenditures

(a) General rule
No deduction shall be allowed for—
(1) Any amount paid out for new buildings or for permanent improvements or betterments made to increase the value of any property or estate.

See also, 26 CFR 1.162-5—Expenses for education

(b) Nondeductible educational expenditures—
(1) **In general.** Educational expenditures described in subparagraphs (2) and (3) of this paragraph are personal expenditures or constitute an inseparable aggregate of personal and capital expenditures and, therefore, are not deductible as ordinary and necessary business expenses even though the education may maintain or improve skills required by the individual in his employment or other trade or business or may meet the express requirements of the individual's employer or of applicable law or regulations.

103. See U.S. Department of the Treasury, Office of Tax Analysis, *Tax Expenditures FY2017*, available online at https://www.treasury.gov/resource-center/tax-policy/Documents/Tax-Expenditures-FY2017.pdf, at 13–16 (exclusion of scholarship and fellowship income, qualified tuition programs, exclusion of interest on student-loan bonds, exclusion of interest on bonds for private nonprofit educational facilities, discharge of student loan indebtedness).
104. Ibid. (deductibility of student loan interest, deduction for higher education expenses, exclusion of interest on savings bonds redeemed to finance educational expenses, parental personal exemption for students age nineteen or over, charitable contributions to educational institutions, special deduction for teacher expenses, qualified school construction bonds).
105. Ibid. (Education Individual Retirement Accounts (IRA)).
106. Ibid. (HOPE tax credit, American Opportunity Tax Credit, Lifetime Learning tax credit, credit for holders of zone academy bonds, exclusion of employer-provided educational assistance).
107. United States Department of the Treasury, *supra* note 98, at 25.
108. The education exclusions include assistances for the following:

(a) Employer provided educational assistance programs such as exclusions from income for employer-paid education expenses up to $5,250 per year (IRC § 127);
(b) Employer provided working condition fringe benefits (IRC § 132);
(c) Income from discharge of student loan debt (IRC § 108);
(d) University employer-paid tuition waivers for employees' dependent children's undergraduate education (IRC § 117 (d)); and
(e) Employer-sponsored scholarships (IRC § 117 (a)).

109. For a discussion of tax credits, see A. J Prigal and M. Howley, *Rabkin and Johnson: Federal Tax Guidebook* (2015), at § 1.04 (credits).
110. The IRC provides three education credits: the American Opportunity Tax Credit (IRC § 25 A (i)); the Hope Scholarship Credit (IRC § 25A (b)); and the Lifetime Learning Credit (IRC § 25A (c)). The American Opportunity Tax Credit is a credit for "qualified education expenses" paid for an "eligible student" for the first four years of higher education. The maximum annual credit is $2,500 per eligible student. If the credit brings the amount of tax to zero, 40 percent of any remaining amount of the credit (up to $1,000) may be refunded to the taxpayer.

111. For a general discussion of deductions, see *Rabkin and Johnson: Federal Income, Gift and Estate Taxation* (2015), at § 1.09. Deductions that support education include: up to $4,000 per year for "qualified education expenses" (IRC § 222); deductions for student loan interest (IRC § 221); business deduction for work-related education (26 USC §162).

112. There are three educational savings plans under the IRC: (1) Coverdell Education Savings Account (IRC § 530 (2)); Qualified Tuition Program Plans (529 plans IRC § 529); and Income from United States Savings Bonds used to Pay Higher Education Tuition and Fees (college savings bonds under Series EE IRC § 135). Coverdell education savings accounts (also known as an Education Savings Account, a Coverdell ESA, a Coverdell Account, or just an ESA and formerly known as an education individual retirement account), is a tax-advantaged investment account in the United States designed to encourage savings to cover future education. Qualified Tuition Program plans do not provide deduction for payments into fund but tax-free growth and tax free withdrawals to pay for education.

113. United States Department of the Treasury, *supra* note 98, at 24–25.
    1. Exclusion of scholarship and fellowship income—$3,200 million
    2. HOPE tax credit—$0
    3. Lifetime Learning tax credit—$2,460 million
    4. American Opportunity Tax Credit—$15,690 million
    5. Education Individual Retirement Accounts (IRA)—$70 million
    6. Deductibility of student-loan interest—$1,760 million
    7. Qualified tuition programs—$2,100 million
    8. Exclusion of interest on student-loan bonds—$620 million
    9. Exclusion of interest on bonds for private nonprofit educational facilities—$2,780 million
    10. Credit for holders of zone academy bonds—$130 million
    11. Exclusion of interest on savings bonds redeemed to finance educational expenses—$30 million
    12. Parental personal exemption for students age 19 or over—$4,540 million
    13. Charitable contributions to educational institutions—$5,480 million
    14. Exclusion of employer-provided educational assistance—$840 million
    15. Special deduction for teacher expenses—$0
    16. Discharge of student loan indebtedness—$90 million
    17. Qualified school construction bonds—$650 million

114. Median income for a family of four is $67,019. United States Census Bureau, *Median Person Income for 4-Person Families, by State*, available online at https://www.census.gov/data/tables/time-series/demo/income-poverty/4-person.html (last visited 19 Sept. 2017).

115. C-C. Huang, *Recent Studies Find Raising Taxes on High-Income Households Would Not Harm the Economy*, 24 Apr. 2012, available online at https://www.cbpp.org/research/recent-studies-find-raising-taxes-on-high-income-households-would-not-harm-the-economy (last visited 19 Sept. 2017) (the value of deductions increases as marginal tax rates increase); R. S. Avi-Yonah, 'Why Tax the Rich?', 111 *Yale Law Journal* (2002), 1391, at 1391 (reviewing J. Slemrod, *Does Atlas Shrug? The Economic Consequences of Taxing the Rich* (2000)).

116. D. Halperin, 'A Charitable Contribution of Appreciated Property and the Realization of Built-In Gains', 56 *Tax Law Review* (2002–2003), 1, at 1.

117. M. A. Hall, 'The Charitable Status of Non-Profit Hospitals: Toward a Donative Theory of Tax Exemption', 66 *Washington Law Review* (1991), 307, at 317, n.33.

118. S. B. Lawsky, 'The Sum of Its Parts: Reforming Charitable Donations of Partial Interests', 64 *Tax Law Review* (2010), 37, at 38.

119. IRC § 213; see also US Tax Center, *Some Deductions Are Better Than Others*, available online at https://www.irs.com/articles/some-deductions-are-better-others (last visited 19 Sept. 2017) ("Above the line" deductions are better than those "below the line," because they reduce your Adjusted Gross Income); IRS, *Topic 502—Medical and Dental Expenses*, available online at https://www.irs.gov/taxtopics/tc502.html (last visited 19 Sept. 2017) (explanation of what is a legitimate medical expense deduction); IRS, *Can I Deduct My Medical and Dental Expenses?*, available

online at https://www.irs.gov/help/ita/can-i-deduct-my-medical-and-dental-expenses (last visited 19 Sept. 2017) (medical expenses must exceed 10 percent of adjusted gross income).

120. United States Department of the Treasury, *supra* note 98, at 25.

121. Ibid.
    1. Exclusion of employer contributions for medical insurance premiums and medical care—$226,860 million
    2. Self-employed medical insurance premiums—$7,270 million
    3. Medical Savings Accounts/Health Savings Accounts—$6,720 million
    4. Deductibility of medical expenses—$7,700 million
    5. Exclusion of interest on hospital construction bonds—$4,770 million
    6. Refundable Premium Assistance Tax Credit— -$3,920
    7. Credit for employee health insurance expenses of small business—$570 million
    8. Deductibility of charitable contributions to health institutions—$5,780 million
    9. Tax credit for orphan drug research—$2,110 million
    10. Special Blue Cross/Blue Shield deduction—$400 million
    11. Tax credit for health insurance purchased by certain displaced and retired individuals—$0

122. IRS, *Section 2: Individual Income Tax Returns, 2014*, available online at https://www.irs.gov/pub/irs-soi/14inintaxreturns.pdf ("In 2014, the number of returns claiming a standard deduction increased 1.7 percent for 2014, accounting for 69.0 percent of all returns filed leaving only 31% of returns with a schedule A) only 8.2% of returns showed a schedule A deduction for charitable contributions.").

123. United States Department of the Treasury, *supra* note 98, at 22–24 (lists the following costs of capital gains preferences by millions).
    1. Capital gains treatment of royalties on coal—$120 million
    2. Capital gains treatment of certain timber—$120 million
    3. Capital gains treatment of certain income—$1.250 billion
    4. Deferral of gain on sales of farm refiners—$20 million
    5. Capital gains exclusion on home sales—$39.560 billion
    6. Capital gains (except agriculture, timber, iron ore, and coal)—$93 million
    7. Capital gains exclusion of small corporation stock—$380 million
    8. Step-up basis of capital gains at death—$66,670 million
    9. Carryover basis of capital gains on gifts—$7,420 million
    10. Empowerment zones—$10 million

124. B. Bittker and L. Lokken, *Federal Taxation of Employee Compensation* (2016), at ¶ 3.14 Taxation of Participants.

125. United States Department of the Treasury, *supra* note 98, at 3 (under the reference tax law baseline, no tax expenditures arise from accelerated depreciation.)

126. J. Zollinger Giele, *Family Policy and the American Safety Net* (2013), at 30, 164; Social Security Administration, *Historical Background and Development of Social Security*, available online at https://www.ssa.gov/history/briefhistory3.html (last visited 29 June 2017).

127. United States Department of Health and Human Services, *United States Life Tables 2006* (National Vital Statistics Reports Vol. 58(21), 2010), available online at https://www.cdc.gov/nchs/data/nvsr/nvsr58/nvsr58_21.pdf. See also Social Security Administration, *supra* note 126 ("The Social Security Act was signed into law by President Roosevelt on August 14, 1935. The age to receive an old age pension in 1935 was 65. The average mortality without regard to race or sex in that year was 61.7").

128. J. Barro, 'We're Living Longer. That's Great, Except for Social Security', *New York Times*, 17 Nov. 2015, available online at http://www.nytimes.com/2015/11/17/upshot/were-living-longer-thats-great-except-for-social-security.html?_r=0 (last visited 29 June 2017).

129. Alan J. Auerbach et al., *How the Growing Gap in Life Expectancy May Affect Retirement Benefits and Reforms* (National Bureau of Economic Research Working Paper No. 23329, 2017); A. Deaton, 'Health, Inequality, and Economic Development', 41(1) *Journal of Economic Literature* (2003), 113, at 114 ("With a few exceptions, the literature does not specify the precise mechanisms through

which income inequality is supposed to affect health. In consequence, there is little guidance on exactly what evidence we should be examining, or whether the propositions are refutable at all").

130. Urban Institute, *Understanding Social Security Disability Insurance* (2016), available online at http://www.urban.org/sites/default/files/publication/77841/2000613-Understanding-Social-Security-Disability-Insurance-Interactions-with-Other-Programs.pdf; Social Security Administration, *Disability Planner: How We Decide if You Are Disabled*, available online at https://www.ssa.gov/planners/disability/dqualify5.html (last visited 29 June 2017); Social Security Administration, *Annual Statistical Report on the Social Security Disability Insurance Program, 2014* (2015), available online at https://www.ssa.gov/policy/docs/statcomps/di_asr/2014/di_asr14.pdf.

131. Auerbach et al., *supra* note 129.

132. United States Department of the Treasury, *supra* note 98, at 26.

133. Social Security Administration, *OASDI and SSI Program Rates and Limits, 2017*, Oct. 2016, available online at https://www.ssa.gov/policy/docs/quickfacts/prog_highlights/RatesLimits2017.html (last visited 20 Sept. 2017) (the maximum wages subject to the Social Security portion of wage taxes in 2017 is $127,200).

134. Ibid., at 2–3. Certain preferences and benefits, such as realization, are not treated as tax expenditures. Further, in relation to capital recovery, under the reference tax law baseline no tax expenditures arise from accelerated depreciation. Under the normal tax baseline, the depreciation allowance for property is computed using estimates of economic depreciation.

135. M. L. Fellows, 'A Comprehensive Attack on Tax Deferral', 88 *Michigan Law Review* (1990), 722.

136. Art. 2, UDHR ("Everyone is entitled to all the rights and freedoms set forth in this Declaration, without distinction of any kind, such as race, colour, sex, language, religion, political or other opinion, national or social origin, property, birth or other status. Furthermore, no distinction shall be made on the basis of the political, jurisdictional or international status of the country or territory to which a person belongs, whether it be independent, trust, non-self-governing or under any other limitation of sovereignty.").

PART 6

BRINGING FISCAL POLICY AND SOCIAL RIGHTS TOGETHER

CHAPTER 23
___

INEQUALITY, TAXATION, AND PUBLIC TRANSFERS IN LATIN AMERICA

MICHAEL HANNI AND RICARDO MARTNER

I. INTRODUCTION

Latin America suffers from some of the highest levels of income concentration and inequality in the world, despite improvements during the recent decade. In contrast with other regions where inequality rose or remained constant, income inequality—as measured by the Gini coefficient, a statistical measure of distribution that is typically used to gauge the extent of income inequality in an economy—fell 9.0 percent in the region between 2000–2004 and 2010–2014.[1] This period was marked by rapid economic growth, bolstered by a positive terms of trade shock brought on by rising international commodities prices and surging demand from developing economies in Asia. With the turn of the economic cycle in the region, however, and the potential for a prolonged period of low growth, Latin American governments and their citizens are understandably concerned about how to capitalize on what has been achieved and make further progress in reducing inequality in the coming years.

While tackling income inequality is a noble goal in its own right, it is also intimately linked to the realization of a wide range of fundamental human rights that continue to be underserved in Latin America. Many of these rights are explicitly recognized in the Universal Declaration of Human Rights, of which all the region's countries are signatories, including: the right to social security (Article 22), to adequate medical care and social services (Article 25) and to education (Article 26), to name but a few.[2] For most Latin Americans, these rights are far from assured, hampered by fragile social protection systems and underdeveloped public health and education services. The full realization of these rights would imply a significant increase in public spending, which in turn would have important implications for the distribution of income in the region's countries.

A key barrier to progress in strengthening public services and tackling income inequality is the generally weak level of tax revenue obtained by Latin American countries. In 2014, the average tax burden in the region was 21 percent of GDP, compared to 34.4 percent among Organisation for Economic Co-operation and Development (OECD) countries.[3] Even accounting for differing levels of development, the region's countries appear to generate lower tax revenues than other countries.[4] Exceptionally low revenues from the personal income tax and social security contributions are a major factor in explaining this result. In turn, the performance of these taxes is reflected in their limited redistributive power. As will be shown below, on average the personal income tax reduces income inequality by just 2 percent in Latin America, compared to 12.5 percent in EU-28 countries.[5]

Unfortunately, poorly designed tax systems, tax evasion, and tax avoidance cost Latin America billions of dollars in unpaid tax revenues—revenues that could and should be invested in ensuring fundamental human rights. Additionally, an archaic and dysfunctional international tax system also provides companies and wealthy individuals with ample scope and opportunity to avoid paying their fair share of taxes. It is therefore incumbent on all governments to take concerted and coordinated action to build tax systems fit for the twenty-first century. Governments must strengthen progressive tax systems at home, and they must bolster global and regional cooperation to reduce harmful tax competition between countries.

Nevertheless, strengthening direct taxation will require addressing the region's frayed fiscal compact. These pacts, either explicit or implicit, outline the rights and obligations of governments and citizens.[6] They can be seen as an agreement between both parties on the amount of taxes to be paid and the services and public goods to be provided. However, given the current state of personal income taxation, characterized by extremely elevated levels of evasion and avoidance, it is clear that the existing fiscal compacts in the region are not meeting expectations. This has also been made manifest in recent years by a rise in protests highlighting the shortcomings, perceived or real, of public services including health and education.

In this context, the adoption of the 2030 Agenda for Sustainable Development offers Latin American countries and their citizens an opportunity to address these concerns and establish a new, stronger, fiscal compact.[7] In particular, governments should seek to fully engage their growing middle classes as part of their attempts to mobilize domestic resources for sustainable development. Research suggests that they often have higher levels of tax morale, defined as a citizen's intrinsic motivation to pay taxes, despite their dissatisfaction with the quality of public services. However, their contribution to the personal income tax remains limited in the region. Indeed, they may be the most likely to heed the call embodied in Article 29 of the Universal Declaration of Human Rights: "Everyone has duties to the community in which alone the free and full development of his personality is possible."

This chapter analyzes inequality in Latin America and the role of fiscal policies in improving the distribution of income. The first section examines current inequality trends in the region and as compared with other developing regions and industrialized countries. The second section investigates the redistributive power of fiscal policies—personal income taxation and cash transfers—in eighteen countries of the region. Finally, the third section explores the region's frayed fiscal compact, in particular as evidenced by rampant tax evasion and an elevated level of opting out of public services, and how a new fiscal compact might be constructed around the 2030 Agenda financed through direct taxation.

II. LATIN AMERICAN INEQUALITY TRENDS
IN CONTEXT

Income inequality levels in Latin America are among the highest in the world. The share of disposable income—after cash transfers and direct taxes—accrued by the top decile relative to that of the bottom decile is significantly elevated in the region compared with the member countries of the OECD (see Figure 23.1, below). On average, the income accrued by the top decile in Latin America is 25.2 times that of the bottom decile, compared to 8.7 times among thirty-three OECD members (excluding Chile and Mexico).[8] Nevertheless, this average belies heterogeneity of results among the region's countries, ranging from a low of 9.1 times in Uruguay to over 30 times in Brazil, Colombia, Bolivia, Dominican Republic, Panama, and Honduras.[9] The vast majority of the region's population lives with levels of income concentration that would be unimaginable for the average citizen of an OECD country.

Nevertheless in contrast to other regions, Latin America recorded a significant reduction in overall income inequality over the past decade. The average Gini coefficient between 2000 and 2004 for seventeen countries in the region fell from 0.54 to 0.49—with a value of 0 representing perfect equality and a value of 1 representing perfect inequality—during 2010 and 2014, or a reduction of 9.0 percent (Figure 23.2, below). These regional figures belie even greater—sometimes much greater—reductions registered in specific countries: Bolivia (20.6 percent), Venezuela (16.7 percent), El Salvador (13.8 percent), Peru (15.0 percent), Ecuador (12.3 percent), Argentina (12.9 percent), Brazil (11.1 percent), and Uruguay (13.5 percent).[10] Of the countries considered here only two experienced an increase in their average Gini: Costa Rica (4.3 percent) and Guatemala (2.0 percent). Of particular note, as Figure 23.2 highlights, between 2000–2004 and 2010–2014 the maximum Gini coefficient recorded in the region also declined, falling from 0.63 to 0.57, suggesting that improvements were also occurring in the most unequal countries. Likewise, the minimum Gini value also registered a decline, from 0.45 to 0.39, which was the lowest level during the entire 1990–2014 period.

The reduction in income inequality during the recent decade has been linked to the combination of a favorable macroeconomic environment and, to a lesser extent, targeted social spending.[11] In particular, there was a significant narrowing of the wage premium for skilled workers, due in part to the surge in employment during the period that resulted in record low unemployment levels and, in turn, higher wages. A decomposition of the change in the income gap between the bottom quintile and the top quintile of the income distribution suggests that higher labor earnings were the principal driver of this trend.[12]

Since 2000, as seen in Figure 23.2, there has also been a modest decline in average income inequality in Developing Asia (–2 percent).[13] Additionally, the gap between the Asian country with the highest Gini coefficient and the country with the lowest has narrowed since the 1990s, suggesting some convergence in inequality levels in the region. China, the largest economy in the region, saw its period average Gini fall slightly between 2000 and 2014 (–1 percent), but in comparison with the early 1990s income inequality remains up sharply (24 percent).[14]

In sub-Saharan Africa there was a 1 percent decline in the period average Gini between 2000–2004 and 2010–2014 (see Figure 23.2, below). Unlike their Latin American and Asian peers, in sub-Saharan African countries, the maximum Gini level has remained high over the entire period, even showing a slight increase over the past decade. This suggests that there has been little progress at reducing inequality in the most unequal countries in the region. Indeed,

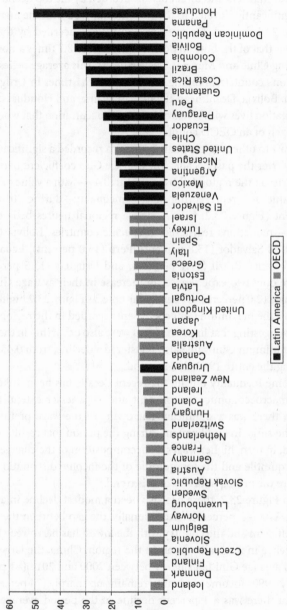

FIGURE 23.1: Latin America (17 countries) and OECD (33 countries): ratio of decile 10 disposable income to decile 1 disposable income (S90/S10 ratio), around 2014 (*ratios*)

Source: Authors' calculations, based on household surveys as processed by the Statistics Division of ECLAC and data from OECD.Stat.

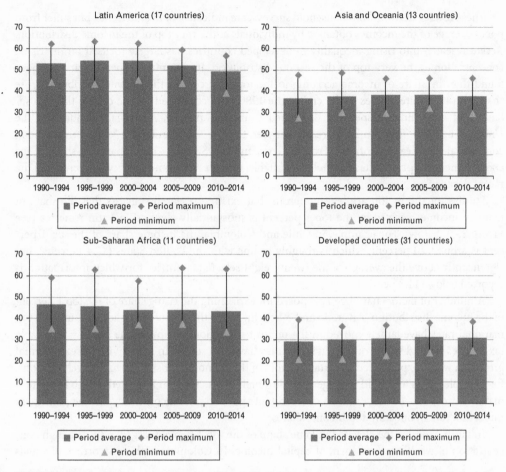

FIGURE 23.2: Selected country groupings: disposable income inequality, 1990–2014 *(Gini coefficients)*

Source: Authors' calculations, based on data from CEPALstat, OECD.Stat, EuroStat and World Development Indicators (World Bank).

the maximum value for the period has been defined by South Africa, which was the most unequal country in the region between 1990 and 2014.[15]

While there has been a very modest increase in average income inequality levels in developed countries between 2000–2004 and 2010–2014 (1 percent) (see Figure 23.2, above), there exist significant differences between countries. This is in keeping with previous research, which has identified evidence of a secular increase in income inequality in some OECD countries over time.[16] Over the period under analysis there has been a steady increase in the minimum period average Gini, which implies that income inequality in even the least unequal country has risen.

For example, the average Gini coefficient of Sweden and Finland, which were respectively the least unequal developed countries in the sample in 1990–1994, rose 30 percent and 23 percent between 1990–1994 and 2010–2014.[17] At the other extreme, the Gini coefficient for the United States, the most unequal country among developed economies in the most recent period, has steadily climbed over time, from a period average of 0.36 in 1990–1994 to 0.39 in 2010–2014.[18]

These results, derived from household surveys, are indicative of overall trends but suffer from poor coverage of the incomes obtained by individuals at the very top of the income distribution. Recent research into rising inequality in developed countries has largely focused on the rising concentration at the very top of the income distribution. In a seminal paper, Piketty and Saez found that the share of income accruing to the top 1 percent of the income distribution rose sharply in the United States at the end of the 1980s and continued to rise during the 1990s.[19] Studies of other English-speaking developed countries—namely, Australia, Canada, and the United Kingdom—find similar increases between the late 1980s and 2010.[20] In contrast among continental European countries—France, Germany, and Sweden—and Japan, the share of income of the top 1 percent has held relatively stable, though with some signs of an increase in the recent decade.[21]

Studies for the region are less numerous, but existing research suggests that the share of national income received by the top 1 percent is substantially elevated in Latin America (see Figure 23.3, below). For example, in Chile and Colombia, the income share of the top 1 percent is around 20 percent, which is roughly in line with the United States (17.4 percent), but significantly above the average of the twenty-eight selected countries for which information is reported below (11.3 percent).

A number of factors have been proposed for explaining the rising share of the top 1 percent of the income distribution. Alvaredo and others highlight the role of tax policy, arguing that top marginal rates have largely moved in the opposite direction of top income shares.[22] Favorable tax policies for high-net-worth individuals may have also served to incentivize the exponential growth in wages experienced in certain sectors of the economy for specific high-level positions, for example CEOs and fund managers. Additionally, an increase in inherited wealth in some—mainly European—countries and a concomitant rise in capital income may also be playing an important role in boosting top income shares.

In Latin America the elevated income share of the top 1 percent largely reflects a high concentration of wealth and, in turn, of capital income. In Colombia high-net-worth individuals

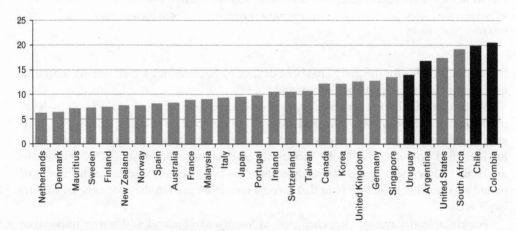

FIGURE 23.3: Selected countries: income share of the top 1% of the income distribution, excluding capital gains, 2013 or latest year *(Percentages)*

Source: Authors' graph, based on data from World Wealth and Income Database and J. C. Gómez Sabaíni and D. Rossignolo, 'La tributación sobre las altas rentas en América Latina', *Serie Estudios y Perspectivas* N° 13, Oficina de la CEPAL en Montevideo (2014).

are largely rentiers, with most of their income coming from returns to capital and rents.[23] López and others find that in Chile the concentration of income in the top 1 percent reflects to a large degree the concentration of wealth in the economy and the income it generates.[24] When these estimates are adjusted for capital gains or for nondistributed profits they find that the top share rises even further, from an average of 21.1 percent between 2005 and 2010 to an average of 32.8 percent when retained earnings are included or an average of 30.5 percent when capital gains are considered.[25]

Incorporating information from tax registers in the calculation of the Gini coefficient reveals that income inequality is generally much higher than household surveys would suggest. In Argentina, the Gini coefficient for 2004 adjusted with information on the top 1 percent rises to 0.56 from an unadjusted 0.47.[26] Likewise, the adjusted Gini coefficient for Chile and Colombia rises significantly when household survey data are adjusted using tax data: from 0.55 to 0.67 in the first country (incorporating retained earnings) and from 0.55 to 0.59 in the second.[27]

Despite the change in level implied by these studies, the overall downward trend largely remains. For example, Burdín and others find that the incorporation of information from tax registers substantially increases the level of income inequality as measured by the Gini coefficient (from 0.46 to 0.56 in 2011),[28] but that the decline in the Gini registered in both the household survey and in tax data is largely consistent, if less pronounced in the latter dataset. This is largely in line with the results found in the previously mentioned studies of Argentina, Chile, and Colombia.

III. INEQUALITY AND FISCAL POLICY: PERSONAL INCOME TAXATION AND PUBLIC CASH TRANSFERS

Research in the region suggests that fiscal policy levers play a limited role in reducing inequality in Latin America. While both Latin American and European countries share a similar initial level of inequality, with a market income Gini of 0.49 in Latin America and 0.50 for the European Union, their "after fiscal action" inequality levels are markedly different. Among countries of the European Union, income inequality fell 42.6 percent after cash transfers and personal income taxes, resulting in a decline of 21.4 basis points in the Gini coefficient (see Table 23.1, below). In contrast, as Table 23.1 highlights, Latin American countries on average achieved only a 5.7 percent decline in inequality after cash transfers and personal income taxes, equivalent to a decrease of 2.8 basis points in the Gini coefficient.

This result, however, belies a significant level of heterogeneity among countries. Some countries of the region were able to achieve greater than average reductions in inequality, including Argentina (–16.0 percent), Uruguay (–15.3 percent), Brazil (–12.1 percent), Chile (–8.9 percent), Mexico (–8.9 percent), Panama (–7.5 percent), Costa Rica (–6.7 percent), and Ecuador (–5.9 percent) (see Table 23.1). These were the exceptions, as ten of the eighteen countries considered registered reductions less than the regional average. In particular, as illustrated in Table 23.1, the smallest decreases were in Honduras (–1.3 percent), Paraguay (–1.3 percent), Colombia (–0.7 percent), and Guatemala (–0.3 percent).

Table 23.1: Reduction in the Gini coefficient due to cash transfers and direct taxes, around 2014 *(percentage points of Gini and percentages)*

	Gini index			Percent reduction		
	Market income (A)	Gross income (A + public cash transfers) (B)	Post-PIT disposable income (B - PIT) (C)	Transfers (B/A)	PIT (C/B)	Total (C/A)
Argentina	0.49	0.43	0.41	−12.5	−4.0	−16.0
Bolivia	0.48	0.47	0.47	−3.0	−0.4	−3.5
Brazil	0.58	0.52	0.51	−9.5	−2.8	−12.1
Chile	0.52	0.49	0.48	−6.6	−2.4	−8.9
Colombia	0.51	0.51	0.51	0.5	−1.1	−0.7
Costa Rica	0.52	0.49	0.48	−5.2	−1.6	−6.7
Dominican Republic	0.54	0.53	0.52	−1.8	−0.9	−2.6
Ecuador	0.49	0.47	0.46	−4.6	−1.4	−5.9
El Salvador	0.44	0.43	0.42	−0.3	−3.2	−3.4
Guatemala	0.50	0.51	0.50	0.4	−0.7	−0.3
Honduras[a]	0.54	0.54	0.54	0.0	−1.3	−1.3
México	0.47	0.45	0.43	−3.2	−5.9	−8.9
Nicaragua	0.44	0.44	0.44	−0.3	−1.7	−2.0
Panama	0.52	0.50	0.48	−5.4	−2.2	−7.5
Paraguay	0.48	0.48	0.48	−1.0	−0.3	−1.3
Peru	0.47	0.46	0.45	−1.5	−1.9	−3.4
Uruguay	0.41	0.36	0.34	−12.4	−3.4	−15.3
Venezuela	0.39	0.39	0.38	−0.9	−1.1	−1.9
AL-18	0.49	0.47	0.46	−3.8	−2.0	−5.7
EU-28	0.50	0.33	0.29	−34.4	−12.5	−42.6

Source: Authors' calculations, based on household surveys as processed by the Statistics Division of ECLAC and data from EUROMOD statistics on Distribution and Decomposition of Disposable Income, G4.0+.

Note: PIT = personal income tax.
[a] No information was obtained on the pensions and subsidies variables in the Honduras household survey, so their effect on the Gini coefficient could not be calculated.

A. THE REDISTRIBUTIVE IMPACT OF CASH TRANSFERS IN LATIN AMERICA IS LIMITED, REFLECTING THE REGION'S LESS DEVELOPED SOCIAL PROTECTION SCHEMES

Cash transfers are the principal redistributive instruments in European countries, the application of which results in a 34.4 percent decrease in market income inequality (see Table 23.1). In contrast, in Latin America the impact of these transfers is nearly 10 times smaller: only a 3.8 percent reduction.[29] In simple terms, the results suggest three groupings of countries within the region: countries with a relatively significant reduction through cash transfers, mainly through public pensions (Argentina, Brazil, and Uruguay); those with a lesser impact but that beat the regional average (Chile, Costa Rica, Ecuador, and Panama); and, the rest (see Figure 23.4,

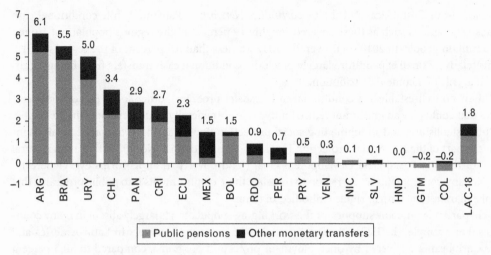

FIGURE 23.4: Latin America (18 countries): reduction in Gini coefficient of market income through cash transfers, around 2014 *(Gini points)*

Source: Authors' graph, based on household surveys as processed by the Statistics Division of ECLAC.

below). The countries in this last group reduced income inequality by only 1.5 Gini points or less through cash transfers, and in some cases the net impact was even an increase in inequality (Colombia and Guatemala).

These results reflect the convergence of a number of factors, including the existence of cash transfer programs in a country, their effective size in terms of budget, and the population they target. In general the single most important cash transfer program in terms of income redistribution is public pensions. These programs are well established among the majority of OECD members, with an average budget of 7.9 percent of GDP, which represents roughly 60 percent of total cash benefits.[30] In contrast, expenditures on public pensions in Latin America are much less, with an average of around 4.7 percent of GDP.[31] While this reflects in part an important difference in demographics between the region and the countries of the OECD, it also highlights the relatively limited reach of public pension programs in a number of Latin American countries. The International Labour Organization (ILO) estimates that recipients of old-age pensions in Latin America account for 56.1 percent of the population above the statutory pension age, compared to 92.4 percent in Western Europe and 93.0 percent in North America.[32]

Even accounting for differences in the relative size of public pension programs there are significant differences across countries in the region. For example, ECLAC estimates that social security outlays in 2013 in Colombia and Costa Rica were roughly similar (7.3 percent and 6.8 percent of GDP, respectively), but their redistributive impact was very different. In the first case, public pensions are largely regressive (with a Kakwani of −0.32), with benefits largely accruing to individuals in higher income deciles.[33] As a result, public pensions in the country increase income inequality in the country by 1.3 percent. In contrast, in Costa Rica public pensions are generally neutral in terms of their regressivity or progressivity (Kakwani of −0.06) and they are bolstered by an important noncontributory component that is highly progressive (Kakwani of 0.52), resulting in an overall reduction of 3.3 percent in income inequality.[34]

Other cash transfers in the region play a lesser role in reducing income inequality, despite being important tools for reducing poverty. Some examples include the *Bolsa Família* program in Brazil, *Oportunidades* (now *Prospera*) in Mexico, *Chile Solidario* (Solidarity Chile),

Avancemos in Costa Rica, and the *Opportunities Network* in Panama. While conditional cash transfer programs such as these covered roughly 19 percent of the region's population, around 113 million people, in 2010 their overall outlay was less than 0.5 percent of the region's GDP.[35] This relatively small expenditure largely precludes conditional cash transfers from being significant agents of income redistribution.

Beyond well-established conditional cash transfer programs, other social protection measures that could play an important redistributive role are generally underdeveloped in the region. While establishing and strengthening social protection floors have been endorsed by all countries as part of the ILO Social Protection Floors Recommendation (No. 202)[36] and as an integral part of the first Sustainable Development Goal ("end poverty in all its forms everywhere")[37], significant work remains in the region to translate these commitments into public programs that make manifest the human rights embodied in them.

In particular, income support for the working-age population is largely absent in many countries. For example, the ILO estimates that only 37.6 percent of workers in Latin America and the Caribbean are covered by unemployment protection programs, compared to 80.3 percent in Western Europe and 86.6 percent in North America.[38] Perhaps more striking, it is estimated that fully 95.4 percent of the unemployed population in the region have not received an unemployment benefit in the form of periodic cash payments.[39] In contrast, only 36.2 percent of the unemployed population in Western Europe failed to receive any form of cash benefit.[40]

B. DESPITE GAINS IN THE LAST DECADE, PERSONAL INCOME TAXATION REMAINS WEAK, LIMITING ITS REDISTRIBUTIVE ROLE

Between 2005 and 2014 personal income tax revenues for eighteen countries of the region—excluding Cuba and Haiti—rose on average from 0.7 percent of GDP to 1.5 percent of GDP, though with significant variation between countries.[41] This increase was strongly influenced by Uruguay (+3.1 percentage points of GDP over the period)—which implemented a personal income tax in 2007—and in Argentina (+1.6 percentage points of GDP)—where strong wage increases have not been matched by changes in the structure of the tax leading to an increasing number of contributors being pushed into higher tax brackets.[42] The majority of the remaining countries registered steady, if slow, improvements, with increases between 0.1 percentage points of GDP and 0.6 percentage points of GDP over the period.[43] Nevertheless, the region remains far from the average of 8.8 percent of GDP for countries of the OECD.[44]

Even taking into account differences in development (as proxied by per capita GDP in purchasing power parity (PPP) terms), a survey of data from 132 countries suggests the region's personal income tax revenues are low (see Figure 23.5, below). As Figure 23.5 illustrates, a significant number of African countries record personal income tax revenues that exceed those registered in Latin America, despite having a much lower per capita GDP in purchasing power terms. Developing countries in Asia and Oceania also tend to see higher personal income tax burden levels, though there is significant heterogeneity among countries as seen in Figure 23.5. Based on the data underlying Figure 23.5, of Latin American countries, only Brazil and Uruguay have personal income tax revenues that come close to reaching a level comparable to developed countries of a similar level of per capita income.

The low level of personal income tax collection is related to its limited redistributive power. In Latin America the personal income tax results in a 2 percent decline in inequality on average, as measured by the Gini coefficient, compared to a 12.5 percent reduction in twenty-eight

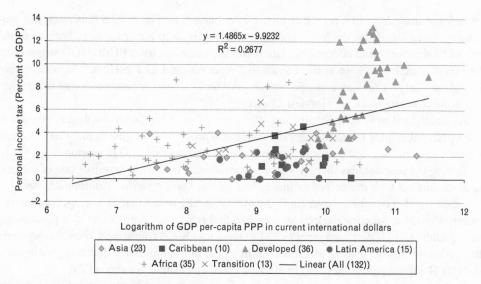

FIGURE 23.5: Personal income tax as a share of GDP and per capita GDP, around 2013 *(percentages of GDP and PPP current international dollars)*

Source: Authors' calculations and graphic based on OECD/Economic Commission for Latin America and the Caribbean/Inter-American Centre for Tax Administrators/Inter-American Development Bank, *Revenue Statistics in Latin America and the Caribbean 1990–2014* (2016); OECD/African Union Commission/African Tax Administration Forum, *Revenue Statistics in Africa 1990–2014* (2016); and IMF, *World Revenue Longitudinal Dataset* (WoRLD) (2015).

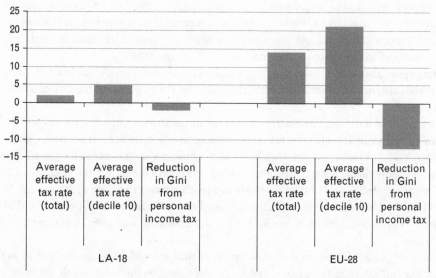

FIGURE 23.6: Latin America (18 countries) and the European Union (28 countries): effective rate of personal income tax and reduction in inequality due to personal income tax, around 2014[a,b] *(percentages)*

Source: Authors' calculations, based on household surveys as processed by the Statistics Division of ECLAC and data from EUROMOD statistics on Distribution and Decomposition of Disposable Income, G4.0+.

[a] Calculated over gross income (market income plus public and private transfers).

[b] Data from EUROMOD include additional direct taxes for some countries, including property taxes and church taxes.

countries of the European Union (see Figure 23.6, below). As Figure 23.6 illustrates, this outcome is driven largely by the lower effective tax rates in Latin America, as in both cases the ratio of Gini reduction to effective tax rate is similar. Estimates from EUROMOD suggest that the overall effective tax rate in the European Union averages 13.9 percent.[45] In contrast, for the eighteen Latin American countries under consideration, ECLAC estimates that the average overall effective rate was a very modest 2 percent.

As highlighted by Gómez Sabaini and others a number of key factors explain the weakness of the personal income tax in the region, including: a progressive decline in marginal tax rates, narrow tax bases that negatively impact equity and an elevated level of tax evasion.[46]

During the past decades there has been a convergence in the top marginal rate of the personal income tax with the corporate income tax rate in Latin America. Additionally, both tax rates have trended downward over time. Data from USAID reveal that on average for nineteen countries in Latin America the average top marginal rate in 2012–2013 was 27.7 percent, excluding Chile and Mexico, compared to 37.1 percent for OECD countries.[47] They also highlight that the lowest income level at which the top marginal rate is imposed is much higher in Latin America (4.5 times per capita GDP) than in the OECD (3.3 times per capita GDP).

In many countries of the region the tax base has been hollowed out by numerous personal deductions as well as preferential treatment, including up to their nontaxation, of capital income sources. Additionally, tax expenditures in the forms of special exemption regimes or other tax benefits significantly erode the income tax base. For example, in 2007 tax expenditures for the personal income tax accounted for 4.4 percent of GDP in forgone revenues in Guatemala, 1.6 percent of GDP in Mexico, 0.8 percent of GDP in Ecuador, and 0.6 percent of GDP in Brazil.[48] Another factor that weakens tax collection in the region is the existence of exceptionally high minimum exempt income levels, which leave many people outside the tax net and serve largely to reduce the taxes paid by the well-off. The lowest income level at which the top marginal rate is imposed is much higher in Latin America (7.34 times per capita GDP) than in Western Europe (3.98 times) and in the United States and Canada (5.56 times).[49]

The region also suffers from very high levels of personal income tax evasion. While this reflects the existence of a significant informal economy, it also points to the lack of a tax culture in the region.

As a result of these deficiencies, the top decile of the income distribution in Latin America pays an exceptionally low effective tax rate compared to countries in North America and Europe (see Figure 23.7, below). Of the eighteen Latin American countries under consideration in Figure 23.7, only three (Brazil, Argentina, and Mexico) have effective rates in excess of 7.5 percent for the top decile, and of these only Mexico reaches a rate in excess of 10 percent. In comparison, in the United States the effective rate for the top quintile is 15.5 percent, and in some European countries the effective rate for the top decile rises to well over 20 percent (see Figure 23.7, below).

These results are based on household surveys that are widely acknowledged to not fully capture the full extent of the income spectrum. For example, high-net-worth individuals with exceptionally high incomes from nontraditional sources—deriving from passive income—are often not represented in these surveys, either because these individuals do not report these incomes or they purposely underreport them, or the survey data has been top-coded to protect the identity of respondents.

Supplementing household survey data with information from tax registers allows for more precise estimations of the effective tax rate paid by the top of the income distribution. Alvaredo and Londoño find that the average effective tax rate of the top 1 percent in Colombia falls with income, from a high of 12 percent for the bottom half of the top percentile to a low of 8 percent

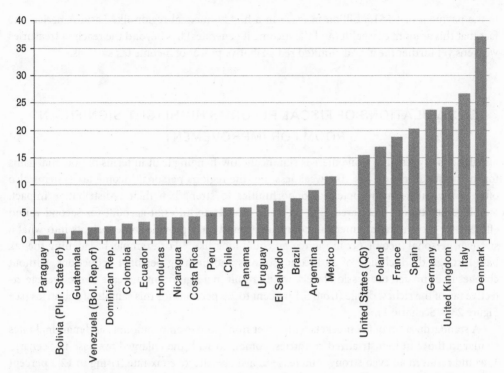

FIGURE 23.7: Selected countries: effective tax rate on the personal income tax of the tenth decile, around 2014[a,b] *(percentages)*

Source: Authors' calculations based on household surveys as processed by the Statistics Division of ECLAC; Congressional Budget Office, 2016; and EUROMOD statistics on Distribution and Decomposition of Disposable Income, G4.0+.

[a] Calculated over gross income (market income plus public and private transfers).

[b] Data from EUROMOD include additional direct taxes for some countries, including property taxes and church taxes.

for the ultra-rich in the top 0.01 percent.[50] In this case the authors highlight the numerous tax benefits that the ultra-rich enjoy, especially as related to capital income.

Low effective tax rates are also reflective of the fact that the region's countries are currently ill-equipped to tackle the glaring concentration of wealth in Latin America. Passive income is largely untaxed or receives preferential treatment such as exemptions or the application of lower tax rates. Despite the introduction of greater taxation of passive income, such as dividends, in recent reforms, their impact continues to be hampered by the fact that a significant share of the region's financial wealth is located offshore and is often undeclared. Zucman estimates that individuals from Latin America hold $700 billion in offshore wealth, representing 22 percent of the region's total financial wealth and that the great bulk of this wealth has not been declared to tax authorities.[51]

Chile's recent experience provides an interesting case study that attests to the extent to which the region's high-net-worth individuals have parked undeclared assets offshore. As part of a tax reform approved in 2014, the government offered a partial tax amnesty to individuals with undeclared assets overseas. The new law stipulated that taxpayers domiciled in Chile with assets or income generated prior to January 1, 2014, who had not paid the relevant taxes could declare them during 2015 and pay 8 percent flat tax on the fair market value of the assets. By the end of 2015, 7,832 declarations were filed, registering roughly US$20 billion in assets, which resulted in the payment of US$1.5 billion in tax.[52] In a highly unequal region like Latin America, the fact that this amount of wealth (and the income it generates) lies beyond the reach of treasuries weakens yet further the already limited redistributive power of income tax systems.

C. SIMULATIONS OF FISCAL REFORMS HIGHLIGHT SIGNIFICANT ROOM FOR IMPROVEMENT

Simulations suggest that while there is significant low-hanging fruit in terms of potential gains for the personal income tax. The weaknesses of the region's personal income tax systems also offer policymakers many potential opportunities to strengthen their redistributive impact. Simple simulations—these are based on static models and do not account for second round effects—for sixteen Latin American countries around 2011 provide some insights into what a stronger personal income tax in the region could look like.[53] For example, broadening the tax base through the inclusion of all income sources and limiting personal deductions, without changes in estimated tax evasion levels, would result in a significant increase of the average effective tax of the richest decile (from 5.1 percent to 7.9 percent) for this sample of countries (see Figure 23.8, Scenario 1).

A standardization of tax brackets with lower minimum exempt amounts and marginal rates similar to those in industrialized countries, combined with the enlarged tax base in Scenario 1, would result in an even stronger increase in average effective tax rate (rising to 12.3 percent for the top decile) (Scenario 2). Leaving structural elements aside, focusing on end results and

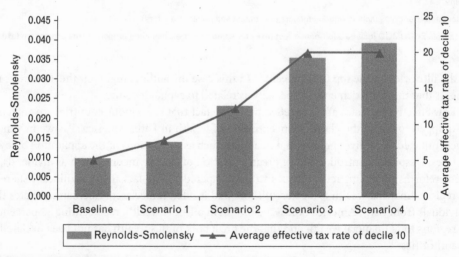

FIGURE 23.8: Latin America (16 countries): estimated effective tax rate under different scenarios, around 2011 *(Gini points)*

Source: Based on M. Hanni, R. Martner and A. Podestá, 'El potencial redistributivo de la fiscalidad en América Latina', 116 *Revista CEPAL* (2015) 7.

Note: Scenario 1: maintain current tax structure but enlarge tax base to include all sources of income; Scenario 2: apply a common tax structure across all countries with lower minimum exempt and progressive rates; Scenario 3: set effective tax rate of individuals in the 10th decile to 20%; Scenario 4: set tax effective rate of individuals in the 9th and 10th deciles to 20%.

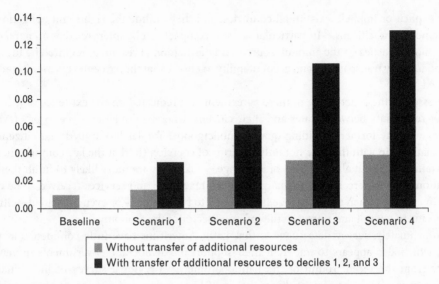

FIGURE 23.9: Latin America (16 countries): reduction in the Gini coefficient due to the personal income tax under different scenarios *(Gini points)*

Source: M. Hanni, R. Martner and A. Podestá, 'El potencial redistributivo de la fiscalidad en América Latina', 116 *Revista CEPAL* (2015) 7.

imposing effective tax rates of 20 percent, it is also possible to imagine a personal income tax that achieves a redistributive impact similar to that in the European Union (Scenarios 3 and 4).

While these latter cases may seem outlandish, especially given the effective tax rates currently paid by these income deciles, the recent tax reform in Chile is illustrative of policies that could increase the tax burden at the top end of the scale. An analysis carried out by Blanco Cossio found that as a result of the measures incorporated in the reform, the effective tax rate of the top 1 percent rose from 12.7 percent to 18.5 percent.[54]

However, these scenarios also highlight a key point for policymakers who aim to tackle income inequality through tax reforms: the targeted use of any additional revenues provides even greater leverage for reducing income inequality. In each of the presented scenarios the additional revenues, relative to the baseline case, were redistributed equally to the individuals in the first three deciles of the income distribution. In each case the subsequent cash transfer reduced income inequality, as measured by the Gini, by more than the improvement in the personal income tax itself (see Figure 23.9). This is especially apparent in the latter scenarios (3 and 4) highlighted in Figure 23.9 where the combined gains due to the change in the tax and the subsequent cash transfer reduced income inequality by upward of 13 Gini points.

IV. THE ROAD AHEAD: FISCAL POLICY CHALLENGES TO MAKING FURTHER GAINS IN THE REDUCTION OF INEQUALITY

Rebuilding fiscal compacts and fostering a greater sense of reciprocity in the region will be key prerequisites to making progress toward the Sustainable Development Goals. These pacts, either explicit or implicit, exist in all countries, and they outline the rights and obligations of governments and citizens.[55] In particular, a fiscal compact can be interpreted as an agreement between both parties on the amount, source, and destination of resources required by the state, accompanied by transparency and accountability to ensure that the agreement is monitored and enforced.[56]

In essence, the functioning of these agreements is predicated on the existence of a certain level of reciprocity between states and their citizens, whereby the latter agree to pay taxes in exchange for the former providing quality public goods. Torgler has argued that citizens see their relationship with the state not only in terms of coercion (in that the law compels them to do certain things) but also in terms of exchange.[57] Taxpayers are more likely to fulfill their tax obligations if they perceive the exchange between taxes paid and services received to be equitable. In contrast, when this exchange is perceived to be unequal—or even one-sided—citizens may decide to opt out and retreat to the informal sector of the economy.[58]

Unfortunately, survey data suggests that Latin Americans have little confidence in their states, which also appears to undercut their support for democratic governments in general. Results from the recent round of the Latinobarómetro, a regional survey of individuals in eighteen countries in the region, shows that in 2015 an average of 63 percent of respondents across the region reported little or no confidence in the state.[59] In the same survey only 57 percent of respondents on average reported that democracy was preferable to any other form of government.[60] For Latin America this is an area of particular concern as researchers have found that support for democracy and trust in government are among the variables with the greatest marginal impact on determining tax morale—more so than other traditional determinants such as gender, religiosity, or educational attainment.[61]

A. TAX EVASION REMAINS RAMPANT IN LATIN AMERICA

This lack of confidence in the state is clearly apparent in the elevated level of tax evasion in Latin American countries. Recent studies of this phenomenon are relatively scarce in the region, but they suggest that Latin American countries on average collect roughly 50 percent of the revenues that their personal income tax systems should theoretically generate (see Table 23.2). However, the situation of individual countries varies significantly, with estimated evasion in excess of 50 percent in Costa Rica, Guatemala, and Ecuador; contrasting with less than 30 percent in Chile and Mexico.

A significant share of this evasion is attributed to self-employed workers who operate in the largely informal economies that characterize the region. For example, while tax evasion by salaried workers and pensioners in Costa Rica was estimated at 11.9 percent of potential revenues in 2012, that of self-employed workers reached 90.9 percent.[62] In Mexico, estimated tax evasion by self-employed workers reached 83.4 percent of potential revenues, while that of salaried workers was 15.5 percent.[63]

Elevated evasion of the personal income tax is often justified in the region by reference to the perception that corporations are not paying their taxes. While corporate tax receipts tend to dominate income tax revenues in the region, studies suggest that tax evasion by enterprises is also significant. As in the case of the personal income tax, Latin America countries are on average realizing only slightly more than 50 percent of their potential corporate income tax revenues (estimated evasion of 27 percent in Brazil, 28 percent in Colombia, 31 percent in Chile, 46 percent in Mexico, 51 percent in El Salvador, 51 percent in Peru, 63 percent in Guatemala,

Table 23.2: Estimated tax evasion in Latin America *(percentages)*

	Personal income tax	Reference year	Corporate income tax	Reference year
Brazil	34.1	2014	26.6	2014
Chile	27.0	2009	31.0	2009
Colombia	n.a.	n.a.	34.4	2012
Costa Rica	53.8	2012	67.5	2012
Ecuador	58.1	2005	65.3	2005
El Salvador	36.3	2005	51.0	2005
Guatemala	69.9	2006	62.8	2006
Mexico	26.3	2012	31.4	2012
Peru	32.6	2006	51.3	2006

Source: Based on J. C. Gómez-Sabaíni and D. Morán, 'Evasión tributaria en América Latina: Nuevos y antiguos desafíos en la cuantificación del fenómeno en los países de la región', *Serie Macroeconomía del Desarrollo* No. 176, CEPAL (2016); and Sindicato Nacional de Procuradores de la Hacienda Nacional (SINPROFAZ), *Sonegação no Brasil: uma estimativa do desvio da arrecadação do exercício de 2014* (2015).

65 percent in Ecuador, and 68 percent in Costa Rica) (see Table 23.2). It is important to note that these estimates of corporate tax evasion make adjustments for often generous tax expenditures that additionally give rise to a sense of tax inequity in the region.

Tax evasion more generally—including that of the personal income tax, the corporate income tax, and the value-added tax—is estimated to have cost the region's governments an estimated $340 billion in potential revenues in 2015.[64] To put that number into context, total central government capital expenditures—including public investment in fixed capital and capital transfers—in Latin America totaled roughly $150 billion in the same year. In a region where a number of countries have an overall tax take of less than 20 percent of GDP—considered to be a minimum level to make progress on the Sustainable Development Goals—these revenue losses threaten to undercut advances in securing fundamental human rights.

B. SIGNIFICANT OPTING OUT OF PUBLIC SERVICES IS SUGGESTIVE OF QUALITY CONCERNS

A key thrust of the Millennium Development Goals and the recently adopted Sustainable Development Goals has been the expansion in access to key public services such as healthcare and education. These services function as key enablers of sustainable development, and access to them is rightly considered a fundamental human right.

Public health and education services represent a large share of total public expenditures in the region. Available data from ECLAC show that education outlays represented between 14 percent and 23 percent of total public expenditures in Brazil (16.4 percent), Chile (20.5 percent), Colombia (17.1 percent), Guatemala (21.9 percent), Nicaragua (23.6 percent), Panama (14.3 percent), and the Bolivarian Republic of Venezuela (18.3 percent).[65] Likewise, health expenditures ranged from 7 percent to 18 percent of total outlays in Brazil (14.6 percent), Chile (17.6 percent), Colombia (10.9 percent), Guatemala (8.1 percent), Nicaragua (18.1 percent), Panama (7.8 percent), and the Bolivarian Republic of Venezuela (12.9 percent).[66]

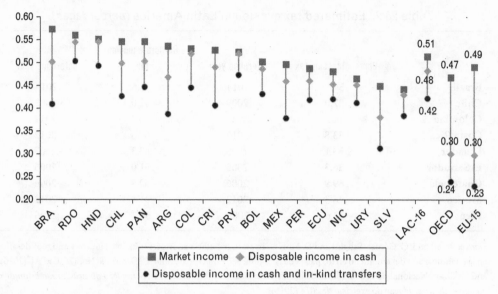

FIGURE 23.10: Latin America (16 countries): inequality of market income and extended disposable income, around 2011 *(Gini coefficients)*

Source: Based on ECLAC-Instituto de Estudios Fiscales, *Los efectos de la política fiscal sobre la redistribución en América Latina y la Unión Europea* (Estudio 8, Serie: Estados de la Cuestión, área: Finanzas Públicas, 2014), available online at http://sia.eurosocial-ii.eu/files/docs/1412088027-Estudio_8_def_final.pdf.

Given the relative size of the public expenditures in these areas, they have the potential to be significant agents of income redistribution. Estimates by ECLAC find that this is indeed the case in Latin America, where the combined impact of public health and education expenditures reduces the Gini coefficient by a further 12.5 percent on average.[67] In contrast to cash transfers the impact of in-kind transfers is much more apparent across the breadth of the region, including in countries where cash transfers and direct taxes have little redistributive role (see Figure 23.10, below). There is, of course, significant heterogeneity in the region, due largely to the differing sizes of education and health budgets.

However, these results obscure a potentially worrying sign for policymakers: a high level of opting out of public services. In the case of OECD countries, the redistributive effect largely stems from the relatively uniform distribution of public spending across income quintiles, which results in a larger increase in the income share at the bottom of the distribution than at the top.[68] In contrast, in Latin America, public spending on education and health is highly concentrated at the bottom of the income distribution (see Table 23.3, below). As Table 23.3 illustrates, on average in Latin America, nearly half of all public education spending (48.5 percent) is concentrated at the bottom 40 percent of the income distribution (quintiles 1 and 2) concentrates, compared to just 13.8 percent of public spending for the top 20 percent of the distribution.

In a number of countries, the ratio of public education spending between the top quintile and the bottom quintile drops significantly. For example, in Argentina, Brazil, Chile, the Dominican Republic, Peru, and Uruguay this ratio is 0.45 or less, implying a significant skew in the distribution of public spending (see Table 23.3). As illustrated in Table 23.3, in these six countries the bottom two quintiles account for between 51.4 percent and 55.5 percent of education outlays. While this result derives in part from the distribution of school-age children within the income distribution, it also reflects a conscious decision by those with means to send their

Table 23.3: Latin America (14 countries): concentration of public education spending, by quintile, around 2011 *(percentages and ratios)*

Countries	Quintiles					Q5/Q1 ratio
	1	2	3	4	5	
Argentina	32.2	22.7	19.5	15.1	10.5	0.3
Brazil	30.4	25.1	19.4	13.6	11.5	0.4
Chile	30.8	24.4	19.3	14.5	10.9	0.4
Colombia	25.3	22.8	20.8	18.1	13.0	0.5
Costa Rica	24.4	22.1	19.5	18.3	15.6	0.6
Dominican Republic	27.7	24.5	19.6	16.6	11.6	0.4
Ecuador	22.5	22.5	20.0	19.1	15.9	0.7
El Salvador	23.0	22.7	20.6	19.4	14.3	0.6
Honduras	19.0	20.6	20.3	20.3	19.7	1.0
Mexico	22.8	22.5	21.5	18.6	14.5	0.6
Panama	22.4	22.5	21.9	19.1	14.1	0.6
Paraguay	22.6	20.0	19.5	19.3	18.4	0.8
Peru	27.2	24.2	21.9	15.9	10.8	0.4
Uruguay	28.8	22.9	18.9	16.4	13.0	0.5
Memorandum:						
Simple average	25.7	22.8	20.2	17.5	13.8	0.6
Min	19.0	20.0	18.9	13.6	10.5	0.3
Max	32.2	25.1	21.9	20.3	19.7	1.0

Source: Authors' calculations, based on data from ECLAC-Instituto de Estudios Fiscales, *Los efectos de la política fiscal sobre la redistribución en América Latina y la Unión Europea* (Estudio 8, Serie: Estados de la Cuestión, área: Finanzas Públicas, 2014), available online at http://sia.eurosocial-ii.eu/files/docs/1412088027-Estudio_8_def_final.pdf.

children to private rather than public institutions. Among these countries, the share of students from the top 50 percent of the income distribution attending a public primary school varies from 47.0 percent in Argentina to 69.8 percent in Brazil.[69] Unsurprisingly, in all countries the share of children in the lower 50 percent of the income distribution that attend public schools nears 100 percent.[70]

This revealed preference on the part of citizens for private educational services appears to reflect a recognition that the region's education systems are not preparing students to participate in an increasingly globalized, services-based knowledge-intensive economy. Results from the OECD's Programme for International Student Assessment (PISA) for 2012 reveal that Latin American countries lag significantly compared to developed countries, as well as other developing economies, in terms of mathematical competencies.[71] Of the sixty-five countries and economies that participated, the eight Latin American countries were all near the bottom of the rankings: Chile (51), Mexico (53), Uruguay (55), Costa Rica (56), Brazil (58), Argentina (59), Colombia (62), and Peru (65).[72] This contrasts sharply with the results for a number of developing economies in Asia, who ranked highly. For example, Vietnam placed seventeenth between Germany (16) and Austria (18).[73]

C. TACKLING THE REGION'S FRAYED FISCAL COMPACTS

High tax evasion and the opting out of public services, especially when viewed from the perspective that taxpayers perceive their relationship to the state as one of exchange, suggests that for many citizens in the region the deal on offer from their governments is not seen as an equitable one. The region finds itself in a suboptimal equilibrium, where many taxpayers do not feel a responsibility to pay their taxes—in part or at all—and where governments lack the necessary revenues to provide public services of the level and the quality that would be more highly valued by their citizens.

Complicating matters, the existing fiscal compacts in the region are largely based on the fiscal conditions that held during the recent period of economic boom. The current macroeconomic environment, defined by weak GDP growth and the need for fiscal consolidation, calls for—indeed will require—new fiscal compacts in order for states to ensure fiscal sustainability while at the same time mobilizing resources to make progress on achieving the Sustainable Development Goals.

While overall regional and country-level forecasts of the resource needs implied by these commitments are lacking, estimates for particular goals are illustrative of the demands that governments will likely face. For example, according to the Social Protection Floor Index, the countries of the region will need to spend on average an additional 5 percent of GDP per year to ensure that all their citizens had access to essential healthcare and basic income security.[74] The actualization of the fundamental human rights embodied in the 2030 Agenda will require a renewed commitment to the provision of largely public services in the region.

Providing these services will only be possible through increases in tax revenues, as resource flows from other sources cannot be depended on to cover recurrent expenditures over time. Given that the region's tax systems are already heavily reliant on indirect taxes, and that the Sustainable Development Goals themselves call for fiscal policies that aim to achieve greater equality (see Goal 10), domestic resource mobilization in Latin America will necessarily require an increase in direct taxation.

As the 2030 Agenda places a premium on the provision of high-quality services, there appears to be an opportunity for governments to tackle low tax morale by proposing a new fiscal compact around attaining the Sustainable Development Goals. Indeed, research in developing countries and in Latin America in particular suggests that the perception of the quality of public services is an important determinant of citizens' willingness to pay taxes, more so than the prospect of upward mobility.[75]

Recent experience in Latin America provides examples of how a holistic approach to fiscal policymaking, taking both revenue raising and public spending into account, could ensure that new reforms will efficiently maximize their redistributive impact. For example, Chile's reform of 2014 called for "advancing in tax equity, improving the distribution of income with the aim to permit the country to advance in a context of social, economic and political stability."[76] The modifications to the tax system, which targeted the top of the income distribution, were planned to generate revenues that would serve to make structural reform of the education system possible. High-quality public education can have an important redistributive impact in the short term, as well as generate an intergenerational dividend in the medium and long term.

Additionally, the Mexican reform of 2013 had as one of its key objectives: "Improve equality: ensure that those that have more pay more, eliminate privileges and establish taxes to achieve a system that is more just, progressive and equitable."[77] Prominent changes to the tax system included the incorporation of new tax brackets and rates at the top end of the income scale, as well as new taxes on certain dividends and capital gains. At the same time the reform called for "the establishment of a universal social security system that guarantees an income for all Mexicans older than 65 years old and an insurance to support the income of workers who lose their jobs."[78]

New fiscal compacts should encourage the region's expanding middle class to play a more active role in financing public spending through the payment of personal income taxes. Daude and Melguizo find that individuals in the middle three quintiles of the income distribution in Latin American countries have higher tax morale, but are not satisfied with the provision of public services, so they suffer from a "dissatisfied customer" relationship with the state.[79] However, they are also less likely to respond that taxes are too high, perhaps reflecting the fact that currently the personal income tax burden in the region is largely carried by the richest decile of the income distribution (88 percent on average for eighteen Latin American countries around 2014).[80]

A well-functioning state that provides public goods of high quality is a benefit for all citizens, even for those who can afford to opt for private services. To that end, to strengthen fiscal compacts in the region there must be a frank public discussion about the tax burden of those individuals in the top 1 percent of the income distribution. For example, Chile's recent reform was crafted to specifically increase the tax burden of those at the very top of the income distribution.[81] Bringing the middle class into the tax net will be much more difficult if they perceive that the wealthy benefit from tax benefits that minimize their effective tax rates. This will require re-examining the taxation of capital income and property, the latter of which is particularly weak in the region.

In the past, governments have hesitated to consider taxing passive income for fear of generating capital flight, among other motives, but with greater international tax cooperation this may become less of a concern. For example, as of November 2016, eighty-seven countries have signed the CRS (common reporting standard) Multilateral Competent Authority Agreement on automatic exchange of financial account information (CRS MCAA), including seven Latin American countries (Argentina, Brazil, Chile, Colombia, Costa Rica, Mexico, and Uruguay).[82] These countries have committed to the automatic exchange of financial account information starting in 2017 or 2018, depending on the country, which will provide tax authorities with detailed information about the foreign financial holdings of their resident taxpayers. This may provide governments with an opportunity to offer these taxpayers a means by which to fully re-engage with their national tax system, while at the same time reforming the overall tax system.

V. CONCLUSION

The full realization of the fundamental human rights embodied in the Universal Declaration of Human Rights in Latin America is still a work in progress. While substantial advances have been made in recent decades, for many of the region's citizens, the enjoyment of their rights is far from ensured. Further progress will require a revisiting of the basic social compact between governments and their citizens with the aim to redefining the balance between the rights and obligations of both parties.

While the region remains the most unequal in the world, income inequality has trended downward during the last decade. Most of this improvement is due to gains in the labor market, assisted in part by the increased prevalence of conditional cash-transfer programs. In general, the redistributive power of the region's fiscal policies has not played a significant role in reducing income inequality. Direct taxation results in a very minor reduction in inequality on average and cash transfers have a limited impact that is highly country specific. Simple tax models constructed over household surveys, however, point to the role the personal income tax could play as a pillar in financing social benefits that would result in a substantial reduction in inequality.

Making further progress in reducing inequality in Latin America will require tackling the frayed fiscal compacts that exist in many of the region's countries. Evidence suggests that many citizens in the region feel that the services on offer from the government are not worth paying taxes for. Tax evasion is rampant, with many countries realizing less than 50 percent of what their systems should theoretically generate. At the same time, while in-kind transfers of health and education services are shown to be highly redistributive, this is due in part to a significant opting out by those with the means to purchase private services.

With the adoption of the 2030 Agenda for Sustainable Development there is an opportunity for the region's governments and their citizens to rebuild these fiscal compacts. The provision of high-quality public services and benefits, as defined in the Sustainable Development Goals, provides the basis for governments to re-engage with their citizens with the aim of reinvigorating sagging tax morale. Bringing more citizens, especially those in the middle class, into the personal income tax system—as well as addressing low taxation of passive income and property—would not only strengthen the system's redistributive power but would provide substantial resources for supporting the realization of fundamental human rights in the region.

NOTES

1. Authors' calculations based on data from CEPALSTAT (Economic Commission for Latin America and the Caribbean, Databases and Statistical Publications), available at http://estadisticas.cepal. org/cepalstat/WEB_CEPALSTAT/Portada.asp?idioma=i (last visited 25 July 2017).
2. GA Res. 217 A (III), 10 Dec. 1948.
3. OECD Centre for Tax Policy and Administration, OECD Development Centre, Inter-American Center for Tax Administration (CIAT), Economic Commission for Latin America and the Caribbean (ECLAC) and the Inter-American Development Bank, *Revenue Statistics in Latin America and the Caribbean 1990–2014* (2016).
4. ECLAC, *Panorama Fiscal de America Latina y el Caribe 2016: las finanzas públicas ante el desafío de conciliar austeridad con crecimiento e igualdad* (LC/L.4140, 2016), available online at http:// www.cepal.org/es/publicaciones/39939-panorama-fiscal-america-latina-caribe-2016-finanzas-publicas-desafio-conciliar (last visited 20 July 2017).
5. See Table 23.1 (presenting the authors' calculations based on household surveys as processed by the Statistics Division of ECLAC and data from EUROMOD statistics on Distribution and Decomposition of Disposable Income, G4.0+, see EUROMOD, *Statistics*, available online at https://www.euromod.ac.uk/using-euromod/statistics (last visited 25 July 2017).
6. ECLAC, *The Fiscal Covenant. Strengths, Weaknesses, Challenges (Summary)* (LC/G.2024, 1998), available online at http://www.cepal.org/en/publications/31007-pacto-fiscal-fortalezas-debilidades-desafios-sintesis-fiscal-covenant-strengths (last visited 25 July 2017).
7. GA Res. 70/1, 25 Sept. 2015.
8. Authors' calculations based on household surveys as processed by the Statistics Division of ECLAC and data from OECD.Stat.
9. See Figure 23.1 (presenting the authors' calculations based on household surveys as processed by the Statistics Division of ECLAC).
10. ECLAC, *CEPALSTAT Income Inequality Statistics Database—Statistics and Indicators*, available online at http://estadisticas.cepal.org/cepalstat/WEB_CEPALSTAT/estadisticasIndicadores. asp?idioma=i (last visited 25 July 2017).

11. L. Gasparini and N. Lustig, *The Rise and Fall of Income Inequality in Latin America* (Tulane Economics Working Paper No. 1110, 2011), available online at http://econ.tulane.edu/RePEc/pdf/tul1110.pdf.

12. ECLAC, *Panorama Social de America Latina 2011* (2012), available online at http://www.cepal.org/es/publicaciones/1241-panorama-social-america-latina-2011 (last visited 20 July 2017).

13. For the purposes of this analysis "Developing Asia" is defined as the countries of Eastern Asia (excluding Japan), Southeastern Asia, and Southern Asia, as classified by the M49 Standard of the United Nations Statistical Division, available online at https://unstats.un.org/unsd/methodology/m49/ (last visited 20 July 2017).

14. World Bank, *World Development Indicators Database*, available online at http://databank.worldbank.org/data/reports.aspx?source=world-development-indicators (last visited 28 Feb. 2017).

15. Ibid.

16. A. B. Atkinson, 'Income Inequality in OECD Countries: Data and Explanations' (2003) (Revised version of paper prepared for CESinfo conference on Globalization, Inequality and Wellbeing, 8–9 Nov. 2002); OECD, *Divided we Stand: Why Inequality Keeps Rising* (2011).

17. *OECD.Stat*, available online at http://stats.oecd.org/ (last visited 25 July 2017).

18. Ibid.

19. T. Piketty and E. Saez, 'Income Inequality in the United States, 1913–1998', 118(1) *Quarterly Journal of Economics* (2003), 1.

20. F. Alvaredo et al., 'The Top 1 Percent in International and Historical Perspective', 27(3) *Journal of Economic Perspectives* (2013), 3.

21. Ibid.

22. Ibid.

23. F. Alvaredo and J. Londoño, *High Incomes and Personal Taxation in a Developing Economy: Colombia 1993–2010* (Commitment to Equity Initiative, Working Paper 12, 2013), available online at http://www.commitmentoequity.org/publications_files/CEQWPNo12%20HighTaxationDevEconColombia1993-2010_19March2013.pdf.

24. R. López, E. Figueroa, and P. Gutiérrez, *La "Parte del León": nuevas estimaciones de la participación de los superricos en el ingreso en Chile (SDT 379)* (Santiago de Chile: Universidad de Chile, Facultad de Economía y Negocios, 2013), available online at http://www.econ.uchile.cl/es/publicacion/la-parte-del-le-n-nuevas-estimaciones-de-la-participaci-n-de-los-s-per-ricos-en-el-ingreso-de-chile (last visited 20 July 2017).

25. Ibid.

26. F. Alvaredo, 'The Rich in Argentina over the Twentieth Century 1932–2004', *in* A. Atkinson and T. Piketty (eds.), *Top Incomes over the Twentieth Century: A Global Perspective* (2010), available online at https://sites.google.com/site/alvaredo/ (last visited 20 July 2017).

27. López et al., *supra* note 24; Alvaredo and Londoño, *supra* note 23.

28. G. Burdín, F. Esponda, and A. Vigorito, *Desigualdad y altos ingresos en Uruguay* (Instituto de Economía-FCEA, Working Paper, 2014), available online at https://cef.org.uy/en/investigaciones/desigualdad-y-altos-ingresos-en-uruguay/ (last visited 20 July 2017).

29. ECLAC, *CEPALSTAT Public Social Expenditures Database, supra* note 10.

30. OECD, *Social Expenditure Update* (2014), available online at https://www.oecd.org/els/soc/OECD2014-SocialExpenditure_Update19Nov_Rev.pdf, at 4.

31. ECLAC, CEPALSTAT Public Social Expenditures Database, *supra* note 10. ECLAC statistics on public social spending do not separately identify public pensions from other social security expenditures (for example, unemployment insurance), but they are assumed to represent the bulk of expenditure in this category. These figures also do not take into account the fact that some countries in the region run private mandatory pension schemes whose outlays are not included in public spending statistics.

32. International Labour Organization, *World Social Protection Report 2014–15* (2014), available online at http://www.ilo.org/global/research/global-reports/world-social-security-report/2014/WCMS_245201/lang--en/index.htm (last visited 20 July 2017).

33. Authors' calculations based on data from ECLAC-Instituto de Estudios Fiscales, *Los efectos de la política fiscal sobre la redistribución en América Latina y la Unión Europea* (Estudio 8, Serie: Estados de la Cuestión, área: Finanzas Públicas, 2014), available online at http://sia.eurosocial-ii.eu/files/docs/1412088027-Estudio_8_def_final.pdf.

34. Ibid.

35. S. Cecchini and A. Madariaga, *Programas de transferencias condicionadas. Balance de la experiencia reciente en América Latina y el Caribe* (2011) (*Cuadernos de la CEPAL*, N° 95 (LC/G.2497- P), Santiago, ECLAC), available online at http://www.cepal.org/es/publicaciones/27854-programas-transferencias-condicionadas-balance-la-experiencia-reciente-america (last visited 20 July 2017).

36. International Labour Organization, Social Protection Floors Recommendation, No. 202, 14 June 2012, available online at http://www.ilo.org/dyn/normlex/en/f?p=NORMLEXPUB:12100:0::NO:: P12100_ILO_CODE:R202 (last visited 29 June 2017).

37. United Nations, *Sustainable Development Goals,* available online at https://sustainabledevelopment.un.org/?menu=1300 (last visited 29 June 2017).

38. International Labour Organization, *supra* note 32.

39. Ibid.

40. Ibid.

41. OECD, CIAT, ECLAC and Inter-American Development Bank, *supra* note 3.

42. Instituto Argentino de Analisis Fiscal (IARAF), *Reporte Mensual de Recaudación Tributaria Nacional: Abril de 2016* (2016), available online at http://www.consejo.org.ar/observatorio/files/ReporteMensualdeRecaudacion_04_16.pdf, at 11.

43. OECD, CIAT, ECLAC and Inter-American Development Bank, *supra* note 3.

44. Ibid.

45. EUROMOD statistics on Distribution and Decomposition of Disposable Income, G4.0+, see EUROMOD, *supra* note 5.

46. J. Gómez Sabaíni, J. P. Jiménez, and D. Rossignolo, *Imposición a la renta personal y equidad en América Latina: Nuevos desafíos* (ECLAC, Serie Macroeconomía del Desarrollo N° 119, 2012), available online at http://www.cepal.org/es/publicaciones/5351-imposicion-la-renta-personal-equidad-america-latina-nuevos-desafios, at 30–36 (last visited 20 July 2017).

47. United States Agency for International Development (USAID), *Collecting Taxes Database 2012–2013* (2013), available online at https://www.usaid.gov/data/dataset/cdeb8a1b-3440-4e88-b6cb-81b2428f8cea (last visited 20 July 2017).

48. L. Villela, A. Lemgruber, and M. Jorratt, *Tax Expenditure Budgets: Concepts and Challenges for Implementation* (Inter-American Development Bank, Working Paper No. IDB-WP-179, 2009), available online at https://www.econstor.eu/bitstream/10419/115368/1/IDB-WP-131en.pdf.

49. ECLAC, *Panorama Fiscal de América Latina y el Caribe 2017: la movilización de recursos para el financiamiento del desarrollo sostenible* (LC/PUB.2017/6-P, 2017), available online at http://www.cepal.org/es/publicaciones/41044-panorama-fiscal-america-latina-caribe-2017-la-movilizacion-recursos (last visited 20 July 2017).

50. Alvaredo and Londoño, *supra* note 23.

51. G. Zucman, *The Hidden Wealth of Nations: The Scourge of Tax Havens* (2015).

52. Press Release, Servicio de Impuestos Internos (SII), SII recibió 7.832 declaraciones voluntarias de capitales en el exterior, 4 Jan. 2016, available online at http://www.sii.cl/pagina/actualizada/noticias/2016/040116noti01jv.htm (last visited 20 July 2017).

53. M. Hanni, R. Martner, and A. Podestá, 'El potencial redistributivo de la fiscalidad en América Latina', 116 *Revista CEPAL* (2015), 7.

54. F. Blanco Cossio, *Chile—Efectos distributivos de la reforma tributaria 2014* (2016) (World Bank), available online at http://documentos.bancomundial.org/curated/es/496131468228282235/Chile-Efectos-distributivos-de-la-reforma-tributaria-2014 (last visited 20 July 2017).

55. ECLAC, *supra* note 6.

56. ECLAC, *Panorama Fiscal de America Latina y el Caribe: reformas tributarias y renovación del pacto fiscal* (LC/L.3580, 2013), available online at http://www.cepal.org/es/publicaciones/

3097-panorama-fiscal-america-latina-caribe-2013-reformas-tributarias-renovacion-pacto   (last visited 20 July 2017).

57. B. Torgler, 'Tax Morale in Latin America', 122(1/2) *Public Choice* (2005), 133.

58. A. O. Hirschman, *Exit, Voice and Loyalty: Responses to Decline in Firms, Organizations and States* (1970).

59. Authors' calculations based on data available from the Latinobarómetro database, available online at http://www.latinobarometro.org/ (last visited 20 July 2017).

60. Ibid.

61. C. Daude, H. Gutiérrez, and A. Melguizo, *What Drives Tax Morale* (OECD Development Centre Working Paper No. 315, 2012), available online at http://www.oecd-ilibrary.org/development/what-drives-tax-morale_5k8zk8m61kzq-en (last visited 29 June 2017).

62. Ministerio de Hacienda de Costa Rica, *Incumplimiento tributario en impuestos sobre la renta y ventas 2010–2012* (2014), available online at http://www.hacienda.go.cr/docs/53ff79e228326_Incumplimiento%20Tributario%20en%20ISR%20e%20IGV%20(2010-2012).pdf.

63. H. J. Fuentes Castro, *Estudio de evasión global de impuestos* (Instituto Tecnologico y de Estudios Superiores de Monterrey 2013), available online at http://sat.gob.mx/administracion_sat/estudios_evasion_fiscal/Documents/ITESM.zip (last visited 20 July 2017).

64. ECLAC, *Estudio Económico de América Latina y el Caribe 2016: La Agenda 2030 para el Desarrollo Sostenible y los desafíos del financiamiento para el desarrollo* (LC/G.2684-P, 2016), available online at http://www.cepal.org/es/publicaciones/40326-estudio-economico-america-latina-caribe-2016-la-agenda-2030-desarrollo (last visited 20 July 2017).

65. ECLAC, *CEPALSTAT Public Social Expenditures Database, supra* note 10.

66. Ibid.

67. ECLAC-Instituto de Estudios Fiscales, *supra* note 33.

68. F. Marical et al., 'Publicly-provided Services and the Distribution of Households' Economics Resources', 44 *OECD Economic Studies* (2008), 9.

69. Authors' calculations based on data from ECLAC-Instituto de Estudios Fiscales, *supra* note 33.

70. Ibid.

71. OECD, *Equations and Inequalities: Making Mathematics Accessible to All* (2016), available online at http://www.oecd.org/publications/equations-and-inequalities-9789264258495-en.htm (last visited 20 July 2017).

72. Ibid.

73. Ibid.

74. M. Bierbaum et al., *A Social Protection Floor Index: Monitoring National Social Protection Policy Implementation* (Maastricht Graduate School of Governance and UNU-Merit/Friedrich-Ebert-Stiftung Discussion Paper, 2016), available online at http://library.fes.de/pdf-files/iez/12490.pdf.

75. Daude, Gutiérrez, and Melguizo, *supra* note 61; C. Daude and A. Melguizo, *Taxation and More Representation? On Fiscal Policy, Social Mobility and Democracy in Latin America* (OECD Development Centre Working Paper No. 294, 2010), available online at http://www.oecd-ilibrary.org/development/taxation-and-more-representation-on-fiscal-policy-social-mobility-and-democracy-in-latin-america_5km5zrrs9bbt-en (last visited 20 July 2017).

76. Republic of Chile, *La Reforma Tributaria: algunas preguntas clave* (2014), available online at http://www.gob.cl/2014/03/31/reforma-tributaria-algunas-preguntas-clave/ (last visited 20 July 2017).

77. United Mexican States, *Reforma de la Hacienda Pública: Resumen Ejecutivo*, available online at https://www.gob.mx/cms/uploads/attachment/file/66458/7_Hacendaria.pdf.

78. Ibid.

79. Daude and Melguizo, *supra* note 75.

80. Authors' calculations based on household surveys as processed by the Statistics Division of ECLAC.

81. Blanco Cossio, *supra* note 54.

82. OECD, *Signatories of the Multilateral Competent Authority Agreement on Automatic Exchange of Financial Account Information*, available online at https://www.oecd.org/ctp/exchange-of-tax-information/MCAA-Signatories.pdf.

CHAPTER 24

BASIC INCOME AS A HUMAN RIGHT?

DANIEL J. HEMEL

I. INTRODUCTION

An emerging literature on tax and human rights emphasizes the obligations of states to confront tax evasion and tax avoidance. The focus is on the flow of funds *from* taxpayers *to* states, and the obligations of states to ensure that taxes are paid. This chapter examines the nature of financial obligations running in the opposite direction: *from* states *to* citizens (and, possibly, to noncitizen residents). It considers whether members of a political community may have a right to a basic income, and symmetrically, whether states may have an obligation to honor such a right.

By "basic income," I mean an income due to all individuals, regardless of whether they work or are capable of work, which comes in cash rather than in kind. Philippe Van Parijs's oft-cited essay arguing for an unconditional basic income is titled "Why Surfers Should Be Fed," but perhaps a more fitting title would be "Why Surfers Should Be *Paid*": Van Parijs and other basic income advocates seek not only redistribution but redistribution in the form of cash.[1] A basic income might be justified on a number of grounds (e.g., utilitarianism or resource egalitarianism[2]). The question considered here is whether a human rights framework can add any force to basic income claims.

By "human rights" framework, I refer to a set of claims phrased in terms that are universal and obligatory. The proposition that human rights are necessarily universal requires little elaboration. The status of a claim as a "right" implies that respect for it is obligatory: it is a claim that all states (and in certain contexts, nonstate actors) are morally or legally bound to honor. The universal and obligatory nature of human rights claims thereby imposes a limit on human rights' scope. If "ought" implies "can," then a human right cannot be one that only the wealthiest states are capable of vindicating; it must be one that all states (or, at least, all states except failed states) are able to vindicate.[3]

From the outset, there are at least two reasons to question whether human rights principles have any bearing on basic income arguments. First, insofar as the existing human rights framework recognizes income security as a right, it generally recognizes claims that are *conditional* on work or on the incapacity to work. Second, the claim that all individuals everywhere in the world have an unconditional right to a "universal basic income" either runs into immediate obstacles of infeasibility or insubstantiality. Any basic allowance that lower- and lower-middle-income countries could possibly provide would be of little significance to lower-income citizens of higher-income countries. Likewise, the allowance envisioned by advocates of a basic income in higher-income countries would be infeasible in lower-income countries. Insofar as feasibility is a constraint on human rights claims, then the idea of a human right to a basic income would seem to be a nonstarter. Perhaps unsurprisingly, many basic income advocates have eschewed claims phrased in rights-based terms.[4]

Yet the idea of a human right to a basic income is (I will argue) more viable than the discussion above would suggest. While I certainly do not claim that nation-states are bound by international human rights law to provide a basic income to their citizens, I will suggest that a basic income can be justified in terms that are universal and obligatory. The core argument is as follows: A state is a collective enterprise that generates a surplus. The income that its members can earn under state protection far exceeds what they can earn in the state of nature, and that difference also far exceeds the cost of state administration. The state's ability to generate such a surplus is predicated upon its members' consent, both as a practical matter and a moral matter. Each law-abiding individual thus contributes to the state's surplus-generating capacity, and from that contribution arises a legitimate claim of entitlement to a share of the surplus. Even an individual who declines to participate in the labor market still participates in the surplus-generating collective enterprise that is the state. The claim to a share of the surplus is in this sense unconditional: it does not depend on whether one participates—or is capable of participating—in the labor market.

That sketch of the argument is far too brief to be of much persuasive force (at least yet), but one feature of the argument merits immediate mention. The argument locates the right to a basic income in the relationship between individual and state; it suggests that the right to a basic income is "political" in that it is a right arising from an individual's membership in a surplus-generating political community. One might question whether a right that arises from an individual's membership in a political community can qualify as a "human right." I will argue that it can (and ought to).

A "human right" can take the form: "If relationship X exists between person A and state B, then person A has a right that state B provide person A with Y (or that state B not prevent person A from doing Z)." Consider Article 21(1) of the Universal Declaration of Human Rights (UDHR): "Everyone has the right to take part in the government of his country, directly or through freely chosen representatives."[5] If relationship X exists between person A and state B (i.e., if state B is "his country"), then person A has a right that state B allow him to take part in B's government. Note that Article 21(1) does not posit that everyone has a right to take part in the government of any country; it posits that everyone has the right to take part in the government of *his* (or *her*) country.[6]

The right to a basic income takes a form similar to the right to vote: If person A is a law-abiding member of state B, then person A has a right to a share of the surplus generated via A's obedience to state B. The right is a human right in that it is a right that all humans can claim when a certain relationship between them and the state obtains. To be sure, the size of the basic income will depend on the surplus generated in the relevant country. The right is nonetheless universal in that it applies whenever a particular relationship between individual and state exists.

Note, moreover, that the argument outlined here is not immediately vulnerable to the critique that a "universal basic income" right will be either infeasible as applied to low-income countries or insubstantial as applied to low-income individuals in high-income countries. The argument is not that all people have a right to a certain monetary income, or even a certain level of subsistence. Rather, the argument is that individuals who contribute to a surplus-generating collective enterprise have a legitimate claim to a share of that surplus. The size of that share may vary in monetary terms from country to country even while the essential claim remains the same.

Before proceeding further, I should clarify the relationship between a "basic income" and the "negative income tax" proposal with which tax scholars may be more familiar.[7] In short, there is no difference. For example, a $10,000 basic income coupled with a 30 percent marginal tax rate on market income is arithmetically equivalent to a negative income tax of the form $T = -\$10,000 + 0.3M$, where T represents the tax due to (transfer due from) the government, and M represents an individual's market income. The clarification is intended to alleviate (though not eliminate) the concern that paying the idle surfer will discourage individuals from working.[8] The surfer's incentive to work is similar to that of anyone who could fund $10,000 of consumption per year from inherited wealth or savings and faces a marginal tax rate in the 30 percent range. This is not to say that the work disincentives generated by a basic income are inconsequential; it is to say that they are not qualitatively different from the work disincentives produced by inherited wealth or income taxation more generally.

Of course, a basic income could be coupled with any of an infinite number of marginal rate schedules. The focus here is on the entitlement of the surfer to a positive transfer from the state, and not on the overall structure of an ideal tax system. Section II briefly examines the support (or lack thereof) for a basic income right in the framework documents of the human rights movement. In section III, I elaborate on the case for a basic income right along the lines sketched above. In section IV, I consider qualifications and objections to the core case. Section V discusses alternative justifications for a basic income and highlights the most important implications of the analysis here.

II. IN SEARCH OF A BASIC INCOME

As emphasized above, the argument here is not that international human rights law recognizes a right to a basic income. Income security makes an appearance in the UDHR, but insofar as it guarantees a "basic income," the guarantee appears to be conditional on work or incapacity to work. Article 23(3) states that "[e]veryone who works has the right to just and favourable remuneration ensuring for himself and his family an existence worthy of human dignity."[9] Article 25(1) states that "[e]veryone has the right to a standard of living adequate for the health and well-being of himself and of his family, including food, clothing, housing and medical care and necessary social services, and the right to security in the event of unemployment, sickness, disability, widowhood, old age or other lack of livelihood in circumstances beyond his control."[10] To be sure, neither Article 23(3) nor Article 25(1) rules out the notion that an individual might have a claim to some sort of remuneration even if he is unemployed voluntarily. Moreover, the first part of Article 25(1) ("[e]veryone has the right to . . . food, clothing, housing and medical care and necessary social services") seems to imply that all individuals are entitled to some level of redistribution *in kind*. Yet it seems fair to infer that Article 25(1) is drawing a distinction between individuals capable of work (who are entitled to food, clothing, housing, medical care, and necessary social services) and individuals incapable of work (who are entitled to all those same things plus "security"). Even if "security" can be equated to income, Article 25(1) confers not a universal right to income but a right limited to those who lack work for reasons beyond their control.

Article 22 of the UDHR might offer more hope to advocates of a basic income searching for support in foundational human rights texts. It begins: "Everyone, as a member of society, has the right to social security. . . ."[11] And Article 9 of the International Covenant on Economic, Social and Cultural Rights reaffirms this point: "The States Parties to the present Covenant recognize the right of everyone to social security, including social insurance."[12] Yet the commentary of the UN Committee on Economic, Social and Cultural Rights on Article 9 clarifies that this "social security" right is not a right to an unconditional basic income. Cash benefits are specified for individuals who are sick, elderly, involuntarily unemployed, or injured in the course of employment, for caregivers to children and adult dependents, for working mothers on maternity leave, for the disabled, and for "survivors and orphans on the death of a breadwinner who was covered by social security or had rights to a pension."[13] The Covenant does posit that the surfer should be *fed*—Article 11 recognizes the "right of everyone to an adequate standard of living," including "adequate food." But the surfer with hope for an income appears to be out of luck—at least until she is injured riding the waves or until she grows old.

All of which is to say that the right to a basic income, if such a right can be justified, will not be based on interpretation of existing international human rights texts. It will be rooted in political theory rather than positive law. It is to the political theory supporting a right to a basic income that this chapter now turns.

III. THE SURFER AS PARTNER

The surfer first enters the basic income debate by way of a footnote in John Rawls's *Political Liberalism*, where Rawls says that "those who surf all day off Malibu must find a way to support themselves" and ought "not be entitled to public funds."[14] (The footnote itself appears to be an outgrowth of a 1987 breakfast conversation between Rawls and Van Parijs.[15]) The focus in basic income debates on the proverbial surfer is in some sense unfortunate, because it diverts our attention from the broader class of individuals whom a basic income would benefit: individuals who—for whatever reason—find themselves near the bottom of the income ladder but who lack any of the visible characteristics (e.g., old age, obvious disability) that would qualify them for income support in a conditional redistributive system. At the same time, the surfer presents us with a useful thought experiment: Does the individual who neither participates in the labor market nor is demonstrably incapable of labor market participation nonetheless "deserve" some share of the surplus generated by the state?

The question, so framed, is concededly a leading one, as it embeds the assumption that there is some state-attributable "surplus." But that assumption strikes me as almost unarguable. Imagine that instead of founding Microsoft in Washington State, Bill Gates and Paul Allen had founded Microsoft in Somalia (or in the Hobbesian state of nature). Of course they would not have accumulated as massive a fortune. Bill Gates's wealth is a product not only of his labor and endowments but also of the rule of law. Without a well-functioning legal system (and, perhaps, a not-so-well-functioning antitrust system), Bill Gates's net worth would not be $90 billion, or even close.[16]

This is not to suggest—to borrow a phrase from the 2012 presidential campaign—that Bill Gates "didn't build that."[17] Bill Gates's wealth is a product of his own labor and endowments combined with the value added by the rule of law. Moreover, the argument here is not that Bill Gates's rightful share is equal to the amount he has earned under a stable legal regime minus the amount he would have earned if he had been born in Somalia. One could just as easily—and no more persuasively—argue that Bill Gates's rightful share is equal to the amount he earned under a stable legal regime minus the amount that someone with lesser endowments who exerted less effort would have earned under the same legal regime. Both the rule of law and the endowments/effort of Bill Gates are necessary conditions for Gates's financial success, and neither is a sufficient condition on its own. To ask what percentage of Bill Gates's wealth is attributable to inputs from the state is to ask the impossible.

The question that I wish to focus on is different: To what share of Bill Gates's wealth does the surfer have a rightful claim? The answer, I believe, is more than none. Bill Gates's wealth is what it is because other members of society—including the Malibu surfer—respect Gates's property rights. They do not trespass on his land; they (generally) do not trade in pirated copies of Windows; and they respect court judgments in Microsoft's favor. They also stand ready to serve on a jury when Microsoft sues for copyright infringement, and stand ready to be conscripted in the event that Bill Gates's property requires defense by a draft army.

The significance of these contributions ought not be understated. Even though Bill Gates could hire a private security force to defend his "Xanadu 2.0" mansion,[18] and even though Microsoft could afford to install armed guards at all of its offices, the size of Bill Gates's fortune is still to a large extent a function of the fact that the surfer (and millions more like her) respect physical—and, perhaps more importantly, intellectual—property rights. How much would you pay for Microsoft Office if bootleg versions were hawked on the street like hot dogs? What would be the value of Microsoft-owned LinkedIn in a world in which the bulk of the population paid no heed to the boundaries of physical and intellectual property? There might be a lot of activity on the site among employers seeking muscle-bound security guards, though probably not enough to offset the decline in the number of recruiters seeking law firm associates and investment bankers.

These observations do not (yet) lead to the conclusion that the surfer ought to be compensated for respecting Bill Gates's property rights. For even if Bill Gates is better off when the surfer respects property rights, the surfer also may be better off when *she* respects property rights. Of course, this is true in the most basic sense because if the surfer trespasses on Bill Gates's property (why she would be wave-riding on Lake Washington is a separate question), the coercive force of the state—if not of Bill Gates's own security guards—will come down upon her. Classical liberals might say that such use of force is legitimate so long as the property-rights arrangement is one that the surfer cannot reasonably reject.[19] They might add that just as Bill Gates benefits from protection against the Lake Washington surfer and other potential trespassers, the surfer benefits from protection against marauding bands on beaches. (And the people who would otherwise be marauders, in turn, are better off employed as police officers, prison guards, and private security personnel in a world with robust property rights.) In economic terms, the move from a state of nature to a world with strong private property rights is Pareto-superior.[20]

Yet the classical liberal response to the surfer's compensation claim proves too much and too little. It proves too much in the following sense: Just as the surfer—when staring at the state of nature as the alternative—sees that she is better off in a world with strong private property rights, Bill Gates—when staring at the state of nature as the alternative—also sees that he is better off in a world in which private property is protected and the surfer is compensated. No reasonable software entrepreneur would prefer a Hobbesian state to a Scandinavian-style social democracy, much less a US-style capitalist economy with a basic income grafted on. Bill Gates might be better off without implementation of a basic income (because a basic income presumably would be funded through higher tax rates on the wealthy), while the surfer would be better off with one. The Pareto frontier includes a range of solutions spanning from the night watchman state to a massively redistributive one.

The classical liberal response also proves too little. That the establishment of private property rights makes the surfer materially better off does not necessarily mean that the surfer cannot reasonably reject the arrangement. Experiments involving "Ultimatum Game" scenarios consistently demonstrate that individuals reject offers they perceive to be lopsided, even if such offers leave them materially better off. In one familiar version of the game, an "Allocator" is told that she can divide $10 between herself and a "Recipient." The Allocator's division of the $10 serves as an offer, which the Recipient can accept or reject. If the Recipient accepts the offer, then the Allocator walks away with the amount that she allocated to herself, and the Recipient walks away with the amount that the Allocator offered to him. If the Recipient rejects the offer, then the Allocator and Recipient both walk away with zero. Note that for any offer greater than zero, the Recipient is better off in material terms if she accepts the offer rather than rejecting it. And yet across countries and cultures, Recipients tend to reject offers that they perceive to be too low (even though above zero). Richard Thaler finds in a review of such studies that Recipients tend to reject offers of less than about a quarter of the pot.[21] Remarkably, Recipients continue to reject lopsided offers even when the stakes are as high as one month's income.[22]

Now, the classical liberal might respond that recipients in the Ultimatum Game who reject nonzero offers are not behaving reasonably. But at that point, the classical liberal argument runs the risk of descending into ad hocery: Pareto superiority is held to be the measure of state legitimacy because no one can reasonably reject a Pareto-improving move, but reasonableness is defined so as to exclude those who reject Pareto-improving moves. Insofar as our account of state legitimacy is based on consent (actual or hypothetical), we either need some reason to disregard the views of individuals who reject lopsided divisions of the surplus or we need to divide the surplus in such a way that is not so lopsided that it would elicit rejections.

To sum up so far: The argument here is that the state is a collective enterprise—a partnership of individuals who, through their consent to the rule of law and private property rights, contribute to the production of surplus. That observation can motivate a rights-based claim to a minimum income in two ways. First, one can argue that individuals who contribute to a surplus-generating collective enterprise are entitled to a share of the surplus from that enterprise—and that a basic income is the dividend to which law-abiding individuals are entitled. Second, one can argue that the legitimacy of the state depends upon the hypothetical consent of the governed, and that consent can be procured only insofar as the surplus generated by the state is broadly shared. The two arguments are inextricably intertwined: the generation of surplus depends on the legitimacy of the state, which in turn depends on how the surplus is distributed.

Translating these abstract arguments into specific dollar amounts is difficult. There is no magic formula to determine what share of the surplus "belongs" to the state and what share "belongs" to hard-working, high-endowment individuals such as Bill Gates who have accumulated large fortunes. The modest claim here is that individuals whose obedience is essential to the legitimacy of the state and the prosperity of its members have a rightful claim to some share. As a lower bound, all members of the collective enterprise have a rightful claim to a share large enough that the bargain is not one they would reasonably reject.

IV. QUALIFICATIONS AND OBJECTIONS

The previous section sought to motivate the idea that the surfer (or, more generally, the member of society who is voluntarily unemployed) is still a partner in a collective enterprise that generates a surplus, such that she acquires a legitimate claim of entitlement to some portion. Here, I will address a handful of anticipated objections, though no doubt will fail to canvass all.

First, and as acknowledged above, the conclusion is indeterminate in that it suggests the surfer has a right to a share of state-generated surplus without specifying *what* share. Yet if we agree that the surfer has a right to a share greater than zero, it cannot be that if we disagree as to the size of the nonzero share, the surfer's right disappears. Subsistence serves as something of a focal point that adds determinacy to the indeterminate claim. Yet the question of amount remains open and variable: a state such as Somalia or South Sudan that has not generated sufficient surplus so as to provide all of its citizens with a basic income would not be obligated to do so, and a state such as Luxembourg or Monaco with far more than enough to provide its members with a subsistence-level income might be obligated to share its surplus more generously.

Second, the skeptic might say that the surfer's contribution (essentially, self-restraint) is minimal relative to the sweat and (perhaps) genius of the software entrepreneur, and that a lopsided allocation of the surplus thus reflects their lopsided contributions. And so it does. Moreover, research in the field of social psychology and related disciplines suggests that individuals across the age spectrum and across cultural contexts are willing to accept lopsided distributions so long as the lopsidedness reflects interpersonal variation in effort, ability, and other attributes.[23] Yet the case for a basic income outlined here does not rest on a rejection of all material inequalities: it posits that grossly lopsided inequalities in the distribution of divisible resources do not command widespread assent. The argument is not that the Malibu surfer should be put on par with Bill Gates; it is that an arrangement that offers *nothing* to the Malibu surfer is one that she can reasonably reject.

Third, the skeptic might say that even if the surfer has a legitimate claim of entitlement to a share of the surplus generated by the state, her claim is satisfied through the provision of government services (roads, parks, museums, police) to her for free. Algebraically, let E be the share of the surplus to which the surfer has a legitimate claim of entitlement by virtue of her role as a partner in a surplus-generating collective enterprise; let G be the value to the surfer of the various government services she enjoys at other taxpayers' expense. So long as $G \geq E$, the state's compensatory obligation to the surfer is satisfied without the provision of a basic income.

Yet the surfer's entitlement to E does not depend on whether she drives on highways, vacations at Yellowstone, frequents the Smithsonian, or calls 911 for help. Her claim arises because she respects Bill Gates's property rights—a contribution not correlated with the extent to which she benefits from government-provided services. To put the point in contractarian terms, the surfer indeed can reasonably reject a bargain whereby she contributes to the surplus-generating collective enterprise in exchange for benefits provided by the state in kind *to others*. Payment in kind through the provision of government services seems like a scattershot way for the state to satisfy its compensatory obligation.

Framing the surfer's claim in rights-based terms also strengthens the argument for providing benefits in cash rather than in kind. One (though not the only) argument for the provision of benefits in kind is that higher-endowment individuals are less likely to collect in-kind government benefits when those benefits are of lower quality than market equivalents (as might be the case for public housing), or when those who claim government benefits suffer from stigma (as might be the case for individuals who use food stamps at grocery store check-out counters). In other words, the provision of in-kind benefits serves a screening function to ensure that the perfectly capable surfer who is poor by choice does not collect benefits intended for the truly needy.[24] The rights-based case for a basic income changes the terms of the debate. No longer is the goal to prevent high-endowment individuals from claiming government benefits intended for individuals in dire need. The surfer who is perfectly capable of working—but chooses not to—still contributes to the collective enterprise. Her consent is still necessary to legitimize the exercise of coercive force against her. On this view, the screening effect of in-kind benefits becomes a bug rather than a feature.

Fourth, the skeptic might point out that the entitlement I have described is not "unconditional" in that it does indeed depend on the surfer respecting the property rights of others. Serial trespassers, larcenists, and criminals of a more serious sort would seem to have no claim. This much I concede. I am open to the notion that one's right to share in the surplus generated by the state might be alienable, just as one's right to participate in the political process may be forfeited by felony. A more concrete proposal for a basic income would delineate the precise conditions under which the entitlement might be lost, and whether there are further conditions under which it might be restored.

Fifth, the skeptic might note the fact that the surfer does *not* reject the present arrangement: we do not see rampant disrespect of property rights on the Malibu beach. And yet we do not know whether the surfer's obedience is generated by her willing participation in a surplus-generating collective enterprise or by fear that if she disobeys, the coercive force of the state will rain down upon her. The failure of a slave population to revolt does not mean that the slaves lack a rightful claim to a share of the surplus generated by their (forced) labor. Which is not to suggest that the surfer's position is analogous to a slave's—only that lack of resistance does not imply that the status quo surplus split is reasonable.

Sixth, some readers will recognize the affinities between this argument and the "partnership theory of taxation," and will object to this argument on the same grounds on which they object to partnership theory. For example, Joseph Dodge writes that "[t]he partnership theory . . . is basically an argument by metaphor, and the characteristic of a metaphor is that, unlike the analogy that the metaphor seeks to mask, it appeals to intuition rather than reason."[25] Yet the entire enterprise of analytic philosophy is an appeal to intuition, using intuitions as data points to test and build reasoned moral claims. The intuition that an individual who contributes to a collective enterprise ought to receive some portion of the surplus generated by that enterprise strikes me as a strong and widely shared one.

Seventh and finally, the skeptic might question whether the argument outlined here actually overcomes the "infeasibility or insubstantiality" objection. While the rule of law at the level of the nation-state contributes to Bill Gates's ability to earn his billions, so too does the rule of law at the international level. Microsoft, after all, is a global corporation benefited by international intellectual property treaties; why does the surfer in Bali or the beggar in Calcutta not have the same claim to a share of the surplus as the surfer in Malibu?

One response is to say that it is the application of coercive force to the surfer that requires justification.[26] In a world without world government, there is no supranational entity that applies coercive force to the surfer in Malibu or in Bali. The government of the United States must procure the consent of the Malibu surfer (or must treat the Malibu surfer on terms to which she would reasonably consent), but it need not procure the consent of the surfer in Indonesia. If the Bali surfer submits a claim for a share of the surplus generated by her respect for Bill Gates's intellectual property rights, she should submit that claim to her own government, not to the United States.[27]

This is not to say that we in the United States should be unconcerned with the plight of individuals abroad. It is to say, though, that the nature of the concern is different from the concern motivating the Malibu surfer's basic income claim. We ought to alleviate the suffering experienced by individuals abroad, especially when such suffering can be alleviated at relatively low cost to ourselves.[28] But for separate reasons, we ought to ensure that the Malibu surfer receives a share of the surplus generated by a collective enterprise of which she is a part and whose legitimacy depends on her consent.

V. ALTERNATIVES AND CONCLUSIONS

I will conclude by distinguishing the argument limned here from two more familiar justifications. One such argument, based on an "equal right to the value of natural resources,"[29] has a long pedigree dating back to Thomas Paine. Paine started from the premise that "the earth, in its natural, uncultivated state, was, and ever would have continued to be, the common property of the human race."[30] From this premise, Paine contended that each individual—as an equal part owner of the global commons—is entitled to a "ground-rent" for the use of his share.[31]

Whatever one thinks of Paine's premise, his argument runs headlong into the "infeasibility or insubstantiality" problem mentioned. The sort of basic income that might be supportable on a "ground-rent" justification would be truly "universal": there is no apparent reason why a citizen of Switzerland would be entitled to a larger ground-rent from her share in the global commons than a citizen of Somalia. The account offered here addresses this problem by framing the substance of the Swiss and Somali citizens' claims in identical terms—each is entitled to a share of the surplus generated by the collective enterprise of which she is a part—while also acknowledging that these claims can result in different dollar amounts because the surplus generated by the Swiss and Somali states is not the same.

To be sure, the very fact that an argument points toward radical transnational redistribution does not mean that the argument is wrong. But an argument along the lines that Paine proposed would point toward a basic income scheme very different from what basic income advocates in rich world countries contemplate. The total value of the world's real estate is, according to one recent estimate, approximately $217 trillion.[32] Other estimates suggest that approximately one-third of that value of real estate is attributable to land (as opposed to improvements on land).[33] Applying the one-third multiplier to the global value figure would suggest that the value of the world's land is roughly $72 trillion. Assuming a ground-rent equal to 5 percent of land value, then the annual ground-rent would be $3.6 trillion, or somewhere in the range of $480 per each of the world's 7.5 billion people.

The argument outlined here, by contrast, would suggest a basic income that varies in size depending on the surplus that each nation-state generates. It could be significantly more than $480 in more advanced countries and potentially less in others. This is because the amount that a state must provide to its poorest citizens in order for them to consent to the state's exercise of coercive force will depend on the size of the surplus. The Recipient might accept an offer of $5 when the Allocator divides a surplus of $10 but reject the same offer when the Allocator divides a surplus of $100. To reiterate: the right not to be subject to coercion except on terms to which one would reasonably consent is universal; the dollar amount to which this universal right translates is not.

The argument here is more straightforwardly distinguishable from the welfarist (i.e., utilitarian) case for a basic income. Optimal tax theories, which posit welfare maximization as their goal, generally produce prescriptions for a basic income (alternatively described as a "demogrant").[34] Given the diminishing marginal utility of income, redistribution under an optimal tax approach serves the purpose of shifting resources from households with a low marginal utility of income to households with a high marginal utility of income.

Welfarist justifications for a basic income encounter two obstacles. First, like Paine's theory, the welfarist justification seems to support a basic income scheme that is transnational in scope. Beneficiaries of a national-level basic income scheme in advanced economies would have an uncertain claim to any net transfer in a worldwide system engineered to maximize global welfare. Insofar as a national-level basic income can be justified on welfarist foundations, it must be justified either as a second-best (behind the first-best of global redistribution) or alongside some rationale for assigning lower weight to the welfare of individuals in poorer countries.[35]

Second, optimal tax theories generally support some sort of "tagging"—i.e., adjusting the size of the demogrant based on the observed capabilities of recipients. The idea is that by only paying the demogrant to low-endowment individuals, or by adjusting the size of the demogrant based on individual endowments, an endowment-conditional transfer system can support larger transfers to the individuals in greatest need.[36] As noted above, tagging arguments also can justify redistribution in kind rather than in cash so that quality and stigma can screen out low-need claimants.[37] The case for tagging thus would seem to suggest that the surfer ought not be paid, at least as long as she can be distinguished from the truly needy whose lack of labor force participation is involuntary. Insofar as the surfer collects the demogrant, that is because the tagging system adopted is an imperfect one.[38]

The argument outlined here, however, requires no apology for payment to the surfer. The surfer should receive a basic income because her obedience to the rule of law contributes to the wealth of the nation-state and its members: she is a participant in a surplus-generating collective enterprise, and that participation entitles her to a share. To be sure, the collective enterprise is not a purely voluntary one—if she disobeyed, she would be the object of coercive force. But the legitimacy of the state's use of force arises from the fact that coercion comes on terms to which all reasonable people would consent. The reasonableness of consent, in turn, depends on the division of the surplus generated by the state: each individual's share need not be equal, but nor can the distribution be so lopsided that surfer would reject the bargain. The notion that the surfer should be denied a basic income because she is "tagged" as not truly needy has no place in this framework because the surfer's claim does not arise from need.

This chapter has presented the sketch of a rights-based justification for a basic income that is distinguishable from the "equal right to the value of natural resources" proposed by Paine, and that supports a national-level basic income scheme more easily than a welfarist justification would. The argument is a "human rights" argument in that it builds off the claim that all individuals have a right to a share of the surplus generated by their participation in the collective enterprise of the state, but the argument does not necessitate the conclusion that all humans are entitled to the same basic income amount regardless of citizenship or nationality.

The argument advanced here also is intended to investigate whether a human rights framework can justify positive claims against the nation-state that overcome the "infeasibility or insubstantiality" problem. On this latter point, the conclusion of the chapter is optimistic. A human rights framework can inform the financial claims that individuals make against the nation-state as well as the financial claims that nation-states make against individuals and entities. The inherent universality of human rights claims does not render the human rights framework irrelevant to basic income arguments. To the contrary, human rights theory can inform—and potentially undergird—powerful arguments for the sharing of income among a nation-state's members.

NOTES

1. P. Van Parijs, 'Why Surfers Should be Fed: The Liberal Case for an Unconditional Basic Income', 20 *Philosophy & Public Affairs* (1991), 101.
2. P. Van Parijs, 'Competing Justifications of Basic Income', *in* P. Van Parijs (ed.), *Arguing for a Basic Income* (1992), 3, 11.
3. J. Tasioulas, *Minimum Core Obligations: Human Rights in the Here and Now* (World Bank, 2017).
4. Van Parijs, possibly the philosopher most closely associated with the basic income idea, has written that "claiming that the right to a basic income is a human right . . . rests on a confusion." P. Van Parijs, *Basic Income: A Radical Proposal for a Free Society and a Sane Economy* (2017), at 281, n.18.
5. General Assembly, Universal Declaration of Human Rights, UN Doc. A/RES/217(III), 10 Dec. 1948, Art. 21(a).
6. What it means for a country to be "his country" is, of course, a topic of considerable debate. The key point is that Article 21(1) clearly sets forth a universal right but does not require every country to allow the entire world population to participate in its government.
7. M. Friedman, *Capitalism and Freedom* (1962), at 191–193.
8. This concern is emphasized in L. Murphy and T. Nagel, *The Myth of Ownership: Taxes and Justice* (2002), at 183.
9. UDHR, *supra* note 5, Art. 23(3).
10. Ibid. at Art. 25(1).
11. Ibid. at Art. 22.
12. Article 9, International Covenant on Economic, Social and Cultural Rights 1966, 993 UNTS 3.
13. Committee on Economic, Social and Cultural Rights, General Comment 19, The Right to Social Security (Art. 9), UN Doc. E/C.12/GC/19, 4 Feb. 2008.
14. J. Rawls, *Political Liberalism* (expanded ed. 2005), at 182, n.9.
15. P. Van Parijs, *Basic Income and Social Justice: Why Philosophers Disagree, Joint Joseph Rowntree Foundation/University of York Annual Lecture 2009*, 13 Mar. 2009, available online at https://www.uclouvain.be/cps/ucl/doc/etes/documents/2009.Rowntree.pdf.
16. D. Pendleton, *Bill Gates's Net Worth Hits $90 Billion: Chart*, 22 Aug. 2016, available online at http://www.bloomberg.com/news/articles/2016-08-22/bill-gates-s-net-worth-hits-record-high-of-90-billion-chart (last visited 25 May 2017).
17. White House Office of the Press Secretary, *Remarks by the President at a Campaign Event in Roanoke, Virginia*, 13 July 2012, available online at https://obamawhitehouse.archives.gov/the-press-office/2012/07/13/remarks-president-campaign-event-roanoke-virginia ("If you've got a business—you didn't build that. Somebody else made that happen.").
18. M. Weinberger and M. Stone, *19 Crazy Facts About Bill Gates' $123 Million Washington Mansion*, 7 Nov. 2014, available online at http://www.businessinsider.com/19-crazy-facts-about-bill-gates-house-2014-11 (last visited 25 May 2017).
19. R. A. Epstein, 'Taxation in a Lockean World', 4 *Social Philosophy & Policy* (1986), 49, at 53.
20. And even better than that. The move is Pareto-superior so long as Bill Gates, the surfer, *or* the marauders are made better off and none are made worse off. The contractarian can argue, plausibly, that the establishment of private property rights makes everyone better off.
21. R. H. Thaler, 'Anomalies: The Ultimatum Game', 2 *Journal of Economic Perspectives* (1988), 195, at 196–198.
22. Cameron, 'Raising the Stakes in the Ultimatum Game: Experimental Evidence from Indonesia', 37 *Economic Inquiry* (1999), 47, at 56 and n.16.
23. C. Starmans, M. Sheshkin, and P. Bloom, 'Why People Prefer Unequal Societies', 1 *Nature Human Behaviour* 0082 (2017).
24. T. Besley and S. Coate, 'Public Provision of Private Goods and the Redistribution of Income', 81 *American Economic Review* (1991), 979.
25. J. M. Dodge, 'Theories of Tax Justice: Ruminations on the Benefit, Partnership, and Ability-to-Pay Principles', 58 *Tax Law Review* (2005), 399, at 444.

26. Miranda Fleischer and I have suggested elsewhere that the Peace of Westphalia might be thought of as "a sort of meta-social contract: each nation-state in the Westphalian system achieves legitimacy so long as it can procure the (hypothetical) consent of its members, and the Westphalian system as a whole is legitimate as long as it can procure the (hypothetical) consent of all member-states. On this view, the state's only concern is to ensure that none of its own members can reasonably reject the forced exchange; there is no need to procure the consent of nonmembers." M. Fleischer and D. Hemel, 'Atlas Nods: The Libertarian Case for a Basic Income', 2017 *Wisconsin Law Review* 1189.

27. For an analogous argument, see T. Nagel, 'The Problem of Global Justice', 33 *Philosophy and Public Affairs* (2005), 113, at 126–130.

28. P. Singer, 'Famine, Affluence, and Morality', 1 *Philosophy and Public Affairs* (1972), 229.

29. Van Parijs, *supra* note 2, at 11.

30. T. Paine, *Agrarian Justice* (3rd ed. 1797), 12 (digitized at: https://books.google.com/books?id=BaU46oFiZnAC).

31. Ibid.

32. I. Fraser, 'What Is All the Property in the World Worth?', *The Telegraph*, 24 Jan. 2016, available online at http://www.telegraph.co.uk/finance/property/news/12116347/What-is-all-the-property-in-the-world-worth.html (last visited 30 May 2017).

33. M. Yglesias, 'What's All the Land in America Worth?', 20 Dec. 2013, available online at http://www.slate.com/blogs/moneybox/2013/12/20/value_of_all_land_in_the_united_states.html (last visited 25 May 2017).

34. L. Batchelder, F. Goldberg, and P. Orszag, 'Efficiency and Tax Incentives: The Case for Refundable Tax Credits', 59 *Stanford Law Review* (2006), 23, 32–33, n.31

35. W. Kopczuk, J. Slemrod, and S. Yitzhaki, 'The Limits of Decentralized World Redistribution: An Optimal Taxation Approach', 49 *European Economic Review* (2005), 1051.

36. As George Akerlof writes in a seminal paper on "tagging" and optimal taxation: "Loosely, it could be said that tagging will in consequence reduce the cost of income redistribution (since, with lower marginal tax rates, there is a smaller gap between social and private returns to work and therefore less loss of consumer's surplus due to redistribution-caused job switching). As a result, it is only natural that tagging increases the optimal transfers to poor people." G. Akerlof, 'The Economics of "Tagging" as Applied to the Optimal Income Tax, Welfare Programs, and Manpower Planning', 68 *American Economic Review* (1978), 8, 11.

37. See Besley and Coate, *supra* note 24.

38. D. Parsons, 'Imperfect "Tagging" in Social Insurance Programs', 62 *Journal of Public Economics* (1996), 183.

CHAPTER 25

TAXATION, HUMAN RIGHTS, AND A UNIVERSAL BASIC INCOME

PHILIP ALSTON

I. INTRODUCTION

Proposals that governments should provide their citizens, and perhaps also other residents of their state, with access to a "universal basic income" (UBI) funded primarily from the receipts of taxation have proliferated rapidly in recent years.[1] To appreciate the significance of a UBI, at least in its comprehensive and ideal form, it is important to note that it is explicitly designed to challenge most of the key assumptions underpinning traditional social security systems. Rather than payments being partial, basic income guarantees a floor; instead of being episodic, payments are regular; rather than being needs-based, they are paid as a flat rate to all; they come in cash, rather than messy in-kind support; they accrue to every individual rather than only to needy households; rather than requiring that various criteria be met, they are unconditional; rather than excluding the well-off, they are universal; and instead of being based on lifetime contributions, they are funded primarily from taxation. Simplicity of design promises minimal bureaucracy and low administrative costs.

Support for giving careful consideration to such an approach has come not just from scholars, including philosophers, economists, and political scientists, but also from governments and trade union representatives.[2] Indeed, so broad is the potential spectrum of support that even the two international organizations that stand for almost diametrically opposed models of social protection seem to agree that a UBI deserves attention. On the one hand, the International Monetary Fund, which has long adopted a minimalist approach that emphasizes narrow targeting of any benefits and the cutting of overall welfare budgets, has suggested that there are circumstances under which some form of UBI might be justifiable and comport with sound fiscal policy.[3] At the other end of the international organizational spectrum, the International Labour Organization (ILO), which is the leading promoter of the much more comprehensive Social Protection Floor Initiative, concluded that "some UBI proposals have the potential to advance equity and social justice, while other proposals may result in a net welfare loss."[4]

The conclusion to be drawn from this diverse array of support is well captured in a report for the Indian government, which observes that if "thinkers on both the extreme left and right" have all become basic income supporters, then it is "a powerful idea" which must be discussed seriously.[5] While that report concludes that the time has not yet come for the implementation of a UBI in India,[6] the proposal should definitely be on the table as a future option for improving existing social protection systems.

This chapter argues that international human rights legal standards are not just relevant to the debate over a UBI but central to it. This is not intended as a concluding chapter in the sense of bringing together all the themes addressed by the various contributors to this volume. Nevertheless, it does illustrate one of the key distinctions between the analyses by human rights proponents and by those whose starting point is tax, domestic law, or even philosophy. While one group assumes that human rights considerations should generally be determinative, the other assumes they are largely irrelevant in this context. Human rights proponents tend to attach great importance to the fact that an array of human rights obligations has been accepted, as a matter of treaty law, by every state in the world. For them, it follows that since these commitments have been undertaken voluntarily and in the knowledge that they are formally binding as a matter of international law, the relevant states should acknowledge their obligations and seek to make their domestic law and practice conform to the greatest extent possible to the relevant international standards. This assumption is bolstered by the fact that the state's obligations stem not only from the one-time action of submitting a formal instrument of accession or ratification to the treaty but also from the government repeatedly subjecting itself over a long period of time to processes of reporting and giving assurances to international monitoring bodies that they would honor their commitments.

In contrast, those who do not take international human rights law as their starting point often tend to dismiss, or more likely simply ignore, the relevance of human rights obligations, especially in contexts that do not involve any "traditional" violations such as killings, torture, or arbitrary imprisonment. In his contribution to this volume, Daniel Hemel provides a cursory survey of the content of the relevant standards, but then moves quickly to dismiss their relevance for the purposes of supporting an argument that there is a human right to a basic income.[7] This chapter is not intended as a comprehensive response to his analysis but rather considers issues raised by his approach that must be addressed to make the case that human rights law is of major relevance to the UBI debate.

Many commentators assume, as does Hemel, that the right to social security should be read in a narrow, traditional sense which gives it limited reach and makes clear that it is not sufficiently expansive to be able to accommodate the notion of a UBI. I argue that the right to social security needs to be read in conjunction with the right to an adequate standard of living, in order to get a sense of the parameters of an umbrella right to social protection that might apply beyond the realm of those who are either employed or are incapable of being so. Notably, the ILO had already used the term "basic income" in 1944 when it adopted its foundational social justice instrument, the Declaration of Philadelphia. In particular, it called for the "extension of social security measures to provide a basic income to all in need of such protection."[8]

Despite the fact that Article 9 of the International Covenant on Economic, Social and Cultural Rights recognizes, *tout court*, "the right of everyone to social security," Hemel bolsters his argument by focusing not on this broad text but on its narrower interpretation by the UN Committee on Economic, Social and Cultural Rights in its General Comment on the article. The Committee confined its focus to the need to guarantee "human dignity for all persons when they are faced with circumstances that deprive them of their capacity to fully realize their Covenant rights."[9] More specifically, it referred to the right to secure protection from:

(a) lack of work-related income caused by sickness, disability, maternity, employment injury, unemployment, old age, or death of a family member; (b) unaffordable access to health care; (c) insufficient family support, particularly for children and adult dependents.[10]

A case could certainly be made that the Committee was excessively influenced by the specific jurisprudence arising out of specialized ILO Conventions in determining that the right to social security does not extend beyond such particular circumstances. But the principal justification for the Committee to have adopted such an approach is that the more expansive, and unconditional, right is defined in a separate provision of the Covenant, the implications of which it was not addressing in this particular General Comment.

Thus, it is Article 11(1) that spells out that "everyone" has the right "to an adequate standard of living for himself and his family, including adequate food, clothing and housing." This provision is not made conditional upon a person working or being able to demonstrate an inability to do so. Hemel actually recognizes this point when he notes that the provision "does posit that the surfer should be *fed*."[11] But singling out the right to food for this purpose can only be either because he misreads the article, which clearly covers clothing and housing as well, or because he does not accept the significance of the right to an adequate standard of living as a stand-alone right.

This overly narrow and thus problematic interpretation of the provisions of the Covenant, leads him to conclude that if the right to a basic income can be justified, it "will not be based on interpretation of existing international human rights texts," but instead "will be rooted in political theory."[12] In this respect, he follows the lead of most non–human rights lawyers in assuming that human rights law not only does not mandate a right to a basic income but that it is of little, if any, relevance to the argument that there should be such a right. He is, of course, on stronger ground if both the reality and the human rights theory applied in the United States are taken as the starting points. Since the US government does not recognize economic and social rights as full-fledged human rights, and since international law–based arguments were of at best marginal relevance even before the advent of the Donald Trump administration, there is little point in trying to invoke such sources to establish the existence of a right to a basic income in the United States.[13] But it is not at all clear that arguments rooted in political theory, no matter how compelling, will fare any better when planted in such barren soil.

Hemel does not confine his dismissal of the relevance of international human rights law to the US context, however. Instead, he goes significantly further and observes that "many basic income advocates have eschewed claims phrased in rights-based terms."[14] But the one authority that he cites for that proposition is worth scrutinizing. He quotes Van Parijs and Vanderborght to the effect that "claiming that the right to a basic income is a human right . . . rests on a confusion."[15] If Van Parijs, the most long-standing and best known of those advocating a basic income, rejects the relevance of human rights in the context of the debate over a basic income, then the position that I am advocating here would presumably be much less tenable. But in fact the argument put forward by these two authors is both more complex and more nuanced than Hemel suggests.

Their argument consists of several parts. The first is their perception that they need to ground their own claim for a universal cash income on the notion of distributive justice, in large part to avoid the sort of claim that Hemel makes, which they would characterize as being grounded in a conception of cooperative justice, or an arrangement among the participants in a cooperative venture.[16] Hemel's notion of an entitlement, or right, is something that is contingent upon the recipient meeting the requirement of being "law-abiding." He analogizes this to the right to vote which, based especially on assumptions that are still widely accepted in the United States (though increasingly challenged), may be denied to individuals who have committed certain offences (those classed as felons, in particular), or who have failed to repay related debts to the state. Van Parijs and Vanderborght, in contrast, recognize that this foundation would make it very easy for their critics to make a basic income contingent upon having made a contribution through work or otherwise, thus undermining the key universalist characteristic of their concept. Accordingly, they reject cooperative justice and insist instead that what is required is "an egalitarian conception of distributive justice."[17] In fact, this is much more consistent with the assumptions reflected in international human rights law that one is entitled to the relevant rights solely on the basis of being human, and not because particular behavioral preconditions are met.

The question then is why Van Parijs and Vanderborght suggest that relying upon a human rights–based argument for basic income is unhelpful and introduces an element of "confusion"? They explain their resistance to the use of human rights–based arguments in the following terms:

> Suppose one can say—on the basis of some ethical theory of human rights or of public international law—that there is something like a human right to an income sufficient, say, to cover basic human needs, or to be lifted out of poverty, or to live in dignity. It does not follow that this sufficient income should be guaranteed to each household through uniform individual cash payments to its members without means test or work requirement. The rhetoric of human rights should not be dismissed, as it is often politically effective, but it is no substitute for a serious philosophical justification.

In other words, human rights are considered to introduce an element of confusion primarily because the relevant standards are seen not to be precisely coterminous with the characteristics that Van Parijs and Vanderborght have identified for their preferred model of a UBI. That model requires that payments be (1) guaranteed, (2) made to each household in cash, and (3) be unconditional. Three responses are in order. The first is that none of these elements is necessarily inconsistent with the standards discussed above, and especially with the right to an adequate standard of living recognized in Article 11 of the Covenant. Even in its General Comment on Article 9 (the right to social security), the UN Committee emphasizes the importance of achieving "universal coverage" of social security, doing so through "non-contributory schemes,"[18] and ensuring that cash payments are a part of the package of benefits.[19]

The second response is to contrast the rigid definitional approach that leads the authors to reject the utility or relevance of human rights with their own subsequent openness to exploring alternatives to their core idea of a *universal* basic income. These alternatives include a categorical basic income, a household basic income, or a tax surcharge. They ultimately express their preference for a partial basic income, "that makes no claim to being sufficient to live on if one lives alone."[20] If such flexibility is in order in terms of moving toward their ideal preferred model, then surely some reliance upon widely accepted human rights standards is appropriate in order to bolster or reinforce the philosophical as well as the legal and political arguments in favor of a UBI.

The third response is to challenge the relationship between what the authors term "the rhetoric of human rights" on the one hand, and "serious philosophical justification" on the other. Almost by definition, the latter is going to be based on one particular theoretical perspective that is unlikely to be very widely shared, or at least unlikely to have significant leverage across different parts of the world. So while it might be helpful to develop a Rawlsian or some other perspective on UBI, a more broadly based and widely accepted set of values would surely strengthen the case rather than just bringing confusion. Similarly, to classify human rights standards as being essentially rhetorical, and thus presumably lacking in serious justificatory power, also seems to be unduly dismissive of the work of many serious philosophers who have engaged constructively and productively in recent years with the philosophical foundations of international human rights norms.[21]

Before exploring further the potentially useful interactions that might result from UBI proponents engaging with aspects of human rights theory and law, it is important to engage with one other issue that many critics of UBI have rightly raised, which concerns the affordability of any such scheme, even in high-income countries, let alone in low-income countries.

II. FEASIBILITY AND AFFORDABILITY

In addition to the central question of affordability of a UBI, Hemel raises a closely related question that stems from a particular understanding of the international human rights legal framework. In chapter 24, he points to the problem that any agreed level of UBI that would be affordable in a low-income country would be insubstantial and thus meaninglessly low in a high-income context. And the reverse means that a UBI level that would be considered adequate in the latter situation would, by definition, be unaffordable for the government of a low-income country. To the extent that a human rights–based UBI would need to translate into a single cash figure to be paid worldwide, he is right that such a universal payment would either be unaffordable in some countries or patently inadequate in others.

From that observation he goes on to conclude that "insofar as feasibility is a constraint on human rights claims," and he clearly believes that they are, "then the idea of a human right to basic income would seem to be a nonstarter."[22] This critique, based on the argument that it is infeasible for low-income countries to ever realize meaningful levels of key economic and social rights has long been used to challenge the very notion that there could actually be such rights. One of the earliest proponents of this argument was Maurice Cranston, who took particular aim at the right to rest and leisure, and the right to social security. Perhaps his primary objection was these rights did not reflect priority concerns for many people around the world. He conceded that they might be admirable as ideals, but insisted that "an ideal belongs to a wholly different logical category from a right. If rights are to be reduced to the status of ideals, the whole enterprise of protecting human rights will be sabotaged." But, feasibility was also a major stumbling block. How, he asked, "can the governments of those parts of Asia, Africa, and South America, where industrialization has hardly begun, be reasonably called upon to provide social security and holidays with pay for the millions of people who inhabit those places and multiply so swiftly?"[23]

But contrary to the assumptions that Hemel, Cranston, and other critics have made, there is nothing in human rights law, notwithstanding its aspiration to set universal standards, which requires that a right be satisfied at identical levels in all countries of the world simultaneously. The reality is that almost all rights are enjoyed at different levels. The fact that prison conditions in Botswana are clearly inferior to those in Norway does not mean that the former cannot meet appropriate international standards which take into account what is feasible in a given society. The same applies to a UBI. An amount of money that would be meaningful in Botswana will be dramatically lower than the amount required in Norway, but both countries might be capable of satisfying the right to a basic income that is compatible with their respective living standards.

Social security and social protection have long been dismissed as unaffordable aspirations, particularly for low-income countries. But this is precisely why the main proponents of the Social Protection Floor Initiative, and especially the ILO, have chosen to emphasize that "[t]here is a wide variety of options to expand fiscal space and generate resources for social protection, even in the poorest countries."[24] Building on policies endorsed by the international financial institutions, the ILO has identified eight financing options which can expand fiscal space to accommodate social protection spending. They are: (1) reallocating public expenditures; (2) increasing tax revenues; (3) expanding social security coverage and contributory revenues; (4) lobbying for aid and transfers; (5) eliminating illicit financial flows; (6) using fiscal and central bank foreign exchange reserves; (7) managing debt, including borrowing or restructuring existing debt; and (8) adopting a more accommodating macroeconomic framework.

In contrast to the detailed studies done in relation to individual countries' options for establishing a social protection floor, UBI proponents have devoted relatively little attention to questions of affordability.[25] The "floor" proposed by Van Parijs and Vanderborght is not "sufficient to cover what would be regarded as basic needs." Although clearly reluctant to put a figure on their proposal, they suggest an amount of 25 percent of current GDP per capita, which is "modest enough [to be] sustainable and generous enough for it to be plausible that it will make a big difference." They calculate that this would have amounted in 2015 to $1,163 per month in the United States, $1,670 in Switzerland, and $9.50 in the Democratic Republic of the Congo. They do not claim that this level is high enough to get every household out of poverty, although the US figure would be higher than the official poverty line. They also emphasize that if individuals currently receive benefits higher than the basic income, it "must be topped up by conditional supplements" so that the total disposable incomes of poor households are not lowered vis-à-vis their current levels.[26]

But how would these expenditures be paid for? Piachaud notes that a full basic income that "replaces social security is far more costly than social security, and this has to be paid from higher taxes on all incomes with far-reaching economic consequences."[27]

The Economist, relying upon the Organisation for Economic Co-operation and Development's (OECD) "universal basic income calculator," concludes that the United States could pay every citizen $6,300 per year if it scrapped all its nonhealth transfer payments.[28] In other words, if it paid its citizens 25 percent of GDP per capita ($13,956 per year) as Van Parijs and Vanderborght propose, it would need to raise taxes to cover the difference between $13,956 and $6,300. The Cato Institute calculated that paying 296 million US citizens the poverty line amount of $12,316 per year would cost $4.4 trillion. Even if all federal and state social assistance spending for the poor (around $1 trillion) and all "middle-class social welfare programs such as Social Security and Medicare" (depending on calculation, ranging between $2.13 trillion and $2.5 trillion) were eliminated, there would still be a funding gap of roughly $1 trillion.[29]

Cost calculations for Canada are also revealing. If existing Canadian "de facto" basic income programs (such as Canada Child Benefit for children, the Guaranteed Income Supplement for the elderly, and sales tax credits for working adults), quasi-basic income programs, earned income tax credits, social assistance, and employment insurance were all canceled, the savings could support a basic income for all Canadians (depending on which programs were scrapped) of between CAN$2,655 and CAN$3,565 per year, with between roughly 1.7 million and 1.9 million Canadians falling below the poverty line. Under a scenario in which all existing programs are kept in place and a supplemental universal basic income is paid to all Canadians of CAN$1,000 per year, 719,000 Canadians would be taken out of poverty, but at a net cost of CAN$29.2 billion (equaling CAN$40,886 per person). To pay for this, the Canadian value-added tax (VAT) rate would have to be increased from 5 percent to 9 percent or income taxes would have to be increased by 20 percent.[30]

Finally, a simulation for the region of Catalonia in Spain suggests that a basic annual income of €7,968 for those older than eighteen and €1,594 for minors would require a 49.57 percent flat tax and extra financing of €7 billion.[31]

Van Parijs and Vanderborght admit that a universal basic income at 25 percent of GDP per capita would result in "far higher rates of taxation because of the need to keep funding other public expenditures." They then proceed to point to some relatively small-scale, basic income experiments, negative-income-tax experiments and econometric models, none of which provides a clear answer on affordability. After discussing alternative financing models such as taxes on capital, nature, money, and consumption, they conclude that "none of these alternative sources offers a panacea, or any robust assurance that a generous basic income is economically sustainable, or any reason to believe that, in the short run at any rate, we can dispense with the income tax."[32] The UBI debate is thus located squarely within the context of fiscal policy.

III. THE FUTURE OF THE UBI DEBATE

Much of the earlier debate about UBI ignored the human rights dimension, and also tended to evaluate it in terms of whether it was per se a good idea or a bad idea. The more recent literature, prompted in part by the realization that something radical might be needed to counter the extreme inequality in both income and wealth that is emerging in many countries around the world, has been more nuanced.

The most committed proponents of UBI proclaim their approach to be utopian,[33] not in the sense of being unrealistic or unachievable, but as providing a highly ambitious, sweeping, and progressive vision. Critics or skeptics who raise objections based on unaffordability, the unacceptability of unconditionality, or the unrealistic change in mentality required will often be dismissed as unimaginative defenders of an obviously unsatisfactory status quo.[34] Perhaps unsurprisingly, these contrasting views accurately reflect the conclusion that emerges from a comprehensive survey of the many different utopias the world has known, which is that "utopias are essential but potentially dangerous."[35] In this case, the danger is that the single-minded pursuit of a UBI as a magic bullet, capable of resolving many deeply troubling challenges, will distract attention from the deeper underlying complexities and values. But the utopian vision may also provide the much needed impetus to rethink the optimal shape of social protection explicitly designed to achieve universal realization of the human right to an adequate standard of living in the twenty-first century. At a comparable watershed moment, Lord Beveridge introduced his 1943 report that laid the groundwork for the British welfare state by insisting that a "revolutionary moment in the world's history is a time for revolutions, not for patching."[36]

Thus the UBI concept should not be rejected out of hand on the grounds that it is utopian. Policymakers at the national and international levels need to develop the sort of creativity in social policy which is capable of matching and responding to the technological innovations and other developments that have brought us to this crossroads. Despite the magnitude of the challenge and the breathtaking scope of the proposed solution, there is an option, which Van Parijs seems to have subtly embraced, to move in an incremental fashion toward the overall goal. As Anthony Atkinson has observed, inspired by Amartya Sen's work, "the aim is progressive reform rather than transcendental optimality."[37]

To the extent that human rights proponents have engaged with the UBI debate to date, the most prominent path chosen has been to focus on ways of better promoting respect for labor rights.[38] But significant questions arise as to whether the tools used to tackle economic insecurity in that context have been, or are likely to be, effective in responding to the emerging conditions in the global labor market. For example, in its General Comment No. 18 (2005) on the right to work, the Committee on Economic, Social and Cultural Rights calls on states "to reduce to the fullest extent possible the number of workers outside the formal economy," "to ensure that privatization measures do not undermine workers' rights," and to ensure that enhanced labor market flexibility does "not render work less stable or reduce the social protection of the worker." All of these important objectives are grounded in human rights law, but the question is how best to respond to the reality that the trends in most industries seem to be heading rapidly in the opposite direction.

Similarly, an ILO report on Decent Work in Global Supply Chains responded to the "negative implications for working conditions" of "the dynamics of production and employment relations within the global economy" by proposing a series of steps such as promoting international labor standards; closing governance gaps; and promoting inclusive and effective social dialogue.[39] Unsurprisingly, after lengthy debate on the report, the 2016 ILO Conference expressed its "concern that current ILO standards may not be fit for purpose to achieve decent work in global supply chains."[40]

It does not follow from the gap between theory and practice that labor rights should be compromised, let alone abandoned. This disconnect, however, does highlight the fact that traditional approaches might not have much traction in the face of the systematic weakening of labor market institutions, the dramatic increase in more flexible working conditions, and the greatly increased insecurity, including the loss of nonwage benefits, for those who remain employed.[41]

This is where the UBI debate comes in. A focus on social protection more broadly defined, including by reference to the right to an adequate standard of living, might be a more propitious entry point to tackle these issues. Governments remain centrally responsible for ensuring appropriate levels of social protection within their borders, they have a self-interest in promoting stability and economic security, and they have the powers needed to promote a more broad-based and ambitious approach.

But it is not only economic and social rights that can, and should, be used to buttress arguments in favor of using taxation policies to achieve a UBI. The sort of extreme poverty that so often accompanies extreme inequality has major implications for the enjoyment of civil and political rights. As illustrated by the case of the United States, rapidly growing inequality facilitates various forms of state capture by economic elites who exercise greatly disproportionate political power. At the same time, the political powerlessness of those living in poverty or on the verge thereof makes them especially vulnerable to policies that not only effectively disenfranchise them but also tend to criminalize poverty by imposing large fees and fines for offences that only low-income people are likely to commit or to be prosecuted for.[42]

One of the most consistent and forceful advocates of a UBI, Guy Standing, has long emphasized the ways in which a basic income would reinforce respect for a range of nonmaterial rights.[43] Although acknowledging that it is primarily "a matter of social justice," he also argues that it would be freedom-enhancing by giving people the financial security to be able to make rational choices and to avoid the vulnerability of poverty and the paternalism of charitable contexts. He thus describes UBI as "the only welfare policy for which the 'emancipatory value' is greater than the monetary value."[44]

Standing's approach highlights the need to clarify the principal objectives a UBI is designed to achieve. At present, it remains conveniently chameleon-like in many of its representations.

Although the same terminology is used, there are in fact many and quite different versions of UBI, and each is supported by a diverse array of actors precisely because they see different attractions in the concept. To assess the utility and acceptability of UBI from a human rights perspective, it is helpful to identify the main categories of motivation. They include at least the following:

Discouraging laziness and incentivizing work.

Efficiency, in terms of avoiding welfare fraud, duplicative programs, double-dipping, and bloated bureaucracies. As one commentator rejoiced: "[W]e get to fire a couple of million bureaucrats."[45]

Adaptation to technological advances, both in terms of compensating for vast numbers of jobs lost in an age of automation and robotization, and to ensure some basic redistribution of wealth in an era characterized by exponential growth in the wealth of "tech entrepreneurs."

The right to work, either in the sense of promoting full employment for the community or of the individual being able to choose satisfying work.

Freedom, in the sense of the ability to make career and related choices, or the ability to exercise political rights, because of a degree of economic security.

Fairness and social justice.

All of these motivations are persuasive on their own terms, but unless they are integrally linked to the last category, the likelihood is that what will emerge will be another strategy designed to promote productivity and efficiency, but without adequate concern for the most important goal.

How then should human rights actors and those concerned with fiscal policy respond to the crisis of economic insecurity and the phenomena associated with it? And where might a campaign to achieve a UBI fit into the overall equation? The starting point is to acknowledge that the forms of economic insecurity that are being promoted by the now dominant neoliberal policies pose a fundamental threat to the enjoyment of a range of human rights. It is not only a threat to the enjoyment of economic and social rights, even though that is a principal concern. Extreme inequality, rapidly increasing insecurity, and the domination of politics by economic elites in many countries, all threaten to undermine support for, and ultimately the viability of, the democratic systems of governance upon which the human rights framework depends.[46]

In the present context, it is also important to acknowledge that these policies have been primarily formulated and justified in terms of the need for balanced and sustainable fiscal policies, which has in turn translated in almost all contexts into demands for forms of "fiscal consolidation." The resulting policies of slashing public expenditures and privatizing many previously public services have facilitated the accumulation of great wealth by small elites and undermined forms of social protection designed to cushion the impact of austerity policies on low-income groups.

In order to tackle these challenges, the human rights community needs to re-evaluate its priorities and ensure that a more prominent place is given to promoting the right to social security, and above all the right to an adequate standard of living. If these rights continue to be marginalized, the overall agenda will become increasingly less relevant to the most pressing and urgent questions of the day. But effective advocacy for these rights will also involve the proponents in debates over redistribution of societal resources, the indispensable role of the state, and the importance of fair, and progressive, fiscal policies which are not premised on the assumption that taxes are inherently bad, either for society or the economy.

There should also be an important gender dimension to UBI advocacy. The growing economic insecurity that is being generated and reinforced by many current macroeconomic policies carries with it almost unremittingly negative implications for gender equality. To this day, "the average woman's career remains shorter, more disrupted, and less remunerative than the average man's,"[47] and the consequences flow through into social security and related arrangements.[48] Again, as various chapters in the present volume have highlighted, fiscal policy has a potentially very large role to play in securing substantive equality for women, but that requires a more effective combination of the tax and human rights agendas than has hitherto been achieved in most societies.

Finally, and most importantly, the debates over social protection floors (SPFs) and UBI need to be brought together. To date, various international organizations have championed the former approach, and a great many governments have been persuaded to implement floors, albeit with content tailored to the specific needs and resource availability of each country. But UBI advocates have tended to more or less ignore this initiative and to debate different basic income schemes as though they have little if anything to do with SPFs. This degree of separation is counterproductive and ultimately self-defeating, since the commonalities between the two agendas are very considerable.

It is also true, of course, that there are points of divergence between the two concepts, but they have vastly more potential if their synergies are recognized, rather than ignored. Among the differences are the following: (1) the SPF mostly draws on experience in developing countries,[49] while UBI advocates tend to emphasize developed countries; (2) SPFs aim to guarantee both income security and access to essential social services, while UBI schemes only guarantee income; (3) the concept of basic income security is broader than basic income cash transfers since it also includes in-kind transfers; (4) SPFs focus not only on achieving social guarantees for all but also on gradually implementing higher standards; (5) SPFs are not viewed as alternatives to social insurance institutions,[50] while some UBI proponents aim to replace existing social insurance institutions; and (6) ILO Recommendation No. 202 is premised upon human rights, unlike most basic income schemes. But the proponents of the two approaches have an immense amount in common, and if it is recognized that UBI is not an idea that can be achieved in a single leap, there could be no better and more elaborate and widely supported program than that for the SPF.

NOTES

1. Parts of this chapter draw on the author's analysis of a UBI contained in Report of the Special Rapporteur on extreme poverty and human rights, Philip Alston, UN Doc. A/HRC/35/26, 22 Mar. 2017.

2. A. Lowrey, *Give People Money: How a Universal Basic Income Would End Poverty, Revolutionize Work, and Remake the World* (2018); P. Van Parijs and Y. Vanderborght, *Basic Income: A Radical Proposal for a Free Society and a Sane Economy* (2017); R. Bregman, *Utopia for Realists: How We Can Build the Ideal World* (2017); T. Straubhaar, *Radikal Gerecht* (2017); and A. Stern, *Raising the Floor: How a Universal Basic Income Can Renew Our Economy and Rebuild the American Dream* (2016).

3. International Monetary Fund, *Tackling Inequality*, Fiscal Monitor (Oct. 2017), 17.

4. I. Ortiz, C. Behrendt, A. Acuña-Ulate, and Q. A. Nguyen, 'Universal Basic Income Proposals in Light of ILO Standards: Key Issues and Global Costing', ESS Working Paper No. 62, Social Protection Department, International Labour Office (2018) 29.

5. Government of India, *Economic Survey 2016–2017* (2017), ch. 7, at 195.
6. Id.
7. Daniel Hemel, chapter 24 in this volume, *supra* at 539–550.
8. Declaration concerning the aims and purposes of the International Labour Organization (ILO), annex to the Constitution of the ILO, Section III (f).
9. Committee on Economic, Social and Cultural Rights, General Comment No. 19 (The right to social security (art. 9)), UN Doc. E/C.12/GC/19, 4 Feb. 2008, at para. 1.
10. Ibid. at para. 2.
11. Hemel, *supra* note 7, 542, emphasis in the original. The term "surfer" is used to connote a person who could be gainfully employed but has opted instead to use his or her days surfing the waves.
12. Ibid.
13. Philip Alston, Report of the Special Rapporteur on extreme poverty and human rights on his mission to the United States of America, UN Doc. A/HRC/38/33/Add.1, 4 May 2018, at para. 12.
14. Hemel, *supra* note 7, at 540.
15. Ibid. at 549 n.4(citing Van Parijs and Vanderborght, *supra* note 2, at 281 n.18).
16. Ibid. at 103.
17. Ibid. at 104.
18. General Comment No. 19, *supra* note 9, at para. 23.
19. See ibid. at paras. 2, 14, 17, and 18.
20. Van Parijs and Vanderborght, *supra* note 2 at 165.
21. In addition to the work of Charles Beitz, James Griffin, John Tasioulas, and Jeremy Waldron, among many others, see Rowan Cruft, S. Matthew Liao, and Massimo Renzo (eds.), *Philosophical Foundations of Human Rights* (2015).
22. Hemel, *supra* note 7, at 540.
23. Cranston, 'Are There Any Human Rights?', 112 *Daedalus* (1983) 1, at 12–13.
24. ILO, *World Social Protection Report 2017–19: Universal social protection to achieve the Sustainable Development Goals* (2017) 184–186.
25. See R. Pereira (ed.), *Financing Basic Income: Addressing the Cost Objection* (2017); J. Mays and G. Marston, 'Reimaging Equity and Egalitarianism: The Basic Income Debate in Australia', *Journal of Sociology & Social Welfare*, Sept. 2016, at 17; A. Major, 'Affording Utopia: The Economic Viability of a Capitalist Road to Communism', 11:2 *Basic Income Studies* (2016), 75; and 'Sighing for Paradise to Come', *The Economist*, 4 June 2016; Lowrey, *supra* note 2.
26. Van Parijs and Vanderborght, *supra* note 2, at 10–12.
27. D. Piachaud, Citizen's Income: Rights and Wrongs (Centre for Analysis of Social Exclusion, London School of Economics, 2016).
28. 'Universal basic income in the OECD', *The Economist*, 3 June 2016.
29. M. Tanner, The Pros and Cons of a Guaranteed National Income (CATO Institute, 12 May 2015), at 15.
30. D. Macdonald, *A Policymaker's Guide to Basic Income* (Canadian Centre for Policy Alternatives, Oct. 2016), 19–21.
31. J. Arcarons, D. Raventos Pañella, and L. Torrens Mèlich, 'Feasibility of Financing a Basic Income', 9(1–2) *Basic Income Studies* (2014), 79–93.
32. Van Parijs and Vanderborght, *supra* note 2, at 137.
33. Ibid. at 245–247; and Bregman, *supra* note 2.
34. For an excellent overview of the practical and principled objections, see Piachaud, *supra* note 27.
35. L. T. Sargent, *Utopianism: A Very Short Introduction* (2010), 127.
36. Beveridge Report, para. 7.
37. A. B. Atkinson, *Inequality: What Can Be Done?* (2015), 236; and A. Sen, *The Idea of Justice* (2009).
38. For an important analysis of the challenges to labor rights in the context of economic reform and austerity measures, see Report of the Independent Expert on the effects of foreign debt and other related international financial obligations of States on the full enjoyment of all human rights, particularly economic, social and cultural rights, Juan Pablo Bohoslavsky, UN Doc. A/HRC/34/57, 27 Dec. 2016.

39. *Decent Work in Global Supply Chains*, Report IV, International Labour Conference, 105th Session, 2016.
40. Resolution concerning decent work in global supply chains, 10 June 2016, at para. 25
41. T. Vlandas and D. Halikiopoulou, *Why Far Right Parties Do Well at Times of Crisis: The Role of Labour Market Institutions*, European Trade Union Institute, Working Paper 2016.07, at 5.
42. See Alston, *supra* note 13.
43. See generally G. Standing, *Basic Income: And How We Can Make It Happen* (2017).
44. G. Standing, 'Why the world should adopt a basic income', Open Future, *The Economist*, 4 July 2018.
45. T. Worstall, 'Krugman's Argument in Favor of a Universal Basic Income', *Forbes*, 5 May 2015.
46. G. Sitaraman, *The Crisis of the Middle-Class Constitution: Why Economic Inequality Threatens Our Republic* (2017).
47. A. L. Alstott, 'Good for Women: A response to 'A Basic Income for All' by Philippe Van Parijs', *Boston Review* (2000), available online at http://bostonreview.net/archives/BR25.5/alstott.html.
48. S. Fredman, 'Substantive Equality Revisited', 14 *International Journal of Constitutional Law* (2016), 712.
49. International Labour Office, *Social Protection Floor for a Fair and Inclusive Globalization: Report of the Social Protection Floor Advisory Group* (2011), at xxii.
50. Ibid. at xxviii.

INDEX

Page numbers followed by *f* indicate figures; page numbers followed by *t* indicate tables; page numbers followed by *b* indicate boxes.